Mobil
Travel Guide

Northwest

2005

Alaska

Idaho

Oregon

Washington

Exx**onMobil**
Travel Publications

Acknowledgements

We gratefully acknowledge the help of our representatives for their efficient and perceptive inspections of the lodging and dining establishments listed; the establishments' proprietors for their cooperation in showing their facilities and providing information about them; and the many users of previous editions who have taken the time to share their experiences. Mobil Travel Guide is also grateful to all the talented writers who contributed entries to this book.

Printing Acknowledgement: North American Corporation of Illinois

www.mobiltravelguide.com

Front cover photo: Mount Rainier, Washington

The information contained herein is derived from a variety of third-party sources. Although every effort has been made to verify the information obtained from such sources, the publisher assumes no responsibility for inconsistencies or inaccuracies in the data or liability for any damages of any type arising from errors or omissions.

Neither the editors nor the publisher assumes responsibility for the services provided by any business listed in this guide or for any loss, damage, or disruption in your travel for any reason.

ISBN: 0-7627-3588-0

ISSN: 1550-0276

Manufactured in the United States of America.

10 9 8 7 6 5 4 3 2 1

Contents

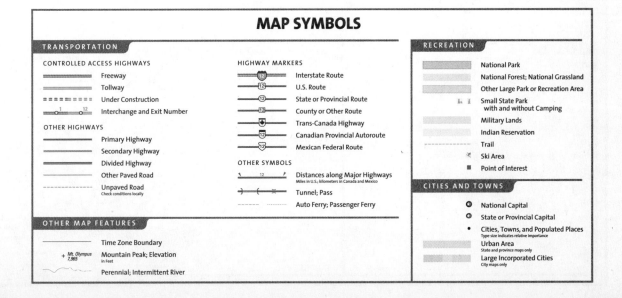

MAP SYMBOLS

TRANSPORTATION

CONTROLLED ACCESS HIGHWAYS

Freeway
Tollway
Under Construction
Interchange and Exit Number

OTHER HIGHWAYS

Primary Highway
Secondary Highway
Divided Highway
Other Paved Road
Unpaved Road
Check conditions locally

HIGHWAY MARKERS

Interstate Route
U.S. Route
State or Provincial Route
County or Other Route
Trans-Canada Highway
Canadian Provincial Autoroute
Mexican Federal Route

OTHER SYMBOLS

Distances along Major Highways
Miles in U.S.; kilometers in Canada and Mexico
Tunnel; Pass
Auto Ferry; Passenger Ferry

OTHER MAP FEATURES

Time Zone Boundary
Mt. Olympus 7,965 Mountain Peak; Elevation
In Feet
Perennial; Intermittent River

RECREATION

National Park
National Forest; National Grassland
Other Large Park or Recreation Area
Small State Park
with and without Camping
Military Lands
Indian Reservation
Trail
Ski Area
Point of Interest

CITIES AND TOWNS

National Capital
State or Provincial Capital
Cities, Towns, and Populated Places
Type size indicates relative importance
Urban Area
State and province maps only
Large Incorporated Cities
City maps only

© MAPQUEST

0	150	300 mi
0	150	300 km

	Interstate Routes
	Other Routes
277	Distance in Miles
1:50	Approximate Driving Time

© MAPQUEST.COM

ALASKA

POP: 626,932, rank 48

AREA: 591,004 sq mi, rank 1

City	Grid
Akutan, 713	F2
Alakanuk, 652	C3
Anchorage, 260283	D5
Angoon, 572	E8
Aniak, 572	D4
Barrow, 4581	A4
Bethel, 5471	D3
Chevak, 765	D3
College, 11402	C5
Cordova, 2454	D6
Craig, 1397	F8
Delta Jct., 840	C6
Dillingham, 2466	E4
Emmonak, 767	C3
Fairbanks, 30224	C5
Ft. Yukon, 595	B6
Galena, 675	C4
Gambell, 649	C2
Haines, 1811	E8
Homer, 3946	E5
Hoonah, 860	E8
Hooper Bay, 1014	D2
Houston, 1202	D5
Juneau, 30711	E8
Kake, 710	E8
Kenai, 6942	D5
Ketchikan, 7922	F9
King Cove, 792	F3
Kipnuk, 644	D3
Kodiak, 6334	E5
Kotzebue, 3082	B3
Kwethluk, 713	D3
Metlakatla, 1375	F9
Naknek, 678	E4
Nome, 3505	C3
N. Pole, 1570	C6
Palmer, 4533	D5
Petersburg, 3224	E8
Pt. Hope, 757	B3
Sand Pt., 952	F3
Savoonga, 643	C2
Selawik, 772	B4
Seward, 2830	D5
Shishmaref, 562	B3
Sitka, 8835	E8
Skagway, 862	D8
Soldotna, 3759	D5
Talkeetna, 772	D5
Togiak, 809	E3
Tok, 1393	C6
Unalakleet, 747	C3
Unalaska, 4283	F2
Valdez, 4036	D6
Wasilla, 5469	D5
Wrangell, 2308	E9
Yakutat, 680	E7

IDAHO
POP: 1,293,953, rank 39
AREA: 83,564 sq mi, rank 13

Aberdeen, 1840 .... E4
American Falls, 4111 .... F4
Ammon, 6187 .... E4
Arco, 1026 .... E3
Ashton, 1129 .... E5
Athol, 676 .... A1
Bancroft, 382 .... F4
Bellevue, 1876 .... E3
Blackfoot, 10419 .... E4
Boise, 185787 .... E1
Bonners Ferry, 2515 .... A2
Bovill, 305 .... B1
Buhl, 3985 .... F2
Burley, 9316 .... F3
Caldwell, 25967 .... E1
Cambridge, 360 .... D1
Carey, 513 .... E3
Cascade, 997 .... D2
Castleford, 277 .... F2
Challis, 909 .... D3
Chubbuck, 9700 .... F4
Clark Fork, 530 .... A2
Coeur d'Alene, 34514 .... B1
Cottonwood, 944 .... C1
Council, 816 .... D1
Craigmont, 556 .... C1
Dayton, 444 .... F4
Deary, 552 .... B1
Declo, 338 .... F3
Downey, 613 .... F4
Driggs, 1100 .... E5
Dubois, 647 .... D4
Eden, 411 .... F3
Emmett, 5490 .... E1
Fairfield, 395 .... E2
Filer, 1620 .... F2
Firth, 408 .... E4
Ft. Hall, 3193 .... F4
Franklin, 641 .... F4
Fruitland, 3805 .... E1
Garden City, 10624 .... E1
Genesee, 946 .... C1
Georgetown, 538 .... F5
Glenns Ferry, 1611 .... E2
Gooding, 3384 .... E2
Grace, 990 .... F4
Grand View, 470 .... E2
Grangeville, 3228 .... C2
Hagerman, 656 .... E2
Hailey, 6200 .... E3
Hayden, 9159 .... B1
Homedale, 2528 .... E1
Horseshoe Bend, 770 .... E2
Idaho City, 458 .... E2
Idaho Falls, 50730 .... E4
Inkom, 738 .... F4
Iona, 1201 .... E4
Jerome, 7780 .... F3
Kamiah, 1160 .... C2
Kellogg, 2395 .... B2
Kendrick, 369 .... C1

Ketchum, 3003 .... E4
Kimberly, 2614 .... F3
Kooskia, 675 .... C2
Kootenai, 441 ....
Kuna, 5382 ....
Lava Hot Sprs., 521 .... E4
Lewiston, 30904 ....
Mackay, 566 ....
Malad City, 2158 ....
Marsing, 890 ....
McCall, 2084 ....
McCammon, 805 ....
Melba, 439 ....
Montpelier, 2785 ....
Moscow, 21291 ....
Mtn. Home, 11143 ....
Moyie Sprs., 656 ....
Nampa, 51867 ....
Newdale, 358 ....
New Meadows, 533 ....
New Plymouth, 1400 ....
Nezperce, 523 ....
Oakley, 668 ....
Orofino, 3247 ....
Osburn, 1545 ....
Paris, 576 ....
Parma, 1771 ....
Paul, 998 ....
Payette, 7054 ....
Pierce, 617 ....
Pinehurst, 1661 ....
Plummer, 990 ....
Pocatello, 51466 ....
Post Falls, 17247 ....
Potlatch, 791 ....
Preston, 4682 ....
Priest River, 1754 ....
Rathdrum, 4816 ....
Rexburg, 17257 ....
Richfield, 412 ....
Rigby, 2998 ....
Riggins, 410 ....
Ririe, 545 ....
Roberts, 647 ....
Rockford, 350 ....
Rockland, 316 ....
Rupert, 5645 ....
Sagle, 425 ....
St. Anthony, 3342 ....
St. Maries, 2652 ....
Salmon, 3122 ....
Sandpoint, 6835 ....
Shelley, 3813 ....
Shoshone, 1398 ....
Soda Sprs., 3381 ....
Spirit Lake, 1376 ....
Sugar City, 1242 ....
Sun Valley, 1427 ....
Troy, 798 ....
Twin Falls, 34469 ....
Ucon, 943 ....
Victor, 840 ....
Wallace, 960 ....
Weippe, 416 ....
Weiser, 5343 ....
Wendell, 2338 ....
Winchester, 308 ....

© MapQuest

EUGENE, OR

MEDFORD, OR

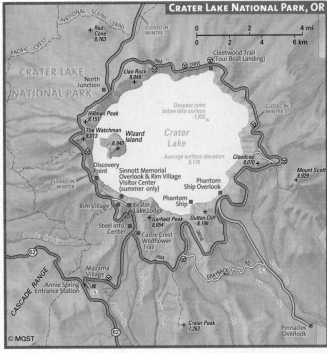

CRATER LAKE NATIONAL PARK, OR

OLYMPIC NATIONAL PARK, WA

TRI-CITIES, WA

JACKSON, WY

GRAND TETON NATIONAL PARK, WY

DOWNTOWN SALT LAKE CITY, UT

Distances in chart are in miles.
To convert miles to kilometers,
multiply the distance in miles
by 1.609.

Example:
New York, NY to Boston, MA
= 215 miles or 346 kilometers
(215 x 1.609)

	ALBUQUERQUE, NM	ATLANTA, GA	BALTIMORE, MD	BILLINGS, MT	BIRMINGHAM, AL	BISMARCK, ND	BOISE, ID	BOSTON, MA	BUFFALO, NY	BURLINGTON, VT	CHARLESTON, SC	CHARLESTON, WV	CHARLOTTE, NC	CHEYENNE, WY	CHICAGO, IL	CINCINNATI, OH	CLEVELAND, OH	DALLAS, TX	DENVER, CO	DES MOINES, IA	DETROIT, MI	EL PASO, TX	HOUSTON, TX	INDIANAPOLIS, IN	JACKSON, MS	KANSAS CITY, MO	LAS VEGAS, NV	LITTLE ROCK, AR	LOS ANGELES, CA	LOUISVILLE, KY	MEMPHIS, TN	MIAMI, FL	MILWAUKEE, WI	MINNEAPOLIS, MN	MONTRÉAL, QC	NASHVILLE, TN	NEW ORLEANS, LA	NEW YORK, NY	OKLAHOMA CITY, OK	OMAHA, NE	ORLANDO, FL	PHILADELPHIA, PA	PHOENIX, AZ	PITTSBURGH, PA	PORTLAND, ME	PORTLAND, OR	RAPID CITY, SD	RENO, NV	RICHMOND, VA	ST. LOUIS, MO	SALT LAKE CITY, UT	SAN ANTONIO, TX	SAN DIEGO, CA	SAN FRANCISCO, CA	SEATTLE, WA	TAMPA, FL	TORONTO, ON	VANCOUVER, BC	WASHINGTON, DC	WICHITA, KS
ALBUQUERQUE, NM		1490	1902	991	1274	1333	966	2240	1808	2178	1793	1568	1649	538	1352	1409	1619	754	438	1091	1608	263	994	1298	1157	894	578	900	806	1320	1033	2155	1426	1339	2172	1248	1276	2015	546	973	1934	1954	466	1670	2338	1395	841	1020	1876	1051	624	818	825	1111	1463	1949	1841	1597	1896	707
ATLANTA, GA	1490		679	1889	150	1559	2218	1100	910	1158	317	503	238	1482	717	476	726	792	1403	967	735	1437	800	531	386	801	2067	528	2237	419	389	661	813	1129	1241	242	473	869	944	989	440	782	1868	676	1197	2647	1511	2440	527	549	1916	1000	2166	2618	2705	455	958	2838	636	989
BALTIMORE, MD	1902	679		1959	795	1551	2401	422	370	481	583	352	441	1665	708	521	377	1399	1690	1031	532	2045	1470	600	1032	1087	2445	1072	2705	602	933	1109	805	1121	564	716	1142	192	1354	1168	904	104	2366	246	520	2830	1626	2623	152	841	2100	1671	2724	2840	2775	960	565	2908	38	1276
BILLINGS, MT	991	1889	1959		1839	413	626	2254	1796	2181	2157	1755	2012	455	1246	1552	1597	1433	554	1007	1534	1255	1673	1432	1836	1088	965	1530	1193	1547	1625	2554	1175	839	1852	1381	2092	2019	1199	1719	2352	889	379	960	2053	1341	548	1500	1302	1176	816	2348	1762	949	1953	1067
BIRMINGHAM, AL	1274	150	795	1839		1509	2170	1039		1039	1846	1388	1773	1749	1347	1604	594	838	1144	1189	1342	693	675	1126	1597	1582	1024	1548	801	1378	1183	1702	1139	1337	2224	767	431	1685	1315	1734	1641	1136	616	2003	1611	1662	1311	1944	1301	320	1372	1645	1053	960	1599	1765	1749	1229	2018	1354	1362	1545	934
BISMARCK, ND	1333	1559	1551	413	1509		1039	1846	1388	1773	1749	1347	1604	594	838	1144	1189	1342	693	675	1126	1597	1582	1024	1548	801	1378	1183	1702	1139	1337	2224	767	431	1685	1315	1734	1641	1136	616	2003	1611	1662	1311	1944	1301	320	1372	1645	1053	960	1599	1765	1749	1229	2018	1354	1362	1545	934
BOISE, ID	966	2218	2401	626	2170	1039		2697	2239	2624	2520	2182	2375	737	1708	1969	2040	1711	833	1369	1977	1206	1952	1852	2115	1376	760	1808	1933	1954	2883	1448	1455	2535	1976	2234	2491	1506	1234	2662	2462	993	2161	2795	432	930	430	2409	1628	342	1761	1096	646	507	2204	633	2395	1346	456	
BOSTON, MA	2240	1100	422	2254	1215	1846	2697		462	214	1003	741	861	1961	1003	862	654	1819	2004	1326	741	2465	1890	940	1453	1427	2757	1493	3046	964	1353	1529	1100	1417	313	1136	1563	215	1694	1463	1324	321	2706	592	107	3126	1921	2919	572	1181	2395	2092	3065	3135	3070	1380	570	3204	458	1616
BUFFALO, NY	1808	910	370	1796		909	1388	2239	462		375	899	431	695	1502	545	442	197	1393	1546	868	277	2039	1513	508	1134	995	2299	1066	2572	545	927	1425	642	958	377	916	1254	400	1262	1005	1221	414	2176	217	560	2667	1463	2460	485	739	1936	1665	2632	2677	2622	1316	106	2745	384	1184
BURLINGTON, VT	2178	1158	481	2181	1039	1773	2624	214	375		1061	782	919	1887	930	817	567	1763	1931	1253	652	2409	1834	878	1479	1366	2684	1437	2957	915	1297	1587	1043	1343	92	1086	1588	299	1632	1390	1383	371	2644	587	233	3052	1848	2845	630	1119	2322	2036	3020	3062	2997	1438	419	3130	517	1554
CHARLESTON, SC	1793	317	583	2157	466	1749	2520	1003	899	1061		468	204	1783	907	622	724	1109	1705	1204	879	1754	1110	721	703	1102	2371	900	2554	610	760	583	1003	1319	1145	543	783	713	1248	1290	379	685	2184	642	1101	2948	1824	2741	428	850	2218	1310	2483	2934	2973	434	1006	3106	539	1291
CHARLESTON, WV	1568	503	352	1755	578	1347	2182	741	431	782	468		265	1445	506	259	255	1072	1367	802	307	1727	1218	356	780	805	2147	731	2420	251	606	994	640	941	1022	386	1014	251	1070	953	790	454	2035	211	822	2610	1422	2603	227	575	2076	1605	2572	2624	2557	890	391	2775	346	953
CHARLOTTE, NC	1649	238	441	2012	389	1604	2375	861	695	919	204	265		1637	761	476	520	1071	1559	1057	675	1677	1041	575	625	956	2225	754	2453	464	614	730	857	1173	1003	397	713	631	1102	1144	525	543	2107	438	959	2802	1678	2595	289	704	2072	1241	2405	2759	2827	581	802	2960	397	1145
CHEYENNE, WY	538	1482	1665	455	1434	594	737	1961	1502	1887	1783	1445	1637		972	1233	1304	979	100	633	1241	801	1220	1115	1382	640	843	1076	1116	1197	1217	2147	1012	881	1799	1240	1502	1755	773	497	1926	1725	1004	1425	2059	1166	305	959	1760	892	436	1046	1179	1176	1234	1941	1468	1368	1659	613
CHICAGO, IL	1352	717	708	1246	667	838	1708	1003	545	930	907	506	761	972		302	346	936	1015	337	283	1543	1088	184	750	532	1768	662	2042	299	539	1382	96	410	837	474	935	797	807	474	1161	768	1809	467	1101	2137	913	1930	802	294	1466	1270	2105	2146	2062	1176	516	2196	701	728
CINCINNATI, OH	1409	476	521	1552		1144	1969	862	442	817	622	259	476	1233	302		253	958	1200	599	261	1605	1079	116	793	591	1955	632	2215	106	493	1141	398	714	815	281	820	636	920	576	1876	292	960	2398	1219	1191	130	1930	802	294	1667	1231	2304	2407	2368	935	484	2501	517	785
CLEVELAND, OH	1619	726	377	1597		1189	2040	654	197	567	724	255	520	1304	346	253		1208	1347	691	175	1809	1283	319	950	806	2100	882	2374	356	742	1251	463	760	581	531	1070	466	1073	806	1045	437	2085	136	751	2683	1481	1487	418	542	1990	1444	2411	2456	2389	1084	288	2518	346	1040
DALLAS, TX	754	792	1399	1433	647	1342	1711	1819	1393	1763	1109	1072	1071	979	936	958	1208		887	752	1218	647	241	913	406	534	1331	327	1446	852	466	1367	1019	999	1772	681	525	1589	209	646	1146	1501	1077	1246	1917	2140	1077	1933	1309	635	1410	271	1375	1827	2208	1161	1441	2342	1362	367
DENVER, CO	438	1403	1690	554	1356	693	833	2004	1546	1931	1705	1367	1559	100	1015	1200	1347	887		676	1284	701	1127	1088	1290	603	756	984	1029	1118	1116	2069	1055	924	1843	1162	1409	1799	681	541	1844	1744	904	1460	2102	1261	404	1054	1688	855	531	946	1092	1271	1329	1862	1512	1463	1686	521
DES MOINES, IA	1091	967	1031	1007		675	1369	1326	868	1253	1204	802	1057	633	337	599	691	752	676		606	1283	931	194	931	194	1429	567	1703	566	540	1411	361	246	1223	728	989	1191	726	135	1624	1176	1252	1106	1600	1807	622	1596	1194	349	1171	964	1755	1807	1822	1426	814	1969	1025	390
DETROIT, MI	1608	735	532	1534	734	1126	1977	741	277	652	879	401	675	1241	283	261	171	1218	1284	606		1799	1338	318	960	751	2037	891	2310	366	752	1401	380	697	564	541	1079	622	1062	743	1180	592	2074	292	838	2605	1398	1470	541	549	1675	1490	2373	2415	2350	1194	233	2483	526	984
EL PASO, TX	263	1437	2045	1255	1292	1597	1206	2465	2039	2409	1754	1718	1677	801	1543	1605	1854	647	701	1283	1799		758	1489	1051	1085	717	974	801	1499	1112	1959	1617	1530	2363	1328	1318	2235	737	1236	1747	2147	432	1893	2767	1505	1315	1955	1242	864	556	730	1181	1434	1910	2013	2087	2008	898
HOUSTON, TX	994	800	1470	1673	675	1582	1952	1890	1513	1834	1110	1218	1041	1220	1088	1079	1283	241	1127	931	1338	758		1033	445	795	1474	447	1598	972	586	1201	1220	1180	980	772	356	1610	449	901	1066	1550	1176	1418	2038	2349	1286	1988	1381	771	1426	199	1479	1938	2449	995	1561	2583	1433	608
INDIANAPOLIS, IN	1298	531	600	1432	481	1024	1852	940	508	878	721	356	575	1115	184	116	319	913	1088	194	318	1489	1033		675	485	1843	587	2104	112	464	1196	279	596	872	287	826	715	752	618	975	655	1764	370	1038	2280	1101	2073	641	239	1549	1186	2122	2290	2249	990	541	2383	596	674
JACKSON, MS	1157	386	1032	1836	241	1548	2115	1453	1134	1479	703	816	625	1382	750	793	950	406	1290	931	960	1051	445	675		747	1735	269	1851	574	211	915	835	1151	1514	423	181	1253	612	935	694	1135	1342	1088	1550	2544	1458	2337	916	548	1880	544	2369	2232	2612	719	1286	2746	996	771
KANSAS CITY, MO	894	801	1087	1088	753	801	1376	1427	995	1366	1102	764	956	640	532	597	806	534	603	194	751	1085	795	485	747		1358	382	1632	516	536	1466	573	441	1359	559	932	1202	348	188	1245	1141	1360	857	1525	1805	510	1598	1085	252	1176	812	1695	1814	1872	1259	1028	2007	1003	192
LAS VEGAS, NV	578	2067	2445	965	1852	1378	760	2757	2299	2684	2371	2122	2225	843	1768	1955	2037	1331	756	1429	2037	717	1474	1843	1735	1358		1478	274	1874	1611	2733	1808	1677	2596	1826	1854	2552	1124	1242	2512	2500	285	2215	2855	1188	1035	442	2444	1610	417	1272	337	575	1256	2526	2265	1390	2441	1276
LITTLE ROCK, AR	900	528	1072	1530	381	1378	1808	1493	1066	1437	900	745	754	1076	662	632	882	327	984	567	891	974	447	587	269	382	1478		1706	526	140	1197	653	871	1355	570	969	1175	347	560	969	1125	1349	967	1635	2312	705	2105	1012	355	1340	551	2012	2305	984	1115	2439	1516	293
LOS ANGELES, CA	806	2237	2705	1241	2092	1702	1033	3046	2572	2957	2554	2374	2453	1116	2042	2215	2374	1446	1029	1703	2310	801	1558	2104	1851	1632	274	1706		1979	1884	2739	2081	1951	2869	2054	1917	2820	1352	1509	2682	2856	369	2476	3144	971	1309	519	2721	1856	691	1356	124	385	1148	2553	2538	1291	2702	1513
LOUISVILLE, KY	1320	419	602	1547	369	1139	1933	964	545	915	610	251	464	1197	299	106	356	852	1118	566	366	1499	972	112	594	516	1874	526	1979		386	1084	394	711	920	175	714	774	863	678	1786	394	1062	2382	1247	2155	172	246	2372	2364	878	1697	596	705	
MEMPHIS, TN	1033	389	933	1625	241	1337	1954	1353	927	1297	760	606	614	1217	539	493	742	466	1116	540	752	1112	586	464	211	536	1611	140	1884	386		1051	624	940	1306	215	396	1123	487	724	830	1035	1500	887	1560	2382	1247	2155	172	246	1652	739	2144	2440	845	975	2574	896	597
MIAMI, FL	2155	661	1109	2554	812	2224	2883	1529	1425	1587	583	994	730	2147	1382	1141	1250	1367	2069	1632	1401	1959	1201	1196	915	1466	2733	1190	2759	1084	1051		1478	1794	1671	907	874	1299	1609	1654	232	1211	2390	1167	1627	3312	2176	3105	954	1214	2581	1401	2688	3140	3370	274	1532	3504	1065	1655
MILWAUKEE, WI	1426	813	805	1175	763	767	1448	1100	642	1027	1003	601	857	1012	96	398	463	1019	1055	361	380	1617	1220	279	835	573	1808	747	2082	394	624	1478		337	939	569	1007	893	416	560	1257	865	1892	563	1122	2160	936	1953	899	375	1489	1361	2128	2169	2085	1199	607	2219	799	769
MINNEAPOLIS, MN	1339	1129	1121	839	1079	431	1465	1417	958	1343	1319	918	1173	881	409	714	760	999	924	246	697	1530	1240	596	1151	441	1677	814	1951	711	940	1794	337		1255	886	1337	1211	793	383	1573	1181	1805	881	1515	1727	606	1839	1216	621	1315	1527	2014	2055	1654	1588	929	1788	1115	637
MONTRÉAL, QC	2172	1241	564	2093	1289	1685	2535	313	397	92	1145	822	1003	1799	841	815	588	1772	1843	1165	564	2363	1892	872	1514	1359	2596	1446	2869	920	1306	1671	939	1255		1094	1632	383	1625	1300	1446	454	2637	607	282	2963	1758	2756	714	1112	2232	2043	2931	2972	2907	1522	330	3041	600	1547
NASHVILLE, TN	1248	242	716	1684	194	1315	1976	1136	596	1088	543	386	397	1240	474	281	531	681	1162	725	541	1328	772	287	423	559	1826	355	2054	175	215	907	569	886	1094		539	906	703	747	686	818	1745	554	1056	2360	2463	701	764	2947	1908	2813	1302	2865	1106	890	
NEW ORLEANS, LA	1276	473	1142	1955	351	1734	2234	1563	1254	1588	783	926	713	1502	935	820	1070	525	1409	1117	1079	1118	360	826	181	932	1854	455	1917	714	396	874	1007	1337	1632	539		1332	731	1011	1225	1548	1108	1660	2663	1643	2431	1002	690	1932	560	1846	2298	2311	668	1302	2865	1106	890
NEW YORK, NY	2015	869	192	2049		859	1431	2491	995	1641	2491	215	299	773	515	631	1755	797	636	1589	1991	672	1221	1287	757	449	752	612	348	131	915	835	1151	378	1469		1469	1260	1094	91	2481	367	313	2920	176	213	2920	1716	1716	2713	346	875	2089	2788	2903	2903	1074	503	3023	228	1350
OKLAHOMA CITY, OK	546	944	1354	1227	729	1136	1506	1694	1262	1632	1248	1022	1102	773	807	863	1073	209	681	546	1062	737	449	752	612	348	1271	347	1352	774	487	1609	880	793	1625	703	731	1469		463	1094	1619	1320	871	1727	1331	505	1204	466	1370	1657	2002	1403	1295	1295	1350	161
OMAHA, NE	973	989	1168	904	941	616	1234	1463	1005	1390	1290	952	1144	497	474	736	806	646	541	135	743	1236	910	618	935	188	1290	570	1567	707	724	1654	514	383	1300	747	1121	1258	463		1440	928	1561	1662	525	1653	440	592	927	1630	1672	1979	1448	971	1853	1162	307
ORLANDO, FL	1934	440	904	2348	606	2018	2662	1324	1283	1383	379	790	525	1926	1161	920	1045	1146	1844	1411	1180	1747	901	975	694	1245	2512	969	2558	863	830	232	1257	1573	1446	686	1011	1094	1388	1440		1006	2169	945	1406	3091	1955	2884	750	993	2360	1327	3283	860	1434
PHILADELPHIA, PA	1954	782	104	2019	897	1611	2462	321	414	371	685	454	543	1725	768	576	437	1501	1744	1091	592	2147	1572	655	1135	1141	2500	1175	2760	678	1035	1211	865	1181	454	818	1245	91	1408	1220	1006		2420	306	419	2890	2683	254	895	2160	1774	2779	2900	2835	1062	527	2968	140	1331
PHOENIX, AZ	466	1868	2366	1199	1723	1662	993	2706	2274	2644	2184	2035	2107	1004	1819	1876	2085	1077	904	1558	2074	432	1188	1764	1482	1360	285	1367	369	1786	1500	2390	1892	1805	2637	1715	1548	2481	1012	1440	2420	2136		1838	2804	1535	1008	883	2343	1517	651	987	376	750	1513	2184	2307	1655	2362	1173
PITTSBURGH, PA	1670	676	246	1779	763	1311	2161	592	217	587	642	211	438	1425	467	130	136	1246	1404	622	292	1893	1418	370	1342	857	2215	920	2476	369	887	1167	563	881	607	569	1108	367	1124	928	963	306	1838		609	2588	1384	1377	372	602	1923	1459	2390	2445	2370	1155	295	2572	240	995
PORTLAND, ME	2338	1197	520	2552	1312	1944	2795	107	560	233	1101	839	959	2059	1101	960	751	1917	2102	1424	838	2563	1988	1038	1550	1525	2855	1591	3144	1062	1451	1627	1198	1515	419	1234	1660	313	1790	1569	1406	419	2804	609		3223	2019	3016	670	1279	2493	2189	3162	3233	3168	1478	668	3301	556	1714
PORTLAND, OR	1395	2647	2830	889	2599	1301	430	3126	2667	3052	2948	2610	2802	1166	2137	2398	2469	2140	1261	1798	2405	1767	2381	2280	2544	1805	1188	2237	971	2362	3312	2063	1883	2963	1757	1908	2663	2920	1935	1663	3091	2890	1408	2890	3223		1262	575	2838	2057	778	2322	1093	1018	642	173	2824	2527	1718	2624	1785
RAPID CITY, SD	841	1511	1626	379	1463	320	930	1921	1463	1848	1824	1422	1678	305	913	1191	1481	1077	404	349	1398	1505	1286	1101	1458	510	1035	705	1309	878	1247	2176	936	621	1758	1255	1643	1716	871	525	1955	1686	1008	1377	2019	1262		963	628	1398	1190	195	1530	1483	1193	1195	2068	1595	1483	1786	712
RENO, NV	1020	2440	2623	960	2392	1372	342	2919	2460	2845	2741	2403	2595	959	1930	1191	1487	1933	1054	1596	1470	1955	1988	2073	2369	1598	442	2030	519	2155	2176	3105	1953	1970	2756	2198	2431	2713	1727	1455	2884	2683	883	2383	3016	578	1151		2718	1850	524	1870	642	217	755	2899	2426	898	2617	1568
RICHMOND, VA	1876	527	152	2053	1611	1662	1311	572	485	630	428	227	289	1760	802	802	418	1309	1688	1511	541	1242	1381	641	916	1085	2444	1012	2724	489	972	232	899	1216	714	764	1071	307	1727	931	750	254	2343	372	670	2838	1635	2718		834	2136	1708	2760	2875	2810	895	534	2943	108	1274
ST. LOUIS, MO	1051	549	841	1341	501	1053	1426	1181	485	1119	850	512	704	892	294	359	542	630	855	349	549	1242	771	239	505	252	1610	355	1856	264	290	1214	367	621	1112	307	690	956	505	440	993	895	1517	611	1279	2057	1483	2050	963	1360	1483	928	1838	1195	1195	1008	782	2259	837	441
SALT LAKE CITY, UT	624	1916	2100	548	1868	960	342	2395	1936	2322	2190	2076	2072	436	1466	1667	1990	1410	531	1171	1675	864	1426	1549	1880	1176	419	1340	691	878	1652	2581	1489	1315	2232	1908	1932	2481	1204	927	2360	2160	651	1923	2493	778	195	524	2136	928		1419	754	740	833	1902	1513	910	2057	1634
SAN ANTONIO, TX	818	1000	1671	1500	878	1599	1761	2092	1665	2036	1310	1605	1241	1046	1270	1231	1444	271	946	1009	1490	556	199	1186	644	812	1272	600	1356	1247	739	1401	1341	1527	2043	954	560	1861	466	927	1327	1774	987	1459	3162	2322	1530	1870	740	1419		1285	1737	2105	2195	1267	1634	2648	1669	843
SAN DIEGO, CA	825	2166	2724	1302	2021	1765	1096	3065	2632	3020	2483	2393	2405	1179	2105	2304	2407	1375	946	1755	2373	730	1479	2122	2369	1812	337	2012	124	596	2144	2688	2128	2014	2972	2865	2360	2788	1295	1653	2824	2900	376	2445	3233	1093	1195	755	2875	1195	740	1285		508	1275	2495	2601	1414	2740	1531
SAN FRANCISCO, CA	1111	2618	2840	1176	2512	1749	646	3135	2677	3062	2934	2624	2759	1176	2146	2407	2456	1827	1092	1755	2415	1181	1938	2290	2232	1872	575	2305	385	705	2440	3140	2169	2055	2972	2865	2298	2788	1350	1853	3283	2900	750	2445	3233	642	1193	217	2810	1275	833	2195	508		808	2734	2617	1050	2769	1784
SEATTLE, WA	1463	2705	2775	816	2657	1229	507	3070	2622	2997	2973	2557	2827	1234	1176	2368	2456	2208	1271	1807	2350	1910	2449	2249	2612	1259	1256	2305	1148	705	845	3370	1199	1588	2907	1106	2311	2903	1295	1853	860	2835	1513	2370	3168	173	1595	755	2810	1008	740	1267	2495	808		3164	2577	140	2769	1843
TAMPA, FL	1949	455	960	2348	606	2018	2677	1380	1276	1438	434	845	581	1941	1176	935	1101	1161	1862	1426	1194	1753	995	990	709	1259	2526	984	2553	878	845	274	1199	1588	1522	701	668	1074	1403	1448	82	1062	2184	1155	1478	1595	1050	2899	895	782	1902	1267	2495	2734	3164		1528	3297	916	1448
TORONTO, ON	1841	958	565	2791		1354	2395	570	106	419	1006	391	802	1468	516	484	288	1441	1512	814	233	2013	1561	541	1286	1028	2265	1516	2538	596	896	1532	607	929	330	890	1302	503	1295	971	1327	527	2307	295	668	2527	1595	2426	534	837	1513	1634	2601	2617	2577	1528		2711	563	1253
VANCOUVER, BC	1597	2838	2908	758	2791	1362	633	3204	2745	3130	3106	2775	2960	1368	2196	2501	2518	2342	1463	1969	2483	2087	2583	2383	2746	2007	1390	2439	1291	705	2574	3504	2219	1788	3041	1106	2865	3023	1350	1853	3283	2968	2362	2572	3301	2624	1786	898	2943	2259	2057	2648	2740	2769	140	3297	2711		2902	1977
WASHINGTON, DC	1896	636	38	1953	758	1545	2395	458	384	517	539	346	397	1659	701	517	346	1362	1686	1025	526	2008	1433	596	996	1083	2441	1036	2702	596	896	1065	799	1115	600	679	1106	228	1350	1162	860	140	2362	240	556	2824	1620	2617	108	837	2057	1669	2740	2769	2769	916	563	2902		1270
WICHITA, KS	707	989	1276	838	934	934	456	1616	1184	1554	1291	953	1145	613	728	785	1040	367	521	390	984	898	608	674	771	192	1276	293	1513	705	597	1655	769	637	1547	890	890	1350	161	307	1434	1331	1173	995	1714	1785	712	1568	1274	441	1634	843	1531	1784	1843	1448	1253	1977	1270	

A Word to Our Readers

Travelers are on the roads in great numbers these days. They're exploring the country on day trips, weekend getaways, business trips, and extended family vacations, visiting major cities and small towns along the way. Because time is precious and the travel industry is ever-changing, having accurate, reliable travel information at your fingertips is critical. Mobil Travel Guide has been providing invaluable insight to travelers for more than 45 years, and we are committed to continuing this service well into the future.

The Mobil Corporation (known as Exxon Mobil Corporation since a 1999 merger) began producing the Mobil Travel Guide books in 1958, following the introduction of the US interstate highway system in 1956. The first edition covered only five Southwestern states. Since then, our books have become the premier travel guides in North America, covering all 50 states and Canada.

Since its founding, Mobil Travel Guide has served as an advocate for travelers seeking knowledge about hotels, restaurants, and places to visit. Based on an objective process, we make recommendations to our customers that we believe will enhance the quality and value of their travel experiences. Our trusted Mobil One- to Five-Star rating system is the oldest and most respected lodging and restaurant inspection and rating program in North America. Most hoteliers, restaurateurs, and industry observers favorably regard the rigor of our inspection program and understand the prestige and benefits that come with receiving a Mobil Star rating.

The Mobil Travel Guide process of rating each establishment includes:

☉ Unannounced facility inspections

☉ Incognito service evaluations for Mobil Four-Star and Mobil Five-Star properties

☉ A review of unsolicited comments from the general public

☉ Senior management oversight

For each property, more than 450 attributes, including cleanliness, physical facilities, and employee attitude and courtesy, are measured and evaluated to produce a mathematically derived score, which is then blended with the other elements to form an overall score. These quantifiable scores allow comparative analysis among properties and form the basis that we use to assign our Mobil One- to Five-Star ratings.

This process focuses largely on guest expectations, guest experience, and consistency of service, not just physical facilities and amenities. It is fundamentally a relative rating system that rewards those properties that continually strive for and achieve excellence each year. Indeed, the very best properties are consistently raising the bar for those that wish to compete with them. These properties proactively respond to consumers' needs even in today's uncertain times.

Only facilities that meet Mobil Travel Guide's standards earn the privilege of being listed in the guide. Deteriorating, poorly managed establishments are deleted. A Mobil Travel Guide listing constitutes a positive quality recommendation; every listing is an accolade, a recognition of achievement. Our Mobil One- to Five-Star rating system highlights its level of service. Extensive in-house research is constantly underway to determine new additions to our lists.

☉ The Mobil Five-Star Award indicates that a property is one of the very best in the country and consistently provides gracious and courteous service, superlative quality in its facility, and a unique ambience. The lodgings and restaurants at the Mobil Five-Star level consistently and proactively respond to consumers' needs and continue their commitment to excellence, doing so with grace and perseverance.

☉ Also highly regarded is the Mobil Four-Star Award, which honors properties for outstanding achievement in overall facility and for providing very strong service levels in all areas. These

Make every tankful count for college.

You need gas. So why not save for college every time you do? ExxonMobil is working with Upromise to help you save for college. You can join for FREE at upromise.com/xom17 and register your check card or credit card. Then every time you buy gas at an Exxon or Mobil location with the card registered with Upromise, ExxonMobil will contribute toward your child's college education. And be sure

to link that same card to your *Speedpass.*™ That way, all your Speedpass gasoline purchases can contribute to your Upromise account. If you don't have a Speedpass device, you can get one, free. Just go to speedpass.com or call toll free 1-87-SPEEDPASS (1-877-733-3727). Upromise is an easy way to help you save for your child's education. How do we know you'd like to make every tankful count? We're drivers too.

We're drivers too.

Welcome

Dear Traveler,

Since its inception in 1958, Mobil Travel Guide has served as a trusted advisor to auto travelers in s value in lodging, dining, and destinations. Now in its 47th year, the Mobil Travel Guide is the hallma our ExxonMobil family of travel publications, and we're proud to offer an array of products and servi from our Mobil, Exxon, and Esso brands in North America to facilitate life on the road.

Whether you're looking for business or pleasure venues, our nationwide network of independent, profes-sional evaluators offers their expertise on thousands of travel options, allowing you to plan a quick family getaway, a full-service business meeting, or an unforgettable Mobil Five-Star celebration.

Your feedback is important to us as we strive to improve our product offerings and better meet today's travel needs. Whether you travel once a week or once a year, please take the time to contact us at www.mobiltravelguide.com. We hope to hear from you soon.

Best wishes for safe and enjoyable travels.

Lee R Raymond

Lee R. Raymond
Chairman and CEO
Exxon Mobil Corporation

award winners provide a distinctive experience for the ever-demanding and sophisticated consumer.

- The Mobil Three-Star Award recognizes an excellent property that provides full services and amenities. This category ranges from exceptional hotels with limited services to elegant restaurants with a less-formal atmosphere.

- A Mobil Two-Star property is a clean and comfortable establishment that has expanded amenities or a distinctive environment. A Mobil Two-Star property is an excellent place to stay or dine.

- A Mobil One-Star property is limited in its amenities and services but focuses on providing a value experience while meeting travelers' expectations. The property can be expected to be clean, comfortable, and convenient.

Allow us to emphasize that we do not charge establishments for inclusion in our guides. We have no relationship with any of the businesses and attractions we list and act only as a consumer advocate. In essence, we do the investigative legwork so that you won't have to.

Keep in mind, too, that the hospitality business is ever-changing. Restaurants and lodgings—particularly small chains and stand-alone establishments—change management or even go out of business with surprising quickness. Although we make every effort to double-check information during our annual updates, we nevertheless recommend that you call ahead to make sure the place you've selected is still open and offers all the amenities you're looking for. We've provided phone numbers; when available, we also list fax numbers and Web site addresses.

We hope that your travels are enjoyable and relaxing and that our books help you get the most out of every trip you take. If any aspect of your accommodation, dining, or sightseeing experience motivates you to comment, please drop us a line. We depend a great deal on our readers' remarks, so you can be assured that we will read your comments and assimilate them into our research. General comments about our books are also welcome. You can write to us at Mobil Travel Guide, 1460 Renaissance Drive, Suite 401, Park Ridge, IL 60068, or send an e-mail to info@mobiltravelguide.com.

Take your Mobil Travel Guide books along on every trip you take. We're confident that you'll be pleased with their convenience, ease of use, and breadth of dependable coverage.

Happy travels!

How to Use This Book

The Mobil Travel Guide Regional Travel Planners are designed for ease of use. Each state has its own chapter, beginning with a general introduction that provides a geographical and historical orientation to the state and gives basic statewide tourist information, from climate to calendar highlights to seatbelt laws. The remainder of each chapter is devoted to travel destinations within the state—mainly cities and towns, but also national parks and tourist areas—which, like the states, are arranged in alphabetical order.

The following sections explain the wealth of information you'll find about those travel destinations: information about the area, things to see and do there, and where to stay and eat.

Maps and Map Coordinates

At the front of this book in the full-color section, we have provided state maps as well as maps of selected larger cities to help you find your way around once you leave the highway. You'll find a key to the map symbols on the Contents page at the beginning of the map section.

Next to most cities and towns throughout the book, you'll find a set of map coordinates, such as C-2. These coordinates reference the maps at the front of this book and help you find the location you're looking for quickly and easily.

Destination Information

Because many travel destinations are close to other cities and towns where travelers might find additional attractions, accommodations, and restaurants, we've included cross-references to those cities and towns when it makes sense to do so. We also list addresses, phone numbers, and Web sites for travel information resources—usually the local chamber of commerce or office of tourism—as well as pertinent statistics and, in many cases, a brief introduction to the area.

Information about airports, ground transportation, and suburbs is included for large cities.

Driving Tours and Walking Tours

The driving tours that we include for many states are usually day trips that make for interesting side excursions, although they can be longer. They offer you a way to get off the beaten path and visit an area that travelers often overlook. These trips frequently cover areas of natural beauty or historical significance.

Each walking tour focuses on a particularly interesting area of a city or town. Again, these tours can provide a break from everyday tourist attractions. The tours often include places to stop for meals or snacks.

What to See and Do

Mobil Travel Guide offers information about nearly 20,000 museums, art galleries, amusement parks, historic sites, national and state parks, ski areas, and many other types of attractions. A white star on a black background ★ signals that the attraction is a must-see—one of the best in the area. Because municipal parks, public tennis courts, swimming pools, and small educational institutions are common to most towns, they generally are not mentioned.

Following an attraction's description, you'll find the months, days, and, in some cases, hours of operation; the address/directions, telephone number, and Web site (if there is one); and the admission price category. The following are the ranges we use for admission fees, based on one adult:

✿ **FREE**

✿ **$** = Up to $5

✿ **$$** = $5.01-$10

✿ **$$$** = $10.01-$15

✿ **$$$$** = Over $15

Special Events

Special events are either annual events that last only a short time, such as festivals and fairs, or longer, seasonal events such as horse racing, theater, and summer concerts. Our Special Events listings also include infrequently occurring occasions that mark certain dates or events, such as a centennial or other commemorative celebration.

Side Trips

We recognize that your travels don't always end where state lines fall, so we've included some side trips that fall outside the states covered in this book but that travelers frequently visit when they're in the region. Nearby national parks, major cities, and other prime tourist draws fall into this category. You'll find side trips for a particular state at the end of that state's section.

Listings

Lodgings, spas, and restaurants are usually listed under the city or town in which they're located. Make sure to check the related cities and towns that appear right beneath a city's heading for additional options, especially if you're traveling to a major metropolitan area that includes many suburbs. If a property is located in a town that doesn't have its own heading, the listing appears under the town nearest it, with the address and town given immediately after the establishment's name. In large cities, lodgings located within 5 miles of major commercial airports may be listed under a separate "Airport Area" heading that follows the city section.

LODGINGS

Travelers have different wants and needs when it comes to accommodations. To help you pinpoint properties that meet your particular needs, Mobil Travel Guide classifies each lodging by type according to the following characteristics.

Mobil Rated Lodgings

○ **Limited-Service Hotel.** A limited-service hotel is traditionally a Mobil One-Star or Mobil Two-Star property. At a Mobil One-Star hotel, guests can expect to find a clean, comfortable property that commonly serves a complimentary continental breakfast. A Mobil Two-Star hotel is also clean and comfortable but has expanded amenities, such as a full-service restaurant, business

center, and fitness center. These services may have limited staffing and/or restricted hours of use.

○ **Full-Service Hotel.** A full-service hotel traditionally enjoys a Mobil Three-Star, Mobil Four-Star, or Mobil Five-Star rating. Guests can expect these hotels to offer at least one full-service restaurant in addition to amenities such as valet parking, luggage assistance, 24-hour room service, concierge service, laundry and/or dry-cleaning services, and turndown service.

○ **Full-Service Resort.** A resort is traditionally a full-service hotel that is geared toward recreation and represents a vacation and holiday destination. A resort's guest rooms are typically furnished to accommodate longer stays. The property may offer a full-service spa, golf, tennis, and fitness facilities or other leisure activities. Resorts are expected to offer a full-service restaurant and expanded amenities, such as luggage assistance, room service, meal plans, concierge service, and turndown service.

○ **Full-Service Inn.** An inn is traditionally a Mobil Three-Star, Mobil Four-Star, or Mobil Five-Star property. Inns are similar to bed-and-breakfasts (see below) but offer a wider range of services, most significantly a full-service restaurant that serves at least breakfast and dinner.

Specialty Lodgings

Mobil Travel Guide recognizes the unique and individualized nature of many different types of lodging establishments, including bed-and-breakfasts, limited-service inns, and guest ranches. For that reason, we have chosen to place our stamp of approval on the properties that fall into these two categories in lieu of applying our traditional Mobil Star ratings.

○ **B&B/Limited-Service Inn.** A bed-and-breakfast (B&B) or limited-service inn is traditionally an owner-occupied home or residence found in a residential area or vacation destination. It may be a structure of historic significance. Rooms are often individually decorated, but telephones, televisions, and private bathrooms may not be available in every room. A B&B typically serves only breakfast to its overnight guests, which is included in the room rate. Cocktails and refreshments may be served in the late afternoon or evening.

✪ **Guest Ranch.** A guest ranch is traditionally a rustic, Western-themed property that specializes in stays of three or more days. Horseback riding is often a feature, with stables and trails found on the property. Facilities can range from clean, comfortable establishments to more luxurious facilities.

Mobil Star Rating Definitions for Lodgings

✪ ★ ★ ★ ★ ★ : A Mobil Five-Star lodging provides consistently superlative service in an exceptionally distinctive luxury environment, with expanded services. Attention to detail is evident throughout the hotel, resort, or inn, from bed linens to staff uniforms.

✪ ★ ★ ★ ★ : A Mobil Four-Star lodging provides a luxury experience with expanded amenities in a distinctive environment. Services may include, but are not limited to, automatic turndown service, 24-hour room service, and valet parking.

✪ ★ ★ ★ : A Mobil Three-Star lodging is well appointed, with a full-service restaurant and expanded amenities, such as a fitness center, golf course, tennis courts, 24-hour room service, and optional turndown service.

✪ ★ ★ : A Mobil Two-Star lodging is considered a clean, comfortable, and reliable establishment that has expanded amenities, such as a full-service restaurant on the premises.

✪ ★ : A Mobil One-Star lodging is a limited-service hotel, motel, or inn that is considered a clean, comfortable, and reliable establishment.

Information Found in the Lodging Listings

Each lodging listing gives the name, address/location (when no street address is available), neighborhood and/or directions from downtown (in major cities), phone number(s), fax number, total number of guest rooms, and seasons open (if not year-round). Also included are details on business, luxury, recreational, and dining facilities at the property or nearby. A key to the symbols at the end of each listing can be found on the page following the "A Word to Our Readers" section.

For every property, we also provide pricing information. Because lodging rates change frequently, we list a pricing category rather than specific prices. The pricing categories break down as follows:

✪ **$** = Up to $150

✪ **$$** = $151-$250

✪ **$$$** = $251-$350

✪ **$$$$** = $351 and up

All prices quoted are in effect at the time of publication; however, prices cannot be guaranteed. In some locations, short-term price variations may exist because of special events, holidays, or seasonality. Certain resorts have complicated rate structures that vary with the time of year; always confirm rates when making your plans.

Because most lodgings offer the following features and services, information about them does not appear in the listings:

✪ Year-round operation

✪ Bathroom with tub and/or shower in each room

✪ Cable television in each room

✪ In-room telephones

✪ Cots and cribs available

✪ Daily maid service

✪ Elevators

✪ Major credit cards accepted

🔍 Although we recommend every lodging we list in this book, a few stand out—they offer noteworthy amenities or stand above the others in their category in terms of quality, value, or historical significance. To draw your attention to these special spots, we've included the magnifying glass icon to the left of the listing, as you see here.

SPAS

Mobil Travel Guide is pleased to announce its newest category: hotel and resort spas. Until now, hotel and resort spas have not been formally rated or inspected by any organization. Every spa selected for inclusion in this book underwent a rigorous inspection process similar to the one Mobil Travel Guide has been applying to lodgings and restaurants for more than four decades. After spending a year and a half researching more than 300 spas and performing exhaustive incognito inspections of more than 200 properties, we narrowed our list to the 48 best spas in the United States and Canada.

Mobil Travel Guide's spa ratings are based on objective evaluations of more than 450 attributes. Approximately half of these criteria assess basic expectations, such as staff courtesy, the technical proficiency and skill of the employees, and whether the facility is maintained properly and hygienically. Several standards address issues that impact a guest's physical comfort and convenience, as well as the staff's ability to impart a sense of personalized service and anticipate clients' needs. Additional criteria measure the spa's ability to create a completely calming ambience.

The Mobil Star ratings focus on much more than the facilities available at a spa and the treatments it offers. Each Mobil Star rating is a cumulative score achieved from multiple inspections that reflects the spa management's attention to detail and commitment to consumers' needs.

Mobil Star Rating Definitions for Spas

✪ ★ ★ ★ ★ ★ : A Mobil Five-Star spa provides consistently superlative service in an exceptionally distinctive luxury environment with extensive amenities. The staff at a Mobil Five-Star spa provides extraordinary service above and beyond the traditional spa experience, allowing guests to achieve the highest level of relaxation and pampering. A Mobil Five-Star spa offers an extensive array of treatments, often incorporating international themes and products. Attention to detail is evident throughout the spa, from arrival to departure.

✪ ★ ★ ★ ★ : A Mobil Four-Star spa provides a luxurious experience with expanded amenities in an elegant and serene environment. Throughout the spa facility, guests experience personalized service. Amenities might include, but are not limited to, single-sex relaxation rooms where guests wait for their treatments, plunge pools and whirlpools in both men's and women's locker rooms, and an array of treatments, including at a minimum a selection of massages, body therapies, facials, and a variety of salon services.

✪ ★ ★ ★ : A Mobil Three-Star spa is physically well appointed and has a full complement of staff to ensure that guests' needs are met. It has some expanded amenities, such as, but not limited to, a well-equipped fitness center, separate men's and women's locker rooms, a sauna or steam room, and a designated relaxation area. It also offers a menu of services that at a minimum includes massages, facial treatments, and at least one other type of body treatment, such as scrubs or wraps.

RESTAURANTS

All Mobil Star rated dining establishments listed in this book have a full kitchen and offer seating at tables; most offer table service.

Mobil Star Rating Definitions for Restaurants

✪ ★ ★ ★ ★ ★ : A Mobil Five-Star restaurant offers one of few flawless dining experiences in the country. These establishments consistently provide their guests with exceptional food, superlative service, elegant décor, and exquisite presentations of each detail surrounding a meal.

✪ ★ ★ ★ ★ : A Mobil Four-Star restaurant provides professional service, distinctive presentations, and wonderful food.

✪ ★ ★ ★ : A Mobil Three-Star restaurant has good food, warm and skillful service, and enjoyable décor.

✪ ★ ★ : A Mobil Two-Star restaurant serves fresh food in a clean setting with efficient service. Value is considered in this category, as is family friendliness.

✪ ★ : A Mobil One-Star restaurant provides a distinctive experience through culinary specialty, local flair, or individual atmosphere.

Information Found in the Restaurant Listings

Each restaurant listing gives the cuisine type, street address (or directions if no address is available), phone and fax numbers, Web site (if available), meals served, days of operation (if not open daily year-round), and pricing category. Information about appropriate attire is provided, although it's always a good idea to call ahead and ask if you're unsure; the meaning of "casual" or "business casual" varies widely in different parts of the country. We also indicate whether the restaurant has a bar, whether a children's menu is offered, and whether outdoor seating is available. If reservations are recommended, we note that fact in the listing. When valet parking is available, it is noted in the description. In many cases, self-parking is available at the restaurant or nearby.

Because menu prices can fluctuate, we list a pricing category rather than specific prices. The pricing categories are defined as follows, per diner, and assume that you order an appetizer or dessert, an entrée, and one drink:

☺ **$** = $15 and under

☺ **$$** = $16-$35

☺ **$$$** = $36-$85

☺ **$$$$** = $86 and up

Again, all prices quoted are in effect at the time of publication, but prices cannot be guaranteed.

Although we recommend every restaurant we list in this book, a few stand out—they offer noteworthy local specialties or stand above the others in their category in terms of quality, value, or experience. To draw your attention to these special spots, we've included the magnifying glass icon to the left of the listing, as you see here.

SPECIAL INFORMATION FOR TRAVELERS WITH DISABILITIES

The Mobil Travel Guide ▣ symbol indicates that an establishment is not at least partially accessible to people with mobility problems. When the ▣ symbol follows a listing, the establishment is not equipped with facilities to accommodate people using wheelchairs or crutches or otherwise needing easy access to doorways and rest rooms. Travelers with severe mobility problems or with hearing or visual impairments may or may not find the facilities they need. Always phone ahead to make sure that an establishment can meet your needs.

AMERICA'S BYWAYS™

Mobil Travel Guide is pleased to announce a new partnership with the National Scenic Byways Program. Under this program, the US Secretary of Transportation recognizes certain roads as National Scenic Byways or All-American Roads based on their archaeological, cultural, historic, natural, recreational, and scenic qualities. To be designated a National Scenic Byway, a road must possess at least one of these six intrinsic qualities. To receive an All-American Road designation, a road must possess multiple intrinsic qualities that are nationally significant and contain one-of-a-kind features that do not exist elsewhere. The road or highway also must be considered a destination unto itself.

America's Byways are a great way to explore the country. From the mighty Mississippi to the towering Rockies to the Historic National Road, these routes take you past America's most treasured scenery and enable you to get in touch with America's past, present, and future. Bringing together all the nationally designated Byways in the Northwest, this bonus section of the book is a handy reference whether you're planning to hop in the car tomorrow or you're simply looking for inspiration for future trips. Look for it at the end of the front section, before page 1.

Understanding the Symbols

What to See and Do

⭐ = One of the top attractions in the area

$ = Up to $5

$$ = $5.01 to $10

$$$ = $10.01 to $15

$$$$ = Over $15

Lodgings

$ = Up to $150

$$ = $151 to $250

$$$ = $251 to $350

$$$$ = Over $350

Restaurants

$ = Up to $15

$$ = $16 to $35

$$$ = $36 to $85

$$$$ = Over $85

Lodging Star Definitions

★ ★ ★ ★ ★ A Mobil Five-Star lodging establishment provides consistently superlative service in an exceptionally distinctive luxury environment with expanded services. Attention to detail is evident throughout the hotel/resort/inn from the bed linens to the staff uniforms.

★ ★ ★ ★ A Mobil Four-Star lodging establishment is a hotel/resort/inn that provides a luxury experience with expanded amenities in a distinctive environment. Services may include, but are not limited to, automatic turndown service, 24-hour room service, and valet parking.

★ ★ ★ A Mobil Three-Star lodging establishment is a hotel/resort/inn that is well appointed, with a full-service restaurant and expanded amenities, such as, but not limited to, a fitness center, golf course, tennis courts, 24-hour room service, and optional turndown service.

★ ★ A Mobil Two-Star lodging establishment is a hotel/resort/inn that is considered a clean, comfortable, and reliable establishment, but also has expanded amenities, such as a full-service restaurant on the premises.

★ A Mobil One-Star lodging establishment is a limited-service hotel or inn that is considered a clean, comfortable, and reliable establishment.

Restaurant Star Definitions

★ ★ ★ ★ ★ A Mobil Five-Star restaurant is one of few flawless dining experiences in the country. These restaurants consistently provide their guests with exceptional food, superlative service, elegant décor, and exquisite presentations of each detail surrounding the meal.

★ ★ ★ ★ A Mobil Four-Star restaurant provides professional service, distinctive presentations, and wonderful food.

★ ★ ★ A Mobil Three-Star restaurant has good food, warm and skillful service, and enjoyable décor.

★ ★ A Mobil Two-Star restaurant serves fresh food in a clean setting with efficient service. Value is considered in this category, as is family friendliness.

★ A Mobil One-Star restaurant provides a distinctive experience through culinary specialty, local flair, or individual atmosphere.

Symbols at End of Listings

🔲 Facilities for people with disabilities not available

🐾 Pets allowed

⛷ Ski in/ski out access

⛳ Golf on premises

🎾 Tennis court(s) on premises

🏊 Indoor or outdoor pool

🏋 Fitness room

✈ Major commercial airport within 5 miles

🏃 Business center

Making the Most of Your Trip

A few hardy souls might look back with fondness on a trip during which the car broke down, leaving them stranded for three days, or a vacation that cost twice what it was supposed to. For most travelers, though, the best trips are those that are safe, smooth, and within budget. To help you make your trip the best it can be, we've assembled a few tips and resources.

Saving Money

ON LODGING

Many hotels and motels offer discounts—for senior citizens, business travelers, families, you name it. It never hurts to ask—politely, that is. Sometimes, especially in the late afternoon, desk clerks are instructed to fill beds, and you might be offered a lower rate or a nicer room to entice you to stay. Simply ask the reservation agent for the best rate available. Also, make sure to try both the toll-free number and the local number. You may be able to get a lower rate from one than from the other.

Timing your trip right can cut your lodging costs as well. Look for bargains on stays over multiple nights, in the off-season, and on weekdays or weekends, depending on the location. Many hotels in major metropolitan areas, for example, have special weekend packages that offer leisure travelers considerable savings on rooms; they may include breakfast, cocktails, and/or dinner discounts.

Another way to save money is to choose accommodations that give you more than just a standard room. Rooms with kitchen facilities enable you to cook some meals yourself, reducing your restaurant costs. A suite might save money for two couples traveling together. Even hotel luxury levels can provide good value, as many include breakfast or cocktails in the price of a room.

State and city taxes, as well as special room taxes, can increase your room rate by as much as 25 percent per day. We are unable to include information about taxes in our listings, but we strongly urge you to ask about taxes when making reservations so that you understand the total cost of your lodgings before you book them.

Watch out for telephone-usage charges that hotels frequently impose on long-distance, credit-card, and other calls. Before phoning from your room, read the information given to you at check-in, and then be sure to review your bill carefully when checking out. You won't be expected to pay for charges that the hotel didn't spell out. Consider using your cell phone if you have one; or, if public telephones are available in the hotel lobby, your cost savings may outweigh the inconvenience of using them.

Here are some additional ways to save on lodgings:

○ Stay in B&B accommodations. They're generally less expensive than standard hotel rooms, and the complimentary breakfast cuts down on food costs.

○ If you're traveling with children, find lodgings at which kids stay free.

○ When visiting a major city, stay just outside the city limits; these rooms are usually less expensive than those in downtown locations.

○ Consider visiting national parks during the low season, when prices of lodgings near the parks drop by 25 percent or more.

○ When calling a hotel, ask whether it is running any special promotions or if any discounts are available; many times reservationists are told not to volunteer these deals unless they're specifically asked about them.

○ Check for hotel packages; some offer nightly rates that include a rental car or discounts on major attractions.

○ Search the Internet for travel bargains. Web sites that allow for online booking of hotel rooms and travel planning, such as *www.mobiltravelguide.com,* often deliver lower rates than are available through telephone reservations.

ON DINING

There are several ways to get a less expensive meal at an expensive restaurant. Early-bird dinners are popular in many parts of the country and offer considerable savings. If you're interested in visiting a Mobil Four- or Five-Star establishment, consider going at lunchtime. Although the prices are probably still relatively high at midday, they may be half of those at dinner, and you'll experience the same ambience, service, and cuisine.

ON ENTERTAINMENT

Although many national parks, monuments, seashores, historic sites, and recreation areas may be visited free of charge, others charge an entrance fee and/or a usage fee for special services and facilities. If you plan to make several visits to national recreation areas, consider one of the following money-saving programs offered by the National Park Service:

⊙ **National Parks Pass.** This annual pass is good for entrance to any national park that charges an entrance fee. If the park charges a per-vehicle fee, the pass holder and any accompanying passengers in a private noncommercial vehicle may enter. If the park charges a per-person fee, the pass applies to the holder's spouse, children, and parents as well as the holder. It is valid for entrance fees only; it does not cover parking, camping, or other fees. You can purchase a National Parks Pass in person at any national park where an entrance fee is charged; by mail from the National Park Foundation, PO Box 34108, Washington, DC 20043-4108; by calling toll-free 888/467-2757; or at www.nationalparks .org. The cost is $50.

⊙ **Golden Eagle Sticker.** When affixed to a National Parks Pass, this hologram sticker, available to people who are between 17 and 61 years of age, extends coverage to sites managed by the US Fish and Wildlife Service, the US Forest Service, and the Bureau of Land Management. It is good until the National Parks Pass to which it is affixed expires and does not cover usage fees. You can purchase one at the National Park Service, the Fish and Wildlife Service, or the Bureau of Land Management fee stations. The cost is $15.

⊙ **Golden Age Passport.** Available to citizens and permanent US residents 62 and older, this passport is a lifetime entrance permit to fee-charging national recreation areas. The fee exemption extends to those accompanying the permit holder in a private noncommercial vehicle or, in the case of walk-in facilities, to the holder's spouse and children. The passport also entitles the holder to a 50 percent discount on federal usage fees charged in park areas, but not on concessions. Golden Age Passports must be obtained in person and are available at most National Park Service units that charge an entrance fee. The applicant must show proof of age, such as a driver's license or birth certificate (Medicare cards are not acceptable proof). The cost is $10.

⊙ **Golden Access Passport.** Issued to citizens and permanent US residents who are physically disabled or visually impaired, this passport is a free lifetime entrance permit to fee-charging national recreation areas. The fee exemption extends to those accompanying the permit holder in a private noncommercial vehicle or, in the case of walk-in facilities, to the holder's spouse and children. The passport also entitles the holder to a 50 percent discount on usage fees charged in park areas, but not on concessions. Golden Access Passports must be obtained in person and are available at most National Park Service units that charge an entrance fee. Proof of eligibility to receive federal benefits (under programs such as Disability Retirement, Compensation for Military Service-Connected Disability, and the Coal Mine Safety and Health Act) is required, or an affidavit must be signed attesting to eligibility.

A money-saving move in several large cities is to purchase a **CityPass.** If you plan to visit several museums and other major attractions, CityPass is a terrific option because it gets you into several sites for one substantially reduced price. Currently, CityPass is available in Boston, Chicago, Hollywood, New York, Philadelphia, San Francisco, Seattle, southern California (which includes Disneyland, SeaWorld, and the San Diego Zoo), and Toronto. For more information or to buy one, call toll-free 888/330-5008 or visit www. citypass.net. You can also buy a CityPass from any participating CityPass attraction.

Here are some additional ways to save on entertainment and shopping:

⊙ Check with your hotel's concierge for various coupons and special offers; they often have two-for-one tickets for area attractions and coupons for discounts at area stores and restaurants.

- Purchase same-day concert or theater tickets for half-price through the local cheap-tickets outlet, such as TKTS in New York or Hot Tix in Chicago.

- Visit museums on their free or "by donation" days, when you can pay what you wish rather than a specific admission fee.

- Save receipts from purchases in Canada; visitors to Canada can get a rebate on federal taxes and some provincial sales taxes.

ON TRANSPORTATION

Transportation is a big part of any vacation budget. Here are some ways to reduce your costs:

- If you're renting a car, shop early over the Internet; you can book a car during the low season for less, even if you'll be using it in the high season.

- Rental car discounts are often available if you rent for one week or longer and reserve in advance.

- Get the best gas mileage out of your vehicle by making sure that it's properly tuned up and keeping your tires properly inflated.

- Travel at moderate speeds on the open road; higher speeds require more gasoline.

- Fill the tank before you return your rental car; rental companies charge to refill the tank and do so at prices of up to 50 percent more than at local gas stations.

- Make a checklist of travel essentials and purchase them before you leave; don't get stuck buying expensive sunscreen at your hotel or overpriced film at the airport.

FOR SENIOR CITIZENS

Always call ahead to ask if a discount is being offered, and be sure to carry proof of age. Additional information for mature travelers is available from the American Association of Retired Persons (AARP), 601 E St NW, Washington, DC 20049; phone 202/434-2277; www.aarp.org.

Tipping

Tips are expressions of appreciation for good service. However, you are never obligated to tip if you receive poor service.

IN HOTELS

- Door attendants usually get $1 for hailing a cab.

- Bell staff expect $2 per bag.

- Concierges are tipped according to the service they perform. Tipping is not mandatory when you've asked for suggestions on sightseeing or restaurants or for help in making dining reservations. However, a tip of $5 is appropriate when a concierge books you a table at a restaurant known to be difficult to get into. For obtaining theater or sporting event tickets, $5 to $10 is expected.

- Maids should be tipped $1 to $2 per day. Hand your tip directly to the maid, or leave it with a note saying that the money has been left expressly for the maid.

IN RESTAURANTS

Before tipping, carefully review your check for any gratuity or service charge that is already included in your bill. If you're in doubt, ask your server.

- Coffee shop and counter service waitstaff usually receive 15 percent of the bill, before sales tax.

- In full-service restaurants, tip 18 percent of the bill, before sales tax.

- In fine restaurants, where gratuities are shared among a larger staff, 18 to 20 percent is appropriate.

- In most cases, the maitre d' is tipped only if the service has been extraordinary, and only on the way out. At upscale properties in major metropolitan areas, $20 is the minimum.

- If there is a wine steward, tip $20 for exemplary service and beyond, or more if the wine was decanted or the bottle was very expensive.

- Tip $1 to $2 per coat at the coat check.

AT AIRPORTS

Curbside luggage handlers expect $1 per bag. Car-rental shuttle drivers who help with your luggage appreciate a $1 or $2 tip.

Staying Safe

The best way to deal with emergencies is to avoid them in the first place. However, unforeseen situations do happen, so you should be prepared for them.

IN YOUR CAR

Before you head out on a road trip, make sure that your car has been serviced and is in good working order. Change the oil, check the battery and belts, make sure that your windshield washer fluid is full and your tires are properly inflated (which can also improve your gas mileage). Other inspections recommended by the vehicle's manufacturer should also be made.

Next, be sure you have the tools and equipment needed to deal with a routine breakdown:

- Jack
- Spare tire
- Lug wrench
- Repair kit
- Emergency tools
- Jumper cables
- Spare fan belt
- Fuses
- Flares and/or reflectors
- Flashlight
- First-aid kit
- In winter, a windshield scraper and snow shovel

Many emergency supplies are sold in special packages that include the essentials you need to stay safe in the event of a breakdown.

Also bring all appropriate and up-to-date documentation—licenses, registration, and insurance cards—and know what your insurance covers. Bring an extra set of keys, too, just in case.

En route, always buckle up! In most states, wearing a seatbelt is required by law.

If your car does break down, do the following:

- Get out of traffic as soon as possible—pull well off the road.
- Raise the hood and turn on your emergency flashers or tie a white cloth to the roadside door handle or antenna.
- Stay in your car.
- Use flares or reflectors to keep your vehicle from being hit.

IN YOUR HOTEL

Chances are slim that you will encounter a hotel or motel fire, but you can protect yourself by doing the following:

- Once you've checked in, make sure that the smoke detector in your room is working properly.
- Find the property's fire safety instructions, usually posted on the inside of the room door.
- Locate the fire extinguishers and at least two fire exits.
- Never use an elevator in a fire.

For personal security, use the peephole in your room door and make sure that anyone claiming to be a hotel employee can show proper identification. Call the front desk if you feel threatened at any time.

PROTECTING AGAINST THEFT

To guard against theft wherever you go:

- Don't bring anything of more value than you need.
- If you do bring valuables, leave them at your hotel rather than in your car.
- If you bring something very expensive, lock it in a safe. Many hotels put one in each room; others will store your valuables in the hotel's safe.
- Don't carry more money than you need. Use traveler's checks and credit cards or visit cash machines to withdraw more cash when you run out.

For Travelers with Disabilities

To get the kind of service you need and have a right to expect, don't hesitate when making a reservation to question the management about the availability of accessible rooms, parking, entrances, restaurants, lounges, or any other facilities that are important to you, and confirm what is meant by "accessible."

The Mobil Travel Guide symbol indicates establishments that are not at least partially accessible to people with special mobility needs (people using wheelchairs or crutches or otherwise needing easy access to buildings and rooms). Further information about these criteria can be found in the earlier section "How to Use This Book."

A thorough listing of published material for travelers with disabilities is available from the Disability Bookshop, Twin Peaks Press, Box 129, Vancouver, WA 98666; phone 360/694-2462; disabilitybookshop.virtualave.net. Another reliable organization is the Society for Accessible Travel & Hospitality (SATH), 347 Fifth Ave, Suite 610, New York, NY 10016; phone 212/447-7284; www.sath.org.

Border-Crossing Regulations

In addition to a photo ID, such as a driver's license or military ID, proof of citizenship—a passport or certified birth certificate—is required for travel into Canada for US citizens ages 18 and over. Children under age 18 traveling with their birth certificates are not required to have photo IDs, but it is highly recommended. A child under age 18 traveling to Canada without both legal guardians must have a notarized letter of consent from the nontraveling parent(s) granting permission for the child to

travel. The notarized letter of consent is not waived even when the minor has his or her own passport.

For stays of up to 180 days, a visa is not required.

Each traveler may bring up to $800 worth of goods purchased in Canada back into the United States duty free. In addition, federal regulations permit each US citizen 21 years of age or older to bring back 1 liter of alcoholic beverage duty free in a 30-day period. Travelers are not permitted to bring in plants, fruits, or vegetables. State regulations vary, so check locally before entering Canada. New regulations may be issued at any time.

For more information about traveling to Canada, including safety information, look for the US State Department's Consular Information Sheet at travel.state.gov/canada.html, or request it by fax by calling 202/647-3000.

Important Toll-Free Numbers and Online Information

Hotels

Adams Mark 800/444-2326
www.adamsmark.com

AmericInn 800/634-3444
www.americinn.com

AmeriHost Inn 800/434-5800
www.amerihostinn.com

Amerisuites 800/833-1516
www.amerisuites.com

Baymont Inns 877/BAYMONT
www.baymontinns.com

Best Inns & Suites 800/237-8466
www.bestinn.com

Best Value Inn 888/315-BEST
www.bestvalueinn.com

Best Western 800/780-7234
www.bestwestern.com

Budget Host Inn 800/BUDHOST
www.budgethost.com

Candlewood Suites 888/CANDLEWOOD
www.candlewoodsuites.com

Clarion Hotels 800/252-7466
www.choicehotels.com

Comfort Inns and Suites 800/252-7466
www.choicehotels.com

Country Hearth Inns 800/848-5767
www.countryhearth.com

Country Inns & Suites 800/456-4000
www.countryinns.com

Courtyard by Marriott 800/321-2211
www.courtyard.com

Cross Country Inns (KY and OH) 800/621-1429
www.crosscountryinns.com

Crowne Plaza Hotels and Resorts 800/227-6963
www.crowneplaza.com

Days Inn 800/544-8313
www.daysinn.com

Delta Hotels 800/268-1133
www.deltahotels.com

Destination Hotels & Resorts 800/434-7347
www.destinationhotels.com

Doubletree Hotels 800/222-8733
www.doubletree.com

Drury Inn 800/378-7946
www.druryinn.com

Econolodge 800/553-2666
www.econolodge.com

Embassy Suites 800/362-2779
www.embassysuites.com

ExelInns of America 800/FOREXEL
www.exelinns.com

Extended StayAmerica 800/EXTSTAY
www.extstay.com

Fairfield Inn by Marriott 800/228-2800
www.fairfieldinn.com

Fairmont Hotels 800/441-1414
www.fairmont.com

Four Points by Sheraton 888/625-5144
www.starwood.com/fourpoints

Four Seasons 800/545-4000
www.fourseasons.com

Hampton Inn 800/426-7866
www.hamptoninn.com

Hard Rock Hotels, Resorts, and Casinos . . 800/HRDROCK
www.hardrock.com

Harrah's Entertainment 800/HARRAHS
www.harrahs.com

Hawthorn Suites 800/527-1133
www.hawthorn.com

Hilton Hotels and Resorts (US) 800/774-1500
www.hilton.com

Holiday Inn Express 800/465-4329
www.hiexpress.com

Holiday Inn Hotels and Resorts 800/465-4329
www.holiday-inn.com

Homestead Studio Suites 888/782-9473
www.homesteadhotels.com

Homewood Suites 800/225-5466
www.homewoodsuites.com

Howard Johnson 800/406-1411
www.hojo.com

Hyatt 800/633-7313
www.hyatt.com

Ian Schrager . . . . Contact individual hotel
www.ianschragerhotels.com

Inns of America 800/826-0778
www.innsofamerica.com

InterContinental 888/567-8725
www.intercontinental.com

Joie de Vivre 800/738-7477
www.jdvhospitality.com

Kimpton Hotels 888/546-7866
www.kimptongroup.com

Knights Inn 800/843-5644
www.knightsinn.com

La Quinta 800/531-5900
www.laquinta.com

Le Meridien 800/543-4300
www.lemeridien.com

Leading Hotels of the World 800/223-6800
www.lhw.com

Loews Hotels 800/235-6397
www.loewshotels.com

MainStay Suites 800/660-6246
www.choicehotels.com

Mandarin Oriental 800/526-6566
www.mandarin-oriental.com

Marriott Hotels, Resorts, and Suites 800/228-9290
www.marriott.com

Microtel Inns & Suites 800/771-7171
www.microtelinn.com

Millennium & Copthorne Hotels 866/866-8086
www.mill-cop.com

Motel 6 . . . . 800/4MOTEL6
www.motel6.com

Omni Hotels 800/843-6664
www.omnihotels.com

Pan Pacific Hotels and Resorts 800/327-8585
www.panpac.com

Park Inn & Park Plaza 888/201-1801
www.parkhtls.com

The Peninsula Group . . . . Contact individual hotel
www.peninsula.com

Preferred Hotels & Resorts Worldwide 800/323-7500
www.preferredhotels.com

Quality Inn 800/228-5151
www.qualityinn.com

Radisson Hotels 800/333-3333
www.radisson.com

Raffles International Hotels and Resorts . . . 800/637-9477
www.raffles.com

Ramada Plazas, Limiteds, and Inns 800/2RAMADA
www.ramada.com

Red Lion Inns 800/733-5466
www.redlion.com

Red Roof Inns 800/733-7663
www.redroof.com

Regal Hotels 800/222-8888
www.regal-hotels.com

Regent International 800/545-4000
www.regenthotels.com

Relais & Chateaux 800/735-2478
www.relaischateaux.com

Renaissance Hotels 888/236-2427
www.renaissancehotels.com

Residence Inn 800/331-3131
www.residenceinn.com

Ritz-Carlton 800/241-3333
www.ritzcarlton.com

Rockresorts 888/FORROCKS
www.rockresorts.com

Rodeway Inn 800/228-2000
www.rodeway.com

Rosewood Hotels & Resorts 888/767-3966
www.rosewood-hotels.com

Select Inn 800/641-1000
www.selectinn.com

Sheraton 888/625-5144
www.sheraton.com

Shilo Inns 800/222-2244
www.shiloinns.com

Shoney's Inn 800/552-4667
www.shoneysinn.com

Signature/Jameson Inns 800/822-5252
www.jamesoninns.com

Sleep Inn 800/453-3746
www.sleepinn.com

Small Luxury Hotels of the World 800/525-4800
www.slh.com

Sofitel 800/763-4835
www.sofitel.com

SpringHill Suites .888/236-2427
www.springhillsuites.com

SRS Worldhotels 800/223-5652
www.srs-worldhotels.com

St. Regis Luxury Collection 888/625-5144
www.stregis.com

Staybridge Suites 800/238-8000
www.staybridge.com

Summerfield Suites by Wyndham 800/833-4353
www.summerfieldsuites.com

Summit International 800/457-4000
www.summithotels.com

Super 8 Motels 800/800-8000
www.super8.com

The Sutton Place Hotels 866/378-8866
www.suttonplace.com

Swissôtel 800/637-9477
www.swissotel.com

TownePlace Suites 888/236-2427
www.towneplace.com

Travelodge 800/578-7878
www.travelodge.com

Vagabond Inns 800/522-1555
www.vagabondinns.com

W Hotels 888/625-5144
www.whotels.com

Wellesley Inn and Suites 800/444-8888
www.wellesleyinnandsuites.com

WestCoast Hotels 800/325-4000
www.westcoasthotels.com

Westin Hotels & Resorts 800/937-8461
www.westin.com

Wingate Inns. 800/228-1000
www.wingateinns.com

Woodfin Suite Hotels 800/966-3346
www.woodfinsuitehotels.com

Wyndham Hotels & Resorts 800/996-3426
www.wyndham.com

Airlines

Air Canada. 888/247-2262
www.aircanada.ca

AirTran. 800/247-8726
www.airtran.com

Alaska Airlines 800/252-7522
www.alaskaair.com

American Airlines. 800/433-7300
www.aa.com

America West 800/235-9292
www.americawest.com

ATA. 800/435-9282
www.ata.com

Continental Airlines 800/523-3273
www.flycontinental.com

Delta Air Lines 800/221-1212
www.delta.com

Frontier Airlines 800/432-1FLY
www.frontierairlines.com

Jet Blue Airways. 800/JET-BLUE
www.jetblue.com

Midwest Express 800/452-2022
www.midwestexpress.com

Northwest Airlines 800/225-2525
www.nwa.com

Southwest Airlines 800/435-9792
www.iflyswa.com

Spirit Airlines 800/772-7117
www.spiritair.com

United Airlines 800/241-6522
www.ual.com

US Airways 800/428-4322
www.usairways.com

Vanguard Airlines. 800/VANGUARD
www.flyvanguard.com

Car Rentals

Advantage 800/777-5500
www.arac.com

Alamo. 800/327-9633
www.goalamo.com

Avis 800/831-2847
www.avis.com

Budget 800/527-0700
www.budgetrentacar.com

Dollar 800/800-4000
www.dollarcar.com

Enterprise 800/325-8007
www.pickenterprise.com

Hertz 800/654-3131
www.hertz.com

National 800/227-7368
www.nationalcar.com

Payless 800/729-5377
www.800-payless.com

Rent-A-Wreck.com 800/535-1391
www.rent-a-wreck.com

Thrifty 800/847-4389
www.thrifty.com

Meet the Stars

Mobil Travel Guide 2005 **Five-Star** *Award Winners*

CALIFORNIA
Lodgings
The Beverly Hills Hotel, *Beverly Hills*
Chateau du Sureau, *Oakhurst*
Four Seasons Hotel San Francisco,
  San Francisco
Hotel Bel-Air, *Los Angeles*
The Peninsula Beverly Hills, *Beverly Hills*
Raffles L'Ermitage Beverly Hills, *Beverly Hills*
The Ritz-Carlton, San Francisco, *San Francisco*

Restaurants
The Dining Room, *San Francisco*
The French Laundry, *Yountville*
Gary Danko, *San Francisco*

COLORADO
Lodgings
The Broadmoor, *Colorado Springs*
The Little Nell, *Aspen*

CONNECTICUT
Lodging
The Mayflower Inn, *Washington*

FLORIDA
Lodgings
Four Seasons Resort Palm Beach, *Palm Beach*
The Ritz-Carlton, Naples, *Naples*
The Ritz-Carlton, Palm Beach, *Manalapan*

GEORGIA
Lodgings
Four Seasons Hotel Atlanta, *Atlanta*
The Lodge at Sea Island Golf Club,
  St. Simons Island

Restaurants
The Dining Room, *Atlanta*
Seeger's, *Atlanta*

HAWAII
Lodging
Four Seasons Resort Maui at Wailea, *Wailea,
  Maui*

ILLINOIS
Lodgings
Four Seasons Hotel Chicago, *Chicago*
The Peninsula Chicago, *Chicago*
The Ritz-Carlton, A Four Seasons Hotel, *Chicago*

Restaurants
Charlie Trotter's, *Chicago*
Trio, *Evanston*

MASSACHUSETTS
Lodgings
Blantyre, *Lenox*
Four Seasons Hotel Boston, *Boston*

NEW YORK
Lodgings
Four Seasons Hotel New York, *New York*
The Point, *Saranac Lake*
The Ritz-Carlton New York, Central Park,
  New York
The St. Regis, *New York*

Restaurants
Alain Ducasse, *New York*
Jean Georges, *New York*
Masa, *New York*

NORTH CAROLINA
Lodging
The Fearrington House Country Inn, *Pittsboro*

OHIO
Restaurant
Maisonette, *Cincinnati*

PENNSYLVANIA
Restaurant
Le Bec-Fin, *Philadelphia*

SOUTH CAROLINA
Lodging
Woodlands Resort & Inn, *Summerville*

Restaurant
Dining Room at the Woodlands, *Summerville*

TEXAS
Lodging
The Mansion on Turtle Creek, *Dallas*

VERMONT
Lodging
Twin Farms, *Barnard*

VIRGINIA
Lodgings
The Inn at Little Washington, *Washington*
The Jefferson Hotel, *Richmond*

Restaurant
The Inn at Little Washington, *Washington*

Mobil Travel Guide has been rating establishments with its Mobil One- to Five-Star system since 1958. Each establishment awarded the Mobil Five-Star rating is one of the best in the country. Detailed information on each award winner can be found in the corresponding regional edition listed on the back cover of this book.

Four- and Five-Star Establishments in the Northwest

Washington

★ ★ ★ ★ Lodgings

Bellevue Club Hotel, *Bellevue*
The Fairmont Olympic Hotel, *Seattle*

★ ★ ★ ★ Restaurants

Brasa, *Seattle*
The Georgian, *Seattle*
The Herbfarm, *Woodinville*
Rover's, *Seattle*

America's Byways™ are a distinctive collection of American roads, their stories, and treasured places. They are roads to the heart and soul of America. In this section, you'll find the nationally designated Byways in Idaho, Oregon, Washington, and Alaska.

Cascade Lakes Scenic Byway
OREGON

The towering Cascade Mountains provide the backdrop for this scenic drive. These mountains also offer fabulous hiking and challenging rock climbing. The Byway climbs into the Deschutes National Forest, where fishing, hiking, rafting, and other outdoor sports are plentiful. This area is also a winter playground; for example, Mount Bachelor's ski resort is filled with snow through June. This Byway also crosses paths with those of early explorers and trappers, such as Kit Carson, John C. Fremont, and Nathaniel J. Wyeth.

QUICK FACTS

Length: 66 miles.

Time to Allow: 3 to 5 hours.

Best Time to Drive: June through October.

Byway Travel Information: Bend Visitor Center and Chamber of Commerce: phone toll-free 800/905-2362; Byway local Web sites: www.fs.fed.us/r6/deschutes; www.ctws.org/museum; www.covisitors.com.

Special Considerations: Winter snowfall closes a portion of the Byway from mid-November until late May each year.

Restrictions: The first 17 miles of the Byway from just outside Bend to Mount Bachelor are open year-round, as are the last 4 miles north of Highway 58. The remaining 48 miles from Mount Bachelor to the Cutoff are closed in the winter due to snow. When parking for more than a few hours near trailhead markers, expect to obtain a permit and pay parking fees. Purchase permits at most outdoor shops, the Bend Chamber of Commerce, and the National Forest Service.

Bicycle/Pedestrian Facilities: This Byway is popular with bicyclists. The section of Byway from Bend to Mount Bachelor is best suited to bicyclists; although narrower, the remaining portions of the Byway are also suited for bicycle travel. The Byway is not suitable for regular pedestrian travel, but the hiking oportunities off the Byway are excellent.

As you drive by many bodies of water along the route, it is easy to see why this route was named after the Cascade Lakes. Some of the lakes that you encounter include Todd Lake, Sparks Lake, Cultus Lake, and Crane Prairie Reservoir. As you can imagine, this is an angler's paradise. Anglers can spend hours at the banks of these lakes, fishing for Atlantic salmon and other freshwater fish. Waterfowl and many species of plants thrive here as well.

The Byway Story

The Cascade Lakes Scenic Byway tells archaeological, historical, natural, recreational, and scenic stories that make it a unique and treasured Byway.

ARCHAEOLOGICAL

The history of how this area was formed is preserved at The High Desert Museum, along with displays and artifacts of the area's Native Americans and original cowboys. Also on display are remakes of prehistoric dwellings.

HISTORICAL

This same scenic drive was once traveled by early mountain men explorers Kit Carson, John C. Fremont, and Nathaniel J. Wyeth. In the days of horse and buggy, this was a well-worn, 100-mile dirt road called the Century Drive. Also, along this Byway in the area of Benham Falls, the classic movies *The Indian Fighter, Rooster Cogburn,* and *Up the Creek* were filmed.

The Lava River Cave, Oregon's longest uncollapsed lava tube, tells the tale of the area's once-active volcanic past. It is closed during winter months, and warm clothing is advised when touring at other times of the year. The Lava

Lands Visitor Center and Lava Butte are also available to observe volcanic cones and formations. There are also other displays and films available on the area's volcanic history.

NATURAL

The geology of the Cascade Lakes Scenic Byway is especially significant. The volcanic Cascade Mountains (unique to the Pacific Northwest) are part of the Ring-of-Fire volcanic mountain chain that borders the Pacific Ocean. Nowhere else in the country (and possibly in the world) is there ready access to such a great diversity of volcanic features.

You can see stratovolcanoes, shield volcanoes, cinder cones, sheets of pumice and ash, sheets of ashflow tuffs, maars, caves, and several kinds of lava flows and domes. Volcanism and glaciation formed more than 150 small and large lakes for which this region is well known.

This area is also featured in geology textbooks and was used as a training ground for the Apollo moon missions in the 1960s. In 1971, astronaut Jim Irwin (aboard *Apollo 15*) placed a rock from Devil's Lake (a lake along this Byway) on the lunar surface—the only Earth rock on the moon!

The route also traverses through the drier forests that include Lodgepole pine and older ponderosa pine. Also, 262 species of birds and animals reside here—including two endangered species: the bald eagle and the northern spotted owl.

RECREATIONAL

You'll find many recreational activities along the Cascade Lakes Scenic Byway. Due to elevation differences and compact geography, six months out of the year, you can ski in the morning and hike, fish, bicycle, or kayak in the afternoon.

Within the Deschutes National Forest and the Three Sisters Wilderness Area, you'll find snow-capped peaks, over 150 lakes, and a Wild & Scenic River. With its dependable, dry powder snow and 3,300-foot elevation drop, Mount Bachelor offers the best downhill skiing in the Northwest. The same snow conditions also provide excellent cross-country skiing, snowmobiling, and dog sledding.

Excellent camping, fishing, boating, bicycling, hiking, backpacking, mountain climbing, and horseback riding are also available. Boaters can motorboat, canoe, sail, or wind surf on the lakes. You can also whitewater raft on the Deschutes River.

SCENIC

As you drive along the Cascade Lakes Scenic Byway, dramatic snow-capped peaks tower over you. These peaks are most often mirrored in crystal-clear alpine lakes.

The Summit Express lift can take you to the 9,065-foot peak of Mount Bachelor in the summer. The dramatic 360-degree view sweeps a volcanic mountain skyline. You can see for hundreds of miles—from Mount Adams in Washington to Mount Shasta in California.

The view from Dutchman Flat (a pumice-covered area at the 6,000-foot base of Mount Bachelor) may look familiar to you. The scenic panorama has been featured in the movies *Homeward Bound, Rooster Cogburn,* and *The Postman.*

The area of Sparks Lake and Meadow (with South Sister Mountain looming in the background) has been chosen as the site to commemorate Ray Atkeson, Oregon's photographer laureate.

Highlights

The following scenic tour gives you a chance to enjoy the highlights of this Byway:

- ☺ Starting from **Bend** and traveling the Cascade Lakes Scenic Byway, you come across **Drake Park,** at the Highway 97 and Franklin Avenue intersection. Park in Mirror Pond Parking Lot (just west of the Franklin and Wall intersection) and explore the charming downtown area. The original site of Bend was selected around this area because it was an easy location for early travelers to cross the Deschutes River.

- ☺ Fifteen miles west of Bend on the Cascade Lakes Highway are hiking, mountain biking, and cross-country skiing opportunities at the **Swampy Lakes** area. From the trailhead at the north end of the parking lot, you can enjoy a variety of marked skiing and hiking trails from 2 to 10 miles in length. The area provides five shelters that are usually stocked with wood in the winter.

- ☺ **Mount Bachelor Ski and Summer Resort** is west of the Swampy Lakes, an area where you can spend a whole day to recreate and ski or fish. Just west of the entrance to Mount Bachelor, a whole

new scenic landscape beckons to be enjoyed and appreciated. By some quirk of nature, the small pumic desert, called **Dutchman Flat,** has not accumulated enough soil nutrients to sustain the growth of many plants. Pusspaws with pink blooms and sulfur flowers with yellow blooms are a few of the hardy plants that grow in this unique area. Stop to take pictures and take note of it as you pass by; this was where the movie *How the West Was Won* was filmed.

- ☺ On the Byway, you pass **Todd Lake, Sparks Lake,** and **Green Lakes Trailhead,** all worthy stops. Continue on west of the Green Lakes Trailhead to a small but scenic area with several springs surfacing from the edge of a huge lava flow, creating a little meadow. Along with the lush meadow grass, you'll find moss, blue lupines, and Indian pictographs, painted on the face of a large dacite boulder, which indicate an ancient Indian trail. This place is **Devils Garden**—recount the legend of the area and explore a bit of the ancient Indian trail.

- ☺ Continue on the Byway to pass picturesque **Devils Lake, Elk Lake, Hosmer Lake, Lava Lake, Little Lava Lake, Cultus Lake,** and **Little Cultus Lake** until you come to the **Osprey Observation Point.** Constructed in 1929, it has become an outstanding fishing area and a breeding ground for the osprey (fish hawk), identified as a potentially endangered species in 1969. From the parking lot, a short walk takes you to an observation area on the west side of the reservoir. Here, you can view snags and artificial nesting poles inhabited by the birds. Many visitors are entertained as osprey dive for fish from more than a hundred feet above the water. Continue south to come to the end of the Byway.

Hells Canyon Scenic Byway

OREGON

Leave the fast pace and fenced-in views of Interstate 84 and follow the contours of the land into slower times and wilder places. Travel this 218-mile journey from river's edge to mountaintop and down to valley floor. Have lunch overlooking a Wild & Scenic River. Share a canyon road with a cattle drive. Pass through lush valleys rimmed by the snow-tipped Wallowa Mountains. Savor the scent of pine on the fresh mountain air. Enjoy panoramic views of rugged basalt cliffs and grassy open ridges. Stand next to the majestic Snake River as it begins its tumbling course through North America's deepest canyon. Place your hand in the weathered track of a wagon wheel. Hear the wind rushing through the forest. This is a journey you won't forget.

QUICK FACTS

Length: 218 miles.

Time to Allow: 8 hours.

Best Time to Drive: Late May to October, when you see spectacular snow-capped mountains, lush green hills, and wildflowers in bloom. High season is in July and August.

Byway Travel Information: Eastern Oregon Visitor's Association: phone 541/856-3272; Byway travel and tourism Web site: www.eova.com.

Special Considerations: You won't find any services beyond Joseph, so make sure you have plenty of gas before leaving Baker City or La Grande. Before starting out, take notice of the travel times as well as mileage between stops and keep your fuel tank as full as possible. Be prepared for temperatures that vary as much as 50 degrees as the day wears on.

Restrictions: Wallowa Mountain Loop USFS Road 39, between Joseph and Halfway, is closed from November through February due to heavy snow.

Bicycle/Pedestrian Facilities: Distances between destinations make pedestrian activity impractical along much of the Byway, except along Highway 351 around Wallowa Lake. Most of the local pedestrian activity occurs in the communities along the Byway, where you find sidewalks and crosswalks.

The route of the Hells Canyon Scenic Byway is a loop that encircles the Wallowa Mountains, intersecting with Interstate 84 at La Grande and Baker City. Small towns scattered along the drive offer visitor services. The entire route is on a paved highway, but plan ahead: you'll find stretches of more than 80 miles without gas stations and with few services. A segment of the Byway between Joseph and Halfway closes due to snow in winter but allows access to winter recreation areas, offering a different kind of northeast Oregon adventure.

The Byway Story

The Hells Canyon Scenic Byway tells archaeological, cultural, historical, natural, recreational, and scenic stories that make it a unique and treasured Byway.

ARCHAEOLOGICAL

Extremes in the land have dictated the course of the area's natural and cultural history. Relatively mild winters and abundant wildlife drew people to the canyon over 7,000 years ago. Archaeological evidence, ranging from rock art to winter "pithouse" villages, can be found in the Snake River corridor. Pictographs and petroglyphs are scattered along the river where Native Americans spent their winters. Please use care when viewing these sites; these national treasures have stood the test of time and will be enjoyed long into the future.

CULTURAL

On the map, northeastern Oregon looks far removed from metropolitan area amenities. However, you may be surprised by the availability of arts and culture. Musical events along the Byway range from old-time fiddling to blues to Beethoven. Plays, concerts, and living-history productions can be enjoyed daily in Baker City. The small town of Joseph has earned a national reputation for its bronze foundries and galleries. Some of the nation's most highly acclaimed artists cast their bronzes at one of the four area foundries or show their work in one of the many galleries that line the town's picturesque main street. Eastern Oregon University, located in La Grande, offers theatrical productions and concerts, including a full season of music from the Grande Ronde Symphony Orchestra. The Historic Elgin Opera House in Elgin is also a crowd pleaser for concerts, movies, and plays.

HISTORICAL

For many centuries, the Grande Ronde Valley was used seasonally by Native Americans. Covered largely by wetlands, the beautiful valley was lush with grass and alive with game. Herds of elk summered in the surrounding high country and wintered in the milder valley. Mule deer, pronghorn antelope, and big-horn sheep browsed the hills and meadows. This bountiful scene was a neutral meeting place for members of the Umatilla, Yakima, Shoshone, Cayuse, and Bannock nations, who came to enjoy the hot springs, hunt, graze their horses, and gather plants for food. The picturesque Wallowa Valley was the beloved home of the Nez Perce Indians. By winter of 1877, settlement conflicts drove young Chief Joseph to make a harrowing attempt to reach Canada with a group of 250 men, women, and children. They struggled to within 24 miles of safety before being captured at Montana and sent to reservations.

This area remains a significant religious and cultural center for the Nez Perce, Umatilla, and Cayuse Indians. Every fall, when leaving the valley to winter in the milder climate along the Columbia plateau, these early residents lit huge fires in the valleys, burning off old grass and allowing for healthy regrowth in the spring.

NATURAL

Millions of years ago, the Wallowa Mountains formed the coast of what would eventually be called Oregon. Uplifted layers of limestone on the peaks harbor fossilized shells that once sat at the bottom of the ocean. Eons of volcanic action and faulting pushed the masses of rock upward while new land formed to the west. The Coast Range, Cascade Mountains, and upland desert of central Oregon now separate the Wallowas from the ocean by hundreds of miles.

Flows of plateau basalt, batholiths of granite, and layers of shale were buckled and folded to form the mountain range. Raging rivers and gigantic glaciers carved the peaks and canyons. In short, nature took a long time to sculpt the dramatic beauty you see along the Byway.

RECREATIONAL

Recreational opportunities along the Hells Canyon Scenic Byway are seemingly endless and range from tranquil to thrilling. Four distinct seasons alter the scenery and determine the activities.

In spring, warm sunshine carpets the hills with green grass and colorful wildflowers. The landscape becomes a patchwork quilt with fields of freshly plowed soil, sprouting crops, and blossoming fruit trees. It's a great time for sightseeing from a car or on a bike. Watch the meadows for frisky new calves and wobbly foals. Along the streams, willows, dogwood, and mock orange create a changing palette of yellows, pinks, and vibrant greens. Fish for steelhead or trout on the Grande Ronde, Minam, Wallowa, and Imnaha rivers. Take a thrilling raft or jet boat ride through the Class III and IV rapids on the Snake River or float the waters of the Grande Ronde and Minam rivers.

Summer bursts with energy. Warm, dry weather and lots of sunshine make the outdoors impossible to resist. Microclimates at different elevations and aspects mean you can always find a cooler or hotter spot within miles. The Wallowa-Whitman National Forest, along with county and state parks departments, operates numerous campgrounds, trail systems, viewpoints, and picnic facilities along or near the route. Hike or mountain bike into the high country. Cast a fishing line on several of the rivers and streams and at Wallowa Lake. Hire a private outfitter to experience horseback riding and pack trips, rafting, parasailing, or jet boat adventures. Cycle the back roads or mountain trails for the amazing views. Watch hang gliders and hot air balloonists catch the breeze high above the Wallowa and Grande Ronde valleys.

In autumn, cooler temperatures and shorter days turn tamarack (western larch) needles to gold and leaves to jewel tones of yellow, orange, and red. Canadian geese are on the move, filling the air with melancholy calls. Hunt for deer, elk, bear, cougar, and bighorn sheep or use them as photo opportunities. Fall is also the time for cattle drives, harvesting, and blue-sky days crisp with the smell of winter. Catch the small-town spirit by watching a high school football game in splendid, scenic surroundings—visitors are always welcome.

Winter's dry, powdery snow opens area ski resorts and turns backcountry side trips and hiking trails into a giant playground for adventurers on skis, snowmobiles, and snowshoes. The FS Road 39 section of the Byway between Joseph and Halfway is closed to auto and truck traffic in winter, when it becomes an especially popular route for snowmobilers. It connects into much larger networks providing access to hundreds of miles of groomed trails in the region. Enjoy winter raptor viewing in Minam and Hells canyons, a horse-drawn sleigh ride in Joseph, or ice fishing on Wallowa Lake. Near the Byway, ride a horse-drawn wagon through a herd of Rocky Mountain elk at the Elkhorn Elk Feeding Site and find out about the majestic animal's history in the area. By day, surround yourself with spectacular scenery topped with fresh white snow. By night, relax before a crackling fire in cozy lodgings.

SCENIC

Travel the Hells Canyon Scenic Byway and see much of the majesty and mystery of the West within a 218-mile corridor. The magnificent Snake River twists and churns over boulders and past towering cliffs. Pungent sagebrush and bunch grasses cover the flats and crouch at the feet of dramatic rock formations. Sparkling streams tumble through thick forests of pine and mixed conifers. Lush valleys lie at the feet of magnificent mountain ranges with peaks that tower to nearly 10,000 feet. Fields of hay, wheat, grass, mint, and canola color the valley floor. Cattle, sheep, and horses graze on a menu of sweet clover and timothy. Historic barns and houses bring human warmth and scale to the dramatic scenery.

Highlights

☸ Start your summer outdoors tour at about midday so you can go to the **Wallowa Mountains Visitor Center** (about half a mile northwest of Enterprise) to get current and detailed information about camps and hikes in the area. Spend the night camping in the Wallowa Mountains or beside the Imnaha River.

☸ Visit **Wallowa Lake** (about 6 miles south of Joseph) and relax for a few hours of swimming, fishing, boating, or hiking. You can also take a tram from here to the peak of Mount Howard and enjoy wonderful views.

☸ Next, visit the **Hells Canyon Overlook.** The overlook is about 30 miles along the Byway from the lake. This is a staggering view, 5,400 feet above the canyon floor.

☸ In Copperfield (about 15 miles south of the Overlook), secure a jet boat tour on the **Snake River.** You can also rent rafts and such here. After a few hours of enjoying the Snake, end your day at the **Hole-in-the-Wall Slide.** The geographically intriguing slide is about 30 miles west on the Byway from Copperfield.

Historic Columbia River Highway

OREGON

The Historic Columbia River Highway (HCRH) is exquisite: drive through the Columbia River Gorge for nearly 50 miles and sweep past majestic waterfalls, including Multnomah Falls, the most visited natural site in Oregon. This Byway also travels through a spectacular river canyon that you often view from the tops of cliffs over 900 feet above the river. During the spring, you experience magnificent wildflower displays, including many plants that exist only in this area.

This is the first scenic highway in the United States to gain the distinction of National Historic Landmark. (To give you an idea of what this means, less than 3 percent of the sites on the National Register of Historic Places become Landmarks.) The construction of this highway was considered one of the greatest engineering feats of the modern age. Its engineer, Samuel C. Lancaster, did "not [want] to mar what God had put there." It was designed in 1913-1914 to take advantage of the many waterfalls and other beautiful spots.

Make sure you travel both the well-known western section of the Byway from Troutdale to Dodson as well as the less-traveled eastern section from Mosier to The Dalles. The difference in vegetation zones and views between the two sections is amazing.

The Byway Story

The Historic Columbia River Highway tells historical, natural, recreational, and scenic stories that make it a unique and treasured Byway.

HISTORICAL

The HCRH has many nationally significant historic features on the National Register of Historic Places—one of which is the highway itself. It is also a National Historic Civil Engineering Landmark that includes 23 unique bridges. The historic district includes not only the highway, but also the Portland Women's Forum State Scenic Viewpoint, Crown Point and Vista House, Multnomah Falls Lodge and

---

QUICK FACTS

Length: 70 miles.

Time to Allow: 3 to 5 hours.

Best Time to Drive: Mid-week sees the fewest crowds along the Byway. Fall has the best weather; spring provides the best time to view the waterfalls. High season is April through September.

Byway Travel Information: US Forest Service–Columbia River Gorge National Scenic Area: phone 541/386-2333; Byway local Web site: www.odot.state .or.us/hcrh.

Special Considerations: Some attractions are closed during the winter months. Also, the Byway is narrow and winding, so you may want to consider traveling in a car instead of an RV.

Restrictions: The Multnomah Falls Lodge is open daily throughout the year. The Vista House is open from April through September.

Bicycle/Pedestrian Facilities: You can bike fairly safely on this highway because of the relatively low volume of automobiles. You'll also find plenty of trails around the Byway on which you can bike. Most notably, portions of the Historic Columbia River Highway that were abandoned during the construction of I-84 are being restored as multi-use trails. Numerous other trailheads are located along the Byway as well. These trails have a good range of length and difficulty, ranging from flat, paved trails to high mountain trails.

Recreation Site, Eagle Creek Recreation Area, and several other waterfall areas.

NATURAL

The Columbia River Gorge is a spectacular river canyon, 80 miles long and up to 4,000 feet deep, cutting the only sea-level route through the Cascade Mountain Range. The Gorge includes 16 endemic plant species (those that exist only within the Gorge) and over 150 rare plant species. Bald eagles, peregrine falcons, Snake River salmon, and Larch Mountain salamanders also reside here. Wildflower tours of the Historic Columbia River Highway are common in the spring.

RECREATIONAL

Recreational facilities in the Columbia River Gorge National Scenic Area are also of national significance, including the three major highways (Historic Columbia River Highway, I-84, and Washington State Route 14) that are used extensively for pleasure driving. The highways provide access to many hiking trails, windsurfing sites, and the Mount Hood Railroad, a scenic and historic passenger and freight route up the Hood River Valley.

SCENIC

The HCRH leaves the Sandy River and climbs to the top of the cliffs, offering spectacular views of the landscape. The Byway was designed in 1913-1914 to take advantage of the many waterfalls and other attractive sites along the route. The corridor contains some of the most dramatic views available anywhere in the country, including the Columbia River, with basalt cliffs and canyon walls; Multnomah Falls, a 620-foot, two-tiered waterfall that is the most visited natural attraction in the state of Oregon; the largest aggregation of high waterfalls outside of Yosemite, including Multnomah Falls, Horsetail Falls, Latourell Falls, Bridal Veil Falls, and Wahkeena Falls, plus numerous small falls; and giant basalt cliffs and monoliths, including Beacon Rock, Rooster Rock, Crown Point (a National Natural Landmark), Oneonta Bluff, and others.

Highlights

Start your must-see tour in Troutdale, the western entry point to the Historic Columbia River Highway. The attractive setting, unique shopping district, and convenient distance from the interstate make this small town a perfect start to your tour of the highway.

○ Drive east. The first stop along the tour is **Sandy River.** An old iron bridge crosses the river at this point. Cross and enjoy. You can even take a side trip to the left to visit Lewis and Clark Park, but be sure to return to the Byway to continue your journey east.

○ If you want a stunning scenic vista, you must stop at **Portland Women's Forum State Scenic Viewpoint.** It is located about 10 minutes from Troutdale (milepost 10.3).

○ **Crown Point** and historic **Vista House** is next, about a mile farther east (milepost 11.5). Take a stroll around the point (carefully—the road curves around the building here) and enjoy yet another wonderful view of the river and the **Columbia River Gorge.**

○ Scattered throughout the next few miles are many waterfalls, each with its own history and qualities. **Latourell Falls, Shepherd's Dell, Wahkeena Falls,** and **Bridal Veil Falls** each whet your appetite for the most visited waterfall on the Byway: **Multnomah Falls.** This beautiful double-cascade falls more than 650 feet. Stop and take the hike up to the bridge, crossing the waterfall for an up-close view.

○ Back on the highway, you shortly encounter **Oneonta Gorge.** This narrow canyon and its associated stream is a cool, dark, and shady hike. To enjoy it fully, follow the path to its river crossing, take off your shoes, and wade in the chilly stream.

© Continuing east, you rejoin the interstate for a while. **The Bridge of the Gods at Cascade Locks** connects Oregon to Washington.

© The city of **Hood River,** at the confluence of the Hood River and the Columbia River, is the wind-surfing capital of the world. Stop and watch expert windsurfers from the riverside or from vantage points at hotels and viewpoints along the river. Or visit the **downtown historic district** and stop by the **Hood River County Museum.**

© Take time to leave your car now and walk a portion of the Historic Columbia River Highway between Hood River and Mosier that has been converted to a **state trail.** Remnants of the original auto highway and railings may still be seen. Or, if you continue in your car along the main highway instead, look for tunnels and roadbed high above you—a visible clue to a tremendous engineering feat.

© As you leave the rain forest of the Gorge and enter the drier, wide rolling plains west of Rowena and The Dalles, stop a moment at the **Memaloose Overlook** near the **Tom McCall Preserve.** Below you, the highway twists in the hairpin turns of the **Rowena Loops.** This engineering achievement remains remarkable even by today's standards.

© After you navigate the switchbacks of the Rowena Loops, catch your breath with a stop at the **Gorge Discovery Center** and **Wasco County Museum.** Opened in 1997, this museum offers interpretive exhibits about the human and natural history of the Columbia River Gorge.

© End your trip on the Historic Columbia River Highway at **The Dalles.** You can view the nearby **Dalles Lock and Dam** or tour the **historic district** of this city.

McKenzie Pass-Santiam Pass Scenic Byway

OREGON

QUICK FACTS

Length: 82 miles.

Time to Allow: 3 to 5 hours.

Best Time to Drive: Spring to fall.

Byway Travel Information: US Forest Service, McKenzie Ranger Station: phone 541/ 822-3381; Oregon Visitors Association: phone toll-free 800/800-8334; McKenzie River Chamber of Commerce: phone 541/896-3330.

Special Considerations: Services are available in the town of McKenzie Bridge.

Restrictions: Because of snow, Highway 242 is closed from mid-November to mid-June. Nearly the entire Byway is in a snow zone, so chains are sometimes required during the winter, especially over the Santiam Pass. Also, due to extremely sharp curves and narrow road width, Highway 242 over McKenzie Pass is closed to vehicles (either single or combined) longer than 35 feet. Trailers are discouraged. Parking passes can be purchased from the ranger station, allowing you to park and hike the trails along this Byway.

Bicycle/Pedestrian Facilities: This Byway is popular with bicyclists during the summer. While the Santiam Pass Highway (US 20) and Clear Lake Cutoff (Oregon 126) are well-traveled routes, they accommodate bicycles with paved shoulders and good sight distances. The McKenzie Pass Highway is narrow and winding, but it accommodates bicycles because no commercial traffic is allowed, recreational traffic is light, and vehicle speeds are low. One section of the Byway is accessible to pedestrians: the 26-mile McKenzie River National Recreational Trail. The remainder of the Byway is not suitable for pedestrian travel.

Experience dramatic, close-up views of the most beautiful of the snowcapped High Cascade Peaks. The panorama of lava fields and six Cascade peaks, as viewed from the summit of McKenzie Pass, is made even more striking by the contrast between the black lava and white snow. The mountains are mirrored in crystal-clear lakes, and the Byway passes spectacular waterfalls, including Sahalie and Koosah falls. Broken Top Mountain and the Three Sisters tower gloriously above the route.

The Byway Story

The McKenzie Pass-Santiam Pass Scenic Byway tells archaeological, cultural, historical, natural, recreational, and scenic stories that make it a unique and treasured Byway.

ARCHAEOLOGICAL

Sahalie Falls and Koosah Falls can be located on the old Clear Lake Cutoff on Highway 126. Sahalie (meaning "heaven") and Koosah (meaning "sky") are Chinook Jargon words—part of a rudimentary trade language that allowed people to exchange news and goods in the area. The Kalapuya, Molala, Sahaptin, and Chinook peoples traveled and traded here, perhaps on their way to obtain obsidian in the high Cascades for tools or to gather huckleberries. Connecting the two waterfalls is a loop trail that offers views of foaming white water, pouring over 3,000-year-old lava flows.

CULTURAL

Communities that reflect rural Western charm anchor the McKenzie Pass-Santiam Pass Scenic Byway and lead you to a variety of cultural events on both sides of the mountains.

The town of Sisters, especially, recalls the Old West with a sophisticated town center that features numerous antique shops, galleries, and Western boutiques. Sisters' annual events include a popular rodeo, an outdoor quilt show, and a Celebration of the Arts.

The town of McKenzie Bridge, known as Strawberry Flat back in 1902, is a small river settlement located on Highway 126 on the east end of the loop. One of several communities spanning the McKenzie River corridor, McKenzie Bridge offers tired travelers a place to hang their hats for the night in much the same tradition as a hundred years ago. Rustic riverside log cabins, natural hot spring pools, and deep forest campgrounds continue to welcome today's visitors.

The Santiam Wagon Road, which once served as a dominant access route over the Cascade Mountains to the Willamette Valley, operated from 1865 until 1939, when Highway 20 and Highways 22 and 126 developments combined to make it obsolete. A segment of this road traverses the Fish Lake Historic Remount Depot on Highway 126, an early roadhouse for wagon road travelers, where lodging, food, and hay were purchased for less than $1 in 1890. Today, vintage pre-1940 vehicles and horse-drawn wagons can travel from here to Tombstone Pass by permit.

The annual John Craig Memorial Race commemorates mail carrier John Craig's journeys across the McKenzie Pass. Craig (1821-1877) died carrying the Christmas mail over this route. Today, Nordic skiers endure winter rain, sleet, hail, and snow to race over Historic Highway 242, which is closed in the winter. This event has been ongoing since the late 1800s and continues to be enjoyed—and endured—today.

HISTORICAL

Travel through the passes was arduous, and development was challenging. The Santiam Pass, one of the major highways crossing the Cascade Range, was discovered in 1859 by Andrew Wiley and was named for the Santiam Indians, a Kalapooian tribe living near the Santiam River. The Byway crosses the route of the Willamette Valley Cascade Mountain Wagon Road, later known as the Santiam Wagon Road. This road is still used today as a secondary road for public access. A portion of the original railroad grade of the Hogg Railroad, constructed as early as 1888, is visible from Santiam Pass near Hogg Rock.

The Fish Lake Work Center, also known as the Fish Lake Remount Station, is a Forest Service administrative site still in use on the northeastern shore of Fish

Lake on Highway 126. Serving as the official Forest Service work center in the early 1900s, structures have been renovated to preserve the history of early horse-packing operations and summer headquarters for patrol and lookout employees.

In Oregon during the 1930s, the Civilian Conservation Corp (CCC) enhanced numerous recreational opportunities along the McKenzie Pass-Santiam Pass National Scenic Byway, including building the lava rock structure at the top of McKenzie Pass and naming it after the group's foreman, Dee Wright. Since its completion in 1935, the observatory has been a favorite attraction for thousands of visitors. Evidence of the CCC's work remains at Clear Lake, located on Highway 126, where a rough-hewn timber shelter is used today by groups that picnic in the area. This shelter stands as a reminder that while journeys through these passes have changed over time, elements of past experiences remain.

NATURAL

The natural qualities of the McKenzie Pass-Santiam Pass Scenic Byway are of national significance. You can find outstanding examples of both ancient and recent volcanoes, cinder cones, lava flows, and deep, glaciated canyons. Forests along the Byway contain rare old-growth fir and ponderosa pine and are home to a great variety of fish and wildlife, including several endangered species, such as the bald eagle, the northern spotted owl, the chinook salmon, the steelhead, and the bull trout.

The geology along the route is especially significant. The McKenzie Pass-Santiam Pass area is the best place in the Pacific Northwest to see how the great bulk of the volcanic Cascade Range has been built. Here, basaltic shield volcanoes are produced on a regular basis. Some have grown into large, steep-sided volcanic cones, such as North Sister and Mount Washington. Glaciers have deeply eroded most of these cones, but a new group of shields, unaffected by glaciers, erupted between 1,500 and 400 years ago. Easily seen from McKenzie Pass, the best example of a new Cascade shield volcano is Belknap Crater, which has long, barren, gentle slopes of lava.

RECREATIONAL

The McKenzie Pass-Santiam Pass Scenic Byway area offers three wilderness areas, two national trails, several lakes, many snow-capped volcanoes, two Wild &

Scenic Rivers, and a major resort. Recreational opportunities include hiking, horseback riding, camping, boating, fishing, swimming, bicycle touring, mountain biking, skiing, golf, and tennis. The Pacific Crest National Scenic Trail provides an opportunity that is unique in the country to hike the crest of a major volcanic mountain range. If you're a boater, you can choose lakes or whitewater rafting and kayaking on the McKenzie River.

The fishing is nationally famous. Anglers come from all over the United States to fly-fish for wild trout on the upper Metolius and to fish for trout, salmon, and steelhead on the upper McKenzie. During the winter, you can downhill ski at the Hoodoo ski area and snowmobile and cross-country ski on miles of marked trails. Because the Byway includes the drier east side of the Cascade Mountains, during several months of the year, you can ski in the morning at higher elevations and then hike, fly-fish, bicycle, or play tennis in the afternoon at lower elevations on the Byway.

SCENIC

Along the McKenzie Pass-Santiam Pass Scenic Byway, you see dramatic, close-up views of the most beautiful snow-capped High Cascade Peaks, two Wild & Scenic rivers, and several waterfalls. The view of the Three Sisters and Broken Top Mountains (found at the start of the Byway on Highway 242 just outside the town of Sisters) represents the greatest concentration of snow-capped volcanoes with glaciers in the lower 48 states. In addition, the panoramic view of lava fields and six Cascade peaks from the summit of McKenzie Pass is made even more striking by the contrast between the black lava and white snow. The mountains are mirrored in crystal-clear lakes.

Highlights

Travelers generally access this Byway from two primary points. If you're heading west from Eugene/Springfield, begin the Byway at the junction of historic Highway 242 and Highway 126, about 5 miles west of the full-service community of McKenzie Bridge. If you're arriving from the east, access the Byway from Sisters, a lively town chock-full of arts and crafts offerings and special events, such as the annual quilt show and jazz festival, following an early Western theme set back in time to the 1800s.

The following list of stops along the Byway indicates milepost numbers, so you can use it regardless of your direction of travel on the Byway.

⊙ **Milepost 2.1—Junction Highway 126 and 242:** Turn right to travel up 242, the McKenzie Pass Route. The forest along the Byway on this portion is dark green, characterized by water-loving species such as hemlocks, cedars, and firs. The climb eastward up Highway 242 is through a thickly vegetated, narrow corridor. Here the road meanders, and travel is slow.

⊙ **Milepost 8.8—Proxy Falls Trailhead:** To take in the beauty of both falls, plan to spend about an hour to hike the 1 1/4-mile loop trail into the Three Sisters Wilderness.

⊙ **Milepost 7.0—Scott Road Historical Marker/ Pulloff:** Take a few moments to get off the highway after your slow wind up Dead Horse Grade. Open views of the Three Sisters Mountains, part of the Cascade Range and originally named Faith, Hope, and Charity in the 1840s, lie to the east. The Scott Road was really an old settler trail named after Felix Scott, Jr. (1829-1879), who pioneered a wagon trail/road over the Cascades northeast of McKenzie Bridge. This route, part of which is maintained trail into the Three Sisters Wilderness, proved to be almost impassible for wagon travel.

☼ **Milepost 2.7—Belknap Crater Viewpoint:** A great photo opportunity awaits you here. You can view Big Belknap Crater and the smaller cone of Little Belknap Crater. Don't let its size fool you—Little Belknap was the origin of the immense lava fields in the foreground. Use caution when walking out onto the lava.

☼ **Milepost 3.5—Dee Wright Observatory:** Plan on an hour to tour the observatory and walk the 1/2-mile Lava River Trail.

☼ **Milepost 3.2—Windy Point Viewpoint:** At an elevation of 4,909 feet, Windy Point offers a picturesque view of the lava flows and volcanic peaks. Although little vegetation grows on the lava fields, as you make your descent down from the summit of the McKenzie Pass, a mixed conifer forest returns, eventually giving way to ponderosa pines at the lower elevation. It is the dramatic transition between these diverse natural environ-ments that defines the uniqueness of this Byway. Geologic interpretive information is available at the viewpoint.

☼ **Milepost 11.5—East Portal, Sisters:** The Santiam Pass Route begins at the Sisters Portal, heading north at the junction of Highways 126/20 and 242.

☼ **Milepost 6.5—Black Butte:** Black Butte is the prominent composite cone north of the highway. In spite of its youthful profile, Black Butte is older than many of the dissected High Cascade peaks. The US Forest Service still operates a lookout on the top.

☼ **Milepost 9.3—Mount Washington Viewpoint:** Geologic and forest interpretive information is available here. For a quick stop, this roadside pull-off offers a spectacular view of the volcanic peak and basin.

☼ **Milepost 19.5 (Sahalie Falls) and milepost 0.4 (Koosah Falls):** The McKenzie River surges over a 70-foot high basalt cliff called Koosah Falls. Plan to spend half an hour here to take pictures and view the interpretive panels featuring geologic history. Then hike for an hour on the Waterfalls Loop trail that connects this site with Sahalie Falls (or drive to the site).

Outback Scenic Byway

OREGON

Outback means "isolated rural country," and this area of Oregon is indeed rugged and remote. This Byway takes you through Oregon's outback, where the agricultural and timber industries employ many of the residents, where the landscape ranges from lush green forests to arid desert, and where the people who live here seek independence yet know each other by first names. While you're here, you'll notice that community is paramount to the people who call this area home.

The Byway Story

The Outback Scenic Byway tells archaeological, cultural, natural, recreational, and scenic stories that make it a unique and treasured Byway.

QUICK FACTS

Length: 171 miles.

Time to Allow: 3 to 4 hours.

Best Time to Drive: Spring to fall.

Byway Travel Information: Lake County Chamber of Commerce: phone 541/947-6040.

Special Considerations: Most supplies should be available in towns near the Byway.

Restrictions: Highway 31 and US Highway 395, along with Country Roads 5-10, 11, and 11A are maintained year-round. On rare occasions, winter snowstorms may slow traffic, but the roads are almost never closed.

Bicycle/Pedestrian Facilities: No special bike paths have been provided along the Byway, but the road has low traffic and a high percentage of straight stretches with good sight distances. Pedestrians are able to stretch their legs or take short hikes at Fort Rock National Landmark, Summer Lake Rest Area, Chandler Wayside, and Gooselake state parks. The town of Lakeview also has sidewalks along Highway 395. Along the rest of the Byway, pedestrians share the shoulder of the road with vehicles.

ARCHAEOLOGICAL

The Outback Scenic Byway transects the Fort Rock Cave National Register Site, the Picture Rock Pass National Register Site, and the Lake Abert National Register District. All these sites contain significant historic and prehistoric cultural values. The districts have one of the highest cultural site densities in the Great Basin Region, and several archaeological papers and reports of regional and national significance have been published regarding the rock art and sagebrush sandals found here.

CULTURAL

Some of this Byway's cultural flavor can be seen in the buildings along the Byway, which reflect the influence of the Old West.

NATURAL

Among the many natural attributes, the Fort Rock State Natural Area is listed as a National Natural Landmark. Fort Rock is a volcanic marr formation that homesteading families of long ago appropriately named for its four-sided towering walls. This ideal natural fort is colored orange/brown.

Abert Rim, another natural attraction, is one of the nation's longest and most continuous fault escarpments. This rim rises more than 2,000 feet above the highway.

The Summer Lake State Wildlife Area is 18,000 acres in size and home to more than 250 species of birds. The marshlike area, located in the high desert, is strategically important for habitat and nesting. Regionally, it is one of the most important stops for migrating birds that use the Pacific Flyway. Many sensitive, threatened, or endangered species, such as bald eagles, American peregrine falcons, western snowy plovers, greater sand hill cranes, and trumpeter swans, can be seen using this habitat. More than 15,000 bird watchers flock here annually. Seasonal access by foot and vehicle is designated. This is truly a bird-watcher's paradise.

RECREATIONAL

The thermal updrafts that are created from the warming of the valley and the mountains make the Lakeview area ideal for hang gliding. In fact, Lakeview has been named the hang gliding capital of the West by many hang-gliding and sport magazines. An annual hang gliding festival around the Fourth of July attracts hundreds of pilots, making it one of the most unique recreational events in Oregon. The US Hang Gliding Association has held two national championships in the Lakeview area. Pilots from around the world come to catch the thermals.

The Byway brings visitors in close proximity to six national designations, including the Gearhart Mountain Wilderness, the Christmas Valley National Back Country Byway, the Lake Abert and the Warner Wetlands Areas of Critical Environmental Concern, the Hart Mountain National Wildlife Refuge, and the Lakeview to Steens Back Country Byway.

SCENIC

The Outback Scenic Byway is one of the most scenic routes in the Great Basin Region. You pass through different environments as you drive the Byway, and the changes between environments are dramatic. The different environments include old-growth ponderosa and lodgepole pine stands found in the Eastern Cascades, the sage brush steppe, the wetlands, and the other high-desert ecosystems.

One of the most striking scenic features along this Byway is the sweeping view of Winter and Abert Rims. These rims are 2,000-foot fault escarpment blocks that tower above the Byway. Abert Rim is Oregon's longest, most dramatic, and most photographed fault escarpment. This rim is also considered one of the most continuous fault escarpments in the United States.

Highlights

Starting at the southern end of the Byway coming out of California on Highway 395, you'll see the following sites. If you start on the other end of the Byway, begin at the bottom of this list and make your way up.

- ○ **Lakeview, Oregon,** is the hang-gliding capital of the West. One mile north of Lakeview is the only active geyser in the West, called **Old Perpetual.** Bring your camera to take a picture of the geyser, which erupts every 90 seconds.

❂ Continue north on the Byway and, if you have an extra 30 to 60 minutes, head east on Highway 395 to the Abert Rim drive and **Lake Abert.** If you don't have that much time, continue north on Highway 31 to the town of **Paisley** and the annual Mosquito Festival that occurs there every July. Continue on past the **Summer Lake Lodge** and wilderness area; if you have a day to spend in the woods, the area is excellent for fishing and hiking.

❂ Just south of Silver Lake is **Picture Rock Pass,** an area named for the ancient Indian petroglyphs that decorate rock within walking distance of the highway.

❂ Continue your drive on Highway 31 to Fort Rock. While there, visit the remnants of an ancient volcano at **Fort Rock State Park,** just 7 miles off the Byway. Nearby is the **Homestead Village Museum,** which takes from 30 to 60 minutes to explore. From Fort Rock, continue on Highway 31, where the Byway ends as it meets Highway 97.

❂ If you end up having extra time to see additional points of interest, from Fort Rock you can travel country road 5-12 past Cougar Mountain to many volcanic formations, such as **Hole-in-the-Ground, Devils Garden, The Blowouts,** and **Derrick Cave.** If you have even more time, from Country Road 5-12, head east to Country Road 5-12B and then south on BLM Road 6109C to **Four Craters Lava Flow** and **Crack in the Ground.** Keep heading south to Christmas Valley, head east on Country Road 5-14, and then go north on Country Road 5-14D to the **Sand Dunes** and the **Lost Forest.**

Pacific Coast Scenic Byway
OREGON

This Byway trots along the full length of the Oregon coast. The northern end starts in the shadow of the impressive Astoria-Megler Bridge, where the mouth of the Columbia River gapes wide (Astoria is the oldest US settlement west of the Rockies). Shining beaches and temperate rain forests govern the following dozens of miles. Parallelling the Lewis and Clark Trail, the route stops by attractive places, such as the resort town of Seaside, famous for its 2-mile beachfront promenade, and the busy Garibaldi fishing port on Tillamook Bay.

QUICK FACTS

Length: 363 miles.

Time to Allow: 10 to 12 hours.

Best Time to Drive: Spring to fall.

Byway Travel Information: Oregon Coast Visitor's Association Oregon Tourism Commission: phone 503/986-0000.

Special Considerations: Services may be several miles apart or closed at night. Slides and floods caused by extreme weather conditions sometimes temporarily disrupt access. With the ocean providing year-round air-conditioning, temperatures are comfortably in the 60s and 70s in the summer and rarely drop below freezing in the winter. Be prepared for fog, drizzle, or rain showers any time of year, but mainly in the winter and spring. Steady breezes are common most of the year. However, winter storms occasionally bring gusts above 50 mph. At the Oregon Dunes National Recreation Area, temperatures are at their highest and winds are at their lowest during the early fall. Be prepared for rapidly changing weather conditions.

Bicycle/Pedestrian Facilities: This Byway is designated by the Oregon Department of Transportation as a state bike route. Signage and stripes are provided for the bike route and pedestrian crossings. Bicycling on the Oregon Coast Bike Route is considered to be the most exciting way to explore the scenery along this Byway.

The southern portion of the Byway changes a little because it is dominated by rugged cliffs, farms, and sandy beaches. This segment maintains some of the most photographed areas in Oregon; photographers often capture Siletz and Depoe Bays, the colorful Oregon skies, lots of dairy land, and the city of Tillamook (the producer of the famous brand of cheese).

The Byway Story

The Pacific Coast Scenic Byway tells archaeological, cultural, historical, natural, recreational, and scenic stories that make it a unique and treasured Byway.

ARCHAEOLOGICAL

The relics and structures located in this area indicate that people have lived and prospered here for several millennia. This Byway's archaeological residue fits into two main categories: relics of a native people that reveal an Eden-like past (such as ancient campsites) and evidences of the activities of a more recent people. Of the ancient people, scientists have found remnants of spears, knives, and other hunting equipment.

Discoveries of bones near campsites indicate the type of food these people ate: fish, large animals (elk and deer), and some birds. The people were largely industrious and thrived in this area for thousands of years.

The sites from a more recent people are mostly historic bridges and lighthouses such as Yaquina Head's 125-year-old lighthouse, the 125-foot Astoria Column in Astoria, and the occasional shipwreck, such as the one known as *Peter Iredale* at Fort Stevens State Park. Some of these impressive structures still stand as landmarks to help guide travelers, while others function as attractions for tourists.

CULTURAL

Appreciate this area more by taking part in everyday activities to familiarize yourself with the area's culture. For instance, go to Lincoln City to soar a colorful kite alongside the locals; after that, visit some of Lincoln City's many art galleries. Another popular destination is Bandon, a charming town famous for its lighthouse, its giant seastacks, its cheese factory, and the cranberry harvest.

You might stop in Tillamook and see Oregon's largest cheese factory for a taste-testing tour: something residents like to do every now and then. This impressive factory has been around for over 100 years. It boasts of continuing to use the time-tested recipe that has made its cheese famous. Other areas of note include North Bend and Coos Bay, cities that compose the coast's largest urban area; here, you'll find cultural activities galore, such as fantastic symphonies, art galleries, and restaurants.

HISTORICAL

The gorgeous and rich Oregon coast has drawn and sustained native people for centuries, and it has done likewise for sightseers and settlers ever since Lewis and Clark highly acclaimed the area. Each new wave of people who came to live around the route added a new facet of culture and history to it and left their mark through historical and archaeological remains.

These remains, shadows of past, are waiting in places like Astoria. Other important historical sites on the Byway include Fort Clatsop National Memorial, a life-size replica of Lewis and Clark's 1805-1806 winter outpost; historic Battle Rock Park in Port Orford, one of Oregon's oldest incorporated towns; and Yaquina Head's lighthouse, a testament to the area's historical shipping industry. The area's history is also evidenced in the many Victorian homes that scale the hillside, the 1883 Flavel House, and the shipwreck of the *Peter Iredale* at Fort Stevens State Park.

NATURAL

The Byway runs along the coastline, bringing highway travelers to the sea and away again, winding by estuarine marshes, clinging to exposed seaside cliffs, passing through gentle agricultural valleys, and brushing against wind-sculpted dunes. Travelers encounter the scenic splendor of sea-stack rock formations that are eroding under constant surf, as well as a plethora of unusual plants and animals that provide natural wonder.

The highest waterfall in the Coast Range is an easy side trip from the Byway. To find this waterfall, go 7 miles south of Tillamook, and then watch for a small sign to Munson Creek Falls. Follow the narrow road 1 1/2 miles to the parking area. A short stroll takes you to the base of this 266-foot cataract.

Many travelers enjoy watching water wildlife along this Byway. Waysides and state parks along the coast make excellent vantage points for watching gray whales that migrate between December and May.

RECREATIONAL

Beaches along the Byway are open to public use. In addition, many state parks run the length of the Byway and provide public access and protection to beaches. An abundance of public campsites, motel rooms, beach houses, and eateries along the Byway corridor ensure a delightful extended stay along Oregon's Pacific Coast Scenic Byway.

Florence is the gateway to the Oregon Dunes National Recreation Area, a 47-mile sandbox with areas designated for bird-watching and dune riding. Honeyman State Park is a popular place to water-ski and camp. As you travel on through the dunes, take a side trip to the Dean Creek Elk Viewing Area at Reedsport. The Oregon Dunes National Recreation Area has more than 31,000 acres. Visitors can camp, arrange a tour, take an exhilarating off-highway vehicle ride, or just walk along tranquil lakes, forest trails, and beaches.

Tucked in among some of the highest coastal dunes in the world, you'll find plenty of fishing and boating opportunities in small communities like Winchester Bay and Lakeside. The dunes end near the cities of North Bend and Coos Bay, the coast's largest urban area. As Oregon's deepest natural harbor, Coos Bay has long been a major shipping port for the timber industry and a haven for sport-fishing enthusiasts.

Depoe Bay also offers fishing and whale-watching excursions from the world's smallest navigable harbor.

Flying large, beautiful kites is a common practice all along the coast, but is especially popular in Lincoln

City, which was recognized by *KiteLines* magazine as the best place to fly a kite in North America. Annual spring and fall kite festivals draw kite enthusiasts from all over. Get out your kite and watch with the crowds as the delicate crafts are lofted up into the sky by the strong coastal winds.

SCENIC

Keep your camera handy so that you can capture the coast's most photographed seascape, Cape Foulweather and the churning waves at Devil's Punch Bowl. The superb scenery continues through Waldport and Yachats to the Cape Perpetua Scenic Area. Here, you can watch the waves rush in and out of Devil's Churn, or you can hike on trails high above it. As the rugged cliffs give way to graceful sand dunes, you'll arrive in Florence, a city that explodes with wild rhododendrons in the spring. The drive into Brookings saves some of the best scenery for last. For example, Samuel Boardman State Park shows off 9 miles of rocky viewpoints and quiet beaches at the base of the Siskiyou Mountains. After crossing the crystal blue Chetco River, the Pacific Coast Scenic Byway ends in redwood country at the California border.

Highlights

Take the Pacific Coast Highway's must-see tour:

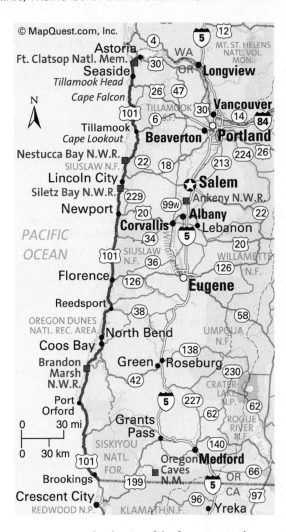

- **Astoria:** You will pass through Long Beach and go on to the city of Astoria, the oldest American settlement west of the Rockies. Astoria offers more points of historical interest than any other place on the Oregon coast.

- **Fort Clatsop National Memorial:** For a glimpse into life on one of the most important expeditions in the nation's history, travel 3 miles east on Alternate (Old) 101 to Fort Clatsop Road and follow signs to the memorial. It is operated by the National Park Service on the site where the Lewis and Clark Expedition spent the winter of 1805-1806.

- **Seaside:** You reach the city of Seaside, which was Oregon's first seashore resort. The Turnaround there is the location of the statue designating the end of the Lewis and Clark Trail. At the south end of the Promenade, you will find the Lewis and Clark Salt Cairn, where members of the expedition made salt from seawater.

- **Cannon Beach:** The site of the famous annual Sandcastle Building Contest in early June. The beach was named for a cannon washed ashore in 1846 after the wreck of the schooner *Shark*.

- **Lincoln County:** Lincoln County has miles of ocean beaches known for fine agates and other minerals, ocean cruises, and whale-watching trips out of Depoe Bay and Newport. Lincoln City also has Oregon's first factory outlet shopping center.

- **Yaquina Bay Lighthouse:** The lighthouse houses a museum and is open during scheduled hours.

- **Devils Churn:** The basalt that forms the shore here is penetrated by a split in the rock that narrows to a few feet before finally disappearing into the cliff. Fascinating in summer, it is awe-inspiring during winter storms and is an excellent spot for photographers.

- **Cape Perpetua Viewpoint:** Just south of Devils Churn you'll find a road going inland. At the branch in the road, turn left and continue climbing sharply to the Cape Perpetua Viewpoint. There is a fine view of the coast both north and south.

- **Heceta Head Lighthouse State Scenic Viewpoint (formerly Devil's Elbow State Park):** This pretty little cove is the place to see Heceta Head Lighthouse up close. Just walk up the trail to the former assistant lighthouse keeper's home, Heceta House, and continue on to the lighthouse.

- **Sea Lion Caves:** These natural caves are home to Steller sea lions.

- **Florence:** There are many delightful shops, restaurants, and galleries in this town near the Siuslaw River.

- **Oregon Dunes National Recreation Area (NRA):** The Oregon Dunes NRA extends from Florence to North Bend with many access points off of the Byway.

- **Umpqua River:** The Umpqua River Bridge is one of the historic coast bridges. The Umpqua is one of the major rivers in Oregon and is navigable by fairly large vessels upstream as far as Scottsburg.

- **Cape Blanco:** Five miles west of the Byway, Cape Blanco was discovered by the Spanish explorer Martin de Aguilar in 1603. The lighthouse is located at the westernmost point in Oregon.

- **Prehistoric Gardens:** In the rain forest atmosphere of the Oregon coast, the developers of Prehistoric Gardens have created life-sized replicas of dinosaurs.

Rogue-Umpqua Scenic Byway
OREGON

More commonly known as the "highway of waterfalls," the Rogue-Umpqua Scenic Byway ascends deep into the Cascades. About 18 miles east of Roseburg, the North Umpqua River meets head-on with the Little River at Colliding Rivers, one of the few places in the world where this head-on phenomenon occurs. The North Umpqua provides whitewater thrills and superb steelhead runs as it tumbles through the Umpqua National Forest.

After passing more than a half dozen waterfalls, the Byway reaches sparkling Diamond Lake, a year-round playground at the base of Mount Thielsen. The paved 11-mile path around the lake is one of the nicest family bike rides anywhere. From here, you're only moments away from Crater Lake's north entrance, which is usually open from June through October, and has attracted people from around the world to view its unusual beauty. Scientists from many places even come here to study the environment. In winter, you can swing through Highway 230 and Highway 62 to the south entrance, which is open year-round.

Whether you're learning about the rich history of the Native Americans, stretching in front of a tranquil lake, or experiencing the rush of whitewater rafting on the river known as an "emerald jewel" of Oregon, this Byway shares one of the state's best-loved areas with you.

QUICK FACTS

Length: 172 miles.

Time to Allow: 7 to 8 hours.

Best Time to Drive: Summer and fall; fall colors are particularly spectacular along this Byway.

Byway Travel Information: Medford Visitors and Convention Bureau: phone 541/779-4847; Upper Rogue Regional Tourism Alliance: phone 541/878-3626; Roseburg Visitors and Convention Bureau: phone 541/672-9731; Byway local Web sites: www.visitroseburg.com; www.upperrogue.org; www.visitmedford.org.

Special Considerations: Check your car's fuel level often. Gas stations are few and far between. Also, during the winter months, the roads may be dangerous.

Bicycle/Pedestrian Facilities: Many trails are available along this Byway, and they vary in levels of difficulty. One of the highlights is a paved 11-mile bike path around Diamond Lake.

The Byway Story

The Rogue-Umpqua Scenic Byway tells archaeological, historical, natural, recreational, and scenic stories that make it a unique and treasured Byway.

ARCHAEOLOGICAL

The North Umpqua and Rogue Wild & Scenic rivers flow through this valley that was inhabited by prehistoric people for more than 8,000 years. Many dating techniques, such as radiocarbon and stratigraphic dating, indicate prehistoric occupations prior to the eruption of the volcano Mount Mazama, approximately 6,800 years ago. The presence of time-sensitive artifacts indicates that occupation may go as far back as 12,500 years.

The route encompasses lands once occupied by the ancestors of the Upland Takelma, Southern Molalla, Klamath, and Cow Creek Bands of the Umpqua and Upper Umpqua rivers. Along the route, interpretative panels are offered at the Colliding Rivers site at Glide, representing an Upper Umpqua village site. There is also a recorded prehistoric fishing locality that is located at the Narrows near Idleyld Park. The Susan Creek archaeological site contains cairns, representing vision questing. A trail provides access to the site, and an interpretive panel provides information on this site.

The nature and habitation of the valley changed with the eruption of Mount Mazama. When the volcano erupted, the Upper North Umpqua and Rogue River drainages were covered with a layer of airborne ash as far downstream as Dry Creek on the Umpqua and Elk Creek on the Rogue. A cloud of superheated gas and ash flowed across Diamond Lake and down the North Umpqua River to the Toketee Falls area and down the Rogue River towards Prospect, denuding the forest and destroying whatever plant and animal life happened to be in the way. Subsequent flood events carried ash and pumice farther downstream, blanketing terraces. Drainages were choked with ash, and their gravel beds became silted over, altering fish habitat. This cataclysmic event forced early inhabitants to adapt to their new surroundings, and archaeological sites within the Rogue and Umpqua corridors preserve a record of these adaptations, including alterations in clothing, food, and hunting techniques.

HISTORICAL
Early settlers to the Rogue-Umpqua Scenic Byway laid a foundation for life in this rugged landscape. The Fort Klamath military wagon road made its way over the formidable Cascades to the settlement of Union Creek. The city doesn't remain today, but the wagon trail was an important trail to get settlers and supplies over the mountains. In the 1850s, the Siskiyou Mountains in the Rogue River National Forest became home to many prospectors who were searching for gold. In the early days of the Byway, Indians, trappers, traders, explorers, and settlers all made their way into the surrounding area and worked or settled there.

The Civilian Conservation Corps (CCC) further developed the area surrounding the Byway during the 1930s. This organization provided work for thousands of people during a time of low employment. The CCC was responsible for a variety of projects, including reforestation, fire prevention, soil conservation, and development of recreational areas. Many structures that stand today along the Byway are a legacy to the CCC.

Stretching across the river near Steamboat is the historic Mott Bridge, a recognized Oregon Historic Civil Engineering Landmark. Constructed by the CCC in 1935-1936, the Mott Bridge is the only surviving example of three such structures built at that time in the Pacific Northwest. The CCC also built Diamond Lake's Visitor Center and guard station, as well as the ranger house at Colliding Rivers. Both of the historic structures at Diamond Lake and Colliding Rivers serve as visitor centers today.

NATURAL
Fisheries play an important role in the ecosystem. The spring-fed rivers flow high amounts of freshwater and support nationally significant fisheries of steelhead and salmon. The Upper Rogue and North Umpqua National Wild & Scenic Rivers sustain critical habitats for a variety of resident and anadromous fish species, including summer and winter steelhead, fall and spring chinook, coho, and sea-run cutthroat. These rivers and others provide large and consistent numbers of native (non-hatchery) fish in the run. In 1997, following the listing of the Umpqua River cutthroat trout as an endangered species, fishing for trout in the mainstream Umpqua and tributaries was prohibited. Additionally, all wild steelhead and coho salmon caught in the North Umpqua River must be released.

Two fish hatcheries are also associated with the Rogue-Umpqua Scenic Byway. Located at the base of Lost Creek Dam on the Rogue River, the Cole M. Rivers Hatchery is the largest hatchery on the West Coast, built in 1973 to mitigate for a lost spawning area when three dams were constructed in the Rogue Valley. The Rock Creek Fish Hatchery, built in lower Rock Creek and 1/2 mile from SH 138, was constructed in the late 1800s. It still operates to supplement the summer steelhead, spring chinook, and coho fisheries of the Umpqua, the North Umpqua, and South Umpqua rivers.

RECREATIONAL
Many come to fish, hike, camp, bike, and soak in the sites. However, the recreational opportunity that's most popular here is whitewater boating, an exhilarating experience that brings people back each year because of its world-class fun. The 33.8-mile Wild & Scenic North Umpqua River offers an array

of whitewater thrills, including rapids of intermediate to advanced experience levels. Averaging a vertical drop of 26 feet per river mile, deep emerald-green pools tail out into whitewater rapids ranging from Class II through Class V (Narrows and Deadline Falls). The Wild & Scenic section has been divided into five segments, each offering put-in and take-out areas that allow you to choose the length and difficulty of your trip. The most frequently used segments are from Boulder Flat Put-in to Gravel Bin Take-Out and Bogus Launch Site to Susan Creek Take-out; each offers a two- to four-hour float trip, depending on water flow.

For the days not spent braving the rapids, Joseph H. Stewart State Park on Lost Creek Reservoir is a water paradise, providing 151 campsites with electrical hook-ups; 50 tent sites with water; two group tent camping areas with the amenities of flush toilets, showers, volleyball and horseshoe pits; and day-use picnic areas. The boating facilities include a marina with a store and café, moorage facility, boat launch, boat rentals, and fish-cleaning facilities. You also find several other recreation sites on the 30 miles of shoreline created by Lost Creek Reservoir, including McGregor Park, a visitor center called "Spirit of the Rogue Nature Center," Takelma Recreation Area, and the Cole M. Rivers Fish Hatchery.

SCENIC

The tremendous diversity of geologic and volcanic formations, coupled with 15 waterfalls, make the Rogue-Umpqua a photographer's paradise. Famous artists and photographers have come from all over the world to capture awe-inspiring images. Nearly every stretch of the route provides serene places to enjoy the beauty of nature.

Volcanic activity ravaged this area, creating many distinctive and stunning landscapes. In the Diamond Lake area, the route is characterized by unique High Cascades volcanic remnants. Some of these include Crater Lake Rim and impressive peaks, such as Mount Thielsen (elevation 9,182 feet), Mount McLoughlin (elevation 9,495 feet), Mount Bailey (elevation 8,363 feet), and others.

The Umpqua Rocks Geologic Area parallels Highway 138 from Marsters Bridge to Soda Springs. Along the Upper Rogue River, the highway is built on pumice and ash flows, which were part of the cataclysmic Mount Mazama eruption. The ash flows overlay 1.25 million-year-old lava flows. The river flows through lava tubes above and below the surface at the Rogue Gorge and Natural Bridge interpretive sites. Sedimentary and marine deposits are evident as the highway enters the Rogue Valley, with the exception of the notable Upper and Lower Table Rocks, which are remnants of High Cascades Province lava flows.

You'll find 15 notable waterfalls along this Byway, ranging in size and accessibility. One of the most popular is the Watson Falls, the third highest in Oregon. The water tumbles down 272 feet, which causes a cool mist to refresh you on a searing day.

Volcanic Legacy Scenic Byway

OREGON

QUICK FACTS

Length: 140 miles.

Time to Allow: 5 to 7 hours.

Best Time to Drive: Spring to fall; summer is the high season.

Byway Travel Information: Klamath County Department of Tourism: phone toll-free 800/445-6728; Byway local Web sites: www.sova.org/volcanic and www.volcaniclegacy.net.

Special Considerations: The portion of the route from the south rim of Crater Lake to the North Park Entrance, including Rim Drive, is closed from mid-October to mid-June each year due to snow. The opening of Rim Drive each year is a locally celebrated event that signals the beginning of summer. Views of Crater Lake are available year-round at the south rim near the visitor facilities. The route generally provides safe winter access.

Restrictions: The Byway from the Oregon/California border to Crater Lake National Park is open year-round. In Crater Lake National Park, the Byway from the south rim of Crater Lake to the North Park Entrance (including the Rim Drive) is closed from mid-October to mid-June.

Bicycle/Pedestrian Facilities: Portions of this Byway are well suited for bicycle travel and pedestrian use (to some extent). The Westside Road (County 531) and the southern portion of Oregon Highway 140 have generous shoulder bikeways and gentle grades. The shared road/bikeways in the Fort Klamath area, the climb to Crater Lake, and the Rim Drive are all popular with touring cyclists. The US Highway 97 segment also has paved shoulders, but it is less desirable for biking due to heavy truck traffic. The northern portion of Oregon Highway 140 over Doak Mountain to the Westside Road needs reconstruction to add bikeway shoulders to safely accommodate bike travel.

This diverse Byway follows the brims of lakes, diverse wetlands, scenic ranches, thriving croplands, and forests full of bald eagles. It passes brilliant Crater Lake National Park and historic Crater Lake Lodge. It also threads its way through volcanic landscapes, craggy mountain reaches, and high-desert wetlands.

As the Byway passes the 90,000-surface-acre Upper Klamath Lake, you can see over 1 million birds during peak migrations in the fall. The Klamath Basin is the largest freshwater ecosystem west of the Great Lakes. Six national wildlife refuges in these wetlands were favorite fishing spots of President Roosevelt.

You can also visit the same Pelican Bay where John Muir (naturalist, writer, conservationist, and founder of the Sierra Club) wrote *The Story of My Boyhood and Youth* in 1908.

The Byway Story

The Volcanic Legacy Scenic Byway tells archaeological, cultural, historical, natural, recreational, and scenic stories that make it a unique and treasured Byway.

ARCHAEOLOGICAL

This Byway was (and still is) littered with ancient Native American artifacts. Most of the artifacts that have been discovered along this route and are displayed among the 100,000 artifacts in the Byway's own Favell Museum of Western Art and Indian Artifacts. This museum focuses on the area's Native American tribes but also spotlights tribes across the country. It covers 12,000 years of history in its collections of basketry, beadwork, stone tools, and pottery.

CULTURAL

The Klamath tribes (more specifically, the Klamaths, Modocs, and Yahooskin) are an integral part of the communities along the Byway because they lived here before anyone can remember. Also, the determination and grit they have demonstrated to survive the changes of years, famine, and new settlers have affected positively the attitudes of other groups who have lived in the area, including the groups who caused their setbacks.

The Klamath tribes have worked hard to maintain their own culture in spite of circumstances. When the tribes were forced to reservations in the 1860s, they turned to cattle ranching and made a profitable living. And even though the tribes were not federally recognized for about 30 years and had to work without supplemental human services or their reservation land, they have sustained the economy of Klamath County for decades; they contribute $12 million per year to the Klamath County economy. They have also instituted training schools to make their enterprises more competitive.

HISTORICAL

This Byway's past dwells in some of its historic buildings. By visiting these buildings, you can learn about the significant historical forces and events that shaped the area. For instance, logging was a major part of the early 20th century, and you can get a feel for the area's logging history at Collier State Park and Logging Museum. Through displays featuring actual equipment and other related items, the incredibly difficult life of a lumberjack is told.

Fort Klamath also tells an important story of early settlement. The fort was built in 1863 to protect Oregon Trail pioneers and southern emigrant trains from the nearby Modoc and Klamath tribes who were inclined to attack on occasion. Two notable events happened at this fort: one was when Captain Jack, a Modoc leader who figured centrally in the war of 1872-1873, was executed at the fort along with three other Modoc warriors in late 1873 (their graves are at the fort); the second was when the fort played an important part in the working out of the 1864 Council Grove peace treaty.

Crater Lake Lodge's historical guest register shows what a popular vacation spot Crater Lake has always been: it has hosted important visitors, such as First Lady Eleanor Roosevelt and author Jack London. It is listed on the National Register of Historic Places.

NATURAL

This Byway sustains masses of wildlife in its several wildlife refuge areas, bulky mountains, and unique geological formations. Six national wildlife refuges have been established in the area: Lower Klamath, Tule Lake, Clear Lake, Bear Valley, Upper Klamath, and Klamath Marsh. These refuges are diverse; they include freshwater marshes, open waters, grassy meadows, coniferous forests, sagebrush, juniper grasslands, agricultural lands, rock cliffs, and slopes. Over 400 different species have been identified in the refuges. In the spring, more than 1 million birds retreat here. This number is added to in the summer, as ducks and Canadian geese join the throng. In the fall, the birds (ducks, geese, swans, and green-winged teal) number in the millions. In addition, the Klamath Basin is home to the largest concentration of wintering bald eagles in the lower 48 states.

Crater Lake, Oregon's only national park, is not only a place for wildlife to refuge, but is also one of the nation's favorite places to retreat. The deepest lake in the United States, it was formed inside the collapsed peak of an ancient volcano, Mount Mazama, that erupted 8,000 years ago. The eruptions were 42 times greater than those of Mount St. Helens in 1980, and the ash spewed over eight states and three Canadian provinces. One of the finest and most accessible examples of a young caldera (a certain kind of volcanic crater) in the world, Crater Lake is recognized worldwide as a scenic wonder.

RECREATIONAL

You can do just about anything outdoorsy on the Volcanic Legacy Scenic Byway. In the summer, you can fish, camp, visit a horse and cattle ranch, whitewater raft, or hike. You can also tour the scenic shores of the Upper Klamath Canoe Trail by canoe. Crater Lake National Park is especially good for camping, hiking, and RV camping. Lake of the Woods is popular for any kind of summer activity and is also great for winter activities, such as cross-country skiing (although cross-country skiing is exceptional in many other areas along the Byway as well). Willamette Ski Lodge and Diamond Lake Resort are particularly good for downhill skiing.

SCENIC

The Volcanic Legacy Scenic Byway is visually diverse: it starts out as 140 miles of craggy volcanic landscape, switches to the high desert, and then transforms to the wetland habitats of the Klamath Basin. Even though these scenes are varied, you'll feel the same surge of grandeur and affection as you experience the croplands' expanse, birds in flight at Upper Klamath Lake, the Wild & Scenic Klamath River, views of the majestic Mount Shasta, and wetlands and rising forests.

Highlights

When traveling the Byway from north to south, consider following this scenic-viewpoints tour. If you're starting from the south, simply read this list from the bottom up:

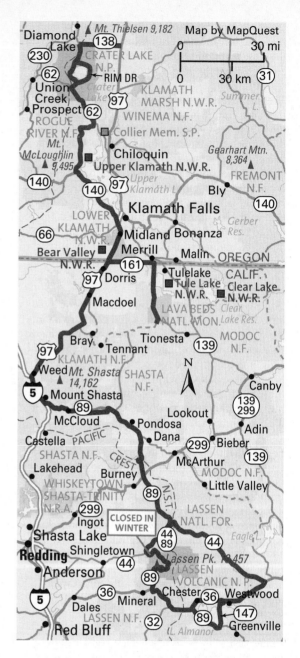

- **Crater Lake National Park:** Located 65 miles north of Klamath Falls on Highways 97 and 62. Here are the world-renowned views you've seen on postcards and in magazines. Many viewpoints are accessible by wheelchair; some are found at the ends of hiking trails.

- **Ouxkanee overlook:** A short drive off Highway 97 leads to a picnic area with a stunning overlook of the Williamson River valley and the surrounding landscape. Scan the horizon as far as Mount Shasta in northern California.

- **Pelican Butte:** The summit offers breathtaking views of Upper Klamath Lake and Sky Lakes Wilderness. Old-growth timber lines the narrow, rough road to the top, which takes about an hour and is accessible only by high-clearance vehicle and by foot.

- **Calimus Butte:** This historic, cupola-style lookout was built by the Bureau of Indian Affairs in 1920 and overlooks the scene of the 48-square-mile Lone Pine fire in 1992, as well as Klamath Marsh and Sprague River Valley. Accessible by high-clearance vehicle only.

- **Herd Peak:** A gravel road off Highway 97 leads to Herd Peak, where a fire lookout is staffed during the summer months and is open to the public. The summit offers breathtaking views of Mount Shasta and the surrounding area.

- **Walker Mountain:** On a clear day, the view from the fire lookout extends from Mount Jefferson in central Oregon to Mount Shasta in northern California. There, you're surrounded by a sea of forest land. Accessible by high-clearance vehicle only.

West Cascades Scenic Byway

OREGON

The West Cascades Scenic Byway isn't the shortest route between Portland and Eugene, but this 220-mile scenic alternative offers some of the best views of thundering waterfalls, lush ancient forests, rushing whitewater, and placid lakes. The Byway frequently intersects major routes that can reconnect you to I-5 or Highway 97, giving you the option of taking shorter loops. The Byway ends near the timber towns of Westfir and Oakridge.

QUICK FACTS

Length: 220 miles.

Time to Allow: 7 to 8 hours.

Best Time to Drive: Late spring through early fall. Late spring offers lush green forests and wildflowers. Summer is the busiest season, but also the best season to visit both high alpine areas adjacent to the Byway and recreation lakes. After Labor Day, the Byway is quieter and less crowded.

Byway Travel Information: Willamette National Forest: phone 541/225-6300; Mount Hood National Forest: phone 503/630-6861.

Special Considerations: Even though Forest Roads 19 and 46 are closed in the winter due to snow, the rest of the route is open during winter months and provides access to cross-country skiing, snowmobiling, snowshoeing, and winter-only cabin rentals at Fish Lake Remount Depot.

Restrictions: Forest Road 46 and Forest Road 19 are generally closed from approximately November 15 to April 30 due to snowfall. You need to buy a $5 day pass to access some of the park.

Bicycle/Pedestrian Facilities: Hundreds of miles of hiking trails are accessible from this Byway, most of which are located on National Forest Service lands. Several trails are also accessible to bicyclists, including the McKenzie River National Recreation Trail and the Breitenbush National Recreation Trail.

The northernmost access to the Byway begins in the historic logging and hydropower city of Estacada, located only 40 minutes from Portland. From the very start, you're immersed in old-growth forest, skimming the edge of the breathtaking Clackamas River. From here, the Byway winds through the Western Cascades and its breathtaking, snowcapped volcanic peaks.

Although two segments of the Byway—Forest Roads 46 and 19—are closed in the winter due to snow, the rest of the Byway offers access to a range of winter sports. These winter sport facilities range from the most rustic, primitive facilities to highly developed, full-service facilities.

The Byway Story

The West Cascades Scenic Byway tells archaeological, historical, natural, recreational, and scenic stories that make it a unique and treasured Byway.

ARCHAEOLOGICAL

Archaeological remains confirm human use of these lands as early as 10,000 years ago. Previous native inhabitants include the Molalla, Kalapuya, Tenino, and Northern Paiute peoples. Even though the Byway has only a relative few archaeological remains, the story of early inhabitants is told well through the Byway's more soft archaeology: rich written and oral histories intertwined with scattered discoveries of tool caches.

For example, a famous oral history is tied with an old trail that formed a natural pass up the Santiam River. The legend says that a fierce battle between the Molalla (of the west hills) and the Paiutes (from the east side) took place on this trail. After the battle was over, the souls of the dead warriors waited to make war on old enemies along both sides of the trail. When white men began to use the pass, they noticed that the Native Americans bypassed gorges along this trail where these souls were believed to be waiting.

Harder archaeological evidence shows that Native Americans hunted, fished, and gathered huckleberries and wild plants in the Santiam Basin at least 10,000 years ago. Gathering obsidian for their tools from the local Obsidian Cliffs, the tools they made (spear points and scraping tools) have been discovered in caches throughout the three major river basins.

HISTORICAL

Early industrial companies and the Civilian Conservation Corps (CCC) both helped shape the Byway as it is today. One such early industrial company that built structures along the route was the Portland General Electric Company (PGEC); the PGEC built a train bed in the 1920s that now serves as a portion of Highway 224. Also, the logging and power companies practically built the city of Estacada, and they specifically left what is now Estacada's Timber Park, featuring a dam that boasts the longest fish tunnel in the Pacific Northwest. Another company built the Hogg Railroad (now listed in the National Register of Historic Places) in the early 1900s, in an effort to connect the Willamette Valley with Eastern Oregon over the Santiam Pass.

In the 1930s, the CCC built many of the structures that are still used for recreation, education, and administration. Some specific places they developed are Camp Belknap (where the CCC workers actually stayed), Clear Lake Cutoff, Clear Lake Shelter, Paradise Campground, and the McKenzie Campgrounds. They also worked to develop the Willamette Valley Cascade Mountain Wagon Road (known today as the Santiam Wagon Road), which now serves as part of Highway 126.

NATURAL

This Byway's interdependent systems of mountains, vegetation, rivers, and wildlife support one another vitally. Wildlife thrives in the volcanic peaks and unique geologic formations of the High Cascades; they also flourish in the Western Cascades' jagged lava flows and smooth glacial valleys. These ranges' old-growth forests of Douglas fir and western red cedar are excellent habitat for the northern spotted owl and the bald eagle (both endangered) and also for the pine marten, pileated woodpecker, Roosevelt elk, black-tailed deer, and mule deer.

The mountains' heavy snow and rain percolates through porous volcanic rocks and reappears as hundreds of springs that feed the Byway's many rivers and lakes, many of which are designated as Wild & Scenic rivers. These rivers support a number of rare and threatened species of fish, including spring chinook, winter and summer steelhead, bull trout, and a rare species of cutthroat trout. This abundant moisture has allowed the development of dense, lush, old-growth forests: some trees measure over 6 feet in diameter and are more than 180 feet tall.

RECREATIONAL

A broad range of recreational activities are available along this Byway. Summer brings horseback riding, picnicking, primitive and rustic camping, and fishing. You can also enjoy any water and watercraft activity: drift and motor boating, canoeing, jet skiing, sailing, water-skiing, kayaking, rafting, and swimming. The hiking here is especially good because the US Forest Service maintains the Byway's three national recreation trails to the highest standard. Hundreds of miles of other trails are also accessed from the Byway. In the winter, you can snowmobile, sled, snowshoe, and downhill and cross-country ski.

SCENIC

As you travel this "scenic alternative to I-5," you absorb immaculate mountainscapes, peer into plush forests, watch the mesmerizing flow of pure waters, and scrutinize each shade of autumn's slow-motion explosion. Spectacular views of snowcapped mountains (Jefferson, Washington, Three Fingered Jack, and the Three Sisters) are omnipresent as you skirt the Cascade Mountain Range and travel through the Mount Hood and Willamette National Forests.

Three Wild & Scenic rivers thread along sections of the Byway. These rivers are associated with other enchanting accumulations of water: glossy lakes, silken pools, rushing whitewater, coarse waterfalls, one-of-a-kind geologic formations, and glacier-carved canyons. One of the most striking and popular of these waters is 120-foot-deep Clear Lake, which is nationally known for its startling clarity.

Highlights

This tour shares the highlights of the West Cascades Scenic Byway. If you're starting at the other end, read this section from the bottom up.

◎ Start your tour at Westfir, which is the southern end of the Byway. In Westfir, take in the **Westfir Covered Bridge.** At 180 feet long, this unique bridge is the longest covered bridge in the state.

◎ Just a few miles north of the Bridge is the **Cougar Reservoir,** a good place to get out and stretch your legs. The dam at the north end of the reservoir is the tallest rock-filled dam in Oregon.

◎ Right near the Reservoir is the **Delta Campground and Nature Trail.** Ancient western red cedar and Douglas fir stretch up to 180 feet here. Walk under them along the nature trail.

◎ End your tour with a picnic lunch at **Box Canyon,** which is adjacent (to the North) of the **Delta Camp and Trail,** right along the McKenzie River.

Northwest Passage Scenic Byway
IDAHO

Follow the footsteps of Meriwether Lewis and William Clark as they searched, at the request of President Thomas Jefferson, for the Northwest Passage—a link between the Missouri River and the Columbia River through the unexplored Rocky Mountains. Lewis and Clark's arduous journey proved that no easy route existed; however, they were led by Sacagawea to the trail through the mountains that had been used by generations of Nez Perce Indians.

Traverse the Northwest Passage Scenic Byway through the winding Clearwater River canyon, and then climb south to the Camas Prairie. Along the way, you will see numerous Nez Perce cultural sites and Lewis and Clark Expedition campsites. View displays, cultural demonstrations, and a historical movie featuring the traditions of the Nez Perce tribe when you visit the Nez Perce National Historical Park Museum at Spalding.

Enjoy the patchwork of wheat, barley, peas, alfalfa, and wildflowers that wave in the gentle breeze of the Camas Prairie. Have your camera ready when you drive this panoramic route between Lewiston and Grangeville; this is scenery you'll definitely want to take with you.

QUICK FACTS

Length: 90 miles.

Time to Allow: 3 hours to 3 days.

Best Time to Drive: Year-round. Summer is the high season.

Byway Travel Information: North Central Idaho Travel Association: phone toll-free 800/473-3543; Byway local Web site: www.northcentralidaho.info.

Special Considerations: Highway 12 above Kooskia is a winding, two-lane road with occasional passing lanes and slow vehicle turnouts.

Restrictions: During winter months, drivers may experience some snow-covered roads near Lolo Pass at the Montana border.

Bicycle/Pedestrian Facilities: Pedestrians, equestrians, and bicyclists all use the Byway. In many cases, however, there may not be a sufficient amount of shoulder room along all portions of the Byway, so nonmotorized travelers use a portion of traffic lanes, making this mode of travel challenging. Beautiful nature and cycling trails can be found all along the Northwest Passage Scenic Byway.

The Byway Story

The Northwest Passage Scenic Byway tells archaeological, cultural, historical, natural, recreational, and scenic stories that make it a unique and treasured Byway.

ARCHAEOLOGICAL

As archaeologists have looked for traces of the past in the land of the Northwest Passage, they have not come up empty-handed. Two significant archaeological sites have been found along the corridor. At Big Eddy, evidence of early native occupation has been discovered. In Eimers Park's Tolo Lake, the remains of mammoths and an extinct species of bison were discovered at the bottom of the lake in 1994. During the excavation, archaeologists determined that the bones excavated were only a fraction of what is actually at the bottom of Tolo Lake. A display of the mammoth is now located at the Idaho Museum of Natural History in Pocatello. When you come upon an archaeological site along the Byway, informational signs point you in the right direction.

CULTURAL

Although a conglomeration of cultures and people make up the Northwest Passage, none of the cultures has preserved its heritage like the Nez Perce. Agriculture and industry, fostered by the coming of homesteaders and gold miners, exist side by side with the customs of the Nez Perce. As the Nez Perce work to restore and preserve their culture, they invite visitors to experience one of their powwows or to visit the Nez Perce National Historic Park, where local arts and crafts are displayed. The Nez Perce commemorate historic events and battles with gatherings and perhaps a pipe ceremony. You can also experience this Northwest Passage culture through events, historical displays, and information centers. Within their reservation, the Nez Perce also offer a language program and have begun to breed Appaloosa horses as they once did in the past.

One of the most significant sites to the Nez Perce is also located along the Byway. A rock formation in the Clearwater River is known to the Nez Perce as the Heart of the Monster in one of their oldest legends. Visitors today can follow a path to the rock formation and listen to its history on an audio program featured here. Keep your eyes open as you drive the rest of the Byway to get the most out of culture on the Northwest Passage.

HISTORICAL

Before the Northwest Passage became a nationally recognized corridor, the route was a home to the Nez Perce, and it remains their home even today. For thousands of years, this native culture built villages and camps along the Clearwater River. The Northwest Passage was a main route for the Nez Perce as they traveled through the mountains and forests of what is now northern Idaho. The society of the Nez Perce met the society of European culture when Lewis and Clark traveled through the area in 1805 and 1806. Known as the Corps of Discovery, the company of Lewis and Clark had a difficult crossing of the Bitteroot Mountains after which they were close to starvation. When three Nez Perce children discovered them, the explorers received help from the Nez Perce and continued their journey.

After the coming of the Lewis and Clark Expedition, new visitors wanted to do more than explore. Trappers, missionaries, and miners soon followed and tried to influence the land and its native people. For a time, people gathered in the area in hopes of discovering gold. The mining districts from this period in history eventually became the towns that are now present on the Byway.

In the 1870s, conflict mounted between the Nez Perce and the US government. Battles occurred as the Nez Perce tried to regain their lands. The conflict ended with many of the Nez Perce dead; the rest were moved to reservations. Today, the Byway travels along the Nez Perce Indian Reservation and passes Nez Perce National Historic Parks in Spalding and Kamiah. As you journey the Byway, you begin to understand why so many people through history have appreciated this beautiful land.

NATURAL

Few evergreen forests and wilderness areas can compete with the Northwest Passage for the grandest of undisturbed nature. Although many of the valleys are now green agricultural fields, the mountainsides are covered in trees, and the sights and smells of the forest still have an overwhelming presence on the Byway. Canyons and valleys appear along the Byway to display the varied topography of the area. Rocks exposed along the Byway are part of basalt lava flows from the Columbia Plateau that formed millions of years ago. Volcanoes in Washington and Oregon made cracks in the Earth's crust that caused an outpouring of molten rock. Some of this rock reached northern Idaho to harden there and remain for geologists and travelers to observe today.

In addition to the scenery, wildlife also thrives here. The rivers are filled with fish, such as steelhead trout and Chinook salmon, and the forests are home to deer, elk, and other species. The variety of tree and plant life that grows along the Byway creates a habitat for all these creatures.

With only small communities along the way, this Byway is far from being urbanized, and the rural, rugged landscape is one of the primary attractions.

RECREATIONAL

If you can canoe down a river, have fresh trout for lunch, and hike to a campsite under a stand of pine trees for a beautiful night under the stars, you might be vacationing along the Northwest Passage Scenic Byway. Sublime outdoor recreation awaits you as you explore this enchanted land that was once known only to native tribes who also loved its forested wilderness. From the rivers to the forests, an outdoor adventure beckons to travelers on the Byway.

The road is surrounded by rivers. Along the Byway, travelers can hardly escape the allure of the Clearwater River and its forks. Nearby, you will also find the Snake, Salmon, Selway, and Lochsa Rivers. And whether you choose to enjoy what's in the water or the water itself, you won't be disappointed. Chinook salmon swim in the waters and fly fishing for steelhead trout is one of the reasons people return again and again to the Northwest Passage.

Whitewater rafting on one of the Byway rivers is also irresistible. From beginning rafters to expert kayakers, the rivers can accommodate everyone, depending on location and the time of year. The Lochsa River is named the Native American word for "rough water," and with good reason; the river boasts 40 rapids that rate 4 or above on the whitewater rafting European rating system. Whether you want to try the extreme river or the swiftly rushing stream, outfitters and guides are available to newcomers and experienced adventurers.

© MapQuest.com, Inc.

If you ever get enough of the water, a walk in the woods may entice you. Travelers take trails through mountains for the sweeping vistas they enjoy along the way. National forests, wilderness areas, and even state parks give you the opportunity to find trails and go exploring. You can hike your way to the top of a mountain or into one of the Byway communities, where the small town atmosphere is sure to make you feel at home. Plenty of campsites, lodges, and bed-and-breakfasts are also available along the Byway.

SCENIC

From canyon to valley to a riverside drive, the Northwest Passage provides a breathtaking variety of scenery. Communities and homesteads provide a pastoral alpine scene against the mountains and deep green forests of the Byway.

Four different landscapes can be found on the Northwest Passage: open canyon, closed canyon, valleys, and panoramic views. From Spalding to Orofino, enjoy the sights of an open canyon, where the water moves along the flat bottom of the canyon between sloping

hills. From the hillsides, you will enjoy panoramic views of the river and surrounding land. Near Orofino and Harpster, closed canyon dominates the landscape with steep canyon walls and dense forests of ponderosa pine and Douglas fir. The closed canyon is where the river moves faster around corners and down hills through the trees. Sometimes, a glimpse of the water is enough to make visitors want to stop and explore this beautiful area. In the closed canyon area, rocky outcroppings add to the rugged mountain atmosphere.

The valley landscape from Kamiah to Stites is characterized by a much calmer river and agricultural fields of green. From Harpster to Eimers, the view from the road is broad and sweeping. National forest lands are perennially beautiful, and the nearby pastoral fields change with the seasons, just as the river does. From colors of crystal turquoise to a demure blue, the Clearwater River changes moods all along the way. On this Byway, views from above and below allow you to truly appreciate the land that makes up the Northwest Passage.

Payette River Scenic Byway
IDAHO

A drive along the Payette River Scenic Byway can be distracting for motorists. Rather than watching the road, you may be more inclined to watch the river as it crashes and tumbles its way over rocks and through the narrow river valley. Be sure to take advantage of the occasional pull-offs that allow you to view wilder parts of the river and treat your senses to the sights, sounds, smells, and rhythms of Idaho's famous white water.

Enjoy the scenic drive along the river through the Boise and Payette national forests before arriving in the high, picturesque mountain valley dotted with the resort towns of Cascade, McCall, and New Meadows. Between the thunderous roll of the whitewater and the quiet serenity of the valley landscapes, you will find a thrilling adventure as you travel this mountain Byway.

The Byway Story

The Payette River Scenic Byway tells historical, natural, recreational, and scenic stories that make it a unique and treasured Byway.

HISTORICAL

The people and events associated with this river stretch thousands of years back in time, creating generational ties between the past and present and between old-timers and new arrivals in Idaho. But most of the recorded history of this area started only a couple hundred years ago. Fur trappers of the early 1800s, working for Hudson's Bay Company, named the Payette River in honor of their comrade, Francois Payette, a French-Canadian who explored much of southwestern Idaho. After explorers mapped the territory, pioneers began to settle the area.

QUICK FACTS

Length: 112 miles.

Time to Allow: 2 days.

Best Time to Drive: Year-round. High season is summer.

Byway Travel Information: Idaho Division of Tourism Development: phone 208/334-2470.

Special Considerations: The roadway is a narrow, winding, two-lane road with occasional passing lanes and slow vehicle turnouts.

Bicycle/Pedestrian Facilities: Numerous hiking trails are available along the Byway.

The city of McCall, built by these early settlers, is well worth a visit. Much of the city's history is on display at the Central Idaho Cultural Center, one of the interpretive centers of the Payette River Scenic Byway. This center occupies the original Southern Idaho Timber Protective Association (SITPA) buildings. The SITPA was a cooperative fire organization established in 1919 to oversee private, state, and federal lands. These buildings were constructed by troops stationed in McCall during the 1930s. Hollywood then discovered McCall in 1936. The famous movie *Northwest Passage*, starring Robert Young and Spencer Tracy, was filmed on the shores of Payette Lake and on the North Fork of the Payette River.

Around that same time, people began the construction of a bridge now called the North Fork Bridge, although locals refer to it as the Rainbow Bridge because of its arch. It crosses the North Fork of the Payette River above Smith's Ferry. Built in 1933, it displays an open-spandrel design introduced to Idaho in the 1920s. Unlike other bridges of this type, the North Fork Bridge has not been altered over the years and is listed on the National Register of Historic Places.

NATURAL

Along the Payette River Scenic Byway rests the Idaho Batholith, which offers a wealth of knowledge for geologists as well as precious samples for gemologists. This unique geological feature covers much of the area and is made up of primarily granite. A lot of this batholith formation began millions of years ago, when magma pushed up on the Earth's crust and created many of the Idaho mountains. The magma eventually hardened below the surface and is now known as the batholith; through erosion, you can see the cooled rock today. Yet much has happened to the land in the last 12,000 years, making Idaho a geologically active place. Quite recently (relatively speaking), magma oozed out of the Earth's crust in many places and has also shot out of volcanoes, warping the land and changing the environment.

Due to differences in the magma's cooling times and conditions, the Idaho Batholith contains many rare and valuable minerals, including the star garnet, jasper, and opal, making Idaho an ideal place for gemologists to collect gems. (Idaho is, after all, known as the Gem State.) The area also boasts many gold, silver, copper, and zinc veins.

This batholith created a unique landscape that interests sightseers as well as geologists. There are mountains made out of solid granite and valleys carved out of this hard mineral. And because many areas near this Byway are still quite new (geologically speaking), several rugged peaks still have not bowed down to the effects of gravity. Furthermore, people can see the traces of glaciers, as these, too, have not yet disappeared with the passing of time.

RECREATIONAL

If you are looking for fun, particularly the lifelong, memorable kind that nature offers, come to Payette River Scenic Byway. Activities are never far away, and the majestic mountains in the background (which offer some of these activities) enhance the recreation. No matter what time of the year, there's always something fun available.

Of all the activities available here, whitewater rafting ranks perhaps as the most popular. People find braving the rapids on the Payette River enjoyable, too: there is a quantity of white water along the Byway, and rafters rarely experience a boring moment. The rapids range in different sizes, so rafters with less adventuresome spirits can usually avoid the more commanding waves. As you raft in the Payette River, you'll witness sparkling, clean water and gorgeous, jagged peaks looming high above the canyon. This privileged view alone is reason enough for many rafters to experience this river.

Other than rafting, you can find numerous places to settle down for a relaxing picnic, enjoy world-class trout fishing, and hike or bike the plentiful mountain trails. Many enjoy viewing wildlife in the wetlands around this area, which attract bald eagles, ospreys, and Canadian geese. During the cold winter months, snowmobiling replaces rafting as the most popular activity, although skiing and snowshoeing follow close behind. Whatever your preference for fun, the Payette River Scenic Byway is sure to offer memorable and exhilarating experiences.

SCENIC

The scenic beauty found along the Payette River Scenic Byway is one of the road's strongest features, an aspect most people remember years after traveling here. For approximately 20 miles, travelers are lulled by the flow of the main Payette River and exhilarated by the turbulent North Fork of the river. Nearly every mile along this stretch makes an ideal setting for pictures.

Driving a little farther along the Byway, Lake Cascade, with its calm serenity and abundant wildlife, can be glimpsed around the corners of the mountains and through the Long Valley surrounding it. Visitors can pull off into access areas, watch the trout anglers,

and gaze at bald eagles and ospreys flying overhead. Several picnic grounds also offer you clean mountain air and an opportunity to soak up the natural scenery. The spectacular view of Payette Lake, nestled among mountains and trees, is a thrill not only for first-time travelers to the city of McCall but also for those who have witnessed it many times before.

Not all scenic features along the Byway are natural, however; manmade features like the Old Tate Barn are reminiscent of old-time America. The agricultural and Finnish culture of the area is preserved on Farm-to-Market Road and Elo Road. An old Finnish church, with a cemetery next to it, still stands today and gives a glimpse of what the area was once like. By seeing man-made attractions such as these, you can experience another aspect of the Byway.

Pend Oreille Scenic Byway

IDAHO

Visit the Pend Oreille Scenic Byway and discover a water-lover's paradise! The Byway follows the shore of Lake Pend Oreille (pronounced PEND oh RAY) for the majority of the length of the Byway, and then winds alongside the Clark Fork River to the Montana state line. You'll find yourself beneath towering mountains that are reflected in the many miles of water along the Byway.

The area is largely undeveloped, ensuring that you are treated to the serene outdoors of Idaho by viewing waterfowl, other species of wildlife, and a variety of plants. Be sure to take advantage of the many pull-outs along the road and experience an uninhibited view of this majestic area.

QUICK FACTS

Length: 33 miles.

Time to Allow: 2 hours.

Best Time to Drive: The Byway can be traveled year-round. High season is summer.

Byway Travel Information: Hope-Clark Fork-Trestle Creek Chamber of Commerce: phone 208-266-1552; Byway local Web site: www.pendoreillescenicbyway.org.

Special Considerations: Highway 200 is a two-lane road with no passing lanes. It can be icy during winter months, so drive with caution. Also remember that the Pend Oreille Scenic Byway and most of northern Idaho is in the Pacific time zone.

Bicycle/Pedestrian Facilities: This Byway is one segment of a national cross-country bicycle tour promoted by Adventure Cycling of Missoula, Montana. Paved shoulders along the highway are narrow, but the Byway does see frequent bicycle users, both local and visiting bikers. The narrow shoulders do not promote a great deal of pedestrian traffic, except along the Byway in Hope and East Hope, where shoulders are noticeably wider.

The area around the Byway has been full of activity for thousands of years. See landscapes formed over 10,000 years ago by the many glacial cycles that created flooding, which reached across Oregon and Washington before hitting the Pacific Ocean. Watch for evidence of the Kalispel people, Native Americans who inhabited the area after the waters receded. Imagine the traders, trappers, and miners who passed through the area, helping to make it what it is today.

These days, there's never a dull moment with Lake Pend Oreille and the Clark Fork River nearby. You can go boating, fishing, sailing, canoeing, kayaking, and swimming in the lake, rivers, and streams that line the Byway. If water sports aren't your thing, spend some time viewing the abundant wildlife, especially waterfowl, or go camping, hiking, biking, horseback riding, or golfing. In the wintertime, hit the slopes at Schweitzer Mountain Ski Resort. Whatever your recreational interests, be assured that you can find plenty to do on the Pend Oreille Scenic Byway.

The Byway Story

The Pend Oreille Scenic Byway tells historical, recreational, and scenic stories that make it a unique and treasured Byway.

HISTORICAL

Throughout time, people have been drawn to water. Towns, roads, and groups of people have been concentrated along rivers and lakes, making water one of the most important factors in the shaping of the land. Lake Pend Oreille and the Clark Fork River have been important in the development of the area that is now the Pend Oreille Scenic Byway. Before humans had an impact on the environment, however, glacial Lake Missoula had a significant impact on the land. Subsequent glacial cycles caused cataclysmic flooding, which began in the area of Cabinet Gorge, near the Idaho/Montana border, and then spread across Oregon and Washington before reaching the Pacific Ocean. This tremendous phenomenon created many of the geological formations seen in the area today.

After the glacial ice abated, the land became habitable, and the native Kalispel people lived in the area. The Clark Fork River was an important aspect of their existence, and the Kalispels hosted an annual regional tribal gathering at the mouth of the river. There, they hunted, fished, picked berries, and traded. The importance of this event and the key location at the mouth of the river continued as traders and trappers moved through the area, exploring the west. One British explorer, David Thompson, established a trading post on the banks of Lake Pend Oreille while he was searching for the headwaters of the Columbia River, and he was instrumental in the settlement of the Pend Oreille region.

As traffic through the West and Northwest continued to grow, new routes of transportation were needed. With the creation of the steamboat in 1866, the waterways in the area of the Pend Oreille Scenic Byway became connected, enabling people to travel efficiently from one place to another. When the Northern Pacific Railroad was being built in the Pend Oreille section, many structures, such as bridges, were built to span the many areas of water. The wooden bridge built to cross the Pack River was the longest structure in the entire transcontinental system.

With each passing era, the water and waterways of the Pend Oreille Scenic Byway continue to shape the history and people of the area.

RECREATIONAL

With unspoiled landscapes and clean country air, it is no wonder that Idaho is known for its many outdoor activities. Pend Oreille Scenic Byway is no exception, and with 100 miles of shoreline along Lake Pend Oreille, water recreational opportunities are never far away and are in great abundance. Boating, fishing, sailing, and other water sports are all available along the Byway. The water is clean and pure, and it draws visitors from around the country and world. In addition to the scenic and recreational Lake Pend Oreille, two rivers are accessible along the Byway. The Clark Fork River stretches across 2 miles of delta and wetland; the river itself is a popular place to go fishing. The Pack River does not create such a vast delta, but it provides wonderful opportunities for canoeing and kayaking. The Byway is located in Bonner County, which accounts for 20 percent of the total surface water in Idaho's 44 counties, so the Byway follows either a lake or river for its entire length.

© MapQuest.com, Inc.

Water sports may dominate the recreational scene along the Byway, but a look toward the forests to the sides of the lake reveal an area rich in other recreational opportunities. A number of trails are accessible through the Kaniksu National Forest, affording you the chance to go hiking, biking, or horseback riding. Hunting, berry picking, and snow-mobiling are additional activities that you can enjoy along the Byway. Every season has its charm along the Byway. Fall colors dazzle visitors in the autumn, winter encourages visits to Schweitzer Mountain Ski Resort, and spring and summer provide the perfect weather for a game of golf on the two courses adjacent to the Byway.

A drive along the Pend Oreille Scenic Byway opens your eyes to the beauty of the outdoors, including many different types of wildlife. The abundance of water along the Byway makes this an ideal route to travel for bird-watching. The delta area at the confluence of the Clark River provides prime opportunity to see different waterfowl up close in the marshes and wetlands. A variety of fish can also be found on the lake and rivers of the Byway, and 20-plus-pound rainbow or mackinaw trout can be caught during week-long fishing derbies that begin in May and end in November. You may also spot deer and moose all along the Byway and near the water.

SCENIC

With over 100 miles of shoreline, Lake Pend Oreille dominates the area. Glassy water reflects the Cabinet Mountains, sunsets, and farming scenes, and the water draws wildlife to its shores. A drive along the Pend Oreille Scenic Byway is a journey into an area that remains largely undeveloped, providing you with the chance to enjoy nature as it was intended to be experienced. You do not have to go far, either, to enjoy breathtaking vistas. Numerous turnouts along the road allow you to experience the outdoors right off of the Byway. Crashing waterfalls and tranquil lake and river scenes await you along the Byway.

Picturesque farms and farmlands are plentiful along the Byway, providing a look at a lifestyle that America was founded on and one that continues to be an important factor in the country's economy. From fields that are almost ready to be harvested to soaring eagles and curious deer, the Pend Oreille Scenic Byway provides a glimpse into a life filled with beauty and serenity.

Every season has its own type of beauty along the Byway, from the explosion of color in the fall to the quiet white world of a northern Idaho winter. Summer may be spent enjoying the water on Lake Pend Oreille or marveling at the brilliance of a sunset. Through every season, you will continually be reminded of the beauty of the area.

Chinook Scenic Byway

WASHINGTON

The Chinook Scenic Byway (also known as the Mather Memorial Parkway) is possibly the most scenic route crossing the Cascade Mountain Range, and it is the most accessible road for viewing Mount Rainier. Mount Rainier National Park (which the Byway travels through) was established in 1890, and the Mather Parkway was established in 1931. Because of its national park status, all features in the park are protected.

The route has a uniquely varied landscape. Traveling east, the route climbs through a closed canopy of Douglas fir. At Chinook Pass, the roadway descends dramatically through the Wenatchee National Forest and along the American River. The road also passes the unique basalt flows of the Columbia Plateau. The Byway ends near the fertile agricultural valleys of Yakima County.

The Byway Story

The Chinook Scenic Byway tells archaeological, historical, natural, recreational, and scenic stories that make it a unique and treasured Byway.

ARCHAEOLOGICAL

Even though only about 2 percent of the park has been systematically surveyed for archaeological remains, it has 79 known sites in the park, of which 62 have been fully documented and recorded.

One prehistoric site dates to between 2,300 and 4,500 years ago. Sites just outside of the park hint at much earlier occupation, perhaps as much as 8,000 years, but most prehistoric archaeological sites are about 1,000 years old.

Later, the area was used on a seasonal basis by lowland tribes for hunting and gathering, and for spiritual and ceremonial events. A few sites were hunting camps (killing and butchering sites), where cedar bark was stripped from trees, rock shelters created, and stone for tools procured.

In more modern centuries, five principal Native American tribes (specifically, the Nisqually, Puyallup, Muckleshoot, Yakama, and Taidnapam) came to the park in the summer and early fall to hunt and to collect resources. These tribes continued to come even after the park was officially designated in 1899. Sites that were used by these tribes are littered with broken weapon points.

Sites from European settlements in the late 19th and early 20th centuries confirm mining, recreation, and early park development. Specifically, sites reveal old campsites, trash dumps, collapsed structures, mine shafts, and other debris.

HISTORICAL

Part of this Byway has a unique historic designation: that of a National Historic Landmark District. This district, called the Mount Rainier National Historic Landmark District, was designated so because it is one of the nation's finest collections of "national park rustic" architecture, both in the park's road system and in its historically developed areas.

In the 1920s, the park developed a plan—the Mount Rainier National Park's Master Plan—that was unusual at the time and is historically significant because it was the first and most complete national park plan developed by the National Park Service Landscape Division.

NATURAL

This Byway's wide range of plants and animals live relatively undisturbed and can, therefore, exist in greater abundance (some 50 species of mammals and 130 species of birds live here) and can attain greater longevity. For example, some high-elevation coniferous stands are over 500 years old. Some of the highest alpine stands are up to 1,000 years old.

In addition, extraordinary geological processes have created this magnificent and unique landscape: Rainier's 25 glaciers form the largest single-peak glacier system in the United States outside of Alaska; the glacier-carved canyon of the Rainier fork of the American River is geologically rare; and mountain parks (lush subalpine meadows encircling the mountain between 5,000 and 7,000 feet) are without parallel in the Cascades or Pacific volcano system.

Mount Rainier has four main glaciers: Nisqually Glacier, Cowlitz-Ingraham Glacier, Emmons Glacier, and Carbon Glacier. Nisqually Glacier is one of the most accessible glaciers on Mount Rainier. It can easily be seen from Nisqually and Glacier Vistas, located less than 1 mile from the Paradise Visitor Center. Emmons Glacier has a surface area of 4.3 square miles, the largest area of any glacier in the contiguous United States. Carbon Glacier is best viewed from a 4-mile trail from Ipsut Creek Campground on the north side of Mount Rainier. This glacier has the greatest measured thickness (700 feet) and volume (0.2 cubic miles) of any glacier in the contiguous United States. Because of the weather patterns in recent years, all of these glaciers are slowly retreating.

Along the Byway and in your forages into Mount Rainier National Park, you can see four distinct life, or vegetation, zones. They are the lowland forest, montane zone, subalpine zone, and alpine zone. Each zone is filled with varied and splendid wildlife and flora.

In the lowland forest zone, a canopy of stately giants allow little sunlight to filter down to the forest floor. Deer browse in the shadows of western hemlock and western red cedar, among others. Hawks and owls perch in the trees waiting for prey to scurry across the shady floor. Bald eagles also thrive in these forests, diving down to grab fish from the water with their talons.

The montane zone is a bit farther up the mountainside and a little wetter and colder. The delicate and elusive calypso orchid blooms here in the spring, and patches of huckleberry bushes abound. Black bears, who really like huckleberries, are one of this area's large predators, although you'll probably never encounter a black bear.

The subalpine zone is typified by tree "islands" mixed with open meadows. The snow lasts longer among the sheltering trees of this zone. By late July, a rainbow of wildflowers carpets the meadow. These flowers include white avalanche lilies, yellow marsh marigolds, purple lupine, magenta paintbrush, and plumed bear grass. Glacier lilies and snowbed buttercups bloom at the treeline. A special feature in the subalpine zone are the krummholzes, trees that are strikingly twisted and stunted due to the severe winds

Map by MapQuest

and snow. Trees only 3 feet in height may be centuries old. The last and highest zone is the alpine zone. It is found above the timberline and is a world of extremes. On a summer day, the sun can shine warm and bright, but in just moments clouds can bring a sudden snow or lightning storm. During storms, the wind knifes across the tundra because there are no trees to break up the wind. Consequently, most alpine plants grow to be only a few inches high.

RECREATIONAL
The area surrounding the Chinook Scenic Byway is rife with recreational activities. Any time of year affords a combination of beautiful scenery and fun things to do. A visit in summer offers great opportunities for fishing, hunting, hiking, biking, and rafting. Summer is not the only time to experience the beauty, however. Mount Rainier and its surrounding area is one of the snowiest places on Earth. In 1972, Paradise received 94 feet of snow, a world record. Naturally, snow sports also abound. Skiing and snowshoeing are the most popular, and plenty of snow-laden slopes and meadows provide remarkable experiences. Although people come here continuously throughout the year, solitude is only a moment away. With over 200 hiking and horse trails, 20 mountain biking trails, 50 Nordic ski trails, six designated wildlife/bird viewing areas, and 24 campgrounds with over 500 campsites, you can still find quiet among nature's majesty.

Spectacular scenery meets the eye with every turn of the Byway, and every stop along the way offers an interesting trail to try out. The grade and length of the trails vary, offering the perfect hike for every person. Many visitors love to hike trails in Mount Rainier National Park. Biking provides a great way to bring you into direct contact with more of the serene area of the Byway a little more quickly than hiking. The Byway itself is equipped to handle bicyclers. The shoulders along the road are paved varying from 2 to 8 feet.

SCENIC
Chinook Scenic Byway takes you through picturesque mountain towns and historical sites and guides you past Mount Rainier, "the shining jewel of the Northwest." The Byway's scenic properties are manifested largely in one of the world's greatest mountains, 14,411-foot Mount Rainier. Rainier is the tallest volcano in the 48 contiguous states and is the largest mountain in the Cascade chain of volcanoes extending from California to the Canadian border. At the numerous developed viewpoints along the roadside, you can enjoy the deep shadowy forests, misty waterfalls, sparkling streams, towering peaks, and snowy rocky ridges that are all a part of Mount Rainier's wonder. Stands of old-growth Douglas fir found in few other places are available at every turn.

A short distance from Highway 410 is the road to Sunrise, the highest point in the park accessible by car. The road to Sunrise winds through forests of cedar, fir, and hemlock, offering glimpses of the four dormant volcanoes, including Mounts Baker and Adams. Mount Rainier rises above alpine meadows profuse with delicate wildflowers to the rocky summit of Little Tahoma Peak visible to the left. Snap a few photographs: Mount Rainier's mountain meadows with their clear icy lakes are among the most visited and photographed areas of the national park. From Sunrise, the views of Emmons Glacier, the largest on Mount Rainier, are breathtaking.

Highlights

Beginning near Naches and traveling northwest on the Byway, you enter the Mount Rainier National Forest a few miles outside of the town of Cliffdell. This national park is known for its scenic, recreational, and natural resources.

After passing through Cliffdell, the road continues for a short space to the Builder Cave National Recreation Trail and Norse Peak, both known for their scenic beauty and recreational value. Here, the road changes to a southwesterly course, enters the Mount Rainier National Park, and passes through old-growth environments that surround Fife Peak. Union Creek Waterfall is also located in this area. Edgar Rock Chinook Pass Historic CCC Work Camp is located at Chinook Pass, where the parkway resumes its northwestern direction. Tipsoo Lake is on the eastern side of the parkway shortly after the pass, followed by the Chinook Pass Overlook and Crystal Mountain Ski Resort.

Leaving the Mount Rainier National Park, the parkway continues through the national forest to the Skookum Flats National Recreation Trail found at the edge of the forest. A popular viewpoint for Mount Rainier is also located here. The parkway travels through the town of Greenwater and the Federation Forest State Park before continuing on to Enumclaw, where the parkway ends.

Mountains to Sound Greenway, I-90

WASHINGTON

QUICK FACTS

Length: 100 miles.

Time to Allow: 1.5 to 2 hours.

Best Time to Drive: Summer and fall. High season includes both summer and winter, when recreational sports are popular.

Byway Travel Information: Washington State Tourism Division: phone toll-free 800/544-1800, extension 036; Washington State Deptartment of Trade and Economic Development: phone 360/753-5601; Byway local Web site: www.mtsgreenway.org.

Special Considerations: Interstate 90 provides a minimum of four lanes of high-speed, limited-access highway for the entire length of the greenway corridor. Road conditions vary during the winter season, lengthening the trip to as long as four hours for the entire route. The greenway is plowed throughout the winter, however, and pull-offs allow you to place chains on your tires. Electronic signs at every highway interchange provide drivers with up-to-the-minute road safety information.

Restrictions: Winter snow conditions on the I-90 Snoqualmie Pass regularly require the use of chains or other traction devices.

Bicycle/Pedestrian Facilities: The I-90 right-of-way is travelable by bicycle for the entire length of the greenway, including separated and landscaped trails along urban portions of the highway. Many recreational trails exist along the corridor in lands managed by the US Forest Service, the State Department of Natural Resources, state parks, and private lands.

Interstate 90 is the primary east/west highway in Washington. It begins at the historic Seattle waterfront and travels east over the Cascade Mountains to the dry plateaus of eastern Washington. As you travel east along this 100-mile Byway, you experience lush green forests, the marine beauty of Puget Sound, pastoral valleys, and a dramatic mountain landscape. You also pass through a complete change in climate, geology, and hometown style.

Each year, more than 20 million vehicles travel this route, making I-90 a popular gateway between Washington's largest city and its diverse and striking landscapes.

The Byway Story

The Mountains to Sound Greenway tells historical, natural, recreational, and scenic stories that make it a unique and treasured Byway.

HISTORICAL

The Byway's historic sites demonstrate different eras of modern history. Some sites possess the soul of the Old West, some seem to still embrace the spirit of early industry, and some retain the more obvious past of the last few decades.

The soul of the Old West is possessed in locations such as Fort Tilton, the site of an 1850s fort (also a wildlife wetland), and Meadowbrook Farm, a preserved historic landscape in the dramatic shadow of towering Mount Si. Meadowbrook Farm was the site of a Native American village that became the world's largest hop ranch at the turn of the century. The Klondike Gold Rush Museum, located in the historic Pioneer Square district, houses photos and memorabilia from Seattle's turn-of-the-century boom days. And what would the Old West be without a few mining operations? Catch a glimpse of a 19th-century coal-mining town at Roslyn. The town hasn't changed much in all these years, except for sprucing up the main street for the 1990s TV series *Northern Exposure*. Roslyn also has a museum that houses photos, mining tools, and historical information; the historic grave-yard is divided into ethnic zones reflecting the many nations that sent miners here.

The spirit of early industry is still embraced in places like Preston, a turn-of-the-century Scandinavian mill town. Presently, Preston consists of the remnants of a small, northwoods logging town along the Raging River, including a number of historic homes and the church. The Thorp Grist Mill, built in 1883, is the oldest industrial artifact in Kittias County. The mill houses a remarkable collection of hand-made wooden mill machinery and is open to the public. In addition, Fall City Waterfront was the final upstream landing for early steamboats on the Snoqualmie River, Reinig Road Sycamore Corridor was the tree-lined main street of a former company town, and Mill Pond was the Snoqualmie Mill's former log-holding pond (and is now home to a variety of fish and wildlife).

NATURAL

The western flanks of the Cascade Mountains, through which the greenway passes, are some of the best conifer tree-growing lands in the world. The combination of temperate climate and ample rainfall produces record growth of Douglas fir, western red cedar, and western hemlock. Lumbering was Washington state's first industry, and trees from this region helped build San Francisco and many other 19th-century cities. You can still find remnants of the massive trees that once grew here: spend an hour in a beautiful old-growth forest just a mile from the interstate at exit 47 on the Asahel Curtis Nature Trail. Named for a founder of the Mountaineers—a natu-ralist, photographer, and conservation leader—the Asahel Curtis Nature Trail provides an excellent glimpse of the ancient forest that once existed. You are surrounded by towering old-growth cedar, pine, and fir trees, as well as underbrush that ranges from devil's club to Canadian dogwood. The atmosphere is completed by rustling streams crossed by log bridges.

RECREATIONAL

Thousands of miles of recreational trails head from the Byway. Most of these trails support hiking, but some of the trails are also great for biking and horseback riding. These trails range in length and difficulty. Some are great for day trips, and others take you deep into the backcountry. Walkers and bicyclists can begin a journey into the mountains from the heart of Seattle on the separated I-90 trail that has its own tunnel and crosses the scenic lake Washington floating bridge. A series of regional trails lead to the John Wayne Pioneer Trail just south of North Bend (38 miles from Seattle). This converted rail/trail crosses the mountains on a wide and gentle slope and includes a 2.3-mile tunnel under the Snoqualmie Summit on its way to the Columbia River. Another of the more fre-quented hiking areas is the Burke Gilman Trail, which begins in Seattle and goes to Bothell, Woodinville, and Redmond, passing through suburban towns and pastoral farmland before arriving at Marymoore Park in the shadow of the Microsoft campus. At the Snoqualmie Summit, exit 52, you can gain access to the Pacific Crest Trail that runs from Mexico to Canada. By taking the trail northward from this exit, you enter the Alpine Lakes Wilderness Area and spectacular high alpine country, dotted with hundreds of small lakes and profuse displays of wildflowers.

Another popular hiking area is in the Cougar Mountain Regional Wildland Park, the largest wild park in an urban area in America at 4,000 acres. This network through wetland and forest passes 19th-century coal-mining shafts and concrete foundations. Another park, the Squak Mountain State Park, offers excellent hiking, because its 2,000 wooded acres are a first-rate wildlife habitat. The Tiger Mountain State Forest has the state's most heavily used trails. This web of trails for hikers, mountain bikers, and eques-trians winds through 13,000 acres of working forest and conservation area. The two access points are just minutes from Seattle suburbs.

At 4,190 feet, Mount Si towers over the town of North Bend and is a favorite hiking destination with its strenuous 8-mile round-trip trail to the summit or its 5-mile round-trip trail to Little Si. Also, the Rattlesnake Ledge Trail climbs steeply (1,175 feet in 1 mile) from Rattlesnake Lake through classic western Washington forests to rock outcrops that provide sweeping views of the Central Cascades and Snoqualmie Valley. The Middle Fork Snoqualmie River Valley, on the edge of the Alpine Lakes Wilderness, has a variety of trails that wind among more than 100,000 acres of both ancient and recently harvested forests. The valley is minutes from North

Bend but is lightly visited. An unpaved, 12-mile road leads to a footbridge, the access to many miles of backcountry trails. Other great places to hike around this Byway are Twin Falls State Park, the Asahel Curtis/Annette Lake Trail, the trail to Denny Creek and Franklin Falls, Snoqualmie Pass Summit, the John Wayne/Iron Horse Trail and Snoqualmie Tunnel, and the Coal Mines Trail.

SCENIC

In 100 miles, the Mountains to Sound Greenway starts in the bustle of a major port city, passes through a suburban town where the interstate highway itself won a national award for highway design, and quickly enters dense forests. The front range of the Cascade Mountains looms over the flat, pastoral Snoqualmie Valley at North Bend and from there, looking eastward, dramatic mountain peaks are continuously visible. From the Snoqualmie Summit eastward, Interstate 90 passes two large lakes, which provide both recreational opportunities and irrigation water for the dryer lands of central Washington. At the end of the 100-mile greenway, you can leave the interstate, drive north a few miles through the historic town of Thorp, and circle back westward on old Highway 10, a dramatic geologic landscape carved and eroded by the Yakima River. Highway 10 rejoins I-90 just east of Cle Elum, where you can head east or west.

All the views along the drive are splendid; however, only a handful of travelers know about an especially magnificent viewpoint. Just west of Snoqualmie Pass, a spot exists where the corridor's diverse richness is most visible. The view extends from the rocky mountaintops of the Cascades to the flourishing green valleys of the Puget Sound lowlands. A little farther west, the view from Snoqualmie Point, a promontory just south of I-90, becomes panoramic—take exit 27, go right up the hill, and park at a gate. A short walk leads to a view that encompasses Mount Si towering nearby; Mount Baker is visible in the far distance on a clear day. The view follows the curve of the corridor past North Bend and on into alpine zones sheathed in silvery snow.

The term "greenway" is particularly applicable to this particular scenic Byway. A sizable portion of this Byway passes through national forests, enabling you to experience the grandeur of many varieties of trees. A blanket of thick forests of Douglas fir, true fir, hemlock, and cedar make this road truly a greenway. Two kinds of trees that can reach enormous proportions are cedars and Sitka spruce. Many of the old cedars were logged, and you can see their disintegrating stumps dotting the landscape around the forests that have since grown in. With a bit of looking and luck, you may find patches of the old trees, which had diameters of more than 15 feet.

Strait of Juan de Fuca Highway, SR 112

WASHINGTON

Reaching farther out into the cold waters of the North Pacific than any other point of mainland in the lower 48 states, this Byway, located in the northwest corner of Washington state, is a remote stretch of coastline with rugged cliffs and forests. The Strait of Juan de Fuca Highway follows the shoreline of a glacial fjord that connects Puget Sound to the Pacific Ocean. Natural wonders that are rare and exciting events in other places of the world are everyday occurrences here. For example, eagles search for food among intertidal rocks, and gray whales feed in the Strait of Juan de Fuca.

This Byway offers an uncommon adventure on an uncrowded stretch of Washington's coast. The highway provides access to Cape Flattery, the farthest northwest point in the continental United States. It also provides access to Olympic National Park beaches. Explore the wild shoreline, stroll windy beaches and fishing towns, fish for salmon and halibut, take a self-guided tour among timber forests, or just set off by foot, bike, boat, or kayak to actively explore the area.

The communities along the highway provide pleasant starting points for exploring the surrounding natural landscape. A boardwalk system provides access to remote shorelines, where Pacific Ocean waves crash against sea stacks and rocky cliffs. Along the route, you'll spy tree-covered hillsides, uncommon sea birds like puffins and auklets, bald eagles, and marine mammals (including sea otters, whales, and sea lions).

Whether you watch the waves break, take a ride on a salmon charter, learn about Native American cultures, or watch whale spouts, the Strait of Juan de Fuca Highway can be an adventure for a day or week.

The Byway Story

The Strait of Juan de Fuca Highway tells archaeological, cultural, historical, natural, recreational, and scenic stories that make it a unique and treasured Byway.

QUICK FACTS

Length: 61 miles.

Time to Allow: 2 to 8 hours.

Best Time to Drive: Spring, when rain keeps the country green and lush, and fall, when the maples turn color and the weather is its mildest. Summer is the high season.

Byway Travel Information: Clallam Bay-Sekiu Chamber of Commerce: phone 360/963-2346.

Special Considerations: Gas is available on Highway 112 at Joyce, Clallam Bay, and Neah Bay. Pets are not allowed on the trails at Lake Ozette. When on the Makah Reservation, follow their request to "take only pictures; leave only footprints." Posted speed limits change frequently depending on the nature of the road, population, and activities.

Restrictions: Flooding and/or landslides occasionally occur and can close the road for short periods. The only fee along the Byway is a nominal one at the Makah Cultural Museum.

Bicycle/Pedestrian Facilities: Bicyclists tend to stay at the east end of the corridor, between Port Angeles and the Highway 113 junction, because it is well suited for bicycle travel. This segment has wider shoulders and good sight distances for much of its length. After the Highway 113 junction, cyclist find either narrower shoulders or no shoulder areas at all, along with many curves and hills.

ARCHAEOLOGICAL

Archaeology is quite prominent in this area because Native American artifacts are unearthed with relative frequency. The many Native American artifacts found here have been gathered into one of the nation's most significant displays of its kind, the Byway's own Makah Cultural and Research Center. This center chronicles the Native American people who have inhabited this region for millennia. Specifically, it features artifacts from two ancient Native American villages that have been unearthed here in recent years. An Ozette village was discovered in 1966; also, a Makah fishing village, estimated to be nearly 3,000 years old, was excavated in the 1980s. Some artifacts from this Makah fishing village include wooden fish-hooks, harpoons, a gill net, and basket fragments.

CULTURAL

The longtime residency of Native American tribes gives distinctive seasoning to this area's already unique culture. The still-thriving Makah tribe contributes particular savor because it resides, continuing in its traditions, at the western end of the Byway. The Makah Cultural and Research Center, which sits on the Makah reservation, tells the story of the Makah. This center also tells the stories of other tribes that had great influence on the area, such as the Klallam and the Quileutes. The Klallam were especially influential; by the late 1700s, they had established 17 villages between Discovery and Clallam Bays and numbered about 2,000 people. The Makah and Ozette, headquartered near Neah Bay and Lake Ozette, also numbered about 2,000 people each. Evidence of the effect of these tribes is prevalent in the overwhelming amount of Native American artifacts that have been found here and are displayed at the center.

HISTORICAL

This Byway's communities treasure their history and have consequently taken care to renovate the buildings that tell the stories of its modern history. For instance, the restored train depot serves as the Joyce Museum, which recounts the area's logging history through logging artifact displays. Another well-preserved building, the Joyce General Store (originally a hotel at the town of Crescent Beach) exudes the spirit of bygone days. The Byway's communities are also continually working to refurbish other structures, such as the West Clallam Schoolhouse. This finely crafted wooden building, built by one of the region's

early timber companies, characterizes the region in that era. Efforts are also being made to restore the warning horn of the unique and well-preserved Slip Point Lighthouse Tender's Residence.

NATURAL

It's no surprise that the Strait of Juan de Fuca's many gorgeous variations—its rocky shorelines, snow-covered mountains, and nationally featured tide pools—support a wide range of remarkable and unique flora and fauna. You need only to walk on the beach or take a sea kayak out on the profound waters to see and feel a kinship with these plants and animals. For example, it wouldn't be atypical to slide past a gray whale, killer whale, or sea otter while on your sea kayak. Olympic National Park's Pacific Beach area offers wild and remote beaches that are yours to discover and are lined with nationally significant old-growth rain forests. Birds and sea mammals crowd around the sea stacks and rocky cliffs and in the waters off Cape Flattery, the most northwestern point in the mainland United States. You can feel close to these animals from your jutting vantage point from Cape Flattery's Cliffside boardwalk system and viewing decks.

These nearly mythic wonders continue as you travel farther inland. The glacier water and deep gorge of the Elwha River were once home to a legendary run of chinook salmon, fish that were large enough that Native American tribes used single skins as ceremonial robes. Unfortunately, these fish no longer exist in this river because populations have been in decline ever since the development of hydroelectric dams at the turn of the century. In fact, no type of salmon has been able to negotiate the dams, but funding has been allocated to begin removing the dams in what is likely to be the highest-profile fish habitat restoration project in the nation.

The Byway's rolling, tree-covered hillsides have been managed for timber production for more than 100 years, meaning that the length of time from harvest to "green-up" is minimal. These forests, consequently, are a dynamic mosaic of newly harvested areas and mature woodlands. Part of the mature woodlands is an area of dense bald eagle nesting, roosting, and feeding. It would be rare to drive through this particular area and not see an eagle hunting or perching. In fact, when the eagle population is at its peak in the spring and fall, it is common to see a dozen eagles in one day.

RECREATIONAL

When driving along the Strait of Juan de Fuca Highway, opportunities to stop and have a good time abound. Every stop affords a dazzling view and also offers a chance to make memories.

Salmon fishers have come here from throughout the country for decades, one of which was the nation's most famous sportsman, Eddie Bauer (of retail and catalog fame); he even had a fishing cabin along this route. Visitors love to fish for salmon, and the fishing is so good that a salmon season exists each summer. Boats of all sizes can be used to fish for mighty Pacific halibut, several kinds of rockfish, resident blackmouth salmon, beautiful coho salmon, and giant chinook salmon. In the area near Neah Bay, the state's record 288-pound flatfish was caught. While fishing is best in the summer, you can also enjoy great fishing in the winter: keep an eye on the wind forecasts, enjoy the solitude, and catch some good-sized fish.

Kayaking and scuba diving are a thrilling way to immerse yourself (quite literally) in the marine life of the area. The Strait of Juan de Fuca from Pillar Point to Cape Flattery offers several places where you can launch and kayak through kelp forests and offshore sea stacks to view the variety of marine life while paddling. There are both freshwater and saltwater kayaking opportunities in the area. For a different kind of adventure, consider scuba diving. The Strait of Juan de Fuca and the Olympic Coast National Marine Sanctuary offer world-class diving. Rocky reefs and kelp forests enable you to catch views of large and colorful invertebrates, including fish-eating anemones,

giant mussels, and the world's largest octopus. Plenty of darting fish also keep you company.

The surrounding area is incredibly diverse. The shores of the Strait of Juan de Fuca and adjacent forests accommodate more than 200 species of birds. Located in the middle of the Pacific flyway, trumpeter swans, falcons, hawks, and sandhill cranes may easily be sighted during the spring and fall migration periods. In addition, expect the excitement of shores crowded with bald eagles in the winter months. Swimming in the waters below the winging birds are a variety of whales for the watching. During the summer, California gray whales and orcas travel the Strait of Juan de Fuca from Tatoosh Island to Clallam Bay. Pilot and humpback whales also frequent the waters south and east of Cape Flattery. Other marine life will catch your eye, including sea lions, porpoises, white-sided dolphins, and harbor seals. In fact, during the winter, you may be able to glimpse an occasional "raft" of up to 100 male sea otters off the shore along the beaches. Female otters with pups reside between Cape Alava and Cape Flattery all year.

SCENIC

The Strait of Juan de Fuca Highway takes you through an incredibly diverse landscape. The Byway travels along the north edge of Washington state right next to the sandy beaches and shoreline of the Strait of Juan de Fuca. The greenery of the Olympic National Forest and Park borders much of the other side of the Byway. The sights and sounds of the culture of various communities in the area add to the rich scenic qualities of this Byway.

The beaches of the Strait of Juan de Fuca themselves are complex and diverse, ranging from rocky coastlines to sandy white beaches. Immense sea stacks—erosion-resistant rock separated from the land by a bit of sea—tower offshore, dwarfing people strolling near the surf. Sea stacks are frequently photographed for their massive yet elegant profiles. The burnished reds of the setting sun cast a delicate light on the sea stacks and the shore, making exquisite photographs. Tide pools abundant in brightly colored marine life dot the rocky shores of this Byway.

A look to the other side of the Byway hides the view of the shoreline and brings into focus the thickly forested mountain knolls and flowering alpine meadows. The world's only coniferous rain forest is near the highway, showcasing a stunning world of gigantic trees and overwhelming greenery. The world's largest specimens of western red cedar and Sitka spruce stalk the terrain, with moss hanging like drapery from their ancient branches. The glacier-capped peaks of Mount Olympus rise in the distance.

Highlights

This tour takes you through some of the highlights of this Byway. If you're starting on the western end, read this list from the bottom up.

○ Start your drive in the early middle of the day at the eastern end of the Byway, which is just west of the city of **Port Angeles.** After 10 miles of enjoying the scenic drive, you'll come upon **Joyce General Store,** where you can get food (like a picnic lunch for later) and other traveling items. This charming establishment was built in the early 1900s and still maintains old-time charm.

○ Adjacent to the store is the **Joyce Museum.** This former railroad station displays early area history; it has general store items from the 1920s through the 1940s, old photos, and more.

○ Twenty miles west of the museum is **Pillar Point,** offering an imposing profile of Pillar Point and a view of the Pysht River estuary.

○ About 15 miles west of the Point is **Clallam Bay County Park,** a gorgeous saltwater agate-strewn beach. You can wade and picnic here and see Seiku Point and Vancouver Island.

○ A few miles west of the Park is Hoko-Ozette road. Take this road for about 10 miles to the southwest to get to **Lake Ozette,** a really large lake in and around which you can backpack for a couple of days or do a little light hiking, bird-watching, and picnicking by the water. Watch the sunset here and travel home in the gentle dusk.

Alaska's Marine Highway

ALASKA

If you want to see Alaska, take the ferry. Alaska's Marine Highway is made up of a state-owned fleet of nine ferries that travel scenic coastal routes totaling more than 8,000 miles. From the southern terminus in Bellingham, Washington, the ferries ply waters lined with the lush, green rain forests of British Columbia and Alaska's Inside Passage. Voyagers pass glaciers and fjords in Prince William Sound and the windswept Aleutian Islands, rich in cultural, archeological, and seismic history.

In southeastern Alaska, northbound travelers can end their sail in Haines or Skagway to connect to the Yukon or other Alaska scenic highways, such as the Haines Highway and the Taylor/Top of the World Highway. The mainline vessels are the Taku, Matanuska, Malaspina, Kennicott, and Columbia. These workhorses of the Inside Passage travel from Bellingham, Washington; Prince Rupert, British Columbia; and southeastern Alaska coastal communities.

The *Bartlett* travels routes in south-central Alaska and Prince William Sound. The *Tustumena* travels the Gulf of Alaska and the Aleutian Islands. During the summer, the state's newest ferry, the M/V *Kennicott,* provides several Gulf of Alaska crossings to the south-central communities of Valdez and Seward.

The Byway Story

Alaska's Marine Highway tells archaeological, cultural, historical, natural, recreational, and scenic stories that make it a unique and treasured Byway.

ARCHAEOLOGICAL

Although you may not see much archaeology from the ferry, stops along the way offer a look at some of Alaska's most intriguing archaeological sites. Much of the archaeological evidence left behind is the work of native Alaskans, and some sites along the Byway are of Russian and American origin.

Petroglyphs can be found on the Byway near Kodiak, near Petersburg in the Tongass National Forest, and in Sitka. In Wrangell, visitors will be delighted to find Petroglyph State Historic Park, where beautiful circles and designs are

---

QUICK FACTS

Length: 8,834 miles.

Time to Allow: Allow one month to take in all the sights.

Best Time to Drive: The highway is beautiful year-round. Summer is the high season, so make reservations early. During the winter months, the frequency of trips to some communities is reduced.

Byway Travel Information: Alaska's Marine Highway: phone toll-free 800/642-0066; Byway local Web sites: www.dot.state .ak.us/amhs/index.html, www.dot.state .ak.us.

Special Considerations: All vehicles, including large trucks, RVs, and trailers, can be accommodated on the highway's ships, provided space is available. Electrical current on board is 110-volt, 60-cycle, AC power.

Restrictions: Fees vary from under $50 to hundreds of dollars depending on how far you go and whether you are bringing your car. Call Alaska's Marine Highway System for a schedule.

Bicycle/Pedestrian Facilities: All ferries accommodate bicycles and walk-on travelers. You must leave your bike on the car deck; access to the deck is prohibited while underway except for specific trips. You also have access to your vehicle while the vessel is in port. Bicycles, kayaks, and very small boats (inflatables under 100 pounds) are charged at the Alternate Means of Conveyance rate, which is limited to one per customer. If the boat exceeds 100 pounds, it will be charged at the "Vehicles to 10 Feet" rate. Larger boats must be on a trailer and will be charged the appropriate amount by length.

carved into large stones. A short hike from the ferry landing takes explorers to a collection of more than 40 petroglyphs from an unknown time and culture, although the native Tlingit people could be descendents of the artists. Archaeologists have made guesses about the significance of the designs on the boulders, but they could be anything from artwork to a record of the past.

In Ketchikan, archaeology and today's cultures come together at the Totem Bight State Historic Park. When native people left their villages to find work in the new towns in Alaska, they also left collections of totem poles behind. During the 1930s, the Civilian Conservation Corps (CCC) came to salvage what was left of these totem poles and re-create what had been lost. An even more recent archaeological excavation began at Sitka in 1995 to uncover Baranof Castle, built in 1837. Work at this site has uncovered many artifacts from the time Russians first began to inhabit Sitka. The occupations and way of life for native Alaskans and new Alaskans become evident through each discovery.

CULTURAL

Three distinct cultures have come to call Alaska their home over the last few centuries, and these cultures are present at every port along Alaska's Marine Highway. The native cultures have been joined over the years by Russian and American cultures to create a rich history and a thriving present.

The lives of residents, along with the industries that allow them to survive in the Land of the Midnight Sun, are around every corner as you enjoy the decks of the ferry or the streets of one of Alaska's towns. Alaska's Marine Highway takes you through fishing villages and historic towns. Watching a fishing boat on the ocean, you may catch a glimpse of one of the huge halibut that fishing boats bring in.

Nearly every stop on the Byway reveals more history of the native Alaskans who have lived here for centuries. The native people celebrate festivals and wear authentic clothing. Feasts and festivals that involve dancing, singing, arts, and crafts traditionally occur during the winter, when all the work of the summer has been done. Many of the festivals are held in honor of animal spirits. Some of the native cultures believe that the hunt will be continually good when the spirits of animals are honored. The festivals and traditions you witness on the Byway may be the most memorable part of your trip.

HISTORICAL

The history of coastal Alaska dates back to unrecorded times, when the first native Alaskans were just getting used to the beautiful, yet extreme, territory they lived in. Over many centuries, Alaska has come to be appreciated by different cultures that wanted to stake a claim in the area. From Russian Orthodox missionaries to American gold miners, the history of Alaska and its coastline is unique and full of stories. As you travel along Alaska's Marine Highway, each port unravels more of the past.

Kodiak Island was the site of the first permanent Russian colony in 1784. The same Russian trappers who were willing to brave the elements in Siberia were also willing to settle the land across the Bering Strait if it meant finding more furs. As settlement progressed, a Russian Orthodox mission was established to keep peace between native peoples and the Russians until the parcel of land was sold to the United States. Today, towns like Sitka, Unalaska, Seldovia, and many others display pieces of Russian history and influence in Alaska.

Development in Alaska really began in 1867 when "Seward's Icebox" became a US territory. News of gold in the arctic spread like wildfire, and prospectors gathered in mining communities to try their luck. Ketchikan became the gateway to the Klondike Gold Rush, and Skagway became the destination. Skagway still maintains its reputation as a gold rush town with the Klondike Gold Rush National Historic Park. All through the Inside Passage and on to south-central Alaska, miners established communities in places that promised wealth. Some were successful, and many were not, but stories of Alaska were told far and wide in the lower 48 states.

The first tourists to Alaska traveled along the coast for a look at the lands that they had heard so much about. They usually took a steamship on a route developed along Alaska's Inside Passage to see the mystical northern territory, and its glaciers and dense forests. Traveling along the coastline remains one of the world's favorite ways to see Alaska—Alaska's Marine Highway preserved the sightseeing tactics of the first Alaskan tourists.

NATURAL

Some of the most unique wonders of the world are clustered in the northern corner—a very large corner—known as Alaska. Filled with majestic sea creatures, geological movements, and land overrun with glaciers and forests, Alaska's scenic coastline abounds with natural wonders. In the daylight, you may see a whale as it splashes its tail against the water. At night, the Northern Lights may fill the sky.

As you travel along the shores of Alaska, you observe the unspoiled natural features of the north. Alaska's Marine Highway travels through the Tongass National Forest and along the Chugach National Forest, allowing you to get a good look at both the land and the sea. These beautiful water passageways display rock outcroppings, forest-covered mountainsides, and even glaciers. Although Norway is known best for having fjords, Alaska has its own collection. The state has 100,000 glaciers, most located on the coast. Also notice the smoldering islands along the Alaska Peninsula. These islands are part of the Pacific "Ring of Fire," where underwater volcanoes create island volcanoes that can be seen from the ferry.

Few Byways offer a view of such fascinating sea creatures. Whales, seals, fish, and seabirds are all an integral part of an experience on Alaska's Marine Highway. Stop in Seward to visit the Alaska Sealife Center, where interactive displays tell all about Alaska's wildlife. The route actually passes through nine wildlife preserves and national parks, where you're sure to catch a glimpse of something interesting. Both baleen whales and killer whales can be spotted at Glacier Bay National Park and Preserve. At Kodiak Island, nearly 2 million seabirds live along the shores, while brown bears roam the spruce forests. As you continue, you may be surprised at the kinds of sights that surface on your voyage.

RECREATIONAL

Recreation and adventure go hand in hand, and what is more adventurous than an ocean voyage? From the decks of the ships to the streets of each town to the trails of the forests, you'll find plenty of places to explore along Alaska's Marine Highway. Nearly 98 percent of the land along the Byway is publicly owned, which makes wilderness experiences and recreational opportunities virtually endless. While you ride the ferry, you can dine, lounge, and even camp on the decks.

One of the benefits of traveling Alaska's Marine Highway is being able to take your favorite recreational activities with you—mountain biking, kayaking, hiking, or whatever other activities beckon along the coast. At each community, you'll find opportunities to get out and explore, with miles of trails, plenty of parks, and places to stay available at every stop. If you're traveling the Byway for a look at local history and culture, spend time in the communities along the way. Stopping in the Tongass National Forest or the Chugach National Forest allows you to see some of Alaska's beautiful forests and perhaps some of its wildlife. If you're an angler, you may want to try salmon fishing in some of Alaska's rivers.

SCENIC

Be sure to bring enough film for your camera. Visiting the coastline of Alaska is like visiting the shores of a fantasy land. Traveling the coast by Alaska's Marine Highway transforms the adventure to a sea voyage, where the wonders of the north are waiting to be discovered. From volcanoes to glaciers, a collection of natural wonders are visible from the decks. You'll see evergreen islands and majestic fjords. Glacier-carved mountains rise up from the shoreline, overshadowing a peaceful fishing village. And at night, the Northern Lights may glide across the black sky.

As you travel among the villages and towns of the three main sections of the marine Byway, the scenery changes, and nature displays different spectacles from her bag of tricks. Along the Alaskan Peninsula, volcanic activity exists on smoldering islands that are still growing and forming. Winding through the Inside Passage, you pass many of the 1,500 islands there. All along the journey, look for Alaskan sea life that can be seen only from the decks of a boat—or on one of television's nature channels.

Each stop on the route takes you to towns and villages with displays of history and culture. Parts of the scenery on the Byway are found in the Russian Orthodox churches and the remnants of booming gold rush towns. Snowcapped mountains in the background and the crisp Alaskan atmosphere only heighten the appeal of each place along the way. And within each city, you are likely to find rivers, trails, or bays, where eagles soar and seals still gather.

Highlights

Alaska's Marine Highway takes you through a variety of towns (listed here alphabetically) along the southern Alaskan coastline.

☼ **Haines:** Located at the northern extent of the Inside Passage route, this community is situated along the Chilkat River. This is a popular port community, linked to the traditional highway system that connects to the Alaska Highway via the Haines state scenic byway. The community is also popular for its bald eagle population in the autumn. In October, the world's largest number of bald eagles gather in Haines to take advantage of the late salmon run. This amazing gathering of eagles is the basis of the Chilkat Bald Eagle Preserve and annual Alaska Bald Eagle Festival held in their honor.

☼ **Homer:** Located on the Kenai Peninsula, Homer is the home port for a large fleet of halibut charter operators fishing the rich and scenic waters of Kachemak Bay. The Spit is where all the action in Homer takes place. Both commercial fishing boats and leisure fishermen gather at The Spit for boating and fishing. Also located in Homer is the Alaska

Maritime National Wildlife Refuge. The refuge is home to seabirds, which find a habitat in the rocks and reefs of Alaskan islands.

☼ **Juneau:** Juneau is the capital of Alaska and a historic community with a range of tourism-oriented services and cultural events. The community was settled as a gold mining district and is now the service hub for southeastern Alaska. It is also the gateway to Glacier Bay National Park.

☼ **Ketchikan:** Ketchikan is known as the Gateway to Alaska and is the state's salmon capital. The community is known for its historic Creek Street district and timber industry.

☼ **Kodiak:** Kodiak, the nation's largest commercial fishing port, was once the capital of Russian America. The community is located on Kodiak Island, a national wildlife preserve, allowing outstanding wildlife viewing opportunities.

☼ **Petersburg:** This town is known as Little Norway due to its Scandinavian roots and has several festivals to celebrate the heritage of its residents. Visitors to the community often believe they are visiting a Norwegian community due to its architecture and commonly spoken language.

☼ **Seward:** If you hear names like "Resurrection Bay" and "Marathon Mountain," you are probably at the romantic town of Seward on the Seward Highway. The town was named to honor William H. Seward, who helped the United States purchase Alaska from Russia. Near Seward, you'll find Kenai Fjords National Park and the Chugach National Forest headquarters. While in Seward, don't miss a visit to the Alaska Sealife Center. Celebrating Independence Day in Seward means running or watching the Mount Marathon Race and participating in events all around the city.

☼ **Sitka:** Numerous volcanic mountains rise out of the ocean and provide a stunning ocean backdrop for this fishing community. Sitka was the Russian capital of North America in the 19th century, as well as the first state capital of Alaska. It still offers visitors a great taste of that period in Alaskan history. The community is also a center for Tlingit native culture.

○ **Skagway:** Skagway is a community with a rich history that includes the Klondike Gold Rush. The history of that period is displayed by a National Park Service site and by the city's historic architecture. The White Pass and Yukon Route historic railway traverses the 3,000-foot mountain pass to the Yukon, Canada.

○ **Unalaska/Dutch Harbor:** Unalaska/Dutch Harbor is the westernmost point of the Marine Highway. Located in the Aleutian Islands, it was the first Russian-American community. The town was invaded by the Japanese during World War II.

○ **Valdez:** Valdez is the terminus of the Trans-Alaskan Pipeline and the Richardson State Scenic Byway. The area is home to the World Extreme Skiing Competitions as well as many other outstanding winter activities. Don't miss the scenic walking trail.

○ **Whittier:** Whittier is an important hub connecting the Marine Highway to the Alaska Railroad and to the rest of Alaska, including Anchorage, Fairbanks, and Denali National Park. The community is also linked by highway to the rest of Alaska.

Glenn Highway

ALASKA

The Glenn Highway is a place where geology, culture, and scenery come together to create a majestic and rugged landscape that can be seen only in Alaska. Winters bring the fascinating Northern Lights among snow-capped mountains. In the spring, hawks, eagles, and falcons can be seen gliding over the Glenn Highway. Summers bring endless days of wildflowers and green forests along the Matanuska River Canyon that runs between the Chugach and Talkeetna Mountains, creating beautiful views all the way.

QUICK FACTS

Length: 135 miles.

Time to Allow: 8 hours.

Best Time to Drive: Summer is beautiful with wildflowers and forests in full bloom. Winter sometimes includes days during which travel is not recommended.

Byway Travel Information: Matanuska-Susitna Convention and Visitor Bureau: phone 907/746-5000; Byway local Web site: www.alaskavisit.com.

Special Considerations: Tour buses travel the Glenn Highway corridor extensively during the summer tourist season. The Glenn Highway is subject to avalanches; when traveling during winter, check road and weather information prior to the trip and carry appropriate winter gear. Pull-offs are plowed and available for viewing in the winter.

Restrictions: The Glenn Highway can be safely traversed by two-wheel-drive vehicles. Most of the state park facilities beyond Sutton are closed during the winter.

Bicycle/Pedestrian Facilities: The Glenn Highway accommodates pedestrians and bicyclists with separated trails between East Anchorage and Chugiak. No pedestrians are allowed on the controlled access facility between Chugiak and the Parks Highway, but tour bikers are. Between the Parks Highway and Sutton, both pedestrians and bicyclists may use the shoulder. Sutton has a new 4-mile separated trail. The road is narrow between Kings River and the end of the Byway at mile 135.

Among the mountains and the unforgettable seasons live a distinct Alaskan culture that has been developing for centuries—beginning with the native Alaskan culture that was altered so much with the arrival of Russian fur traders and, later, gold miners from the lower 48. The history of all of Alaska's cultures can be seen along the Byway in museums and historic places.

The Byway Story

The Glenn Highway tells archaeological, cultural, historical, natural, recreational, and scenic stories that make it a unique and treasured Byway.

ARCHAEOLOGICAL

Although pieces of archaeology can be found all over the ancient lands along the Glenn Highway, many of them are so delicate that few people know about them. From studying small tools made of flint and other materials, archaeologists are slowly becoming acquainted with societies that are long forgotten in Alaska. In Knik, south of Wasilla, archaeologists are uncovering a village and many artifacts. The Knik town-site became a Euro-American trading and supply post in the late 1800s. Archaeologists have uncovered an old blacksmith shop, an assayer's house, and tools used for refining gold. When the townsite has been excavated, the discoveries and artifacts will go on display in a nearby museum.

As you travel the Glenn Highway, you may also want to explore Anthracite Ridge near Sutton. The ridge was formed when a warmer climate existed on the lands that are now Alaska. Ginkgo trees and other warm vegetation were buried here to create the coal resources and the fossils that attract both miners and paleontologists. Bones from a dinosaur known as the Hadrosaur were also found near the Byway at Gunsight Mountain in the Talkeetna Mountains. The dinosaur has been affectionately dubbed "Lizzie."

CULTURAL

Cultures from all over the world have combined along the Glenn Highway. They join to make the winter a little warmer and communities a little brighter. The native cultures of Alaska changed and developed over many centuries before they were joined by fur traders from Russia and miners from the United States. Amid gold rush history, native tradition, and Russian influence, Alaska has emerged as a diverse state in more than just its natural resources.

Although many different cultures are gathered along the Byway, museums, architecture, and historic districts celebrate the unique history of each culture. To discover the original cultures of Alaska, visit the Anchorage Museum of History and Art or the Alaska Native Heritage Center. Historic villages of Eklutna and Chickaloon also house buildings and places that are reminiscent of days gone by.

Native society was structured around the family unit, and the bigger the family, the better. Families hunted together and when fishing, hunting, or trapping was good, the entire family experienced prosperity. But survival in the arctic was always a challenge. This way of life remained unchanged for many years, until a new culture emerged during the late 1700s.

When people from Russia began to come to Alaska, they brought their religion with them. Their goal was to introduce the native people of Alaska to Christianity, and one of the rules was that the people could accept the religion only of their own free will. Because of this, the Russian priests who lived in Alaska were extremely dedicated to supporting their parishes during the 100 years they were in Alaska. Yet native Alaskans often combined cultural beliefs: native people who converted to Orthodoxy would bury the remains of their dead, but also build a small "spirit house" above the grave. The St. Nicholas Russian Orthodox Church located in Eklutna is an example of the Russian Orthodox influence in Alaska. In fact, Eklutna provides some of the most striking examples of the mix of Russian Orthodoxy and native tradition in its buildings and even the cemetery.

An economic culture began to grow in Alaska during the 1870s. Rumors of coal, timber, and especially gold brought another significant culture to the land. Mining towns sprung up all over the land, and Alaska embarked on another great change. Many of those mining towns became the central cities of Alaska; descendents of gold miners became coal miners. Today, Independence Mine State Historic Park allows visitors to explore the lifestyle of the early gold miners in Alaska.

During the 20th century, people continued to gather in Alaska for relief from the Depression or for military strategy during World War II. It was during wartime that the Glenn Highway was constructed as an attempt to better connect Alaska with the lower 48 states. You can still see roadhouses along the Glenn Highway that offered shelter to early travelers.

HISTORICAL

Alaska's history in the United States has been shorter than that of the rest of the lower 48, but it is a romanticized land with history of gold camps, dogsled races, and native Alaskans. The roots of these historical ideas were established long before Alaska became a part of the US. Native people with the courage and endurance to establish their culture in this rugged territory settled here nearly 35,000 years ago. Since then, Alaska has maintained its pristine wildernesses, unique wildlife, and exotic atmosphere.

A people known as the Athabascans came from Asia to be the first inhabitants in the lands where the Glenn Highway is now located. The village of Eklutna is a settlement that has been inhabited since the late 1600s by these people, and the Athabascan languages are still preserved in the names of places along the Glenn Highway. It was not until the 1700s that the land and its people were recorded by Europeans. Explorers James Cook and Vitus Bering opened up European trade between native people in Alaska and their own countries. After the Russian-American Company began to establish missions, trade, and government here in the late 1790s, the people of Russia and Alaska interacted for nearly 100 years, for better or for worse, until another country began to take interest in Alaska.

In 1867, the United States purchased Alaska from Russia and caused a scandal among the American people. They were mortified at the $7.2 million price tag that the government was willing to pay for a frozen wasteland. But with the continued wealth achieved from fur trapping and gold discovered in Alaska, the area's reputation improved in the eyes of Americans, and people from the states began to flock to the territory. The need for roads in Alaska came with the expanding population of miners and trappers; during

World War II, Alaska's strategic position also made it a candidate for improved roads. As Alaska's roads improved, communities grew up and were able to have contact with each other. In fact, the Glenn Highway is known for connecting Alaska's history and culture.

NATURAL

Dramatic natural events formed the landscape along the Glenn Highway, and many of these events continue today. This is a land where melting glaciers, winds, and rivers are the moving forces. They create the scenery and, in many ways, have determined the history of the Byway. Without the rich soils and, of course, the gold that was found here, Alaska may still be unknown to Americans. Fortunately, even with the coming of settlers and roads, the wildlife and wildlands are preserved in Alaska as the defining features.

Earthquakes and the movement of the Earth's plates thousands of years ago created the Chugach and the Talkeetna mountain ranges, and the rich minerals found in the mountains have been drawing people to Alaska for more than 100 years. It was just off the Glenn Highway where some of Alaska's first gold was discovered. Today, mining is still occurring in the mountains, as geologists search the sediment for fossils and other geological remnants. Rivers, wind, and ice have played a role in the formation of the mountains since the beginning of their existence, moving the rich sediment from one end of the landscape to the other.

Although the Glenn Highway runs through the tundra, this ecosystem is far from a frozen wasteland. You may see salmon and trout swimming in the rivers while a moose wanders by the riverside. Flowers, trees, bushes, and meadow grasses are an array of different colors. Accumulating meltwater forms wetlands and marshes where birds and waterfowl gather. And when all the land is blanketed with snow, spruce, aspen, and other trees create a winter wonderland.

RECREATIONAL

Getting a good dose of nature isn't difficult when you visit the Glenn Highway for recreation. From winter sports to summer pastimes, the Byway provides plenty of places where scenery and activity come together. Chugach State Park is accessible from the Byway, and places like the Palmer Hayflats and the Matanuska

Glacier provide opportunities to spot wildlife or get a closer look at a glacier. With the Chugach and Talkeetna mountains surrounding the Byway, you have many opportunities for hiking and exploring these ancient landforms.

In a place where winter engulfs a large part of the year, winter recreation has been perfected. The lodges and roadhouses along the Glenn Highway are the perfect place to stop in the winter and enjoy cross-country skiing, snowmobiling, and snowshoeing. You can hardly help enjoying a winter night in Alaska, where the short days lead to extra-long nights. You may want to do some stargazing here or watch for the Northern Lights. You've never seen so many stars!

But even in Alaska, the snow melts and summer activities become available to travelers and residents. Alaska is the Land of the Midnight Sun, where, in summer, the long, sunny days make up for the nights of winter. Many people come just to see the wildflowers and watch for wildlife. During March, April, and early May, the air is filled with birds, migrating and moving. A stop at milepost 118 provides an excellent opportunity for viewing birds of prey. The melting rivers and streams are another source of activity. Of course, the fishing in Alaska is superb, but anglers aren't the only ones who enjoy the rivers; rafters and kayakers find places on Alaska rivers to test their skills. In Anchorage, a biking trail is located along the Byway for cyclists and in-line skaters to make their way from Anchorage to Chugiak. The city of Anchorage holds many diversions, including museums and nature centers. Whether you're drawn to the mountains or to cities, the Glenn Highway is a great way to see it all.

SCENIC

Along the Glenn Highway, scenery is just waiting to be noticed out of every car window. Drivers wish they were passengers as they drive among mountain ranges, crystal-clear waterways, and tundra where moose and bear wander. And just when you feel that you've reached the edge of civilization, a historic lodge or village comes into view.

The Byway is bordered by the Chugach Mountain Range from beginning to end. Majestic rock formations rise in between the glaciers that are so prevalent in this area. When the day is clear, you can look to the north and catch a glimpse of Mount McKinley, the highest mountain in the United States. Just past Palmer, Alaska, the Chugach Mountains are joined by the Talkeetna Mountains. Fields of wild irises decorate the Palmer Hayflats and follow the Knik River back to a glacier of the same name. Knik Glacier is located in the shadow of Mount Marcus Baker, one of the highest peaks in the Chugach Mountains.

Glaciers have formed much of Alaska, carving great masses of rock and stone. You can see the Matanuska Glacier from the road and feel the cool air that surrounds it. This huge mass of slow-melting ice displays the blue, gray, and white colors it has collected over the hundreds of years it has been retreating. When glaciers retreat, they leave streams and lakes behind: The Matanuska River is a collection of melted glacier water that runs among a bed of gray silt, creating a braided appearance. In summer, you can see where meltwater goes.

Alaska may not have as many April showers as other places in the nation, but what it doesn't get in rain it makes up in glacial meltwater. The water brings entire fields of wildflowers in the late spring and summer. Flowers of every color and kind decorate the valleys beneath the mountains, inviting travelers to take a closer look or try some nature photography. Wetland areas like the Palmer Hay Flats create views of marshy reeds and willows, where a tundra swan or a Canadian goose may be swimming. All along the Byway, sights of moose or Dall sheep are a reminder that this scenic country still belongs to nature.

Highlights

The Glenn Highway takes you through several Alaskan towns and villages (listed here alphabetically).

- **Anchorage:** The city of Anchorage began as a ramshackle community of rail workers living in tents. The community, settled in 1915, has grown and evolved into the largest city in Alaska, with 260,000 people. For a look at Alaskan culture, Anchorage is the place to be. Explore the Anchorage Museum of History and Art or the Alaska Native Heritage Center for a taste of what Alaska has to offer.

- **Chickaloon Village:** This native community is nestled above the confluence of Moose Creek and the Matanuska River in the Talkeetna Mountains. It is the home of Alaska's first native-maintained school and Katie's Wall, built 60 years ago by Katie Wade to stop the cut slope from eroding. Many of the perennial shrubs she planted are still alive today and bloom brightly in the spring.

- **Eagle River:** This community, within the municipality of Anchorage, is nestled in the foothills of the Chugach Mountains and provides access to the Old Glenn Highway.

- **Eklutna Village:** The Athabascan Village of Eklutna has a museum, a Russian Orthodox church, and a cemetery with spirit houses that provide visitors a look into native life.

- **Glacier View Community:** The Glacier View Community provides several views of the Matanuska Glacier. The Matanuska Glacier Park Campground allows you to walk up next to—or even onto—the glacier.

- **Palmer:** Palmer is the seat of government for the Matanuska Susitna Borough, the home of the Alaska State Fair, the center of colonial history, and the heart of Alaska's breadbasket.

- **Sutton:** This quaint residential community is located in the Talkeetna Mountains. The Alpine Heritage and Cultural Center provides a look into Sutton's past.

The Seward Highway

ALASKA

The Seward Highway, linking Anchorage with Seward, passes through some of the most spectacular scenery in the country. The landscape varies from the muddy waters of Turnagain Arm to the icy blue glaciers that hang almost to the sea. Wildflowers and waterfalls brighten every corner of the road as it glides below rough mountains that pierce thick, heavy clouds. Only Alaska's Seward Highway can offer this particular mix created by climate, geography, and geology.

QUICK FACTS

Length: 127 miles.

Time to Allow: 3 to 5 hours.

Best Time to Drive: From May to mid-October, salmon fishing is at its peak, and you can see whales along the shore and sheep on the mountainsides. The off-season consists of winter and spring. Avalanches may cause the road to be closed for short periods of time throughout the winter.

Byway Travel Information: Alaska Public Lands Information Center: phone 907/271-2737; Alaska Deptartment of Transportation and Public Facilities: phone 907/465-6975; Chugach National Forest: phone 907/743-9500; Byway local Web site: www.dot.state.ak.us/ stwdplng/scenic/bsewardhwy.html.

Special Considerations: The only significant seasonal problem facing the Seward Highway is adverse winter conditions. The Alaska Department of Transportation and Public Facilities has made a serious and effective commitment to keeping the Seward Highway passable during the winter months, however, because it is the principal highway serving the Kenai Peninsula.

Restrictions: Due to extreme conditions during the winter, the road is closed by avalanches an average of five times a year for approximately four hours.

Bicycle/Pedestrian Facilities: Bicyclists can take advantage of existing wide shoulders and many miles of separated bike paths. Pedestrians are accommodated at most of the highway's pullouts and along many of the trails paralleling the route.

The Seward Highway is located in a richly varied and highly diverse corridor. Its character changes over the course of its length. Roadside topography, the proximity of water, the types of views, the levels and types of development, and the width and character of the road are some of the ways in which the Seward Highway expresses different moods and landscapes between Anchorage and Seward. Each of these distinctive landscapes is uniquely spectacular.

For 127 miles, the road winds through a land of remarkable beauty, a land of saltwater bays, frigid-blue glaciers, knife-edged ridges, and alpine valleys. From the reflective waters of Turnagain Arm, you rapidly ascend 1,000 feet above sea level to an alpine meadow. Within the hour, you find yourself back at sea level surrounded by fjords, having just passed through a district of rivers and lakes.

Whether you drive for pleasure or you fish, hunt, backpack, camp, or ski, the Seward Highway can take you there. And it's all against a backdrop of spruce forests, wildflowers, and extraordinary wildlife.

The Byway Story

The Seward Highway tells historical, natural, recreational, and scenic stories that make it a unique and treasured Byway.

HISTORICAL

Far removed from the rest of the world sits Alaska, perched above the fast-paced industry of the world below. The route from Resurrection Bay to Alaska's Interior has been in existence for thousands of years; even Russian explorers searched the area for gold and fur in the 1700s. Following the same early routes used by native Alaskans, sled dogs, miners, and trains, the Seward Highway has evolved into a modern transportation system.

Natives first used an area along the Seward Highway 9,000 years ago as a hunting camp. In this area, now known as Beluga Point on Turnagain Arm, Tanaina Indians also discovered abundant game in the region over 8,000 years after the first natives inhabited the area. The region finally received its name in 1778 when Captain Cook sailed along the coast in his quest for the Northwest Passage. When shallow water forced him to turn around, he christened the sound Turnagain River. South of Anchorage, Highway 1 now follows the shore of Turnagain Arm.

In 1895, prospectors discovered gold in Hope, Alaska, in the Kenai Peninsula, and the rush began. One miner panned 385 ounces of gold from the river in one day. (Now, fishermen line the stream with hopes of catching salmon.) This gold rush of the late 1800s brought several thousand gold seekers to the area. Suddenly, the tiny towns of Hope and Sunrise grew into booming gold mining towns. Sunrise became the largest town in the Cook Inlet area and was even considered as a potential state capital. Scattered findings of gold all over the Kenai Mountains established the need for improved transportation routes from the ice-free port of Seward to Turnagain Arm.

Today's Byway traces several historic routes that miners used to cross the Kenai Mountains. The route from Seward to Snow River was used by hikers, dog teams, and horse parties. These travelers crossed Kenai Lake and landed at Cooper Landing, or they continued on to Moose Pass. The route from Moose Pass to Tern Lake and Cooper Landing was used when Kenai Lake was impassable, and it was used by northbound travelers from Kenai and Cooper Landing. Johnson Pass was the route of choice from Moose Pass to Sunrise and Hope. The Trail Creek to Placer River route was a direct path from Moose Pass to Portage Valley. This route was later chosen for the Alaska Central Railroad, which was in use by 1909.

By 1910, most miners had left the area in order to follow prospects of gold farther north. Sunrise dwindled into nothing more than a few residences, and mining activity in Hope came almost to a standstill. However, Cooper Landing's economy was soon influenced not by mining but by interest in big game hunting and fishing.

Today, the mining legacy of the Kenai Peninsula lives on through stories, museum photos, and weathered wood remains scattered throughout the Kenai Mountains. The privately owned townsite of Sunrise is a historic archaeological district. The Hope Historical Society operates a small museum that includes photographs, journals, mine buildings, and equipment from the gold rush.

NATURAL

As you travel the Seward Highway, watch for wildlife along the highway. You may hear the honking of Canadian geese in the wetlands, the whistle of hoary marmots in the alpine valleys, and the cry of bald eagles in the dense coastal forests. Just south of Anchorage, Potter's Marsh Wildlife Viewing Area offers a temporary home to ducks, geese, and other nesting water birds as they raise their young. Along Turnagain Arm, you may spot Dall sheep as they scale rugged mountainsides or bring their young near the highway to forage. Bald eagles, moose, bears, mountain goats, salmon, and a variety of birds thrive along the highway as well. Many species of wildflowers help beautify the road corridor. Two of the most common and colorful are the blue-purple arctic lupine and the pink-red fireweed.

Spotting Alaska's wildlife isn't always easy. Catching a glimpse of wildlife usually means being in the right place at the right time, but you can increase your chances by taking time to stop and scan hillsides and valleys, using binoculars to search for movement. Knowing where and why animals frequent can increase your chances of seeing them.

RECREATIONAL

From the beginning of human habitation in Alaska, people have been aware of the great natural resources of the land. In more recent years, people have come to discover another resource besides good hunting and gold mining: recreation. Although the activities offered on the Byway are unique and diverse, you will find camping, hiking, and picnicking spots in abundance all along the highway.

The section of the Seward Highway adjacent to Turnagain Arm provides scenic vistas across the Arm to the Kenai Mountains. Most of the lands above the highway are within Chugach State Park and provide you with a collection of things to see and ways to see them: windsurfing on the Arm, rock climbing on roadside rock cuts, rafting or canoeing on the Russian River, kite-flying at Beluga Point, angling at Bird Creek, and bicycling the highway. Two hundred miles of trails are in the forest alone.

Once a mining town, Girdwood is now home to a world-famous ski resort that offers excellent scenery and plenty of challenges. This town combines the best of today's recreation with classic activities of the past, like panning for gold—try your luck! During the summer, the community celebrates a Forest Fair with arts, crafts, food, and entertainment. Other Byway towns like Hope and Cooper Landing offer havens for fishing. In Anchorage, you can stroll the streets and browse in shops or visitor centers.

SCENIC

The trip from Anchorage to Seward is one of the most scenic 127-mile drives you can take. Frequent pullouts offer vistas of snow-capped mountains, glaciers, wildlife, and wildflowers at almost every turn, and side trips and hiking trails beckon adventurous explorers. With such an impressive "menu" of vacation selections, you don't want to rush between appetizer and dessert.

The road up Portage Valley leads into the 5.8-million-acre Chugach National Forest and past three "hanging" glaciers that are perched in the cleavage of mountain canyons. Portage Glacier pokes its nose through the mountains at the head of a valley that it cut a long time ago. Since 1890, it has receded 1 mile and will be out of view by 2020, so don't procrastinate taking a trip to see it. Last year, the glacier finally withdrew from the lake and stopped calving. Now, only a few bergs float in water that was once brimming with ice. The visitor center offers excellent descriptive displays of glaciers and the best chance to see ice worms, pin-sized critters that burrow into glaciers and eat algae. Temperatures above freezing kill them.

If the many sights along the road to Seward make up the appetizer and main course, a boat trip along the rugged coast of Kenai Fjords National Park offers a high-calorie dessert. You can take a day cruise to see wildlife and tidewater glaciers that calve into the sea. Along the way, you may see orcas breach at boatside or a humpback whale with young swimming placidly along. At Chiswall Islands, thousands of puffins and kittywakes circle the boat. Just when you think you've seen the best, the boat stops at the foot of Holgate Glacier. With the engines cut, the cracking and pop-

ping of the 500-foot wall of aquamarine ice thunders through the frigid air like cannons firing. A slab of ice silently slips from the face of the glacier and crashes into the water. Seconds later, the blast reaches your ears. This is no dainty wildflower beside a trickling stream; you're witnessing the raw power of nature that carves valleys through mountains and determines the weather of the entire planet.

Highlights

The Seward Highway is in a richly varied and highly diverse area of Alaska. Over the length of its route, the character of the Byway continually changes with its proximity to water, mountains, and towns. The Seward Highway begins in the town of Seward nestled among the fjords surrounding Resurrection Bay. Nearby Kenai Fjords National Park offers the chance to see puffins, otters, eagles, arctic terns, whales, seals, and other marine life.

✪ As you travel north, the landscape surrounding the Byway becomes one of alpine meadows dotted with rivers and lakes. During late July and early August, **Ptarmigan Creek Recreation Site,** 23 miles from Seward, is an excellent place to stop and watch the incredible salmon run when thousands of red salmon can be seen in this creek heading upstream to spawn.

○ Farther north, approximately 75 miles from Seward, is **Twentymile Flats,** an expanse of lowlands and intertidal mudflats where three river valleys empty their silt-laden waters into Turnagain Arm and provide unobstructed views of the surrounding mountain peaks and glaciers. The view here is breathtaking, definitely worth stopping and taking in for a few minutes at the very least.

○ Another 5 miles along the Byway is Portage Lake. **Portage Glacier,** located on the far side of Portage Lake, is rapidly receding out of the lake and provides an incredible opportunity to watch glacial action on fast-forward. One-hour boat tours are available to better witness the action.

○ The remaining portion of the Seward Highway travels along the **Turnagain Arm** and offers you a plethora of things to see, both on and off the water. Turnagain Arm experiences the second highest tides in the world, often up to a 38-foot change in water level. Bore tides, a rare natural phenomenon in which the front of an incoming tide is a moving wall of water from 3 to 5 feet high, can be witnessed during extremely low tides in Turnagain Arm.

○ The city of **Anchorage** is located at the northern terminus of the Seward Highway. With its rich history as a city on the edge of one of the final frontiers, Anchorage offers a wealth of historic and cultural sites that you can enjoy, whether you have an hour or a day to spend.

Idaho

When the Idaho Territory was created (it included much of Montana and Wyoming as well), President Abraham Lincoln had difficulty finding a governor who was willing to come to this wild and rugged land. Some appointees, including Gilman Marston and Alexander H. Conner, never appeared.

They had good reason to be timorous—the area was formidable and still is. For there is not just one Idaho; there are at least a half-dozen: a land of virgin rain forests (more than one-third of the state is wooded); a high desert covering an area bigger than Rhode Island and Delaware combined; gently sloping farmland, where soft Pacific winds carry the pungency of growing alfalfa; an alpine region of icy, isolated peaks and densely forested valleys hiding more lakes and streams than have been named, counted, or even discovered; an atomic energy testing station as modern as tomorrow, only a few miles from the Craters of the Moon, where lava once poured forth and congealed in fantastic formations; and the roadless, nearly uninhabited, 2.3 million-acre Frank Church-River of No Return Wilderness, where grizzly bear, moose, and bighorn sheep still run wild.

Stretching southward from Canada for nearly 500 miles and varying dramatically in terrain, altitude, and climate, Idaho has the deepest canyon in North America (Hell's Canyon, 7,913 feet), the largest stand of white pine in the world (in Idaho Panhandle National Forests), the finest big game area in the country (Chamberlain Basin and Selway), the largest wilderness area in the United States (the Frank Church-River of No Return Wilderness), and the largest contiguous irrigated area in the United States (created by American Falls and several lesser dams). Idaho's largest county,

---

Population: 1,293,593

Area: 83,557 square miles

Elevation: 710-12,662 feet

Peak: Borah Peak (Custer County)

Entered Union: July 3, 1890 (43rd state)

Capital: Boise

Motto: Let It Be Perpetual

Nickname: Gem State

Flower: Syringa

Bird: Mountain Bluebird

Tree: White Pine

Fair: Eastern, August in Blackfoot; Western, August in Boise

Time Zone: Mountain and Pacific

Web site: www.visitid.org

Fun Facts:

- Rivers flow across 3,100 miles of Idaho, more than any other state.
- Idaho's Hells Canyon is the deepest river gorge (7,913 feet) in North America.
- Ernest Hemingway finished *For Whom the Bell Tolls* while living in Sun Valley, and he is buried in Ketchum.

---

named after the state itself, would hold the entire state of Massachusetts; its second-largest county, Owyhee, would hold New Jersey.

In addition to superlative scenery, fishing, and hunting, visitors find such diversions as buried bandit treasure, lost gold mines, hair-raising boat trips down the turbulent Salmon River (the "River of No Return"), and ghost mining towns. For those who prefer less strenuous activities, Sun Valley and Coeur d'Alene have luxurious accommodations.

Millions of years ago herds of mammoth, mastodon, camels, and a species of enormous musk ox roamed the Idaho area. When Lewis and Clark entered the region in 1805, they found fur-bearing animals in such great numbers that they got in each other's way. The promise of riches in furs

Calendar Highlights

FEBRUARY

Lionel Hampton Jazz Festival *(Moscow). Phone 208/885-6765. University of Idaho.* Four-day festival hosted by Lionel Hampton featuring all-star headliners and student performers.

Pacific Northwest Sled Dog Championship Races *At Priest Lake Airport. Phone Chamber of Commerce, 208/263-2161.* Approximately 100 teams from the US and Canada compete in various races from 1/2 mile to 35 miles.

APRIL

Cowboy Poet Festival *(St. Anthony). Phone South Fremont Chamber of Commerce, 208/624-4870.* Entertainment, clogging demonstrations.

JUNE

Boise River Festival *(Boise). Phone 208/338-8887.* Nighttime parade, contests, entertainment, and fireworks.

National Oldtime Fiddlers' Contest *(Weiser). Phone 800/437-1280.* One of the oldest such contests in the country, attracting some of the nation's finest fiddlers. Also parade, barbecue, and arts and crafts.

Western Days *(Twin Falls). Phone 208/733-3974.* Three-day event features a shoot-out, barbecue contests, dances, and a parade.

JULY

The Festival at Sandpoint. *(Sandpoint) Phone 208/265-4554.* Since 1982, thousands have gathered in this arts town to enjoy music performed by internationally acclaimed musicians representing just about every genre imaginable. Past artists include the likes of B.B. King, Shawn Colvin, Tony Bennett, Wynton Marsalis, and Johnny Cash.

smART Festival *St. Marie's City Park. Phone 208/245-3417.* Paintings and crafts by local and regional artists. Food, entertainment, and swimming.

Snake River Stampede *(Nampa). Phone 208/466-4641.* Among the nation's top professional rodeos. All seats reserved.

AUGUST

Shoshone-Bannock Indian Festival *(Blackfoot). Phone 208/238-3700. Fort Hall Indian Reservation.* Tribes from many western states and Canada gather for this festival. Dancing, parades, rodeo, Native American queen contest, buffalo feast, and other events.

Western Idaho Fair *(Boise). Phone 208/376-3247.* Largest fair in the state. Four entertainment stages, grandstand for nationally known musicians. Livestock, rodeo, agricultural pavilion, antique tractors, indoor and outdoor commercial exhibits, and midway rides.

SEPTEMBER

Eastern Idaho State Fair *(Blackfoot). Phone 208/785-2480.* 70-acre fairground. Livestock, machinery exhibits, four-, six-, and eight-horse hitch competition, racing (pari-mutuel betting), rodeo, tractor pull, demolition derby, parade, and nightly outdoor musical shows.

---

brought trappers, who fought the animals, the Native Americans, the country, and each other with equal gusto. They were aided and abetted by the great fur companies, including the legendary Hudson's Bay Company. The first gold strike in the Clearwater country in 1860, followed by rich strikes in the Salmon River and Florence areas, the Boise Basin, and Coeur d'Alene (still an important mining area in the state) brought hordes of miners who were perfectly willing to continue the no-holds-barred way of life initiated by fur trappers. Soon afterward the shots of warring sheepmen and cattlemen mingled with those of miners.

Mining, once Idaho's most productive and colorful industry, has yielded its economic reign, but the state still produces large amounts of silver, zinc, pumice, antimony, and lead. It holds great reserves (268,000 acres) of phosphate rock. Copper, thorium, limestone, asbestos, graphite, talc, tungsten, cobalt, nickel, cinnabar, bentonite, and a wealth of other important minerals are found here. Gems, some of the finest quality, include agate, jasper, garnets, opals, onyx, sapphires, and rubies.

Today, Idaho's single largest industry is farming. On more than 3.5 million irrigated acres, the state produces an abundance of potatoes, beets, hay, vegetables, fruit, and livestock. The upper reaches of the Snake River Valley, once a wasteland of sagebrush and greasewood, are now among the West's most fertile farmlands. Manufacturing and processing of farm products, timber, and minerals is an important part of the state's economic base. Tourism is also important to the economy.

When to Go/Climate

Summer and fall are usually pleasant times to visit Idaho, although it can snow at almost any time of year here. The state's varied topography makes for a wide range of weather conditions. Winter temperatures are cold but not so cold as to make outdoor activities uncomfortable.

AVERAGE HIGH/LOW TEMPERATURES (° F)

Boise

Jan 36/22	**May** 71/44	**Sept** 77/48
Feb 44/28	**June** 81/58	**Oct** 65/39
Mar 53/32	**July** 90/58	**Nov** 49/31
Apr 61/37	**Aug** 88/57	**Dec** 38/23

Pocatello

Jan 32/14	**May** 68/40	**Sept** 75/43
Feb 38/20	**June** 78/53	**Oct** 63/34
Mar 47/26	**July** 88/53	**Nov** 45/26
Apr 58/32	**Aug** 86/51	**Dec** 34/16

Parks and Recreation

Water-related activities, hiking, riding, various other sports, picnicking, visitor centers, and camping are available in most of Idaho's state parks. Camping: $16/site per night with all hookups; $12/site per night with water; $10/site per night for primitive site. Extra vehicle $7/night. Fifteen-day maximum stay at most parks. Reservations available only at Bear Lake, Farragut, Hells Gate, Ponderosa and Priest Lake parks (fee $$). Motorized vehicle entrance fee (included in camping fee), $3/day or $35 annual pass; no entrance fee for persons walking, riding a bicycle, or horseback riding. All camping parks in the Idaho system feature at least one site designed for use by the disabled. Most visitor centers and restrooms also accommodate the disabled. For further information, contact the Idaho Dept of Parks & Recreation, PO Box 83720, Boise 83720-0065; phone 208/334-4199 or toll-free 800/847-4843.

FISHING AND HUNTING

Nowhere in Idaho is the outdoor enthusiast more than an hour's drive from a clearwater fly-fishing stream. From 2,000 lakes, 90 reservoirs, and 16,000 miles of rivers and streams, anglers take several million fish each year. Kokanee, trout (steelhead, rainbow, Kamloops, cutthroat, brown, brook, Dolly Varden, and Mackinaw), bass, perch, channel catfish, and sunfish are the most common varieties, with trout the most widespread and certainly among the scrappiest. Big game includes whitetail and mule deer, elk, antelope, bighorn sheep, mountain goat, and black bear. There are 12 kinds of upland game birds, plus ducks, Canada geese, and doves in season.

Nonresident fishing license: season $53; one-day $10; each additional day $4/day; three-day salmon/steelhead $31.50. Nonresident hunting license: game $110; turkey tag $40; deer tag $240; elk tag $340; other tag fees required for some game. There are nonresident quotas for deer and elk; apply mid-Dec. State permit validation is required for hunting waterfowl and some upland bird species, $6.50; archery and muzzleloader permits, $16.50. Prices may vary; for full information contact the Idaho Dept of Fish and Game, 600 S Walnut St, Box 25, Boise 83707; phone 208/334-3700 or toll-free 800/635-7820.

Driving Information

Safety belts are mandatory for all persons in the front seat of a vehicle. Children under 4 years must be in an approved safety seat anywhere in the vehicle. For further information, phone 208/334-8100.

INTERSTATE HIGHWAY SYSTEM
The following alphabetical listing of Idaho towns in this book shows that these cities are within 10 miles of the indicated interstate highways. Check a highway map for the nearest exit.

Highway Number Cities/Towns within 10 Miles

Highway Number	Cities/Towns within 10 Miles
Interstate 15	Blackfoot, Idaho Falls, Lava Hot Springs, Pocatello.
Interstate 84	Boise, Burley, Caldwell, Jerome, Mountain Home, Nampa, Twin Falls.
Interstate 86	American Falls, Pocatello.
Interstate 90	Coeur d'Alene, Kellogg, Wallace.

Additional Visitor Information

Idaho Travel Council, PO Box 83720, 700 W State St, Boise 83720-0093, publishes a number of attractive and helpful pamphlets, among them an Idaho Travel Guide. Phone 208/334-2470 or 800/71-IDAHO.

Visitor centers in Idaho are located in or near the Oregon/Idaho, Washington/Idaho, and Utah/Idaho borders, as well as throughout the state. Visitors who stop by will find information and brochures helpful in planning stops at points of interest.

ICE-AGE LAKES AND DEEP RIVER CANYONS

This tour starts at a gold rush town at the heart of the Rockies, passes an ice-age glacial lake, and drops down through farm country to the desert canyons of the Snake River.

Stately Wallace sits in the shadows of a steep Rocky Mountain valley that contains some of the richest silver and lead veins in the world. There has been extensive industrial mining here since the 1880s, and the town of Wallace possesses one of the best-preserved Victorian town centers in Idaho. The entire town is listed on the National Historic Register. Visit the Wallace District Mining Museum, which tells the story of the region's silver boom. Then walk to the Northern Pacific Depot Railroad Museum, located in the town's lovely old depot.

A number of silver mines still operate in the Wallace area. If you're interested in what goes on underground in a silver mine, take a tour of the Sierra Silver Mine. From downtown Wallace, old trolleys drive you to the mine, where underground tours demonstrate the techniques and equipment of hard-rock mining.

Continue west on I-90 to Cataldo. The Mission of the Sacred Heart, now a state park, is Idaho's oldest building. Built by Catholic "Blackrobe" Jesuits in 1848, this simple church, constructed of mortised and tenoned beams, sits above a bluff on the Coeur d'Alene River. For decades this was the spiritual and educational center of northern Idaho. The state park now includes a visitor center with interpretive information, picnic area, and a self-guiding nature trail.

Continue west on I-90, climbing up over the Fourth of July Pass before dropping down onto Lake Coeur d'Alene, a large glacier-dug lake flanked by green forested mountains. The town of Coeur d'Alene sits at the west end of the lake and is the center of a large resort community. The heart of Coeur d'Alene is City Park and Beach at the edge of downtown. During summer a crush of people enjoy the sun and water here, indulging in such pastimes as swimming, sailing, jet-skiing, and windsurfing. From the marina in front of the Coeur d'Alene Resort, lake cruises depart to explore the lake. The streets behind the beachfront preserve period storefronts with good casual restaurants and shops.

From Coeur d'Alene, turn south on Highway 95 and pass through the Coeur d'Alene Indian Reservation. The landscape transforms from pine and fir forests to rolling farmland. Amid the wheat fields are more curious crops: this is the center of lentil production in the United States. Moscow is home to the University of Idaho. The compact downtown area has a pleasant alternative feel, with bookstores, coffee shops, food co-ops, and brew pubs.

From Moscow south on Highway 95, the farmland begins to fall away and the road begins to wind down the Snake River Canyon. During the early settlement days, the canyon wall north of Lewiston was an impediment to transport and commerce with farms in the Moscow area. Finally in 1914, with improved engineering and technology, a road was devised that snaked down Lewiston Hill, slowly dropping 2,000 feet in 9 1/2 miles, with 64 switchbacks, to reach the valley floor. Nowadays, a freeway zips up and down the hill, but the old road is preserved as the Old Spiral Highway. Take this side road for more leisurely and scenic views onto Lewiston and the confluence of the Snake and Clearwater rivers.

Lewiston is the departure point for jet boat trips up the Hells Canyon of the Snake River, the deepest river canyon in North America. The tours depart from Hells Gate Park, south of the city on Snake River Avenue. **(Approximately 164 miles)**

THE WILDS OF IDAHO

This route begins in the Snake River Canyon and follows a series of dramatic river valleys into the very heart of the Rockies, finally climbing up to crest the Continental Divide. Lewiston sits at the junction of the Snake and Clearwater rivers, which meet beneath 1,000-foot desert cliffs. (Lewiston is the starting point for jet boat trips to popular Hell's Canyon, the gorge formed by the Snake River.) Highway 30 follows the Clearwater River east, where the valley quickly turns forested and green. This portion of the route passes through the Nez Perce National Historic Park, where several sites of mythic and historic interest to the Nez Perce people are highlighted and interpreted. As the route continues east, the valley becomes more narrow and dramatic, with small, venerable fishing resorts clinging to the rocky river bank. East from Kooskia, Highway 12 wedges into the canyon of the Lochsa River, a mountain terrain so formidable (and scenically dramatic) that completion of this section of the highway was not possible until 1962, when modern engineering and construction processes became available. This near-wilderness area is popular with experienced whitewater rafters, who are often seen on the coursing river. Near the pass into Montana, easy hiking trails lead to undeveloped, natural hot springs. **(Approximately 172 miles)**

American Falls (F-4)

See also Pocatello

Population 3,757
Elevation 4,404 ft
Area Code 208
Zip 83211
Information Chamber of Commerce, 239 Idaho St, PO Box 207; phone 208/226-7214

After a party of American Fur Company trappers was caught in the current of the Snake River and swept over the falls here, the fur company gave its name to both the community and the falls. American Falls boasts an important hydroelectric plant and is the capital of a vast dry-farming wheat belt; agricultural reclamation projects stretch westward for 170 miles.

What to See and Do

American Falls Dam. *239 Idaho St, American Falls (83211). I-86 exit 40, follow signs on ID 39 Bypass. Phone 208/226-7214.* Impounds 25-mile-long lake; Willow Bay Recreation Area has swimming (beaches), fishing, boating (ramp; fee); picnicking, camping (hookups; fee).

Indian Springs. *3249 Indian Springs Rd, American Falls (83211). 4 miles S on Hwy 37. Phone 208/226-2174.* Hot mineralized springs, pools, and baths; camping. (May-Labor Day, daily) **$$**

Massacre Rocks State Park. *3592 Park Ln, American Falls (83211). 12 miles SW on I-86 at exit 28. Phone 208/548-2672.* Covers 995 acres. Along the Old Oregon Trail, emigrants carved their names on Register Rock. Nearby, at Massacre Rocks, is the spot where a wagon train was ambushed in 1862. River, juniper-sagebrush area; extensive bird life. Waterskiing, fishing, boating (ramps); hiking, bird-watching, picnicking. 52 tent and trailer sites (dump station). Interpretive programs; info center. (Daily) **$**

Trenner Memorial Park. *Near Idaho Power Company plant, SW of dam.* Honors an engineer who played a key role in the development of the area; includes a miniature power station, fountain, and lava terrace. **FREE**

Special Event

Massacre Rocks Rendezvous. *Massacre Rocks State Park, 3592 Park Ln, American Falls (83211). Phone 208/548-2672.* Reenactment of Wild West past with black powder shoots and knife-throwing contest. First weekend in June.

Arco (E-3)

Settled 1879
Population 1,016
Elevation 5,318 ft
Area Code 208
Zip 83213

Arco, the seat of Butte County, was the first town to be lighted by power derived from atomic energy. Wildcat Peak casts its shadow on this pleasant little community located in a bend of the Big Lost River. Visitors pause here while exploring the Craters of the Moon National Monument, 20 miles southwest.

What to See and Do

Experimental Breeder Reactor Number 1 (EBR-1). *Hwy 20/26, Arco (83213). 18 miles SE via Hwy 20/26. Phone 208/526-0050.* The first nuclear reactor developed to generate electricity (Dec 20, 1951). Visitor center exhibits include the original reactor and three other nuclear reactors, equipment, and control room, as well as displays on the production of electricity. Self-guided or one-hour tours (Memorial Day weekend-Labor Day: daily; rest of year: by appointment). Contact INEL Tours, PO Box 1625, Idaho Falls 83415-3695. **FREE**

Ashton (E-5)

See also Driggs, Rexburg, St. Anthony

Population 1,114
Elevation 5,260 ft
Area Code 208
Zip 83420
Information Chamber of Commerce, City Hall, 64 N 10th St, PO Box 689; phone 208/652-3987
Web site www.ashtonidaho.com

Ashton's economy is centered on the flow of products from the rich agricultural area that extends to Blackfoot. Equally important to the town, which has a view of the Twin Teton Peaks in Wyoming, is the influx of vacationers bound for the Targhee National Forest, Warm River recreation areas, and Bear Gulch winter sports area. A Ranger District office of the forest is located here.

What to See and Do

Harriman State Park. *3489 Hwy 20, Ashton (83420). 19 miles N on Hwy 20/191, S of Island Park. Phone 208/558-7368.* Located in the heart of a 16,000-acre wildlife refuge; home of the rare trumpeter swan. Nature is the main attraction here with Golden and Silver lakes, wildflowers, lodgepole pines, and thriving wildlife. The world-famous fly-fishing stream, Henry's Fork of the Snake River, winds through the park. Historic Railroad Ranch. Hiking, horseback riding, cross-country skiing. (Daily) **$**

Henry's Lake State Park. *3489 Hwy 20, Ashton (83420). 37 miles N on Hwy 20, then 1 mile W; N of Island Park, on the S shore of famous fishing area, Henry's Lake. Phone 208/558-7368.* This 586-acre park offers waterskiing, boating (ramp); hiking, picnicking, 50 campsites (26 with hookups, 24 without hookups; dump station). (Mid-May-Oct, daily) **$**

⭐ **Targhee National Forest.** *505 Lindsay Blvd, Idaho Falls (83402). Phone 208/524-7500.* Approximately 1.8 million acres included two wilderness areas: Jedediah Smith (W slope of the Tetons, adjacent to Grand Teton National Park) and Winegar Hole (grizzly bear habitat, bordering Yellowstone National Park); no motorized vehicles allowed in wilderness areas. Fishing (including trout fishing on Henry's Fork of the Snake River and Henry's Lake Reservoir); big game hunting, camping (fee), picnicking, winter sports; Grand Targhee Resort (see DRIGGS) ski area. Float trips on the Snake River; boating, sailing, waterskiing, and canoeing on the Palisades Reservoir; outfitters and guides for the Jedediah Smith Wilderness. Closed Sat-Sun. In the forest are

Big Springs. *33 miles N on Hwy 20/191 to Mack's Inn, then 5 miles E on paved road.* Source of the north fork of the Snake River, which gushes from a subterranean cavern at a constant 52° F; it quickly becomes 150 feet wide. Schools of salmon and rainbow trout can be seen from the bridge. The stream was designated the first National Recreation Water Trail. Moose, deer, sandhill cranes, trumpeter swans, and bald eagles can be seen along the banks.

Lower Mesa Falls. *14 miles NE on Hwy 47.* N Fork drops another 65 feet here; scenic overlook; camping.

Upper Mesa Falls. *18 miles NE on Hwy 47 on Forest Service land.* North Fork of Snake River takes a 114-foot plunge here; scenic overlook.

Bellevue (E-3)

See also Shoshone, Sun Valley Area

Population 1,275
Elevation 5,190 ft
Area Code 208
Zip 83313

What to See and Do

Sawtooth National Forest. *2647 Kimberly Rd E, Twin Falls (83301). Phone 208/737-3200.* Elevations from 4,500-12,100 feet. Swimming, water sports, fishing, boating; nature trails, downhill and cross-country skiing, snowmobiling, picnicking, saddle and pack trips, hunting, camping. Fee at certain designated campgrounds. **FREE**

Blackfoot (E-4)

See also Idaho Falls, Pocatello

Founded 1878
Population 9,646
Elevation 4,504 ft
Area Code 208
Zip 83221
Information Chamber of Commerce, Riverside Plaza, #1, PO Box 801; phone 208/785-0510
Web site www.blackfootidaho.net

Blackfoot is situated in southeastern Idaho, halfway between Idaho Falls and Pocatello. The community bills itself as the "Potato Capital of the World," a boast supported by the downtown presence of the Idaho Potato Expo, a museum celebrating the state's most famous export. Blackfoot was originally called Grove City, an homage to the town's abundance of trees. Its present name is derived from the Blackfoot River, which flows through town. The Fort Hall Indian Reservation sprawls across 544,000 acres to the south. Authentic Shoshone and Bannock arts and crafts are available at nearby stores, a favorite being the Clothes Horse, a marketplace located on the reservation.

What to See and Do

Airport Park. *Parkway Dr, 1/2 miles N via I-15 exit 93.* Racetrack; picnicking, playground, golf, BMX track.

Bingham County Historical Museum. *190 N Shilling Ave, Blackfoot (83221). Phone 208/785-8065.* Restored 1905 homestead of Brown family containing gun collection, Native American artifacts, early 20th-century furnishings and kitchen utensils. (Mar-Nov, Wed-Fri; closed holidays) **DONATION**

Jensen Grove Park. *Airport Rd, on Snake River.* Boating, waterskiing, paddleboat rentals, varied water activities, disc golf, skateboard park, hockey.

Special Events

Blackfoot Pride Days. *Phone 208/785-0510.* Late June.

Eastern Idaho State Fair. *Phone 208/785-2480. 70-acre fairground, N of town.* Livestock, machinery exhibits, four-, six-, and eight-horse hitch competition, racing (pari-mutuel betting), rodeo, tractor pull, demolition derby, parade, nightly outdoor musical shows. Sept.

Shoshone-Bannock Indian Festival. *Fort Hall Indian Reservation, S on I-15, Simplot Rd exit 80, then 2 miles W.* Tribes from many western states and Canada gather for this festival. Dancing, parades, rodeo, Native American queen contest, buffalo feast, and other events. Early Aug.

Boise (E-2)

See also Nampa

Settled 1862
Population 125,738
Elevation 2,726 ft
Area Code 208
Information Convention and Visitors Bureau, 312 S 9th St, Suite 100, 83701; phone 208/344-7777 or toll-free 800/635-5240
Web site www.boise.org

Capital and largest city in Idaho, Boise (BOY-see) is also the business, financial, professional, and transportation center of the state. It is home to Boise State University (1932) and the National Interagency Fire Center, the nation's logistical support center for wildland fire suppression. Early French trappers labeled this still tree-rich area as *les bois* (the woods). Established during gold rush days, Boise was overshadowed by nearby Idaho City until designated the territorial capital in 1864. Abundant hydroelectric power stimulated manufacturing, with electronics, steel fabrication, and mobile homes the leading industries. Several major companies have their headquarters here. Lumber, fruit, sugar beets, and livestock are other mainstays of the economy; the state's main dairy region lies to the west of Boise. Natural hot water from the underground springs (with temperatures up to 170° F) heats some of the homes in the eastern portion of the city. A Ranger District office and the headquarters of the Boise National Forest are located here.

Extending alongside the Boise River is the Greenbelt, a trail used for jogging, skating, biking, and walking. When complete, the 22-mile trail will connect Eagle Island State Park on the west side of the city with Lucky Peak State Park on the east side of the city.

Boise Fun Fact

- Idaho's statehouse in Boise is geothermally heated by underground hot springs.

Public Transportation

Buses ValleyRide, phone 208/846-8547, www.valleyride.org

Airport Boise Airport.

Information Phone 208/383-3110

Airlines Alaska Airlines, America West Airlines, Big Sky Airlines, Delta Air Lines, Frontier Airlines, Horizon Air, Northwest Airlines, Salmon Air, SkyWest Airlines, Southwest Airlines, United Airlines

What to See and Do

Basque Museum and Cultural Center. *611 Grove St, Boise (83702). Phone 208/343-2671.* (1864) The only museum in North America dedicated solely to Basque heritage; historical displays, paintings by Basque artists, changing exhibits, restored boarding house used by Basque immigrants in 1900s. (Tues-Sat, limited hours) **$$**

Exploring Downtown Boise

Boise is a high-spirited city that manages to meld the vestiges of the cowboy Old West with the sophistication of the urban Pacific Northwest. The downtown core is relatively small, which makes it fun to explore on foot. There's plenty of street life and activity, and much of the late-19th-century architecture—born of a gold rush—is still intact.

Begin at the state capitol building, at Capitol Boulevard and Jefferson Street. This vast structure is constructed of local sandstone and faced on the interior with four kinds of marble and mahogany paneling. On the first floor, wander across the rotunda and gaze upward at the interior of the 200-foot dome, ringed with 43 stars (Idaho was the 43rd state in the Union). The legislative chambers are on the third floor. The Idaho capitol is the only geothermally heated statehouse in the country: water from hot springs five blocks away is pumped into the building's radiators.

From the capitol, proceed down Capitol Boulevard to Main Street. From this corner east on Main Street to about 3rd Street is a district of fine old homes—many renovated into shops and restaurants—that recalls Boise's early-20th-century opulence. Referred to as Old Boise, this street is home to the Egyptian Theatre (at Main and Capital Boulevard), an architecturally exuberant early vaudeville theater and movie palace in full King Tut drag.

One block farther west, at Grove and 8th Street, is The Grove, Boise's unofficial city center. The grove is a brick-lined plaza with a large fountain, public art, and a pedestrian area. Summer concerts are held here, and it's the place to gather for skateboarders, cyclists, and lunchtime office workers.

Continue down Grove to 6th Street to the Basque Museum and Cultural Center (611 Grove St). Idaho contains one of the largest Basque settlements outside of Europe, and this interesting museum tells the story of their culture and settlement in southwest Idaho. Next door, and part of the museum, is the Cyrus Jacobs-Uberuaga House, built as a boarding house for Basque immigrants in 1864.

Continue up Capitol Boulevard to Julia Davis Park, a large park along the Boise River that contains many of the city's important museums and cultural institutions. Follow the posted sign trails to the Idaho Historical Museum (610 N Julia Davis Dr), which gives an excellent overview of the state's rich historic heritage. Especially good are the exhibits devoted to Idaho native Indian history and to Oregon Trail pioneers. Immediately next door is Pioneer Village, a re-created town with vintage buildings dating from the late 19th century. Also in the park is the Boise Art Museum (670 Julia Davis Dr), with a permanent collection that focuses on American Realism.

At the center of Julia Davis Park is Zoo Boise. In addition to the traditional exotic zoo animal favorites from Africa, the zoo is home to a collection of large Rocky Mountain mammals like moose, mountain lions, elk, and bighorn sheep. Zoo Boise has the largest display of birds of prey in the Northwest. Return to the downtown area along 5th Street.

Bogus Basin Ski Resort. *2405 Bogus Basin Rd, Boise (83702). 16 miles N on Bogus Basin Rd. Phone 208/342-2100 (snow conditions); toll-free 800/367-4397 (except ID). www.bogusbasin.com.* Four double chairlifts, two high-speed quad, paddle tow; patrol, school, rentals; two lodges, restaurants, bar; day care. Longest run 1 1/2 miles; vertical drop 1,800 feet. Night skiing. (Nov-Apr, daily) Cross-country trails. **$$$$**

Boise National Forest. *1387 S Vinnell, Boise (83709). Phone 208/373-4007.* This 2,646,341-acre forest includes the headwaters of the Boise and Payette rivers, two scenic byways, abandoned mines and ghost towns, and access to the Sawtooth Wilderness and the Frank Church—River of No Return Wilderness. Trout fishing, swimming, rafting; hunting, skiing, snowmobiling, mountain biking, motorized trail biking, hiking, picnicking, camping. Visitor Center.

Bronco Stadium. *1400 Bronco Ln, Boise (83725). Phone 208/385-1600.* Although it is not one of the largest or most hallowed arenas in college football, Boise State University's Bronco Stadium has one thing that few other places (if any at all) have: blue turf. The trademark blue Astroturf makes this stadium unique not only to the Western Athletic Conference, but to stadiums in general. Fans can see teams from places like the University of Hawaii on the mainland in Boise in one of the most unique places to watch a sporting event of any kind.

Discovery Center of Idaho. *131 Myrtle St, Boise (83702). Phone 208/343-9895. www.scidaho.org.* Hands-on exhibits explore various principles of science; large bubblemaker, catenary arch, magnetic sand. (Tues-Sun; closed holidays) **$$**

Eagle Island State Park. *2691 Mace Rd, Eagle (83616). 8 miles W via Hwy 20/26 to Linder Rd. Phone 208/939-0696.* This 546-acre park was once a prison farm. Situated between the north and south channels of the Boise River, the park has cottonwoods, willows, and a variety of native flowers, as well as an abundance of wildlife including the great blue heron, eagle, hawk, beaver, muskrat, fox, and weasel. Facilities include a 15-acre man-made lake (no fishing), swimming beach, water slide (fee); picnicking, concession. No pets. No glass beverage bottles. (Memorial Day-Labor Day, daily) **$$**

Idaho Botanical Gardens. *2355 N Penitentiary Rd, Boise (83712). Phone 208/343-8649.* Twelve theme and display gardens include meditation, cactus, rose, water, and butterfly/hummingbird gardens; 3/4-mile nature trail, plaza. (Daily) **$$**

⭐ **Julia Davis Park.** *1104 Royal Blvd, Boise (83706). Between Capitol Blvd and Broadway on the Boise River. Phone 208/384-4240.* Rose garden, tennis courts, picnicking, (shelters), playground. Boat rentals, Gene Harris bandshell. On grounds are

Boise Art Museum. *670 S Julia Davis Dr, Boise (83702). Phone 208/345-8330.* Northwest, Asian, and American art featured in changing and permanent exhibits. (Tues-Sun; closed holidays) **$$**

Boise Tour Train. *9824 Gurdon Ct, Boise (83704). Phone 208/342-4796.* Narrated, one-hour tour of the city and historical areas aboard motorized 1890s-style tour train. Departure point in Julia Davis Park. (Memorial Day-Labor Day: daily; early May-Memorial Day and after Labor Day-Oct: weekends) **$$$**

Idaho Black History Museum. *508 N Julia Davis Dr, Boise (83702). Phone 208/443-0017. www. ibhm.org.* Changing exhibits highlight the history and culture of African Americans, with special emphasis on Idaho African Americans. Lectures, films, workshops, storytelling, and musical performances. (Summer: Tues-Sun 10 am-4 pm; winter: Wed-Sat 10 am-4 pm)

Idaho Historical Museum. *610 N Julia Davis Dr, Boise (83702). Phone 208/334-2120.* History of Idaho and Pacific Northwest. Ten historical interiors; Native American exhibits; fur trade, mining, ranching, forestry displays. (Daily) **$**

Zoo Boise. *355 N Julia Davis Dr, Boise (83702). Phone 208/384-4260.* Home to 285 animals; large birds of prey area; otter exhibit, primates, variety of cats, petting zoo. Education center; gift shop. (Daily; closed Jan 1, Thanksgiving, Dec 25) **$$**

Lucky Peak State Park. *10 miles SE on Hwy 21. Phone 208/334-2679.* A 237-acre park comprised of three units: Spring Shores Marina (boating, day use), Sandy Point (swimming beach below dam), and Discovery unit (picnicking, three group shelters, river). **$$**

M-K Nature Center. *600 S Walnut St, Boise (83712). Phone 208/334-2225.* River observatory allows visitors to view activities of fish life; aquatic and riparian ecology displays; also visitor center with hands-on computerized exhibits; nature trails. (Tues-Sun) **$$**

Old Idaho Penitentiary. *2445 Old Penitentiary Rd, Boise (83712). 2 1/2 miles E via Warm Springs Ave (Hwy 21). Phone 208/368-6080.* (1870) Self-guided tour through the cells, compounds, and other areas of the prison. Guided tours by appointment (Memorial Day-Labor Day). Displays about famous inmates, lawmen, and penal methods. Slide show on history. (Daily; closed holidays) Under 13 only with adult. **$$**

St. Michael's Episcopal Cathedral. *518 N 8th St, Boise (83702). Phone 208/342-5601. www. stmichaelscathedral.org.* (1900) The Tiffany window in the south transept is a fine example of this type of stained glass. (Mon-Fri, call for schedule)

State Capitol. *8th and Jefferson sts, Boise. Phone 208/334-5174.* (1905-1922) Neoclassical design, faced with Boise sandstone; mounted statue of George Washington in lobby on second floor. Murals on fourth floor symbolically tell state's past, present, and future. Changing exhibits. Self-guided tours (Mon-Sat). Guided tours (Mon-Fri, by appointment). **FREE**

Table Rock. *4 miles E at end of Shaw Mountain Rd.* Provides panoramic view of entire valley, 1,100 feet below. Road may be closed in winter.

World Center for Birds of Prey. *5668 W Flying Hawk Ln, Boise (83709). I-84, exit 50 to S Cole Rd, then 6 miles S. Phone 208/362-TOUR.* Originally created to prevent extinction of peregrine falcon; scope has been expanded to incl national and international conservation of birds of prey and their environments. Visitors can see breeding chamber of California condors and other raptors at interpretive center; gift shop. (Daily; closed Jan 1, Thanksiving, Dec 25) **$$**

Special Events

Boise River Festival. *7032 S Eisenman Rd, Boise (83716). Phone 208-338-8887.* Night parade, contests, entertainment, fireworks. Last full weekend in June.

Idaho Shakespeare Festival. *Amphitheater, 520 9th St, Boise (83702). Phone 208/429-9908.* Repertory theater. June-Sept.

Thoroughbred racing. *Les Bois Park, 5610 Glenwood St, Boise (83714). Phone 208/376-7223.* Wed and Sat evenings; matinees Sun. Simulcast racing year-round (daily). May-mid-Aug.

Western Idaho Fair. *Les Bois Park, 5610 Glenwood St, Boise (83714). Phone 208/376-3247.* The largest fair in the state. Aug.

Limited-Service Hotels

★ **BEST WESTERN SAFARI MOTOR INN.** *1070 Grove St, Boise (83702). Phone 208/344-6556; toll-free 800/541-6556; fax 208/344-7240. www. bestwestern.com.* 103 rooms, 3 story. Complimentary continental breakfast. Check-out 1 pm. Fitness room. Pool, whirlpool. Airport transportation available. **$**

★ ★ **DOUBLETREE HOTEL.** *475 Parkcenter Blvd, Boise (83706). Phone 208/345-2002; toll-free 800/222-8733; fax 208/345-8354. www.doubletree.com.* Near the Boise River and just minutes from the airport, this property offers guest rooms with large workstations and data ports. Shopping and dining options of downtown Boise can be found nearby. 158 rooms, 6 story. Check-in 3 pm, check-out noon. Restaurant, bar. Fitness room. Pool. Airport transportation available. Business center. **$**

★ ★ **DOUBLETREE HOTEL.** *2900 Chinden Blvd, Boise (83714). Phone 208/343-1871; toll-free 800/222-8733; fax 208/344-4994. www.doubletree.com.* Right on the banks of the Boise River, this hotel is only 1 mile from the city center, near golf, white water rafting, and the Bogus Basin Ski Area. 304 rooms, 2 story. Pets accepted, some restrictions; fee. Check-in 3 pm, check-out noon. Restaurant, bar. Fitness room. Outdoor pool, children's pool, whirlpool. Airport transportation available. **$**

★ ★ **HOLIDAY INN.** *3300 Vista Ave, Boise (83705). Phone 208/344-8365; toll-free 800/465-4329; fax 208/343-9635. www.holiday-inn.com.* 265 rooms, 2 story. Pets accepted; fee. Check-out noon. Restaurant, bar. Fitness room. Pool. Airport transportation available. **$**

★ ★ **OWYHEE PLAZA HOTEL.** *1109 Main St, Boise (83702). Phone 208/343-4611; toll-free 800/233-4611; fax 208/336-3860. www.owyheeplaza.com.* This historic property in the Owyhee Mountains offers an outdoor pool, two restaurants, and a complimentary airport shuttle, making the beauty of Idaho accessible. 100 rooms, 3 story. Pets accepted, some restrictions; fee. Check-in 3 pm, check-out noon. Two restaurants, bar. Outdoor pool. Airport transportation available. **$**

★ ★ **RED LION.** *1800 Fairview Ave, Boise (83702). Phone 208/344-7691; toll-free 800/733-5466; fax 208/336-3652. www.redlion.com.* 182 rooms, 7 story. Check-out noon. Restaurant, bar. Fitness room. Pool. Airport transportation available. **$**

★ **SHILO INN.** *3031 Main St, Boise (83702). Phone 208/344-3521; toll-free 800/222-2244; fax 208/384-1217. www.shiloinns.com.* 112 rooms, 3 story. Pets accepted, some restrictions; fee. Complimentary continental breakfast. Check-in 3 pm, check-out noon. Fitness room. Indoor pool, whirlpool. Airport transportation available. **$**

★ ★ **STATEHOUSE INN.** *981 Grove St, Boise (83702). Phone 208/342-4622; toll-free 800/243-4622; fax 208/344-5751. www.statehouse-inn.com.* 112 rooms, 6 story. Complimentary full breakfast. Check-in 1 pm, check-out 1 pm. Restaurant, bar. Fitness room. Whirlpool. Airport transportation available. **$**

Full-Service Hotel

★ ★ ★ **GROVE HOTEL.** *245 S Capitol Blvd, Boise (83702). Phone 208/333-8000. www.grovehotelboise.com.* Steps from the Boise Convention Center, this hotel situates guests in the heart of the downtown area. Rooms are comfortably appointed with modern furnishings. With over 17,000 square feet of flexible meeting space, The Grove Hotel has much to offer business travelers. The hotel is attached to the 5,000-seat Bank of America Centre, which hosts a variety of sporting and entertainment events. Fine dining is available at Emilio's, which offers a menu of New American cuisine. Julia Davis Park and the Boise River are a short stroll away. 154 rooms. Check-in 3 pm, check-out noon. High-speed Internet access. Restaurant, bar. Fitness room (fee). Indoor pool, whirlpool. Airport transportation available. **$$**

Specialty Lodging

The following lodging establishment is approved by Mobil Travel Guide, but due to its unique and individualized nature has not been given a traditional Mobil Star rating. Included in this listing you may find bed-and-breakfasts, limited-service inns, guest ranches, and other unique hotel properties.

IDAHO HERITAGE INN. *109 W Idaho St, Boise (83702). Phone 208/342-8066; toll-free 800/342-8445; fax 208/342-3325. www.idheritageinn.com.* 6 rooms, 3 story. Complimentary full breakfast. Check-in 3 pm, check-out 11 am. Built in 1904. **$**

Restaurants

★ ★ **MILFORD'S FISH HOUSE.** *405 S 8th St #100, Boise (83702). Phone 208/342-8382; fax 208/345-6112.* Seafood menu. Dinner. Bar. Children's menu. Former railroad freight warehouse. Casual attire. Outdoor seating. **$$$**

★ **RICK'S CAFE AMERICAN AT THE FLICKS.** *646 Fulton St, Boise (83702). Phone 208/342-4288; fax 208/345-2668. www.theflicksboise.com.* International menu. Lunch, dinner. Bar. Casual attire. Outdoor seating. **$$**

Bonners Ferry (A-2)

See also Sandpoint

Settled 1864
Population 2,193
Elevation 1,777 ft
Area Code 208
Zip 83805
Information Visitors Center, PO Box X; phone 208/267-5922
Web site www.bonnersferrychamber.com

E. L. Bonner offered ferry service from this point on the Kootenai River, near the northern tip of the state, and gave this community its name. Today, Bonner's Ferry services the agricultural and lumbering districts of Boundary County, of which it is the county seat. From here the broad, flat, and fertile Kootenai Valley stretches north to British Columbia. This scenic area features many lakes and streams; fishing, hunting, and hiking are popular pastimes. A Ranger District office of the Idaho Panhandle National Forest-Kaniksu is located here.

What to See and Do

Kootenai National Wildlife Refuge. *Riverside Rd, Bonners Ferry (83805). 5 miles W on Riverside Rd. Phone 208/267-3888.* This 2,774-acre refuge was created as a resting area for waterfowl during migration. Its wide variety of habitat supports many species of birds and mammals, including bald eagles. Auto tour (4 1/2 miles). Hunting, fishing. **FREE**

Moyie Falls. *9 miles E on Hwy 2, then N at Moyie Springs on small road; watch for sign for overlook just E of first bridge over Moyie River.* Park and look down into 400-foot canyon at spectacular series of plunges. Greater flow during the spring runoff.

Special Event

Kootenai River Days. *Phone 208/267-3888.* June.

Limited-Service Hotels

★ **KOOTENAI VALLEY MOTEL.** *Hwy 95, Bonners Ferry (83805). Phone 208/267-7567; fax 208/267-2600. www.visitidaho.org.* 22 rooms, 1 story. Pets accepted, some restrictions; fee. Check-in 1 pm, check-out 11 am. Whirlpool. **$**

★ **TOWN & COUNTRY MOTEL.** *Hwy 95 S, Bonners Ferry (83805). Phone 208/267-7915.* 12 rooms. Pets accepted; fee. Complimentary continental breakfast. Check-in noon, check-out 11 am. Whirlpool. **$**

Restaurant

★ **PANHANDLE RESTAURANT.** *230 Main St, Bonners Ferry (83805). Phone 208/267-2623.* American menu. Breakfast, lunch, dinner, brunch. Children's menu. Casual attire. **$$**

Buhl (F-2)

See also Twin Falls

Population 3,516
Elevation 3,793 ft
Area Code 208
Zip 83316
Information Chamber of Commerce, 716 Hwy 30 E; phone 208/543-6682

Named for Frank Buhl, an early empire builder, this community processes the outpouring of farm goods produced in the farmlands of "Magic Valley." A Ranger District office of Nevada's Humboldt National Forest is located here.

What to See and Do

Balanced Rock. *12 miles SW on local roads.* This 40-foot rock tower, resembling the mushroom cloud of an atomic bomb, rests on an 18-by-36-inch base; picnic area nearby.

Special Events

Farmers Market. *Phone 208/733-3974.* Last week in June-Sept.

Sagebrush Days. *Phone 208/543-6682.* Sidewalk sales, arts in the park, fireworks, parade. Early July.

Twin Falls County Fair and Magic Valley Stampede. *215 Fair Ave, Filer (83328). 6 miles E in Filer. Phone 208/326-4396.* Carnival, 4-H exhibits, flower, art, and antique shows; RCA rodeo. First weekend in Sept.

Burley (F-3)

See also Twin Falls

Population 8,702
Elevation 4,165 ft
Area Code 208
Zip 83318
Information Mini-Cassia Chamber of Commerce, 324 Scott Ave, Rupert, 83350; phone 208/678-7230 or toll-free 800/333-3408

Burley was created by a 210,000-acre irrigation project that turned a near-desert area into a thriving agricultural center ideal for alfalfa, grain, sugar beet, and potatoes. The town is a center for potato processing and has one of the largest sugar beet processing plants in the world. A Ranger District office of the Sawtooth National Forest is located here.

What to See and Do

Boating. Thirty miles of the Snake River, with constant water levels, provide great boating opportunities throughout the summer.

Cassia County Historical Museum. *E Main St and Highland Ave, Burley (83318). Phone 208/678-7172.* Railroad cars, pioneer cabins, wagon collection, other pioneer relics. (Apr-mid-Nov, Tues-Sat; closed July 4) **DONATION**

City of Rocks National Reserve. *3010 Elba Almo Rd, Almo (83312).* 22 miles S on Hwy 27 to Oakley, then 16 miles S and follow signs; or 32 miles S on Hwy 77 to Almo, then 2 miles W and follow signs. Phone 208/824-5519. A pioneer stopping place, this 25-square-mile area of granite spires and sculptured rock formations resembles a city carved from stone; granite walls are inscribed with messages and names of westward-bound settlers, and remnants of the California Trail are still visible. Well known for technical rock climbing. Hiking, picnicking, primitive camping.

Sawtooth National Forest. *2647 Kimberly Rd, Twin Falls (83301).* 9 miles E on Hwy 30 to Declo, then 15 miles S on Hwy 77; other areas E and W. Phone 208/737-3200. Fishing, camping, hiking, horseback riding, snowmobiling, cross-country and downhill skiing, scenic views. Includes Howell Canyon, Lake Cleveland and four other glacial lakes. Fee for certain designated campgrounds. In forest is

> **Pomerelle Ski Area.** *25 miles SE on Hwy 77, off I-84 Exit 216.* Phone 208/638-5599 (office). Double, triple chairlifts, rope tow; patrol, school, rentals; cafeteria. Longest run 2.2 miles; vertical drop 1,000 feet. (Mid-Nov-Mar: daily; Apr: weekends) Night skiing (Jan-mid-Mar, Tues-Sat). **$$$$**

Special Events

Cassia County Fair and Rodeo. *County Fairgrounds, E end of E 10th and E 12th sts. Burley.* Phone 208/678-9150. Racing, pari-mutuel betting. Third week in Aug.

Idaho Powerboat Regatta. *Burley Marina.* Phone 208/436-4793. Boat racers from throughout the western US compete in this American Power Boat Association's national championship series event. Last weekend in June.

Limited-Service Hotel

★ ★ **BEST WESTERN BURLEY INN & CONVENTION CENTER.** *800 N Overland Ave, Burley (83318).* Phone 208/678-3501; toll-free 800/599-1849; fax 208/678-9532. www.bestwestern.com. 126 rooms, 2 story. Pets accepted, some restrictions. Check-out noon. Restaurant, bar. Pool. **$**

Caldwell (E-1)

See also Boise, Nampa

Founded 1883
Population 18,400
Elevation 2,369 ft
Area Code 208
Zip 83605
Information Chamber of Commerce, 300 Frontage Rd, PO Box 819, 83606; phone 208/459-7493
Web site www.caldwellonline.org

Caldwell, seat of Canyon County, is situated in the triangle formed by the confluence of the Snake and Boise rivers. Founded by the Idaho and Oregon Land Improvement Company, the town was named for the company's president, C. A. Caldwell. Livestock, diversified agriculture, and vegetable-processing plants are mainstays of the economy.

What to See and Do

Albertson College of Idaho. *2112 Cleveland Blvd, Caldwell (83605).* At 20th St. Phone 208/459-5500. (1891) (800 students) Oldest four-year college in the state. Private liberal arts college. Evans Mineral Collection, the Orma J. Smith Natural Science Museum, and a planetarium are in Boone Science Hall; Blatchley Hall houses the Rosenthal Gallery of Art (Sept-May, inquire for hours).

Ste. Chapelle Winery and Vineyards. *12 miles S via Hwy 55.* Phone 208/459-7222. Vineyards spread over slopes of the beautiful Snake River Valley. Reception area; tasting room; 24-foot cathedral windows offer spectacular view of valley and distant Owyhee Mountains. 30-minute tours. (Daily) **FREE**

Succor Creek Canyon. *33 miles W on Hwy 19, just across Oregon line.* Two-mile stretch of spectacular canyon scenery and interesting earth formations. An abundance of prehistoric fossils has been found here.

Warhawk Air Museum. *Caldwell Industrial Airport, 4917 Aviation Way, Caldwell (83605).* Phone 208/465-6446. Displays World War II aviation artifacts. (Tues-Sun; call for schedule) **$$**

Special Events

Caldwell Exchange Youth Rodeo. *2024 Blaine St, Caldwell (83605). Phone 208/459-7493.* Second week in July.

Canyon County Fair. *111 S 22nd Ave, Caldwell (83605). Phone 208/455-8500. www.canyoncountyfair.org.* Late July.

Night Rodeo. *Phone 208/459-2060.* Second or third week in Aug.

Limited-Service Hotels

★ **LA QUINTA INN.** *901 Specht Ave, Caldwell (83605). Phone 208/454-2222; fax 208/454-9334.* 65 rooms, 3 story. Pets accepted, some restrictions. Complimentary continental breakfast. Check-in 2 pm, check-out noon. Fitness room. Indoor pool, whirlpool. **$**

★ **SUNDOWNER MOTEL.** *1002 Arhtur, Caldwell (83605). Phone 208/459-1585; toll-free 800/588-5268; fax 208/467-5268.* 66 rooms, 2 story. Pets accepted; fee. Complimentary continental breakfast. Check-in 2 pm, check-out 11 am. **$**

Challis (D-3)

Founded 1876
Population 1,073
Elevation 5,288 ft
Area Code 208
Zip 83226
Web site www.challisidaho.com

Cloud-capped mountains, rocky gorges, and the Salmon River make this village one of the most picturesque in the Salmon River "Grand Canyon" area. Challis is the seat of Custer County and the headquarters for Challis National Forest. Two Ranger District offices of the forest are located here.

What to See and Do

Challis National Forest. *Hwy 93 S and Hwy 75, Challis (83226). Phone 208/879-2285.* More than 2 1/2 million acres of forestland surrounds Challis on all sides, crossed by Hwy 93 and Hwy 75. Hot springs, ghost towns, nature viewing via trails; portion of the Frank Church—River of No Return Wilderness; trout fishing; camping, picnicking, hunting. Guides, outfitters available in Challis and vicinity. Idaho's highest point is here—Mount Borah (12,665 feet). For further info contact the Recreation Staff Officer, Forest Supervisor Bldg, HC 63, Box 1671. Flowing through the forest is the

Middle Fork of the Salmon Wild and Scenic River. *Hwy 93 S, Challis (83226). Phone 208/879-4101. www.nps.gov/rivers/wsr-salmon-middle.html.* One of the premier whitewater rafting rivers in the US. Permits are required to float this river (apply Oct-Jan, permits issued June-Sept by lottery; fee). For permit information, contact the Middle Fork Ranger, PO Box 750.

Grand Canyon in miniature. *13 miles S and SE on Hwy 93.* Walls cut 2,000 feet down on either side. Best seen at dusk.

Limited-Service Hotels

★ **NORTHGATE INN.** *Hwy 93, Challis (83226). Phone 208/879-2490; fax 208/879-5767.* 60 rooms, 3 story. Pets accepted, some restrictions; fee. Check-in 3 pm, check-out 11 am. **$**

★ ★ **VILLAGE INN.** *Hwy 93, Challis (83226). Phone 208/879-2239; fax 208/879-2813.* 54 rooms, 2 story. Pets accepted, some restrictions; fee. Check-in 2 pm, check-out 11 am. Restaurant. Whirlpool. **$**

Coeur d'Alene (B-1)

See also Kellogg

Settled 1878
Population 24,563
Elevation 2,152 ft
Area Code 208
Zip 83814
Information Coeur d'Alene Area Chamber of Commerce, PO Box 850, 83816; phone 208/664-3194
Web site www.coeurdalene.org

Nestled amid lakes and rivers, Coeur d'Alene (cor-da-LANE) is a tourist and lumbering community, but particularly a gateway to a lush vacation area in the

Idaho Panhandle. Irrigation has opened vast sections of nearby countryside for agricultural development; grass seed production is of major importance. The city is the headquarters for the three Idaho Panhandle National Forests, and there are three Ranger District offices here.

Coeur d'Alene Fun Fact

- The world's longest floating boardwalk surrounds the marina at the Coeur d'Alene Resort in Coeur d'Alene, Idaho. Built in 1986, it is 12-feet wide and 3,300 feet long.

What to See and Do

Coeur d'Alene Greyhound Park. *5100 W Riverbend Rd, Post Falls (83854). 11 miles W via I-90, at Idaho/ Washington state line. Phone 208/773-0545.* Pari-mutuel betting; clubhouse, restaurant, concessions. (Daily) **FREE**

Farragut State Park. *13400 E Ranger Rd, Athol (83801). 20 miles N on Hwy 95, then 4 miles E on Hwy 54. Phone 208/683-2425.* Comprised of 4,000 acres on south end of Lake Pend Oreille; some open landscape, heavy woods. Swimming, bathhouse, fishing, boating (ramps); hiking and bicycle route, cross-country skiing, sledding, and snowshoeing in winter. Model airplane field. Picnicking. Tent and trailer sites (hookups Apr-mid-Oct, dump station; reservations recommended). Campfire programs; interpretive displays and talks; information center. (Daily) **$**

Idaho Panhandle National Forests–Coeur d'Alene. *3815 Schreiber Way, Coeur d'Alene (83815). Other national forests that lie in the panhandle are Kaniksu and St. Joe. Phone 208/765-7223. www.fs.fed.us/ipnf.* Boating, fishing; camping (fee), cabins, picnicking, hiking, cross-country skiing, snowmobiling trails. Visitors are welcome at the Coeur d'Alene Tree Nursery, 1 mile NW on Ramsey Rd.

Lake Coeur d'Alene. *1201 W Ironwood Dr, Coeur d'Alene (83814).* Partially adjacent to the Idaho Panhandle National Forest. This lake, 26 miles long with a 109-mile shoreline, is considered one of the loveliest in the country and is popular for boating, fishing, and swimming. Municipal beach, picnic grounds at point where lake and town meet. At south end of lake is

Lake Coeur d'Alene Cruises, Inc. *1115 S Second St, Coeur d'Alene (83814). Phone 208/765-4000.* Makes a 6-hour trip up Lake Coeur d'Alene into the St. Joe River (Mid-June-early Sept: Wed and Sun; late Sept-Oct: Sun only). Also 90-minute lake cruises (Mid-May-mid-Oct, daily). Dinner cruises (June-mid-Sept, Sun-Thurs). Sun brunch cruises (Mid-June-Sept). **$$$$**

St. Joe River. One of the rivers that feed Lake Coeur d'Alene. Trout and lovely scenery abound. Stretch between Lake Chatcolet and Round Lake is said to be the world's highest navigable river.

Museum of North Idaho. *115 Northwest Blvd, Coeur d'Alene (83814). Adjacent to City Park, near the waterfront. Phone 208/664-3448. www.museumni.org.* Exhibits at this museum feature steamboating, the timber industry, and Native American history. There is also a big game trophy collection. (Apr-Oct, Tues-Sat 11 am-5 pm) **$** Admission includes entrance to

Fort Sherman Museum. *On the North Idaho College campus. Phone 208/664-3448. www. museumni.org.* Housed in the old powder house of Fort Coeur d'Alene (circa 1880). Exhibits include a log cabin once used by US Forest Service firefighters, as well as logging, mining, and pioneer implements. (May-Sept, Tues-Sat 1-4:45 pm)

⭐ **Scenic drives.** *In any direction from city.* Some of the most spectacular drives are S on Hwy 97, along E shore of Lake Coeur d'Alene; E on Hwy 10, through Fourth of July Canyon; and N, along Hwy 95.

Silverwood Theme Park. *26225 N Hwy 95, Athol (83801). 15 miles N on I-95. Phone 208/683-3400.* Turn-of-the-century park and village with Victorian buildings includes restaurants, saloon, general store, theater featuring old newsreels and classic movies, aircraft museum, air shows, and entertainment; adjacent to amusement park with rides and attractions. (Memorial Day weekend-Labor Day, daily) **$$$$**

Special Events

Art on the Green. *Hubbard St and Rosenberry Dr, Coeur d'Alene (83814). Phone 208/667-9346.* First weekend in Aug.

Northern Idaho Fair. *4060 N Government Way, Coeur d'Alene (83815). Phone 208/765-4969.* Late Aug.

Limited-Service Hotels

★ **AMERITEL INN.** *333 Ironwood Ave, Coeur D'Alene (83814). Phone 208/665-9000; toll-free 800/600-6001; fax 208/665-9900.* 114 rooms, 4 story. Complimentary continental breakfast. Check-in 3 pm, check-out 11 am. High-speed Internet access. Fitness room. Indoor pool, whirlpool. **$**

★ ★ **BEST WESTERN COEUR D'ALENE INN.** *414 W Appleway Ave, Coeur d'Alene (83814). Phone 208/765-3200; toll-free 800/251-7829; fax 208/664-1962. www.bestwestern.com.* 122 rooms, 2 story. Pets accepted; fee. Check-out noon. Restaurant, bar. Fitness room, spa. Pool. Airport transportation available. **$**

★ **DAYS INN.** *2200 Northwest Blvd, Coeur d'Alene (83814). Phone 208/667-8668; fax 208/765-0933. www.daysinn.com.* 62 rooms, 2 story. Pets accepted; fee. Complimentary continental breakfast. Check-in 3 pm, check-out noon. Fitness room. Whirlpool. **$**

★ ★ **RED LION TEMPLINS HOTEL ON THE RIVER.** *414 E 1st Ave, Post Falls (83854). Phone 208/773-1611; fax 208/773-4192. www.redlion.com.* 167 rooms, 3 story. Pets accepted, some restrictions; fee. Check-in 2 pm, check-out noon. Restaurant, bar. Fitness room. Indoor pool, whirlpool. Tennis. Airport transportation available. **$**

★ **RIVERBEND INN.** *4105 W Riverbend Ave, Post Falls (83854). Phone 208/773-3583; toll-free 800/243-7666; fax 208/773-1306.* 71 rooms, 2 story. Complimentary continental breakfast. Check-in 3 pm, check-out noon. Outdoor pool, whirlpool. **$**

★ **SHILO INN.** *702 W Appleway Ave, Coeur f'Alene (83814). Phone 208/664-2300; toll-free 800/222-2244; fax 208/667-2863. www.shiloinns.com.* 139 rooms, 4 story. Pets accepted; fee. Complimentary continental breakfast. Check-in 4 pm, check-out noon. Fitness room. Indoor pool, whirlpool. **$**

Full-Service Resort

★ ★ ★ **COEUR D'ALENE RESORT.** *115 S 2nd St, Coeur d'Alene (83814). Phone 208/765-4000; toll-free 800/688-5253; fax 208/664-7276. www.cdaresort.com.* Northern Idaho's Coeur d'Alene Resort is a superb destination for active travelers. This lakeside resort enjoys a parklike setting filled with a multitude of outdoor activities. From boat cruises, water-skiing, and marina access to downhill skiing, championship golf, and nearby shopping, this resort has something to satisfy every guest. This spot is particularly notable for its golf, both for its premier golf academy and its amazing floating green, accessible by a small boat. A European-style spa primps and pampers, while five lounges and bars entertain. Sophisticated Northwestern regional cuisine is highlighted at Beverly's restaurant (see), and Tito Macaroni's enjoys a lively Italian spirit. 336 rooms, 18 story. Pets accepted; fee. Check-in 4 pm, check-out noon. Three restaurants, bar. Children's activity center. Fitness room, spa. Beach. Indoor pool, outdoor pool, children's pool, whirlpool. Golf, 18 holes. Tennis. Airport transportation available. Business center. **$**

Specialty Lodging

The following lodging establishment is approved by Mobil Travel Guide, but due to its unique and individualized nature has not been given a traditional Mobil Star rating. Included in this listing you may find bed-and-breakfasts, limited-service inns, guest ranches, and other unique hotel properties.

THE ROOSEVELT. *105 E Wallace Ave, Coeur d'Alene (83814). Phone 208/765-5200; toll-free 800/290-3358; fax 208/664-4142. www.therooseveltinn .com.* 15 rooms, 4 story. Take one look at this inn's charming red brick exterior and you won't be at all surprised to learn that it originally served as a schoolhouse. Built in 1905 and listed on the National Register of Historic Places, the four-story building was converted into a cozy bed-and-breakfast in 1994. The inn—named in honor of Theodore Roosevelt—features 15 antique-furnished rooms. A complimentary gourmet breakfast awaits guests each morning. Pets accepted, some restrictions; fee. Children over 6 years only. Check-in 3 pm, check-out noon. Fitness room. Whirlpool. Airport transportation available. Pets accepted, some restrictions; fee. Children over 6 years only. Complimentary full breakfast. Check-in 3 pm, check-out noon. Fitness room. Whirlpool. Airport transportation available. **$**

Restaurants

★ ★ ★ **BEVERLY'S.** *115 S 2nd St, Coeur d'Alene (83816). Phone 208/765-4000; toll-free 800/688-5253; fax 208/664-7276. www.cdaresort.com.* This 7th-floor restaurant is the signature dining room at the Coeur d'Alene Resort (see). Enjoy great lake views, a fine wine cellar, and Northwest-inspired cuisine that includes the popular firecracker prawns with angel hair pasta. Fusion menu. Breakfast, lunch, dinner, late-night, brunch. Bar. Children's menu. Casual attire. Valet parking. **$$$**

★ **IRON HORSE.** *407 Sherman Ave, Coeur d'Alene (83814). Phone 208/667-7314.* American menu. Breakfast, lunch, dinner, brunch. Bar. Children's menu. Casual attire. Valet parking. Outdoor seating. **$$**

Craters of the Moon National Monument

(18 miles W of Arco on Hwy 20)

Web site: www.nps.gov/crmo

So named because it resembles the surface of the moon as seen through a telescope, this 83-square-mile monument has spectacular lava flows, cinder cones, and other volcanic creations. Geologists believe a weak spot in the earth's crust permitted outbursts of lava at least eight times during the last 15,000 years. These eruptions produced the lava flows, the 25 cinder cones, spatter cones, lava tubes, natural bridges, and tree molds within the monument. Geological and historical exhibits are on display at the visitor center (daily 8 am-4:30 pm, until 6 pm in summer; closed winter holidays). Autos may follow the 7-mile loop drive, which is closed by snow in winter. Interpretive programs of nature walks, campfire talks (mid-June-Labor Day). Campsites (no hookups, showers, or dump station) are found near the entrance (mid-May-Oct; fee). Golden Eagle, Golden Age, and Golden Access passports are accepted (see MAKING THE MOST OF YOUR TRIP), and pets on leash are allowed. Per vehicle **$**

Driggs (E-5)

See also Ashton, Rexburg, St. Anthony

Population 846
Elevation 6,116 ft
Area Code 208
Zip 83422

This mountain town sits in eastern Idaho, a short drive from the Wyoming state line and Grand Teton National Park. The Teton Basin Ranger Station of the Targhee National Forest is located here.

What to See and Do

Grand Targhee Ski and Summer Resort. *1200 E Ski Hill Rd, Alta (83422). 12 miles E on county road. Phone 307/353-2300; toll-free 800/827-4433.* Three chairlifts, surface lift; patrol, school, rentals; three lodges, three restaurants, cafeteria, bar; nursery; hot tubs, heated outdoor pool. Longest run 2.7 miles; vertical drop 2,200 feet. (Mid-Nov-early Apr, daily) Second mountain for powder skiing only. Cross-country trails; snowboard half-pipe. Summer activities incl fishing, rafting; horseback riding, biking, hiking, golf, tennis, music festivals (July-Aug); chairlift rides (June-Aug, daily). Half-day rates. **$$$$**

Limited-Service Hotel

★ **BEST WESTERN TETON WEST.** *476 N Main St, Driggs (83422). Phone 208/354-2363; toll-free 800/ 780-7234; fax 208/354-2962. www.bestwestern.com.* 40 rooms, 2 story. Pets accepted; fee. Complimentary continental breakfast. Check-in 3 pm, check-out noon. Indoor pool, whirlpool. **$**

Specialty Lodging

The following lodging establishment is approved by Mobil Travel Guide, but due to its unique and individualized nature has not been given a traditional Mobil Star rating. Included in this listing you may find bed-and-breakfasts, limited-service inns, guest ranches, and other unique hotel properties.

TETON RIDGE RANCH. *200 Valley View Rd, Tetonia (83452). Phone 208/456-2650; fax 208/456-2218. www.tetonridge.com.* More of a lodge or guest house than a dude ranch, this casually elegant property offers well appointed guest rooms, incredible views of the Grand Tetons, and gourmet dining on 4,000 private acres. Horseback riding and fishing are available. 5 rooms. Closed Nov-mid-Dec, Apr-May. Pets accepted. Children over 12 years only. Complimentary full breakfast. Check-in 1 pm, check-out 11 am. Airport transportation available. **$$$$**

Grangeville (C-2)

Founded 1876
Population 3,226
Elevation 3,390 ft
Area Code 208
Zip 83530
Information Chamber of Commerce, Hwy 95 and Pine St, PO Box 212; phone 208/983-0460
Web site www.grangevilleidaho.com

Grangeville is a light industrial and agricultural community. It was a focal point in the Nez Perce Indian War and a gold rush town in the 1890s, when rich ore was found in the Florence Basin and the Elk City areas. The seat of Idaho County, it is also the gateway to several wilderness areas. The headquarters and two Ranger District offices of the Nez Perce National Forest are located here.

What to See and Do

Hells Canyon National Recreation Area. *Access approximately 16 miles S on Hwy 95 to White Bird, then W on County Rd 493 to Pittsburg Landing; access also from Riggins, from Hwy 95 take Rd 241 (Race Creek) N of Riggins; paved access via Hwy 71 from Cambridge (see WEISER). Phone 541/426-4978. www.fs.fed.us/hellscanyon.* Created by the Snake River, at the Idaho/Oregon border, Hell's Canyon is the deepest gorge in North America—1 1/2 miles from He Devil Mountain (elevation 9,393 feet) to the Snake River at Granite Creek (elevation 1,408 feet). Overlooks at Heaven's Gate, W of Riggins, and in Oregon (see JOSEPH, OR). The recreation area includes parts of the Nez Perce and Payette National Forests in Idaho and the Wallowa-Whitman National Forest in Oregon. Activities include float trips, jet boat tours; auto tours, backpacking, and horseback riding; boat trips into canyon from Lewiston, Grangeville, and Riggins, also via Pittsburg Landing or the Hells Canyon Dam. Developed campgrounds in Oregon and Idaho; much of the area is undeveloped, some is designated wilderness. Be sure to inquire about road conditions before planning a trip; some roads are rough and open for a limited season. For further information, contact Hells Canyon National Recreation Area, 88401 Hwy 82, Enterprise, OR 97828; or 2535 Riverside Dr, Box 699, Clarkston, WA 99403, phone 509/758-0616. For river information and float reservations, phone 509/758-1957.

⭐ **Nez Perce National Forest.** *Main St and E Hwy 13, Grangeville (83530). S on Hwy 95. Phone 208/983-1950.* More than 2.2 million acres with excellent fishing; camping, cabins (fee at some campgrounds), picnicking, cross-country skiing, and snowmobiling. The Salmon (the River of No Return), Selway, South Fork Clearwater, and Snake rivers, all classified as wild and scenic, flow through or are adjacent to the forest. Pack and float trips are available; contact the Idaho Outfitters and Guides Association, PO Box 95, Boise 83701; Phone 208/342-1438. High elevations are open only in summer and fall; low elevations are open Mar-Nov. For further info contact Office of Information, Hwy 2, Box 475.

Snowhaven. *7 miles SE via Fish Creek Rd. Phone 208/983-3866.* T-bar, rope tow; patrol, school, rentals; cafeteria. Vertical drop 400 feet. (Dec-early Mar, Fri-Sun) Night skiing; half-day rates. **$$$$**

White Bird Hill. *5 miles S on Hwy 95. Phone 208/983-0460.* Site of the famous Whitebird Battle of the Nez Perce Indian Wars. View of Camas Prairie, canyons, mountains, and Seven Devils Peaks. Self-guided tour brochures available from Chamber of Commerce.

Special Events

Border Days. *Hwy 95, Grangeville (83530). Phone 208/983-0460.* Three-day rodeo and parades, dances. Art-in-the-park; food. July 4 weekend.

Oktubberfest. *Hwy 95, Grangeville (83530). Phone 208/983-0460.* Three-day event features tub races on Main St, arts and crafts, street dance, entertainment. Last weekend in Sept.

Hope

Restaurant

★ ★ **FLOATING RESTAURANT.** *Hwy 200 E, Hope (83836). Phone 208/264-5311.* Enjoy panoramic views of Lake Pend Oreille while dining on the restaurant's floating deck or in the indoor dining room. Seafood menu. Dinner, Sun brunch. Closed Mon-Tues; also Nov-Mar. Bar. Children's menu. Outdoor seating. **$$**

Idaho City (E-2)

See also Boise

Settled 1862
Population 322
Elevation 3,906 ft
Area Code 208
Zip 83631
Information Chamber of Commerce, PO Box 70; phone 208/392-4148
Web site www.idahocitychamber.com

Flecks of gold persist in the gravel beneath most of Idaho City, and the community is steeped in gold rush lore. From the 18-square-mile Boise Basin, said to have produced more gold than all of Alaska, Idaho City's fame once spread far and wide. Idaho City also is home to the state's first Pioneer Lodge (established in 1864) and the birthplace of the Grand Lodge of Idaho (established in 1867).

What to See and Do

Boise Basin Museum. *313 Main St, Idaho City (83631). Montgomery and Wall sts. Phone 208/392-4550.* (1867) Restored building houses artifacts of gold rush era. Walking tours of Idaho City available (fee). (Memorial Day-Labor Day: daily; May and Sept: weekends only; rest of year: by appointment) **$**

Boise National Forest. *1750 Front St, Idaho City (87302).* Fishing, hunting, swimming; camping, skiing, and snowmobiling. A Ranger District office of the forest is located here.

Boot Hill. *Phone 208/392-4148.* Restored 40-acre cemetery, last resting place of many gunfight victims.

Gold Hill. *1 mile N on Main St. Phone 208/392-4148.* Rich Boise Basin placer ground.

Idaho Falls (E-2)

See also Blackfoot, Pocatello, Rexburg

Population 43,929
Elevation 4,710 ft
Area Code 208
Information Chamber of Commerce, 505 Lindsay Blvd, PO Box 50498, 83405; phone 208/523-1010 or toll-free 800/634-3246
Web site www.visitidahofalls.com

An industrial, transportation, and trading center in the upper Snake River Valley, Idaho Falls is a center of potato production and headquarters for the Idaho Operations Office of the Department of Energy. The Idaho National Engineering Laboratory is located on the Lost River Plains, 30 miles west on Highway 20. Potato processing is important; the stockyards here are the state's largest; and one of the nation's leading safety research centers for nuclear reactors is located here. A Ranger District office of Targhee National Forest (see ASHTON) can be found in Idaho Falls.

What to See and Do

Bonneville Museum. *200 N Eastern Ave, Idaho Falls (83402). Phone 208/522-1400.* Displays of early county, state, and city history; natural history; Native American artifacts; early settler and mountain-man relics; replica of early (circa 1890) Idaho Falls (Eagle Rock); 30-minute video on county history and other subjects of local interest. Art exhibits featuring works of area artists; special and traveling exhibits. (Mon-Fri; also Sat afternoons; closed Jan 1, Thanksgiving, Dec 25) **$**

Heise Hot Springs. *5116 E Heise Rd, Ririe (83443). 23 miles E on Hwy 26. Phone 208/538-7312.* Mineral water pool, freshwater pools, water slide, fishing; golf, camping. (Mid-May-Sept) Fee for activities.

Idaho Falls. *On river downtown, Idaho Falls (83409). Phone 208/523-1010.* Falls run for 1,500 feet along the Snake River. Picnic tables nearby.

The Lavas. *10 miles S via Hwy 91 to Shelley, then 4 miles W on local road. Phone 208/523-1010.* Lava-created caves, fissures, and rock flows, fringed by dwarf trees. Native American relics are also plentiful.

Tautphaus Park. *2725 Carnival Way, Idaho Falls (83405). Rollandet Ave or South Blvd. Phone 208/528-5552.* Zoo (fee); amusement rides (Memorial Day weekend-Labor Day weekend, fee); picnic and barbecue areas; lighted tennis courts and softball diamonds; horseshoe pits; ice skating, hockey (seasonal). Park (Daily; closed Jan 1, Thanksgiving, Dec 25). **FREE**

Special Event

War Bonnet Roundup. *Sandy Downs Park Rodeo Grounds, 6855 S 15 E, Idaho Falls (83404). Phone 208/523-1010.* Rodeo. Four nights in early Aug.

Limited-Service Hotels

★ **AMERITEL INN IDAHO FALLS.** *645 Lindsay Blvd, Idaho Falls (83402). Phone 208/523-1400; toll-free 800/600-6001; fax 208/523-0004. www.ameritelinns.com.* 126 rooms, 4 story. Complimentary full breakfast. Check-in 3 pm, check-out noon. Fitness room. Indoor pool, whirlpool. Airport transportation available. **$**

⊠ 🕴 ⌨

★ ★ **RED LION HOTEL ON THE FALLS.** *475 River Pkwy, Idaho Falls (83402). Phone 208/523-8000; toll-free 800/733-5466; fax 208/529-9610. www.redlion.com.* 142 rooms. Pets accepted; fee. Check-in 3 pm, check-out noon. High-speed Internet access. Restaurant, bar. Fitness room. Outdoor pool. **$**

🐾 🕴 ⌨

★ **SHILO INN.** *780 Lindsay Blvd, Idaho Falls (83402). Phone 208/523-0088; toll-free 800/222-2244; fax 208/522-7420. www.shiloinns.com.* 162 rooms, 4 story. Pets accepted, some restrictions. Complimentary full breakfast. Check-in 2 pm, check-out noon. Restaurant, bar. Fitness room. Indoor pool, whirlpool. Airport transportation available. **$**

⊠ 🐾 🕴 ⌨

Restaurant

★ **JAKERS.** *851 Lindsay Blvd, Idaho Falls (83402). Phone 208/524-5240; fax 208/524-1937. www.jakers.com.* American menu. Lunch, dinner. Closed

Thanksgiving, Dec 25; also Super Bowl Sun. Bar. Children's menu. Casual attire. **$$**

Jerome (F-3)

See also Shoshone, Twin Falls

Population 6,529
Elevation 3,781 ft
Area Code 208
Zip 83338
Information Chamber of Commerce, 101 W Main St, Suite 6; phone 208/324-2711

What to See and Do

Jerome County Historical Museum. *220 N Lincoln, Jerome (83338). Phone 208/324-5641.* Located in historic Pioneer Hall building. Changing displays. Guided tours. (May-Sept: Mon-Sat; rest of year: Tues-Sat) **FREE**

Malad Gorge State Park. *1074 E 2350 S, Jerome (83332). Phone 208/837-4505.* More than 650 acres with the 2 1/2-mile-long, 250-feet-deep Malad Gorge. A footbridge spans a waterfall at Devil's Washbowl. Interpretive trails, picnicking. (Schedule varies)

Special Events

Chariot Races. *Jerome County Fairgrounds, 200 N Fir St, Jerome (83338). Phone 208/324-7211.* Weekends, Dec-Feb.

Horse racing. *Jerome County Fairgrounds, 200 N Fir St, Jerome (83338). Phone 208/324-7211.* Pari-mutuel racing. Two weekends in mid-June.

Jerome County Fair & Rodeo. *Jerome County Fairgrounds, 200 N Fir St, Jerome (83338). Phone 208/324-7211.* Concert, rodeo, carnival, parade. First week in Aug.

Limited-Service Hotel

★ **BEST WESTERN SAWTOOTH INN & SUITES.** *2653 S Lincoln Ave, Jerome (83338). Phone 208/324-9200; toll-free 800/780-7234; fax 208/324-9292. www.bestwestern.com.* 57 rooms, 2 story. Pets accepted; fee. Complimentary continental breakfast. Check-out noon. Fitness room. Indoor pool, whirlpool. **$**

🐾 🕴 ⌨

Kellogg (B-2)

See also Coeur d'Alene, Wallace

Population 2,591
Elevation 2,308 ft
Area Code 208
Zip 83837
Information Greater Kellogg Area Chamber of Commerce, 608 Bunker Ave; phone 208/784-0821
Web site www.kellogg-idaho.com

In this rich mining region are the country's largest silver and lead mines. One of the state's most violent miners' strikes took place here in 1899. Today, the former mining town is being transformed into a ski resort.

What to See and Do

Old Mission State Park. *10 miles W off I-90, exit 39, in Cataldo. Phone 208/682-3814. www.idahoparks.org.* (1850) A 100-acre park. Tours of the Coeur d'Alene Mission of the Sacred Heart, a restored Native American mission, which is the oldest existing building in the state. Information center, interpretive programs, history trail. (Daily 9 am-5 pm)

Silver Mountain Ski Area. *610 Bunker Ave, Kellogg (83837). 1/2 mile SW, off I-90 exit 49. Phone 208/783-1111; toll-free 800/204-6428. www.silvermt.com.* Double, quad, three triple chairlifts, surface lift; patrol, school, rentals; lodges, restaurants, cafeteria, bar, nursery. Fifty trails, longest run 2 1/2 miles; vertical drop 2,200 feet. (Mid-Nov-Apr, Wed-Sun) **$$$$**

Sunshine Mine Disaster Memorial. *Frontage Rd, Hwy 90 exit 54, Kellogg (83837). 3 miles E on I-90, exit 54, Big Creek. Phone 208/784-0821.* Double-life-size statue constructed of steel is memorial to all miners; created by Kenn Lonn, a native of Kellogg. The helmet's light burns perpetually and the miner holds a typical jackleg drill.

Special Event

Christmas Dickens Festival. *608 Bunker Ave, Kellogg (83837). Phone 208/784-0821.* Entire town dressed in period costume. Plays, skits, puppet shows, parade. Second weekend in Dec.

Limited-Service Hotel

★ **SUPER 8.** *601 Bunker Ave, Kellogg (83837). Phone 800/785-5443; toll-free 800/800-8000; fax 208/784-0461. www.super8.com.* 61 rooms, 2 story. Pets accepted, some restrictions; fee. Complimentary continental breakfast. Check-in 3 pm, check-out 11 am. Indoor pool, whirlpool. Ski in/ski out. **$**

Ketchum (E-3)

See Sun Valley Area

Lava Hot Springs (F-4)

See also Pocatello

Population 420
Elevation 5,060 ft
Area Code 208
Zip 83246
Web site www.lavahotsprings.org

Hot water pouring out of the mountains and bubbling up in springs, believed to be the most highly mineralized water in the world, makes Lava Hot Springs a busy year-round resort. Fishing, swimming; hunting, camping, and golf are available in the surrounding area.

What to See and Do

Lava Hot Springs. *430 E Main, Lava Hot Springs (83246). 1/2 mile E on Hwy 30 N. Phone 208/776-5221. www.lavahotsprings.org.* Outdoor mineral pools, fed by 30 different springs, range from 104-112°F. Olympic-size swimming pool with diving tower (Memorial Day-Labor Day). (Daily; closed Thanksgiving, Dec 25) **$$**

South Bannock County Historical Center. *110 Main St, Lava Hot Springs (83246). Phone 208/776-5254.* Museum artifacts, photographs, transcripts, and memorabilia trace history of town from the era of Native American and fur trappers to its development as a resort area. Slide show and guided walking tour (by appointment). (Daily) **DONATION**

Lewiston (C-1)

See also Moscow

Founded 1861
Population 28,082
Elevation 739 ft
Area Code 208
Zip 83501
Information Chamber of Commerce, 111 Main St, Suite 120; phone 208/743-3531 or toll-free 800/473-3543
Web site www.lewistonchamber.org

The Clearwater River, starting in the Bitterroot Mountains and plunging through the vast Clearwater National Forest, joins the Snake River at Lewiston. The two rivers and the mountains that surround the town give it one of the most picturesque settings in the state. A thriving tourist trade supplements Lewiston's grain, lumber, and livestock industries.

What to See and Do

⭐ **Auto tours.** The Lewis and Clark Highway (Hwy 12) parallels the famous Lewis and Clark Trail east to Montana. Interpretive signs along the way explain the human and natural history of the canyon. A Forest Service Information Station is at Lolo Pass on the Idaho/Montana border. The Chamber of Commerce has maps for other tours.

Castle Museum. *202 State St, Juliaetta (83535). 23 miles N on Hwy 3; 1 block off main hwy. Phone 208/276-3081.* 3 story, handmade cement block house built in 1906 and patterned after Scottish castle; embossed metal ceilings, antiques. (By appointment) **DONATION**

Clearwater National Forest. *12730 Hwy 12, Orofino (83544). Phone 208/476-4541.* About 1,850,000 acres with trout fishing; hunting, skiing and snowmobiling trails, camping (fee for some developed campsites), cabins, picnicking, lookout towers (fee). Pack trips. Higher elevations accessible July-Sept; lower elevations accessible Mar-Oct or Nov. Lolo Pass Visitor Center and Lochsa Historical Ranger Station on Highway 12 (Mid-May-mid-Sept; daily).

Hells Gate State Park. *4 miles S on Snake River Ave. Phone 208/799-5015.* 960 acres on Snake River, 40 miles N of Hells Canyon National Recreation Area. Swimming, fishing, boating (marina, concession, ramp); hiking and paved bicycle trails, horseback riding area, picnicking, playground, tent and trailer campsites (hookups, dump station; 15-day maximum). Info center, interpretive programs, exhibits; excursion boats. Park (Mar-Nov).

Hells Canyon excursions. Jet boat trips and fishing charters into Hells Canyon National Recreation Area (see GRANGEVILLE). For information, contact the Chamber of Commerce.

Luna House Museum. *0306 3rd St, Lewiston (83501). 3rd and C sts. Phone 208/743-2535.* On site of first hotel in town (1861). Exhibits on Nez Perce and pioneers; displays on town and county history. (Tues-Sat; closed holidays) **FREE**

Nez Perce National Historical Park. *Hwy 95 S, Spalding (83541). Headquarters has visitor center and museum, 39063 Hwy 95, Lapwai, ID 83540. Phone 208/843-2261.* The park is composed of 38 separate sites scattered throughout Washington, Oregon, Montana, and Idaho. All of the sites relate to the culture and history of the Nez Perce; some relate to the westward expansion of the nation into homelands. **FREE**

Special Events

Lewiston Round-Up. *Lewiston Round-Up grounds, 7000 Tammany Creek Rd, Lewiston (83501). Phone 208/746-6324.* Weekend after Labor Day.

Nez Perce County Fair. *1229 Burrell Ave, Lewiston (83501). Phone 208/743-3302.* Four days in late Sept.

Limited-Service Hotels

⭐ ⭐ **INN AMERICA.** *702 21st St, Lewiston (83501). Phone 208/746-7756; toll-free 800/469-4667; fax 208/746-7756. www.lewiston.innamerica.com.* 61 rooms, 3 story. Check-in 2 pm, check-out 1 pm. Restaurant. Pool. **$**

⭐ ⭐ **RED LION HOTEL LEWISTON.** *621 21st St, Lewiston (83501). Phone 208/799-1000; toll-free 800/232-6730. www.redlionlewiston.com.* 183 rooms, 4 story. Pets accepted, some restrictions. Check-in 3 pm, check-out noon. Restaurant, bar. Pool, whirlpool. Airport transportation available. **$**

★ **RIVERVIEW INN.** *1325 Main St, Lewiston (83501). Phone 208/746-3311; toll-free 800/806-7666; fax 208/746-7955.* 75 rooms, 4 story. Pets accepted. Check-in 3 pm, check-out noon. Fitness room. Pool. **$**

⊞ ⬚ ⬚

★ ★ **SACAJAWEA SELECT INN.** *1824 Main St, Lewiston (83501). Phone 208/746-1393; toll-free 800/333-1393; fax 208/743-3620. www.selectinn.com.* 90 rooms, 2 story. Pets accepted, some restrictions; fee. Complimentary continental breakfast. Check-in 1 pm, check-out noon. Restaurant, bar. Fitness room. Outdoor pool, whirlpool. Airport transportation available. **$**

⊞ ⬚ ⬚

McCall (D-2)

Population 2,005
Elevation 5,030 ft
Area Code 208
Zip 83638
Information Chamber of Commerce, PO Box D; phone 208/634-7631 or toll-free 800/260-5130
Web site www.mccall.id.us

At the southern tip of Payette Lake, McCall is a resort center for one of the state's chief recreational areas. Fishing, swimming, boating, and waterskiing are available on Payette Lake. McCall is also the head-quarters for Payette National Forest, and three Ranger District offices of the forest are located here.

What to See and Do

Brundage Mountain Ski Area. *8 miles NW via Hwy 55, unnumbered road. Phone 208/634-4151; toll-free 888/255-7669 (snow conditions). www. brundage.com.* Two triple chairlifts, Quadlift, Pomalift, platter tow; patrol, school, rentals; bar, cafeteria; nursery. (Mid-Nov-mid-Apr, daily) **$$$$**

Cascade Dam Reservoir. *25 miles S on Hwy 55. Phone 208/382-4258.* Situated alongside the West Mountains, this 30,000-acre body of water offers exceptional fishing and boating opportunities. Notable fish species include smallmouth bass, rainbow trout, yellow perch, and coho salmon. Open year-round, ice fishermen dot the frozen reservoir in the winter.

Pack trips into Idaho primitive areas. *Phone 208/634-7631.* Check with the Chamber of Commerce for a list of outfitters.

Payette National Forest. *800 W Lakeside, McCall (83638). Phone 208/634-0700.* More than 2.3 million acres surrounded by the Snake and Salmon rivers, the River of No Return Wilderness, Hell's Canyon National Recreation Area, and the Boise National Forest. Trout and salmon fishing in 300 lakes and 3,000 miles of streams, boating; 2,100 miles of hiking trails, hunting, camping, and picnic areas; winter sports.

Ponderosa State Park. *Miles Standish Rd, McCall. 2 miles NE, on Payette Lake. Phone 208/634-2164.* Approximately 1,280 acres. Large stand of ponderosa pines. Swimming, waterskiing, fishing, boating (ramps); hiking; cross-country skiing, picnicking, camping (except winter; reservations accepted Memorial Day-Labor Day); tent and trailer sites (hookups; 15-day maximum; dump station). Park (Daily). Contact Park Manager, PO Box A.

River rafting. *Salmon River Outfitters, 1734 W Roseberry Rd, Donnelly (83615). Phone toll-free 800/346-6204. www.salmonriveroutfitters.com.* Offers five- and six-day guided raft trips along the Salmon River. **$$$$**

Special Events

McCall Folk Music Festival. *University of Idaho Field Campus Ponderosa State Park, McCall (83638). Phone 208/634-7631.* Fiddle music; Western, swing, Irish, folk, blues, and jazz; square dancing. Third weekend in July.

Winter Carnival. *Phone 208/634-7631.* Parades, fireworks; ice sculptures, snowmobile and ski races, snowman-building contest, carriage and sleigh rides, ball. Ten days in early Feb.

Limited-Service Hotel

★ **BEST WESTERN MCCALL.** *415 N 3rd St, McCall (83638). Phone 208/634-6300; toll-free 800/ 780-7234; fax 208/634-2967. www.bestwestern.com.* 79 rooms, 2 story. Pets accepted, some restrictions. Check-in 2 pm, check-out 11 am. Fitness room. Indoor pool, whirlpool. **$**

⊞ ⬚ ⬚

Specialty Lodging

The following lodging establishment is approved by Mobil Travel Guide, but due to its unique and individualized nature has not been given a traditional Mobil Star rating. Included in this listing you may find bed-and-breakfasts, limited-service inns, guest ranches, and other unique hotel properties.

HOTEL MCCALL. *1101 N 3rd St, McCall (83638). Phone 208/634-8105; toll-free 866/800-1183; fax 208/634-8755.* 32 rooms, 3 story. Complimentary full breakfast. Check-in 2 pm, check-out 11 am. **$**

Restaurant

★ ★ **MILL STEAKS & SPIRITS.** *324 N 3rd St, McCall (83638). Phone 208/634-7683. www. themillmccallidaho.com.* Steak menu. Dinner. Closed Thanksgiving, Dec 25. Bar. Children's menu. Photo collection of history of the Northwest. **$$$**

🅳

Montpelier (F-5)

Founded 1864
Population 2,656
Elevation 5,964 ft
Area Code 208
Zip 83254
Information Bear Lake Convention & Visitors Bureau, PO Box 26, Fish Haven 83287; phone 208/945-2072 or toll-free 800/448-2327

Located in the highlands of Bear Lake Valley, Montpelier is surrounded by lakes, rivers, creeks, and grazing ranges. The average yearly temperature is 46° F. First called Clover Creek, then Belmont, it was finally designated by the Mormon leader, Brigham Young, as Montpelier, after the capital of Vermont. There are Mormon tabernacles throughout this area. Phosphate is mined extensively nearby. A Ranger District office of the Caribou National Forest is located here.

What to See and Do

Bear Lake. *20 miles S on Hwy 89.* Covering 71,000 acres, this 20-mile-long, 200-foot-deep body of water lies across the Idaho/Utah border. Fishing for Mackinaw, cutthroat, whitefish, and the rare Bonneville cisco. On the north shore is

Bear Lake State Park. *181 S Main, Montpelier (83261). Phone 208/945-2790.* Provides swimming beach, waterskiing, fishing, boating (ramp); picnicking, park (Mid-May-mid-Sept), camping on east shore (dump station, hookups).

Bloomington Lake. *12 miles S on Hwy 89, then W on local road, W of Bloomington.* Spring-fed lake of unknown depth. Camping, fishing.

Caribou National Forest. *322 N 4th St, Montpelier (83254) Phone 208/847-0375.* Fishing; camping (fee at certain designated campsites), hunting, picnicking, winter sports. Within the forest is

Minnetonka Cave. *10 miles W of St. Charles off Hwy 89. Phone 208/847-0375.* Cave is 1/2 mile long and has 9 rooms; 40° F. Guided tours (Mid-June-Labor Day, daily). **$$**

Special Events

Bear Lake County Fair and Rodeo. *Phone 208/945-2072.* Third weekend in Aug.

Oregon Trail Rendezvous Pageant. *Phone toll-free 800/448-2327.* Fri closest to July 24.

Limited-Service Hotel

★ ★ **BEST WESTERN CLOVER CREEK INN.** *243 N 4th St, Montpelier (83254). Phone 208/847-1782; toll-free 800/528-1234; fax 208/847-3519. www. bestwestern.com.* 65 rooms, 2 story. Pets accepted, some restrictions; fee. Complimentary continental breakfast. Check-in 2 pm, check-out 11 am. Restaurant. Fitness room. Whirlpool. **$**

🐾 🏃

Moscow (B-1)

See also Lewiston

Population 18,519
Elevation 2,583 ft
Area Code 208
Zip 83843
Information Chamber of Commerce, PO Box 8936; phone 208/882-1800 or toll-free 800/380-1801
Web site www.moscowchamber.com

This northern Idaho town is nestled between Moscow Mountain and the scenic rolling hills of the Palouse. A quaint college town, Moscow is home to the University of Idaho, and Washington State University is only a 15-minute drive west, just across the state line in Pullman. Moscow bills itself as the "Heart of the Arts," an appropriate moniker given the town's well-attended arts festivals, renowned summer theater program, and vibrant live music scene. The nearby Palouse hills possess rich soils, producing high yields of dry peas and lentils. The USA Dry Pea and Lentil Council is headquartered in Moscow.

What to See and Do

Appaloosa Museum and Heritage Center. *5070 Hwy 8 W, Moscow (83843). Moscow-Pullman Hwy. Phone 208/882-5578.* Exhibit of paintings and artifacts relating to the appaloosa horse; early cowboy equipment; saddle collection; Nez Perce clothing, tools. (June-Aug: Mon-Sat; rest of year: Mon-Fri; closed holidays) Also houses national headquarters of the Appaloosa Horse Club, Inc. **FREE**

Latah County Historical Society. *110 S Adams St, Moscow (83843). Mc Connell Mansion (1886). Phone 208/882-1004.* Historic rooms, exhibits, and artifacts depicting local history. Local history and genealogy library, children's activities. Museum (Tues-Sat, limited hours; closed holidays); library, 327 E 2nd St (Tues-Fri). **DONATION**

University of Idaho. *415 W 6th St, Moscow (83843). W off Hwy 95. Phone 208/885-6424.* (1889) (11,000 students) Graduate and undergraduate programs. On campus is a major collection of big game specimens from the estate of well-known hunter Jack O'Connor; art gallery and performing arts center; mining, forestry, and wildlife exhibits in the mining and forestry bldgs; 18,000-seat, covered Kibbie-ASUI Activities Center with award-winning barrel-arch dome. Tours (daily).

Special Events

Idaho Repertory Theater. *E.W. Hartung Theater, University of Idaho, 6th St and Stadium Dr, Moscow (83843). Phone 208/885-7986.* Shakespeare, musicals, dramas, comedies. June-early Aug.

Latah County Fair. *Fairgrounds, 1021 Harold St, Moscow (83843). E of town. Phone 208/883-5722.* Second week in Sept, after Labor Day.

Lionel Hampton Jazz Festival. *University of Idaho, Perimeter Dr and Rayburn St, Moscow (83843). Phone 208/885-6765.* 4-day festival hosted by Lionel Hampton featuring all-star headliners and student performers. Late Feb.

Rendezvous in the Park. *East City Park, 1021 Harold St, Moscow (83843). Phone 208/882-1178.* Arts and crafts festival, juried art shows, silent movies, concerts under the stars. Two weekends in July.

Limited-Service Hotels

★ ★ **BEST WESTERN UNIVERSITY INN.** *1516 Pullman Rd, Moscow (83843). Phone 208/882-0550; toll-free 800/325-8765; fax 208/883-3056. www.bestwestern.com.* 173 rooms, 2 story. Pets accepted; fee. Check-in 4 pm, check-out noon. Restaurant, bar. Fitness room. Indoor pool, children's pool, whirlpool. Airport transportation available. **$**

★ ★ **MARK IV MOTOR INN.** *414 N Main St, Moscow (83843). Phone 208/882-7557; toll-free 800/833-4240; fax 208/883-0684.* 86 rooms, 2 story. Pets accepted; fee. Check-in 3 pm, check-out noon. Restaurant, bar. Indoor pool, whirlpool. Airport transportation available. **$**

★ **SUPER 8.** *175 Peterson Dr, Moscow (83843). Phone 208/883-1503; toll-free 800/800-8000; fax 208/883-4769. www.super8.com.* 60 rooms, 3 story. Check-in 2 pm, check-out 11 am. **$**

Mountain Home (E-2)

See also Boise

Population 7,913
Elevation 3,143 ft
Area Code 208
Zip 83647
Information Desert Mountain Visitor Center, 2900 American Legion Blvd, PO Box 3; phone 208/587-4464
Web site www.mountain-home.org/chamber/tour/index.htm

A transportation center in the Boise-Owyhee Valley of southwest Idaho, Mountain Home affords a fine starting point for side trips. Within a few hours' drive are forested ranges of the Boise National Forest, sand dunes, ghost towns, reservoirs, and canyons; a Ranger District office of the forest (see BOISE) is located here.

What to See and Do

Bruneau Canyon. *Hwy 78, Mountain Home. 20 miles S on Hwy 51 to Bruneau, then SE on local road. Phone 208/366-7919. www.idahoparks.org.* A 61-mile gorge, 800 feet deep but narrow enough in places to toss a rock across. Bruneau Dunes State Park (4,800 acres) has small lakes, sand dunes, and the highest single- structured dune in North America (470 feet). Fishing for bass and bluegill, boating (ramps; no motors); nature trails, picnicking, tent and trailer sites (15-day maximum; hookups, dump station). Info center, public observatory, interpretive programs (by appointment).

Elmore County Historical Foundation Museum. *180 S 3rd St E, Mountain Home (83647). Phone 208/587-2104.* Contains historical info about Mountain Home and Elmore County. (Mar-Dec, Fri and Sat afternoons) **DONATION**

Fishing, swimming, boating, camping. *Strike Reservoir, 23 miles S on Hwy 51; or Anderson Ranch Reservoir, 22 miles NE on Hwy 20.*

Soldier Mountain Ski Area. *NE on Hwy 20 to Fairfield, then 10 miles N on Soldier Creek Rd. Phone 208/764-2300.* Two double chairlifts, rope tow; patrol, school, rentals; snowmaking; cafeteria, concession. Longest run 2 miles; vertical drop 1,400 feet. Half-day rates. (Mid-Nov-Apr: Thurs-Sun and holidays; Christmas and Easter weeks: daily) **$$$$**

Three Island Crossing State Park. *W Madison St, Mountain Home (83623). 35 miles SE in Glenns Ferry, I-84 at Glenns Ferry exit. Phone 208/366-2394. www. idahoparks.org.* On 513 acres. The site was once a river crossing on the Oregon Trail. Camping (reservations recommended; fee). Interpretive center; gift shop.

Limited-Service Hotel

★ **BEST WESTERN FOOTHILLS MOTOR INN.** *1080 Hwy 20, Mountain Home (83647). Phone* 208/587-8477; toll-free 800/604-8477; fax 208/587-5774. www.bestwestern.com/foothillsmotorinn. 76 rooms, 2 story. Pets accepted; fee. Complimentary continental breakfast. Check-in 3 pm, check-out noon. Pool, whirlpool. **$**

Nampa (E-1)

See also Boise, Caldwell

Founded 1885
Population 28,365
Elevation 2,490 ft
Area Code 208
Information Chamber of Commerce, 1305 3rd St S, PO Box A, 83653; phone 208/466-4641
Web site www.nampa.com

Nampa, the most populous city in Canyon County, is located in southwestern Idaho's agriculturally rich Treasure Valley. Crops such as sweet corn, onions, mint, and potatoes thrive in the area's sun soaked, high desert climate. Nampa is a short drive west of Boise on I-84, a few miles north of the Snake River Birds of Prey National Conservation Area, home to North America's largest concentration of nesting raptors.

What to See and Do

Canyon County Historical Society Museum. *1200 Front St, Nampa (83651). Phone 208/467-7611.* Historical artifacts and memorabilia inside a 1903 train depot once used as offices of the Union Pacific Railroad. (Tues-Sat, limited hours) **DONATION**

Deer Flat National Wildlife Refuge. *13751 Upper Embankment, Nampa (83686). 5 miles SW off I-84. Phone 208/467-9278.* Thousands of migratory waterfowl pause at this 10,500-acre refuge while on their journey (Oct-Dec). Wildlife observation. Fishing, hunting in season. Visitor center (Mon-Fri; closed holidays). **FREE** Within the refuge is

Lake Lowell. Approximately 8,800 acres. Boating, sailing, water-skiing; picnicking (mid-Apr-Sept, daily).

Lakeview Park. *Garrity Blvd and 16th Ave, Nampa (83686). Phone 208/465-2215.* A 90-acre park with gardens, sports facilities, tennis, picnic areas.

Pool (June-Labor Day; fee). Antique fire engine, locomotive, steam roller, jet fighter plane on display. Amphitheater. Park (Daily). **FREE**

Special Event

Snake River Stampede. *109 12th Ave S, Nampa (83651). Phone 208/466-8497.* Among nation's top professional rodeos. All seats reserved. For tickets contact PO Box 231, 83653; Tues-Sat, third week in July.

Limited-Service Hotels

★ **HAMPTON INN AT IDAHO CENTER.** *5750 E Franklin Rd, Nampa (83687). Phone 208/442-0036; toll-free 800/426-7866; fax 208/442-0037. www. hamptoninn.com.* 101 rooms. Complimentary continental breakfast. Check-in 3 pm, check-out noon. Fitness room. Indoor pool. **$**

★ **SHILO INN.** *1401 Shilo Dr, Nampa (83687). Phone 208/466-8993; toll-free 800/222-2244; fax 208/ 465-5929. www.shiloinns.com.* 84 rooms, 3 story. Pets accepted; fee. Complimentary continental breakfast. Check-in 3 pm, check-out noon. Pool, whirlpool. **$**

Pocatello (F-4)

See also American Falls, Blackfoot, Idaho Falls, Lava Hot Springs

Founded 1882
Population 46,080
Elevation 4,464 ft
Area Code 208
Information Greater Pocatello Chamber of Commerce, 343 W Center St, PO Box 626, 83204; phone 208/233-1525
Web site www.ci.pocatello.id.us

At the heart of the intermontane transportation system is Pocatello. Once the site of a reservation, the city was named for the Native American leader who granted the railroad rights of way and building privileges. A Ranger District office and the headquarters of the Caribou National Forest are located here.

What to See and Do

Caribou National Forest. *1405 Hollipark Dr, Pocatello (83201). S, W, and E of city. Phone 208/523-3278.* Scenic drives, pack trips, camping (fee in some designated developed campgrounds), picnic grounds, hunting, fishing, downhill and cross-country skiing, snowmobiling. For further info contact the Forest Supervisor, 670 Broadway Ave, Idaho Falls, 83401. In the forest is

Pebble Creek Ski Area. *3340 E Green Canyon Rd, Inkom (83245). 10 miles SE on I-15 to Inkom, then 5 miles E on Green Canyon Rd. Phone 208/775-4452. www.pebblecreekskiarea.com.* Two triple, one double chairlifts; beginner-to-expert trails; patrol, school, rentals; restaurant, bar. Longest run 1 1/2 miles; vertical drop 2,200 feet. Night skiing. Half-day rates. (Second week in Dec-early Apr; daily) **$$$$**

Idaho State University. *92 S 8th Ave, Pocatello (83209). Phone 208/236-3620.* (1901) (13,500 students) Undergraduate and graduate programs. Art gallery in Fine Arts Building has changing exhibits (academic year, daily; summer by appointment, phone 208/236-3532); art gallery in Student Union Building (daily); both galleries free. On campus is 12,000-seat Holt Arena, indoor football stadium and sports arena. Tours. Also here is

Idaho Museum of Natural History. *1066 S 5th Ave, Pocatello (83209). Phone 208/282-3168.* Exhibits on Idaho fossils, especially large mammals of the Ice Age; Native American basketry and beadwork; "Discovery Room" for educational activities; museum shop. (Mon-Sat; closed holidays) **$$**

Rocky Mountain River Tours. *314 Stevens Ave, Pocatello (83707). Middlefork Salmon River Canyon. Phone 208/345-2400.* Six-day wilderness rafting tours; equipment provided.

Ross Park. *911 N 7th Ave, Pocatello (83201). S 2nd Ave. Phone 208/234-6232.* Zoo; swimming pool (June-Aug), water slide; playground, picnic area with shelter, band shell. Park (Daily). Fee for some activities. On upper level are

Bannock County Historical Museum. *3000 Alvord Loop, Pocatello (83204). Phone 208/233-0434.* Relics of the early days of Pocatello and Bannock County; Bannock and Shoshone display.

(Memorial Day-Labor Day: daily; rest of year: Tues-Sat, limited hours; closed holidays, also mid-Dec-mid-Jan) **$**

Old Fort Hall Replica. Reproduction of 1834 Hudson's Bay Trading Post; period displays. (June-mid-Sept: daily; Apr-May: Tues-Sat) **$**

Special Events

Bannock County Fair and Rodeo. *10588 Fairgrounds Rd, Pocatello (83201). Phone 208/237-1340.* North: Bannock County Fairgrounds. South: Downey Fairgrounds. Carnival, rodeo, exhibits, food booths, livestock and horse shows. Mid-Aug.

Shoshone-Bannock Indian Festival. *10588 Fairgrounds Rd, Pocatello (83201). Phone 208/237-1340.* Begins the second Wed in Aug.

Summer Band Concert Series. *Guy Gates Memorial Band Shell, in lower level of Ross Park, 2901 S 2nd Ave, Pocatello. Phone 208/234-6232.* Sun, July-Aug.

Limited-Service Hotels

★ ★ **HOLIDAY INN.** *1399 Bench Rd, Pocatello (83201). Phone 208/237-1400; toll-free 800/200-8944; fax 208/238-0225. www.holiday-inn.com.* 205 rooms, 2 story. Pets accepted, some restrictions. Complimentary continental breakfast. Check-in 3 pm, check-out noon. Restaurant, bar. Fitness room. Indoor pool, whirlpool. Airport transportation available. **$**

⊡ ⬤ 𝕏 ⩳

★ ★ **RED LION.** *1555 Pocatello Creek Rd, Pocatello (83201). Phone 208/233-2200; toll-free 800/325-4000; fax 208/234-4524. www.redlion.com.* 150 rooms, 2 story. Pets accepted, some restrictions. Check-out noon. Restaurant, bar. Fitness room. Indoor pool, children's pool, whirlpool. Airport transportation available. Business center. **$**

𝕏 ⬤ 𝕏 ⩳ 𝕏

Priest Lake Area

See also Sandpoint

(25 miles N of Priest River via Hwy 57)

Among the few remaining unspoiled playgrounds of the Pacific Northwest are lovely and spectacular

Priest Lake and the Idaho Panhandle National Forest. North of the confluence of the Pend Oreille and Priest rivers, giant lake trout, big game, towering mountains, waterfalls, lakes, and tall trees make this area one of the most attractive in the country. Mountain ranges and Pacific breezes keep the climate moderate.

This entire water and forest domain was explored by a Jesuit priest, Father Peter John DeSmet, also known as "great black robe" and the "first apostle of the Northwest." Priest Lake and Priest River were both named in his honor. A Ranger District office of the Idaho Panhandle National Forests-Kaniksu is located at Priest Lake.

What to See and Do

Idaho Panhandle National Forests–Kaniksu. *Nordman Hwy, Priest River. Phone 208/443-2512. Surrounds Priest Lake and Lake Pend Oreille; other areas NE.* Rich with huge trees, wildflowers, fishing streams. Boating, swimming, fishing in Pend Oreille and Priest lakes; big game hunting, cross-country skiing, snowmobiling trails, picnicking, 12 forest-run campgrounds on the west side of Priest Lake; other state-run campgrounds in the area. For more information, contact the Priest Lake Ranger District, 32203 Hwy 57, Priest River 83856.

Priest Lake. *32203 Hwy 57, Priest River (83856). 22 miles N of town of Priest River via Hwy 57, then approximately 6 miles E on East Shore Rd; or approximately 6 miles farther on Hwy 57, then 1 mile E on Outlet Bay Rd.* Lower Priest, the main lake, is 18 1/2 miles long and about 4 miles wide and has a 63-mile shoreline. Upper Priest (inaccessible by road; best reached by boat) is 3 1/4 miles long and 1 mile wide and has an 8-mile shoreline. The area is popular for picnics, overnight cruises, and campouts. There are three state-run campgrounds on the east side: Dickensheet, Indian Creek, and Lionhead; the US Forest Service operates other campgrounds in the area, on the west side. Nearby is the Roosevelt Grove of ancient cedars with 800-year-old trees standing as tall as 150 feet. Granite Falls is within the grove. Priest Lake is famous for its giant lake trout (Mackinaw trout) and cutthroat trout. The main lake contains six islands ideal for picnicking and camping (ten-day maximum). Recreation around the lake includes swimming, boating (ramp), ice fishing, cross-country skiing, snowmobiling, ice skating, and sledding. On the east side of the lake is

Priest Lake State Park. *423 Indian Creek Bay, Priest Lake Area (83821). Phone 208/443-6710.* This park comprises three state-run campgrounds: the Dickensheet unit is 1 mile off Highway 57, on the Coolin Rd (46 acres; 11 campsites); the Indian Creek unit is 11 miles N of Coolin, on Eastshore Rd (park headquarters; 295 acres; 93 campsites, two camper cabins, store, boating facilities, RV hookups, trails); and the Lionhead unit is 23 miles N of Coolin, on Eastshore Rd (415 acres; 47 tent sites, group camp, boating facilities, trails). Reservations are available for Indian Creek campsites; reservations are required for the group camp at Lionhead.

Priest River. *Priest Lake. Winds for 44 miles S of the lake through wild, forested country.* Old logging roads parallel much of it. Only at the north and south stretches is it easily reached from Highway 57. Long whitewater stretches provide adventure for canoe experts; riffles, big holes, smooth-flowing sections make it a tantalizing trout stream (fishing: June-Oct).

Special Events

Pacific Northwest Sled Dog Championship Races. *On Hwy 57 at Priest Lake Airport, W shore.* Last weekend in Jan.

Spring Festival. *Phone 208/443-3191.* Auction, parade. Memorial Day weekend.

Full-Service Resorts

★ ★ **ELKINS ON PRIEST LAKE.** *404 Elkins Rd, Nordman (83848). Phone 208/443-2432; fax 208/443-2527. www.elkinsresort.com.* 31 rooms. Closed Mar-Apr. Pets accepted, some restrictions; fee. Check-in 4 pm, check-out 11 am. Restaurant, bar. **$**

★ ★ **HILLS RESORT.** *4777 W Lakeshore Rd, Priest Lake (83856). Phone 208/443-2551; fax 208/443-2363. www.hillsresort.com.* 77 rooms, 2 story. Pets accepted; fee. Check-in 4:30 pm, check-out 10:30 am. Restaurant, bar. Tennis. **$**

Rexburg (E-4)

See also Ashton, Driggs, Idaho Falls, St. Anthony

Founded 1883
Population 14,302
Elevation 4,865 ft
Area Code 208
Zip 83440
Information Chamber of Commerce Tourist & Information Center, 420 W 4th St; phone 208/356-5700
Web site www.rexcc.com

Rexburg enjoys its position as a farm and trading center. Founded on instructions of the Mormon Church, the community was named for Thomas Ricks; common usage changed it to Rexburg.

What to See and Do

Beaver Dick. *7 miles W on Hwy 33.* A 12-acre preserve on west bank of the north Fork of Snake River. Fishing, boating, ramp; picnic facilities, primitive camping. (Mar-Dec)

Idaho Centennial Carousel. *Porter Park, 12 N Center St, Rexburg (83440). Phone 208/359-3020.* Restored Spillman Engineering carousel. (June-Labor Day, daily) **$**

Teton Flood Museum. *51 N Center, Rexburg (83440). Phone 208/359-3063.* Artifacts, photographs, and films document the 1976 flood caused by the collapse of the Teton Dam, which left 11 persons dead and $1 billion in damage. Also various historical displays. (May-Aug: Mon-Sat; rest of year: Mon-Fri, limited hours; closed holidays except July 4) **$**

Twin Bridges. *13 miles SE on Archer-Lyman Rd. Phone 208/356-3102.* A 30-acre preserve on the north bank of the south Fork of Snake River. Fishing, boating, ramp; picnic facilities, camping. (Apr-Nov)

Yellowstone Bear World. *6010 S 4300 W, Rexburg (83440). 5 miles S on Hwy 20. Phone 208/359-9688.* Drive-through preserve near Yellowstone National Park features bears, wolves, other wildlife; "Cub Yard" shows bear cubs at play; "Duck Deck" waterfowl observation/feeding deck. (May-Oct, daily) 5 miles S on Hwy 20. **$$$**

Special Event

Idaho International Folk Dance Festival. *Phone 208/356-5700.* Dance teams from around the world, events. Last week in July-first weekend in Aug.

Limited-Service Hotels

★ ★ **BEST WESTERN COTTONTREE INN.** *450 W 4th St S, Rexburg (83440). Phone 208/356-4646; toll-free 800/662-6886; fax 208/356-7461. www. bestwestern.com.* 98 rooms, 2 story. Pets accepted, some restrictions. Check-in 2 pm, check-out noon. Restaurant. Indoor pool, whirlpool. **$**

★ **COMFORT INN.** *1565 W Main St, Rexburg (83440). Phone 208/359-1311; toll-free 800/228-5150; fax 208/359-1387. www.choicehotels.com.* 52 rooms, 2 story. Pets accepted. Complimentary continental breakfast. Check-in 3 pm, check-out 11 am. Fitness room. Indoor pool, whirlpool. **$**

Restaurant

★ **FRONTIER PIES RESTAURANT.** *460 W 4th St, Rexburg (83440). Phone 208/356-3600; fax 208/356-3673.* American menu. Breakfast, lunch, dinner, brunch. Children's menu. **$$**

St. Anthony (E-4)

See also Ashton, Driggs, Idaho Falls, Rexburg

Population 3,010
Elevation 4,972 ft
Area Code 208
Zip 83445
Information Chamber of Commerce, City Hall, 114 N Bridge St; phone 208/624-3494

Seat of Fremont County, headquarters for the Targhee National Forest and a center of the seed potato industry, Saint Anthony is named for Anthony Falls, Minnesota. Tourists make it a base for exploring Idaho's tiny (30 miles long, 1 mile wide) "sahara desert," the Saint Anthony Sand Dunes.

What to See and Do

Fort Henry Trading Post Site. *7 miles W along Henry's Fork of Snake River.* (1810) First fort on what early voyageurs called the "accursed mad river."

St. Anthony Sand Dunes. *12 miles W. Phone 208/624-3494.* More than 10,000 acres of ever-shifting white quartz sand dunes. The area is popular among dune buggy, ATV, and horseback riders. During the winter months, kids—and kids at heart—arrive to sled and tube down the snow-covered dunes.

Special Events

Cowboy Poet Festival. *Phone 208/624-4870.* Entertainment, clogging demonstrations. Apr.

Fremont County Fair. *Fairgrounds, St. Anthony. Phone 208/624-4870.* Features demolition derby. Aug.

Fremont County Pioneer Days. *Phone 208/624-4870.* Rodeo, parade, carnival. Late July.

Summerfest. *Phone 208/624-4870.* Main Street Booth fair. Aug.

St. Marie's (B-1)

See also Coeur d'Alene

Population 2,442
Elevation 2,216 ft
Area Code 208
Zip 83861
Information Chamber of Commerce, 906 Main St, PO Box 162; phone 208/245-3563

St. Marie's (St. Mary's) is a center for lumbering and the production of plywood, a crossroads for lake, rail, and road transportation, and the jumping-off place for exploring the shadowy St. Joe River country. A Ranger District office of the Idaho Panhandle National Forests-St. Joe is located in St. Marie's.

What to See and Do

Benewah, Round, and Chatcolet lakes. *Along the St. Joe River.* Famous as one of the state's best bass fishing and duck hunting areas. The three lakes became one with the construction of the Post Falls Dam. Also here is

Heyburn State Park. *1291 Chatcolet Rd, Plummer (83851). 7 miles W on Hwy 5. Phone 208/686-1308.* More than 7,800 acres. Swimming beach, fishing, boating (ramps, fee), ice skating, ice fishing; hiking and bridle trails, mountain biking, self-guided nature walks, picnicking, concession, tent and trailer campsites (15-day maximum; hookups), dump station. Campfire and interpretive programs. Dinner and interpretive cruises. Park (Daily).

Idaho Panhandle National Forests–St. Joe. *Access from Hwy 95 and I-90; other areas E on local roads. Phone 208/245-2531.* Hunting, fishing, hiking, camping, cabins, picnicking, summer and winter sports areas, cross-country skiing, snowmobiling trails; digging for garnets; scenic drives. For more information, contact the Avery Ranger District, HC Box 1, Avery 83802, phone 208/245-4517; or the Supervisor, 3815 Schreiber Way, Coeur d'Alene 83815, phone 208/765-7223.

St. Joe Baldy Mountain. *8 miles E on St. Joe River Rd (Forest Hwy 50).* Lookout at top has view of Washington and Montana.

St. Joe River. *Just E on Hwy 5.* Called "the river through the lakes," one of the world's highest navigable rivers. Connects St. Marie's with Lake Coeur d'Alene.

Special Events

Paul Bunyan Days. *Phone 208/245-3563.* Includes parade, fireworks, logging events, water show, carnival. Labor Day weekend.

smART Festival. *St. Marie's City Park, 827 Main Ave, St. Marie's (83861). Phone 208/245-3417.* Paintings and crafts by local and regional artists. Food, entertainment, swimming. Third weekend in July.

Salmon (D-3)

Settled 1866
Population 2,941
Elevation 4,004 ft
Area Code 208
Zip 83467
Information Salmon Valley Chamber of Commerce, 200 Main St, Suite 1; phone 208/756-2100 or toll-free 800/727-2540
Web site www.salmonidaho.com

This town, at the junction of the Salmon and Lemhi rivers, serves as a doorway to the Salmon River country. It has towering mountains, lush farmland, timberland, and rich mines. The Salmon River runs through the town on its way to the Columbia River and the Pacific Ocean. Fishing and boating are available along the Salmon and Lemhi rivers and in more than 250 lakes. The headquarters and two Ranger District offices of the Salmon National Forest are located here.

What to See and Do

River rafting, backpack, fishing, and pack trips. Trips along the Lemhi, Salmon, Middle Fork, and other rivers can be arranged. Contact the Chamber of Commerce for a list of outfitters in the area.

Salmon National Forest. *50 Hwy 93 S, Salmon (83467). N, E, and W of town along Hwy 93. Phone 208/756-2215.* Approximately 1.8 million acres. Boat trips, fishing; hunting, picnicking, camping. Includes portion of the Frank Church—River of No Return Wilderness.

Special Events

The Great Salmon BalloonFest. *Phone 208/727-2540.* Hot-air balloon festival. Aug.

High School Rodeo. *Phone 208/756-2100.* First weekend in June.

Lemhi County Fair & Rodeo. Third week in Aug.

Salmon River Days. *Phone 208/756-2100.* July 4.

Limited-Service Hotel

★ **STAGECOACH INN MOTEL.** *201 Hwy 93 N, N Salmon (83467). Phone 208/756-4251; fax 208/756-3456.* 100 rooms, 3 story. Complimentary continental breakfast. Check-in 3 pm, check-out 11 am. Beach access. Pool. Airport transportation available. **$**

✈ ⛱

Restaurant

★ **SALMON RIVER COFFEE SHOP.** *606 Main St, Salmon (83467). Phone 208/756-3521.* American menu. Breakfast, lunch, dinner, brunch. Closed Jan 1, Thanksgiving, Dec 25. Bar. Children's menu. **$$**

Sandpoint (A-1)

See also Bonners Ferry, Priest Lake Area

Population 5,203
Elevation 2,085 ft
Area Code 208
Zip 83864
Information Chamber of Commerce, 900 N 5th, PO Box 928; phone 208/263-2161 or toll-free 800/800-2106
Web site www.sandpointchamber.com

At the point where the Pend Oreille River empties into Lake Pend Oreille (pon-da-RAY, from a Native American tribe given to wearing pendant ear ornaments), Sandpoint straddles two major railroads and three US highways. All of these bring a stream of tourists into town. In the surrounding area are dozens of smaller lakes and streams. A Ranger District office of the Idaho Panhandle National Forests-Coeur d'Alene is located here.

What to See and Do

Bonner County Historical Society Museum. *611 S Ella St, Sandpoint (83864). In Lakeview Park, at Ontario and Ella sts. Phone 208/263-2344. www. sandpoint.com/museum.* Exhibits depict the history of Bonner County. There is also a research library with a newspaper collection dating from 1899. (Tues-Sat 10 am-4 pm; closed holidays) **$**

Coldwater Creek on the Cedar Street Bridge. *334 N 1st Ave, Sandpoint (83864). Phone 208/263-2265.* Shopping mall built on a bridge over Sand Creek. Inspired by the Ponte Vecchio in Florence, Italy, the Coldwater Creek shops provide panoramic views of Lake Pend Oreille and nearby mountains. (Daily)

Lake Pend Oreille. The largest lake in Idaho, and one of the largest natural lakes wholly within the US, Lake Pend Oreille is more than 43 miles long and 6 miles wide, with more than 111 miles of shoreline. Anglers catch approximately 14 varieties of game fish, including the famous Kamloops, the largest rainbow trout in world (they average 16 to 26 pounds). Boating, swimming, water-skiing; camping, picnicking.

Round Lake State Park. *Sagle. 10 miles S on Hwy 95, then 2 miles W. Phone 208/263-3489.* Approximately 140 acres of coniferous woods. Swimming, skin diving, fishing, ice fishing, ice-skating, boating (ramp, no motors); hiking, cross-country skiing, sledding, tobogganing, snowshoeing in winter, picnicking. Camping (15-day maximum; no hookups), dump station. Campfire programs. Park (Daily).

Sandpoint Public Beach. *Foot of Bridge St, E edge of town.* Nearly 20 acres. Bathhouse, swimming, water-skiing, boat docks, ramps; picnic tables, fireplaces, volleyball and tennis courts; concession (seasonal). Park (Daily). **FREE**

Schweitzer Mountain Resort. *10000 Schweitzer Mountain Rd, Sandpoint (83864). 11 miles NW off Hwy 2 and Hwy 95, in Selkirk Mts of Idaho Panhandle National Forests. Phone toll-free 800/831-8810.* Five chairlifts, high-speed quad; school, rentals; lodging, restaurants, bars, cafeteria; nursery. Longest run 2.7 miles; vertical drop 2,400 feet. (Nov-Apr, daily) Summer chairlift rides (fee).

Special Events

The Festival at Sandpoint. *Phone 208/265-4554.* Since 1982, thousands have gathered in this arts town to enjoy music performed by internationally acclaimed musicians representing just about every genre imaginable. Past artists have included the likes of B.B. King, Shawn Colvin, Tony Bennett, Wynton Marsalis, and Johnny Cash. Aug.

Winter Carnival. *Phone 208/263-2161.* Two weekends of festivities include snow sculpture, snowshoe softball, and other games, races, torchlight parade. Mid-Jan.

Limited-Service Hotels

★ ★ **BEST WESTERN EDGEWATER RESORT.** *56 Bridge St, Sandpoint (83864). Phone 208/263-3194; toll-free 800/635-2534; fax 208/263-3194. www.sandpointhotels.com/edgewater.* 55 rooms, 3 story. Pets accepted; fee. Complimentary full breakfast. Check-in 3 pm, check-out noon. Restaurant, bar. Indoor pool, whirlpool. **$**

★ ★ **LA QUINTA INN.** *415 Cedar St, Sandpoint (83864). Phone 208/263-9581; toll-free 800/282-0660; fax 208/263-3395. www.laquinta.com.* 70 rooms, 3 story. Check-out 1 pm. Restaurant, bar. Fitness room. Outdoor pool, whirlpool. **$**

★ ★ **SELKIRK LODGE AT SCHWEITZER MOUNTAIN.** *10000 Schweitzer Mountain Rd, Sandpoint (83864). Phone 208/265-0257.* 78 rooms. Check-in 3 pm, check-out noon. Restaurant, bar. Ski in/ski out. **$**

★ ★ **WHITE PINE LODGE AT SCHWEITZER MOUNTAIN.** *10000 Schweitzer Mountain Lodge, Sandpoint (83864). Phone 208/265-0257.* 42 rooms. Check-in 3 pm, check-out noon. Restaurant, bar. Ski in/ski out. **$$**

Specialty Lodging

The following lodging establishment is approved by Mobil Travel Guide, but due to its unique and individualized nature has not been given a traditional Mobil Star rating. Included in this listing you may find bed-and-breakfasts, limited-service inns, guest ranches, and other unique hotel properties.

THE COIT HOUSE B&B. *502 N Fourth Ave, Sandpoint (83864). Phone 208/265-4035; toll-free 866/265-2648; fax 208/265-5558.* This charming B&B is located in downtown Sandpoint, steps away from shopping, restaurants, and the City Beach at Lake Pend Oreille. Antiques and handmade crafts can be found throughout this restored 1907 Victorian manor. Each of the four bedrooms has a private bath. The upstairs master suite charms guests with a beautiful sleigh bed and clawfoot tub. A mural of an English garden graces the wall alongside the staircase. A cheery sun room is the perfect place to relax before or after a day of outdoor fun in this year-round vacation community. 4 rooms. Complimentary full breakfast. Check-in 3 pm, check-out 11 am. **$**

Restaurants

★ ★ **BANGKOK CUISINE.** *202 N 2nd Ave, Sandpoint (83864). Phone 208/265-4149. www.bangkokcuisine.com.* Thai menu. Lunch, dinner. Closed Sun. **$$**

★ **HYDRA.** *115 Lake St, Sandpoint (83864). Phone 208/263-7123.* American menu. Lunch, dinner, Sun brunch. Closed Thanksgiving, Dec 25. Bar. **$$**

★ ★ **IVANO'S RISTORANTE.** *102 S First Ave, Sandpoint (83864). Phone 208/263-0211; fax 208/255-4225. www.ivanos.com.* Italian menu. Lunch, dinner. Bar. Children's menu. Outdoor seating. Cathedral ceiling in main dining room. **$$**

★ **JALAPENO'S.** *314 N 2nd Ave, Sandpoint (83864). Phone 208/263-2995; fax 208/265-9000.* Mexican menu. Lunch, dinner. Children's menu. Outdoor seating. Wall murals. **$$**

Shoshone (E-3)

See also Bellevue, Jerome, Twin Falls

Founded 1882
Population 1,249
Elevation 3,970 ft
Area Code 208
Zip 83352
Information City Hall, 207 S Rail St W, Box 208; phone 208/886-2030

Located in the Magic Valley region of south-central Idaho, Shoshone serves as the seat of Lincoln County. The town is surrounded by ranches and farms, and the area retains an aura of the untamed Old West. Popular recreational activities include boating, fishing, and big-game hunting. Shoshone marks the beginning of the Sawtooth Scenic Route, a stretch of State Highway 75 leading northward to the resort community of Sun Valley.

What to See and Do

Mary L. Gooding Memorial Park. *300 N Rail St, Shoshone (83324). Phone 208/886-2030.* Playground, pool (May-Aug, daily), picnic area along Little Wood River. (Daily)

✪ **Shoshone Indian Ice Caves.** *1561 N Hwy 75, Shoshone (83352). 17 miles N on Hwy 75. Phone 208/886-2058.* The caves function as a natural refrigerator, with temperatures ranging from 18 to 33° F. The cave is three blocks long, 30 feet wide, and 40 feet high, and local legend has it that long ago a princess named Idahow was buried under the ice. To this day, visitors report hearing strange voices and footsteps that seem to come from nowhere. On the grounds are a statue of Shoshone Chief Washakie and a museum of Native American artifacts, as well as minerals and gems (free). The caves are a good place to take children. 45-minute guided tours (May-Sept, daily). **$$$**

Special Events

Arts in the Park. Arts and crafts fair. Second weekend in July.

Lincoln County Fair. *Phone 208/886-2030.* Third week in July.

Manty Shaw Fiddlers' Jamboree. *Phone 208/886-2030.* Second weekend in July.

Stanley (D-2)

Population 71
Elevation 6,260 ft
Area Code 208
Zip 83278
Information Chamber of Commerce, PO Box 8; phone 208/774-3411
Web site www.stanleycc.org

Situated on the Salmon River (the famous "river of no return"), Stanley is located at the center of the Sawtooth Wilderness, Sawtooth Valley, and scenic Stanley Basin. A Ranger District office of the Sawtooth National Forest is located here.

What to See and Do

Salmon River. *Phone 208/879-4101.* Rafting, kayaking, fishing; camping.

River expeditions. *Hwy 21, Stanley. Phone 208/774-3411.* Many outfitters offer wilderness float trips on the Middle Fork of the Salmon River. Along the river are Native American pictographs, caves, abandoned gold mines, and abundant wildlife. Activities include boating, fishing, hiking, natural hot water springs, and photography. For a list of outfitters contact the Chamber of Commerce or the Idaho Company Outfitters and Guides Association.

Sawtooth National Recreation Area. *In Sawtooth National Forest. Phone 208/727-5000.* Fishing, boating, waterskiing; hiking, biking, camping (fee). Many lakes are here, including Stanley, Redfish, and Alturas. Contact Area Ranger, HC 64, Box 8291, Ketchum 83340. In recreation area are

Redfish Lake Visitor Center. *5 miles S on Hwy 75, then 2 miles SW. Phone 208/774-3376.* Historical, geological, naturalist displays and dioramas. Self-guided trails. Campfire programs, guided tours. (Memorial Day-Labor Day, daily) **FREE**

Sawtooth Wilderness. *8 miles N. Phone 208/727-5000.* Many lakes; wilderness hiking, backpacking, and mountain climbing.

Sawtooth Valley and Stanley Basin. *Phone 208/774-3411.* Fishing; cross-country skiing, snowmobiling, mountain biking, backpacking, hunting. Dude ranches featuring pack trips; big game guides. Contact Chamber of Commerce.

Special Events

Sawtooth Mountain Mamas Arts and Crafts Fair. *Phone 208/774-3411.* Third weekend in July.

Sawtooth Quilt Festival. *Community Building, Stanley. Phone 208/774-3411.* Third weekend in Sept.

Limited-Service Hotel

★ ★ **MOUNTAIN VILLAGE LODGE.** *Hwy 75 and 21, Stanley (83278). Phone 208/774-3661; fax 208/774-3761. www.mountainvillage.com.* 54 rooms, 2 story. Pets accepted; fee. Check-in 3 pm, check-out 11 am. Restaurant, bar. Airport transportation available. **$**
✈ 🐾

Specialty Lodging

The following lodging establishment is approved by Mobil Travel Guide, but due to its unique and individualized nature has not been given a traditional Mobil Star rating. Included in this listing you may find bed-and-breakfasts, limited-service inns, guest ranches, and other unique hotel properties.

IDAHO ROCKY MOUNTAIN RANCH. *HC 64, Box 9934, Stanley (83278). Phone 208/774-3544; fax 208/774-3477. www.idahorocky.com.* View of Sawtooth Mountains. 21 rooms. Complimentary full breakfast.

Check-in 3 pm, check-out 11 am. Restaurant. Outdoor pool. **$**

Sun Valley Area

See also Bellevue

Elevation 5,920 ft
Area Code 208
Information Sun Valley/Ketchum Chamber of Commerce, PO Box 2420, Sun Valley 83353; phone 208/726-3423 or toll-free 800/634-3347
Web site www.visitsunvalley.com

In a sun-drenched, bowl-shaped valley, this is one of the most famous resorts in the world. Developed by the Union Pacific Railroad, this area was established after an extensive survey of the West. Sheltered by surrounding ranges, it attracts both winter and summer visitors and offers nearly every imaginable recreational opportunity. Powder snow lasts until late spring, allowing long skiing seasons, and there is hunting, mountain biking, and superb fly fishing. Two Ranger District offices of the Sawtooth National Forest are located in Ketchum.

What to See and Do

Sawtooth National Recreation Area. *NW via Hwy 75, in Sawtooth National Forest. Phone 208/727-5000.* Fishing, boating, waterskiing; hiking, camping (fee). Many lakes are here, including Stanley, Redfish, and Alturas. Contact Area Ranger, HC 64, Box 8291, Ketchum 83340. In recreation area on Highway 75 is

Headquarters Visitor Information Center.
Hwy 75 and Chocolate Gulch, Sun Valley Area. Phone 208/727-5013. Orientation exhibits, maps, brochures, interpretive material. Evening programs (summer). Center (Daily; schedule may vary)
FREE

Sun Valley Resort. *1 Sun Valley Rd, Sun Valley (83353). Phone 208/622-4111. www.sunvalley.com* Sports director, supervised recreation for children; three outdoor pools (two glass-enclosed) lifeguard; sauna, massage, bowling, indoor and outdoor ice-skating, movies, dancing; Sun Valley Center for the Arts and Humanities. Special activities. Contact Sun Valley Resort.

Summer. Three outdoor pools, fishing, boating, whitewater river raft trips; tennis (school), 18-hole

Robert Trent Jones golf course (pro), Olympic ice show, skeet and trap shooting, lawn games, horseback riding (school), mountain biking, hiking, pack trips, hay rides. Auto trips may be arranged to Redfish Lake near Stanley.

Winter. Seventeen ski lifts to slopes for every level of skier; ski school, rentals. Longest run 3 miles; vertical drop 3,400 feet. Ice-skating, sleigh rides, and groomed cross-country trails. (Thanksgiving-Apr, daily)

Special Event

Wagon Days. *Phone 208/726-3423.* Celebration of the area's mining history; large, non-motorized parade, band concerts, entertainment, arts and crafts fair, dramas. Labor Day weekend.

Limited-Service Hotels

★ ★ **BEST WESTERN KENTWOOD LODGE.**
180 S Main St, Ketchum (83340). Phone 208/726-4114; toll-free 800/805-1001; fax 208/726-2417. www. bestwestern.com. 57 rooms, 3 story. Check-in 3 pm, check-out 11 am. Restaurant. Fitness room. Indoor pool, whirlpool. **$$**

★ **TAMARACK LODGE.** *291 Walnut Ave N, Ketchum (83340). Phone 208/726-3344; toll-free 800/ 521-5379; fax 208/726-3347. www.tamaracksunvalley .com.* 26 rooms, 3 story. Check-in 3 pm, check-out noon. Indoor pool, whirlpool. **$**

Full-Service Resort

★ ★ ★ **SUN VALLEY LODGE.** *1 Sun Valley Rd, Sun Valley (83353). Phone 208/622-2001; toll-free 800/786-8259; fax 208/622-2015. www. sunvalley.com.* Everyone from Ernest Hemingway to Clark Gable came to Sun Valley to rusticate in luxury, and the Sun Valley Lodge has been this resort town's shining star since 1936. The guest rooms and suites are decorated in a French country style with oak furnishings and cozy fabrics, and modern amenities make guests feel at home. A heated pool, fitness center, day spa and salon, bowling alley, and game room are among the many features at this property, while Sun Valley's legendary skiing and fishing lure visitors away from the sophisticated confines of the hotel. The Duchin Lounge's hot buttered rum hits the spot after a day on the slopes; Gretchen's (see) pleases with

Wandering the Sun-Drenched Sun Valley Area

Begin a tour of the resort towns of Ketchum and Sun Valley at the Ketchum-Sun Valley Heritage and Ski Museum, in Ketchum's Forest Service Park at 1st Street and Washington Avenue. The museum tells the story of the indigenous Tukudeka tribe, the early mining settlement, and the building of Sun River Resort. There is also information on past and present residents like Ernest Hemingway, Olympic athletes, and the Hollywood glitterati who come here to ski. Walk north along Washington Ave, passing coffee shops and gift boutiques, to the Sun Valley Center for the Arts and Humanities (191 5th St E), the hub of the valley's art world. The center presents exhibits, lectures, and films and is a great place to find out what's going on in Ketchum.

Walk one block east to Main Street. Downtown Ketchum has, for a city of its size, an enormous number of art galleries, restaurants, and high-end boutiques. It would be easy to spend a day wandering the small town center, looking at art, trying on sheepskin coats, and stopping for lattes. While you wander, be sure to stop at the Chapter One Bookstore (160 Main), which offers a good selection of regional titles. Charles Stuhlberg Furniture (571 East Ave N) is filled with the faux-rustic New West furniture and accessories popular with the area's upscale residents. For art galleries, go to the corner of Sun Valley Rd and Walnut Ave. The Walnut Avenue Mall (620 Sun Valley Rd) is a boutique development with four independent galleries. Directly across the street is the Colonnade Mill (601 Sun Valley Rd) with four more top-notch galleries.

Continue east on Sun Valley Rd, picking up the walking and biking trail north of the road. Follow

the trail one mile east through forest to the Sun Valley Resort, a massive complex with an imposing central lodge, condominium developments, home tracts, and golf courses. The lodge was built in 1936 by Averill Harriman, chairman of the Union Pacific Railroad, and was modeled after European ski resorts in Switzerland and Austria. Harriman hired an Austrian count to tour the western United States in search of a suitable locale; the count chose the little mining town of Ketchum for the resort.

Wander the interior of the vast lodge, looking at the photos of the celebrities who have skied here. In its heyday, Sun Valley hosted the likes of Lucille Ball, the Kennedys, Gary Cooper, and dozens of other stars of film and politics. Just west of the lodge, and easily glimpsed through the windows that look out onto the Bald Mountain ski area, is an outdoor skating rink. Kept frozen even in summer, the rink is usually a-spin with novice ice-skaters. On Saturday evenings, professional ice-skaters take to the ice to perform.

For a longer hike, return to Sun Valley Road and walking trail, and continue east up Trail Creek, past golf courses and meadows. In a mile, the valley narrows. Here, in a grove of cottonwoods overlooking the river, is the Hemingway Memorial, a simple stone bust that commemorates the author who died in Ketchum in 1961. Etched in the stone are the words Hemingway wrote at the death of a friend: "Best of all he loved the fall. The leaves yellow on the cottonwoods. Leaves floating on the trout streams. And above the hills the high blue windless skies . . . now he will be a part of them forever."

---

casual fare; and the Lounge Dining Room is a standout with its epicurean delights. 148 rooms, 4 story. Check-in 4 pm, check-out 11 am. Two restaurants, bar. Children's activity center. Fitness room. Outdoor pool, children's pool. Golf, 18 holes. Tennis. Ski in/ski out. Airport transportation available. **$$**

Full-Service Inn

★ ★ ★ **KNOB HILL INN.** *960 N Main St, Ketchum (83340). Phone 208/726-8010; toll-free 800/526-8010; fax 208/726-2712. www.knobhillinn.com.* This charming country-style inn draws skiers who flock to Sun Valley for its top-notch slopes, as well as summer vacationers who come here take advantage of the area's golf courses, hiking trails, and river rafting. Each guest room has a balcony, enabling guests to revel in the mountain views. You'll also find a dressing room and a separate tub and shower. The inn prides itself on serving a healthy breakfast using no artificial ingredients; coffee, tea, wine, and pastries are available at the Knob Hill Cafe in the afternoons. 26 rooms, 4 story. Check-in 3 pm, check-out noon. Fitness room. Indoor pool, whirlpool. **$$**

⊡ ⟨⟩ ⊠

Restaurants

★ ★ **CHANDLER'S RESTAURANT.** *200 S Main St, Ketchum (83340). Phone 208/726-1776. www.chandlersrestaurant.com.* American menu. Dinner. Closed Sun. Children's menu. Outdoor seating. **$$$**

★ ★ ★ **GRETCHEN'S.** *Sun Valley Rd, Sun Valley (83353). Phone 208/622-2144. www.sunvalley.com.* After a day on the slopes, guests can relax and unwind at this beautifully decorated restaurant. Serving a variety of specialty salads, pastas, seafood, and poultry, there is also a full bar and friendly staff. Continental menu. Breakfast, lunch, dinner, brunch. Bar. Children's menu. Valet parking. Outdoor seating. **$$$**

★ ★ **WARM SPRINGS RANCH RESTAURANT.** *1801 Warm Springs Rd, Ketchum (83340). Phone 208/726-2609; fax 208/726-4582.* American menu. Dinner. Bar. Children's menu. Valet parking. Outdoor seating. **$$$**

Twin Falls (F-3)

See also Buhl, Burley, Jerome, Shoshone

Founded 1904
Population 27,591
Elevation 3,745 ft
Area Code 208
Zip 83301
Information Chamber of Commerce, 858 Blue Lakes Blvd N; phone 208/733-3974 or toll-free 800/255-8946

After rising "like magic" on the tide of irrigation that reached this valley early in the century, Twin Falls has become the major city of south central Idaho's "Magic Valley" region. Seat of agriculturally rich Twin Falls County, it is also a tourist center, boasting that visitors in the area can enjoy almost every known sport.

The headquarters and a Ranger District office of the Sawtooth National Forest are located here.

What to See and Do

Fishing. In the Snake River and numerous other rivers and lakes. Sturgeon of up to 100 pounds may be caught, but by law cannot be removed from the water. The Twin Falls Chamber of Commerce can provide detailed information.

Herrett Center. *315 Falls Ave, Twin Falls (83301). On College of Southern Idaho campus. Phone 208/733-9554.* Exhibits on archaeology of North, Central, and South America; gallery of contemporary art; Faulkner Planetarium. (Tues-Sat; closed holidays)

Perrine Memorial Bridge. *1 1/2 miles N on Hwy 93. Phone 208/733-3974.* Bridge, 486 feet high and 1,500 feet long, crosses the Snake River canyon.

Sawtooth Twin Falls Ranger District. *2647 Kimberly Rd, Twin Falls (83301). 9 miles E on Hwy 30 to Hansen, then 28 miles S on local roads, in Sawtooth National Forest. Phone 208/737-3200.* Fishing; camping (fee at some designated campgrounds), picnicking, hiking trails, snowmobile trails, downhill and cross-country skiing.

⭐ **Shoshone Falls.** *5 miles NE, on Snake River.* "Niagara of the West" drops 212 feet (52 feet more than Niagara Falls). During irrigation season, the flow is limited; it is best during spring and fall. Access to the falls is available through

> **Shoshone Falls Park.** *136 Maxwell Ave, Twin Falls (83301). S bank of river. Phone 208/736-2265.* Picnic tables, stoves, fireplace, trails, waterskiing. (Mar-Nov, daily) **$$**

Twin Falls. *5 1/2 miles NE.* These 132-foot falls are accessible via

> **Twin Falls Park.** *3593 Twin Falls Grade, Twin Falls (83301). S bank of river. Phone 208/423-4223.* Boating (dock, ramp), fishing, waterskiing; picnic area. (Daily)

Special Events

Twin Falls County Fair and Magic Valley Stampede. *County Fairgrounds, 215 Fair Ave, Filer (83328). Phone 208/326-4396. 6 miles W via Hwy 30.* One week starting the Wed before Labor Day.

Western Days. *Phone toll-free 800/255-8946.* Three-day event featuring shoot-out, barbecue contests, dances, parade. Dates may vary, call for schedule; usually the weekend following Memorial Day.

Limited-Service Hotels

★ **AMERITEL INN TWIN FALLS.** *1377 Blue Lakes Blvd N, Twin Falls (83301). Phone 208/736-8000; toll-free 800/600-6001; fax 208/734-7777. www.ameritelinns .com.* 118 rooms, 3 story. Complimentary continental breakfast. Check-out 11 am. Fitness room. Indoor pool, whirlpool. Airport transportation available. **$**

★ ★ **RED LION HOTEL CANYON SPRINGS.** *1357 Blue Lakes Blvd N, Twin Falls (83301). Phone 208/734-5000; toll-free 800/733-5466; fax 208/734-3813. www.redlion.com.* 112 rooms, 2 story. Check-out 1 pm. Restaurant, bar. Fitness room. Pool. Airport transportation available. **$**

★ **SHILO INN.** *1586 Blue Lakes Blvd N, Twin Falls (83301). Phone 208/733-7545; toll-free 800/222-2244; fax 208/736-2019. www.shiloinns.com.* 128 rooms, 4 story. Pets accepted; fee. Complimentary continental breakfast. Check-out noon. Fitness room. Indoor pool, whirlpool. **$**

Restaurant

★ ★ **JAKER'S.** *1598 Blue Lakes Blvd, Twin Falls (83301). Phone 208/733-8400. www.jakers.com.* American menu. Lunch, dinner. Bar. Children's menu. Outdoor seating. **$$**

Wallace (B-2)

See also Coeur d'Alene, Kellogg

Founded 1884
Population 1,010
Elevation 2,744 ft
Area Code 208
Zip 83873
Information Chamber of Commerce, 10 River St, PO Box 1167; phone 208/753-7151

Gold was discovered in streams near here in 1882; lead, zinc, silver, and copper deposits were found in 1884. A Ranger District office of the Idaho Panhandle National Forests-Coeur d'Alene is located in nearby Silverton.

What to See and Do

Auto tour. A 15-mile drive through spectacular scenery in Idaho Panhandle National Forests—Coeur d'Alene and St. Joe. Local roads follow Nine Mile Creek, Dobson Pass, and Two Mile Creek to Osburn. This trip may be extended by traveling north and east out of Dobson Pass along Beaver and Trail creeks to Murray, then west to Prichard; then follow Coeur d'Alene River west and south to Kingston; return to Wallace on Highway 10, I-90.

Lookout Pass Ski Area. *73888 Lookout Pass Rd, Mullan.* 12 miles E on I-90, in Idaho Panhandle National Forests. *Phone 208/744-1301. www.skilookout .com.* Chairlift, rope tow; patrol, school, rentals; cafeteria; bar. Longest run 1 mile; vertical drop 850 feet. Half-day rate. (Mid-Nov-mid-Apr, Thurs-Sun) Cross-country skiing is also available. Snowmobiling. **$$$$**

Northern Pacific Depot Railroad Museum. *219 6th St, Wallace (83873). Phone 208/752-0111.* (1901) Houses artifacts, photographs, and memorabilia that portray railroad history of the Coeur d'Alene Mining District; display of railroad depot (circa 1910). (May-Oct, hours vary) **$**

Oasis Bordello Museum. *605 Cedar St, Wallace (83873). Phone 208/753-0801.* Former bordello (circa 1895); moonshine still. (May-Oct, daily) **$$**

Sierra Silver Mine Tour. *420 5th St, Wallace (83873). Phone 208/752-5151.* Offers 1 1/4-hour guided tour through actual silver mine. Demonstrations of mining methods, techniques, and operation of modern-day equipment. Departs every 30 minutes. (May-mid-Oct, daily) **$$$**

Wallace District Mining Museum. *509 Bank St, Wallace (83873). Phone 208/556-1592.* Material on the history of mining, 20-minute video, old mining machinery. Information on mine tours and old mining towns in the area. (May-Sept: daily; rest of year: Mon-Sat) **$**

Limited-Service Hotel

★ ★ **BEST WESTERN WALLACE INN.** *100 Front St, Wallace (83873). Phone 208/752-1252; toll-free 800/643-2386; fax 208/753-0981. www.bestwestern.com.* 63 rooms, 2 story. Pets accepted; fee. Check-out noon. Restaurant, bar. Fitness room. Indoor pool, whirlpool. **$**

⊠ ➦ ⌘ ⎙

Weiser (D-1)

See also Ontario, OR

Founded 1888
Population 4,571
Elevation 2,117 ft
Area Code 208
Zip 83672
Information Chamber of Commerce, 8 E Idaho St; phone 208/549-0452 or toll-free 800/437-1280

Located at the confluence of the Weiser and Snake rivers, the town of Weiser (WEE-zer) is both a center for tourism for Hells Canyon National Recreation Area to the north and a center for trade and transportation for the vast orchards, onion, wheat, and sugar beet fields of the fertile Weiser Valley to the east. Lumbering, mining, the manufacture of mobile homes, and the raising of cattle also contribute to the town's economy. A Ranger District office of the Payette National Forest is located in Weiser.

What to See and Do

Fiddlers' Hall of Fame. *10 E Idaho St, Weiser (83672). Phone 208/549-0452.* Mementos of past fiddle contests, pictures of champion fiddlers, state winners; collection of old-time fiddles; state scrapbook on view. (Mon-Fri; also weekend during Fiddlers' Contest; closed holidays)

Hells Canyon National Recreation Area. *Stretching N for 100 miles; access approximately 55 miles NW via Hwy 95 to Cambridge, then via Hwy 71.* Spanning the Idaho/Oregon border, this canyon, the deepest in North America, was created by the Snake River, which rushes nearly 8,000 feet below Seven Devils rim on the Idaho side. Three dams built by the Idaho Power Company have opened up areas that were once inaccessible and created man-made lakes that provide boating, fishing, and water-skiing. Whitewater rafting and jet boat tours are available below the dams, on the Snake River. Also here are

Brownlee Dam. The southernmost dam of the three, at end of Hwy 71. This 395-foot rockfill dam creates Brownlee Lake, 57 1/2 miles long, reaching to 10 miles north of Weiser. Woodhead Park, a short distance south, and McCormick Park, a short distance north, provide picnicking, boat ramps; tent and trailer sites, showers. **$$$**

Hells Canyon Dam. *23 miles N of Oxbow Dam.* This structure (330 feet high) creates a water recreation area. The improved Deep Creek trail, Idaho side, provides angler and other recreational access to the Snake River below Hells Canyon Dam.

Oxbow Dam. *12 1/2 miles N of Brownlee Dam.* This 205-foot-high barrier makes a 12 1/2-mile-long reservoir. Copperfield Park, just below the dam on the Oregon side, has trailer and tent spaces, showers, and day-use picnicking; 9 miles north of dam on the Idaho side is Hell's Canyon Park, offering boat ramp; tent and trailer sites, showers, picnicking. **$$$**

Snake River Heritage Center. *2295 Paddock Ave, Weiser (83672). In Hooker Hall. Phone 208/549-0205.* Artifacts and memorabilia portray the history of Snake River Valley. (By appointment only) **$**

Trips into Hells Canyon. Several companies offer river rafting, jet boat, and pack trips into and around Hells Canyon National Recreation Area. For information on additional outfitters, contact the Chamber of Commerce.

Hells Canyon Adventures. *Phone 503/785-3352; toll-free 800/422-3568. www.hellscanyonadventures .com.* Jet boat and whitewater rafting trips down the Snake River. For more information, contact PO Box 159, Oxbow, OR 97840.

Hughes River Expeditions. *95 First St, Cambridge (83610). 26 miles N on Hwy 95. Phone 208/257-3477.* Outfitters for whitewater and fishing trips on backcountry rivers of Idaho and eastern Oregon, including three-, four-, and five-day trips on the Snake River through Hell's Canyon. (May-Oct, several dates) Advance reservations required. **$$$$**

Special Event

National Oldtime Fiddlers' Contest. *Phone toll-free 800/437-1280.* One of the oldest such contests in the country, attracting some of the nation's finest fiddlers. Also parade, barbecue, arts and crafts. Mon-Sat, third full week in June.

Side Trips

When wandering around the Boise area, be sure to schedule a few days to take in some amazing sites in Wyoming and Utah. One of America's most awe-inspiring national parks is located in Wyoming—Grand Teton—and it is just a day's drive from Boise. Similarly, Salt Lake City, where you can hear the world-famous Mormon Tabernacle Choir or swoosh down some slopes, is just a day away from Boise. If you are in the mood for a little bit of country flavor, Jackson, Wyoming, will satisfy that craving.

Salt Lake City, UT

5 1/2 hours, 340 miles from Boise, ID

Founded 1847
Population 181,743
Elevation 4,330 ft
Area Code 801
Information Convention & Visitors Bureau, 90 S West Temple, 84101-1406; 801/521-2822 or 801/534-4927
Web site www.saltlake.org

On a hill at the north end of State Street stands Utah's classic capitol building. Three blocks south is Temple Square, with the famed Mormon Temple and Tabernacle. The adjacent block houses the headquarters of the Church of Jesus Christ of Latter-day Saints, whose members are often called Mormons. Salt Lake City, with its 10-acre blocks, 132-foot-wide, tree-lined streets, and mountains rising to the east and west, is one of the most beautifully planned cities in the country.

Once a desert wilderness, Salt Lake City was built by Mormon settlers who sought refuge from religious persecution. Neither the barrenness of the land, drought, nor a plague of crickets swayed these people from their purpose. Followers of Brigham Young arrived and named their new territory "Deseret." In these early days, the Mormons began a variety of experiments in farming, industry, and society, many of which were highly successful. Today, Salt Lake City is an industrious, businesslike city, a center for electronics, steel, missiles, and a hundred other enterprises.

West of the city is the enormous Great Salt Lake, stretching 48 miles one way and 90 miles the other. It is less than 35 feet deep and between 15 and 20 percent salt—almost five times as salty as the ocean. Humans bob like corks and cannot sink in the water. The lake is what remains of ancient Lake Bonneville, once 145 miles wide, 350 miles long, and 1,000 feet deep. As Lake Bonneville water evaporated over thousands of years, a large expanse of perfectly flat, solid salt was left. Today, the Bonneville Salt Flats stretch west almost to Nevada.

Salt Lake City was laid out in grid fashion, with Temple Square at the center. Most street names are coordinates on this grid: 4th South Street is four blocks south of Temple Square, 7th East is seven blocks east. These are written as 400 South and 700 East.

Headquarters and a Ranger District office of the Wasatch-Cache National Forest are located in Salt Lake City.

Additional Visitor Information

For additional information contact the Salt Lake Convention & Visitors Bureau, 90 S West Temple, 84101-1406; phone 801/521-2822; or the Utah Travel Council and Visitor Information Center, Council Hall, 300 N State St, 84114; phone 801/538-1030.

Public Transportation

Buses (Utah Transit Authority), phone 801/287-4636.

What to See and Do

Alta. *26 miles SE on Hwy 210 in Little Cottonwood Canyon (see). Phone 801/742-3333.*

Arrow Press Square. *165 S West Temple St, Salt Lake City (84101). Phone 801/531-9700.* Once the city's printing district, now buildings such as Arrow Press

Salt Lake City's Mormon Heritage

The centerpiece of downtown Salt Lake City is Temple Square, the city block bordered by three streets named Temple—West, North, and South—and Main Street on the east side. Utah's top tourist attraction, Temple Square, is the hub for the Church of Jesus Christ of the Latter-Day Saints, where guests are invited to join a free guided tour that offers a glimpse of several architectural and cultural landmarks, including the Mormon Tabernacle, the Museum of Church History and Art, and the Joseph Smith Memorial Building. (Tours start at the flagpole every few minutes.) If your timing is right, you can also take in a film, choir rehearsal, or organ recital here. From Temple Square, head east on South Temple to a pair of historic homes, the Lion House (63 East South Temple) and the Beehive House (67 East South Temple). No tours are available of the Lion House, which served as Brigham Young's abode during the mid-19th century, but there is a restaurant on the lower level that is a good spot for a lunch break. Next door, the Beehive House, another former Young residence and a National Historic Landmark, offers free tours every day. Just east of these houses on South Temple is Eagle Gate (at the intersection of State Street), an impressive arch capped by a two-ton sculpture of an eagle with a 20-foot wingspan. Just south of Eagle Gate on the east side of State Street are two of Salt Lake City's standout cultural facilities, the Hansen

Planetarium (15 South State Street) and the Social Hall Heritage Museum (39 South State Street). The former features daily star shows and a free space museum with hands-on exhibits; the latter includes remnants of Utah's first public building and the West's first theater. From the museum, it's best to reverse course and walk north on State Street, passing under Eagle Gate. Just beyond North Temple, hop on the paths that run through the lush City Creek Park for a break from the urban bustle and head north to the adjoining Memory Grove Park. From here, it's only a two-block walk west to the Utah State Capitol (just north of the intersection of State Street and 300 North Street), an exemplary Renaissance Revival-style structure built from Utah granite in 1915. The building is open to the public daily and guided tours are offered on weekdays. Two blocks west of the State Capitol is the Pioneer Memorial Museum (300 North Main Street), a majestic replica of the original Salt Lake Theater (demolished in 1928) with 38 rooms of relics from the area's past, including photographs, vehicles, dolls, and weapons. The museum is on the eastern edge of one of the city's oldest neighborhoods, the tree-lined Marmalade District (between 300 and 500 North streets to the north and south and Center and Quince streets to the east and west), a good place to meander and gaze at historic homes.

Building (1890), Upland Hotel (1910), and Midwest Office Building Supply (1910) have been reconstructed into a retail/restaurant complex.

Brigham Young Monument. *At N side of intersection of Main and South Temple sts. Phone 801/531-9700.* (1897) This statue, first seen at the Chicago's World's Fair in 1893, honors the church leader.

Brighton Resort. *12601 E Big Cottonwood, Big Cottonwood Canyon (84121). 25 miles SE via I-215, exit 6 in Big Cottonwood Canyon. Phone 801/532-4731. www.skibrighton.com.* Three high-speed quad, one triple, three double chairlifts; patrol, school, rentals;

lodge, restaurant, cafeteria. Sixty-four runs; longest run 3 miles, vertical drop 1,745 feet. (Mid-Nov-late-Apr, daily) Night skiing (Mon-Sat). Half-day rates. **$$$$**

The Canyons. *4000 The Canyons Resort Dr, Park City (84098). 28 miles E and S via I-80, Hwy 224 in Park City (see). Phone 435/649-5400. www.thecanyons.com.*

Clark Planetarium. *110 S 400 W, Salt Lake City (84101). Phone 801/538-2104. www.hansenplanetarium.net.* Space science museum and library. Seasonal star shows, stage plays (fee; schedule varies). (Daily at 11 am; closed Thanksgiving, Dec 25) **$$**

Council Hall. *300 N State St, Salt Lake City (84114). S of Capitol Hill. Phone 801/538-1900.* (1864-1866) Council Hall was once the meeting place of territorial legislature and city hall for 30 years. It was dismantled and then reconstructed in 1963 at its present location; Federal/Greek Revival-style architecture. Visitor information center and office; memorabilia. (Daily; closed Jan 1, Thanksgiving, Dec 25) **FREE**

Deer Valley Resort. *2250 Deer Valley Dr S, Park City (84060). 34 miles E and S via I-80, Hwy 224. Phone 435/649-1000; toll-free 800/424-3337. www.deervalley.com.*

Fort Douglas Military Museum. *32 Potter St, Salt Lake City (84113). 3 miles NE, Building 32. Phone 801/581-1251. www.fortdouglas.org.* Army museum features history of military in Utah from arrival of Johnston's Army during the 1857 "Utah War" through Vietnam. Also tours of fort (self-guided or guided, by appointment). (Tues-Sat noon-4 pm; closed Jan, holidays) **FREE**

Governor's Mansion. *603 E S Temple St, Salt Lake City (84102). Phone 801/538-1005.* (1902) Restored mansion of Thomas Kearns, wealthy Utah senator of early 1900s; decorated with Italian marble. Tours. (Apr-mid-Dec, Tues and Thurs 2-4 pm; closed holidays) **FREE**

Hogle Zoological Garden. *2600 E Sunnyside Ave, Salt Lake City (84108). Phone 801/582-1631.* Wildlife exhibits; Discovery Land; bird show; miniature train (summer). Picnicking, concession. (Daily; closed Jan 1, Dec 25) **$$$**

InnsBrook Tours. *3359 S Main St, Suite 804, Salt Lake City (84115). Phone 801/534-1001; toll-free 877/210-5637. www.saltlakecitytours.org.* This is the best way to see all the famous sites in Salt Lake City. Pick-up begins at 9:15 am, and then you're off to see landmarks like the Mormon Tabernacle, the Salt Lake Temple, and the Olympic Stadium and Village. (Daily) **$$$$**

Kennecott Bingham Canyon Mine. *Hwy 48 (7200 S), Magna. 25 miles SW of Salt Lake City. Phone 801/569-6248.* Open-pit copper mine 2 1/2 miles wide and 1/2 mile deep. Visitor center, observation deck, and audio presentation explain mining operations, which date from 1906. Gift shop.(Apr-mid-Oct, daily) **$**

Lagoon Amusement Park, Pioneer Village and Water Park. *PO Box 696, Salt Lake City (84025). 17 miles N on I-15, exit 325, then N to Lagoon Dr. Phone toll-free 800/748-5246. www.lagoonpark.com.* Rides, water slides; re-creation of 19th-century Utah town; stagecoach and steam-engine train rides. Camping, picnicking. (Memorial Day-Aug: daily; mid-Apr-late May and Sept: Sat-Sun only) **$$$$**

Liberty Park. *1300 South St, Salt Lake City (84105). Between 500 and 700 E and 900 and 1300 S. Phone 801/972-7800 (park).* In 100-acre park are Chase Mill (1852), Tracy Aviary, children's garden playground (Apr-Sept), amusement park. Swimming; lighted tennis, horseshoe courts, picnicking. Park (daily 6 am-11 pm). Aviary (daily 9 am-6 pm; Nov-Mar: daily 9 am-4:30 pm). **FREE**

Lion House. *67 E South Temple, Salt Lake City (84111). South Temple and State St. Phone 801/363-5466 (Lion House).* Lion House(1856) and Beehive House. (1854), family residences, offices, and social centers for Brigham Young and his wives and children. Guided tours of Beehive House. (Mon-Sat 9 am-6 pm; closed Jan 1, Thanksgiving, Dec 25) **FREE**

Maurice Abravanel Concert Hall. *123 W South Temple, Salt Lake City (84101). Phone 801/533-6683.* The home of the Utah Symphony, this building is adorned with more than 12,000 square feet of 24-karat gold leaf and a mile of brass railing. It has been rated one of the best halls in the US, acoustically. Free tours (by appointment). The symphony has performances most weekends.

Park City Mountain Resort. *1310 Lowell Ave, Park City (84060). 32 miles E and S via I-80, Hwy 224. Phone 435/649-8111; toll-free 800/222-7275. www.pcski.com.*

Pioneer Memorial Museum. *300 N Main St, Salt Lake City (84103). W side of capitol grounds. Phone 801/538-1050.* Manuscripts, pioneer relics. Also here is Carriage House, with exhibits relating to transportation, including Brigham Young's wagon, mule-drawn vehicles, Pony Express items. One-hour guided tours (by appointment). (Mon-Sat 9 am-5 pm; June-Aug: Mon-Sat 9 am-5 pm, Sun 1-5 pm; closed holidays) **FREE**

River trips. *Moki Mac River Expeditions, 6006 S 1300 E, Salt Lake City (84121). Phone 801/268-6667; toll-free 800/284-7280. www.mokimac.com.* Offers 1-14-day whitewater and canoeing trips on the Green and Colorado rivers. **$$$$**

Salt Lake Art Center. *20 S West Temple, Salt Lake City (84101). In the Salt Palace complex. Phone 801/328-4201.* Changing exhibits featuring photographs, paintings, ceramics, and sculptures; school; lectures, seminars, films. (Tues-Thurs, Sat 10 am-5 pm, Fri 10 am-9 pm; closed holidays) **FREE**

Sightseeing USA. *553 W and 100 S sts, Salt Lake City (84101). Phone 801/521-7060.*

Snowbird. *Little Cottonwood Canyon, Hwy 210, Snowbird (84092). 25 miles E and S via I-215, Hwy 210 in Little Cottonwood Canyon. Phone 801/742-2222 (resort information). www.snowbird.com.*

Solitude Resort. *12000 Big Cottonwood Canyon, Salt Lake City (84121). SE via I-215. Phone 801/534-1400. www.skisolitude.com.* Detachable quad, two triple, four double chairlifts; race course, patrol, school, rentals; day lodge, cafeteria, restaurants, bar. Longest run 3 1/2 miles, vertical drop 2,047 feet. (Nov-Apr, daily) Cross-country center. **$$$$**

State Capitol. *350 N Main St, Salt Lake City (84103). Phone 801/538-1563; toll-free 800/200-1160. www.utah .com/culture/capitol.htm.* (1914) Constructed of Utah granite and Georgia marble, with a modern annex, the capitol has a commanding view of the valley and Wasatch Mountains. The Gold Room is decorated with bird's-eye marble and gold from Utah mines. The ground floor has exhibits. Guided tours every 30 minutes (Mon-Fri 9 am-4 pm). Building (Sept-May: daily 6 am-6 pm; June-Aug: daily 6 am-8 pm). **FREE**

⭐ **Temple Square.** *Main and N,S, and W Temple sts, Salt Lake City (84101). Phone 801/240-1245; toll-free 800/537-9703.* Visitor centers provide information, exhibits and guided tours (1/2- to 1-hour; daily, every 10 minutes). (Daily 9 am-9 pm) **FREE** Tour includes

Assembly Hall. *SW corner of Temple Square. Phone 801/521-2822.* (1880) Tours (daily), concerts (Fri, Sat evenings).

Family History Library. *35 N West Temple, Salt Lake City (84150). Phone 801/240-2331.* Largest genealogy library in the world aids in compilation of family histories. (Mon 7:30 am-5 pm, Tues-Sat 7:30 am-10 pm) **FREE**

Museum of Church History and Art. *45 N West Temple St, Salt Lake City (84150). Phone 801/240-3310.* Exhibits of Latter-Day Saints church history from 1820 to present. (Mon-Fri 9 am-9 pm, Sat-Sun 10 am-7 pm; closed holidays) **FREE**

Seagull Monument. *Phone 801/521-2822.* (1913) The monument commemorates the seagulls that saved the crops from crickets in 1848.

Tabernacle. *Phone 801/240-2534.* (1867) The self-supporting roof, an elongated dome, is 250 feet long and 150 feet wide. The tabernacle organ has 11,623 pipes, ranging from 5/8 inch to 32 feet in length. The world-famous Tabernacle Choir may be heard at rehearsal (Thurs 8 pm) or at broadcast time (Sun 9:30 am, be seated by 9:15 am). Organ recitals (Mon-Sat noon, Sun afternoon). **FREE**

Temple. *Phone 801/240-2534.* (1893) Used for sacred ordinances, such as baptisms and marriages. Closed to non-Mormons.

This Is the Place Heritage Park. *2601 Sunnyside Ave (800 S), Salt Lake City (84108). Phone 801/584-8392. www.thisistheplace.org.* Day-use museum park at mouth of Emigration Canyon, where Mormon pioneers first entered the valley. In the park are This Is the Place Monument (1947), commemorating Brigham Young's words upon first seeing the Salt Lake City site; a visitor center with an audio presentation and murals of the Mormon migration; and the Old Deseret Pioneer Village, a living museum that depicts the 1847-1869 era and pioneer life. Admission to the monument and visitor's center is free. (Monument and grounds (daily, dawn-dusk). Visitor center (Mon-Sat 9 am-6 pm). Village (late May-early Sept: Mon-Sat 10 am-6 pm)) **$$**

Trolley Square. *600 S 700 East St, Salt Lake City (84102). Bounded by 500 and 600 S sts and 600 and 700 E sts. Phone 801/521-9877.* This 10-acre complex of trolley barns has been converted into an entertainment/shopping/dining center. (Daily)

University of Utah. *200 South St, Salt Lake City (84101). 2 1/2 miles E, at head of 200 S St. Phone 801/581-6515. www.utah.edu.* (1850) (25,900 students) On campus are

J. Willard Marriott Library. *University of Utah, 295 S 1500 E, Salt Lake City (84112). Phone 801/581-8558. www.lib.utah.edu.* Western Americana collection, rare books, manuscripts. (Mon-Thurs 7 am-midnight, Fri 7 am-8 pm, Sat 9 am-8 pm,

Sun 11 am-midnight; closed holidays, also July 24) **FREE**

Pioneer Theatre Company. *300 S and 1400 E sts, Salt Lake City (84112). Phone 801/581-6270. www. pioneertheatre.org.* Two auditoriums; dramas, musicals, comedies. (Sept-May; closed holidays) **$$$$**

Red Butte Garden and Arboretum. *300 Wakara Way, Salt Lake City (84108). Phone 801/581-4747. www.redbuttegarden.org.* More than 9,000 trees on 150 acres, representing 350 species; conservatory. Self-guided tours. Special events in summer. (Apr: daily 9 am-5 pm; May-Sept: Mon-Sat 9 am-8 pm, Sun 9 am-5 pm; Oct: daily 9 am-5 pm; Nov-Mar: Tues-Sun 10 am-5 pm; closed Dec 25) **$**

Utah Museum of Fine Arts. *University of Utah, 410 Campus Center Dr, Salt Lake City (84112). Art & Architecture Center, S of library. Phone 801/581-7332. www.umfa.utah.edu.* Representations of artistic styles from Egyptian antiquities to contemporary American paintings; 19th-century French and American paintings, furniture. (Mon-Fri 10 am-5 pm, Sat-Sun noon-5 pm; closed holidays) **FREE**

Utah Museum of Natural History. *University of Utah, 1390 E Presidents Cir, Salt Lake City (84112). Phone 801/581-6927. www.umnh.utah.edu.* Halls of anthropology, biology, mineralology, paleontology, geology; traveling exhibits. (Mon-Sat 9:30 am-5:30 pm, Sun noon-5 pm; closed holidays, also July 24) **$$**

Utah Fun Dome. *4998 S 360 W, Murray (84123). Located 20 minutes S of Salt Lake City. S on I-15, 53rd St S exit, W to 700 West, then N. Phone 801/265-3866. www.fundome.com.* Enclosed mall with entertainment, rides, bowling, roller skating, baseball, arcades, miniature golf; cafés. Fee for activities. (Mon-Sat) **$**

Utah Jazz (NBA). *Delta Center, 301 W South Temple, Salt Lake City (84101). Professional basketball. Phone 801/355-3865. www.nba.com/jazz.*

Utah Opera Company. *Capitol Theatre, 50 W 200 South St, Salt Lake City (84101). Phone 801/533-5626. www.utahopera.org.* Grand opera. (Oct-May)

Utah Starzz (WNBA). *Delta Center, 301 W South Temple, Salt Lake City (84101). Women's professional basketball team. Phone 801/355-3865. www.utah .com/sports/starzz.htm.*

Wasatch-Cache National Forest. *82306 Federal Building, 125 S State St, Salt Lake City (84138). E via I-80; or N via Hwy 89; Lone Peak Wilderness Area, 20 miles SE. Phone 801/524-3900. www.fs.fed.us/r4/wcnf.* High Uintas Wilderness Area has alpine lakes and rugged peaks; Big Cottonwood, Little Cottonwood, and Logan canyons. Forest (1 million acres) has fishing, boating, deer and elk hunting, winter sports, and camping (fees). **FREE**

Wheeler Historic Farm. *6351 S 900 E St, Salt Lake City (84121). 15 miles SE on I-15, exit I-215. Phone 801/264-2241. www.wheelerfarm.com.* Living history farm (75 acres) depicts rural life from 1890 to 1918. Farmhouse, farm buildings; animals, crops; hay rides (fee). Tour (fee). Visitors can feed animals, gather eggs, milk cows. There is a small fee for various activities and events. (Daily from dusk to dawn; no rides Sun) **FREE**

ZCMI (Zion's Co-operative Mercantile Institution) Center. *Main and South Temple, Salt Lake City (84101). Phone 801/321-8745.* Department store established in 1868 by Brigham Young anchors this 85-store, enclosed, downtown shopping mall. (Mon-Sat) **FREE**

Special Events

Days of '47 Celebration. *300 N Main St, Salt Lake City (84103).* Mid-July.

Utah Arts Festival. *Library Square, 400 S 200 E, Salt Lake City (84101). Phone 801/322-2428. www.uaf.org.* More than 1,000 participants, 90 performing groups; Children's Art Yard, juried show with demonstrations. Ethnic food. Last week in June.

Utah State Fair. *Utah State Fairpark, 155 N 1000 W, Salt Lake City (84116). Phone 801/538-8400. www. utah-state-fair.com.* Mid-Sept.

Limited-Service Hotels

★ ★ **COMFORT INN.** *200 N Admiral Byrd Rd, Salt Lake City (84116). Phone 801/746-5200; toll-free 800/535-8742; fax 801/532-4721. www. slccomfortinn.com.* 155 rooms, 4 story. Pets accepted; fee. Complimentary continental breakfast. Check-in 3 pm, check-out 11 am. Restaurant, bar. Fitness room. Outdoor pool, whirlpool. Airport transportation available. **$**

★ **DAYS INN.** *1900 W North Temple, Salt Lake City (84116). Phone 801/539-8538; fax 801/595-1041. www.daysinn.com.* 110 rooms, 2 story. Pets accepted, some restrictions. Complimentary continental breakfast. Check-out 11 am. Fitness room. Indoor pool. Airport transportation available. **$**

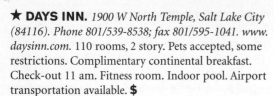

★ ★ **EMBASSY SUITES.** *110 W 600 S, Salt Lake City (84101). Phone 801/359-7800; toll-free 800/325-7643; fax 801/359-3753. www.embassysuites.com.* Located in the heart of Salt Lake City, this downtown hotel offers guests spacious rooms, a relaxing atmosphere, and friendly service. Nearby attractions include the LDS Mormon Temple, Salt Lake City Convention Center, and guests are just 1/2 mile to the historic Trolley Square Plaza. 241 rooms, 9 story, all suites. Complimentary full breakfast. Check-in 3 pm, check-out noon. Restaurant, bar. Fitness room. Indoor pool, whirlpool. Airport transportation available. **$**

★ ★ **HILTON SALT LAKE CITY AIRPORT.** *5151 Wiley Post Way, Salt Lake City (84116). Phone 801/539-1515; toll-free 800/999-3736; fax 801/539-1113. www.hilton.com.* With views of the Wasatch and Oquirrh Mountains, this hotel is minutes from the airport. Amenities include an outdoor swimming pool and whirlpool. Other activities are paddle boats, a putting green, jogging path, fitness center and indoor pool. Grill 114 is a full-service restaurant with seating outside and great panoramas. 188 rooms, 5 story. Pets accepted; fee. Check-in 3 pm, check-out noon. Restaurant, bar. Fitness room. Indoor pool, outdoor pool, whirlpool. Airport transportation available. Business center. **$**

★ ★ **HOLIDAY INN.** *999 S Main St, Salt Lake City (84111). Phone 801/359-8600; toll-free 800/933-9678; fax 801/359-7186. www.saltlakeholidayinn.com.* 292 rooms, 3 story. Pets accepted. Check-in 3 pm, check-out noon. Restaurant, bar. Fitness room. Indoor pool, whirlpool. Tennis. Airport transportation available. Business center. **$**

★ ★ **INN AT TEMPLE SQUARE.** *71 W S Temple, Salt Lake City (84101). Phone 801/531-1000; toll-free 800/843-4668; fax 801/536-7272. www.theinn.com.* Nestled in the heart of downtown Salt Lake City and just blocks from the Symphony Hall and Temple Square, this Edwardian landmark offers guests a truly unique stay. From the warm and personal service to the elegant guest rooms, this hotel offers style and personal service that immediately welcomes guests and relaxes them. 90 rooms, 7 story. Complimentary full breakfast. Check-in 3 pm, check-out noon. Restaurant. Airport transportation available. **$**

★ ★ **PEERY HOTEL.** *110 W 300 S, Salt Lake City (84101). Phone 801/521-4300; toll-free 800/331-0073; fax 801/364-3295. www.peeryhotel.com.* Historic building (1910). 73 rooms, 3 story. Check-in 3 pm, check-out noon. Restaurant, bar. Fitness room. Airport transportation available. **$**

★ ★ **WYNDHAM SALT LAKE CITY HOTEL.** *215 W S Temple, Salt Lake City (84101). Phone 801/531-7500; toll-free 800/553-0075; fax 801/328-1289. www.wyndham.com.* Adjacent to Delta Center. 381 rooms, 15 story. Check-out noon. Restaurant, bar. Fitness room. Indoor pool, whirlpool. Airport transportation available. Business center. **$**

Full-Service Hotels

★ ★ ★ ★ **THE GRAND AMERICA HOTEL.** *555 S Main St, Salt Lake City (84111). Phone 801/258-6000; toll-free 800/453-9450; fax 801/258-6911. www.grandamerica.com.* Set against the beautiful backdrop of the Wasatch Mountains, The Grand America is a tribute to the glory of old-world Europe. This esteemed hotel is the pinnacle of refinement. The details make the difference here, from intuitive service to extraordinary amenities. The guest rooms are classically French, with plush carpets, resplendent fabrics, fine art, and Richelieu furniture. Private balconies draw guests' attention to the splendid mountain views. Several dining establishments tantalize tastebuds in a variety of atmospheric settings. Afternoon tea, with its delicate sandwiches and flaky pastries, is particularly notable here, and the seasonally-inspired cuisine of the Garden Café is matched by its lovely outdoor venue. The hotel's convenient location is perfect for exploring Utah's famous great outdoors, yet the two pools, spa, salon, and fine shopping persuade many to remain within this temple of luxury.

775 rooms, 24 story. Check-in 3 pm, check-out noon. Restaurant, bar. Fitness room, spa. Indoor pool, outdoor pool, whirlpool. Business center. **$$$**

★ ★ ★ **HILTON SALT LAKE CITY CENTER.** *255 S W Temple, Salt Lake City (84101). Phone 801/ 328-2000; fax 801/532-1953. www.hilton.com.* Located in the heart of downtown, guests can enjoy all the comforts of home with spacious rooms and friendly service. 499 rooms, 18 story. Pets accepted, some restrictions; fee. Check-in 3 pm, check-out noon. Restaurant, bar. Fitness room, spa. Indoor pool, whirlpool. Airport transportation available. Business center. **$$**

★ ★ ★ **HOTEL MONACO SALT LAKE CITY.** *15 W 200 S, Salt Lake City (84101). Phone 801/595-0000; toll-free 877/294-9710; fax 801/990-9754. www. monaco-saltlakecity.com.* The Hotel Monaco stands out for its haute décor and personalized services. Located in the heart of downtown Salt Lake City, this boutique hotel makes a smashing first impression with its dazzling décor. At once classic and irreverent, the rooms and suites blend a panoply of colors and designs. Creature comforts abound, from beds piled high with luxurious sheets to high-speed technology for business travelers. Pets are more than welcome to share in the high style at this hotel, and those guests who left their furry friends behind may request a goldfish to join them in their rooms. Bambara's design and menu reflect the contemporary panache of the hotel, delighting diners with flavorful and creative concoctions. 225 rooms, 15 story. Pets accepted, some restrictions. Check-in 3 pm, check-out noon. Restaurant, bar. Fitness room. Tennis. **$$**

★ ★ ★ **LITTLE AMERICA HOTEL.** *500 S Main St, Salt Lake City (84101). Phone 801/363-6781; toll-free 800/453-9450; fax 801/596-5911. www. littleamerica.com.* This hotel provides every possible amenity, along with elegant and spacious rooms. 850 rooms, 17 story. Check-in 3 pm, check-out noon. Restaurant, bar. Fitness room. Indoor pool, outdoor pool, children's pool, whirlpool. Airport transportation available. **$$**

★ ★ ★ **MARRIOTT SALT LAKE CITY DOWNTOWN.** *75 S West Temple, Salt Lake City (84101). Phone 801/531-0800; fax 801/532-4127. www. marriott.com.* Located across from the Salt Palace Convention Center, this hotel caters to the business traveler and is close to the airport and major ski resorts. 515 rooms, 15 story. Check-in 3 pm, check-out noon. Restaurant, bar. Fitness room. Indoor pool, whirlpool. Airport transportation available. Business center. **$$**

★ ★ ★ **MARRIOTT SALT LAKE CITY-CITY CENTER.** *220 S State St, Salt Lake City (84111). Phone 801/961-8700; toll-free 866/961-8700; fax 801/ 961-8704. www.marriott.com.* 359 rooms, 12 story. Check-in 3 pm, check-out noon. Restaurant, bar. Fitness room. Indoor pool, whirlpool. Business center. **$$**

Full-Service Inns

★ ★ ★ **ARMSTRONG MANSION.** *667 E 100 S, Salt Lake City (84102). Phone 801/531-1333; toll-free 800/708-1333; fax 801/531-0282. www. armstrongmansion.com.* This bed-and-breakfast, built in 1893, is tastefully decorated with antiques and carved wood, creating a relaxing setting for guests. 13 rooms, 3 story. Complimentary full breakfast. Check-in 3 pm, check-out 11 am. **$$**

★ ★ ★ **BRIGHAM STREET INN.** *1135 E S Temple St, Salt Lake City (84102). Phone 801/364-4461; fax 801/521-3201. www.brightonstreetinn.citysearch .com.* This appealing bed-and-breakfast is located just blocks from the scenic area of downtown Salt Lake City. This remarkable inn offers guests a relaxing stay amidst elegant surroundings. 9 rooms, 3 story. Complimentary continental breakfast. Check-in 3 pm, check-out 11 am. **$**

★ ★ ★ **LA EUROPA ROYALE.** *1135 Vine, Salt Lake City (84121). Phone 801/263-7999; toll-free 800/523-8767; fax 801/263-8090. www.laeuropa.com.* Tucked away in a residential area, the large floor-to-ceiling windows in the public areas overlook the lovely landscaped grounds punctuated with fountains and small ponds. 9 rooms, 2 story. Complimentary full breakfast. Check-in 2 pm, check-out 11:30 am. Restaurant, bar. Fitness room. Airport transportation available. Business center. **$$**

Restaurants

★ ★ **ABSOLUTE.** *52 W 200 S, Salt Lake City (84101). Phone 801/359-0899; fax 801/359-0559.* American menu. Lunch, dinner. Closed Sun. Bar. Children's menu. Casual attire. Outdoor seating. **$$$**

★ **ARGENTINE GRILL.** *6055 S 900 E, Salt Lake City (84121). Phone 801/265-0205; fax 801/265-0760. www.argentinegrill.citysearch.com.* Latin American menu. Lunch, dinner. Outdoor seating. **$$**

★ ★ **BABA AFGHAN.** *55 E 400 S, Salt Lake City (84111). Phone 801/596-0786.* Middle Eastern menu. Lunch, dinner. Closed Sun; holidays. Casual attire. **$**

★ ★ **BACI TRATTORIA.** *134 W Pierpont Ave, Salt Lake City (84101). Phone 801/328-1500; fax 801/539-8783. www.gastronomyinc.com.* Large stained-glass partitions. Italian menu. Lunch, dinner. Closed Sun; holidays. Bar. Children's menu. Casual attire. Outdoor seating. **$$**

★ ★ **BAMBARA.** *202 S Main St, Salt Lake City (84101). Phone 801/363-5454; fax 801/363-5888. www. kimptongroup.com.* American menu. Breakfast, lunch, dinner. Bar. Children's menu. Casual attire. **$$$**

★ ★ **CREEKSIDE AT SOLITUDE.** *12000 Big Cottonwood Canyon, Solitude (84121). Phone 435/649-8400; fax 435/649-5276. www.skisolitude.com.* Overlooks a pond and the ski slopes. American menu. Dinner, brunch. Closed May, late Sept-mid-Nov. Bar. Casual attire. Outdoor seating. **$$**

★ ★ ★ **FRESCO ITALIAN CAFÉ.** *1513 S 1500 E, Salt Lake City (84105). Phone 801/486-1300.* A winding brick walkway lined with flowers leads the way to this charming neighborhood bistro, which offers a roaring fireplace indoors and alfresco dining during the summer. Guests will enjoy the fresh and authentic flavors of Italy. Italian menu. Dinner. **$$$**

★ **LITZA'S FOR PIZZA.** *716 E 400 S St, Salt Lake City (84102). Phone 801/359-5352; fax 801/359-5352.* Italian menu. Lunch, dinner. Closed Sun; Thanksgiving, Dec 25. **$$**

★ ★ ★ **LOG HAVEN.** *6451 E 3800 S, Salt Lake City (84109). Phone 801/272-8255; fax 801/272-6173. www.log-haven.com.* Chef David Jones revived this rustic log mansion into Utah's most innovative and elegant restaurant. His sophisticated and excellent fresh specialties change daily. Check out the wine and dine program. American menu. Dinner. Closed Jan 1, July 4, Dec 25. Casual attire. Valet parking. Outdoor seating. **$$$**

★ ★ **MARKET STREET BROILER.** *260 S 1300 E, Salt Lake City (84102). Phone 801/583-8808; fax 801/582-8107. www.gastronomyinc.com.* American menu. Lunch, dinner. Bar. Modern décor in historic former fire station. Casual attire. Outdoor seating. **$$**

★ ★ **MARKET STREET GRILL.** *48 Market St, Salt Lake City (84101). Phone 801/322-4668; fax 801/531-0730. www.gastronomyinc.com.* Located in a renovated 1906 hotel. Seafood menu. Breakfast, lunch, dinner, Sun brunch. Closed Labor Day, Thanksgiving, Dec 25. Bar. Children's menu. Casual attire. **$$**

★ ★ **MELTING POT.** *340 S Main St, Salt Lake City (84101). Phone 801/521-6358; fax 801/521-7001. www. meltingpot.com.* Fondue menu. Dinner. Bar. Casual attire. **$$**

★ ★ ★ **METROPOLITAN.** *173 W Broadway, Salt Lake City (84110). Phone 801/364-3472; fax 801/364-8671.* American menu. Dinner. Closed Sun; Jan 1, Thanksgiving, Dec 25. Bar. Casual attire. **$$$**

★ ★ **MIKADO AT COTTONWOOD.** *6572 S Big Cottonwood Canyon Rd, Salt Lake City (84121). Phone 801/947-9800.* Zashiki rooms. Japanese menu. Lunch, dinner. Closed holidays. Casual attire. Outdoor seating. **$$$**

★ ★ ★ **NEW YORKER CLUB.** *60 W Market St, Salt Lake City (84101). Phone 801/363-0166; fax 801/363-0588. www.gastronomyinc.com.* Appetizers (including fruit, cheese, and seafood) are offered as guests arrive. American menu. Lunch, dinner. Closed Sun; holidays. Bar. Casual attire. Valet parking. **$$$**

★ ★ **PIERPONT CANTINA.** *122 W Pierpont Ave, Salt Lake City (84101). Phone 801/364-1222; fax 801/539-8783. www.gastronomyinc.com.* Mexican menu. Lunch, dinner. Closed Jan 1, Thanksgiving, Dec 25. Bar. Children's menu. Outdoor seating. **$$**

★ ★ **RINO'S.** *2302 Parleys Way, Salt Lake City (84109). Phone 801/484-0901.* Bistro-style café. Italian menu. Dinner. Closed holidays. Casual attire. Outdoor seating. **$$$**

★ **RIO GRANDE CAFE.** *270 S Rio Grande St, Salt Lake City (84101). Phone 801/364-3302; fax 801/364-1857. www.riograndecafe.citysearch.com.* In historic Rio Grande Depot also housing train museum and displays. Mexican menu. Lunch, dinner. Closed holidays. Bar. Children's menu. Casual attire. Outdoor seating. **$$**

★ ★ **SAMBA GRILL.** *162 South 400 West, Salt Lake City (84101). Phone 801/456-2200. www.sambagrill.net.* Brazilian menu. Lunch, dinner. Casual attire. **$$**

★ **SQUATTERS PUB BREWERY.** *147 W Broadway, Salt Lake City (84101). Phone 801/363-2739; fax 801/359-5426. www.squatters.com.* American menu. Lunch, dinner, late-night. Closed Thanksgiving, Dec 25. Bar. Casual attire. Outdoor seating. **$**

★ ★ **TUCCI'S CUCINA ITALIA.** *515 S 700 E, Salt Lake City (84102). Phone 801/533-9111; fax 801/531-9633. www.tuccisitalian.com.* Italian menu. Lunch, dinner. Closed Thanksgiving, Dec 25. Bar. Children's menu. Casual attire. Outdoor seating. **$$**

★ ★ ★ **TUSCANY.** *2832 E 6200 S, Salt Lake City (84121). Phone 801/277-9919; fax 801/277-0980. www.tuscanyslc.com.* This tremendously popular place maintains a high quality of service. Italian menu. Lunch, dinner. Bar. Children's menu. Casual attire. Outdoor seating. **$$$**

★ ★ **XIAO LI.** *307 W 200 S #1000, Salt Lake City (84101). Phone 801/328-8688; fax 801/328-9488.* Chinese menu. Lunch, dinner. Closed July 4, Dec 25. Casual attire. **$**

Grand Teton National Park, WY

7 1/2 hours, 388 miles from Boise, ID

Web site www.nps.gov/grte/

These rugged, block-faulted mountains began to rise about 9 million years ago, making them some of the youngest on the continent. Geologic and glacial forces combined to buckle and sculpt the landscape into a dramatic setting of canyons, cirques, and craggy peaks that cast their reflections across numerous clear alpine lakes. The Snake River winds gracefully through Jackson Hole ("hole" being the old fur trapper's term for a high-altitude valley surrounded by mountains).

John Colter passed through the area during 1807-1808. French-Canadian trappers in the region thought the peaks resembled breasts and applied the French word teton to them.

Entering from the north, from Yellowstone National Park, Highway 89/191/287 skirts the eastern shore of Jackson Lake to Colter Bay, continuing to Jackson Lake Junction, where it turns eastward to the entrance at Moran Junction (at Hwy 26). The Teton Park Road begins at Jackson Lake Junction and borders the mountains to Jenny Lake, and then continues to park headquarters at Moose. Highway 89/191/26 parallels Teton Park Road on the east side of the Snake River to the south entrance from Moran Junction. All highways have a continuous view of the Teton Range, which runs from north to south. Highway 26/89/191 is open year-round from Jackson to Flagg Ranch, 2 miles south of Yellowstone National Park's South Gate, as is Hwy 26/287 to Dubois. Secondary roads and Teton Park Road are open May-Oct.

The park is open year-round (limited in winter), with food and lodging available in the park from mid-May through September and in Jackson. There are three visitor centers with interpretive displays: Moose Visitor Center (daily; closed Dec 25), Colter Bay Visitor Center & Indian Arts Museum (mid-May-late Sept, daily), and Jenny Lake Visitor Center (June-Labor Day). Ranger-led hikes are available (mid-June-mid-Sept, daily; inquire for schedule), and self-guided trails are marked. A 24-hour recorded message gives information about weather; phone 307/739-3611.

The park can be explored by various means. There is hiking on more than 200 miles of trails. Corrals at Jackson Lake Lodge and Colter Bay have strings of horses accustomed to rocky trails; pack trips can be arranged. Boaters and anglers can enjoy placid lakes or wild streams; the Colter Bay, Signal Mountain, and Leek's marinas have ramps, guides, facilities, and rentals. Climbers can tackle summits via routes of varying difficulty; the more ambitious may take advantage of Exum School of Mountaineering and Jackson Hole Mountain Guides classes that range from a beginner's course to an attempt at conquering the 13,770-foot Grand Teton, considered a major North American climbing peak.

Horses, boats, and other equipment can be rented. Bus tours, an airport, auto rentals, general stores, and guide services are available. Five National Park Service campgrounds are maintained: Colter Bay, Signal Mountain, Jenny Lake, Lizard Creek, and Gros Ventre (fee). Slide-illustrated talks on the park and its features are held each night (mid-June-Labor Day) at the amphitheaters at Colter Bay, Signal Mountain, and Gros Ventre.

Many river and lake trips are offered, including 5-, 10-, and 20-mile trips on rubber rafts on the Snake River. Visitors can choose an adventure to suit their individual tastes. A self-guided trail tells the story of Menor's Ferry (1894) and the Maude Noble Cabin. Jenny Lake has boat trips and boat rentals. Jackson Lake cruises are available, some reaching island hideaways for breakfast cookouts. Boat rentals also are available at Jackson Lake. The Grand Teton Lodge Company offers a full-day guided bus and boat trip covering major points of interest in the park (June-mid-Sept); phone 307/543-2811.

A tram with a vertical lift of 4,600 feet operates at Teton Village, rising from the valley floor to the top of Rendezvous Peak, just outside the park's southern boundary.

The Chapel of the Transfiguration, located in Moose, is a log chapel with a large picture window over the altar framing the mountains (daily; services held late May-Sept).

The park is home to abundant wildlife, including pronghorn antelopes, bighorn sheep, mule deer, elk, moose, grizzly and black bears, coyotes, beavers, marmots, bald eagles, and trumpeter swans. Never approach or feed any wild animal. Do not pick wildflowers.

A park boat permit is required. A Wyoming fishing license is required for any fishing and may be obtained at several locations in the park. Camping permits are required for backcountry camping.

Grand Teton and Yellowstone national parks admission is $20 per car. Contact the Superintendent, PO Drawer 170, Moose 83012; phone 307/739-3399 or 307/739-3600 (recording).

CCInc Auto Tape Tours. This 90-minute cassette offers a mile-by-mile self-guided tour of the park. Written by informed guides, it provides information on history, points of interest, and flora and fauna of the park. Tapes may be purchased directly from CCInc, PO Box 227, 2 Elbrook Dr, Allendale, NJ 07401; phone 201/236-1666 or from the Grand Teton Lodge Company, phone 307/543-2811. **$$$**

Limited-Service Hotel

★ ★ **COWBOY VILLAGE RESORT.** *Hwy 26/287, Moran (83013).* Phone 307/543-2847; toll-free 800/962-4988. www.cowboyvillage.com. 89 rooms, 3 story. Check-out 11 am. Restaurant, bar. **$**

Full-Service Resorts

★ ★ ★ **JACKSON LAKE LODGE.** *N Hwys 89 and 1191, Moran (83013).* Phone 307/543-3100; fax 307/543-3143. www.gtlc.com. This lodge is located in Grand Teton National Park. It features a grand lobby with two fireplaces and a 60-foot picture window, and a view across Jackson Lake. 385 rooms, 3 story.

Closed early Oct-mid-May. Check-in 4 pm, check-out 11 am. Two restaurants, bar. Outdoor pool. Airport transportation available. **$$**

★ ★ ★ **JENNY LAKE LODGE.** *Inner Loop Rd-Box 240, Moose (83012). Phone 307/733-2811; fax 307/543-3046. www.gtlc.com.* Nestled at the base of the Tetons in Grand Teton National Park, this rustic, all-inclusive retreat is actually a cluster of 37 western-style cabins outfitted with down comforters and handmade quilts. The pine-shaded property welcomes visitors from June through October for elegantly rustic accommodations and back-to-nature recreation including Jackson Hole Golf & Tennis Club, numerous hiking trails, and three lakes. 37 rooms. Closed early Oct-May. Check-in 4 pm, check-out 11 am. Restaurant, bar. Airport transportation available. **$$$$**

Specialty Lodgings

The following lodging establishment is approved by Mobil Travel Guide, but due to its unique and individualized nature has not been given a traditional Mobil Star rating. Included in this listing you may find bed-and-breakfasts, limited-service inns, guest ranches, and other unique hotel properties.

GROS VENTRE RIVER RANCH. *18 Gros Ventre Rd, Moose (83011). Phone 307/733-4138; fax 307/733-4272. www.grosventreriverranch.com.* Guests stay in a log cabin or lodge, each with a magnificent view of the Teton Mountains. 8 rooms. Closed Oct-mid-May. Complimentary full breakfast. Check-in 3 pm, check-out 10 am. High-speed Internet access. Restaurant. Fitness room. Airport transportation available. No credit cards accepted. **$$$$**

LOST CREEK RANCH. *#1 Old Ranch Rd, Grand Teton National Park (83012). Phone 307/733-3435; fax 307/733-1954. www.lostcreek.com.* It's difficult to imagine a place more awe-inspiring than Lost Creek Ranch, where majestic snow-capped mountain peaks tower over a pristine wilderness of gurgling streams and flourishing wildlife. This guest ranch occupies a spectacular location, bordered by Grand Teton National Park and Bridger Teton National Forest and just 20 miles south of the resort town of Jackson Hole.

One- and two-bedroom log cabins provide comfortable accommodations, and the authentic Western décor puts a smile on visitors' faces. Recreational opportunities abound, with horseback riding, tennis, hiking, auto tours to nearby Yellowstone National Park, and float trips down the Snake River. The spa presents a more sybaritic experience, offering mineral wraps, sea salt body scrubs, and Dead Sea Fango mud massages. Guests forge new friendships over the family-style meals and traditional cookouts, and in the evenings, they revisit the Old West with swing dancing, cowboy poetry, and cowboy serenades. 30 rooms. Closed Oct-mid-May. Check-in 3 pm, check-out 10 am. Restaurant, bar. Children's activity center. Fitness room, spa. Outdoor pool, whirlpool. Tennis. Airport transportation available. **$$$$**

Restaurants

★ **DORNAN'S CHUCK WAGON.** *10 Moose Jct, Moose (83012). Phone 307/733-2415; fax 307/733-3544. www.dornans.com.* Barbecue menu. Breakfast, lunch, dinner. Bar. Outdoor seating. Closed mid-Sept-mid-June. **$**

★ ★ ★ **JENNY LAKE LODGE DINING ROOM.** *Inner Loop Rd-Box 240, Moose (83012). Phone 307/543-2811; fax 307/543-3029. www.gtlc.com.* American menu. Breakfast, dinner. Dining in restored cabin. Jacket required. Reservations recommended. Closed early Oct-May. **$$$$**

Jackson, WY

7 hours, 369 miles from Boise, ID

Population 4,472
Elevation 6,234 ft
Area Code 307
Zip 83001
Information Jackson Hole Area Chamber of Commerce, 990 W Broadway, PO Box 550; phone 307/733-3316
Web site jacksonholechamber.com

Jackson, uninhibitedly western, is the key town for the mountain-rimmed, 600-square-mile valley of Jackson Hole, which is surrounded by mountain scenery, dude ranches, national parks, big game, and other vacation attractions. Jackson Hole is one of the most famous ski resort areas in the country, known for its spectacular views and its abundant ski slopes. It has three Alpine ski areas, five Nordic ski areas, and miles of groomed snowmobile trails. Annual snowfall usually exceeds 38 feet, and winter temperatures average around 21° F. The Jackson Hole area, which includes Grand Teton National Park, the town of Jackson, and much of the Bridger-Teton National Forest, has all the facilities and luxuries necessary to accommodate both the winter and summer visitor. Jackson Hole offers winter sports, boating, chuck wagon dinner shows, live theater productions, symphony concerts, art galleries, rodeos, horseback riding, mountain climbing, fishing, and several whitewater and scenic float trips. Two Ranger District offices of the Bridger-Teton National Forest are located in Jackson.

What to See and Do

Aerial Tramway. *Phone 307/733-2291.* Makes a 2 1/2-mile ride to top of Rendezvous Mountain for spectacular views. Free guided nature hike. (Late May-early Oct) **$$$$**

Barker-Ewing Float Trips. *Grand Teton National Park Rd, Moose. Phone 307/733-1800; toll-free 800/365-1800.* Ten-mile scenic trips on the Snake River, within Grand Teton National Park. Reservations necessary. **$$$$**

Bridger-Teton National Forest. *Phone 307/739-5500.* With more than 3.3 million acres, the forest literally surrounds the town of Jackson. Bridger-Teton was the site of one of the largest earth slides in US history, the Gros Ventre Slide (1925), which dammed the Gros Ventre River (to a height of 225 ft and a width of nearly 1/2 mile), forming Slide Lake, which is approximately 3 miles long. There are scenic drives along the Hoback River Canyon, the Snake River Canyon, and in Star Valley. Unspoiled backcountry includes parts of Gros Ventre, Teton, and Wind River ranges along the Continental Divide and the Wyoming Range. Teton Wilderness (557,311 acres) and Gros Wilderness (247,000 acres) are accessible on foot or horseback. Swimming, fishing, rafting; hiking, mountain biking, winter sports areas, camping (fee). Also in the forest is Bridger Wilderness. Fishing, boating; big-game hunting. For further information contact Forest Supervisor, 340 N Cache, PO Box 1888.

Gray Line bus tours. *1680 W Matrin Ln, Jackson (83001). Phone 307/733-4325; toll-free 800/443-6133. www.grayline.com.* Tours in Jackson, Grand Teton, and Yellowstone national parks.

Jackson Hole Historical Society & Museum. *105 Mercill Ave, Jackson (83001). Phone 307/733-9605.* Fur trade exhibit. Research library. (Daily) **FREE**

Jackson Hole Mountain Resort. *3395 McCollister Dr, Teton Village. 12 miles NW. Phone 307/733-2292; toll-free 800/333-7766 (snow report). www.jacksonhole.com.* Easily Wyoming's highest-profile ski resort, Jackson Hole Mountain Resort is set on the eastern flank of the Teton Range, south of Grand Teton National Park and northwest of Jackson itself. Spread across two mountains (Apres Vous and Rendezvous), the resort's ski terrain features the longest continuous rise in the US—4,139 feet—and 2,500 acres geared toward the skilled skier (10% beginner/40% intermediate/50% expert). There is also a superpipe and a terrain park for the snowboarding set, as well as a Nordic Center for cross-country enthusiasts. Among the 11 lifts are an aerial tram (which also runs in summer) and an eight-person gondola. The booming base village is abuzz with activity, with a number of new hotels and time-share complexes opening in the 21st century, as well as restaurants, stores, and a ski school. While not as well known for warm weather recreation, the resort also is a good base for hiking, golf, and horseback riding. (Dec-mid-Apr, daily) **$$$$**

Jackson Hole Museum. *105 N Glenwood, Jackson (83001). Phone 307/733-9605.* Regional museum of early West, local history and archaeology. (Late May-Sept, daily) **$$**

Lewis and Clark Expeditions. *335 N Cache, Jackson (83001). Phone 307/733-4022; toll-free 800/824-5375.* Scenic 3 1/2 and 6-hour whitewater float trips through Grand Canyon of Snake River. (June-mid-Sept, daily) **$$$$**

Mad River Boat Trips, Inc. *1255 S Hwy 89, Jackson (83001). Phone 307/733-6203; toll-free 800/458-7238.* Three-hour whitewater Snake River Canyon trips (daily). Also combination scenic/whitewater trips, lunch/dinner trips. Reservations suggested. **$$$$**

National Elk Refuge. *2 miles N of town. Phone 307/733-9212.* This 25,000-acre refuge is the winter home of thousands of elk and many waterfowl. Visitor center with slide show, exhibits, and horse-drawn sleigh rides (mid-Dec-Mar, daily).

National Museum of Wildlife Art. *2820 Rungius Rd, Jackson (83001). N of town. Phone 307/733-5771; toll-free 800/313-9553. www.wildlifeart.org.* Nearly blending into the hillside across from the National Elk Refuge, this organic-looking structure (made of red sandstone from Arizona) houses an impressive collection of wildlife art: more than 2,000 works dating from 2000 BC, the 21st century, and just about every artistic era in between. The museum is the largest arts facility dedicated to the theme of wildlife, and includes galleries dedicated to the American bison and legendary wildlife impressionist Carl Rungius. Among the other artists represented here are bird specialist John James Audubon, Dutch master Rembrandt, and cowboy artist Charles M. Russell. The kid's program is excellent, with many interactive exhibits and a strong educational component; there is a restaurant and a gift shop onsite. In winter, sleigh tours of the National Elk Refuge originate here, and combination admission/sleigh tour packages are available. (Daily 9 am-5 pm; Sun from 1 pm in the spring and fall) **$$**

Snow King Ski Resort. *400 E Snow King Ave, Jackson (83001). Six blocks S of Town Square. Phone toll-free 800/522-5464. www.snowkind.com.* Triple, two double chairlifts, surface tow; school, rental/repair shop; snack bar, resort facilities. Longest run nearly 1 mile; vertical drop 1,571 feet. (Nov-Mar, daily) **$$$$**

Solitude Float Trips. *110 E Karns Ave, Jackson (83001). Phone 307/733-2871.* Five- and ten-mile scenic trips within Grand Teton National Park. Reservations suggested.

Teton Mountain Bike Tours. *Phone toll-free 800/733-0788.* Guided mountain bike tours for all ability levels. Mountain bike, helmet, transportation, and local guides. Day, multiday, and customized group tours available.

Teton Wagon Train & Horse Adventure. *820 Cache Creek Rd, Jackson (83001). Phone 307/734-6101.* Four-day guided covered wagon trip between Yellowstone and Grand Teton national parks. Activities include hiking, horseback riding, swimming, and canoeing. Meals, tents, and sleeping bags included. (Mid-June-late Aug) **$$$$** Also available is

Covered Wagon Cookout & Wild West Show. *Phone 307/733-5386.* Ride covered wagons to outdoor dining area; eating area covered in case of rain. Western entertainment. Departs from Bar-T-Five Corral (late May-mid-Sept, Mon-Sat).

Triangle X Float Trips. *2 Triangle X Ranch Rd, Moose (83012). On the Snake River in Grand Teton National Park. Phone 307/733-5500.* Trips include 10-mile floats; sunrise and evening wildlife floats; also cookout supper floats. Most trips originate at Triangle X Ranch. (May-Oct) **$$$$**

Wagons West. *Phone 307/886-9693; toll-free 800/447-4711.* Covered wagon treks through the foothills of the Tetons. Gentle riding horses, chuck-wagon meals, campfire entertainment. Special guided horseback treks and hiking trips into surrounding mountains. Two-, four-, and six-day furnished trips. (June-Labor Day, Mon-Sat) Reservations necessary. Depart from motels in Jackson. **$$$$**

Special Events

Grand Teton Music Festival. *4015 W Lake Creek Dr, Jackson (83001). Phone 307/733-3050. 12 miles NW in Teton Village.* Symphony and chamber music concerts. Virtuoso orchestra of top professional musicians from around the world. Many different programs of chamber music and orchestral concerts. Early July-late Aug.

Jackson Hole Fall Arts Festival. *Phone 307/733-3316.* Three-week celebration of the arts featuring special exhibits in more than 30 galleries, demonstrations, special activities. Also dance, theater, mountain film festival, Native American arts, and culinary arts. Mid-Sept-early Oct.

Jackson Hole Rodeo. *447 W Snow King Dr, Jackson (83001). Phone 307/733-2805.* Memorial Day weekend-late Aug.

The Shootout. *Phone 307/733-3316.* Town Square. Real-life Western melodrama. Mon-Sat evenings, Memorial Day weekend-Labor Day.

Limited-Service Hotels

★ ★ **BEST WESTERN INN AT JACKSON HOLE.** *3345 W Village Dr, Teton Village (83025). Phone 307/733-2311; toll-free 800/842-7666; fax*

307/733-0844. www.innatjh.com. In the Teton Village part of the Jackson Hole ski area, about 12 miles from Jackson, this rustic lodge is a good base for touring Grand Teton National Park, Jackson Hole, and Yellowstone National Park. It has a nice pool and is close to the aerial tram, shops, and restaurants. 83 rooms, 4 story. Check-in 4 pm, check-out 11 am. Restaurant, bar. Outdoor pool, whirlpool. **$$**

★ **BEST WESTERN THE LODGE AT JACKSON HOLE.** *80 Scott Ln, Jackson (83002). Phone 307/739-9703; toll-free 800/458-3866; fax 307/739-9168. www.lodgeatjh.com.* 153 rooms, 3 story. Complimentary continental breakfast. Check-in 4 pm, check-out 11 am. Indoor, outdoor pool; whirlpool. **$$**

★ ★ **JACKSON HOLE LODGE.** *420 W Broadway, Jackson Hole (83001). Phone 307/733-2992; toll-free 800/556-4638; fax 307/739-2144. www.skijacksonhole .com.* 59 rooms. Check-in 4 pm, check-out 11 am. Ski in/ski out. **$**

★ ★ **QUALITY INN.** *330 W Pearl St, Jackson (83001). Phone 307/733-7550; toll-free 800/451-2980; fax 307/733-2002. www.qualityinn.com.* 142 rooms, 3 story. Pets accepted, some restrictions. Complimentary continental breakfast. Check-in 3 pm, check-out 11 am. Fitness room. Whirlpool. **$**

★ **RED LION WYOMING INN.** *930 W Broadway, Jackson (83002). Phone 307/734-0035; toll-free 800/844-0035; fax 307/734-0037. www.wyoming-inn .com.* 73 rooms, 3 story. Complimentary continental breakfast. Check-in 4 pm, check-out 11 am. Airport transportation available. Business center. **$$**

★ ★ ★ **SPRING CREEK RANCH.** *1800 Spirit Dance Rd, Jackson (83001). Phone 307/733-8833; toll-free 800/443-6139; fax 307/733-1524. www. springcreekranch.com.* Offering a great view of the Teton Mountain Range, surrounded by two national parks and tons of wildlife, this resort features great accommodations, and is located near many attrac-

tions. 130 rooms. Check-in 4 pm, check-out 11 am. Restaurant, bar. Fitness room. Outdoor pool, whirlpool. Tennis. Airport transportation available. **$$**

★ ★ ★ **THE WORT HOTEL.** *50 N Glenwood St, Jackson (83001). Phone 307/733-2190; toll-free 800/322-2727; fax 307/733-2067. www.worthotel.com.* Reflecting the history and culture of Jackson Hole, this popular country inn is decorated with fabrics and furnishings of the Old West. 61 rooms, 2 story. Check-in 4 pm, check-out 11 am. Restaurant, bar. Fitness room. Whirlpools. **$$**

Full-Service Resort

★ ★ ★ **TETON PINES.** *3450 N Clubhouse Dr, Wilson (83014). Phone 307/733-1005; toll-free 800/ 238-2223; fax 307/733-2860. www.tetonpines.com.* 16 rooms. Complimentary continental breakfast. Check-in 3 pm, check-out 11 am. Restaurant. Fitness room. Pool, whirlpool. Golf. Tennis. Airport transportation available. **$$**

Full-Service Inns

★ ★ ★ **THE ALPINE HOUSE COUNTRY INN & SPA.** *285 N Glenwood St, Jackson (83001). Phone 307/739-1570; toll-free 800/753-1421. www.alpinehouse .com.* 22 rooms. Closed Apr and Nov. Check-in 3 pm, check-out 11 am. Ski in/ski out. **$$**

★ ★ ★ **PARKWAY INN.** *125 N Jackson St, Jackson (83001). Phone 307/733-3143; toll-free 800/247-8390; fax 307/733-0955. www.parkwayinn.com.* 49 rooms. Complimentary continental breakfast. Check-in 3 pm, check-out 11 am. Fitness room. Indoor pool, whirlpool. Ski in/ski out. No credit cards accepted. **$$**

★ ★ ★ **RUSTY PARROT LODGE.** *175 N Jackson St, Jackson (83001). Phone 307/733-2000; toll-free 800/458-2004; fax 307/733-5566. www. rustyparrotlodge.com.* Just minutes from Grand Teton and Yellowstone national parks and Jackson Hole, the lodge is also just three blocks from Town Square. Rustic rooms are filled with mountain-style touches:

antler chandeliers, hand-made furniture, and goose-down comforters. A hearty breakfast is included in the rates. To rejuvenate the body and the spirit after a day on the slopes, try one of the many treatments available at the The Body Sage, the on-site day spa. 31 rooms, 3 story. Complimentary full breakfast. Check-in 4 pm, check-out 11 am. Restaurant, bar. Spa. Whirlpool. **$$$**

D

★ ★ ★ **THE WILDFLOWER INN.** *3725 N Teton Village Rd, Jackson (83002). Phone 307/733-4710; fax 307/739-0914. www.jacksonholewildflower.com.* This log bed-and-breakfast is located just outside of town and only 5 minutes from the Jackson Hole Mountain ski area. 5 rooms, 2 story. Complimentary full breakfast. Check-in 3-5 pm, check-out 11 am. **$$**

D

Specialty Lodgings

The following lodging establishments are approved by Mobil Travel Guide, but due to their unique and individualized nature have not been given a traditional Mobil Star rating. Included in this listing you may find bed-and-breakfasts, limited-service inns, guest ranches, and other unique hotel properties.

DAVY JACKSON. *85 Perry Ave, Jackson (83001). Phone 307/739-2294; toll-free 800/584-0532. www.davyjackson.com.* 12 rooms, 3 story. Complimentary full breakfast. Check-in 4 pm, check-out 11 am. Victorian décor. **$$**

D

THE HUFF HOUSE INN BED & BREAKFAST. *240 E Deloney, Jackson (83001). Phone 307/733-4164; fax 307/739-9091. www.jacksonwyomingbnb.com.* Each room of this 1917 Victorian house features lovely appointments that help provide a warm and relaxing atmosphere. 7 rooms, 2 story. Complimentary full breakfast. Check-in 3-5 pm, check-out 11 am. Whirlpool. **$**

D

INN ON THE CREEK. *295 N Millward, Jackson (83001). Phone 307/739-1565. www.innonthecreek.com.* 9 rooms. Closed three weeks in Apr. Complimentary full breakfast. Check-in 4-6 pm, check-out 11 am. **$$**

THE PAINTED PORCH. *3755 Moose-Wilson Rd, Wilson (83014). Phone 307/733-1981. www.jacksonholebedandbreakfast.com.* 3 rooms. Complimentary full breakfast. Check-in 3 pm, check-out 11 am. **$**

Restaurants

★ ★ **ANTHONY'S.** *62 S Glenwood St, Jackson (83001). Phone 307/733-3717.* Italian menu. Dinner. Closed Thanksgiving, Dec 25. Children's menu. Casual attire. **$$**

D

★ ★ ★ **BLUE LION.** *160 N Millward St, Jackson (83001). Phone 307/733-3912; fax 307/733-3915. www.bluelionrestaurant.com.* Housed in a charming old home, this restaurant offers creative preparations of many dishes. American menu. Dinner. Closed Thanksgiving. Bar. Children's menu. Outdoor seating. **$$$**

D

★ ★ ★ **CADILLAC GRILLE.** *55 N Cache Dr, Jackson (83001). Phone 307/733-3279; fax 307/739-0110.* Aglow with neon lights, this energetic restaurant is on the town square's west side and has been open since 1983. The creative dishes are served in a fun, casual atmosphere. American menu. Dinner. Closed Thanksgiving, Dec 25. Bar. Casual attire. **$$$**

★ ★ **CALICO.** *2650 Teton Village Rd, Jackson (83025). Phone 307/733-2460; fax 307/734-0451. www.calicorestaurant.com.* Italian menu. Dinner. Closed Thanksgiving. Bar. Casual attire. Outdoor seating. **$$**

D

★ **JEDEDIAH'S.** *135 E Broadway, Jackson (83001). Phone 307/733-5671.* American menu. Dinner. Closed Thanksgiving, Dec 25; also Super Bowl Sun, children's menu. Casual attire. Outdoor seating. **$$**

D

★ ★ **MILLION DOLLAR COWBOY STEAK HOUSE.** *25 N Cache St, Jackson (83001). Phone 307/733-4790.* Steak menu. Dinner. Closed Thanksgiving; also Apr and Nov. Bar. Casual attire. **$$$**

★ ★ **OFF BROADWAY.** *30 S King St, Jackson (83001). Phone 307/733-9777.* American menu.

Dinner. Closed Thanksgiving, Dec 25. Children's menu. Casual attire. Outdoor seating. **$$$**
🄳

★ ★ ★ **SNAKE RIVER GRILL.** *84 E Broadway, Jackson (83001). Phone 307/733-0557; fax 307/733-5767. www.snakerivergrill.com.* With hardwood floors and a cozy fireplace set in the center of this rustic restaurant, diners will appreciate the charm of the Northwest. American menu. Dinner. Closed Dec 25; also Apr and Nov. Bar. Children's menu. Outdoor seating. **$$$**
🄳

★ ★ ★ **STRUTTING GROUSE.** *5000 N Spring Gulch Rd, Jackson (83001). Phone 307/733-7788; fax 307/733-8473. www.gtlc.com.* Just outside the southern border of Grand Teton National Park, this restaurant and lounge is part of the Jackson Hole Golf and Tennis Club. The dining room overlooks the golf course and mountains. American menu. Dinner. Closed mid-Oct-mid-May. Bar. Outdoor seating (lunch). **$$**

★ ★ ★ **SWEETWATER.** *85 S King St, Jackson (83001). Phone 307/733-3553; toll-free 800/222-4700; fax 307/739-4580.* In log house built by pioneers. Mediterranean menu. Dinner. Closed Thanksgiving, Dec 25. Children's menu. Casual attire. Outdoor seating. **$$$**

★ ★ ★ **TETON PINES.** *3450 N Clubhouse Dr, Wilson (83014). Phone 307/733-1005; toll-free 800/238-2223; fax 307/733-2860. www.tetonpines.com.* American menu. Dinner. Closed Sun; Dec 25. Bar. Children's menu. Casual attire. Outdoor dining. **$$$**

★ ★ **VISTA GRANDE.** *2550 Teton Village Rd, Jackson (83001). Phone 307/733-6964.* Mexican menu. Dinner. Closed Dec 25. Bar. Children's menu. Casual attire. Outdoor seating. **$$**

Oregon

This is the end of the famous Oregon Trail, over which came scores of pioneers in covered wagons. The state abounds in the romance of the country's westward expansion. Meriwether Lewis and William Clark, sent by President Thomas Jefferson to explore the vast area bought in the Louisiana Purchase, ended their explorations here. This was also the scene of John Jacob Astor's fortune-making fur trade and that of Hudson's Bay Company, which hoped to keep the area for England, as well as gold rushes and the traffic of stately clippers of the China trade.

English Captain James Cook saw the coast in 1778. Others had seen it before him and others after him, but it remained for Lewis and Clark to discover what a prize Oregon was. On their return to St. Louis in 1806, they spread the word. In 1811, Astor's Pacific Fur Company built its post at Astoria, only to be frightened into selling to the British North West Company during the War of 1812. (In 1818, it again became US territory.) Other fur traders, missionaries, salmon fishermen, and travelers followed them, but the Oregon country was far away and hard to reach. The first true settlers did not make their way there until 1839, four years before a great wagon train blazed the Oregon Trail.

Cattle and sheep were driven up from California and land was cleared for farms. Oregon was settled not by people hungry for gold but by pioneers looking for good land that could support them. The Native Americans resented the early settlers and fought them until 1880. The Oregon Territory, established in 1848, received a flood of immigrants; they continued to arrive after statehood was proclaimed under President James Buchanan 11 years later.

Population: 3,421,399
Area: 97,073 square miles
Elevation: 0-11,235 feet
Peak: Mount Hood (between Clackamas and Hood River counties)
Entered Union: February 14, 1859 (33rd state)
Capital: Salem
Motto: She Flies With Her Own Wings
Nickname: Beaver State
Flower: Oregon Grape
Bird: Western Meadowlark
Tree: Douglas Fir
Fair: August-September in Salem
Time Zone: Mountain and Pacific
Web site: www.traveloregon.com
Fun Facts:
- At 1,932 feet, Crater Lake is the deepest lake in the United States.
- Oregon has more ghost towns than any other state.

The rich forests grew rapidly in the moist climate west of the mountains called the Cascades, and lumber was an early product of this frontier. The streams were full of fish, the woods offered nuts and berries, and the lush, green scenery lifted hearts and hopes at the end of the weary journey. The rivers—Columbia, Willamette, Rogue, and many others—offered transportation to the sea. Steamboats plied the Willamette and Columbia as early as 1850. The first full ship's cargo of wheat went from Portland to Liverpool in 1868, and when the railroad reached Portland in 1883, the world began receiving the fish, grain, lumber, and livestock that Oregon was ready to deliver.

Vast rivers provide more than transportation. Dammed, they are the source of abundant electric power and water to irrigate farms east of the Cascades. Timber is still important; a quarter of

Calendar Highlights

MAY

Boatnik Festival (*Grants Pass*). *Riverside Park. Phone toll-free 800/547-5927.* Parade, concessions, carnival rides, boat races, and entertainment. A 25-mile whitewater hydroboat race from Riverside Park to Hellgate Canyon and back. Square dance festival at Josephine County Fairgrounds.

JUNE

Bach Festival (*Eugene*). *Phone toll-free 800/457-1486; www.bachfest.uoregon.edu.* Numerous concerts by regional and international artists; master classes; family activities.

Portland Rose Festival (*Portland*). *Phone 503/227-2681; www.rosefestival.org.* Held for more than 90 years, this festival includes the Grand Floral Parade (reservations required for indoor parade seats) and two other parades; band competition; rose show; championship auto racing; hotair balloons; air show; carnival; Navy ships.

Return of the Sternwheeler Days (*Hood River*). *Phone 541/374-8619.* Celebration of the sternwheeler Columbia Gorge's return to home port for the summer. Wine and cheese tasting, crafts, food.

Sandcastle Contest (*Cannon Beach*). *Phone 503/436-2623.* Nationally known event features sand sculptures on beach.

SCANDINAVIAN MIDSUMMER FESTIVAL

Scandinavian Midsummer Festival (*Astoria*). *Astoria Warrenton Chamber of Commerce, phone 503/325-6311.* Parade, folk dancing, display booths, arts and crafts demonstrations, Scandinavian food.

JULY

Da Vinci Days (*Corvallis*). *Phone 541/757-6363.* Festival celebrating the relationship between art, science, and technology.

Oregon Coast Music Festival (*Coos Bay*). *Phone toll-free 877/897-9350.* Variety of musical presentations ranging from jazz and dance to chamber and symphonic music.

Salem Art Fair & Festival (*Salem*). *Bush's Pasture Park. Phone 503/581-2228.* Arts and crafts booths and demonstrations, children's art activities and parade, ethnic folk arts, performing arts, street painting, 5K run, food; tours of historic Bush House.

AUGUST

Oregon State Fair (*Salem*). *Fairgrounds. Phone 503/378-FAIR.* Horse racing, wine competition and tastings, agricultural exhibits, horse show, livestock, food, carnival, entertainment.

SEPTEMBER

Pendleton Round-Up (*Pendleton*). *Stadium. Phone toll-free 800/457-6336.* Rodeo and pageantry of the Old West, held annually since 1910. Gathering of Native Americans, PRCA working cowboys, and thousands of visitors.

Oregon is national forest land. Sustained yield practices by the big lumber companies ensure a continuing supply.

One of the most beautiful drives in Oregon extends from Portland (see) to The Dalles (see) along the Columbia River. Here is the spectacular Columbia Gorge, designated a National Scenic Area, where waterfalls, streams, and mountains abound. The area offers many recreational activities such as camping—the Cascade Locks Marina Park lies 4 miles east of the Bonneville Dam (see also HOOD RIVER), skiing (see also MOUNT HOOD NATIONAL FOREST), snowmobiling, windsurfing, and hiking.

Whether your taste is for an ocean beach, a ski slope, a mountain lake, or ranch life with riding and rodeos, the visitor who loves the outdoors or the American West loves Oregon. Each year, millions of tourists enjoy the state's magnificent coastline, blue lakes, mountains, and forests.

When to Go/Climate

Temperatures along the Pacific coast are mild, while Portland and the Willamette Valley experience more extreme weather conditions. Heavy snow falls in the Cascades, and to the east there's a high desert area that experiences typical desert heat and dry conditions.

AVERAGE HIGH/LOW TEMPERATURES (° F)

Burns

Jan 34/13	May 66/36	Sept 74/36
Feb 40/19	June 74/42	Oct 62/28
Mar 48/25	July 85/47	Nov 45/22
Apr 57/29	Aug 83/45	Dec 35/15

Portland

Jan 45/34	May 67/47	Sept 75/52
Feb 51/36	June 74/53	Oct 64/45
Mar 56/39	July 80/57	Nov 53/40
Apr 61/41	Aug 80/57	Dec 46/35

Parks and Recreation

Water-related activities, hiking, riding, various other sports, picnicking, and visitor centers, as well as camping, are available in many of Oregon's state parks. Many camping facilities in these parks stay open year-round, while others remain open as long as the weather permits, usually March through October. All campgrounds are open from mid-April to late October. Campers are limited to ten days in any 14-day period from May 15 to September 14, and 14 days out of 18 the rest of the year. Discount rates are available at most campgrounds from October to April. Fees per night are as follows: primitive campsites $4-$6; tent sites $10-$13; electrical sites $12-$17; full hookup sites $12-$18; extra vehicle $5-$7. Firewood is available. Campsites may be reserved at 25 state parks throughout the year with a $6 fee plus the first night's camping rate. A day-use fee of $3 is charged for each motor vehicle entering 24 state parks. For more information, contact the Oregon Parks and Recreation Department, 725 Summer St, Suite C, Salem 97301; phone 503/378-6305 or toll-free 800/551-6949; www. oregonstateparks.org. For campsite reservations, phone toll-free 800/452-5687.

FISHING AND HUNTING

Oregon has 15,000 miles of streams, hundreds of lakes, and surf and deep-sea fishing. Fishing is good for Chinook and coho salmon, steelhead, rainbow and cutthroat trout, striped bass, perch, crappie, bluegill, catfish, and many other varieties. Hunters will find mule and black-tailed deer, elk, ring-necked pheasant, Hungarian and chukar partridge, quail, blue and ruffed grouse, band-tailed pigeons, mourning doves, waterfowl, jackrabbits, coyotes, foxes, and bears.

Nonresident fishing license, annual $61.50; seven-day license $43.75; combined angling harvest tag, $21.50; one-day license, $12. Nonresident hunting license, annual $76.50. Special tags are required in addition to a license for big game. All licenses include an agent-writing fee.

For synopses of the latest angling and big-game regulations, contact Oregon Department of Fish and Wildlife, PO Box 59, Portland 97207; phone 503/872-5268; www.dfw.state.or.us.

Driving Information

Safety belts are mandatory for all persons anywhere in a vehicle. Children under age 4 (or 40 pounds in weight) must use approved safety seats anywhere in a vehicle. For more information, phone 503/986-4190 or toll-free 800/922-2022 (in Oregon).

INTERSTATE HIGHWAY SYSTEM

The following alphabetical listing of Oregon towns in this book shows that these cities are within 10 miles of the indicated interstate highways. Check a highway map for the nearest exit.

Highway Number	Cities/Towns within 10 Miles
Interstate 5	Albany, Ashland, Beaverton, Corvallis, Cottage Grove, Eugene, Grants Pass, Jacksonville, Medford, Oregon City, Portland, Roseburg, Salem.
Interstate 84	Baker City, Beaverton, Biggs, Hermiston, Hood River, La Grande, Ontario, Oregon City, Pendleton, Portland, The Dalles, Umatilla.

Additional Visitor Information

The Oregon Tourism Commission, 775 Summer St NE, Salem 97301 (phone toll-free 800/547-7842; www.traveloregon.com) will provide visitors with an Oregon travel guide and other informative brochures upon request.

There are nine staffed state welcome centers in Oregon (April-October): Astoria (downtown); Brookings (OR-CA border, S on Hwy 101); Lakeview (downtown); Siskiyou (OR-CA border, S on I-5); Ontario (OR-ID border, E on I-84); Seaside (at the Chamber of Commerce on Hwy 101); Umatilla (on Brownell Blvd); Jantzen Beach-Portland (I-5, exit 308); and Klamath Falls (OR-CA border, S on Hwy 97).

DRIVING OREGON'S CENTRAL COAST

Oregon's central coast has some of the state's most dramatic scenery, with volcanic mountains dropping into the pounding Pacific surf. Along this route, you'll encounter many enchanting small towns, as well as an excellent aquarium and a sand dune recreation area.

Begin in Newport, Oregon's second-largest commercial port. Dominated by the high-arching Yaquina Bay Bridge, old downtown Newport is still a very lively seafront, complete with seafood markets, the smells of a working port, and the bark of seals. Bay Boulevard is lined with fish-processing plants on one side, chandlers, fish restaurants, art galleries, and brew pubs on the other. A number of ship owners offer boat excursions around Yaquina Bay and trips out into the Pacific to view whales.

Besides Newport's mile-long beaches, the city's biggest draw is the Oregon Coast Aquarium. Exhibits are grouped by ecosystem with interactive displays to explain the dynamics of the various forms of life found there. Outside, trails lead around natural-looking enclosures for seals, sea lions, and sea otters; the seabird aviary includes puffins and murres.

Drive south along Highway 101 to Seal Rock State Park, where a massive hump of rock protects a beach and tide pools, making this a good place for young children to explore the coast. Waldport is a quiet town on the mouth of the Alsea River with an unusual museum of transport. Travel along Oregon's rugged coast was not always simple, as The Alsea Bay Bridge Historical Interpretive Center makes evident. The facility traces the history of transportation routes along the coast, beginning with trails used by Native Americans and moving on to the sea, rail, and road routes now in use. From Waldport south to Yachats (pronounced Ya-HOTS) are more wide sandy beaches, easily accessed at state park access points.

Some of Oregon's most spectacular shoreline begins at Yachats and continues south about 20 miles. This entire area was once a series of volcanic intrusions, which resisted the pummeling of the Pacific long enough to rise as oceanside peaks and promontories. Tiny beaches lined by cliffs seem almost serendipitous; acres of tide pools appear and disappear according to the fancy of the tides and are home to starfish, sea anemones, and sea lions. Picturesque lighthouses rise above the surf.

Cape Perpetua, 2 miles south of Yachats, was first sited and named by England's Captain James Cook in 1778. This volcanic remnant is one of the highest points on the Oregon coast. Views from the cape are incredible, taking in coastal promontories from Cape Foulweather to Cape Arago. Deep fractures in the old volcano allow waves to erode narrow channels into the headland, creating the compelling Devils Churn. Waves race up a deep trench between basalt ledges, then shoot up the 30-foot inlet only to explode against the narrow sides of the channel. From the base of the Devils Churn trail, turn south to explore acres of tide pools.

To continue, follow Highway 101 south. Stop at Devils Elbow State Park and the Heceta Head Lighthouse, complete with an 1893 lighthouse keeper's house. From here, the road tunnels through mountains and edges along cliffs to reach Sea Lion Caves, an enormous natural sea grotto filled with smelly, shrieking sea lions. A 208-foot elevator drops down a small natural shaft that opens onto the larger grotto. From this observation point 50 feet above the surging waves, watch Steller's sea lions clambering onto rocks, jockeying for position at the top of ledges, and letting loose with mighty roars.

From the Sea Lion Caves, Highway 101 drops down from the volcanic peaks to a broad sandy plain fronted by extensive beaches preserved in state parks. Florence is an old fishing port that boomed in the 1890s. Detour from the unlovely Highway 101 strip to Old Town Florence, the historic port area on the Siuslaw River. The town's small fishing fleet ties at the base of restored Victorian storefronts, now filled with restaurants, coffee shops, and galleries.

From Florence southward to Reedsport is the Oregon Dunes National Recreation Area. These massive dunes front the Pacific Ocean but undulate east as much as 3 miles to meet coastal forests, with a succession of curious ecosystems and formations between. A number of hiking trails, bridle paths, and boating and swimming areas have been established throughout this unique place, and the entire region is noted for its abundant wildlife, especially birds.

Reedsport, once an important fishing and log milling town, is home to the Umpqua Lighthouse State Park. The still-operating lighthouse was built in 1894 and is open for tours. Directly opposite the lighthouse is a whale-watching platform, with displays that explain various whale species and their habits.
(Approximately 75 miles)

THE COLUMBIA RIVER HIGHWAY AND BEYOND

The magnificent canyon of the Columbia River slices through the spine of the Cascade Range just east of Portland. The Columbia, over a mile wide, winds through a 3,000-foot-deep gorge flanked by volcanic peaks and austere bands of basalt. The gorge contains one of the greatest concentrations of waterfalls in North America—chutes of water tumble from its edge to fall hundreds of feet to the river.

Begin in Portland, driving east on I-84. As the walls of the river canyon rise in the distance, take exit 22 and climb up the forested valley to join Highway 30, the Historic Columbia River Highway, atop the gorge wall. Modeled on European mountain roads, the Columbia River Highway was built in the 1910s as a scenic automobile route through the Gorge—quite an engineering feat at that time.

Famous as the western entry to the Gorge, Crown Point is a viewpoint and interpretive center atop a craggy 800-foot-high point of basalt. To the east, as far as the eye can see, the Columbia River unfurls between green cliffs. The famed Columbia Gorge waterfalls start almost immediately. Latourell Falls is the first major falls, a chute of water dropping 249 feet into a misty pool. To see churning Bridal Veil Falls requires a mile round-trip walk through deep forest and odd rock formations. Hike up the trail at Wahkeena Falls to see why it is named after an Indian term meaning "the most beautiful."

Half a mile east of Oneonta Gorge is Horsetail Falls, which drops out of a notch in the rock to fall 176 feet. While the waterfall is easily seen from the turnout along Highway 30, hikers should consider the 3-mile Horsetail-Oneonta Loop Trail, an easy hike that takes in another waterfall and the narrow Oneonta chasm.

From there, continue east on Highway 30, rejoining I-84 at Dodson. Built in 1937 at the height of the Depression, Bonneville Dam was one of the largest of the New Deal projects and was the first major hydropower dam on the Columbia. The visitor center, at exit 40, has a good collection of Native American artifacts, as well as exhibits about the building of the dam. From the lower floors of the visitor center, you can watch through underwater windows as fish negotiate the dam's fish ladders. Walk to the Bonneville Fish Hatchery, where salmon and sturgeon are reared to restock the Columbia River. Nearby, the Columbia River Sternwheeler offers cruises through the Columbia River Gorge departing from Cascade Locks Marine Park.

Continue on I-84 to Hood River, an old orchard town on the Columbia River that has found new life as a world capital of windsurfing. From Hood River, turn south on Highway 35. As you climb out of the Gorge, Mount Hood—Oregon's highest peak at 11,240 feet—fills the skyline, a slim white incisor towering above a valley filled with apple, pear, and cherry orchards. As the orchards thin, Highway 35 winds up around the base of Mount Hood, through fir forests and along rushing streams. At Government Camp, turn north into Timberline Lodge and climb 6 steep miles to 6,000 feet. Here, at the foot of soaring Mount Hood, sits one of the unquestioned masterpieces of WPA-funded Depression-era public works, Timberline Lodge (phone 503/272-3311). The interior of this 43,700-square-foot lodge is spectacular: the central stone fireplace rises 92 feet through three open stories of lobby. The third floor bar and café is a wonderful place to take in the inspiring handiwork that created this architectural gem.

The ski lifts at Timberline operate almost all year, so strap on skis or a snowboard and head to the lifts. Hiking trails lead out from the lodge in almost all directions. For food, check out the Blue Ox Pub, tucked away in a cavernlike corner, or splurge at the wood-beamed Cascade Dining Room.

Return to Highway 30, and continue west to the Portland suburbs. **(Approximately 75 miles)**

Albany

See also Corvallis, Salem, Sweet Home

Founded 1848
Population 29,462
Elevation 212 ft
Area Code 541
Zip 97321
Information Visitors Convention & Association, 300 SW 2nd Ave, PO Box 965; phone 541/928-0911 or toll-free 800/526-2256
Web site www.albanyvisitors.com

The gateway to Oregon's covered bridge country, Albany was founded by Walter and Thomas Monteith and named for their former home, Albany, New York. The city boasts the state's largest collection of Victorian homes. The seat of Linn County, Albany is nestled in the heart of the Willamette Valley along the I-5 corridor of the Cascades. The Calapooia River joins the Willamette here.

What to See and Do

Flinn's Heritage Tours. *222 First Ave W, Albany (97321). Phone 541/928-5008; toll-free 800/636-5008.* Twenty different narrated tours take visitors through historic areas in the Mid Willamette Valley. Tours range from 45 minutes to 6 hours and feature the covered bridges of Linn County, Albany's three historic districts, ghost towns, a 100-year-old apple orchard, and historic homes. (Daily; closed Dec 25) **$$$$**

Special Events

Historic Interior Homes Tours. *300 2nd Ave SW, Albany (97321). Phone 541/928-0911or toll-free 800/526-3356.* Summer and late Dec.

Veteran's Day Parade. *626 Harrison St, Albany (97321). Phone 541/367-8323.* One of the nation's largest. Mid-Nov.

Limited-Service Hotel

★ **LA QUINTA INN.** *251 Airport Rd SE, Albany (97321). Phone 541/928-0921; fax 541/928-8055. www. laquinta.com.* 62 rooms, 2 story. Pets accepted, some restrictions. Complimentary continental breakfast. Check-out 1 pm. Fitness room. Indoor pool, whirlpool. **$**

Ashland (E-2)

See also Jacksonville, Medford

Founded 1852
Population 16,234
Elevation 1,951 ft
Area Code 541
Zip 97520
Information Chamber of Commerce, 110 E Main St, PO Box 1360; phone 541/482-3486
Web site www.ashlandchamber.com

When the pioneers climbed over the Siskiyou Mountains and saw the green expanse of the Rogue River Valley ahead of them, many decided to go no further and settled here. Later, when mineral springs were found, their Lithia water was piped in; it now gushes from fountains on this city's plaza. Tourism, education, and small industry support the town. Southern Oregon University College (1926) makes Ashland a regional education center. The Rogue River National Forest is on three sides; a Ranger District office is located here.

What to See and Do

Lithia Park. *E Main St and Winburn Way, Ashland (97520). Adjacent to City Plaza. Phone 541/488-5340.* Has 100 acres of woodlands and ponds. Nature trails, tennis, picnicking, sand volleyball. Rose and Japanese gardens. Concerts. (Daily) **FREE**

Mount Ashland Ski Area. *8 miles S on I-5, then 9 miles W on access road. Phone 541/482-2897. www.mtashland .com.* Area has two triple, two double chairlifts; patrol, school, rentals; cafeteria, bar. Longest run 1 mile vertical drop 1,150 feet. (Thanksgiving-Apr)

Special Events

Oregon Cabaret Theatre. *241 Hargadine St, Ashland (97520). Phone 541/488-2902. 1st and Hargadine sts.* Musicals, revues, and comedies in dinner club setting. Schedule varies. Feb-Dec.

Oregon Shakespeare Festival. *15 S Pioneer St, Ashland (97520). Phone 541/482-4331.* You wouldn't expect to find world-class theater productions in a quiet town of 20,000 people, but that's exactly what you get with the Oregon Shakespeare Festival (OSF). From its humble beginnings with a 1935 staging of

Twelfth Night, this repertory theater has evolved in size and scope, earning a reputation for consistently excellent productions and making Ashland a must-stop destination for drama lovers. *Time* magazine recognized OSF in 2003, heralding the company as one of the five best regional theaters in the United States. The name is something of a misnomer, as Shakespeare's plays, though featured prominently, are not the only offerings here. Running from February to early November, the 2003 season featured four Shakespeare productions, including *A Midsummer Night's Dream* and *Romeo and Juliet,* while seven works from other playwrights also were staged, ranging from the Ibsen classic *Hedda Gabler* to August Wilson's modern masterpiece, *The Piano Lesson.* OSF actually consists of three separate theaters: the intimate New Theatre, the versatile Angus Bowmer Theatre, and the open-air Elizabethan Stage, which is fashioned after the Bard's legendary Globe Theatre. Feb-early Nov.

Limited-Service Hotels

★ ★ **ASHLAND SPRINGS HOTEL.** *212 E Main St, Ashland (97520). Phone 541/488-1700; toll-free 888/795-4545; fax 541/488-1701. www.ashlandspringshotel.com.* With a stately exterior that employs gothic and Beaux Arts architectural elements, the nine-story Ashland Springs Hotel towers impressively over the intersection at Main and 1st streets. The elegant hotel serves as the perfect home base for exploring the Rogue River Valley. Listed on the National Register of Historic Places, the hotel has been a southern Oregon landmark since opening its doors as the Lithia Hotel in 1925. After years of ups and downs, the hotel was closed and abandoned in 1997, only to be exhaustively renovated a few years later and reopened as the Ashland Springs Hotel. The hotel now includes modern amenities, but it retains many original details, including six chandeliers in the ballroom and the original stained glass that bears the LH crest. 70 rooms. Complimentary continental breakfast. Check-in 3 pm, check-out 11 am. High-speed Internet access. Restaurant, bar. **$**

★ **BEST WESTERN BARD'S INN.** *132 N Main St, Ashland (97520). Phone 541/482-0049; toll-free 800/528-1234; fax 541/488-3259. www.bestwestern.com.* Near Shakespeare Festival theater. 91 rooms, 3 story. Pets accepted; fee. Complimentary continental breakfast. Check-in 3 pm, check-out 11 am. Outdoor pool, whirlpool. **$**

★ **STRATFORD INN.** *555 Siskiyou Blvd, Ashland (97520). Phone 541/488-2151; toll-free 800/547-4741; fax 541/482-0479.* 55 rooms, 3 story. Complimentary continental breakfast. Check-out 11 am. Indoor pool, whirlpool. **$**

★ ★ **WINDMILL INN AND SUITES OF ASHLAND.** *2525 Ashland St, Ashland (97520). Phone 541/482-8310; toll-free 800/547-4747; fax 541/488-1783. www.windmillinns.com.* Easily accessible from Interstate 5, this downtown hotel features a hair salon, lending library, and bikes available for guests to enjoy. 230 rooms, 3 story. Pets accepted. Complimentary continental breakfast. Check-out 11 am. Restaurant, bar. Fitness room. Pool, whirlpool. Tennis. Airport transportation available. **$**

Full-Service Inns

★ ★ ★ **MT. ASHLAND INN.** *550 Mt. Ashland Rd, Ashland (97520). Phone 541/482-8707; toll-free 800/830-8707. www.mtashlandinn.com.* With slopes and cliffs on one side and the mountain ranges on the other, guests are guaranteed a breathtaking view no matter where they look. Whatever the season, guests will enjoy such activities as hiking, skiing, rafting, sledding, and fishing. A truly exciting getaway. 5 rooms, 4 story. Children over 10 years only. Complimentary full breakfast. Check-in 3-5 pm, check-out 11 am. **$$**

★ ★ ★ **THE WINCHESTER INN & RESTAURANT.** *35 S Second St, Ashland (97520). Phone 541/488-1113; toll-free 800/972-4991; fax 541/488-4604. www.winchesterinn.com.* Located just one block from downtown Ashland, this restored Victorian house once served as the area's first hospital. 18 rooms, 3 story. Complimentary full breakfast. Check-in 3 pm, check-out 11 am. Restaurant. **$$**

Specialty Lodgings

The following lodging establishments are approved by Mobil Travel Guide, but due to their unique and individualized nature have not been given a traditional Mobil Star rating. Included in this listing you may find bed-and-breakfasts, limited-service inns, guest ranches, and other unique hotel properties.

CHANTICLEER INN. *120 Gresham St, Ashland (97520). Phone 541/482-1919; toll-free 800/898-1950; fax 541/488-4810. www.ashlandbnb.com.* This inn is convenient to many area attractions such as the Shakespeare Festival, Cascade volcanoes, and the Oregon Caves. Antiques, fine art, and a beautifully manicured garden welcome guests for a romantic getaway. 6 rooms, 3 story. Complimentary full breakfast. Check-in 3-6 pm, check-out 11 am. Wireless Internet access. **$$**

COUNTRY WILLOWS BED & BREAKFAST INN. *1313 Clay St, Ashland (97520). Phone 541/488-1590; toll-free 800/945-5697; fax 541/488-1611. www.willowsinn.com.* This restored 1890s farmhouse is surrounded by 5 acres of farmland in the Siskiyou and Cascade Mountain Ranges. Breakfast is served every morning at your own private table. 9 rooms, 2 story. Children over 12 years only. Complimentary full breakfast. Check-in 3-5 pm, check-out 11 am. High-speed Internet access. Outdoor pool, whirlpool. **$$**

OAK HILL BED & BREAKFAST. *2190 Siskiyou Blvd, Ashland (97520). Phone toll-free 800/888-7434; fax 541/482-1378. www.oakhillbb.com.* 6 rooms, 2 story. Children over 12 years only. Complimentary full breakfast. Check-in 3-6 pm, check-out 11 am. **$**

ROMEO INN BED & BREAKFAST. *295 Idaho St, Ashland (97520). Phone 541/488-0884; toll-free 800/915-8899; fax 541/488-0817. www.romeoinn.com.* Established in 1982, this property has all the amenities to help guests relax and enjoy their time away from the hustle and bustle of life. Whether your idea of relaxing is swinging in the hammock amid the garden, unwinding in the jacuzzi, or swimming in the pool, this bed-and-breakfast has it all. 6 rooms, 2 story. Children over 12 years only. Complimentary full breakfast. Check-in 3-6 pm, check-out 11 am. Pool, whirlpool. **$**

Restaurants

★ **ASHLAND BAKERY & CAFE.** *38 E Main St, Ashland (97520). Phone 541/482-2117. www.ashlandbakery.com.* American, vegetarian menu. Breakfast, lunch, dinner. Closed Thanksgiving, Dec 25. **$$**

★ ★ **CHATEAULIN.** *50 E Main St, Ashland (97520). Phone 541/482-2264. www.chateaulin.com.* French menu. Dinner. Closed Thanksgiving, Dec 24-25. Bar. Children's menu. **$$$**

★ **MACARONI'S.** *58 E Main St, Ashland (97520). Phone 541/488-3359.* Italian menu. Dinner. Closed Jan 1, Thanksgiving, Dec 25. Bar. **$$**

★ ★ **WINCHESTER COUNTRY INN.** *35 S Second St, Ashland (97520). Phone 541/488-1113; toll-free 800/972-4991. www.winchesterinn.com.* Built in 1886. Continental menu. Dinner, Sun brunch. Outdoor seating. **$$**

Astoria (A-0)

See also Cannon Beach, Fort Clatsop National Memorial, Seaside

Settled 1811
Population 10,069
Elevation 18 ft
Area Code 503
Zip 97103
Information Astoria-Warrenton Chamber of Commerce, 111 W Marine Dr, PO Box 176; phone 503/325-6311 or toll-free 800/875-6807
Web site www.oldoregon.com

John Jacob Astor's partners sailed around Cape Horn and picked this point of land 10 miles from the Pacific, overlooking the mouth of the Columbia River, for a fur-trading post. The post eventually lost its importance, but the location and natural resources attracted immigrants, and the town continued to grow. A 4-mile-long bridge crosses the mouth of the Columbia here.

What to See and Do

Astoria Column. *Follow scenic drive signs to Coxcomb Hill. Phone 503/325-7275.* (1926) A 125-foot tower commemorates first settlement; observation deck at top. Gift shop. (Daily) Information booth (Memorial Day-Labor Day, daily). **FREE**

Columbia River Maritime Museum. *1792 Marine Dr, Astoria (97103). Phone 503/325-2323. www.crmm.org.* Rare maritime artifacts and memorabilia of the Columbia River, its tributaries, and the Northwest coast. Columbia, Lightship 604 at moorage in Maritime Park. Fishing industry, discovery and exploration, steamship, shipwreck, navigation, and steamboat exhibits. Coast Guard and Navy exhibits. (Daily 9:30 am-5 pm; closed Thanksgiving, Dec 25) **$$**

Flavel House. *441 8th St, Astoria (97103). Phone 503/325-2203.* (1883-1887) Built by Captain George Flavel, pilot and shipping man; outstanding example of Queen Anne architecture. Restored Victorian home houses antique furnishings and fine art; collection of 19th- and 20th-century toys. Carriage house, museum store, orientation film. (Daily; closed holidays) **$$**

⭐ **Fort Clatsop National Memorial.** *6 miles SW on Hwy 101A. www.nps.gov/focl/.* (see).

Fort Stevens State Park. *5 miles W on Hwy 101, then 5 miles N on Ridge Rd. Phone 503/861-1671.* A 3,763-acre park adjacent to old Civil War fort. Wreck

Sleepy Astoria

The oldest American settlement in the Pacific Northwest, Astoria was founded as a fur-trading fort in 1811. Thereafter, thanks to its fortuitous location at the mouth of the mighty Columbia River, the town became a prosperous shipping and fishing port. During the 1880s, sea captains and other captains of industry built magnificent homes overlooking the Columbia River. Astoria contains some of the most lovingly restored and precipitously poised Victorian homes outside of San Francisco.

Begin a walking tour of Astoria at the Columbia River Maritime Museum (1792 Marine Dr), a modern 25,000-square-foot facility that tells the story of the city's two centuries of seafaring history. The galleries explore Astoria's maritime past with exhibits on the salmon-packing industry, local lighthouses, the evolution of boat design, and delicate ivory scrimshaw work. There is also a creepy display on harpoons.

From the museum, follow Highway 30/Marine Drive to the west, and turn south on 16th Street. Housed in the former City Hall building, the Astoria Heritage Museum (1618 Exchange St) contains a commemoration of Astoria's fishing past, as well as an exhibit dedicated to the various ethnic communities that came together to form the city; take note of the Tong shrine. Another room is dedicated to the Clatsop Indians and the early days of exploration.

A block to the west, at 15th and Exchange streets, is the site of old Fort Astoria, founded in 1811 by the Pacific Fur Company. While nothing remains of the original structure, volunteers have rebuilt the blockhouse and stockade to original drawings.

Astoria's landmark Victorian mansions line the steep hills behind downtown. Climb up 16th Street to Grand Avenue. One block east is the Foard House (690 17th St), an elaborate Queen Anne mansion that is now a wildly painted bed-and-breakfast. Walk back west, past more restored mansions and below the St. Mary's Catholic Church (1465 Grand Ave), built in 1902.

Drop down to Franklin Street and continue walking westward past street after street of mammoth Victorian homes. At 137 Franklin Avenue is the oldest surviving house in Astoria, built in 1853. Other notable homes, now bed-and-breakfasts, include the Columbia River Inn (1681 Franklin St) and the Rosebriar Hotel (636 14th St), formerly a convent.

At 8th Street, turn north and walk downhill to Duane Street. Captain George Flavel, one of Astoria's leading citizens during the 1870s and 1880s, built a highly ornamented mansion, Flavel House (441 8th St), with great views over the harbor (especially from the three-story corner tower) to keep an eye on his ships. The house is now a museum that has been restored throughout and repainted with its original colors; the grounds have been returned to Victorian-era landscaping. Tours are offered daily.

From the Flavel House, drop down to Commercial Street, and walk west through sleepy downtown Astoria to again reach the Maritime Museum.

of the Peter Iredale (1906) is on the ocean shore. Fort Stevens is the only military post in the lower 48 states to be fired upon by foreign forces since 1812. On June 21, 1942, a Japanese submarine fired several shells from its 5-inch gun; only one hit land while the others fell short. Visitor center and self-guided tour at the Old Fort Stevens Military Complex. Ocean beach, lake swimming, fishing, clamming on beach, boating (dock, ramp); bicycling, picnicking at Coffenbury Lake. Improved tent and trailer sites (daily; standard fees, dump station).

Special Events

Astoria Regatta. *1609 E Habor Dr, Astoria (97146).* *Phone 503/325-2353.* Parade, arts festival, public dinner, barbecue, boating competition. Mid-Aug.

Astoria-Warrenton Crab and Seafood Festival. *1090 1st Ave, Hammond (97121). Phone 503/325-6311. Hammond Mooring Basin on Columbia River.* Crab feast, Oregon wines, food and craft booths. Carnival, water taxi, crabbing and fishing boats. Last weekend in Apr.

Great Columbia Crossing Bridge Run. *Port of Astoria, 1 Portway, Astoria (97103). Phone 503/325-6311.* One of the most unusual and scenic runs; 8 mile course begins at Chinook, WA, and ends at Astoria port docks. Mid-Oct.

Scandinavian Midsummer Festival. *Phone 503/325-4600.* Parade, folk dancing, display booths, arts and crafts demonstrations, Scandinavian food. Mid-June.

Limited-Service Hotels

★ **BEST WESTERN ASTORIA INN.** *555 Hamburg Ave, Astoria (97103). Phone 503/325-2205; toll-free 800/621-0641; fax 503/325-5550. www. bestwestern.com.* 76 rooms, 4 story. Pets accepted; fee. Complimentary continental breakfast. Check-out 11 am. Indoor pool, whirlpool. **$**

★ ★ **RED LION.** *400 Industry St, Astoria (97103). Phone 503/325-7373; fax 503/325-8727. www.redlion .com.* Overlooks harbor; on Columbia River. 124 rooms, 2 story. Pets accepted; fee. Check-out noon. Restaurant, bar. Airport transportation available. **$**

★ ★ **SHILO INN.** *1609 E Harbor Dr, Warrenton (97146). Phone 503/861-2181; toll-free 800/222-2244; fax 503/861-2980. www.shiloinns.com.* 63 rooms, 4 story. Pets accepted, some restrictions; fee. Check-out noon. Restaurant, bar. Fitness room. Indoor pool, whirlpool. Airport transportation available. **$**

Specialty Lodging

The following lodging establishment is approved by Mobil Travel Guide, but due to its unique and individualized nature has not been given a traditional Mobil Star rating. Included in this listing you may find bed-and-breakfasts, limited-service inns, guest ranches, and other unique hotel properties.

ROSEBRIAR HOTEL. *636 14th St, Astoria (97103). Phone 503/325-7427; toll-free 800/487-0224; fax 503/325-6937. www.rosebriarhotel.com.* Built in 1902 as a residence; was also used as a convent. 10 rooms, 2 story. Complimentary full breakfast. Check-in 3 pm, check-out 11 am.

Restaurants

★ ★ **PIER 11 FEED STORE.** *77 11th St, Astoria (97103). Phone 503/325-0279; fax 503/325-6101.* Old feed store on pier (late 1800s); natural beamed ceilings. Seafood, steak menu. Lunch, dinner. Closed Thanksgiving, Dec 25. Bar. **$$**

★ ★ **SHIP INN.** *1 2nd St, Astoria (97103). Phone 503/325-0033.* Seafood menu. Lunch, dinner. Closed holidays. Bar. **$$**

★ ★ **SILVER SALMON GRILLE.** *1105 Commercial St, Astoria (97103). Phone 503/338-6640. www.silversalmongrille.com.* Located on the beautiful Oregon coast in a 1924 commercial building with a renovated interior and featuring an abundance of regional specialties. American, seafood menu. Lunch, dinner. **$$**

★ ★ **T. PAUL'S URBAN CAFÉ.** *1119 Commercial St, Astoria (97103). Phone 503/338-5133. www. tpaulsurbancafe.com.* Located on the north coast in the heart of Astoria, this restaurant features eclectic, local cuisine; regional wines; and microwbrew beer. American menu. Lunch, dinner. Closed Sun. **$**

Baker City (C-5)

See also LaGrande

Population 9,140
Elevation 3,443 ft
Area Code 541
Zip 97814
Information Baker County Visitor & Convention Bureau, 490 Campbell St; phone 541/523-3356 or toll-free 800/523-1235
Web site www.visitbaker.com

The Baker City Historic District includes more than 100 commercial and residential buildings, many built from stone quarried in town at the same place where gold was found. A 15-block area, from the Powder River to 4th Street and from Estes to Campbell streets, has many structures built between 1890 and 1910 that are being restored. Baker City, on the "old Oregon trail," is also the home of the Armstrong Gold Nugget found by George Armstrong on June 19, 1913. It weighs more than 80 ounces. A Ranger District office and the office of the supervisor of the Wallowa-Whitman National Forest are located here.

What to See and Do

Eastern Oregon Museum. *610 3rd St, Baker City (97814). 9 miles NW on old Hwy 30.* Phone 541/856-3233. A large collection of relics and implements used in the development of the West; turn-of-the-century logging and mining tools; period rooms; doll collection; children's antique furniture. On the grounds is an 1884 railroad depot. (Mid-Apr-Labor Day, daily) **$**

National Historic Oregon Trail Interpretive Center. *Hwy 86, Baker City (97814). 5 miles E on Hwy 86, at summit of Flagstaff Hill.* Phone toll-free 800/523-1235. Exhibits, living history presentations, multimedia displays. (Daily; closed Jan 1, Dec 25) **$$$**

Oregon Trail Regional Museum. *2490 Grove St, Baker City (97814).* Phone 541/523-9308; toll-free 800/523-1235. Houses one of the most outstanding collections of rocks, minerals, and semiprecious stones in the West. Also, an elaborate sea-life display; wildlife display; period clothing and artifacts of early Baker County. (Late Mar-Oct, daily) **$**

Sumpter Valley Railway. *30 miles SW on Hwy 7.* Phone 541/894-2268; toll-free 800/523-1235. www.svry .com. A restored gear-driven Heisler steam locomotive and two observation cars travel 7 miles on a narrow-gauge track through a wildlife game habitat area where beavers, muskrats, geese, waterfowl, herons, and other animals can be seen. The train also passes through the Sumpter mining district, the location of the Sumpter Dredge, which brought up more than $10 million in gold between 1913 and 1954 from as far down as 20 feet. (Memorial Day-Sept, weekends and holidays) **$$**

Unity Lake State Park. *Hwy 26, Mount Vernon. 45 miles SW on Hwy 245, near junction Hwy 26.* Phone 541/575-2773. A 39-acre park with swimming, fishing, boat ramp on Unity Lake; picnicking, tent and improved-site camping.

Wallowa-Whitman National Forest. *47794 Oregon Hwy 244, Baker City (97850). Sections W, NE, and S.* Phone 541/523-6391. More than 2 million acres with 14,000-acre North Fork John Day Wilderness; 7,000-acre Monument Rock Wilderness; 358,461-acre Eagle Cap Wilderness; 215,500-acre Hells Canyon Wilderness. Snowcapped peaks, Minam River; alpine meadows, rare wildflowers; national scenic byway, scenic drive Hells Canyon Overlook, which overlooks deepest canyon in North America—Hells Canyon National Recreation Area; Buckhorn Lookout; Anthony Lake and Phillips Lake. Stream and lake trout fishing; elk, deer, and bear hunting; float and jet boat trips; saddle and pack trips. Picnic area. Camping. For further information contact Supervisor, PO Box 907. In the forest is

Anthony Lakes Ski Area. *47500 Anthony Lake Hwy, North Powder (97867). 35 miles NW, off I-84.* Phone 541/856-3277. www.anthonylakes.com. Triple chairlift, Pomalift; patrol, school, rentals; nursery; day lodge, cafeteria, concession area, bar. Longest run 1 1/2 miles; vertical drop 900 feet. Cross-country trails. (Mid-Nov-mid-Apr, Thurs-Sun) Fishing, hiking, cabin rentals, store (summer). **$$$$**

Special Event

Miner's Jubilee. *490 Campbell St, Baker City (97814).* Phone 541/523-5855. Third weekend in July.

Limited-Service Hotels

★ ★ **BEST WESTERN SUNRIDGE INN.**
1 Sunridge Ln, Baker City (97814). Phone 541/
523-6444; toll-free 800/233-2368; fax 541/523-6446.
www.bestwestern.com. 155 rooms, 2 story. Check-out
noon. Restaurant. Pool, whirlpool. Airport transportation available. **$**

★ ★ **GEISER GRAND HOTEL.** *1996 Main St,*
Baker City (97814). Phone 541/488-1889; toll-free 888/
434-7374; fax 541/523-1800. www.geisergrand.com.
30 rooms. Check-in 3 pm, check-out noon.
Restaurant, bar. **$**

Bandon (D-1)

See also Coos Bay, North Bend, Port Orford

Population 2,215
Elevation 67 ft
Area Code 541
Zip 97411
Information Chamber of Commerce, PO Box 1515;
phone 503/347-9616

A fine beach, known for its picturesque beauty,
legendary rocks, and a harbor at the mouth of the
Coquille River attracts many travelers to Bandon.
From November through March, the town is known
for its short-lived storms followed by sunshine; it
even has a group called the Storm Watchers. Popular
seashore activities include beachcombing, hiking, fishing from the south jetty, and crabbing from the docks.
Summer and early autumn bring the salmon run
in the Coquille River. Rockhounds search for agate,
jasper, and petrified wood.

What to See and Do

Bandon Museum. *300 2nd St, Bandon (97411). Hwy*
101 and Filmore Ave. Phone 541/347-2164. Exhibits
on maritime activities of early Bandon and Coquille
River; coastal shipwrecks, Coast Guard operations;
extensive collection of Native American artifacts; old
photos. (Schedule varies) **$**

Bullards Beach State Park. *52470 Hwy 101, Bandon*
(97411). 2 miles N on Hwy 101. Phone 541/347-3501.

A 1,266-acre park with 4 miles of ocean beach.
Fishing; boating (dock, ramp with access to Coquille
River). Picnicking. Improved trailer campsites (dump
station). Coquille River Lighthouse (1896); interpretive plaques (May-Oct, daily). **FREE**

Face Rock State Park. *4 miles S on Hwy 101, then 1*
mile W on Bradley Lake Rd. Phone 541/347-3501. An
879-acre park on coastal dune area with access to
beach; fishing. Picnicking. **FREE**

West Coast Game Park. *7 miles S on Hwy 101. Phone*
541/347-3106. A 21-acre park with more than 450
exotic animals and birds. Visitors meet and walk with
free-roaming wildlife. Animal keepers demonstrate
the personalities of many large predators residing at
the park. (Mar-Nov: daily; rest of year: weekends and
holidays) **$$$**

Special Events

Cranberry Festival. *Phone 541/347-9616.* Parade,
barbecue, square dances, harvest ball, sports events.
Sept.

Wine & Food Festival. *300 2nd, Bandon (97121).*
Phone 541/347-9616. Memorial Day weekend.

Limited-Service Hotels

★ ★ **BEST WESTERN INN AT FACE ROCK**
RESORT. *3225 Beach Loop Rd, Bandon (97411).*
Phone 541/347-9441; toll-free 800/638-3092; fax 541/
347-2532. www.facerock.net. 74 rooms. Pets accepted,
some restrictions; fee. Check-in 4 pm, check-out
11 am. Restaurant. Children's activity center. Fitness
room. Beach. Indoor pool, whirlpool. Golf, 9 holes.
Business center. **$$**

★ ★ **SUNSET OCEANFRONT LODGING.** *1865*
Beach Loop Dr, Bandon (97411). Phone 541/347-2453;
toll-free 800/842-2407; fax 541/347-3636. www.sunset-
motel.com. Located on Bandon's scenic Beach Loop
Drive just south of the mouth of the Coquille River,
this hotel offers exceptional views of the Pacific and
its rugged coastline. The large family-owned property
is made up of a motel-like structure as well as cabins,
houses, and studios, many of which have kitchen
facilities. With easy access to a private beach, all

outdoor activities here are oriented toward the ocean. 71 rooms, 2 story. Pets accepted; fee. Check-in 4 pm, check-out 11 am. Restaurant, bar. Indoor pool, whirlpool. **$**

Full-Service Resort

★ ★ ★ **BANDON DUNES GOLF RESORT.**
57744 Round Lake Rd, Bandon (97411). Phone 541/347-4380; toll-free 888/345-6008; fax 541/347-8161. www.bandondunesgolf.com. The Bandon Dunes Golf Resort sits alongside the windswept coast of the Pacific Ocean. The property offers luxurious accommodations for the Bandon Dunes Golf Resort, home to two of the Northwest's premiere 18-hole golf courses. All rooms feature scenic views, and some have fireplaces and private balconies. Just off the lobby, The Gallery Restaurant serves three meals a day, specializing in fresh Pacific Northwest seafood. 153 rooms. Check-in 4 pm, check-out 11 am. High-speed Internet access. Two restaurants, two bars. Fitness room. Beach. Whirlpool. Golf, 36 holes. Airport transportation available. Business center. **$$**

Restaurants

★ ★ **BANDON BOATWORKS.** *275 Lincoln Ave SW, Bandon (97411). Phone 541/347-2111.* Seafood menu. Lunch, dinner. Closed Dec 25. Children's menu. Casual attire. Valet parking. **$$**

★ ★ **LORD BENNETT'S.** *1695 Beach Loop Dr, Bandon (97411). Phone 541/347-3663; fax 541/347-9032. www.lordbennetts.com.* Come relish this restaurant's spectacular Pacific Ocean view and fresh, straightforward preparations of pasta, beef, pork, veal, chicken, and seafood. The atmosphere is refined but casual with a slightly nautical feel, and the adjacent lounge offers great cocktails and live entertainment. Seafood, steak menu. Lunch, dinner, late-night, Sun brunch. Bar. Children's menu. Casual attire. **$$**

★ ★ **WHEELHOUSE.** *125 Chicago Ave, Bandon (97411). Phone 541/347-9331.* In restored fish warehouse. Seafood, steak menu. Lunch, dinner. Bar. Children's menu. Casual attire. **$$**

Beaverton (B-2)

See also Forest Grove, Hillsboro, Newburg, Oregon City, Portland

Population 53,310
Elevation 189 ft
Area Code 503
Zip 97005
Information Beaverton Area Chamber of Commerce, 4800 SW Griffith Dr, Suite 100; phone 503/644-0123
Web site www.beaverton.org

Nestled amid the scenic rolling hills and lush forests of the Tualatin Valley, Beaverton appeals to those who love to explore the great outdoors, with more than 100 public parks, 30 miles of hiking trails, and a 25-mile network of bike paths. In fact, every home in the city is within a half mile of a park. Beaverton is situated midway between the beaches of the Pacific Ocean and the ski slopes at Mount Hood, an enviable location to find oneself, allowing for either destination to be reached in an hour's drive. Oregon's 5th most populous city, Beaverton boasts strong public schools and close-knit residential neighborhoods. Economically, the city has been strengthened by the tremendous success of Nike, which is headquartered here. Each July, Beaverton's SummerFest features a parade, live music, freshly prepared food, and an arts and crafts marketplace. The event draws thousands to this friendly community 7 miles west of Portland.

Limited-Service Hotels

★ ★ **BEST WESTERN GREENWOOD INN & SUITES.** *10700 SW Allen Blvd, Beaverton (97005). Phone 503/643-7444; toll-free 800/289-1300; fax 503/626-4553. www.greenwoodinn.com.* Located minutes from downtown Portland, this modern hotel is known best for its design and service. 250 rooms, 2 story. Pets accepted; fee. Check-out 1 pm. Restaurant, bar. Outdoor pool, whirlpool. Business center. **$**

★ ★ **COURTYARD BY MARRIOTT.** *8500 SW Nimbus Dr, Beaverton (97008). Phone 503/641-3200; toll-free 800/831-0224; fax 503/641-1287. www.courtyard.com.* 149 rooms, 3 story. Check-out noon. Bar. Fitness room. Indoor pool, whirlpool. **$**

★ **FAIRFIELD INN.** *15583 NW Gateway Ct, Beaverton (97006). Phone 503/972-0048; fax 503/972-0049. www.fairfieldinn.com/pdxfh.* 106 rooms, 4 story. Complimentary continental breakfast. Check-out noon. Fitness room. Indoor pool, whirlpool. **$**

🧍 ⛵

Restaurants

★ ★ ★ **PAVILION TRATTORIA.** *10700 SW Allen Blvd, Beaverton (97005). Phone 503/626-4550. www. paviliontrattoria.citysearch.com.* American menu. Breakfast, lunch, dinner, Sun brunch. Bar. Children's menu. Outdoor seating. **$$**

★ ★ **SAYLER'S OLD COUNTRY KITCHEN.** *4655 SW Griffith Dr, Beaverton (97005). Phone 503/644-1492; fax 503/644-5424.* American menu. Dinner. Closed holidays. Bar. Children's menu. **$$**

Bend (C-3)

See also Prineville, Redmond

Settled 1900
Population 20,469
Elevation 3,628 ft
Area Code 541
Information Chamber of Commerce, 63085 N Hwy 97, 97701; phone 541/382-3221 or toll-free 800/905-2363
Web site www.bendchamber.org

The early town was named Farewell Bend after a beautiful wooded area on a sweeping curve of the Deschutes River, where pioneer travelers had their last view of the river. The Post Office Department short-ened it, but there was good reason for this nostalgic name. As westward-bound settlers approached, they found the first lush, green forests and good water they had seen in Oregon.

Tourists are attracted year-round to the region by its streams, lakes, mountains, great pine forests, ski slopes, and golf courses. There is also much of interest to geologists and rockhounds in this area. Movie and television producers often take advantage of the wild western scenery.

Two Ranger District offices of the Deschutes National Forest are located here.

What to See and Do

Deschutes National Forest. *1645 Hwy 20 E, Bend (97701). Phone 541/383-5300. www.fs.fed.us/r6/centraloregon/index.shtml.* The Deschutes National Forest encompasses 1.6 million acres of ruggedly scenic wilderness, a broad and diverse expanse of land marked by snow-capped mountains, craggy volcanic formations, old-growth forests, and deep rivers knifing through high-desert canyons. Established as a national forest in 1908, Deschutes has become one of the Pacific Northwest's most popular year-round tourist destinations, attracting over 8 million visitors annually. The winter months bring hordes of skiers and snowmobilers. Oregon's largest ski resort can be found alongside the 9,065-foot-high Mt. Bachelor. Hikers arrive after the spring thaw, eager to take advantage of the area's 1,388 miles of trails—including 60 miles of the Pacific Crest National Scenic Trail. Cars carrying strapped-down canoes and kayaks are a common sight, with paddlers headed to the Deschutes River, which has been designated both a National Scenic River and a National Recreational River. Anglers are drawn to the forest's 157 trout-filled lakes and reservoirs. Situated on the eastern side of the Cascade Mountains, the Deschutes National Forest gets significantly more sunshine than the rainier western side, but drier conditions also create a greater risk for forest fires. In the summer of 2003, the Booth and Bear Butte fires burned nearly 91,000 acres over the course of 39 days. The rapidly growing town of Bend lies just to the east of Deschutes, offering visitors a return to civilization after an exhausting day of outdoor adventure.

⭐ **Driving Tour in Deschutes National Forest.** *1645 Hwy 20 E, Bend (97701). Phone 541/388-2715.* An 89-mile paved loop (Century Dr, Cascade Lakes Hwy) provides a clear view of Three Sisters peaks, passes many mountain lakes and streams. Go west on Franklin Ave past Drake Park, follow the signs. Continue south past Mt. Bachelor, Elk Lake, Lava Lakes, and Cultus Lake. After passing Crane Prairie Reservoir, turn left (east) on Forest Rd 42 to Highway 97, then left (north) for return to Bend. Also in the forest are Newberry National Volcanic Monument, the Lava Cast Forest and Lava Butte Geological Area, Mt. Bachelor Ski Area, Crane Prairie Osprey Management Area, as well as Mt. Jefferson, Diamond Peak, Three Sisters, and Mt. Washington wildernesses. Fishing, hiking, camping, picnicking, and rafting are popular.

The forest includes 1.6 million acres with headquarters in Bend. Ten miles south of Bend, at the base of Lava Butte, is Lava Lands Visitor Center, operated by the US Forest Service, with dioramas and exhibits on history and geology of volcanic area. For further information contact Supervisor, 1645 Hwy 20 E, 97701.

The High Desert Museum. *59800 S Hwy 97, Bend (97702). 6 miles S on Hwy 97. Phone 541/382-4754. www.highdesert.org.* A regional museum with indoor/outdoor exhibits featuring live animals and cultural history of Intermountain Northwest aridlands; hands-on activities; ongoing presentations. The galleries house wildlife, Western art, and Native American artifacts; landscape photography; and walk-through dioramas depicting the opening of the American West. The desertarium showcases seldom-seen bats, burrowing owls, amphibians, and reptiles. (Daily 9 am-5 pm; closed Jan 1, Thanksgiving, Dec 25) **$$**

LaPine. *15800 State Recreation Rd, Bend (97739). 22 miles S on Hwy 97, then 4 miles W. Phone 541/388-6055.* A 2,333-acre park on Deschutes River in Ponderosa pine forest. Scenic views. Swimming, bathhouse, fishing, boating; picnicking, improved trailer campsites (dump station).

Lava Butte and Lava River Cave. *58201 Hwy 97 S, Bend (97707). 11 miles S on Hwy 97. Phone 541/593-2421.* Lava Butte is an extinct cinder cone. Paved road to top provides view of Cascades; interpretive trails through pine forest and lava flow. One mile south, Lava River Cave offers a lava tube 1.2 miles long (fee); ramps and stairs ease walking. Visitor center has audiovisual shows (May-Sept, daily). **$$**

Mount Bachelor Ski Area. *22 miles SW on Century Dr. Phone 541/382-2442; toll-free 800/829-2442 (reservations). www.mtbachelor.com.* Panoramic, scenic view of forests, lakes, and Cascade Range. Facilities at base of 6,000 feet; 6,000 acres. Ten chairlifts; patrol, school, rentals; cafeterias, concession areas, bars, lodges; day care. Longest run 1 1/2 miles; vertical drop 3,365 feet. 56 miles of cross-country trails. (Mid-Nov-May, daily) **$$$$**

Newberry National Volcanic Monument. *1645 Hwy 20 E, Bend (97701). 24 miles S on Hwy 97, then 14 miles E on Forest Rd 21, in Deschutes National Forest. Phone 541/383-5300. www.fs.fed.us/r6/centraloregon/newberrynvm/index.shtml.* This monument, an active volcano, has a wide range of volcanic features

and deposits similar to Mount Etna; obsidian flow, pumice deposits. On same road are East and Paulina lakes, both of which have excellent fishing as well as boat landings; hiking, picnicking (stoves, fireplaces), resorts, tent and trailer sites. You can get a view of the entire area from Paulina Peak, at nearly 8,000 feet. **$$**

Pilot Butte. *2880 NE 27th St, Bend (97701). 1 mile E on Hwy 20. Phone 541/388-6055.* A 101-acre park noted for a lone cinder cone rising 511 feet above the city. Summit affords an excellent view of the Cascade Range. No water, no camping.

Pine Mount Observatory. *26 miles SE near Millican, via Hwy 20, then 9 miles S. Phone 541/382-8331 (for appointment).* University of Oregon astronomical research facility. Visitors may view stars, planets, and galaxies through telescopes. (Memorial Day-Sept, Fri and Sat) **$$**

Tumalo. *5 1/2 miles NW off Hwy 20. Phone 541/382-3586.* A 320-acre park situated along the banks of the Deschutes River; swimming nearby, fishing; hiking, picnicking, tent and trailer campsites; solar-heated showers.

Tumalo Falls. *Skyliner Rd and Tumalo Falls, Bend (97701). W via Franklin Ave and Galveston Ave, 12 miles beyond city limits, then 2 miles via unsurfaced forest road. Phone 541/383-5300.* A 97-foot waterfall deep in pine forest devastated by 1979 fire.

Whitewater Rafting. *Sun Country Tours, 531 SW 13th St, Bend (97702). Phone 541/382-6277. www.suncountrytours.com.* Choose from 2-hour or all-day trips. Also canoeing and special programs. (May-Sept) **$$$$**

Limited-Service Hotels

★★ **MOUNT BACHELOR VILLAGE RESORT.** *19717 Mount Bachelor Dr, Bend (97701). Phone 541/389-5900; toll-free 800/452-9846; fax 541/388-7820. www.mountbachelorvillage.com.* Woodland setting along Deschutes River. 130 rooms, 2 story. Check-out noon. Restaurant. Pool. Tennis. Business center. **$$**

★★ **RED LION.** *1415 NE 3rd St, Bend (97701). Phone 541/382-7011; fax 541/382-7934. www.redlion.com.* 75 rooms, 2 story. Pets accepted. Check-out noon. Restaurant. Pool, whirlpool. **$**

★ ★ **THE RIVERHOUSE.** *3075 N Hwy 97, Bend (97701). Phone 541/389-3111; toll-free 800/547-3928; fax 541/389-0870. www.riverhouse.com.* This resort is located on the Deschutes River and features such amenities as refrigerators and microwaves, an indoor/outdoor pool, and golfing and skiing packages. 220 rooms, 2 story. Pets accepted. Check-out noon. Restaurant. Indoor, outdoor pool. Golf. **$**

★ ★ **SHILO INN.** *3105 NE O. B. Riley Rd, Bend (97701). Phone 541/389-9600; toll-free 800/222-2244; fax 541/382-4310. www.shiloinns.com.* On Deschutes River. 151 rooms, 2 story. Pets accepted, some restrictions; fee. Check-out noon. Restaurant, bar. Fitness room. Indoor pool, outdoor pool, whirlpool. Airport transportation available. **$**

Full-Service Resorts

★ ★ ★ **INN OF THE SEVENTH MOUNTAIN.** *18575 SW Century Dr, Bend (97702). Phone 541/ 382-8711; toll-free 800/452-6810; fax 541/382-3517. www.7thmtn.com.* With breathtaking views both in summer and winter, this beautiful oasis is set in Deschutes National Forest. Activities such as whitewater rafting, horseback riding, golfing, and canoeing make it Oregon's premier resort destination. 300 rooms, 3 story. Check-out noon. Restaurant, bar. Children's activity center. Two pools, children's pool, whirlpool. Tennis. **$**

★ ★ ★ **SUNRIVER RESORT.** *1 Center Dr, Sunriver (97707). Phone 541/593-1000; toll-free 800/801-8765; fax 541/593-4167. www.sunriverresort .com.* Central Oregon's Sunriver Resort is one of the state's best vacation destinations. This full-service, all-season resort on the sunny side of the scenic Cascade Mountain Range offers visitors a complete getaway with an endless supply of recreational opportunities, including sparkling pools, three 18-hole golf courses, a state-of-the-art fitness center, and an elegant spa. Recreational opportunities run the gamut from canoe and kayak trips to 30 miles of biking trails to a challenge ropes course, while the Sunriver Nature Center and Observatory offers stargazing, a botanical garden, and nature trails. Whether you plan to stay for just a few days or enjoy a longer visit, the accommodations range from deluxe rooms in the River Lodges and rooms and suites in the Lodge Village to private home and condominium rentals. Several restaurants entice diners with distinctive Northwestern cuisine or classic pub-food favorites, and regional beers and wines are a special highlight. 441 rooms, 2 story. Check-in 4 pm, check-out 11 am. Three restaurants, bar. Children's activity center. Fitness room, fitness classes available, spa. Three pools, children's pool, whirlpool. Golf, 54 holes. Tennis. Airport transportation available. Business center. **$**

Specialty Lodgings

The following lodging establishments are approved by Mobil Travel Guide, but due to their unique and individualized nature have not been given a traditional Mobil Star rating. Included in this listing you may find bed-and-breakfasts, limited-service inns, guest ranches, and other unique hotel properties.

DIAMOND STONE GUEST LODGE. *16693 Sprague Loop, LaPine (97739). Phone 541/536-6263; toll-free 800/600-6263. www.diamondstone.com.* This lodge sits adjacent to Quail Run Golf Course, at the gateway to Newberry National Volcanic Monument, with the Cascade Mountains as a backdrop. Surrounded by open meadows and pines, there are plenty of trails for hiking and exploring. 3 rooms, 2 story. **$**

ROCK SPRINGS GUEST RANCH. *64201 Tyler Rd, Bend (97701). Phone 541/382-1957; toll-free 800/ 225-3833; fax 541/382-7774. www.rocksprings.com.* 26 rooms. Check-in 4:30 pm, check-out 11 am. Restaurant. Children's activity center. Fitness room. Pool, whirlpool. Tennis. Airport transportation available. **$$**

Restaurants

★ ★ **COWBOY DINNER TREE.** *4 miles S on Hager Mountain Rd, Silver Lake (97638). Phone 541/576-2426. www.cowboydinnertree.homestead.com.* A very traditional Old West restaurant with a very limited menu and hours, but worth a visit, for the great food and atmosphere. Located in a turn-of-the-century ranch. American menu. Dinner. Closed Mon, Tues, Thurs. No credit cards accepted. **$$**

★ ★ ★ **ERNESTO'S ITALIAN RESTAURANT.**
*1203 NE 3rd St, Bend (97701). Phone 541/389-7274;
fax 541/389-1686.* This former church is now a family
restaurant featuring basic Italian fare. Service is courteous and helpful, but the food may be a little heavy at
times. Italian menu. Dinner. Bar. Children's menu. **$$**
🐕

★ ★ ★ **MEADOWS.** *1 Center Dr, Sunriver
(97707). Phone 541/593-1000. www.sunriver-resort
.com.* American menu. Dinner. Bar. **$$**

★ ★ **PINE TAVERN.** *967 NW Brooks St, Bend
(97701). Phone 541/382-5581. www.pinetavern.com.*
100-foot pine tree in dining room. Seafood, steak
menu. Lunch, dinner. Bar. Children's menu. Outdoor
seating. **$$**

★ **ROSZAK'S FISH HOUSE.** *1230 NE 3rd St,
Bend (97701). Phone 541/382-3173.* Seafood, steak
menu. Lunch, dinner. Closed Memorial Day, Labor
Day. Bar. Children's menu. **$$**

★ **TONY'S.** *415 NE 3rd St, Bend (97701). Phone
541/389-5858.* American, Italian menu. Breakfast,
lunch, dinner. Closed Dec 25. Bar. Children's menu.
$$

★ **WESTSIDE BAKERY & CAFE.** *1005 NW
Galveston Ave, Bend (97701). Phone 541/382-3426.*
American menu. Breakfast, lunch. Closed
Thanksgiving, Dec 25. Children's menu. **$**

Biggs

See also The Dalles

Population 30
Elevation 173 ft
Area Code 541
Zip 97065

What to See and Do

John Day Locks and Dam. *5 miles E off I-84 N.* A
$487-million unit in the US Army Corps of Engineers
Columbia River Basin project. Visitors may view
turbine generators from powerhouse observation
room; fish-viewing stations. Self-guided tours (daily;
guided tours by appointment; closed holidays). **FREE**
The dam creates

Lake Umatilla. A 100-mile reservoir. The eastern
part of the lake is a national wildlife management
area for the preservation of game waterfowl and fish.

Brookings (E-1)

See also Coos Bay, Gold Beach

Population 4,400
Elevation 130 ft
Area Code 541
Zip 97415
Information Brookings-Harbor Chamber of
Commerce and Information Center, 16330 Lower
Harbor Rd, PO Box 940; phone 541/469-3181 or
toll-free 800/535-9469
Web site www.brookingsor.com

Beachcombers, whale-watchers, and fishermen find
this coastal city a haven for their activities. A commer-
cial and sportfishing center, Brookings lies in an area
that produces a high percentage of the nation's Easter
lily bulbs. A Ranger District office of the Siskiyou
National Forest is located here.

What to See and Do

Azalea Park. *Hwy 101 and N Bank Chetco River
Rd, Brookings (97415). Just E off Hwy 101. Phone 541/
469-2021.* A 36-acre city park with five varieties of
large native azaleas, some blooming twice a year.
Observation point. Hiking. Picnicking.

Harris Beach. *1655 Hwy 101 N, Brookings (97415).
2 miles N on Hwy 101. Phone 541/469-2021.* A
171-acre park with scenic rock cliffs along ocean.
Ocean beach, fishing; hiking trails, observation point,
picnicking, improved tent and trailer campsites
(dump station).

Loeb. *1601 Hwy 101 N, Brookings (97415). 10 miles
NE off Hwy 101. Phone 541/469-2021.* A 320-acre
park on the Chetco River with an area of beautiful
old myrtle trees; also redwoods. Swimming, fishing;
picnicking, improved camping.

Samuel H. Boardman. *4655 Hwy 101 N, Brookings
(97415). 4 miles N on Hwy 101. Phone 541/469-2021.*
A 1,473-acre park with observation points along
11 miles of spectacular coastline. Fishing, clamming;
hiking, picnicking.

Special Event

Azalea Festival. *Azalea Park, Brookings. Phone 541/469-2021.* Parade, seafood, art exhibits, street fair, crafts fair, music. Memorial Day weekend.

Limited-Service Hotel

★ ★ **BEST WESTERN BROOKINGS INN.** *1143 Chetco Ave, Brookings (97415). Phone 541/469-2173; toll-free 800/822-9087; fax 541/469-2996. www.bestwestern.com.* 68 rooms. Check-in 3 pm, check-out noon. Restaurant, bar. Indoor pool, whirlpool. Business center. **$**

Burns (D-5)

Population 2,913
Elevation 4,170 ft
Area Code 541
Zip 97720
Information Harney County Chamber of Commerce, 18 W D St; phone 541/573-2636
Web site www.harneycounty.com

This remote trading center and county seat serves a livestock-raising and forage production area bigger than many eastern states. Ranger District offices of the Malheur National Forest and Ochoco National Forest are located here.

What to See and Do

Harney County Historical Museum. *18 West D St, Burns (97720). Phone 541/573-5618.* Displays include arrowheads, quilts, wildlife, artifacts, furniture, clothing, cut glass, old-fashioned kitchen, Pete French's safe and spurs. The Hayes Room contains a bedroom and dining room furnished in antiques. Also old wagons, tools, and machinery. (Apr-Oct, Mon-Sat; closed July 4) **$$**

Malheur National Wildlife Refuge. *36391 Sodhouse Ln, Princeton (97721). 32 miles S on Hwy 205. Phone 541/493-2612. pacific.fws.gov/malheur.* Established in 1908 by Theodore Roosevelt, the 185,000-acre refuge was set aside primarily as a nesting area for migratory birds. It is also an important fall and spring gathering point for waterfowl migrating between the northern breeding grounds and the California wintering grounds. More than 320 species of birds and 58 species of mammals have been recorded on the refuge. The headquarters has a museum. (Daily dawn-dusk) **FREE**

Special Events

Harney County Fair, Rodeo and Race Meet. *Phone 541/573-6166.* Includes rodeo and pari-mutuel racing. Tues-Sun after Labor Day.

John Scharff Migratory Bird Festival. *76 E Washington St, Burns (97720). Phone 541/573-2636.* Includes bird-watching and historical tours, films, arts and crafts. First weekend in Apr.

Steens Mountain Rim Run. *Phone 541/573-2636. In Frenchglen, approximately 48 miles S on Hwy 205.* Features a 6-mile run at high elevation, pit barbecue, all-night street dance, team-roping, horse cutting. First Sat in Aug.

Limited-Service Hotel

★ **DAYS INN.** *577 W Monroe St, Burns (97720). Phone 541/573-2047; toll-free 800/303-2047; fax 541/573-3828. www.daysinn.com.* 52 rooms, 2 story. Pets accepted; fee. Complimentary continental breakfast. Check-out 11 am. Pool. **$**

Restaurant

★ ★ **PINE ROOM CAFE.** *543 W Monroe, Burns (97720). Phone 541/573-6631.* American menu. Dinner. Closed Sun-Mon; holidays. Bar. **$$**

Cannon Beach (A-1)

See also Astoria, Rockaway, Seaside

Population 1,588
Elevation 25 ft
Area Code 503
Zip 97110
Information Cannon Beach Chamber of Commerce Visitor Information Center, 207 N Spruce, PO Box 64; phone 503/436-2623
Web site www.cannonbeach.org

The cannon and capstan from the survey schooner USS *Shark,* which washed ashore near here in 1846, are now on a small monument 4 miles south of this resort town. Swimming (with a lifeguard on duty in summer), surfing, and surf fishing can be enjoyed here, and the 7-mile stretch of wide beach is wonderful for walking. Among the large rocks offshore is the 235-foot Haystack Rock, the third-largest monolith in the world. Migrating gray whales often can be spotted heading south from mid-December to early February and then heading back north in early to mid-spring.

What to See and Do

Ecola State Park. *Ecola Rd, Cannon Beach. 2 miles N off Hwy 101. Phone 503/861-1671.* End of the trail for Lewis and Clark expedition. A 1,303-acre park with 6 miles of ocean frontage; sea lion and bird rookeries on rocks and offshore islands; Tillamook Lighthouse. Beaches, fishing; hiking (on the Oregon Coast Trail), picnicking at Ecola Point. Whale-watching at observation point.

Oswald West State Park. *9500 Sandpiper Ln, Nehalem (97131). 10 miles S on Hwy 101. Phone 503/368-5943. www.oregonstateparks.org/park_195.php.* A 2,474-acre park with outstanding coastal headland, towering cliffs, low dunes, and rain forest with massive spruce and cedar trees. The road winds 700 feet above sea level and 1,000 feet below the peak of Neahkahnie Mountain. Surfing (at nearby Short Sands Beach), fishing; hiking trails (on the Oregon Coast Trail), picnicking, primitive campgrounds accessible only by a 1/4-mile foot trail. **FREE**

Special Event

Sandcastle Contest. *Phone 503/436-2623.* Nationally known event features sand sculptures on beach. Early June.

Limited-Service Hotels

★ **HALLMARK RESORT.** *PO Box 547, Cannon Beach (97110). Phone 503/436-1566; toll-free 800/ 345-5676; fax 503/436-0324. www.hallmarkinns.com.* Located in Cannon Beach, this property overlooks Haystack Rock. 137 rooms, 3 story. Pets accepted, some restrictions; fee. Check-in 4 pm, check-out noon. Fitness room. On beach. Indoor pool, children's pool, whirlpool. **$**

★ ★ **SURFSAND RESORT.** *Oceanfront, Cannon Beach (97110). Phone 503/436-2274; toll-free 800/547-6100; fax 503/436-9116. www.surfsand.com.* 82 rooms, 2 story. Pets accepted, some restrictions; fee. Check-out noon. Restaurant, bar. On ocean, beach. Indoor pool, whirlpool. **$$**

★ **TOLOVANA INN.** *3400 S Hemlock, Cannon Beach (97145). Phone 503/436-2211; toll-free 800/ 333-8890; fax 503/436-0134. www.tolovanainn.com.* 175 rooms, 3 story. Pets accepted, some restrictions; fee. Check-out noon. Indoor pool, whirlpool. **$**

Restaurant

★ ★ **DOOGER'S.** *1371 S Hemlock, Cannon Beach (97110). Phone 503/436-2225.* Seafood, steak menu. Breakfast, lunch, dinner. Closed Thanksgiving Dec 25. Bar. Children's menu. **$$$**

Cave Junction (E-1)

See also Grants Pass, Oregon Caves National Monument

Population 1,126
Elevation 1,295 ft
Area Code 541
Zip 97523
Information Illinois Valley Chamber of Commerce, 201 Caves Hwy, PO Box 312; phone 541/592-3326
Web site www.cavejunction.com

This small rural community in the picturesque Illinois Valley is the gateway to the Oregon Caves National Monument. Surrounding forest lands offer opportunities for fishing, hiking, and backpacking. A Ranger District office of the Siskiyou National Forest is located here.

What to See and Do

Kerbyville Museum. *24195 Redwood Hwy, Kerby (97531). 2 miles N on Hwy 199. Phone 541/592-2076.* Home (circa 1870) furnished in the period; outdoor display of farm, logging, and mining tools; Native American artifacts; rock display; log schoolhouse, blacksmith shop, general store. Picnic tables. (Mar-Dec, daily) **$$**

Special Events

Annual Moon Tree Country Run. *Siskiyou Smoke Jump Base, Cave Junction. Phone 541/596-2621.* Mid-June.

Wild Blackberry Festival. *Phone 541/592-3326.* Blackberry foods, cooking, games, crafts and music. Mid-Aug.

Limited-Service Hotel

★ ★ **OREGON CAVES LODGE.** *20000 Caves Hwy, Cave Junction (97523). Phone 541/592-3400; fax 541/592-3800.* 22 rooms, 3 story. Closed Nov-Apr. Check-out 11 am. Restaurant. Business center. **$**
🔲 🏃

Coos Bay (D-1)

See also Bandon, Brookings, North Bead, Reedsport

Founded 1854
Population 15,374
Elevation 11 ft
Area Code 541
Zip 97420
Information Bay Area Chamber of Commerce, 50 E Central, PO Box 210; phone 541/269-0215 or toll-free 800/824-8486
Web site www.oregonsbayareachamber.com

This charming port town borders a bay that shares its name. The bay itself is the largest natural harbor between San Francisco and Seattle, and since the earliest pioneer days it has served as a key means of commercial passage to and from the sea. Coos Bay is the state's second busiest maritime center, supported by such industries as forestry, shipbuilding, and fishing. Outdoor enthusiasts appreciate the area's mild climate (the temperature rarely falls below 45 degrees F) and the terrific recreational opportunities available at three local state parks: Cape Arago, Shore Acres, and Sunset Bay. Anglers flock to the shores of the nearby Coos River, which is considered one of best places in Oregon to catch salmon and steelhead.

What to See and Do

Cape Arago. *Cape Arago Hwy, Coos Bay. 14 miles SW off Hwy 101 on Cape Arago Hwy. Phone 541/888-8867.*

www.oregonstateparks.org. This 134-acre promontory juts 1/2 mile into the ocean. Two beaches, fishing; hiking (on Oregon Coast Trail), picnicking. Observation point (whale and seal watching).

Charleston Marina Complex. *63534 Kingfisher Dr, Charleston (97420). 9 miles SW. Phone 541/888-2548. www.charlestonmarina.com.* Charter boats; launching and moorage facilities (fee); car and boat trailer parking (free); dry boat storage, travel park; motel; marine fuel dock; tackle shops; restaurants. Office (Mon-Fri).

The Oregon Connection/House of Myrtlewood. *1125 S 1st St, Coos Bay (97420). Just off Hwy 101 in S Coos Bay. Phone 541/267-7804.* Manufacturing of myrtlewood gift items. Tours. (Daily; closed holidays) **FREE**

Shore Acres. *89814 Cape Arago Hwy, Coos Bay (97420). 13 miles SW off Hwy 101 on Cape Arago Hwy. Phone 541/888-3732. www.shoreacres.net.* Former grand estate of Coos Bay lumberman, noted for its unusual botanical and Japanese gardens and spectacular ocean views (743 acres). Ocean beach; hiking (on the Oregon Coast Trail), picnicking.

South Slough National Estuarine Research Reserve. *61907 Seven Devils Rd, Charleston (97420). 4 miles S on Seven Devils Rd. Phone 541/888-5558. www. southsloughestuary.org.* A 4,400-acre area reserved for the study of estuarine ecosystems and life. Previous studies here include oyster culture techniques and water pollution. Special programs, lectures, and exhibits at Interpretive Center. Trails and waterways (Daily); guided trail walks and canoe tours (June-Aug; fee). Interpretive Center (June-Aug: daily; rest of year: Mon-Fri). **FREE**

Sunset Bay. *Cape Arago Hwy, Coos Bay. 12 miles SW off Hwy 101 on Cape Arago Hwy. Phone 541/888-4902. www.oregonstateparks.org.* A 395-acre park with swimming beach on sheltered bay, fishing; hiking, picnicking, tent and trailer sites. Observation point.

Special Events

Bay Area Fun Festival. *Phone 541/267-3341; toll-free 800/738-4849.* Third weekend in Sept.

Blackberry Arts Festival. *Phone 541/267-1022.* Fourth weekend in Aug.

Oregon Coast Music Festival. *Phone toll-free 877/897-9350.* Variety of musical presentations ranging from jazz and dance to chamber and symphonic music. Also free outdoor picnic concerts. Last two full weeks in July.

Limited-Service Hotel

★ ★ **RED LION HOTEL.** *1313 N Bayshore Dr, Coos Bay (97420). Phone 541/267-4141; toll-free 800/733-5466; fax 541/267-2884. www.redlion.com.* Located at the north end of downtown Coos Bay on busy Highway 101, this motel-style facility offers nicely renovated guest rooms. Most have refrigerators and microwaves. For entertainment, there's an on-site putting green, and the lounge hosts stand-up comedy shows on weekend nights. 143 rooms, 2 story. Pets accepted. Check-in 3 pm, check-out noon. Restaurant, bar. Fitness room. Outdoor pool, whirlpool. Airport transportation available. **$**

Restaurant

★ ★ **PORTSIDE.** *8001 Kingfisher Rd, Charleston (97420). Phone 541/888-5544. www.portsidebythebay.com.* Seafood menu. Lunch, dinner. Bar. Children's menu. Outdoor seating. **$$**

Corvallis (C-2)

See also Albany, Eugene, Salem

Settled 1845
Population 44,757
Elevation 225 ft
Area Code 541
Information Convention & Visitors Bureau, 420 NW 2nd, 97330; phone 541/757-1544 or toll-free 800/334-8118
Web site www.visitcorvallis.com

Located in the heart of Oregon's fertile Willamette Valley and built on the banks of the Willamette River, Corvallis is a center for education, culture, and commerce. It is the home of Oregon State University, the state's oldest institution of higher education. The Siuslaw National Forest headquarters is here.

What to See and Do

Avery Park. *1310 SW Avery Pk Dr, Corvallis (97331). S 15th St and Hwy 20. Phone 541/757-6918.* A 75-acre park on the Marys River. Bicycle, cross-country, and jogging trails. Picnicking, playground, ballfield. Rose and rhododendron gardens, community gardens; 1922 Mikado locomotive. Playground (accessible to the disabled). (Daily) **FREE**

Benton County Historical Museum. *1101 Main St, Philomath (97370). 6 miles W. Phone 541/929-6230. www.bentoncountymuseum.org.* Located in the former Philomath College building. Features displays on history of the county; art gallery. Reference library (by appointment). (Tues-Sat) **FREE**

Oregon State University. *Oregon State University, Corvallis (97331). Phone 541/737-2416. oregonstate.edu.* (1868) (14,500 students) On its 400-acre campus are Memorial Union Concourse Gallery (daily). **FREE**

Siuslaw National Forest. *4077 Research Way, Corvallis (97333). W via Hwy 34. Phone 541/750-7000.* Includes 50 miles of ocean frontage with more than 30 campgrounds; public beaches, sand dunes and overlooks; visitor center and nature trails in the Cape Perpetua Scenic Area. Mary's Peak, highest peak in the Coast Range, has a road to picnic grounds and campground near the summit. Swimming; ocean, lake, and stream fishing; hunting for deer, bear, elk, and migratory birds; clam digging; boating. Hiking. Picnicking. Camping (fee in most areas); dune buggies (in designated areas). Forest contains 630,000 acres including the Oregon Dunes National Recreation Area.

Tyee Wine Cellars. *26335 Greenberry Rd, Corvallis (97333). 7 miles S via Hwy 99 W, 3 miles W on Greenberry Rd. Phone 541/753-8754.* Located on 460-acre Century farm. Offers tastings, tours, interpretive hikes, picnicking. (July-Aug: Fri-Mon; Apr-June and Oct-Dec: weekends; also by appointment) **FREE**

Special Events

Benton County Fair and Rodeo. *110 SW 53rd St, Corvallis (97333). Phone 541/757-1521.* Late July-early Aug.

Da Vinci Days. *760 SW Madison Ave, Corvallis (97333). Phone 541/757-6363.* Festival celebrating the relationship between art, science, and technology. Third weekend in July.

Fall Festival. *Phone 541/752-9655.* Last weekend in Sept.

Oregon Folklife Festival. *Phone 541/754-3601.* Traditional and contemporary folk music; crafts. Late June.

Limited-Service Hotel

★ **BEST WESTERN GRAND MANOR INN.** *925 NW Garfield Ave, Corvallis (97330). Phone 541/758-8571; toll-free 800/626-1900; fax 541/758-0834. www.bestwestern.com.* 55 rooms, 3 story. Complimentary continental breakfast. Check-out 11 am. Fitness room. Pool. **$**

🕴 🛌

Specialty Lodging

The following lodging establishment is approved by Mobil Travel Guide, but due to its unique and individualized nature has not been given a traditional Mobil Star rating. Included in this listing you may find bed-and-breakfasts, limited-service inns, guest ranches, and other unique hotel properties.

HARRISON HOUSE B&B. *2310 NW Harrison Blvd, Corvallis (97330). Phone 800/233-6248; toll-free 800/233-6248; fax 541/754-1353. www.corvallis-lodging .com.* Located within walking distance to Oregon State University, this bed-and-breakfast is convenient to such area activities as kayaking, rafting, and hiking. 4 rooms, 2 story. Complimentary full breakfast. Check-in 4 pm, check-out 11 am. **$**

🔖

Restaurants

★ ★ **GABLES.** *1121 NW 9th St, Corvallis (97330). Phone 541/752-3364; toll-free 800/815-0167; fax 541/757-0351.* Continental menu. Dinner. Bar. Children's menu. **$$**

★ ★ **MICHAEL'S LANDING.** *603 NW Second St, Corvallis (97330). Phone 541/754-6141. www. michaelslanding.com.* Old train depot overlooking river, built 1909. American menu. Lunch, dinner. Closed Dec 25. Bar. Children's menu. **$$**

Cottage Grove (D-2)

See also Eugene

Population 7,402
Elevation 641 ft
Area Code 541
Zip 97424
Information Cottage Grove Area Chamber of Commerce, 330 Hwy 99 S, PO Box 587; phone 541/942-2411
Web site www.cottagegrove.org

Cottage Grove is the lumber, retail, and distribution center for south Lane County. A Ranger District office of the Umpqua National Forest is located here.

What to See and Do

Chateau Lorane Winery. *27415 Siuslaw River Rd, Lorane (97451). 12 miles W on Cottage Grove-Lorane Rd to Siuslaw River Rd. Phone 541/942-8028.* A 30-acre vineyard is located on this 200-acre wooded estate. Features a lakeside tasting room in which to enjoy great variety of traditional, rare and handmade wines. (June-Oct: daily; Mar-May and Nov-Dec: weekends and holidays; also by appointment). **FREE**

Cottage Grove Lake. *75819 Short Ridge Hill Rd, Cottage Grove (97424). S via I-5, Cottage Grove Lake exit 170, turn left, then 5 miles S on London Rd. Phone 541/942-8657.* A 3-mile-long lake. Lakeside (west shore) and Wilson Creek (east shore) parks have swimming, boat launch, and picnicking. Shortridge Park (east shore) has swimming, waterskiing, fishing, and picnicking. Primitive and improved camping (showers, dump station) at Pine Meadows on east shore (mid-May-mid-Sept, 14-day limit; no reservations; fee). **$$$**

Cottage Grove Museum. *147 H St, Cottage Grove (97424). Birch Ave and H St. Phone 541/942-3963.* Displays of pioneer homelife and Native American artifacts housed in a former Roman Catholic Church (1897), octagonal, with stained-glass windows made in Italy. Adjacent to annex houses model of ore stamp mill showing how gold was extracted from the ore; working model of a green chain; antique tools. (Mid-June-Labor Day: Wed-Sun afternoons; rest of year: weekends) **FREE**

Covered Bridges. *710 Row River Rd, Cottage Grove (97424). Phone 541/942-2411.* Five old-time covered bridges within 10-mile radius of town. Inquire at Chamber of Commerce.

Dorena Lake. *34979 Shoreview Dr, Cottage Grove (97424). 5 miles E on Row River Rd. Phone 541/942-1418.* A 5-mile-long lake. Schwarz Park (camping fee), on Row River below the dam, has fishing, picnicking, and camping (dump station). Lane County maintains Baker Bay Park, on the south shore, and offers swimming, waterskiing, fishing, boating (launch, marina, rentals); picnicking, concession, camping (fee). Harms Park, on the north shore, offers boat launching and picnicking. For further information, inquire at the Cottage Grove project office. **$$$**

Special Event

Bohemia Mining Days Celebration. *Phone 541/942-5064.* Commemorates area's gold-mining days; parades; flower, art shows; rodeo, entertainment. Third week in July.

Limited-Service Hotel

★ ★ **VILLAGE GREEN RESORT.** *725 Row River Rd, Cottage Grove (97424). Phone 541/942-2491; toll-free 800/343-7666; fax 541/942-2386. www.bestwestern.com.* 96 rooms. Pets accepted. Check-out 11 am. Restaurant, bar. Pool, whirlpool. Tennis. **$**

Restaurant

★ **COTTAGE.** *2915 Row River Rd, Cottage Grove (97424). Phone 541/942-3091.* American menu. Lunch, dinner. Closed Sun; week of Thanksgiving. Bar. Children's menu. **$$**

Crater Lake (D-3)

What to See and Do

Crater Lake National Park. *Crater Lake National Park, PO Box 7, Crater Lake (97604). 57 miles N of Klamath Falls on Hwy 97, Hwy 62. Phone 541/594-2211. www.nps.gov/crla/.* One of Crater Lake's former names, Lake Majesty, probably comes closest to

describing the feeling visitors get from the deep blue waters in the caldera of dormant Mount Mazama. More than 7,700 years ago, following climactic eruptions, this volcano collapsed and formed a deep basin. Rain and snow accumulated in the empty caldera, forming the deepest lake in the United States (1,932 feet). Surrounded by 25 miles of jagged rim rock, the 21-square-mile lake is broken only by Wizard and Phantom Ship islands. Entering by road from any direction brings you to the 33-mile Rim Drive (July-mid-Oct or the first snow), leading to all observation points, park headquarters, and a visitor center at Rim Village (June-Sept, daily). The Sinnott Memorial Overlook with a broad terrace permits a beautiful view of the area. On summer evenings, rangers give campfire talks at Mazama Campground (late June-Sept, phone 541/594-2211). The Steel Center located at Park Headquarters (open daily) has exhibits about the natural history of the park and shows a movie daily.

The park can be explored on foot or by car following spurs and trails extending from Rim Drive. Going clockwise from Rim Village to the west, The Watchman Peak is reached by a trail almost 1 mile long that takes hikers 1,800 feet above the lake with a full view in all directions; Mount Shasta in California, 105 miles away, is visible on clear days. The road to the north entrance passes through the Pumice Desert, once a flood of frothy debris from the erupting volcano.

On the northeast side, Cleetwood Trail descends 1 mile to the shore and a boat landing, where 2-hour launch trips depart hourly each day in summer (fee). From the boats, Wizard Island, a small volcano, and Phantom Ship, a craggy mass of lava, can be seen up close.

Six miles farther on Rim Drive, going clockwise, is the start of a 2 1/2-mile hiking trail, 1,230 feet to Mount Scott, soaring 8,926 feet, the highest point in the park. Just to the west of the beginning of this trail is a 1-mile drive to the top of Cloudcap, 8,070 feet high and 1,600 feet above the lake. Four miles beyond this point, a road leads 7 miles from Rim Drive to The Pinnacles, pumice spires rising like stone needles from the canyon of Wheeler Creek.

Back at Rim Village, two trails lead in opposite directions. Counterclockwise, a 1 1/2-mile trek mounts the top of Garfield Peak. The other trail goes to Discovery Point, where in 1853 a young prospector, John Hillman, became the first settler to see the lake.

In winter, the south and west entrance roads are kept clear in spite of the annual 45-foot snowfall; the north entrance road and Rim Drive are closed from mid-Oct-June, depending on snow conditions. A cafeteria is open daily at Rim Village for refreshments and souvenirs.

Depending on snow, the campground (fee) is open from late June-mid-October. Mazama, at the junction of the south and west entrance drives, has a camp store, fireplaces, showers, laundry facilities, toilets, water, and tables; no reservations. There are six picnic areas on Rim Drive. The wildlife includes black bears—keep your distance and never feed them. There are also deer, golden-mantled ground squirrels, marmots, and coyotes. Do not feed any wildlife in park.

The park was established in 1902 and covers 286 square miles. For park information, contact Superintendent, Crater Lake National Park, PO Box 7, Crater Lake 97604; phone 541/594-2211 ext 402. Golden Eagle Passports are accepted (see MAKING THE MOST OF YOUR TRIP).

Note: Conservation measures may dictate the closing of certain roads and recreational facilities. In winter, inquire locally before attempting to enter the park. **$$$**

Full-Service Resort

★ ★ ★ **CRATER LAKE LODGE.** *565 Rim Village Dr, Crater Lake (97604). Phone 541/594-2255; fax 541/594-2342. www.crater-lake.com.* This grand lodge has been welcoming guests to its lakeside location since 1915. The lodge captures the essence of Pacific Northwest beauty and rusticity. Guests can relax with a good book in front of the Great Hall's massive stone fireplace. The Dining Room restaurant prepares dishes using Oregon-grown ingredients. It's also the perfect place to enjoy a cup of coffee as you watch the sun rise over Crater Lake, the morning light reflecting on the placid blue surface of the second deepest lake in the Western Hemisphere. Guest rooms are without TVs and phones, but, at a destination as blissful as this, you won't miss them. 71 rooms, 4 story. Closed mid-Oct-mid-May. Check-out 11 am. Restaurant. **$**

The Dalles (B-3)

See also Biggs, Hood River, Mount Hood National Forest

Founded 1851
Population 10,200
Elevation 98 ft
Area Code 541
Zip 97058
Information Chamber of Commerce, 404 W 2nd St; phone 541/296-2231 or toll-free 800/255-3385
Web site www.thedalleschamber.com

At one time The Dalles was the end of the wagon haul on the Oregon Trail. Here the pioneers loaded their goods on boats and made the rest of their journey westward on the Columbia River. The falls and rapids that once made the river above The Dalles unnavigable are now submerged under water backed up by the Columbia River dams. The Dalles Dam is part of a system of dams extending barge traffic inland as far as Lewiston, Idaho, and Pasco, Washington. The port has berthing space for all types of shallow draft vessels. The chief source of income in the area is agriculture. The Dalles is noted for its cherry orchards and wheat fields located in the many canyons along the river.

What to See and Do

⭐ **Columbia Gorge Discovery Center.** *5000 Discovery Dr, The Dalles (97058). 3 miles NW at Crate's Point. Phone 541/296-8600.* Over 26,000-square-feet building is official interpretive center for the Columbia River Gorge National Scenic Area. Hands-on and electronic exhibits detail the volcanic upheavals and raging floods that created the Gorge, describe the history and importance of the river, and look to the Gorge's future. Also Early Explorers, Steamboats and Trains, Industry and Stewardship exhibits. Guided tours, seminars, classes, and workshops (some fees). Library and collections (by appointment). Café. (Daily; closed Jan 1, Thanksgiving, Dec 25) **$$$** Admission includes

Oregon Trail Living History Park. Includes 80,000 square feet of outdoor exhibits and gardens. Costumed interpreters demonstrate life of Oregon Trail emigrants, members of Lewis and Clark expedition, and Native Americans. Footpaths wind through park; offers stunning views of river from high bluff. (Schedule and phone same as Center)

Wasco County Historical Museum. Reveals colorful history of over 10,000 years of county's occupation and importance of Columbia River on area history. Artifacts and exhibits feature Native Americans, missionaries, early pioneers and explorers; history of area railroad industry, farming, and shipping. Interactive displays include a late-19th-century town, railroad depot and barn. (Schedule and phone same as Center)

The Dalles Dam and Reservoir. *3 miles E of town off I-84 and 1 mile E of The Dalles Hwy Bridge, which crosses the Columbia just below the dam (use I-84 exit 87 in summer, exit 88 off-season). Phone 541/296-1181.* Two-mile train tour with views of historic navigation canal, visitor center, petroglyphs, and fish ladder facilities (Memorial Day-Labor Day: daily; Apr-May and Oct-Mar: Wed-Sun). **FREE** On south shore, 8 1/2 miles east of dam is

Celilo Park. *Adjacent to ancient fishing grounds, now submerged under waters backed up by The Dalles Dam.* Swimming, sailboarding, fishing, boating (ramp); picnicking, playground. Comfort station. Recreational areas with similar facilities also are on north and south shores.

Fort Dalles Museum. *500 W 15th St, The Dalles (97058). Phone 541/296-4547. At Garrison St.* Only remaining building of the 1856 outpost is the Surgeon's Quarters. Rare collection of pioneer equipment; stagecoaches, covered wagons. (Mar-Oct: daily; rest of year: Wed-Sun; closed holidays, also first two weeks in Jan)

Mayer State Park. *10 miles W, off I-84, exit 77. Phone 541/695-2261. www.oregonstateparks.org/park_161.php.* A 613-acre park comprised of an undeveloped area with an overlook on Rowena Heights and a developed area on the shores of the Columbia River, with a swimming beach, dressing rooms, and boat ramp. Windsurfing, fishing. Wildflowers bloom in March/April. Picnicking. **$**

Mount Hood National Forest. (see). *W of city.*

Sorosis Park. This 15-acre park overlooks the city from the highest point on Scenic Drive, with view of the Columbia River, Mt. Adams, and Mt. Hood. Located on part of the bottom of ancient Lake

Condon. The bones of three types of camels, the ancient horse, and mastodons were found near here. Jogging trail; tennis courts. Picnic area. Rose Garden.

Riverfront Park. *Off I-84, exit 85.* Swimming beach, windsurfing, fishing, boating (launch), jet boat excursions; picnicking.

Special Events

Fort Dalles Rodeo. *Phone 541/296-2231.* CASI sanctioned. Thurs-Sun, third week in July.

Northwest Cherry Festival. *Phone 541/296-5481.* Fourth weekend in Apr.

Limited-Service Hotel

★ ★ **COUSINS COUNTRY INN.** *2114 W 6th St, The Dalles (97058). Phone 541/298-5161; fax 541/298-6411.* 85 rooms, 2 story. Pets accepted; fee. Check-out 11 am. Restaurant. Pool, whirlpool. **$**

Restaurant

★ **COUSIN'S.** *2115 W 6th St, The Dalles (97058). Phone 541/298-2771. www.cousins-restaurant.com.* American menu. Breakfast, lunch, dinner. Closed Dec 25. Bar. Children's menu. **$$**

Depoe Bay (B-1)

See also Lincoln City, Newport

Population 870
Elevation 58 ft
Area Code 541
Zip 97341
Information Chamber of Commerce, PO Box 21; phone 541/765-2889
Web site www.depoebaychamber.org

The world's smallest natural navigable harbor, with six acres, Depoe Bay is a base for the US Coast Guard and a good spot for deep-sea fishing. The shoreline is rugged at this point. Seals and sea lions inhabit the area, and whales are so often seen that Depoe Bay claims to be the "whale watching capital of the Oregon coast." In the center of town are the "spouting horns," natural rock formations throwing geyserlike sprays high in the air. There are nine state parks within a few miles of this resort community.

What to See and Do

Depoe Bay Park. *Hwy 101 and Shell Ave, Depoe Bay (97341). N on Hwy 101.* Phone 541/765-2361. Covers three acres. Ocean observation building with view of bay, spouting horn, and fishing fleets. Small picnic area.

Fogarty Creek State Park. *2 miles N on Hwy 101.* Phone 541/265-9278. A 142-acre park with beach area and creek, swimming (dressing rooms), fishing; hiking, picnicking. **$$**

Thundering Seas. *Point Ave, Depoe Bay.* Phone 541/765-2604. (Oregon State University School for the Crafts). Professional school for goldsmiths and silversmiths lies 60 feet above the Pacific Ocean; unusual museum. Tours (Daily). **FREE**

Special Events

Classic Wooden Boat Show and Crab Feed. *Phone 541/765-2889.* Last weekend Apr.

Fleet of Flowers Ceremony. *Phone 541/765-2889.* After services on shore, flowers are cast on the water to honor those who lost their lives at sea. Memorial Day.

Salmon Bake. *Depoe Bay Park, Depoe Bay.* Phone 541/765-2889. Salmon prepared in the Native American manner. Third Sat in Sept.

Limited-Service Hotels

★ ★ **INN AT OTTER CREST.** *301 Otter Crest Loop Rd, Otter Rock (97369).* Phone 541/765-2111; toll-free 800/452-2101; fax 541/765-2047. *www.innatottercrest.com.* 120 rooms. Check-out noon. Restaurant, bar. Fitness room. Pool, whirlpool. Tennis. **$**

★ ★ **SURFRIDER RESORT.** *3115 NW Hwy 101, Depoe Bay (97341).* Phone 541/764-2311; toll-free 800/662-2378; fax 541/764-4634. *www.surfriderresort.com.* 52 rooms, 2 story. Check-out 11 am. Restaurant, bar. Indoor pool, whirlpool. Airport transportation available. **$**

Specialty Lodging

The following lodging establishment is approved by Mobil Travel Guide, but due to its unique and individualized nature has not been given a traditional Mobil Star rating. Included in this listing you may find bed-and-breakfasts, limited-service inns, guest ranches, and other unique hotel properties.

CHANNEL HOUSE. *35 Ellingson St, Depoe Bay (97341).* Phone 541/765-2140; toll-free 800/447-2140; fax 541/765-2191. *www.channelhouse.com.* Modern oceanfront building overlooking Depoe Bay. 14 rooms, 3 story. Children over 16 years only. Complimentary full breakfast. Check-in 4 pm, check-out 11 am. **$$**

Eugene (C-2)

See also Corvallis, Cottage Grove

Settled 1846
Population 112,669
Elevation 419 ft
Area Code 541
Information Lane County Convention & Visitors Association, 115 W 8th, Suite 190, PO Box 10286, 97440; phone 541/484-5307 or toll-free 800/547-5445
Web site www.cvalco.org/travelguide/travelguide.html

Eugene sits on the west bank of the Willamette (Wil-AM-et) River, facing its sister city Springfield on the east bank. The Cascade Range rises to the east, mountains of the Coast Range to the west. Bicycling, hiking, and jogging are especially popular here, with a variety of trails to choose from. Forests of Douglas fir support a lumber industry that accounts for 40 percent of the city's manufacturing. Eugene-Springfield is at the head of a series of dams built for flood control of the Willamette River Basin. Willamette National Forest headquarters is located here.

What to See and Do

Armitage County Park. *90064 Coburg Rd, Eugene (97408). 6 miles N off I-5 on Coburg Rd.* Phone 541/682-2000. A 57-acre park on partially wooded area on the south bank of the McKenzie River. Fishing, boating (ramp); hiking, picnicking.

Camp Putt Adventure Golf Park. *4006 Franklin Blvd, Eugene (97403). Phone 541/741-9828.* An 18-hole course with challenging holes like "Pond O' Peril," "Thunder Falls," and "Earthquake." Lakeside patio with ice cream bar. (Late Mar-mid-Nov, daily) **$$**

Fall Creek Dam and Lake. *40386 W Boundary Rd, Lowell (97452). 20 miles SE on Hwy 58 to Lowell, then follow signs to Big Fall Creek Rd. Phone 541/937-2131.* Winberry Creek Park has swimming beach, fishing, boating (ramp); picnicking. (May-Sept) Some fees. North Shore Ramp has fishing, boat launching facilities; picnicking. (Daily with low-level ramp) Cascara Campground has swimming, fishing, boating (ramp); camping (May-Sept). Some fees.

Hendricks Park Rhododendron Garden. *Summit and Skyline drs, Eugene (97401). Phone 541/682-5324.* A 20-acre, internationally known garden features more than 6,000 aromatic plants, including rare species and hybrid rhododendrons from the local area and around the world (peak bloom mid-Apr-mid-May). Walking paths, hiking trails, picnic area. (Daily) **FREE**

Hult Center. *1 Eugene Ctr, Eugene (97401). 7th Ave and Willamette St. Phone 541/682-5000 (tickets).* Performing arts center offering more than 300 events each year ranging from Broadway shows and concerts to ballet.

Lane County Historical Museum. *740 W 13th Ave, Eugene (97402). Phone 541/682-4242. www.lchmuseum .org.* Changing exhibits depict history of county from mid-19th century to 1930s; includes artifacts of pioneer and Victorian periods; textiles; local history research library. (Wed-Fri 10 am-4 pm, Sat-Sun noon-4 pm) **$**

Lookout Point and Dexter Dams and Lakes. *40386 W Boundary Rd, Lowell (97452). 20 miles SE on Hwy 58. Phone 541/937-2131.* The 14-mile-long Lookout Point Lake has Black Canyon Campground (May-Oct; fee) with trailer parking. Fishing; picnicking. Hampton Boat Ramp with launching facilities and four camp sites (all year; fee) with trailer parking, picnicking; fishing, closed to launching during low water (usually Oct-Apr). Lowell Park on 3-mile-long Dexter Lake has swimming, waterskiing, boating (moorage, ramp), sailboating; picnicking. Dexter Park has waterskiing, fishing, boating (ramp), sailboating; picnicking. The Powerhouse at Lookout Point Dam is open to the public (by appointment).

Owen Municipal Rose Garden. *North Jefferson at the river, Eugene. N end of Jefferson St, along the Willamette River. Phone 541/682-5025.* A 5-acre park with more than 300 new and rare varieties of roses, as well as wild species (best blooms late June-early July); a recognized test garden for experimental roses. Also here is a collection of antiques and miniatures. Picnic area. (Daily) **FREE**

Spencer Butte Park. *Ridgeline and Willamette St, Eugene. 2 miles S of city limits on Willamette St. Phone 541/682-4800.* Park has 305 acres of wilderness, with Spencer Butte Summit, at 2,052 feet, dominating the scene. Hiking trails. Panoramic views of Eugene, Cascade Mountains. (Daily) **FREE** Starting at edge of park is

South Hills Ridgeline Trail. *52nd St and Spencers Butte Park, Eugene (97405). Begins at 52nd St and Willamette St. Phone 503/325-7275.* A 5-mile trail extending from Blanton Road east to Dillard Road; a spur leads to top of Butte. The trail offers magnificent views of the Cascade Mountains, Coburg Hills, and Mount Baldy; the wildflowers along the trail reach their peak bloom in late Apr.

University of Oregon. *1205 University of Oregon, Eugene (97403). Bounded by Franklin Blvd and Agate St, Alder and 18th sts. Phone 541/346-3014. www. uoregon.edu.* (1876) (19,000 students) The 250-acre campus includes more than 2,000 varieties of trees. Points of interest include the Museum of Natural History, Robinson Theatre, Beall Concert Hall, Hayward Field, and the Erb Memorial Union. Campus tours depart from Information and Tour Services, Oregon Hall (Mon-Sat). Also on campus are

Jordan Schnitzer Museum of Art. *1430 Johnson Ln, Eugene (97403). Phone 541/346-3027. uoma. uoregon.edu.* Diverse collections include large selection of Asian art representing cultures of China, Japan, Korea, Cambodia, and American and British works of Asian influence; official court robes of the Ch'ing dynasty (China, 1644-1911); Russian icon paintings from the 17th-19th centuries; Persian miniatures and ceramics; photography; works by contemporary artists and craftsmen from the Pacific Northwest, including those of Morris Graves. Special exhibits. Gift shop. (Wed-Sun afternoons; closed holidays). **FREE**

Knight Library. *University of Oregon Library, 1299 University of Oregon, Eugene (97403). Phone 541/346-3054. www.libweb.uorgon.egu.* With more than 2 million volumes, this is the largest library in Oregon. Main lobby features changing exhibits of rare books, manuscripts; Oregon Collection on second floor. Fine arts pieces, wrought iron gates and carved panels. (Daily)

Whitewater rafting. *Phone toll-free 800/547-5445.* Numerous companies offer trips on the McKenzie, Deschutes, and Willamette rivers. Trips range from two hours to five days. Contact Convention and Visitors Association for details.

Willamette National Forest. *211 E 7th Av, Eugene (97401). E via Hwy 20, Hwy 126. Phone 541/225-6300.* More than 1 1/2 million acres. Home to more than 300 species of wildlife; including Cascade Mountain Range summit; Pacific Crest National Scenic Trail with views of snowcapped Mt. Jefferson, Mt. Washington, Three Fingered Jack, Three Sisters, Diamond Peak; Koosah and Sahalie Falls on the Upper McKenzie River; Clear Lake; the lava beds at summit of McKenzie Pass; Waldo Lake near summit of Willamette Pass. Fishing; hunting, hiking, skiing, snowmobiling, camping (fee at some sites).

Willamette Pass Ski Area. *Cascade Summit. S via I-5, E on Hwy 58. Phone 541/345-7669. www.willamettepass .com.* Double, three triple chairlifts; patrol, school, rentals (ski and snowboard). Lodge, restaurant, lounge. Longest run 2.1 miles; vertical drop 1,583 feet. Also 20 kilometers of groomed nordic trails. (Late-Nov-mid-Apr) Night skiing (late Dec-late Feb, Fri-Sat). **$$$$**

Willamette Science and Technology Center. *2300 Leo Harris Pkwy, Eugene (97401). Phone 541/682-7888.* Participatory science center encourages hands-on learning; features exhibits illustrating physical, biological, and earth sciences and related technologies. Planetarium shows. (Wed-Sun) **$$**

Special Events

Bach Festival. *Phone toll-free 800/457-1486.* Numerous concerts by regional and international artists; master classes; family activities. Mid-June-early July.

Lane County Fair. *796 W 13th Ave, Eugene (97402). Phone 541/682-4292.* Mid-Aug.

Limited-Service Hotels

★ **PHOENIX INN SUITES EUGENE.** *850 Franklin Blvd, Eugene (97403). Phone 541/344-0001; toll-free 800/344-0131; fax 541/686-1288. www. phoenixinn.com.* 97 rooms, 4 story. Complimentary continental breakfast. Check-out noon. Fitness room. Indoor pool, whirlpool. **$**

★ ★ **RED LION.** *205 Coburg Rd, Eugene (97401). Phone 541/342-5201; toll-free 800/733-5466; fax 541/485-2314. www.redlion.com.* 137 rooms, 2 story. Pets accepted. Check-out noon. Restaurant, bar. Fitness room. Pool, whirlpool. Airport transportation available. **$**

Full-Service Hotels

★ ★ ★ **HILTON EUGENE AND CONFERENCE CENTER.** *66 E 6th Ave, Eugene (97401). Phone 541/342-2000; toll-free 800/445-8667; fax 541/342-6661. www.eugene.hilton.com.* In the heart of downtown Eugene, the Hilton is adjacent to the Hult Center for the Performing Arts (see), which holds Broadway shows, concerts, and other performances throughout the year. It's within walking distance of shops and restaurants. At the hotel, the Big River Grille serves Pacific Northwest cuisine, and the lobby bar offers local microbrews. 272 rooms, 12 story. Pets accepted, some restrictions; fee. Check-in 3 pm, check-out noon. High-speed Internet access. Restaurant, bar. Fitness room. Indoor pool, whirlpool. Airport transportation available. Business center. **$$**

★ ★ ★ **VALLEY RIVER INN.** *1000 Valley River Way, Eugene (97401). Phone 541/587-0123; toll-free 800/543-8266; fax 541/687-0289. www.valleyriverinn .com.* This hotel is conveniently located downtown and minutes from the airport, shopping, the University of Oregon, and the convention center. Some rooms have views of the Willamette River. 257 rooms, 3 story. Pets accepted, some restrictions. Check-out 11 am. Restaurant, bar. Fitness room. Pool, children's pool, whirlpool. Airport transportation available. Logging memorabilia. **$$**

Specialty Lodging

The following lodging establishment is approved by Mobil Travel Guide, but due to its unique and individualized nature has not been given a traditional Mobil Star rating. Included in this listing you may find bed-and-breakfasts, limited-service inns, guest ranches, and other unique hotel properties.

THE CAMPBELL HOUSE, A CITY INN. *252 Pearl St, Eugene (97401). Phone 541/343-1119; toll-free 800/264-2519; fax 541/343-2258. www.campbellhouse .com.* Comfort and elegance await you at this intimate bed-and-breakfast, which offers views of the city from a hill. Each room is tastefully and uniquely furnished. 19 rooms, 3 story. Complimentary full breakfast. Check-in 4 pm, check-out noon. **$$**

Restaurants

★ ★ **AMBROSIA.** *174 E Broadway, Eugene (97401). Phone 541/342-4141.* Italian menu. Lunch, dinner. Closed holidays. Bar. Outdoor seating. **$$**

★ ★ ★ **CHANTERELLE.** *207 E 5th Ave, Eugene (97401). Phone 541/484-4065.* European cuisine set in an intimate, relaxed atmosphere. Chef Ralf Schmidt creatively uses fresh, local ingredients to create such flawless dishes as lamb Provencale, tournedo of beef "Chanterelle," and sautéed prawns Maison. Continental menu. Dinner. Closed Sun, Mon; holidays. Service bar. **$$**

★ **EXCELSIOR INN.** *754 E 13th, Eugene (97401). Phone 541/342-6963. www.excelsiorinn.com.* Continental menu. Breakfast, lunch, dinner, Sun brunch. Bar. Children's menu. Outdoor seating. **$$**

★ **GOVINDA'S VEGETARIAN BUFFET.** *270 W 8th Ave, Eugene (97401). Phone 541/686-3531.* Vegetarian menu. Lunch, dinner. Closed Sun; Jan 1, July 4, Dec 25. Bar. Children's menu. **$**

★ ★ **NORTH BANK.** *22 Club Rd, Eugene (97401). Phone 541/343-5622.* Seafood, steak menu. Lunch, dinner. Closed Dec 25. Bar. **$$**

★ ★ **OREGON ELECTRIC STATION.** *27 E 5th Ave, Eugene (97401). Phone 541/485-4444; fax 541/484-6149. www.oesrestaurant.com.* Former train station (1912); memorabilia. American menu. Lunch, dinner. Closed July 4, Dec 25. Bar. Children's menu. Outdoor seating. **$$**

★ ★ ★ **SWEETWATERS.** *1000 Valley River Way, Eugene (97401). Phone 541/687-0123. www. valleyriverinn.com.* With a beautiful view of the Willamette River, this casually elegant restaurant delights guests with ample portions of Northwest cuisine and Mediterranean-inspired dishes. Fresh seafood, game meats, exotic fruits, and seasonal, local ingredients make up the majority of the menu. Breakfast, lunch, dinner, Sun brunch. Bar. Children's menu. Outdoor seating. **$$**

★ ★ **ZENON CAFE.** *898 Pearl St, Eugene (97401). Phone 541/343-3005.* American menu. Breakfast, lunch, dinner, Sun brunch. Closed Thanksgiving, Dec 25. Outdoor seating. **$$**

Florence (C-1)

See also Reedsport, Yachats

Settled 1876
Population 5,162
Elevation 23 ft
Area Code 541
Zip 97439
Information Florence Area Chamber of Commerce, PO Box 26000; phone 541/997-3128
Web site www.el.com/to/florence

At the northern edge of the National Dunes Recreation Area, with some of the highest sand dunes in the world, Florence is within reach of 17 lakes for fishing, swimming, and boating. River and ocean fishing, crabbing, and clamming are also popular. Along the Siuslaw River is "Old Town," an historic area with galleries, restaurants, and attractions.

What to See and Do

C&M Stables. *90241 Hwy 101, Florence (97439). 8 miles N on Hwy 101. Phone 541/997-7540.* Experience spectacular scenery of Oregon coast on horseback. Beach (1 1/2-2 hours), dune trail (1-1 1/2 hours), sunset (2 hours, with or without meal), and coast range (1/2-day or all day) rides. Must be 8 years or older. (Daily; closed Thanksgiving, Dec 25) **$$$$**

Carl G. Washburne Memorial. *93111 Hwy 101, Florence (97439). 14 miles N on Hwy 101. Phone 541/547-3416.* This 1,089-acre park is a good area for study of botany. Features a 2-mile-long beach, swimming, fishing, clamming; hiking, picnicking, tent and trailer campsites with access to beach. Elk may be seen in campgrounds and nearby meadows.

Darlingtonia. *84505 Hwy 101 S, Florence (97439). 5 miles N on Hwy 101. Phone 541/997-3641.* An 18-acre park with short loop trail through bog area noted for Darlingtonia, a carnivorous, insect-eating plant also known as cobra lily. Picnicking, viewing deck.

Devils Elbow. *84505 Hwy 101, Florence (97439). 13 miles N on Hwy 101, below Heceta Head Lighthouse. Phone 541/997-3641.* A 545-acre park. Ocean beach, fishing; hiking, picnicking. Observation point. **$$**

Heceta Head Lighthouse. *92072 Hwy 101 S, Yachats (97498). 12 miles N on Hwy 101. Phone 541/547-3696.* (1894) Picturesque beacon set high on rugged cliff.

Jessie M. Honeyman Memorial. *84505 Hwy 101, Florence (97439). 3 miles S on Hwy 101. Phone 541/ 997-3641.* Park has 522 coastal acres with wooded lakes and sand dunes, an abundance of rhododendrons and an excellent beach. Swimming, waterskiing, fishing, boat dock and ramps; hiking, picnicking, improved camping, tent and trailer sites (dump station). (Daily)

Sand Dunes Frontier. *83960 Hwy 101, Florence (97439). 3 1/2 miles S on Hwy 101. Phone 541/997-3544.* Excursions aboard 20-passenger dune buggies or drive-yourself Odysseys; miniature golf; flower garden; gift shop, snack bar. (Daily) **$$$$**

⭐ **Sea Lion Caves.** *91560 Hwy 101, Florence (97439). 12 miles N on Hwy 101. Phone 541/547-3111. www. sealioncaves.com.* Descend 208 feet under basaltic headland into a 1,500-foot-long cavern that is home to wild sea lions. These mammals (up to 12 feet long) are generally seen on rocky ledges outside the cave in spring and summer and inside the cave in fall and winter. Self-guided tours; a light jacket and comfortable shoes are suggested. (Daily from 9 am; closed Dec 25) **$$**

Siuslaw Pioneer Museum. *85294 Hwy 101 S, Florence (97439). 1 mile S. Phone 541/997-7884.* Exhibits preserve the history of the area; impressive display of artifacts and items from early settlers and Native Americans. Library room; extensive genealogy records; hundreds of old photographs. (Jan-Nov, Tues-Sun; closed holidays) **$**

Westward Ho! Sternwheeler. *Bay and Maple, Florence. Phone 541/997-9691.* One-hour historical cruise, half-hour afternoon cruises; Sun brunch cruises (Apr-Oct, daily).

Special Event

Rhododendron Festival. *Phone 541/997-3128.* Third weekend in May.

Limited-Service Hotels

★ **BEST WESTERN PIER POINT INN.** *85625 Hwy 101, Florence (97439). Phone 541/997-7191; fax 541/997-3828. www.bestwestern.com.* Overlooks Siuslaw River. 55 rooms, 3 story. Complimentary continental breakfast. Check-out 11 am. Whirlpool. **$**

★ ★ **DRIFTWOOD SHORES RESORT & CONFERENCE CENTER.** *88416 1st Ave, Florence (97439). Phone 541/997-8263; fax 541/997-5857. www.driftwoodshores.com.* 128 rooms. Check-in 3 pm, check-out noon. Restaurant, bar. Indoor pool, whirlpool. **$$**

Restaurant

★ ★ **CLAWSON WINDWARD INN.** *3757 Hwy 101 N, Florence (97439). Phone 541/997-8243; fax 541/997-8243.* American menu. Breakfast, lunch, dinner. Closed Dec 25. Bar. Children's menu. **$$**

Forest Grove (B-2)

See also Beaverton, Hillsboro, Oregon City, Portland

Settled 1845
Population 13,559
Elevation 175 ft
Area Code 503
Zip 97116
Information Chamber of Commerce, 2417 Pacific Ave; phone 503/357-3006
Web site www.grovenet.org/ForestGrove/forestgrove .html

Forest Grove traces its beginning to missionaries who brought religion to what they called the "benighted Indian." The town is believed to have been named for a forest of firs which met a grove of oaks.

What to See and Do

Pacific University. *2043 College Way, Forest Grove (97116). Main entrance on College Way. Phone 503/357-6151. www.pacific.edu.* (1849) (1,600 students) Founded as Tualatin Academy, it is one of the Northwest's oldest schools. On campus is art gallery and Old College Hall (academic year, Tues, Thurs; also by appointment). Tours of campus.

Scoggin Valley Park and Hagg Lake. *50250 SW Scoggins Valley Rd, Gaston (97119). 7 miles SW via Hwy 47, Scoggin Valley Rd exit. Phone 503/359-5732.* Features 11 miles of shoreline. Swimming, windsurfing, fishing, boating (ramps); picnic sites. (Feb-Nov)

Special Events

Barbershop Ballad Contest. *Pacific University, 2331 Main St, Forest Grove (97116). Phone 503/357-3006.* First weekend in Mar.

Concours d'Elegance. *Pacific University, 2043 College Way, Forest Grove (97116). Phone 503/357-2300.* Classic and vintage auto display. Third Sun in June.

Founders Day Corn Roast. *2417 Pacific Ave, Forest Grove (97116). Phone 503/357-3006.* Late Sept.

Hawaiian Luau. *Pacific University, 2043 College Way, Forest Grove (97116). Phone 503/357-6151.* Hawaiian traditions celebrated in food, fashions, and dance. Mid-Apr.

Limited-Service Hotel

★ **BEST WESTERN UNIVERSITY INN AND SUITES.** *3933 Pacific Ave, Forest Grove (97116). Phone 503/992-8888; toll-free 800/780-7234; fax 503/992-8444. www.bestwestern.com.* 54 rooms. Complimentary continental breakfast. Check-in 3 pm, check-out noon. Fitness room. Indoor pool, whirlpool. **$**

Fort Clatsop National Memorial

See also Astoria

(6 miles SW of Astoria off Hwy 101A)

Web site *www.nps.gov/focl/*

This site marks the western extremity of the territory explored by Meriwether Lewis and William Clark in their expedition of 1804-1806. The fort is a reconstruction of their 1805-1806 winter quarters. The original fort was built here because of its excellent elk hunting grounds, its easy access to ocean salt, its protection from the westerly coastal storms, and the availability of fresh water.

The expedition set out on May 14, 1804, to seek "the most direct and practicable water communication across this continent" under orders from President Thomas Jefferson. The first winter was spent near Bismarck, North Dakota. In April, 1805, the party, then numbering 33, resumed the journey. On November 15, they had their first view of the ocean from a point near McGowan, Washington. The company left Fort Clatsop on March 23, 1806, on their return trip and was back in St. Louis on September 23 of the same year. The Lewis and Clark Expedition was one of the greatest explorations in the history of the United States, and its journals depict one of the most fascinating chapters in the annals of the American frontier. The visitor center has museum exhibits and provides audiovisual programs. The canoe landing has replicas of dugout canoes of that period. Ranger talks and living history demonstrations are presented mid-June-Labor Day. (Daily; closed Dec 25) For further information contact Superintendent, Hwy 3, Box 604 FC, Astoria 97103; phone 503/861-2471. Apr-Sept; **$$** Rest of year **FREE**

Gold Beach (E-1)

See also Brookings, Port Orford

Population 1,546
Elevation 51 ft
Area Code 541
Zip 97444
Information Chamber of Commerce & Visitors Center, 29279 Ellensburg Ave #3; phone 541/247-7526 or toll-free 800/525-2334
Web site www.goldbeach.org

Until floods in 1861 washed the deposits out to sea, placer mining in the beach sands was profitable here; hence the name. There is still some mining farther up the Rogue River. Gold Beach is at the mouth of the Rogue River, on the south shore; Wedderburn is on the north bank. Agate hunting is popular at the mouth of the Rogue River. The river is also well-known for steelhead and salmon fishing. Surf fishing and clamming are possible at many excellent beaches. The Siskiyou National Forest is at the edge of town and a Ranger District office of the forest is located here.

What to See and Do

Cape Sebastian State Park. *7 miles S on Hwy 101. Phone 541/469-2021.* Approximately 1,143 acres of open and forested land. Cape Sebastian is a precipitous headland, rising more than 700 feet above the tide with a view of many miles of coastline. One-and-a-half-mile trail to the tip of the cape; beach access. A short roadside through the forest area is marked by wild azaleas, rhododendrons, and blue ceanothus in season. Trails; no rest rooms or water.

Curry County Historical Museum. *29984 Ellensburg Ave, Gold Beach (97444). Phone 541/247-6113.* Collections and interpretive displays of early life in Curry County. (Feb-Dec, Tues-Sat afternoons) **DONATION**

Jerry's Rogue River Jet Boat Trips. *S end of Rogue River Bridge at port of Gold Beach Boat Basin. Phone 541/247-4571; toll-free 800/451-3645.* A 6-hour (64-mile) round trip into wilderness area; 2-hour lunch or dinner stop at Agness. Also 8-hour (104-mile) and 6-hour (80-mile) round-trip whitewater excursions.

Rogue River Museum and Gift Shop (all year). (May-Oct, daily). **$$$$**

Mail Boat Whitewater Trips. *94294 Rouge River Rd, Gold Beach (97444). Mail Boat Dock. Phone 541/247-7033; toll-free 800/458-3511.* A 104-mile round trip by jet boat into wilderness and whitewater of the upper Rogue River. Narrated 7 1/2-hour trip. (Mid-May-mid-Oct, daily) Also 80-mile round trip to the middle Rogue River. Narrated 6 3/4-hour trip departs twice daily. (Mid-June-Sept) Reservations advised for all trips. **$$$$**

Official Rogue River Mail Boat Hydro-Jet Trips. *94294 Rogue River Rd, Gold Beach (97444). Mail Boat Dock, 1/4 mile upstream from N end of Rogue River Bridge. Phone 541/247-7033; toll-free 800/458-3511.* A 64-mile round trip by jet boat up the wild and scenic Rogue River; 2-hour lunch stop at Agness. (May-Oct, daily) Reservations advised. **$$$$**

Prehistoric Gardens. *36848 Hwy 101, Port Orford (97465). 14 miles N on Hwy 101, located in Oregon's rain forest. Phone 541/332-4463.* Life-size sculptures of dinosaurs and other prehistoric animals that disappeared more than 70 million years ago are set among primitive plants, which have survived. (Daily) **$$$**

Special Events

Curry County Fair. *29392 Ellensburg Ave, Gold Beach (97444).* Last weekend in July.

Festival of Quilts. *Phone 541/247-7526.* Sept.

Spring Flower, Art, & Clam Chowder Festival. *Phone 541/247-6550.* First weekend in May.

Whale of an Art and Wine Festival. *Phone 541/247-7526.* Mid-May.

Limited-Service Hotel

★ **SHORE CLIFF INN.** *29346 Ellensburg Ave, Gold Beach (97444). Phone 541/247-7091; toll-free 888/663-0608; fax 541/247-0225. www.shorecliffinn.com.* On Highway 101, this rather nondescript but well maintained hotel has a beautiful location to recommend it. Most guest rooms overlook the ocean, as does the hotel's balcony. Beachcombing for driftwood is popular here. 40 rooms, 2 story. Pets accepted; fee.

Complimentary continental breakfast. Check-in 2 pm, check-out 11 am. Beach. **$**

Full-Service Inn

 ★ ★ ★ **TU TU' TUN LODGE.** *96550 N Bank Rogue, Gold Beach (97444). Phone 541/247-6664; toll-free 800/864-6357; fax 541/247-0672. www. tututun.com.* Tu Tu' Tun Lodge corners the market on sophisticated rustication. From its flower-filled gardens to its scenic spot on the banks of the Rogue River, this place seems to ooze serenity. Entered from covered walkways, the guest rooms and suites are true havens from the outside world with wood-burning fireplaces, deep-soaking tubs, overstuffed furnishings, and luxuriously soft bed linens. A peaceful slumber is virtually guaranteed here, where romantics enjoy the blissful quietude. Nature is the inspiration behind this great resort, where large windows bring the outdoors in, and river rock fireplaces and distinctive wood furnishings celebrate nature's bounty. Don't miss a boat ride on the Rogue River, which can be arranged through the lodge. There's also a four-hole pitch-and-putt course and horseshoe courts. Inventive Pacific Northwest cuisine accounts for memorable dining experiences at this unique lodge. 18 rooms. Closed Jan 1, Thanksgiving, Dec 25. Check-in 3 pm, check-out 11 am. Restaurant, bar. Outdoor pool. Airport transportation available. **$$**

Specialty Lodging

The following lodging establishment is approved by Mobil Travel Guide, but due to its unique and individualized nature has not been given a traditional Mobil Star rating. Included in this listing you may find bed-and-breakfasts, limited-service inns, guest ranches, and other unique hotel properties.

INN AT NESIKA BEACH. *33026 Nesika Rd, Gold Beach (97444). Phone 541/247-6434.* A romantic getaway in a large Victorian-style house, this oceanfront inn is just a mile from Highway 101. Rooms are individually decorated with antiques, fireplaces, and feather beds; two have private decks and in-room Jacuzzi tubs for two overlooking the ocean. Guests can relax on the large wraparound porch or on the brick patio at the side of the house. 4 rooms, 2 story. Complimentary full breakfast. Check-in 2 pm, check-out 11 am. No credit cards accepted. **$**

Grants Pass (E-2)

See also Cave Junction, Jacksonville, Medford, Oregon Caves National Monument

Population 17,488
Elevation 948 ft
Area Code 541
Information Visitor & Convention Bureau, PO Box 1787, 97528; phone 541/476-5510 or toll-free 800/547-5927;
Web site www.visitgrantspass.org

Grants Pass was named by the rail constructors who were here when news reached them of General Grant's victorious siege of Vicksburg in 1863. On the Rogue River, Grants Pass is the seat of Josephine County. Tourism is the chief source of income; agriculture and electronics are next in importance. Fishing in the Rogue River is a popular activity. A Ranger District office and headquarters of the Siskiyou National Forest is located here.

What to See and Do

Grants Pass Museum of Art. *229 SW G St, Grants Pass (97527). Phone 541/479-3290.* Permanent and changing exhibits of photography, paintings, art objects. (Tues-Sat afternoons; closed holidays) **FREE**

Rogue River Raft Trips. *Phone toll-free 800/547-5927.* One- to five-day whitewater scenic or fishing trips through the wilderness, past abandoned gold-mining sites; overnight lodges or camping en route. Some of these are seasonal; some all year. For details, contact the Visitor and Convention Bureau. Also available is

Hellgate Jetboat Excursions. *966 SW 6th St, Grants Pass (97526). Depart from Riverside Inn. Phone 541/479-7204; toll-free 800/648-4874.* Interpretive jet boat trips down the Rogue River: 2-hour scenic excursion (May-Sept, daily); 4-hour country dinner excursion (Mid-May-Sept); 4-hour champagne brunch excursion (Mid-May-Sept, weekends); 5-hour whitewater trip (May-Sept, daily). **$$$$**

Siskiyou National Forest. *N, S, and W off Hwy 199 or W of I-5. Phone 541/471-6516.* Over 1 million acres. Famous for salmon fishing in lower Rogue River gorge and early-day gold camps. Many species of trees and plants are relics of past ages; a botanist's paradise. An 84-mile stretch of Rogue River between Applegate

River and Lobster Creek Bridge is designated a National Wild and Scenic River; nearly half is in the forest. Boat, pack, and saddle trips into rugged backcountry. Picnic sites. Camping. For further information contact Visitor Information Office, PO Box 440, 200 NE Greenfield Rd.

Valley of the Rogue State Park. *3792 N River Rd, Grants Pass (97525). 8 miles S on I-5. Phone 541/582-1118.* A 275-acre park with fishing, boat ramp to Rogue River; picnicking, improved tent and trailer sites. (Daily; dump station)

Special Events

Amazing May. *Phone 541/476-7717.* Eclectic mixture of events heralding the arrival of spring. May.

Boatnik Festival. *Riverside Park, Grants Pass. Phone 541/474-2361.* Parade, concessions, carnival rides, boat races; entertainment. A 25-mile whitewater hydroboat race from Riverside Park to Hellgate Canyon and back. Square dance festival at Josephine County Fairgrounds. Memorial Day weekend.

Heritage Days. *Phone 541/476-7717.* Historical and ethnic related events of the pioneers that settled the southern Oregon territory. Sept-mid-Oct.

Jedediah Smith Mountain Man Rendezvous. *Sportsman Park, Grants Pass. Phone 541/476-5020.* Muzzleloader/black powder shoots, costume contests, exhibits. Early Aug.

Josephine County Fair. *Fairgrounds, 1451 Fairgrounds Rd, Grants Pass (97527). Redwood Hwy and W Park St. Phone 541/476-3215.* Mid-Aug.

Pari-mutuel horse racing. *Fairgrounds, 1451 Fairgrounds Rd, Grants Pass (97527). Phone 541/476-3215.* Late May-early July.

Limited-Service Hotels

★ **BEST WESTERN INN AT THE ROGUE.** *8959 Rogue River Hwy, Grants Pass (97527). Phone 541/582-2200; toll-free 800/238-0700; fax 541/582-1415. www.bestwestern.com.* Easily accessible from I-5, this hotel is a convenient overnight stopover. It's also a destination unto itself; the nearby Rogue River offers fishing, rafting, and jet boat excursions. Guest rooms have microwaves and small refrigerators, and VCRs are available. 54 rooms, 2 story. Pets accepted; fee. Complimentary continental breakfast. Check-in 2 pm, check-out 11 am. Fitness room. Outdoor pool, whirlpool. **$**

★ **COMFORT INN.** *1889 NE 6th St, Grants Pass (97526). Phone 541/479-8301; toll-free 800/626-1900; fax 541/955-9721. www.choicehotels.com.* 59 rooms, 2 story. Pets accepted; fee. Complimentary continental breakfast. Check-in 2 pm, check-out 11 am. Outdoor pool. **$**

★ **HOLIDAY INN EXPRESS.** *105 NE Agness Ave, Grants Pass (97526). Phone 541/471-6144; toll-free 800/838-7666; fax 541/471-9248. www.hiexpress.com.* 81 rooms, 4 story. Pets accepted, some restrictions; fee. Complimentary continental breakfast. Check-in 3 pm, check-out 11 am. Outdoor pool, whirlpool. Airport transportation available. Business center. **$**

★ ★ **MORRISON'S ROGUE RIVER LODGE.** *8500 Galice Rd, Merlin (97532). Phone 541/476-3825; toll-free 800/826-1963; fax 541/476-4953. www.morrisonslodge.com.* 22 rooms. Closed Dec-Apr. Check-out 11 am. Restaurant. Pool. Tennis. Business center. **$**

Specialty Lodgings

The following lodging establishments are approved by Mobil Travel Guide, but due to their unique and individualized nature have not been given a traditional Mobil Star rating. Included in this listing you may find bed-and-breakfasts, limited-service inns, guest ranches, and other unique hotel properties.

FLERY MANOR. *2000 Jumpoff Joe Creek Rd, Grants Pass (97526). Phone 541/476-3591; fax 541/471-2303. www.flerymanor.com.* Set on 7 rural acres about 10 miles north of Grants Pass, Flery Manor is an elegant country bed-and-breakfast. The grounds include gardens, three ponds, a small waterfall, and a gazebo. True to the period of the home, the unique guest rooms are furnished with antiques, canopied feather beds with lots of pillows, and clawfoot tubs. Breakfast is a highlight here: three gourmet courses are served on fine china and heirloom linens. 5 rooms, 3 story. Children over 11 years only. Complimentary full breakfast. Check-in 4 pm, check-out 11 am. **$**

PINE MEADOW INN. *1000 Crow Rd, Grants Pass (97532). Phone 541/471-6277; toll-free 800/554-0806; fax 541/471-6277. www.pinemeadowinn.com.* Situated on 9 acres of meadow and private forest, this Midwest-style farmhouse is furnished with turn-of-the-century antiques. 4 rooms, 2 story. Closed Nov-Jan. Children over 11 years only. Complimentary full breakfast. Check-in 4 pm, check-out 11 am. Whirlpool. **$**

WEASKU INN. *5560 Rogue River Hwy, Grants Pass (97527). Phone 541/471-8000; toll-free 800/493-2758; fax 541/471-7038. www.weasku.com.* A secluded setting on the Rogue River amid towering pine trees lends this 1924 inn an air of tranquility. Originally a vacation spot for Hollywood stars, including Clark Gable, Bing Cosby, and Carole Lombard, the Weasku is a high-end lodge that offers guests the opporunity to fish for salmon, go river rafting, or simply relax on the expansive lawn. Choose from five rooms in the main lodge, with its rustic great room complete with roaring fire, and the surrounding cabins, which have river rock fireplaces of their own. All accommodations feature pine furnishings, homey quilts, and beamed ceilings with ceiling fans. Guests enjoy an evening wine-and-cheese reception, nightly milk and cookies, and summertime barbecues. 17 rooms, 2 story. Complimentary continental breakfast. Check-in 4 pm, check-out noon. High-speed Internet access. **$$**

Restaurant

★ ★ **YANKEE POT ROAST.** *720 NW Sixth St, Grants Pass (97526). Phone 541/476-0551. www.yankee-potroast.com.* Restored historic home; built in 1905. American menu. Lunch, dinner. Closed Mon-Tues; Dec 25. Service bar. Children's menu. **$$**

Hermiston (A-4)

See also Pendleton, Umatilla

Population 10,040
Elevation 457 ft
Area Code 541
Zip 97838
Information Greater Hermiston Chamber of Commerce, 415 S US Hwy 395, PO Box 185; phone 541/567-6151 or 541/564-9109
Web site www.el.com/to/hermiston/

Centrally located between the major cities of the Northwest, Hermiston offers an abundant array of recreational opportunities. The Columbia River, second largest river in the country, flows 5 miles to the north and the Umatilla River skirts the city limits; both are popular for fishing. The nearby Blue Mountains offer a variety of summer and winter activities. Agriculture, processing, and production form the economic base of this community, which has become a trading center for this area of the Columbia River Basin.

Special Event

Stock Car Racing. *Race City, USA, on Hwy 395. Phone 541/564-8674.* Apr-Oct.

Limited-Service Hotel

★ **BEST WESTERN HERMISTON INN.** *2255 S Hwy 395, Hermiston (97838). Phone 541/564-0202; toll-free 800/780-7234; fax 541/567-5512. www.best western.com.* 54 rooms. Complimentary continental breakfast. Check-in 2 pm, check-out 11 am. Fitness room. Indoor pool. **$**

Hood River (B-3)

See also Mount Hood National Forest, The Dalles

Settled 1854
Population 4,632
Elevation 155 ft
Area Code 541
Zip 97031
Information Chamber of Commerce Visitor Center, 405 Portway Ave; phone 541/386-2000 or toll-free 800/366-3530
Web site www.hoodriver.org

Hood River, located in the midst of a valley producing apples, pears, and cherries, boasts a scenic view of Oregon's highest peak, Mount Hood; its slopes are accessible in all seasons by road. Highway 35, called the Loop Highway, leads around the mountain and up to the snowline. The Columbia River Gorge provides perfect conditions for windsurfing in the Hood River Port Marina Park.

What to See and Do

Bonneville Lock & Dam. *US Army Corp of Engineers Bonneville Lock & Dam Cascade Locks, Cascade Locks (97014). 23 miles W on I-84. Phone 541/374-8820.* The dam consists of three parts, one spillway and two powerhouses. It has an overall length of 3,463 feet and extends across the Columbia River to Washington. It was a major hydroelectric project of the US Army Corps of Engineers. On the Oregon side is a five-story visitor center with underwater windows into the fish ladders and new navigation lock with viewing facilities. Audiovisual presentations and tours of fish ladders, and the original powerhouse (June-Sept, daily or by appointment; closed Jan 1, Thanksgiving, Dec 25). State salmon hatchery adjacent. Fishing (salmon and sturgeon ponds); picnicking. Powerhouse II and Visitor Orientation Building on Washington side, Highway 14; underwater fish viewing, audiovisual presentations, fish ladder and powerhouse tours (June-Sept, daily or by appointment; closed Jan 1, Thanksgiving, Dec 25); accessible via Bridge of the Gods from I-84. **FREE**

Columbia Gorge. *Port of Cascade Locks. 10 miles W on I-84, exit 44. Phone 541/374-8427.* Sternwheeler makes daytime excursions, sunset dinner and brunch cruises, harbor tours, and special holiday cruises. Reservations required except for daily excursions (mid-June-Sept).

Flerchinger Vineyards. *4200 Post Canyon Dr, Hood River (97031). Phone 541/386-2882.* Tours; tasting room. (Daily) **FREE**

Hood River County Museum. *300 E Port Marina Dr, Hood River (97031). Port Marina Park. Phone 541/386-6772.* Items from early settlers to modern residents. An outdoor display includes a sternwheeler paddle wheel, beacon light used by air pilots in the Columbia Gorge, steam engine from the *Mary.* (Apr-Oct, daily) **DONATION**

Hood River Vineyards. *4693 Westwood Dr, Hood River (97031). Phone 541/386-3772.* Tours; tasting room. (Mar-Dec, daily) **FREE**

Lost Lake. *Hwy 26 and LoLo Pass, ZigZag. 28 miles SW off I-84 on Dee Secondary Hwy and paved Forest Service road in Mount Hood National Forest. Phone 541/386-6366.* Swimming, fishing, boat rentals; hiking, picnicking, concession, day lodge, camping.

Mount Hood National Forest. (see). *S and W of city.*

Mount Hood Scenic Railroad. *110 Railroad Ave, Hood River (97031). Phone 541/386-3556; toll-free 800/872-4661. www.mthoodrr.com.* This historic railroad (1906) makes 44-mile round-trip excursions. Dinner, brunch, and murder mystery and comedy excursions are available. Reservations are recommended. (Mar-Dec, schedule varies) **$$$$**

Panorama Point. *Hwy 35 S and Eastside Rd, Hood River (97031). 1/2 mile S on Hwy 35 to Eastside Rd. Phone toll-free 800/366-3530.* Observation point for Hood River Valley and Mount Hood.

Special Events

Blossom Festival. Third weekend in Apr.

Cross Channel Swim. *405 Portway Ave, Hood River (97031). Phone toll-free 800/366-3530.* Labor Day.

Hood River County Fair. *3020 Wyeast Rd, Hood River (97031). Phone 541/354-2865.* July.

Hood River Valley Harvest Fest. *Phone toll-free 800/366-3530.* Fresh local fruit, art and crafts, wine tasting, contests. Third weekend in Oct.

Hood River Valley Sternwheeler Days. *355 Wanapa St, Hood River (97031). Phone 541/386-2000.* Celebration of the sternwheeler Columbia Gorge's return to home port for the summer. Wine and cheese tasting, crafts, food. June.

Limited-Service Hotel

★ ★ **BEST WESTERN HOOD RIVER INN.** *1108 E Marina Way, Hood River (97031). Phone 541/386-2200; toll-free 800/828-7873; fax 541/386-8905. www.hoodriverinn.com.* In Columbia River Gorge. 149 rooms, 3 story. Pets accepted, some restrictions; fee. Check-out noon. Restaurant, bar. Pool. **$**

Full-Service Hotels

★ ★ ★ **COLUMBIA GORGE HOTEL.** *4000 Westcliff Dr, Hood River (97031). Phone 541/386-5566; toll-free 800/345-1921; fax 541/386-9141.*

www.columbiagorgehotel.com. Nestled in the Columbia Gorge National Scenic Area, trees and mountain peaks surround this hotel, which features a waterfall, beautiful scenic gardens, and a Jazz Age atmosphere. 40 rooms, 3 story. Pets accepted, some restrictions; fee. Complimentary full breakfast. Check-out noon. Restaurant, bar. **$$**

★ ★ ★ **HOOD RIVER HOTEL.** *102 Oak St, Hood River (97031). Phone 541/386-1900. www. hoodriverhotel.com.* Charm and elegance await guests at the Hood River Hotel, which is listed on the National Register of Historic Places. Each room is uniquely decorated with antique reproductions and artwork evoking the hotel's history, dating back to its construction as an annex to the Mt. Hood Hotel in 1913. The hotel graces downtown Hood River, a stone's throw from the Columbia River Gorge. Pasquale's Ristorante can be found in the hotel, specializing in Italian and Pacific Northwest cuisines. 41 rooms. Complimentary continental breakfast. Check-in 3 pm, check-out noon. Restaurant, bar. **$$**

Full-Service Resort

★ ★ ★ **DOLCE SKAMANIA LODGE.** *1131 SW Skamania Lodge Way, Stevenson, WA (98648). Phone 509/427-7700; toll-free 800/376-9116; fax 509/427-2547. www.skamania.com.* At once rugged and sophisticated, the Dolce Skamania Lodge is a perfect mountain get-away. Tucked among the mountain peaks, waterfalls, and canyons of the Columbia River Gorge, just 45 minutes north of Portland, Oregon, this resort enjoys a picture-perfect setting. Comprehensive yet intimate, this hideaway is an ideal spot for large groups or couples escaping the daily grind. From golf and tennis to hiking and biking, this resort offers an endless supply of recreational opportunities. The guest rooms and suites pay tribute to the area's Native American heritage with unique decorative accents, while the clean lines of Pacific Northwestern architecture come shining through here. Three restaurants enchant diners with refined renditions of American classics. 254 rooms, 4 story. Check-in 4 pm, check-out noon. Wireless Internet access. Three restaurants, bar. Fitness room. Indoor pool, whirlpool. Golf, 18 holes. Tennis. Business center. **$**

Specialty Lodging

The following lodging establishment is approved by Mobil Travel Guide, but due to its unique and individualized nature has not been given a traditional Mobil Star rating. Included in this listing you may find bed-and-breakfasts, limited-service inns, guest ranches, and other unique hotel properties.

INN OF THE WHITE SALMON. *172 W Jewett Blvd, White Salmon, WA (98672). Phone 509/493-2335; toll-free 800/972-5226. www.innofthewhitesalmon .com.* European-style inn built in 1937; antique décor, original art. 16 rooms, 2 story. Pets accepted, some restrictions; fee. Complimentary full breakfast. Check-in 3 pm, check-out noon. Outdoor pool. **$**

Restaurant

★ ★ ★ **COLUMBIA GORGE DINING ROOM.** *4000 Westcliff Dr, Hood River (97031). Phone 541/386-5566; fax 541/386-9141. www.columbiagorgehotel.com.* Located in the historic Columbia Gorge Hotel. Visitors are urged to try the signature "farm" breakfast, a five-course extravaganza. Evening meals focus on Northwest cuisine, especially salmon, lamb, and venison. Continental menu. Breakfast, lunch, dinner, brunch. Bar. **$$**

Jacksonville (E-2)

See also Ashland, Grants Pass, Medford

Founded 1852
Population 1,896
Elevation 1,569 ft
Area Code 541
Zip 97530
Information Historic Jacksonville Chamber of Commerce, PO Box 33; phone 541/899-8118
Web site www.jacksonvilleoregon.org

Gold was discovered here in 1851 and brought prospectors by the thousands. An active town until the gold strike played out in the 1920s, Jacksonville lost its county seat to the neighboring town of Medford in 1927. Now a national historic landmark, the town is one of the best preserved pioneer communities in the Pacific Northwest. Approximately 80 original buildings can be seen and some visited. A Ranger District office of the Rogue River National Forest is located about 20 miles southwest of town, in Applegate Valley.

What to See and Do

⭐ **Jacksonville Museum.** *206 N 5th St, Jacksonville (97530). Phone 541/773-6536.* In Old County Courthouse (1883), has exhibits of southern Oregon history, pioneer relics, early photographs, Native American artifacts, quilts, natural history. (Wed-Sun; closed Jan 1, Thanksgiving, Dec 25) Children's Museum is in Old County Jail. (1911) **$$** Also maintained by the Southern Oregon Historical Society is

Beekman House. *352 E California St, Jacksonville (97530).* (1875) Country Gothic house; former home of a prominent Jacksonville citizen. Living history exhibit. (Memorial Day-Labor Day, Wed-Sun) **$$**

The Oregon Vortex Location of the House of Mystery. *4303 Sardine Creek L Fork Rd, Gold Hill (97525). Approximately 10 miles NW on county road. Phone 541/855-1543. www.oregonvortex.com.* The Vortex is a spherical field of force half above the ground, half below. Natural, historical, educational, and scientific phenomena are found in former assay office and surrounding grounds. Guided lecture tours (Mar-Oct, daily). **$$**

Special Event

Britt Musical Festivals. *517 W 10th St, Jacksonville (97530). Phone 541/779-0847 or toll-free 800/882-7488.* Hillside estate of pioneer photographer Peter Britt forms a natural amphitheatre. Festivals in classical, jazz, folk, country, dance, and musical theater. Mid-June-Sept.

Specialty Lodging

The following lodging establishment is approved by Mobil Travel Guide, but due to its unique and individualized nature has not been given a traditional Mobil Star rating. Included in this listing you may find bed-and-breakfasts, limited-service inns, guest ranches, and other unique hotel properties.

JACKSONVILLE INN. *175 E California St, Jacksonville (97530). Phone 541/899-1900; toll-free 800/321-9344; fax 541/899-1373. www.jacksonvilleinn.com.*

Built in 1860s; gold-rush era atmosphere. 12 rooms, 2 story. Pets accepted, some restrictions. Complimentary full breakfast. Check-in 4 pm, check-out 11:30 am. High-speed Internet access. Two restaurants, bar. Airport transportation available. **$$**

Restaurants

★ ★ ★ **JACKSONVILLE INN.** *175 E California St, Jacksonville (97530). Phone 541/899-1900. www.jacksonvilleinn.com.* Set in a gold rush-era guesthouse, this nationally recognized restaurant serves hearty country fare seasoned with fresh herbs from the inn's garden. Continental menu. Breakfast, lunch, dinner. Closed Thanksgiving, Dec 24-25. Bar. Outdoor seating. **$$**

⬛

★ ★ ★ **MCCULLY HOUSE.** *240 E California St, Jacksonville (97530). Phone 541/899-1942. www.mccullyhouseinn.com.* Housed in a historic Gothic Revival mansion—one of the first houses built in town—that is now the McCully House Inn, the dining room features contemporary Pacific Northwest cuisine. Emphasizing only the freshest ingredients, chef Mark Bender provides tempting selections, including pan-seared scallops with cilantro crème fraîche and an extensive wine list. American menu. Dinner. Bar. Outdoor seating. Rose garden. **$$**

John Day (C-5)

Population 1,836
Elevation 3,085 ft
Area Code 541
Zip 97845
Information Grant County Chamber of Commerce, 281 W Main; phone 541/575-0547 or toll-free 800/769-5664

John Day, named for a heroic scout in the first Astor expedition, was once a Pony Express stop on trail to The Dalles. Logging and cattle raising are the major industries in the area. Headquarters for the Malheur National Forest is located here; two Ranger District offices of the forest are also located here.

What to See and Do

Grant County Historical Museum. *101 S Canyon City Blvd, Canyon City (97820). 2 miles S on Hwy 395.* Phone 541/575-0362. Mementos of gold-mining days, Joaquin Miller cabin, Greenhorn jail (1910). (Mid-May-Sept, Mon-Sat, also Sun afternoons) **$**

John Day Fossil Beds National Monument. *Hwys 19 and 26, John Day (97848). 40 miles W on Hwy 26, then 2 miles N on Hwy 19.* Phone 541/987-2333. The monument consists of three separate units in Wheeler and Grant counties of north central Oregon; no collecting within monument. Wayside exhibits at points of interest in each unit. **FREE** These units include

Clarno Unit. *Hwy 218 and Hwy 19, Fossil (97830). 20 miles W of Fossil on Hwy 218.* Phone 541/763-2203. Consists of hills, bluffs, towering rock palisades, and pinnacles. Self-guided Trail of the Fossils features abundant plant fossils visible in the 35-50 million-year-old rock. Picnicking.

Painted Hills Unit. *37375 Bear Creek Rd, Mitchell (97750). 9 miles NW of Mitchell, off Hwy 26 on a county road.* Phone 541/462-3961. Displays a colorful, scenic landscape of buff and red layers in the John Day Formation. Self-guided Painted Cove Trail and Leaf Hill Trail. Exhibits; picnicking.

Sheep Rock Unit. *Hwys 19 and 26, Kimberly (97848). 7 miles W of Dayville on Hwy 19.* Phone 541/987-2333. Here are outstanding examples of the buff and green layers of the fossil-bearing John Day Formation, Mascall Formation, and Rattlesnake Formation. Visitor center offers picnicking and browsing among fossil displays. Self-guided Island in Time Trail and Story in Stone Trail includes exhibits.

Kam Wah Chung and Co Museum. *250 NW Canton, John Day (97845). Adjacent to city park.* Phone 541/575-0028. Originally constructed as a trading post on The Dalles Military Rd (1866-1867). Now houses Chinese medicine herb collection, shrine, kitchen, picture gallery, Doc Hay's bedroom. (May-Oct, Mon-Thurs, Sat and Sun)

Malheur National Forest. *431 Patterson Bridge Rd, John Day (97845). N and S on Hwy 395; E and W on Hwy 26.* Camping. Phone 541/575-3000. Nearly 1 1/2 million acres in southwestern part of Blue Mountains include Strawberry Mountain and Monument Rock wilderness areas. Trout fishing in Magone and Yellowjacket Lakes, stream fishing, elk and deer hunting. Hiking. Winter sports. Picnicking. **FREE**

Special Events

"62" Day Celebration. Phone 541/575-0329. *Canyon City, 1 mile S.* Celebrates the discovery of gold in 1862. Medicine wagon and fiddling shows, parade, booths, barbecue, dancing, selection of queen. Second weekend in June.

Grant County Fair and Rodeo. *Grant County Fairgrounds, 411 NW Bridge St, John Day (97845).* Phone 541/575-1900. Oregon's oldest continuous county fair. Early Aug.

Limited-Service Hotel

★ **BEST WESTERN JOHN DAY INN.** *315 W Main St, John Day (97845).* Phone 541/575-1700; toll-free 800/780-7234; fax 541/575-1558. www.bestwestern .com. 39 rooms. Complimentary continental breakfast. Check-in 3 pm, check-out noon. **$**

Joseph

Population 1,073
Elevation 4,190 ft
Area Code 541
Zip 97846
Information Wallowa County Chamber of Commerce, 107 SW First St, PO Box 427, Enterprise 97828; phone 541/426-4622 or toll-free 800/585-4121
Web site www.josephoregon.com

Joseph is located in the isolated wilderness of northeast Oregon. Remote from industry, the town attracts vacationers with its beautiful surroundings. There are fishing lakes here and hunting in the surrounding area. At the north end of Wallowa Lake is Old Joseph Monument, a memorial to the Nez Perce chief who resisted the US government. A Ranger District office of the Wallowa-Whitman National Forest is located in nearby Enterprise.

What to See and Do

Hells Canyon National Recreation Area. *612 SW 2nd St, Enterprise (97828). 30 miles NE on County Rd 350 in Wallowa-Whitman National Forest.* Phone 541/426-5546. www.fs.fed.us/hellscanyon. Created by the Snake

River at the Idaho/Oregon border, Hells Canyon is the deepest river-carved gorge in North America— 1 1/2 miles from Idaho's He Devil Mountain (elevation 9,393 feet) to the Snake River at Granite Creek (elevation 1,408 feet). Overlooks at Hat Point, southeast of Imnaha, and in Idaho (see GRANGEVILLE); both are fire lookouts. The recreation area includes parts of the Wallowa-Whitman National Forest in Oregon and the Nez Perce and Payette national forests in Idaho. Activities include float trips, jet boat tours, boat trips into the canyon from Lewiston, ID (see) or the Hells Canyon Dam (see WEISER, ID), as well as auto tours, backpacking, and horseback riding. There are developed campgrounds in Oregon and Idaho; much of the area is undeveloped, and some is designated wilderness. Be sure to inquire about road conditions before planning a trip; some roads are rough and open for a limited season. For a commercial outfitters guide list and further information, contact Hells Canyon National Recreation Area Office, 88401 OR 82, Enterprise 97828.

Valley Bronze of Oregon. *307 W Alder St, Joseph (97846). Phone 541/432-7445. www.valleybronze.com.* Company produces finished castings of bronze, fine and sterling silver, and stainless steel. Showroom displays finished pieces. Tours of foundry depart from showroom (by reservation). (May-Nov: daily; rest of year: by appointment) **$$**

Wallowa Lake State Park. *72214 Marina Ln, Joseph (97846). 6 miles S on Hwy 82. Phone 541/432-4185.* Park has 201 forested acres in an alpine setting formed by a glacier at the base of the rugged Wallowa Mountains. Swimming, water sport equipment rentals, fishing, boating (dock, motor rentals); picnicking, concession, improved tent and trailer sites (dump station). Park at edge of Eagle Cap wilderness area; hiking and riding trails begin here. Horse stables nearby.

Wallowa Lake Tramway. *6 miles S on Hwy 82. Phone 541/432-5331.* Gondola rises from valley to Mt. Howard summit. Snack bar at summit. (June-Sept: daily; May: weekends, weather permitting) **$$$$**

Special Event

Chief Joseph Days. *102 E 1st, Joseph (97846). Phone 541/432-1015.* PRCA rodeo, parades, Native American dances, cowboy breakfasts. Contact Chamber of Commerce. Last full weekend in July.

Limited-Service Hotel

★ **INDIAN LODGE MOTEL.** *201 S Main, Joseph (97846). Phone 541/432-2651; toll-free 888/286-5484; fax 541/432-4949.* 16 rooms. Pets accepted, some restrictions; fee. Check-out 11 am. **$**

★ ★ **WALLOWA LAKE LODGE.** *60060 Wallowa Lake Hwy, Joseph (97846). Phone 541/432-9821; fax 503/432-4885. www.wallowalake.com.* 30 rooms, 3 story. Check-out 11 am. Restaurant. **$**

Specialty Lodging

The following lodging establishment is approved by Mobil Travel Guide, but due to its unique and individualized nature has not been given a traditional Mobil Star rating. Included in this listing you may find bed-and-breakfasts, limited-service inns, guest ranches, and other unique hotel properties.

CHANDLERS BED BREAD TRAIL INN. *700 S Main St, Joseph (97846). Phone 541/432-9765; toll-free 800/452-3781; fax 541/432-4303. www.eoni.com/ chanbbti.* Cedar and log interiors with high vaulted ceilings. 5 rooms, 2 story. Children over 11 years only. Complimentary full breakfast. Check-in 2 pm, check-out 11 am. **$**

Klamath Falls (E-3)

Settled 1867
Population 17,737
Elevation 4,105 ft
Area Code 541
Information Klamath County Department of Tourism, 1451 Main St, 97601; phone 541/884-0666 or toll-free 800/445-6728
Web site www.klamathcountytourism.com

The closest sizable town to Crater Lake National Park with more than 100 good fishing lakes nearby, Klamath Falls is host to sports-minded people. Upper Klamath Lake, the largest body of fresh water in Oregon, runs north of town for 30 miles. White pelicans, protected by law, nest here each summer, and a large concentration of bald eagles winter in the Klamath Basin. Headquarters and a Ranger District office of the Winema National Forest are located here.

What to See and Do

Collier Memorial State Park and Logging Museum.
46000 Hwy 97, Chiloquin (97624). 30 miles N, on both sides of Hwy 97. Phone 541/783-2471. www. collierloggingmuseum.org. A 655-acre park located at the confluence of Spring Creek and Williamson River. Open-air historic logging museum with display of tools, machines, and engines; various types of furnished 1800s-era pioneer cabins; gift shop (daily; free). Fishing; hiking, picnicking. Tent and trailer campsites (hookups, dump station).

Favell Museum of Western Art and Native American Artifacts. *125 W Main, Klamath Falls (97601). Phone 541/882-9996.* Contemporary Western art; working miniature gun collection; extensive display of Native American artifacts. Also art and print sales galleries. Gift shop. (Tues-Sat) **$$**

Jackson F. Kimball State Recreation Site. *46000 Hwy 97, Chiloquin (97624). 40 miles N on Hwy 97, Hwy 62 to Fort Klamath, then 3 miles N on Hwy 232. Phone 541/783-2471. www.oregonstateparks.org/park_229.php.* A 19-acre pine- and fir-timbered area at the headwaters of the Wood River, noted for its transparency and deep blue appearance. Fishing, picnicking, ten primitive campsites (mid-Apr-Oct; no water). **FREE**

Klamath County Baldwin Hotel Museum. *31 Main St, Klamath Falls (97601). Phone 541/883-4208.* Restored turn-of-the-century hotel contains many original furnishings. Guided tours (June-Sept, Tues-Sat; closed holidays). **$$**

Klamath County Museum. *1451 Main St, Klamath Falls (97601). Phone 541/883-4208.* Local geology, history, wildlife, and Native American displays; research library has books on history, natural history, and anthropology of Pacific Northwest. (Tues-Sat; closed holidays) **$**

Migratory Bird Refuge. *4009 Hill Rd, Tulelake (96134). S on Hwy 39 and Hwy 139 to Tulelake, CA, then 5 miles W on East-West Rd. Phone 530/667-2231.* (In OR and CA) Major stopover on Pacific Flyway. There are six national wildlife refuges in the Klamath Basin. Upper Klamath and Klamath Marsh refuges lie to the north, and Lower Klamath, Bear Valley, Tule Lake, and Clear Lake lie to the south of the city. There is a visitor center with exhibits at refuge headquarters at Tule Lake (Daily). Waterfowl (Mar-Apr, Oct-Nov); bald eagles (Dec-Mar); migratory birds (Mar-Apr); waterfowl and colonial bird nesting (summer). **FREE**

Winema National Forest. *2819 Dahlia, Klamath Falls (97601). N, E, and W, reached by Hwy 97, Hwy 62 or Hwy 140. Phone 541/883-6714.* This forest (more than 1 million acres) includes former reservation lands of the Klamath Tribe; high country of Sky Lakes; portions of Pacific Crest National Scenic Trail; recreation areas in Lake of the Woods, Recreation Creek, Mountain Lakes Wilderness, and Mt. Theilson Wilderness. Swimming, boating; picnicking, camping (some areas free). **$$$**

Special Events

Bald Eagle Conference. *Phone toll-free 800/445-6728.* Mid-Feb.

Jefferson State Stampede. *Phone 541/883-3796.* Early Aug.

Klamath County Fair. *3531 S 6th St, Klamath Falls (97603). Phone 541/883-3796.* Early Aug.

Klamath Memorial Powow and Rodeo. *Phone toll-free 800/524-9787.* Late May.

Limited-Service Hotels

★ **BEST WESTERN OLYMPIC INN.** *2627 S 6th St, Klamath Falls (97603). Phone 541/882-9665; toll-free 800/600-9665; fax 541/884-3214. www. klamathfallshotelmotel.com.* 92 rooms, 3 story. Complimentary full breakfast. Check-in 4 pm, check-out 11 am. Outdoor pool, whirlpool. Airport transportation available. Business center. **$**

★ **HOLIDAY INN EXPRESS.** *2500 S 6th St, Klamath Falls (97601). Phone 541/884-9999; toll-free 800/465-4329; fax 541/882-4020. www.hiexpress.com.* 58 rooms, 2 story. Complimentary continental breakfast. Check-in 2 pm, check-out noon. High-speed Internet access. Fitness room. Indoor pool, whirlpool. Business center. **$**

Full-Service Resort

★ ★ ★ **THE RUNNING Y RANCH RESORT.** *5500 Running Y Rd, Klamath Falls (97601). Phone 541/850-5500; toll-free 888/850-0275. www.runningy.com.* This 3,600-acre resort is a nature lover's paradise, set amid wooded hills and open meadows at the edge of the Cascade Range. The Running Y Ranch overlooks Klamath Lake, the largest natural lake in the Northwest. The resort's lodge has comfortably appointed rooms with golf course views. Also offered are 2- and 3-bedroom townhouses and chalets, each equipped with a full kitchen, washer and dryer, fireplace, and private deck. Guests can take advantage of the resort's fitness center, pool complex, and Sandhill Spa. The Ranch House Restaurant serves up steak, seafood, and pasta dishes, while the Sugar Pine Café provides lighter fare and snack foods. An on-site Arnold Palmer-designed golf course is among the best public links in the nation. 350 rooms. Check-in 3 pm, check-out noon. Two restaurants, bar. Fitness room. Indoor pool, whirlpool. Airport transportation available. **$**

Restaurant

★ ★ **FIORELLA'S.** *6139 Simmer Ave, Klamath Falls (97603). Phone 541/882-1878.* Italian menu. Dinner. Closed Sun-Mon; Dec 25. Bar. Children's menu. **$$**

La Grande (B-5)

See also Baker City, Pendleton

Settled 1861
Population 11,766
Elevation 2,771 ft
Area Code 541
Zip 97850
Information La Grande/Union County Visitors & Conventions Bureau, 1912 Fourth Ave, #200; phone 541/963-8588 or toll-free 800/848-9969
Web site www.el.com/to/lagrande/

Located in the heart of Northeast Oregon amid the Blue and Wallowa mountains, La Grande offers visitors breathtaking scenery and numerous exhilarating activities. Rafting and fishing enthusiasts enjoy the Grande Ronde River; hikers and mountain bikers navigate the Eagle Cap Wilderness and the tracks of the Oregon Trail. A Ranger District office of the Wallowa-Whitman National Forest is located here.

What to See and Do

Catherine Creek State Park. *8 miles SE on Hwy 203. Phone 541/963-0430; toll-free 800/551-6949. www. oregonstateparks.org/park_17.php.* A 160-acre park in a pine forest along the creek. Fishing, biking, hiking, picnicking. Twenty primitive campsites (mid-Apr-Oct). **FREE**

Eastern Oregon University. *1 University Blvd, La Grande (97850). Phone 541/962-3672.* (1929) (2,000 students) Campus overlooks the town. Liberal arts college. Rock and mineral collection displayed in science building (Mon-Fri; closed holidays; free). Nightingale Gallery, concerts, theatrical productions, in Loso Hall; changing exhibits.

Hilgard Junction State Park. *8 miles W off I-84 N. Phone 541/963-0430. www.oregonstateparks.org/park_20.php.* A 233-acre park on the old Oregon Trail. Fishing, picnicking, 18 primitive campsites (mid-Apr-Oct). Exhibits at the Oregon Trail Interpretive Center (Memorial Day-Labor Day, daily). **FREE**

Turns of the Brick. *105 Fir, Suite 321, La Grande (97850). Phone 503/963-2411.* Self-guided walking tour of 30 turn-of-the-century buildings and ghost signs. Approximately one-hour tour includes McGlasson's Stationery (1890), Masonic Lodge and JC Penney Company (circa 1900), Fire Station Building (1898) and Helm Building (1891). Unique brickwork and architecture explained in brochure available from La Grande Downtown Development Association. **FREE**

Special Event

Union County Fair. *Union County Fairgrounds, 3604 N 2nd St, La Grande (97850). Phone toll-free 800/848-9969.* Early Aug.

Specialty Lodging

The following lodging establishment is approved by Mobil Travel Guide, but due to its unique and individualized nature has not been given a traditional Mobil Star rating. Included in this listing you may find bed-and-breakfasts, limited-service inns, guest ranches, and other unique hotel properties.

STANG MANOR BED & BREAKFAST. *1612 Walnut St, La Grande (97850). Phone 541/963-2400; toll-free 888/286-9463. www.stangmanor.com.* 4 rooms, 2 story. Children over 10 years only. Complimentary full breakfast. Check-in 3 pm, check-out 11 am. **$**

Lakeview (E-4)

Founded 1876
Population 2,526
Elevation 4,798 ft
Area Code 541
Zip 97630
Information Lake County Chamber of Commerce, 126 N E St; phone 541/947-6040

General John C. Fremont and Kit Carson passed through what is now Lake County in 1843. There are antelope and bighorn sheep in the area, many trout streams, and seven lakes nearby. A supervisor's office of the Fremont National Forest is located here; also here is a district office of the Bureau of Land Management and an office of the US Department of Fish and Wildlife.

What to See and Do

Drews Reservoir. *15 miles W on Dog Lake Rd. Phone 541/947-3334.* Fishing, boating (launch); camping.

Fremont National Forest. *1301 S G St, Lakeview (97630). E and W via Hwy 140, N and S via Hwy 395 and Hwy 31. Phone 541/947-2151.* More than 5 million acres. Includes remnants of ice-age lava flows and the largest and most defined exposed geologic fault in North America, Abert Rim, on east side of Lake Abert. Abert Rim is most spectacular at the east side of Crooked Creek Valley. Many of the lakes are remnants of post-glacial Lake Lahontan. Gearhart Mountain Wilderness is rough and forested with unusual rock formations, streams and Blue Lake. Fishing; hunting, picnicking, camping.

Geyser and Hot Springs. *1 mile N on Hwy 395. Phone 541/947-2817.* "Old perpetual," said to be largest continuous hot water geyser in the Northwest. Spouts as high as 70 feet occur approximately every 90 seconds. Hot springs nearby.

Paisley. *303 Hwy 31, Paisley (97636). 45 miles N on Hwy 31. Phone 541/943-3114.* Unspoiled old Western town.

Schminck Memorial Museum. *128 South E St, Lakeview (97630). Phone 541/947-3134.* Pressed-glass goblets, home furnishings, dolls, toys, books, clothing, quilts, guns, saddles, tools, and Native American artifacts. (Feb-Nov, Tues-Sat; also by appointment; closed holidays) **$**

Special Events

Festival of Free-Flight. *Phone toll-free 877/947-6040.* July 4 weekend.

Irish Days. *Phone toll-free 877/947-6040.* Mid-Mar.

Junior Rodeo. *Phone toll-free 877/947-6040.* Last weekend in June.

Lake County Fair and Roundup. *1900 N 4th St, Lakeview (97630). Phone toll-free 877/947-6040.* Labor Day weekend.

Limited-Service Hotel

★ **BEST WESTERN SKYLINE MOTOR LODGE.** *414 N G St, Lakeview (97630). Phone 541/947-2194; toll-free 800/528-1234; fax 541/947-3100. www.bestwestern.com.* 38 rooms, 2 story. Pets accepted, some restrictions; fee. Complimentary continental breakfast. Check-out 11 am. Indoor pool, whirlpool. **$**

Specialty Lodging

The following lodging establishment is approved by Mobil Travel Guide, but due to its unique and individualized nature has not been given a traditional Mobil Star rating. Included in this listing you may find bed-and-breakfasts, limited-service inns, guest ranches, and other unique hotel properties.

HERYFORD HOUSE INN. *108 S F St, Lakeview (97630). Phone 541/947-4727; toll-free 888/295-3402.* Located in a 1911 brick Queen Anne Victorian mansion in downtown Lakeview. 6 rooms, 3 story. **$**

Restaurant

★ **HOMESTEAD.** *Hwy 31 N, Paisley (97636). Phone 541/943-3187.* Classic American food is served at this restaurant in a historic location. American menu. Breakfast, lunch, dinner. **$**

Lincoln City (B-1)

See also Depoe Bay, Newport, Tillamook

Population 5,892
Elevation 11-115 ft
Area Code 541
Zip 97367
Information Visitor & Convention Bureau, 801 SW Hwy 101, Suite #1; phone 541/994-8378 or toll-free 800/452-2151
Web site www.el.com/to/lincolncity/

Nicknamed the "kite capital of the world," Lincoln City is a popular recreation, art, and shopping area offering many accommodations with ocean view rooms.

What to See and Do

Alder House II. *611 Immonen Rd, Lincoln City (97367). 1/2 mile E off Hwy 101.* Set in a grove of alder trees, this is the oldest glass-blowing studio in Oregon. Watch molten glass drawn from a furnace and shaped into pieces of traditional or modern design. (Mid-Mar-Nov; daily) **FREE**

Chinook Winds Casino & Convention Center. *1777 NW 44th St, Lincoln City (97367). Phone 541/996-5825; toll-free 888/244-6665. www.chinookwindscasino.com.* About 80 miles south of the Washington border on the scenic Oregon coast, Chinook Winds is the largest convention facility between Seattle and San Francisco. With more than 1,200 machines and tables, the modern casino has all the requisite games—slots, blackjack, keno, poker, roulette, craps, and even bingo—with a betting limit of $500. The cavernous showroom sees regular performances by classic rock bands, country artists, and comedians, many of them household names. There are also three restaurants (an upscale room, a buffet, and a deli), a lounge, and childcare services and an arcade for the kids, but no hotel rooms. (There are plenty of the latter in Lincoln City, however.) Best of all, the casino's beachfront location is serene, and there's plenty of public access in the area.

Devils Lake State Park. *1645 SE East Devils Lake Rd, Lincoln City (97367). S of town, off Hwy 101. Phone 541/994-2002.* A 109-acre park with swimming, fishing, boating (ramp on east side of Devil's Lake). Tent and trailer sites (on northwest side of lake).

Theatre West. *3536 SE Hwy 101, Lincoln City (97367). Phone 541/994-5663.* Community theater featuring comedy and drama. (Thurs-Sat)

Limited-Service Hotels

★ BEST WESTERN LINCOLN SANDS SUITES. *535 NW Inlet Ave, Lincoln City (97367). Phone 541/994-4227; toll-free 800/445-3234; fax 541/994-2232. www.bestwestern.com.* 33 rooms, 3 story. Complimentary continental breakfast. Check-out 11 am. Fitness room. On beach. Pool, whirlpool. **$**

★ ★ CHINOOK WINDS RESORT & CASINO. *1501 NW 40th Pl, Lincoln City (97367). Phone 541/994-3655; fax 541/994-2199. www.shiloinn.com.* 247 rooms, 4 story. Pets accepted, some restrictions; fee. Check-out noon. Restaurant, bar. Fitness room. Indoor pool, whirlpool. Airport transportation available. Business center. **$**

★ COHO INN. *1635 NW Harbor Ave, Lincoln City (97367). Phone 541/994-3684; toll-free 800/848-7006; fax 541/994-6244. www.thecohoinn.com.* 50 rooms, 3 story. Pets accepted, some restrictions; fee. Check-out 11 am. Whirlpool. **$**

★ ★ INN AT SPANISH HEAD. *4009 S Hwy 101, Lincoln City (97367). Phone toll-free 800/452-8127; fax 541/996-4089. www.spanishhead.com.* Built on side of cliff; oceanfront. Colorful sunsets and sandy beaches are the setting for this oceanfront hotel on the Oregon coast. 120 rooms, 10 story. Restaurant, bar. Check-out noon. Fitness room. Pool, whirlpool. **$$**

Full-Service Resort

★ ★ ★ SALISHAN LODGE & GOLF RESORT. *7760 Hwy 101 N, Gleneden Beach (97388). Phone 541/764-2371; toll-free 800/452-2300; fax 541/764-3663. www.salishan.com.* Carved out of a scenic stretch of Oregon coastline, the Salishan Lodge & Golf Resort is paradise for nature lovers who love their creature comforts. This traditional Pacific Northwest lodge knows how to pamper its guests with fireside massages, fine dining, and a multitude of recreational pursuits, but it is perhaps best loved for

its magnificent views of the region's ruggedly beautiful landscape. Private beach access and an 18-hole Scottish-style golf course rank among the property's favorite amenities, which also include an indoor tennis center, fitness center, and two indoor pools. Diners enjoy laid-back sophistication at the resort's eateries, where fresh, flavorful Pacific Northwest cuisine and classic American favorites provide rewarding ways to end the day. 205 rooms, 3 story. Pets accepted; fee. Check-out noon. Restaurant, bar. Fitness room. Indoor pool, whirlpool. Golf. Tennis. **$**

Specialty Lodging

The following lodging establishment is approved by Mobil Travel Guide, but due to its unique and individualized nature has not been given a traditional Mobil Star rating. Included in this listing you may find bed-and-breakfasts, limited-service inns, guest ranches, and other unique hotel properties.

THE O'DYSIUS HOTEL. *120 NW Inlet Ct, Lincoln City (97367). Phone 541/994-4121; toll-free 800/869-8069; fax 541/994-8160.* The O'dysius Hotel appeals to water lovers, with the Pacific Ocean to the immediate west, the D-River (the world's shortest river) bordering to the south, and Devil's Lake a short walk to the east. Each room has a fireplace, whirlpool tub, and custom décor. Select rooms have balconies overlooking a sandy beach and the ocean's pounding surf. Nightly wine tastings are offered in the lobby and parlor. Antique furnishings and lacquer-finished wainscoted walls evoke warmth and sophistication throughout the hotel. 30 rooms. No children allowed. Complimentary continental breakfast. Check-in 4 pm, check-out noon. Whirlpool. **$$**

Restaurants

★ ★ ★ **BAY HOUSE.** *PO Box 847, Lincoln City (97367). Phone 541/996-3222. www.bayhouserestaurant.com.* Located at the south end of the city, this romantic restaurant offers spectacular views of Siletz Bay. American menu. Dinner, brunch. **$$**

★ ★ **THE DINING ROOM AT SALISHAN.** *7760 N Hwy 101, Gleneden Beach (97388). Phone 541/764-2371. www.salishan.com.* American menu. Breakfast, lunch, dinner, Sun brunch. Children's menu. Valet parking. **$$$**

★ **DORY COVE.** *5819 Logan Rd, Lincoln City (97367). Phone 541/994-5180. www.dorycove.com.* Seafood menu. Lunch, dinner. Children's menu. **$$**

Madras (C-3)

See also Prineville, Redmond

Population 3,443
Elevation 2,242 ft
Area Code 541
Zip 97741
Information Chamber of Commerce, 197 SE 5th St, PO Box 770; phone 541/475-2350 or toll-free 800/967-3564

Although the area was explored as early as 1825, settlement here was difficult because of Native American hostility. Settlement east of the Cascades, considered a wall of separation between the Native Americans and the settlers, was officially forbidden in 1856. In 1858 the order was revoked, and in 1862 the first road was built across the Cascades to provide a passage for traders. Shortly thereafter, settlement began in earnest.

What to See and Do

The Cove Palisades State Park. *7300 SW Jordan Rd, Madras (97734). 15 miles SW off Hwy 97. Phone 541/546-3412. www.oregonstateparks.org/park_32.php.* A 4,130-acre park on Lake Billy Chinook behind the Round Butte Dam; scenic canyon of geological interest; spectacular views of the confluence of the Crooked, Deschutes, and Metolius rivers forming Lake Billy Chinook in a steep basaltic canyon. Swimming, fishing, boating (ramp, dock, rentals, marina with restaurant, groceries), houseboat rentals; hiking (nearly 10 miles of trails), picnicking, tent and trailer sites (dump station). **$**

Jefferson County Museum. *34 SE D St, Madras (97741). 1 block off Main St. Phone 541/475-3808.* Located in the old courthouse; old-time doctor's equipment; military memorabilia; homestead and farm equipment. (May-Oct, Mon-Fri) **$**

Rockhounding. *Richardson's Recreational Ranch, Mile Post 81 on Hwy 87, Madras (97741). 11 miles N on Hwy 97, then right 3 miles to ranch office. Phone*

541/475-2680. All diggings accessible by road; highlight of ranch are famous agate beds, featuring Thunder Eggs and ledge agate material. Rockhound campground area (no hookups). Digging fee.

Special Event

Collage of Culture. *Friendship Park, Madras. Phone 541/475-2350.* Music and balloon festival celebrating cultural diversity. Mid-May.

Limited-Service Hotel

★ **SONNY'S MOTEL.** *1539 SW Hwy 97, Madras (97741). Phone 541/475-7217; fax 541/475-6547. www. sonnysmotel.com.* 44 rooms, 2 story. Pets accepted; fee. Complimentary continental breakfast. Check-out 11 am. Pool, whirlpool. **$**

Full-Service Resort

★ ★ ★ **KAH-NEE-TA LODGE.** *100 Main St, Warm Springs (97761). Phone 541/553-1112; toll-free 800/554-4786; fax 541/553-1071. www.kah-nee-taresort .com.* Overlooking the Warm Springs River, this resort gives each guest a view of the sunrise from each room. For the guests who enjoy testing their luck, this resort features a casino on site. 139 rooms, 4 story. Pets accepted, some restrictions. Check-in 4:30 pm, check-out 11:30 am. Restaurant, bar. Fitness room. Pool. Golf. Tennis. Casino. Authentic Native American dances, Sun (May-Sept). **$**

McKenzie Bridge

Population 200
Elevation 1,337 ft
Area Code 541
Zip 97413
Information McKenzie River Chamber of Commerce and Information Center, MP 24 McKenzie Hwy East (Hwy 126), PO Box 1117, Leaburg 97489; phone 541/896-3330 or -9011
Web site www.el.com/to/Mckenzierivervalley

McKenzie Bridge and the neighboring town of Blue River are located on the beautiful McKenzie River, with covered bridges, lakes, waterfalls, and wilderness trails of the Cascades nearby. Fishing, float trips,

skiing, and backpacking are some of the many activities available. Ranger District offices of the Willamette National Forest (see EUGENE) are located here and in Blue River.

What to See and Do

Blue River Dam and Lake. *51668 Blue River Dr, Vida. 7 miles W on Hwy 126, then N on Forest Rd 15 in Willamette National Forest. Phone 541/822-3317 (Blue River Ranger Station).* Saddle Dam Boating Site offers boat ramp. Mona Campground offers swimming; fishing. Picnicking (fee). Dam is a US Army Corps of Engineers project. Recreation areas administered by the US Forest Service. Camping (mid-May-mid-Sept; fee).

Carmen-Smith Hydroelectric Development. *14 miles NE on Hwy 126, on Upper McKenzie River. Phone 541/484-2411.* Salmon spawning facility near Trail Bridge Dam; three stocked reservoirs—Trail Bridge, Smith and Carmen (daily). Boat launching (free). Picnicking. Camping at Lake's End, north end of Smith Reservoir, at Ice Cap Creek on Carmen Reservoir and at Trail Bridge (10-day limit). **$$$**

Cougar Dam and Lake. *51668 Blue River Dr, Vida. 5 miles W on Hwy 126, then S on Forest Rd 19 (Aufderheide Forest Dr), in Willamette National Forest. Phone 541/822-3317.* A 6-mile-long reservoir. Echo Park is a day-use area with boat ramp (free). Slide Creek campground offers swimming, water-skiing, fishing, and a boat ramp. Picnicking; camping (fee). Delta and French Pete campgrounds offer fishing and picnicking. The campgrounds are maintained and operated by the US Forest Service. The dam is a US Army Corps of Engineers project. For further information, inquire at Blue River Ranger Station. (May-Sept; most areas closed rest of year, inquire)

Limited-Service Hotels

★ **ALL SEASONS MOTEL.** *130 Breitenbush Rd, Detroit (97342). Phone 503/854-3421.* Situated on 2 1/2 acres of wooded land in the foothills of central Oregon, the location is ideal for hiking, boating, and recreation. 10 rooms, 1 story. **$**

★ ★ **HOLIDAY FARM RESORT.** *54455 McKenzie River Dr, Blue River (97413). Phone 541/822-3715; toll-free 800/823-3715.* Located on 90 acres of woods and streams with guides for fishing and rafting available. 15 rooms, 2 story. Restaurant. **$$**

★ **SUTTLE LAKE RESORT & MARINA.** *Hwy 20, Sisters (97759). Phone 541/595-6662.* Historic 1920s cabins and houseboat are available for rental featuring a full-service marina with boat and bike rental. 15 rooms, 1 story. **$**

Specialty Lodgings

The following lodging establishments are approved by Mobil Travel Guide, but due to their unique and individualized nature have not been given a traditional Mobil Star rating. Included in this listing you may find bed-and-breakfasts, limited-service inns, guest ranches, and other unique hotel properties.

BELKNAP LODGE & HOT SPRINGS. *59296 N Belknap Springs Rd, Blue River (97413). Phone 541/822-3512.* Extensive grounds and perennial gardens make this mountain retreat on the banks of the McKenzie River one of the state's most enjoyable. 24 rooms, 2 story. **$$**

MCKENZIE RIVER INN. *49164 McKenzie River Hwy, Vida (97488). Phone 541/822-6260. www. mckenzieriverinn.com.* Built in 1929, this inn is one of the oldest bed-and-breakfasts on the river. All special needs are catered to. 6 rooms, 2 story. **$**

MCKENZIE RIVER TROUT HOUSE BED & BREAKFAST. *41496 McKenzie Hwy, Springfield (97478). Phone 541/896-9819. www. mckenzierivertrouthouse.com.* Located on the McKenzie River, this gated 3 1/2-acre estate offers beautifully landscaped grounds with in-room fireplaces. 5 rooms, 2 story. **$$**

METOLIUS RIVER RESORT. *2551 SW F.S. Rd, #1419, Camp Sherman (97730). Phone toll-free 800/818-7688. www.metolius-river-resort.com.* Located on one of Oregon's premier fly fishing rivers, this area offers fully furnished cabins with kitchens and private decks. All linens are provided. 12 rooms, 2 story. **$$**

WAYFARER RESORT. *46725 Goodpasture Rd, Vida (97488). Phone 541/896-3613; toll-free 800/627-3613. www.wayfarerresort.com.* Located on the banks of the McKenzie River with fully applianced cabins, open-beamed ceilings, spacious decks, and fireplaces. 13 rooms, 2 story. **$$**

Restaurants

★ ★ **BRONCO BILLY'S RANCH GRILL.** *190 E Cascade, Sisters (97759). Phone 541/549-7427. www. broncobillysranchgrill.com.* Located in the historic Sisters Hotel, this establishment serves up modern interpretations of Old West cooking in a unique period environment. American menu. Dinner. **$**

★ **THE CEDARS RESTAURANT & LOUNGE.** *200 Detroit Ave, Detroit (97432). Phone 503/854-3636.* Serving authentic local cuisine for over 52 years in beautiful downtown Detroit. American menu. Breakfast, lunch, dinner. **$**

★ **KORNER POST RESTAURANT.** *100 S Detroit Ave, Detroit (97342). Phone 503/854-3735. www. kornerpost.com.* Located in a former post office, this restaurant and gift shop serves classic American cuisine with a kitschy atmosphere. Breakfast, lunch, dinner. American menu. **$**

★ **THE LAKESIDE BISTRO.** *13653 Hawks Beard Rd, Black Butte Ranch (97759). Phone toll-free 800/452-7455. www.blackbutteranch.com.* This country-style Western barbecue restaurant features ingredients from the Northwest. American menu. Lunch, dinner. **$**

★ ★ **THE LODGE RESTAURANT.** *13653 Hawks Beard Rd, Black Butte Ranch (97759). Phone toll-free 800/452-7455. www.blackbutteranch.com.* Located in an elegant setting with incredible views of the surrounding mountains and lake, this restaurant serves modern French cuisine utilizing Northwest products. French menu. Dinner. **$**

★ ★ **LOG CABIN INN.** *56483 McKenzie Hwy, McKenzie Bridge (97413). Phone 541/822-3432; toll-free 800/355-3432; fax 541/822-6173. www.logcabininn .com.* Situated in the deep woods in an 1886 river house, this restaurant features an extensive menu of Northwestern specialties. American menu. Lunch, dinner. Bar. Children's menu. Outdoor seating. **$$**

★ **MARION FORKS RESTAURANT.** *Mile 66, Hwy 22, Marion Forks (97350). Phone 503/854-3669.* Offering classic American road food in a family-oriented environment. American menu. Lunch, dinner. **$**

★ **SEASON'S CAFÉ AND WINE SHOP.** *411 E Hood, Sisters (97759). Phone 541/549-8911.* The freshly unique sandwiches and light fare here are complemented by a great by-the-glass wine selection. American menu. Lunch. Closed Mon. **$**

McMinnville (B-2)

See also Newberg, Oregon City, Salem

Population 17,894
Elevation 160 ft
Area Code 503
Zip 97128
Information Chamber of Commerce, 417 N Adams; phone 503/472-6196
Web site www.mcminnville.org

McMinnville is in the center of a wine-producing area. Many of the wineries offer tours.

What to See and Do

Community Theater. *210 2nd Ford St, McMinnville (97128). Phone 503/472-2227.* Musical, comedy and drama productions by the Gallery Players of Oregon (Fri-Sun).

Linfield College. *900 SE Baker St, McMinnville (97128). Phone 503/883-2200.* (1849) (2,100 students) Liberal arts. On the 100-acre campus are Miller Fine Arts Center, Linfield Anthropology Museum and the Linfield Theater. The music department offers concerts. Lectures and events throughout the year.

Special Events

Turkey Rama. *417 NW Adams St, McMinnville (97128). Phone 503/472-6196.* Mid-July.

Wine & Food Classic. *Phone 503/472-6196.* Mid-Mar.

Yamhill County Fair & Rodeo. *2070 NE LaFayette Ave, McMinnville (97128). Phone 503/434-7524.* Late July-early Aug.

Limited-Service Hotel

★ **BEST WESTERN VINEYARD INN.** *2035 S Hwy 99 W, Mcminnville (97128). Phone 503/472-4900;* *toll-free 800/285-6242; fax 503/434-9157. www. bestwestern.com.* 65 rooms. Complimentary continental breakfast. Check-in 4 pm, check-out noon. Fitness room. Indoor pool, whirlpool. **$**

Specialty Lodgings

The following lodging establishments are approved by Mobil Travel Guide, but due to their unique and individualized nature have not been given a traditional Mobil Star rating. Included in this listing you may find bed-and-breakfasts, limited-service inns, guest ranches, and other unique hotel properties.

FLYING M RANCH. *23029 NW Flying M Rd, Yamhill (97148). Phone 503/662-3222; fax 503/ 662-3202. www.flying-m-ranch.com.* 31 rooms. Pets accepted. Check-in 4 pm, check-out 11 am. Restaurant, bar. **$**

STEIGER HAUS BED & BREAKFAST. *360 SE Wilson St, McMinnville (97128). Phone 503/472-0821; fax 503/472-0100. www.steigerhaus.com.* Northern European country-style house; stained-glass windows. 5 rooms, 3 story. Children over 10 years only. Complimentary full breakfast. Check-in 3-6 pm, check-out 11 am. **$**

YOUNGBERG HILL VINEYARDS INN. *10660 SW Youngberg Hill Rd, McMinnville (97128). Phone 503/472-2727; toll-free 888/657-8668; fax 503/472-1313.* Set on a hillside high above the Willamette Valley, this cozy inn possesses an idyllic location in Oregon's wine country. The inn overlooks Youngberg Hill's award-winning Pinot Noir vineyards. Accommodations are nicely appointed with elegant furnishings. The Martini room has a fireplace and Jacuzzi tub, as well as French doors leading to a private deck. Guests are welcome to relax in the library and lounging salon. Covered decks wrap around the perimeter of the inn, affording breathtaking views of the valley below and mountain peaks on the horizon. 7 rooms. Check-in 4 pm. Whirlpool. **$$**

Medford (E-2)

See also Ashland, Grants Pass, Jacksonville

Founded 1885
Population 46,951
Elevation 1,380 ft
Area Code 541
Information Visitors and Convention Bureau, 101 E 8th St, 97501; phone 541/779-4847 or toll-free 800/469-6307
Web site www.el.com/to/medford/

Medford is a name known throughout the US for pears: Comice, Bartlett, Winter Nellis, Bosc, and d'Anjou. The city, on Bear Creek 10 miles from its confluence with the Rogue River, is surrounded by orchards. Trees make the city parklike; lumbering provides a large share of the industry. Mild winters and warm summers favor outdoor living and also encourage outdoor sports: boating and fishing on the Rogue River, fishing in 153 stocked streams and 17 lakes; camping and hunting in 56 forest camps within an 80-mile radius. The Rogue River National Forest headquarters is here.

What to See and Do

Butte Creek Mill. *402 Royal Ave N, Eagle Point (97524). 10 miles N on Hwy 62. Phone 541/826-3531.* Water-powered gristmill (1872) grinds whole grain products with original millstones. Museum (summer, Sat). Mill (Mon-Sat; closed holidays). **FREE**

Crater Rock Museum. *2002 Scenic Ave, Central Point (97502). N on I-5, exit 35, then S on Hwy 99. Phone 541/664-6081.* Gem and mineral collection; Native American artifacts; fossils, geodes and crystals. Gift shop. (Tues, Thurs, and Sat; closed holidays) **DONATION**

Joseph H. Stewart State Park. *35251 Hwy 62, Trail (97451). 35 miles NE on Hwy 62. Phone 541/560-3334. www.oregonstateparks.org/park_30.php.* A 910-acre park located on a lake formed by the Lost Creek Dam. Swimming, fishing (trout, bass); boat dock and ramp to the Rogue River. Hiking, bike trails (11 miles). Picnicking. Tent and improved campsites (dump station). **FREE**

★ Rogue River National Forest. *333 W 8th St, PO Box 520, Medford (97501). S off I-5 and NE on Hwy 62, 140. Phone 541/776-3600.* Forest has 632,045 acres with extensive stands of Douglas fir, ponderosa, and sugar pine. Rogue-Umpqua National Forest Scenic Byway offers a day-long drive through southern Oregon's dramatic panorama of mountains, rivers, and forest; viewpoints. A part of the Pacific Crest National Scenic Trail and portions of three wilderness areas are included in the forest. For fishermen, the upper reaches of the Rogue River, and other streams and lakes yield rainbow, cutthroat, and brook trout. Union Creek Historic District, on Hwy 62 near Crater Lake National Park. Forest is in two separate sections, located in the Siskiyou Mountains (W of I-5) and Cascade Range (E of I-5). Swimming; hiking, backpacking, downhill and cross-country skiing, picnic areas, camping. Some fees.

Southern Oregon Historical Society. *106 N Central Ave, Medford (97501). Phone 541/773-6536. www. sohs.org.* More than 2,000 items from Southern Oregon Historical Society's cultural history collection. Exhibits, public programs, research library. (Mon-Fri) **FREE**

TouVelle State Recreation Site. *3 miles NE on I-5, then 6 miles N on Table Rock Rd. Phone 541/582-1118. www.oregonstateparks.org/park_106.php.* A 51-acre park. Fishing on the Rogue River; boat ramp. Swimming, hiking, bird-watching, picnicking. **$**

Special Events

Jackson County Fair. *Jackson County Fairgrounds, Medford. Phone 541/774-8270.* Entertainment, dance, music, 4-H fair. Third weekend in July.

Pear Blossom Festival. *Phone 541/779-4847.* Parade; 10-mile run; band festival. Second weekend in Apr.

Limited-Service Hotels

★ ★ RED LION. *200 N Riverside Ave, Medford (97501). Phone 541/779-5811; toll-free 800/733-5466; fax 541/779-7961. www.redlion.com.* 185 rooms, 2 story. Pets accepted; fee. Check-in 3 pm, check-out noon. High-speed Internet access. Two restaurants, bar. Fitness room. Outdoor pool. Airport transportation available. Business center. **$**

★ ★ **ROGUE REGENCY INN.** *2345 Crater Lake Hwy, Medford (97504). Phone 541/770-1234; toll-free 800/535-5805; fax 541/770-2466. www.rogueregency .com.* 203 rooms, 4 story. Complimentary continental breakfast. Check-in 3 pm, check-out 11 am. High-speed Internet access. Restaurant, bar. Fitness room. Indoor pool, whirlpool. Airport transportation available. Business center. **$**

★ **WINDMILL INN OF MEDFORD.** *1950 Biddle Rd, Medford (97504). Phone 541/779-0050; toll-free 800/547-4747; fax 541/779-0050. www. windmillinns.com.* 123 rooms, 2 story. Pets accepted. Complimentary continental breakfast. Check-in 3 pm, check-out 11 am. Fitness room. Outdoor pool, whirlpool. Airport transportation available. Business center. **$**

Restaurant

★ ★ **MON DESIR DINING INN.** *4615 Hanrick Rd, Central Point (97502). Phone 541/664-7558.* Continental menu. Lunch, dinner. Closed Sun-Mon. Bar. Converted mansion; fireplace, antiques; garden. Outdoor seating. **$$**

Mount Hood National Forest

See also Hood River, The Dalles

Web site www.mthood.org

Mount Hood (11,235 feet) is the natural focal point of this 1,064,573-acre forest with headquarters in Sandy. Its white-crowned top, the highest point in Oregon, can be seen for miles on a clear day. It is also popular with skiers, who know it has some of the best slopes in the Northwest. There are five winter sports areas. Throughout the year, however, visitors can take advantage of the surrounding forest facilities for camping (1,600 camp and picnic sites), hunting, fishing, swimming, mountain climbing, golfing, horseback riding, hiking and tobogganing. The Columbia Gorge, which cuts through the Cascades here, has many spectacular waterfalls, including Multnomah (620 feet). There are nine routes to the summit, which has fumed and

smoked several times since the volcanic peak was discovered. Only experienced climbers should try the ascent and then only with a guide. For further information contact the Mount Hood Information Center, 65000 E Hwy 26, Welches 97067; phone 503/622-7674, 503/622-4822, or toll-free 888/622-4822.

What to See and Do

Mount Hood Meadows. *11 miles NE of Government Camp on Hwy 35. Phone 503/337-2222. www.skihood .com.* Quad, triple, seven double chairlifts, free rope tow; patrol, school, rentals; restaurant, cafeteria, concession, bar, daycare, two day lodges. Longest run 3 miles; vertical drop 2,777 feet. Also 550 acres of expert canyon skiing. (Nov-May, daily) Groomed, ungroomed cross-country trails; night skiing (Wed-Sun).

River cruise. *Cascade Locks. 45 miles E of Portland via I-84. Phone 503/223-3928.* 2-hour narrated cruise of Columbia Gorge aboard the 599-passenger *Columbia Gorge,* an authentic sternwheeler. (Mid-June-Sept, three departures daily; reservations required for dinner cruise) Also here: museum; marina; travel information; picnicking; camping. **$$$$**

Timberline Lodge. *Timberline Ski Area, Timberline (97028). 6 miles N of Hwy 26. Phone 503/272-3311. www.timberlinelodge.com.* Four Quads, triple, one double chairlift; patrol, school, rentals; restaurant, cafeteria, concession, bar, lodge. Longest run more than 2 miles; vertical drop 3,580 feet. (Mid-Nov-June, daily) Chairlift also operates (Daily, weather permitting; fee). **$$$$**

Limited-Service Hotels

★ **MOUNT HOOD INN.** *87450 E Government Camp Loop, Government Camp (97028). Phone 503/ 272-3205; toll-free 800/443-7777; fax 503/272-3307. www.mounthoodinn.com.* 56 rooms, 2 story. Pets accepted, some restrictions; fee. Complimentary continental breakfast. Check-out noon. Whirlpool. **$**

★ ★ **TIMBERLINE LODGE.** *Timberline, Timberline Lodge (97028). Phone 503/272-3311; fax 503/272-3710. www.timberlinelodge.com.* 70 rooms, 4 story. Check-in 4 pm, check-out 11 am. Restaurant, bar. Children's activity center. Pool, whirlpool. Ski in/ski out. **$**

Staying in a Fire Lookout in the Cascades

The Cascades possess a majestic beauty rivaling that of any other mountain range in the lower 48. To fully appreciate the splendor of the Cascades, you must set off on foot and spend several days navigating your way through dense forests and across open meadows, up and over rocky ridges and alongside deep alpine lakes. Most trekkers choose to sleep in tents, which means bringing along a tarp, rainfly, poles, and stakes, along with the tent itself, all of which must be assembled and disassembled, as well as kept clean and dry. But a tent is not your only option when it comes to shelter. In the Pacific Northwest, the US Forest Service (www.fs.fed.us) rents out dozens of fire lookouts to the public. Lookout amenities are wide-ranging. Some are furnished with just a cot and table, while others have such luxuries as propane-powered heaters, refrigerators, and stoves. With all fire lookouts, a spectacular view comes standard.

If you're ready to leave the tent behind and stay in a fire lookout, here are several worthy of consideration:

Pickett Butte Lookout stands on a ridge near the southern Oregon town of Tiller, a short drive north of Medford and west of Crater Lake. Nestled amid the pines of Umpqua National Forest, the lookout is well equipped with a heater, lantern, stove, and refrigerator, all of which are powered by complimentary propane. The lookout can be rented for up to three consecutive nights from early November through May. The fee is $40 per night. To make a reservation, contact the Tiller Ranger Station at phone 541/825-3100.

Set high above Hidden Lake in Willamette National Forest, **Indian Ridge Lookout** offers breathtaking views of the Three Sisters mountain peaks. An hour's drive east of Eugene, the lookout is surrounded by pine trees, beargrass, and huckleberries. Amenities are minimal; you'll find two twin beds and a table but no heat, so bring your flannel pajamas. The 16 x 16 structure is available from July through September for $40 a night. Make a reservation by calling the ranger station in McKenzie Bridge at phone 541/822-3381.

East of Portland, **Clear Lake Lookout** is perched on a 40-foot tower in Mount Hood National Forest. The lookout rents for $30 per night and accommodates four people. This one's a good option for those who love snow, as it's available only from November through May. Nearby, the Timberline Lodge offers year-round skiing on the shoulders of 11,239-foot-high Mount Hood. To reserve the lookout, contact the Barlow Ranger Station at phone 541/467-2291.

Evergreen Mountain Lookout sits atop a mountain ridge at an elevation of 5,587 feet. A two-hour drive east of Seattle in Mount Baker-Snoqualmie National Forest, the structure was used to detect fires from 1935 until the early 1980s, and even served as an Air Warning Station during World War II. After nearly 20 years of neglect, the lookout was renovated in 2001 and made available for public rental. Furnishings include a stove, two lanterns, four mattresses, a table, and folding chairs. The lookout can be rented from early August until mid-November, depending on the weather, at a fee of $40 per night. Contact the Skykomish Ranger Station at phone 360/677-2414 for more information.

While a lookout may offer more protection than a tent, you still need to bring along such essentials as flashlights, bedding, and ample food and water. It also must be noted that reaching a fire lookout typically involves driving on an unpaved Forest Service road to an unattended parking area, followed by a mile-plus hike, and finishing with a climb up a narrow switchback of stairs to the enclosed lookout. Those willing to make the effort are rewarded with a unique and enchanting experience that will make their travels in the Cascades all the more memorable.

Full-Service Resort

★ ★ ★ THE RESORT AT THE MOUNTAIN.

68010 E Fairway Ave, Welches (97067). Phone 503/622-3101; toll-free 800/669-7666; fax 503/622-2222. www.theresort.com. Situated on 300 acres of forest at Salmon River. Scottish amenities reminiscent of Highlands. 160 rooms, 2 story. Check-in 4 pm, check-out noon. Restaurant, bar. Fitness room. Pool, whirlpool. Golf. Tennis. **$**

Restaurants

★ ★ DON GUIDO'S ITALIAN CUISINE. *73330 E Hwy 26, Rhododendron (97049). Phone 503/622-5141. www.donguidos.com.* Italian menu. Dinner. Closed holidays. Bar. Children's menu. **$$**

★ ★ ★ HIGHLANDS DINING ROOM. *68010 E Fairway Ave, Welches (97067). Phone 503/622-2214; fax 503/622-2222. www.theresort.com.* Continental menu. Breakfast, lunch, dinner, Sun brunch. Bar. Children's menu. Outdoor seating. **$$**

Newberg (B-2)

See also Beaverton, Hillsboro, McMinnville, Oregon City, Portland, Salem, Silverton

Founded 1889
Population 13,086
Elevation 176 ft
Area Code 503
Zip 97132
Information Chamber of Commerce, 115 N Washington; phone 503/538-2014
Web site ci.newberg.or.us/page.asp

Quakers made their first settlement west of the Rockies here and established Pacific Academy in 1885. Herbert Hoover was in its first graduating class (1888).

What to See and Do

Champoeg State Historic Area. *7679 Champoeg Rd NE, Saint Paul (97137). 5 miles W off I-5. Phone 503/678-1251.* A 615-acre park on site of early Willamette River settlement, site of settlers' vote in 1843 for a provisional territorial government, swept away by flood of 1861. Fishing, boat dock on Willamette River; hiking, picnicking, improved camping (dump station). Visitor information, interpretive center; monument. French Prairie Loop 40-mile auto or bike tour begins and ends here. (See SPECIAL EVENT) **$$** In the area are

Newell House Museum. *8089 Champoeg Rd NE, Newberg (97132). Just W of park entrance. Phone 503/678-5537.* Reconstructed home of Robert Newell, one-time mountain man and friend of the Native Americans. Contains period furnishings, quilts, coverlets and examples of fine handiwork; collection of inaugural gowns worn by wives of Oregon governors; Native American artifacts. Old jail (1850) and typical pioneer one-room schoolhouse. (Feb-Nov, Wed-Sun; closed Thanksgiving) **$**

Pioneer Mother's Memorial Log Cabin. *8035 Champoeg Rd NE, Newberg (97132). Located in the park, on the banks of the Willamette River. Phone 503/633-2237.* A replica, much enlarged, of the type of log cabin built by early pioneers. Constructed of peeled hand-hewn logs, with a shake roof, it has a massive stone fireplace in the living room, a sleeping loft and two small bedrooms; many pioneer items include an old Hudson's Bay heating stove, collection of guns and muskets dating from 1777-1853, a fife played at Lincoln's funeral, china and glassware and original furnishings from pioneer homes. (Feb-Nov, Wed-Sun; closed Thanksgiving) **$**

Visitor Center. *8239 Champoeg Rd NE, Newberg. Phone 503/678-1251.* Interpretive historical exhibits tell the story of "Champoeg: Birthplace of Oregon"; films; tours. (Daily) **DONATION**

George Fox University. *414 N Meridian, Newberg (97132). Phone 503/538-8383.* (1891) (2,600 students) Founded as Friends Pacific Academy; renamed in 1949 for English founder of the Society of Friends. Herbert Hoover was a student here; Hoover Building has displays. Brougher Museum has Quaker and pioneer exhibits. Campus tours.

Hoover-Minthorn House Museum. *115 S River St, Newberg (97132). Phone 503/538-6629.* Herbert Hoover lived here with his uncle, Dr. Henry Minthorn. Quaker house built in 1881 contains many original furnishings, photographs, and souvenirs of Hoover's boyhood. (Mar-Nov: Wed-Sun; Dec and Feb: Sat-Sun; closed Jan) **$**

Special Event

Vintage Celebration. *115 N Washington St, Newberg (97132). Phone 503/538-2014.* Classic automobiles and airplanes, arts and crafts, wine tasting. Sat, Sun after Labor Day.

Limited-Service Hotel

★ **SHILO INN.** *501 Sitka Ave, Newberg (97132). Phone 503/537-0303; fax 503/537-0442. www.shiloinn .com.* 60 rooms, 3 story. Pets accepted, some restrictions; fee. Complimentary continental breakfast. Check-out noon. Fitness room. Pool, whirlpool. **$**

Newport (C-1)

See also Depoe Bay, Lincoln City, Yachats

Settled 1882
Population 8,437
Elevation 160 ft
Area Code 541
Zip 97365
Information Chamber of Commerce, 555 SW Coast Hwy; phone 541/265-8801 or toll-free 800/262-7844
Web site www.newportchamber.org

This fishing port at the mouth of the Yaquina River has been a resort for more than 100 years. Crabbing is a popular activity here; Dungeness crabs can be caught in the bay year-round.

What to See and Do

Beverly Beach. *198 NE 123rd St, Newport (97365). 7 miles N on Hwy 101. Phone 541/265-9278; toll-free 800/452-5687.* A 130-acre park with beach access; fishing. Hiking. Picnicking. Tent and trailer sites (dump station).

Devils Punch Bowl. *8 miles N off Hwy 101. Phone 541/265-9278.* An 8-acre park noted for its bowl-shaped rock formation that fills at high tide; ocean-carved caves, marine gardens. Beach. Trails. Picnicking. Observation point.

Hatfield Marine Science Center of Oregon State University. *2030 S Marine Science Dr, Newport (97365). S side of Yaquina Bay, just E of Newport Bridge, off Hwy 101. Phone 541/867-0100.* Conducts research on oceanography, fisheries, water quality, marine science education and marine biology; research vessel Wecoma; nature trail; aquarium-museum; films; special programs in summer. Winter and spring grey whale programs. Braille text and other aids for the hearing and visually impaired. (Daily; closed Dec 25) **DONATION**

Lincoln County Historical Society Museums. *Log Cabin Museum, 545 SW 9th St, Newport (97365). Also Burrows House Museum. Victorian-era household furnishings, clothing; history of Lincoln County. (Same days as log cabin museum) 579 SW 9th St. Phone 541/265-7509.* Artifacts from Siletz Reservation; historical, pioneer and maritime exhibits. (Tues-Sun; closed Jan 1, Thanksgiving, Dec 25) **FREE**

Marine Discovery Tours. *345 SW Bay Blvd, Newport (97365). Phone 541/265-6200; toll-free 800/903-2628.* Whale-watching and river cruises. Hands-on activities. (Hours vary seasonally; closed Dec 25) **$$$$**

Mineral collecting. *Phone toll-free 800/262-7844.* Gemstones, marine fossils, other stones are found on beaches to north and south of Newport, particularly at creek mouths.

Ona Beach. *8 miles S on Hwy 101. Phone 541/867-7451.* A 237-acre day-use park with ocean beach, swimming; fishing, boat ramp on creek. Picnicking.

Oregon Coast Aquarium. *2820 SE Ferry Slip Rd, Newport (97365). S side of Yaquina Bay. Phone 541/867-3474.* Houses 15,000 animals representing 500 species in unique habitats. (Daily; closed Dec 25) **$$$**

Ripley's—Believe It or Not. *250 SW Bay Blvd, Newport (97365). Phone 541/265-2206.* Exhibits include replicas of a backwards fountain; King Tut's tomb; the *Titanic;* the Fiji mermaid. (Daily; closed Dec 25) **$$$**

South Beach. *5580 S Coast Hwy, South Beach (97366). 2 miles S on Hwy 101. Phone 541/867-7451 (reservations).* Over 400 acres. Botanically interesting area, sandy beach, dunes. Fishing. Hiking. Picnicking. Improved campsites (dump station).

Undersea Gardens. *250 SW Bay Blvd, Newport (97365). On Yaquina Bay just off Hwy 101 in the Bay Front district. Phone 541/265-2206.* Visitors descend beneath the sea for underwater show. Watch native sea life through viewing windows; guides narrate as scuba divers perform; features Armstrong, the giant octopus. (Daily; closed Dec 25) **$$$**

Wax Works. *250 SW Bay Blvd, Newport (97365). Phone 541/265-2206.* Events of the past and future shown with animation and special effects. (Daily; closed Dec 25) **$$$**

Yaquina Bay. *5580 S Coast Hwy, Newport (97365). N end of bridge on Hwy 101. Phone 541/867-7451.* Over 30 acres. Ocean beach, fishing, picnicking. Agate beaches nearby. Old Yaquina Bay Lighthouse (1871) has been restored; exhibits. (Memorial Day-Labor Day: daily; rest of year: weekends) **DONATION**

Yaquina Head. *Lighthouse Dr and Hwy 101, Newport (97365). 1/2 mile N on Hwy 101. Phone 541/574-3100.* Lighthouse here is a popular spot for whale-watching and fully accessible tidal pool viewing. Also interpretive center.

Special Events

Loyalty Days and Sea Fair Festival. *555 SW Coast Hwy, Newport (97365). Phone 541/867-3798.* Military ships, parade, sailboat races; entertainment. First weekend in May.

Seafood and Wine Festival. *Phone 541/265-8801.* Last full weekend in Feb.

Limited-Service Hotels

★ ★ **EMBARCADERO RESORT HOTEL.** *1000 SE Bay Blvd, Newport (97365). Phone 541/265-8521; toll-free 800/547-4779; fax 541/265-7844. www. embarcadero-resort.com.* View of bay. 85 rooms, 3 story. Check-out 11 am. Restaurant, bar. Fitness room. Indoor pool, whirlpool. Airport transportation available. **$**

★ ★ **SHILO INN.** *536 SW Elizabeth St, Newport (97365). Phone 541/265-7701; fax 541/265-5687. www. shiloinns.com.* 179 rooms, 4 story. Pets accepted, some restrictions; fee. Check-out noon. Restaurant, bar. Indoor pool. **$**

★ **WHALER MOTEL.** *155 SW Elizabeth St, Newport (97365). Phone 541/265-9261; toll-free 800/433-9444; fax 541/265-9515. www.whalernewport.com.* 73 rooms,

3 story. Complimentary continental breakfast. Check-out noon. Fitness room. Ocean view. Indoor pool, whirlpool. Airport transportation available. **$**

Restaurant

★ **WHALE'S TALE.** *452 SW Bay Blvd, Newport (97365). Phone 541/265-8660.* Seafood menu. Breakfast, lunch, dinner, brunch. Closed Wed. Children's menu. **$$**

North Bend (D-1)

See also Bandon, Coos Bay, Reedsport

Settled 1853
Population 9,614
Elevation 23 ft
Area Code 541
Zip 97459
Information Bay Area Chamber of Commerce, PO Box 210, Coos Bay 97420; phone 541/269-0215 or toll-free 800/824-8486. North Bend Info Center is located at 1380 Sherman Ave in town, phone 541/756-4613

This town sits on the "north bend" of Coos Bay, one of the largest and deepest ports in the Northwest. Forestry has long been the town's lifeblood industry, followed by shipbuilding and fishing. Situated at the southern edge of Oregon Dunes National Recreation Area, the town is intersected by Highway 101. The Conde B. McCullough Memorial Bridge stands as North Bend's most prominent landmark, a 5,300-foot-long expanse of steel, constructed during the Depression and bearing the name of its architect. Commercial fisheries, lumbering, and manufacturing thrive in this city on a peninsula in Coos Bay.

What to See and Do

Coos County Historical Society Museum. *1220 Sherman Ave, North Bend (97459). In Simpson Park, on Hwy 101, N edge of town. Phone 541/756-6320.* Local history; permanent and changing exhibits. (Tues-Sat) **$**

Oregon Dunes National Recreation Area. *855 Hwy 11, Reedsport (97467). Phone 541/271-3611.* Area is 2 miles wide and 40 miles long. One of largest bodies of sand outside of the Sahara. (See REEDSPORT)

The Real Oregon Gift. *68794 Hauser Depot Rd, North Bend (97459). 5 miles N on Hwy 101. Phone 541/756-2220.* Manufacturers of myrtlewood products. Tour of factory; gift shop. (Daily) **FREE**

Limited-Service Hotel

★ ★ **RAMADA INN NORTH BEND.** *1503 Virginia Ave, North Bend (97459). Phone 541/756-3191; toll-free 888/298-2054; fax 541/756-5818. www.ramada.com.* 96 rooms. Check-in 3 pm, check-out noon. Restaurant, bar. Fitness room. Whirlpool. **$**
🧖

Restaurant

★ ★ **HILLTOP HOUSE.** *166 N Bay Dr, North Bend (97459). Phone 541/756-4160.* Continental menu. Lunch, dinner. **$$**

Ontario (C-6)

See also Caldwell, ID; Weiser, ID

Founded 1883
Population 9,392
Elevation 2,154 ft
Area Code 541
Zip 97914
Information Visitors & Convention Bureau, 88 SW 3rd Ave; phone 541/889-8012 or toll-free 888/889-8012
Web site www.el.com/to/Ontario/

Ontario, the largest town in Malheur County, is a trading center at the eastern border of Oregon. Irrigation from the Snake River has made possible the cultivation of sugar beets, potatoes, onions, corn, hay, and alfalfa seed, but there is still a vast wilderness of rangeland, lakes and reservoirs, mountains, and canyons. Quartz crystals, jaspers, thundereggs, marine fossils, petrified wood, and obsidian are abundant in the area.

What to See and Do

Farewell Bend. *23751 Old Hwy 30, Huntington (97907). 25 miles NW on I-84. Phone 541/869-2365.* A 72-acre park named by pioneers who left the Snake River at this point in their trek west. Swimming beach (bathhouse); fishing; boat ramp. Picnicking. Primitive and improved camping (dump station).

Fishing and hunting. *Phone 541/384-3300.* Rainbow trout, crappie, and bass are plentiful. Mallard and Canada geese are found on the Snake River; sage grouse, chukars, antelope, mule deer in the sagebrush areas; pheasant on irrigated land.

Lake Owyhee. *33 miles SW off Hwy 201. Phone 541/339-2331.* A 730-acre park with a 52-mile-long lake created by the Owyhee Dam. Fishing; boating (ramp). Picnicking. Improved camping (dump station).

Ontario. *On I-84 at N end of town. Phone 541/869-2365.* A 35-acre day-use area. Fishing; boat ramp. Picnicking.

Owyhee Canyon. *Rome. Phone 541/384-3300.* Fossils and utensils of Native Americans; petroglyphs. Boating. Fishing and hunting. Contact office, 3948 Development Ave, Boise, ID 83705.

Special Events

American Musical Jubilee. *Phone toll-free 888/889-8012.* Early June.

Malheur County Fair. *795 NW 9th St, Ontario (97914). Phone 541/889-3431.* First week in Aug.

Obon Festival. *Phone toll-free 888/889-8012.* Japanese dancing, food; art show. Mid-July.

Limited-Service Hotel

★ **BEST WESTERN INN & SUITES.** *251 Goodfellow St, Ontario (97914). Phone 541/889-2600; fax 541/889-2259. www.bestwestern.com.* 61 rooms, 2 story. Pets accepted, some restrictions; fee. Complimentary continental breakfast. Check-out 11 am. Fitness room. Indoor pool, whirlpool. **$**
🍴 🧖 🏊

Restaurant

★ ★ **NICHOLS STEAK HOUSE.** *411 SW 3rd St, Fruitland (83619). Phone 541/452-3030.* Steak menu. Lunch, dinner. Closed Mon; holidays. Children's menu. **$$**

Oregon Caves National Monument

See also Cave Junction, Grants Pass

(20 miles E of Cave Junction on Hwy 46)

This area was discovered in 1874, when hunter Elijah Davidson's dog followed a bear into the cave. After a visit in 1907, frontier poet Joaquin Miller called this "The Marble Halls of Oregon." In 1909, the cave and 480 acres of the Siskiyou Mts were made a national monument.

The cave has many chambers—Paradise Lost, Joaquin Miller's Chapel, Ghost Room, and others. Guide service is required. The average temperature is 42° F. Evening talks are given by National Park Service naturalists in summer.

On the surface, the area is covered with a beautiful old growth forest with abundant wildlife, birds, wildflowers, and an interesting variety of trees and shrubs. A maintained and marked system of trails provides access to these areas; stay on the trail. Dogs aren't allowed on trails.

Forest Service campgrounds (fee) are located 4 miles and 8 miles NW on Hwy 46 in Siskiyou National Forest (see GRANTS PASS). (Mid-May-Labor Day) Phone 541/592-3400.

Cave tours (daily; closed Thanksgiving, Dec 25). Children must be at least 3' 6" (42 inches) in height and complete a step test to be permitted into the cave. Cave tours are strenuous; recommended only for those in good physical condition. A jacket and walking shoes with nonslip soles should be worn. Lodge, dining room (May-mid-Oct). For further information contact Oregon Caves Co, 19000 Caves Hwy, Cave Junction 97523; phone 541/592-2100. Cave tours **$$$**.

Oregon City (B-2)

See also Beaverton, Forest Grove, Hillsboro, McMinnville, Newberg, Portland, Salem, Silverton

Settled 1829
Population 14,698
Elevation 55 ft
Area Code 503
Zip 97045
Information Oregon City Chamber of Commerce and Visitors Center, PO Box 226; phone 503/656-1619 or toll-free 800/424-3002
Web site www.oregoncity.org

Below Willamette Falls, where the river spills over a 42-foot drop, is historic Oregon City. Steamers were built here in the 1850s and locks around the falls opened the upriver to navigation in 1873. Salmon fishing in the Willamette and Clackamas rivers is from early Mar-mid-May. The city is built on terraces and there is an enclosed elevator to an observation platform.

What to See and Do

End of the Oregon Trail Interpretive Center. *1726 Washington St, Oregon City (97045). Phone 503/657-9336.* Exhibits on journey made by early settlers over the Oregon Trail. (Daily; closed holidays) **$$$**

Holmes Family Home. *Holmes Ln and Rilance St, Oregon City (97045). Phone 503/656-5146.* (Rose Farm). Oldest standing American home in Oregon City, built in 1847. First Territorial governor gave his first address here in 1849; the upstairs ballroom was the scene of many social events. (Apr-Oct, Sun; closed holidays and rest of year) **$**

John Inskeep Environmental Learning Center. *19600 S Molalla, Oregon City (97045). On N side of Clackamas Community College's campus. Phone 503/657-6958.* Eight acres developed on former industrial site to demonstrate wildlife habitat in an urban setting. Includes extensive birds of prey exhibits, various plant and wildlife displays, and plant nursery. Haggart Astronomical Observatory (Wed, Fri-Sat; fee). **$**

McLoughlin House National Historic Site. *713 Center St, Oregon City (97045). Between 7th and 8th sts. Phone 503/656-5146.* Georgian frame building built in 1845-1846 by Dr. John McLoughlin, chief factor of the Hudson's Bay Company, who ruled the Columbia River region from 1824-1846. Period furnishings; many are original pieces, most having come around Cape Horn on sailing ships. (Tues-Sun; closed holidays, also Jan) **$$**

Milo McIver State Park. *24101 S Entrance Rd, Estacada (97023). 4 miles N on Hwy 213, then 12 miles SE via Hwys 212, 211. Phone 503/630-7150. www.oregonstateparks.org/park_142.php.* On the Clackamas River, this 937-acre park offers a panoramic view of Mount Hood. Fishing; boating (ramp to the river). Hiking, horseback trails. Disc golf course. Interpretive programs. Picnicking. Improved campsites (dump station, electric hook-ups, showers). **$**

The Old Aurora Colony Museum. *212 2nd St NE, Aurora (97002). 15 miles SW via Hwy 99 E. Phone 503/678-5754. www.auroracolonymuseum.com.* Complex of buildings forming historical museum of the Aurora Colony, a German religious communal society, founded by Dr. William Keil (1856-1883). Includes Kraus House (1863), a colony house with original artifacts; Steinbach Cabin (1876); wash house used by colony women for washing, soapmaking and canning; herb garden divided into various uses—teas, cooking, medicinal, fragrances. Exhibits of furniture, musical instruments, quilts, tools. Tours. (May-mid-Oct: Tues-Sun; mid-Oct-Dec and Mar-Apr: Fri-Sun; Jan-Feb: by appointment only) **$$**

Stevens Crawford Heritage House. *603 6th St, Oregon City (97045). Phone 503/655-2866.* (Mertie Stevens Residence, 1908). Fifteen fully furnished period rooms. Working kitchen, bedrooms, living room, dining room; doll collection. (Feb-Dec, Wed-Sun) **$$**

Willamette Falls Locks. *On Willamette River, West Linn. Phone 503/656-3381.* National Historical site; oldest multilift navagation lock, built 1873. Four locks, canal basin and guard lock operated by US Army Corps of Engineers. Picnic areas. Information Center. (Daily) **FREE**

Limited-Service Hotel

★ ★ **RIVERSHORE HOTEL.** *1900 Clackamette Dr, Oregon City (97045). Phone 503/655-7141; toll-free 800/443-7777; fax 503/655-1927. www.rivershore.com.*

120 rooms, 4 story. Pets accepted, some restrictions; fee. Check-out noon. Restaurant, bar. Pool, whirlpool. **$**

Pendleton (B-5)

See also Hermiston, La Grande, Umatilla

Founded 1868
Population 15,126
Elevation 1,068 ft
Area Code 541
Zip 97801
Information Chamber of Commerce, 501 S Main; phone 541/276-7411 or toll-free 800/547-8911
Web site www.pendleton-oregon.org

Located on the old Oregon Trail, Pendleton is a trading center for the extensive cattle, wheat, and green pea production in the area. Seat of Umatilla County, it is famous for its annual Round-up.

What to See and Do

Emigrant Springs State Park. *26 miles SE off I-84. Phone 541/983-2277.* A 23-acre park near summit of Blue Mountains (nearly 4,000 feet); ponderosa pine forest. Winter sports. Picnicking, lodge. Tent and trailer sites. Oregon Trail display.

Pendleton Woolen Mills. *1307 SE Court Pl, Pendleton (97801). Phone 541/276-6911.* Woolen manufacturing; carding, spinning, rewinding and weaving processes. Guided tours (30 minutes; Mon-Fri; closed holidays). **FREE**

Ukiah-Dale Forest State Park. *50 miles S on Hwy 395, 3 miles SW of Ukiah. Phone 541/983-2277; toll-free 800/551-6949. www.oregonstateparks.org/park_22.php.* A 3,000-acre scenic forest canyon extending along Camas Creek and the north fork of the John Day River. Fishing for trout, steelhead, and salmon. Twenty-seven primitive campsites. **FREE**

✪ **Umatilla Indian Reservation.** *51 Umatilla Loop, Pendleton (97801). 5 miles E via Mission Hwy (Hwy 30). Phone 541/276-3873.* Created by the Walla Walla Valley Treaty of 1855. Firsthand view and understanding of a Native American community in transition.

Historic significance as well as a lifestyle different from modern-day, American-style development. One of the first Catholic missions in the US is here. Reservation always open for unguided touring. Indian Lake has good fishing, camping and beautiful scenery. The foothills and lowlands of the Blue Mountains provide excellent upland game and waterfowl hunting. In addition, the Umatilla Tribes have reestablished runs of chinook salmon and steelhead within the Umatilla River. Some fees.

Umatilla National Forest. *2517 SW Hailey Ave, Pendleton (97801). NE and S of Pendleton. Reached by I-84, Hwys 395, 11, 204, 82, 244, 207, and 12. Phone 541/276-3811.* More than 1 million acres, partly in Washington. Lewis and Clark passed through this region on the Columbia River in 1805. Includes spectacular views of the Tucannon, Umatilla, Grande Ronde, North Fork John Day, and Wenaha River canyons. Remnants of historic gold mining can be found in the Granite, OR, area in sight of the Greenhorn Mountain Range. North Fork John Day, North Fork Umatilla and the Wenaha-Tucannon wilderness areas may be reached on horseback or on foot. Stream fishing (steelhead, rainbow trout), big-game hunting (elk, deer); boating, river rafting. Hiking. Skiing, snowmobiling. Picnicking. Camping (fee at some campgrounds). In forest are

> **Spout Springs.** *Ski Bluewood. Hwy 204 to Mile Post 22, Pendleton. 21 miles NE on Hwy 11 to Weston, then 20 miles E on Hwy 204 to Tollgate. 45 miles NE to Walla Walla, WA, 29 miles NE on Hwy 12 to Dayton, then 23 miles SE on country road. Phone 541/276-7411. www.bluewood.com.*

Special Event

Pendleton Round-up. *Stadium, Pendleton. Phone toll-free 800/457-6336.* Rodeo and pageantry of Old West, annually since 1910. Gathering of Native Americans, PRCA working cowboys and thousands of visitors. Mid-Sept.

Limited-Service Hotel

★ ★ **RED LION.** *304 SE Nye Ave, Pendleton (97801). Phone 541/276-6111; fax 541/278-2413. www.redlionhotel.com.* 168 rooms, 3 story. Pets accepted, some restrictions; fee. Check-out noon. Restaurant, bar. Pool. Airport transportation available. **$**

Restaurant

★ ★ **CIMMIYOTTI'S.** *137 S Main St, Pendleton (97801). Phone 541/276-4314.* American menu. Dinner. Closed Sun. Bar. Children's menu. **$$**

Port Orford

See also Bandon, Gold Beach

Founded 1851
Population 1,025
Elevation 56 ft
Area Code 541
Zip 97465
Information Chamber of Commerce, 502 Battle Rock City Park, PO Box 637; phone 541/332-8055
Web site www.portorfordoregon.com

The westernmost incorporated city in the contiguous United States, Port Orford overlooks the Pacific Ocean with spectacular views. This was the first settlement in Coos and Curry counties. Captain George Vancouver sighted this area in 1792 and named it for the Earl of Orford. The cedar trees that grow in the area (sometimes called Lawson cypress and later named for the Earl) are highly favored for boat construction.

What to See and Do

Battle Rock Wayside. *520 Jefferson, Port Orford (97465). S edge of town on Hwy 101. Phone 541/332-4106.* Site of one of the fiercest Native American battles on the Oregon Coast (1851); explanation of battle is inscribed on a marker in the park. Battle Rock offers one of the best seascapes in the state and has an ocean beach, surfing. Hiking trail.

Cape Blanco State Park. *91814 Cape Blanco Rd, Port Orford (97465). 9 miles N off Hwy 101. Phone 541/332-6774.* A 1,880-acre park with an ocean beach, observation point, and historic lighthouse (1870). Fishing; river access for boats. Hiking, picnicking. Horse camp, beach access/horse trails. Rustic cabins, improved campsites. **FREE** In the park is the

> **Historic Hughes House.** *Hwy 101 and Cape Blanco Rd, Port Orford (97465). Phone 541/332-4106.* (1898). Restored Victorian house. (May-Sept, Thurs-Mon and holidays) **DONATION**

Fishing. *300 Dock Rd, Port Orford (97465). Phone 541/332-7121.* Ocean fishing provides salmon, ling cod, perch, snapper, and crabs. Fall fishing in the Elk and Sixes rivers provides catches of chinook salmon and trout. Garrison Lake, at the northwest edge of town, is open all year for trout and bass fishing. Also swimming, waterskiing; boat ramp.

Humbug Mountian State Park. *6 miles S on Hwy 101. Phone 541/332-6774. www.oregonstateparks. org/park_56.php.* A 1,842-acre park with a winding trail leading to the summit of Humbug Mountain (elevation 1,756 feet); the peak looks out on virgin forest, trout streams, and a sand beach. Windsurfing, scuba diving. Fishing, hiking, picnicking. Tent and trailer sites (dump station). **FREE**

Portland (B-2)

See also Beaverton, Forest Grove, Hillsboro, Newberg, North Plains, Oregon City

Founded 1851
Population 437,319
Elevation 77 ft
Area Code 503
Information Portland Oregon Visitors Association, 26 SW Salmon St, 97204; phone 503/222-2223 or toll-free 877/678-5263
Web site www.pova.com

Suburbs Beaverton, Forest Grove, Hillsboro, Newburg, Oregon City; also Vancouver, WA.

Oregon's largest city sprawls across both banks of the Willamette River, just south of its confluence with the Columbia. The lush and fertile Willamette Valley brings it beauty and riches. Portland's freshwater harbor is visited by more than 1,400 vessels annually from throughout the world. The city enjoys plentiful electric power, captured from river waters, which drives scores of industries with minimal amounts of smoke or smog.

Portland is surrounded by spectacular scenery. The Columbia River Gorge, Mount Hood, waterfalls, forests, ski slopes, fishing streams, and hunting and camping areas are within easy access. It attracts many conventions, for which it is well equipped, with four large auditoriums: the Memorial Coliseum Complex, the Metropolitan Exposition Center, and the Oregon Convention Center. Portland's reputation as "The City of Roses" is justified by its leadership in rose culture,

as seen in its International Rose Test Garden and celebrated during the annual Portland Rose Festival, which attracts visitors worldwide. Mount St. Helens, in Washington's Gifford Pinchot National Forest, 50 miles to the northeast, can be seen from numerous vantage points in Portland.

Portland is also an educational center, with Portland State University, the University of Portland (1901), Lewis & Clark College (1867), and Reed College (1911).

Additional Visitor Information

For further information, contact the Portland Oregon Visitors Association, 26 SW Salmon, 97204, phone 503/222-2223. For a recorded message describing major theater, sports, and music events in Portland for the current month, phone 503/225-5555.

Public Transportation

Buses MAX light rail trains (Tri-County Metropolitan Transportation District), phone 503/238-7433, www. trimet.org

Airport Portland International Airport (PDX). NE of the city off I-205.

Information Phone 503/460-4234, toll-free 877/739-4636

Lost and Found Phone 503/460-4277; toll-free 800/547-8411, ext 4272

Airlines Air Canada Jazz, Alaska Airlines, America West Airlines, American Airlines, Continental Airlines, Delta Air Lines, Frontier Airlines, Hawaiian Air, Horizon Air, Lufthansa, Mexicana Airlines, Northwest Airlines, Skywest Airlines, Southwest Airlines, Sun Country Airlines, United Airlines

What to See and Do

American Advertising Museum. *211 NW 5th Ave, Portland (97209). Phone 503/226-0000.* This museum is devoted to the history and evolution of advertising and its impact on culture. Boasting the industry's most comprehensive collection of advertising and business artifacts, the American Advertising Museum features permanent as well as changing exhibits. (Thurs-Sat, 11 am-5 pm) **$**

Portland's Outstanding Parks

The glory of Portland is its parks. Settled by idealistic New Englanders, Portland had an extensive park system in the 1850s, decades before other West Coast cities were even founded. Begin at Portland State University in the North Park Blocks, a swath of twenty blocks of parkland that cuts right through the heart of the city. The park was established in the 1850s and for generations was the best address for civic structures. Numerous historic churches, plus the Portland Art Museum, the Oregon History Center, the Portland Center for the Performing Arts, and the Schnitzer Concert Hall (home to the Oregon Symphony) flank the park. The park is also home to the largest remaining stand of American elm (killed elsewhere by Dutch elm disease), numerous heroic statues, and a farmers market (on Wednesdays and Saturdays).

Drop down to Pioneer Courthouse Square at 6th and Morrison, often referred to as Portland's living room. This is where many outdoor festivals, concerts, and demonstrations take place. (Dan Quayle got such a raucous reception here that he thenceforward refused to visit Portland, referring to the city as "America's Beirut.") The Square is a great place for people-watching and sunbathing, and there are many food carts and cafés here. In the blocks around Pioneer Courthouse Square are many of Portland's major shopping venues. Adjacent is the Pioneer Courthouse itself, built in 1875.

Follow 5th Avenue south, noting the abundance of public art along the pedestrian friendly bus mall.

At 5th Avenue and Main Street is the Portland Building, a noted postmodern structure designed by Michael Graves. The front is surmounted by a massive statue called Portlandia. This is the second-largest hammered copper statue in the world, the largest being the Statue of Liberty.

Head over to the Willamette River waterfront. The park that runs the length of downtown along the river is recent. In the 1970s, the city ripped out a freeway that ran along the river and replaced it with this park, which in summer is loaded with joggers, sun worshipers, and any number of summer festivals. Also along the river are boat tour operators, a large marina with some shops and cafés, and, at the north end, a memorial to Japanese-American internment during World War II. Under the Burnside Bridge, adjacent to Waterfront Park, is the Portland Saturday Market (open both Saturday and Sunday), which is reputed to be the largest open-air crafts market in the nation.

Turn north along 3rd Avenue and walk through Portland's Old Town (most buildings date from the 1880s) to Chinatown. Here, between 2nd and 3rd avenues and Everett and Flanders streets is the Portland Chinese Garden, a traditional Chinese garden that is a joint project of Portland and the city of Suzhou. It is the largest Chinese-style garden outside of China itself.

Benson State Recreation Area. *30 miles E on I-84, exit 30. Phone 503/695-2261. www.oregonstateparks .org/park_147.php.* Thirty miles east of Portland, near Multnomah Falls, the Benson State Recreation Area has a lake that's perfect for fishing, swimming, and boating (non-motorized boats only). Picnicking is also popular here, and the park even has a disc golf course. (Daily) **$**

Children's Museum 2nd Generation. *4015 SW Canyon Rd, Portland (97221). Off Hwy 26 opposite the Oregon Zoo. Phone 503/223-6500. www.portlandcm2.org.* CM2

offers plenty of hands-on play spaces, including the Vroom Room, where kids can race in a variety of wheeled objects, and KidCity Market, a children-sized grocery store with miniature carts and aisles of fake food. The museum also features temporary exhibits, a recent example being a replica of the television set of *Mister Rogers' Neighborhood.* (Sun 11 am-5 pm; Mon-Thurs, Sat 9 am-5 pm; Fri 9 am-8 pm; closed holidays) **$**

Council Crest Park. *SW Council Crest Dr, Portland (97201). S on SW Greenway Ave (follow the blue and* *white scenic tour signs). Phone 503/823-2223. www. parks.ci.portland.or.us/parks/councilcrest.htm.* Council Crest Park is not just the city's highest park, it's the site of Portland's highest point, topping off at 1,073 feet above sea level. That may not sound all that high, but it's high enough to afford wonderful views of the Tualatin Valley, the Willamette River, Mount St. Helens, and the truly high and mighty Mount Hood. **FREE**

Crown Point. *40700 Historic Columbia River, Corbett (97019). E on I-84, exit 22; on Hwy 30. Phone 503/695-2230. www.oregonstateparks.org/park_150.php.* This 307-acre park possesses a 725-foot-high vantage point alongside the Columbia River Gorge, allowing for spectacular views of the gorge's rock walls, which rise 2,000 feet above the river. The historic Vista House, an octagonal building with a copper dome, can be found here, though it was recently closed indefinitely while restoration work is performed. **FREE**

Crystal Springs Rhododendron Garden. *SE 28th Ave, Portland (97202). N of SE Woodstock Blvd. Phone 503/823-2223. www.parks.ci.portland.or.us/parks/crysspringrhodgar.htm.* The pathways at Crystal Springs wind through a woodland setting, passing by some 2,500 rhododendrons, azaleas, and companion plants. A spring-fed lake attracts many species of birds and waterfowl. Admission is free from Labor Day through February. (Daily) **$**

Dabney State Recreation Area. *19 miles E off I-84 exit 18, at Stark St Bridge on Hwy 30. Phone 503/695-2261. www.oregonstateparks.org/park_151.php.* East of Portland, this 135-acre park is a popular summertime destination, thanks to its idyllic swimming hole and picnic area. The park even offers electric cooking stations to fry up those hamburgers and tofu dogs. Other amenities include a reservable group shelter, walking trails, beach, boat ramp, and disc golf course. Many visitors enjoy fishing for salmon and steelhead in the Sandy River. **$**

Forest Park. *NW Skyline and Helens Rd, Portland. Off Hwy 30, NW of Fremont Bridge. Phone 503/228-8733. www.parks.ci.portland.or.us/parks/forestpark.htm.* Park encompasses over 5,000 wooded acres, making it the largest wilderness park within city limits in the US. Visitors can take advantage of 74 miles of hiking, bicycling, and equestrian trails. Wildwood Trail begins at the Vietnam Veterans Living Memorial in Hoyt Arboretum and extends 27 miles, ending deep in the park, beyond Germantown Road. Some 100 bird species and 60 mammal species inhabit the park. (Daily) **FREE**

Gray Line bus tours. *4320 N Suttle Rd, Portland (97217). Phone 503/285-9845; toll-free 800/422-7042. www.grayline.com.* Gray Line offers seven tours that originate in Portland, including a three-hour tour of the city and a nine-hour tour that retraces Lewis and Clark's journey along the Columbia River. **$$$$**

The Grotto. *8840 N E Skidmore, Portland (97220). NE 85th Ave at Sandy Blvd, on Hwy 30. Phone 503/254-7371. www.thegrotto.org.* The National Sanctuary of Our Sorrowful Mother—commonly called The Grotto—is a 62-acre Catholic shrine and botanical garden. Created in 1924, The Grotto cuts into the side of a 110-foot cliff and is surrounded by beautiful plants and flowers. An elevator takes visitors to the Natural Gallery in the woods, where you'll find more than 100 statues. The landscaped upper level has a meditation chapel overlooking the Columbia River, with Mount St. Helens visible in the distance. (Daily; closed Thanksgiving, Dec 25) **DONATION**

Guy W. Talbot State Park. *Columbia River Hwy, Troutdale (97062). E on I-84, exit 27; on Hwy 30. Phone 503/695-2261. www.oregonstateparks.org/park_154.php.* These 371 lush acres served as the estate of Guy Webster Talbot and his family until the property was donated to the state in 1929. The park is regarded as a wonderful picnicking destination, as it's rarely crowded and features beautiful natural surroundings, including 250-foot-high Latourell Falls, the second-highest falls along the Columbia River Gorge. **FREE**

Howell Territorial Park and the Bybee House. *13901 NW Howell Park Rd, Portland (97231). 12 miles N via Hwy 30, cross bridge to Sauvie Island, 1 mile W to Howell Territorial Park Rd. Phone 503/222-1741.* The Howell Territorial Park, occupying 93 pastoral acres on Sauvie Island, is home to the Bybee House, an impressive example of Greek Revival architecture. Originally a private home, the Bybee House was purchased in 1961 by Multnomah County and soon after restored to appear as it would have at the time of its construction in 1858. Guided tours of the home are conducted on the half-hour. (Park open daily year-round; Bybee House open weekend afternoons from June-Labor Day) **DONATION**

Portland's Passion for Microwbrews

San Francisco has wine and Seattle has coffee, but in unpretentious and easygoing Portland, the beverage of choice is beer. And if you appreciate fresh, handcrafted beer, you're certain to enjoy your stay here. Portland has been dubbed "America's Microbrew Capital," an appropriate moniker given the city's numerous thriving microbreweries. Portland stakes claim to having more microbreweries and brewpubs per capita than any other city in the nation. Beer drinkers flock daily to brewpubs such as the Laurelwood Public House (1728 NE 40th Ave) and BridgePort BrewPub (1313 NW Marshall St), where they enjoy a variety of ales crafted in the old-world tradition, often using locally grown barley and hops.

Portland's beer history dates to 1852, when German brewer Henry Saxer moved to the Oregon Territory, opening Liberty Brewery in the village of Portland near First and Davis streets. Saxer's brewery experienced immediate success, and other breweries opened soon after to tap into the locals' seemingly insatiable thirst for beer. The city's enthusiasm for beer continued into the 20th century, although it slowed during the Prohibition period. In the mid-1980s, Portland's brew tastes focused on European-style microbrews, a trend driven by a law passed by the Oregon state legislature that enabled brewers to sell beer directly to the public. Suddenly, microbreweries and brewpubs were popping up all over the state. Nobody took better advantage of the new law than Mike and Brian McMenamin, who in 1984 opened the Hillsdale Brewery and Public House (www.mcmenamins.com), the state's first brewpub since Prohibition. The McMenamins admit that their first brew, Hillsdale Ale, needed improvement, but after experimenting with different recipes—one doomed effort included Mars Bars—they were able to concoct colorfully named beers (Hammerhead, Terminator) that quickly became popular. The McMenamin brothers parlayed these early successes into a brewmeisting empire, opening more than 50 breweries and brewpubs in the Northwest, as well as seven theater pubs and six hotels.

A fun and safe way to experience the city's many microbrews is to book a trip on the Portland Brew Bus (www.brewbus.com). The five-hour tour aboard the Brew Bus takes you to three or four local brewers, where you'll sample 15 to 25 beers, recording your impressions of each on a complimentary sampling scorecard. The bus often stops at Widmer Brothers Gasthaus Restaurant & Pub (955 N Russell), founded by siblings Kurt and Rob in 1984. Widmer Brothers Brewing Company has emerged as one of the most successful brewers in the Northwest, thanks largely to the popularity of its Hefeweizen, a strongly aromatic beer that goes unfiltered from the lagering tank to the bottle, creating a golden-hued cloudy appearance.

Another way to enjoy beer in Portland is to attend the Oregon Brewers Festival (OBF). Since 1987, OBF (www.oregonbrewfest.com) has been attracting tens of thousands of beer drinkers to Tom McCall Waterfront Park in downtown Portland, where the annual event is held on the last full weekend in July. Whatever your favored beer style, be it a pale ale, robust porter, or a Bavarian-style lager, you're certain to find a brew—or two or three—that appeals to your tastes.

Hoyt Arboretum. *4000 SW Fairview Blvd, Portland (97221). Phone 503/228-8733. www.hoytarboretum.org.* Within its 175 acres, the Hoyt Arboretum boasts more than 900 species of trees and shrubs, including one of the largest collections of conifers in the US. The arboretum sits upon a ridge overlooking the Oregon Zoo. Guided tours are offered April-October on Saturdays and Sundays at 2 pm. The park and visitor center are open daily. **FREE**

Lewis and Clark College. *0615 SW Palatine Hill Rd, Portland (97219). 3 miles E of I-5 Terwilliger Exit. Phone 503/768-7000. www.lclark.edu.* The campus at Lewis and Clark College is simply gorgeous, highlighted by the floral display at the Memorial Rose Garden. Established in 1867, the college has an enrollment of about 3,000 students. Two campus buildings, the Manor House and Gatehouse, are listed in the National Register of Historic Places.

Lewis and Clark State Recreation Area. *16 miles E on I-84, exit 18. Phone 503/695-2261. www. oregonstateparks.org/park_159.php.* Situated near the confluence of the Columbia and Sandy rivers, this park offers picnic tables, a beach, and a boat ramp. Anglers and swimmers are a common sight in the cool waters of the Sandy River. Hiking also is popular here, particularly along a trail that leads to Broughton's Bluff. The park's namesakes camped and explored the area in November 1805. **FREE**

Lloyd Center. *2201 Lloyd Center, Portland (97232). Phone 503/282-2511. www.lloydcentermall.com.* Billing itself as the biggest mall in Oregon, the trilevel Lloyd Center features anchor stores such as Nordstrom and Meier & Frank, discount stores like Marshalls, numerous eateries, and an 18-screen movie theater.

Mount Hood-Columbia Gorge Loop Scenic Drive. *Phone toll-free 877/678-5263.* This 163-mile scenic drive along the Columbia River and through Mount Hood National Forest offers splendid views of the river basin, visits to waterfalls, many state parks, and spectacular mountain scenery. Drive east 17 miles on Highway 30, I-84 to Troutdale. At this point, for approximately 24 miles, there are two routes: you may turn right and take the mountainous upper-level scenic route or continue on the main river-level freeway. The two roads rejoin about 10 miles west of Bonneville Dam. Continue east on Highway 30, I-84 for 23 miles to Hood River, turning south on Highway 35 for 47 miles through Mount Hood National Forest to Highway 26. Drive northwest on Highway 26, 56 miles back to Portland. A description of this tour may be found in a free visitors guide from the Portland Visitors Association.

Mount Tabor Park. *SE 60th Ave and Salmon St, Portland (97215). Phone 503/823-2223. www.parks .ci.portland.or.us/Parks/MtTabor.htm.* This 195-acre park has something for everyone, with a basketball court, volleyball court, horseshoe pit, playground, picnic shelter, and tennis courts, as well as an off-leash area for dogs. The park contains an extinct volcano, making Portland one of only two US cities to have an extinct volcano within its city limits. (Daily)

Multnomah Falls. *I-84 to Multnomah Falls turnoff, Bridal Veil. 32 miles E on I-84. Phone 503/695-2372.* Chief among the 11 waterfalls along 11 miles of this highway; 620-foot drop in two falls, fourth-highest in US. Hiking. Restaurant. Visitor center.

Oaks Park. *SE Spokane St, Portland (97202). SE Oaks Park Way, E end of Sellwood Bridge. Phone 503/233-5777. www.oakspark.com.* Opened in 1905, Oaks Park is one of the oldest continuously operating amusement parks in the US. It features thrill rides, a children's area, a roller rink (Tues-Sun; rentals available), miniature golf, and waterfront picnicking. (Spring and fall: weekends; summer: daily).

Oregon Convention Center. *777 NE Martin Luther King Jr. Blvd, Portland (97232). Phone 503/235-7575; toll-free 800/791-2250. www.oregoncc.org.* Located within Portland's city center, the Oregon Convention Center (OCC) hosts conferences, exhibitions, and parties year round within its 255,000-square-foot facility. OCC provides Wi-Fi access throughout the property, a big plus for visitors seeking a high-speed connection to the Internet. The MAX light rail stops at OCC's front door.

Oregon Historical Society. *1200 SW Park Ave, Portland (97205). Phone 503/222-1741. www.ohs.org.* The Oregon Historical Society features a broad range of exhibits and collections within its museum and research library. The history of Oregon and the Pacific Northwest is documented through photographs, audio recordings, artifacts, and books. The library houses a book collection exceeding 35,000 titles (Wed-Sat). The museum offers permanent and changing exhibits. (Tues-Sun; closed holidays) **$$**

Oregon Museum of Science and Industry. *1945 SE Water Ave, Portland (97214). Phone 503/797-4000. www.omsi.edu.* The museum has six exhibit halls and labs, with an emphasis on putting the fun in such topics as astronomy, electronics, Earth science, biology, and dinosaurs. The museum is also home to a planetarium and OMNIMAX Theater (daily, fee), as well as the USS *Blueback*, the Navy's last non-nuclear, fast attack submarine. (Labor Day-Memorial Day: Tues-Sun; rest of the year: daily; closed Dec 25) **$$**

Oregon Zoo. *4001 SW Canyon Rd, Portland (97221). Phone 503/226-1561. www.zooregon.org.* Specializing in breeding and protecting rare and endangered species, the Oregon Zoo has about 1,029 living specimens, 54 of which are considered either endangered or threatened. Opened as the Washington Park Zoo in 1887, the Oregon Zoo houses creatures large and small, ranging from elephants and giraffes to millipedes and scorpions. The botanical gardens have more than 1,000 species of exotic plants. The zoo is a five-minute ride from downtown Portland on the MAX light rail. A separate zoo railway links to the popular Washington Park. (Daily; closed Dec 25) **$$**

Peninsula Park and Community Center. *700 N Portland Blvd, Portland (97217). N Portland Blvd and Albina Ave. Phone 503/823-2223. www.parks .ci.portland.or.us/parks/peninsulapkrosegar.htm.* Home to Portland's first public rose garden and community center, Peninsula Park has extensive facilities, including softball, football, and soccer fields; a basketball court; an outdoor swimming pool; tennis courts; a horseshoe pit; a playground; and a picnic shelter. An amazing 8,900 plantings grow in the 2-acre rose garden. The park's community center (Mon-Fri; closed most holidays) is impressively fashioned as an Italian villa. (Daily) **FREE**

PGE Park. *1844 SW Morrison, Portland (97205). Take I-405 to the Salmon St exit. www.pgepark.com.* PGE Park serves as the home for two professional sports teams, the Portland Beavers and the Portland Timbers, as well as the football team at Portland State University. The Beavers are the AAA affiliate of the San Diego Padres, while the Timbers compete in the USL's A-League, soccer's highest level of play in the US and Canada. PGE Park sits on a plot of land that has been used for athletic events since 1893, a time when it was known as Multnomah Field. Over the years, the versatile facility has hosted a wide range of athletic events, including tennis, cricket, and ski jumping. In 2001, PGE Park underwent a $38.5 million renovation, turning it into one of the most modern and comfortable stadiums of its size. Tickets may be purchased at the PGE Park box office or by calling Ticketmaster at 503/224-4400. **$$$**

Pittock Mansion. *3229 NW Pittock Dr, Portland (97210). Phone 503/823-3624. www.pittockmansion .com.* This restored and furnished French Chateauesque mansion, dating to 1914, is surrounded by 46 forested and landscaped acres. Spectacular views of rivers, the city, and snowcapped mountains, including Mount St. Helens and Mount Hood, are an added bonus. (Summer, daily 11 am-4 pm; noon-4 pm rest of year; closed holidays) **$$**

Police Historical Museum. *16th floor of Justice Center, 1111 SW 2nd Ave, Portland (97204). Phone 503/823-0019.* The museum features a collection of police uniforms, badges, photos, confiscated weapons, and other police memorabilia. One of the most popular museum pieces is a police motorbike with sidecar. (Mon-Thu; closed holidays) **FREE**

⭐ **Portland Art Museum.** *1219 SW Park Ave, Portland (97205). At Jefferson St. Phone 503/226-2811. www. portlandartmuseum.org.* Founded in 1892, the Portland Art Museum holds a collection of more than 32,000 works of art, including European paintings and sculptures from the Renaissance to the present; 19th- and 20th-century American works; a noted collection of Northwest Coast Native American art; Asian, pre-Columbian, West African, and classical Greek and Roman art; British silver; and creative photography. The museum hosts lectures, films, concerts, and other arts-related special events. (Tues-Sun; closed holidays) **$$$**

Portland Fire (WNBA). *One Center Ct, Portland (97227). Phone 503/797-9622.* Team plays in the Rose Garden.

Portland Saturday Market. *108 W Burnside, Portland (97209). Under the Burnside Bridge. Phone 503/222-6072. www.portlandsaturdaymarket.com.* One of largest, oldest open-air community markets in the US. More than 350 vendor booths feature arts and crafts made by Pacific Northwest artisans and a wide variety of foods, from sushi to curry. Street entertainers, face painters, and the like enliven the atmosphere and keep kids smiling. (Sat 10 am-5 pm, Sun 11 am-4:30 pm, Mar-Dec 24)

Portland State University. *724 SW Harrison St, Portland (97201). Visitor information center at SW Broadway and College sts. Phone 503/725-3000. www. pdx.edu.* Located in the woodsy South Park Blocks area, the university enrolls more than 21,000 students in its undergraduate and graduate programs. Art exhibits are often featured in the Smith Memorial Center and Neuberger Hall.

Portland Trail Blazers (NBA). *Rose Garden, 1 Center Ct, Portland (97227). Phone 503/797-9600. www.nba .com/blazers.* Portland loves its Trail Blazers, the city's lone major sports franchise. The Blazers, as they're better known, compete in the Pacific Division of the National Basketball Association, playing their home games in the 19,980-seat Rose Garden. Founded in 1970, the Blazers have made it to the NBA Finals on three occasions, taking home the championship in 1977 behind the stellar play of center Bill Walton and forward Maurice Lucas. The Blazers host 41 regular-season games, beginning in late October and finishing in mid-April. **$$$$**

Powell's City of Books. *1005 W Burnside, Portland (97209). Phone toll-free 866/201-7601. www.powells .com.* A must-stop for bibliophiles, Powell's City of Books stocks more than a million new and used titles within a sprawling 68,000-square-foot facility that occupies an entire city block in downtown Portland. First-time visitors should pick up a complimentary store map to help them navigate through nine color-coded rooms, perusing an inventory that's divided into 122 major subject areas and approximately 3,500 subsections. If you're a collector looking for, say, a signed first edition of *The Hobbit,* be sure to check out the Rare Book Room, which houses autographed first editions and other collectible volumes. (Daily 9 am-11 pm)

Rooster Rock State Park. *E on I-84, milepost 25. Phone 503/695-2261. www.oregonstateparks.org/ park_175.php.* A short drive east of Portland, Rooster Rock offers 3 miles of sandy beaches along the Columbia River. The park is a popular destination for windsurfing, boating, fishing, swimming, hiking, and picnicking. One of Oregon's two designated nude beaches is located at the park's eastern edge. The nude beach is secluded, and it cannot be seen from the clothing-required area. **$**

Rose Quarter. *One Center Ct, Portland (97227). Phone 503/231-8000. www.rosequarter.com.* The Rose Quarter is Portland's home for big-name live entertainment. Two venues comprise the Rose Quarter: the Memorial Coliseum, which seats a shade under 13,000, and the Rose Garden, a modern arena with a capacity near 20,000. The Rose Garden serves as the home court for the NBA's Trail Blazers. The Portland Winter Hawks, a minor-league hockey team, take to the ice in both

venues. Musical acts also perform in both venues, with more popular artists taking to the stage in the Rose Garden.

Sternwheeler *Columbia Gorge.* *1200 NW Naito Pkwy, Portland (97209). Cruises leave from Marine Park in Cascade Locks, E on I-84, exit 44. Phone 503/223-3928. www.sternwheeler.com.* Climb aboard the Sternwheeler *Columbia Gorge,* an authentic triple-deck paddle wheeler, and enjoy spectacular views as you journey along the Columbia River. A variety of excursions are offered, including champagne brunch cruises and dinner cruises. **$$$$**

★ **Washington Park.** *400 S W Kingston, Portland (97211). Accessible via W Burnside St, SW Park Place, or Canyon Rd. Phone 503/823-2223 (weekdays). www.parks.ci.portland.or.us/Parks/Washington.htm.* Washington Park encompasses 129 scenic acres on a hill overlooking the city. On a clear day, the views are simply spectacular, with Mount Hood towering majestically in the east and Mount St. Helens visible in the northern horizon. The Shakespeare Garden, Lewis and Clark Memorial, and Sacajawea Memorial Statue can be found in the park, as well as the popular International Rose Test Garden and Japanese Garden. Washington Park facilities include softball and soccer fields, lighted tennis courts, covered picnic areas, a playground, and hiking trails. The MAX light rail stops at Washington Park. Also here are

International Rose Test Garden. *Phone 503/ 823-7529. www.parks.ci.portland.or.us/Parks/ IntRoseTestGarden.htm.* In a city rich with natural wonders, perhaps no Portland location can match the beauty found at the International Rose Test Garden. The garden sits on a hillside in Washington Park, with a clear view of snowcapped Mount Hood rising majestically in the distance. The garden was created in 1917 by three prominent nurserymen, established, in part, to serve as a safe haven for hybrid roses grown in war-torn Europe. Today, the garden features more than 8,000 rosebushes, enhancing the city's reputation as the "City of Roses." Near the garden's parking lot, the Rose Garden Store offers an impressive array of rose-related arts and crafts. (Daily 7:30 am-9 pm)

Japanese Garden. *611 SW Kingston Ave, Portland (97205). Phone 503/223-1321. www.japanesegarden .com.* This 5-acre enclave of tranquility is considered one of the most authentic Japanese gardens outside of Japan. Masterly designed by Professor Takuma Tono, the garden opened in 1967 as a place for reflection and serenity within an environment of natural beauty and quietude. The Japanese Garden possesses five formal garden styles: Natural Garden, Sand and Stone Garden, Tea Garden, Strolling Pond Garden, and Flat Garden. The Japanese Garden Gift Store offers an eclectic array of arts and crafts merchandise, most of which comes from Japan. (Daily; closed holidays) **$$**

The Water Tower at Johns Landing. *5331 SW MacAdam Ave, Portland (97239). Phone 503/242-0022.* Once a three-story furniture factory with a water tower used for fighting fires, this structure now houses specialty shops and restaurants. A cobblestone courtyard and rustic beamed ceilings make for a unique shopping experience. (Daily; closed holidays)

Willamette Stone State Heritage Site. *Skyline Blvd and W Burnside, Portland (97229). 4 miles W. Phone toll-free 877/678-5263. www.oregonstateparks.org/ park_246.php.* The land in the US is divided into a grid, and markers such as Willamette Stone are used as starting points from which grid lines are established. Willamette Stone serves as the "zero point" for the Willamette Meridian region, encompassing all of the land west of the Cascade Mountains in Oregon and Washington. A 500-foot trail cuts through dense forest as it leads to the actual marker and a plaque describing its relevance. **FREE**

World Forestry Center. *4033 SW Canyon Rd, Portland (97221). Phone 503/228-1367. www.worldforestry.org.* The World Forestry Center is highlighted by the Forest Discovery Center, a museum celebrating the importance and diversity of tree life. Opened in 1971, the museum features educational programs, gallery shows, and exhibits. The museum's most popular exhibit is a 70-foot-high talking tree, a replica Douglas fir that teaches tree biology in five different languages: English, French, Japanese, Spanish, and German. (Daily; closed Dec 25) **$$**

Special Events

Chamber Music Northwest. *Catlin Gabel School and Reed College, 522 SW 5th Ave # 725, Portland (97204). Phone 503/294-6400.* Nationally acclaimed summer chamber music festival offers 25 concerts featuring 40-50 artists (Mon, Tues, Thurs-Sat). A catered picnic precedes each concert. Children under 7 only permitted at Family Concert. Mid-June-late July.

Elephant Garlic Festival. *Jessie Mayes Community Center, 30955 NW Hillcrest, North Plains (97133). Phone 503/647-2207. www.funstinks.com.* How can you go wrong with a festival whose motto is "Where fun stinks"? Garlic ice cream, garlic beer, and other delicacies dominate this yearly extravaganza that is almost surely devoid of vampires. Elephant garlic has been the theme only since 1998, when it was made the focus after almost ten years of lackluster attendance at "North Plains Days." Since then, the festival has blossomed, and attendance (which is still free) has increased almost every year. Third weekend in Aug.

Greyhound Racing. *Multnomah Greyhound Park, 944 NE 223rd Ave, Wood Village (97060). NE 223rd Ave between NE Halsey and Glisan Sts, 12 miles E off I-84, exit 13 or 16A. Phone 503/667-7700.* Parimutuel betting. Matinee and evening races. Under 12 years not permitted at evening races. May-Oct.

Holiday Parade of Christmas Ships. *Along Willamette and Columbia rivers. Phone 503/225-5555.* More than 50 boats cruise the two rivers in a holiday display. Early-mid-Dec.

Horse racing. *Portland Meadows, 1001 N Schmeer, Portland (97217). 6 miles N on I-5. Rd, Portland. Phone 503/285-9144.* Parimutuel betting. Thoroughbred and quarter horse racing. (Fri evenings, Sat and Sun matinee) Under 12 years not permitted at evening races. Late Oct-Apr.

Mount Hood Jazz Festival. *Main and Powell sts, Portland (97030). 15 miles E on I-84, in Gresham. Phone 503/219-9833.* International, national and local jazz acts presented in outdoor festival. First weekend in Aug.

Multnomah County Fair. *Phone 503/761-7577.* Agricultural and horticultural exhibits; entertainment. Mid-July.

Portland Center Stage. *Portland Center for the Performing Arts, 1111 SW Broadway, Portland (97205). For fees, performance and title schedules phone 503/ 274-6588.* Series of contemporary and classical plays. Daily except Mon. Sept-Apr.

Portland Marathon. *1221 SW 4th Ave, Portland (97204). Phone 503/226-1111. www.portlandmarathon .org.* World-class running event featuring international competition. Early Oct.

Portland Rose Festival. *220 NW 2nd Ave # 99, Portland (97209). Phone 503/227-2681.* Held for more than 90 years, this festival includes the Grand Floral Parade (reservations required for indoor parade seats) and two other parades; band competition; rose show; championship auto racing; hot-air balloons; air show; carnival; Navy ships. Late May-June.

Portland Scottish Highland Games. *26000 SE Stark St, Portland (97030). 15 miles E at Mt. Hood Community College in Gresham. Phone 503/293-8501.* Mid-July.

St. Patrick's Irish Festival. *Phone 503/227-4057.* One of the largest Irish festivals in the Pacific Northwest. Three days in Mar.

Limited-Service Hotels

★ ★ **DAYS INN.** *1414 SW 6th Ave, Portland (97201). Phone 503/221-1611; toll-free 800/544-8313; fax 503/226-0447. www.daysinn.com.* 173 rooms, 5 story. Check-out noon. Restaurant, bar. Pool. **$**

★ **DAYS INN PORTLAND SOUTH.** *9717 SE Sunnyside Rd, Clackamas (97015). Phone 503/654- 1699; toll-free 800/241-1699; fax 503/659-2702. www.daysinn.com.* This hotel on the south side of Portland is across the street from the Clackamas Town Center Mall, which includes a movie theater. Several restaurants are within walking distance, and there's a public golf course one block away. 110 rooms, 3 story. Complimentary continental breakfast. Check-in 4 pm, check-out noon. Bar. Outdoor pool, whirlpool. **$**

★ ★ **DOUBLETREE COLUMBIA RIVER HOTEL.** *1401 N Hayden Island Dr, Portland (97217).*

Phone 503/283-2111; toll-free 800/222-8733; fax 503/283-4718. www.doubletree.com. This hotel is located on the banks of the Columbia River. Located just 15 minutes from the Portland International Airport, free shuttle service is provided. 352 rooms, 3 story. Pets accepted; fee. Check-in 3 pm, check-out noon. Restaurant, bar. Fitness room, spa. Golf. Business center. **$$**

★ ★ **DOUBLETREE HOTEL.** *909 N Hayden Island Dr, Portland (97217). Phone 503/283-4466; toll-free 800/222-8733; fax 503/283-4743. www. doubletree.com.* This facility is conveniently located just 12 minutes from the Portland International Airport and provides guests with complimentary shuttle service. It is a sister property of the Doubletree Columbia River Hotel (see). 320 rooms, 4 story. Pets accepted; fee. Check-in 3 pm, check-out noon. Restaurant, bar. Fitness room. Outdoor pool, whirl-pool. Tennis. Business center. **$$**

★ ★ **DOUBLETREE HOTEL.** *1000 NE Multnomah St, Portland (97232). Phone 503/281-6111; toll-free 800/222-8733; fax 503/284-8553. www. doubletree.com.* Located across from the Lloyd Center Mall and over 200 stores, 18 movie theaters, and an ice skating rink. 476 rooms, 15 story. Check-in 3 pm, check-out noon. Restaurant, bar. Fitness room. Outdoor pool. Airport transportation available. Business center. **$**

★ **FAIRFIELD INN.** *11929 NE Airport Way, Portland (97220). Phone 503/253-1400; toll-free 800/228-2800; fax 503/253-3889. www.fairfieldinn. com.* 106 rooms, 3 story. Complimentary continental breakfast. Check-in 3 pm, check-out noon. Fitness room. Outdoor pool, whirlpool. **$**

★ **HAWTHORN SUITES.** *2323 NE 181st Ave, Portland (97230). Phone 503/492-4000; toll-free 800/527-1133; fax 503/492-3271. www.hawthorn.com.* 71 rooms, 3 story. Pets accepted, some restrictions; fee. Complimentary full breakfast. Check-out 1 pm. Fitness room. Indoor pool, whirlpool. **$**

★ ★ **HOLIDAY INN.** *1441 NE 2nd Ave, Portland (97232). Phone 503/233-2401; toll-free 800/465-4329; fax 503/238-7016. www.holiday-inn.com.* 238 rooms, 10 story. Check-out noon. Restaurant, bar. Pool. Airport transportation available. Business center. **$**

★ ★ **HOTEL LUCIA.** *400 SW Broadway at Stark, Portland (97205). Phone 503/228-7221; fax 503/223-4551.* 128 rooms, 9 story. Pets accepted. Check-out 2 pm. Restaurant, bar. **$**

★ ★ **MALLORY HOTEL.** *729 SW 15th Ave, Portland (97205). Phone 503/223-6311; toll-free 800/228-8657; fax 503/223-0522. www.malloryhotel.com.* 136 rooms, 8 story. Pets accepted; fee. Check-out 1 pm. Restaurant, bar. **$**

★ ★ **SWEET BRIER INN & SUITES.** *7125 SW Nyberg Rd, Tualatin (97062). Phone 503/692-5800; toll-free 800/551-9167; fax 503/691-2894. www.sweetbrier .com.* 131 rooms. Pets accepted; fee. Complimentary continental breakfast. Check-out noon. Restaurant, bar. Fitness room. Pool. **$**

Full-Service Hotels

★ ★ ★ **5TH AVENUE SUITES HOTEL.** *506 SW Washington St, Portland (97204). Phone 503/222-0001; toll-free 888/207-2201; fax 503/417-3386. www.5thavenuesuites.com.* This centrally located, full-service historic hotel dating to 1912 was once the Lipman, Wolf & Co. department store. It has been renovated, and its guest rooms feature upholstered headboards, fluffy bedspreads, and Egyptian cotton robes to snuggle up in. The accommodations are decorated in soft colors, with subtle lighting and comfortable furniture adding to the cozy feel. The elegant lobby features soaring ceilings of molded plaster and wood, floor-to-ceiling windows, and a large corner fireplace surrounded by marble and topped with an antique mirror. Dine on Pacific Northwest cuisine at the Red Star Tavern & Roast House (see). 221 rooms, 10 story. Pets accepted, some restrictions. Check-in 2 pm, check-out noon. Restaurant, bar. Fitness room, spa. Business center. **$$**

★ ★ ★ **AVALON HOTEL & SPA.** *0455 SW Hamilton Ct, Portland (97239). Phone 503/802-5800; toll-free 888/556-4402; fax 503/802-5820. www. avalonhotelandspa.com.* Carefree yet sophisticated, Portland's Avalon Hotel & Spa is a unique destination. On the edge of downtown, this boutique hotel offers guests the best of both worlds. Its proximity to the city's attractions lures cosmopolitan travelers, while its location on the Willamette River draws those seeking a tranquil retreat. Blending styles from Asia and the Pacific Northwest, the hotel is a splendid contemporary showpiece. Dark and light woods combine to create a soothing space, while large windows capitalize on the superior setting. The two-story lobby is an inviting place to take in local artwork displays or to rest by the fire. When you enter the guest accommodations, an instant calm washes over you, largely due to the floor-to-ceiling windows that showcase the river's beautiful surroundings. Standard rooms feature marble baths, plush bathrobes, CD players, cordless phones, and private balconies; suites add fireplaces and double vanities. The Avalon Spa captures the essence of the region while paying tribute to Asian and European traditions. Dedicated to well-being, the spa's carefully selected treatment menu utilizes natural ingredients, ancient wisdom, and innovative therapies to completely relax you. The excellent Avalon Fitness Club offers cutting-edge classes like Pilates, kickboxing, and Neuromuscular Integrative Action (NIA) in addition to free weights and cardio equipment, with personal trainers on duty to help customize workous for optimum results. 99 rooms, 6 story. Check-in 3 pm, check-out noon. High-speed Internet access. Restaurant. Fitness room (fee), fitness classes available, spa. **$$**

★ ★ ★ **THE BENSON HOTEL.** *309 SW Broadway, Portland (97205). Phone 503/228-2000; toll-free 888/523-6766; fax 503/471-3924. www.bensonhotel .com.* Presidents and celebrities alike have stayed in this landmark downtown hotel, whose owners have spared no expense since it was built in 1912. Feast your eyes on the lobby's paneling and Russian pillars, Austrian crystal chandeliers, and Italian marble staircase. The guest rooms are equally elegant, offering pleasantries like complimentary coffee, tea, and apples. With the hotel's one-to-one ratio of employees to guests, expect top service—from wine tastings to afternoon tea to the hotel's jazz club (the first ever to open in Portland). Don't miss the popular London Grill (see) restaurant, which offers an extensive wine collection and live jazz. 287 rooms, 14 story. Pets accepted; fee. Check-in 3 pm, check-out 1 pm. Restaurant, bar. Fitness room. Airport transportation available. Business center. **$$$**

★ ★ ★ **CROWNE PLAZA.** *14811 Kruse Oaks Blvd, Lake Oswego (97035). Phone 503/624-8400; toll-free 800/227-6963; fax 503/684-8324. www.crowne-plaza.com.* Located just minutes from the downtown area, this hotel is quite convenient to the convention center as well as many of the area universities. 161 rooms, 6 story. Pets accepted; fee. Check-out noon. Restaurant, bar. Fitness room. Indoor, outdoor pool; whirlpool. Business center. **$$**

★ ★ ★ **EMBASSY SUITES DOWNTOWN.** *319 SW Pine St, Portland (97204). Phone 503/279-9000; toll-free 800/362-2779; fax 503/497-9051. www.embassyportland.com.* Unlike a typical Embassy Suites, the downtown Portland location is a historic hotel, originally opened in 1912. The restored lobby remains true to its origins, adorned with gold-leafed columns, marble stairways, and crystal chandeliers. The two-room suites have comfortable, traditional-style furnishings, as well as refrigerators and microwaves. Guests dine at Portland Steak and Chophouse, which offers more than 100 fine scotches and whiskies. Also onsite is the Salon Nyla Day Spa. 276 rooms, 8 story, all suites. Complimentary full breakfast. Check-in 4 pm, check-out noon. High-speed Internet access. Restaurant. Children's activity center. Fitness room, spa. Indoor pool, whirlpool. Airport transportation available. Business center. **$**

★ ★ ★ **GOVERNOR HOTEL.** *611 SW 10th Ave, Portland (97205). Phone 503/224-3400; toll-free 800/554-3456; fax 503/241-2122. www.govhotel.com.* The historic building sports a unique Lewis & Clark theme, with Native American flair throughout. The lobby, for example, features a totem pole, wood-burning fireplace, panoramic murals retracing Lewis & Clark's expedition, and turn-of-the-century frescoes. Some guest rooms have fireplaces, wet bars, and balconies offering panoramic city views. The clubby

Jake's Grill (see) serves American food. 100 rooms, 6 story. Check-in 4 pm, check-out noon. Restaurant. Fitness room. Indoor pool, whirlpool. Business center. **$$**

★ ★ ★ **THE HEATHMAN HOTEL.** *1001 SW Broadway, Portland (97205). Phone 503/241-4100; toll-free 800/551-0011; fax 503/790-7110. www.heathmanhotel.com.* Dating to 1927, this grand "Arts Hotel of Portland" features a mix of artwork—from Art Deco mirrors in the Marble Bar to 18th-century French canvases in the historic Tea Court to silk-screens by Andy Warhol in the Heathman Restaurant (see). It's worth a tour for art lovers of any style and period. The guest rooms also have varied pieces of art. Personalized service at the front desk adds a warm and inviting touch. Distinguishing touches include a 400+ film library, afternoon tea, and nightly jazz in the Tea Court. 150 rooms, 10 story. Pets accepted; fee. Check-in 3:30 pm, check-out noon. Restaurant, bar. Fitness room. **$$**

★ ★ ★ **HILTON PORTLAND.** *921 SW Sixth Ave, Portland (97204). Phone 503/226-1611; toll-free 800/774-1500; fax 503/220-2565. www.portland.hilton.com.* Located in Portland's entertainment and cultural district, this hotel features fine dining and an athletic club with an indoor pool, tanning beds, sauna, and more. It is near the Performing Arts Center, shopping, and over 60 restaurants. 782 rooms, 23 story. Check-in 4 pm, check-out noon. Restaurant, bar. Children's activity center. Fitness room. Indoor pool. Business center. **$$**

★ ★ ★ **HOTEL VINTAGE PLAZA.** *422 SW Broadway, Portland (97205). Phone 503/228-1212; toll-free 800/263-2305; fax 503/228-3598. www.vintageplaza.com.* What started out as the Imperial Hotel in 1894 is now the elegant Hotel Vintage Plaza, listed on the National Register of Historic Places. The hotel celebrates local winemaking by offering tastings of Oregon vintages in the evenings in the warm and inviting lobby. Guest accommodations feature Tuscan wine country décor, with Italian tapestries, ornately carved wooden mirrors, and bright colors and textures. Special rooms include the Garden Spa rooms, with their own outdoor patios and private spa tubs; and Starlight rooms, with slanted skylights and power shades. Pazzo Ristorante (see) offers fine Italian cuisine and wines. 107 rooms, 10 story. Pets accepted. Check-in 3 pm, check-out noon. Restaurant. Fitness room. Business center. **$**

★ ★ ★ MARRIOTT PORTLAND CITY
CENTER. *520 SW Broadway, Portland (97205). Phone 503/226-6300; toll-free 800/228-9290; fax 503/227-7515. www.marriott.com.* 249 rooms, 20 story. Pets accepted; fee. Check-in 4 pm, check-out noon. Restaurant, bar. Fitness room. Whirlpool. Business center. **$**

★ ★ ★ MARRIOTT PORTLAND
DOWNTOWN. *1401 SW Naito Parkway, Portland (97201). Phone 503/226-7600; toll-free 800/228-9290; fax 503/221-1789. www.marriott.com.* Enjoy a convenient location, lovely river views, and easy access to the waterfront in this friendly, stylish chain hotel that offers more than your typical Marriott. The guest rooms are decorated in warm tones of green, gold, and rust, and the lobby is equally inviting with its comfortable furniture and soft lighting. 503 rooms, 16 story. Check-in 4 pm, check-out noon. Restaurant, bar. Fitness room. Indoor pool, whirlpool. Business center. **$$**

★ ★ ★ PARAMOUNT HOTEL.
808 SW Taylor St, Portland (97205). Phone 503/223-9900; toll-free 800/ 663-1144; fax 503/223-7900. www.paramounthotel.net. Fashioned in the neoclassical style, this 15-story boutique hotel is located smack dab in the middle of downtown Portland, within walking distance of Pioneer Square and the Center for the Performing Arts. The hotel's marble-tiled lobby creates a favorable first impression, with soaring ceilings, hand-loomed Persian rugs, and original artwork. Rooms are colored in warm tones, the walls adorned by black-and-white photography. Jetted tubs and private balconies are available in some rooms. Just off the hotel lobby, the Dragonfish Asian Café melds flavors and styles from all across East Asia, creating an eclectic Pan-Asian cuisine. 154 rooms. Pets accepted, some restrictions; fee. Check-in 3 pm, check-out noon. Wireless Internet access. Restaurant, bar. Fitness room. Business center. **$$**

★ ★ ★ RIVERPLACE HOTEL.
1510 SW Harbor Way, Portland (97201). Phone 503/228-3233; toll-free 800/227-1333; fax 503/295-6190. www.riverplacehotel .com. Offering a full-service restaurant and bar, valet parking, and room service, this hotel is located in a quiet neighborhood next to a park and near downtown and its attractions. Also nearby is an athletic club and pool, for which guests receive passes. 84 rooms, 4 story. Pets accepted; fee. Complimentary continental breakfast. Check-out 1 pm. Restaurant, bar. Spa. Whirlpool. **$$**

★ ★ ★ SHERATON PORTLAND AIRPORT
HOTEL. *8235 NE Airport Way, Portland (97220). Phone 503/281-2500; toll-free 800/325-3525; fax 503/249-7602. www.sheratonpdx.com.* This hotel is conveniently located on the grounds of the airport and offers many services and amenities. 218 rooms, 5 story. Pets accepted, some restrictions; fee. Check-in 3 pm, check-out noon. Restaurant, bar. Fitness room. Indoor pool, whirlpool. Business center. **$**

★ ★ ★ THE WESTIN PORTLAND.
750 SW Alder St, Portland (97205). Phone 503/294-9000; toll-free 800/937-8461; fax 503/241-9565. www.westin .com. Located in the center of downtown Portland, this hotel is within walking distance to such area attractions as the Portland Convention Center. This facility offers guests Internet access, coffee makers, in-room safes, and dual-line direct-dial telephones with fax and data ports. 205 rooms, 18 story. Pets accepted; fee. Check-in 3 pm, check-out noon. Restaurant, bar. Fitness room. Business center. **$$**

Specialty Lodgings

The following lodging establishments are approved by Mobil Travel Guide, but due to their unique and individualized nature have not been given a traditional Mobil Star rating. Included in this listing you may find bed-and-breakfasts, limited-service inns, guest ranches, and other unique hotel properties.

HERON HAUS. *2545 NW Westover Rd, Portland (97210). Phone 503/274-1846; fax 503/248-4055. www. heronhaus.com.* Restored house (1904) in the northwest hills overlooking city; library, morning room. 6 rooms, 3 story. Complimentary continental breakfast. Check-in 4-6 pm, check-out 11 am. High-speed Internet access. Pool. **$$**

MCMENAMINS EDGEFIELD. *2126 SW Halsey St, Troutdale (97060). Phone 503/669-8610; toll-free 800/669-8610; fax 503/665-4209. www.mcmenamins .com/edge.* Renovated in the style of a European village complete with theater, winery, distillery, and brewery. 103 rooms, 3 story. Complimentary full breakfast. Check-out 11 am. Restaurant, bar. Golf. **$**

PORTLAND'S WHITE HOUSE BED AND BREAKFAST. *1914 NE 22nd Ave, Portland (97212). Phone 503/287-7131; toll-free 800/272-7131; fax 503/ 249-1641. www.portlandswhitehouse.com.* Located in a historic neighborhood within walking distance to shopping, dining, fitness facilities and local attractions, this bed-and-breakfast offers finely furnished rooms, each with a full bath. A white southern colonial mansion with Greek columns and a fountain at the entrance, it bears a striking resemblance to Washington, DC's White House. 9 rooms, 2 story. Complimentary full breakfast. Check-in 2 pm, check-out 11 am. Airport transportation available. **$**

Spa

★ ★ ★ **AVALON SPA.** *455 SW Hamilton Ct, Portland (97239). Phone 503/802-5900; toll-free 888/ 556-4402. www.avalonhotelandspa.com.* The Avalon Spa captures the essence of the Pacific Northwest while paying tribute to Asian and European traditions. Dedicated to well-being, the spa's carefully selected treatment menu utilizes natural ingredients, ancient wisdom, and innovative therapies to relax you. Warm and attentive, the exceptional staff enhances the experience. Whether you need help with a fitness machine or require more information to select the right spa treatment, the staff is there to assist you in every possible way. If you would like to run on a treadmill or to join a group exercise class, the state-of-the-art fitness center warrants a visit. The juice bar welcomes you to catch your breath and refuel yourself with a fresh

drink. Pamper yourself with an Ayurvedic ritual or a body care therapy. Choose from rose, coastal evergreen, aromatherapy, chamomile, and Turkish aroma for your exfoliation treatment, or take advantage of the detoxifying benefits of a natural spirulina or moor mud body wrap. Relish a renew or a revitalize facial. Traditional European kurs, including Hungarian thermal mineral, thalasso, and Kräuter, are available to experience, or surrender to the heated waters of a themed bath. If stress has you tied up in knots, a heated stone, Swedish, sports, or reflexology massage can help melt away your tension. Expectant mothers in their second or third trimesters enjoy customized massages designed for them. The spa also offers salon services, including hair care, manicures, pedicures, waxing, and makeup instruction and applications.

Restaurants

★ ★ **AL-AMIR LEBANESE RESTAURANT.** *223 SW Stark St, Portland (97204). Phone 503/274-0010. www.alamirrestaurant.com.* Lebanese menu. Lunch, dinner. Bar. Children's menu. Casual attire. Reservations recommended. Valet parking. **$$**

★ **ALESSANDRO'S.** *301 SW Morrison, Portland (97204). Phone 503/222-3900; fax 503/224-9613.* Italian menu. Lunch, dinner. Closed Sun; holidays. Bar. **$$$**

★ **ALEXIS.** *215 W Burnside, Portland (97209). Phone 503/224-8577; fax 503/224-9354.* Greek menu. Lunch, dinner. Closed Sun. Bar. **$$**

★ ★ **BREWHOUSE TAP ROOM & GRILL.** *2730 NW 31st Ave, Portland (97210). Phone 503/228-5269. www.macsbeer.com.* American, German menu. Lunch, dinner. Closed holidays. Bar. Children's menu. Outdoor seating. **$$**

★ ★ **BUGATTI'S.** *18740 Willamette Dr, West Linn (97068). Phone 503/636-9555.* Italian menu. Dinner. Closed holidays. Children's menu. Outdoor seating. **$$**

★ ★ **BUSH GARDEN.** *900 SW Morrison, Portland (97205). Phone 503/226-7181; fax 503/226-7184.* Japanese menu. Lunch, dinner. Closed holidays. Bar. **$$$**

★ ★ **CAFE AZUL.** *112 NW 9th Ave, Portland (97209).* Phone 503/525-4422. Mexican menu. Dinner. Closed Sun-Mon; holidays. Bar. Outdoor seating. **$$$**

★ ★ ★ **CAFE DES AMIS.** *1987 NW Kearney St, Portland (97209).* Phone 503/295-6487. A quiet, intimate atmosphere with classic French bistro cuisine, offering excellent cooking, service, and wine selection. Try the not-to-be-missed steak or grilled scallops. Country French menu. Dinner, late-night. Closed Mon. **$**

★ ★ **CAPRIAL'S BISTRO.** *7015 SE Milwaukee Ave, Portland (97202).* Phone 503/236-6457; fax 503/238-8554. www.caprial.com. Fusion menu. Lunch, dinner. Closed Sun-Mon; holidays. Reservations recommended. **$$$**

★ ★ **CHART HOUSE.** *5700 SW Terwilliger Blvd, Portland (97201).* Phone 503/246-6963. www.chart-house.com. Seafood, steak menu. Lunch, dinner. Bar. Children's menu. Valet parking. **$$**

★ **DAN & LOUIS OYSTER BAR.** *208 SW Ankeny St, Portland (97204).* Phone 503/227-5906. Seafood menu. Lunch, dinner. Closed holidays. Children's menu. **$$**

★ **ESPARZA'S TEX MEX CAFE.** *2725 SE Ankeny St, Portland (97214).* Phone 503/234-7909; fax 503/232-3589. Tex-Mex menu. Lunch, dinner. Closed Sun-Mon; holidays. Bar. Children's menu. **$$**

★ ★ **FERNANDO'S HIDEAWAY.** *824 SW First Ave, Portland (97204).* Phone 503/248-4709; fax 503/248-0798. www.fernandosportland.com. Spanish menu. Lunch, dinner, late-night. Bar. Casual attire. Outdoor seating. **$$**

★ ★ ★ **GENOA.** *2832 SE Belmont St, Portland (97214).* Phone 503/238-1464; fax 503/238-9786. www.genoarestaurant.com. Housed in a windowless, unassuming storefront that offers outsiders no clue as to the wonders just beyond the front door, Genoa is a hidden gem where glorious Italian feasts are served nightly. However, if you require predictability and control in your life, this restaurant may not be the place for you. There is no printed menu at Genoa. Your gracious waiter will offer you a choice of three entrées, but all other decisions rest with the chef. The menu is seven courses, prix fixe, and includes antipasto, soup, pasta, fish or salad, your chosen entrée, dessert, and then fruit. (A trip to the gym should be scheduled for the following day.) With this much food to consume, dinner at Genoa is a lengthy, leisurely, and lovely affair. The service is hospitable and knowledgeable, and nothing is rushed (a terrific concept), giving you time to savor the food and your company. *Secret Inspector's Notes: Definitely go for the food at this just slightly out-of-the-way spot; the décor is quite understated and underwhelming. But between the food and the service, you'll be carried away just the same.* Italian menu. Dinner. Casual attire. Reservations recommended. **$$$**

★ ★ ★ **HEATHMAN.** *1001 SW Broadway, Portland (97205).* Phone 503/241-4100; fax 503/790-7110. www.heathmanhotel.com. Executive chef Philippe Boulot offers classic French cooking, with an emphasis on Normandy, in a three-level dining room with a kitchen on one side and views of Broadway Street on the other. A $19.99 prix fixe menu is offered for hurried theatergoers. American, French menu. Breakfast, lunch, dinner, late-night, brunch. Bar. Children's menu. Casual attire. Valet parking. Outdoor seating. **$$**

★ ★ ★ **HIGGINS.** *1239 SW Broadway, Portland (97205).* Phone 503/222-9070; fax 503/222-1244. Elegantly designed like a French bistro, this trilevel restaurant has taken special efforts to create an inviting atmosphere. Passionate about using local, organic ingredients, the chef creates a menu that leaves palates pleased. Northwestern regional cuisine. Lunch, dinner, late-night. Closed holidays. Bar. Children's menu. Casual attire. **$$$**

★ ★ **HUBER'S CAFE.** *411 SW 3rd Ave, Portland (97204).* Phone 503/228-5686; fax 503/227-3922. www.hubers.com. Originally a saloon established in 1879 that became a restaurant during Prohibition. Arched stained-glass skylight, mahogany paneling, and terrazzo floor. American menu. Breakfast, lunch, dinner, late-night. Closed Sun. Bar. Children's menu. Casual attire. Outdoor seating. **$$**

★ ★ **IL FORNAIO.** *115 NW 22nd Ave, Portland (97210).* Phone 503/248-9400; fax 503/248-5678. www.ilfornaio.com. Italian menu. Lunch, dinner, Sun brunch. Bar. Children's menu. Casual attire. Outdoor seating. **$$**

★ ★ ★ **JAKE'S FAMOUS CRAWFISH.** *401 SW 12th Ave, Portland (97205). Phone 503/226-1419; fax 503/220-1856. www.jakesfamouscrawfish.com.* At more than 110 years old, this downtown landmark restaurant doesn't hide its age; dark woods, turn-of-the-century décor, and scenes of old-time Portland give it a classic feel. An upbeat mood pervades the place, especially in the lively bar area, which is a local favorite. Jake's serves fresh regional seafood dishes as well as several varieties of the crawfish that made it famous. If you're feeling especially adventurous (not to mention hungry), try the 1-pound crawfish platter. Seafood menu. Breakfast, lunch, dinner, late-night. Bar. Children's menu. Casual attire. Outdoor seating. **$$**

★ ★ ★ **JAKE'S GRILL.** *611 SW 10th St, Portland (97205). Phone 503/220-1850; fax 503/226-8365. www.jakesgrill.com.* American menu. Breakfast, lunch, dinner, late-night, brunch. Bar. Children's menu. Casual attire. Valet parking. Outdoor seating. **$$$**

★ ★ **L'AUBERGE.** *2601 NW Vaughn St, Portland (97210). Phone 503/223-3302; fax 503/243-6600. www.laubergepdx.com.* French menu. Dinner. Closed holidays. Bar. Outdoor seating. **$$$**

🅳

★ ★ ★ **LONDON GRILL.** *309 SW Broadway, Portland (97205). Phone 503/295-4110; fax 503/471-3924. www.bensonhotel.com.* With quiet elegance, this restaurant is set in The Benson Hotel. The chef prepares regional specialties such as Northwest salmon, rack of lamb, and ostrich. Continental menu. Breakfast, lunch, dinner, Sun brunch. Bar. Children's menu. Casual attire. Valet parking. **$$**

★ ★ **MANDARIN COVE.** *111 SW Columbia, Portland (97201). Phone 503/222-0006; fax 503/274-9800.* Mandarin, Chinese menu. Lunch, dinner. Bar. Casual attire. **$**

★ ★ **MARRAKESH MOROCCAN RESTAURANT.** *1201 NW 21st Ave, Portland (97209). Phone 503/248-9442; fax 503/294-7191.* Moroccan menu. Dinner. Children's menu. Casual attire. **$$**

★ ★ **MURATA.** *200 SW Market St, Portland (97201). Phone 503/227-0080.* Japanese menu. Lunch, dinner. Closed Sun. Casual attire. Reservations recommended. Valet parking. **$$**

★ ★ **NOHO'S HAWAIIAN CAFE.** *2525 SE Clinton, Portland (97202). Phone 503/233-5301. www.nohos.com.* Hawaiian menu. Lunch, dinner. Casual attire. Outdoor seating. **$$**

★ ★ ★ **PALEY'S PLACE.** *1204 NW 21st Ave, Portland (97209). Phone 503/243-2403; fax 503/223-8041. www.paleysplace.citysearch.com.* Bistro fare featuring imaginative and beautifully presented entrées, using only the freshest local ingredients. Homemade chocolates arrive with the bill. Wine Wednesdays include wine tastings and a menu to match. French Bistro menu. Dinner. Bar. Casual attire. Outdoor seating. **$$$**

🅳

★ ★ **PAPA HAYDN.** *5829 SE Milwaukie, Portland (97202). Phone 503/232-9440; fax 503/236-5815. www.papahaydn.com.* American Bistro. Lunch, dinner, late-night, brunch. Children's menu. Casual attire. Outdoor seating. No credit cards accepted. **$$**

★ ★ ★ **PAZZO RISTORANTE.** *627 SW Washington, Portland (97205). Phone 503/228-1515; fax 503/228-5935. www.kimptongroup.com.* A cozy, friendly atmosphere is the setting for an authentically northern Italian restaurant that is a favorite among the locals. The open kitchen gives guests a preview of what's to come: handmade pastas and hearty dishes such as leg of lamb with goat cheese. Italian menu. Breakfast, lunch, dinner, brunch. Bar. Children's menu. Casual attire. Valet parking. Outdoor seating. **$$$**

★ ★ **PERRY'S ON FREMONT.** *2401 NE Fremont, Portland (97212). Phone 503/287-3655; fax 503/287-6216.* American menu. Dinner. Closed Sun. Bar. Children's menu. Casual attire. Valet parking. Outdoor seating. **$$**

★ ★ ★ **PLAINFIELD'S MAYUR.** *852 SW 21st Ave, Portland (97205). Phone 503/223-2995. www.plainfields.com.* Located in a historic Victorian house near Civic Stadium, this restaurant features East Indian food, an extensive wine list, and vegan and vegetarian entrées. Indian menu. Dinner. Casual attire. Reservations recommended. Outdoor seating. **$$$**

★ **POOR RICHARDS.** *3907 NE Broadway, Portland (97232). Phone 503/288-5285; fax 503/493-1449. www.poorrichardstwofer.com.* Seafood, steak menu. Lunch, dinner. Closed holidays. Bar. Children's menu. **$$**

★ ★ ★ **RED STAR TAVERN & ROAST HOUSE.** *503 SW Alder St, Portland (97204). Phone 503/222-0005; fax 503/417-3334. www.kimptongroup.com.* With views overlooking downtown Portland, this tavern turns out Northwestern fare that centers on spit-roasted meats, fresh seafood (especially shellfish) and great flatbread appetizers. Diners can watch their food being prepared in the semi-exposed kitchen. American menu. Breakfast, lunch, dinner, late-night, brunch. Bar. Children's menu. Casual attire. Valet parking. **$$**

★ ★ **RHEINLANDER.** *5035 NE Sandy Blvd, Portland (97213). Phone 503/288-5503. www.gutenfoods.com.* German menu. Lunch, dinner. Closed July 4, Dec 24-25. Bar. Children's menu. **$$**

★ ★ ★ **RINGSIDE.** *2165 W Burnside St, Portland (97210). Phone 503/223-1513; fax 503/223-6908. www.ringsidesteakhouse.com.* Seafood, steak menu. Dinner, late-night. Bar. Casual attire. Valet parking. **$$$**

★ **RINGSIDE EAST.** *14021 NE Glisan, Portland (97230). Phone 503/255-0750.* Seafood, steak menu. Lunch, dinner. Closed holidays. Bar. **$$$**

★ ★ **SALTY'S ON THE COLUMBIA.** *3839 NE Marine Dr, Portland (97211). Phone 503/288-4444; fax 503/288-3426. www.saltys.com.* Seafood, steak menu. Lunch, dinner, Sun brunch. Bar. Children's menu. Casual attire. Valet parking. Outdoor seating. **$$$**

★ ★ **SAUCEBOX.** *214 SW Broadway, Portland (97205). Phone 503/241-3393. www.saucebox.com.* Pan-Asian menu. Lunch, dinner. Closed Sun-Mon. Bar. Outdoor seating. **$$**

★ **SAYLER'S OLD COUNTRY KITCHEN.** *10519 SE Stark, Portland (97216). Phone 503/252-4171.* American menu. Dinner. Closed holidays. Bar. Children's menu. **$$$**

★ **SYLVIA'S.** *5115 NE Sandy Blvd, Portland (97213). Phone 503/288-6828. www.sylvias.net.* Italian menu. Dinner. Closed Thanksgiving, Dec 24-25. Bar. Children's menu. **$$**

★ **TASTE OF BALI.** *947 SW Broadway, Portland (97205). Phone 503/224-2254.* Indonesian, Malaysian menu. Lunch, dinner. Casual attire. Outdoor seating. **$**

★ ★ **TYPHOON!.** *2310 NW Everett St, Portland (97210). Phone 503/243-7557; fax 503/243-7144.* Thai menu. Lunch, dinner. Closed holidays. Outdoor seating. **$$**

★ **WIDMER GASTHAUS.** *955 N Russell St, Portland (97227). Phone 503/281-3333. www.widmer.com.* German menu. Lunch, dinner. Closed Jan 1, Thanksgiving, Dec 25. Bar. Outdoor seating. **$$**

★ ★ ★ **WILDWOOD.** *1221 NW 21st Ave, Portland (97209). Phone 503/248-9663; fax 503/222-5153. www.wildwoodrestaurant.com.* This acclaimed Oregon restaurant serves the freshest seafood and seasonal Northwest ingredients in elegant combinations that highlight the indigenous flavors. A wood-burning oven turns out crisp pizzas and adds warmth to the dining room's comforting natural tones. American menu. Lunch, dinner, Sun brunch. Bar. Outdoor seating. **$$**

★ ★ **WINTERBORNE.** *3520 NE 42nd, Portland (97213). Phone 503/249-8486.* French menu. Dinner. Closed Sun-Tues; Dec 25. Children's menu. **$$**

Prineville (C-3)

See also Bend, Madras, Redmond

Founded 1868
Population 5,355
Elevation 2,864 ft
Area Code 541
Zip 97754
Information Prineville-Crook County Chamber of Commerce, 390 N Fairview; phone 541/447-6304

Two-thirds of the population of Crook County lives in or near Prineville. Livestock, alfalfa, wheat, mint, sugar beets, and lumbering are important in this county. Hunting, fishing, and rockhounding are popular. The City of Prineville Railroad, 19 miles of main line connecting the Union Pacific and Oregon Trunk Railway, is one of the few municipally-owned railroads in the US. Two Ranger District offices and headquarters of the Ochoco National Forest are located here.

What to See and Do

Mineral collecting. *Phone 541/447-6304.* Agates of various types, obsidian, petrified wood, geodes and other stones. More than 1,000 acres of digging space in Eagle Rock, Maury Mountain, White Rock Springs and other areas. Obtain info from Chamber of Commerce.

Ochoco Lake Campground. *7 miles E on Hwy 26. Phone 541/447-1209.* A 10-acre juniper-covered promontory on the N shore of Ochoco Reservoir. Fishing; boating (ramp). Hiking. Picnicking. Improved tent and trailer sites.

Ochoco National Forest. *3160 NE 3rd St, Prineville (97754). E on Hwy 26. Phone 541/416-6500. www.fs.fed .us/r6/centraloregon/.* An approximately 848,000-acre forest, plus the 111,000-acre Crooked River National Grassland. Central Oregon high desert, thunderegg deposits, and stands of ponderosa pine. Fishing in streams, Walton and Delintment lakes, Haystack and Antelope reservoirs; also hunting. Hiking trails. Winter sports. Picnicking. Camping (fee).

Redmond (C-3)

See also Bend, Madras, Prineville

Population 7,163
Elevation 2,997 ft
Area Code 541
Zip 97756
Information Chamber of Commerce, 446 SW 7th St; phone 541/923-5191 or toll-free 800/574-1325
Web site www.el.com/to/redmond

Popular with sports enthusiasts and tourists, this is also the agricultural, lumbering, and industrial center of central Oregon. A Ranger District office of the Deschutes National Forest is located here. The US Forest Service Redmond Regional Air Center is located at Roberts Field.

What to See and Do

Cline Falls. *4 miles W on Hwy 126. Phone 541/388-6055.* A 9-acre park on the banks of the Deschutes River. Fishing. Picnicking.

Firemen's Lake. *Lake Rd and Sisters Ave, Redmond (97756). Phone 541/548-6068.* Children's fishing pond. Three-acre lake stocked with bass and bluegill. Children under 14 and disabled persons only. (Mid-Apr-mid-Oct, daily) **FREE**

Petersen Rock Gardens. *7930 SW 77th St, Redmond (97756). 7 miles S on Hwy 97, then 2 1/2 miles W. Phone 541/382-5574.* Model castles and bridges built with rock specimens; lagoons and flower beds; picnicking, fireplaces; museum. (Daily) **$$**

Peter Skene Ogden Wayside. *9241 NE Crooked River Rd, Terrebonne (97760). 9 miles N on Hwy 97. Phone 541/548-7501.* A 98-acre park with canyon 400 feet wide, 304 feet deep. Picnicking. Observation point.

Smith Rock. *9241 NE Crooked River Rd, Terrebonne (97760). 9 miles NE off Hwy 97. Phone 541/548-7501.* A 623-acre park with views of unusual multicolored volcanic and sedimentary rock formations and the Crooked River Canyon. The Crooked River Gorge (403 feet deep) is 3 miles north. Fishing. Hiking, rock climbing. Picnicking.

Special Event

Deschutes County Fair and Rodeo. *3800 SW Airport Way, Redmond (97756). Phone 541/548-2711.* First week in Aug.

Limited-Service Hotel

★ **COMFORT SUITES INN.** *2243 SW Yew Ave, Redmond (97756). Phone 541/504-8900; toll-free 800/ 517-4000; fax 541/504-1316. www.choicehotels.com.* 92 rooms. Complimentary continental breakfast. Check-in 3 pm, check-out noon. Fitness room. **$**
🖈

Full-Service Resort

★ ★ INN AT EAGLE CREST RESORT.

1522 Cline Falls Rd, Redmond (97756). Phone 541/923-2453; toll-free 800/682-4786; fax 541/923-1720. www.eagle-crest.com. This central Oregon getaway is a haven for golfers with its two 18-hole championship courses, par-63 challenge course, and an 18-hole live-turf putting course. Its low elevation means that one of the courses can be kept open year-round, and an average of 300 days of sunshine makes it likely that you'll enjoy nice weather during your round. Some guest rooms have views of the 16th green and 17th tee. The resort also features an equestrian center offering guided rides and lessons. Sizable conference facilities make this a great choice for active-minded business travelers. 100 rooms, 2 story. Check-in 4 pm, check-out noon. Restaurant, bar. Children's activity center. Outdoor pool, whirlpool. Golf, 36 holes. Tennis. Airport transportation available. **$**

✈ 🏊 🎣

Restaurant

★ ★ MRS. BEASLEY'S. *1555 S Hwy 97, Redmond (97756). Phone 541/548-4023.* American menu. Breakfast, lunch, dinner, Sun brunch. Closed Dec 25. Bar. Children's menu. **$**

Reedsport (D-1)

See also Coos Bay, Florence, North Bend

Population 4,796
Elevation 10 ft
Area Code 541
Zip 97467
Information Chamber of Commerce, PO Box 11; phone 541/271-3495 or toll-free 800/247-2155
Web site www.reedsportcc.org

Surrounded by rivers, lakes, and the ocean, the area has an abundance and variety of fish, particularly striped bass, steelhead, and salmon. Two of the best bass fishing lakes in Oregon are nearby. Reedsport was originally marshland subject to flooding at high tides, so the earliest buildings and sidewalks were built 3-8 feet above ground. A dike was built after the destructive Christmastime flood of 1964 to shield the lower part of town.

What to See and Do

Dean Creek Elk Viewing Area. *3 miles E on Hwy 38. Phone 541/756-0100.* Area has 440 acres of pasture and bottomland where Roosevelt elk (Oregon's largest land mammal) and other wildlife can be viewed. Interpretive center. No hunting. Contact Bureau of Land Management, 1300 Airport Ln, North Bend 97459. (Daily) **FREE**

Oregon Dunes National Recreation Area. *855 Hwy 101, Reedsport (97467). W off Hwy 101. Phone 541/271-3611.* Large coastal sand dunes, forests and wetlands comprise this 32,000-acre area in Siuslaw National Forest (see CORVALLIS). Beachcombing; fishing; boating. Hiking, horseback riding, off-road vehicle areas. Picnicking. Camping (fee; some campgrounds closed Oct-May). Visitors center and headquarters in Reedsport at Hwy 101 and Hwy 38 (Daily).

Salmon Harbor. *100 Ork Rock Rd, Winchester Bay (97495). Phone 541/271-3407.* Excellent boat basin for charter boats and pleasure and fishing craft. Fishing for silver and chinook salmon in the ocean, a short run from the mouth of the Umpqua River (May-Sept: daily; rest of year: Mon-Fri).

Umpqua Discovery Center. *409 Riverfront Way, Reedsport (97467). Phone 541/271-4816.* Interpretive displays centering on cultural and natural history of area. (Daily; closed Jan 1, Thanksgiving, Dec 25) **$$**

Umpqua Lighthouse State Park. *460 Lighthouse Rd, Reedsport (97467). 6 miles S off Hwy 101. Phone 541/271-4118.* This 450-acre park touches the mouth of the Umpqua River, borders the Umpqua Lighthouse Reservation, and skirts the ocean shore for more than 2 miles, with sand dunes rising 500 feet (highest in US). Noted for its marvelous, seasonal display of rhododendrons. Swimming; fishing. Hiking; trail to beach and around Lake Marie. Picnicking. Tent and trailer sites. Whale watching area.

William M. Tugman State Park. *8 miles S on Hwy 101 in Lakeside. Phone 541/759-3604.* A 560-acre park in scenic coastal lake region. Swimming, bathhouse; fishing; boating (ramp to Eel Lake). Picnicking. Improved tent and trailer sites (dump station).

Rockaway Beach (B-2)

See also Cannon Beach, Seaside, Tillamook

Population 970
Elevation 16 ft
Area Code 503
Zip 97136
Information Rockaway Beach Chamber of Commerce 103 S First St, PO Box 198; phone 503/355-8108 or toll-free 800/331-5928
Web site www.rockawaybeach.net

Once an extremely popular resort town for Portland residents, Rockaway Beach is quieter now, though its 7-mile stretch of sandy beach still attracts a crowd on weekends in the summer. It's not uncommon to see a cluster of colorful kites darting and diving in the sky above the shoreline. The town hosts a kite flying festival each spring. Rockaway Beach is located on Highway 101, a short drive north of Tillamook.

Limited-Service Hotel

★ **SURFSIDE MOTEL.** *101 NW 11th Ave, Rockaway Beach (97136). Phone 503/355-2312; toll-free 800/243-7786.* 79 rooms, 2 story. Pets accepted, some restrictions; fee. Check-out noon. Indoor pool. **$**

Roseburg (D-2)

Settled 1853
Population 17,032
Elevation 459 ft
Area Code 541
Zip 97470
Information Visitors and Convention Bureau, 410 Spruce St, PO Box 1262; phone 541/672-9731 or toll-free 800/444-9584
Web site www.visitroseburg.com

Roseburg is in one of Oregon's big stands of virgin timber that supports lumbermills and plywood plants. Although roses were the local pride, the town's name came not from the flower but from Aaron Rose, an early settler. This is the seat of Douglas County and headquarters for Umpqua National Forest.

What to See and Do

Callahan Ridge Winery. *340 Busenbark Ln, Roseburg (97470). W of I-5; Garden Valley exit 125, 2 miles W to Melrose then 1 mile S to Busenbark Ln, then right. Phone 541/673-7901; toll-free 888/946-3487.* Tasting room. (Apr-Oct, daily; other times call for appointment) **FREE**

Douglas County Museum of History and Natural History. *1020 Lighthouse Rd, Roseburg (97467). 1 mile S via I-5, exit 123 at fairgrounds. Phone 541/440-4507.* Exhibits include early history and natural history displays of the region; photographic collection; research library. Also Regional Tourist Information. (Daily) **$$**

Henry Estate Winery. *687 Hubbard Creek Rd, Umpqua (97486). 13 miles NW via I-5, 1 mile W of Umpqua on County 6. Phone 541/459-5120; toll-free 800/782-2686.* Tours, tasting room; picnic area. (Daily; closed holidays) **FREE**

Hillcrest Vineyard. *240 Vineyard Ln, Roseburg (97470). Approximately 10 miles W; I-5 exit 125, W on Garden Valley Rd, Melrose Rd, Doerner Rd then N on Elgarose and follow signs. Phone 541/673-3709; toll-free 800/736-3709.* Wine tastings; tours. (Daily; closed holidays) **FREE**

Umpqua National Forest. *2900 NW Stewart Pkwy, Roseburg (97470). Direct access from Hwy 138, along North Umpqua River. Phone 541/672-6601.* Paved scenic byway takes visitors through magnificent scenery to Diamond Lake, which offers fishing (rainbow, steelhead trout) and forest camps. Mount Thielsen (9,182 feet) and Mount Bailey (8,363 feet) tower above the lake. The Colliding Rivers Visitor Information Center (daily) is located along Highway 138 in Glide; the Diamond Lake Visitor Center (summer) is located opposite the entrance to Diamond Lake Campground. The forest (nearly 1 million acres), named for Native Americans who once fished in the rivers, includes three wilderness areas: Boulder Creek, 19,100 acres; Mount Thielsen, 22,700 acres; and Roque-Umpqua Divide, 29,000 acres. Also the Oregon Cascades Recreation Area, 35,500 acres. Picnicking, lodging, hiking, camping (fee).

Wildlife Safari. *1790 Safari Rd, Winston (97496). 6 miles S on I-5, exit 119 to Hwy 42 for 4 miles. Phone 541/679-6761; toll-free 800/355-4848.* A 600-acre drive-through animal park; 600 exotic specimens of African, Asian and North American wildlife in natural habitats; petting zoo; elephant and train rides (seasonal); guided and walk-through tours by reservation; restaurant. (Daily) **$$$$**

Special Events

Douglas County Fair. *2110 Frear St, Roseburg (97470). Phone 541/957-7010.* Early Aug.

Greatest of the Grape. *Phone 541/672-9731.* Mid-Feb.

Roseburg Graffiti Week. *Phone 541/672-9731.* 1950s car show and activities. First week in July.

Spring Craft Fair. *2110 Frear St, Roseburg (97470). Phone 541/672-9731.* Late Mar.

Umpqua Valley Roundup. *2110 Frear St, Roseburg (97470). Phone 541/672-5777.* Weekend in mid-June.

Wildlife Safari Wildlights. *Phone 541/679-9210.* Dec.

Limited-Service Hotels

★ **QUALITY INN.** *427 NW Garden Valley Blvd, Roseburg (97470). Phone 541/673-5561; toll-free 800/424-6423; fax 541/957-0318. www.qualityinn.com.* 70 rooms, 2 story. Pets accepted, some restrictions; fee. Complimentary continental breakfast. Check-in 2 pm, check-out 11 am. Fitness room. Outdoor pool. **$**

★ ★ **WINDMILL INN OF ROSEBURG.** *1450 NW Mulholland Dr, Roseburg (97470). Phone 541/673-0901; toll-free 800/547-4747; fax 541/673-0901. www.windmillinns.com.* 128 rooms, 2 story. Pets accepted. Complimentary continental breakfast. Check-in 4 pm, check-out 11 am. Restaurant, bar. Fitness room. Outdoor pool, whirlpool. Business center. **$**

Specialty Lodgings

The following lodging establishments are approved by Mobil Travel Guide, but due to their unique and individualized nature have not been given a traditional Mobil Star rating. Included in this listing you may find bed-and-breakfasts, limited-service inns, guest ranches, and other unique hotel properties.

STEAMBOAT INN. *42705 N Umpqua Hwy, Steamboat (97447). Phone 541/498-2230; toll-free 800/840-8825. www.thesteamboatinn.com.* Located inside the Umpqua National Forest along the banks of the North Umpqua River, this inn offers spectacular views of the local scenery. 3 rooms, 2 story. **$$**

STEELHEAD RUN BED & BREAKFAST. *23049 N Umpqua Hwy, Glide (97443). Phone 541/496-0563; toll-free 800/348-0563. www.steelheadrun.com.* Located on a bluff overlooking the North Umpqua River with private beach, picnic area, trails, and fishing. 6 rooms, 2 story. Pets accepted. Complimentary full breakfast. Check-in 1 pm, check-out 11 am. **$**

Restaurants

★ ★ **JIN GAI INTERNATIONAL RESTAURANT.** *805 SE Stephens, Roseburg (97638). Phone 541/673-8373.* Modern and traditional sushi and Japanese specialties are served at this unlikely location. Sushi menu. Lunch, dinner. **$$**

★ ★ **MCMENAMINS ROSEBURG STATION.** *700 SE Sheridan St, Roseburg (97470). Phone 541/672-1934. www.mcmenamins.com.* Situated in an 87-year-old railway station, this restaurant offers a fine selection of local specialties and microbrews. American menu. Lunch, dinner. **$**

Salem (B-2)

See also Albany, Corvallis, McMinnville, Newberg, Oregon City, Portland, Silverton

Settled 1840
Population 107,786
Elevation 154 ft
Area Code 503
Information Convention & Visitors Association, 1313 Mill St SE, 97301; phone 503/581-4325 or toll-free 800/874-7012
Web site www.scva.org

The state capital and the third largest city in Oregon, Salem's economy is based on the state government, food processing, light manufacturing, agriculture, and wood products. Salem shares Oregon's sports attractions with other cities of the Willamette Valley.

What to See and Do

A.C. Gilbert's Discovery Village. *116 Marion St, Salem (97301). Phone 503/371-3631. www.acgilbert.org.* Hands-on exhibits related to art, drama, music, science and nature. (Mon-Sat, also Sun afternoons) **$$**

Bush House. *600 Mission St SE, Salem (97302). Bush's Pasture Park. 6 blocks S of capitol. Phone 503/363-4714.* Victorian mansion (1878) with authentic furnishings. (Tues-Sun; closed holidays) **$$** Also here is

> **Bush Barn Art Center.** *Phone 503/581-2228.* Remodeled barn houses two exhibit galleries with monthly shows and a sales gallery featuring Northwest artists. (Tues-Sun; closed holidays) **FREE**

Enchanted Forest. *8462 Enchanted Way SE, Turner (97392). 7 miles S, off I-5 Sunnyside-Turner exit 248. Phone 503/363-3060. www.enchantedforest.com.* Features storybook theme. Other exhibits include reproduction of early mining town, haunted house (fee), log flume ride (fee), ice mountain bobsled ride (fee), kiddie bumper boats and kiddie ferris wheel (fee), old world village, theater featuring live comedy and children's shows, water and light show. Picnic area; refreshments; gift stores. (Mid-Mar-Mar 31, May 1-Labor Day: daily; Apr and Sept: weekends only) **$$$**

Historic Deepwood Estate. *1116 Mission St SE, Salem (97302). Phone 503/363-1825.* (1894) Queen Anne-style house and carriage house designed by W. C. Knighton. Povey Brothers stained-glass windows, golden oak woodwork; solarium; Lord and Schryver gardens with wrought-iron gazebo from 1905, boxwood gardens, perennial garden with English teahouse; nature trail. House (May-Sept: Mon-Fri, Sun; rest of year: Tues-Sat; closed holidays). **$$**

Honeywood Winery. *1350 Hines St SE, Salem (97302). Phone 503/362-4111.* Oregon's oldest producing winery. Tours, tasting room, gift shop. (Daily; closed Thanksgiving, Dec 25) **FREE**

Mission Mill Museum. *1313 Mill St SE, Salem (97301). Phone 503/585-7012.* Thomas Kay Woolen Mill Museum (1889) shows process of processing fleece into fabric. Jason Lee House (1841), John D. Boon House (1847), Methodist Parsonage (1841) and Pleasant Grove-Presbyterian Church (1858) help interpret missionary family life. Shops, park, picnicking. Tours of woolen mill, historic houses (Mon-Sat, daily; closed Jan 1, Thanksgiving, Dec 25). **$$$**

State Capitol. *900 Court St NE, Salem (97301). Phone 503/986-1388.* (1938). Marble, of modern Greek design. Atop the capitol is a fluted tower topped by a bronze, gold-leafed statue symbolic of the pioneers who carved Oregon out of the wilderness. Tours of capitol (June-Aug: daily; rest of year: by appointment). Capitol building (Daily; closed Thanksgiving, Dec 25). Video; gift shop. **FREE** North of here is the

> **Capitol Mall.** Flanked by four state buildings in modern Greek style, including the Public Service, Transportation, Labor and Industries and State Library buildings. The grounds are an arboretum with historical statuary and monuments.

Willamette University. *900 State St, Salem (97301). Between 12th and Winter sts. Phone 503/370-6300. www.willamette.edu.* (1842) (2,500 students) Oldest institution of higher learning west of Missouri River, with several historic buildings on campus including Waller Hall (1867) and the Art Building (1905) with the Hallie Brown Ford Art Gallery. The Mark O. Hatfield Library has a special area for research and viewing of Senator Hatfield's public papers. Campus tours; picnic area.

Special Events

Oregon State Fair. *Fairgrounds, 2330 17th St NE, Salem (97303). Phone 503/947-3247.* Horse racing, wine competition and tasting, agricultural exhibits, horse show, livestock, food, carnival, entertainment. End of Aug through first week of Sept.

Salem Art Fair and Festival. *Bush's Pasture Park, 600 Mission St SE, Salem (97302). Phone 503/581-2228.* Arts and crafts booths and demonstrations, children's art activities and parade, ethnic folk arts, performing arts, street painting, 5K run, food; tours of historic Bush House. Late July.

West Salem Waterfront Parade. *Phone 503/362-3601.* Mid-Aug.

Limited-Service Hotels

★ **BEST WESTERN NEW KINGS INN.** *1600 Motor Court NE, Salem (97301). Phone 503/581-1559; fax 503/364-4272. www.bestwestern.com.* 101 rooms, 2 story. Pets accepted, some restrictions; fee. Check-out noon. Fitness room. Indoor pool, whirlpool. Tennis. **$**

⬛🐾🕴️〰️⛱️

★ ★ **RED LION.** *3301 Market St, Salem (97301). Phone 503/370-7888; toll-free 800/248-6273; fax 503/370-6305. www.redlion.com.* 150 rooms, 4 story. Pets accepted; fee. Check-out 11 am. Restaurant, bar. Fitness room. Indoor pool, whirlpool. **$**

⬛🐾🕴️〰️

Specialty Lodging

The following lodging establishment is approved by Mobil Travel Guide, but due to its unique and individualized nature has not been given a traditional Mobil Star rating. Included in this listing you may find bed-and-breakfasts, limited-service inns, guest ranches, and other unique hotel properties.

A CREEKSIDE INN THE MARQUEE HOUSE. *33 Wyatt Ct NE, Salem (97301). Phone 503/391-0837; toll-free 800/949-0837; fax 503/391-1713. www. marqueehouse.com.* 5 rooms. Children over 14 years only. Check-in 4-6 pm, check-out 11 am. Airport transportation available. **$**

⬛

Restaurants

★ ★ ★ **ALESSANDRO'S.** *120 NE Commercial St, Salem (97301). Phone 503/370-9951; fax 503/375-3412. www.alessandros120.com.* This family-owned northern Italian restaurant and bar has been in business for over 22 years, serving specialties such as baked salmon, various veal dishes, and a splendid tiramisu. Staff is friendly and attentive, and the historic store-front location is a simple, quiet retreat. Italian menu. Lunch, dinner. Closed Sun. Bar. Children's menu. Casual attire. **$$**

★ ★ **KWAN ORIGINAL CUISINE.** *835 Commerical St SE, Salem (97302). Phone 503/362-7711; fax 503/373-5818. www.kwanscuisine.com.* Chinese menu. Lunch, dinner. Closed holidays. Bar. Children's menu. **$$**

Seaside (A-1)

See also Astoria, Cannon Beach, Rockaway

Population 5,359
Elevation 13 ft
Area Code 503
Zip 97138
Information Chamber of Commerce, 7 N Roosevelt, PO Box 7; phone 503/738-6391 or toll-free 800/444-6740
Web site www.el.com/to/seaside/

Seaside is the largest and oldest seashore town in Oregon. It has a concrete promenade 2 miles long; ocean beaches provide clam digging, surfing, surf fishing, and beachcombing.

What to See and Do

Saddle Mountain State Park. *13 miles SE on Hwy 26, then 9 miles N. Phone 503/368-5154. www. oregonstateparks.org/park_197.php.* A 2,922-acre park with a 2 1/2-mile trail to the 3,283-foot summit of Saddle Mountain, one of the highest peaks in the Coastal Range. Hiking, picnicking. Ten primitive campsites (Mar-Nov). **FREE**

Seaside Aquarium. *200 N Prom, Seaside (97138). On beach. Phone 503/738-6211.* Deep-sea life and trained seals; seal feeding (fee); (Mar-Nov: daily; rest of year: Wed-Sun; closed Thanksgiving, Dec 24, 25) **$$$**

Limited-Service Hotels

★ ★ **BEST WESTERN OCEAN VIEW RESORT.** *414 N Prom, Seaside (97138). Phone 503/738-3334; toll-free 800/234-8439; fax 503/738-5959. www.oceanviewresort.com.* 104 rooms, 5 story. Pets accepted, some restrictions; fee. Check-out 11 am. Restaurant, bar. Beach. Indoor pool, whirlpool. **$**

🐾〰️

★ ★ **GEARHART BY THE SEA RESORT.** *1157 N Marion Ave, Gearhart (97138). Phone 503/738-8331; toll-free 800/547-0115; fax 503/738-0881. www. gearhartresort.com.* 80 rooms, 5 story. Pets accepted, some restrictions; fee. Check-out 11 am. Restaurant, bar. Indoor pool. Golf. **$**

⬛🐾〰️🏌️

★ ★ **SHILO INN.** *30 N Prom, Seaside (97138).*
Phone 503/738-9571; toll-free 800/222-2244; fax 503/
738-0674. www.shiloinns.com. 112 rooms, 5 story.
Check-out noon. Restaurant, bar. Indoor pool, whirlpool. Airport transportation available. **$**

Specialty Lodgings

The following lodging establishments are approved by
Mobil Travel Guide, but due to their unique and individualized nature have not been given a traditional
Mobil Star rating. Included in this listing you may
find bed-and-breakfasts, limited-service inns, guest
ranches, and other unique hotel properties.

CUSTER HOUSE BED & BREAKFAST. *811 1st*
Ave, Seaside (97138). Phone 503/738-7825; toll-free 800/
738-7852; fax 503/738-4324. www.clatsop.com/custer.
6 rooms, 2 story. Complimentary full breakfast.
Check-in 3 pm, check-out 11 am. **$**

GILBERT INN BED & BREAKFAST. *341 Beach*
Dr, Seaside (97138). Phone 503/738-9770; toll-free 800/
410-9770; fax 503/717-1070. www.gilbertinn.com. This
Queen Anne Victorian home, built in 1892, features
a large fireplace in the parlor and a rich and warm
atmosphere. It is located near shops, restaurants,
beaches and other attractions of the Northwest
coast. 10 rooms, 3 story. Closed Jan. Complimentary
full breakfast. Check-in 3-11 pm, check-out 11 am.
Airport transportation available. **$**

Restaurants

★ **CAMP 18.** *42362 Hwy 26, Seaside (97138). Phone*
503/755-1818. American menu. Breakfast, lunch,
dinner, Sun brunch. Closed Dec 25. Bar. Children's
menu. **$$**

★ ★ **DOOGER'S SEAFOOD & GRILL.** *505*
Broadway, Seaside (97138). Phone 503/738-3773.
Seafood, steak menu. Lunch, dinner. Children's menu.
$$

Silverton (B-2)

See also Newberg, Oregon City, Salem

Population 5,635
Elevation 249 ft
Area Code 503
Zip 97381
Information Chamber of Commerce, City Hall,
421 S Water St, PO Box 257; phone 503/873-5615
Web site www.silverton.or.us

What to See and Do

Cooley's Gardens. *11553 Silverton Rd NE, Silverton*
(97381). Phone 503/873-5463. Largest producer of
bearded iris in the world. Display gardens feature
many varieties; over 1 million blossom in fields (Mid-
May-early June). **FREE**

Country Museum/Restored Train Station. *428 S Water*
St, Silverton (97381). Ames-Warnock House (1908)
contains local historical items dating from 1846.
Southern Pacific Station (1906) contains larger items.
(Mar-Dec, Thurs and Sun) Contact Chamber of
Commerce. **DONATION**

Silver Falls State Park. *15 miles SE on Hwy 214.*
Phone 503/873-8681. www.oregonstateparks.org/
park_211.php. Oregon's largest state park, at 8,706
acres, has ten waterfalls, five of which are more than
100 feet high; four may be viewed from road, the
others from a forested canyon hiking trail. Swimming.
Bridle, bicycle trails. Picnicking. Tent and improved
sites (dump station), cabins. Pets allowed on leash only.

Sweet Home (C-2)

See also Albany

Population 6,850
Elevation 525 ft
Area Code 541
Zip 97386
Information Chamber of Commerce, 1575 Main St;
phone 541/367-6186
Web site www.sweet-home.or.us

Gateway to Santiam Pass and the rugged Oregon Cascades, the area around Sweet Home is popular for fishing, boating, skiing, hiking, and rock hounding. A Ranger District office of Willamette National Forest is located here.

What to See and Do

East Linn Museum. *746 Long St, Sweet Home (97386). At junction Hwy 228, Hwy 20. Phone 541/367-4580.* Nearly 5,000 artifacts of pioneer life in the area (1847). Period rooms; rock collection and mining equipment; logging tools; maps, photos, portraits; guns, dolls, bottles; saddlery and blacksmith shop. (May-Sept: Tues-Sun; rest of year: Thurs-Sun; also by appointment; closed holidays) **DONATION**

Foster Lake. *Hwy 20 and Foster, Foster (97345). 2 miles E on Hwy 20 at Foster. Phone 541/367-5124.* Swimming, water sports; fishing; boating.

Special Events

The Oregon Jamboree. *1331 Main St, Sweet Home (97386). Phone 541/367-8800.* Three-day country music and camping festival. Second weekend in Aug.

The Sweet Home Rodeo. *1575 Main St, Sweet Home (97386). Phone 541/367-6186.* Bull riding, barrel racing, bronc riding, mutton bustin'. Second weekend in July.

Tillamook (B-1)

See also Lincoln City, Rockaway

Founded 1851
Population 4,001
Elevation 16 ft
Area Code 503
Zip 97141
Information Tillamook Chamber of Commerce, 3705 Hwy 101 N; phone 503/842-7525
Web site www.tillamookchamber.org

Located at the southern end of Tillamook Bay, this is the county seat. Dairying, cheese and butter making, timber, and fishing are the main industries. There are many beaches for swimming, crabbing, clamming, and beachcombing; boat landings, camping, picnicking, and fishing sites are also in the area.

What to See and Do

Cape Lookout State Park. *13000 Whiskey Creek Rd, Tillamook (97141). 12 miles SW off Hwy 101 on Whiskey Creek Rd. Phone 503/842-4981.* A 1,974-acre park with virgin spruce forest and an observation point; it's one of most primitive ocean shore areas in the state. Hiking trail to the end of the cape. Picnicking. Tent and trailer sites (dump station). **$**

★ Capes Scenic Loop Drive to Cape Meares and Oceanside. (Approximately 10 miles) West on 3rd Street, northwest on Bay Ocean Road to Cape Meares; go south on Loop Road to Cape Meares State Park. See Tillamook Bay County Boat Landing, Cape Meares Lake, beach with beachcombing; also Cape Meares Lighthouse; Native American burial Sitka spruce tree known as "Octopus Tree." Continue south to Oceanside, site of Three Arch Rocks Federal Sea Lion and Migratory Bird Refuge, and beach area with beachcombing and agates. Continue south to Netarts; see Netarts Bay Boat Landing and Whiskey Creek Fish Hatchery. Go south on Cape Lookout Road to Pacific City and Cape Kiwanda, then back to Highway 101 S. (Or take Whiskey Creek Rd from Netarts boat launching site, continue over Cape Lookout Mountain through Sandlake, Tierra Del Mar to Pacific City. Exceptionally scenic, it also avoids traffic on Highway 101.)

Tillamook County Pioneer Museum. *2106 2nd St, Tillamook (97141). At Pacific Ave. Phone 503/842-4553.* Possessions of early settlers, replica of pioneer home and barn; blacksmith shop; logging displays, war relics; relics from Tillamook Naval Air Station and Blimp Base; minerals, guns, books, vehicles, natural history and wildlife exhibits including nine dioramas; "great grandma's kitchen." (Daily; closed Thanksgiving, Dec 25) **$$**

Special Events

Tillamook County Fair. *Fairgrounds, 4603 3rd St, Tillamook (97141). Phone 503/842-2272.* First full week in Aug.

Tillamook Dairy Parade and Rodeo. *Fairgrounds, 4603 3rd St, Tillamook (97141). Phone 503/842-7525.* Fourth weekend in June.

Limited-Service Hotels

★ **BEST WESTERN INN & SUITES.** *1722 N Makinster Rd, Tillamook (97141). Phone 503/842-7599; toll-free 800/780-7234; fax 503/842-7930. www.bestwestern.com.* 52 rooms. Check-in 3 pm, check-out noon. Fitness room. Indoor pool, whirlpool. **$**

⛷ ⌷

★ ★ **SHILO INN.** *2515 N Main St, Tillamook (97141). Phone 503/842-7971; toll-free 800/222-2244; fax 503/842-7960. www.shiloinns.com.* 101 rooms, 2 story. Pets accepted; fee. Check-out noon. Restaurant, bar. Fitness room. Indoor pool, whirlpool. **$**

🐾 ⛷ ⌷

Specialty Lodging

The following lodging establishment is approved by Mobil Travel Guide, but due to its unique and individualized nature has not been given a traditional Mobil Star rating. Included in this listing you may find bed-and-breakfasts, limited-service inns, guest ranches, and other unique hotel properties.

SANDLAKE COUNTRY INN. *8505 Galloway Rd, Cloverdale (97112). Phone 503/965-6745; fax 503/965-7425. www.sandlakecountryinn.com.* Farmhouse built of timbers washed ashore from a shipwreck in 1890. 4 rooms, 2 story. Complimentary full breakfast. Check-in 3 pm, check-out 11 am. **$**

Troutdale

What to See and Do

Columbia Gorge Premium Outlets. *450 NW 257th Ave, Troutdale (97060). Phone 503/669-8060. www.premiumoutlets.com/columbiagorge.* More than 40 factory outlet stores, including Adidas, Gap, and Samsonite.

Restaurant

★ ★ **BLACK RABBIT.** *2126 SW Halsey, Troutdale (97060). Phone 503/492-3086. www.mcmenamins.com.* American menu. Breakfast, lunch, dinner. Bar. Children's menu. Outdoor seating. **$$**

Umatilla (A-4)

See also Hermiston, Pendleton

Founded 1863
Population 3,046
Elevation 296 ft
Area Code 541
Zip 97882
Information Chamber of Commerce, PO Box 67; phone 541/922-4825 or toll-free 800/542-4944
Web site www.umatilla.org

What to See and Do

Columbia Crest Winery. *Columbia Crest Dr Hwy 221, Paterson, WA (99345). 18 miles NW via Hwy 14. Phone 509/875-2061. www.columbia-crest.com.* Located amidst 2,000 acres of European-style vinifera grapes. Tours, including wine production, cellar and tastings. Picnicking; gardens. (Self-guided tours, Mon-Fri; guided tours, Sat-Sun; closed holidays) **FREE**

Hat Rock State Park. *Hat Rock, Hermiston. 9 miles E off Hwy 730 near junction Hwy 207. Phone 541/567-5032. www.oregonstateparks.org/park_19.php.* A 735-acre park on a lake formed by the McNary Dam. Hat Rock is a large monolith that looks like a man's top hat; this landmark is often referred to in the diaries of early explorers and travelers. Swimming beach, fishing (pond stocked with rainbow trout); boat ramp to the Columbia River. Hiking, picnicking. **FREE**

McNary Lock and Dam. *3rd St, Umatilla. 2 miles E on Hwy 730. Phone 541/922-4388.* Single lift navigation lock. Dam is 7,365 feet long, 92 feet high. The Columbia River forms Lake Wallula, a 61-mile waterway partly in Washington. Swimming, waterskiing; fishing, hunting; boating (marinas). Picnicking. Primitive camping (two areas; free). Tours of power, navigation and fish passage facilities (June-Sept, daily). **FREE**

Umatilla Marina Park. *1710 Quincy Ave, Umatilla (97882). NE edge of town on Columbia River. Phone 541/922-3939.* Swimming beach; boating (launch, storage, gas, oil). Picnicking. RV trailer camping (fee). (Daily)

Special Event

Sage Riders Rodeo. *Phone 541/922-4825.* NRA sanctioned, Second weekend in June.

Yachats (C-1)

See also Florence, Newport

Population 533
Elevation 15 ft
Area Code 541
Zip 97498
Information Yachats Area Chamber of Commerce, US 101; PO Box 728; phone 541/547-3530
Web site www.yachats.org

Yachats (YA-hots) is a resort area on the central Oregon coast, west of Siuslaw National Forest. Derived from a Native American phrase meaning "waters at the foot of the mountain," Yachats is along a rocky shore with a fine sandy beach.

What to See and Do

Cape Perpetua Campground. *2400 Hwy 101 S, Yachats (97498). 3 miles S on Hwy 101. Phone 541/563-3211.* Beachcombing; fishing. Hiking. Camping. Summer campfire programs (Sat, Sun). **$$$** Nearby is

Cape Perpetua Visitor Center. *In Suislaw National Forest. Phone 541/547-3289.* Interpretive displays of oceanography, natural history of coastal area, movies. Nature trails, auto tour. (May: Wed-Sun; Memorial Day-Labor Day: daily; closed winter) **$$**

Neptune State Scenic Viewpoint. *3 miles S on Hwy 101. Phone 541/547-3416. www.oregonstateparks .org/park_126.php.* This 302-acre park features Cook's Chasm (near the north end), a long, narrow, deep fissure where the sea falls in with a spectacular fury; wind-depressed forest trees (near the north end); and slopes covered with huckleberry shrubs. A community of harbor seals makes its home on the rocks below Strawberry Hill; whales are also spotted here. Bird-watching. Surf fishing, windsurfing. Hiking, picnicking. Observation point. **FREE**

Tillicum Beach Campground. *8199 Hwy 101 N, Yachats (97498). 3 1/2 miles N on Hwy 101. Phone 541/563-3211.* Ocean view, beachcombing. Camping. Summer evening campfire programs Sat and Sun. Camping. **$$$**

Yachats State Recreation Area. *On Hwy 101. Phone 541/997-3851.* A 93-acre day-use park bordering the Yachats River, in the shadow of Cape Perpetua. Small picnic area. Observation point.

Limited-Service Hotel

★ **OVERLEAF LODGE.** *2055 Hwy 101 N, Yachats (97498). Phone 541/547-4880; toll-free 800/338-0507. www.overleaflodge.com.* The Overleaf Lodge is situated alongside central Oregon's rugged coast. All rooms have ocean views. Select rooms have fireplaces, whirlpool tubs, and private balconies. The property's location is ideal for exploring the state's coastline; nearby, you'll find great hiking trails at Cape Perpetua Recreation Area, wildlife at Sea Lion Caves, and dramatic scenery at Heceta Head Lighthouse, the most photographed lighthouse in the US. 39 rooms. Complimentary continental breakfast. Check-in 3 pm, check-out noon. Fitness room. **$$**
🏃

Specialty Lodging

The following lodging establishment is approved by Mobil Travel Guide, but due to its unique and individualized nature has not been given a traditional Mobil Star rating. Included in this listing you may find bed-and-breakfasts, limited-service inns, guest ranches, and other unique hotel properties.

SEA QUEST BED & BREAKFAST. *95354 Hwy 101 S, Yachats (97498). Phone 541/547-3782; toll-free 800/341-4878; fax 541/547-3719. www.seaq.com.* 5 rooms, 2 story. Children over 14 years only. Complimentary full breakfast. Check-in 3 pm, check-out 11am. **$$**

If volcanoes and lava pique your interest, two places in California are must-sees: Lassen Volcanic National Park and Lava Beds National Monument. From Medford, both are a little over three hours of driving time. You'll need to have a couple of days for exploring both attractions. Another amazing natural site to see in California is the Redwood National Park. Be sure to check out the General when you are there.

Crescent City, CA

2 hours 15 minutes, 111 miles from Medford, OR

Founded 1852
Population 4,006
Elevation 44 ft
Information Chamber of Commerce, Visitor Information Center, 1001 Front St; phone 707/464-3174 or toll-free 800/343-8300.
Web site www.northerncalifornia.net

The crescent-shaped beach that gives the city its name outlines a busy harbor. A party of treasure seekers discovered the harbor, and the city was laid out a year later.

What to See and Do

Battery Point Lighthouse. *577 H St, Crescent City (95531). Phone 707/464-3089. (1856) On Battery Point, at the end of A St.* Accessible only at low tide. Museum. (Apr-Sept, Wed-Sun, call for times) **$**

Del Norte County Historical Society Main Museum. *577 H St, Crescent City (95531). Phone 707/464-3922.* Research center for local history; two-story lighthouse lens (1892), Native American and pioneer exhibits housed in former county jail. (May-Sept, daily 10 am-4 pm) **$**

Elk Valley Casino. *2500 Howland Hill Rd, Crescent City (95531). Phone 707/464-1020. www.elkvalleycasino.com.* Just south of the Oregon-California border in Crescent City, the Tolowa Tribe's Elk Valley Casino features blackjack and poker tables, a bingo gallery, and 275 gambling machines. Poker tournaments are held four nights a week, and a prime rib buffet is available on Wednesdays. There is a 24-hour restaurant, but no hotel rooms onsite.

Ocean World. *304 Hwy 101 S, Crescent City (95531). Phone 707/464-4900. www.oceanworldonline.com.* Aquarium, shark-petting tank, sea lion show. Gift shop. (Daily) **$$$**

Point St. George. *N of beach.* The Brother Jonathan, a side-wheeler, was wrecked here in 1865. Of 232 persons aboard, 203 died; they are buried in Brother Jonathan Cemetery, Pebble Beach Dr and 9th St.

⭐ **Redwood National and State Parks.** *1111 2nd St, Crescent City (95531). S of town. Phone 707/464-6101. www.nps.gov/redw.* The venerable redwoods that dominate the northwestern-most corner of California are some of the tallest and oldest trees in the world—topping out at about 350 feet in height and 2,000 years in age. To protect the redwoods from decimation by logging, the federal and California state governments created a checkerboard of four parks—three state and one national—containing more than 100,000 acres of redwood forest. Hiking and backpacking are the most popular out-of-the-car pursuits here, in part because of the sheer scale of the trees and other super-sized flora; boaters, bikers, equestrians, and fishermen are also frequent visitors. A number of long backcountry trails, including the 37-mile Coastal Trail connecting the parks along the coast, make for great multi-day backpacking routes. There are also several beaches—great spots for watching the gray whale migration in winter and spring, but quite cold for swimming year-round. A large herd of elk also calls the parks home. **FREE** The three state parks located within the national park boundaries are

Del Norte Coast Redwoods State Park. *7 miles S on Hwy 101. Phone 707/464-6101; toll-free 800/444-7275 (reservations).* Redwood trees grow on steep slopes just above the surf. Rhododendrons blanket the slopes, blooming in May and June. Nature, hiking trails; picnicking, camping (dump station). **$**

Jedediah Smith Redwoods State Park. *9 miles NE off Hwy 101 on Hwy 199. Phone 707/464-6101; toll-free 800/444-7275 (reservations).* Stout Memorial Grove, at the center of Mill Creek Flat, is about 4 miles from the park entrance. Swimming, fishing; nature and hiking trails, picnicking, camping (dump station). **$**

Prairie Creek Redwoods State Park. *33 miles S on Hwy 101. Phone 707/464-6101; toll-free 800/444-7275 (reservations).* These 14,000 acres are adorned by magnificent groves of coast redwoods. Gold Bluffs Beach was worked for gold in 1851, but most of it remained hopelessly mixed in vast amounts of sand and rock. Lush ferns cover the 50-foot walls of Fern Canyon and moss carpets the fallen tree trunks. Fishing; hiking on 75 miles of nature trails, picnicking. Educational displays in visitor center. Frequent campfire programs and ranger-conducted hikes in summer. Two campgrounds: Elk Prairie, tent and trailer (reservations recommended); Gold Bluffs Beach, approximately 3 1/2 miles south via Highway 101 to Davison Rd (unpaved road; vehicle size and weight restriction). **$**

Trees of Mystery. *15500 Hwy 101 N, Klamath (95548). Phone toll-free 800/638-3389. www.treesofmystery.net.* A giant Paul Bunyan and Babe the Blue Ox greet visitors to this tacky-but-fun landmark south of Klamath on Highway 101. The touristy complex includes a trail that runs through thick redwood forest, with more than a few trees carved into the form of Paul Bunyan's legendary cohorts, as well as a "SkyTrail" gondola that takes riders to an observation platform. A motel, restaurant, and kitschy souvenir shop round out the ever-expanding facilities. Museum (June-Aug: daily 8:30 am-7:30 pm; Sept-May: daily 9:30 am-4:30 pm). **$$$**

Special Event

World Championship Crab Races. *Del Norte County Fairgrounds, 1001 Front St, Crescent City (95531). Phone 707/464-3174.* Sun before President's Day.

Limited-Service Hotels

★ ★ **BEST WESTERN NORTHWOODS INN.** *655 Redwood Hwy 101 S, Crescent City (95531). Phone 707/464-9771; toll-free 800/557-3396; fax 707/464-9461. www.bestwestern.com.* 89 rooms, 2 story. Complimentary full breakfast. Check-in 3 pm, check-out 11 am. Restaurant, bar. Fitness room. Indoor pool, whirlpool. **$**

★ **COMFORT INN & SUITES.** *100 Walton St, Crescent City (95531). Phone 707/464-3885; toll-free 800/228-5160; fax 707/464-5311. www.choicehotels.com.* Adjacent to bay. 46 rooms, 2 story. Complimentary continental breakfast. Check-in 1 pm, check-out 11 am. **$**

Restaurant

★ ★ **HARBOR VIEW GROTTO.** *150 Starfish Way, Crescent City (95531). Phone 707/464-3815.* Lunch, dinner. Closed Jan 1, Thanksgiving, Dec 24-25. Bar. **$$**

Lassen Volcanic National Park, CA

3 hours 35 minutes, 207 miles from Medford, OR

(44 miles E of Redding via Hwy 44; 51 miles E of Red Bluff via Hwy 36, 89)

Web site www.nps.gov/lavo/

This 165-square-mile park was created to preserve the area including 10,457-foot Lassen Peak, a volcano last active in 1921. Lassen Park, in the southernmost part of the Cascade Range, contains glacial lakes, virgin forests, mountain meadows, and snow-fed streams. Hydrothermal features, the Devastated Area, and Chaos Jumbles can be seen from Lassen Park Road. Boiling mud pots and fumaroles (steam vents) can be seen a short distance off the road at Sulphur Works. At Butte Lake, colorful masses of lava and volcanic ash blend with the forests, meadows, and streams. The peak is named for Peter Lassen, a Danish pioneer who used it as a landmark in guiding immigrant trains into the northern Sacramento Valley.

After being denuded in 1915 by a mudflow and a hot blast, The Devastated Area is slowly being reclaimed by small trees and flowers. The Chaos Crags, a group of lava plugs, were formed some 1,100 years ago. Bumpass Hell, a colorful area of mud pots, boiling pools, and steam vents, is a 3-mile round-trip hike from Lassen Park Road. Clouds of steam and sulfurous gases pour from vents in the thermal areas. Nearby is Lake Helen, named for Helen Tanner Brodt, the first white woman to climb Lassen Peak, in 1864. At the northwest entrance is a visitor center (late June-Labor Day, daily) where you can find information about the park's human, natural, and geological history. There are guided walks during the summer; self-guided nature trails; and evening talks at some campgrounds. Camping (fee) is available at eight campgrounds; there's a two-week limit, except at Lost Creek and Summit Lake campgrounds, which impose a seven-day limit; check at a ranger station for regulations.

Lassen Park Road is usually open mid-June-mid-Oct, weather permitting. The Sulphur Works entrance to the south and the Manzanita Lake entrance to the northwest are open during the winter months for winter sports.

There are facilities for the disabled, including the visitor center, comfort station, and amphitheater at Manzanita Lake.

Lava Beds National Monument, CA

3 hours, 119 miles from Medford, OR

(30 miles SW of Tulelake, off Hwy 139)

Web site www.nps.gov/labe

Seventy-two square miles of volcanic formations are preserved here in the extreme northeastern part of the state. Centuries ago, rivers of molten lava flowed here. In cooling, they formed a strange and fantastic region. Cinder cones dot the landscape, one rising 476 feet from its base. Winding trenches mark the collapsed roofs of lava tubes, an indicator of the 380 caves beneath the surface. Throughout the area are masses of lava hardened into strange shapes. Spatter cones may be seen where vents in the lava formed vertical tubelike channels, some only 3 feet in diameter but reaching downward 100 feet.

Outstanding caves include Sentinel Cave, named for a lava formation in its passageway; Catacombs Cave, with passageways resembling Rome's catacombs; and Skull Cave, with a broad entry cavern reaching approximately 80 feet in diameter. (The name comes from the many skulls of mountain sheep that were found here.) The National Park Service provides ladders and trails in the 24 caves that are easily accessible to the public.

One of the most costly Native American campaigns in history took place in this rugged, otherworldly setting. The Modoc War of 1872-1873 saw a small band of Native Americans revolt against reservation life and fight a series of battles with US troops. Although they were obliged to care for their families and live off the country, the Modocs held off an army almost ten times their number for more than five months.

There is a campground at Indian Well (fee, water available mid-May-Labor Day), and there are picnic areas at Fleener Chimneys and Captain Jack's Stronghold (no water). Guided walks, audiovisual programs, cave trips, and campfire programs are held daily, mid-June-Labor Day. Park headquarters has a visitor center (daily). No gasoline is available in the park, so fill your gas tank before entering. Golden Eagle, Golden Age, and Golden Access passports accepted (see MAKING THE MOST OF YOUR TRIP).

Washington

The Stillaguamish, Steilacoom and Hoh, Puyallup, Tulalip and La Push, the Duckabush, the Dosewallips and the Queets, the Skookumchuck, the Sol Duc and the Pysht—all these are Washington towns and rivers. There are many more like them, named by Native Americans.

Ruggedly handsome Washington is like a bank in which nature has deposited some of her greatest resources. In addition to dramatic mountain ranges, expansive forests, and inviting harbors, it is a cornerstone of American hydroelectric technology. Here are the majestic spectacles of mighty Mount Rainier—revered as a god by the Native Americans—and the Olympic Peninsula, where one of the wettest and one of the driest parts of the country are only a mountain away from each other; also here is Puget Sound, a giant inland sea where 2,000 miles of shoreline bend into jewel-like bays.

Although British and Spanish navigators were the first Europeans to explore Washington's serrated shoreline, the first major discoveries were made in 1792, when an American, Captain Robert Gray, gave his name to Grays Harbor and the name of his ship, *Columbia,* to the great river. An Englishman, Captain George Vancouver, explored and named Puget Sound and christened Mount Baker and Mount Rainier, which he could see far inland. Fort Vancouver was the keystone of the British fur industry, dominating a Northwest empire. After conflicting US and British claims were resolved, Americans surged into this area by ship and wagon train.

Part of the Oregon Territory until separated in 1853, the state's eastern boundary was established in 1863, when Idaho became a territory. Entering the last decade of the 19th century as a state of the Union, Washington found itself no longer America's last territorial frontier.

Population: 5,894,121
Area: 70,637 square miles
Elevation: 0-14,410 feet
Peak: Mount Rainier (Pierce County)
Entered Union: November 11, 1889 (42nd state)
Capital: Olympia
Motto: Al-ki (By and By)
Nickname: Evergreen State
Flower: Rhododendron
Bird: Willow Goldfinch
Tree: Western Hemlock
Time Zone: Pacific
Web site: www.tourism.wa.gov
Fun Facts:
- Washington has more glaciers than the other 47 contiguous states combined.
- More than half of all apples grown in the United States for fresh eating come from orchards in Washington.

Civilization has not dissipated Washington's natural wealth. On the contrary, after more than a century of logging operations, Washington retains 24 million acres of superb forests, and miracles of modern engineering have almost completely erased the wastelands through which the wagon trains of the pioneers passed on their way to the sea.

The mighty but capricious Columbia River meanders through the heart of northeast and central Washington, then runs for 300 miles along the Oregon-Washington border. Through a series of dams and the Grand Coulee Reclamation Project, the energies of the Columbia have been harnessed and converted into what is presently one of the world's great sources of water power. Irrigation and a vast supply of inexpensive power gave a tremendous push to Washington's economy, sparking new industries and making possible the state's production of huge crops of grains, vegetables, and fruit.

Calendar Highlights

MARCH

Chocolate Fantasy (*Yakima*). *Phone 509/966-6309.* Chocolate manufacturers from across the nation showcase candy, cookies, and pies; sampling, "chocolate bingo."

APRIL

Daffodil Festival (*Tacoma*). *In Tacoma and Puyallup Valley. Phone 253/627-6176.* Flower show, coronation, four-city floral parade of floats, marine regatta, and bowling tournament.

MAY

Ski to Sea Festival (*Bellingham*). *Phone 360/734-1330.* Parades, carnival, art show, and special events. Ski to Sea race; starts on Mount Baker, ends in Bellingham Bay and involves skiers, runners, canoeists, bicyclists, and kayakers. Memorial Day weekend.

Wooden Boat Festival (*Olympia*). *Percival Landing in Harbor. Phone 360/943-5404.* Wooden boats on display, some open for public viewing. Wooden crafts fair.

JULY

San Juan Island Jazz Festival (*San Juan Islands*). *Friday Harbor. Phone 360/378-5509.* Indoor/outdoor jazz festival featuring Dixieland, swing, zydeco, and blues/jazz.

AUGUST

Seafair (*Seattle*). *Phone 206/728-0123; www.seafair.com.* Citywide marine festival. Regattas, speedboat races, shows at Aqua Theater, parades, sports events, exhibits.

Stampede and Suicide Race (*Omak*). *Phone 509/826-1002.* Rodeo events; horses and riders race down a cliff and across the Okanogan River. Western art show. Native American dance contests. Encampment with more than 100 teepees.

Southwest Washington Fair (*Centralia*). *Phone 360/736-6072.* First held in 1909, this is the state's second oldest fair and one of the largest.

SEPTEMBER

Central Washington State Fair and Rodeo (*Yakima*). *Fairgrounds. Phone 509/248-7160.* Thoroughbred racing. Pari-mutuel wagering.

Northeast Washington Fair (*Colville*). *Stevens County Fairgrounds. Phone 509/684-2585.* Parade, livestock and horse shows, arts and crafts exhibits, and carnival.

Western Washington Fair (*Puyallup*). *Phone 253/841-5045.* The Pacific Northwest's largest fair; includes three statewide youth fairs, livestock shows, agricultural and commercial exhibits, free entertainment, midway, rodeo, and top-name grandstand acts.

Central Washington is the apple barrel of the country; dairying is a big industry in the western valleys. Forestry and wood products as well as the production of paper and allied products are of major importance in the western and northern sections of the state; one-third of the state is covered by commercial forests. In recent years, Washington wines have enjoyed great popularity around the nation.

Since 1965, more than 25 percent of Washington's total manufacturing effort has been devoted to the production of transportation equipment, of which a large portion is involved in commercial jet aircraft. Along Puget Sound, industry means canning plants, lumber mills, and pulp and paper plants; but even here there is a new economic dimension: petroleum refineries of four major companies have a daily capacity of 366,500 barrels of crude oil and gasoline; biotechnology and software development are growing industries. Tourism is the state's fourth largest industry, amounting to more than $8.8 billion a year.

When to Go/Climate

Moist air off the Pacific Ocean and Puget Sound creates rainy conditions in western Washington and heavy snowfall in the Cascades. While the western slopes of the Cascades and Olympic Mountains are soaked with moisture, the eastern slopes and, indeed, the entire eastern part of the state are almost desert dry. Temperatures are seasonally mild except for high in the mountains.

AVERAGE HIGH/LOW TEMPERATURES (° F)

Seattle

Jan 46/36	**May** 64/48	**Sept** 69/53
Feb 51/38	**June** 70/53	**Oct** 60/47
Mar 54/40	**July** 74/56	**Nov** 52/41
Apr 58/43	**Aug** 74/57	**Dec** 46/37

Spokane

Jan 33/21	**May** 66/42	**Sept** 72/46
Feb 41/26	**June** 75/49	**Oct** 59/36
Mar 48/30	**July** 83/54	**Nov** 41/29
Apr 57/35	**Aug** 83/54	**Dec** 34/22

Parks and Recreation

Water-related activities, hiking, riding, various other sports, picnicking, and visitor centers, as well as camping, are available in many of Washington's state parks. The 248,882 acres owned or managed by the Washington State Parks & Recreation Commission provide unusually good camping and trailer facilities at most locations, with a camping fee of $15 per site; hookups $21; ten-day limit in summer; 20 days rest of year. Most parks are open daily: April-mid-October, 6:30 am-dusk; some are closed the rest of the year. Pets are allowed on leash only. For further information, contact the Washington State Parks & Recreation Commission, 7150 Cleanwater Ln, PO Box 42650, Olympia 98504-2650, phone 360/902-8844 or toll-free 888/226-7688.

FISHING AND HUNTING

With 10,000 miles of bay and Pacific shoreline, 8,000 lakes, and rivers that stretch from Oregon to Canada, Washington provides something for every angler's whim. Fish hatcheries dot the state, stocking nature's waterways and those artificially created by irrigation and navigation dams. If you like salmon and steelhead, Washington is the state to try your luck.

Nonresident freshwater fishing license $40; two-day license $6. A food fish license is required for salmon and saltwater bottomfish; nonresident food fish license, $20; nonresident saltwater fish license, $36; nonresident combination fresh water/saltwater fish license, $72. A shellfish/seaweed license is required for shellfish; nonresident license, $20. Razor clam season varies; contact the Department of Fish & Wildlife for season dates, phone 360/902-2200. Nonresident small-game hunting license $165; three-day $50; big game, $200-$725. Get hunting and freshwater fishing regulations and a complete list of license fees from the Department of Fish & Wildlife, 500 Capitol Way N, Olympia 98504. Fishing and hunting regulation pamphlets are available at local sporting goods stores.

Driving Information

Safety belts are mandatory for all persons anywhere in a vehicle. Children under 40 pounds in weight must be in approved safety seats anywhere in a vehicle. For more information, phone 360/753-6197.

INTERSTATE HIGHWAY SYSTEM

The following alphabetical listing of Washington towns in this book shows that these cities are within 10 miles of the indicated interstate highways. Check a highway map for the nearest exit.

Highway Number	Cities/Towns within 10 Miles
Interstate 5	Bellingham, Blaine, Centralia, Chehalis, Everett, Kelso, Longview, Marysville, Mount Vernon, Olympia, Puyallup, Seattle, Sedro Woolley, Snohomish, Tacoma, Vancouver.
Interstate 82	Ellensburg, Kennewick, Pasco, Richland, Sunnyside, Toppenish, Yakima.
Interstate 90	Bellevue, Ellensburg, Issaquah, Moses Lake, North Bend, Ritzville, Seattle, Spokane.
Interstate 182	Pasco, Richland.

Additional Visitor Information

Washington travel information and brochures are available from the Washington State Tourism Department of Community, Trade, and Economic Development, 101 General Administration Building, PO Box 42500, Olympia 98504-2500.

Phone toll-free 800/544-1800 for a copy of *Washington State Lodging and Travel Guide;* phone 360/586-2088 or toll-free 800/638-8474 for tourism information.

There are 180 visitor information centers in Washington; most are open May-September. Visitors who stop by will find information and brochures helpful in planning stops at points of interest. The locations for the official state visitor centers at points of entry are as follows: 7 miles south of Blaine, near the Canadian border; east of Spokane at the Idaho/Washington border, I-90 exit 299 westbound; 404 E 15th St, Vancouver; in Oroville on Hwy 97, near the Canadian border; at the Oregon border on Hwy 97, near Maryhill State Park and Sam Hill Bridge; and on Hwy 401 near the Astoria Bridge.

MOUNTAIN WATERWAYS IN THE CASCADES

This route passes through spectacular mountain scenery in one of the West's most rugged national parks. Starting on the moist Pacific side of the Cascade range at Sedro-Woolley, Highway 20 follows the increasingly narrow Skagit River valley inland through dripping fir and cedar forests. Near Rockport, the landscape becomes wilder and steeper; this is a major wintering area for bald eagles, which come here to dine on migrating salmon. As the route enters the park near Marblemount, the Skagit is dammed in quick succession in a precipitous canyon by three early-20th-century hydrodams (this is where Seattle gets its power). Tours of the largest dam are the most popular activity in the park; getting up to the dam itself involves riding an incline railroad up a sheer cliff face. Around the dams are hikes to waterfalls and mist gardens. After climbing Rainy Pass, which has incredible views of tooth-edged mountain ranges and volcanoes in good weather, Highway 20 drops onto the dry side of the Cascades, where the forests are suddenly dominated by ponderosa pines and juniper. The highway follows the Methow River, a lovely semiarid valley that was once the province of cattle ranches but is now lined with resort homes and golf courses. The town of Winthrop, which just 20 years ago was filled with feed stores and tractor dealerships, now epitomizes the wealthy New West culture with its art galleries, fine restaurants, and home décor boutiques. From the delightfully named town of Twisp, follow Highway 153 through ranch land, which slowly gives way to apple orchards as the route joins Highway 97 and the Columbia River at Pateros. **(Approximately 168 miles)**

MOUNT RAINIER AND NORTHWEST WILDLIFE

A popular day trip from Seattle, this route rounds the imposing volcanic cone of Mount Rainier, the centerpiece of Mount Rainier National Park. Take Highway 410 east and climb along the White River with the towering white cone of 14,412-foot Mount Rainier rising above the forest. The park itself has a number of different viewpoints for taking in the peak, and each has its own personalities. Sunrise—the highest point reached by road in the park—is on the drier, east side of the peak; there are hikes to wildflower meadows and glacial overlooks, and mountain goats are often seen in the area. The aptly named Paradise area—on the southern side of the mountain atop a broad timberline shoulder—shares postcard views of the peak with the Paradise Inn, a vast historic stone-and-log lodge built in classic Arts-and-Crafts style. An extensive trail system explores flower-filled meadows and tumbling waterfalls. Other highlights of this route are Ohanapecosh, a riparian wetland with a stand of massive old-growth cedar trees, and Longmire, the original park headquarters with several turn-of-the-20th-century structures and another heritage hotel. A highlight of the return trip near Eatonville (on Highway 161) is the Northwest Trek Wildlife Park, a private refuge that rehabilitates wolves, cougars, and other wildlife native to the area that have been injured or must be removed from the wild for other reasons. **(Approximately 142 miles)**

Aberdeen (C-1)

See also Hoquiam, Ocean Shores, Westport

Settled 1878
Population 16,461
Elevation 19 ft
Area Code 360
Zip 98520
Information Grays Harbor Chamber of Commerce, 506 Duffy St; phone 360/532-1924 or toll-free 800/321-1924
Web site www.graysharbor.org

Aberdeen and Hoquiam (see) are twin cities on the eastern tip of Grays Harbor. Born as a cannery named for the city in Scotland, Aberdeen later blossomed as a lumber town, with one of the greatest stands of Douglas fir ever found in the Pacific Northwest at its back. Many Harbor residents are descendants of Midwestern Scandinavians who came here to fell the forests. Today, the town's commerce consists of wood processing, fishing, and shipbuilding. The Port of Grays Harbor is located along the waterfront of the two towns.

What to See and Do

Aberdeen Museum of History. *111 E 3rd St, Aberdeen (98520). Phone 360/533-1976.* Special exhibits with 1880s-1940s furnishings and implements include kitchen and bed, general mercantile store, one-room school; farm and logging equipment and displays; blacksmith shop; pioneer church; fire trucks. Slide show, photographs. (June-Labor Day: Wed-Sun; rest of year: weekends) **DONATION**

Grays Harbor Historical Seaport. *813 E Heron St, Aberdeen (98520). Phone 360/532-8611. www. graysharbor.org.* Historical interpretive center; classes in long boat building. Includes a museum with informational and active exhibits on the history of sailing in the Pacific Northwest. Also a replica of Robert Gray's tall ship *Lady Washington* (seasonal; fee). (Daily; closed holidays) **FREE**

Lake Sylvia State Park. *1812 Lake Sylvia Rd N, Montesano (98563). 10 miles E on Hwy 12, then 1 mile N on an unnumbered road. Phone 360/249-3621. www. parks.wa.gov.* An old logging camp, this park contains approximately 233 acres of protected timber on the freshwater shoreline of Lake Sylvia. Activities include boating (non-motorized), swimming, fishing, hiking (5 miles of trails), mountain biking, and bird-watching. Camping (Mar-Oct). Picnicking, concession. (Daily 8 am-dusk)

Samuel Benn Park. *E 9th and N I sts, Aberdeen (98520). Phone 360/533-4100.* Named for pioneer settler. Rose and rhododendron gardens; picnic facilities, playground, tennis. (Daily) **FREE**

Schafer State Park. *13 miles E on Hwy 12, then 10 miles N on an unnumbered road. Phone 360/482-3852. www.parks.wa.gov.* Approximately 120 acres on the Satsop River. Activities include swimming, fishing (steelhead, cutthroat trout, and salmon), hiking (2 miles of trails), and bird-watching. Abundant wildlife. Picnicking, camping (hookups; dump station; late Apr-Oct). (Daily 8 am-dusk)

Limited-Service Hotel

★ **RED LION HOTEL.** *521 W Wishkah St, Aberdeen (98520). Phone 360/532-5210; toll-free 800/733-5466; fax 360/533-8483. www.redlion.com.* This motel is located just off Highway 101 near the tall ship *Lady Washington*, just five blocks from the city center. 67 rooms, 2 story. Pets accepted. Complimentary continental breakfast. Check-out noon. **$**

Specialty Lodging

The following lodging establishment is approved by Mobil Travel Guide, but due to its unique and individualized nature has not been given a traditional Mobil Star rating. Included in this listing you may find bed-and-breakfasts, limited-service inns, guest ranches, and other unique hotel properties.

ABERDEEN MANSION BED AND BREAKFAST. *807 N M St, Aberdeen (98520). Phone 360/533-7079; toll-free 888/533-7079. www. aberdeenmansionbb.com.* This sunny yellow Victorian furnished with antiques was built in 1905 for a local lumber baron. Two libraries and a large wraparound porch encourage reading, conversation, or quiet contemplation; the game room contains a pool table and board games for guests' use. All five guest rooms have king-size beds and TVs, and the carriage house also has two twin beds and a small kitchen. 5 rooms,

2 story. Children over 10 years only. Complimentary full breakfast. Check-in 4-7 pm, check-out 11 am. **$** 🅱

Restaurants

★ ★ **BILLY'S RESTAURANT.** *322 E Heron, Aberdeen (98520). Phone 360/533-7144.* In 1904 building with antique furnishings. American menu. Lunch, dinner. Closed Thanksgiving, Dec 25. Bar. Children's menu. **$$**

★ ★ **BRIDGES RESTAURANT.** *112 N G St, Aberdeen (98520). Phone 360/532-6563; fax 360/532-5490.* American menu. Lunch, dinner. Bar. Children's menu. **$$**

Anacortes (A-2)

See also Coupeville, La Conner, Mount Vernon, Oak Harbor, Sedro Woolley

Settled 1860
Population 14,557
Elevation 24 ft
Area Code 360
Zip 98221
Information Visitor Information Center at the Chamber of Commerce, 819 Commercial Ave; phone 360/293-3832
Web site www.anacortes.org

Anacortes, at the northwest tip of Fidalgo Island, houses the San Juan Islands ferries. The town's name honors Anna Curtis, the wife of one of its founders.

What to See and Do

Deception Pass State Park. *41229 Hwy 20, Anacortes (98277). 9 miles S on Hwy 20. Phone 360/675-2417. www.parks.wa.gov.* More than 4,100 acres of sheltered bays and deep old-growth forests with fjordlike shoreline. Four lakes provide ample opportunities for swimming (lifeguards in summer), scuba diving, fishing, clamming, boating (eight ramps, saltwater and freshwater dock). More than 170 varieties of birds make this a popular bird-watching spot. You'll also find 38 miles of hiking trails, some accessible for the disabled. Picnicking, camping (with showers). Pets on leash only. (Summer: 6:30 am-dusk; winter: 8 am-dusk)

⭐ **San Juan Island.** Friday Harbor on eastern shore serves as base for salmon fleet; major commercial center of islands. Fishing lakes; camping facilities; golf, International Seaplane Base, and two airstrips are here. Also on San Juan is

San Juan Island National Historical Park. *Phone 360/378-2240. www.nps.gov/sajh.* Commemorates the settlement of the boundary issue between the US and Great Britain. English Camp, 10 miles northwest of Friday Harbor on Garrison Bay, has a restored blockhouse, commissary, hospital, formal garden, and barracks built during the British occupation. American Camp, 6 miles southeast of Friday Harbor, has remains of redoubt, the American defensive earthwork; laundresses' and officers' quarters. Picnicking; information specialist at both camps (June-Sept: daily; rest of year: Thurs-Sun). Office and information center in Friday Harbor, 1st and Spring sts (June-Aug: daily; May and Sept: Mon-Fri; closed rest of year; closed holidays)

San Juan Islands trip. *Phone 360/293-3832.* Ferry boats leave several times daily for Lopez Island, Shaw Island, Orcas Island, Friday Harbor, and Sidney, British Columbia. Either leave your car at the dock in Anacortes or take your vehicle with you, disembark at any point, and explore from paved roads. For schedules and fares, contact Washington State Ferries, phone 206/464-6400 or toll-free 888/808-7977 (in state), www.wsdot.wa.gov/ferries.

Swinomish Northern Lights Casino. *12885 Casino Dr, Anacortes (98221). Phone 360/293-2691. www.swinomishcasino.com.* The largest Washington casino north of Seattle has tables, machines, off-track betting, and a large poker room. Lower-key gamblers can hit the bingo hall or keno lounge. The Starlight Lounge features live comedy; you'll also find pro boxing, musical entertainment, and a family-style restaurant with both buffets and table service. (Daily)

Washington Park. *End of Sunset Ave, Anacortes (98221). 4 miles W on 12th St (Oakes Ave). Phone 360/293-1927. www.anacortes.org.* With more than 100 species of birds, this 220-acre park is popular with bird-watchers; it also draws whale-watchers in season. Sunset Beach; saltwater fishing, boating (ramps); picnicking, camping (14-day limit; electricity and water; showers).

Special Events

Barbershop Concert and Salmon Barbecue.
Phone 360/293-1282. Last weekend in July.

Shipwreck Day. *819 Commercial Ave, Anacortes (98221). Phone 360/293-7911.* Mid-July.

Waterfront Festival. *1019 Q Ave, Anacortes (98221). Phone 360/293-7911.* Mid-May.

Limited-Service Hotel

★ **SHIP HARBOR INN.** *5316 Ferry Terminal Rd, Anacortes (98221). Phone 360/293-5177; toll-free 800/852-8568; fax 360/299-2412. www.shipharborinn .com.* 16 rooms, 2 story. Pets accepted, some restrictions; fee. Complimentary continental breakfast. Check-out 11 am. Bar. **$**

✈ 🦮

Arlington (B-3)

What to See and Do

Possession Point Fishing Charters. *2807 Freestad Rd, Arlington (28223). Phone 360/652-3797. www. possessionpointfishing.com.* Based out of the Port of Everett marina—about 30 miles north of downtown Seattle—Possession Point Fishing Charters offers a variety of seven-hour trips. Most expeditions focus on King, Coho, and silver salmon or bottom fish, but the company also offers crabbing tours. Tackle, bait, and fishing licenses are all available on board.

Ashford

Specialty Lodging

The following lodging establishment is approved by Mobil Travel Guide, but due to its unique and individualized nature has not been given a traditional Mobil Star rating. Included in this listing you may find bed-and-breakfasts, limited-service inns, guest ranches, and other unique hotel properties.

ALEXANDER'S COUNTRY INN. *37515 Hwy 706 E, Ashford (98304). Phone 360/569-2300; toll-free 800/654-7615. www.alexanderscountryinn.com.*
14 rooms, 3 story. Complimentary full breakfast. Check-in 3 pm, check-out 11 am. Restaurant. **$**
🐕

Auburn (C-2)

See also Seattle, Tacoma

Founded 1891
Population 40,314
Web site www.ci.auburn.wa.us

What to See and Do

Auburn Golf Course. *29630 Green River Rd, Auburn (98092). Phone 253/833-2350.* This excellent 18-hole public course abuts the Green River in Auburn, about 25 miles southeast of downtown Seattle. Well known for its lush vegetation and challenging greens, the course is alternately flat (the front nine) and hilly (after the turn). It is widely regarded as one of the best golf values in the state, and is accordingly crowded on weekends. **$$$$**

Emerald Downs. *2300 Emerald Downs Dr, Auburn (98001). Phone 253/288-7000. www.emdowns.com.* The only live thoroughbred horse racing venue in the Seattle area, Emerald Downs features a full slate of races from spring to late summer. The esteemed Longacres Mile, an area tradition since the 1930s with an ever-growing purse ($250,000 in 2003), is the schedule's highlight, held in August. Built in 1996, the grandstand is thoroughly modern, with a wide range of seating on six levels and numerous food stands, restaurants, and bars. The 1-mile oval track hosts a number of special events and concerts (including an Independence Day celebration with fireworks). Sundays bring "family fun days," with clowns, face painting, pony rides, and other kid-friendly diversions. **$**

Muckleshoot Casino. *2402 Auburn Way S, Auburn (98002). Phone toll-free 800/804-4944. www. muckleshootcasino.com.* Located between Seattle and Tacoma in Auburn, Muckleshoot Casino sports a tropical theme and more than 2,000 gaming machines, as well as the usual array of Vegas-style tables. The distinguishing features here are a piano lounge/cigar bar and a sushi bar. Entertainment includes a "Legends" show (with impersonators aping Elvis, Madonna, and other stars) and pro boxing matches on Saturday nights. (Sat-Tues 24 hours, Wed-Fri 10 am-5:45 am)

White River Valley Museum. *918 H St SE, Auburn (98002). Phone 253/288-7433. www.wrvmuseum.org.* Situated in Les Gove Park, this historically rich museum celebrates the settlement of the White River Valley during the early part of the 20th century. Visitors can explore a Japanese-American farmhouse, climb aboard a Northern Pacific caboose, and tour a replica of downtown Auburn complete with public market, drugstore, and hat shop. Admission is free on Wednesdays. (Wed-Sun noon-4 pm) **$**

Bellevue (B-3)

See also Issaquah, Seattle

Population 109,569
Elevation 125 ft
Information Bellevue Chamber of Commerce, 10500 NE 8th St #212, 98004; phone 425/454-2464
Web site www.bellevuechamber.org

Incorporated in 1953, Bellevue has rapidly become the state's fourth largest city. It is linked across Lake Washington to Seattle by the Evergreen Floating Bridge.

What to See and Do

Bellevue Botanical Garden. *12001 Main St, Bellevue (98005). Phone 425/452-2749. www.bellevuebotanical. org.* Features 36 acres of woodlands, meadows, and display gardens including Waterwise Garden, Japanese Gardens, and Fuchsia Display. Garden shop. Visitor Center. (Daily) **FREE**

Bellevue Square. *575 Bellevue Sq, Bellevue (98004). Phone 425/454-2431. www.bellevuesquare.com.* One of the biggest and most posh shopping centers in metro Seattle, Bellevue Square is located 8 miles east of the city in suburban Bellevue, on the eastern shore of Lake Washington. Well-heeled locals love the place for its eye-catching design, climate-controlled corridors, and 200 high-end stores: anchors such as Nordstrom and the Bon Marché, specialty stores like Pottery Barn and Williams-Sonoma, and upscale eateries including P.F. Chang's China Bistro and Ruth's Chris Steak House. This is not to mention the non-shopping facilities and services, which are head and shoulders above that of the typical mall, with a concierge, valet parking, a local shuttle bus, and a pair of kids' play areas. An Eastside institution since the 1940s, Bellevue Square underwent

a major redevelopment in the 1990s that transformed it into the shopper's paradise it is today.

Rosalie Whyel Museum of Doll Art. *1116 108th Ave NE, Bellevue (98004). Phone 425/455-1116. www. dollart.com.* Features curated collection of dolls, teddy bears, toys, and miniatures. Museum shop. (Daily; closed holidays) **$$$**

Limited-Service Hotels

★ ★ **DOUBLETREE HOTEL.** *300 112th Ave, Bellevue (98004). Phone 425/455-1300; toll-free 800/222-8733; fax 425/450-4119. www.doubletree.com.* Convenient to downtown and numerous shopping and dining choices, this hotel caters equally well to business travelers—with up-to-date amenities and an executive level—and families, although you probably wouldn't choose it for a romantic getaway. The guest rooms surround a dramatic seven-story atrium. Open-air balconies let guests get a feel for the great outdoors. 353 rooms, 10 story. Pets accepted, some restrictions. Check-in 3 pm, check-out noon. High-speed Internet access. Restaurant, bar. Fitness room, spa. Outdoor pool, whirlpool. Business center. **$$**
🐾 👟 🏊 🏃

★ ★ **RED LION BELLEVUE INN.** *11211 Main St, Bellevue (98004). Phone 425/455-5240; toll-free 800/421-8193; fax 425/455-0654. www.redlion.com.* Located just six blocks from Bellevue Square Mall, and convenient to the city's attractions, the hotel has a warm, lodge-like feel with overstuffed furniture and comforters on the extra-long double or king-size beds. It's a car-friendly place, with ample free parking and rental cars available on the premises. 181 rooms, 2 story. Pets accepted, some restrictions; fee. Check-in 4 pm, check-out noon. High-speed Internet access. Restaurant, bar. Fitness room. Outdoor pool. **$**
🐾 👟 🏊

★ **SILVER CLOUD INN BELLEVUE.** *10621 NE 12th St, Bellevue (98004). Phone 425/637-7000; toll-free 800/205-6937; fax 425/455-0531. www.scinns.com.* This hotel is within walking distance of area attractions, including Bellevue Square Mall, the Meydenbauer Convention Center, and the Rosalie Whyel Museum of Doll Art. Perhaps the best attraction nearby is the small park across the street, where you can jog before a day of meetings or relax afterward. Guest rooms have refrigerators and microwaves, and the hotel's guest laundry facilities are complimentary. 97 rooms, 4 story. Complimentary continental breakfast. Check-in 3 pm, check-out noon. High-speed Internet access. Fitness room. Outdoor pool, whirlpool. **$$**

Full-Service Hotels

★ ★ ★ BELLEVUE CLUB HOTEL. *11200 SE 6th St, Bellevue (98004). Phone 425/454-4424; toll-free 800/579-1110; fax 425/688-3101. www. bellevueclub.com.* You instantly feel the hush of the Bellevue Club Hotel when you walk through the vine-covered entrance to this exquisite hotel. Visitors are instantly welcomed to this temple of serenity and contemporary elegance set on 9 acres in the center of Bellevue. While the Bellevue Club feels very private and exclusive, hotel guests are warmly greeted with thoughtful touches and deluxe amenities. Each room has an inviting atmosphere, complete with luxurious bedding and baths crafted of marble, limestone, or granite. Stone fireplaces, oversized baths, or private balconies set each room apart from another. An Olympic-size pool, state-of-the-art equipment, racquet courts, and spa make the fitness facility a true sanctuary. Quick bites are provided at two other establishments for those on the go. 67 rooms, 4 story. Pets accepted, some restrictions; fee. Complimentary continental breakfast. Check-in 3 pm, check-out 1 pm. Restaurant, bar. Children's activity center. Fitness room, spa. Indoor pool, outdoor pool, children's pool, whirlpool. Tennis. Business center. **$$$**

★ ★ ★ HYATT REGENCY BELLEVUE. *900 Bellevue Way NE, Bellevue (98004). Phone 425/462-1234; toll-free 800/233-1234; fax 425/646-7567. www. bellevue.hyatt.com.* Located in the fashionable Eastside area and directly across from Bellevue Square Mall, this hotel is situated within Bellevue Place, a mixed-use development that includes retail stores, a fitness center, and plenty of dining options. The hotel makes the most of its location and, instead of maintaining its own fitness facilities, encourages guests to use the Bellevue Place Club (for a fee) and to dine at one of the many nearby restaurants (the hotel restaurant isn't open for dinner). 381 rooms, 24 story. Check-in 3 pm, check-out noon. High-speed Internet access. Restaurant, bar. Business center. **$$**

Restaurants

★ ★ SEASTAR RESTAURANT AND RAW BAR. *205 108th Ave NE, Bellevue (98004). Phone 425/456-0010. www.seastarrestaurant.com.* American menu. Lunch, dinner. Bar. Casual attire. Reservations recommended. Valet parking. **$$$**

★ ★ SPAZZO ITALIAN GRILL. *10655 NE 4th St, Bellevue (98004). Phone 425/454-8255; fax 425/453-8462. www.schwartzbros.com.* Views of Lake Washington and downtown from the ninth floor of the Key Bank Building add a serene touch to this formerly Mediterranean restaurant that recently went Italian. Changing weekly, the menu features house-made pastas, grilled meats and seafood, and traditional Italian desserts like cannoli and tiramisu. The new wine bar features 175 selections, including an impressive 75 by the glass. Italian menu. Dinner. Closed Thanksgiving, Dec 25. Bar. Children's menu. Casual attire. **$$$**

Bellingham (A-2)

See also Blaine, Sedro Woolley; also see Vancouver, BC; Victoria, BC

Founded 1853
Population 67,171
Elevation 68 ft
Area Code 360
Information Bellingham/Whatcom County Convention & Visitors Bureau, 904 Potter St, 98226; phone 360/671-3990 or toll-free 800/487-2032 (order information). The Bureau operates a Visitor Information Center off I-5 exit 253 (daily; closed holidays).
Web site www.bellingham.org

This small city, located on Bellingham Bay, has the impressive Mount Baker as its backdrop and is the last major city before the Washington coastline meets the Canadian border. The broad curve of the bay was charted in 1792 by Captain George Vancouver, who named it in honor of Sir William Bellingham. When the first settlers arrived here, forests stretched to the edge of the high bluffs along the shoreline. Timber and coal played major roles in the town's early economy.

Today, Bellingham has an active waterfront port, which supports fishing, cold storage, boat building, shipping, paper processing, and marina operations.

Squalicum Harbor's commercial and pleasure boat marina accommodates more than 1,800 vessels, making it the second largest marina on Puget Sound. The marina is a pleasant area to dine, picnic, and watch the fishermen at work. Fairhaven, the downtown area, contains a mix of restaurants, art galleries, and specialty shops. Bellingham is also home to Western Washington University, located on Sehome Hill, which affords a scenic view of the city and bay.

What to See and Do

Chuckanut Drive. *S from Fairhaven Park on Hwy 11 along Chuckanut Bay to Larrabee State Park.* A 10-mile drive, mostly along highway cut into mountain sides; beautiful vistas of Puget Sound and San Juan Islands.

City recreation areas. *3424 Mindian, Bellingham (98225). Phone 360/676-6985.* More than 2,000 acres of parkland offer a wide variety of activities. (Daily) Fee for some activities. Areas include

Arroyo Park. *Chuckanut Dr and Old Samish Rd, Bellingham.* Approximately 40 acres of dense, second-growth forest in a canyon setting. Creek fishing. Hiking, nature, and bridle trails.

Bloedel Donovan Park. *2214 Electric Ave, Bellingham (98229). NW area of Lake Whatcom.* Swimming beach, fishing, boat launch (fee); picnicking, playground, concession (summer). Community center with gym.

Boulevard Park. *S State St and Bayview Dr, Bellingham.* Fishing, boat dock; bicycle paths, picnicking, playground. Craft studio.

Civic Field Athletic Complex. *Lakeway Dr and Orleans St, Bellingham. Phone 360/676-6976.* Contains multiple athletic fields and indoor community pool.

Cornwall Park. *2800 Cornwall Ave, Bellingham (98225).* Approximately 65 acres. Wading pool, steelhead fishing in Squalicum Creek; fitness trail, tennis, other game courts and fields, picnicking, playground. Extensive rose garden in park.

Fairhaven Park. *107 Chuckanut Dr, Bellingham (98229).* Wading pool; hiking trails, tennis, picnicking, playground.

Lake Padden Park. *4882 Samish Way, Bellingham (98229).* Approximately 1,000 acres with a 152-acre lake. Swimming beach, fishing, boat launch (no motors), hiking and bridle trails, 18-hole golf course (fee), tennis, athletic fields, picnicking, playground.

Sehome Hill Arboretum. *25th St and McDonald Pkwy, Bellingham.* The 165-acre native plant preserve contains hiking and interpretive trails; scenic views of city, Puget Sound, San Juan Islands, and mountains from observation tower atop hill.

Whatcom Falls Park. *1401 Electric Ave, Bellingham (98229). Near Lake Whatcom.* Approximately 240 acres. Children's fishing pond, state fish hatchery; hiking trails, tennis, athletic fields, picnicking, playground.

⭐ **Fairhaven District.** *107 Chuckanut Dr, Bellingham (98229).* In the late 1800s, this area was a separate city that had hopes of becoming the next Chicago. The 1890s buildings are now restaurants and shops. Brass plaques detail the history of the area. Walking tour brochures at the information gazebo, 12th and Harris.

Ferndale. *Approximately 9 miles NW off I-5, exit 262. Phone 360/384-3444.* Community founded in mid-1800s, with several preserved areas. Hovander Homestead, on Neilson Road, is a county park with working farm and museum; interpretive center with nature trails and observation tower. **$$**

Larrabee State Park. *245 Chuckanut Dr, Bellingham (98226). 7 miles S on Hwy 11. Phone 360/676-2093.* Approximately 2,000 acres. Scuba diving, fishing, clamming, crabbing, tide pools, boating (ramp); hiking, picnicking, camping (hookups). Mountain viewpoints.

Lynden Pioneer Museum. *217 Front St, Lynden (98264). Approximately 12 miles N via Hwy 539. Phone 360/354-3675.* Exhibits on history of this Dutch community; antique car and buggy, farm equipment. (Mon-Sat) **$**

Maritime Heritage Center. *1600 C St, Bellingham (98225). Phone 360/676-6806.* Salmon life-cycle facility and learning center. Outdoor rearing tanks; indoor displays detail development from egg to adult. Park (daily). Learning Center (Mon-Fri; closed holidays). **FREE**

Mount Baker Ski Area. *55 miles E on Hwy 542. Phone 360/734-6771. www.mtbakerskiarea.com.* Four quad, three double chairlifts, rope tow; patrol, school, rentals; restaurant, cafeteria, bar; lodge. Longest run

1 1/2 miles; vertical drop 1,500 feet. Also cross-country trails. Half-day rates (weekends, holidays). (Nov-Mar: daily; Apr: Fri-Sun; closed Dec 25)

Mount Baker-Snoqualmie National Forest. *21965 64th Ave W, Mountlake Terrace (98043). Phone 425/775-9702; toll-free 800/627-0062. www.fs.fed.us/r6/mbs.* The Mount Baker and Snoqualmie national forests were combined under a single forest supervisor in July 1974. Divided into five ranger districts, the combined forest encompasses nearly 2 million acres. The Snoqualmie section lies east and southeast of Seattle; the Mount Baker section lies east on Highway 542 and includes the Mount Baker Ski Area. The forest extends from the Canadian border south to Mount Rainier National Park and includes rugged mountains and woodlands on the western slopes of the Cascades, the western portions of the Glacier Peak and Alpine Lakes, Henry M. Jackson, Noisy-Diobsud, Boulder River, Jackson, Clearwater, and Norse Peak wildernesses; seven commercial ski areas; 1,440 miles of hiking trails; and picnic areas and campsites. Mount Baker rises 10,778 feet in the north, forming a center for recreation all year, famous for deep-powder snow skiing and snowboarding. Snoqualmie Pass (via I-90) and Stevens Pass (via Hwy 2) provide year-round access to popular scenic destinations; Baker Lake provides excellent boating and fishing. East of the forest is

> **North Cascades National Park.** *www.nps.gov/noca/.* (See SEDRO WOOLLEY)

Western Washington University. *516 High St, Bellingham (98225). Phone 360/650-3963.* (1893) (11,500 students) A 189-acre campus; internationally acclaimed outdoor sculpture collection; contemporary art at Western Gallery.

Whatcom Museum of History and Art. *121 Prospect St, Bellingham (98225). Phone 360/676-6981.* Regional and historic displays; also changing art exhibits; in former city hall (1892) and three adjacent buildings. Fee for special exhibitions. (Tues-Sun; closed holidays) **FREE**

Special Events

Deming Logging Show. *3295 Cedarville Rd, Bellingham (98226). Phone 360/592-2423. Log show grounds, in Deming.* Log chopping, tree climbing, logger rodeo, salmon barbecue. Second weekend in June.

Lummi Stommish. *Lummi Reservation, 15 miles NW via I-5, exit 260 to Hwy 540, Bellingham. Phone 360/384-1489.* Water carnival with war canoe races, arts and crafts; salmon bake, Native American dancing. June.

Ski to Sea Festival. *1435 Railroad Ave, Bellingham (98225). Phone 360/734-1330.* Parades, carnival, art show, special events. Ski to Sea race starts on Mt. Baker, ends in Bellingham Bay and involves skiers, runners, canoeists, bicyclists, and kayakers. Memorial Day weekend.

Limited-Service Hotels

★ ★ **BEST WESTERN HERITAGE INN.** *151 E Mcleod Rd, Bellingham (98226). Phone 360/647-1912; toll-free 800/780-7234; fax 360/671-3878. www.bestwestern.com.* 90 rooms, 3 story. Complimentary continental breakfast. Check-out noon. Restaurant. Pool, whirlpool. Airport transportation available. **$**

★ ★ **BEST WESTERN LAKEWAY INN.** *714 Lakeway Dr, Bellingham (98226). Phone 360/671-1011; toll-free 888/671-1011; fax 360/676-8519. www.bellingham-hotel.com.* Just off I-5 at the south end of Bellingham, the Best Western Lakeway Inn is a great base from which to explore this lovely area. Golf and ski packages are available. It's also a nice place to host a meeting, with ample meeting space, a grand ballroom, and a 24-hour business center. Restaurants and shops are nearby, although you'll need to drive to the city's historic Fairhaven District. 132 rooms, 4 story. Pets accepted, some restrictions; fee. Check-in 3 pm, check-out noon. Two restaurants, bar. Fitness room. Indoor pool, whirlpool. Business center. **$**

★ **HAMPTON INN BELLINGHAM AIRPORT.** *3985 Bennett Dr, Bellingham (98225). Phone 360/676-7700; toll-free 800/426-7866; fax 360/671-7557. www.hamptoninn.com.* If you need to stay near the airport, this is your best option. This well-maintained hotel has a nice pool area and a sunken atrium dining room, where breakfast is served each morning. 132 rooms, 4 story. Complimentary full breakfast. Check-in 3 pm, check-out noon. Fitness room. Outdoor pool. **$**

★ **QUALITY INN.** *100 E Kellogg Rd, Bellingham (98226). Phone 360/647-8000; toll-free 800/900-4661; fax 360/647-8094. www.qualityinn.com.* 85 rooms, 3 story. Pets accepted; fee. Complimentary continental breakfast. Check-in 3 pm, check-out noon. Fitness room. Outdoor pool, whirlpool. **$**

Full-Service Hotel

★ ★ ★ **HOTEL BELLWETHER.** *One Bellwether Way, Bellingham (98225). Phone 360/392-3100; toll-free 877/411-1200; fax 360/392-3101. www.hotelbellwether.com.* 68 rooms. Pets accepted; fee. Check-in 3 pm, check-out noon. High-speed Internet access. Restaurant, bar. Fitness room. Airport transportation available. Business center. **$$**

Full-Service Inn

★ ★ ★ **THE CHRYSALIS INN & SPA.** *804 10th St, Bellingham (98225). Phone 360/756-1005; toll-free 888/808-0005. www.thechrysalisinn.com.* 43 rooms. Check-in 3 pm, check-out noon. Restaurant, bar. **$$**

Specialty Lodging

The following lodging establishment is approved by Mobil Travel Guide, but due to its unique and individualized nature has not been given a traditional Mobil Star rating. Included in this listing you may find bed-and-breakfasts, limited-service inns, guest ranches, and other unique hotel properties.

FAIRHAVEN VILLAGE INN. *1200 10th St, Bellingham (98225). Phone toll-free 877/733-1100. www.fairhavenvillageinn.com.* 22 rooms. Complimentary continental breakfast. Check-in 3 pm, check-out noon. High-speed Internet access. Business center. **$$**

Restaurants

★ ★ **CHUCKANUT MANOR.** *3056 Chuckanut Dr, Bow (98232). Phone 360/766-6191. www.chuckanutmanor.com.* Seafood, steak menu. Lunch, dinner, Sun brunch. Closed Mon. Bar. Children's menu. Valet parking. **$$**

★ ★ **MARINA.** *7 Bellwetherway, Bellingham (98225). Phone 360/733-8292.* American menu. Lunch, dinner. Closed Dec 25. Bar. Children's menu. Outdoor seating. **$$**

Blaine (A-2)

See also Bellingham

Population 3,770
Elevation 41 ft
Area Code 360
Zip 98231
Information Visitor Information Center, 215 Marine Dr, PO Box 4680; phone 360/332-4544 or toll-free 800/487-2032
Web site www.blaine.net

Blaine sits just south of the Canadian border on I-5.

What to See and Do

Birch Bay State Park. *5105 Helwig Rd, Blaine (98230). 10 miles SW via I-5, exit 266, then 7 miles W via Grandview Rd, N via Jackson Rd to Helwig Rd. Phone 360/371-2800.* Approximately 190 acres. Swimming, scuba diving, fishing, crabbing, clamming, picnicking, camping; (hookups; dump station) (Daily, reservations advised Memorial Day-Labor Day).

International Peace Arch. *N at point where I-5 reaches Canadian border.* (1921) The 67-foot-high arch is on the boundary line between the US and Canada and marks more than a century of peace and friendship between the two countries. The surrounding park is maintained by the state of Washington and Province of British Columbia; gardens, picnicking, playground.

Semiahmoo Park. *9565 Semiahmoo Pkwy, Blaine (98230). Off I-5, exit 274, on Semiahmoo Sandspit, Drayton Harbor. Phone 360/371-2000.* A cannery once located on this 1 1/2-mile-long spit was the last port of call for Alaskan fishing boats on Puget Sound. Restored buildings now house museum, gallery, and gift shop (June-mid-Sept, Sat and Sun afternoons). Park (daily) offers clam digging, picnicking, bird watching. **$$**

Special Event

Peace Arch Celebration. *International Peace Arch, I-5 exit 276, Anacortes (98230). Phone 360/332-4544.* Ceremony celebrates the relationship between the US and Canada; scouts and veterans from both nations. Second Sun in June.

Full-Service Resort

★ ★ ★ **RESORT SEMIAHMOO.** *9565 Semiahmoo Pkwy, Blaine (98230). Phone 360/318-2000; toll-free 800/770-7992; fax 360/318-2087. www. semiahmoo.com.* Spellbinding views are the calling card of Resort Semiahmoo. This cottage-style resort, located on a wildlife preserve at the tip of a peninsula stretching into Puget Sound, enjoys one of the most scenic spots in the state. Wherever the eye looks, views of snow-capped peaks, the Gulf Islands, Drayton Harbor, or Semiahmoo Bay captivate and enchant. Blond woods and clean lines create an uncluttered look throughout the resort, while fireplaces, patios, and balconies enhance the exceedingly comfortable guest rooms and suites. Relaxation is the order of the day here, where golf, water activities, and a terrific spa compete for attention. Dining is especially memorable, with creative and artfully presented cuisine tempting even the most demanding taste buds. 261 rooms, 4 story. Pets accepted, some restrictions; fee. Check-in 3 pm, check-out noon. Restaurant, bar. Fitness room, spa. Indoor pool, outdoor pool, whirlpool. Golf. Tennis. **$**

Bow

What to See and Do

Skagit Valley Casino Resort. *5984 N Darrk Ln, Bow (98232). Phone 360/724-7777. www.svcasinoresort.com.* Positioned midway between Seattle and Vancouver, British Columbia, the Skagit Valley Casino Resort is swank and full of facilities. Beyond the casino (with 600 machines and numerous tables), there are 103 hotel rooms, a pool, and three restaurants (a fine dining room, a buffet, and a deli). The entertainment is varied, with country stars, dance troupes, and tribute acts among the performers gracing the Pacific Showroom's stage. (Daily)

Bremerton (B-2)

See also Seattle, Union

Founded 1891
Population 37,259
Elevation 60 ft
Information Bremerton Chamber of Commerce, 301 Pacific Ave, Port Gamble, 98364; phone 360/479-3579
Web site www.bremertonwa.com

The tempo of the Puget Sound Naval Shipyard is the heartbeat of Bremerton, a community surrounded on three sides by water. The six dry docks of the Naval Shipyard make Bremerton a home port for the Pacific fleet.

What to See and Do

Belfair. *3151 NE Hwy 300, Belfair (98529). 15 miles SW via Hwy 3. Phone 360/275-0668.* Approximately 80 acres. Swimming; picnicking, camping (hookups). (Reservations Memorial Day-Labor Day, by mail only).

Blake Island. *6 miles SE, accessible only by boat. Phone 360/731-8330.* More than 475 acres. Saltwater swimming beach, scuba diving, fishing, boating (dock); hiking, picnicking, primitive camping.

Bremerton Naval Museum. *130 Washington Ave, Bremerton (98337). Phone 360/479-7447.* Ship models, pictures, display of navy and shipyard history. Naval artifacts. (Tues-Sun; closed holidays) **FREE**

Illahee. *3 miles NE off Hwy 306. Phone 360/478-6460.* Approximately 75 acres. Swimming, scuba diving; fishing, clamming; boating (ramp, dock). Hiking. Picnicking. Primitive camping.

Kitsap County Historical Society Museum. *280 4th St, Bremerton (98337). Phone 360/692-1949.* Re-creation of 1800s pioneer settlements. Photos and documents of history to World War II era. (Tues-Sat; closed holidays) **$**

Scenic Beach. *12 miles NW on Hwy 3. Phone 360/830-5079.* Approximately 90 acres. Swimming, scuba diving; limited fishing, oysters in season. Nature trail. Picnicking. Primitive camping.

USS *Turner Joy.* *300 Washington Beach Ave, Bremerton (98337). Phone 360/792-2457.* Tours of Vietnam War-era US Navy destroyer. (May-Sept: daily; rest of year: Mon, Thurs-Sun; closed Dec 25)

Special Events

Armed Forces Day Parade. *301 Pacific, Bremerton (98337). Phone 360/479-3579.* Mid-May.

Blackberry Festival. *2nd and Washington, Bremerton (98337). Phone 360/479-3579.* Late Aug.

Kitsap County Fair and Stampede. *Fairgrounds in Tracyton, 1200 Fairgrounds Rd, Bremerton (98311). Phone 360/337-5376.* Late Aug.

Mountaineers' Forest Theater. *Phone 206/284-6310. 8 miles W via Hwy 3, Kitsap Way, Seabeck Hwy, watch for signs.* Oldest outdoor theater in the Pacific Northwest. Natural amphitheater surrounded by hundreds of rhododendrons beneath old-growth Douglas fir and hemlock. Log terraced seats. Family-oriented plays. The 1/3-mile walk to the theater is difficult for the physically disabled or elderly (assistance available). Picnicking; concession. Contact 300 Third Ave W, Seattle 98119. Late May-early June.

Limited-Service Hotels

★ **BEST WESTERN BREMERTON INN.** *4303 Kitsap Way, Bremerton (98312). Phone 360/405-1111; toll-free 800/780-7234; fax 360/377-0597. www. bestwestern.com.* 103 rooms, 3 story. Complimentary continental breakfast. Check-out 11 am. Fitness room. Pool, whirlpool. **$**

🚶 ☕

★ ★ **RED LION.** *3073 NW Bucklin Hill Rd, Silverdale (98383). Phone 360/698-1000; fax 360/682-0932. www.redlion.com.* 150 rooms, 3 story. Check-out noon. Restaurant, bar. Fitness room. Indoor pool, whirlpool. Tennis. **$**

🚶 ☕ 🎿

Restaurants

★ ★ **BOAT SHED.** *101 Shore Dr, Bremerton (98310). Phone 360/377-2600; fax 360/377-1345.* American menu. Lunch, dinner. Closed Jan 1, Thanksgiving, Dec. 25, outdoor seating. **$$**

★ ★ **YACHT CLUB BROILER.** *9226 Bay Shore Dr, Silverdale (98383). Phone 360/698-1601; fax 360/ 692-1348.* Seafood, steak menu. Breakfast, lunch, dinner, Sun brunch. Bar. Children's menu. Valet parking. Outdoor seating. **$$$**

Cashmere (B-4)

See also Leavenworth, Wenatchee

Founded 1881
Population 2,965
Elevation 853 ft
Area Code 509
Zip 98815
Information Chamber of Commerce, PO Box 834; phone 509/782-7404
Web site www.visitcashmere.com

Cashmere's history dates to the 1860s, when a Catholic missionary came to the area to set up a school for Native Americans. The town is located in the Wenatchee Valley in the center of the state on the North Cascade Loop. It has strong timber and fruit industries.

What to See and Do

Cashmere Museum. *600 Cotlets Way, Cashmere (98815). E edge of town. Phone 509/782-3230. www. cashmeremuseum.com.* Pioneer relics, Native American artifacts; Columbia River archaeology exhibit; water wheel (1891); mineral exhibit; "pioneer village" with 21 cabins, mining displays. Great Northern Railroad depot, passenger car and caboose. (Mar-Nov: daily; rest of year: by appointment) **$$**

Liberty Orchards Company, Inc. *117 Mission St, Cashmere (98815). Off Hwy 2. Phone 509/782-2191.* Makes fruit-nut confections known as "aplets," "cotlets," "grapelets," and "fruit festives." Tour, samples. (May-Dec: daily; rest of year: Mon-Fri; closed holidays) Children with adult only.

Special Events

Apple Days. *Chelan County Historical Museum, 600 Cotlets Way, Cashmere (98815). Phone 509/782-3230.* Apple pie contest, old-time crafts, Pioneer Village in operation, cider making. First weekend in Oct.

Chelan County Fair. *5700 Westcott Dr, Cashmere (98815). Phone 509/782-0708.* First weekend after Labor Day.

Founders' Day. *Chelan County Historical Museum, 600 Cotlets Way, Cashmere (98815). Phone 509/782-3230.* Last weekend in June.

Centralia (C-2)

See also Chehalis, Olympia

Founded 1875
Population 14,742
Elevation 189 ft
Area Code 360
Zip 98531
Information The Centralia, Chehalis, and Greater Lewis County Chamber of Commerce, 500 NW Chamber of Commerce Way, Chehalis 98532; phone 360/748-8885 or toll-free 800/525-3323
Web site www.chamberway.com

Centralia was founded by a former slave named George Washington. The town's George Washington Park is named for the founder, not for the country's first president.

What to See and Do

Schaefer County Park. *822 Hwy 507, Centralia (98531). 1/2 mile N on Hwy 507. Phone 360/740-1135.* Swimming in the Skookumchuck River; fishing; hiking trails, picnicking (shelter), playground, horseshoe pits, volleyball. **FREE**

Special Event

Southwest Washington Fair. *2555 N National Ave, Chehalis (98532). 1 mile S on I-5. Phone 360/736-6072.* First held in 1909, this is the state's second-oldest fair and one of the largest. Third week in Aug.

Limited-Service Hotel

★ **HOLIDAY INN EXPRESS.** *1233 Alder St, Centralia (98531). Phone 360/330-9441; toll-free 800/ 465-4329; fax 360/330-1467. www.holiday-inn.com.* 75 rooms. Complimentary continental breakfast. Check-in 3 pm, check-out noon. Indoor pool, whirlpool. **$**

Chehalis (C-2)

See also Centralia, Longview

Settled 1873
Population 7,057
Elevation 226 ft
Area Code 360
Zip 98532
Information The Centralia, Chehalis, and Greater Lewis County Chamber of Commerce, 500 NW Chamber of Commerce Way; phone 360/748-8885 or toll-free 800/525-3323
Web site www.chamberway.com

First called Saundersville, this city takes its present name, Native American for "shifting sands," from its position at the point where the Newaukum and Chehalis rivers meet. Farms and an industrial park give economic sustenance to Chehalis and neighboring Centralia (see).

What to See and Do

Historic Claquato Church. *125 Water St, Chehalis (98532). 3 miles W on Hwy 6, on Claquato Hill. Phone 360/748-4551.* (1858) Oldest church in state, original building on original site; handmade pews, pulpit. (Schedule varies)

Lewis County Historical Museum. *599 NW Front Way, Chehalis (98532). Phone 360/748-0831.* Restored railroad depot (1912). Pioneer displays; Native American exhibits. Cemetery, genealogical history; artifacts, newspapers, books, photographs, written family histories, oral histories of pioneers. (Tues-Sun; closed holidays) **$**

Rainbow Falls State Park. *18 miles W on Hwy 6. Phone 360/291-3767.* Approximately 125 acres of woodland. Fishing; hiking trails, picnicking, camping (dump station).

Special Event

Music and Art Festival. *Phone 360/748-8885.* Arts and craft vendors, food. Late July.

Restaurant

★ **MARY MC CRANK'S DINNER HOUSE.** *2923 Jackson Hwy, Chehalis (98532). Phone 360/748-*

3662; fax 360/740-9222. www.marymccranks.com. American menu. Lunch, dinner. Closed Mon. Children's menu. **$$**

Chelan (B-4)

See also Wenatchee

Settled 1885
Population 3,552
Elevation 1,208 ft
Area Code 509
Zip 98816
Information Lake Chelan Chamber of Commerce, 102 E Johnson; phone 509/682-3503 or toll-free 800/424-3526
Web site www.lakechelan.com

Located in an apple-growing region, Chelan is a gateway to Lake Chelan and the spectacular northern Cascade Mountains. A Ranger District office of the Wenatchee National Forest is located here.

What to See and Do

Alta Lake. *191 Alta Lake Rd, Chelan (98846). 20 miles N on Hwy 97, then 2 miles W on Hwy 153. Phone 509/923-2473.* More than 180 acres. Swimming, fishing, boating (ramps); hiking, snowmobiling, ice skating, camping (hookups).

Lake Chelan. *Phone 360/902-8844.* This fjordlike lake, the largest and deepest in the state, stretches northwest for approximately 55 miles through the Cascade Mountains to the community of Stehekin in the North Cascades National Park; the lake is nearly 1,500 feet deep in some areas. There are two state parks and several recreation areas along the lake.

Lake cruises. *1418 W Woodin Ave, Chelan (98816). Phone 509/682-4584; toll-free 888/424-3526. www.ladyofthelake.com.* The passenger boats *Lady of the Lake II* and *Lady Express* and the *High-Speed Lady Cat* make daily cruises on Lake Chelan to Stehekin, Holden Village, and North Cascades National Park. (Call or visit Web site for schedule) **$$$$**

Lake Chelan State Park. *7544 S Lakeshore Dr, Chelan (98816). 9 1/2 miles W via Hwy 97 and South Shore Dr or Navarre Coulee Rd. Phone toll-free 800/452-5687.* Approximately 130 lakefront acres. Swimming, fishing, boating (ramps, dock); picnicking, camping (hookups; reservations required late May-Aug). (Apr-Oct: daily; rest of year: weekends and holidays)

Twenty-Five Mile Creek. *20530 S Lakeshore, Chelan (20530). 18 miles NW on S Shore Dr. Phone toll-free 800/452-5687.* Approximately 65 acres. Fishing, boating (launch, mooring, gas); hiking, concession, camping (hookups).

Special Events

Apple Blossom Festival. *516 Washington St, Chelan (98801). Phone 509/687-3071. 8 miles W via Hwy 150 in Manson.* Second weekend in May.

Lake Chelan Rodeo. *5700 Wescott Dr, Chelan (98815). Phone 509/682-5526.* Last weekend in July.

Taste of Chelan Street Fair. *Phone 509/682-9384.* Late June.

Limited-Service Hotels

★ **BEST WESTERN LAKESIDE LODGE AND SUITES.** *2312 W Woodin Ave, Chelan (98816). Phone 509/682-4396; toll-free 800/468-2781; fax 509/682-3278. www.lakesidelodge.net.* Although the in-season rates can be high for a limited-service hotel, this is the place to stay in Chelan. With a private beach and boat dock, accessing lovely Lake Chelan is easy, and the heated outdoor pool has a truly majestic view. Small pets are allowed, but access is very restricted, so call ahead for details if you plan to bring your pet along. 67 rooms. Pets accepted, some restrictions; fee. Complimentary continental breakfast. Check-in 3 pm, check-out 11 am. Indoor pool, outdoor pool, whirlpool. **$**

★ ★ **CAMPBELL'S RESORT AND CONFERENCE CENTER.** *104 W Woodin Ave, Chelan (98816). Phone 509/682-2561; toll-free 800/553-8225; fax 509/682-2177. www.campbellsresort.com.* Lovely Lake Chelan is the centerpiece at this 8-acre resort in central Washington, where families and groups come to work and play. Every guest room is on the water, and private balconies enable guests to enjoy the stunning views of the Cascades looming beyond the lake. Summer brings all kinds of activities, from drawing and fishing classes to outdoor barbecues to magicians and jugglers on weekend evenings. The resort's meeting facilities can accommodate groups of up to 325 people, making this a popular spot for weddings and business meetings. 170 rooms, 4 story. Check-in 3 pm, check-out 11 am. High-speed Internet access. Two restaurants, bar. Fitness room, spa. Two outdoor pools, two whirlpools. Business center. **$$**

Cheney (B-6)

See also Spokane

Population 8,832
Elevation 2,350 ft
Area Code 509
Zip 99004
Information Chamber of Commerce, 201 First St; phone 509/235-8480
Web site www.westplainschamber.org

Cheney, on a rise of land that gives it one of the highest elevations of any municipality in the state, has been a university town since 1882. It is also a farm distribution and servicing center.

What to See and Do

Cheney Historical Museum. *614 3rd St, Cheney (99004). Phone 509/235-4343.* Features pioneer artifacts. (Mar-Nov, Tues and Sat afternoons) **FREE**

Eastern Washington University. *Phone 509/359-2397.* (1882) (9,000 students) Tours of campus. On campus are a theater, recital hall, and

Gallery of Art. *526 Fifth St, Cheney (99004). Phone 509/359-2493.* Changing exhibits. (Academic year, Mon-Fri; closed holidays) **FREE**

Museum of Anthropology. *Phone 509/359-2433.* Teaching-research facility concerning Native Americans of North America. **FREE**

Turnbull National Wildlife Refuge. *4 miles S on Cheney-Plaza Rd, then 2 miles E. Phone 509/235-4723.* Located on the Pacific Flyway; more than 200 species of birds have been observed in the area; also a habitat for deer, elk, coyotes, beaver, mink, chipmunks, red squirrels, and Columbia ground squirrels. Refuge named after Cyrus Turnbull, an early settler. A 2,200-acre public use area (daily).

Special Event

Rodeo Days. *Phone 509/235-4848.* Rodeo, parade. Second weekend in July.

Clarkston (D-6)

See also Pullman; also see Lewiston, ID

Founded 1896
Population 7,337
Elevation 736 ft
Area Code 509
Zip 99403
Information Chamber of Commerce, 502 Bridge St; phone 509/758-7712 or toll-free 800/933-2128
Web site www.clarkstonchamber.org

Clarkston is located on the Washington-Idaho boundary at the confluence of the Clearwater and Snake rivers. The town became a shipping center when the construction of four dams on the lower Snake River brought barge transportation here. Many recreation areas are located near Clarkston, especially along the Snake River and in the Umatilla National Forest. River trips are available into Hell's Canyon.

What to See and Do

Asotin County Museum. *215 Filmore St, Asotin (99402). Approximately 6 miles S on Hwy 129. Phone 509/243-4659.* Main museum contains sculptures, pioneer equiptment, pictures, and clothing. On the grounds are a furnished pioneer house, shepherd's cabin, one-room schoolhouse, 1882 log cabin, blacksmith shop, a windmill, and Salmon River barge. (Tues-Sat; closed holidays) **FREE**

Fields Spring State Park. *30 miles S on Hwy 129. Phone 509/256-3332.* Approximately 800 forested acres in the Blue Mountains. A 1-mile uphill hike from parking lot to Puffer Butte gives view of three states. Wide variety of wildflowers and birdlife. Picnicking, primitive camping.

Petroglyphs. *Phone toll-free 800/933-2128.* Ancient writings inscribed in cliffs of Snake River near Buffalo Eddy. Near town of Asotin.

Umatilla National Forest. *S of Hwy 12, access near Pomeroy. Phone 503/276-3811. www.fs.fed.us/r6/uma.* Approximately 319,000 acres of heavily forested mountain area extending into Oregon. Many recreation areas offer fishing, hunting, hiking, camping, and downhill skiing. For further information, contact the Supervisor, 2517 SW Hailey Ave, Pendleton, OR 97801.

Valley Art Center. *842 6th St, Clarkston (99403).* *Phone 509/758-8331.* Various types of art and crafts; changing monthly exhibits with featured artists and special showings. (Mon-Fri, closed holidays) Northwest Heritage Show is held for two months in summer. **FREE**

Special Events

Asotin County Fair. *Phone 509/758-7712.* Includes cowboy breakfast, barbecue, parade. Last Thurs-Sun in Apr.

Sunflower Days. *Phone 509/758-7712.* Second Fri-Sat in Aug.

Limited-Service Hotels

★ **BEST WESTERN RIVERTREE INN.** *1257 Bridge St, Clarkston (99403). Phone 509/758-9551; toll-free 800/597-3621; fax 509/758-9551. www.bestwestern .com.* Many rooms with spiral staircase to loft. 61 rooms, 2 story. Check-out noon. Fitness room. Pool, whirlpool. **$**

★ ★ **QUALITY INN.** *700 Port Dr, Clarkston (99403). Phone 509/758-9500; fax 509/758-5580. www. qualityinn.com.* 75 rooms, 3 story. Check-out noon. Restaurant, bar. Fitness room. Pool. **$**

Restaurant

★ **ROOSTER'S LANDING.** *1550 Port Dr, Clarkston (99403). Phone 509/751-0155; fax 509/751-8706. www.roosterslanding.com.* American menu. Lunch, dinner. Bar. Children's menu. Outdoor seating. **$$**

Colville (A-6)

See also Spokane

Population 4,988
Elevation 1,635 ft
Area Code 509
Zip 99114
Information Chamber of Commerce, 121 E Astor; phone 509/684-5973
Web site www.colville.com

Once a brawling frontier town, Colville, the seat of Stevens County, has quieted down and now reflects the peacefulness of the surrounding hills and mountains. Many towns flourished and died in this area—orchards, mills, and mines all had their day. The portage at Kettle Falls, a fort, and the crossing of several trails made Colville a thriving center.

What to See and Do

Colville National Forest. *765 S Main St, Colville (99114). Phone 509/684-7000.* This million-acre forest is located in the northeast corner of Washington, bordering Canada. The forest extends along its western boundary from the Canadian border south to the Colville Reservation and east across the Columbia River to Idaho. Comprising conifer forest types, small lakes, and winding valleys bounded by slopes leading to higher mountainous areas, the forest offers good hunting and fishing and full-service camping. Also here is Sullivan Lake, offering such recreational opportunities as boating, fishing, swimming, and hiking trails, and developed and dispersed campground settings. The bighorn sheep that inhabit adjacent Hall Mountain can be viewed at a feeding station near the lake, which is cooperatively managed by the forest and the Washington Department of Wildlife. Also located here are a Ranger District office and

> **Lake Gillette Recreation Area.** *2430 Hwy 20 E, Colville (99114). E via Tiger Hwy (Hwy 20). Phone 509/684-5657.* Boating, swimming, fishing; picnicking, amphitheater with programs, camping (fee). (Mid-May-Sept) **FREE**

Keller Heritage Center. *700 N Wynne St, Colville (99114). Phone 509/684-5968.* Site of three-story Keller home (1910), carriage house; blacksmith shop; farmstead cabin; gardens; museum; schoolhouse; machinery building; lookout tower. Local records, Native American artifacts. (May-Sept; daily) **DONATION**

St. Paul's Mission. *12 miles NW, near intersection of Columbia River and Hwy 395. Phone 509/738-6266.* A chapel was built by Jesuit Priests assisted by Native Americans near here in 1845, followed by the hand-hewn log church in 1847. It fell into disuse in the 1870s and in 1939 was restored to its original state. Self-guided tour. Located at Kettle Falls in Lake Roosevelt National Recreation Area. (All year)

Special Events

Colville PRCA Rodeo. *Phone 509/684-4849.* Father's Day weekend.

Northeast Washington Fair. *Stevens County Fairgrounds, Colville. Phone 509/684-2585.* Parade, livestock and horse shows; arts and crafts exhibits; carnival. Aug.

Rendezvous. *Phone 509/684-5973.* Arts and crafts, entertainment. First weekend in Aug.

Coulee Dam

See also Soap Lake

Founded 1934
Population 1,044
Elevation 1,145 ft
Area Code 509
Zip 99116
Information Grand Coulee Dam Area Chamber of Commerce, 306 Midway Ave, PO Box 760, Grand Coulee, 99133-0760; phone 509/633-3074 or toll-free 800/268-5332
Web site www.grandcouleedam.org

Established as a construction community for workers on the Grand Coulee Dam project, this town is now the home of service and maintenance employees of the dam and the headquarters for the Lake Roosevelt National Recreation Area.

What to See and Do

Colville Tribal Museum. *512 Mead Way, Coulee Dam (99116). Phone 509/633-0751.* More than 8,000 years of history on 11 tribes. (Late May-Sept: daily; rest of year: schedule varies) **FREE**

★ **Grand Coulee Dam.** *306 Midway Ave, Grand Coulee (99116). Near jct Hwy 155, 174. Phone 509/633-3838.* Major structure of multipurpose Columbia Basin Project, built by Bureau of Reclamation. Water is diverted from the Columbia River to what in prehistoric days was its temporary course down the Grand Coulee (a deep water-carved ravine). The project will reclaim more than a million acres through irrigation and already provides a vast reservoir of electric power.

One of the largest concrete structures in the world, the dam towers 550 feet high, has a 500-foot-wide base and a 5,223-foot-long crest. Power plants contain some of world's largest hydro-generators. **FREE**

Lake Roosevelt National Recreation Area. *1008 Crest Dr, Coulee Dam (99116). Phone 509/633-9441. www.nps.gov/laro.* Totals 100,059 acres, including Franklin D. Roosevelt Lake. The lake, formed by the Grand Coulee Dam, serves as a storage reservoir with a 630-mile shoreline and extends 151 miles northeast, reaching the Canadian border. The southern part is semi-arid; the northern part is mountainous, forested with ponderosa pine, fir, and tamarack. Excellent for all sizes of motorboats with a 151-mile waterway along the reservoir and 200 miles of cruising water in Canada provided by Arrow Lakes, reached from Lake Roosevelt by the Columbia River. Thirty-eight areas have been specially developed; most provide camping (fee), picnicking; swimming, boating and launching sites (fee). Visitors can fish all year in Roosevelt Lake. Within the area is

Fort Spokane. *Phone 509/725-2715.* One of the last frontier military outposts of the 1800s. Four of 45 buildings remain; brick guardhouse is now a visitor center and small museum. Built to maintain peace between the settlers and Native Americans; no shot was ever fired. Self-guided trail around old parade grounds; interpretive displays. (Mid-June-Labor Day; daily) Living history programs performed on weekends in summer. Nearby are beach and camping (fee).

Steamboat Rock State Park. *11 miles S of Electric City on Hwy 155. Phone 509/633-1304; toll-free 800/452-5687 (reservations).* Approximately 900 acres. Swimming, fishing, boating (launch); hiking, picnicking, camping (hookups; reservations recommended Memorial Day-Labor Day weekends).

Special Events

Colorama Festival & PWRA Rodeo. *306 Midway Ave, Coulee Dam (99133). Phone toll-free 800/268-5332.* Second weekend in May.

Laser Light Festival. *Phone toll-free 800/268-5332.* Memorial Day weekend.

Limited-Service Hotel

★ **COLUMBIA RIVER INN.** *10 Lincoln Ave, Coulee Dam (99116). Phone 509/633-2100; toll-free 800/633-6421. www.columbiariverinn.com.* View of dam. 34 rooms, 2 story. Check-out 11 am. Pool, whirlpool. **$**
🅿 ⊠

Coupeville

See also Anacortes, Oak Harbor, Port Townsend

Population 1,723
Elevation 80 ft
Area Code 360
Zip 98239
Information Visitor Information Center, 107 S Main St; phone 360/678-5434

One of the oldest towns in the state, Coupeville was named for Thomas Coupe, a sea captain and early settler, the only man ever to sail a full-rigged ship through Deception Pass. Fortified to protect the settlers and for the defense of Puget Sound, Coupeville was once the home of the only seat of higher education north of Seattle, the Puget Sound Academy. Today it is near Whidbey Island Naval Air Station, home of naval aviation for the Pacific Northwest.

What to See and Do

Alexander Blockhouse. *Near Front St, on waterfront. Phone 360/678-5434.* (1855) One of four such buildings built on Whidbey Island to protect settlers' homes from Native Americans during the White River Massacre.

Fort Casey State Park. *3 miles S. Phone 360/678-4519.* Approximately 140 acres. Scuba diving, saltwater fishing, boating (launch); picnicking, camping. Museum (early May-mid-Sept).

Full-Service Inn

★ ★ ★ **INN AT LANGLEY.** *400 First St, Langley (98260). Phone 360/221-3033; fax 360/221-3033. www. innatlangley.com.* A tranquil retreat awaits guests at this exquisitely designed inn. Guest rooms are luxurious with water views, an outdoor porch, and an oversized whirlpool jet tub. 24 rooms, 4 story. Children over 12 years only. Complimentary continental breakfast. Check-in 3 pm, check-out noon. Restaurant. **$$**

Specialty Lodgings

The following lodging establishments are approved by Mobil Travel Guide, but due to their unique and individualized nature have not been given a traditional Mobil Star rating. Included in this listing you may find bed-and-breakfasts, limited-service inns, guest ranches, and other unique hotel properties.

CAPTAIN WHIDBEY INN. *2072 W Captain Whidbey Inn Rd, Coupeville (98239). Phone 360/678-4097; toll-free 800/366-4097. www.captainwhidbey.com.* This turn-of-the-century log inn (1907) is situated on a sheltered cove. 32 rooms. Complimentary full breakfast. Check-in 4 pm, check-out noon. Bar. **$**

GUEST HOUSE BED & BREAKFAST COTTAGES. *24371 Hwy 525, Greenbank (98253). Phone 360/678-3115. www.guesthouselogcottages.com.* This inn is located on 25 acres of forest and features a scenic wildlife pond and marine and mountain views. 6 rooms, 2 story. No children allowed. Complimentary full breakfast. Check-in 4 pm, check-out 11 am. Fitness room. Outdoor pool. **$$**
🅿 🧍 ⊠

Dayton (D-6)

See also Walla Walla

Settled 1859
Population 2,655
Elevation 1,613 ft
Area Code 509
Zip 99328
Information Chamber of Commerce, 166 E Main St; phone 509/382-4825 or toll-free 800/882-6299
Web site www.historicdayton.com

Once an important stagecoach depot and stopping-off place for miners, Dayton is now the center of a farm area in which sheep, cattle, wheat, apples, peas, asparagus, and hay are raised. Little Goose Lock and Dam, a multipurpose federal project and one of four such developments on the Snake River, is about 35 miles north of town. Vegetable canning and lumbering are key local industries.

Dayton has many historic homes and buildings, including the Columbia County Courthouse (1886), the oldest courthouse in the state, which is still used for county government; and the Dayton Historic Depot (the oldest in the state).

What to See and Do

Kendall Skyline Drive. *South of town.* Scenic route through the Blue Mountains and Umatilla National Forest. Usually open by July. Contact Chamber of Commerce for details.

Lewis and Clark Trail State Park. *36149 Hwy 12, Dayton (Columbia Co) (99328). 5 miles SW on Hwy 12.* Phone 509/337-6457. Approximately 40 acres. Swimming, fishing; hiking, picnicking, camping.

Palouse River Canyon. *18 miles N on Hwy 12, then 22 miles NW on unnumbered roads.* Deeply eroded gorge pierces wheatlands of region; cliffs rise hundreds of feet above river. At Palouse Falls, river roars over 198-foot cliff into deep ravine of basaltic rock, continues south to join Snake River. Nearby are Lyons Ferry and Palouse Falls state parks.

Ski Bluewood. *262 E Main, Dayton (99328). 22 miles S via 4th St (North Touchet Rd), in Umatilla National Forest.* Phone 509/382-4725. www.bluewood.com. Two triple chairlifts, platter pull, half pipe; patrol, school, rentals; cafeteria, bar. Longest run 2 1/4 miles; vertical drop 1,125 feet. Snowboarding. Half-day rates. (Jan-Feb: daily; mid-Nov-Dec and Feb-Apr: Tues-Sun) **$$$$**

Special Events

Columbia County Fair. *Dayton Fairgrounds, Dayton.* Phone toll-free 800/882-6299. Second weekend in Sept.

Dayton Depot Festival. *222 E Commercial St, Dayton (Columbia Co) (99328).* Phone 509/382-2026. Third weekend in July.

Ellensburg (C-4)

See also Quincy, Yakima

Settled 1867
Population 12,361
Elevation 1,508 ft
Area Code 509
Zip 98926
Information Chamber of Commerce, 609 N Main; phone 509/925-3137 or toll-free 888/925-2204
Web site www.ellensburg-wa.com

Although this community has long abandoned its first name, Robber's Roost, it cherishes the tradition and style of the West, both as a center for dude ranches and as the scene of one of the country's best annual rodeos. At the geographic center of the state, Ellensburg processes beef and dairy products. The county ranges from lakes and crags in the west through irrigated farmlands to sagebrush prairie along the Columbia River to the east.

A Ranger District office of the Wenatchee National Forest is located here.

What to See and Do

Central Washington University. *262 E Main, Dayton (Columbia Co) (99328). 8th Ave and Walnut St.* Phone 509/963-1111. www.cwu.edu. (1890) (7,000 students) Liberal arts and sciences, business, technology, education.

  CWU Library. *14th Ave and D St, Ellensburg (98926).* Phone 509/963-1777. Regional depository for federal documents; collection of microforms, maps, general materials. (Daily) **FREE**

  Sarah Spurgeon Art Gallery. *400 E 8th Ave, Ellensburg (98926). In Randall Hall.* Phone 509/963-2665. Features national, regional, and advanced students' art exhibits in all media. (Sept-June, Mon-Fri; closed school holidays) **FREE**

Clymer Museum of Art. *416 N Pearl, Ellensburg (98926).* Phone 509/962-6416. Changing gallery exhibits; local artists. (Daily; Sat, Sun afternoons) **$$**

Ginkgo/Wanapum State Park. *4511 Huntzinger Rd, Vantage (98950). 28 miles E on I-90 exit 136.* Phone 509/856-2700. One of world's largest petrified forests (7,600 acres), with more than 200 species of petrified wood, including a prehistoric ginkgo tree. Waterskiing, fishing, boating; hiking, picnicking, camping (hookups). **FREE**

⭐ **Olmstead Place State Park-Heritage Site.** *4 miles E via Kittitas Hwy on Squaw Creek Trail Rd.* Phone 509/925-1943. This turn-of-the-century Kittitas Valley farm, originally homesteaded in 1875, is being converted to a living historical farm. Eight buildings; wildlife, flowers and trees; 1/2-mile interpretive trail. Farm machinery. Tours. (June-Sept: weekends; rest of year: by appointment). **FREE**

Wanapum Dam Heritage Center. *15655 Wanapum Village Ln SW, Ellensburg (99321). 29 miles E on I-90, then 3 miles S on Hwy 243. Phone 509/754-5088.* Self-guided tour of center; fish-viewing; petroglyph rubbings; exhibits detail life of the Wanapum, fur traders, ranchers, miners. (Daily) **FREE**

Special Events

Kittitas County Fair & Rodeo. *512 N Poplar, Ellensburg (98926). Phone 509/962-7639.* Carnival, exhibits, livestock, crafts, contests, entertainment. Labor Day weekend.

National Western Art Show and Auction. *Phone 509/962-2934.* Third weekend in May.

Threshing Bee and Antique Equipment Show. *Olmstead Place State Park, Ellensburg. Phone 509/925-1943.* Steam and gas threshing, blacksmithing demonstrations, horse-drawn equipment, old-time plowing. Third weekend in Sept.

Limited-Service Hotel

★ ★ **ELLENSBURG INN.** *1700 Canyon Rd, Ellensburg (98926). Phone 509/925-9801; toll-free 800/321-8791; fax 509/925-2093. www.ellensburginn.com.* 105 rooms, 2 story. Pets accepted, some restrictions; fee. Check-in 4 pm, check-out noon. Restaurant, bar. Indoor pool, whirlpool. **$**

Restaurant

★ ★ **CASA DE BLANCA.** *1318 S Canyon Rd, Ellensburg (98926). Phone 509/925-1693; fax 509/962-5222.* American, Mexican menu. Lunch, dinner. Closed Thanksgiving, Dec 25. Bar. Children's menu. **$$**

Enumclaw (C-3)

See also Puyallup, Tacoma

Population 7,227
Elevation 750 ft
Area Code 360
Zip 98022
Information Chamber of Commerce/Visitor Information, 1421 Cole St; phone 360/825-7666
Web site chamber.enumclaw.wa.us

A Ranger District office of the Mount Baker-Snoqualmie National Forest is located here.

What to See and Do

Federation Forest State Park. *49201 Hwy 410 E, Enumclaw (98022). 18 miles SE on Hwy 410. Phone 360/663-2207.* Approximately 620 acres of old-growth timber. Catherine Montgomery Interpretive Center has displays on the state's seven life zones. Three interpretive trails, hiking trails, and part of the Naches Trail, one of the first pioneer trails between eastern Washington and Puget Sound. Fishing; hiking, picnicking. **FREE**

Green River Gorge Conservation Area. *29500 SE Green River Gorge, Enumclaw (98022). 12 miles N on Hwy 169.* Protects a unique 12-mile corridor of the Green River, which cuts through unusual rock areas, many with fossils. Views of present-day forces of stream erosion through caves, smooth canyon walls. **FREE** One of the many areas in the gorge is

Flaming Geyser State Park. *23700 SE Flaming Geyser Rd, Auburn (98002). Phone 253/931-3930.* Two geysers (actually old test holes for coal), one burning about 6 inches high and the other bubbling methane gas through a spring. Fishing, boating, rafting; hiking, picnicking, playground. Abundant wildlife, wildflowers. No camping. (Daily)

Mud Mountain Dam. *7 miles SE via Hwy 410. Phone 360/825-3211.* One of the world's highest earth core and rock-fill dams.

Special Events

King County Fair. *Fairgrounds, 45224 284th Ave SE, Enumclaw (98022). Phone 360/825-7777.* Third week in July.

Pacific NW Scottish Highland Games. *Fairgrounds, 45224 284th Ave SE, Enumclaw (98022). Phone 360/825-7777.* Fourth weekend in July.

Pickles & Ice Cream Festival Street Fair. *Downtown, Enumclaw. Phone 360/825-1448.* Fourth weekend in July.

Limited-Service Hotel

★ ★ **BEST WESTERN PARK CENTER HOTEL.** *1000 Griffin Ave, Enumclaw (98022). Phone*

360/825-4490; fax 360/825-3686. www.bestwestern.com. 40 rooms, 2 story. Pets accepted; fee. Check-out 11 am. Restaurant, bar. Fitness room. **$**

Ephrata (C-4)

See also Moses Lake, Quincy, Soap Lake

Settled 1882
Population 5,349
Elevation 1,275 ft
Area Code 509
Zip 98823
Information Chamber of Commerce, 90 Alder NW; phone 509/754-4656
Web site www.ephratawachamber.com

The growth of this area is the result of the development of surrounding farmland, originally irrigated by wells, now supplied by the Columbia Basin irrigation project. Ephrata is the center of an area containing a series of lakes that offer fishing and water sports. There is excellent upland game bird hunting as well.

What to See and Do

Grant County Historical Museum and Village. *742 Basin St NW, Ephrata (98823). Phone 509/754-3334.* Displays trace natural history and early pioneer development of area. Native American artifacts. Pioneer homestead and country village with 31 buildings (some original, restored), including church, schoolhouse, saloon, barbershop, Krupp-Marlin Jail, photography studio, bank, firehouse, livery stable, blacksmith shop; farm machinery exhibit. Guided tour. (Early May-Sept: Mon-Tues, Thurs-Sun; rest of year: guided tour by appointment) **$**

Oasis Park. *2541 Basin St SW, Ephrata (98823). 1 1/2 miles SW on Hwy 28. Phone 509/754-5102.* Picnicking; nine-hole, par-three golf (fee); children's fishing pond; playground; miniature golf (fee). Camping (fee); swimming pool (free to campers). (Daily)

Special Event

Sage and Sun Festival. *Phone 509/754-4656.* Parade, sports events, arts and crafts shows. Second weekend in June.

Limited-Service Hotel

★ **BEST WESTERN RAMA INN.** *1818 Basin St SW, Ephrata (98823). Phone 509/754-7111; toll-free 888/726-2466; fax 509/754-7171. www.bestwestern.com.* 45 rooms. Complimentary continental breakfast. Check-in 3 pm, check-out noon. High-speed Internet access. Indoor pool, whirlpool. **$**

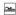

Specialty Lodging

The following lodging establishment is approved by Mobil Travel Guide, but due to its unique and individualized nature has not been given a traditional Mobil Star rating. Included in this listing you may find bed-and-breakfasts, limited-service inns, guest ranches, and other unique hotel properties.

IVY CHAPEL INN BED & BREAKFAST. *164 D St SW, Ephrata (98823). Phone 509/754-0629. www.ivychapelinn.com.* Built in 1948; was first Presbyterian church in Ephrata. 6 rooms, 3 story. Children over 10 years only. Complimentary full breakfast. Check-in 3 pm, check-out 11 am. **$**

Everett (B-3)

See also Marysville, Oak Harbor, Port Townsend, Seattle, Snohomish

Founded 1890
Population 91,488
Elevation 157 ft
Area Code 425
Information Everett/Snohomish County Convention and Visitor Bureau, 11400 Airport Rd, Suite B; phone 425/438-1487
Web site www.everettchamber.com

This lumber, aircraft, electronics, and shipping city is on a sheltered harbor where the Snohomish River empties into Port Gardner Bay. To the east is the snowcapped Cascade Mountain Range; to the west are the Olympic Mountains. Developed by Eastern industrial and railroad money, Everett serves as a major commercial fishing port and receives and dispatches a steady stream of cargo vessels. The Boeing 747 and 767 are assembled here.

Along the waterfront is an 1890s-style seaside marketplace, the Everett Marina Village.

What to See and Do

Boat tours. *Phone 425/438-1487.* For information on companies offering sightseeing, dinner, and whale-watching cruises, contact the Convention and Visitors Bureau.

 Boeing Everett Facility. *3003 W Casino, Everett (98203). I-5 exit 189, approximately 3 miles W on Hwy 526. Phone toll-free 800/464-1476.* Audiovisual presentation; bus tour of assembly facility. Gift shop. (Mon-Fri; closed holidays) No children under 10. **$$$**

Harbour Pointe Golf Club. *11817 Harbour Pointe Blvd, Mukilteo (98275). Phone toll-free 800/233-3128. www.harbourpointegolf.com.* Harbour Pointe is really a tale of two nines, with the front a very flat, target-oriented layout and the back lined with tall evergreen trees and narrower fairways, which force players to work their way around each hole for the best approach to each green. Opened in 1991, Harbour Pointe has won awards as one of America's best public courses. It's better to play on a day when it hasn't rained for at least a week; otherwise, the course plays considerably longer due to the moisture. **$$$$**

Mukilteo. *Phone 425/347-1456.* This town, just west of Everett, is the major ferry point from the mainland to the southern tip of Whidbey Island. Its name means "good camping ground." A lighthouse built in 1905 is open for tours (Sat).

Recreation areas. *802 Mukilteo Blvd, Everett (98203). Phone 425/257-8300.* There are many recreation areas in and near the city that offer swimming (fee), fishing, boat launch; hiking, picnicking, camping, nature centers, tennis, golf (fee). **FREE**

Totem Pole. *Rucker Ave and 44th St, Everett.* 80 feet high, carved by Tulalip Chief William Shelton.

Special Events

Auto racing. *Evergreen Speedway, 17901 Hwy 2, Monroe (98272). Phone 360/805-6100. 15 miles SE via Hwy 2, exit 194 off I-5.* NASCAR super and mini stocks, SVRA modifieds, hobby stocks, figure eights; demolition events. Apr-Sept.

Salty Sea Days. *2520 Colby Ave, Everett (98201). Phone 425/339-1113.* Festival, parade, displays, food and carnival. Early June.

Limited-Service Hotel

★ **BEST WESTERN CASCADIA INN.** *2800 Pacific Ave, Everett (98201). Phone 425/258-4141; toll-free 800/822-5876; fax 425/258-4755. www.bestwesterncascadia.com.* 134 rooms, 3 story. Complimentary continental breakfast. Check-out noon. Bar. Pool, whirlpool. **$**
⌷

Specialty Lodging

The following lodging establishment is approved by Mobil Travel Guide, but due to its unique and individualized nature has not been given a traditional Mobil Star rating. Included in this listing you may find bed-and-breakfasts, limited-service inns, guest ranches, and other unique hotel properties.

MARINA VILLAGE INN. *1728 W Marina View Dr, Everett (98201). Phone 425/259-4040; toll-free 800/281-7037; fax 425/252-8419. www.marinavillageinn.net.* This waterfront property is located within walking distance to shops, a large marina, restaurants, and other attractions. 26 rooms, 2 story. Complimentary continental breakfast. Check-out noon. **$**
⌷

Forks (B-1)

See also Olympic National Park

Population 3,120
Elevation 375 ft
Area Code 360
Zip 98331
Information Chamber of Commerce, 1411 S Forks Ave; phone 360/374-2531 or toll-free 800/443-6757

The major town in the northwest section of the Olympic Peninsula, Forks takes its name from the nearby junction of the Soleduck, Bogachiel, and Dickey rivers. Timber processing is a major industry. A Ranger District office of the Olympic National Forest is located here.

What to See and Do

Bogachiel State Park. *185983 Hwy 101, Forks (98331). 6 miles S on Hwy 101. Phone 360/374-6356.* Approximately 120 acres, on the shores of the Bogachiel River with swimming, fishing; hiking, camping (hookups, dump station). (Daily)

Limited-Service Hotel

★ **FORKS MOTEL.** *351 S Forks Ave, Forks (98331). Phone 360/374-6243; toll-free 800/544-3416; fax 360/374-6760. www.forksmotel.com.* 73 rooms, 2 story. Check-out 11 am. Pool, children's pool. **$**

Goldendale (D-4)

Settled 1863
Population 3,760
Elevation 1,633 ft
Area Code 509
Zip 98620
Information Greater Goldendale Area Chamber of Commerce, Box 524; phone 509/773-3400

Agriculture, aluminum smelting, and an assortment of small industries comprise the major business of Goldendale, named for John J. Golden, a pioneer settler.

What to See and Do

Brooks Memorial State Park. *2465 Hwy 97, Goldendale (98620). 12 miles N on Hwy 97. Phone 509/773-4611.* More than 700 acres. Fishing; hiking, picnicking, camping (hookups).

Goldendale Observatory. *1602 Observatory Dr, Goldendale (98620). Phone 509/773-3141.* Nation's largest amateur-built Cassegrain telescope for public use; tours, demonstrations, displays, audiovisual programs. (Apr-Sept: Wed-Sun; rest of year: schedule varies) **FREE**

Klickitat County Historical Museum. *127 W Broadway, Goldendale (98620). Phone 509/773-4303.* Furniture and exhibits from early days of Klickitat County, in 20-room restored mansion. Gift shop. (Apr-Oct: daily; rest of year: by appointment) **$$**

Maryhill Museum of Art. *35 Maryhill Museum Dr, Goldendale (98620). 11 miles S on Hwy 97, then 2 miles W on Hwy 14. Phone 509/773-3733.* Constructed by Samuel Hill. Permanent exhibits include a Rodin sculpture, European and American paintings, Russian icons, chess collection, French fashion mannequins, Native American baskets and artifacts. (Mid-Mar-mid-Nov, daily) **$$**

Mount Adams Recreation Area. *NW of town.* Lakes, streams, forests; excellent fishing, bird hunting.

Special Event

Klickitat County Fair and Rodeo. *228 W Main St, Goldendale (98620). Phone 509/773-3900.* Fourth weekend in Aug.

Limited-Service Hotel

★ ★ **FARVUE MOTEL.** *808 E Simcoe Dr, Goldendale (98620). Phone 509/773-5881; toll-free 800/358-5881.* 48 rooms, 2 story. Check-out 11 am. Restaurant, bar. Pool. Airport transportation available. **$**

Hoquiam (C-1)

See also Aberdeen, Ocean Shores, Westport

Settled 1859
Population 9,097
Elevation 10 ft
Area Code 360
Zip 98550
Information Grays Harbor Chamber of Commerce, 506 Duffy St, Aberdeen 98520; phone 360/532-1924 or toll-free 800/321-1924
Web site www.graysharbor.org

Twin city to Aberdeen (see), Hoquiam is the senior community of the two and the pioneer town of the Grays Harbor region. A deepwater port 12 miles from the Pacific, it docks cargo and fishing vessels, manufactures wood products and machine tools, and cans the harvest of the sea.

What to See and Do

Hoquiam's "Castle". *515 Chenault Ave, Hoquiam (98550). Phone 360/533-2005.* A 20-room mansion built in 1897 by lumber tycoon Robert Lytle; antique furnishings; oak-columned entry hall; authentic Victorian atmosphere. (Summer, Wed through Sat) **$**

Polson Park and Museum. *1611 Riverside Ave, Hoquiam (98550). Phone 360/533-5862.* (1924) Restored 26-room mansion; antiques; rose garden. (June-Aug: Wed-Sun; rest of year: weekends)

Issaquah

See also Bellevue, North Bend, Seattle

Population 11,212
Elevation 100 ft
Area Code 425
Zip 98027
Information Chamber of Commerce, 155 NW Gilman Blvd; phone 425/392-7024
Web site www.issaquahchamber.com

Historic buildings and homes of Issaquah have been renovated and moved to a 7-acre farm site, called Gilman Village, where they now serve as specialty shops.

What to See and Do

Boehm's Chocolate Factory. *255 NE Gilman Blvd, Issaquah (98027). Phone 425/392-6652.* The home of Boehm's Candies was built here in 1956 by Julius Boehm. The candy-making process and the Edelweiss Chalet, filled with artifacts, paintings, and statues, can be toured. The Luis Trenker Kirch'l, a replica of a 12th-century Swiss chapel, was also built by Boehm. Tours by appointment (July-Aug). **FREE**

Lake Sammamish State Park. *20606 SE 56th St, Issaquah (98027). 2 miles W off I-90. Phone 425/455-7010.* Approximately 430 acres. Swimming, fishing, boating (launch); hiking, picnicking.

Special Event

Salmon Days Festival. *155 NW Gilman Blvd, Issaquah (98027). Phone 425/392-0661.* Welcomes return of Northwest salmon to original home. First full weekend in Oct.

Limited-Service Hotel

★ ★ **HOLIDAY INN.** *1801 12th Ave NW, Issaquah (98027). Phone 425/392-6421; fax 425/391-4650. www. holiday-inn.com.* 100 rooms, 2 story. Check-out noon. Restaurant, bar. Pool, children's pool. **$**

Kelso (D-2)

See also Longview

Founded 1847
Population 11,895
Elevation 40 ft
Information Chamber of Commerce, 105 Minor Rd; phone 360/577-8058
Web site www.kelso.gov

Kelso straddles the Cowlitz River and is an artery for the lumber industry. The river also yields a variety of fish from giant salmon to tiny smelt.

What to See and Do

Cowlitz County Historical Museum. *405 Allen St, Kelso (98626). Phone 360/577-3119.* Exhibits depict history of the area. (Tues-Sun; closed holidays) **DONATION**

Seaquest State Park. *3030 Spirit Lake Hwy, Kelso (98611). 10 miles N on I-5 exit 49, then 5 miles E on Hwy 504. Phone 360/274-8633.* Approximately 300 acres. Hiking, picnicking, camping (hookups). Nearby is Silver Lake with fishing (about 10,000 fish are caught here every summer).

Volcano Information Center. *105 Minor Rd, Kelso (98626). Off I-5 exit 39. Phone 360/577-8058.* Pictorial and scientific exhibits on the eruption of Mount St. Helens; 3-D narrated topographical display of the devastation. Also visitor information on surrounding area. (Daily) **FREE**

Limited-Service Hotels

★ **COMFORT INN.** *440 Three Rivers Dr, Kelso (98626). Phone 360/425-4600; fax 360/423-0762. www. choicehotels.com.* 57 rooms, 2 story. Complimentary continental breakfast. Check-out noon. Indoor pool, whirlpool. **$**

★ **MT. ST. HELENS MOTEL.** *1340 Mount Saint Helens Way, Castle Rock (98611). Phone 360/274-7721; fax 360/274-7721. www.mtsthelensmotel.com.* 32 rooms, 2 story. Check-in 3 pm, check-out 11 am. **$**

★ ★ **RED LION.** *510 Kelso Dr, Kelso (98626). Phone 360/636-4400; fax 360/425-3296. www.redlion.com.* 162 rooms, 2 story. Pets accepted; fee. Check-out noon. Restaurant, bar. Fitness room. Pool, children's pool, whirlpool. **$**

Kennewick (D-5)

See also Pasco, Richland

Founded 1892
Population 54,693
Elevation 380 ft
Area Code 509
Information Chamber of Commerce, 3180 W Clearwater Ave, Suite F, 99336; phone 509/736-0510
Web site www.ci.kennewick.wa.us/home/

Huge hydroelectric dams harnessing the lower stem of the Columbia River have brought economic vitality to the "Tri-Cities" of Kennewick, Pasco, and Richland (see both). On the south bank of Lake Wallula and near the confluence of the Columbia, Snake, and Yakima rivers, Kennewick has chemical and agricultural processing plants. Irrigation of the 20,500-acre Kennewick Highland project has converted sagebrush into thousands of farms, producing three cuttings of alfalfa annually, plus corn and beans. Appropriately enough, this city with the Native American name meaning "winter paradise" enjoys a brief winter and is the center of the state's grape industry.

What to See and Do

Columbia Park. *6515 Columbia Dr Trail, Kennewick (99336). 2 1/2 miles W on Hwy 12 on Lake Wallula, formed by McNary Dam. Phone 509/585-4529.* Approximately 300 acres. Waterskiing, fishing, boating (ramps); 18-hole golf, driving range (fee), tennis, picnicking, camping (hookups; fee). Park open all year (daily). **FREE**

Two Rivers Park. *213316 E Finley Rd, Kennewick (99337). 5 miles E, off Finley Rd. Phone 509/783-3118.* Picnicking; boating (ramp), swimming, fishing. Park open all year (daily). **FREE**

Limited-Service Hotels

★ ★ **RED LION.** *1101 N Columbia Center Blvd, Kennewick (99336). Phone 509/783-0611; fax 509/735-3087. www.redlion.com.* 162 rooms, 2 story. Pets accepted; fee. Check-out noon. Restaurant, bar. Pool, whirlpool. Airport transportation available. **$**

★ **SILVER CLOUD INN KENNEWICK.** *7901 W Quinault Ave, Kennewick (99336). Phone 509/735-6100; toll-free 800/205-6938; fax 509/735-3084. www.scinns.com.* 125 rooms, 4 story. Complimentary continental breakfast. Check-out noon. Fitness room. Indoor pool, outdoor pool, whirlpool. **$**

Kirkland (B-2)

Full-Service Hotel

★ ★ ★ **THE WOODMARK HOTEL ON LAKE WASHINGTON.** *1200 Carillon Point, Kirkland (98033). Phone 425/822-3700; toll-free 800/822-3700; fax 425/822-3699. www.thewoodmark .com.* With the blinking lights of Seattle's skyline only 7 miles in the distance, the Woodmark Hotel gently rests on the shores of scenic Lake Washington. Convenient to Bellevue and Redmond, the Woodmark is an ideal stop for travelers to the pristine Pacific Northwest. Set within a complex of specialty shops, restaurants, and marina, the hotel is a true getaway enhanced by a marvelous destination spa. Characterized by the serenity and casual elegance of the region, the Woodmark instills a sense of belonging in its guests. From the friendly staff to the cozy furnishings, a relaxed, residential style pervades the hotel. The 100 rooms are luxurious without being pretentious and feature lake, marina, or creek views. The region's fresh, delicious cuisine is the highlight at Waters Lakeside Bistro, and the Library Bar serves a wonderful afternoon tea, complete with a special menu and china service for children. 100 rooms, 4 story. Pets accepted; fee. Check-in 4 pm, check-out noon. Restaurant, bar. Fitness room, spa. Pool. **$$**

Specialty Lodging

The following lodging establishment is approved by Mobil Travel Guide, but due to its unique and individualized nature has not been given a traditional Mobil Star rating. Included in this listing you may find bed-and-breakfasts, limited-service inns, guest ranches, and other unique hotel properties.

SHUMWAY MANSION. *11410 99th Pl NE, Kirkland (98033). Phone 425/823-2303; fax 425/822-0421. www.shumwaymansion.com.* This inn is located near Waneada Beach, many restaurants and shops, and walking distance to a nature park with hiking trails. 9 rooms, 2 story. Children over 12 years only. Complimentary full breakfast. Check-in 3 pm, check-out 1 pm. **$**

Restaurants

★ ★ ★ **CAFE JUANITA.** *9702 120th Pl NE, Kirkland (98034). Phone 425/823-1505; fax 425/823-8500. www.cafejuanita.com.* The dining destination for the Puget Sound region since 1979, Cafe Juanita serves some of the best northern Italian food around. The wine list complements the cafe's chalkboard menu of well-executed cuisine. Italian menu. Dinner. Closed Mon. Casual attire. **$$$**

★ ★ **THIRD FLOOR FISH CAFE.** *205 Lake St S, Kirkland (98033). Phone 425/822-3553; fax 425/827-1364. www.fishcafe.com.* This restaurant features excellent service, breathtaking views of Lake Washington and the Seattle skyline, and upscale cuisine. Seafood menu. Dinner. Closed Jan 1, Dec 25. Bar. Casual attire. **$$$**

La Conner

See also Anacortes, Mount Vernon

Population 761
Area Code 360
Zip 98257
Information Chamber of Commerce, PO Box 1610; phone 360/466-4778 or toll-free 888/642-9284
Web site www.laconnerchamber.com

A picturesque town along the Swinomish Channel, La Conner is a popular destination for weekend travelers. Many of the town's homes and businesses are housed in the clapboarded structures built by its founders around the turn of the century. Numerous boutiques, galleries, and antique shops, some containing the works of local artists and craftspeople, line its streets.

What to See and Do

Museum of Northwest Art. *121 S 1st St, La Conner (98257). Phone 360/466-4446. www.museumofnwart.org.* Exhibits artist of the "Northwest School." (Tues-Sun; closed Jan 1, Thanksgiving, Dec 25) **$$**

Skagit County Historical Museum. *501 4th St, La Conner (98257). Phone 360/466-3365.* Exhibits depicting history of Skagit County. (Tues-Sun afternoons; closed Jan 1, Thanksgiving, Dec 25) **$**

Specialty Lodgings

The following lodging establishments are approved by Mobil Travel Guide, but due to their unique and individualized nature have not been given a traditional Mobil Star rating. Included in this listing you may find bed-and-breakfasts, limited-service inns, guest ranches, and other unique hotel properties.

THE HERON. *117 Maple Ave, La Conner (98257). Phone 360/466-4626; toll-free 877/883-8899; fax 360/466-3254. www.theheron.com.* 12 rooms, 3 story. Children over 12 years only. Complimentary full breakfast. Check-in 3-6 pm, check-out 11 am. Spa. Country-style inn. **$**
🗋

LACONNER COUNTRY INN. *107 S Second St, La Conner (98257). Phone 360/466-3101; toll-free 888/466-4113; fax 360/466-0199. www.laconnerlodging.com.* 28 rooms, 2 story. Pets accepted; fee. Complimentary continental breakfast. Check-in 3 pm, check-out noon. High-speed Internet access. Restaurant, bar. **$**
🐾

Langley

Restaurant

★ ★ **CAFE LANGLEY.** *113 1st St, Langley (98260). Phone 360/221-3090; fax 360/221-8542. www.langley-wa.com/cl.* Greek, Mediterranean menu. Lunch, dinner. Closed Dec 25. **$$**

Leavenworth (B-4)

See also Cashmere, Wenatchee

Founded 1892
Population 2,074
Elevation 1,165 ft
Area Code 509
Zip 98826
Information Chamber of Commerce, PO Box 327;
phone 509/548-5807
Web site www.leavenworth.org

Surrounded by the Cascade Mountains, Leavenworth has an old-world charm enhanced by authentic Bavarian architecture. Less than three hours from Seattle, the village is a favorite stop for people who enjoy river rafting, hiking, bicycling, fishing, golf, and skiing. Two Ranger District offices of the Wenatchee National Forest are located here.

What to See and Do

The Leavenworth Nutcracker Museum. *735 Front St, Leavenworth (98826). Phone 509/548-4573; toll-free 800/892-3989. www.nutcrackermuseum.com.* Spanning the wall and floor space of a beautiful Bavarian-style house is the Nutcracker Museum, born out of Arlene Wagner's love of the Tchaikovsky ballet of the same name. Wagner now has more than 4,000 nutcrackers in her museum, having traveled the world over in search of the most exotic specimens she and her husband could find. Some of the examples housed in the museum date as far back as the 15th century and detail the history of these very functional, yet ornamental items. (May-Oct: daily 2-5 pm; rest of year: weekends only; also by appointment) **$**

National Fish Hatchery. *3 1/2 miles S on Icicle Creek Rd. Phone 509/548-7641.* Raises chinook salmon and steelhead. Educational exhibits. Fishing, boat ramp; hiking, interpretive trails, picnicking, cross-country skiing. (Daily; closed Dec 25)

Stevens Pass Ski Area. *Summit Stevens Pass, Hwy 2, Leavenworth (98288). 36 miles NW on Hwy 2. Phone 206/812-4510. www.stevenspass.com.* Quad, four triple, six double chairlifts; patrol, school, rentals; snowboarding; tubing; restaurant, cafeteria, bar; nursery. (Late Nov-mid-Apr, daily) **$$$$**

Special Events

Autumn Leaf Festival. *Front and 8th sts, Leavenworth (98826). Phone 509/548-6348.* Late Sept and Early Oct.

Bavarian Ice Fest. *Phone 509/548-5807.* Snowshoe races, dogsled rides. Fireworks. Mid-Jan.

Bavarian Maifest. *Phone 509/548-5807.* Bandstand music, grand march, Maypole dance, art, chuck wagon breakfast. Early May.

Chamber Music Festival. *Icicle Creek Music Center, 9286 Icicle Rd, Leavenworth (98826). Phone 509/548-6800.* Professional chamber music festival featuring classical, jazz, bluegrass. Kayak and raft races. Tours, booths, and more. May.

Christmas Lighting. *Phone 509/548-5807.* Sleigh rides, sledding. Early and mid Dec.

Limited-Service Hotels

★ ★ **BEST WESTERN ICICLE INN.** *505 Hwy 2, Leavenworth (98826). Phone 509/548-7000; toll-free 800/558-2438; fax 509/548-7050. www.bestwestern.com.* Set right on the main highway through town, this hotel has been a landmark property in Leavenworth. As expected in a city that celebrates its German heritage, a Bavarian theme dominates the hotel, especially the lobby. Next door is the Icicle Junction Family Fun Center, with miniature golf, bumper boats, arcade, and movie theater, making the Icicle Inn a great choice for families. 93 rooms, 3 story. Pets accepted, some restrictions; fee. Complimentary full breakfast. Check-in 3 pm, check-out 11 am. High-speed Internet access. Restaurant. Fitness room, spa. Outdoor pool, whirlpool. **$**

★ **ENZIAN INN.** *590 Hwy 2, Leavenworth (98826). Phone 509/548-5269; toll-free 800/223-8511; fax 509/548-9319. www.enzianinn.com.* 104 rooms, 4 story. Complimentary full breakfast. Check-in 3 pm, check-out noon. Fitness room. Indoor pool, outdoor pool, whirlpool. **$**

★ ★ **SLEEPING LADY MOUNTAIN RETREAT.** *7375 Icicle Rd, Leavenworth (98826). Phone 509/548-6344; toll-free 800/574-2123; fax 509/548-6312. www.sleepinglady.com.* 46 rooms, 2 story. Check-in 3 pm, check-out noon. Restaurant, bar. Fitness room. Indoor pool. **$**

Full-Service Inn

★ ★ ★ **MOUNTAIN HOME LODGE.** *8201 Mountain Home Rd, Leavenworth (98826). Phone 509/ 548-7077; toll-free 800/414-2378; fax 509/548-5008. www.mthome.com.* In a picturesque, serene setting, this great escape is a wonderful mix of luxury, comfort, and style. Some guests come for relaxation and seclusion while others enjoy the activities. 12 rooms, 4 story. No children allowed. Complimentary full breakfast. Check-in 3 pm, check-out noon. Restaurant. Pool, whirlpool. Tennis. **$$$**

Specialty Lodgings

The following lodging establishments are approved by Mobil Travel Guide, but due to their unique and individualized nature have not been given a traditional Mobil Star rating. Included in this listing you may find bed-and-breakfasts, limited-service inns, guest ranches, and other unique hotel properties.

ALL SEASONS RIVER INN. *8751 Icicle Rd, Leavenworth (98826). Phone 509/548-1425; toll-free 800/254-0555. www.allseasonsriverinn.com.* Located 80 feet above the Wenatchee River, this serene bed-and-breakfast feels more like a private home than a hotel. Guest rooms lack TVs and telephones, but lovely water views and Jacuzzi tubs provide their own form of entertainment. Passionate about antiques, the innkeeper has meticulously furnished each room with unique pieces. The inn makes bicycles available for the 1/2-mile ride to downtown Leavenworth. 6 rooms, 2 story. No children allowed. Complimentary full breakfast. Check-in 3 pm, check-out 11 am. **$$**

BOSCH GARTEN. *9846 Dye Rd, Leavenworth (98826). Phone 509/548-6900; toll-free 800/535-0069. www.boschgarten.com.* 3 rooms. Children over 12 years only. Complimentary full breakfast. Check-in 3 pm, check-out 11 am. Whirlpool. **$**

RUN OF THE RIVER BED & BREAKFAST. *9308 E Leavenworth Rd, Leavenworth (98826). Phone 509/548-7171; toll-free 800/288-6491; fax 509/548-7547. www.runoftheriver.com.* This small, quiet inn on

the Icicle River is tucked among the towering Cascade Mountains. Visitors will enjoy hiking, walking, or mountain biking through forest trails. 6 rooms. No children allowed. Complimentary full breakfast. Check-in 3 pm, check-out 11 am. Whirlpool. **$$**

Restaurant

★ ★ **LORRAINE'S EDEL HAUS.** *320 Ninth St, Leavenworth (98826). Phone 509/548-4412. www. edelhaus.com.* Continental menu. Lunch, dinner. Children's menu. Outdoor seating. **$$$**

Long Beach

Population 1,283
Elevation 10 ft
Area Code 360
Zip 98631
Information Peninsula Visitors Bureau, PO Box 562; phone 360/642-2400 or toll-free 800/451-2542
Web site www.funbeach.com

This seashore resort is on one of the longest hard-sand beaches in the world, stretching 28 miles along a narrow peninsula just north of where the Columbia River empties into the Pacific Ocean.

What to See and Do

Fort Canby. *2 miles S on Hwy 100, in Ilwaco. Phone 360/642-3078; toll-free 800/452-5687 (reservations).* (1864) More than 1,880 acres overlooking mouth of Columbia River. Strategic base from pioneer days through World War II. The Lewis and Clark Interpretive Center, built near an artillery bunker on a hillside, has exhibits depicting the historic expedition and the contributions made by Native American tribes; also multimedia presentations (daily). Fishing; hiking, picnicking, camping (hookups). (Daily)

Fort Columbia. *11 miles SE on Hwy 101. Phone 360/777-8755.* More than 580 acres. Site of former coastal artillery corps post with Endicott-period fortifications that protected mouth of Columbia River. Interpretive center in former barracks (Apr-Sept, daily) Also here is Columbia House, a former commander's residence. Hiking, picnicking. Grounds (daily).

Oysterville. *Hwy 101 and 103, Seaview. 15 miles N via Sandridge Rd. Phone 360/642-2400; toll-free 800/451-2542.* Community founded in 1854; original settlers were lured by oysters found on tidal flats of Willapa Bay. Many original homes remain, as well as church and schoolhouse.

Seascape scenic drive. *14 miles N from Seaview on Hwy 103, through Long Beach to Ocean Park.*

Limited-Service Hotels

★ **CHAUTAUQUA LODGE.** *304 14th St NW, Long Beach (98631). Phone 360/642-4401; toll-free 800/869-8401; fax 360/642-2340. www.chautauqualodge.com.* 180 rooms, 3 story. Pets accepted; fee. Check-out 11 am. Bar. Indoor pool, whirlpool. **$**

★ ★ **EDGEWATER INN.** *409 10th St, Long Beach (98631). Phone 360/642-2311; toll-free 800/561-2456; fax 360/642-8018.* 84 rooms, 3 story. Pets accepted, some restrictions; fee. Check-out 11 am. Restaurant, bar. **$**

★ **SUPER 8.** *500 Ocean Beach Blvd, Long Beach (98631). Phone 360/642-8988; toll-free 888/478-3297; fax 360/642-8986. www.super8.com.* 50 rooms, 3 story. Complimentary continental breakfast. Check-out noon. **$**

Specialty Lodgings

The following lodging establishments are approved by Mobil Travel Guide, but due to their unique and individualized nature have not been given a traditional Mobil Star rating. Included in this listing you may find bed-and-breakfasts, limited-service inns, guest ranches, and other unique hotel properties.

BOREAS BED & BREAKFAST. *607 Ocean Beach Blvd N, Long Beach (98631). Phone 360/642-8069; toll-free 888/642-8069. www.boreasinn.com.* This scenic oceanfront bed-and-breakfast comes well equipped with many personal touches. Each of the suites is designed to reflect the style and fun-loving personalities at the inn. 5 rooms, 2 story. Complimentary full breakfast. Check-in 4 pm, check-out 11 am. **$**

THE INN AT ILWACO. *120 Williams Ave NE, Ilwaco (98642). Phone 360/642-8686; toll-free 888/244-2523;*

fax 360/642-8642. www.longbeachlodging.com. Originally built as a church, this renovated inn provides a comfortable haven overlooking the Port of Ilwaco. Each room has stylish touches. 9 rooms, 1 story. Complimentary full breakfast. Check-in 3 pm, check-out 11 am. Airport transportation available. **$**

SCANDINAVIAN GARDENS INN BED & BREAKFAST. *1610 California Ave SW, Long Beach (98631). Phone 360/642-8877; toll-free 800/988-9277; fax 360/642-8764. www.longbeachwa.com.* Each room decorated to theme of different Scandinavian country. 5 rooms, 2 story. Children over 2 years only. Complimentary full breakfast. Check-in 3-6 pm, check-out 11 am. **$**

Restaurants

★ ★ **SANCTUARY.** *794 Hwy 101, Chinook (98631). Phone 360/777-8380. www.sanctuaryrestaurant.com.* This reataurant was a former church built in 1906. Seafood menu. Dinner. Closed Mon-Thurs. Children's menu. Outdoor seating. **$$**

★ ★ **SHOALWATER.** *4503 Pacific Hwy, Seaview (98644). Phone 360/642-4142. www.shoalwater.com.* Seafood menu. Lunch, dinner. Closed Dec 25. Bar. Children's menu. Outdoor seating. **$$**

Longview (D-2)

See also Chehalis, Kelso

Settled 1923
Population 34,660
Elevation 21 ft
Area Code 360
Zip 98632
Information Longview Area Chamber of Commerce, 1563 Olympia Way; phone 360/423-8400

Situated between Seattle, Washington and Portland, Oregon, Longview is the home of one of the largest forest products mills in the world. Factories produce pulp, fine and kraft papers, paper boxes, plywood, glassine, pig aluminum, concrete paint, caustic soda, and chlorine. The first planned city in the West, Longview is a deepwater port fed by six railroad systems and several highways. Fishing for steelhead, smelt, and salmon is excellent.

What to See and Do

Lake Sacajawea Park. *Between Kessler and Nichols blvds, Hwy 30 and Hwy 432.* A 120-acre park with 60-acre lake; picnic areas, playgrounds; gardens, jogging, bike and fitness trail. Fishing, wildlife refuge. (Daily)

Monticello Convention Site. *Olympia Way and Maple St, Longview.* Here residents of Washington met to petition the federal government to separate Washington Territory from Oregon.

Mount St. Helens Visitor Center. *10 miles N on I-5 to Castle Rock, then 5 miles E on Hwy 504.*

Special Events

Cowlitz County Fair. *Cowlitz County Expo Center, 7 Washington St, Longview (98632). Phone 360/577-3121.* Exhibits, entertainment, carnival, pro rodeo. Last week in July.

Rain Fest. *Cowlitz County Expo Center, 7 Washington St, Longview (98632). Phone 360/577-3121.* Wine tasting, exhibit booths, music. Early Oct.

Marysville (B-3)

See also Everett, Snohomish

Settled 1872
Population 25,315
Area Code 360
Information The Greater Marysville Tulalip Chamber of Commerce, 4411 76th St NE, 98270; phone 360/659-7700

Natural surroundings, including lakes, rivers, and wooded countryside, make Marysville a popular spot for outdoor recreation.

What to See and Do

Tulalip Casino. *6410 33rd Ave NE, Marysville (98271). Phone 360/651-1111. www.tulalipcasino.com.* Just off I-5 about 35 miles north of downtown Seattle is the Tulalip Casino, with an array of Vegas-style tables, a bingo parlor, and more than 1,000 gaming machines. Hunger is sated at three eateries (a steak and seafood restaurant and two delis), and the waters of Puget Sound—just a stone's throw away—beckon non-gamblers outdoors. (Mon-Tues 10-6 am, Wed-Sun 24 hours)

Tulalip Reservation. *6700 Totem Beach Rd, Marysville (98271). 6 miles NW via Hwy 506. Phone 360/651-4000.* Within the community are St. Anne's Church (1904) with old mission bell, the Native American Shaker Church, and tribal community center.

Wenberg State Park. *15430 Lake Goodwin Rd, Stanwood (98292). N via I-5 exit 206, 2 miles W to Lakewood Rd, then 3 miles N to E Lake Goodwin Rd, then S. Phone 360/652-7417.* A 46-acre park. Swimming, fishing, boating (launch); picnicking, concession (summer), camping (some hookups).

Special Events

Home-Grown Festival. *3rd and State sts, Marysville. Phone 360/659-4997.* Open-air market, arts and crafts booths, street fair. Early Aug.

Merrysville for the Holidays. *Phone 360/651-5085.* Water-tower lighting, lighted holiday parade. Early Dec.

Strawberry Festival. *1624 Grove St, Marysville (98270). Phone 360/659-7664.* Parade, art show, races. Third week in June.

Limited-Service Hotel

★ ★ **BEST WESTERN TULALIP INN.** *3228 Marine Dr NE, Marysville (98271). Phone 360/659-4488; toll-free 800/780-7234; fax 360/659-5688. www.bestwestern.com.* 69 rooms. Check-in 3 pm, check-out noon. Restaurant, bar. Indoor pool, whirlpool. **$**
🖾

Restaurant

★ **VILLAGE.** *220 Ash Ave, Marysville (98270). Phone 360/659-2305; fax 360/659-6661.* Seafood, steak menu. Breakfast, lunch, dinner. Closed Dec 25. Bar. Children's menu. **$$**

Moses Lake (C-5)

See also Ephrata, Othello, Ritzville

Settled 1910
Population 14,953
Elevation 1,060 ft
Area Code 509
Zip 98837
Information Chamber of Commerce, 324 S Pioneer Way; phone 509/765-7888
Web site www.moses-lake.com

Because of the water impounded by Grand Coulee Dam, the recreational and agricultural resources of this area have blossomed. Swimming, fishing, and hunting abound within a 25-mile radius. The city is also an important shipping and processing point for agricultural products.

What to See and Do

Moses Lake Museum and Art Center. *122 W 3rd Ave, Moses Lake (98837). Phone 509/766-9395.* Native American artifacts; regional artwork; local history. (Tues-Sat afternoons; closed holidays) **FREE**

Moses Lake Recreation Area. *401 S Balsam St, Moses Lake (98837). Phone 509/766-9240.* South and west of city. **FREE** Includes

Cascade Park. *Valley Rd and Cascade Valley, Moses Lake (98837). Phone 509/766-9240.* Swimming, boating (launch), fishing, waterskiing; camping (fee). Park (Mid-Apr-mid-Oct, daily).

Moses Lake. *401 S Balsam St, Moses Lake (98837). NW off I-90, Hwy 17. Phone 509/766-9240.* 18 miles long.

Moses Lake State Park. *111 W Shore, Moses Lake (98837). 2 miles W on I-90. Phone 509/766-9240.* A 78-acre park with swimming, fishing, boating (launch); picnicking. (Daily)

Potholes Reservoir. *14 miles SW off Hwy 17, I-90 on Hwy 170.* Formed by O'Sullivan Dam (10 miles S). Swimming, boating, waterskiing, fishing.

Potholes State Park. *14 miles SW on Hwy 17 to Hwy 170.* Approximately 2,500 acres. Water sports, fishing, boat launch; hiking, picnicking, camping (hookups).

Special Events

Grant County Fair. *Fairgrounds, 3953 Airway Dr NE, Moses Lake (98837). Phone 509/765-3581.* Rodeo. Five days in mid-Aug.

Spring Festival. *Phone 509/765-8248.* Memorial Day weekend.

Limited-Service Hotels

★ **BEST VALUE INN.** *1214 S Pioneer Way, Moses Lake (98837). Phone 509/765-9173; toll-free 888/315-2378; fax 509/765-1137. www.bestvalueinn.com.* 20 rooms. Pets accepted, some restrictions. Check-out 11 am. Pool. **$**

★ ★ **BEST WESTERN HALLMARK INN & CONFERENCE CENTER.** *3000 Marina Dr, Moses Lake (98837). Phone 509/765-9211; toll-free 800/235-4255; fax 509/766-1214. www.hallmarkinns.com.* 161 rooms, 3 story. Pets accepted, some restrictions; fee. Check-in 3 pm, check-out noon. Restaurant, bar. Fitness room. Outdoor pool, whirlpool. Airport transportation available. **$**

★ **SHILO INN.** *1819 E Kittleson, Moses Lake (98837). Phone 509/765-9317; fax 509/765-5058. www.shiloinn.com.* 100 rooms, 2 story. Pets accepted, some restrictions; fee. Check-in 3 pm, check-out noon. Fitness room. Indoor pool, whirlpool. Airport transportation available. **$**

Mount Rainier National Park

See also Packwood

Web site www.nps.gov/mora

Majestic Mount Rainier, towering 14,411 feet above sea level and 8,000 feet above the Cascade Range of western Washington, is one of America's outstanding tourist attractions. More than 2 million people visit this 378-square-mile park each year to picnic, hike, camp, climb mountains, or simply admire the spectacular scenery along the many miles of roadways.

The park's various "life zones," which change at different elevations, support a wide array of plant and animal life. Douglas fir, red cedar, and western hemlock, some rising 200 feet into the air, thrive in the old-growth forests. In the summer, the subalpine meadows come alive with brilliant, multicolored wildflowers. These areas are home to more than 130 species of birds and 50 species of mammals. Mountain goats, chipmunks, and marmots are favorites among visitors, but deer, elk, bears, mountain lions, and other animals can also be seen here.

Mount Rainier is the largest volcano in the Cascade Range, which extends from Mount Garibaldi in southwestern British Columbia to Lassen Peak in northern California. The eruption of Mount St. Helens in 1980 gives a clue to the violent history of these volcanoes. Eruptions occurred at Mount Rainier as recently as the mid-1800s. Even today, steam emissions often form caves in the summit ice cap and usually melt the snow along the rims of the twin craters.

A young volcano by geologic standards, Mount Rainier was once a fairly symmetrical mountain rising about 16,000 feet above sea level. But glaciers and further volcanic activity shaped the mountain into an irregular mass of rock. The sculpting action of the ice gave each face of the mountain its own distinctive profile. The glaciation continues today, as Mount Rainier supports the largest glacier system in the contiguous United States, with 35 square miles of ice and 26 named glaciers.

Much of the park's beauty can be attributed to the glaciers, which at one time extended far beyond the park boundaries. The moving masses of ice carved deep valleys separated by high, sharp ridges or broad plateaus. From certain vantages, the valleys accentuate the mountain's height. The glaciers are the source of the many streams in the park, as well as several rivers in the Pacific Northwest. The meltwaters also nourish the various plants and animals throughout the region.

Winters at Mount Rainier are legendary. Moist air masses moving eastward across the Pacific Ocean are intercepted by the mountain. As a result, some areas on the mountain commonly receive 50 or more feet of snow each winter. At 5,400 feet in elevation, Paradise

made history in 1971-1972, when it received 93 feet of snow, the heaviest snowfall ever recorded in this country; the 3-story Paradise Inn is often buried up to its roof in snow. Because the mountain's summit is usually above the storm clouds, the snowfall there is not as great.

The park's transformation from winter wonderland to summer playground is almost magical. Beginning in June or July, the weather becomes warm and clear, although the mountain is occasionally shrouded in clouds. The snow at the lower elevations then disappears; meltwaters fill stream valleys and cascade over cliffs; wildflowers blanket the meadows; and visitors descend on the park for its many recreational activities.

There are several entrances to the park. The roads from the Nisqually entrance to Paradise and from the southeast boundary to Ohanapecosh are usually open year-round but may be closed temporarily during the winter. Following the first heavy snow, around November 1, all other roads are closed until May or June. The entrance fee is $10 per vehicle. For further information, contact Mount Rainier National Park, Tahoma Woods, Star Rte, Ashford 98304; phone 360/569-2211.

What to See and Do

Camping. *Tahoma Woods, Ashford. Phone toll-free 800/365-2267.* Major campgrounds are located at Cougar Rock, Ohanapecosh, and White River, and have fireplaces, tables, water, and sanitary facilities. Smaller campgrounds are at Sunshine Point and Ipsut Creek. No hookups; dump stations at Cougar Rock and Ohanapecosh only. All areas closed during winter except Sunshine Point. **$$$$**

Carbon River. Located on the Pacific side of Mount Rainier, the Carbon River area receives the most rainfall and contains the most luxurious forests. In fact, much of the woodland here is considered temperate rainforest. The main road into the Carbon River and the northwestern corner of the park leads from Carbonado into Ipsut Creek, a seasonal ranger station and campground.

Crystal Mountain Resort. *33914 Crystal Mountain Blvd, Crystal Mountain (98022). E via Hwy 410, then 6 miles E, on NE boundary of Mount Rainier National Park, in Mount Baker-Snoqualmie National*

Forest. *Phone 360/663-2265. www.crystalmt.com.* Located 75 miles south of Seattle in the shadows of Mount Rainier, Crystal Mountain is a ski resort with an impressive 3,100-foot vertical drop and equally impressive 340 inches of average annual snowfall. During the December-to-April ski season, ten lifts service 1,300 acres of skiable terrain on Silver King Mountain, a nice balance of beginner, intermediate, and advanced trails; there are an additional 1,000 acres of backcountry terrain for diehards. The place is known for its family-friendly perks, such as free children's passes with an adult purchase and a "Kids Club" that offers supervision, skiing classes, and lunch while parents enjoy the slopes. The resort also encompasses several hotels (ranging from a basic room to a slope-side honeymoon cabin) and restaurants, as well as a rental shop, skiing and snowboarding school, and a day spa.

Fishing. No license required. Fishing season is open in lakes and ponds late April-October, in rivers and streams late May-November. Heavy snowfall restricts access to all water November-May. Most lakes are usually not ice-free until early July; ice-fishing not permitted. Specific regulations and details on special closure areas are available at ranger stations.

Hiking. More than 250 miles of trails wind throughout the park, offering unspoiled views of Mount Rainier, glaciers, meadows, lakes, waterfalls, and deep valleys; many trails converge at Paradise and Sunrise; trails vary in degree of difficulty. The Wonderland Trail, a 93-mile trail that circles the mountain, is linked with several other trails in the park. A Pictorial Map (1986) of the park's topography and 50 Hikes in Mount Rainier National Park, an illustrated book with maps and hiking details, are available for purchase. Hiking information centers (summer, daily) are located at Longmire and White River. Permit is required year-round for overnight backpacking; available at ranger stations and visitor centers (fee).

Interpretive programs and walks. Programs, including nature walks and evening slide shows, are offered at several locations. Schedules are posted in visitor centers and at other locations. (Late June-Labor Day)

Longmire. *Near the Nisqually entrance, in SW corner of park.* Longmire is often the first stop for visitors in this area of the park. Visitor center; lodging; cafe, limited groceries. Facilities usually open year-round.

Mountain climbing-Mount Rainier. *Phone 360/569-2211. www.nps.gov/mora.* The park has many opportunities for climbers; one of the most popular climbs is the two-day trek to the summit of Mount Rainier. The guide service at Paradise conducts various programs for new and experienced climbers. Climbs should be attempted only by persons who are in good physical condition and have the proper equipment; deep crevasses and unstable ridges of lava are dangerous. All climbers must register with a park ranger (fee).

Ohanapecosh. *SE corner of park. Phone 360/569-2211.* A preserve of rushing waters and dense old growth forest. Some of the largest trees in the park—many over 1,000 years old—are here. The Grove of the Patriarchs, a cluster of massive conifers on an island in the Ohanapecosh River, is reached by bridge along a popular trail that starts near the Steven's Canyon Entrance Station. At the Ohanapecosh Visitor Center, exhibits tell the story of the lowland forest ecosystem, where Douglas fir, western hemlock, and red cedar trees reign supreme.

Paradise. *Accessible from Nisqually entrance at SW corner of park, and from Stevens Canyon entrance at SE corner of park (summer only). Phone 360/569-2211.* This is the most visited area of the park, featuring subalpine meadows covered with wildflowers, and hiking trails that provide views of Nisqually, Paradise, and Stevens glaciers. Visitor center with slide programs and films (May-mid-Oct: daily; rest of year: weekends only); lodging (see LIMITED-SERVICE HOTELS); café (summer, daily); snack bar (summer, daily; winter, weekends and holidays only). The nearby Narada Falls drop 168 feet to Paradise River Canyon; viewpoints along stairway.

Paradise area. *Phone 360/569-2211.* Cross-country skiing is popular here; equipment rentals and lessons available at Longmire. For further information contact park headquarters.

Sunrise. On northeast side of mountain; accessible only July-mid-September. This is the highest point reached by a paved road within Washington (6,400 feet). The drive to Sunrise is worth the time; the crowds are smaller, and this area offers spectacular views of the mountain and Emmons Glacier, the largest in the US outside Alaska. Visitor center, snack bar, picnic area.

⭐ **Visitor centers.** Located at Longmire; at Paradise; at Sunrise (summer only); and at Ohanapecosh (summer only), near the Stevens Canyon entrance, in southeastern corner of park. All offer exhibits and publications.

White Pass Village. *White Pass, Naches. On Hwy 12, 12 miles E of Stevens Canyon (SE) entrance to the park. Phone 509/672-3100. www.skiwhitepass.com.* Quad, triple, two double chairlifts, Pomalift, rope tow; patrol, school, rentals; accommodations, restaurant, bar, daycare, general store, service station. Longest run 2 1/2 miles; vertical drop 1,500 feet. (Mid-Nov-mid-Apr, daily) Cross-country trails. **$$$$**

Limited-Service Hotels

★ ★ **THE NISQUALLY LODGE.** *31609 Hwy 706, Ashford (98304). Phone 360/569-8804; toll-free 888/674-3554; fax 360/569-2435. www.escapetothemountains .com.* This chalet-style lodge is near the entrance to Mount Rainier National Park, making it a great place from which to explore the outdoors. The accommodations are simple but do provide telephones and TVs; laundry facilities, an outdoor hot tub, and a great room with fireplace round out the amenities. 24 rooms, 2 story. Complimentary continental breakfast. Check-out 11 am. Restaurant. Whirlpool. **$**

★ ★ **PARADISE INN.** *PO Box 108, Ashford (98304). Phone 360/569-2275; fax 360/569-2770.* This shake-shingle mountain lodge, part of the Mount Rainier National Park system, was built with onsite timber in 1917. The decorative woodwork inside, including the rustic piano and 14-foot grandfather clock, was added shortly thereafter. But the real reason to come here is the outdoors, as attested by the lack of telephones and TVs in the guest rooms. In the shadow of majestic Mount Rainier, guests enjoy miles of hiking trails, flowering meadows, and the many other activities afforded by the nearby national park. Fuel up after a busy day at the Paradise Inn Dining Room, which serves classic American cuisine with a Pacific Northwest twist. If you'd like to visit the park between mid-October and mid-May, when the inn is closed, try its sister property, the National Park Inn, which is open year-round. (Their contact information is the same.)117 rooms, 4 story. Closed mid-Oct-mid-May. Check-out 11 am. Restaurant, bar. **$**

Mount St. Helens National Volcanic Monument

See also Amboy

(From I-5 exit 68: 48 miles E on Hwy 12 to Randle, then S on Forest Service Rd 25; from I-5 exit 21: approximately 35 miles NE on Hwy 503, Forest Service rds 90, 25)

Web site www.fs.fed.us/gpnf/mshnvm

In 1978, two geologists who had been studying Mount St. Helens warned that this youngest volcano in the Cascade Range could erupt again by the end of the century. On March 27, 1980, the volcano did just that, ending 123 years of inactivity. Less than two months later, on May 18, a massive eruption transformed this beautiful snow-capped mountain and the surrounding forest into an eerie, desolate landscape with few signs of life.

The eruption sent a lateral blast of hot ash and gases out across the land at speeds up to 670 miles per hour, flattening 150 square miles of forest north of the volcano. An ash plume rising 13 miles into the atmosphere was spread eastward by the wind, coating many cities in Washington, Idaho, and Montana with a fine grit. Rivers were choked with logs and mud, huge logging trucks were toppled like small toys, and the mountain, having lost 1,300 feet of its summit, was left with a gaping crater 2,000 feet deep, 1/2 mile wide, and a mile long.

Among the 57 people missing or killed by the eruption was 83-year-old Harry Truman, who for many years owned a lodge on Spirit Lake, just north of the mountain. Truman refused to heed evacuation warnings, believing his "beloved mountain" would not harm him; he and his lodge are now beneath hundreds of feet of mud and water.

The Monument, established in 1982, covers 110,000 acres within the Gifford Pinchot National Forest and provides a rare, natural laboratory in which scientists and visitors can view the effects of a volcanic eruption. Despite the destruction, the return of vegetation and wildlife to the blast zone has been relatively rapid. Within just weeks of the eruption, small plants and insects had begun to make their way through the ash. Today, herds of elk and other animals, as well as fir trees and wildflowers, have taken a strong foothold here.

Forest Service Road 25, which runs north-south near the eastern boundary, provides access to views of the volcano. The roads are usually closed from approximately November-May because of snow; some roads are narrow and winding.

Visitors are advised to phone ahead for current road conditions. Although volcanic activity at Mount St. Helens has decreased greatly in the last few years, some roads into the Monument could be closed if weather conditions dictate.

For further information, including a map with the locations of various facilities and attractions, contact the Monument Headquarters, 42218 NE Yale Bridge Rd, Amboy 98601; phone 360/247-3900.

What to See and Do

Ape Cave. *Amboy. On Forest Service Rd 8303, in southern part of monument. Phone 360/247-3900.* At 12,810 feet in length, the cave is said to be one of the longest intact lava tubes in the continental US. Downslope portion of cave, extending approximately 4,000 feet, is the most easily traveled. Upslope portion, extending nearly 7,000 feet, is recommended only for visitors carrying the proper equipment. All visitors are advised to carry three sources of light and wear sturdy shoes or boots and warm clothing; cave is a constant 42° F. An information station is also here; lantern rentals available seasonally.

Camping. There are no campgrounds within the Monument, but many public and private campgrounds are located nearby. Primitive camping is usually allowed throughout the Gifford Pinchot National Forest (see VANCOUVER).

Coldwater Ridge Visitor Center. *3029 Spirits Lake Hwy, Mount St. Helens National Volcanic Monument (98611). 45 miles E of Castle Rock. Phone 360/274-2131.* Major interpretive center at 3,100 feet offers views directly into mouth of crater. Lodgelike building overlooks Coldwater Lake created by eruption

landslide. Films and viewing area; displays focus on rebirth of nature. Bookstore, cafeteria, interpretive hikes. (Daily)

Hiking. An extensive system of trails offers hikers impressive views of the volcano and surrounding devastated areas. Trails vary in degree of difficulty. Some trails are accessible to wheelchairs. Temperatures can be very warm along the trails due to a lack of shade; hikers are advised to carry water.

Interpretive walks and programs. Presented at several locations. Details are available at the information stations, Monument headquarters, or visitor centers.

Johnson Ridge Obervatory. *3029 Spirit Lake Hwy, Mount St. Helens National Volcanic Monument (98611). 52 miles E of Castle Rock. Phone 360/274-2131.* At 4,200 feet. State-of-the-art interpretive displays focus on sequence of geological events that drastically altered the landscape and opened up a new era in the science of monitoring an active volcano and forecasting eruptions. Wide-screen theater presentation, interpretive exhibits, staffed information desk, bookstore. Views of the lava dome, crater, pumice plain, and landslide deposit. Visitors can take a 1/2-mile walk on Eruption Trail. Interpretive talks and hikes in summer. (Daily) **$**

⭐ **Mount St. Helens Visitor Center.** *Outside the Monument, off I-5 exit 49, 5 miles east of Castle Rock on Hwy 504. Phone 360/274-2100.* (Center cannot be reached directly from the northeast side Monument.) The center houses exhibits that include a walk-through model of the volcano, displays on the history of the mountain and the 1980 eruption, and volcano monitoring equipment. A 10-minute slide program and a 22-minute movie are shown several times daily, and special programs are held throughout the year. Also here are volcano viewpoints and a nature trail along Silver Lake. Contact 3029 Spirit Lake Hwy, Castle Rock 98611. (Daily; closed holidays) **$**

Summit climb. *Phone 360/247-3961.* Climbers are allowed to hike to the summit; free climbing permits are issued on a limited basis. Climb should be attempted only by persons in good physical condition. For climbing information contact the headquarters.

Visitor information stations. Located at Pine Creek, on Forest Service Road 90 near the southeast side of the Monument; at Woods Creek, at the junction of

Forest Service roads 25 and 76 near the northeast side of the Monument; and at Ape Cave. (Summer, daily; may remain open until Labor Day)

Volcano viewpoints. *Off Forest Service Rd 99.* There are several viewpoints throughout the eastern side of the Monument, particularly along Forest Service Road 99; this road leads to Windy Ridge, with a spectacular view of the volcano and Spirit Lake. Lahar Viewpoint, on Forest Service Road 83, provides an excellent view of mud flow activity on the south side of the mountain.

Mount Vernon (A-2)

See also Anacortes, La Conner, Sedro Woolley

Settled 1870
Population 26,232
Elevation 31 ft
Area Code 360
Zip 98273
Information Chamber of Commerce, 117 N 1st St #4; phone 360/428-8547
Web site www.ci.mount-vernon.wa.us

Developed by farmers and loggers, Mount Vernon is a major commercial center. Centrally located between Puget Sound and the North Cascades, the Skagit Delta's deep alluvial soil grows 125 varieties of produce, including flowers and bulbs, fruit, and vegetables. Spring brings fields of daffodils, tulips, and irises to the country; a map of the fields is available at the Chamber of Commerce. The city is named for George Washington's plantation in Virginia.

What to See and Do

Bay View State Park. *10905 Bay View Edison Rd, Mount Vernon (98273). 7 miles W via Hwy 20, then right on Bay View Edison Rd. Phone 360/757-0227.* Approximately 25 acres. Sand beach (no swimming), picnicking, camping (hookups). Interpretive center nearby.

Hillcrest Park. *1717 S 13th St, Mount Vernon (98274). Phone 360/336-6213.* Approximately 30 acres with playgrounds, tennis and basketball courts, hiking trails, covered and open picnic facilities, barbecue pits. **FREE**

Little Mountain. *SE of city on Blackburn Rd W. Phone 360/336-6213.* Observation area atop 934-foot mountain, providing view of Skagit Valley, Olympic Mountains, Mount Rainier, and San Juan Islands; surrounded by 480-acre forested park. Hiking, picnicking. (Daily)

Special Events

Awesome Autumn Festival. *Phone 360/428-8547.* Six weeks of events including a 4-acre corn maze, arts and crafts fair, pumpkin festival. Sept-Oct.

Prime Outlets at Burlington. *448 Fashion Way, Burlington (98233). I-5 to exit 229. Phone 360/757-3549.* If you're a bargain shopper who wants to take a drive out of the city, the Prime Outlets at Burlington is your place. Just about 65 miles north of Seattle, this shopper's paradise houses nearly 50 stores, like Tommy Hilfiger, Gap, Reebok, Farberware, and Samsonite. On the drive here, you'll be able to enjoy some of the Northwest's breathtaking scenery.

Skagit County Fair. *1410 Virginia St, Mount Vernon (98273). Phone 360/336-9453.* Second week in Aug.

Skagit Valley Tulip Festival. *PO Box 1784, Mount Vernon (98273). Phone 360/428-5959. www.tulipfestival.org.* This annual festival gives the county's two primary tulip growers, the Skagit Valley Bulb Farm and the Washington Bulb Company, a chance to display their beautiful blooms at sites throughout the county. Each grower invites visitors to tour its gardens, which feature hundreds of thousands of bulbs and more than 60 varieties of the famous Dutch export. But this month-long festival is about more than just flowers: the many events include the Anacortes Quilt Walk, Art in a Pickle Barn, and a bald eagle and birding float trip. Apr.

Full-Service Hotels

★ ★ **BEST WESTERN COTTONTREE INN.** *2300 Market St, Mount Vernon (98273). Phone 360/428-5678; toll-free 800/662-6886; fax 360/428-1844. www.bwcottreeinn.com.* Just off I-5 and near Mount Vernon College, this hotel is close to a variety of restaurants, making it a convenient stopover. Recently renovated guest rooms have refrigerators and microwaves, and wireless Internet access is availble throughout the property. The hotel doesn't have its own fitness room, but guests receive complimentary privileges at the nearby Riverside Health Club. 120 rooms, 3 story. Pets accepted, some restrictions; fee. Complimentary full breakfast. Check-in 3 pm, check-out noon. Wireless Internet access. Restaurant, bar. Outdoor pool. **$**

Specialty Lodging

The following lodging establishment is approved by Mobil Travel Guide, but due to its unique and individualized nature has not been given a traditional Mobil Star rating. Included in this listing you may find bed-and-breakfasts, limited-service inns, guest ranches, and other unique hotel properties.

THE WHITE SWAN GUEST HOUSE. *15872 Moore Rd, Mount Vernon (98273). Phone 360/445-6805. www.thewhiteswan.com.* Queen Anne-style farmhouse (circa 1890). 3 rooms. Complimentary continental breakfast. Check-in 3-6 pm, check-out 11 am. **$$**

Neah Bay

See also Port Angeles, Sequim

Settled 1791
Population 794
Elevation 0 ft
Area Code 360
Zip 98357
Web site www.olympicpeninsula.com/index.htm

What to See and Do

Makah Cultural and Research Center. *Hwy 112 and Bay View Ave, Neah Bay. Hwy 112, 1 mile E. Phone 360/645-2711.* Exhibits on Makah and Northwest Coast Native Americans; 500-year-old artifacts uncovered at the Ozette archaeological site, a Makah village dating back 2,000 years. Craft shop; dioramas; canoes; complete longhouse. (Memorial Day-mid-Sept: daily; rest of year: Wed-Sun; closed Jan 1, Thanksgiving, Dec 25) **$$**

Specialty Lodgings

The following lodging establishments are approved by Mobil Travel Guide, but due to their unique and individualized nature have not been given a traditional Mobil Star rating. Included in this listing you may find bed-and-breakfasts, limited-service inns, guest ranches, and other unique hotel properties.

CHITO BEACH RESORT. *7639 Hwy 112, Clallam Bay (98326). Phone 360/963-2581. www.chitobeach .com.* Long regarded as one of the state's best waterfront accommodations, Chito Beach is home to an amazingly beautiful stretch of Washington State's rugged coastline. 4 rooms, 2 story. **$**

KING FISHER INN. *1562 Hwy 112, Neah Bay (98357). Phone toll-free 888/622-8216. www. kingfisherenterprises.com.* Overlooking the Straight of San Juan de Fuca and international shipping lanes with views of Vancouver Island in the background, this inn is perfect for year-round hiking, surfing, and kayaking. 4 rooms, 3 story. **$$**

STRAITSIDE RESORT. *241 Front St, Sekiu (98381). Phone 360/963-2100.* Located on the Strait of Juan de Fuca with waterfront views, full kitchens, and plenty of outdoor excursions available. 7 rooms, 2 story. **$**

Newport (A-6)

See also Spokane

Settled 1890
Population 1,921
Area Code 509
Zip 99156
Information Chamber of Commerce, 325 W 4th St; phone 509/447-5812
Web site www.newport-wa.org

A shopping, distribution, and lumbering center, Newport was born in Idaho. For a while, there was a Newport on both sides of the state line, but the US Post Office interceded on behalf of the Washington community, which was the county seat of Pend Oreille County. Newport is known as "the city of flags"; flags from around the world are displayed on the main streets. A Ranger District office of the Colville National Forest is located here.

What to See and Do

Historical Society Museum. *402 S Washington Ave, Newport (99156). Phone 509/447-5388.* In old railroad depot; houses historical artifacts of Pend Oreille County; two reconstructed log cabins. (Mid-May-Sept, daily) **DONATION**

Big Wheel. *Centennial Plaza, Newport. Phone 509/447-5812.* Giant Corliss steam engine that for years powered the town's foremost sawmill. Flag display. A visitor information center is located here.

North Bend (B-3)

See also Issaquah, Seattle

Founded 1889
Population 4,746
Elevation 442 ft
Area Code 425
Zip 98045
Information The Upper Snoqualmie Valley Chamber of Commerce, PO Box 357, 98045; phone 425/888-4440
Web site ci.north-bend.wa.us

A gateway to Mount Baker-Snoqualmie National Forest—Snoqualmie section—and a popular winter sports area, North Bend also serves as a shipping town for this logging, farming, and dairy region. A Ranger District office of the Mount Baker-Snoqualmie National Forest is located here.

What to See and Do

Alpental. *1001 Hwy 906, North Bend (98068). 17 miles SE on I-90, then 1 mile N on Alpental Rd. Phone 425/434-7669.* Three double chairlifts, quad, three rope tows, platter pull; patrol, school, rentals; cafeteria, bar. Longest run 1 1/2 miles; vertical drop 2,200 feet. (Hours, fees same as Summit West) Shuttle bus to Summit West, Summit East, and Summit Central (Fri nights, weekends and holidays); tickets interchangeable. **$$$$**

North Bend Outlet Stores. *461 S Fork Ave SW, North Bend (98045). 31 miles E of Seattle; I-90 to exit 31. Phone 425/888-4505.* Located just 40 minutes from Seattle, this complex of outlet stores offers amazing bargains from names such as Eddie Bauer, Gap, the Naturalizer, KB Toys, and many more. The mall, itself, doesn't have many choices for satiating the appetite you're sure to work up after power shopping, (just a lone Subway), but there are many options across the street.

Snoqualmie Falls. *6501 Railroad Ave SE, Snoqualmie (98109). 4 miles NW via Hwy 202. www.snoqualmiefalls.com.* Perpetual snow in the Cascade Mountains feeds the 268-foot falls. Power plant; park area; trail to bottom of falls.

Snoqualmie Valley Historical Museum. *320 Bendigo Blvd S, North Bend (98045). Phone 425/888-3200.* Displays, room settings of early pioneer life from 1890s; photos, Native American artifacts; logging exhibits; farm shed; reference material. Slide shows; changing exhibits. (Apr-mid-Dec, Thurs-Sun; tours by appointment) **DONATION**

Summit Central. *1001 Hwy 906, North Bend (98068). 18 miles SE on I-90 at Snoqualmie Pass. Phone 425/434-7669.* Two triple, six double chairlifts, five rope tows; patrol, school, rentals; cross-country center; cafeteria, bar; day care center. Vertical drop 1,020 feet. (Mid-Nov-Apr, daily) Shuttle bus to Summit West, Summit East, and Alpental (Fri nights, weekends, and holidays); tickets interchangeable. **$$$$**

Summit East. *1001 Hwy 906, North Bend (98068). 19 miles SE on I-90, at Snoqualmie Pass. Phone 425/434-7669.* Two double chairlifts; patrol, school, rentals; cafeteria, bar. Vertical drop 1,055 feet. Shuttle bus to Summit Central, Summit West, and Alpental. (Late Dec-mid-Mar, Fri-Sat, and Sun) Tickets interchangeable. **$$$$**

Summit West. *1001 Hwy 906, North Bend (98068). 17 miles SE on I-90. Phone 425/434-7669. www.summit-at-snoqualmie.com.* Six double, two triple, quad chairlifts; two rope tows; 15 slopes and trails. Patrol, school, rentals; bar, restaurant, cafeteria; day care center. Vertical drop 900 feet. (Mid-Nov-Apr, daily) Intermediate chairs; half-day and evening rates. **$$$$**

Oak Harbor (A-2)

See also Anacortes, Coupeville, Everett, Port Townsend

Settled 1849
Population 19,795
Elevation 115 ft
Area Code 360
Zip 98277
Information Chamber of Commerce Visitor Information Center, 5506 Hwy 20; phone 360/675-3535
Web site www.whidbey.net/islandco

This trading center on Whidbey Island was first settled by sea captains and adventurers and then in the 1890s by immigrants from the Netherlands who developed the rich countryside. The town's name was inspired by the oak trees that cloaked the area when the first settlers arrived, which have been preserved. Side roads lead to secluded beaches and excellent boating and fishing, with marinas nearby.

What to See and Do

Holland Gardens. *SE 6th Ave W and Ireland St, Oak Harbor.* Gardens of flowers and shrubs surround blue and white windmill; Dutch provincial flags, tulips, and daffodils decorate gardens during Holland Happening. (Daily) **FREE**

Oak Harbor Beach Park. *Phone 360/679-5551.* Authentic Dutch windmill; picnicking, barbecue pit; 1,800-foot sand beach, lagoon swimming, bathhouse, wading pools; tennis, baseball diamonds, playground; illuminated trails. Camping (hookups, dump station; fee). (Daily) **FREE**

Whidbey Island Naval Air Station. *1170 W Lexington Ave, Oak Harbor (98278). Approximately 5 miles N on Hwy 20. Phone 360/257-2286.* Only active naval air station in the Northwest. Guided group tours (minimum ten persons); reservations required several months in advance. **FREE**

Special Events

Holland Happening. *Phone 360/675-3755.* Tulip show, arts and crafts, Dutch buffet, carnival, culture food-fest, square dance exhibition, parade. Late Apr.

Whidbey Island Jazz Festival. *302 N Main St, Oak Harbor (98239). Phone toll-free 888/747-7777.* Mid-Aug.

Limited-Service Hotels

★ ★ **AULD HOLLAND INN.** *33575 Hwy 20, Oak Harbor (98277). Phone 360/675-2288; toll-free 800/ 228-0148; fax 360/675-2817. www.auldhollandinn.com.* 34 rooms. Complimentary continental breakfast. Check-out 11 am. Restaurant, bar. Fitness room. Pool, whirlpool. Tennis. **$**

★ **BEST WESTERN HARBOR PLAZA.** *33175 Hwy 20, Oak Harbor (98277). Phone 360/679-4567; toll-free 800/927-5478; fax 360/675-2543. www. bestwestern.com.* 80 rooms, 3 story. Pets accepted, some restrictions; fee. Complimentary continental breakfast. Check-out noon. Bar. Pool, whirlpool. **$**

Ocean Shores (C-1)

See also Aberdeen, Hoquiam, Westport

Population 3,836
Elevation 21 ft
Area Code 360
Zip 98569
Information Chamber of Commerce, Box 382; phone 360/289-2451 or toll-free 800/762-3224
Web site www.oceanshores.org

This 6,000-acre area at the southern end of the Olympic Peninsula is a seaside resort community with 6 miles of ocean beaches, 23 miles of lakes and canals, and 12 miles of bay front. Clamming, crabbing, and trout and bass fishing are popular.

What to See and Do

Pacific Paradise Family Fun Center. *767 Minard Ave, Ocean Shores (98569). Phone 360/289-9537; fax 360/289-9566.* 36-hole miniature golf (fee); entertainment center; Paradise Lake (fee).

Limited-Service Hotels

★ **CANTERBURY INN.** *643 Ocean Shores Blvd, Ocean Shores (98569). Phone 360/289-3317; toll-free 800/562-6678; fax 360/289-3420. www.canterburyinn .com.* 44 rooms, 3 story. Check-out noon. Indoor pool, whirlpool. **$**

★ ★ **SHILO INN.** *707 Ocean Shores Blvd NW, Ocean Shores (98569). Phone 360/289-4600; fax 360/289-0355. www.shiloinns.com.* 113 rooms, 4 story. Check-out noon. Restaurant, bar. Fitness room. Indoor pool, whirlpool. **$**

Olympia (C-2)

See also Centralia, Tacoma

Founded 1850
Population 42,514
Elevation 100 ft
Area Code 360
Information Olympia/Thurston County Chamber of Commerce, 521 Legion Way SE, 98507-1427; phone 360/357-3362
Web site www.thurstonchamber.com

As though inspired by the natural beauty that surrounds it—Mount Rainier and the Olympic Mountains on the skyline and Puget Sound at its doorstep—Washington's capital city is a carefully groomed, parklike community. Although concentrating on the business of government, Olympia also serves tourists and the needs of nearby military installations. It is a deep-sea port and a manufacturer of wood products, plastics, and mobile homes. The tiny village of Smithfield was chosen in 1851 as the site for a customhouse. The US Collector of Customs prevailed on the citizens to rename the community for the Olympic Mountains. Shortly afterward, agitation to separate the land north of the Columbia from Oregon began. In 1853, the new territory was proclaimed, with Olympia as territorial capital. The first legislature convened here in 1854, despite Native American unrest that forced construction of a stockade ringing the town. (The 15-foot wall was later dismantled and used to plank the capital's streets.) The Olympia metropolitan area also includes the communities of Lacey and Tumwater, the oldest settlement in the state (1845) north of the Columbia River. The city today has a compact 20-square-block business section and a variety of stores that attract shoppers from a wide area.

What to See and Do

★ **Capitol Group.** *Capitol Way and 11th Ave, Olympia. On Capitol Way between 11th and 14th aves. Phone 360/586-8687.* In 35-acre park overlooking Capitol Lake and Budd Inlet of Puget Sound are

Capitol grounds. Grounds lined with Japanese cherry trees attract hundreds of visitors in the spring; plantings are changed seasonally. Also here is a replica of Tivoli Gardens Fountain in Copenhagen, Denmark; sunken gardens, state conservatory (Memorial Day-Labor Day, daily); World War I and Vietnam memorials. Grounds (daily).

Legislative Building. *Phone 360/586-8687.* A 287-foot dome with 47-foot lantern; Neoclassical architecture; lavishly detailed interior.

Library Building. Houses rare books; murals, mosaics. (Mon-Fri; closed holidays)

Temple of Justice. Houses State Supreme Court. (Mon-Fri; closed holidays)

Capitol Lake. *14th and Capitol Way, Olympia (98409). Phone 360/586-8687.* Formed by a dam at the point where fresh water of the Deschutes River empties into salt water of Budd Inlet. From the top of the dam, thousands of salmon can be seen making their way upstream during spawning season starting in mid-Aug. Boating, bicycle and running trails, playground and picnic tables. (Daily) **FREE**

Millersylvania State Park. *12245 Tilley Rd S, Olympia (98512). 10 miles S off I-5. Phone 360/753-1519.* More than 800 acres along Deep Lake. Swimming, fishing, boating; hiking, picnicking, camping (hookups).

Mima Mounds Natural Area. *1405 Rush Rd, Olympia (98506). I-5 S to exit 95 toward Littlerock (Hwy 121), then 128th Ave SW 1 mile to t-jct with Waddell Creek Rd. Turn N 1 mile to preserve. Phone 360/748-2383.* Mounds 8 to 10 feet high and 20 to 30 feet in diameter spread across miles of meadows west of Olympia. Once thought to be ancient burial chambers, they are now believed to be the result of Ice Age freeze-thaw patterns. Trails wind through 500-acre site. Information kiosk, picnic area. Contact Washington Department of Natural Resources. **FREE**

Olympic National Forest. *1835 Black Lake Blvd SW, Olympia (98502). NW of city, reached via Hwy 101, exit 104. Phone 360/956-2400. www.fs.fed.us/r6/olympic.* More than 632,000 acres. Picturesque streams and rivers, winding ridges, rugged peaks, deep canyons, tree-covered slopes; rain forest, the world's largest stand of Douglas fir, public-owned oyster beds; populous herd of Roosevelt elk. Swimming, fishing; hiking, hunting, picnicking, camping (May-Sept).

Oyster beds. Big Skookum, Little Skookum, Mud, Oyster bays. Beds of rare Olympia oyster found only in South Puget Sound.

Percival Landing Park. *Waterfront, Olympia. Between Thurston St and 4th Ave.* Pleasant 1/2-mile walk along marina filled with pleasure crafts and seals. Observation tower; at south end is statue of *The Kiss.* Also Heritage Fountain, popular with children on summer days. **FREE**

Priest Point Park. *E Bay Dr, overlooks Budd Inlet.* Playgrounds, hiking trails, picnic facilities in heavily wooded area with view of Olympic Mountains. (Daily) **FREE**

State Capital Museum. *212 21st Ave SW, Olympia (98501). Phone 360/753-2580.* A 1920 Spanish-style stucco mansion houses art gallery; Native American art and culture exhibits; pioneer exhibits. (Tues-Sun; closed holidays) **$$**

State Capitol Campus. *14 Capitol Way, Olympia (98409). On Capitol Way between 11th and 14th aves. Phone 360/586-8687.*

Tumwater Falls Park. *S of city off I-5, 15 acres. Phone 360/943-2550.* Gentle walk (1 mile) follows spectacular falls of the Deschutes River. Landscaped grounds, picnicking, playground. Good view of fall salmon run on man-made fish ladder. (Daily) Adjacent is

Tumwater Valley Athletic Club. *4833 Tumwater Valley Dr, Tumwater (98501). Phone 360/943-9500.* Indoor swimming pools. Tennis and racquetball courts. 18-hole golf course. Fee for activities. (All year)

Wolf Haven International. *3111 Offut Lake Rd, Tenino (98589). Phone 360/264-4695.* Wolf Sanctuary center on 75 acres; also home to 40 wolves no longer able to live in the wild. Interpretive center, tours, and ecology center. (May-Sept: daily; rest of year: Wed-Sun; closed Jan and Feb) **$$$**

Yahiro Gardens. *Plum St and Union Ave, Olympia.* A cooperative project between Olympia and its sister city, Yashiro, Japan. The gardens include a pagoda, bamboo grove, pond, and waterfall. (Daily during daylight hours) **FREE**

Special Events

Capital City Marathon and Relay. *2139 Lakemoor Dr SW, Olympia (98512). Phone 360/786-1786.* Features an 8-kilometer run, children's run, 5-10-kilometer walk, wheelchair division. Weekend before Memorial Day weekend.

Lakefair. *Capitol Lake, 612 5th Ave, Olympia (98501). Phone 360/943-7344.* Parade, carnival midway, boating and swimming competition, naval vessel tours, flower shows. Mid-July.

Olympia Farmers Market. *700 Capitol Way N, Olympia (98501). Phone 360/352-9096.* Includes fresh produce, baked goods, food booths, seafood, crafts. First weekend in Apr through Dec; weekends only in Apr, Nov, and Dec.

Super Saturday. *Evergreen State College, 2700 Evergreen Pkwy, Olympia (98505). Phone 360/867-6000.* Arts, crafts, food fair. Early June.

Thurston County Fair. *Fairgrounds in Lacey. 3054 Carpenter Rd SE, Olympia (98503). Phone 360/786-5453.* Late July-early Aug.

Limited-Service Hotels

★ **BEST WESTERN TUMWATER INN.** *5188 Capitol Blvd, Tumwater (98501). Phone 360/956-1235; fax 360/956-1235. www.bestwestern.com.* 89 rooms, 2 story. Pets accepted; fee. Complimentary continental breakfast. Check-out 11 am. Fitness room. **$**

★ ★ **RAMADA INN GOVERNOR HOUSE.** *621 S Capitol Way, Olympia (98501). Phone 360/352-7700; toll-free 888/298-2054; fax 360/943-9349. www.ramada.com.* 125 rooms, 8 story. Pets accepted; fee. Complimentary full breakfast. Check-in 3 pm, check-out noon. Restaurant, bar. Fitness room. Outdoor pool, whirlpool. **$**

★ ★ **RED LION.** *2300 Evergreen Park Dr, Olympia (98502). Phone 360/943-4000; toll-free 800/733-5466; fax 360/357-6604. www.redlion.com.* This state capital property is near the beautiful Cascade Mountains and many recreational activities. 190 rooms, 3 story. Pets accepted; fee. Complimentary continental breakfast. Check-in 3 pm, check-out 11 am. High-speed Internet access. Restaurant, bar. Fitness room. Outdoor pool, whirlpool. Business center. **$**

Restaurant

★ ★ **BUDD BAY CAFE.** *525 N Columbia St, Olympia (98501). Phone 360/357-6963. www. buddbaycafe.com.* American menu. Lunch, dinner, Sun brunch. Closed Dec 25. Bar. Children's menu. Outdoor seating. **$$**

Olympic National Park

See also Forks, Port Angeles, Sequim

(119 miles NW of Olympia on Hwy 101)

Web site: www.nps.gov/olym

In these 1,442 square miles of rugged wilderness are such contrasts as the wettest climate in the contiguous United States (averaging 140-167 inches of precipitation a year) and one of the driest, seascapes and snow-cloaked peaks, glaciers and rain forests, elk and seals. With Olympic National Forest, State Sustained Yield Forest No. 1, much private land, and several American Indian reservations, the national park occupies the Olympic Peninsula, due west of Seattle and Puget Sound.

The Spanish explorer Juan Perez was the first European explorer to spot the Olympic Mountains in 1774. However, the first major western land exploration did not take place until more than a century later. Since then, generations of adventurous tourists have redis-covered Mount Olympus, the highest peak (7,965 feet); several other 7,000-foot peaks; and hundreds of ridges and crests between 5,000 and 6,000 feet high. The architects of these ruggedly contoured mountains are glaciers, which have etched these heights for thousands of years. About 60 glaciers are still actively eroding these mountains; the largest three are on Mount Olympus.

From approximately November through March, the west side of the park is soaked with rain and mist, while the northeast side is the driest area on the West Coast except southern California. The yearly deluge creates a rain forest in the western valleys of the park. Here Sitka spruce, western hemlock, Douglas fir, and western red cedar grow to heights of 250 feet with 8-foot diameters. Mosses carpet the forest floor and climb tree trunks. Club moss drips from the branches.

Some 50 species of mammals inhabit this wilderness, including several thousand elk, Olympic marmots, black-tailed deer, and black bears. On the park's 60-mile strip of Pacific coastline wilderness, deer, bears, raccoons, and skunks can be seen; seals sun on the offshore rocks or plow through the water beyond the breakers. Mountain and lowland lakes sparkle everywhere. Lake Crescent is among the largest. Some roads are closed in winter.

What to See and Do

Fishing. *3002 Mount Angeles Rd, Olympic National Park (98362). Phone 360/565-3130.* Streams and lakes have game fish including salmon, rainbow, Dolly Varden, eastern brook trout, steelhead, and cutthroat. No license required in the park; permit or punch card is necessary for steelhead and salmon. Contact Park Headquarters for restrictions.

Hiking. Over 600 miles of trails. Obtain maps and trail guides in the park. Guided walks conducted July and Aug.

Mountain climbing. Something for everyone, from the novice to the experienced climber. Climbing parties must register at a ranger station.

Rain forests. Along Hoh, Queets, and Quinault river roads. Hall of Mosses and Spruce Nature Trails and trail to Mount Olympus start at end of Hoh River Road.

★ **Visitor Center.** *3002 Mount Angeles Rd, Olympic National Park (98362).* Has information, natural history exhibits, displays of American Indian culture, orientation slideshow. (Daily) From here, one can enter the park on Heart O' the Hills Pkwy to Hurricane Ridge (there is limited access Nov-Apr). 600 E Park Ave in Port Angeles. **$$$$$** Here is

Hurricane Ridge Winter Use Area. Pomalift, intermediate, and beginner's runs; school, rentals; snack bar. (Late Dec-late Mar, Sat-Sun) Also snowshoeing and cross-country ski trails.

Full-Service Resorts

★ ★ **KALALOCH LODGE.** *157151 Hwy 101, Forks (98331). Phone 360/962-2271; fax 360/962-3391. www. visitkalaloch.com.* No room phones. 65 rooms, 2 story. Pets accepted, some restrictions; fee. Check-in 4 pm, check-out 11 am. Restaurant. Beach. **$**

★ ★ **SOL DUC HOT SPRINGS RESORT.** *Sol Duc Rd and Hwy 101, Port Angeles (98362). Phone 360/327-3583; fax 360/327-3593. www.northolympic. com/solduc.* Originally conceived as a European-style health spa (circa 1912), the Sol Duc Resort is a haven for nature lovers. The natural mineral pools for which the resort is named range in temperature from 98° F to 106° F. Rates include use of the pools. At the northern end of Olympic National Park, next to the Sol Duc River, the resort is the perfect place from which to explore the area's rain forests and waterfalls. Studio cabins, some with kitchens, house those guests who choose not to rough it in tents. In addition to The Springs, a casual but upscale restaurant, you'll find a deli and a grocery store. 32 rooms. Closed Oct-late Mar. Check-in 4 pm, check-out 11 am. Restaurant. Outdoor pool, children's pool. **$**

Omak (A-4)

See also Winthrop

Settled 1900
Population 4,721
Elevation 837 ft
Area Code 509
Zip 98841
Information Tourist Information Center, 401 Omak Ave; phone 509/826-4218 or toll-free 800/225-6625
Web site www.omakchamber.com

This lumber town is the largest in the north-central part of Washington and is also known for its production of apples and its many orchards. The name of the town and nearby lake and mountain is derived from a Native American word meaning "good medicine." Omak is the "baby's breath capital of the world," a flower much used by florists.

What to See and Do

Conconully State Park. *5 miles N on Hwy 97, then 10 miles NW on Conconully Hwy (unnumbered road). Phone 509/826-7408.* Approximately 80 acres along Conconully Reservoir; swimming, fishing, boating; picnicking, snowmobiling, camping. (Daily)

Okanogan National Forest. *1240 Second Ave S, Okanogan (98840). NE and NW of town, reached via Hwy 97, Hwy 20. Phone 509/826-3275. www.fs.fed.us/r6 /oka.* Nearly 1.75 million acres. In the northern part

of the forest is the 530,031-acre Pasayten Wilderness. In the southwestern part is the 95,976-acre Lake Chelan-Sawtooth Wilderness. Hunting and fishing are plentiful; picnicking and camping at 41 sites, most of which have trailer spaces; eight boating sites. 38 miles west of town at Methow Valley Airport, between Winthrop and Twisp, is the North Cascades Smokejumper Base; visitors are welcome. There is a 1-mile paved wheelchair trail to Rainy Lake at Rainy Pass.

Special Event

Stampede and Suicide Race. *Phone 509/826-1002.* Rodeo events; horses and riders race down a cliff and across the Okanogan River. Western art show. Native American dance contests. Encampment with more than 100 teepees. Second weekend in Aug.

Limited-Service Hotel

★ ★ **CEDARS INN.** *1 Apple Way, Okanogan (98840). Phone 509/422-6431; fax 509/422-4214. www. cedarsinn.com.* 78 rooms, 3 story. Pets accepted; fee. Check-out noon. Restaurant, bar. Pool. **$**

Othello (C-5)

See also Moses Lake

Population 5,847
Area Code 509
Zip 99344
Information Chamber of Commerce, 33 E Larch; phone 509/488-2683 or toll-free 800/684-2556
Web site www.televar.com/chambers/othello

Another beneficiary of the Grand Coulee project, Othello had a population of only 526 in 1950. The Potholes Canal runs by the town, linking the Potholes Reservoir and the smaller Scooteney Reservoir.

Special Events

Adams County Fair. *831 S Reynolds, Othello (99344). Phone 509/488-2871.* Carnival, entertainment, tractor pull, exhibits. Mid-Sept.

Sandhill Crane Festival. *Wildlife Refuge, 735 E Main St, Othello (99344). Phone 509/488-2668.* View migrating birds. Guided tours, wildlife workshops. Late Mar-early Apr.

Limited-Service Hotel

★ ★ **BEST WESTERN LINCOLN INN.** *1020 E Cedar, Othello (99344). Phone 509/488-5671; toll-free 800/240-7865; fax 509/488-5084. www.bestwestern.com.* 50 rooms, 2 story. Pets accepted; fee. Complimentary continental breakfast. Check-out 11 am. Restaurant. Fitness room. Pool. **$**

🐾 ⬅ 🚶 🏊

Packwood

See also Mount Rainer National Park

Population 950
Elevation 1,051 ft
Area Code 360
Zip 98361

Named for William Packwood, a colorful explorer who helped open this region, this town is a provisioning point for modern-day explorers of Mount Rainier National Park and Snoqualmie and Gifford Pinchot national forests. A Ranger District office of the Gifford Pinchot National Forest is located here. The area abounds in edible wild berries and mushrooms; no permit is needed for picking. Winter and spring are popular with game-watchers; elk, deer, bears, and goats can be spotted in the local cemetery as well as in nearby parks.

What to See and Do

Goat Rocks Wilderness. *E and S of town, in Gifford Pinchot National Forest.* 105,600 acres of alpine beauty with elevations from 3,000-8,200 feet. Jagged pinnacles rising above snowfields, cascading streams, mountain meadows with wildflowers; this is the home of the pika and mountain goat.

Limited-Service Hotels

★ **COWLITZ RIVER LODGE.** *13069 Hwy 12, Packwood (98361). Phone 360/494-4444; toll-free 888/305-2185; fax 360/494-2075. www.escapetothemountains.com.* If you plan to explore Mount St. Helens, this simple lodge will put you right in the heart of the action, providing a clean, simple place from which to set off on hikes and nature tours. Mount Rainier National Park is also close by. 32 rooms, 2 story. Complimentary continental breakfast. Check-out 11 am. Whirlpool. **$**

★ **CREST TRAIL LODGE.** *12729 Hwy 12, Packwood (98361). Phone 360/494-4944; toll-free 800/477-5339; fax 360/494-6629.* 27 rooms, 2 story. Complimentary continental breakfast. Check-out 11 am. Airport transportation available. **$**

Pasco (D-5)

See also Kennewick, Richland

Founded 1880
Population 32,066
Elevation 381 ft
Area Code 509
Zip 99301
Information Greater Pasco Area Chamber of Commerce, 1600 N 20th, Suite A; phone 509/547-9755
Web site www.pascochamber.org

One of the "tri-cities" (see KENNEWICK and RICHLAND), Pasco has been nurtured by transportation throughout its history. Still a rail, air, highway, and waterway crossroads, Pasco is enjoying increased farm and industrial commerce thanks to the Columbia Basin project.

What to See and Do

Kahlotus. *42 miles NE via Hwy 395 and Hwy 260.* Town redone in Old West atmosphere. Many of the businesses and buildings are museums in themselves. Near Palouse Falls and Lower Monumental Dam.

McNary Lock and Dam. *3 miles S of Hwy 14 in Umatilla, OR. Phone 541/922-4388.* Single-lift navigation lock. Dam is 7,365 feet long, 92 feet high, and is the easternmost of four multipurpose dams on the lower Columbia River between Portland, OR and Pasco. The Columbia River forms Lake Wallula here. The 61-mile-long lake reaches beyond the tri-cities up to Ice Harbor Dam on Snake River. Developed parks with boating, marinas, waterskiing, swimming, fishing; picnicking and camping nearby. For information contact Park Ranger, PO Box 1441, Umatilla, OR 97882. (Daily)

Preston Premium Wines. *502 E Vineyard Dr, Pasco (99301). 5 miles N via Hwy 395, watch for road sign. Phone 509/545-1990.* Self-guided tour of tasting room, oak aging casks, storage tanks, and bottling line; park with picnic and play area, amphitheater, gazebo, pond. (Daily; closed holidays) **FREE**

Sacajawea State Park. *2501 Sacajawea Park Rd, Pasco (99301). 2 miles SE off Hwy 12. Phone 509/545-2361.* Site where Lewis and Clark camped in 1805. Approximately 280 acres. Swimming, fishing, boating (launch, dock); picnicking. (Daily)

Special Events

Fiery Food Festival. *Phone 509/545-0738.* Weekend after Labor Day.

Jazz Unlimited. *Columbia Basin Community College, 2600 N 20th Ave, Pasco (99301). Phone 509/547-0511.* Usually the second and third weekend in Apr.

Tri-Cities Water Follies. *1313 W Clark St, Pasco (99301). Phone 509/547-5563.* Events scheduled throughout month of July leading to hydroplane races on Columbia River on last weekend of month. July.

Limited-Service Hotel

★ ★ **RED LION.** *2525 N 20th Ave, Pasco (99301). Phone 509/547-0701; toll-free 800/733-5466; fax 509/547-4278. www.redlion.com.* Located in the heart of Washington State wine country, this hotel is close to plenty of shopping and many attractions. 279 rooms, 3 story. Pets accepted. Check-out noon. Restaurant, bar. Fitness room. Pool, whirlpool. Airport transportation available. Business center. **$**

Port Angeles (B-2)

See also Neah Bay, Olympic National Park, Sequim

Population 18,397
Elevation 32 ft
Area Code 360
Zip 98362
Information Chamber of Commerce, 121 E Railroad; phone 360/452-2363
Web site www.portangeles.org

Sitting atop the Olympic Peninsula, Port Angeles has the Olympic Mountains at its back and the Juan de Fuca Strait at its shoreline; just 17 miles across the strait is Victoria, British Columbia. Ediz Hook, a sandspit, protects the harbor and helps make it the first American port of entry for ships coming to Puget Sound from all parts of the Pacific; there is a US Coast Guard Air Rescue Station here. A Spanish captain who entered the harbor in 1791 named the village he found here Port of Our Lady of the Angels, a name that has survived in abbreviated form. The fishing fleet; pulp, paper and lumber mills; and tourism are its economic mainstays today.

Port Angeles is the headquarters for Olympic National Park. It is an excellent starting point for expeditions to explore the many faces of the peninsula.

What to See and Do

Ferry service to Victoria, BC, Canada. *Phone 206/622-2222.* A 90-minute trip; departs from Coho ferry terminal to Victoria's Inner Harbour. (Daily; summer, four trips; spring and fall, two trips; rest of year, one trip) Contact Black Ball Transport Inc, 10777 Main St, Suite 106, Bellevue 98004. **$$$$**

Olympic Raft and Guide Service. *123 Lake Aldwell Rd, Port Angeles (98363). Phone 360/452-1443.* River rafting in Olympic National Park.

Olympic Van Tours, Inc. *731 W 4th St, Port Angeles (98363). Phone 360/457-3545.* Unique, interpretive sightseeing tours into Olympic National Park (eight hours). Reservations required. For schedule and fees contact PO Box 2201.

Special Event

Clallam County Fair. *1608 W 16th St, Port Angeles (98363). Phone 360/417-2551.* Mid-Aug.

Limited-Service Hotels

★ **PORT ANGELES INN.** *111 E 2nd St, Port Angeles (98362). Phone 360/452-9285; toll-free 800/421-0706; fax 360/452-7935. www.portangelesinn.com.* 23 rooms, 3 story. Check-out 11 am. **$**

★ ★ **RED LION HOTEL.** *221 N Lincoln, Port Angeles (98362). Phone 360/452-9215; fax 360/452-4734. www.redlion.com.* Overlooks harbor. 186 rooms, 2 story. Pets accepted, some restrictions; fee. Check-out noon. Restaurant. Pool, whirlpool. **$**

Specialty Lodgings

The following lodging establishments are approved by Mobil Travel Guide, but due to their unique and individualized nature have not been given a traditional Mobil Star rating. Included in this listing you may find bed-and-breakfasts, limited-service inns, guest ranches, and other unique hotel properties.

DOMAINE MADELEINE. *146 Wildflower Ln, Port Angeles (98362). Phone 360/457-4174; toll-free 888/ 811-8376; fax 360/457-3037. www.domainemadeleine .com.* The guest rooms at this intimate bed-and-breakfast are individually decorated. The views of Victoria, British Columbia, and the San Juan Islands are magnificent. 5 rooms, 2 story. Children over 12 years only. Complimentary full breakfast. Check-in 4-6 pm, check-out 11 am. Airport transportation available. **$$**

🈳

FIVE SEASUNS BED & BREAKFAST. *1006 S Lincoln St, Port Angeles (98362). Phone 360/452-8248; toll-free 800/708-0777; fax 360/417-0465. www.seasuns .com.* Restored Dutch Colonial inn built in 1920s; pond, waterfall. 5 rooms, 2 story. Children over 12 years only. Complimentary full breakfast. Check-in 4-6 pm, check-out 11 am. **$**

🈳

TUDOR INN BED & BREAKFAST. *1108 S Oak St, Port Angeles (98362). Phone 360/452-3138; fax 360/457-9360. www.tudorinn.com.* This European, Tudor-style bed-and-breakfast offers guests a historical location from which to enjoy the Pacific Northwest. Visitors can relax in the living room, the library, or the inn's natural surroundings while enjoying the view of the Strait of Juan de Fuca. 5 rooms, 2 story. Children over 12 years only. Complimentary full breakfast. Check-in 4-6 pm, check-out 11 am. **$**

🈳

Restaurants

★ ★ **BELLA ITALIA.** *118 E 1st St, Port Angeles (98362). Phone 360/457-5442. www.bellaitaliapa.com.* Italian menu. Lunch, dinner. Closed Thanksgiving, Dec 25. Bar. Children's menu. **$$**

★ ★ **BUSHWHACKER.** *1527 E 1st St, Port Angeles (98362). Phone 360/457-4113.* American menu. Dinner. Closed Thanksgiving, Dec 24-25. Bar. Children's menu. **$$**

★ ★ ★ **C'EST SI BON.** *23 Cedar Park Dr, Port Angeles (98362). Phone 360/452-8888. www.cestsibon-frenchcuisine.com.* Elaborate paintings and floral wall coverings and fabrics give this restaurant its classic French feel. A gracious host and talented chef deliver a delightful dining experience. French menu. Dinner. Closed Mon. Bar. Children's menu. Outdoor seating. **$$**

★ **LANDINGS.** *115 E Railroad Ave, Port Angeles (98362). Phone 360/457-6768.* American menu. Breakfast, lunch, dinner. Closed Jan 1, Dec 25. Bar. Outdoor seating. **$$**

★ ★ ★ **TOGA'S INTERNATIONAL CUISINE.** *122 W Lauridsen Blvd, Port Angeles (98362). Phone 360/452-1952.* The menu at this quaint, intimate restaurant shows influences from all over Europe and highlights Northwest ingredients. The dining room is located in a remodeled, 1943 home and boasts beautiful Olympic Mountain Range views from its back window. Continental menu. Dinner. Closed Sun, Mon; holidays; also Sept. Children's menu. Reservations recommended. Outdoor seating. **$$**

Port Gamble

See also Port Ludlow, Seattle

Settled 1853
Area Code 360
Zip 98364

Captain William Talbot, a native of Maine, discovered the vast Puget Sound timberlands and located what has become the oldest continuously operating sawmill in North America here. Spars for the ships of the world were a specialty. The community, built by the company and still owned by it, gradually developed a distinctive appearance because of its unusual (to this part of the country) New England-style architecture.

The company, realizing an opportunity to preserve a bit of the past, has rebuilt and restored more than 30 homes, commercial buildings, and St. Paul's Episcopal Church. Replicas of gas lamps and underground wiring have replaced street lighting. The entire town has been declared a historic district.

What to See and Do

Hood Canal Nursery. *4110 Carver Dr, Port Gamble (98364). W edge of town. Phone 360/297-7555.* Self-guided tour covers storage and maintenance building, soil mixing, pump house, and chemical storage, water reservoir, greenhouses with a capacity of 3 1/2 million seedlings. (Mon-Fri) **FREE**

Kitsap Memorial State Park. *202 NE Park St, Port Gamble (98370). 4 miles S on Hwy 3. Phone 360/779-3205.* Over 50 acres. Saltwater swimming, scuba diving, fishing, boating (mooring); hiking, picnicking, shelters, camping (dump station).

Of Sea and Shore Museum. *General Store Building, 3 Ranier Ave, Port Gamble (98364). Phone 360/297-2426.* One of the largest shell collections in the country. Gift, book shop. (Daily; closed Jan 1, Thanksgiving, Dec 25) **FREE**

Port Gamble Historic Museum. *3 Rainier Ave, Port Gamble (98364). Downhill side of the General Store. Phone 360/297-8074.* Exhibits trace the history of the area and the timber company. Displays arranged in order of time: replica of old saw filing room; San Francisco office, captain's cabin from ship; individual rooms from hotels and houses; Forest of the Future exhibit. (May-Oct, daily) **$$**

Port Ludlow (A-0)

See also Port Gamble, Sequim

Settled 1878
Population 1,968
Elevation 0-30 ft
Area Code 360
Zip 98365
Information Port Ludlow Olympic Peninsula Gateway Visitor Center, 93 Beaver Valley Rd; phone 360/437-0120
Web site www.portludlowchamber.org

Full-Service Inn

★ ★ ★ **INN AT PORT LUDLOW.** *1 Heron Rd, Port Ludlow (98365). Phone 360/437-0411; fax 360/437-0310. www.heronbeachinn.com.* This inn, resting on the shores of the Olympic Peninsula, offers its own brand of charm. Built to resemble an estate in Maine, the inn features rooms with exquisite views, comfortable amenities, and tasteful touches. 39 rooms, 3 story. Complimentary continental breakfast. Check-in 4 pm, check-out noon. Restaurant. **$$**

Restaurant

★ ★ ★ **HERON BEACH INN DINING ROOM.** *1 Heron Rd, Port Ludlow (98365). Phone 360/437-0411. www.heronbeachinn.com.* Reminiscent of the East Coast's charming summer homes, this veranda-wrapped inn provides a serene setting for waterfront dining at its best. Seafood menu. Dinner. Closed Mon-Tues (winter). Bar. Children's menu. **$$**

Port Townsend (B-2)

See also Coupeville, Everett, Oak Harbor, Sequim

Settled 1851
Population 8,334
Elevation 100 ft
Area Code 360
Zip 98368
Information Tourist Information Center, 2437 E Sims Way; phone 360/385-2722
Web site www.ptchamber.org

Located on the Quimper Peninsula at the northeast corner of the Olympic Peninsula, this was once a busy port city served by sailing vessels and sternwheelers. Captain George Vancouver came ashore in 1792 and named the spot Port Townshend, after an English nobleman. Port Townsend is a papermill town with boat building and farming.

What to See and Do

Fort Flagler. *20 miles SE on Marrowstone Island. Phone 360/385-3701.* More than 780 acres. Saltwater swimming, scuba diving, fishing, boating (launch, mooring); hiking, picnicking, camping (reservations required Memorial Day-Labor Day). Nature study; forested areas, some military areas.

Fort Worden. *200 Battery Way, Port Townsend (98368). 1 mile N. Phone 360/385-3102.* Approximately 430 acres. Home of Centrum Foundation, with poetry and visual arts symposiums; fiction writer's workshop; fiddletune, jazz, and folk dance festivals; **FREE**

Old Fort Townsend. *3 miles S on Hwy 20. Phone 360/385-4730.* Approximately 380 acres. Posted site of a fort established in 1856, abandoned in 1895. Swimming, scuba diving, bank fishing; hiking, picnicking, camping. (Mid-Apr-mid-Sept)

Rothschild House. *Franklin and Taylor sts, Port Townsend. Phone 360/379-8076.* (1868) Furnished in original style; flower and herb gardens. (May-Sept: daily; rest of year: Sat-Sun, and holidays only) **$**

Special Events

House Tours. *2437 E Sims Way, Port Townsend (98368). Phone 360/385-2722.* Third weekend in Sept.

Jefferson County Fair. *4907 Landes St, Port Townsend (98368). Phone 360/385-1013.* Agricultural and 4-H displays, livestock shows. Weekend in mid-Aug.

Wooden Boat Festival. *103 Hudson St, Port Townsend (98368). Phone 360/385-3628.* Displays, classes, and lectures. First weekend after Labor Day.

Limited-Service Hotels

★ **BISHOP VICTORIAN GUEST SUITES.** *714 Washington St, Port Townsend (98368). Phone 360/ 385-6122; toll-free 800/824-4738. www.bishopvictorian .com.* Built in 1890 as an office/warehouse; converted to English inn. 14 rooms, 3 story, all suites. Pets accepted, some restrictions; fee. Complimentary continental breakfast. Check-in 3 pm, check-out 11 am. **$**

🅿️ 🐾

★ ★ **INN AT PORT HADLOCK.** *310 Alcohol Loop Rd, Port Hadlock (98339). Phone 360/385-7030; toll-free 800/785-7030; fax 360/385-6955. www.innatporthadlock .com.* A former alcohol plant built in 1910, the Inn at Port Hadlock is a half-hour drive or ferry ride from Seattle. If you're bringing your own boat, the inn has a 164-slip marina to accommodate it. 33 rooms, 3 story. Pets accepted, some restrictions; fee. Check-in 3 pm, check-out 11 am. Wireless Internet access. Restaurant, bar. **$**

🐾

★ ★ **PALACE.** *1004 Water St, Port Townsend (98368). Phone 360/385-0773; toll-free 800/962-0741. www.palacehotelpt.com.* 15 rooms, 2 story. Pets accepted; fee. Complimentary continental breakfast. Check-out noon. Restaurant. **$**

🅿️ 🐾

Specialty Lodgings

The following lodging establishments are approved by Mobil Travel Guide, but due to their unique and indi-
vidualized nature have not been given a traditional Mobil Star rating. Included in this listing you may find bed-and-breakfasts, limited-service inns, guest ranches, and other unique hotel properties.

ANN STARRETT MANSION VICTORIAN BED & BREAKFAST. *744 Clay St, Port Townsend (98368). Phone 360/385-3205; toll-free 800/321-0644; fax 360/385-2976. www.starrettmansion.com.* Overlooking the mountains and waters of Puget Sound, this bed-and-breakfast was built in 1889 using Victorian architecture. It is furnished with antiques and decorated with carvings and fine art work, and features a winding staircase and frescoed ceilings. 11 rooms, 4 story. Complimentary full breakfast. Check-in 3-8 pm, check-out 11 am. **$$**

🅿️

CHANTICLEER INN. *1208 Franklin St, Port Townsend (98368). Phone 360/385-6239; toll-free 800/858-9421; fax 360/385-3377. www.chanticleerinnbb .com.* In the heart of the historic district lies this quaint bed-and-breakfast built circa 1876 and decorated with grand style and rich furnishings. The gourmet breakfast is a special treat. 5 rooms, 2 story. Children over 12 years only. Complimentary full breakfast. Check-in 3-6 pm, check-out 10:30 am. **$**

🅿️

F. W. HASTINGS HOUSE OLD CONSULATE. *313 Walker St, Port Townsend (98368). Phone 360/385-6753; toll-free 800/300-6753; fax 360/385-2097. www. oldconsulateinn.com.* This is an elegant and tastefully stylish inn with the feel of an old Victorian Manor home. Attention to all details have been taken care of by the staff. 8 rooms, 3 story. Children over 12 years only. Complimentary full breakfast. Check-in 3-6 pm, check-out 11 am. Airport transportation available. **$$**

🅿️

HOLLY HILL HOUSE B&B. *611 Polk St, Port Townsend (98368). Phone 360/385-5619; toll-free 800/ 435-1454; fax 360/385-4610. www.hollyhillhouse.com.* This guest house is located only a short walk from downtown, antique shops, museums, art galleries, and restaurants. Some rooms offer a view of the water. 5 rooms. Children over 12 years only. Complimentary full breakfast. Check-in 3-6 pm, check-out 10:30 am. **$**

🅿️

JAMES HOUSE. *1238 Washington St, Port Townsend (98368). Phone 360/385-1238; toll-free 800/385-1238; fax 360/379-5551. www.jameshouse.com.* Built in 1889, this grand Victorian mansion sits on a bluff overlooking Puget Sound and mountains. Featuring fine woodwork, furnishings, and well-kept gardens, this bed-and-breakfast is a perfect place for a getaway. 12 rooms, 4 story. Complimentary full breakfast. Check-in 3 pm, check-out 11 am,**$**

RAVENSCROFT. *533 Quincy St, Port Townsend (98368). Phone 360/385-2784; toll-free 800/782-2691; fax 360/385-6724. www.ravenscroftinn.com.* A seaport inn built in the style of Charleston, SC, this property offers guest rooms with views of Puget Sound, Mt. Baker and Mt. Rainer. 8 rooms. Children over 12 years only. Complimentary full breakfast. Check-in 3-6 pm, check-out 11 am. Airport transportation available. **$**

Restaurants

★ ★ **KHU LARB THAI.** *225 Adams St, Port Townsend (98368). Phone 360/385-5023. www. khularbthai.com.* Thai menu. Lunch, dinner. Closed Mon. **$$**

★ ★ ★ **LONNY'S.** *2330 Washington St, Port Townsend (98368). Phone 360/385-0700. www.lonnys .com.* Dine by soft candlelight in the warm, grotto-like atmosphere of this elegant Italian bistro. The open kitchen turns out innovative favorites, and an unusual assortment of desserts completes the meal. American, Italian menu. Dinner. Closed Tues; Thanksgiving, Dec 25. Bar. Children's menu. **$$**

★ ★ ★ **MANRESA CASTLE.** *7th and Sheridan sts, Port Townsend (98368). Phone 360/385-5750. www.manresacastle.com.* This century-old, European-inspired castle is the home of an elegant yet casual dining room with spectacular views of the Olympic and Cascade Mountains. Continental menu. Dinner, Sun brunch. Closed Jan 1, Dec 25. Bar. **$$**

★ ★ **ORIGINAL OYSTER HOUSE.** *280417 Hwy 101, Port Townsend (98368). Phone 360/385-1785.* Seafood menu. Dinner, Sun brunch. Bar. Children's menu. Outdoor seating. **$$**

★ **SILVERWATER CAFE.** *237 Taylor St, Port Townsend (98368). Phone 360/385-6448. www. silverwatercafe.com.* Seafood, vegetarian menu. Lunch, dinner. Closed Thanksgiving, Dec 25. Bar. Children's menu. **$$**

Pullman (C-6)

See also Clarkston

Settled 1881
Population 24,675
Elevation 2,351 ft
Area Code 509
Zip 99163
Information Chamber of Commerce, 415 N Grand Ave; phone 509/334-3565 or toll-free 800/365-6948
Web site www.pullman-wa.com

A university town and an agricultural storage and shipping center in the fertile Palouse Hills, this community is named for George M. Pullman, the inventor/tycoon who gave his name to the railroad sleeping car.

What to See and Do

Kamiak Butte County Park. *10 miles N on Hwy 27. Phone 509/397-6238.* A timbered area with a rocky butte rising 3,641 feet high, trails leading to the summit. Approximately 300 acres. Picnicking, hiking, interpretive programs (summer). Camping (Apr-Oct; fee). Park (all year). **FREE**

Washington State University. *E of town center. Guided tours at admission office, Lighty Building, Room 370 (afternoon, daily). Phone 509/335-8633. www.wsu.edu.* (1890) (17,000 students) On campus are

Museum of Art. *Fine Arts Center. Phone 509/335-1910.* Exhibitions, lectures, films. (Sept-July, daily, hours vary) **FREE**

Wawawai County Park. *11 miles N on Hwy 27.* Boating, fishing; picnicking, hiking. Earth-sheltered home (afternoon tours, call for dates). Camping (Apr-Oct; fee). Park (all year).

Special Event

National Lentil Festival. *Phone 509/334-3565.* Food booths, arts and crafts, musical entertainment, parade. Late Aug.

Limited-Service Hotels

★ **HOLIDAY INN EXPRESS HOTEL & SUITES PULLMAN.** *SE 1190 Bishop Blvd, Pullman (99163). Phone 509/334-4437; toll-free 800/465-4329; fax 509/334-4447. www.holiday-inn.com.* 130 rooms. Complimentary continental breakfast. Check-in 3 pm, check-out noon. Wireless Internet access. Fitness room. Indoor pool, whirlpool. Business center. **$**

★ **QUALITY INN.** *SE 1400 Bishop Blvd, Pullman (99163). Phone 509/332-0500; toll-free 800/228-5151; fax 509/334-4271. www.qualityinn.com.* 66 rooms, 2 story. Pets accepted, some restrictions; fee. Check-out noon. Pool, whirlpool. Airport transportation available. **$**

Puyallup (C-2)

See also Enumclaw, Tacoma

Founded 1877
Population 33,011
Elevation 40 ft
Area Code 253
Information Chamber of Eastern Pierce County, 417 E Pioneer, 98371; phone 253/845-6755
Web site www.puyallupchamber.com

Puyallup freezes the farm produce from the fertile soil and mild climate of the valley between Mount Rainier and Tacoma. A $2 million bulb industry (irises, daffodils, and tulips) was born in 1923, when it was discovered that the valley was ideal for growing. Ezra Meeker crossed the plains by covered wagon and named this city Puyallup (meaning "generous people") after a tribe that lived in the valley; Puyallups still live in the area.

What to See and Do

Ezra Meeker Mansion. *312 Spring St, Puyallup (98372). Phone 253/848-1770.* (1890) The 17-room Victorian house of Ezra Meeker, pioneer, farmer, first town mayor, author, and preserver of the Oregon Trail. Six fireplaces, period furnishings, stained-glass windows, and hand-carved woodwork. (Mar-mid-Dec, Wed-Sun; closed Easter, Thanksgiving) **$**

Pioneer Park. *324 S Meridian, Puyallup (98371). Phone 253/841-5457.* Life-size statue of Ezra Meeker. Playground; wading pool (summer). **FREE**

Special Events

Ezra Meeker Community Festival. *312 Spring St, Puyallup (98372). Phone 253/848-1770.* Fine arts show, arts and crafts, entertainment; ice cream social at Meeker Mansion. Late June.

Pierce County Fair. *21802 Meridian Ave E, Graham (98338). Phone 253/847-4754.* 6 miles S in Graham. Early Aug.

Puyallup Fair. *110 9th Ave SW, Puyallup (98371). Phone 253/841-5045. www.thefair.com.* An annual tradition every September since 1900, the Puyallup Fair is held on fairgrounds about 40 miles south of downtown Seattle for a period of nearly three weeks. The event includes all sorts of entertainment (including racing pigs, hypnotists, and local and national musical acts), as well as rodeo competitions, a full carnival with thrill rides and a midway, and a petting farm. There is also a three-day Spring Fair held here in April. Seventeen days in Sept.

Sumner Summer Festival. *Phone 253/845-3182.* Early Aug.

Quinault

Population 350
Elevation 221 ft
Area Code 360
Zip 98575
Information Grays Harbor Chamber of Commerce, 506 Duffy St, Aberdeen 98520; phone 360/532-1924 or toll-free 800/321-1924
Web site www.graysharbor.org

Quinault, on the shore of Lake Quinault, is the south entrance to Olympic National Park. In the heart of the Olympic National Forest, it is the gateway to any of three valleys—the Hoh, Queets, and Quinault—that make up the rain forest, a lush green ecological phenomenon. It also provides an entrance to the Enchanted Valley area of the park. The Quinault Reservation is 2 miles west.

A Ranger District office of the Olympic National Forest is located here.

Limited-Service Hotel

★ ★ **LAKE QUINAULT LODGE.** *345 South Shore Rd, Quinault (98525). Phone 360/288-2900; toll-free 800/562-6672; fax 360/288-2901. www.visitlakequinault .com.* 92 rooms, 3 story. Check-out 11 am. Restaurant, bar. Beach. Indoor pool. **$**

Quincy (C-4)

See also Ellensburg, Ephrata, Wenatchee

Settled 1892
Population 5,044
Elevation 1,301 ft
Area Code 509
Zip 98848
Information Quincy Valley Chamber of Commerce, 119 F St SE; phone 509/787-2140
Web site www.quincyvalley.org

Although this area gets only about 8 inches of rain a year, irrigation has turned the surrounding countryside green. Quincy processes and markets farm produce; more than 80 crops are grown in the area. Deposits of diatomaceous earth (soft, chalky material used for fertilizers, mineral aids, and filters) are mined in the area and refined in Quincy. Fishing and game-bird hunting are good in the surrounding area.

What to See and Do

Crescent Bar Park. *8 miles W off Hwy 28. On Wanapum Reservoir in the Columbia River.* Swimming, bathhouse, beaches, waterskiing, boating, fishing, marina; playground, picnicking, camping (Apr-Oct; hookups; fee), restaurants, putting green, shops, pro shop, grocery, nine-hole golf (fee), four tennis courts (fee). Park (all year).

Special Event

Farmer Consumer Awareness Day. *Quincy High School, 16 Sixth Ave SE, Quincy (98848). Phone 509/ 787-3501.* Free tours to dairies, processing plants, packing houses, farms, harvesting operations. Exhibits, food booths, arts and crafts, petting zoo,

antique autos, farm equipment, games, parade, 2K and 5K run, entertainment. Second Sat in Sept.

Limited-Service Hotel

★ **TRADITIONAL INNS.** *500 F St SW, Quincy (98848). Phone 509/787-3525; fax 509/787-3528. www. traditionalinns.com.* 24 rooms, 2 story. Pets accepted, some restrictions; fee. Check-out 11 am. **$**

Redmond (B-3)

Settled 1871
Population 45,256
Elevation 50 ft
Area Code 425
Information Redmond Chamber of Commerce, 16210 NE 80th St, 98073; phone 425/885-4014
Web site www.redmondchamber.org

Redmond experienced dramatic change over the course of the 20th century, evolving from a sleepy logging town to a high-tech hub, a transformation driven by the exponential growth of Microsoft, which is headquartered here. Situated at the northern tip of Lake Sammamish, Redmond boasts safe neighborhoods, excellent schools, and a public park system that covers 1,350 acres and more than 25 miles of trails. A wide variety of shops and restaurants can be found at Redmond Town Center. The city is a short drive east of Seattle on Highway 520.

What to See and Do

Celtic Bayou Brewpub. *7281 W Lake Sammamish Pkwy NE, Redmond (98052). Phone 425/869-5933. www.celticbayou.com.* An Irish pub with a laid-back vibe, a Cajun menu, and an in-house brewery, Celtic Bayou is a pleasant place to unwind, with walls clad in mellow-toned wood, booths and tables, and an outdoor beer garden. Located east of Seattle in suburban Redmond, the place attracts its fair share of Microsoft employees and other high-tech types. Live music is featured on Saturday nights. (Sun-Mon 11:30 am-10 pm, Tues-Thurs 11:30 am-midnight, Fri-Sat 11:30 am-1 am)

Marymoor Park. *6046 W Lake Sammamish Pkwy, Redmond (98052). Phone 206/205-3661.* Located in Redmond in Seattle's Eastside suburbs, Marymoor

Park is the largest, and likely the busiest, park in metro Seattle. With 640 acres of parkland around a historic farmhouse, it is home to the area's only velodrome, as well as a climbing rock, a model airplane field, and numerous sports fields. Marymoor is also home to a very popular off-leash dog park, about 100 acres of forest and meadow on the shores of a slow-moving river.

Redmond Town Center. *16495 NE 74th St, Redmond (98052). Phone 425/867-0808. www. shopredmondtowncenter.com.* This 120-acre, open-air shopping and entertainment hub is in Redmond, the Eastside home of Microsoft and numerous other high-tech companies. National chains such as Gap, REI, Borders, and Eddie Bauer dominate the retail landscape, and there are also a number of restaurants (including national chains) and an eight-screen movie theater. Every Saturday from May though October, a farmers' market offers fresh produce and flowers, and on Tuesday evenings in summer, live music can be enjoyed. There are also a number of events for children on the Redmond Town Center calendar. (Mon-Sat 10 am-8 pm, Sun 11 am-6 pm)

Sammamish River Trail. A 10-mile paved trail running southeast from Bothell to Redmond, the Sammamish River Trail connects with the Burke-Gilman Trail, forming a 27-mile route that leads to Gas Works Park in Seattle. This peaceful, mostly level trail follows alongside the gentle current of the Sammamish River, passing through Woodinville, with its two wineries and the Redhook Ale Brewery a short jaunt off the trail. The trail is popular with joggers, walkers, cyclists, and in-line skaters. At the north end of the trail, start your journey at Bothell Landing Park (9919 NE 180th St). Down south in Redmond, begin your trek at Marymoor Park (6046 W Lake Sammamish Parkway NE).

Willows Run Golf Club. *10402 Willows Rd NE, Redmond (98052). Phone 425/883-1200. www. willowsrun.com.* Willows Run offers an intriguing mix of golf getaway and closeness to civilization during your round. Much of the back nine is built next to an industrial park, but the course has few trees and resembles British Open layouts. There are two 18-hole tracks and a 9-hole par-three course as well. The holes are closely packed, but they are challenging, with plenty of water along either 18. The facility's signature hole is the 17th on the Eagle's Talon course, a long hole with a nearly island green that slopes to

the front, assuring those who do not hit the ball far enough will go fishing. **$$$$**

Renton (B-2)

What to See and Do

Spirit of Washington Dinner Train Tour. *626 S 4th St, Renton (98055). Phone 425/227-7245; toll-free 800/ 876-7245. www.spiritofwashingtondinnertrain.com.* All aboard for breathtaking scenery, gourmet dining, and a winery tour! The Spirit of Washington Dinner Train takes passengers back in time to an era when railway travel was considered a luxury. Riders aboard the Spirit of Washington's vintage train cars are treated to a three-course gourmet meal, feasting on such delicacies as cherry smoke roasted salmon and crab enchiladas, during a 3 1/4-hour excursion that begins and ends in the city of Renton. The views are often spectacular, particularly in the cars offering glass dome ceilings, as the train winds along the shores of Lake Washington and passes through the Sammamish River Valley. A highlight of the trip is when it passes over the 102-foot-high Wilburton Trestle, a local landmark since its construction in 1891. The ride includes a 45-minute stop in Woodinville at the Columbia Winery, where guests tour the cellar and enjoy a wine tasting. The Spirit of Washington operates year-round, with daily trips during the summer months. **$$$$**

Limited-Service Hotel

★ **SILVER CLOUD.** *1850 Maple Valley Hwy, Renton (98055). Phone 425/226-7600; toll-free 800/551-7207; fax 425/271-1296. www.silvercloud.com.* 105 rooms. Complimentary continental breakfast. Check-in 3 pm, check-out noon. High-speed Internet access. Fitness room. Whirlpool. Business center. **$**

🚶 🏃

Richland (D-5)

See also Kennewick, Pasco, Sunnyside

Population 38,708
Elevation 360 ft
Area Code 509
Zip 99352
Information Chamber of Commerce, 710A George Washington Way; phone 509/946-1651
Web site www.ci.richland.wa.us

Although it's one of the "tri-cities" (see KENNEWICK and PASCO), Richland has an entirely different personality due to the 560-square-mile Hanford Works of the Department of Energy (DOE)—formerly the US Atomic Energy Commission. In 1943, Richland was a village of 250, dedicated to fruit cultivation. A year later, Hanford was established by the government as one of four main development points for the atomic bomb, along with Oak Ridge, Tennessee; Los Alamos, New Mexico; and the Argonne Laboratory, near Chicago. Hanford no longer is involved in the production of plutonium, and the more than 16,000 employees are now dedicated to environmental cleanup and safe disposal of nuclear and hazardous wastes.

Once largely desert area, Richland today is surrounded by vineyards and orchards thanks to irrigation from the Grand Coulee Dam and the Yakima River Irrigation Projects. The city is at the hub of an area of spectacular scenery and outdoor activities within a short drive in any direction.

What to See and Do

CRESHT Museum. *95 Lee Blvd, Richland (99352). Phone 509/943-9000.* Displays, models, computer exhibits relating to US energy, science, and environmental topics. (Mon-Sat, Sun afternoon; closed holidays) **$$**

Special Events

Benton-Franklin Fair and Rodeo. *Franklin County Fairgrounds, Richland. Phone 509/586-9211.* Fair, parade, carnival. Aug.

Columbia Cup. *5111 Columbia Dr SE, Richland (99336). Phone 509/547-2203.* Hydroplane races. July.

Cool Desert Nights Car Show. *515 Lee Blvd, Richland (99352). Phone 509/697-5898.* June.

NASCAR Auto Racing. June-Sept.

Limited-Service Hotels

★ **DAYS INN.** *615 Jadwin Ave, Richland (99352). Phone 509/943-4611; fax 509/946-2271. www. daysinn.com.* 98 rooms, 2 story. Pets accepted; fee. Complimentary continental breakfast. Check-out noon. Pool. **$**

★ ★ **RED LION.** *802 George Washington Way, Richland (99352). Phone 509/946-7611; fax 509/ 943-8564. www.redlion.com.* 149 rooms, 2 story. Pets accepted; fee. Check-out noon. Restaurant, bar. Pool. Airport transportation available. **$**

★ ★ **ROYAL HOTEL AND CONFERENCE CENTER.** *1515 George Washington, Richland (99352). Phone 509/946-4121; toll-free 800/635-3980; fax 509/ 946-2222. www.bestwestern.com.* 195 rooms, 6 story. Pets accepted; fee. Complimentary full breakfast. Check-out noon. Restaurant, bar. Pool, children's pool, whirlpool. Airport transportation available. **$**

Restaurant

★ **R. F. MCDOUGALL'S.** *1705 Columbia Park Trail, Richland (99352). Phone 509/735-6418; fax 509/ 737-8010.* American menu. Lunch, dinner. Closed Thanksgiving, Dec 25. Bar. Outdoor seating. **$$**

Ritzville

See also Moses Lake

Settled 1878
Population 1,736
Elevation 1,815 ft
Area Code 509
Zip 99169
Information Chamber of Commerce, 201 W Railroad; phone 509/659-1936

Special Events

Ritzville Blues Festival. *Phone 509/659-1936.* Second Sat in July.

Wheat Land Communities Fair. *Phone 509/659-0141.* Parade, rodeo. Labor Day weekend.

Limited-Service Hotel

★ **LA QUINTA INN.** *1513 S Smittys Blvd, Ritzville (99169). Phone 509/659-1007; fax 509/659-1025. www.laquinta.com.* 54 rooms, 2 story. Pets accepted. Complimentary continental breakfast. Check-out 11 am. Pool, whirlpool. **$**

Restaurant

★ ★ **CIRCLE T INN.** *214 W Main Ave, Ritzville (99169). Phone 509/659-0922.* American menu. Breakfast, lunch, dinner. Bar. **$$**

San Juan Islands (A-2)

See also Orcas Island

Area Code 360
Information San Juan Islands Visitor Information Service, PO Box 65, Lopez Island, 98261; phone 360/468-3663 or toll-free 888/468-3701
Web site www.guidetosanjuans.com

These 172 islands nestled between the northwest corner of Washington and Vancouver Island, British Columbia, Canada, compose a beautiful and historic area. Secluded coves, giant trees, freshwater lakes, fishing camps, modest motels, numerous bed-and-breakfasts, and plush resorts characterize the four major islands. Over 500 miles of paved or gravel roads swing through virgin woodlands and along lovely shorelines. The islands are accessible by ferry from Anacortes.

San Juan Island gave birth in 1845 to the expansionist slogan "fifty-four forty or fight" and was the setting for the "pig war" of 1859, in which a British pig uprooted an American potato patch. The subsequent hostilities between the islands' 7 British and 14 American inhabitants reached such proportions that eventually Kaiser Wilhelm I of Germany was called in to act as arbiter and settle the boundaries. During the 13 years of controversy, the pig was the only casualty. This island was the last place the British flag flew within the territorial United States. Friday Harbor, most westerly stop in the United States on San Juan Islands ferry tour, is county seat of San Juan.

What to See and Do

⭐ **San Juan Island.** Friday Harbor on eastern shore serves as base for salmon fleet; major commercial center of islands. Fishing lakes; camping facilities, golf, International Seaplane Base, and two airstrips are here. Also on San Juan is

San Juan Island National Historical Park. *Phone 360/378-2240. www.nps.gov/sajh.* Commemorates the settlement of the boundary issue between the US and Great Britain. English Camp, 10 miles northwest of Friday Harbor on Garrison Bay, has a restored blockhouse, commissary, hospital, formal garden, and barracks built during the British occupation. American Camp, 6 miles southeast of Friday Harbor, has remains of redoubt, the American defensive earthwork; laundresses' and officers' quarters. Picnicking; information specialist at both camps (June-Sept: daily; rest of year: Thurs-Sun). Office and information center in Friday Harbor, 1st and Spring sts (June-Aug: daily; May and Sept: Mon-Fri; closed rest of year; closed holidays)

The Whale Museum. *62 1st St N, Friday Harbor (98250). Phone 360/378-4710.* Art and science exhibits document the lives of whales and porpoises in this area. (Daily; closed holidays) **$$**

Special Event

San Juan Jazz Festival. *Friday Harbor and Roche Harbor. Phone 360/378-5240.* Last weekend in July.

Limited-Service Hotel

★ **HOTEL DE HARO AT ROCHE HARBOR SEASIDE VILLAGE.** *248 Reuben Memorial Dr, Roche Harbor (98250). Phone 360/378-2155; toll-free 800/451-8910; fax 360/378-6809. www.rocheharbor .com.* 29 rooms, 3 story. Check-in 3 pm, check-out 11 am. Bar. Pool. Tennis. Business center. **$**

Full-Service Resort

★ ★ ★ **ROSARIO RESORT.** *1400 Rosario Rd, East Sound (98245). Phone 360/376-2222; toll-free 800/562-8820; fax 360/376-2289. www. rosarioresort.com.* Few places induce an adrenalin rush upon arrival, yet Rosario Resort is one spot that bears that distinction. Located at the tip of Orcas Island in Washington's picturesque San Juan Islands, visitors land directly in front of the resort via a thrilling and scenic seaplane ride (less adventurous types may opt for the ferry). This resort is a veritable Eden for outdoor enthusiasts, with a variety of recreational opportunities available both on- and off-resort. From whale-watching and sea kayaking to nature hikes in Moran State Park, Rosario's backdrop serves as a playground for visitors. Back at the resort, the Avanyu

Spa soothes frayed nerves and four restaurants satisfy hearty appetites. Fanning out across Cascade Bay, the welcoming guest accommodations reflect the resort's dedication to casual elegance. 86 rooms, 2 story. Check-in 4 pm, check-out 11 am. Restaurant, bar. Fitness room. Indoor pool, two outdoor pools, whirlpool. Tennis. Airport transportation available. Music room; piano, organ concerts. **$$**

Specialty Lodgings

The following lodging establishments are approved by Mobil Travel Guide, but due to their unique and individualized nature have not been given a traditional Mobil Star rating. Included in this listing you may find bed-and-breakfasts, limited-service inns, guest ranches, and other unique hotel properties.

ARGYLE HOUSE BED & BREAKFAST. *685 Argyle Ave, Friday Harbor (98250). Phone 360/378-4084; toll-free 800/624-3459. www.argylehouse.net.* Built in 1910; country setting, gardens. 4 rooms, 2 story. Children over 10 years only. Complimentary full breakfast. Check-in 3 pm, check-out 11 am. **$**

FRIDAY'S HISTORIC INN. *35 First St, San Juan Island (98250). Phone 360/378-5848; toll-free 800/352-2632; fax 360/378-2881. www.friday-harbor.com.* Found only a short walk from this bed-and-breakfast are Friday Harbor's waterfront, town shops, and restaurants. The property features limited-edition wildlife art, soundproof rooms, and a large parlor. 15 rooms, 3 story. Complimentary continental breakfast. Check-in 3:30 pm, check-out 11 am. **$$**

HILLSIDE HOUSE BED AND BREAKFAST. *365 Carter Ave, Friday Harbor (98250). Phone 360/378-4730; toll-free 800/232-4730; fax 360/378-4715. www.hillsidehouse.com.* A contemporary home among acres of fir and pine trees. Some rooms overlook the atrium; others have a view of the harbor. 7 rooms, 3 story. Complimentary full breakfast. Check-in 3 pm, check-out 11 am. **$**

INN AT SWIFTS BAY. *856 Port Stanley Rd, Lopez Island (98261). Phone 360/468-3636; toll-free 888/903-*

9536; fax 360/468-3637. www.swiftsbay.com. Incredible comfort and unsurpassed amenities are on the top of the list at this Tudor-style bed-and-breakfast. It lies in the San Juan Islands away from busy city life and offers amazing bedrooms and a great living area, dining room, and library. 5 rooms, 2 story. Complimentary full breakfast. Check-in 3-7 pm, check-out 11 am. Fitness room. **$$**

TUCKER HOUSE BED & BREAKFAST. *260 B St, Friday Harbor (98250). Phone 360/378-2783; toll-free 800/965-0123; fax 360/378-8775. www.tuckerhouse.com.* Victorian home built in 1898. 6 rooms, 2 story. Pets accepted; fee. Complimentary full breakfast. Check-in 3 pm, check-out 11 am. **$**

TURTLEBACK FARM INN. *1981 Crow Valley Rd, East Sound (98245). Phone 360/376-4914; toll-free 800/376-4914; fax 360/376-5329. www.turtlebackinn.com.* The inn is a country farmhouse located on Orcas Island overlooking the clear waters of the Puget Sound. It features spacious guest rooms decorated with antiques and contemporary pieces. Fine dining and unique shopping are nearby. 11 rooms, 2 story. Complimentary full breakfast. Check-out 11 am. **$$**

Restaurants

★ ★ ★ **CHRISTINA'S.** *310 Main, East Sound (98245). Phone 360/376-4904. www.christinas.net.* Christina's is one of the most highly regarded establishments in the Northwest. Photos of the owners' Hollywood connections adorn the wall of the small bar. The innovative treatments of meat, fresh Northwest seafood, and fowl keep devotees returning. Seafood menu. Dinner. Closed Dec 25; first 3 weeks in Nov and Jan. Bar. Children's menu. Outdoor seating. **$$**

★ ★ **DOWNRIGGERS.** *10 Front St, San Juan Islands (98250). Phone 360/378-2700; fax 360/378-3026. www.downriggerssanjuan.com.* Seafood, steak menu. Breakfast, lunch, dinner. Bar. Outdoor seating. **$$**

Seattle (B-2)

See also Auburn, Bellevue, Bremerton, Everett, Issaquah, Lynwood, North Bend, Port Gamble

Founded 1852
Population 563,374
Elevation 125 ft
Area Code 206
Information Seattle-King County Convention & Visitors Bureau, 520 Pike St, Suite 1300, 98101; phone 206/461-5840
Web site www.seeseattle.org

Suburbs Bellevue, Bremerton, Everett, Federal Way, Issaquah, Marysville, Port Gamble, Tacoma. (See individual alphabetical listings.)

Seattle has prospered from the products of its surrounding forests, farms, and waterways, serving as a provisioner to Alaska and the Orient. Since the 1950s, it has acquired a new dimension from the manufacture of jet airplanes, missiles, and space vehicles—which, along with tourism, comprise the city's most important industries.

The Space Needle, which dominated Seattle's boldly futuristic 1962 World's Fair, still stands, symbolic of the city's forward-looking character. The site of the fair is now the Seattle Center. Many features of the fair have been made permanent.

Seattle is on Elliott Bay, nestled between Puget Sound, an inland-probing arm of the Pacific Ocean, and Lake Washington, a 24-mile stretch of fresh water. The city sprawls across hills and ridges, some of them 500 feet high, but all are dwarfed by the Olympic Mountains to the west and the Cascades to the east. Elliott Bay, Seattle's natural harbor, welcomes about 2,000 commercial deep-sea cargo vessels a year. From Seattle's piers, ships wind their way 125 nautical miles through Puget Sound and the Strait of Juan de Fuca, two-thirds of them Orient-bound, the others destined for European, Alaskan, and Eastern ports.

On the same latitude as Newfoundland, Seattle is warmed by the Japan Current, shielded by the Olympics from excessive winter rains, and protected by the Cascades from midcontinent winter blasts. Only twice has the temperature been recorded at 100°F; there isn't a zero on record.

Five families pioneered here and named the town for a friendly Native American chief. The great harbor and the timber surrounding it made an inviting combination; shortly thereafter, a sawmill and a salmon-canning plant were in operation. Soon wagon trains were rolling to Seattle through Snoqualmie Pass, a tempting 3,022 feet, lower than any other in the Northwest.

Isolated at the fringe of the continent by the vast expanse of America, Seattle enjoyed great expectations but few women, an obvious threat to the community's growth and serenity. Asa Mercer, a civic leader and the first president of the Territorial University, went east and persuaded 11 proper young women from New England to sail with him around the Horn to Seattle to take husbands among the pioneers. This venture in long-distance matchmaking proved so successful that Mercer returned east and recruited 100 Civil War widows. Today, many of Seattle's families proudly trace their lineage to these women.

When a ship arrived from Alaska with a "ton of gold" in 1897, the great Klondike Gold Rush was on, converting Seattle into a boomtown—the beginning of the trail to fortune. Since then, Seattle has been the natural gateway to Alaska because of the protected Inside Passage; the commercial interests of the two remain tightly knit. Another major event for Seattle was the opening of the Panama Canal in 1914, a tremendous stimulant for the city's commerce.

Additional Visitor Information

For additional accommodations, see SEATTLE-TACOMA INTERNATIONAL AIRPORT AREA, which follows SEATTLE.

Public Transportation

Metro Transit System phone 206/553-3000. Web transit.metrokc.gov

What to See and Do

5th Avenue Theater. *1305 5th Ave, Seattle (98101). Phone 206/625-1418. www.fifthavenuetheater.org.* This historic theater, which opened as a vaudeville house in 1926, now features musicals, concerts, films, and lectures. Its ornate interior, modeled after some of China's architectural treasures, may well distract you from whatever's taking place onstage. Free tours Mon-Fri.

ACT Theatre. *700 Union St, Seattle (98101). Phone 206/292-7660. www.acttheatre.org.* ACT Theatre presents contemporary (read: edgy and daring) pieces as well as classic plays and musicals. Performances are held in two main theaters in Kreielsheimer Place, a renovation of the historic Eagles Auditorium completed in 1996. The Allen, a theater in the round, was carved out of the old auditorium's floor; the top row of seats is actually at ground level. The Falls features a restored Joshua Green Foundation Vault, used by the Eagles as a bank vault.

Alderwood Mall. *3000 184th St, Lynwood (98037). Phone 425/771-1211. www.alderwoodmall.com.* The largest shopping center in north Seattle, the Alderwood Mall is undergoing a major redevelopment slated for completion in November 2004. The goal is to transform the mall into an upscale retail and entertainment destination with shops in an indoor "village" and on outdoor "terraces," as well as a 16-screen movie theater. Of the 120-plus stores, Alderwood's anchors include Nordstrom and the Bon Marché. (Daily)

Alki Beach. *1100 Alki Ave SW, Seattle (98116). Phone 206/684-4075.* Skirting the northwestern waterfront of the South Seattle neighborhood, the 2.5-mile Alki Beach is a Mecca for outdoor types of all kinds—joggers, divers, bicyclists, beach volleyball players, sunbathers, and rollerbladers. The beach, administered by the Seattle Parks Department, runs from Duwamish Head to Alki Point on Elliot Bay and offers stunning views of Puget Sound and the city skyline. Facilities are a notch above the norm, with scads of picnic tables, a playground, small boat access, and a wide, multi-use path. At Alki Point (the southern end of the beach), there is a bathhouse/art studio and a plaque commemorating the landing of the first settlers here in 1851. At Duwamish Head (the northern tip of the beach) are the sea-walled site of a former amusement park and a miniature version of the Statue of Liberty.

Argosy Harbor Cruise. *1100 Alaskan Way, Seattle (98101). From Pier 55, at the foot of Seneca St. Phone 206/623-1445. www.argosycruises.com.* Boasting a 50-year history in Seattle's harbors, the family-owned Argosy Cruises is in proud possession of a fleet of nine cruise ships, ranging in size from the 77-foot *Champagne Lady* to the 180-foot *Royal Argosy*. The company operates from piers at the Seattle waterfront, Lake Union, and suburban Kirkland (on the eastern shore of Lake Washington). The most basic Argosy outing is a one-hour Harbor Cruise, which explores Seattle's downtown shoreline and offers some nice skyline views. Longer options include the Locks Cruise, which meanders from the salty waters of Puget Sound to Lake Union via the Ballard Locks, and a pair of lake cruises that explore Lake Union and Lake Washington. Snacks and beverages are offered on every Argosy cruise, but food is not included in the ticket price—the exceptions being ritzy lunch and dinner trips on the *Royal Argosy.* (Daily) **$$$$**

Bainbridge Island. *www.bainbridgeisland.org.* A half-hour ferry trip from downtown Seattle (ferries depart regularly throughout the day), Bainbridge Island is the size of Manhattan but a world apart. In the late 1800s, the island boasted the world's largest sawmill and a substantial shipbuilding industry, but its economy stumbled. It has recently regained footing as a tourist destination. With about 20,000 residents, the city of Bainbridge Island is now known for its delightful Victorian architecture and abundant shops and galleries. Densely wooded and lush with greenery, the island also attracts outdoor enthusiasts of all stripes—kayaking, golfing, fishing, and hiking are all popular—and boasts an active arts and entertainment scene. The Bainbridge Island Historical Museum is a great starting point, presenting displays on the island's geology, history, and industry in a converted 1908 schoolhouse.

Ballard Locks. *3015 NW 54th St, Seattle (98107). Phone 206/783-7059.* Popularly known as the Ballard Locks because of their location in Seattle's Ballard neighborhood, the Hiram M. Chittenden Locks are a marvel of engineering. Built in the early 20th century by the US Army Corps of Engineers, the locks are part of the canal system that connects salty Puget Sound (and, by extension, the Pacific Ocean) to Seattle's freshwater, providing a link for safe passage of watercraft. Salmon use a manmade "fish ladder" here to navigate their annual spawn through the locks. Underwater observation windows afford visitors a firsthand look at the migrating fish (and the seals and sea lions that feast on them, which workers struggle to keep out), but only at certain times of the year; the coho and chinook runs peak in midsummer. A visitor center presents exhibits that detail the locks' history and ecology, and an impressively vibrant botanical garden is also onsite. (May-Sept: daily; Oct-Apr: Thurs-Mon) **FREE**

⭐ **Boeing Field–King County International Airport.**
7277 Perimeter Rd, Seattle (98108). Phone 206/296-7380. Observation Park has viewing, picnicking facilities. Southeast Side. Also here is

Museum of Flight. *9404 E Marginal Way S, Seattle (98108). Phone 206/764-5700. www.museumofflight.org.* As a major hub for plane-maker Boeing—even since the aviation giant's headquarters bolted for Chicago in 2001—Seattle is the ideal location for this impressive air and space museum. The facility is highlighted by the soaring Great Gallery, home of more than 50 vintage aircraft, many of which are suspended in formation six stories above the ground. On display here are the original presidential *Air Force One* and a replica of the Wright Brothers' biplane from Kitty Hawk, North Carolina, alongside mint-condition models of the first fighter jet (a 1914 Caproni Ca 20) and the first jumbo jet (a prototype Boeing 747); many planes are open for visitors to sit in the cockpit or explore the hold. Located near Seattle-Tacoma International Airport in southern Seattle, the museum is also home to the restored "Red Barn" where the Boeing Company was founded nearly a century ago and several space-themed exhibits. (Daily; closed Thanksgiving, Dec 25) **$$$**

Capitol Hill. *12th Ave to Boren Ave and E Madison St to Denny Way.* Melding metropolitan chic, Victorian elegance, and urban grunge just east of downtown, Capitol Hill is one of Seattle's oldest and grandest neighborhoods and, today, is the nexus of the city's youth culture and gay scene. Broadway, the heart of Capitol Hill and one of the city's liveliest thoroughfares, has hip nightclubs, eateries, and tattoo parlors to spare. The neighborhood also features an eclectic mix of stores that cater to fashion plates, tattooed punks, antique lovers, and everyone in between. The primary shopping areas here are on Broadway (home to a bevy of youth fashion and resale shops, music retailers, and unusual bookstores), 15th Street (plenty of home and garden stores with a more upscale slant than Broadway), and Pike and Pine streets (a mix of antique stores, florists, coffee shops, and funky specialty retailers).

Carkeek Park. *950 NW Carkeek Park Rd, Seattle (98177).* Approximately 190 acres on Puget Sound. Beach, picnic area; model airplane meadow, hiking trail (1 mile). (Daily) **FREE**

The Center for Wooden Boats. *1010 Valley St, Seattle (98109). Phone 206/382-2628. www.cwb.org.* Located north of downtown on the southern tip of Lake Union, this is a "hands-on maritime heritage museum" where the focus is squarely set on historic wooden sailboats, kayaks, and canoes. Visitors can learn time-tested boat-building skills from master craftsmen, take sailing lessons, or rent a classic sailboat for a spin around the lake. The center also provides the setting for numerous annual festivals and boat shows. **FREE**

Central Library. *1000 Fourth Ave, Seattle (98104). Phone 206/386-4100. www.spl.org.* The new Central Library opened to much acclaim in 2004. The library was designed by famed Dutch architect Rem Koolhaas, winner of the 2000 Pritzker Prize, his profession's highest honor. With a transparent exterior of diamond-shaped panes of glass, the library stands as a marvel of contemporary architecture. The interior is equally amazing, highlighted by the Books Spiral, a series of tiers and ramps winding through four floors of book stacks. The library features more than 400 public computers, and wireless Internet access is available throughout the facility. Built at a cost of $165.5 million, the 11-level library exemplifies Seattle's passion for books and learning. **FREE**

Century Ballroom. *915 E Pine, 2nd Floor, Seattle (98122). Phone 206/324-7263. www.centuryballroom.com.* Home to one of Seattle's largest dance floors (2,000 square feet of refinished wood), the stylishly restored Century Ballroom is the place to go for swing and salsa dancing in the Emerald City. Many nights are themed (tango night, salsa night, and swing night). For those with two left feet, lessons are offered; while most are multi-week endeavors, there are occasional one-shot workshops. With a full bar, seating at comfortable tables, and a cavernous downtown location, the venue also hosts a number of concerts every month, with the talent tending to be jazz acts and singer/songwriters. There is also a popular restaurant here serving lunch, dinner, and Sunday brunch. The cuisine is eclectic, with a menu that melds the Far East with the Deep South (i.e. potpies and Vietnamese noodle bowls). (Mon-Tue 11 am-2 pm, Wed-Fri 8:30 am-2 pm, 5 pm-1 am, Sat 8:30 am-3 pm, 5 pm-1 am, Sun 8:30 am-3 pm) **$$$**

Charles and Emma Frye Art Museum. *704 Terry Ave, Seattle (98104). At Cherry St, downtown. Phone*

The Buzz on Seattle's Caffeine Culture

Seattle is known worldwide for its eclectic and innumerable mix of coffee establishments, ranging from chic espresso bars in trendy downtown hotels to tin-roofed java huts in grocery store parking lots. But for most of the 20th century, Seattle was regarded as a great place to partake in fresh fish, not fresh coffee. The emergence of Seattle's coffee scene corresponded with the spectacular success of a local company bearing a now familiar name, Starbucks. Founded in 1971, Starbucks' first coffeehouse opened in the city's Pike Place Market. It wasn't until the mid-1980s—when Starbucks employee Howard Schultz convinced the company's founders to develop a coffee bar culture similar to that found in Milan's espresso bars—that Starbucks' fortunes took off. At that time, it became a cultural and commercial phenomenon in Seattle and around the globe. Attempting to take advantage of the coffee craze, the likes of Seattle's Best Coffee and Tully's opened numerous Seattle locations, and now it's almost impossible to walk a city block without passing a franchise coffeehouse.

To fully appreciate Seattle's coffee culture, you should visit a few of the city's many independent coffee shops, one of the best being Espresso Vivace Roasteria (901 E Denny Way). Situated on Capitol Hill near the Seattle Center, Espresso Vivace has taken espresso preparation to an art form, having spent 15 years perfecting the roasting process for their signature beverage. Espresso Vivace even offers an intensive three-day espresso preparation course.

Artists like to gather downtown at the stylish and hip Zeitgeist Coffee (171 S Jackson St). Zeitgeist is particularly crowded on the first Thursday of each month, when the art galleries in and around Pioneer Square stay open late and hundreds of art lovers congregate in the area. Coffee is not the only thing on the menu; Zeitgeist also serves fresh pastries and grilled sandwiches.

Visitors to the Queen Anne neighborhood should stop by Uptown Espresso (525 Queen Anne Ave N). Weekends are particularly crowded at this casual coffeehouse situated at the bottom of Queen Anne Hill. Uptown Espresso's "velvet foam lattes" are a local favorite. The coffeehouse features vintage décor and the artwork of local painters.

Before you venture into one of the city's hundreds of coffee shops, it behooves you to study up on your coffee lexicon, which means that, if you don't want to sound like an instant-coffee drinker while ordering a small decaf espresso to go, you should know to request a short harmless espresso on a leash. At the very least, you should know these key terms:

Americano: An espresso mixed with hot water.

Barista: An individual who makes coffee drinks.

Cappuccino: An espresso with foamed milk on top.

Espresso: A roughly 1-ounce shot of espresso. Espresso is made from Arabica beans rather than the Robusta beans used to make regular coffee.

Latte: An espresso mixed with steamed milk, then topped by foamed milk.

Mochaccino: A cappuccino flavored with chocolate.

Ristretto: The strongest espresso; it is made using less water and more coffee.

206/622-9250. www.fryeart.org. In a city where abstract and postmodern art are the norm, the conservative Frye Art Museum bucks the trend by focusing solely on representational art: contemporary and classic landscapes and portraits. The works are both dark and bright (in both tint and theme), and are all bathed in natural light in simple, classic settings. Among the artists represented here are Winslow Homer and Andrew Wyeth. The café and the bookstore here are both excellent, and worth a visit. (Tue-Sun; closed holidays) **FREE**

Crocodile Cafe. *2200 2nd Ave, Seattle (98121). Phone 206/441-5611. www.thecrocodile.com.* Established just as the Seattle rock scene was exploding onto the national scene in 1991, a concert at the Crocodile

Café is a feast for both the ears and the eyes. Beyond the varnished driftwood tables and psychedelic décor, the Belltown venue doubles as a gallery, with rotating exhibits by local artists. As Seattle has been the center of the grunge scene for more than a decade, most of the performers who take the Crocodile's stage are up and coming rock bands (including past shows by homegrown acts like Pearl Jam and Nirvana), but some nights feature electronic acts and lighter pop bands. There is also a café here that serves a menu of burgers and other pub grub, and is an especially popular breakfast destination for eggs and a Crocodile Mary ("a bloody Mary with a bite"). (Tues-Sat 8-2 am, Sun 9 am-3 pm; open Sun and Mon nights for special shows)

Dimitriou's Jazz Alley. *2033 6th Ave, Seattle (98121). Phone 206/441-9729. www.jazzalley.com.* Jazz aficionados descend on Dimitriou's Jazz Alley in droves on a near-nightly basis to enjoy top musicians in an intimate setting. Widely considered the best jazz club in Seattle, the downtown venue originally opened in the University District in 1979, then moved downtown in 1985, and has seen performances by such big names as Taj Mahal and Eartha Kitt in the time since. The atmosphere is refined, with chairs and tables surrounding the circular stage and a mezzanine overlooking it. A renovation in 2002 expanded Jazz Alley's capacity and bolstered the sound system while retaining the heralded ambiance. A restaurant here serves a varied menu with an Italian thrust, with options ranging from calamari and salmon to manicotti and rib eye steak. (Daily; doors open Mon-Sat 6 pm, Sun 4:30 pm)

Discovery Park. *3801 W Government Way, Seattle (98119). Phone 206/386-4236.* An in-city wildlife sanctuary and nature preserve, the 534-acre Discovery Park is the largest park in Seattle, located on the western shores of the swanky Magnolia neighborhood. It is centered on a tall bluff that formerly served as a post for the US Army, making for great views of the Olympic Mountains to the west and the Cascades to the east, with waterfront access to the north and west. An extensive trail system lures joggers, bikers, and other fitness buffs from all over the city, but the educational program is at the heart of the park's mission, hence the 'Discovery' tag. School buses and day campers frequent the park year-round, but the events calendar has something for every age and interest. A diverse population of flora and fauna—including wildflowers, owls, hummingbirds, and crustaceans—

calls the park's dunes, thickets, forests, and tide pools home. **FREE**

Downtown Shopping District. *1st Ave to 7th Ave, Madison St to Pine St. www.downtownseattle.com.* Downtown is undoubtedly the heart of Seattle's vibrant shopping scene, with a who's who of national department stores alongside fun and funky retailers of all stripes. Prime window-shopping corridors include First and Second avenues, populated by fashionable boutiques, upscale galleries, and a few quirky curiosities to boot; and Fifth and Sixth avenues, brimming with jewelers, kitchen stores, and clothing stores ranging from small boutiques to mega-sized versions of national staples. There ia also a pair of malls on Pine Street: Westlake (between Fourth and Fifth avenues), a fairly typical enclosed shopping center; and the ritzy Pacific Place Mall, downtown Seattle's newest (and most stylish) retail destination. The centerpiece of the whole shopping district is Nordstrom (500 Pine St), the flagship store for the Seattle-based department store chain.

Druids Glen Golf Course. *29925 207th Ave SE, Covington (98042). Phone 253/638-1200. www. druidsglengolf.com.* Completed in June 2003, Druids Glen offers affordable prices and the backdrop of Mount Rainier on a sparkling new course. The second hole offers a view of the majestic mountain from the tee box, and several holes require difficult shots over water right off the tee or on the approach to the green. Four different pros are available for private lessons, and the practice facility is unblemished. **$$$$**

Evergreen Floating Bridge. *On Hwy 520, near Montlake Pl, SE Side.* Almost 1 1/2 miles long; connects downtown Seattle with Bellevue (see).

Experience Music Project. *325 5th Ave, Seattle (98109). Phone 206/770-2700. www.emplive.com.* More than 30 years after his death, legendary rock guitarist Jimi Hendrix remains Seattle's favorite native son, and this thoroughly modern museum is a tribute to the huge impact of his short life. Financed by Microsoft co-founder and Hendrix fanatic Paul Allen, the $200 million museum opened in 2000 as an archive of rock and roll memorabilia and a tribute to musical innovation. The striking architecture, all sharp angles, contrasting textures, and bright hues, intentionally evokes the image of a smashed guitar and the rhythms of rock and roll. The facilities within are similarly cutting-edge, from the grand hall/musical venue dubbed the "Sky Church" to Crossroads, an exhibit space that meshes historical artifacts with multimedia to present the history of American music, to Sound Lab, a recording studio that's as high-tech as it gets. Food and drink (and live music) are available at the highly stylized Turntable Restaurant and Liquid Lounge. (Mon-Thurs 10 am-5 pm, Fri-Sat 10 am-9 pm, Sun 10 am-6 pm; closed Dec 25) **$$$$**

Ferry trips. *Seattle Ferry Terminal, Colman Dock, foot of Madison St. Phone 206/464-6400; toll-free 800/843-3779 (WA).* Access to Olympic Peninsula; a number of interesting ferry trips. Contact Washington State Ferries, Colman Dock, 98104. **$$$$**

Floyd's Place. *521 1st Ave N, Seattle (98109). Phone 206/522-4454.* A beer and barbecue joint across from Key Arena in the Queen Anne neighborhood, Floyd's is jammed with SuperSonic fans before and after games, but the succulent brisket and ribs lure locals year-round. There are 27 beers on tap here (many of them local microbrews), and a game room with pinball, pool tables, and dartboards. (Daily noon-2 am)

Freeway Park. *6th and Seneca, Seattle. Downtown.* This 5-acre park features dramatic water displays. Free concerts (summer, Mon). (Daily)

Fremont District. Undoubtedly Seattle's funkiest neighborhood, Fremont wears its eccentricity like a badge: the self-proclaimed "Center of the Universe" went as far as to declare facetious independence from Seattle in 1994. North of downtown and the Lake Washington Ship Canal, the former lumber-mill center is now an artist's paradise, well known for such public sculptures as a towering statue of Vladimir Lenin, a post-Cold War import from the former Soviet Union; the Fremont Troll, gobbling a VW Beetle under Aurora Bridge; and "Waiting for Interurban," six cast aluminum figures waiting for the bus. The area is also home to an unusually high concentration of brewpubs, coffee shops, and secondhand stores. In an afternoon, shoppers can comb vintage stores for Space Age décor, browse unusual galleries, try on all kind of interesting clothing, and shop for bulk foods. Atypical shopping strips line Fremont Avenue, Fremont Place, and 34th and 35th streets.

***Gallant Lady* Cruises.** *Depart from Lake Union. For prices, schedule, contact PO Box 1250, Vashon 98070. Phone 206/463-2073.* Offers 6-day inclusive summer cruises to San Juan Islands; also extended cruises along British Columbia.

Under and Above Ground in Downtown Seattle

Begin in Seattle's Pioneer Square district, the city's original downtown, which was built in the 1890s (after a disastrous fire) as money from the Yukon Gold Rush started pouring in. The architecture is amazingly harmonious (one architect was responsible for nearly 60 major buildings in a ten-block radius) and graciously restored. The area also features the underground tour and many galleries, cafes, and antique shops. A collection of totem poles can be found in tree-lined Occidental Park and in Pioneer Square itself.

Continue across Alaskan Way (or take Waterfront Trolley, a vintage street car that runs from Pioneer Square to the waterfront to Pike Place Market) to the waterfront. Walk along the harbor, watching ferries dart to and fro, or take a boat tour (see FERRY TRIPS AND CRUISES). Stop at the Seattle Aquarium, located in Waterfront Park at Pier 59,

then stop for clam chowder at Ivar's, located at Pier 54.

Continue north, recrossing Alaskan Way, and climb to Pike Place Market, eight stories above the harbor on a bluff. There are two ways to do this: there's an elevator hidden at the base of the market, or you can take the Harbor Stairs, a new cascade of steps flanked by shops and gardens. The Pike Place Market is Seattle's most interesting destination, an old-fashioned public market (built around 1910) in a warrenlike building with three floors of food, baked goods, ethnic shops, fresh fish, and crafts. You could spend hours here. Also in the Market are some of Seattle's best-loved restaurants; many of them have great views over the harbor to the islands and Olympic Mountains to the west. Just down the street is the new Seattle Art Museum, with its excellent collection of Northwest Native Art.

Gas Works Park. *3300 Meridian Ave N, Seattle (98103). Phone 206/684-4075.* A former gas-processing plant on the north side of Lake Union, the 20-acre Gas Works Park is a model for urban renewal and a magnet for kite-flyers. The plant's facilities have been nicely converted for recreational use: the boiler house is now a picnic area and the exhauster-compressor building is now the "Play Barn," a brightly painted playground for kids. The 12.5-mile Burke-Gilman trail begins here, offering a paved route north to suburban Kirkland for joggers and bikers. (Daily) **FREE**

Golden Gardens. *8499 Seaview Pl NW, Seattle (98117). Phone 206/684-4075.* Nestled on the bluffs that front Puget Sound in Seattle's Ballard neighborhood, Golden Gardens Park attracts sunbathers and fishermen to its beach and pier, and all sorts of outdoor buffs to its myriad of recreational opportunities. The park's trail system connects the beach with the forested bluffs above, with a leash-optional dog park at the summit. A teen center called the "Brick House" is on the beach, which features concerts and other events year-round. **FREE**

Golf Club at Newcastle. *15500 Six Penny Ln, Newcastle (98059). Phone 425/793-4653. www.newcastlegolf.com.* Some of the best views in the Seattle area can be found at Newcastle, which includes sightlines of the city's skyline and nearby Mount Rainier. There are two courses, the Coal Creek and the China Creek, with the latter the more difficult of the two. There is a putting course and a practice facility for warming up before your round and an excellent restaurant and bar for afterwards. **$$$$**

Graceland. *109 Eastlake Ave E, Seattle (98109). Phone 206/381-3094.* Features live bands and DJs; Monday is bargain night, where admission is $5 and gives you access to the live music in the front room and a DJ in the back lounge.

Gray Line bus tours. *4500 W Marginal Way SW, Seattle (98106). Phone 206/624-5077; toll-free 800/426-7505. www.graylineofseattle.com.*

Green Lake Park. *7201 E Green Lake Dr N, Seattle (98103). Phone 206/684-4075.* Ground zero for jogging in fitness-crazy Seattle, Green Lake is the heart of a bustling 320-acre park of the same name. Two paved trails encircle the lake and see a good deal of use from a cross-section of ages and speeds. Each trail is about 3 miles around the lake, and there are separate lanes for bikers, walkers, and runners. The trails aside, the lake itself is a recreation destination: a private company provides boat rentals, and the Green Lake Small Craft Center offers rowing, sailing, and canoe classes, and organizes several annual regattas. The lush park surrounding Green Lake is home to a "Pitch and Putt" golf course (with nine par-three holes) and an indoor pool, as well as a community center, tennis courts, picnic tables, and a children's playground. **FREE**

International District. *SE of Downtown, 4th Ave to I-5 and Yesler to S Dearborn sts. www.internationaldistrict.org.* Southeast of downtown, the colorful International District is home to one of the largest and most vibrant Asian communities in the US. Its roots took seed in the late 19th century, and the neighborhood is now one of the most diverse ethnic populations in the world. Asian markets and eateries of all kinds dot the streets; top attractions include the Wing Luke Asian Museum, the Nippon Kan Theatre, and Uwajimaya, a huge food market and cooking school.

Jefferson Park Golf Club. *4101 Beacon Ave S, Seattle (98108). Phone 206/762-4513. www.jeffersonparkgolf.com.* Seattle's Jefferson Park offers a shorter par-70 layout, but at least it doesn't cost quite as much as some of the other courses in the area. There is also a par-three course on the grounds, but it's the big course people come for, with a hilly layout that is challenging at times but still playable for just about any golfer. Go for the views as much as the golf. Bring your camera to take pictures of the long putt you made and then smile in front of Mount Rainier for the subsequent photo. **$$$$**

Klondike Gold Rush National Historical Park. *117 S Main St, Seattle (98104). Phone 206/553-7220.* The 1897 gold strike in the Canadian Yukon triggered an influx of tens of thousands of prospectors to Seattle and its commercial district, Pioneer Square. Motivated by dreams of riches, they arrived here to purchase food, equipment, and pack animals in preparation for the arduous six-month trip to the frozen wilderness of the Klondike Gold Fields. While the gold rush provided an economic boost to the city, it was an economic failure for nearly all of the prospectors. Only a handful struck it rich. Most discovered no gold, and many lost their lives during the trek across the steep, snow-covered trail leading to the Klondike. The stampede of prospectors spurred commercial development in Pioneer Square, where the Klondike

Gold Rush National Historical Park is located. The National Historical Park offers exhibits, audiovisuals, and ranger programs that document the gold rush and its impact on Seattle. (Daily from 9 am-5 pm; closed Jan 1, Thanksgiving, Dec 25)

Lake Union. *Seen from George Washington Memorial Bridge, NW side.* There are boatyards, seaplane moorages, and houseboat colonies on the lake.

Lake Washington Canal. *Can be seen from Seaview Ave NW or NW 54th St, NW side.* Chittenden Locks raise and lower boats to link saltwater and freshwater anchorages. More than 400,000 passengers and 6 million tons of freight pass through annually. Commodore Park and a salmon ladder with viewing windows are on the south side.

Lake Washington Floating Bridge. *Lake Washington Blvd and Lakeside Ave, Seattle.* Connects downtown Seattle with Mercer Island via I-90.

Lincoln Park. *8011 Fauntleroy Way SW, Seattle (98102). SW Side.* Trails, picnic areas, tennis; beach, bathhouse, saltwater pool (Mid-June-early Sept, daily; fee), wading pool (June-Sept, daily); fitness trail. (Daily) **FREE**

Mount Baker-Snoqualmie National Forest. *Outdoor Recreation Information Center, 915 2nd Ave, Suite 442, Seattle (98174). Phone 425/775-9702.* Snoqualmie section. Includes several ski areas; eight wilderness areas; picnic and campsites, fishing, hunting. More than 1 million acres. East and south of city, reached via I-90.

Museum of History and Industry. *2700 24th Ave E, Seattle (98112). On N side of Hwy 520, just S of Husky Stadium, SE side. Phone 206/324-1126. www.seattlehistory.org.* The showcase of the Seattle Historical Society, this excellent facility (popularly known as MOHAI) tracks the people and events that have shaped Seattle over the course of its 150-year history. With a collection of more than a million photographs and historical artifacts, MOHAI is a treasure trove for history buffs, giving visitors a comprehensive look into the social and economic roots of the Puget Sound area. The Great Seattle Fire is documented by an exhibit complete with a historic fire engine, murals, and other relics of the disaster that razed the city in 1889; a mock-up of an 1880s street scene gives visitors a glimpse into the pre-fire Emerald City. Another highlight is the comprehensive collection of souvenirs

from the 1962 World's Fair. (Daily 10 am-5 pm; closed Thanksgiving, Dec 25) **$$**

Myrtle Edwards/Elliott Bay. *North of Pier 70, NW Side.* One mile of shoreline; paved bike trail; views of Puget Sound, the Olympic Peninsula, and oceangoing vessels; Seamen's Memorial and a granite and concrete sculpture.

Nordic Heritage Museum. *3014 NW 67th St, Seattle (98117). NW Side. Phone 206/789-5707. www.nordicmuseum.org.* Center for Scandinavian community in Pacific Northwest. Represents all five Scandinavian countries. Historical exhibits; art gallery; performing arts. (Tues-Sat, also Sun afternoon) **$$**

Northwest Outdoor Center. *2100 Westlake Ave N, Suite 1, Seattle (98109). Phone 206/281-9694.* A 20-year-old Seattle institution on the docks of Lake Union, the Northwest Outdoor Center is a major hub for the Pacific Northwest's paddling community. A combination school/store/guide service, the place has over 100 kayaks available for rental (starting at $10 for an hour on Lake Union) and a full slate of whitewater and sea kayaking classes, ranging from a 2.5-hour session to a 6-day immersion. The center's guided tours include day trips spent sea kayaking in Puget Sound and multi-day wildlife-watching adventures that take participants to the San Juan Islands and beyond. A bit off the beaten path, sunset and nighttime excursions explore Lake Union and—via the Lake Washington Ship Canal and the water elevator known as the Ballard Locks—Puget Sound. The Northwest Outdoor Center is also the best source of paddling information and advice in the city. **$$$$**

Paramount Theatre. *911 Pine St, Seattle (98101). Phone 206/682-1414. www.theparamount.com.* This 75-year-old theater brings a wide range of entertainment to Seattle: Broadway plays and musicals, ballet and modern dance performances, jazz and rock-and-roll concerts, and comedy acts. It also shows silent films and hosts family-oriented entertainment. Check out the Publix theater organ, one of only three remaining, which has been magnificently restored.

⭐ **Pike Place Market.** *85 Pike St, Seattle (98101). First Ave and Pike St, in 9-acre historical district, downtown. Phone 206/587-0351. www.pikeplacemarket.org.* Area that farmers established the Pike Place Market in 1907 because they were tired of middlemen taking more than their fair share. Today, the indoor/outdoor market is a Seattle landmark and a cornucopia for the senses, with burly guys tossing fresh fish back and forth at the fish market, bin after bin of fresh, colorful fruits, vegetables, and flowers, the sounds and sights of street performers, and the wares of hundreds of artists on display. But it doesn't stop there: the astoundingly comprehensive Pike Place Market has dozens of restaurants and food stands, a day spa, a barbershop, a tattoo parlor, and a dating service onsite. Just two blocks east of the waterfront, the market is a quick walk from the center of downtown and surrounded by eateries and bars. Guided tours are available Wednesday to Sunday year-round, but there is a fee ($7 adults, $5 seniors and children). (Daily; closed holidays) **FREE**

Pioneer Square. *Bounded by 1st Ave, James St, and Yesler Way.* Seattle's oldest neighborhood, the original Pioneer Square saw its beginnings in the early 1850s but soon met a blazing fate in the Great Seattle Fire of 1889. Today's Pioneer Square was built atop the scorched remains, resulting in a ghostlike underground beneath the city streets. (The Underground Tour allows visitors to explore this buried history.) The area boomed again after the lure of gold began attracting miners during the following decade, and a seedy underbelly (that remains to this day) followed in their wake. Now dominated by stately (and inflammable) Victorian and Romanesque redbricks above cobblestone squares, the neighborhood is a commercial and social hub: a melting pot of offices, stores, galleries, restaurants, and nightclubs wedged between downtown and a pair of major stadiums, SAFECO Field (baseball) and Seahawks Stadium (football).

Queen Anne Neighborhood. Named for its predominant architectural style, the Queen Anne neighborhood dates from the 1880s and is one of Seattle's most scenic spots. Built on the 456-foot slope of Queen Anne Hill, the ritzy area is dotted with overlooks that are perfect perches for views of the Space Needle, downtown, and Mount Rainier. The neighborhood's top attraction is the Seattle Center, with the Space Needle, the Experience Music Project, and KeyArena, the pyramidal home court of the National Basketball Association's Seattle SuperSonics.

Rock Bottom Brewery. *1333 Fifth Ave, Seattle (98101). Phone 206/623-3070. www.rockbottom.com.* This brewpub in the heart of downtown Seattle is one of the flagships of the Rock Bottom chain, which consists of about 30 breweries in the US. At any given time, at least six beers are on tap, all of which are brewed onsite with Washington-grown hops. The menu is varied, with burgers, pizzas, salads, and steaks, served inside in an upstairs dining room and a downstairs bar/poolroom or outside on a breezy patio.

SAFECO Field. *1250 1st Ave S, Seattle (98134). Phone 306/346-4000. www.mariners.mlb.com.* First opening in 1999, SAFECO Field replaced the much-maligned Kingdome as the home of Major League Baseball's Seattle Mariners. It's easy to see why the $517 million ballpark quickly won the hearts of the Emerald City's sports fans, based on nostalgic architecture, stunning views of the Seattle skyline and the Puget Sound sunset, and a one-of-a-kind umbrella for the city's infamous rainstorms: a retractable roof that weighs 22 million pounds and covers nine acres. Hour-long tours of the facility are available on a near-daily basis (except Mondays during baseball's off-season and day game days during the season), and cover a walking distance of about 1 mile. Aside from the roof and old-time ironwork, some of SAFECO's can't-miss features are the works of public art integrated into its design, a playground for kids, and the official Mariners team store.

Schmitz Park. *Admiral Way SW and SW Stevens St, Seattle.* Section of forest as it was when first settlers arrived. **FREE**

The Seattle Aquarium. *1483 Alaskan Way, Seattle (98101). Pier 59, Waterfront Park, downtown. Phone 206/386-4300. www.seattleaquarium.org.* A Waterfront mainstay at Pier 59 since 1977, the Seattle Aquarium is an engrossing educational experience for curious minds of all ages. The top facility of its kind in the region, the aquarium is home to nearly 400 species of fish, birds, marine mammals, and other sea life. Staff here have celebrated several breakthroughs over the years, including the first live births of sea otters in North American captivity, which has happened six times here, and the rearing of a giant Pacific octopus to adulthood, another first. (The 50-pound octopus, "Dudley," is still an aquarium resident and visitor favorite.) Another highlight is the underwater dome, which allows guests to immerse themselves in a transparent bubble on the bottom of a fish-filled, 400,000-gallon tank. An IMAX theater is adjacent, charging separate entry fees. Plans are in the works to build a new aquarium on the Waterfront in coming years. (Daily) **$$$$**

Seattle Art Museum. *100 University St, Seattle (98101). Downtown. Phone 206/654-3255. www. seattleartmuseum.org.* Its entrance guarded by an animated, 48-foot-tall sculpture named "Hammering Man," the Seattle Art Museum (known locally as SAM) is the premiere facility of its kind in the Pacific Northwest. There is something for everybody here, from ancient Greek sculpture to modern Russian decorative art. Held in particularly high regard are the collections of contemporary art (with pieces by Andy Warhol, Jackson Pollock, and Roy Lichtenstein) and Northwest Coast Native American art (comprised of nearly 200 masks, sculptures and household items). SAM's temporary exhibitions are similarly diverse. A dynamic events calendar helps distinguish the museum, offering up a bevy of concerts, films, lectures, demonstrations, family programs, and classes. Admission is waived on the first Thursday of every month, and a restaurant and two gift shops are onsite. (Tues-Sun; closed holidays) **$$$**

Seattle Asian Art Museum. *1400 E Prospect St, Seattle (98112). Phone 206/654-3100. www.seattleartmuseum .org.* Sitting atop a hill in Volunteer Park in the swank Capitol Hill neighborhood, an ornate Art Deco structure houses one of the top collections of Asian art in the Western Hemisphere. The Seattle Asian Art Museum, under the umbrella of the Seattle Art Museum, is known for its outstanding Chinese, Japanese and Korean pieces—a wide-ranging assortment that includes everything from calligraphy and ink paintings to tomb figures and Buddha sculptures. The Japanese collection is particularly renowned, as experts consider it among the top five in the entire US. Out front is Isamu Noguchi's "Black Sun," a shelllike sculpture with a peephole in the center perfect for framing the Space Needle at sunset. Admission is free on the first Thursday and first Saturday of each month. (Wed-Sun 10 am-5 pm, Thurs to 9 pm; closed holidays) **$$**

★ **Seattle Center.** *305 Harrison St, Seattle (98109). Phone 206/684-7200; fax 206/684-7366.* Site of 1962 World's Fair. Its 74 acres include

Center House. Three floors of specialty shops, restaurants, conference facilities, administrative offices. (Daily)

Fun Forest Amusement Park. *Phone 206/728-1585.* Rides (fees), games in parklike setting. (June-Labor Day: daily; Mar-June and early Sept-Nov: Fri-Sun) **FREE**

International Fountain. *www.seattlecenter.com/ attractions/int_fountain.asp.* Like the Space Needle, the International Fountain is a remnant of the 1962 World's Fair, but unlike that other Seattle icon, it was demolished and rebuilt in 1995. More inviting than its rocky, sunflower-inspired predecessor, the new fountain is interactive: visitors can play aside its sleek silver globe in the path of splashing arcs of water, which go off hourly and shoot up to 150 feet in the air. The spot is the site of several festival events. (Daily)

Marion Oliver McCaw Hall. *Phone 206/443-2222.* The Opera House is home of the Seattle Opera Association, Pacific Northwest Ballet, and Seattle Symphony. Bagley Wright Theatre is home of Seattle Repertory Theatre.

Monorail. Provides a scenic 90-second ride between Center House and Westlake Center, Downtown. Legacy of 1962 World's Fair, the Swedish-built train makes frequent runs throughout the day. (Daily, closed Jan 1, Thanksgiving, Dec 25) **$$**

Pacific Science Center. *200 2nd Ave N, Seattle (98109). Phone 206/443-2001. www.pacsci.org.* This educational museum in downtown Seattle is aimed at young minds, but the exhibits tend to engage every age group. With subject matter that balances cutting-edge technology and natural history, the center features such permanent exhibits as an indoor butterfly house, a room-sized model of Puget Sound, and "Dinosaurs: A Journey through Time," complete with seven robotic dinosaurs; on the other side of the science spectrum is "Tech Zone," where visitors can challenge a robot to a game of tic-tac-toe or create art on a computer. Beyond the permanent and seasonal exhibits, there are movies on a pair of giant-sized IMAX screens (one of which is coupled with a 3-D projector), astronomy demonstrations in the onsite planetarium, and dazzling light displays with rock and roll soundtracks in the Adobe Laser Dome. **$$$$**

Space Needle. *400 Broad St, Seattle (98109). Phone toll-free 800/937-9582. www.spaceneedle.com.* First a sketch on a placemat, then the centerpiece of the 1962 World's Fair, and now Seattle's face to the world, the Space Needle is one of the most distinctive structures in the US. Capping the 605-foot tower, the flying saucer-inspired dome is symbolic of both the Seattle World's Fair's theme—Century 21—and the coinciding national push into space. The dome houses an observation deck (with stunning city views) and SkyCity, a revolving restaurant that goes full circle every 48 minutes. There is also a banquet facility 100 feet above street level and a gift shop at the tower's base, where visitors board an elevator for the 43-second journey to the top. The Space Needle is the setting for one of the West Coast's premiere New Year's Eve celebrations every Dec 31. **$$$**

Seattle Mariners (MLB). *1250 1st Ave S, Seattle (98134). Phone 206/346-4000. www.mariners.mlb.com.* The city's Major League Baseball franchise has been a Seattle sports stalwart since 1977, its inaugural season playing in the American League. The Mariners played home games at the now-demolished (and often criticized) Kingdome, but the team got new digs in 1999—the state-of-the-art SAFECO Field (with a retractable roof to thwart Seattle's notorious rainstorms), located just south of downtown. In recent years, the Mariners have enjoyed a nice resurgence in fan support, thanks to the new ballpark, a competitive team, and a fitting Asian flair—thanks to Japanese stars like Ichiro Suzuki and a sushi bar just beyond SAFECO's outfield fences. The season runs from March to October; the team's schedule includes 81 home games every year.

Seattle Opera. *1020 John St, Seattle (98109). Phone 206/389-7676. www.seattleopera.org.* This renowned company presents five operas per season (Aug-May). After a year and a half of renovation of the historic Opera House, performances return to their old home, now called Marian Oliver McCaw Hall. **$$$$**

Seattle Seahawks (NFL). *800 Occidental Ave S, Seattle (98134). Phone 425/827-9777; toll-free 888/635-4295; fax 425/893-5066. www.seahawks.com.* The Seattle Seahawks have been competing in the National Football League since the franchise's inaugural season of 1976. The team takes to the gridiron at 67,000-seat Seahawks Stadium, a state-of-the-art facility that opened for play in 2002. Seventy percent of the seats are covered by a pair of arcing roofs that shield spectators from the rain—and also serve to amplify crowd noise. The stadium's Ring of Honor celebrates the on-field accomplishments of Seahawk greats such as wide receiver Steve Largent and running back Curt Warner. The Seahawks were originally owned by department-store giant John Nordstrom, but today the franchise is owned by billionaire Paul Allen, who co-founded Microsoft with Bill Gates.

Seattle Sounders (USL). *406 N Logan, Seattle (98055). Phone 206/622-3415. www.seattlesounders.net.* The Seattle Sounders play professional soccer in the United Soccer Leagues' A-League and have had many players go on to play in Major League Soccer. The team has had a successful run, winning the league championship during the 1990s. The 28-game schedule runs from May to September, with the Sounders playing 14 home games at Seahawks Stadium, just south of downtown Seattle.

Seattle Storm (WNBA). *305 Elliott Ave W, Seattle (98109). Phone 206/684-7200. www.wnba.com/storm.* The Emerald City's entry in the Women's National Basketball Association, the Storm plays 16 home games at Key Arena between May and August. The team's inaugural season was in 2000, making it the newest professional sports franchise in Seattle. After floundering for the first two years of its existence, the Storm made the playoffs in 2002 behind rookie phenomenon Sue Bird.

Seattle SuperSonics (NBA). *305 Elliott Ave W, Seattle (98109). First Ave N between Thomas and Republican. Phone 206/283-3865. www.supersonics. com.* Longtime Seattleites still wax nostalgic about the 1979 SuperSonics. Guided by legendary coach Lenny Wilkens and featuring balanced scoring from the likes of Gus Williams and "Downtown" Freddie Brown, the Sonics, as they're better known, won the NBA Championship, upsetting a talented Washington Bullets squad. Unfortunately for Seattle hoops fans, the franchise has never repeated its 1979 championship performance. Nonetheless, the city's support for the team remains strong. The Sonics play home games at KeyArena, a 17,000-seat facility on the grounds of the Seattle Center. In 2004, the team was shuffled into the newly created Northwest Division of the NBA's Western Conference.

Seattle Thunderbirds (WHL). *305 Elliott Ave W, Seattle (98109). Phone 206/448-7825. www. seattle-thunderbirds.com.* While a National Hockey League franchise is noticeably absent from town, Seattle's hockey fans get their fix in the form of the Thunderbirds of the Western Hockey League. An Emerald City fixture since 1977, the team garners good fan support and won the WHL's Western Conference championship in 1997. The Thunderbirds play 36 home games at Key Arena during the September-to-March regular season.

Seattle University. *900 Broadway, Seattle (98122). Phone 206/296-6000.* (1891) (4,800 students) Landscaped urban campus with more than 1,000 varieties of exotic flowers, trees and shrubs; water fountain sculpture by George Tsutakawa. Tours of campus.

Seward Park. *Occupies peninsula off Lake Washington Blvd S and S Orcas St, SE Side.* Swimming beach (Mid-June-early Sept, daily), bathhouse; picnic and play areas, tennis; amphitheater; Japanese lantern and torii (Japanese arch); fish hatchery. (Daily) **FREE**

Shilshole Bay Marina. *7001 Seaview Ave NW, Seattle (98117). NW Side. Phone 206/728-3385.* Moorage for 1,500 boats, fuel, repairs, launching ramp, marine supplies; restaurants.

Six Arms. *300 E Pike St, Seattle (98122). Phone 206/223-1698.* McMenamins, the tycoons of Portland, Oregon's bar scene, have also dipped their toes in the Seattle waters with this brewpub on the western slope of Capitol Hill. It's a pleasant space, the décor blending Seattle's ever-present grunge with a pseudo-European feel and a Hindu motif. The oversized wooden booths are a bonus, as is the menu of international pub standards. McMenamins also owns Dad Watson's in Fremont and McMenamins Queen Anne Hill in Queen Anne. (Mon-Sat 11-1 am; Sun noon-midnight)

Smith Cove. *Elliott Ave and W Garfield St, Seattle.* Navy ships at anchor; Seattle Annex, Naval Supply Center along north side of West Garfield Street.

Sur La Table. *84 Pine St, Seattle (98101). Phone 206/448-2244. www.surlatable.com.* In the 1970s, Seattle spawned this clearinghouse for hard-to-find kitchen gear, and it soon became known as a source for cookware, small appliances, cutlery, kitchen tools, linens, tableware, gadgets, and specialty foods. Sur La Table has since expanded to include cooking classes ($$$$), chef demonstrations, and cookbook author signings, as well as a catalog and online presence. Cooking connoisseurs discover such finds as cool oven mitts, zest graters, copper whisks, onion soup bowls, and inspired TV dinner trays. (Daily)

Teatro ZinZanni. *2301 6th Ave, Seattle (98121). Phone 206/802-0015. www.teatrozinzanni.org.* An avant-garde dinner theater with a sister facility in San Francisco, Teatro ZinZanni offers entertainment like nothing else in town: a hyper-imaginative circus/nightclub act hybrid of music, comedy, trapeze, Kabuki, and magic. The food is similarly enchanting—an eclectic fusion of culinary traditions—as is the venue itself, a beautifully restored antique circular pavilion with a hazy, opulent vibe, complete with reams of velvet, crystal chandeliers, and hand-carved wooden columns. **$$$$**

Tillicum Village. *Blake Island State Park, 2992 SW Avalon Way, Seattle (98126). Excursion from Pier 55/56, foot of Seneca St. Phone toll-free 800/426-1205. www.tillicumvillage.com.* Narrated harbor cruise; baked salmon dinner; stage show. (May-mid-Oct: daily; rest of year: Sat; hours vary) Reservations advised. **$$$$**

Underground Tour. *608 First Ave, Seattle (98104). Phone 206/682-4646; toll-free 888/608-6337. www.undergroundtour.com.* A fun and funny look at Seattle's colorful past, Bill Speidel's Underground Tour takes guests on a journey under the streets of Pioneer Square, where remnants of the frontier town that met its fiery end here in 1889 still remain. The tour begins in a bar (Doc Maynard's Public House) and lasts about an hour and a half, with Speidel dishing enough humorous insight into Seattle's history to fill a book. (Daily; closed holidays; advance reservations recommended) **$$**

University of Washington. *17th Ave NE and NE 45th St, NE side, Seattle. Phone 206/543-9198.* (1861) (34,400 students) Visitor Information Center, 4014 University Way NE. A 694-acre campus with 128 major buildings and a stadium. Special exhibits in Henry Art Gallery (daily except Mon; closed holidays; fee); Henry Suzzallo Library. Meany Hall for the Performing Arts, three theaters; health sciences research center and teaching hospital; Waterfront Activities Center; Washington Park Arboretum. Parking fee. Located here are

Burke Museum of Natural History and Culture.
Phone 206/543-5590. www.washington.edu/burkemuseum. Located on the campus of the University of Washington, the Burke Museum is Washington State's official museum of natural and cultural history, and a research hub for the entire Pacific Northwest. Between its collections in four areas—anthropology, geology, zoology and botany—the museum is in possession of 5 million specimens in all. The facility houses a pair of notable permanent exhibits (in addition to a number of rotating temporary displays each year):

"The Life and Times of Washington State," a look at the last 500 million years of the state's geology and biology (with fossils and skeletons galore), and "Pacific Voices," which delves into the rich melting pot of cultures present in the Pacific Northwest. Also on site is the Erna Gunther Ethnobotanical Garden, alive with hundreds of plants used by the region's natives, as well as a café and a gift shop. (Daily; closed Thanksgiving, Dec 25) **$$**

University of Washington Huskies. *101 Graves Bldg, Seattle (98195). Phone 206/543-2200. gohuskies.ocsn.com.* During the school year, the University of Washington Huskies play NCAA Division I-A schedules in a wide variety of men's and women's sports, including football, basketball, track and field, swimming, baseball, and swimming. The school's teams play in the Pac-10 conference, competing against the likes of UCLA and Arizona, as well as cross-state rival Washington State. The University of Washington football team plays its home games at picturesque Husky Stadium, situated on the western shores of Lake Washington. Because of the stadium's lakefront location, many fans travel to and from games by boat, and traditionally throw tailgate parties in the water prior to kickoff. The men's and women's basketball teams play on a home court at the 10,000-seat Clarence S. "Hec" Edmundson Pavilion. Most venues for other UW sports are also on the Seattle campus.

University Village Shopping. *45th St, Seattle (98105). Phone 206/461-5840. www.uvillage.com.* Located near the University of Washington campus in northeast Seattle, University Village has a rare balance of national and local establishments. Chains are well represented here, with Abercrombie & Fitch, Pottery Barn, and Restoration Hardware, but there is also a nice sampling of homegrown retailers and eateries—about 50 in all. The area also has banking, insurance, childcare centers, and day spa services onsite.

Victoria Clipper Charters. *2701 Alaskan Way, Pier 69, Seattle (98121). Phone 206/448-5000. www. victoriaclipper.com.* This tour company operates a fleet of high-speed, passenger-only ferries on routes between Seattle, the San Juan Islands in Puget Sound, and Victoria, Canada. The trip to Victoria takes about two hours, and VCC offers many packages that integrate hotel stays, recreational excursions and other transportation. There are also narrated whale-watching cruises, and the clippers have basic cafés and duty-free shops on board. **$$$$**

Volunteer Park. *1247 15th Ave E, Seattle (98112). NE Side.* Tennis, play area, wading pool (June-Sept, daily), picnic area; conservatory (daily), formal gardens; observation deck in water tower (520 feet) with view of mountains, city, Puget Sound (daily). **FREE**

Warren G. Magnuson Park. *NE 65th and Sand Point Way NE, Seattle. NE Side.* Approximately 200 acres; 1-mile shoreline. Swimming beach (Mid-July-early Sept, daily); picnicking, playfield, small boat launch ramp, concessions. Fee for some activities. (Daily)

Washington Park Arboretum. *2300 Arboretum Dr E, Seattle (98112). On both sides of Lake Washington Blvd, between E Madison and Montlake, SE Side. Phone 206/543-8800.* Arboretum Drive East winds over 200 acres containing more than 5,000 species of trees and shrubs from all parts of world. Rhododendrons, cherries, azaleas (Apr-June). Arboretum open daily all year. Tours (Jan-Nov, Sun). **FREE** Within is

Japanese Garden. *1502 Lake Washington Blvd E, Seattle (98122). Phone 206/684-4725.* Ornamental plants, glassy pools, 12-tier pagoda, and teahouse. Tea ceremony. **$$**

The Waterfront. The most tourist-trafficked spot in all of Seattle, the downtown Waterfront bustles with activity year-round. Abutting Puget Sound on the western fringe of downtown, such landmarks as the Pike Place Market and the Seattle Aquarium reel in visitors by the thousands. Then there are the crowds drawn in by the boats—including the ferry to Bainbridge Island and Victoria Clipper Charters—that depart from the piers, encrusted with touristy shops, seafood restaurants, and oyster bars. One particularly kitschy retailer that's worth a peek is Ye Olde Curiosity Shop on Pier 54, with a circus-meets-harbor atmosphere accentuated by the mummies and jar-encased, two-headed calves on display. As for recreation, some people fish here; others engage in a pursuit that is distinctly Seattle: jigging for squid.

Waterfront Drive. Follow Alaskan Way along Elliott Bay to see ships of many nations docked at piers. Or take higher level Alaskan Way Viaduct along a parallel route to view the harbor, sound, and mountains. A trolley runs the length of the waterfront and continues into Pioneer Square and the International District.

Wawona. *Northwest Seaport Maritime Heritage Center, 1002 Valley St, Seattle (98109). Phone 206/447-9800. www.nwseaport.org.* The largest sailing schooner ever built in North America, the *Wawona* was launched as a lumber ship in 1897, then later saw 30 years of cod-fishing action in the Bering Sea. Now docked permanently at Lake Union, this 165-foot, three-masted beauty is open to the public and the subject of ongoing volunteer restoration. Out of 300 that were built, only two such ships still exist: the *Wawona* and the *C. A. Thayer* in San Francisco.

West Seattle Golf Course. *4470 35th Ave SW, Seattle (98126). Phone 206/935-5187. www.westseattlegolf.com.* This public course, designed by course architect H. Chandler Eagan and opened in 1940, has drawn good reviews over the years. You can usually get on for less than $30, and early-bird specials make it even cheaper. With a recent change in ownership, the course has undergone a resurgence in popularity and is now one of the more heavily played courses in the area. Still, it's a good course on which to learn, something the course staff realizes and is willing and able to help with. **$$$$**

The Wing Luke Asian Museum. *407 7th Ave S, Seattle (98104). Phone 206/623-5124. www.wingluke.org.* An apt counterpart to the Seattle Asian Art Museum, the Wing Luke Asian Museum in Seattle's busy International District illuminates the Asian American experience in a historical and cultural light. A collection of diverse artifacts details the 200-year history of Asians in the Pacific Northwest. Another permanent exhibit, the Densho Project, allows visitors to access oral histories recorded by Japanese Americans who were detained in Word War II-era internment camps. (Tue-Fri 11 am-4:30 pm, Sat-Sun noon-4 pm; closed Mon) **$**

Woodland Park Zoo. *5500 Phinney Ave N, Seattle (98103). Phone 206/684-4800 (recording). www.zoo.org.* One of the biggest and best zoos in the country sits in the park of the same name in north Seattle. The exhibits focus on ecosystems instead of single species: the Alaska enclosure is home to Kodiak bears that catch live trout out of a stream; "Tropical Asia" inhabitants include elephants, tapirs, and orangutans; and the African Savannah features giraffes, hippos, and zebras—as well as a plaque dedicated to Seattle native son Jimi Hendrix. There is also a Komodo dragon display, a petting zoo, "Bug World" (with such spine-chilling denizens as millipedes, scorpions, and

tarantulas), and an enclosed aviary housing hawks, falcons, and owls. The special events calendar is dense and varied, with breakfasts and overnighters for kids, as well as lectures, festivals, and holiday happenings. (Daily) **$$$**

Special Events

A Contemporary Theatre (ACT). *700 Union St, Seattle (98101). Phone 206/292-7676.* One of the major resident theaters in the country, ACT is a professional (Equity) theater. Tues-Sun, May-Nov. Shows *A Christmas Carol* in Dec.

Bumbershoot. *305 Harrison St, Seattle (98109). Phone 206/281-7788. www.bumbershoot.com.* This annual 4-day music fest is the largest of its kind on the West Coast. Legendary artists and rising stars alike perform in more than 30 different indoor and outdoor venues, stages, and galleries. Bumbershoot also features poetry, dance, comedy, and contemporary art exhibits. Labor Day weekend. **$$$$**

Chilly Hilly Bicycle Classic. *6310 NE 7th St, Building 30, Seattle (98115). Phone 206/522-3222. www.cascade.org.* One of *Bicycle Magazine's* top four recreational bike rides in the US, this 33-mile course on Bainbridge Island attracts thousands of riders for a one-day organized ride in February. The course starts at the ferry dock and makes many gains and losses in elevation (with 2,700 feet of elevation change in all) before skidding to a stop at a finish line festival with a huge chili feast. Mid-Feb.

Fremont Oktoberfest. *35th and Fremont Ave N, Seattle (98103). Phone 206/633-0422. www.fremontoktoberfest.org.* The eccentric Fremont neighborhood puts its own stamp on the traditional Bavarian beer-drinking festival, with a rambunctious chainsaw pumpkin-carving contest, a street dance, polka-dancing lessons, and live bands that run the gamut from mainstream to bizarre. Held in the shadows of the Aurora Avenue Bridge, this street fair is considered one of the top Oktoberfest festivals outside of Germany, taking place over the course of the third weekend in September. The rowdy beer garden here is quite a sight, serving up a wide variety of beers (including root beer for kids), with an emphasis on local microbrews. The street fair is free and open to the public, but admission is charged to enter the beer garden; six beer tokens and a souvenir cup are included. Mid-Sept. **FREE**

Opening Day Regatta. *1807 E Humlin St, Seattle (98112). Phone 206/325-1000. www.seattleyachtclub .org.* A Seattle tradition since the 1910s, the opening day of yachting season takes place every year on the first Saturday in May, with such featured events as a boat parade and a rowing regatta. Most of the action is centered on the Montlake Cut that links Lake Washington and Lake Union, and there are a number of great viewpoints on and near the campus of the University of Washington. May.

Pacific Northwest Arts Fair. *Bellevue. 4 miles E. Phone 206/363-2048.* Art exhibits, handicrafts. Late July.

Seafair. *2200 6th Ave, #400, Seattle (98121). Phone 206/728-0123.* Citywide marine festival. Regattas, speedboat races, shows at Aqua Theater, parades, sports events, exhibits. Late July-early Aug.

Seattle International Film Festival. *600 Pine St, Seattle (98101). Phone 206/464-5380. www.seattlefilm.com.* Held annually from late May to mid-June, Seattle's top-notch film fest is one of the largest cinema show-cases in the US, and perhaps the preeminent event of its kind held in a major city. While the content tends toward documentaries and international independent films, Hollywood is also well represented. **$$**

Seattle Marathon. *1101 N Northlake Way, Seattle (98103). Phone 206/729-3660. www.seattlemarathon .org.* Held annually in late November, the Seattle Marathon is open to runners and walkers of all skill levels and registers more than 10,000 entrants each year. Much of the hilly, scenic route runs along the Lake Washington shoreline, taking entrants from the Seattle Center to Seward Park in southeast Seattle, and back again. A kids marathon, a half marathon, and a marathon walk are also held. Late Nov. **$$$$**

Seattle Rep. *155 Mercer St, Seattle (98109). Phone 206/443-2222. www.seattlerep.org.* Short for Seattle Repertory Theatre, the award-winning Seattle Rep is one of the top regional non-profit theatre companies in the US. Two stages host six to ten productions a year, with the emphasis on challenging dramatic works and time-tested classics injected with fresh perspectives. Recent performances staged by the Rep include *Romeo and Juliet, Wit,* and *The Search for Signs of Intelligent Life in the Universe.* Sept-June.

Seattle to Portland Bicycle Classic. *6310 NE 74th St, Seattle (98115). Phone 206/522-3222. www.cascade.org.*

This 200-mile road race draws up to 8,000 riders each year for a one- or two-day tour through Washington and Oregon's forests and farmlands. Mid-July. **$$$$**

Summer Nights at the Pier. *1901 Alaskan Way, Seattle (98101). Phone 206/281-8111. www.summernights.org.* The location of this music venue—at Pier 62/63 on the downtown Seattle waterfront—is exceedingly picturesque, rivaling the Gorge Amphitheater with great views of the downtown skyline, ferries cruising Puget Sound, and sunsets over the looming Olympic Mountains to the west. Owned by the city's Parks Department, the 3,800-seat amphitheater hosts touring rock and rhythm and blues acts during its summer season, with such performers as the Flaming Lips, Billy Idol, and the Roots taking its stage in recent years. Many locals moor their sailboats around the pier at show time—and take in the concert without buying a ticket in the process. Beer, wine, fast food, and coffee are all available on the premises; visitors can also bring their own outside food and non-alcoholic beverages. June-Aug.

Limited-Service Hotels

★ ★ **COURTYARD BY MARRIOTT.** *925 Westlake Ave N, Seattle (98109). Phone 206/213-0100; fax 206/213-0101. www.courtyard.com.* Many area attractions are nearby, including the Space Needle, Woodland Park Zoo, and the Seattle Waterfront. 250 rooms, 7 story. Check-in 3 pm, check-out noon. Restaurant, bar. Fitness room. Indoor pool. Business center. **$**

★ **HAMPTON INN & SUITES.** *700 Fifth Ave N, Seattle (98109). Phone 206/282-7700; toll-free 800/ 426-7866; fax 206/282-0899. www.hamptoninn.com.* Each suite boasts a full kitchen, fireplace, and balcony. The hotel is near the Seattle Center, putting you close to opera, ballet, and theater, as well as the Space Needle and a wide range of shopping and dining options. 198 rooms, 6 story. Complimentary conti-nental breakfast. Check-in 3 pm, check-out noon. High-speed Internet access. Fitness room. Business center. **$$**

★ **HOMEWOOD SUITES DOWNTOWN SEATTLE.** *206 Western Ave W, Seattle (98119). Phone 206/281-9393; toll-free 800/225-5466; fax 206/283-5022. www.homewoodsuites.com.* 161 rooms. Check-in

3 pm, check-out noon. Wireless Internet access. Fitness room. **$**

🏃

Full-Service Hotels

★ ★ ★ **ALEXIS HOTEL.** *1007 First Ave, Seattle (98104). Phone 206/624-4844; toll-free 800/426-7033; fax 206/621-9009. www.alexishotel.com.* This historic hotel has been offering fine accommodations in downtown Seattle since the turn of the century. The rooms are all finely decorated and furnished with European décor. 109 rooms, 6 story. Pets accepted, some restrictions. Check-out noon. Restaurant, bar. **$$$**

🐾

★ ★ ★ **ELLIOTT GRAND HYATT SEATTLE.** *721 Pine St, Seattle (98101). Phone 206/774-1234; fax 206/774-6120. www.hyatt.com.* The Elliott Grand Hyatt brings contemporary dash to Seattle's bustling financial and business district. From the wired public spaces ideal for meetings and conferences to the fantastic in-room digital concierges, this hotel is a technology aficionado's paradise. Earth tones and Asian inspiration create a sanctuary-like ambience in the guest rooms and suites, where well-defined workspaces are a boon to business travelers. Large windows frame striking city or Puget Sound views, while oversized bathrooms implore guests to enjoy some quiet time. The Elliott Grand Hyatt understands the needs of modern travelers, with a comprehensive fitness center and a variety of dining options. Starbucks appeals to those on the go, while others enjoy comfort food at the Cheesecake Factory or linger over gourmet fare at 727 Pine. 425 rooms, 30 story. Pets accepted, some restrictions; fee. Check-in 3 pm, check-out noon. Restaurant, bar. Fitness room, spa. Whirlpool. Business center. **$$$**

🐾 🏃 🏃

★ ★ ★ ★ **THE FAIRMONT OLYMPIC HOTEL.** *411 University St, Seattle (98101). Phone 206/621-1700; fax 206/623-2271. www.fairmont.com.* The Fairmont Olympic Hotel (formerly Four Seasons Olympic Hotel) brings grand tradition and pampering service to downtown Seattle. Carefully blending its 1920s Italian Renaissance heritage with 21st-century hospitality, The Fairmont is a premier destination. The hotel is conveniently located in Rainier Square, only minutes from the city's top attractions. The rooms and suites

are tasteful retreats with floral draperies, soft pastel colors, and period furnishings, while fresh fruit and flowers make guests feel at home. Guests are cosseted throughout the hotel whether enjoying room service or visiting the full-service salon and spa. The bounty of the Pacific Northwest is the focus at The Georgian (see), where pale yellow walls and crystal chandeliers set a refined tone. Shuckers is a popular oyster bar at which Seattle's famous microbrews are savored, and a selection of cocktails is available at The Terrace. 450 rooms, 13 story. Pets accepted, some restrictions; fee. Check-in 3 pm, check-out noon. Restaurant, bar. Fitness room, spa. Indoor pool, whirlpool. Airport transportation available. Business center. **$$$**

🐾 🏃 🛏 🏃

★ ★ ★ **HOTEL ANDRA.** *2000 Fourth Ave, Seattle (98121). Phone 206/448-8600; fax 206/441-7140. www.hotelandra.com.* The Hotel Andra combines Northwest and Scandinavian design influences, creating a warm and inviting retreat in Seattle's vibrant Belltown neighborhood. Situated near art galleries, boutiques, and restaurants, the hotel appeals to travelers who like to be out and about, getting a taste for the local scene. Guests are greeted by a dramatic lobby fireplace built from split-grain granite and bookended by a pair of golden maple bookcases. Above the fireplace, a plasma screen projects a collection of electronic fine art. Rooms include such luxuries as 300-thread-count cotton linens, goose down pillows, and alpaca headboards. 119 rooms. Check-in 3 pm, check-out noon. Wireless Internet access. Restaurant, bar. Fitness room. Airport transportation available. **$$**

🏃

★ ★ ★ **HOTEL MONACO.** *1101 Fourth Ave, Seattle (98101). Phone 206/621-1770; toll-free 800/945-2240; fax 206/621-7779. www.monaco-seattle.com.* A hip hotel decorated with imagination. Guests will enjoy the intimate feel here. For lonely pet owners, the hotel will even provide a temporary pet goldfish in each guest suite upon request. 189 rooms, 11 story. Pets accepted. Check-out noon. Restaurant, bar. Fitness room. Business center. **$$$**

🐾 🏃 🏃

★ ★ ★ **HOTEL VINTAGE PARK.** *1100 Fifth Ave, Seattle (98101). Phone 206/624-8000; toll-free 800/624-4433; fax 206/623-0568. www.vintagepark.com.* This hotel offers well-appointed and finely furnished guest rooms, each named after a local winery or vineyard. Visitors can enjoy the comfortable lobby while sitting by the fireplace and tasting local wines and microbeers. 127 rooms, 11 story. Pets accepted, some restrictions. Check-in 3 pm, check-out noon. Restaurant. **$$$**

★ ★ ★ **INN AT THE MARKET.** *86 Pine St, Seattle (98101). Phone 206/443-3600; toll-free 800/446-4484; fax 206/448-0631. www.innatthemarket .com.* Seattle's renowned creative spirit is perhaps best felt at the delightful Inn at the Market. This boutique hotel enjoys a prime location at the vibrant Pike Place Market overlooking the pristine waters of Elliott Bay. Picturesque views and cultural attractions are just outside the door at this country chic home-away-from-home. The spacious and stylish accommodations are the last word in comfort, with in-room massages and special Tempur-Pedic mattresses ensuring restful sleep. The rooftop garden provides the perfect place to daydream or keep watch on the goings-on at the market below. From guest privileges at the Seattle Club's state-of-the-art fitness facility to in-room dining provided by two favorite establishments, guests reap the rewards of the inn's market location. 70 rooms, 8 story. Check-in 4 pm, check-out noon. Restaurant, bar. **$$**

★ ★ ★ **MAYFLOWER PARK HOTEL.** *405 Olive Way, Seattle (98101). Phone 206/623-8700; toll-free 800/426-5100; fax 206/382-6996. www.mayflowerpark .com.* This hotel, near Pike Place Market, is located in the downtown Seattle shopping district. 201 rooms, 12 story. Check-in 3 pm, check-out noon. Restaurant, bar. **$**

★ ★ ★ **THE PARAMOUNT.** *724 Pine St, Seattle (98101). Phone 206/292-9500; fax 206/292-8610. www.paramounthotelseattle.com.* This European-style hotel is in a great location near theaters, shopping, and entertainment, as well as the Washington State Convention and Trade Center. 148 rooms, 11 story. Check-in 3 pm, check-out noon. Restaurant, bar. Fitness room. **$$**

★ ★ ★ **RENAISSANCE SEATTLE HOTEL.** *515 Madison St, Seattle (98104). Phone 206/583-0300; toll-free 800/278-4159; fax 206/447-0992. www. renaissancehotels.com.* Located in the heart of Seattle, this hotel manages to combine contemporary décor

of marble and glass with earth-toned colors that convey a warm, rich ambience. Guests have a great view of the city from the 25th floor, where the indoor pool is located. Nearly everything that defines Seattle is less than a mile away—Pike Place Market and the waterfront, Pioneer Square, and Safeco Field (where the Mariners play) and Seahawks Stadium. 553 rooms, 28 story. Check-in 3 pm, check-out noon. High-speed Internet access. Two restaurants, bar. Fitness room. Indoor pool, whirlpool. Business center. **$$**

★ ★ ★ **SEATTLE MARRIOTT WATERFRONT.** *2100 Alaskan Way, Seattle (98121). Phone 206/443-5000; toll-free 800/228-9290; fax 206/256-1100. www. marriott.com.* 358 rooms. Check-in 3 pm, check-out noon. High-speed Internet access. Restaurant, bar. Fitness room. Indoor pool, outdoor pool, whirlpool. Airport transportation available. **$$$**

★ ★ ★ **THE SHERATON SEATTLE HOTEL AND TOWERS.** *1400 Sixth Ave, Seattle (98101). Phone 206/621-9000; toll-free 800/204-6100; fax 206/ 621-8441. www.sheraton.com/seattle.* In the heart of Seattle's most popular attractions. 840 rooms, 35 story. Check-in 3 pm, check-out noon. Restaurant, bar. Fitness room. Indoor pool, whirlpool. Business center. **$$$**

★ ★ ★ **SORRENTO HOTEL.** *900 Madison St, Seattle (98104). Phone 206/622-6400; toll-free 800/ 426-1265; fax 206/343-6159. www.hotelsorrento.com.* Drawing on its namesake Italian village for inspiration, the Sorrento Hotel is a classic Mediterranean masterpiece. This historic Seattle hotel remains close to the attractions of downtown while maintaining an unparalleled intimacy. Jewel tones, stunning fabrics, and rich mahogany furnishings set a regal ambience throughout this traditional hotel. The guest accommodations are the very definition of elegance, with marble baths, plush amenities, and distinctive artwork. From knowledgeable concierges to shiatsu massage therapists, the hotel's seamless service makes it a perfect place for business and leisure travelers alike. Home to the Hunt Club (see), one of Seattle's revered landmarks, the Sorrento whets the appetite of its visitors with two other dining establishments, including the cozy Fireside Room and the seasonal outdoor Piazza Capri. 76 rooms, 7 story.

Pets accepted; fee. Check-in 4 pm, check-out noon. Restaurant, bar. Fitness room. Airport transportation available. **$$**

★ ★ ★ **W SEATTLE HOTEL.** *1112 Fourth Ave, Seattle (98101). Phone 206/264-6000; fax 206/264-6100. www.whotels.com.* The W Seattle Hotel combines cutting-edge style with top-notch comfort and cute and quirky touches—like a candy necklace in the in-room munchies box. Since this hotel is designed for tech-savvy business travelers, rooms offer CD players, high-speed Ethernet access, and cordless phones at well-equipped workstations. Young children may not be the best fit for the decidedly upscale atmosphere, but if you want your every business need catered to or are looking for a romantic getaway, look no further than the bright colors and cool leather of W Seattle. The lobby, adjacent bar, and dining room are contenders in the "now" scene of Seattle. 426 rooms, 26 story. Pets accepted, some restrictions; fee. Check-in 3 pm, check-out noon. High-speed Internet access. Restaurant, bar. Fitness room. Business center. **$$$$**

Full-Service Inn

★ ★ ★ **INN AT HARBOR STEPS.** *1221 First Ave, Seattle (98101). Phone 206/748-0973; toll-free 888/728-8910; fax 206/748-0533. www.foursisters.com.* Near Seattle's waterfront, this inn offers all the amenities of residential living. Nestled in a 25-story apartment complex, guests can enjoy a 40-foot lap pool. 25 rooms, 2 story. Complimentary full breakfast. Check-in 3 pm, check-out noon. Restaurant. Indoor pool, whirlpool. **$$**

Specialty Lodgings

The following lodging establishments are approved by Mobil Travel Guide, but due to their unique and individualized nature have not been given a traditional Mobil Star rating. Included in this listing you may find bed-and-breakfasts, limited-service inns, guest ranches, and other unique hotel properties.

ACE HOTEL. *2423 First Ave, Seattle (98121). Phone 206/448-4721. www.acehotel.com.* The ultra-hip Ace Hotel bills itself as "the ultimate lodging for the urban nomad on a mission of experience." Modeled after European hotels, Ace presents a stylish décor, with modern furnishings and clean white walls throughout. Rooms feature exposed brick walls, lofted ceilings, and hardwood floors. Half of the hotel's accommodations have private bathrooms, while the other half utilize shared facilities. Each private bathroom is entered through a revolving door that's hidden in the wall. All rooms include a sink and vanity. 28 rooms. Check-in 3 pm, check-out noon. Wireless Internet access. **$$**

CHAMBERED NAUTILUS BED & BREAKFAST. *5005 22nd Ave NE, Seattle (98105). Phone 206/522-2536; toll-free 800/545-8459; fax 206/528-0898. www.chamberednautilus.com.* Built in 1912 by a professor at the University of Washington, this quaint Georgian colonial B&B offers cozy and distinctive rooms just a short walk from campus. Each antique-filled guest room offers a private bath and phone as well as its own resident teddy bear; there's also a library/sitting room with a fireplace and a sundeck. The plentiful steps make the Chambered Nautilus inappropriate for those in wheelchairs and those who have trouble climbing. 10 rooms, 3 story. Children over 4 years only. Complimentary full breakfast. Check-in 4-6 pm, check-out 11 am. Wireless Internet access. **$**

CHELSEA STATION ON THE PARK. *4915 Linden Ave N, Seattle (98103). Phone 206/547-6077; toll-free 800/400-6077; fax 206/632-5107.* Near Woodland Park Zoo. 9 rooms, 3 story. Children over 12 years only. Complimentary full breakfast. Check-in 3-6 pm, check-out 11 am. **$**

GASLIGHT INN. *1727 15th Ave, Seattle (98122). Phone 206/325-3654; fax 206/328-4803. www.gaslight-inn.com.* Two buildings; one built in 1906. 22 rooms, 3 story. Complimentary continental breakfast. Check-in 3-6 pm, check-out 11 am. Pool. **$**

HILL HOUSE BED & BREAKFAST. *1113 E John St, Seattle (98102). Phone 206/720-7161; toll-free 800/720-7161; fax 206/323-0772. www.seattlebnb .com.* Restored 1903 Victorian inn. 9 rooms, 3 story. Children over 12 years only. Complimentary full breakfast. Check-in by appointment, check-out 11 am. **$**

SALISBURY HOUSE BED & BREAKFAST.
750 16th Ave E, Seattle (98112). Phone 206/328-8682; fax 206/720-1019. www.salisburyhouse.com. Built in 1904, this house has been carefully renovated to preserve its charm while adding modern conveniences. Be aware that these conveniences don't extend to a TV in every room, though—only the Suite has one. Each of the five rooms has at least one distinctive feature: the Blue Room has a private deck, the Suite a private entrance and fireplace, the Rose Room a bay window and window seat, the Lavender Room a 6-foot-long soaking tub, and the Garden Room a country French and wicker décor. 5 rooms, 4 story. Children over 12 years only. Complimentary full breakfast. Check-in 4-6 pm, check-out 11 am. Wireless Internet access. **$**
▣

Restaurants

★ ★ ★ **AL BOCCALINO.** *1 Yesler Way, Seattle (98104). Phone 206/622-7688; fax 206/622-1798. www. boccalino.com.* This intimate Italian restaurant features muted antique lighting and candlelit tables that set the stage for many marriage proposals. Italian menu. Lunch, dinner. Closed holidays. Casual attire. **$$**

★ ★ ★ **ANDALUCA.** *407 Olive Way, Seattle (98101). Phone 206/382-6999; fax 206/382-6996. www. andaluca.com.* Mediterranean menu. Breakfast, lunch, dinner. Bar. **$$$**
▣

★ ★ ★ **ASSAGGIO RISTORANTE.** *2010 Fourth Ave, Seattle (98121). Phone 206/441-1399. www. assaggioseattle.com.* Italian menu. Lunch, dinner. Closed Sun; holidays. Casual attire. Outdoor seating. **$$$**

★ **ATLAS FOODS.** *2820 NE University Village, Seattle (98105). Phone 206/522-6025; fax 206/988-8763. www.chowfoods.com.* International menu. Breakfast, lunch, dinner. Children's menu. Casual attire. **$$**

★ ★ **BANDOLEONE.** *2241 Eastlake Ave E, Seattle (98102). Phone 206/329-7559; fax 206/583-0133. www. bandoleone.net.* Latin American menu. Dinner, late-night. Closed Thanksgiving, Dec 25. Bar. Casual attire. Outdoor seating. **$$**

★ ★ ★ **BRASA.** *2107 Third Ave, Seattle (98121). Phone 206/728-4220; fax 206/728-8067. www.brasa .com.* Seattle's trendy residents gather at Brasa on a regular basis to indulge in this hotspot's robust, Mediterranean-inspired fare. While the crowd at the bar tends to be young and hip, the folks filling the rustic but sleek dining room, decorated with terrazzo floors, black and tan accented wood, and wrought-iron railings, are a stylish set of 30- and 40-somethings. No matter what your age, however, the vibrant cuisine at Brasa is easy for all to love. Two of the signature dishes show off the kitchen's culinary brilliance: the roast suckling pig and the mussels and clams served oven-steamed in a cataplana, a double-domed copper pot that's used to cook stews in Portugal. All dishes are layered with the bold flavors of Spain, Portugal, France, and Brazil. Brasa serves wonderful food that dazzles the palate and the eye and expertly balances the rustic and the sophisticated. Iberian, Mediterranean menu. Dinner, late-night. Closed holidays. Bar. Casual attire. **$$$**

★ ★ **BROOKLYN SEAFOOD, STEAK & OYSTER HOUSE.** *1212 Second Ave, Seattle (98101). Phone 206/224-7000; fax 206/224-7008.* In 1890s building; artwork. Seafood, steak menu. Lunch, dinner. Closed Jan 1, Dec 25. Bar. Children's menu. Valet parking. Outdoor seating. **$$$**

★ **BURRITO LOCO.** *9211 Holman Rd NW, Seattle (98117). Phone 206/783-0719.* Mexican menu. Lunch, dinner. Closed July 4, Thanksgiving, Dec 25, Children's menu. Outdoor seating. **$$**

★ ★ ★ **CAFE CAMPAGNE.** *1600 Post Alley, Seattle (98101). Phone 206/728-2233.* With its no-fuss French cuisine, this restaurant proves to be a popular jaunt for casual dining. Visitors come in droves for the Sunday brunch, which includes French toast made with brioche. French menu. Breakfast, lunch, dinner, Sun brunch. Closed holidays. Bar. **$$**

★ ★ ★ **CAFE FLORA.** *2901 E Madison, Seattle (98112). Phone 206/325-9100; fax 206/324-9783. www.cafeflora.com.* Vegetarian menu. Lunch, dinner, brunch. Closed Mon; holidays. Children's menu. **$$**

★ ★ **CAFE LAGO.** *2305 24th Ave E, Seattle (98112). Phone 206/329-8005.* A hotspot among locals, this casual Italian eatery has great food and a welcoming atmosphere. Italian menu. Dinner. Closed holidays. Bar. Children's menu. Casual attire. **$$$**

★ ★ **CAMPAGNE.** *86 Pine St, Seattle (98101). Phone 206/728-2800.* French menu. Dinner. Closed

Jan 1, Thanksgiving, Dec 25. Bar. Outdoor seating. **$$$**

★ ★ **CANLIS.** *2576 Aurora Ave N, Seattle (98109). Phone 206/283-3313; fax 206/283-1766. www. canlis.com.* Guests come for the serene and spectacular views of Lake Union and the Cascade Mountains, but the ever-attentive service keeps them coming back. Pacific Northwest menu. Dinner. Closed Sun; holidays. Bar. Jacket required. Valet parking. **$$$**

★ ★ **CARMELITA.** *7314 Greenwood Ave N, Seattle (98103). Phone 206/706-7703. www.carmelita.net.* Vegan, vegetarian menu. Dinner, brunch. Closed Mon; Jan 1, Dec 24-25. Bar. Children's menu. Outdoor seating. **$$**

★ ★ ★ **CASCADIA.** *2328 First Ave, Seattle (98121). Phone 206/448-8884; fax 206/448-2242. www. cascadiarestaurant.com.* Continental menu. Dinner. Closed Sun; holidays. Children's menu. Casual attire. **$$$**

★ ★ ★ **CHEZ SHEA.** *94 Pike St, Seattle (98101). Phone 206/467-9990. www.chezshea.com.* Tucked into Pike Place Market, you'll discover Chez Shea, an old-world charmer featuring the finest ingredients of the Northwest prepared with French technique and regional gusto. The intimate, candlelit dining room boasts picture-perfect views of the sun setting over the Puget Sound and is usually filled with couples well versed in the art of cross-table handholding, lingering stares, and soft whispers. But locals in the know about cuisine dine here as much for the food as for the cozy ambience. The four-course prix fixe menu features hearty, home-style regional fare that makes beautiful use of local produce as the seasons dictate. A simple salad ends the meal; dessert comes at an extra charge. The chocolate torte and the ginger-steeped bread pudding are worth the splurge. Contemporary American menu. Dinner. Closed Mon; holidays. Bar. Children's menu. Valet parking. **$$$**

★ ★ **CHUTNEY'S.** *519 First Ave N, Seattle (98109). Phone 206/284-6799.* Indian menu. Lunch, dinner. Bar. **$$**

★ ★ ★ **DAHLIA LOUNGE.** *2001 Fourth Ave, Seattle (98121). Phone 206/682-4142. www.tomdouglas .com.* Chef/owner Tom Douglas and his wife Jackie Cross (both also of Palace Kitchen and Etta's Seafood)

oversee this artsy eatery in the heart of downtown. Red walls, yellow pillars, and upholstered booths create a colorful, playful backdrop for boldly flavored Northwest cuisine. American menu. Dinner. Closed holidays. Children's menu. Casual attire. **$$$**

★ **DOONG KONG LAU.** *9710 Aurora Ave N, Seattle (98103). Phone 206/526-8828; fax 206/526-8828.* Chinese menu. Lunch, dinner. **$**

★ ★ **DRAGON FISH ASIAN CAFE.** *722 Pine St, Seattle (98101). Phone 206/467-7777; fax 206/467-8891. www.dragonfishcafe.com.* Pan-Asian menu. Breakfast, lunch, dinner. Closed Thanksgiving, Dec 25. **$$**

★ ★ **DULCES LATIN BISTRO.** *1430 34th Ave, Seattle (98122). Phone 206/322-5453. www. dulceslatinbistro.com.* Continental menu. Dinner. Closed Sun-Mon. Bar. **$$$**

★ ★ ★ **EARTH AND OCEAN.** *1112 Fourth Ave, Seattle (98101). Phone 206/264-6060; fax 206/264-6070. www.whotels.com.* A trendy, chic clientele match the restaurant's New York-inspired scene, with its ultrahip decor and fusion cuisine. Artfully prepared and creatively named French/Asian dishes make up the tasting-style menu. American menu. Breakfast, lunch, dinner. Children's menu. Casual attire. **$$$**

★ ★ ★ **EL GAUCHO.** *2505 First Ave, Seattle (98121). Phone 206/728-1337; fax 206/728-7744. www. elgaucho.com.* This swanky dinner-only restaurant—a former union hall for merchant seamen—is known mainly for its martinis and meat. Continental menu. Dinner. Closed holidays. Bar. Casual attire. Valet parking. **$$$**

★ ★ ★ **ETTA'S SEAFOOD.** *2020 Western Ave, Seattle (98121). Phone 206/443-6000. www.tomdouglas .com.* With an atmosphere as colorful as the food, Etta's brings in droves of hungry patrons both day and night. Northwestern seafood menu. Lunch, dinner. Closed holidays. Bar. Children's menu. Casual attire. **$$**

★ ★ **F.X. MCRORY'S STEAK, CHOP & OYSTER HOUSE.** *419 Occidental Ave S, Seattle (98104). Phone 206/623-4800. www.mickmchughs.com.* Steak menu. Lunch, dinner. Closed holidays. Bar. Children's menu. Outdoor seating. **$$$**

★ ★ ★ **FLYING FISH.** *2234 First Ave, Seattle (98121). Phone 206/728-8595. www.flyingfishseattle .com.* Guest will find Asian-influenced fish dishes that are artfully presented. Seafood menu. Dinner. Closed holidays. Bar. Casual attire. Outdoor seating. **$$**

★ **FOUR SEAS.** *714 S King St, Seattle (98104). Phone 206/682-4900. www.fourseasrestaurant.com.* Chinese menu. Lunch, dinner. Bar. **$$**

★ ★ ★ **GENEVA.** *1106 Eighth Ave, Seattle (98101). Phone 206/624-2222; fax 206/624-2519. www.genevarestaurant.com.* Possibly the best kept secret in Seattle, this romantic restaurant is decorated with European style and elegance. The chef creates his continental masterpieces using fresh, Northwest ingredients. Continental menu. Dinner. Closed Sun, Mon; holidays. Bar. Casual attire. Outdoor seating. **$$$**

★ ★ ★ ★ **THE GEORGIAN.** *411 University St, Seattle (98101). Phone 206/621-7889; fax 206/682-9633. www.fairmont.com.* With its creamy butterscotch walls, vaulted ceilings, exquisite chandeliers, and live piano, The Georgian has the romantic and elegant allure of an Italian Renaissance house. The innovative New American menu highlights the incredible array of seasonal ingredients found in the Northwest, flawlessly executed with artistry and style. The Georgian's menu may be considered haute cuisine in that it is beautifully presented and prepared, but this food is not over the top. The dishes tend to be more of the stylish comfort food variety than of the intricate, overfussed fare of the traditional French type. This food is simply easy to love. An impressive regional wine list highlights California, Oregon, and Washington State; it is the perfect compliment to the restaurant's sophisticated, homespun cuisine. Set in the Fairmont Olympic Hotel (see), The Georgian has become a destination for power breakfasts, although it is also a popular spot for business lunches and intimate, special-occasion dining. Breakfast, lunch, dinner. Bar. Children's menu. Casual attire. Valet parking. **$$$**

★ ★ ★ **HUNT CLUB.** *900 Madison St, Seattle (98104). Phone 206/343-6156. www.hotelsorrento.com.* An elegant and intimate dining experience awaits guests here. American menu. Breakfast, lunch, dinner. Bar. Valet parking. **$$$**

★ ★ **IL BISTRO.** *93A Pike St, Seattle (98101). Phone 206/682-3049. www.savvydiner.com.* Set on a quiet cobblestone street, this intimate hideaway, with its low ceilings and arched doorways, is dimly lit and cozy. Italian menu. Dinner. Closed holidays. Bar. Valet parking. Outdoor seating. **$**

★ ★ ★ **IL TERRAZZO CARMINE.** *411 First Ave S, Seattle (98104). Phone 206/467-7797.* High standards and a faithful clientele make this the darling of Italian restaurants in Seattle. While guests enjoy relaxing in the beautifully designed dining area, it's the fresh fare, well-selected wine list, and impeccable service that is truly appreciated here. Italian menu. Dinner. Closed Sun; holidays. Bar. Casual attire. Outdoor seating. **$$$**

★ **IVAR'S ACRES OF CLAMS.** *Pier 54, Seattle (98104). Phone 206/624-6852. www.ivars.net.* Seafood menu. Lunch, dinner. Closed Thanksgiving, Dec 25. Bar. Casual attire. **$$**

★ **IVAR'S INDIAN SALMON HOUSE.** *401 NE Northlake Way, Seattle (98105). Phone 206/632-0767; fax 206/632-0715. www.ivars.net.* Northwest seafood menu. Lunch, dinner, brunch. Closed Thanksgiving, Dec 25. Bar. Children's menu. Casual attire. Outdoor seating. **$$$**

★ **JITTERBUG.** *2114 N 45th St, Seattle (98103). Phone 206/547-6313; fax 206/548-1069. www. chowfoods.com.* Breakfast, lunch, dinner. Closed Thanksgiving, Dec 25. Bar. Children's menu. **$$**

★ ★ ★ **KASPAR'S.** *19 W Harrison St, Seattle (98119). Phone 206/298-0123; fax 206/298-0146. www. kaspars.com.* Hints of European, Asian, and local cuisine paired with unusual seasonings and spices are the essence of the ever-changing menu at this contemporary restaurant. Regulars opt for the appetizer "towers" for an array of new and inspired selections. Meats and seafood are smoked on the premises for the freshest flavor. Contemporary Northwest menu. Dinner. Closed Sun-Mon; first week in Jan, first week in July. Bar. Casual attire. **$$$**

★ ★ ★ **LAMPREIA RESTAURANT.** *2400 First Ave, Seattle (98121). Phone 206/443-3301.* You can taste the Italian influence of chef Scott Carsberg's Mediterranean cooking in everything from the fresh pasta to the hearty game dishes. The dining room is sleek and elegant, and the service is friendly and helpful. Italian, Mediterranean menu. Dinner. Closed Sun, Mon; Thanksgiving, Dec 25. Bar. **$$$**

★ ★ ★ **LE GOURMAND.** *425 NW Market St, Seattle (98107). Phone 206/784-3463.* It's no wonder this is one of the best French restaurants in town, with delectable cuisine and magnificent desserts. Each dish is prepared with fresh ingredients and imagination. American, French menu. Dinner. Closed Sun-Tues; holidays. **$$$**

🎟

★ ★ ★ **MADISON PARK CAFE.** *1807 42nd Ave E, Seattle (98112). Phone 206/324-2626; fax 206/328-0432. www.madisonparkcafe.citysearch.com.* French Bistro menu. Dinner, brunch. Closed Mon; holidays. Casual attire. Reservations recommended. Outdoor seating. **$$**

🎟

★ **MALAY SATAY HUT.** *212 12th Ave S, Seattle (98144). Phone 206/324-4091. www.malaysatayhut.com.* Indian menu. Lunch, dinner. Reservations recommended. **$$**

★ ★ **MARCO'S SUPPER CLUB.** *2510 First Ave, Seattle (98121). Phone 206/441-7801.* International menu. Dinner. Closed holidays. Bar. Casual attire. Outdoor seating. **$$**

★ ★ **MAXIMILIEN-IN-THE-MARKET.** *81A Pike Pl, Seattle (98101). Phone 206/682-7270. www.maximilienrestaurant.com.* French menu. Breakfast, lunch, dinner, Sun brunch. Closed Jan 1, Thanksgiving, Dec 25. Bar. Casual attire. Valet parking. **$$**

★ ★ ★ **MCCORMICK'S FISH HOUSE AND BAR.** *722 4th Ave, Seattle (98104). Phone 206/682-3900. www.msmg.com.* Seafood menu. Lunch, dinner. Closed Memorial Day, Thanksgiving, Dec 25. Bar. Casual attire. Outdoor seating. **$$**

★ ★ **MELTING POT.** *14 Mercer St, Seattle (98109). Phone 206/378-1208; fax 206/283-7571. www.meltingpotnw.com.* Fondue menu. Dinner, late-night. Bar. Casual attire. Valet parking. **$$**

★ ★ **METROPOLITAN GRILL.** *820 Second Ave, Seattle (98104). Phone 206/624-3287; fax 206/389-0042. www.themetropolitangrill.com.* Seafood, steak menu. Lunch, dinner. Closed Thanksgiving. Bar. Children's menu. Casual attire. **$$**

★ ★ ★ **NIKKO RESTAURANT.** *1900 5th Ave, Seattle (98101). Phone 206/322-4641; fax 206/441-2946. www.nikkorestaurant.com.* Japanese menu. Lunch, dinner. Closed Sun; holidays. **$$$**

🎟

★ ★ **NISHINO.** *3130 E Madison, Seattle (98112). Phone 206/322-5800.* Heralded as one of Seattle's best, Nishino is known for having the freshest fish around. Set in an impeccably refined space, it serves perfectly prepared sashimi and sushi. Japanese menu. Dinner. Closed holidays. Children's menu. Casual attire. Outdoor seating. **$$$**

★ ★ ★ **PALACE KITCHEN.** *2030 5th Ave, Seattle (98121). Phone 206/448-2001. www.tomdouglas.com.* This theatrical restaurant/saloon caters to a drinking crowd in search of imaginative rustic food. American menu. Lunch, dinner. Closed holidays. Bar. Children's menu. Casual attire. **$$**

★ ★ **PALISADE.** *2601 W Marina Pl, Seattle (98199). Phone 206/285-1000; fax 206/285-7087. www.palisaderestaurant.com.* Seafood menu. Lunch, dinner, Sun brunch. Bar. Casual attire. **$$$**

★ ★ ★ **PALOMINO.** *1420 Fifth Ave, Seattle (98101). Phone 206/623-1300; fax 206/467-1386. www.palominoseattle.com.* Mediterranean menu. Lunch, dinner. Closed holidays. Casual attire. **$$$**

★ ★ **PARAGON.** *2125 Queen Anne Ave N, Seattle (98109). Phone 206/283-4548; fax 206/283-0919. www.paragonseattle.com.* Northwest Rustic menu. Lunch, dinner, late-night, brunch. Closed Dec 25. Bar. Casual attire. **$$**

★ ★ **PIATTI RESTAURANT.** *2800 NE University Village, Seattle (98105). Phone 206/524-9088. www.piatti.com.* Italian menu. Lunch, dinner. Closed Dec 25. Bar. Children's menu. Casual attire. Reservations recommended. Outdoor seating. **$$**

★ ★ **PINK DOOR.** *1919 Post Alley, Seattle (98101). Phone 206/443-3241; fax 206/443-3341.* Italian menu. Lunch, dinner. Closed Mon; holidays. Bar. Children's menu. Casual attire. Outdoor seating. **$$**

🎟

★ ★ ★ **PLACE PIGALLE.** *81 Pike St, Seattle (98101). Phone 206/624-1756.* Crisp linens and a black-and-white parquet floor create a truly romantic setting alongside the bustling Puget Sound. Northwest regional menu. Lunch, dinner. Closed Sun; holidays. Bar. Casual attire. **$$**

🅳

★ ★ ★ **PONTI SEAFOOD GRILL.** *3014 3rd Ave N, Seattle (98109). Phone 206/284-3000; fax 206/284-4768. www.pontiseafoodgrill.com.* Pacific Rim menu. Lunch, dinner. Closed Jan 1, July 4, Dec 25. Bar. Children's menu. Casual attire. Valet parking. Outdoor seating. **$$**

★ **PORTAGE BAY CAFE.** *4130 Roosevelt Way NE, Seattle (98105). Phone 206/547-8230.* American menu. Breakfast, lunch. Closed Jan 1, Dec 25. Children's menu. Outdoor seating. **$$**

★ ★ **PREGO.** *515 Madison St, Seattle (98104). Phone 206/583-0300.* Downtown views and an intimate atmosphere are the setting for this restaurant. Customers like the attentive service and tasty food. Italian menu. Dinner. Closed Sun-Mon; Dec 25. Bar. **$$$**

★ ★ **QUEEN CITY GRILL.** *2201 First Ave, Seattle (98121). Phone 206/443-0975. www.queencitygrill.com.* One of Belltown's longest-running restaurants, the Queen City Grill stays young with hip service and fresh seafood. Seafood, steak menu. Lunch, dinner. Closed holidays. Bar. Children's menu. Casual attire. **$$$**

★ ★ ★ **RAY'S BOATHOUSE.** *6049 Seaview Ave NW, Seattle (98107). Phone 206/789-3770; fax 206/781-1960. www.rays.com.* For fresh Northwest seafood, this favorite on the water is a sure bet. Whether you're sitting in the Boathouse dining room or the outside deck at the café, spectacular views of Puget Sound and the Olympic Mountains are a commanding force. Seafood menu. Lunch, dinner. Closed Jan 1, Dec 25. Bar. Children's menu. Casual attire. Valet parking. **$$$**

★ ★ ★ ★ **ROVER'S.** *2808 E Madison St, Seattle (98112). Phone 206/325-7442; fax 206/325-1092. www.rovers-seattle.com.* A small, white clapboard cottage houses Rover's, an intimate restaurant serving innovative and amazing contemporary cuisine. Thierry Rautureau, the chef and owner, stays true to the regional ingredients of the Northwest while paying homage to impeccable French technique, perhaps because he hails from France. The restaurant's modest but lovely décor does little to tip you off to the extraordinary culinary masterpieces that await you. Presented like precious little works of art, the portions are perfect in size, taste, and appearance. The miraculous part of Rautureau's menu is that as soon as you finish the course in front of you, you are ready and salivating for the next. (The restaurant offers five-course and eight-course tasting menus in addition to a five-course vegetarian menu.) Not only is Rautureau a gifted chef, but he is also a gregarious and witty host who makes a point of visiting and welcoming every guest personally. *Secret Inspector's Notes: Don't be put off by the odd location and old-fashioned décor when you arrive at Rover's. The graciously accommodating service and brilliant food will transport you within minutes of being seated in the intimate dining room.* Northwest Contemporary menu. Dinner. Closed Sun-Mon; holidays. Casual attire. **$$$$**

★ ★ **ROY'S.** *1900 Fifth Ave, Seattle (98101). Phone 206/256-7697; fax 206/728-2007. www.roysrestaurant.com.* Pacific-Rim menu. Breakfast, lunch, dinner. Bar. Children's menu. Casual attire. **$$$**

★ ★ ★ **RUTH'S CHRIS STEAK HOUSE.** *800 5th Ave, Seattle (98104). Phone 206/624-8524; fax 206/624-6268. www.ruthschrissteakhouse.com.* Seafood, steak menu. Dinner. Closed holidays. Bar. Valet parking. **$$$**

★ ★ ★ **SAZERAC.** *1101 Fourth Ave, Seattle (98101). Phone 206/624-7755; fax 206/624-0054. www.sazerac-seattle.com.* Nestled in Hotel Monaco, Sazerac serves reliably satisfying, Southern-inspired food. It is also a particular hit with the happy-hour crowd. Southern menu. Breakfast, lunch, dinner. Bar. Children's menu. Valet parking. **$$**

🅳

★ ★ **SERAFINA.** *2043 Eastlake Ave E, Seattle (98102). Phone 206/323-0807; fax 206/325-2766. www.serafinaseattle.com.* Italian menu. Lunch, dinner. Closed holidays. Bar. Casual attire. Outdoor seating. **$$**

★ ★ **SHIRO'S.** *2401 Second Ave, Seattle (98121). Phone 206/443-9844.* Japanese menu. Lunch, dinner. Closed Sun; holidays. **$$**

★ ★ ★ **SPENCER'S FOR STEAKS AND CHOPS.** *17620 Pacific Hwy S, Seattle (98188). Phone 206/248-7153; fax 206/248-4495.* Steak menu. Breakfast, lunch, dinner. Bar. Children's menu. Casual attire. Outdoor seating. **$$**

★ ★ **STELLA'S TRATTORIA.** *4500 9th Ave NE, Seattle (98105). Phone 206/633-1100.* Italian menu. Breakfast, lunch, dinner. Closed Thanksgiving, Dec 25. Children's menu. Casual attire. Outdoor seating. **$$**

★ ★ ★ **SZMANIA'S MAGNOLIA.** *3321 W McGraw, Seattle (98199). Phone 206/284-7305. www. szmanias.com.* A favorite neighborhood hangout, guests here can always see the German chef at work in the open kitchen. Continental menu. Dinner. Closed Mon; holidays. Bar. Children's menu. **$$**

★ **TRATTORIA MITCHELLI.** *84 Yesler Way, Seattle (98104). Phone 206/623-3883; fax 206/682-5029.* Italian menu. Breakfast, lunch, dinner. Closed Dec 25. Bar. Children's menu. Casual attire. Outdoor seating. **$$**

★ ★ ★ **TULIO RISTORANTE.** *1100 Fifth Ave, Seattle (98101). Phone 206/624-5500; toll-free 800/624-4433; fax 206/623-0568. www.vintagepark.com.* An intimate dining room with dark wood paneling and dim chandeliers creates a cozy setting for a classic Tuscan trattoria. The food is inventive yet unpretentious, highlighted by ample tomatoes, cheeses, and fresh pasta. A knowledgeable and gracious staff completes the inviting experience. Italian menu. Breakfast, lunch, dinner. Closed holidays. Bar. Children's menu. Casual attire. Valet parking. Outdoor seating. **$$$**
🄳

★ ★ ★ **UNION BAY CAFE.** *3515 NE 45th St, Seattle (98105). Phone 206/527-8364.* Fans still flock to chef/owner Mark Manley's mostly Italian eatery, now occupying a romantic space a few doors from his original storefront location. Italian, seafood menu. Dinner. Closed Mon; holidays. Casual attire. Outdoor seating. **$$**

★ ★ ★ **UNION SQUARE GRILL.** *621 Union St, Seattle (98101). Phone 206/224-4321.* Comfortable booth seating, a busy, Art Deco-inspired design, and quick service make this eatery, with a bistrolike menu, a popular stop for business lunches and pre-theater meals. Seafood, steak menu. Lunch, dinner. Closed holidays. Bar. Casual attire. Valet parking. **$$$**

★ ★ ★ **WILD GINGER.** *1401 Third Ave, Seattle (98101). Phone 206/623-4450.* One of Seattle's premier restaurants, Wild Ginger is a hotspot for celebrities who sometimes come for Monday night jazz sessions. Chinese menu. Lunch, dinner. Closed Thanksgiving, Dec 25. Bar. Casual attire. **$$$**

Seattle-Tacoma International Airport Area

Web site www.portseattle.org/seatac

Airport Information

Airport Seattle-Tacoma International Airport.

Information Phone 206/433-5388

Lost and Found Phone 206/433-5312

Airlines Aeroflot Airlines, Air Canada, Alaska Airlines, America West, American Airlines, American Trans Air, Asiana Airlines, Big Sky, British Airways, Continental Airlines, Delta Air Lines, EVA Air, Frontier Airlines, Hawaiian Airlines, Horizon Air, Iberia Airlines, jetBlue Airways, KLM Royal Dutch, Lufthansa, Mesa Airlines, Northwest Airlines, Scandinavian Airlines (SAS), Skywest Airlines, Sun Country Airlines, United Airlines, United Express, US Airways

Limited-Service Hotels

★ ★ **BEST WESTERN FEDERAL WAY EXECUTEL.** *31611 20th Ave S, Federal Way (98003). Phone 253/941-6000; toll-free 800/648-3311; fax 253/941-9500. www.bestwestern.com.* Just half a mile from Sea-Tac Mall, this hotel sits amid a wide variety of dining and shopping options. Business travelers appreciate the high-speed Internet access in every room and the ample meeting facilities. Vacation travelers find themselves within easy reach of Wild Waves Enchanted Village water park and other area attractions, and the hotel provides shuttle service to and from Sea-Tac Airport as well as area business headquarters and attractions. 112 rooms, 3 story. Complimentary continental breakfast. Check-in 3 pm, check-out noon. High-speed Internet access.

Restaurant, bar. Outdoor pool, whirlpool. Airport transportation available. Business center. **$**

⌷ ⌷

★ ★ ★ **MARRIOTT SEA-TAC AIRPORT.** *3201 S 176th St, Seattle (98188). Phone 206/241-2000; toll-free 800/228-9290; fax 206/248-0789. www.marriotthotels .com.* This large Marriott is located across from the airport. The indoor pool under an atrium is a nice touch, with screening plants to give swimmers a sense of privacy. The business center caters to every need of business travelers, and the small spa offers opportunities for pampering. Try the concierge level for services beyond the ordinary. 459 rooms, 7 story. Pets accepted. Check-in 3 pm, check-out 1 pm. High-speed Internet access. Restaurant, bar. Children's activity center. Fitness room, spa. Indoor pool, whirlpool. Airport transportation available. **$**

⌷ ⌷ ⌷ ⌷

Restaurant

★ ★ **SEAPORTS.** *18740 Pacific Hwy S, Seattle (98188). Phone 206/246-8600.* Continental menu. Lunch, dinner, Sun brunch. Closed Dec 25. Bar. Children's menu. Casual attire. Valet parking. **$$**

Sedro-Woolley (A-2)

See also Anacortes, Bellingham, Mount Vernon

Founded 1889
Population 8,658
Elevation 509 ft
Area Code 360
Zip 98284
Information Chamber of Commerce, 714-B Metcalf St; phone 360/855-1841 or toll-free 888/225-8365
Web site www.sedro-woolley.com

A thick growth of cedar once cloaked the Skagit River Valley, but it has been replaced with fertile farms, for which Sedro Woolley is the commercial center. Lumbering is still one of the main industries. The town represents the merger of the town of Sedro (Spanish for "cedar") and its onetime rival, Woolley, named for its founder.

A Ranger District station of the Mount Baker-Snoqualmie National Forest is located here.

What to See and Do

Lake Whatcom Railway. *4180 S Bay Dr, Wickersham (98284). 11 miles N on Hwy 9. Phone 360/595-2218.* A 7-mile, round-trip steam train ride in antique Northern Pacific passenger cars through countryside. (July-Aug: Sat and Tues; Dec: Sat only; rest of year: charter trips) **$$$**

North Cascades National Park. *810 Hwy 20, Sedro-Woolley (98284). 50 miles E on Hwy 20 (portions of this road are closed in winter). Phone 360/856-5700. www. nps.gov/noca/.* Authorized in 1968, this 504,781-acre area has beautiful alpine scenery, deep glaciated canyons, more than 300 active glaciers, and hundreds of jagged peaks and mountain lakes. It is adjacent to the 576,865-acre Glacier Peak Wilderness dominated by 10,541-foot-high Glacier Peak and to Ross Lake and Lake Chelan National Recreation Areas. Camping along Highway 20 in Ross Lake area (June-Sept, fee); fishing; climbing, hiking, backpacking (by permit).

Seattle City Light Skagit Hydroelectric Project. *500 Newhalem St, Diablo (98283). 62 miles E of I-5/Mt Vernon on Hwy 20 (North Cascades Hwy), in Ross Lake National Recreation Area. Phone 206/684-3030.* The 4 1/2-hour tours includes a 560-foot ride up the mountain on an incline lift, a 4 1/2-mile boat ride to Ross Dam and Powerhouse (tour) and return by boat to Diablo; family-style dinner. (Late June-Labor Day, Mon, Thurs-Sun) Reservations and advance payment required. Single 90-minute tour also available. Contact Skagit Tours, Seattle City Light, 1015 3rd Ave, Seattle 98104. (July-Labor Day, Thurs-Mon) **$$$$** Self-guided mini-tours at Ross Lake National Recreation Area include

Gorge Powerhouse/Ladder Creek Falls and Rock Gardens. Begins at Gorge Powerhouse, Newhalem; self-guided tour of powerhouse, walk through Gorge Rock Gardens to Ladder Creek Falls. Gardens lighted at night. (Late June-Labor Day, daily) **FREE**

Newhalem Visitor Information Center. Information on Skagit Project and National Park/Recreation Area. (Mid-June-Labor day, daily) **FREE**

Trail of the Cedars. *Begins at end of Main St.* (45 minutes) Informative nature walk on south bank of Skagit River. **FREE**

Swimming, hiking, camping, boating, fishing, windsurfing. *Clear Lake. 3 miles S on Hwy 9. RV sites in town.* Also fishing in Skagit River.

Special Events

Loggerodeo. *Phone 360/855-1129.* Logging contests, rodeos, parades. One week in late June-early July.

Santa's City of Lights. *Phone 360/855-1841.* Parade, tree lighting. First weekend in Dec.

Woodfest. *1235 3rd St, Sedro Woolley (98284). Phone 360/855-1841.* Woodcarvers displaying their craft. Second weekend in May.

Sequim (B-2)

See also Neah Bay, Port Angeles, Port Ludlow, Port Townsend

Population 4,334
Elevation 183 ft
Area Code 360
Zip 98382
Information Sequim-Dungeness Valley Chamber of Commerce, 1192 E Washington St; phone 360/683-6197 or toll-free 800/737-8462
Web site www.cityofsequim.com

Sequim (pronounced SKWIM) is a Native American name meaning "quiet water."

What to See and Do

Dungeness Recreation Area. *Clallam County Park, 554 Voice of America W, Sequim (98382). 6 miles NW. Phone 360/683-5847.* Approximately 200 acres. Camping (Feb-Oct; fee). Access to Dungeness National Wildlife Refuge. (Daily)

Olympic Game Farm. *1423 Word Rd, Sequim (98382). 6 miles NW. Phone 360/683-4295.* Wild animals; guided walking tour (summer; drive-through rest of year). Endangered species breeding program. (Daily)

Sequim Bay State Park. *269035 Hwy 101, Sequim (98382). 4 miles SE on Hwy 101. Phone 360/683-4235.* Along Sequim Bay. Swimming, scuba diving, fishing, clamming, boating (dock); hiking, tennis, ballpark, picnicking, camping (hookups).

Special Event

Irrigation Festival. *1192 E Washington, Sequim (98382). Phone 360/683-6197. www.irrigationfestival .com.* Irrigation may not sound like a very exciting reason to hold a festival, but the city of Sequim has been celebrating the gift of water for more than 100 years. The bringing of water to the parched Sequim Prairie enabled pioneer settlers to build a farming community here, and today's citizens remain thankful for the efforts that brought their hometown into existence. Festival events include parades, carnivals, flower shows, contests, and an arts and crafts street fair. First full week in May.

Limited-Service Hotel

★ **ECONO LODGE.** *801 E Washington St, Sequim (98382). Phone 360/683-7113; fax 360/683-7343. www. econolodge.com.* 43 rooms, 2 story. Pets accepted; fee. Complimentary continental breakfast. Check-out 11 am. **$**

Specialty Lodging

The following lodging establishment is approved by Mobil Travel Guide, but due to its unique and individualized nature has not been given a traditional Mobil Star rating. Included in this listing you may find bed-and-breakfasts, limited-service inns, guest ranches, and other unique hotel properties.

GREYWOLF INN. *395 Keeler Rd, Sequim (98382). Phone 360/683-5889; toll-free 800/914-9653; fax 360/683-1487.* This is a perfect inn for a romantic getaway. This bed-and-breakfast has a secluded location near Olympic National Park, the Pacific Ocean, and great beaches. 5 rooms, 2 story. Children over 12 years only. Complimentary full breakfast. Check-in 4 pm, check-out 11:30 am. Fitness room. **$**

GROVELAND COTTAGE BED & BREAKFAST. *4861 Sequim Dungeness Way, Sequim (98382). Phone 360/683-3565; toll-free 800/879-8859; fax 360/683-5181.* 4 rooms, 2 story. Pets accepted, some restrictions; fee. Children over 12 years only. Complimentary full breakfast. Check-in 3 pm, check-out noon. **$**

Restaurants

★ ★ **DUNGENESS INN.** *1965 Woodcock, Sequim (98382). Phone 360/683-3331. www.dungenessgcc.com.* Seafood, steak menu. Breakfast, lunch, dinner, brunch. Closed Dec 25. Bar. Children's menu. **$$**
🅳

★ **MOON PALACE.** *323 E Washington, Sequim (98382). Phone 360/683-6898.* Chinese menu. Lunch, dinner. Closed Mon; holidays. Bar. **$$**

★ ★ **PARADISE.** *703 N Sequim Ave, Sequim (98382). Phone 360/683-1977.* Seafood, steak menu. Lunch, dinner. Closed Mon; July 4, Thanksgiving, Dec 25. Bar. **$$**

Snohomish (B-3)

See also Everett, Marysville

Settled 1853
Population 8,494
Elevation 64 ft
Area Code 360
Zip 98290
Information Chamber of Commerce, 127 Ave A, Waltz Building, 98291; phone 360/568-2526
Web site www.ci.snohomish.wa.us

Snohomish is sustained by dairy farms, tourism, and retail trade. The Boeing plant that manufactures 747s and 767s is nearby. Snohomish claims to be the antique capital of the Pacific Northwest, boasting 450 dealers and many specialty shops.

What to See and Do

Blackman Museum. *118 Ave B, Snohomish (98290). Phone 360/568-5235.* Restored 1878 Victorian house; vintage furnishings. (June-Sept: daily; Mar-May and Oct-Dec: Wed-Sun afternoons; closed rest of year) **$**

Old Snohomish Village. *2nd and Pine sts, Snohomish (98290). Phone 360/568-5235.* Six authentic pioneer buildings moved here including the general store (circa 1910) and weaver's shop, which displays antique looms. (June-Sept: daily; rest of year: by appointment) **$**

Star Center Antique Mall. *829 2nd St, Snohomish (98290). Phone 360/568-2131.* More than 165 antique shops housed in a former armory. Restaurant, children's play area. (Daily)

Stevens Pass Ski Area. *53 miles E on Hwy 2.* Road goes past Eagle Falls. Downhill, cross-country skiing; snowboarding, tubing. **$$$$**

Walking tour of historical houses. *116 Ave B, Snohomish (98290). Phone 360/568-2526.* Contact Chamber of Commerce Waltz Building, for brochure. **FREE**

Snoqualmie

What to See and Do

Mount Si Golf Course. *9010 Boalch Ave SE, Snoqualmie (98065). Phone 425/391-4926. www.mtsigolf.com.* Mount Si used to be the world's largest field for growing hops for beer before being turned into an 18-hole course in the 1930s. Since then, it has undergone several renovations, most recently in 1994, when eight of the holes were completely changed. The change upped the length of the course to more than 6,300 yards, as well moving or adding more than 100 trees. The course has several leagues and sessions for younger golfers to learn the game, making it one of the better organized courses in the Seattle area. **$$$$**

Full-Service Resort

🔍 ★ ★ ★ **SALISH LODGE & SPA.** *6501 Railroad Ave, Snoqualmie (98065). Phone 425/888-2556; toll-free 800/272-5474; fax 425/888-2420. www.salishlodge.com.* Just 30 miles east of Seattle, the Salish Lodge & Spa is a celebration of the rugged beauty of the Pacific Northwest. Nestled in the foothills of the Cascade Mountains, this understated lodge enjoys a majestic setting amid lush evergreen forests and the roaring whitewater of the Snoqualmie Falls. World-weary travelers quickly adopt a gentle pace here, whether hiking the serene mountain trails or enjoying a hot rock massage in the Asian-inspired spa. A rustic simplicity pervades the accommodations, while luxurious details such as wood-burning fireplaces, whirlpool tubs, and pillow menus ensure maximum comfort and large windows focus attention on the serene views.

Three exceptional restaurants delight the palates of discriminating diners with a focus on fresh, regional cuisine. 91 rooms, 4 story. Check-in 4 pm, check-out noon. Restaurant, bar. Fitness room, spa. Whirlpool. **$$$**

⧖

Restaurant

★ ★ ★ **SALISH LODGE & SPA DINING ROOM.** *6501 Railroad Ave, Snoqualmie (98065). Phone 425/888-2556; toll-free 800/272-5474; fax 425/888-2553. www.salishlodge.com.* With views overlooking the magnificent Snoqualmie Falls, the word is casual elegance at this rustic lodge restaurant. New World menu. Breakfast, lunch, dinner, brunch. Closed Mon. Bar. Casual attire. Valet parking. **$$$**

Snoqualmie Pass

What to See and Do

Summit at Snoqualmie. *1001 State Rd 906, Snoqualmie Pass (98068). Phone 425/434-7669. www.summit-at-snoqualmie.com.* About an hour's drive east of downtown Seattle, the Summit at Snoqualmie is the top winter sports destination for the city's skiers and snowboarders. The mountain has four distinct base areas—Summit West, Central, and East, as well as the daunting Alpental—each with its own amenities and lifts. Between the four, the resort has varied terrain with ample acreage for every skill level. Of special note: the snowboarding paradise called the Nissan Terrain Park and Halfpipe at Summit West and the Nordic Center at Summit East, the starting point for more than 30 miles of groomed trails. Restaurant and ski rental services are at all four base areas; the repair shop is at Summit Central. Lodging is available in the area at hotels, motels, and vacation home rentals.

Soap Lake

See also Coulee Dam, Ephrata

Population 1,733
Elevation 1,075 ft
Area Code 509
Zip 98851
Information Soap Lake Chamber of Commerce, PO Box 433; phone 509/246-1821
Web site www.soaplakecoc.org

The minerals and salts in Soap Lake (from the Native American name Smokiam, which means "healing waters") give the community status as a health resort. They also whip into a soaplike foam that lines the shore on windy days. This is the south entrance to the Grand Coulee, the 50-mile channel of the prehistoric Columbia River.

Limited-Service Hotel

★ ★ **NOTARAS LODGE.** *13 Canna St, Soap Lake (98851). Phone 509/246-0462; fax 509/246-1054. www.notaraslodge.com.* Four log buildings make up this historic lodge, the original of which was destroyed by fire in 1998. Each guest room has a different theme, but all feature rustic furnishings, kitchenettes, and dual plumbing systems that allow visitors to choose between regular and Soap Lake mineral water. Five of the rooms have whirlpool tubs. 15 rooms, 2 story. Pets accepted; fee. Check-out 11 am. Restaurant. **$**

Restaurant

★ ★ **DON'S.** *14 Canna St, Soap Lake (98851). Phone 509/246-1217; fax 509/246-1054.* Greek, seafood, steak menu. Lunch, dinner. Closed Dec 25. Bar. **$$**

Spokane (B-6)

See also Cheney, Colville, Newport; also see Coeur d'Alene, ID, Sandpoint, ID

Settled 1871
Population 195,629
Elevation 1,898 ft
Area Code 509
Information Spokane Area Visitor Information Center, 801 W Riverside, #301, 99201; phone 509/624-1341
Web site www.visitspokane.com

Spokane (spo-KAN) is the booming center of the vast, rich "Inland Northwest," an area that includes eastern Washington, northern Idaho, northeastern Oregon, western Montana, and southern British Columbia. A large rail center, the Spokane area also produces wheat, apples, hops, silver, gold, zinc, and lead. Thanks to the surrounding mountain ranges, Spokane enjoys what it likes to term New Mexico's climate in the winter and Maine's in the summer. The city itself is in a saucerlike setting amid pine-green hills, with the Spokane River running through its 52 square miles.

Long a favorite Native American hunting and fishing ground, Spokane began as a sawmill, powered by Spokane Falls. This village, the name meaning "children of the sun," was the only point in a 400-mile-long north-south range of mountains where railroads could cross the Rockies and reach the Columbia Basin. Railroading sparked the city's early growth. The Coeur d'Alene gold fields in Idaho helped finance Spokane's continuing development and helped it survive an 1889 fire that nearly leveled the city. Farming, lumbering, mining, and railroading aided Spokane's growth during the first decade of the century.

In 1974, the Havermale and Cannon islands in the Spokane River were the site of EXPO 74. The area has since been developed as Riverfront Park.

Public Transportation

Spokane Transit Authority Phone 509/328-7433, information 509/455-6455. www.spokanetransit.com

Airport Spokane International Airport. SW of the city off Hwy 2.

Airlines Air Canada, Alaska Airlines, America West Airlines, Big Sky Airlines, Delta Air Lines, Horizon Air, Northwest Airlines, Southwest Airlines, United Airlines

What to See and Do

Cathedral of St. John the Evangelist. *127 E 12th Ave, Spokane (99202). Phone 509/838-4277.* (Episcopal) Magnificent sandstone Gothic structure; stained-glass windows by Boston's Connick Studios; wood and stone carvings. Tours (Mon, Tues, Thurs, Sat; Sun after services). Recitals on 49-bell carillon (Thurs, Sun); also recitals on Aeolian-Skinner organ (schedule varies).

Cheney Cowles Museum. *2316 W 1st Ave, Spokane (99204). Phone 509/456-3931.* Houses collections of regional history and Native American culture. Fine Arts Gallery has changing art exhibits. Adjacent is Campbell House (1898), a restored mansion of Spokane's "age of elegance." **$$**

Children's Museum. *110 N Post, Spokane (99201). Phone 509/624-5437.* Children are permitted to touch, encouraged to make noise, and create. Weather exhibit; hydroelectric power station; music, art; regional and cultural history. (Tues-Sat) **$$**

Cliff Park. *13th Ave and Grove St, Spokane (99204).* Built around old volcanic island; Review Rock, half acre at base, offers highest point in city for viewing. (Daily) **FREE**

Comstock Park. *29th Ave and Howard St, Spokane (99203).* Picnicking, tennis courts. Pool (Mid-June-Aug, daily; fee). Park (daily). **FREE**

Finch Arboretum. *3404 W Woodland Blvd, Spokane (99224). Off Sunset Blvd. Phone 509/624-4832.* Approximately 70 acres; includes Corey Glen Rhododendron Gardens, creek, 2,000 specimen plantings of ornamental trees and shrubs. (Daily) **FREE**

Flour Mill. *621 W Mallon, Spokane (99201). Adjacent to Riverfront Park N entrance.* (1890) When it was built it was the most modern mill west of the Mississippi River. Today it is the home of boutiques, designer shops, galleries, and restaurants. Overlooks Spokane River. (Daily) **FREE**

Gonzaga University. *Boone Ave and Addison St, Spokane (99201). Phone 509/328-4220.* (1887) (4,700 students) Rodin sculptures on display. In center of campus is Bing Crosby's gift to his alma mater, the Crosby Student Center; Academy Award Oscar, gold records, certificates, trophies on display in Crosbyana Room (daily). Tours of campus (including Crosby Center and St. Aloyisius Church; by appointment).

⭐ **Loop drive.** *Sprague Ave and Stevens St, Spokane (99201).* A 33-mile city drive to major points of interest; route, marked with "city drive" signs, begins at Sprague Ave and Stevens St.

Manito Park. *Grand Blvd and 18th Ave, Spokane (99203). Phone 509/625-6622.* Duncan Formal Gardens (May-Sept, daily); conservatory (Daily; closed Jan 1, Dec 25). Davenport Memorial Fountain with changing formations in 10-minute cycle (May-Sept, daily); Japanese, lilac, and rose gardens (Apr-Oct, daily). Duck pond; picnicking. **FREE**

Mount Spokane. *30 miles NE on Hwy 206, in Mount Spokane State Park. Phone 509/238-2220. www.mtspokane.com.* Five double chairlifts; patrol, school, rentals; cafeteria, bar; lodge, daycare. Longest run 1 1/2 miles; vertical drop 2,000 feet. (Dec-mid-Apr, Wed-Sun)

Mount Spokane State Park. *25 miles NE on Hwy 206. Phone 509/456-4169.* More than 13,000 acres; includes

Mount Spokane (5,881 feet), with excellent view from summit, and Mount Kit Carson (5,306 feet). Hiking and bridle trails, downhill skiing, cross-country skiing, snowmobiling (special parking permit required), picnicking, camping.

Riverfront Park. *Spokane Falls Blvd and Howard St, Spokane (99201). Phone 509/625-6600. www.spokaneriverfront.com.* A 100-acre recreational park features outdoor amphitheater, IMAX theater, opera house, game room. Spokane River runs through park; suspension bridges over Spokane River; foot bridges; skyride over falls. Miniature golf; roller coaster, carousel. Children's petting zoo. Ponds; ice rink. Restaurant, vending carts, picnicking. Fees for some activities. **FREE**

Riverside State Park. *Rutter Pkwy, Spokane. 6 miles NW via Downriver Dr. Phone 509/456-3964.* Approximately 7,300 acres along the Spokane River. Fishing, boating (launch); hiking, equestrian area, snowmobiling, picnicking, camping. Also 600-acre off-road vehicle area; outdoor stoves; interpretive center.

Spokane Falls. Viewed from Bridge Avenue at Monroe Street or foot of Lincoln Street. Spokane River roars over rocks in series of cascades; illuminated at night.

Wyvern Cellars. *7217 W Westbow, Spokane (99224). Phone 509/455-7835.* Tour and tasting of Gold Medal wines. Picnicking. (Daily; closed Jan 1, Dec 25) **FREE**

Special Events

Ag Expo. *Convention Center, 334 W Spokane Falls Blvd, Spokane (99201). Phone 509/459-4108.* Agricultural fair. Mid-Jan.

Horse racing. *Playfair Race Course, 202 N Altamont St, Spokane (99202). N Altamont and E Main sts. Phone 509/534-0505.* Wed, Fri-Sun, holidays. July-mid-Nov.

Spokane Civic Theatre. *1020 N Howard St, Spokane (99201). Phone 509/325-1413.* Live productions. Thurs-Sun, Oct-mid-June.

Spokane Interstate Fair. *Interstate Fairgrounds, 404 N Havana St, Spokane (99202). Broadway and Havana sts. Phone 509/477-1766.* Nine days in mid-Sept.

Limited-Service Hotels

★ **COMFORT INN.** *905 N Sullivan Rd, Veradale (99037). Phone 509/924-3838; toll-free 800/252-*

7466; fax 509/921-6976. www.choicehotels.com. 76 rooms, 2 story. Pets accepted, some restrictions; fee. Complimentary continental breakfast. Check-out 11 am. Pool, whirlpool. **$**

★ ★ **COURTYARD BY MARRIOTT.** *N 401 Riverpoint Blvd, Spokane (99202). Phone 509/456-7600; toll-free 800/321-2211; fax 509/456-0969. www.courtyard.com.* 149 rooms, 3 story. Check-in 3 pm, check-out noon. Restaurant, bar. Fitness room. Indoor pool, whirlpool. **$**

★ ★ **DOUBLETREE HOTEL SPOKANE-CITY CENTER.** *322 N Spokane Falls Ct, Spokane (99201). Phone 509/455-9600; toll-free 800/222-8733; fax 509/455-6285. www.doubletree.com.* Located on the Spokane River in Riverfront Park, this hotel is convenient to the convention center and arena, making it a frequent choice of business travelers. Shopping, restaurants, and entertainment are also nearby, as is the Centennial Trail. The Doubletree's restaurant, Spencer's, is a steakhouse that appeals to locals as well as hotel guests. 375 rooms, 15 story. Pets accepted, some restrictions. Check-in 4 pm, check-out noon. High-speed Internet access. Two restaurants, bar. Fitness room. Outdoor pool, whirlpool. Airport transportation available. Business center. **$**

★ ★ **HAMPTON INN.** *2010 S Assembly Rd, Spokane (99224). Phone 509/747-1100; toll-free 800/426-7866; fax 509/747-8722. www.hamptoninn.com.* Complimentary continental breakfast. Check-in 4 pm, check-out noon. High-speed Internet access. Restaurant, bar. Fitness room. Indoor pool, whirlpool. Airport transportation available. Business center. **$**

★ **QUALITY INN VALLEY SUITES.** *8923 E Mission Ave, Spokane (99212). Phone 509/928-5218; toll-free 800/777-7355; fax 509/928-5211. www.spokanequalityinn.com.* You get a full hot breakfast every morning and a complimentary wine reception Monday through Friday. In-room kitchen facilities—microwave, refrigerator, and bar sink—allow you to prepare your own meals. Add to this a handsome Mediterranean décor, a 24-hour business center, and exceptional cleanliness, and you get real value from this motel. 128 rooms, 4 story. Pets accepted, some restrictions; fee. Complimentary full breakfast. Check-in 3 pm, check-out 11 am. Fitness room. Indoor pool, whirlpool. Business center. **$**

★ ★ **RED LION HOTEL AT THE PARK.** *303 W North River Dr, Spokane (99201). Phone 509/326-8000; toll-free 800/733-5466; fax 509/325-7329. www.redlion .com.* 400 rooms. Pets accepted, some restrictions. Check-in 3 pm, check-out 11 am. High-speed Internet access. Two restaurants, bar. Children's activity center. Fitness room, spa. Indoor pool, outdoor pool, whirlpool. Airport transportation available. Business center. **$**

★ ★ **WESTCOAST.** *N 700 Division St, Spokane (99202). Phone 509/326-5577; fax 509/326-1120. www. westcoasthotels.com.* 245 rooms, 2 story. Pets accepted. Complimentary continental breakfast. Check-in 3 pm, check-out noon. Restaurant, bar. Fitness room. Outdoor pool, whirlpool. Tennis. Airport transportation available. **$**

Full-Service Hotels

★ ★ ★ **THE DAVENPORT HOTEL.** *10 S Post St, Spokane (99201). Phone 509/455-8888; toll-free 800/899-1482; fax 509/624-4455. www. thedavenporthotel.com.* Step back in time at this grand downtown hotel that opened in 1914 and recently underwent a massive renovation to restore it to its original grandeur. As soon as you step into the soaring two-story lobby, you can see the attention to design and detail that has been put into this property. The guest rooms feature hand-carved mahogany furniture, imported Irish linens (made by the same company that supplied the hotel when it first opened), and travertine marble bathrooms with spacious walk-in showers. Some suites and deluxe rooms have fireplaces, wet bars, and jetted tubs for extra comfort and luxury. Exquisite ballrooms provide magical settings for special events, making the Davenport a popular site for weddings and other important celebrations. The upscale Palm Court restaurant serves Euro-Asian cuisine, while the Peacock Room serves cocktails and a light menu. The hotel also offers a cigar bar, espresso bar, candy shop, flower shop, and art gallery. 284 rooms, 14 story. Pets accepted. Check-in 3 pm,

check-out noon. High-speed Internet access. Three restaurants, two bars. Fitness room, spa. Indoor pool, whirlpool. Airport transportation available. Business center. **$$**

★ ★ ★ **HOTEL LUSSO.** *N 1 Post, Spokane (99201). Phone 509/747-9750; fax 509/363-2389. www.hotellusso.com.* 48 rooms. Complimentary continental breakfast. Check-in 3 pm, check-out noon. High-speed Internet access. Restaurant, bar. Airport transportation available. **$$**

Specialty Lodgings

The following lodging establishments are approved by Mobil Travel Guide, but due to their unique and individualized nature have not been given a traditional Mobil Star rating. Included in this listing you may find bed-and-breakfasts, limited-service inns, guest ranches, and other unique hotel properties.

FOTHERINGHAM HOUSE. *2128 W 2nd Ave, Spokane (99204). Phone 509/838-1891; fax 509/838-1807. www.fotheringham.net.* Recently restored to its original grandeur, the charming Queen Anne-style bed-and-breakfast has a wraparound porch and stunning gardens. In the evening, guests can relax with Scottish tea and hazelnut truffles. It's simply a worthwhile stay. 4 rooms. Children over 12 years only. Complimentary full breakfast. Check-in 2 pm, check-out 11 am. **$**

MARIANNA STOLTZ HOUSE BED & BREAKFAST. *427 E Indiana Ave, Spokane (99207). Phone 509/483-4316; toll-free 800/978-6587; fax 509/ 483-6773. www.mariannastoltzhouse.com.* Built in 1908, this homey bed-and-breakfast reflects the era's tradition of craftsmanship. Each guest suite is unique and handsomely decorated. Guests awake to scents from the kitchen, where puffy Dutch pancakes or peach Melba parfait are served up. 4 rooms, 2 story. No children allowed. Complimentary full breakfast. Check-in 3-6 pm, check-out 11 am. **$**

Restaurants

★ **CHAPTER XI.** *105 E Mission Ave, Spokane (99202). Phone 509/326-0466.* American menu. Lunch, dinner. Closed Thanksgiving, Dec 25. Bar. **$$$**

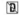

★ ★ **CLINKERDAGGER.** *621 W Mallon, Spokane (99201). Phone 509/328-5965; fax 509/327-4653.* Seafood, steak menu. Lunch, dinner. Closed Thanksgiving, Dec 25. Bar. Children's menu. Casual attire. Outdoor seating. Converted flour mill; shops inside. **$$$**

Stevenson

See Hood River, OR

Sunnyside (D-4)

See also Richland, Toppenish

Founded 1893
Population 13,905
Elevation 743 ft
Area Code 509
Zip 98944
Information Chamber of Commerce, 520 S 7th St; phone 509/837-5939 or toll-free 800/457-8089
Web site www.sunnysidechamber.com

This is the home of one of the first irrigation projects of more than 100,000 acres in the state. Its selection as a site for a large settlement of the Christian Cooperative movement brought growth and prosperity to this community. Irrigation continues to bring rich crops to the fields that circle the city.

The town is aptly named. Sunnyside averages over 300 days of sunshine every year, with mild winters and dry summers.

What to See and Do

Darigold Dairy Fair. *400 Alexander Rd, Sunnyside (98944). Phone 509/837-4321.* Tours of cheese-making plant. (Daily; closed holidays) **FREE**

Tucker Cellars Winery. *70 Ray Rd, Sunnyside (98944). Yakima Valley Hwy and Ray Rd. Phone 509/837-8701.* Wine tasting. (Daily)

Washington Hills Cellar. *111 E Lincoln, Sunnyside (98944). Phone 509/839-9463.* Wine tasting. (Daily)

Tacoma (C-2)

See also Auburn, Enumclaw, Olympia, Puyallup

Settled 1868
Population 193,556
Elevation 250 ft
Area Code 253
Information Tacoma-Pierce County Visitor & Convention Bureau, 1119 Pacific Ave, 5th floor, PO Box 1754, 98402; phone 253/627-2836 or toll-free 800/272-2662
Web site www.traveltacoma.com

In its gemlike setting on Puget Sound, midway between Seattle and Olympia, Tacoma maintains its wood and paper industries and its shipping traditions. Its harbor is a port of call for merchant vessels plying the oceans of the world. Backed by timber, shipping facilities, and low-cost water and power, more than 500 industries produce lumber, plywood, paper, millwork, furniture, foodstuffs, beverages, chemicals, and clothing. Major railroad and shipbuilding yards are also located here. Healthcare is a major employer, and the high-tech industry continues to grow rapidly. The nearest metropolitan center to Mount Rainier National Park, Tacoma is a base for trips to Olympic National Park and Puget Sound. Mild weather keeps parks and gardens green throughout the year.

In 1833, the Hudson's Bay Company built its second post (Fort Nisqually) on the North Pacific Coast in the forest, 18 miles south of the present site of Tacoma. In 1841, Charles Wilkes, commander of a US expedition, began a survey of Puget Sound from this point and named the bay around which Tacoma is built Commencement Bay. When the rails of the Northern Pacific reached tidewater here late in 1873, they sparked the industrial growth of the city.

What to See and Do

Emerald Queen Casino. *2102 Alexander Ave, Tacoma (98421). Phone toll-free 888/831-7655. www.emeraldqueen.com.* A Cajun-themed, Native American-owned riverboat in the Port of Tacoma with 180,000 square feet of gaming space, the Emerald Queen Casino is big and bright, brimming with antiques and Vegas-style tables (including blackjack, Caribbean stud poker, roulette, craps, and others), as well as 1,500 slots and video poker machines. (The place has some nice touches: a smoke-free gaming floor on the first deck and dealers in period costumes.) The stage here regularly attracts national rock and country acts, some of them household names. In addition to the requisite casino buffet, the boat has a pair of restaurants, one a casual café and the other an Asian eatery with regular surf-and-turf specials. A second, newer location in Tacoma nixes the riverboat and Deep South themes, operating from a landlocked building near I-5 (2024 E 29th St). (Daily)

Enchanted Village. *36201 Enchanted Pkwy S, Tacoma (98003). S in Federal Way. Phone 253/661-8000; fax 253/661-8065. www.sixflags.com.* Family entertainment park with rides for all ages; wax museum, antique toy and doll museum. Live entertainment. Concessions. (Mid-May-Labor Day: daily; early Apr-mid-May and Sept after Labor Day: weekends) **$$$$** Also here is

Wild Waves Water Park. *Phone 253/661-8000 or 253/661-8065. www.sixflags.com.* A 24,000-square-foot wave pool with body and mat surfing in ocean-size waves; raging river ride; adult activity pool; four giant water slides with flashing lights and music, two speed slides; spas; children's pool. Game room; raft rentals. (Memorial Day weekend-Labor Day weekend, daily) Admission includes entry to Enchanted Village. **$$$$**

Ferry. *Phone 206/464-6400.* Point Defiance to Vashon Island. Contact Washington State Ferries, Seattle Ferry Terminal, Colman Dock, Seattle 98104. **$$$**

Fort Lewis. *11 miles SW on I-5. Phone 253/967-7206.* Army center of the Northwest, home of I Corps, the Seventh Infantry Division, and associated support units. Approximately 86,000 acres with military buildings and living quarters. Museum with exhibits on Northwest military history (Wed-Sun).

McChord AFB. *8 miles SW on I-5. Phone 253/982-2485.* The 62nd Airlift Wing and 446th Aircraft Wing (Reserves) are based here. Tours (Tues and Thurs; reservations required one month in advance). Museum (Tues-Sun, afternoons).

Mount Rainier National Park. (see). *Nisqually entrance, approximately 56 miles SE on Hwy 7. www.nps.gov/mora/.*

Narrows Bridge. *W on Olympic Blvd; Hwy 16.* Fifth-longest span for a suspension bridge in US (2,800 feet). Total length: 5,450 feet between anchorages. Successor to "Galloping Gertie," which collapsed in 1940, four months and seven days after it had officially opened.

Northwest Trek. *32 miles SE via I-5, Hwy 512, 161. Phone 360/832-6117. www.nwtrek.org.* One-hour naturalist-guided and narrated tram tour takes visitors on a 5 1/2-mile ride through a 600-acre wilderness and wildlife preserve, where native Northwest animals may be seen roaming free in their natural habitat; self-guided nature walks through wetlands and forest animal exhibits; nature trails include barrier-free trail; children's discovery center. Theater with 14-minute film on history of facility. (Mar-Oct: daily; rest of year: Fri-Sun and selected holidays) **$$$**

Pacific Lutheran University. *11 miles SW on I-5. Off I-5, exit 127. Phone 253/535-7430. www.plu.edu.* (1890) (3,500 students) Swimming pool. Nine-hole golf course open to public. On campus are

Robert Mortvedt Library. *S 121st and Park, Tacoma (98447). Phone 253/535-7500.* African tribal art. (Mon-Sat) **FREE**

University Gallery. *Ingram Hall. Phone 253/535-7573.* Changing art exhibits (Mon-Fri). Rune stones sculpture on campus mall.

Pioneer Farm. *7716 Ohop Valley Rd E, Tacoma (98328). 35 miles SE via Hwy 7, in the Ohop Valley. Phone 360/832-6300.* Replica of an 1887 homestead with animals; log cabin, barn, trading post, and other outbuildings; furnished with turn-of-the-century antiques. "Hands on" program; guided tours. (Mid-June-Labor Day: daily; Mar-mid-June and after Labor Day-Thanksgiving: Sat and Sun only)

⭐ **Point Defiance Park.** *54th and Pearl sts, Tacoma (98407). 6 miles N.* Approximately 700 acres of dense forest, clay cliffs, driftwood-covered gravel beaches, and formal gardens. On bold promontory, nearly surrounded by water. Boating, fishing, swimming; hiking, picnicking. Park (daily). **FREE** In the park are

Boathouse Marina. *5912 N Waterfront Dr, Tacoma (98407). Phone 253/591-5325.* Bait and tackle shop. Boat and motor rentals. Moorage. Restaurant. Gift shop. (Daily; closed Thanksgiving, Dec 25)

Camp Six Logging Exhibit (Western Forest Industries Museum). *Phone 253/752-0047.* Reconstructed steam logging camp set amid virgin timber. Dolbeer Donkey steam engine (one of two in existence), 110-foot spar pole, restored water wagon, bunkhouses. (Jan-Oct, Wed-Sun) Logging train ride (Apr-Sept, Sat-Sun, and holidays). A 90-ton shay steam locomotive operates in summer (weekends and holidays). Santa train (three weekends in Dec). **$**

Five Mile Drive. Around Point Defiance Park. Contains old growth forest with some 200-foot-high Douglas firs, variety of other evergreens, deciduous trees, shrubs. Scenic views of Puget Sound, Olympic and Cascade mountains, Narrows Bridge. Drive closed to motor vehicles Saturday mornings for cycling and walking.

Fort Nisqually. *Phone 253/591-5339.* (1833) Restored fur-trading outpost of Hudson's Bay Company reflects period of English control when fur pelts were used as currency. Purchased by the US in 1869, moved to this site in 1937. Two remaining buildings of original outpost are the Factor's House (1853) and the Granary (1843), oldest existing building in state; eight other buildings reconstructed according to original specifications using handmade hardware, lumber. Living history presentations. Fee for some special events. (Memorial Day-Labor Day: daily; rest of year: Wed-Sun) **$**

Gardens. Formal gardens in park include an AARS rose garden, Japanese Garden, Northwest Native garden, Pacific Northwest dahlia trial garden, rhododendron garden, and seasonal annual displays. **FREE**

Never Never Land. *Phone 253/591-5845. www. metroparkstacoma.org.* Sculptured storybook characters in 10-acre forest setting. Each weekend storybook characters visit and special events take place. (May-Aug: daily; Apr and Sept: weekends only) **$$**

Point Defiance Zoo & Aquarium. *Phone 253/591-5337. www.pdza.org.* The zoo has a polar bear complex, a musk ox habitat, tundra waterfowl, elephants, beluga whales, walrus, seals, and otters. The 38 perimeter displays show off hundreds of Pacific Northwest marine specimens, and 2003 brought a special showing called "Project Seahorse" to the aquarium. The Reef Aquarium features sharks and other South Pacific sea life, and the Simpson lab shows how humans can affect the ecosystem of animals like sea urchins and hermit crabs. (Opens daily at 9:30 am; closing times vary by season; closed July 18, Thanksgiving, Dec 25) **$$**

Seattle Museum of Glass. *1801 E Dock St, Tacoma (98402). Phone 253/396-1768. www.museumofglass.org.* The only museum in the US focusing on contemporary glass art, the Museum of Glass first opened its doors at the waterfront in downtown Tacoma (35 miles south of Seattle) in 2001. The collection includes works by some of the best-known glass artists in the world, including Dale Chiluly, whose 500-foot Chiluly Bridge of Glass here is one of the largest outdoor glass installations in existence anywhere. Visitors can watch glass artists ply their trade at an amphitheater onsite. (Tues-Sat 10 am-5 pm; Sun noon-5 pm; 3rd Tues of month 10 am-8 pm; closed Mon, holidays) **$$$**

St. Peter's Church. *2910 Starr St, Tacoma (98403). At N 29th St. Phone 253/272-4406.* (1873) (Episcopal) Oldest church in the city; the organ came around Cape Horn in 1874; half-ton bell, also shipped around the Horn, is mounted on tower beside church. (Sun; also by appointment)

Tacoma Art Museum. *1123 Pacific Ave, Tacoma (98402). 12th St and Pacific Ave. Phone 253/272-4258. www.tacomaartmuseum.org.* Permanent collection; changing exhibits; children's gallery with hands-on art activities. (Tues-Sun; closed Jan 1, Dec 25) **$$**

Tacoma Nature Center. *1919 S Tyler St, Tacoma (98405). Phone 253/591-6439.* Approximately 50 acres of marshland, forest, thickets, and ponds providing a wildlife haven in heart of urbanized Tacoma. Nature trails, observation shelters; natural science library. Interpretive center; lectures and workshops. Park (daily). **FREE**

Totem Pole. *9th and A sts, Tacoma (98401).* One of the tallest in the US, carved from 105-foot cedar tree by Alaskan Native Americans; located in Firemen's Park with view of Commencement Bay and the Port of Tacoma.

University of Puget Sound. *1500 N Warner St, Tacoma (98416). Phone 253/879-3100. www.ups.edu.* (1888) (2,800 students) Includes 37 Tudor Gothic buildings on a 72-acre campus. Many free cultural events, art gallery, theater, recital hall. University is older than state. Also here is

James R. Slater Museum of Natural History.
Thompson Hall. Displays research specimens, particularly of Pacific Northwest flora and fauna;

more than 11,000 birds, 4,600 egg sets; reptiles, amphibians, mammals, and pressed plants. (Mon-Fri by appointment; closed holidays) **FREE**

Washington State History Museum. *1911 Pacific Ave, Tacoma (98402). Phone toll-free 888/238-4373. www. wshs.org.* Exhibits include collections of pioneer, Native American, and Alaskan artifacts, and detail the history of the state and its people. Interactive, introductory, and changing exhibits. Indoor and outdoor theaters. Museum café and shop. (Memorial Day-Labor Day: daily; rest of year: Tues-Sun; closed holidays) **$$** Adjacent is

> **Union Station.** *Phone 253/396-1768.* Built in 1911 by Northern Pacific Railroad, the station, with its 98-foot-high dome, has been restored. Now home to the federal courthouse. The rotunda houses the largest single exhibit of sculptured glass by Tacoma native Dale Chihuly. (Mon-Fri; closed holidays) **FREE**

Wright Park. *316 S G St, Tacoma (98405). 6th Ave and I St. Phone 253/591-5330.* More than 800 trees of 100 varieties in one of finest arboretums in the Pacific Northwest. W. W. Seymour Botanical Conservatory, located in the park at S 4th and G streets, contains tropical plants, seasonal displays, and a botanical gift shop. Lawn bowling and horseshoe courts; playground, wading community center pool. (Daily) **FREE**

Special Events

Daffodil Festival. *741 Saint Helens Ave, Tacoma (98402). Phone 253/627-6176. In Tacoma and Puyallup Valley.* Flower show, coronation, four-city floral parade of floats, marine regatta, bowling tournament. Two weeks in Apr.

Tacoma Little Theater. *210 N I St, Tacoma (98403). Phone 253/272-2281.* Five shows, including comedies, dramas, and musicals. Sept-June.

Tacoma Symphony Orchestra. *727 Commerce St, #210, Tacoma (98402). Phone 253/272-7264.* Late Sept-early Apr.

Taste of Tacoma. *Point Defiance Park, 5400 N Pearl St, Tacoma (98407). Phone 206/232-2982.* Entertainment, arts and crafts. Early July.

Limited-Service Hotels

★ ★ BEST WESTERN TACOMA INN.
8726 S Hosmer St, Tacoma (98444). Phone 253/535-2880; toll-free 800/937-8376; fax 253/537-8379. www. bwtacomainn.com. 149 rooms, 2 story. Pets accepted; fee. Complimentary continental breakfast. Check-in 2 pm, check-out noon. Restaurant, bar. Outdoor pool. **$**

★ ★ LA QUINTA INN.
1425 E 27th St, Tacoma (98421). Phone 253/383-0146; toll-free 800/531-5900; fax 253/627-3280. www.laquinta.com. View of both Mount Rainier and Commencement Bay. 155 rooms, 7 story. Pets accepted. Complimentary continental breakfast. Check-in 3 pm, check-out noon. High-speed Internet access. Restaurant, bar. Fitness room. Indoor pool, whirlpool. Business center. **$**

★ SHILO INN.
7414 S Hosmer, Tacoma (98408). Phone 253/475-4020; toll-free 800/222-2244; fax 253/475-1236. www.shiloinns.com. Retaining a bit of 1970s ambience with the lobby's tile floor and overstuffed furniture, this motel is nonetheless well maintained and inviting. Although there's no on-site restaurant, you can get to-your-room delivery from a nearby restaurant or reserve a guest room with a refrigerator and microwave oven. The sauna, steam rooms, and indoor pool are available 24 hours. 132 rooms, 4 story. Pets accepted. Complimentary continental breakfast. Check-in 3 pm, check-out noon. Fitness room. Indoor pool, whirlpool. **$**

Full-Service Hotel

★ ★ ★ SHERATON TACOMA HOTEL.
1320 Broadway Plz, Tacoma (98402). Phone 253/572-3200; toll-free 800/325-3535; fax 253/591-4105. www. sheratontacoma.com. The restaurant level overlooks the three-story, skylight-lit lobby, decorated with glass work by world-renowned local artist Dale Chihuly. At the very top of the hotel is Altezzo, the hotel's rooftop restaurant, where you can enjoy fine Italian cuisine and check out views of Mount Rainier and Commencement Bay. Make use of the fitness facilities at the YMCA next door for free. The hotel welcomes your small pet (under 30 pounds) and provides a doggie bed if desired. 319 rooms, 26 story. Pets accepted, some restrictions. Check-in 3 pm, check-out noon.

Point Defiance Park

One of Tacoma's preeminent attractions, this 700-acre park, flanked by the waters of Puget Sound, contains a wealth of gardens, the city zoo and aquarium, and a number of recreational and historical sites. The park includes 14 miles of hiking trails, which wind through groves of old-growth forests and lead to sheltered beaches. The main paved road through the park is called Five Mile Drive; on Saturdays this scenic road remains closed to motor vehicles until 1 pm, though it's open to cyclists, joggers, and inline skaters.

Enter the park at Pearl Street and follow signs to the parking area at the Vashon Island Ferry. From here, watch as the ferries cross to and from Vashon Island, an agricultural island in the misty distance. Walk past the tennis courts, and follow the path to the garden area.

Formal gardens are abundant at Point Defiance Park and are maintained cooperatively by members of local garden clubs, with help from Tacoma's Metropolitan Park District. Park gardens include the Japanese Garden, with a Torii Gate and Shinto Shrine received as a gift from Kitakyushu, Tacoma's sister city in Japan. Also found here are iris gardens, dahlia test gardens, herb gardens, and a rhododendron garden that is a blaze of color in May. Just past the zoo entrance on Five Mile Drive is the civic Rose Garden, established in 1895, with more than an acre of bushes, many of heirloom varieties. The Northwest Native Garden, located near the Pearl Street entrance, presents a collection of indigenous plants ranging from trees to grasses.

Just past the main garden area is the Point Defiance Zoo & Aquarium. Often considered one of the best in the United States, the Point Defiance Zoo is unusual in that it focuses primarily on species from the Pacific Rim, including polar bears, musk ox, and Arctic fox. Peer at coastline mammals through the underwater windows at Rocky Shores. No less than 30 huge sharks swim among tropical fish and eels in the lagoon at Discovery Reef Aquarium. Elephants and apes and other zoo favorites are housed in the Southeast Asia complex.

From the zoo, follow trails north into the wild heart of the park. Point Defiance has been a public park for almost 125 years, and vast sections of it preserve old-growth forest and virgin meadowlands. Heading north, stop at Owens Beach to explore the shoreline or take in the sun along the sandy strand. Farther west, past a viewpoint onto Vashon Island, is Mountaineer Tree, a massive fir tree nearly 450 years old. The western edge of the park is at Gig Harbor Viewpoint, which overlooks the Tacoma Narrows, a constricted, surging strait between Point Defiance and the Kitsap Peninsula.

Round the cap and walk south along the western flank of the park. From here, watch for vistas onto the Tacoma Narrows Bridge. At a mile in length, it is the fifth longest span in North America. The present bridge replaced the infamous "Galloping Gertie" bridge that collapsed at this site during a wind storm in 1940.

At the southwest corner of the park are a number of attractions. If you have kids in tow, they may enjoy Never Never Land, a 10-acre, storyland theme park in an outdoor forest setting. Wooded paths lead to oversized sculpted figures of nursery-rhyme characters. On summer weekends, kids can meet real costumed characters.

Adjacent is Fort Nisqually Historic Site. In 1833, the Hudson's Bay Company trading post at Fort Nisqually was established 17 miles south of Tacoma, near DuPont. This restoration of the original fort includes the factor's house, granary, trade store, blacksmith shop, laborer's quarters, and stockade, all furnished to reflect life on the frontier in the 1850s. Docents in period clothing demonstrate blacksmithing, spinning, beadwork, and black powder.

Walk back toward the main park entrance, stopping by Camp 6 Logging Museum, an open-air logging museum and reconstruction of a pioneer logging camp. On spring and summer weekends, hitch a ride on a logging train with a steam locomotive.

Back at the ferry terminal, refresh yourself with a stop at the Boathouse Grill, located above the marina with views over Vashon Island and the Olympic mountain peaks.

High-speed Internet access. Two restaurants, two bars. Spa. Business center. **$**

Specialty Lodgings

The following lodging establishments are approved by Mobil Travel Guide, but due to their unique and individualized nature have not been given a traditional Mobil Star rating. Included in this listing you may find bed-and-breakfasts, limited-service inns, guest ranches, and other unique hotel properties.

CHINABERRY HILL. *302 Tacoma Ave N, Tacoma (98403). Phone 253/272-1282; fax 253/272-1335. www. chinaberryhill.com.* Nestled among century-old trees on a steep hill overlooking Puget Sound, this quaint 1889 Victorian mansion oozes old-world charm. Convenient to nearby shops, restaurants, theaters, and galleries, as well as the university and the Tacoma Dome, this inn has lovely multiroom suites furnished with antiques and an inviting wraparound porch. In addition to five standard rooms, the two-story carriage house sleeps six to seven guests, with two full baths and a private Jacuzzi. 6 rooms, 3 story. Complimentary full breakfast. Check-in 4-6 pm, check-out 11 am. **$**

VILLA BED & BREAKFAST. *705 N 5th St, Tacoma (98403). Phone 253/572-1157; toll-free 888/572-1157; fax 253/572-1157. www.villabb.com.* Stunning décor and sumptuous hospitality are only two reasons to check out this Italianate Villa, built in 1925. Each guest room offers distinctive décor and some special feature, ranging from a private veranda to a spa or claw-foot tub large enough for two to a gas fireplace. Relax in the beautifully landscaped and maintained gardens next to the gentle burble of a fountain. The full breakfast includes scrumptious gourmet offerings. 6 rooms, 2 story. Children over 12 years only. Complimentary full breakfast. Check-in 3 pm, check-out 11 am. High-speed Internet access. Whirlpool. **$**

Restaurants

★ ★ ★ **ALTEZZO RISTORANTE.** *1320 Broadway Plaza, Tacoma (98402). Phone 253/591-4155. www.sheratontacoma.com.* This restaurant offers breathtaking panoramic views of Puget Sound, Commencement Bay, and Mount Rainier. Italian menu. Dinner. Bar. Valet parking. **$$**

★ ★ ★ **CLIFF HOUSE.** *6300 Marine View Dr, Tacoma (98422). Phone 253/927-0400. www. cliffhouserestaurant.com.* Visitors will find Northwest-influenced cuisine at this dusty rose and floral-accented dining room. Northwest menu. Lunch, dinner. Closed Jan 1, Dec 25. Bar. Casual attire. Reservations recommended. **$$$**

★ ★ **HARBOR LIGHTS.** *2761 Ruston Way, Tacoma (98402). Phone 253/752-8600.* Seafood menu. Lunch, dinner, brunch. Closed holidays. Bar. Children's menu. Casual attire. Reservations recommended. **$$**

★ ★ **JOHNNY'S DOCK.** *1900 E D St, Tacoma (98421). Phone 253/627-3186. www.johnnysdock.com.* Seafood menu. Breakfast, lunch, dinner, brunch. Bar. Children's menu. Casual attire. Reservations recommended. Outdoor seating. **$**

★ ★ ★ **LOBSTER SHOP SOUTH.** *4015 Ruston Way, Tacoma (98402). Phone 253/759-2165. www. lobstershop.com.* This Commencement Bay restaurant has a bright look, boat moorage, and outdoor dining (during spring and summer). The coastline location affords beautiful views. Seafood, steak menu. Lunch, dinner, Sun brunch. Closed Dec 25. Bar. Children's menu. Casual attire. Outdoor seating. **$$$**

Toppenish (D-4)

See also Sunnyside, Yakima

Population 8,946
Elevation 755 ft
Area Code 509
Zip 98948
Information Chamber of Commerce, PO Box 28; phone 509/865-3262 or toll-free 800/569-3982

Toppenish is a Native American word meaning "people from the foot of the hills." The Yakama Indian Agency is here, and the nearby million-acre Yakama Reservation is an important tourist attraction. The cultural differences offer good opportunities for sightseeing and dining. The Toppenish area produces hops, fruits, vegetables, and dairy products. Average rainfall is only about 8 inches a year, but irrigation makes the countryside bloom.

What to See and Do

Fort Simcoe Historical State Park. *28 miles W on Hwy 220, Fort Rd. Phone 509/874-2372.* 200 acres. A restoration of a fort established in 1856 to protect treaty lands from land-hungry settlers and to guard military roads. Five original buildings have been restored; the interpretive center displays army and Native American relics. Picnicking, hiking. (Apr-Sept: daily; rest of year: weekends and holidays)

Historical Murals. *5 S Toppenniski Ave, Toppenish (98948). Phone 509/865-6516.* Painted on downtown buildings. For map or guided tour contact Mural Society.

Yakama Nation Cultural Center. *Hwy 97, Toppenish (98948). S on Hwy 97. Phone 509/865-2800.* Located on ancestral grounds of the Yakamas. Includes a museum depicting history of the Yakama Nation, library, theater, and restaurant. (Daily; closed Dec 25) **$$**

Special Events

Native American Celebrations. *Phone 509/865-2800. Most at Yakama Reservation in White Swan, 23 miles W on Hwy 220.* Call for details and locations. Yakama Nation Treaty Day, Powwow Rodeo. Early June at fairgrounds. Bull-O-Rama. Early July.

Old-Fashioned Melodrama. *Yakama Nation Cultural Center Theatre, 280 Buster Rd, Toppenish (98948). Phone 509/865-5719.* Boo and hiss at the villain, cheer the hero. Late July-early Aug.

Silver Spur PRCA Rodeo. *Phone 509/248-7160.* Early July.

Western Art Show. *Downtown. Phone toll-free 800/569-3982.* Three-day art show, cowboy poetry. Late Aug.

Tukwila

What to See and Do

Southcenter Mall. *633 Southcenter, Tukwila (98188). Phone 206/246-7400.* The nexus of a same-named office/retail/residential development in south suburban Tukwila (about a 15-minute drive from downtown Seattle), the Southcenter Mall opened in 1968 and continues to lure hordes of shoppers to its mix of national department stores and specialty shops. With more than 150 stores and restaurants in the mall—and countless more in the surrounding area—this is a retail destination that is entering middle age quite gracefully.

Union (C-2)

See also Bremerton

Settled 1858
Population 600
Elevation 10 ft
Area Code 360
Zip 98592

This resort town at the curve of the Hood Canal almost became the saltwater terminus of the Union Pacific Railroad, but the failure of a British bank was a blow to Union's commercial future. There are public beaches, a marina, free launching sites, and a golf course in town.

What to See and Do

Lake Cushman State Park. *7211 N Lake Cushman Rd, Hoodsport (98548). 5 miles SW via Hwy 106, 5 miles N via Hwy 101 to Hoodsport, then 7 miles NW via Lake Cushman Rd. Phone 360/877-5491; toll-free 800/233-0321 (information).* Approximately 600 acres. Swimming, fishing, boating (launch, fee); hiking trails, picnicking, camping (Apr-Nov; hookups).

Tollie Shay Engine and Caboose #7. *230 W Railroad One, Shelton (98584). 5 miles W on Hwy 106, 10 miles S on Hwy 101. Phone 360/426-2021.* Refurbished three-cylinder locomotive and Simpson logging caboose with coal-burning stove and unique side-door design. Caboose is used by Shelton-Mason County Chamber of Commerce as an office and tourist information center. (Daily; closed holidays) **FREE**

Twanoh State Park. *12190 E Hwy 106, Union (98592). 12 miles E on Hwy 106, off Hwy 101. Phone 360/275-2222.* 182 acres along Hood Canal. Swimming, scuba diving, boating (launch, dock), fishing, clamming; hiking, picnicking, camping (hookups).

Vancouver (E-2)

See also Portland, OR

Founded 1824
Population 143,560
Elevation 89 ft
Area Code 360
Information Greater Vancouver Chamber of Commerce, 1101 Broadway, Suite 120, 98660; phone 360/694-2588
Web site www.vancouverusa.com

Vancouver treasures a national historic site, Fort Vancouver, now completely encircled by the city. The fort served as a commercial bastion for the Hudson's Bay Company, whose vast enterprises stretched far to the north and across the sea to Hawaii, bringing furs from Utah and California and dominating coastal trade well up the shoreline to Alaska. Around the stockaded fort, the company's cultivated fields and pastures extended for miles; drying sheds, mills, forges, and shops made it a pioneer metropolis. This community was a major stake in Britain's claim for all the territory north of the Columbia River, but by the treaty of 1846, Fort Vancouver became American. Settlers began to take over the Hudson's Bay Company lands, and an Army post was established here in 1849, continuing to the present day. In 1860, all of Fort Vancouver was turned over to the US Army.

The city is on the Columbia River, just north of Portland, Oregon. Vancouver has a diversified industrial climate, which includes electronics, paper products, fruit packing, malt production, and the manufacture of textiles, furniture, and machinery. The Port of Vancouver, one of the largest on the West Coast, is a deepwater seaport handling a wide range of commodities.

What to See and Do

Clark County Historical Museum. *1511 Main St, Vancouver (98660). Phone 360/695-4681.* Exhibits include 1890s store, doctor's office, printing press, doll collection, dioramas of area history, Native American artifacts; railroad exhibit; genealogical and historical research libraries. (Tues-Sat; closed holidays) **FREE**

Downtown Historic Railway. Two refurbished train cars take passengers between Granville Island and Science World. (May-Sept, Sat-Sun 1-5 pm; also holidays) **$**

★ Fort Vancouver National Historic Site. *612 E Reserve St, Vancouver (98661). Phone 360/696-7655; toll-free 800/832-3599. www.nps.gov/fova.* Over 150 acres. After extensive research and excavation, the fort has been partially reconstructed by the National Park Service. Now at the fort site are Chief Factor's house, a kitchen, wash house, stockade wall, gates, bastion, bake house, blacksmith shop, and trade shop-dispensary. The visitor center has a museum exhibiting artifacts, an information desk, and video presentations. Tours, interpretive talks, and living history programs are also offered. (Daily, hours vary by season; closed holidays)

Gifford Pinchot National Forest. *10600 NE 51st Cir, Vancouver (98682). NE of the city, reached via Hwys 14, 25, 503. Phone 360/891-5000. www.fs.fed.us/gpnf.* The forest's 1,379,000 acres include the 12,326-foot Mount Adams; the 8,400-foot Mount St. Helens; and 180,600 acres distributed among seven wilderness areas. Picnicking, hiking, swimming, fishing, boating; camping, hunting.

Officers' Row. Self-guided walking tour of 21 turn-of-the-century houses; two open to public.

Pearson Air Museum. *1115 E 5th St, Vancouver (98661). Phone 360/694-7026.* At M. J. Murdock Aviation Center, one of the oldest operating airfields in the nation. Vintage aircraft and flying memorabilia. (Tues-Sun; closed holidays) **$**

Limited-Service Hotels

★ COMFORT INN. *4714 NE 94th Ave, Vancouver (98662). Phone 360/253-3100; toll-free 800/252-7466; fax 360/253-7998. www.choicehotels.com.* 68 rooms, 2 story, all suites. Complimentary continental breakfast. Check-in 3 pm, check-out noon. Indoor pool, whirlpool. **$**
🛏

★ HOLIDAY INN EXPRESS. *9107 NE Vancouver Mall Dr, Vancouver (98662). Phone 360/253-5000; toll-free 800/465-4329; fax 360/253-3137. www.hiexpress .com.* 56 rooms, 2 story. Complimentary continental breakfast. Check-in 2 pm, check-out noon. Indoor pool, whirlpool. **$**
🛏

Full-Service Resort

 ★ ★ ★ THE HEATHMAN LODGE. *7801 NE Greenwood Dr, Vancouver (98662). Phone 360/254-3100; toll-free 888/475-3100; fax 360/254-*

6100. www.heathmanlodge.com. For travelers who like a little sophistication when retreating to the woods, the Heathman Lodge is just the place. This restful resort is just 15 minutes from downtown Vancouver and only a short distance from Portland, Oregon, yet it maintains a peaceful, mountain-retreat ambience. Part woodsy, part elegant, the guest rooms and suites have an inimitable charm with Pendleton blankets and leather lampshades. Guests never leave behind the conveniences of the 21st century when visiting this property; a complete fitness center and business center are among the many amenities offered here. Hudson's elevates simple comfort food to a new level with its delightful riffs on favorite dishes, and the casual setting perfectly complements the laid-back attitude of this resort. 143 rooms, 4 story. Check-out noon. Restaurant, bar. Fitness room. Indoor pool, whirlpool. Business center. **$**

🏃 ⛴ 🎿

Walla Walla (D-5)

See also Dayton

Founded 1859
Population 29,686
Elevation 949 ft
Area Code 509
Zip 99362
Information Chamber of Commerce, 29 E Sumach, PO Box 644; phone 509/525-0850 or toll-free 877/998-4748
Web site www.wwchamber.com

Walla Walla Valley was first the site of a Native American trail and then an avenue for exploration and settlement of the West. Lewis and Clark passed through the area in 1805. Fur traders followed, and Fort Walla Walla was established in 1818 as a trading post at the point where the Walla Walla and Columbia rivers meet. One of the key figures in the area's history was Dr. Marcus Whitman, a medical missionary, who in 1836 founded the first settler's home in the Northwest—a mission 7 miles west of present-day Walla Walla. The Whitmans were killed by Native Americans in 1847. No successful settlement was made until after the Indian Wars of 1855-1858.

In 1859, the city became the seat of Walla Walla County, which then included half of present-day Washington, all of Idaho, and a quarter of Montana.

It also had the first railroad in the Northwest, the first bank in the state, the first meat market and packing plant, and the first institution of higher learning.

Walla Walla means "many waters," but local enthusiasts will tell you that this is "the city they liked so much they named it twice." Agriculture is the major industry, with wheat the most important crop and green peas the second. Industries concentrate chiefly on food processing. The Walla Walla onion is known nationwide for its sweetness; a festival is held each July to honor the important crop. A Ranger District office of the Umatilla National Forest is located here.

What to See and Do

Fort Walla Walla Park. *Dalles Military Rd. 1 mile W of Hwy 125, W edge of town. Phone 509/527-3770.* Camping (dump station; fee). (Apr-Sept, daily; limited facilities rest of year) Also in park is Audubon Society Nature Walk, outdoor amphitheater, and

Fort Walla Walla Museum. *755 Myra Rd, Walla Walla (99362). Phone 509/525-7703. www.fortwallawallamuseum.org.* The largest horse-era agricultural museum in the West. Twelve original and replica buildings from the mid-1800s, including a schoolhouse, homestead cabin, railroad depot, blockhouse, doctor's office, and blacksmith shop. Living history programs by more than 40 characters make the period come alive on summer weekends. (Apr-Oct, daily 10 am-5 pm) **$$**

Pioneer Park. *Division and Alder sts, Walla Walla (99362). Phone 509/527-4527.* A 58-acre park with horticultural displays, including a rose garden; exotic bird aviary; playground; tennis courts and ball fields; and picnic tables and shelter. **FREE**

Whitman Mission National Historic Site. *328 Whitman Mission Rd, Walla Walla (99362). 7 miles W, just off Hwy 12. Phone 509/522-6360. www.nps.gov/whmi.* The memorial shaft, erected in 1897, overlooks the site of the mission established by Dr. Marcus and Narcissa Whitman in 1836. A self-guided trail with audio stations leads to the mission grounds, Old Oregon Trail, memorial shaft, and grave. The visitor center has a ten-minute slide presentation and a museum. In summer, there are cultural demonstrations Sat-Sun 1-4 pm. (Daily; summer: 8 am-6 pm, rest of year: 8 am-4:30 pm; closed Jan 1, Thanksgiving, Dec 25) **$**

Limited-Service Hotel

★ **BEST WESTERN WALLA WALLA INN & SUITES.** *7 E Oak St, Walla Walla (99362). Phone 509/525-4700; toll-free 800/780-7234; fax 509/525-2457. www.bestwestern.com.* 78 rooms. Complimentary continental breakfast. Check-in 3 pm, check-out noon. Fitness room. Indoor pool, whirlpool. **$**

Specialty Lodging

The following lodging establishment is approved by Mobil Travel Guide, but due to its unique and individualized nature has not been given a traditional Mobil Star rating. Included in this listing you may find bed-and-breakfasts, limited-service inns, guest ranches, and other unique hotel properties.

GREEN GABLES INN. *922 Bonsella St, Walla Walla (99362). Phone 509/525-5501; toll-free 888/525-5501. www.greengablesinn.com.* Built in 1909; period antiques. 5 rooms. Children over 11 years only. Complimentary full breakfast. Check-in 3 pm, check-out 11 am. High-speed Internet access. **$**

Wenatchee (B-4)

See also Cashmere, Chelan, Leavenworth, Quincy

Founded 1888
Population 27,856
Elevation 727 ft
Area Code 509
Information Wenatchee Chamber of Commerce, 300 S Columbia, 98807; phone 509/662-2116 or toll-free 800/572-7753
Web site www.wenatchee.org

The apple blossoms in the spring and the sturdy red of grown fruit in the fall are the symbols of this community. Nestled among towering mountains are fertile irrigated valleys where residents care for orchards. Cherries, pears, peaches, and apricots are also grown here. With the establishment in 1952 of a huge aluminum smelter and casting plant, Wenatchee no longer has an economy based only on agriculture. The headquarters of the Wenatchee National Forest is located here.

What to See and Do

Mission Ridge Ski Area. *7500 Mission Ridge Rd, Wenatchee (98801). Phone 509/663-6543. www.missionridge.com.* Four double chairlifts, two rope tows; patrol, school, rentals; snowmaking; cafeteria; childcare. Vertical drop 2,200 feet. Half-day rates. Limited cross-country trails. (Dec-mid-Apr) **$$$$**

Rocky Reach Dam. *7 miles N on Hwy 97A, on the Columbia River. Phone 509/663-7522.* The Visitor Center has an underwater fish viewing gallery and a theater. The Powerhouse has the Gallery of the Columbia and the Gallery of Electricity, plus changing art exhibits. Landscaped grounds; picnic and play areas. (Daily; closed Dec 25, also Jan-mid-Feb) **FREE**

Squilchuck State Park. *9 miles SW on Squilchuck Rd. Phone 509/664-6373. www.parks.wa.gov.* This 287-acre park at an elevation of 4,000 feet offers day use and group camping, 10 miles of hiking and biking trails, and ample opportunities for winter sports like skiing and snowshoeing. (May-late Sept, 6:30 am-dusk)

Wenatchee National Forest. *Forest Headquarters, 215 Melody Ln, Wenatchee (98801). N, S, and W of town. Phone 509/662-4335. www.fs.fed.us/r6/wenatchee.* Approximately 2 million forested, mountainous acres lying west of Columbia River. A trail system leads to jagged peaks, mountain meadows, and sparkling lakes. Fishing, hunting, horseback riding, winter sports, many developed campsites (some fees). A forest map is available (fee).

Wenatchee Valley Museum & Cultural Center. *127 S Mission St, Wenatchee (98801). Phone 509/664-3340. www.wenatcheevalleymuseum.com.* This regional history museum includes a restored, operational 1919 Wurlitzer pipe organ; a Great Northern Railway model; a fine-art gallery; an apple industry exhibit; an exhibit on the first trans-Pacific flight (Japan to Wenatchee); and archaeological and Native American exhibits. (Tues-Sat 10 am-4 pm; closed holidays) **$**

Special Event

Washington State Apple Blossom Festival. *516 Washington St, Wenatchee (98801). Phone 509/662-3616. www.appleblossom.org.* Parades, carnival, arts and crafts, and musical productions; Ridge to River Relay. Last weekend in Apr-first weekend in May.

Limited-Service Hotels

★ ★ **BEST WESTERN CHIEFTAIN INN.** *1017 N Wenatchee Ave, Wenatchee (98801). Phone 509/665-8585; toll-free 800/937-8376; fax 509/665-8585. www.bestwestern.com.* 74 rooms. Complimentary continental breakfast. Check-in 3 pm, check-out noon. Restaurant, bar. Fitness room. Outdoor pool. Business center. **$**

★ ★ **RED LION.** *1225 N Wenatchee Ave, Wenatchee (98801). Phone 509/663-0711; toll-free 800/733-5466; fax 509/662-8175. www.redlion.com.* 149 rooms, 3 story. Pets accepted. Check-in 3 pm, check-out noon. High-speed Internet access. Restaurant, bar. Fitness room. Outdoor pool, whirlpool. Airport transportation available. **$**

Westport (C-1)

See also Aberdeen, Hoquiam, Ocean Shores

Settled 1858
Population 2,137
Elevation 12 ft
Area Code 360
Zip 98595
Information Westport-Grayland Chamber of Commerce, 2985 S Montesano St, 98595-0306; phone 360/268-9422 or toll-free 800/345-6223
Web site www.ci.westport.wa.us

Near the tip of a sandy strip of land separating Grays Harbor from the Pacific, Westport is home to probably the largest sports fishing fleet in the Northwest. Pleasure and charter boats take novice and experienced anglers alike across Grays Harbor Bay into the Pacific for salmon fishing in the summer and deep-sea fishing nearly all year. In the winter, commercial fleets set their pots for crab and have their catch processed at one of Westport's large canneries. Whale-watching excursions operate from March to May.

What to See and Do

Grays Harbor Lighthouse. *Ocean Ave, Westport.* (1898) At 107 feet, this is the tallest lighthouse on the West Coast.

Twin Harbors State Park. *420 State Hwy 105, Westport (98595). 3 miles S on Hwy 105. Phone 360/268-9717.*

www.parks.wa.gov. 172 acres. Surf fishing, clamming, bird- and whale-watching; hiking, picnicking, camping (hookups; reservations advised Memorial Day-Labor Day). Ocean swimming is permitted, but hazardous. (Daily; summer 6:30 am-10 pm, winter 8 am-5 pm)

Westport Aquarium. *321 E Harbor St, Westport (98595). Phone 360/268-0471.* This small aquarium has large tank aquariums and performing seals. (Feb-Oct: daily; Nov: weekends; closed holidays) **$$**

Westport Maritime Museum. *2201 Westhaven Dr, Westport (98595). Phone 360/268-0078. www.westportmuseum.org.* This museum complex features exhibits on the Coast Guard, shipwrecks and rescue operations, whales, and the area's cranberry and logging industries. The Children's Room has educational games and displays designed for elementary students. Also on the grounds are two Whale Houses, which exhibit sea mammal skeletons and other items, and the Lens Building, which contains a 100-year-old, 18-foot-high rotating lens with 1,176 glass prisms. (Memorial Day-Labor Day: daily 10 am-4 pm; rest of year: Thurs-Mon noon-4 pm) **$**

White Salmon (D-3)

See Hood River, OR

Winthrop (A-4)

See also Omak

Population 349
Elevation 1,760 ft
Area Code 509
Zip 98862
Information Chamber of Commerce, Information Office, 202 Hwy 20; phone 509/996-2125 or toll-free 888/463-8469
Web site www.winthropwashington.com

Redesigning the entire town on an Old West theme has transformed it into the "Old Western town of Winthrop," complete with annual events in the same vein.

Fifty-five miles west on the North Cascades Highway (Hwy 20) is North Cascades National Park. A Ranger District office of the Okanogan National Forest is located here.

What to See and Do

Shafer Museum. *285 Castle Ave, Winthrop (98862). Phone 509/996-2712. www.ghosttownsusa.com/shafer/ shafer.htm.* This log house built in 1897 by the town's founder, Guy Waring, has been redecorated as a turn-of-the-century pioneer home and includes early farming and mining implements from the nearby gold and silver mines. Also on-site are a schoolhouse, stagecoach, and early print shop. (Memorial Day-Labor Day, Thurs-Mon 10 am-5 pm) **FREE**

Limited-Service Hotel

★ **BEST WESTERN CASCADE INN.** *960 Hwy 20, Winthrop (98862). Phone 509/996-3100; toll-free 800/444-1972; fax 509/996-3317. www.bestwestern.com.* 30 rooms, 2 story. Pets accepted, some restrictions; fee. Check-out 11 am. Pool, whirlpool. **$**

Full-Service Resort

★ ★ ★ **SUN MOUNTAIN LODGE.** *Patterson Lake Rd, Winthrop (98862). Phone 509/996-2211; toll-free 800/572-0493; fax 509/996-3133. www. sunmountainlodge.com.* Whether carpeted in wildflowers or blanketed in snow, Sun Mountain Lodge is a perfect year-round destination. Active families take advantage of the endless opportunities for recreation on the resort's 3,000 acres, located east of Seattle. During the summer months, hiking, biking, and fly fishing are popular pursuits, while winter months draw cross-country skiers, ice skaters, and sleigh riders. Antler chandeliers, wood beams, and massive stone fireplaces lend a sense of place to the interiors, and the guest rooms and suites continue the rustic theme with regional decorative objects and handcrafted furnishings. Firmly rooted in mountain traditions, yet forward-thinking, Sun Mountain Lodge is far from backwoods, with impressive dining complete with a 5,000-bottle wine cellar and a full-service spa. 102 rooms, 3 story. Check-in 4 pm, check-out noon. Restaurant, bar. Children's activity center. Fitness room. Two pools, whirlpool. **$$**

Restaurant

★ ★ ★ **THE DINING ROOM.** *Patterson Lake Rd, Winthrop (98862). Phone 509/996-2211; fax 509/996-3133. www.sunmountainlodge.com.* A casual, rustic

setting overlooking towering snow-capped mountains is the backdrop for a hearty meal of fresh regional cuisine. The kitchen skillfully combines fish, seafood and meat with a local blend of herbs and vegetables that accentuate the natural flavors. American menu. Breakfast, lunch, dinner, brunch. Bar. Children's menu. **$$$**

Woodinville

Settled 1871
Population 9,194
Area Code 425
Zip 98072
Information Woodinville Chamber of Commerce, 17301 133rd Ave NE; phone 425/483-8100.
Web site www.ci.woodinville.wa.us/visitorguide.asp

Woodinville sits at the northern end of the Sammamish River Valley, a short drive northeast of Seattle on either Highway 522 or Interstate 405. Woodinville's main artery, NE 175th Avenue, cuts through a downtown area occupied by shops and restaurants, as well as small offices. South of downtown, in the Tourist District, highlights include two wineries, a brewery, and romantic accommodations and lodging at the Willows Lodge and its two restaurants, The Herbfarm and Barking Frog. Once a community of loggers, the city retains much of its Pacific Northwest woodland charm, though today its residents are much more likely to work at the nearby Microsoft headquarters than at a sawmill.

What to See and Do

Chateau Ste. Michelle. *14111 NE 145th St, Woodinville (98072). Phone 425/415-3632; toll-free 800/267-6793. www.ste-michelle.com.* Washington state's oldest winery offers free tours and tastings at its 87-acre estate. The winery's grapes are grown east of the Cascade Mountains in the sunny and dry Columbia Valley. Chateau Ste. Michelle utilizes two distinct winemaking operations, one devoted to white wines and the other focusing exclusively on reds. During the busy summer season, arrive early to avoid the post-lunch throng of wine aficionados. The winery welcomes 250,000 visitors annually. Premium tastings are available for a nominal fee. (Daily 10 am-5 pm; closed holidays) **FREE**

Columbia Winery. *14030 NE 145th St, Woodinville (98072). Phone 425/488-2776; toll-free 800/488-2347.*

www.columbiawinery.com. Columbia Winery's humble beginnings can be traced back to a garage in the Seattle neighborhood of Laurelhurst. It was in that garage in 1962 that the winery first began making wines. Founded by ten friends, the operation has grown steadily over the years, helping to launch Washington's wine industry, which now ranks behind only California in premium wine production. The winery's grapes are grown east of the Cascades, amid a climate of sunny days and cool nights in the Columbia and Yakima valleys of eastern Washington. On weekends, tours and tastings are available at the winery's Victorian-style manor in Woodinville. Group tours on weekdays are available by appointment. Retail shop (daily 10 am-7 pm). **FREE**

Molbak's. *13625 NE 175th St, Woodinville (98072). Phone 425/483-5000.* Each year more than a million green thumbs pay a visit to Molbak's, a garden shop located 20 miles northeast of Seattle. Egon and Laina Molbak emigrated from Denmark to Woodinville in 1956, purchasing a small greenhouse and becoming a wholesaler of cut flowers. Ten years later, the Molbaks expanded their business by opening a 700-square-foot retail shop. Their business has flourished ever since, and today Molbak's employs 200 people to oversee garden, gift, and floral shops, as well as a store selling Christmas items and patio furniture. (Sun-Fri 10 am-6 pm, Sat 9 am-9 pm)

Redhook Ale Brewery. *14300 NE 145thSt, Woodinville (98072). Phone 425/483-3232. www.redhook.com.* In the early 1980s, Paul Shipman and Gordon Bowker identified two market trends: import beers were becoming increasingly popular, and the Pacific Northwest held the nation's highest per capita draft beer consumption rate. The pair responded by founding the Redhook Brewing Company, producing their ale at a brewery in the Ballard area of Seattle. They sold their first pint in 1982. Sales took off with the 1984 release of Ballard Bitter, and Redhook grew to become one of the most successful microbreweries in the US. To keep pace with demand, a brewery was built in Woodinville, opening in 1994. Here, for a mere $1, visitors can tour the brewery, sample several of Redhook's eight ales, receive a free tasting glass, and learn about the company's history. After the tour, sidle up to the bar in the Forecasters Public House and partake in pub-style food and, of course, fresh Redhook ale. (Daily) **$**

Full-Service Hotel

★ ★ ★ **WILLOWS LODGE.** *14580 NE 145th St, Woodinville (98072). Phone 425/424-3900; toll-free 877/424-3930; fax 425/424-2585. www.willowslodge.com.* Bordering the Sammamish River in Washington's western wine country, The Willows Lodge is an exceptional getaway. Industrial chic meets Native American sensibilities at this former hunting lodge where guests rusticate in style. Stained concrete, slate, and sleek lines reveal a modern slant in the accommodations, while dynamic artwork crafted by Northwest Coast Native Americans showcases local pride. Luxuries are not lost on this country escape, where Frette linens and 300-thread-count bedding pamper guests. Lush, landscaped gardens complete with hidden courtyards create a veritable Eden, and the herb and edible plant gardens serve as the inspiration behind the excellent menus at The Herbfarm and Barking Frog restaurants (see). The resort's sanctuary-like atmosphere is enhanced by a full-service spa that offers a host of soothing and beautifying treatments. 86 rooms, 2 story. Pets accepted, some restrictions. Complimentary continental breakfast. Check-in 4 pm, check-out noon. Restaurant, bar. Fitness room, spa. Whirlpool. **$$$**

Restaurants

★ ★ ★ **BARKING FROG.** *14580 NE 145th St, Woodinville (98072). Phone 425/424-2999; fax 425/424-2585.* Located in the Willows Lodge (see). Northwestern menu. Lunch, dinner, brunch. Children's menu. Casual attire. Outdoor seating. **$$**

★ ★ ★ ★ **THE HERBFARM.** *14590 NE 145th St, Woodinville (98072). Phone 425/485-5300; fax 425/424-2925. www.theherbfarm.com.* Set in an enchanted old farmhouse on the Willows Lodge property (see), The Herbfarm Restaurant is a place where nature rules the dinner table. Each evening's gourmet nine-course menu is finalized only hours before the meal to best reflect the harvest of the season. (Dinner is served with five or six matched wines; nonalcoholic beverages and beers are available upon request.) But it's not just the last-minute nature of the menu that is impressive. The really wild and wonderful thing about The Herbfarm is that for most of the year, the harvest used for your dinner comes directly from The Herbfarm's own house-run gardens and farm, as well as from small, local growers and producers of

wild mushrooms, heritage fruits, handmade cheeses, and rare ingredients like water-grown wasabi root and artisanal caviars. This is a gourmet's dream. In the summer, bocce ball is played on the restaurant's grass court and a pre-dinner outdoor hosted garden tour (weather permitting) begins 30 minutes before service each evening. This unique and spectacular dining experience will stay with you well after you have licked your plates clean. *Secret Inspector's Notes: Be prepared: meals at The Herbfarm last an average of four hours, and the restaurant has relocated itself a significant distance from downtown Seattle.* Seasonal Pacific Northwest menu. Dinner. Closed Mon-Wed; holidays; one week in Feb or March. Casual attire. Reservations recommended. **$$$$**

Yakima (C-4)

See also Ellensburg, Toppenish

Settled 1861
Population 71,845
Elevation 1,068 ft
Area Code 509
Information Yakima Valley Visitors & Convention Bureau, 10 N 9th St, 98901; phone 509/248-2021
Web site www.yakima.org

Yakima (YAK-e-ma) County ranks first in the United States in production of apples, hops, sweet cherries, and winter pears. Irrigation was started as early as 1875, when early settlers dug crude canals. Orchards and farms replaced sagebrush and desert. The city takes its name from the Yakama Nation, whose reservation lies to the south. There are about 300 days of sunshine annually, with an average yearly rainfall of 8 inches.

What to See and Do

Ahtanum Mission. *9 miles SW on unnumbered roads.* Founded in 1852, destroyed by fire in the Yakama Native American Wars, and rebuilt in 1867, the Ahtanum Mission was the site of the oldest irrigated apple orchards in the valley (1872).

H. M. Gilbert Homeplace. *2109 W Yakima Ave, Yakima (98902). Phone 509/248-0747. www. yakimavalleymuseum.org.* This late Victorian farmhouse, a restored orchard home, features period furnishings. (Apr-Dec, by appointment) **$**

Historic North Front Street. Called "the birthplace of Yakima," this two-block section of downtown has restaurants and shopping.

Painted Rocks. *7 miles NW on Hwy 12.* Historic Yakima Nation pictographs.

White Pass Village. *55 miles NW on Hwy 12.* A ski area in Mount Baker-Snoqualmie National Forest. (See Mount Rainier National Park.)

Yakima Interurban Trolley Lines. *307 W Pine St, Yakima (98902). Phone 509/575-1700. www. yakimavalleytrolleys.com.* Trolley cars make trips around the city and the surrounding countryside on a historic railroad line. Board the trolley at the car barns at 3rd Avenue and W Pine Street. (Mid-May-mid-Oct, weekends at 10 am, noon, and 2 pm) **$**

Yakima Sportsman State Park. *904 Keys Rd, Yakima (98901). 3 miles E on Hwy 24. Phone 509/575-2774. www.parks.wa.gov.* Approximately 250 acres of "green zone" on the floodplain of the Yakima River. Bird-watching, fishing, picnicking, and camping (hookups; **$$$$**). (Summer: daily 6:30 am-10 pm; winter: daily 8 am-5 pm)

Yakima Valley Museum. *2105 Tieton Dr, Yakima (98902). In Franklin Park. Phone 509/248-0747. www. yakimavalleymuseum.org.* Exhibits relate to the history of Yakima Valley, the Yakima Nation, pioneer life, and the area's fruit industry. The museum's collection of horse-drawn vehicles is a highlight. Children's Underground is an area designed just for kids ages 5 to 15, with a working replica of a 1930s soda fountain built from salvaged and restored parts. The Great Hall hosts concerts throughout the year. (Tues-Sun 11 am-5 pm; closed holidays) **$**

Yakima Valley Wine Tours. *Phone toll-free 800/258-7270. www.yakimavalleywine.com.* The river-carved Yakima Valley, about 100 miles southeast of Seattle, has a climate that is nearly ideal for grape growing. The abundance of great wine is reminiscent of northern California's Napa Valley, as is the requisite armada of B&Bs, but Yakima Valley is not nearly as exclusive or expensive. Almost all of the wineries here offer free tours and tasting, and the area draws big crowds for such annual traditions as the Red Wine and Chocolate festival over President's Day weekend and Merlotfest in May.

Special Events

Central Washington State Fair and Rodeo. *Fairgrounds, Yakima. Phone 509/248-7160. www. fairfun.com.* Late Sept-early Oct.

Chocolate Fantasy. *Phone 509/575-6062.* Chocolate manufacturers from across the nation showcase candy, cookies, and pies. Visitors can sample the goodies and play "chocolate bingo." Mid-Mar.

Spring Barrel Tasting. *Various local wineries, Yakima. Phone toll-free 800/258-7270. www.yakimavalleywine .com/springbarrel.html.* Area wineries open their doors to visitors eager for a taste of the latest vintages. Last full weekend in Apr.

Yakima Meadows Racetrack. *Fairgrounds, Yakima. Phone 509/248-7160.* Thoroughbred racing. Pari-mutuel wagering.

Limited-Service Hotels

★ ★ **CLARION HOTEL.** *1507 N First St, Yakima (98901). Phone 509/248-7850; toll-free 800/252-7466; fax 509/576-4940. www.choicehotels.com.* This hotel is located near the city center, wineries, the Yakima Mall, Sundome, and Mount Rainier National Park. 208 rooms, 2 story. Pets accepted; fee. Check-out noon. Restaurant, bar. Fitness room. Two pools, whirlpool. **$**

★ **OXFORD INN YAKIMA.** *1603 E Yakima Ave, Yakima (98901). Phone 509/457-4444; fax 509/453-7593. www.oxfordsuites.com.* View of river. 96 rooms, 4 story. Complimentary continental breakfast. Check-out noon. Bar. Pool, whirlpool. **$**

★ ★ **RED LION.** *607 E Yakima Ave, Yakima (98901). Phone 509/248-5900; fax 509/575-8975. www. redlion.com.* 153 rooms, 2 story. Pets accepted; fee. Check-out noon. Restaurant, bar. Two pools. Airport transportation available. Business center. **$**

Restaurant

★ ★ **DELI DE PASTA.** *7 N Front St, Yakima (98901). Phone 509/453-0571.* Italian menu. Dinner. Closed Sun; holidays. **$$**

Alberta offers many activities for outdoor enthusiasts, as well as plenty of cultural activities and bustling nightlife. For a bit of English-flare, take a trip to Victoria "City of Gardens", British Columbia. Victoria also offers a thriving nightlife and arts scene. All of Vancouver's charms are just two-and-a-half hours from Seattle. Vancouver offers many art museums, boutiques, cafes, food markets—treats for just about everyone.

Vancouver, BC

2 hours 30 minutes, 140 miles from Seattle, WA

Settled 1886
Population 572,000
Elevation 38 ft (12 m)
Area Code 604
Information Tourism Vancouver—The Greater Vancouver Convention and Visitors Bureau, 200 Burrard St V6C 3L6; phone 604/682-2222
Web site www.tourismvancouver.com

Surrounded by the blue waters of the Strait of Georgia and backed by the mile-high peaks of the Coast Range, Vancouver enjoys a natural setting surpassed by few other cities on this continent. The waters that wash the city's shores protect it from heat and cold, making it a pleasant place to visit year-round.

Captain George Vancouver, searching these waters for the Northwest Passage, sailed into Burrard Inlet and landed here in 1792. Fur traders, gold prospectors, and other settlers soon followed. In 1886, Vancouver was incorporated as a city, only to be destroyed by fire several months later. The city was rebuilt by the end of that same year. In the next four years, rail transportation from the east, along with the traffic of sailing vessels of the Canadian Pacific fleet, assured its future growth. Today,

Vancouver is one of Canada's largest cities—a major seaport, cultural center, tourist spot, and gateway to Asia.

Vancouver's population is primarily English, but its large number of ethnic groups—including Germans, French, Scandinavians, Dutch, Chinese, and Japanese—give the city an international flavor. Tourism, logging, mineral extraction equipment, marine supplies, chemical and petroleum products, and machine tools are among the city's major industries.

Vancouver is on the Canadian mainland, not on Vancouver Island as some people think. The downtown area, which includes many of the points of interest which follow, is a "peninsula on a peninsula": it juts out from the rest of Vancouver into Burrard Inlet, making it an especially attractive spot with beaches and marinas within easy walking distance of the city's busy heart. To the north across Burrard Inlet is North Vancouver; to the south is the mouth of the Fraser River and the island municipality of Richmond; to the east is Burnaby, and beyond that, the Canadian mainland.

For border crossing regulations, see MAKING THE MOST OF YOUR TRIP.

Additional Visitor Information

There are many more interesting things to see and do in Vancouver and the suburbs of Burnaby and New Westminster to the east, Richmond to the south, North Vancouver, and West Vancouver. The Tourism Vancouver InfoCentre has pamphlets, maps, ferry schedules, and additional information at Plaza Level, Waterfront Centre, 200 Burrard St, V6C 3L6; phone 604/683-2000.

Public Transportation

TransLink Phone 604/953-3333, www.translink.bc.ca

Airport Vancouver International Airport (YVR). S of the city off Hwy 99.

Lost and Found Phone 604/276-6104, toll-free 866/817-5243

Airlines Aeromexico, Air Canada, Air China, Air New Zealand, Air North, Air Pacific, Air Transat, Alaska Airlines, Alitalia, All Nippon Airways, Aloha Airlines, America West, American Airlines, Amigo Airways, ATA, Baxter Aviation, Belair, Britannia Airways, British Airways, British Midland, Canadian Western Airlines, Cathay Pacific Airways, Central Mountain Air, Champion Air, China Air, Condor Fuugdienst, Continental Airlines, Delta Air Lines, Delta Connector, EVA Air, Edelweiss Air, El Al, Finnair, HMY Airways, Harbor Airlines, Horizon Air, Japan Airlines, Jetsgo, KLM Royal Dutch, Korean Air, Lignum Air, Lufthansa, Martinair, Mexicana, Northwest Airlines, Philippine Airlines, Qantas Airways, Quikair, Regency North Vancouver Air, Scandinavian Airlines (SAS), Singapore Airlines, Skywest Airlines, Skyservice Airlines, Thai Airlines, Thomas Cook Airlines, Tofino Air, United Airlines, Varig Airlines, WestJet, Western Express Airlines, Whistler Air Services, Zip, Zoom

What to See and Do

Arts Club Theatre Company. *1585 Johnston St, Vancouver (V6H 3R9). Phone 604/687-5315. www.artsclub.com.* Having helped launch the careers of actors Michael J. Fox and Brent Carver, The Arts Club Theatre steals the Vancouver stage spotlight. In addition to its four annual mainstage productions at Stanley Theatre (Granville and 12th), the company mounts four productions at the Granville Island Stage. Bills range from musicals like *My Fair Lady* to contemporary dramas such as *Burn This.* The Revue Stage, adjacent to the Granville, presents popular musicals and comedies, including the likes of *A Closer Walk with Patsy Cline.* **$$$$**

Ballet British Columbia. *677 Davie St, Vancouver (V6B 2G6). Phone 604/732-5003. www.balletbc.com.* With a strong company of 14 dancers, Ballet BC reigns as Vancouver's top dance troupe. Directed by John Alleyne, former dancer with the Stuttgart Ballet and the National Ballet of Canada, the company's repertoire includes dances by famed choreographers like William Forsythe and John Cranko as well as commissioned works by Canadian talents. Ballet BC's home stage is the Queen Elizabeth Theatre (Hamilton at Dunsmuir). (Nov-May) **$$$$**

Barbara Jo's Books to Cooks. *1128 Mainland St, Vancouver (V6B 2T4). Phone 604/688-6755. www.bookstocooks.com.* Books to Cooks incarnates owner Barbara Jo McIntosh's passion for both food and books. A former restaurateur and cookbook author with many credits, McIntosh runs the Yaletown shop as bookstore-cum-cooking school. Beyond the stacks, which include both new releases and out-of-print finds, a demonstration kitchen enables a staff cooking teacher and visiting authors to whip up their favorites. Regularly scheduled two-hour classes on topics from slow roasting to Chinese food require pre-registration. (Mon-Sat 10 am-6 pm, Sun 11:30 am-5 pm)

BC Lions (CFL). *777 Pacific Blvd, Vancouver (V6B 4Y8). Phone 604/589-7627. www.bclions.com.* The Canadian Football League's BC Lions, along with eight other CFL teams, contend for the season-winning Grey Cup. In contrast to American football, the Canadian game consists of only three downs per possession rather than four and takes place on a longer and wider field, which proponents say makes for more exciting, pass-driven games. Although the summer season may appeal to fair-weather fans, Vancouver's Lions play under the BC Place dome. (June-Nov)

Bites-On Salmon Charter. *200-1128 Hornby St, Vancouver (V6H 3S4). On Granville Island. Phone 604/688-2483. www.bites-on.com.* Coho, sockeye, and chinook salmon school in the waters around Vancouver, which is convenient for urban-bound fishing fans. Granville Island-based Bites-On offers day trips of five or eight hours, during which you can sink a line into the Strait of Georgia on a yacht up to 40 feet (12 meters) long. The charters serve parties of 1 to 12 people. Peak fishing months are April through October, although charters operate year-round. Boat trips also acquaint fishermen with the region's abundant sea lion, porpoise, and whale populations. (Daily) **$$$$**

British Columbia Ferry Corp. *1112 Fort St, Victoria (V8V 4V2). Phone 250/386-3432 (Victoria). www.bcferries.bc.ca.* Trips to Nanaimo (2 hours) or to Swartz Bay near Victoria (1 1/2 hours); both destinations are on Vancouver Island. Terminals at Horseshoe Bay, north of Vancouver via Trans-Canada Highway 1 and Tsawwassen near US border, south of Vancouver via Highways 99, 17. **$$$$**

Burnaby Village Museum. *6501 Deer Lake Ave, Vancouver (V5G 3T6). Phone 604/293-6500.* Living museum of the period before 1925 with costumed attendants; more than 30 full-scale buildings with displays and demonstrations. (Daily 11 am-4:30 pm; closed early Jan-early May) **$$$**

Capilano Suspension Bridge. *3735 Capilano Rd, Vancouver (V7R 4J1). Phone 604/985-7474. www.capbridge.com.* Want to get the kids to hold your hand again? Take them across the 400-foot-long (122 meters) Capilano Suspension Bridge strung some 230 feet (70 meters) above the Capilano River gorge. Originally constructed in 1889 and rebuilt in 1956, the wooden bridge is engineered of wire rope cemented at either end. In addition to the bridge, the surrounding park provides walking trails, gardens, a totem pole collection, and audiences with First Nations carvers at work. Arrive early in high season to best appreciate the thrill of the feat without the aggravation of the hordes. (Summer: daily 8:30 am-8 pm; spring-fall: daily 9 am-6 pm; winter: daily 9 am-5 pm; closed Dec 25) **$$$$**

The Centre in Vancouver for Performing Arts. *77 Homer St, Vancouver (V6B 2W1). Phone 604/602-0616. www.centreinvancouver.com.* Acclaimed Canadian architect Moshe Safdie designed the dramatic Centre in Vancouver with an arched glass facade and, punctuating the entry, a spiraling glass cone. Inside, polished marble floors and sweeping curved stairways heighten the pre-curtain lobby buzz. The auditorium seats 1,800, accommodating major Broadway tours including past productions of *Cabaret, Sunset Boulevard, The Phantom of the Opera, Joseph and the Amazing Technicolor Dreamcoat, Riverdance,* and *Ragtime.*

Chan Centre for the Performing Arts. *University of British Columbia, 6265 Crescent Rd, Vancouver (V6T 1Z1). Phone 604/822-9197. www.chancentre.com.* In the University of British Columbia district, the Chan houses three venues for theater and music, all sharing the same light-flooded lobby. Built in 1997, the distinctive zinc-clad cylindrical building stands out amid the verdant campus. With superior acoustics, this is one of the best spots in town to hear concerts by touring soloists, UBC musicians, and the Vancouver Symphony.

Chinatown. *E Pender and Gore sts, Vancouver.* This downtown area is the nucleus of the third-largest Chinese community in North America (only those in San Francisco and New York are larger). At the heart lies the Chinese Market where 100-year-old duck eggs may be purchased; herbalists promise cures with roots and powdered bones. The Dr. Sun Yat-Sen Classical Chinese Garden (see) provides a beautiful centerpiece. Chinese shops display a variety of items ranging from cricket cages to cloisonné vases. Offices of three Chinese newspapers and one of the world's narrowest buildings are located within the community's borders. Resplendent Asian atmosphere offers fine examples of Chinese architecture, restaurants, and nightclubs.

Dr. Sun-Yat-Sen Classical Chinese Garden. *578 Carrall St, Vancouver (V6B 5K2). Phone 604/662-3207. www.vancouverchinesegarden.com.* Unique to the Western Hemisphere, this garden was originally built in China circa 1492 and transplanted to Vancouver for Expo '86. (Daily) **$$**

CN IMAX Theatre. *201-999 Canada Pl, Vancouver (V6A 3Z7). Phone 604/682-2384. www.imax.com/vancouver.* Under the white sails that distinguish waterfront Canada Place, CN IMAX screens wide-format documentary films on subjects ranging from space travel to wildlife conservation. Several shows are screened throughout the day, with a new film starting approximately every hour. A food court and shops join the cinema at Vancouver's convention center. (Daily noon-10 pm) **$$$**

The Commodore Ballroom. *868 Granville St, Vancouver (V6Z 1K3). Phone 604/739-4550. www.hob .com/venues/concerts/commodore.* It's been swinging since the big band era, and the Commodore flaunts its age with brass chandeliers and polished wood stairs. A $3.5 million renovation in 1999 restored its elegance (and kept the spring-loaded dance floor) while modernizing its stage wizardry. US-based House of Blues now programs the acts that come through the ballroom, ranging primarily from rock to blues with a smattering of world talent. HOB also operates a kitchen on site, making food as well as drinks available.

Cypress Mountain. *Cypress Bowl and Hwy 1, Vancouver. 7 1/2 miles (12 kilometers) NW via Hwy 99, in Cypress Provincial Park. Phone 604/419-7669. www.cypressmountain.com.* Covering two mountains with 34 runs and five lifts, Cypress Mountain claims the region's biggest vertical drop at 1,750 feet (533 meters). But the ski area's bigger claim to fame is its cross-country skiing facilities, which span 12 miles (19 kilometers) of groomed trails, nearly five of which are lit for night gliding. The region's most popular Nordic destination also offers private and group lessons as well as rental equipment. Snowshoers can tramp on designated trails solo or take a guided tour. (Winter: daily 9 am-10 pm) **$$$$**

Dubrulle International Culinary & Hotel Institute of Canada. *1522 W 8th St, Vancouver (V6J 4R8). Phone 604/738-3155; toll-free 800/667-7288. www.homechef .ca.* Graduates of Canada's largest private cooking school have gone on to work worldwide and at home, opening top-notch local restaurants like Lumiere (see). For keen locals and visitors, its "serious amateur" division offers evening and weekend training that ranges from stock prep to knife skills, Indian bread-making to do-it-yourself pasta. With a maximum enrollment of 16, courses are hands-on in a professional kitchen, capped by dining on the meal prepared in the prior three hours. (Call for class schedules) **$$$$**

Ecomarine Ocean Kayak Centre. *1668 Duranleau St, Vancouver (V6H 354). On Granville Island. Phone 604/689-7575. www.ecomarine.com.* To get the full impact of Vancouver's magnificent setting on the coast, troll the waterways under paddle power with a kayak from Ecomarine. The outfitter rents both single and double kayaks at its Granville Island headquarters and at an outpost on Jericho Beach (Jericho Sailing Center, 1300 Discovery St), where first-timers can take a three-hour lesson before getting started. Navigate from placid False Creek to more rugged inlets up the shore. (Sept-May: daily 10 am-6 pm; June-Aug: Sun-Wed 9 am-6 pm, Thurs-Sat 9 am-9 pm; closed Jan 1, Dec 25) **$$$$**

Exhibition Park. *2901 E Hastings St, Vancouver (V5K 5J1). Between Renfrew and Cassiar sts. Phone 604/253-2311.* Approximately 165 acres (70 hectares). Concert, convention, entertainment facilities. Thoroughbred racing (late spring-early fall) and Playland Amusement Park (Apr-June: weekends; July-Oct: daily; also evenings).

Gallery at Ceperley House. *6344 Deer Lake Ave, Vancouver (V5G 2J3). Phone 604/205-7332.* Monthly exhibitions of local, national, and international artists. Collection of contemporary Canadian works on paper. Housed in Ceperley Mansion, overlooking Deer Lake and the surrounding gardens. (Tues-Fri 10 am-4:30 pm, to 8 pm first Thurs of month; Sat-Sun noon-5 pm; closed Mon) **DONATION**

⭐ **Gastown.** *Roughly bounded by Burrard Inlet on the N, Dunsmuir St on the S, Carrall St to the E, and Richards St to the W. Phone 604/683-5650. www. gastown.org.* So gabby was the Brit-born barman Jack

Discovering Downtown Vancouver

Vancouver is one of the most cosmopolitan cities in the world, and part of its considerable charm is the wonderful mix of people from all around the globe. Downtown Vancouver remains very dynamic, and a wander through the people-thronged streets is a great way to catch the energy of this city. Start at the Vancouver Art Gallery, which is the old City Hall. Walk up Robson Street, the city's primary boutique street, lined with all sorts of tiny shops, cafés, galleries, and food markets: this is a very busy place, and you'll hear dozens of languages in the bustle of the crowds. Grab a table at a coffee shop, and watch the world—literally—go by. Continue to Denman Street, and turn south (left). Denman is another busy commercial street, but less international. Here you'll find remnants of aging hippie Vancouver-bookstores, veggie restaurants,

and little corner markets—rubbing shoulders with upscale 20-something cocktail bars and tattoo parlors for middle-class teenagers. Denman terminates at English Beach, where you can relax on the sand and enjoy the views of Vancouver's West Side across English Bay. Follow the seawall west (right) and, after a couple of blocks, enter Stanley Park, Vancouver's fantastic 1,000-acre (405-hectare) park filled with old-growth forests, winding paths, and a number of tourist destinations. Of these, Vancouver Aquarium, reached by a forest path from the southern part of the park, is a must-see. One of the best in North America, it features performing orcas and porpoises, as well as ecosystem tanks from waters around the world. Nearby is Vancouver's small zoo, mostly of interest to children; stop and watch the sea otters play.

Deighton that patrons of his shoreside 1867 saloon called him Gassy. Thus, when the city started to grow around the joint south of the Burrard Inlet, the district came to be known as "Gassy's Town," hence "Gastown." Vancouver's historic nucleus consists of a series of Victorian buildings rehabbed to shelter an array of shops, clubs, and eateries. Among the highlights, the Gastown Steam Clock pipes up every 15 minutes and the Vancouver Police Centennial Museum covers the most notorious local crimes. To fully appreciate the neighborhood, show up for a free tour sponsored by the Gastown Business Improvement Society in Maple Tree Square at 2 pm daily in summer. **FREE** Adjacent is

Harbour Centre-The Lookout. *555 W Hastings St, Vancouver (V6B 4N4).* Phone 604/689-0421. Glass elevators take you to a 360° viewing deck 553 feet (167 meters) above street level; multimedia presentation, historical displays, tour guides. (Daily; closed Dec 25) **$$$**

Gordon Southam Observatory. *Phone 604/738-7827.* Fri-Sat evenings and holidays, weather permitting **FREE**

⭐ **Granville Island.** *1661 Duranleau St, 2nd Fl, Vancouver (V6H 3S3).* A 37-acre (15-hectare) area

in the heart of the city, beneath the S end of Granville Bridge. Phone 604/666-5784. www.granvilleisland.bc.ca. A former industrial isle, Granville Island is an urban renewal case study, fashioning markets, shops, homes, and entertainment out of decaying wharf warehouses beginning in the 1970s. Its hub is the Public Market, a prime picnic provisioner teeming with fishmongers, produce vendors, butchers, cheese shops, bakeries, and chef demonstrations. A specialized Kid's Market and a free outdoor Water Park (May-Sept) appeal to children. The Maritime Market on the southwest shore serves as a dock for boat owners as well as those looking to hire a fishing charter, hop on a ferry, or rent a kayak. Three Granville Island museums showcase miniature trains, ship models, and sport fishing. Dozens of bars and restaurants, many with views back across the water to the downtown skyline, drive the after-dark trade. An art school, artists' studios, and several galleries lend bohemian flare to the Granville, abetted by several theaters and a panoply of street musicians. (Daily) **FREE**

Granville Island Kids Market. *1465 Cartwright St, Vancouver (V6A 2S4). Phone 604/689-8447. www. kidsmarket.ca.* Vancouver's open food market turns its third floor into something kids can enjoy—beyond pastries on the market floor, that is. Twenty-five children's shops, including eight selling toys and another seven selling clothes, take aim at junior consumers, many of whom, of course, prefer Kids Market's indoor play area. Strolling clowns and face-painters amplify the carnival-like setting. (Daily 10 am-6 pm) **FREE**

Gray Line sightseeing tours. *Phone 604/879-3363. www.grayline.ca/vancouver.* Pickup at all major Vancouver hotels; call for reservations.

Great Canadian Casino. *Holiday Inn Vancouver-Centre, 711 W Broadway, Vancouver (V6Z 3Y2). Phone 604/303-1000. www.greatcanadiancasino.com.* The Great Canadian Casino runs the two major gambling dens in town, one in the downtown financial district at the Renaissance Vancouver (1133 W Hastings) and the other on the south shore of False Creek, Holiday Inn Vancouver-Centre (711 W Broadway). Roulette and blackjack join many games popular in the Asian community, such as baccarat and pai gow poker, on the gaming floors (note that there are no slot machines at either casino). Dress is casual, and the minimum gambling age in Canada is 19. (Daily 10 am-4 pm) **FREE**

Greater Vancouver Zoo. *5048-264th St, Aldergrove (V4W 1N7). Phone 604/856-6825. www.greater vancouverzoo.com.* Explore 120 acres housing more than 700 animals. Miniature train ride; bus tour of North American Wild exhibit. (Apr-Sept: daily 9:30 am-7 pm; Oct-Mar: daily 9:30 am-4 pm; closed Dec 25) **$$$**

Grouse Mountain. *6400 Nancy Greene Way, Vancouver (V7R 4K9). Phone 604/984-0661. www.grousemountain .com.* For skiing in winter, hiking in summer, and sightseeing year-round, Grouse Mountain draws legions of visitors to Vancouver's North Shore. The area's first ski mountain is still its most convenient, with ski and snowboard runs that overlook the metropolis, as well as a skating rink and sleigh rides available. Hikers have loads of trails to choose from, but the one to boast about is the Grouse Grind, a 1.8-mile (2.9 kilometers) hike straight up the 3,700-foot (1128 meter) peak, thus accounting for the "grind" ("grouse" is for "bird," not "complaint"). Look for mountain bike trails on the backside of the slopes. The Skyride gondola takes the easy route up in an eight-minute ride. At the top, seasonless attractions include Theater in the Sky, a high-definition aerial film, and several panoramic-view restaurants starring

the Strait of Georgia and the twinkling lights of Vancouver. (Daily 10 am-10 pm) **$$$$**

Harbour Cruises Ltd. *Departures from northern foot of Denman St. Phone 604/688-7246 (schedule and fees). www.boatcruises.com.* Boat/train excursion (6 1/2 hours); also sunset dinner cruises; harbor tours, private charters. (May-Sept)

Hastings Park Racecourse. *Renfrew and Dundas sts, Vancouver (V5K 3N8). Phone toll-free 800/677-7702. www.hastingspark.com.* Thoroughbreds run in Vancouver at Hastings Park on the city's east side. Although the lengthy racing season runs late Apr-Nov, most races are held on Saturday and Sunday, with extra meets scheduled for major holidays like Canada Day and Labor Day. Two-dollar-bet minimums encourage cheap dates, while self-service betting terminals patiently acquaint you with the track lingo. **$$**

HR MacMillan Space Centre. *1100 Chestnut St, Vancouver (V6J 3J9). Phone 604/738-7827. www. hrmacmillanspacecentre.com.* One of several museums in Vanier Park tucked between Kitsilano Beach and Granville Island, the MacMillan Space Centre appeals to would-be astronauts with a space flight simulator, planetarium, and interactive games. After hours, laser light shows depart from the scientific and delve into the psychedelic, dramatizing music by the likes of Pink Floyd and Led Zeppelin. (Tues-Sun 10 am-5 pm) **$$$**

Inuit Gallery of Vancouver. *206-220 Cambie St, Vancouver (V6B 2M9). Phone 604/688-7323. www. inuit.com.* From the moment you enter the gallery, Inuit immerses you in the rich artistic tradition of coastal natives with soapstone sculptures, native prints, ceremonial masks, and bentwood boxes. One of Vancouver's best sources for First Peoples art, Inuit represents tribes up and down the Pacific Northwest. Because many of its pieces are large, including totem poles, the gallery ships worldwide. In the Gastown district, Inuit is a short walk from the convention center and cruise ship terminal. (Mon-Sat 10 am-6 pm, Sun 11 am-5 pm; closed Jan 1, Dec 25)

Irving House Historic Centre. *302 Royal Ave, New Westminster (V3L 1H7). Phone 604/527-4640.* (1864) Fourteen rooms of period furniture from 1864-1890. Adjacent is the New Westminster Museum, on the back of the property, which has displays on local history, household goods, and May Day memorabilia. (May-mid-Sept: Tues-Sun; rest of year: Sat-Sun; closed Jan 1, Dec 25-26) **DONATION**

The Marine Building. *355 Burrard St, Vancouver (V6C 2G8).* Vancouver's Art Deco gem, the ornate 25-story Marine Building was the tallest building in the British Empire when it was completed in 1929. But if the icon brought the international Deco style home to Canada, it also uniquely hailed the region. Exterior terra-cotta reliefs pay homage to the city's marine heritage in images of starfish, crabs, seashells, and snails as well as sail- and steam-powered boats. The office building's lobby continues the motif in ornate coffered ceilings.

Metrotown Centre. *4700 Kingsway, Burnaby (V5H 4M1). Between Boundary Rd and Royal Oak. Phone 604/430-0501. www.metropolisatmetrotown .com.* Three connected shopping centers make up Metrotown, BC's largest shopping center, counting nearly 500 shops in the near suburb of Burnaby. Among its tenants are well-known chains like menswear's Massimo, clothier Roots, outdoor outfitter Coast Mountain Sports, and Chapters bookstore. Several video game arcades and dozens of movie screens provide entertainment. (Mon-Fri 10 am-9 pm, Sat 9:30 am-6 pm, Sun 11 am-6 pm)

Murchie's Tea. *970 Robson St, Vancouver (V6Z 2E7). Phone 604/669-0783. www.murchies.com.* Gourmet coffee and high-grade tea are Murchie's considerable claims to fame. At it since 1894, the company blends its own offerings with the care and sophistication normally associated with winemakers. In addition to the Robson Street shop, Murchie's operates five other stores in BC, as well as a mail-order business. Whether you're a fan of the drinks or not, the atmospheric shop makes it fun to peruse tea blends from Sri Lanka and Costa Rican Arabica whole beans. (Mon-Wed 6 am-6:30 pm, Thurs-Fri 9 am-7 pm, Sat 9 am-6 pm, Sun 10 am-6 pm; closed Jan 1, Dec 25)

Oakridge Shopping Centre. *650 W 41st Ave, Vancouver (V5Z 2M9). Phone 604/261-2511. oakridge.shopping.ca.* With 150 shops and services, a children's play area, movie theaters, and a walking club, Oakridge serves its community with more than just sales. One of the city's original malls, built in 1959, Oakridge has grown to house magnet tenants such as The Bay

department store, Eddie Bauer, Banana Republic, French Connection, MAC, MaxMara, and Swarovski. (Mon-Wed 6 am-6:30 pm, Thurs-Fri 9 am-7 pm, Sat 9 am-6 pm, Sun 10 am-6 pm; closed Jan 1, Dec 25)

Old Hastings Mill. *1575 Alma Rd, Vancouver (V6R 3P3). Phone 604/734-1212.* (Circa 1865) One of the few buildings remaining after the fire of 1886, it now houses indigenous artifacts and memorabilia of Vancouver's first settlers. (June-mid-Sept: daily; rest of year: Sat and Sun afternoons) **FREE**

Pacific Centre. *550-700 W Georgia St, Vancouver (V7Y 1A1). Phone 604/688-7236. www.pacificretail.ca.* Downtown Vancouver's major shopping destination, the three-block-long Pacific Centre runs a shopping arcade underground between Granville and Howe streets from Robson to Pender streets. National and international mid-range and upscale clothiers, including the Gap, Club Monaco, and Canada's trendsetter Holt Renfrew, dominate the tenant types. Its central locale makes it an easy pedestrian destination from many major hotels. (Mon-Wed 9:30 am-7 pm, Thurs-Fri to 9 pm, Sat to 6 pm, Sun noon-6 pm; closed Jan 1, Dec 25)

Pacific Institute of Culinary Arts. *1505 W 2nd Ave, Vancouver (V6H 3Y4). Phone 604/734-4488. www. picularts.bc.ca.* In addition to offering culinary and baking degrees to professionals-in-training, the Pacific Institute customizes instruction for individuals and groups in evening and weekend sessions. Course topics are determined by arrangement with a staff chef and may include specialty sessions like cake decorating or the preparation of an entire gourmet meal. Full-time advanced students also staff the on-site restaurant and bakeshop serving lunch, tea, and dinner to the public. (Restaurant Mon-Fri 11 am-2 pm, 3-5 pm, 6-9 pm; Sat 6-9 pm; Bakeshop Mon-Fri 9 am-9 pm, Sat from noon)

Park Royal Shopping Centre. *2002 Park Royal S, West Vancouver (V7T 2W4). At the N end of the Lions Gate Bridge at Taylor Way and Marine Dr. Phone 604/925-9576. www.shopparkroyal.com.* A short hop over the Lion Gate Bridge lands shoppers at the Park Royal Shopping Centre, which reflects the affluence of the West Vancouver community in fashionable shops. Anchor department store The Bay joins other big-box retailers such as Linens 'n Things, along with an interesting selection of specialty stores, including

Aveda, Roots, the Disney Store, and Guess. (Mon-Wed 10 am-6 pm, Thurs-Fri to 9 pm, Sat 9:30 am-5:30 pm, Sun noon-6 pm; closed Jan 1, Dec 25)

Queen Elizabeth Park. *Cambie St and W 33rd Ave, Vancouver. Phone 604/257-8570 (recording).* Observation point affords a view of the city, harbor, and mountains; Bloedel Conservatory has more than 100 free-flying birds, plus tropical, desert, and seasonal displays. (Daily; closed Dec 25) **$$**

Queen Elizabeth Theatre and Playhouse and Orpheum Theatre. *Hamilton at Dunsmuir, Vancouver. Phone 604/683-2000.* A symphony orchestra, opera company, and many theater groups present productions around town, especially at the Queen Elizabeth Theatre and Playhouse and Orpheum Theatre. Consult the local paper for details.

Robson Street. *Robson Street Business Association, 412-1155 Robson St, Vancouver (V6E 1B5). www.robsonstreet.ca.* The epicenter of Vancouver's street chic, Robson makes a nice window-shopping stroll. A string of shops and sidewalk cafés runs several blocks in either direction from the intersection of Robson and Burrard streets. Retailers range from the tony Giorgio Armani and Salvatore Ferragamo to the playful Benetton on down to the bovine-mad T-shirt shop Cows. Jewelry stores, chocolatiers, and craft galleries round out the offerings.

Royal City Star Riverboat Casino. *788 Quayside Dr, New Westminster (V3M 6Z6). Docked on the Fraser River in downtown New Westminster, SW of Vancouver. Phone 604/519-3660. www.royalcitystar.bc.ca.* The late-model paddlewheeler *Queen of New Orleans*, once stationed on the Mississippi, now calls the Fraser River its home port as the Royal City Star. On-board games of chance include pai gow poker, mini baccarat, blackjack, roulette, and Caribbean stud poker. Several bars, a deli, and a restaurant feed and water patrons. Between May and October, the boat schedules regular sailings. (Daily 10-4 am) **FREE**

Samson V Maritime Museum. *New Westminster. Moored on the Fraser River at the Westminster Quay Market in New Westminster, 12 miles (19 kilometers) S via Hwy 1A. Phone 604/522-6891.* The last steam-powered paddlewheeler to operate on the Fraser River now functions as a floating museum. Displays focus on the various paddlewheelers and paddlewheeler captains that have worked the river, and on river-

related activities. (May-June: Sat-Sun, holidays; July-Labor Day: daily; Labor Day-mid-Oct: Sat-Sun, holidays)

Science World British Columbia. *1455 Quebec St, Vancouver (V6A 3Z7). Phone 604/443-7443. www.scienceworld.bc.ca.* The massive golf ball-shaped Science World attracts both architecture and museum fans. Modeled on the geodesic domes of F. Buckminster Fuller, the aluminum ball was erected for Expo '86 and now houses a science center devoted to interactive exhibits on nature, invention, ecology, and optical illusions. A play space with a water table and giant building blocks engages the 3-to-6 set, while the dome-projection Omnimax theater entertains the whole brood. (Mon-Fri 10 am-5 pm, Sat-Sun to 6 pm) **$$$**

SeaBus Harbour Ride. *13401 18th Ave, Vancouver. Operates between Waterfront Station and Lonsdale Quay, across Burrard Inlet. Phone 604/953-3333.* Makes 15-minute crossing on twin-hulled catamaran vessels every 15 minutes (30 minutes evenings and Sun). Part of regional public transit system. **$$**

Seymour Ski Country. *1700 Mount Seymour Rd, Vancouver (V7J 2L8). 9 miles (15 kilometers) NE off Mount Seymour Pkwy, in Mount Seymour Provincial Park. Phone 604/736-4431.* Three double chairlifts, rope tow; night skiing; patrol, school, rentals; cafeteria. (Mid-Nov-Apr, daily) Cross-country and snowshoe trails (Dec-Mar, daily). Chairlift also operates July-Aug (daily). Mount Seymour Provincial Park is a large semiwilderness with scenic roadside viewpoints overlooking Vancouver; picnic areas; hiking, self-guided interpretive trails. Park (all year, daily). **$$$$**

Shaughnessy. *Between 16th and 41st aves, W of Granville St.* Originally developed by the Canadian Pacific Railway in 1907 for Vancouverites in search of urban escape, the elite Shaughnessy neighborhood housed (and still houses) the city's well-to-do in mansions of Tudor and colonial styles, among others. A prime neighborhood for biking or strolling, Shaughnessy's quiet streets are curved, its lots large, its homes impressive, and its gardens lush.

Simon Fraser University. *Gaglardi Way and University Dr W, Burnaby. 10 miles (16 kilometers) E off Hwy 7A (Hastings St). Phone 604/291-3210.* (1965) (20,000 students.) Located on Burnaby Mountain; architecturally outstanding buildings. Original campus was completed in only 18 months. Hourly guided tours (July-Aug, daily; free)

Sinclair Centre. *757 W Hastings St, Vancouver (V6C 1A1). Phone 604/666-4438. www.sinclaircentre.com.* This one-square-block mall cobbles together four restored Victorian-era buildings into a shopping center with personality. Centered around a glass-topped atrium, the multilevel Sinclair preserves the limestone walls and archways of the original buildings retrofitted with contemporary retailers. Designer boutiques like Plaza Escada, Leone, and clothier A'Wear join several restaurants, including Morton's of Chicago, among the top shops. (Mon-Fri 9:30 am-6 pm, Sat to 5:30 pm, Sun noon-5 pm; closed Jan 1, Dec 25)

Spokes Bicycle Rentals. *1789 W Georgia St, Vancouver (V6G 2V7). Phone 604/688-5141. www. vancouverbikerental.com.* For bike rides along the Stanley Park seawall and interior trails, Spokes couldn't be better located. Just across from the park entrance on Georgia Street, the cycle shop rents from a vast fleet that includes cruisers, tandems, mountain bikes, and hybrid models. Spokes also offers bike tours of the Stanley Park perimeter (1 1/2 hours) and Granville Island (3 1/2 hours). (Daily) **$$$**

⭐ **Stanley Park.** *2099 Beach Ave, Vancouver (V6G 3E2). A peninsula between English Bay and Burrard Inlet at the foot of W George St. Phone 604/257-8400. www.seestanleypark.com.* One thousand acres of native British Columbia in the heart of the city, Stanley Park, the largest city park in Canada, is a green haven with few peers. Towering forests of cedar, hemlock, and fir spill onto sand beaches, immersing visitors and residents alike in the wild just minutes from the civilized. Come shod to explore. Park-goers recreate along forest hiking trails, on three beaches, and along the 5.5-mile (8.9-kilometers) 1920s vintage seawall, where in-line skaters, runners, and cyclists admire skyline and ocean views. Man's hand distinguishes the park in gardens devoted to roses and rhododendrons and in a vivid stand of First Nations totem poles. Providing an appeal for every interest, Stanley Park also hosts the Vancouver Aquarium (see), Children's Farmyard, Miniature Railway, Theatre Under the Stars, and several worth-the-trip restaurants. (May-mid-Oct)

Vancouver Aquarium Marine Science Centre. *845 Avison Way, Stanley Park, Vancouver (V6B 3X8). Phone 604/659-3474. www.vanaqua.org.* With inviting, hands-on exhibits, Vancouver Aquarium in sylvan Stanley Park explores the undersea world from Amazon to Arctic, assembling 300 species of fish, their invertebrate tank mates (sea stars, jellyfish, and octopuses), and food-chain-higher-ups (sea mammals). For all its globetrotting interests, the aquarium is a top spot to study the local environment as well. In outdoor pools, graceful beluga whales, frisky sea lions, and playful otters prove comfortable with the changeable Pacific Northwest climate (private encounters with the belugas and dolphins run $125 to $175 per parent/child pair). Progeny of salmon released by the aquarium in 1998 from a park river return each winter, roughly November to February, illustrating BC's rich salmon spawning waterways. Behind-the-scenes tours with trainers (an extra $15 to $20) provide visitors a glimpse of the marine mammal rescue and rehab program for which the aquarium is lauded. (Sept-June: daily 10 am-5:30 pm; July-Aug: daily 9:30 am-7 pm) **$$$$**

University of British Columbia. *2329 West Mall, Vancouver (V6T 1Z4). 8 miles (13 kilometers) SW via Burrard St, 4th Ave. Phone 604/822-2211. www.ubc.com.* (1915) (34,869 students) The 990-acre (401-hectare) campus features museums, galleries (some fees), many spectacular gardens; almost 400 buildings complement the natural grandeur of the area. Free guided campus tours (May-Aug). Beautifully situated on scenic Point Grey. Includes

Frederic Wood Theatre. *6354 Crescent Rd, Vancouver (V6T 1Z2). Phone 604/822-2678.* Summer stock and winter mainstage productions.

Museum of Anthropology at the University of British Columbia. *6393 NW Marine Dr, Vancouver (V6T 1Z2). Phone 604/822-3825 (recording). www. moa.ubc.ca.* Built to reference a First Nations longhouse, the glass and concrete Museum of Anthropology makes a fitting shrine for the art and artifacts of West Coast natives. The Great Hall surrounds visitors in immense totem poles, canoes, and feast dishes of the Kwakwaka'wakw, Nisga'a, Gitksan, and Haida peoples, among others. An outdoor sculpture garden sets tribal houses and totem poles, many carved by the best known contemporary artists, against a backdrop of sea and mountain views. In its mission to explore all the cultures of the world, the Anthro also catalogs 600 ceramics works from 15th- to 19th-century Europe. (Winter: Wed-Sun 11 am-5 pm, Tues to

9 pm; Summer: daily 10 am-5 pm, Tues to 9 pm; closed Mon in winter) **$$**

UBC Botanical Garden. *6804 SW Marine Dr, Vancouver (V6T 1Z4). Phone 604/822-3928. www.ubcbotanicalgarden.org.* Seven separate areas include Asian, Physick, BC Native, Alpine, and Food gardens. (Daily; closed Jan 1, Dec 25) Nitobe Garden, authentic Japanese tea garden located behind Asian Centre (mid-Mar-early Oct: daily; rest of year: Mon-Fri). **$$**

Vancouver Art Gallery. *750 Hornby St, Vancouver (V6Z 2H7). Phone 604/662-4700. www.vanartgallery.bc.ca.* Most visitors bound up to the Vancouver Art Gallery's fourth floor for a look at the largest collection of works by British Columbia's best known painter, Emily Carr. But the other galleries in western Canada's largest art museum, housed in an early 20th-century courthouse, warrant a poke around; subjects range from Group of Seven landscapes to photography and conceptual art. A cozy café, sculpture garden, and intriguing museum shop bid you to linger a bit longer. (Daily 10 am-5:30 pm, Thurs to 9 pm; closed Mon in winter) **$$$**

Vancouver Canadians. *Nat Bailey Stadium in Queen Ellizabeth Park, 4601 Ontario St, Vancouver (V5V 2H4). Phone 604/872-5232. www.canadiansbaseball.com.* In the 76-game short season, the single-A Minor League Baseball Canadians compete in the Northwest League. Most games start at 7 pm in order to draw the after-work crowd, although "nooners," or weekday afternoon starts, make popular ex-office outings. Team talent is often secondary to fans who come out for the low ticket prices, comic stadium antics, and park setting. The University of British Columbia's baseball team calls Nat Bailey its home field as well. (Mid-June-early Sept)

Vancouver Canucks (NHL). *800 Griffiths Way, Vancouver (V6B 6G1). Phone 604/820-4400. www.canucks.com.* Canada's love of hockey comes alive in black and blue at rowdy Vancouver Canucks matches, where joining the beer-fueled fans may be as close as you can get to feeling like a local. The National Hockey League franchise came to town in the mid-1970s, launching an industry of boosters and media wags. Having won the Stanley Cup in 1995, the Canucks are perennially in the hunt for the sport's top prize. (Sept-Apr)

Vancouver Giants. *Pacific Colosseum, 100 North Renfrew St, Vancouver (V5K 3N7). Phone 604/444-2687. www.vancouvergiants.com.* As training grounds for National Hockey League hopefuls, the Western Hockey League vets young players, ages 15 to 20, in a hardscrabble league cheered on largely by the friends and families of players. The Giants, Vancouver's local boys new to the WHL in 2001, play 36 games at home at Pacific Colosseum (Hastings and Renfrew) and another 36 on the road against a 19-team field. (Sept-Mar)

Vancouver Griffins. *1st and 3rd aves, New Westminster. Phone 604/669-3169. www.vancouvergriffins.com.* One of the newest members of the National Women's Hockey League (NWHL), the Vancouver Griffins compete against nine other Canadian women's pro teams. Olympic silver medalist, five-time world champion, and seven-time national champion Nancy Drolet leads the Griffins on the ice in the 3,500-seat Queens Park Arena. Hockey is popular enough in the region that the Griffins often join the NHL Canucks, or at least their mascot, in promotional appearances. (Oct-Mar)

Vancouver Maritime Museum. *1905 Ogden Ave, Vancouver (V6J 3J9). Phone 604/257-8300. www.vmm.bc.ca.* Built around the *St. Roch*, the first ship to navigate Canada's Inside Passage from west to east, Vanier Park's Maritime Museum lets seafaring fans explore the 1928 supply ship from wheelhouse to captain's quarters. In addition to the series of historic model ships housed inside the museum, several historic craft are tethered outside its waterfront Heritage Harbour, including two tugs, a rescue boat, and the 1927 seiner once featured on Canada's $5 bill. (Daily 10 am-5 pm; winter Tues-Sat 10 am-5 pm, Sun from noon) **$$**

Vancouver Museum. *1100 Chestnut St, Vancouver (V6J 3J9). 1 1/2 miles (2 1/2 kilometers) SW via Burrard, Cypress sts. Phone 604/736-4431. www.vanmuseum.bc.ca.* Keeper of city history, and another Vanier Park attraction, Vancouver Museum takes a sweeping view of civilization, collecting everything from Egyptian mummies to local vintage swimming togs. In addition to the urban story, told in lifelike re-creations of an Edwardian parlor, ship's berth, and trading post, the museum examines First Nations artifacts, the contributions of Asian Rim cultures, and world history. (Tues-Wed, Fri-Sun 10 am-5 pm, Thurs to 9 pm; closed Mon) **$$$**

Vancouver Opera. *500-845 Cambie St, Vancouver (V6B 4Z9). Phone 604/683-0222. www.vanopera.bc.ca.* From the frolic of Mozart's "Figaro! Figaro! Figaro!" to the passion of Carmen, Vancouver Opera stages four productions annually. Established in 1958, the company has hosted a roster of greats, including guest singers Placido Domingo, Joan Sutherland, and Marilyn Horne. Performances take place at the Queen Elizabeth Theatre (Hamilton at Dunsmuir) with subtitles projected above the stage. (Oct-May, Tues, Thurs, Sat 8 pm) **$$$$**

Vancouver Police Centennial Museum. *240 E Cordova St, Vancouver (V6A 1L3). Phone 604/665-3346. www.city.vancouver.bc.va/police/museum.* For fans of the macabre, the Vancouver Police Centennial Museum in Gastown not only supplies the gruesome details of the city's most lurid crimes (such as bodies found in Stanley Park and the man who tried to murder his wife with arsenic-laced milkshakes) but also dramatizes them crime-scene style. Run by the city's police department, the museum tells the history of local law-keeping and ushers visitors into an eerie mock-forensics lab in the former city morgue. (Mon-Fri 9 am-3 pm, also Sat from 10 am May-Aug; closed holidays) **$$**

Vancouver Ravens. *800 Griffiths Way, Vancouver (V6B 6G1). Phone 604/899-5300. www.vancouverravens.com.* Vancouver's entry in the National Lacrosse League, the Ravens play a spirited four-month schedule at the indoor General Motors Place. The town's newest professional team, the Ravens franchise got the green light with the 2001/2002 season, competing in the Northern division against Toronto, Calgary, and Ottawa. Eight more US teams vie in the Eastern and Central divisions. (Dec-Apr)

Vancouver Symphony Orchestra. *601 Smithe St, Vancouver (V6B 5G1). Phone 604/684-9100. www.vancouversymphony.ca.* Canada's third largest orchestra, the Vancouver Symphony presents more than 140 concerts annually, most of them at the ornate 1927-built Orpheum Theatre (Granville at Smithe Street) downtown. Under the direction of Bramwell Tovey, the symphony's featured programs broadly encompass classical, light classical, pops, and children's works. Most of the concerts cluster around weekends (Fri-Mon) and include family-oriented matinees. (Sept-June)

Vancouver Trolley Company Ltd. *875 Terminal Ave, Vancouver (V6A 2M9). Phone 604/801-5515. www.vancouvertrolley.com.* Narrated trolley tours to top attractions and neighborhoods throughout the city. Get on and off at designated stops throughout the day. **$$$$**

Vancouver Whitecaps. *Kingsway and Boundary Rd, Burnaby (V3J 1A1). Phone 604/669-9283. www.whitecapssoccer.com.* Named for the whitecaps on the surrounding waters and mountains, the men's professional soccer team competes in the United Soccer League's A-League. In suburban Burnaby, Swangard Stadium entertains up to 6,500 fans with both on-field activity and a pine-forested backdrop. A Whitecaps-affiliated women's team, The Breakers, plays here in the USL's W-League. (May-Aug)

VanDusen Botanical Garden. *5251 Oak St, Vancouver (V6M 4H1). Phone 604/878-9274. www.vandusen-garden.org.* Approximately 55 acres (22 hectares) of flowers and exotic plants. Seasonal displays, mountain views, restaurant. (Daily; closed Dec 25) **$$$**

Vogue Theatre. *918 Granville St, Vancouver (V6Z 1L2). Phone 604/331-7900. www.voguetheatre.com.* A soaring neon marquee is found outside this well-preserved 1941 Art Deco Vogue Theatre. Updated sound and light systems enable the vintage stage to produce 1,200-seat shows that range from local rockers to percussion groups and stand-up comedy reviews. Though largely a concert venue, the Vogue also screens movies throughout the Vancouver International Film Festival held each September.

Whale-watching tours. *950 Wharf St, Victoria (V8W 1T3).* Whale-watching boats line both the Wharf Street waterfront and Inner Harbour. Half-day tours display marine life, including orcas, sea lions, seals, and porpoises. Victoria Marine Adventures (phone 250/995-2211) and Prince of Whales (phone 250/383-4884) are two of the finer tour companies.

Windsure Windsurfing School. *1300 Discovery St, Vancouver (V6R 4L9). Phone 604/224-0615. www.windsure.com.* Head to Jericho Beach to catch the offshore drafts in English Bay aboard a windsurfer. Windsure Windsurfing School, operating out of the Jericho Sailing Center, rents both boards and wetsuits, including rigs suitable for children. Just starting out? Two-hour introductory group lessons go for $39, and three-hour semi-private tutorials (meaning no more than three students per teacher) cost $99. (Early Apr-early Oct, 9 am-8 pm)

The Yale Hotel. *1300 Granville St, Vancouver (V6Z 1M7). Phone 604/681-9253. www.theyale.ca.* Built in 1889 as a hotel for rough-and-tumble miners, fishermen, and loggers, The Yale, née The Colonial, prizes its working-class roots and makes a fitting home for the city's best blues club. The mansard-roofed Yale stages nightly shows from a pool of local talent as well as touring acts. Past headliners include John Lee Hooker, Clarence "Gatemouth" Brown, Jeff Healey, and Jim Byrnes. (Nightly 9:30 pm)

Yaletown. *Hamilton St, Vancouver. From False Creek to Burrard Inlet on the NW and Georgia St on the NE.* A former rail yard, Yaletown once held the world record for the most bars per acre. With time and prosperity, the warehouse district is now one of Vancouver's hippest, drawing urban dwellers with an arty bent. The former loading docks along Hamilton and Mainland teem with cafés disgorging umbrella-shaded tables onto concrete terraces. Tucked in between are a slew of shops, galleries, and clothiers.

Special Events

Alcan International Dragon Boat Festival. *Festival Office, 401-788 Beatty St, Vancouver (V6B 1A2). Phone 604/688-2382. www.canadadragonboat.com.* Vancouver's considerable Asian community imports an eastern rite in dragon boat racing, the traditional Chinese rain ceremony that is equal parts pageant and competition. But don't tell that to the 100 or so crews that enter the False Creek event paddling boats with dragon figureheads representing the Asian water deity. Bring loads of film to the colorful event, which, in addition to racing, features a Taoist blessing of the fleet and, on land, Asian entertainment, crafts, and food. Mid-June. **FREE**

Bard on the Beach Shakespeare Festival. *1100 Chestnut St, Vancouver (V6J 3J9). Phone 604/739-0559. www.bardonthebeach.org.* The works of Shakespeare take the outdoor stage at Vanier Park's permanent seasonal theater, Bard on the Beach. Elizabethan-style tents cover the audience and actors, who play against an open backdrop of BC coastal landscape. The company mounts approximately three plays each summer, performed in repertory with several shows slated daily on two stages. June-Sept. **$$$$**

Caribbean Days Festival. *Waterfront Park, North Vancouver. Take the Seabus from Canada Place to Lonsdale Quay, which borders Waterfront Park. Phone 604/515-2400. www.caribbeandaysfestival.com.* The Trinidad and Tobago Cultural Society of BC throws the province's biggest island jump-up at this North Vancouver park. Its highlight parade kicks off Saturday morning with a slow, carnival-like promenade of bands and costumes, drawing crowds of pan-Caribbean expats. Head to the park festival grounds for calypso, steel drum, soca, and reggae music as well as island food and crafts. Late July. **FREE**

Christmas events. *Vancouver Tourism Infocenter, 200 Burrard St, Vancouver. Phone 604/683-2000.* Christmas Carol Ship and lighted ship parade; New Year's Day Polar Bear swim.

HSBC Powersmart Celebration of Light.
English Bay, Vancouver. Phone 604/641-1193. www. celebration-of-light.com. On four nights spread over two weeks, pyrotechnic fans ooh and ah as the world's best fireworks designers compete for bragging rights in Vancouver's Celebration of Light. Teams from Italy, Canada, and Spain have competed on the basis of originality, rhythm, musical synchronization, and color, leading up to the grand finale night on which all competitors restage their shows. For best viewing, park your beach towel along English Bay at Stanley or Vanier parks, Kitsilano or Jericho beaches. Come prepared for very large crowds, especially for the finale. Late July-early Aug. **FREE**

Hyack Festival. *1st and 3rd aves, New Westminster. Phone 604/522-6894. www.hyack.bc.ca. 12 miles (19 kilometers) S via Hwy 1A in New Westminster.* Commemorates the birthday of Queen Victoria, held yearly since 1871; 21-gun salute; band concerts, parade, carnival, sports events. Ten days in mid-May.

International Bathtub Race. *Front St and Terminal Ave, Nanaimo. Phone toll-free 800/663-7337.* Thirty-four-mile (55-kilometers) race from Nanaimo to Vancouver. Third or fourth Sun in July.

Molson Indy Vancouver. *Mailbox #20, 8103-750 Pacific Blvd, Vancouver (V6B 5E7). Phone 604/280-4639. www.molsonindy.com/vancouver.* For three days in July, Indy cars skirt False Creek near Concord Pacific Place, racing around a 1.8-mile (2.9-kilometer) course on Vancouver streets posted temporarily with pit stops and grandstands. Counting more than 161,000 fans in recent attendance, the Molson Indy considers itself Vancouver's biggest summer sporting event, a CART Champ Car World Series race. Late July. **$$$$**

Pacific National Exhibition Annual Fair. *Exhibition Park, 2901 E Hastings St, Vancouver (V5K 5J1). Phone 604/253-2311. www.pne.bc.ca.* Second-largest fair in Canada. Hundreds of free exhibits, major theme event, concerts, thrill shows, world championship timber show; petting zoo, thoroughbred horse racing, commercial exhibits, roller coaster, agricultural shows, horse shows, livestock competitions, horticultural exhibits. Usually mid-Aug–early Sept.

Theatre Under the Stars. *Stanley Park, Malkin Bowl, 2099 Beach Ave, Vancouver (V6G 3E2). Phone 604/687-0174. www.tuts.bc.ca.* Theatre Under the Stars puts the outdoors in outdoor theater. Towering forests of Douglas fir surround the 1,200-seat open-air Malkin Bowl theater in Stanley Park, binding art and nature in nightly performances. The short summer season generally presents two shows in every-other-night rotation, an annual repertory that hews to comedies and musicals. July-Aug.

Vancouver Fringe Festival. *1402 Anderson St, Vancouver (V6H 3R6). Phone 604/257-0350. www. vancouverfringe.com.* From comedies to musical acts to full-on drama, Vancouver Fringe trains the spotlight on fledgling theater troupes who come from around the globe to participate in the 11-day annual arts festival. Modeled on the oft-copied fringe festival in Edinburgh, Scotland, the Canadian organization mounts about 100 productions in a variety of venues—theaters, yes, but also garages and even the Aquabus. Mid-Sept. **$$$$**

Vancouver International Children's Festival. *Vanier Park, 1100 Chestnut St, Vancouver (V6J 3J9). Phone 604/708-5655. www.vancouverchildrensfestival.com.* Although the seven-day slate of events programmed by the annual Children's Festival aims at school group audiences, its talent warrants broader attention. In a program ranging from music to theater, the performance lineup for young audiences might include Japanese dancers, Australia's teen troupe Flying Fruit Fly Circus, Aboriginal storytellers, and clown companies. Aside from showtime, the festival engages kids with more than two dozen hands-on arts activities. Late May. **$$$$**

Vancouver International Jazz Festival. *Coastal Jazz and Blues Society, 316 W 6th Ave, Vancouver (V5Y 1K9). Phone 604/872-5200. www.jazzvancouver.com.* The Coastal Jazz and Blues Society runs this annual jazz festival over a ten-day span in several venues, climaxing in the headlining stage at the Orpheum Theatre. Past performers range from greats like Dizzy Gillespie to New Age interpreters like Pat Metheny to crooners such as Diana Krall. In addition to the main event, CJBS also sponsors 40 concerts between September and May each year (its 24-hour jazz hotline delivers a useful "what's-on-now" club report year-round). June. **$$$$**

Limited-Service Hotels

★ ★ **BEST WESTERN SANDS.** *1755 Davie St, Vancouver (Z6G 1W5). Phone 604/682-1831; toll-free 800/663-9400; fax 604/682-3546. www.bestwestern.com.* 121 rooms, 5 story. Pets accepted; fee. Complimentary continental breakfast. Check-in 4 pm, check-out noon. Restaurant, bar. Fitness room. Beach. **$$**

⊠ ◗ ⼊

★ ★ **DELTA TOWN AND COUNTRY INN.** *6005 Hwy 17 at Hwy 99, Delta (V4K 5B8). Phone 604/946-4404; toll-free 888/777-1266; fax 604/946-4404. www. deltainn.com.* 48 rooms, 2 story. Check-out 11 am. Restaurant. Fitness room. Tennis. **$**

▣ ⼊ ⽓

★ ★ **EXECUTIVE HOTEL.** *4201 Lougheed Hwy, Burnaby (V5C 3Y6). Phone 604/298-2010; toll-free 800/590-3932; fax 604/298-1123. www.executivehotels .net.* 125 rooms, 4 story. Check-out noon. Restaurant, bar. Fitness room. Outdoor pool, whirlpool. Business center. **$**

⼊ ⊨ ⼊

★ ★ **GOLDEN TULIP GEORGIAN COURT HOTEL.** *773 Beatty St, Vancouver (V6B 2M4). Phone 604/682-5555; toll-free 800/663-1155; fax 604/682-8830. www.georgiancourt.com.* This hotel's handsome exterior, with its overhead terraced brick garden boxes, leads guests into a lobby full of old-world charm. The grandfather clock is just one of several antique pieces amid the rich mahogany furnishings. Just steps away from many downtown attractions and dining options, the Georgian Court offers its own appealing restaurants, including the well-known William Tell (see), open for dinner each evening.

180 rooms, 12 story. Pets accepted; fee. Check-in 3 pm, check-out 1 pm. High-speed Internet access. Restaurant, bar. Fitness room. Whirlpool. **$$**

★ HAMPTON INN VANCOUVER AIRPORT.

8811 Bridgeport Rd, Richmond (V6X 1R9). Phone 604/232-5505; toll-free 800/HAMPTON; fax 604/232-5508. www.hamptoninn-vancouver.com. 111 rooms, 5 story. Complimentary continental breakfast. Check-in 3 pm, check-out noon. Fitness room. Golf. Business center. **$**

Full-Service Hotels

★ ★ ★ CLUB INTRAWEST VANCOUVER.

1088 Burrard St, Vancouver (V6Z 2R9). Phone 604/689-8816; toll-free 800/663-9255; fax 604/689-9534. 733 rooms, 25 story. Pets accepted; fee. Check-in 3 pm, check-out noon. Restaurant, bar. Fitness room, spa. Indoor pool, whirlpool. Business center. **$$$**

★ ★ ★ COAST PLAZA SUITE HOTEL.

1763 Comox St, Vancouver (V6G 1P6). Phone 604/688-7711; toll-free 800/663-1144; fax 604/688-5934. www.coasthotels.com. This hotel overlooks English Bay and is near Stanley Park and other major attractions in the Vancouver area. 269 rooms, 35 story. Check-out noon. Restaurant, bar. Fitness room. Indoor pool. **$$$**

★ ★ ★ DELTA VANCOUVER SUITES.

550 W Hastings St, Vancouver (V6B 1L6). Phone 877/814-7706; fax 604/605-8881. www.deltahotels.com. 225 rooms, 22 story, all suites. Check-out noon. Restaurant. Fitness room. Indoor pool. Business center. **$$**

★ ★ ★ THE FAIRMONT HOTEL VANCOUVER.

900 W Georgia St, Vancouver (V6C 2W6). Phone 604/684-3131; toll-free 800/441-1414; fax 604/662-1929. www.fairmont.com. The Fairmont Hotel echoes the vibrancy of its home city. This gracious hotel offers guests the perfect blend of history and cosmopolitan panache. Grand and inviting, it has been a preeminent destination since 1939, when it opened to celebrate the royal visit of King George VI and Queen Elizabeth. The guest rooms employ rich jewel tones and sumptuous fabrics to create a wonderful English castle ambience. The décor gives a nod to the past, but the dining and entertainment venues are cutting edge and are hotspots on the local scene. Business and fitness centers keep guests focused on goals, while world-renowned boutiques, including Louis Vuitton and St. John, tempt shoppers. 550 rooms, 14 story. Pets accepted; fee. Check-out noon. Restaurants, bars. Fitness room. Indoor pool, children's pool, whirlpool. **$$**

★ ★ ★ THE FAIRMONT VANCOUVER AIRPORT.

3111 Grant McConachie Way, Vancouver (V7B 1X9). Phone 604/207-5200; toll-free 800/676-8922; fax 604/248-3219. www.fairmont.com. It doesn't get much more convenient than The Fairmont Vancouver Airport. Located right inside this international gateway, the stylish hotel is easily accessed by a quick escalator ride. Popular with those making connections, this hotel provides a gracious home-away-from-home for those visitors exploring Vancouver's cultural and natural treasures. The rooms and suites are the very definition of modern sophistication with elegant furnishings and thoughtful amenities. Airport dining is elevated to new levels at the Globe@YVR, where diners marvel at the soaring jets while enjoying cosmopolitan cuisine, and the Jetside Bar makes delayed departures seem like a godsend. 392 rooms, 14 story. Pets accepted, some restrictions; fee. Check-in 3 pm, check-out noon. Restaurant, bar. Fitness room. Indoor pool, whirlpool. Business center. **$$**

★ ★ ★ THE FAIRMONT WATERFRONT.

900 Canada Way, Vancouver (V6C 3L5). Phone 604/691-1991; fax 604/691-1828. www.fairmont.com. Guests stay at The Fairmont Waterfront for its gracious accommodations, central location, and complete range of services, but they keep returning for its views. This contemporary glass tower showcases the finest view in all of Vancouver. From its superior harborfront location, this hotel gives guests a bird's eye view of the city's renowned sparkling waters and majestic, misty mountains. The modern exterior belies its warm interiors, where rooms and suites are outfitted with all the comforts of home. Room service is available throughout the day for those who prefer to remain in their elegant accommodations, while the Herons Restaurant and Lounge serves up more of the hotel's signature views along with its regionally influenced menu. 489 rooms, 23 story. Pets accepted, some restrictions; fee. Check-out noon. Restaurant, bar. Fitness room. Pool, whirlpool. Business center. **$$**

★ ★ ★ ★ **FOUR SEASONS HOTEL VANCOUVER.** *791 W Georgia St, Vancouver (V6C 2T4). Phone 604/689-9333; fax 604/689-3466. www.fourseasons.com.* Impeccable service and an ideal location make the Four Seasons Hotel a natural choice in Vancouver. The city's vibrant arts and entertainment area is just a short walk from this hotel, situated above the shops of the Pacific Centre. The guest rooms are comfortably elegant. Moods are instantly brightened in the accommodations, where plaid and floral fabrics add a cheery feel. Unencumbered views of the city, mountains, and harbor delight visitors. Fitness and business centers assist travelers with their needs, and the indoor-outdoor pool is an urban oasis with its flower-filled outdoor terrace. The signature restaurant, Chartwell, looked to Winston Churchill's favorite country home for its design influences, and the walnut-paneled walls, clubby furnishings, and parquet floors capture that spirit perfectly. Blooming plants and large windows impart a greenhouse atmosphere at the Garden Terrace, where patrons enjoy informal dining. *Secret Inspector's Notes: The concierge service at the Four Seasons is impeccable; the staff is capable of suggesting such a variety of options for your pleasure that you may find it difficult to decide what to do. The bar makes for an excellent spot to enjoy an evening cocktail or beer.* 385 rooms, 28 story. Pets accepted. Check-out noon. Restaurant, bar. Fitness room. Pool, whirlpool. Business center. **$$$**

★ ★ ★ **HILTON VANCOUVER METROTOWN.** *6083 McKay Ave, Vancouver (V5H 2W7). Phone 604/438-1200; fax 604/431-7782. www.hilton.com.* 750 rooms, 32 story. Check-in 4 pm, check-out noon. Restaurant, bar. Fitness room. Indoor pool, whirlpool. Business center. **$$**

★ ★ ★ **HYATT REGENCY VANCOUVER.** *655 Burrard St, Vancouver (V6C 2R7). Phone 604/683-1234; fax 604/689-3707. www.vancouver.hyatt.com.* This hotel is adjacent to the Royal Center shopping complex and near Pacific Centre, Robson Street, theaters, Granville Island, and other attractions.

644 rooms, 34 story. Check-in 3 pm, check-out noon. Restaurant, bar. Fitness room. Outdoor pool. Business center. **$$$**

★ ★ ★ **LE SOLEIL HOTEL AND SUITES.** *567 Hornby St, Vancouver (V6C 2E8). Phone 604/632-3000; toll-free 877/632-3030; fax 604/632-3001. www.lesoleilhotel.com.* In the heart of the city's financial and business districts sits this charming 122-suite boutique hotel. The stunning lobby boasts 30-foot gilded ceilings, crystal chandeliers, and a Louis XVI-style collection of imported Italian furniture. Complimentary bottled water and fruit upon arrival are welcome surprises, and the property's restaurant, a cool hotspot, offers an eclectic Asian-Mediterranean cuisine. 122 rooms. Restaurant. Fitness room. Indoor pool. Business center. **$$**

★ ★ ★ ★ **METROPOLITAN HOTEL VANCOUVER.** *645 Howe St, Vancouver (V6C 2Y9). Phone 604/687-1122; toll-free 800/667-2300; fax 604/643-7267. www.metropolitan.com.* Wired for the new millennium, the Metropolitan Hotel Vancouver is the hotel of choice for executives, VIPs, and technology aficionados. This contemporary hotel makes it easy to stay in touch, with dual-line telephones and broadband Internet connections in all accommodations, even in public spaces. Contemporary artwork adorns the walls of the guest rooms. Light woods and neutral colors result in a soothing ambience in the private spaces, and luxurious bed linens ensure a good night's sleep. Guests enjoy views of this beautiful city from the privacy of their rooms, and many of the suites feature balconies. A fitness center, indoor pool, and squash court are available, and the hotel's convenient location makes it popular with joggers and walkers who want to experience the city by foot. Diva at the Met earns bravos from diners who feast on sensational regional specialties. 197 rooms, 18 story. Pets accepted. Check-out 1 pm. Restaurant, bar. Fitness room. Indoor pool, whirlpool. Business center. **$$$**

★ ★ ★ **PACIFIC PALISADES HOTEL.** *1277 Robson St, Vancouver (V6E 1C4). Phone 604/688-0461; toll-free 800/663-1815; fax 604/688-0461. www.pacificpalisadeshotel.com.* So many attractions in the lobby alone! Look up in wonder at the striking Murano chandelier and gaze in awe at the stainless-steel floating fireplace. Relax in the courtyard that connects the two towers, or while away some time in the Art + Soul Gallery. This hotel underwent a total makeover in 2001 and is now among the trendiest locations on the very hip Robson Street with a lively, citrus-colored motif. Roomy guest accommodations owe their largesse to the fact that the building started life as an apartment complex. Fitness-minded guests enjoy complimentary yoga kits and a designated yoga channel on the TV; personal trainers are available for private yoga and Pilates sessions. Pets are welcomed here (the hotel even donates part of the pet deposit to the local Society for the Prevention of Cruelty to Animals), and dogs rate a special goodie bag. 233 rooms, 23 story. Pets accepted; fee. Check-in 3 pm, check-out noon. High-speed Internet access. Restaurant, bar. Fitness room, spa. Indoor pool, whirlpool. Business center. **$**

★ ★ ★ **PAN PACIFIC VANCOUVER.** *300-999 Canada Pl, Vancouver (V6C 3B5). Phone 604/662-8111; toll-free 800/937-1515; fax 604/685-8690. www. panpacific.com.* Awe-inspiring views take center stage at Vancouver's Pan Pacific Hotel, located on the waterfront. This contemporary hotel enjoys a serene setting on the harbour, yet is only minutes from the alluring shopping of Robson Street. The guest rooms are a testament to subtle luxury, with clean lines and neutral tones. Large windows look out over unobstructed, picture-perfect views of the mountains and sea, and many accommodations include private balconies for further enjoyment. Whether taking advantage of the fitness center or relaxing in the privacy of their accommodations, guests reap the rewards of the hotel's commitment to the latest technology. Diners traverse the world in the four distinctive restaurants, where sushi, Italian, and other international dishes tantalize taste buds. 504 rooms, 23 story. Pets accepted, some restrictions. Check-in 3 pm, check-out noon. Restaurant, bar. Fitness room, spa. Outdoor pool, whirlpool. Business center. **$$$**

★ ★ ★ **RENAISSANCE VANCOUVER HARBOURSIDE HOTEL.** *1133 W Hastings, Vancouver (V6E 3T3). Phone 604/689-9211; fax 604/689-4358. www.renaissancevancouver.com.* This hotel, located on the waterfront overlooking Vancouver Harbor, Burrard Inlet, and the North Shore Mountains, is within easy walking distance to Robson Street and the Pacific Centre shopping area. 438 rooms, 19 story. Pets accepted; fee. Check-in 3 pm, check-out noon. Restaurant, bar. Fitness room. Indoor pool, whirlpool. **$$**

★ ★ ★ **SHERATON GUILDFORD HOTEL.** *15269 104th Ave, Surrey (V3R 1N5). Phone 604/582-9288; fax 604/582-9712. www.sheraton.com.* 278 rooms, 18 story. Check-out noon. Restaurant. Fitness room. Business center. **$**

★ ★ ★ ★ **THE SUTTON PLACE HOTEL.** *845 Burrard St, Vancouver (V6Z 2K6). Phone 604/682-5511; toll-free 800/961-7555; fax 604/682-5513. www. suttonplace.com.* The Sutton Place Hotel is a little slice of Europe transplanted to Vancouver's city center. Located one block from Robson Conference Center and only a short distance from the energetic cultural scene, this hotel is ideal for business travelers or vacationers. Spacious and elegant, the guest rooms reflect the grace of the continent with unique decorative accents and traditional furnishings, yet all modern amenities are included to maximize guests' comfort. This hotel epitomizes full service, from the intuitive personal attention to the complete business and fitness centers. A European-style spa features wonderful options, including the popular La Stone therapy. Patrons sink into the large club chairs and relax by the fire at the English-style Gerard Lounge, while diners relish French classics in the warm setting of Fleuri. 397 rooms, 21 story. Check-out noon. Restaurant, bar. Fitness room. Indoor pool, whirlpool. Business center. **$$**

★ ★ ★ **WEDGEWOOD HOTEL.** *845 Hornby St, Vancouver (V6Z 1V1). Phone 604/689-7777; toll-free 800/663-0666; fax 604/608-5348. www.wedgewoodhotel .com.* Tradition abounds at this independent boutique hotel. The public areas are richly furnished and appointed with original artwork, handsome antiques, and fresh flower arrangements. The lobby boasts a large fireplace. Renovations completed in 2003 gave each bathroom separate shower and soaking-tub areas and added a small but full-service spa and an up-to-date business center. Bachus (see), the on-site restaurant, offers a full menu plus sumptuous weekend brunch menus and traditional high tea served from 2-4 pm daily. 83 rooms, 14 story. Check-in 3 pm, check-out 12:30 pm. Restaurant, bar. Fitness room, spa. Business center. **$$$**

★ ★ ★ **THE WESTIN GRAND.** *433 Robson St, Vancouver (V6B 6L9). Phone 604/602-1999; toll-free 888/680-9393; fax 604/647-2502. www. westingrandvancouver.com.* All of Vancouver is within reach of the Westin Grand. This high-rise tower is perfectly located for business travelers conducting meetings or leisure visitors absorbing the local culture. Sleek and stylish, this property introduces visitors to the hip side of this western Canadian city. The accommodations define city chic with modern, polished-wood furnishings and floor-to-ceiling windows with skyline vistas. Guests never leave behind the comforts of home here, where all rooms feature well-stocked kitchenettes. The hotel caters to the sophisticated, and many services, including the fitness center, are offered 24 hours daily. Diners feast on Pacific Rim dishes at the Aria Restaurant & Lounge and dance the night away at the fashionable Club Voda. 207 rooms, 31 story. Pets accepted; fee. Check-in 3 pm, check-out noon. Restaurant, bar. Fitness room. Beach access. Outdoor pool, whirlpool. Business center. **$$**

Full-Service Resort

★ ★ **PARK PLAZA VANCOUVER AIRPORT.** *10251 St. Edwards Dr, Richmond (V6X 2M9). Phone 604/278-9611; toll-free 800/268-1133; fax 604/276-1121.* 438 rooms, 21 story. Pets accepted, some restrictions; fee. Check-out noon. Restaurant, bar. Children's activity center. Fitness room. Indoor pool, two outdoor pools, whirlpool. Tennis. Business center. **$$**

Full-Service Inns

★ ★ **ENGLISH BAY INN.** *1968 Comox St, Vancouver (V6G 1R4). Phone 604/683-8002. www. englishbayinn.com.* This relaxing, Tudor-style escape is a short walk from the West End's Stanley Park and the sea. All guest rooms are decorated with Ralph Lauren linens and antiques. 7 rooms. Complimentary full breakfast. **$**

★ ★ ★ **RIVER RUN COTTAGES.** *4551 River Rd W, Ladner (V4K 1R9). Phone 604/946-7778; fax 604/940-1970. www.riverruncottages.com.* Kayaking, canoeing, and rowboats are available for guests to venture out to watch the eagles, seals, otters, and beavers in their natural environment. Guests can pack a picnic and enjoy a romantic getaway on No Name Island. 4 rooms, 1 story. Pets accepted; fee. Complimentary full breakfast. Check-in 4 pm, check-out noon. **$**

Specialty Lodgings

The following lodging establishments are approved by Mobil Travel Guide, but due to their unique and individualized nature have not been given a traditional Mobil Star rating. Included in this listing you may find bed-and-breakfasts, limited-service inns, guest ranches, and other unique hotel properties.

BARCLAY HOUSE IN THE WEST END. *1351 Barclay St, Vancouver (V6E 1H6). Phone 604/605-1351; toll-free 800/971-1351; fax 604/605-1382. www. barclayhouse.com.* Guests staying in this restored 1904 late Victorian home sleep in large two-room suites complete with TV/VCRs and CD players. Videos and classical music CDs are on hand, as are four soaking tubs, hot three-course breakfasts, and private bathrooms. Vancouver attractions such as Stanley Park, Gastown, and Granville are close by. 5 rooms. Complimentary full breakfast. Check-in noon-3 pm, check-out 11 am. **$$**

BEAUTIFUL BED AND BREAKFAST. *428 W 40th Ave, Vancouver (V5Y 2R4). Phone 604/327-1102; fax 604/327-2299. www.beautifulbandb.bc.ca.* 5 rooms, 2 story. Children over 14 years only. Complimentary full breakfast. Check-in 5-6 pm, check-out 11 am. **$**

O CANADA HOUSE. *1114 Barclay St, Vancouver (V6E 1H1). Phone 604/688-0555; toll-free 877/688-1114; fax 604/488-0556. www.ocanadahouse.com.* Housed in a historic home built in 1897, this bed-and-breakfast gives guests personalized service with the convenience of a location close to attractions such as Stanley Park, Granville Island, and Gastown. This home is where owner Ewing Buchan and his brother penned the Canadian anthem "O Canada" in

1909. The wraparound porch and English garden give guests plenty of space to unwind outdoors. Inside, guests are treated to a three-course daily breakfast and have access to a 24-hour stocked pantry. Evening sherry in the front parlor and a video library and book collection make guests feel at home. 7 rooms. Complimentary full breakfast. Check-out 11 am. **$$**

WEST END GUEST HOUSE. *1362 Haro St, Vancouver (V6E 1G2). Phone 604/681-2889; toll-free 888/546-3327; fax 604/688-8812. www. westendguesthouse.com.* 8 rooms, 3 story. Children over 12 years only. Complimentary full breakfast. Check-in 3 pm, check-out 11 am. **$**

Restaurants

★ ★ **ALLEGRO CAFE.** *888 Nelson St, Vancouver (V6Z 2H1). Phone 604/683-8485.* Mediterranean, seafood menu. Lunch, dinner, late-night. Closed holidays. Bar. Outdoor seating. **$$**

★ ★ **AQUA RIVA.** *30-200 Gramble St, Vancouver (V6C 1S4). Phone 604/683-5599. www.aquariva.com.* Seafood menu. Lunch, dinner, brunch. Closed holidays. **$$$**

★ ★ ★ **BACCHUS.** *845 Hornby St, Vancouver (V6Z 1V1). Phone 604/689-7777; fax 604/608-5348. www.wedgewoodhotel.com.* This luxurious restaurant, tucked inside the Wedgewood Hotel (see), is adorned with richly upholstered furniture, light fixtures from Venice, and of course, a large canvas depicting Bacchus, Greek god of wine and revelry. French, seafood menu. Breakfast, lunch, dinner, late-night, Sun brunch. Bar. Children's menu. Valet parking. **$$$**

★ ★ ★ **THE BEACH HOUSE.** *150 25th St, Vancouver (V7B 4H8). Phone 604/922-1414; fax 604/922-7971.* Originally built in 1912, this multilevel waterfront restaurant affords all diners beautiful views of Burrard Inlet. Seafood menu. Lunch, dinner, brunch. Bar. Valet parking. Outdoor seating. **$$$**

★ ★ ★ ★ **BISHOP'S.** *2183 W 4th Ave, Vancouver (V6K 1N7). Phone 604/738-2025; fax 604/738-2025. www.bishopsonline.com.* If your radar is set for one of the most coveted tables in Vancouver, you will find it at Bishop's. Intimate, modern, and airy, with a lofty, homelike yet upscale feel, this chic duplex restaurant is known for West Coast continental cuisine—a menu that emphasizes seasonal, organic produce and British Columbia seafood. The kitchen serves high art in the form of food. It isn't uncommon to spy celebrities and VIPs nibbling on these delicious culinary wares. For those who like to sample lots of different wines with dinner, Bishop's offers a nice selection of wines by the glass and an outstanding range of wines by the half-bottle. In addition to being a visionary chef, owner John Bishop is a gracious host, which makes Bishop's a hotspot, so call ahead to secure your very own coveted table. *Secret Inspector's Notes: The food at Bishop's is a flavor fantasy. Local and seasonal ingredients are expertly prepared in a style that focuses on the ingredients, bringing out their inherently wonderful qualities. John Bishop makes for such a warm host that Bishop's should certainly be a stop on your Vancouver eating calendar: it is a uniquely enjoyable dining experience. He will gladly autograph his cookbook for you and provide many other outstanding dining recommendations in the area.* Eclectic/International menu. Dinner. Closed Dec 24-26. Reservations recommended. **$$$**

★ ★ ★ **C RESTAURANT.** *1600 Howe St, Vancouver (V6O 2L9). Phone 604/681-1164; fax 604/605-8263.* Seafood menu. Lunch (summer only), dinner. Bar. Outdoor seating. **$$$**

★ ★ **CAFE DE PARIS.** *761 Denman St, Vancouver (V6G 2L6). Phone 604/687-1418; fax 604/464-3359.* French Bistro menu. Lunch, dinner, brunch. Closed Dec 25. Bar. **$$$**

★ ★ **CAFFE DE MEDICI.** *1025 Robson St, Vancouver (V6E 1A9). Phone 604/669-9322.* Italian menu. Dinner. Closed Jan 1, Dec 25. **$$**

★ ★ **CANNERY.** *2205 Commissioner St, Vancouver (V5L 1A4). Phone 604/254-9606; fax 604/254-1820. www.canneryseafood.com.* Seafood menu. Lunch, dinner. Closed Dec 24-26. Bar. Children's menu. Outdoor seating. **$$$**

★ ★ ★ **CINCIN ITALIAN WOOD GRILL.** *1154 Robson St, Vancouver (V6E 1V5). Phone 604/688-7338. www.cincin.net.* Italian menu. Lunch, dinner. Bar. Children's menu. Outdoor seating. **$$$**

★ ★ **CLOUD 9.** *1400 Robson St, Vancouver (V6G 1B9). Phone 604/687-0511.* Seafood menu. Dinner, brunch. Bar. **$$$**

★ ★ **DELILAH'S.** *1789 Comox St, Vancouver (V6G 1P5). Phone 604/687-3424.* Eclectic/International menu. Dinner. Closed Dec 24-26. Bar. **$$**

★ **DOCKSIDE BREWING COMPANY.** *1253 Johnston St, Vancouver (V6H 3R9). Phone 604/685-7070; fax 604/685-7079. www.docksidebrewing.com.* International menu. Breakfast, lunch, dinner, brunch. Bar. Outdoor seating. **$$**

★ ★ **FISH HOUSE IN STANLEY PARK.** *8901 Stanley Park Dr, Vancouver (V6G 3E2). Phone 604/681-7275; toll-free 877/681-7275; fax 604/681-3137. www.fishhousestanleypark.com.* Seafood menu. Lunch, dinner. Bar. Children's menu. Outdoor seating. **$$$**

★ ★ **FIVE SAILS.** *300-999 Canada Pl, Vancouver (V6C 3B5). Phone 604/662-8111; fax 604/891-2864. www.dinepanpacific.com.* Exceptional views of the harbor and neighboring mountains, a talented kitchen that produces creative Northwest/Asian fusion food, and good service make this restaurant a favorite destination among locals. French, Pacific Rim/Pan-Asian menu. Dinner. Bar. Children's menu. Valet parking. **$$$**

★ ★ **GOTHAM STEAKHOUSE AND COCKTAIL BAR.** *615 Seymour St, Vancouver (V6B 3K3). Phone 604/605-8282; fax 604/605-8285. www.gothamsteakhouse.com.* It's worth the splurge for truly excellent steaks, smooth, friendly service, and a sleek crowd at this downtown destination. The dining room, actually a converted bank, is modern and opulent with main floor and balcony dining and a large, comfortable bar. Steak menu. Dinner, late-night. Closed Dec 25. Bar. Children's menu. Outdoor seating. **$$$**

★ ★ **GRANVILLE SUSHI.** *2526 Granville St, Vancouver (V6H 3G8). Phone 604/738-0388; fax 604/738-0399.* Sushi menu. Lunch, dinner. **$$**

★ ★ **HART HOUSE ON DEER LAKE.** *6664 Deer Lake Ave, Burnaby (V5E 4H3). Phone 604/298-4278; fax 604/298-0124. www.harthouserestaurant.com.* French menu. Lunch, dinner. Closed Mon. Children's menu. Outdoor seating. **$$**

★ ★ ★ **IL GIARDINO DI UMBERTO RISTORANTE.** *1382 Hornby St, Vancouver (V6Z 1W5). Phone 604/669-2422. www.umberto.com.*

Part of Umberto Menghi's local restaurant empire, this rustic room, neighboring the original Umberto's, transports its young, established clientele to a Tuscan villa. Italian menu. Lunch, dinner. Closed Sun; holidays. Valet parking. **$$$**

★ ★ **IMPERIAL CHINESE SEAFOOD RESTAURANT.** *355 Burrard St, Vancouver (V6C 2G8). Phone 604/688-8191; fax 604/688-8466. www.imperialrest.com.* Chinese menu. Lunch, dinner. Bar. **$$**

★ ★ ★ ★ **LA BELLE AUBERGE.** *4856 48th Ave, Ladner (V4K 1V2). Phone 604/946-7717; fax 604/276-2651. www.labelleauberge.com.* If you can't be bothered to fly to Paris for dinner but crave the glorious food of France's best kitchens, you can opt for a 30-minute drive from Vancouver to Ladner and settle in for dinner at La Belle Auberge. Set in a charming 1902 country inn, La Belle Auberge is an intimate restaurant made of up five antique-filled, salon-style dining rooms. Refined service adds to the restaurant's unbeatable charm. The kitchen, led by chef/owner Bruno Marti, offers spectacular, authentic French cuisine. Marti is a masterful culinary technician who serves impeccable classics that will please the most discerning Francophile. Close your eyes, and you will feel like you're dining along the Seine. Open them, and you won't care that you aren't. *Secret Inspector's Notes: Be aware that La Belle Auberge is a considerable distance from downtown Vancouver and traveling there via taxi is not practical. If you're traveling by car, be sure to follow carefully the driving directions to this culinary destination hidden in a quiet suburb.* French menu. Lunch, dinner. Closed Mon. **$$$$**

★ ★ ★ **LA TERRAZZA.** *1088 Cambie St, Vancouver (V6B 6J5). Phone 604/899-4449; fax 604/899-9179. www.laterrazza.ca.* This impressive restaurant feels like a classical villa, with burnt-sienna walls, murals, massive windows, and vaulted ceilings. The wine library, cellar and private dining room are signs of the owners' commitment to stocking many fine, unique bottles. Italian menu. Dinner. Closed holidays. Children's menu. Outdoor seating. **$$$**

★ ★ **LE BISTRO CHEZ MICHEL.** *1373 Marine Dr, Vancouver (V7T 1B6). Phone 604/926-4913. www.chezmichelvancouver.com.* French menu. Lunch, dinner. Closed Sun; holidays. Children's menu. **$$**

★ ★ ★ **LE CROCODILE.** *909 Burrard St, Vancouver (V6Z 2N2). Phone 604/669-4298. www. lecrocodilerestaurant.com.* A wonderful dress-up place, this downtown French bistro is worth a trip for the food alone. French menu. Lunch, dinner. Closed Sun; holidays. Bar. Valet parking. Outdoor seating. **$$$**

★ ★ ★ ★ **LUMIERE.** *2551 W Broadway, Vancouver (V6K 2E9). Phone 604/739-8185; fax 604/739-8139. www.lumiere.ca.* Lumiere is a glossy, stunning, and elegant restaurant that offers European-style dining of the most divine order. The inspired and innovative fare is French with Asian accents and a respect for regional ingredients. Plates are beautiful and balanced and come in eights—as in eight courses—and each of the eight-course chef's, signature, and vegetarian menus changes with the seasons. While eight courses could be overkill, each portion is perfectly sized so that you don't finish dinner feeling perilously inflated and exhausted from the exercise. Instead, you feel deliciously satiated and utterly pampered by the experience. The global wine list is in sync with the kitchen's style, but attention should also be paid to the classic cocktails served at Lumiere's slick and sexy bar. The bartenders here recall a pre-Prohibition era, where the craft of cocktail was taken as seriously as the mastery of the plate. *Secret Inspector's Notes: Lumiere is a spot that Vancouver notables and VIP visitors alike frequent with loyalty. The crowd at this modern dining room raises curiosity about who exactly the diners are at the table next to or across from yours. The food is unbelievably good, and the staff is both professional and entertaining. The bar is indeed a destination in itself for expertly mixed cocktails and uniquely selected wines by the glass or bottle.* French menu. Dinner. Closed holidays. Bar. Reservations recommended. Outdoor seating. **$$$$**

★ ★ **MONK MCQUEENS.** *601 Stamps Landing, Vancouver (D5Z 3Z1). Phone 604/877-1351. www. monkmcqueens.com.* Eclectic/International menu. Lunch, dinner. Children's menu. Outdoor seating. **$**

★ ★ **MONTRI'S THAI.** *3629 W Broadway, Vancouver (3V6 R2B). Phone 604/738-9888.* Thai menu. Dinner. Closed Mon. Bar. **$$**

★ ★ ★ **PICCOLO MONDO.** *850 Thurlow St, Vancouver (V6E 1W2). Phone 604/688-1633; fax 604/682-4875.* Italian menu. Lunch, dinner. Closed Sun. **$$$**

★ ★ **PINK PEARL.** *1132 E Hastings St, Vancouver (V6A 1S2). Phone 604/253-4316. www.pinkpearl.com.* Chinese menu. Lunch, dinner. Bar. **$$**

★ ★ **PROVENCE MEDITERRANEAN GRILL.** *4473 W 10th Ave, Vancouver (V6R 2H2). Phone 604/222-1980; fax 604/222-1908. www.provencevancouver.com.* Mediterranean menu. Lunch, dinner. Children's menu. Casual attire. Outdoor seating. **$$**

★ ★ ★ **QUATTRO ON FOURTH.** *2611 W 4th, Vancouver (V6K 1P8). Phone 604/734-4444.* Italian menu. Dinner. Closed Dec 24-27. **$$$**

★ ★ ★ **RAINCITY GRILL.** *1193 Denman St, Vancouver (V6G 2N1). Phone 604/685-7337. www.raincitygrill.com.* Eclectic/International menu. Dinner, brunch. Closed Dec 24-25. Outdoor seating. **$$$**
🅳

★ ★ ★ **SEASON IN THE PARK RESTAURANT.** *33rd and Cambie, Vancouver (V6G 3E7). Phone 604/874-8008; toll-free 800/632-9422; fax 604/874-7101.* Eclectic/International menu. Lunch, dinner. Closed Dec 25. Bar. Children's menu. Reservations recommended. Outdoor seating. **$$$**

★ ★ **SHANGHAI CHINESE BISTRO.** *1124 Alberni St, Vancouver (V6E 1A5). Phone 604/683-8222; fax 604/683-8847.* Handmade noodle show. Chinese menu. Lunch, dinner. Closed Dec 25. Bar. **$$**

★ ★ **SHIJO JAPANESE RESTAURANT.** *1926 W 4th Ave, Suite 202, Vancouver (V6J 1M5). Phone 604/732-4676.* Japanese menu. Lunch, dinner. **$$**

★ ★ ★ **STAR ANISE.** *1485 W 12th Ave, Vancouver (V6H 1M6). Phone 604/737-1485. www.staranise.ca.* Eclectic/International menu. Lunch, dinner. Closed Dec 25, Jan 1. Bar. **$$$**

★ ★ ★ **SUN SUI WAH SEAFOOD RESTAURANT.** *3888 Main St, Vancouver (V5V 3N9). Phone 604/872-8822; toll-free 866/872-8822; fax 604/876-1638. www.sunsuiwah.com.* Grab an egg tart from the dim sum cart even if you're not ready for dessert; they sell out quickly at this huge, widely acclaimed chain restaurant. Chinese menu. Lunch, dinner. Bar. Reservations recommended. **$$**

★ ★ **TAMA SUSHI.** *1595 W Broadway, Suite 200, Vancouver (V6J 1W6). Phone 604/738-0119.* Japanese-style rooms. Sushi menu. Lunch, dinner. **$$**

★ **TAPASTREE.** *1829 Robson St, Vancouver (V6G 1E4). Phone 604/606-4680; fax 604/682-6509.* Tapas menu. Dinner. Bar. Outdoor seating. **$$**

★ ★ **TEAHOUSE.** *7501 Stanley Park Dr, Vancouver (V6G 3E7). Phone 604/669-3281; fax 604/687-5662. www.sequoiarestaurants.com.* Eclectic/International menu. Lunch, dinner, brunch. Closed Dec 25. Outdoor seating. **$$$**

★ ★ **TOJO'S.** *777 W Broadway #202, Vancouver (V5Z 4J7). Phone 604/872-8050; fax 604/872-8060. www.tojos.com.* Frequented by entertainment industry insiders, this popular Japanese restaurant serves great food with friendly service. Menu items keep the hip and cool crowd coming back time and time again. Japanese menu. Dinner. Closed Sun; also mid-Jan. Bar. Outdoor seating. **$$$**

★ ★ **TOP OF VANCOUVER.** *555 W Hastings, Vancouver (V6B 4N6). Phone 604/669-2220.* Seafood menu. Lunch, dinner, Sun brunch. Bar. **$$$**

★ **TRUE CONFECTIONS.** *866 Denman St, Vancouver (V6G 2L8). Phone 604/682-1292. www.trueconfections.ca.* Dessert menu. Lunch, dinner, late-night. Casual attire. Outdoor seating. **$**

★ ★ **VILLA DEL LUPO.** *869 Hamilton St, Vancouver (V6B 2R7). Phone 604/688-7436. www.villadellupo.com.* Tiny white lights and sparkling bay windows attract attention at this classic Italian restaurant housed in a charming, turn-of-the-century home. The menu highlights different regions of Italy using fresh, local ingredients in dishes such as osso bucco with risotto Milanese. Italian menu. Dinner. **$$**
🅿

★ ★ ★ **WEST.** *2881 Granville St, Vancouver. Phone 604/738-8938. www.westrestaurant.com.* West is one of those sleek, heavenly spots that makes sipping cocktails for hours on end an easy task—they use fresh juices and know how to mix a serious drink. It is also one of those restaurants that makes the act of eating an art and a delight. It is an ideal choice for gourmets in search of an inventive, eclectic meal, as well as for simple eaters who crave local flavor and seasonal ingredients that are seamlessly married on the plate. Whatever your appetite and whatever the occasion—if you are entertaining colleagues, in need of a night out with friends, or just searching for a place to have dinner with your significant other—look no further than West, a restaurant with an inspiring menu and a stylish, contemporary urban setting. Located in Vancouver's chic South Granville neighborhood, West offers diners the chance to sample the vibrant cuisine of the Pacific Northwest region. Stunning, locally sourced ingredients are on display here, and the masterful kitchen staff offers a glorious show. Eclectic/International menu. Lunch, dinner. Bar. **$$$**

★ ★ ★ **THE WILLIAM TELL.** *765 Beatty St, Vancouver (V6B 2M4). Phone 604/688-3504; fax 604/683-8810. www.thewilliamtellrestaurant.com.* Named after a Swiss mountain hero, this restaurant has been in business for more than 40 years under the direction of restaurateur Erwin Doebeli. French, Swiss menu. Dinner. Closed Mon. Bar. Valet parking. **$$$**

Victoria, BC

5 hours 15 minutes, 109 miles from Seattle, WA

Founded 1843
Population 64,379
Elevation 211 ft (64 m)
Area Code 250
Information Tourism Victoria, 812 Wharf St, V8W 1T3; phone 250/953-2033 or toll-free 800/663-3883
Web site www.tourismvictoria.com

Bordered by the Juan de Fuca Strait on one side, and majestic mountains on the other, Victoria is situated on the southeast tip of Vancouver Island. Established in 1843 as a trading post of the Hudson's Bay Company, the city was later called Fort Victoria. In the late 1850s, Victoria became the provisioning and outfitting base for miners on their way to British Columbia's goldfields. In 1866, Vancouver Island was administratively linked with the mainland; Victoria became the provincial capital in 1871.

A major port with two harbors—the outer for ocean shipping and cruising and the inner for coastal shipping, pleasure boats, ferries to the US mainland, amphibian aircraft, and fishing—Victoria has a distinctly British flavor with many Tudor-style buildings and a relaxed way of life. It is a center of Pacific Northwest indigenous culture.

Victoria is a city of parks and gardens; even the five-globed Victorian lampposts are decorated with baskets of flowers in summer. Visitors may take a horse-drawn carriage or double-decker bus tour through many historic and scenic landmarks; inquire locally for details. In winter, temperatures rarely go below 40°F (4°C). Victoria's climate is Canada's most moderate, making it a delightful place to visit any time of year.

Public Transportation

Airport Victoria International Airport.

Lost and Found Phone 250/953-7511

Airlines Air Canada, Air Canada Jazz, Helijet International, Horizon Air, Pacific Coastal Airlines, WestJet, Zip

What to See and Do

Art Gallery of Greater Victoria. *1040 Moss St, Victoria (V8V 4P1). Phone 250/384-4101. aggv.bc.ca.* This gallery is said to have the finest collection of Japanese art in Canada; it includes major holdings of Asian ceramics and paintings. Also housed here are collections of Canadian and European art, with a focus on prints and drawings, and decorative arts. The gallery is home to the only Shinto shrine outside of Japan and is the site of many lectures, film screenings, and concerts. (Mon-Sat 10 am-5 pm, Thurs to 9 pm, Sun 1-5 pm; closed Good Fri, Nov 11, Dec 25) **$$**

BC Forest Museum. *40 miles (64 kilometers) N on Hwy 1, near Duncan. Phone 250/715-1113.* Logging museum; old logging machines and tools, hands-on exhibits, logging camp, 1 1/2 miles (2.4 kilometers) steam railway ride, sawmill, films, nature walk, picnic park, snack bar, gift shop. (May-Sept, daily)

Beacon Hill Park. *From Douglas St to Cook St, between Superior St and waterfront. Phone 250/361-0370.* Approximately 180 acres (75 hectares) with lakes, wildfowl sanctuary, children's petting farm, walks and floral gardens, cricket pitch; world's second-tallest totem pole; beautiful view of the sea. For a list of additional recreational areas, contact Tourism Victoria. **FREE**

Butchart Gardens. *800 Benvenuto, Brentwood Bay (V8M 1J8). 13 miles (21 kilometers) N on Benvenuto Ave, near Brentwood Bay. Phone 250/652-4422. www. butchartgardens.com.* Approximately 50 acres (20 hectares). The Sunken Garden was created in the early 1900s by the Butcharts on the site of their depleted limestone quarry with topsoil brought in by horse-drawn cart. Already a tourist attraction by the 1920s, the gardens now include the Rose, Japanese, and Italian gardens; also Star Pond, Concert Lawn, Fireworks Basin, Ross Fountain, and Show Greenhouse. The gardens are subtly illuminated at night (mid-June-mid-Sept), and on Saturday evenings in July and August, visitors enjoy fireworks displays. Restaurants; seed and gift store. Fees vary by season. **$$$$**

Capital City Tally-Ho and Sightseeing Company. *7450 Veyaness Rd, Saanichton (V8M 1V9). Phone 250/383-5067.* English horse-drawn carriage sightseeing tours of city highlights, departing from Inner Harbour beside Parliament Buildings; or past Victorian homes and through 200-acre (81-hectare) Beacon Hill Park and its extensive flower gardens (departs from Menzies and Belleville sts). Fully narrated. (Apr-Sept, daily)

Carr House. *207 Government St, Victoria (V8V 2K8). Phone 250/383-5843.* (1863) Italianate birthplace of famous Canadian painter/author Emily Carr. Ground floor restored to period. (Mid-May-Oct: daily; rest of year: by appointment) **$$**

Centennial Square. *Douglas and Pandora sts, Victoria.* Includes fountain plaza; Elizabethan knot garden of herbs and flowers. Occasional noontime concerts.

Chinatown. Chinese immigrants, used for railroad labor, established Canada's oldest Chinatown in 1858. Two key attractions are Fan Tan Alley, the narrowest street in North America and the Gate of Harmonious Interest, guarded by hand-carved stone lions from Szuchou, China. Visit shops with exotic merchandise and restaurants.

Craigdarroch Castle. *1050 Joan Crescent, Victoria (V8S 3L5). Phone 250/592-5323. www.craigdarrochcastle.com.* (1890) Historic house museum with beautifully crafted wood, stained glass; furnished with period furniture and artifacts. (Daily 10 am-4:30 pm; mid-June-Labor Day 9 am-7 pm; closed Jan 1, Dec 25-26) **$$$**

Craigflower Farmhouse & Schoolhouse Historic Site. *2709 Manor and Schoolhouse, Victoria (V9B 1M5). Phone 250/383-4627.* This farmhouse was built in

Cycling

Victoria's mild climate and natural beauty inspire locals and visitors to get out and enjoy the great outdoors. Year-round outdoor adventure includes access to miles of scenic trails and sites that incorporate old growth rainforests, ocean shores, and mountains. In the Greater Victoria Region, cycling accounts for 6.2 percent of commuter travel—more than any other city in Canada. In Victoria, most people live within a 30-minute bike ride of their workplace and, from some neighborhoods, up to 20 percent of trips to work are made by bicycle. Bike lanes on many of Victoria's downtown streets and bike racks on city buses that travel to the suburban communities also promote cycling.

One of the best routes to cycle is the Galloping Goose Trail—a linear park that stretches 44 miles (70 kilometers) from Victoria to Sooke. Built on abandoned railway tracks and trestles, and named after a 1920's rail car, the Galloping Goose is part of the Trans Canada Trail. The Galloping Goose trail surface is wide, mostly flat, and leads through a wonderful diversity of landscapes. Many local cyclists use the Galloping Goose Trail to get around southern Vancouver Island. The Galloping Goose Trail connects with the Lochside Trail and Seaside Cycling Route to create the first bicycle touring route in the southern Vancouver Island region. For more information visit www.crd.bc.ca/parks/galloping_goose.htm.

1856 in simple Georgian style. The adjoining 1854 schoolhouse is the oldest in western Canada. Some original furnishings. (Daily; guided tours June 10-Labor Day, Wed-Sun noon-4 pm) **$$**

Crystal Garden. *713 Douglas St, Victoria (V8W 2B4). Phone 250/953-8800. www.bcpcc.com/crystal.* Glass building formerly housed the largest saltwater pool in the British Empire. Tropical gardens, waterfall, fountain, aviary, monkeys, free-flying butterflies, exotic fish pool; restaurant, shops. (Daily) **$$$**

Dominion Astrophysical Observatory. *5071 W Saanich Rd, Victoria (V9E 2E7). Phone 250/363-0001. www.hia-iha.nrc-gc.ca.* The observatory contains three telescopes, two of which are used for research by professional astronomers. The 72-inch Plaskett Telescope is used for public viewing on Saturday nights during "Star Parties" (Apr-Oct 31, 7-11 pm). Interactive exhibits, film presentations, and other special programs are designed to entertain visitors while educating them about the universe. (Daily 10 am-6 pm; to 11 pm Fri, May 1-Aug 31, and Sun, July 1-Aug 31; closed Mon from Nov-Apr) **$$$**

Empress Hotel. *721 Government St, Victoria (V8W 1W5).* This historically famous building was constructed by Canadian Pacific Railroad in 1908 and restored in 1989 (see The Fairmont Empress). Victorian in tradition, afternoon tea and crumpets are

served in the lobby—an impressive, if expensive affair. Guests leave with a full stomach and a canister of tea as a souvenir.

Ferry trips. *430 Bellville St, Victoria (V8W 1W5).* Black Ball Transport, Inc: between Victoria, BC, and Port Angeles, WA, car ferry, phone 250/386-2202; Washington State Ferries: between Sidney, BC, and Anacortes, WA (see), phone 250/381-1551; British Columbia Ferry Corp: between Victoria and British Columbia mainland or smaller island destinations, car ferry, phone 250/386-3431 or 604/669-1211 (Vancouver).

Fort Rodd Hill and Fisgard Lighthouse National Historic Site. *603 Fort Rodd Hill Rd, Victoria (V9C 2W8). 8 miles (13 km) W, then 1/2 mile (1 km) S of Hwy 1A. Phone 250/478-5849. www.pc.gc.ca.* A coastal artillery fort from 1895 to 1956; casemated barracks, gun and searchlight positions, loopholed walls. Grounds (daily; closed Dec 25). Historic lighthouse (1860) adjacent. **$$**

Gray Line bus tours. *700 Douglas St, Victoria (V8W 2B3). Phone 250/388-5248.* Several bus tours of Victoria and vicinity are offered (all year). **$$$$**

Hatley Castle. *2005 Sooke Rd, Colwood (V9B 5Y2). 6 miles (10 km) W via Trans-Canada Hwy 1 and 1A, Colwood exit, on Hwy 14 (Sooke Rd). Phone 250/391-*

2600. www.royalroads.ca. (Royal Roads University, 1908) Once the private estate of James Dunsmuir, former Lieutenant Governor of British Columbia. Buildings are noted for their beauty, as are the grounds, with their Japanese, Italian, and rose gardens. Grounds (daily). **$$**

Helmcken House. *10 Elliot Sq, Victoria (V8V 2P8). Phone 250/361-0021.* (1852) Second-oldest house in British Columbia; most furnishings are original. Extensive 19th-century medical collection. (May-Oct: daily; rest of year: by appointment) **$$**

Maritime Museum. *28 Bastion Sq, Victoria (V8W 1H9). Phone 250/385-4222. Located in Old Provincial Courthouse.* Depicts the rich maritime heritage of the Pacific Northwest from early explorers through age of sail and steam; Canadian naval wartime history; large collection of models of ships used throughout the history of British Columbia. The *Tilikum*, a converted dugout that sailed from Victoria to England during the years 1901 to 1904, is here. Captain James Cook display. (Daily; closed Jan 1, Dec 25) **$$**

Miniature World. *649 Humboldt St, Victoria (V8W 1A6). Phone 250/385-9731. www.miniature-world.com.* More than 80 miniature, 3-D scenes of fact, fiction, and history. Two large doll houses; very large rail diorama; villages; world's smallest operational sawmill. (Daily; closed Dec 25) **$$$**

Pacific Undersea Gardens. *490 Belleville St, Victoria (V8V 1W9). Phone 250/382-5717.* Underwater windows for viewing of more than 5,000 marine specimens; scuba diver shows. (Daily; closed Dec 25) **$$$**

Parliament Buildings. *501 Belleville St, Victoria (V8W 1A1). Phone 250/387-3046.* Built from 1893 to 1897 mostly of native materials, beautifully illuminated at night; houses British Columbia's Legislative Assembly. Guided tours (mid-June-Labor Day: daily; rest of year: Mon-Fri; closed holidays except summer). Foreign language tours. Advance notice suggested for group tours. **FREE**

Point Ellice House Museum. *2616 Pleasant St, Victoria (V8T 4V3). Phone 250/380-6506.* (1861) Original Victorian setting, furnishings. Afternoon tea served in restored garden. (May-mid-Sept; daily) **$$**

Royal British Columbia Museum. *675 Belleville St, Victoria (V8W 1A1). Phone 250/356-7226; toll-free 888/447-7977. www.royalbcmuseum.bc.ca.* Three-dimensional exhibits include natural and human history, indigenous history, and art; also a re-creation of a turn-of-the-century town. In the natural history gallery, the "Living Land-Living Sea" exhibit depicts the natural history of British Columbia from the Ice Age to the present. (Daily 9 am-5 pm; closed Jan 1, Dec 25) **$$$** While here, see

Carillon. Bells made in Holland; presented to the province by citizens of Dutch descent. Concerts; inquire locally for private tour.

National Geographic IMAX Theatre. *Phone 250/480-4887. www.imaxvictoria.com.* A selection of acclaimed films on topics from nature to exotic destinations appears larger than life on this giant IMAX screen. Purchase tickets in the museum's lobby; combination tickets are available. (Shows daily 10 am-9 pm; closed Jan 1, Dec 25) **$$**

Gardens

Vancouver Island's mild climate and British ancestry are two of the reasons Victoria is known as the "City of Gardens." Early British settlers planted roses to remind them of their home. Their love of gardening translated into the multitude of gardens in and around Victoria today, including Butchart Gardens, Hatley Park Gardens, and Abkhazi Garden. Throughout downtown Victoria, notice the flower baskets hanging from lampposts. Every June for the past 65 years, over 1,000 baskets are hung to herald the beginning of summer. The baskets remain up until mid-September. Even in inclement weather, visitors can enjoy the wealth of flowers and shrubs by visiting the Crystal Garden Conservation Centre downtown. Hundreds of tropical plants, endangered species of birds and mammals, and exotic butterflies, are housed in a building designed by famous Victoria architect Francis Rattenbury.

Whale-watching

Vancouver Island is known as one of the best places to view migrating and resident whales. Whale-watching tours leave from Victoria and other large city centers on the island. View migrating gray whales during March and April, while Orcas (killer) whales are best observed between May and October, with July and August as the key months for whale sightings. Three Orcas pods totaling more than 80 whales make their home in the waters off of Victoria. North of Vancouver Island, a resident community of 217 whales patrol the Johnstone Strait in 16 pods. Other whales and marine mammals that can be seen off of Vancouver Island include humpback whales, Minke whales, otters, seals, sea lions, and dolphins.

Thunderbird Park. Collection of authentic totem poles and indigenous carvings, representing the work of the main Pacific Coastal tribes. Indigenous carvers may be seen at work in the Carving Shed. (May-Sept).

Royal London Wax Museum. *470 Belleville St, Victoria (V8V 1W9). Phone 250/388-4461. www.waxworld.com.* More than 250 figures in theatrical settings. (Daily; closed Dec 25) **$$$**

Scenic Drives. Malahat Drive (Trans-Canada Hwy 1), a continuation of Victoria's Douglas Street, through Goldstream Park over Malahat Drive to Mill Bay, Cowichan Bay, Duncan, and the BC Forest Museum. **North.** On the continuation of Victoria's Blanshard Street (Hwys 17 and 17A) through rural communities, pastoral valleys known as the Saanich Peninsula where on 50 acres (20 hectares) of manicured lawns, ponds, fountains, and formal gardens bloom the world-famous Butchart Gardens. **North.** Around the seashore along Dallas Road through beautiful, traditionally English residential areas to Beach Drive, Oak Bay, and beyond to Cordova Bay. **West.** Leave the city behind on Trans-Canada Highway 1 to Highway 14, which winds through rural communities to the village of Sooke, where the population is still engaged in fishing, clamming, and logging. Unspoiled beaches, hiking trails, rocky seashores are accessible from this West Coast road. Continuation on Highway 14 will lead to Jordan River and to Port Renfrew, with its beautiful Botanical Beach.

Limited-Service Hotels

★ ★ **BEDFORD REGENCY HOTEL.** *1140 Government St, Victoria (V8W 1Y2). Phone 250/384-6835; toll-free 800/665-6500; fax 250/386-8930. www.* *bedfordregency.com.* Built around 1910, this building started its life as a bookstore and stationery shop. Today, it combines its old-world ambience with modern conveniences—window boxes outside every room and high-speed Internet access within. Nestled in Victoria's business district, it's just a short walk to the Parliament Buildings, museums, and other attractions. No recent renovation has marred the traditional feel or the size of the guest rooms, although the bathrooms are a bit on the small side. 40 rooms, 6 story. Check-in 3 pm, check-out 11 am. High-speed Internet access. Restaurant, bar. **$$**

✈

★ ★ **BEST WESTERN CARLTON PLAZA HOTEL.** *642 Johnson St, Victoria (V8W 1M6). Phone 250/388-5513; toll-free 800/663-7241; fax 250/388-5343. www.bestwesterncarlton.com.* Choose your entrance—from the street or through the Carlton Plaza shopping center, which shares this historic building. Although the building is heritage, the hotel is contemporary, with wireless Internet access in the lobby and complimentary bottled water in the guest rooms. Make use of the in-house fitness room or get a pass to the nearby YMCA/YWCA for a range of exercise and spa options. The on- site pancake house is open for breakfast and lunch. 103 rooms, 6 story. Pets accepted; fee. Check-in 3 pm, check-out 11 am. Restaurant. Fitness room. **$**

🐾 🏋

★ ★ **CHATEAU VICTORIA HOTEL AND SUITES.** *740 Burdett Ave, Victoria (V8W 1B2). Phone 250/382-4221; toll-free 800/663-5891; fax 250/380-1950. www.chateauvictoria.com.* Its location atop a hill, across the street from the Victoria Conference Centre, gives this hotel's Vista 18 restaurant on the top floor prime position for spectacular views of the city and the Inner Harbour. The fairly large lobby is a bright and comfortable place for meeting or relaxing. The hotel offers nearly twice as many suites as regular guest rooms; all the rooms boast recent-renovation touches such as duvets and writing desks. With its secure storage area for bicycles, Chateau Victoria is a good choice for cyclists. 177 rooms, 19 story. Pets accepted, some restrictions; fee. Check-in 3 pm, check-out 11 am. Restaurant, bar. Fitness room. Indoor pool, whirlpool. **$$**

★ ★ **EXECUTIVE HOUSE HOTEL.** *777 Douglas St, Victoria (V8W 2B5). Phone 250/388-5111; toll-free 800/663-7001; fax 250/385-1323. www.executivehouse .com.* This family-owned hotel has an excellent location across from the Victoria Conference Centre and just one block from the Inner Harbour and its many attractions. The original artwork in both public spaces and guest rooms is one of the advantages of staying at this independent hotel, as is a friendly staff. The guest accommodations are spacious and comfortable; executive suites boast a full kitchen. The Executive Club and Executive Level cater to business travelers, and pet-friendly policies let families feel at home away from home. 181 rooms, 17 story. Pets accepted, some restrictions; fee. Check-in 3 pm, check-out noon. Restaurant, bar. Fitness room. Whirlpool. **$**

★ ★ **HARBOUR TOWERS HOTEL & SUITES.** *345 Quebec St, Victoria (V8V 1W4). Phone 250/385-2405; toll-free 800/663-5896; fax 250/360-2313. www. harbourtowers.com.* Convenient to downtown, this hotel's comfortable contemporary décor includes solid dark woods and soothing neutral colors in the overstuffed sofas and chairs. You can relax in front of the fire in the lobby, swim laps in the indoor pool, or make use of the facilities at the independently operated spa. A full-service restaurant can take care of your dining needs, and a children's activity center and babysitting services are helpful for families. 195 rooms, 12 story. Pets accepted, some restrictions; fee. Complimentary continental breakfast. Check-out 11 am. Restaurant, bar. Children's activity center. Fitness room, spa. Indoor pool, whirlpool. Airport transportation available. Business center. **$$**

★ ★ **ROYAL SCOT SUITE HOTEL.** *425 Quebec St, Victoria (V8V 1W7). Phone 250/388-5463; toll-free 800/663-7315; fax 250/388-5452. www.royalscot.com.* Most of the guest rooms at this hotel—about 80 percent—are suites. but even the regular rooms are spacious and inviting. The inn has a billiards room with a full-size table as well as a game room stocked with board games, puzzles, playing cards, and a TV. Although the hotel is located on a street filled with commercial businesses, it backs up to a quiet residential area and takes on some of that ambience. The extensive and beautifully landscaped grounds help give guests the feeling of being in an oasis in the middle of the city. 176 rooms, 4 story. Check-in 3 pm, check-out noon. Restaurant, bar. Children's activity center. Fitness room. Indoor pool, whirlpool. **$**

Full-Service Hotels

★ ★ ★ **COAST HARBOURSIDE HOTEL & MARINA.** *146 Kingston St, Victoria (V9B 5X3). Phone 250/360-1211; toll-free 800/663-1144; fax 250/360-1418. www.coasthotels.com.* A contemporary high-rise built in 1991, this hotel has its own marina where you can dock overnight or stay for a month. Marine-life and whale-watching tours leave directly from the marina. Additional water-based attractions include the indoor/outdoor pool and whirlpool, both with views of the harbor. Take a shuttle, water taxi, or a scenic stroll into downtown and the attractions there. Well-appointed guest rooms provide large writing desks, Web TV, and two phone lines for business travelers, and the Blue Crab Bar and Grill (see) provides a full-service grill and fantastic views. 140 rooms, 10 story. Pets accepted; fee. Check-in 4 pm, check-out 11 am. High-speed Internet access. Restaurant, bar. Fitness room. Indoor pool, outdoor pool, whirlpool. **$$$**

★ ★ ★ **THE FAIRMONT EMPRESS.** *721 Government St, Victoria (V8W 1W5). Phone 250/384-8111; toll-free 800/441-1414; fax 250/389-2747. www. fairmont.com.* The Fairmont Empress is one of British Columbia's most cherished landmarks. Nearly a century old, this storybook castle resting on the banks of Victoria's Inner Harbour enjoys a legendary past. Royals and celebrities have long favored this graceful hotel, where a walk through the doors returns guests to the grace of a bygone era. Classic and elegant, the public and private spaces reflect Victorian-era styling with mahogany furnishings and floral fabrics. Afternoon tea at The Fairmont Empress is a local institution and is a must for all visitors to Victoria. Additional dining options include the exotic Bengal Lounge, the sophisticated Empress Room (see), and the casual Kipling's. Steeped in tradition while embracing the 21st century, the hotel has recently added a spa to its list of amenities. 477 rooms, 7 story. Pets accepted, some restrictions; fee. Check-in 4 pm, check-out 11 am. Restaurant, bar. Fitness room, spa. Indoor pool, children's pool, whirlpool. **$$$**

★ ★ ★ HOTEL GRAND PACIFIC.

463 Belleville St, Victoria (V8V 1X3). Phone 250/386-0450; toll-free 800/663-7550; fax 250/380-4473. www.hotelgrandpacific.com. Located at the southern tip of Vancouver Island, Victoria is a tiny slice of England on a ruggedly beautiful island. Its quaint downtown and beautiful Inner Harbour is home to the sophisticated Hotel Grand Pacific, one of the city's best hotels. Its location is superb, with serene water views and easy access to historic Old Town and area businesses. The rooms and suites are light and airy, with pastel colors rounding out the sun-filled spaces. Fine dining is one of Victoria's hallmarks, and this hotel is no exception. The Pacific Northwest cuisine at The Pacific is a stand-out, while The Mark's regionally influenced dishes are equally delicious. Extra calories aren't a worry here, where a large fitness center and spa help guests work off any dietary indiscretions. 304 rooms, 10 story. Pets accepted, some restrictions; fee. Check-in 3 pm, check-out noon. Restaurant, bar. Fitness room, spa. Indoor pool, whirlpool. **$$**

★ ★ ★ LAUREL POINT INN. *680 Montreal St,*
Victoria (V8V 1Z8). Phone 250/386-8721; toll-free 800/663-7667; fax 250/386-9547. www.laurelpoint.com. Every room of this hotel has a balcony and a fabulous view of either the Inner Harbour or the Upper Harbour. Or you can check out the view as you stroll along the paved harbor walkway. The grounds include a Japanese-style garden, and the Asian influence is felt in the décor of the hotel's public rooms (which include 11 meeting rooms) and, to a lesser extent, its guest rooms. Relax in the cozy piano lounge, the fragrant garden, or the outdoor patio. 200 rooms,

3 story. Pets accepted, some restrictions; fee. Check-in 3 pm, check-out 11:30 am. Restaurant, bar. Beach. Indoor pool, whirlpool. **$$$**

★ ★ ★ MAGNOLIA HOTEL AND SPA. *623*
Courtney St, Victoria (V8W 1B8). Phone 250/381-0999; toll-free 877/624-6654; fax 250/381-0988. www.magnoliahotel.com. This luxury boutique hotel provides comfort and pampering throughout. The cherry-paneled walls and oversized chairs and sofas of blue, taupe, and gold tones in the lobby immerse you in an old-world ambience and touch on the contemporary with excellent photographs of area landmarks. The cherry wood carries through in the guest room appointments—a large work desk, an armoire housing the TV, and two armchairs. The spa offers a full range of beauty and relaxation regimens and prides itself on using natural products from renewable resources. 63 rooms, 7 story. Pets accepted, some restrictions; fee. Complimentary continental breakfast. Check-in 3 pm, check-out noon. Restaurant, bar. Fitness room, spa. **$$$**

★ ★ ★ SWANS SUITE HOTEL. *506 Pandora*
Ave, Victoria (V8W 1N2). Phone 250/361-3310; toll-free 800/668-7926; fax 250/361-3491. www.swanshotel.com. Built in 1913, this hotel holds 30 one- and two-bedroom suites that sleep up to six adults. It's a lively place with its own brewery and two popular eating and drinking establishments that serve ales brewed in the British tradition. Most of the guest rooms have a loft that contributes a spacious feeling, and various rooms have a variety of features, including skylights and private patios. All room boast full kitchens, duvets, and original artwork. 30 rooms, 4 story, all suites. Check-in 4 pm, check-out noon. Restaurant, bar. **$$**

Full-Service Resorts

★ ★ ★ DELTA VICTORIA OCEAN POINTE
RESORT AND SPA. *45 Songhees Rd, Victoria (V9A 6T3). Phone 888/778-5050; toll-free 888/244-8666; fax 250/360-2999. www.oprhotel.com.* Located on a point between Victoria's Inner and Upper harbours, this elegant, modern hotel offers wonderful views of the waterfront, Parliament Buildings, and the Royal

BC Museum—just choose a vantage point. Everything is prime, from the high-end amenities in the guest rooms to the full range of services in the European-style spa to the food served in the restaurants. Taking advantage of the full resort experience may include participating in water aerobics and other fitness classes, booking a tee time on a nearby golf course, and playing tennis on one of the hotel's two lighted courts. 242 rooms, 8 story. Pets accepted; fee. Check-in 3 pm, check-out noon. High-speed Internet access. Restaurant, bar. Children's activity center. Fitness room, spa. Indoor pool, whirlpool. Tennis. Business center. **$$**

★ ★ ★ **OAK BAY BEACH AND MARINE RESORT.** *1175 Beach Dr, Victoria (V8S 2N2). Phone 250/598-4556; toll-free 800/668-7758; fax 250/598-6180. www.oakbaybeachhotel.com.* Almost all of this resort's individually decorated guest rooms have a spectacular view of Oak Bay and beyond to Mount Baker. The Tudor-style inn offers plenty of activities and amenities for the adventuresome, including the loan of a tennis racquet or mountain bike. Start the day with a continental breakfast and then pursue hiking, kayaking, golfing, or whale-watching activities. Or choose a day cruise to Roche Harbour or a rail ride to take in the magnificent scenery. You can choose pub fare for your meals or go the fine-dining route at Bentley's Seaside Patio. End the day by gathering around the fireplace for hot chocolate and cookies. 49 rooms, 3 story. Complimentary continental breakfast. Check-in 3 pm, check-out noon. Restaurant, bar. Beach. **$$**

Full-Service Inns

★ ★ ★ **ENGLISH INN & RESORT.** *429 Lampson St, Victoria (V9A 5Y9). Phone 250/388-4353; toll-free 866/388-4353; fax 250/382-8311. www.englishinnresort.com.* This unique resort was built to echo an English country village. The main manor is a replica of Anne Hathaway's cottage, and the names of the satellite houses continue the Shakespearean theme. The buildings are set amidst 5 acres of beautifully landscaped English-style gardens—the perfect setting for a wedding, the hosting of which is one of the resort's specialties. Renovations in 2003 gave the resort a more modern feel, with hardwood floors and contemporary colors, although plenty of antiques still grace the guest rooms and public spaces. The lack of elevators may dissuade some guests. 40 rooms, 3 story.

Pets accepted, some restrictions; fee. Complimentary continental breakfast. Check-in 3 pm, check-out 11 am. High-speed Internet access. Restaurant, bar. Children's activity center. Business center. **$$**

★ ★ ★ ★ **HASTINGS HOUSE.** *160 Upper Ganges Rd, Salt Spring Island (V8K 2S2). Phone 250/537-2362; toll-free 800/661-9255; fax 250/537-5333. www.hastingshouse.com.* Snuggled on a sylvan knoll on Canada's Salt Spring Island, the Tudor-style Hastings House captures the essence of the English countryside. This charming country estate delights its visitors, who retreat to this inn for a taste of the good life. Scattered throughout the lovely grounds, the rooms and suites are housed within ivy-covered garden cottages and the timber-framed barn. The accommodations are full of character and distinguished by wood-burning fireplaces, beamed ceilings, window seats, and overstuffed furnishings. All feature enchanting views of the estate's verdant lawns or the sparkling harbor. Guests don jackets for the formal setting and refined cuisine of the Dining Room, while the Verandah offers the same menu in a more casual garden setting. The Snug, adjacent to the wine cellar, provides an inviting spot for informal fare. While outdoor enthusiasts will find a bevy of athletic pursuits, many choose to remain within this storybook setting. 18 rooms. Closed mid-Nov-mid-Mar. Check-in 3 pm, check-out 11 am. Restaurant. **$$$$**

★ ★ ★ **SHOAL HARBOUR INN.** *2308 Harbour Rd, Sidney (V8L 2P8). Phone 250/656-6622; toll-free 877/956-6622; fax 250/656-6212. www.shoalharbourinn.com.* Here, guests stay in either the Shoal Harbour Inn suites or the historic Latch guest rooms. The Latch Mansion, built in the 1920s, was the summer residence for the lieutenant governor of British Columbia. It is located in Sidney, just 20 minutes from downtown Victoria and five minutes from ferries and the airport. Guest rooms are decorated with Canadian furnishings and artwork. Dine in the intimate small dining rooms in the Latch Mansion after watching the sun set over the harbor from the terrace. 26 rooms. Check-in 3 pm, check-out 11 am. High-speed Internet access. Restaurant, bar. Fitness room. Whirlpool. Business center. **$$**

★ ★ ★ **SOOKE HARBOUR HOUSE.** *1528 Whiffen Spit Rd, Sooke (V0S 1N0). Phone 250/642-*

3421; toll-free 800/889-9688; fax 250/642-6988. www.
sookeharbourhouse.com. Located on Vancouver Island
by the sea, this bed-and-breakfast features 28 beautifully designed guest rooms with fireplaces and
spectacular ocean views. Guests can enjoy such area
activities as hiking, whale watching and cross-country
skiing. Ideal for a romantic getaway or honeymoon-
ers. 28 rooms, 4 story. Closed 3 weeks in Jan. Pets
accepted; fee. Complimentary continental breakfast.
Check-in 3 pm, check-out noon. Restaurant. **$$$**

Specialty Lodgings

The following lodging establishments are approved by
Mobil Travel Guide, but due to their unique and indi-
vidualized nature have not been given a traditional
Mobil Star rating. Included in this listing you may
find bed-and-breakfasts, limited-service inns, guest
ranches, and other unique hotel properties.

ABIGAIL'S HOTEL. *906 McClure St, Victoria (V8V
3E7). Phone 250/388-5363; toll-free 800/561-6565; fax
250/388-7787. www.abigailshotel.com.* This colorfully
painted inn consists of a historic Tudor mansion and
converted carriage house. The quiet setting belies
the inn's location just three blocks from Victoria's
Inner Harbour and main tourist attractions. Enjoy
afternoon tea in the book-lined library while sinking
into a leather armchair or sofa in front of a blazing
fire. A full gourmet breakfast is served overlooking the
patio and English-style gardens. The guest rooms are
well appointed, with down-filled duvets and private
baths, many with Jacuzzi tubs. 23 rooms, 4 story.
Complimentary full breakfast. Check-in 3 pm, check-
out 11 am. **$$**

ANDERSEN HOUSE. *301 Kingston St, Victoria
(V8V 1V5). Phone 250/388-4565; fax 250/388-4563.
www.andersenhouse.com.* This sprawling Queen
Anne Victorian home successfully blends old-world
charm with contemporary excitement. The guest
rooms' hardwood floors are covered with Persian
rugs, and the walls are decorated with lively modern
artwork. Individual rooms may have a Jacuzzi for
two, European stained-glass windows, a microwave
and fridge, or a private sundeck; all rooms have
feather beds, TVs, CD players, and Calvin Klein
robes. Spotless cleanliness, a full breakfast, and several
outdoor lounging areas make this inn worth checking

into. 5 rooms, 3 story. Children over 12 years only.
Check-in 1 pm, check-out 11 am. Wireless Internet
access. **$$**

BEACONSFIELD INN. *998 Humboldt St, Victoria
(V8V 2Z8). Phone 250/384-4044; toll-free 888/884-
4044; fax 250/384-4052. www.beaconsfieldinn.com.*
Built around 1905 by a local financier, this three-story
Edwardian mansion on Victoria's south side, not far
from the water, is a Registered Heritage Property.
The inn makes the most of its British heritage both
in appearance and attitude. Rich wood paneling is
complemented by antique furnishings and period
décor. The gardens are kept in the English style, and
high tea and sherry are served each afternoon. Each
guest room boasts unique décor and features, among
them canopied beds, skylights, beamed ceilings,
leaded and stained-glass windows, and wood-burning
fireplaces. 9 rooms, 3 story. Complimentary continen-
tal breakfast. Check-in 3 pm, check-out 11 am. **$$**

GATSBY MANSION B&B. *309 Belleville St,
Victoria (V8V 1X2). Phone 250/388-9191; toll-free
800/663-7557; fax 250/382-7666. www.bellevillepark
.com.* Soak up the sunshine off of Victoria's Inner
Harbour from the bay windows of the Gatsby
Mansion. Victorian décor enhances the 20 guest suites.
Chandeliers, stained-glass windows, and hand-frescoed
ceilings in the public rooms take guests back in time.
Rooms face the harbor, a rose garden, or the topiary.
20 rooms. Complimentary continental breakfast.
Check-in 3 pm, check-out noon. Restaurant, bar. **$$**

HATERLEIGH HERITAGE INN. *243 Kingston
St, Victoria (V8V 1V5). Phone 866/234-2244; toll-free
866/234-2244; fax 250/384-1935. www.haterleigh.com.*
This seven-room inn was converted from a private
residence built in 1901. The city designated it a
heritage property, and the neighborhood surrounding
it and the antiques decorating it—including remark-
able leaded stained-glass windows—tell you why. The
innkeepers reflect traditional values by providing
locally made soaps along with plush robes in the guest
rooms and using local organic produce in preparing a
full gourmet breakfast each morning. The afternoon
social hour provides an opportunity to mingle,
browse the Internet, or relax on the covered veranda.
7 rooms, 2 story. Complimentary full breakfast.
Check-in 4-5 pm, check-out 11 am. **$$**

PRIOR HOUSE B&B INN. *620 St. Charles, Victoria (V8S 3N7). Phone 250/592-8847; toll-free 877/924-3300; fax 250/592-8223. www.priorhouse.com.* This English-manor-style home features antique-filled rooms, some with ocean and mountain views. The property's stone staircases and beautiful gardens are within walking distance of many local historic sites and antique shops. 6 rooms, 3 story. Complimentary full breakfast. Check-in 4-6 pm, check-out 11 am. **$$**

ROSEWOOD INN. *595 Michigan St, Victoria (V8V 1S7). Phone 250/384-6644; toll-free 866/986-2222; fax 250/384-6117. www.rosewoodvictoria.com.* Each suite in this English-style inn boasts a distinctive decorating style. Some rooms are done up in traditional English floral patterns, while other rooms reflect contemporary colors and style. Most rooms have a fireplace, some have a patio or veranda, and all have a private bath and sitting room with TV and telephone. The quiet, residential location is a short walk to the Inner Harbour, restaurants and shopping, and ferry terminals. The grounds are beautifully landscaped, and the courtyard boasts a goldfish pond. 17 rooms, 3 story. Children over 10 years only. Complimentary full breakfast. Check-in 3 pm, check-out 11 am. **$**
✈

Restaurants

★ ★ ★ **ANTOINE'S.** *2 Centennial Sq, Victoria (V8V 1P7). Phone 250/384-7055.* Adjacent to City Hall, this restaurant overlooks Centennial Square's beautiful fountain. French menu. Dinner. Closed Jan 1. Bar. Reservations recommended. **$$$**
🅳

★ ★ **BLUE CRAB BAR AND GRILL.** *146 Kingston, Victoria (V8V 1V4). Phone 250/480-1999; fax 250/360-1418. www.coasthotels.com.* Seafood menu. Breakfast, lunch, dinner, Sun brunch. Bar. Children's menu. **$$$**

★ ★ **CAFE BRIO.** *944 Fort St, Victoria (V8V 3K2). Phone 250/383-0009; fax 250/383-0063. www.cafe-brio .com.* Eclectic menu. Dinner. Closed Dec 25; first week in Jan. Bar. Outdoor seating. **$$$**

★ ★ **CAMILLE'S.** *45 Bastion Sq, Victoria (V8W 1J1). Phone 250/381-3433. www.camillesrestaurant.com.* Eclectic menu. Dinner. Closed Jan 1, Dec 24-25. **$$**

★ ★ ★ **DEEP COVE CHALET.** *11190 Chalet Rd, Sidney (V8L 4R4). Phone 250/656-3541; fax 250/656-2601. www.deepcovechalet.com.* This charming and historic country inn has a great view overlooking the waters of the inside passage. Built in 1914, it originally was a teahouse for a railroad station. French menu. Lunch, dinner. Closed Mon. Bar. Children's menu. Outdoor seating. **$$$**

★ ★ ★ **EMPRESS ROOM.** *721 Government St, Victoria (V8W 1W5). Phone 250/384-8111; fax 250/381-5939. www.fairmont.com.* Dine on classic cuisine in this richly appointed room of tapestries, intricately carved ceilings, and live harp music. The 100-year-old hotel's waterfront location is full of European style, a great spot for a romantic meal. Eclectic menu. Dinner. Closed Mon, Tues in Nov and Feb. Children's menu. Jacket required. Reservations recommended. Outdoor seating. **$$$**

★ ★ **GATSBY MANSION.** *309 Belleville St, Victoria (V8V 1X2). Phone 250/388-9191; toll-free 800/563-9656. www.gatsbymansion.com.* French menu. Breakfast, lunch, dinner. Children's menu. Outdoor seating. **$$$**
🅳

★ ★ ★ **HERALD STREET CAFFE.** *546 Herald St, Victoria (V8W 1S6). Phone 250/381-1441; fax 250/ 381-1093. www.heraldstreetcaffe.com.* This restaurant has a consistently great menu, served up in a casual, lively atmosphere, providing exceptionally good service. California, seafood, eclectic menu. Lunch, dinner, Sun brunch. Bar. Outdoor seating. **$$**

★ ★ **HUGO'S.** *619 Courtney St, Victoria (V8W 1B8). Phone 250/920-4844; fax 250/920-4842. www. hugoslounge.com.* Eclectic menu. Lunch, dinner, late-night. Closed Dec 25. Bar. Outdoor seating. **$$$**

★ ★ **IL TERRAZZO.** *555 Johnson St, Victoria (V8W 1M2). Phone 250/361-0028; fax 250/360-2594. www.ilterrazzo.com.* Italian menu. Lunch, dinner. Closed Jan 1, Dec 25. Bar. Outdoor seating. **$$$**

★ **J & J WONTON NOODLE HOUSE.** *1012 Fort St, Victoria (V8V 3K4). Phone 250/383-0680. www. jjnoodlehouse.com.* Chinese menu. Lunch, dinner. Closed Sun-Mon; holidays; also 2 weeks (time varies). **$$**

★ ★ **JAPANESE VILLAGE STEAK AND SEAFOOD HOUSE.** *734 Broughton St, Victoria (V8W 1E1). Phone 250/382-5165. www.japanesevillage .bc.ca.* Japanese menu. Lunch, dinner. Closed holidays. Children's menu. Outdoor seating. **$$**

★ ★ **THE MARINA.** *1327 Beach Dr, Victoria (V8S 2N4). Phone 250/598-8555; fax 250/598-3014. www.obmg.com.* Seafood menu. Lunch, dinner, Sun brunch. Closed Dec 25. Bar. Children's menu. **$$$**

★ ★ ★ **RESTAURANT MATISSE.** *512 Yates St, Victoria (V8W 1K8). Phone 250/480-0883; fax 250/480-0886. www.restaurantmatisse.com.* Right smack in the heart of downtown Victoria, you will discover a delightful retreat for authentic French fare. Warmed with yellow brick walls, colorful floral arrangements, and country-style charm, Restaurant Matisse is a gem of a dining room that has become a destination for simple, traditional French fare among Vancouver's dining elite. Many dishes taste as though they've been beamed over from a Parisian kitchen. House specialties include duck palette and Marseilles-style bouillabaisse. In addition to the à la carte selections, the chef offers a nine-course prix fixe menu for those who have penciled excess and indulgence into the evening. While French wines dominate the list, a great selection of California bottles is also included. Classic French menu. Dinner. Closed Mon, Tues; also two weeks in May. Children's menu. **$$$**

★ ★ ★ **SOOKE HARBOUR HOUSE.** *1528 Whiffen Spit Rd, Sooke Harbour (V0S 1N0). Phone 250/ 642-3421; fax 250/642-6988. www.sookeharbourhouse .com.* Considered one of the most unique restaurants in Canada. Here, guests will find a new menu daily. Fresh, local organic seafood, meat, and produce are the focus. Meals have special flavors with edible herbs and flowers from the garden. Eclectic menu. Multicourse menu. Dinner. Closed Mon-Wed in Jan and Dec. **$$$**

★ ★ **SPINNAKER'S BREW PUB.** *308 Catherine St, Victoria (V9A 3S8). Phone 250/386-2739; fax 250/ 384-3246. www.spinnakers.com.* Eclectic menu. Breakfast, lunch, dinner. Bar. Children's menu. Outdoor seating. **$$**

★ ★ ★ **THE VICTORIAN.** *45 Songhees Rd, Victoria (V9A 6T3). Phone 250/360-5800; fax 250/360-1041. www.deltahotels.com.* Located in the Ocean Pointe Resort Hotel, this fine restaurant has wonderful panoramic views of Victoria. Eclectic menu. Dinner. Closed Sun-Mon; also Jan. Bar. Valet parking. **$$$**

★ **WHITE HEATHER TEA ROOM.** *1885 Oak Bay Ave, Victoria (V8R 1C6). Phone 250/595-8020; fax 250/598-4667. www.whiteheathertearoom.com.* Scottish menu. Lunch. Closed Sun-Mon. Reservations recommended. **$**

Alaska

The breathtaking beauty of million-year-old glaciers, a rugged landscape, and exotic wildlife make Alaska a paradise for nature lovers. Its national forests and parks are America's largest, and the abundant coastal waters provide some of the best salmon and halibut fishing in the world. Veteran rock and ice climbers routinely assault Mount McKinley, the highest peak in North America at 20,320 feet, and the truly intrepid compete in the annual Iditarod sled dog race. Surprisingly cosmopolitan and comfortable, Anchorage is home to about half of the state's population and offers first-class restaurants, nightclubs, and entertainment.

The great Yukon River cuts the Alaskan interior almost in half, carving tremendous valleys along the way as it makes its 1,265-mile journey from the state's border to the Bering Sea. The mazelike convergence of land and water in the famed Inside Passage of the panhandle was sculpted into its present form by thousands of years of glacial ice scoring its way toward the sea and eventually melting.

Population: 626,932
Area: 586,412 square miles
Elevation: 0-20,320 feet
Peak: Mount McKinley
Entered Union: January 3, 1959 (49th state)
Capital: Juneau
Motto: North to the Future
Nickname: The Last Frontier
Flower: Forget-Me-Not
Bird: Willow Ptarmigan
Tree: Sitka Spruce
Fair: August in Palmer
Time Zone: Alaska, Hawaii-Aleutian
Information: Alaska Travel Industry Association, 2600 Cordova St, Suite 201, Anchorage, 99503
Web site: www.travelalaska.com
Fun Facts:
- Alaska's state gem is jade. An entire mountain of jade is located on the Seward Peninsula.
- Alaska has almost twice as many caribou as people.
- More than 450,000 cruise ship passengers visit Juneau between May and September each year.
- Alaska contains the northernmost, westernmost, and easternmost points in the United States. (The Aleutian Chain extends into the Eastern Hemisphere.)

When to Go/Climate

Befitting its vastness, Alaska experiences a huge range of temperatures throughout the year. In the far north, average daily high temperatures never reach 50 degrees, even in summer, while southeastern Alaska enjoys temperatures in the 60s and higher between June and August. Obviously, summer is peak travel season, with hours of sunlight nearing 20 hours per day. Only a few hardy souls venture here in the colder, darker months.

AVERAGE HIGH/LOW TEMPERATURES (° F)

Anchorage

Jan 22/9	**May** 55/39	**Sept** 55/41
Feb 26/12	**June** 62/47	**Oct** 40/28
Mar 34/18	**July** 65/52	**Nov** 28/16
Apr 44/29	**Aug** 63/49	**Dec** 24/11

Juneau

Jan 31/21	**May** 56/40	**Sept** 56/44
Feb 34/24	**June** 62/46	**Oct** 47/38
Mar 39/28	**July** 64/49	**Nov** 38/29
Apr 48/33	**Aug** 63/48	**Dec** 33/24

Calendar Highlights

FEBRUARY

Fur Rendezvous (*Anchorage*). *Phone 907/274-1177. www.furrondy.net.* Winter festival and carnival that leads into the Iditarod.

MARCH

Iditarod and Sled Dog Races (*Anchorage*). *Phone 907/376-5155. www.iditarod.com.* The sled dog races are short-distance events beginning downtown. The Iditarod, a separate event run by a different group, caps off the week. This famous dogsled race covers more than 1,150 miles from Anchorage to Nome and usually takes 9 to 12 days.

MAY

Kachemak Bay Shorebird Festival (*Homer*). *Contact the Chamber of Commerce, phone 907/235-7740. www.homeralaska.org/shorebird.htm.* A popular festival celebrating the arrival of hundreds of thousands of migratory birds each spring.

JUNE

Copper River Wild! Salmon Festival (*Cordova*). *Contact the Chamber of Commerce, phone 907/424-7260.* Celebrates the annual arrival of Copper River Reds (red salmon)—a major Alaskan export.

Last Frontier Theatre Conference (*Valdez*). One of the largest theatric conferences in America, with 400 to 800 participants, depending on which famous people agree to take part. Features playwrights, authors, actors, and wannabes. The honorary founder is playwright Edward Albee.

Summer Solstice Festival (*Fairbanks*). Considered the biggest and best in a state in which nearly every town celebrates the summer solstice.

JULY

Fourth of July Festival and Mount Marathon Race (*Seward*). *Contact the Chamber of Commerce, phone 907/224-8051.* Considered by many to be the best Independence Day festival in Alaska. Thousands of people flood into town for parades, food booths, music, and craft fairs. The festival is capped off by the Mount Marathon Race, one of the oldest and toughest footraces in America (a 3.25-mile run from just above sea level to the top of Mount Marathon—3,020 feet—and crashing back down again).

Moose Dropping Festival (*Talkeetna*). *Phone 907/733-2487.* This festival ranks high in terms of small-town charm: food and craft booths, slow-pitch softball tournaments, a mini parade, a footrace, pancake breakfasts, and the Mountain Mother Contests, where local women compete for the title of Mountain Mother (crossing a "stream" with a baby doll on their backs, shooting an arrow, casting a fishing pole, cutting firewood, etc.).

AUGUST

Alaska State Fair (*Palmer*). *Phone 907/745-4827. www.alaskastatefair.org.* Giant veggies, including cabbages the size of beanbag chairs, lots of farm animals, and rides all in the beautiful setting of the Matanuska Valley, 40 minutes north of Anchorage.

NOVEMBER

Haines Bald Eagle Festival (*Haines*). *Phone 907/766-3094. baldeagles.org/festival.* Tens of thousands of bald eagles descend on Haines for the late salmon run.

Parks and Recreation

Alaska's state parks are concentrated in the southern half of the state, with a large number on the Kenai Peninsula. Water-related activities, hiking, camping, and picnicking are available in many of Alaska's state parks on a seasonal basis. Daily parking fees are $3-$5 per vehicle, while camping fees range from $10-$15 a night. Cabins are available at more than 15 parks. The Alaska Trails System, established in 2001, includes 41 land- and water-based trails notable for their scenic, historic, and recreational value, such as the Iditarod National Historic Trail. For more information or to reserve a cabin, contact the Alaska Department of Natural Resources, Division of Parks and Outdoor Recreation, at 550 W 7th Ave, Suite 1260, Anchorage, 99501 (phone 907/269-8400) or 3700 Airport Way, Fairbanks, 99709 (phone 907/451-2705); or visit the Web site www.dnr.state.ak.us/parks.

FISHING AND HUNTING

Fishing and hunting in Alaska are legendary. From salmon to moose to brown and black bears, the state's wildlife is plentiful and thriving. Because hunting here is so different than in other states, nonresidents must be accompanied by a registered Alaskan guide or by close relatives who are residents. Conditions are rugged and excursions are expensive, so casual hunters may want to opt for wildlife viewing instead. A nonresident hunting license costs $85, a small game license costs $20, and a state waterfowl stamp is $5. For more information, contact the Division of Wildlife Conservation, PO Box 25526, Juneau, 99802; phone 907/465-4190.

Saltwater and freshwater fishing charters can be arranged throughout the state; you can find a list of registered businesses on the Web at www. sf.adfg.state.ak.us. An annual nonresident sport fishing license costs $100, while a seven-day license runs $50, a three-day license is $20, and a one-day license is $10. A one-day king salmon stamp costs $10. For more information, contact the Division of Sport Fish headquarters, 1255 W 8th St, Juneau, 99801; phone 907/465-4180.

A combination nonresident hunting and seven-day sport fishing license can be obtained for $115. For more information about fishing, hunting, and wildlife viewing in Alaska, contact the Alaska Department of Fish and Game, PO Box 25526, Juneau, 99802; phone 907/465-4100; www.wildlife. alaska.gov.

Driving Information

Travelers should note that most rental car agencies do not permit their vehicles to be driven on unpaved roads in Alaska, including, but not limited to, the Dalton, Denali, Elliott, Steese, and Taylor highways and the road from Chitina to McCarthy inside Wrangell-St. Elias National Park & Preserve.

Additional Visitor Information

Coast Magazine, which focuses on outdoor recreation, is published monthly and distributed free throughout the state. Visit their Web site at www. coast-magazine.com. Alaska's *Official State Guide and Vacation Planner* is available by contacting: Alaska Vacation Planner, Mailing Center, Dept. 501, PO Box 3728, Portland, OR, 972078; phone 907/465-2010. For a calendar of events and state and campground maps, contact Division of Tourism, Dept AP, PO Box 110801, Juneau, AK 99811-0801; phone 907/465-2010.

A number of visitor bureaus and tourist boards are located throughout the state and can provide information on planning stops at points of interest. Their locations are as follows: Anchorage, Delta Junction, Fairbanks, Haines, Homer, Juneau, Kenai, Ketchikan, Kodiak, Matanuska-Susitna Valleys, Nome, Palmer, Petersburg, Sitka, Skagway, Talkeetna, Tok, and Valdez.

CRUISING SOUTHEASTERN ALASKA

Alaska is at its most beautiful along the state's pristine southeastern coast, a spectacular stretch of densely forested islands, snowcapped mountains, ancient glaciers, and abundant wildlife. Aside from a few historic port towns, the region is undeveloped, and as such it cannot be navigated by car. The coastal area can be explored by watercraft, however, sheltered by the thousand-plus islands just off the mainland, most notably those of the Alexander Archipelago. The straits and channels between the islands enable boats of all sizes to weave their way through the Northwest's Inside Passage, protected from the open, choppy seas of the Pacific Ocean. Cruises have become a popular way to experience the splendor of Alaska's southeastern coast.

For those seeking a luxurious voyage, Princess Cruises offers Alaska vacations aboard ships with such amenities as swimming pools, day spas, movie theaters, casinos, and art galleries. The Voyage of the Glaciers Cruise travels between Vancouver, British Columbia, and Whittier, Alaska. The seven-day journey includes stops in scenic Glacier Bay and College Fjord, as well as the gold-rush town of Skagway and the state capital, Juneau. For more information, contact Princess Cruises toll-free at 800/774-6237 or visit www.princess.com.

Holland America features cruises coupled with land tours, a great choice for travelers who want the conveniences of a cruise but still want to experience the magnificence and enormity of Alaska's interior. The 14-day Alyeska Denali Adventure involves varied means of travel, including seven days of ship-based exploration within the Inside Passage, a drive up the Seward Highway for a two-night stay at the Alyeska Prince Hotel overlooking Glacier Valley, a train ride between Anchorage and Fairbanks aboard a domed railcar, and a tundra wilderness tour in Denali National Park. Call Holland America toll-free at 877/724-5425 or visit www.hollandamerica.com for details.

The elegant sternwheeler *Empress of the North* (www.empressofthenorth.com) harkens back to the 19th century, when paddlewheel riverboats plied the waterways of the Northwest. The 112-stateroom *Empress* is smaller than most cruise ships, enabling it to sail closer to shore and pass through narrow inlets and fjords. The 11-night Inside Passage Cruise travels between Seattle to the south and Sitka to the north, with ports of call in Victoria, Ketchikan, and Glacier Bay National Park. The cruise is offered by the American West Steamboat Company, which can be reached toll-free at 800/434-1232.

Budget-minded travelers should consider booking a trip with the Alaska Marine Highway System (www.dot.state.ak.us/amhs), which travels between Skagway and Bellingham, Washington, on its Inside Passage route. While not nearly as posh as the major cruise lines, the vessels in Alaska's fleet have cafeterias, recliner lounges, solariums, and private cabins with bathroom facilities. More adventurous travelers choose to pitch tents on the ship's exposed upper deck. Perhaps the main advantage of using the Marine Highway System is that each vessel has a deck for the storage of passenger cars, bikes, and kayaks—perfect for travelers who want to continue their adventures when the ship comes ashore.

Anchor Point

Population 1,845
Area Code 907

Anchor Point is located in the southwestern corner of the Kenai Peninsula. The main claim to fame of this tiny community is that it is the westernmost point on the US highway system, but its spectacular setting is what really makes it so appealing. The town is nestled in the middle of an untamed landscape of rugged, windswept beaches, densely wooded hills, and icy rivers and streams. It's a popular destination for fishermen, who have the option of freshwater fishing in the Anchor River for salmon and steelhead trout or saltwater fishing for halibut and salmon on one of the many charter boats based at the local harbor. The town also has a number of public campgrounds that provide primitive camping facilities along with easy access to the Anchor River and nearby beaches.

What to See and Do

Anchor River State Recreation Area. *5 miles N. Phone 907/262-5581. www.dnr.state.ak.us/parks/ units/anchoriv.htm.* In the 1770s, this area got its name when Captain James Cook lost an anchor at the mouth of the river. Today, people venture here to catch glimpses of moose, beaver, mink, and bald eagles, along with the beluga whales, harbor seals, and sea otters that hang around near the shore of Cook Inlet. You also can see three volcanoes across the inlet: Mount Augustine to the south and Mount Iliamna and Mount Redoubt to the north. Fishing is quite popular here; anglers can hope to catch salmon, Dolly Varden, and steelhead in the summer months. Nine campsites are available (dump stations).

Camping. RV and tent campers will find a range of private and public camping areas along Anchor River Road, all within easy walking distance of the Anchor River, Cook Inlet, and most local hiking trails. Prices and amenities vary by location. To get to the river from the Sterling Highway, turn onto Old Sterling Highway at the Visitor Information Center at mile marker 156. Continue downhill and across the Anchor River Bridge, and then turn right onto Anchor River Road.

Fishing. Known for excellent silver and king salmon runs, the Anchor River is also a popular spot to catch steelhead and rainbow trout. Anglers heading out to Cook Inlet for halibut, salmon, and rockfish can launch their own boats for a fee at the end of Anchor River Road or can join one of the fishing charters that depart on most days during the summer. Several companies offer charters to anglers, including Alaska Sport Fishing Tours (phone 907/235-2556) and Tall Tales Charters (phone 907/235-6271). Most fishing charter companies in the area are based on Anchor River Road. For more information about fishing and charters in the Anchor Point area, contact the Anchor Point Chamber of Commerce at phone 907/235-2600.

Limited-Service Hotel

★ ★ **ANCHOR RIVER INN.** *34350 Old Sterling Hwy, Anchor Point (99556). Phone 907/235-8531; toll-free 800/435-8531; fax 907/235-2296. www. anchorriverinn.com.* From its location on a bluff overlooking the north fork of the Anchor River, the Anchor River Inn offers quiet, rustic lodging for visitors to the southern Kenai Peninsula. Picturesque views, reasonable prices, and close proximity to fishing charters, wildlife viewing, and some of the best steelhead fishing in the world make the Inn a perennial favorite with seasoned travelers on the peninsula. 20 rooms. Pets accepted. Check-in 2 pm, check-out 11 am. Restaurant, bar. Fitness room. **$**

Restaurant

★ ★ **ANCHOR RIVER INN.** *34350 Old Sterling Hwy, Anchor Point (99556). Phone 907/235-8531; toll-free 800/435-8531; fax 907/235-2296. www. anchorriverinn.com.* For 38 years, the Anchor River Inn Restaurant has been providing family dining in a cozy room with bluff-top views of the Anchor River. The menu selection is varied enough to appeal to most tastes, with classic steak and seafood dishes along with lighter fare like hamburgers, soups, and sandwiches. American, seafood menu. Breakfast, lunch, dinner. Closed Dec 25. Bar. Children's menu. Casual attire. **$$**

Anchorage (D-5)

Population 260,283
Area Code 907
Information Anchorage Convention & Visitors Bureau, 524 W Fourth Ave, 99501; phone 907/276-4118
Web site www.anchorage.net

With a population of about 260,000, Anchorage is the largest city in Alaska and one of the most ethnically and culturally diverse. In 1915, three years after Alaska became an official US territory, the site of present day Anchorage was selected as a construction base and supply depot for the rail line being built from Seward into the Interior. With the railroad came people attracted by the lure of jobs, adventure, and uncharted wilderness. The city grew steadily the first few decades after its founding and by 1950 had surpassed Juneau as the largest city in the Territory of Alaska. Upon Alaska's admission to the Union in 1959, Anchorage's population stood at 83,000.

In March of 1964, a massive earthquake in the Chugach Range nearby caused widespread damage throughout the state and left some parts of Anchorage devastated, particularly the downtown area, the international airport, and the Turnagain Arm neighborhood. With turmoil came prosperity as thousands of tradesmen arrived soon after to help rebuild, many of whom ultimately chose to settle in Alaska.

Although it's located farther north than St. Petersburg, Russia, Anchorage's weather is surprisingly mild, the result of Japanese currents pushing warm, moisture laden air up into the Gulf of Alaska. Winter daytime highs hover around 20 degrees with an average of 69 inches of snow falling each year. Summer daytime highs average 65 degrees with over 19 hours of daylight on the summer solstice. Geographically, the city is bounded by the Chugach Range and the waters of Knik Arm, Turnagain Arm, and Cook Inlet. Downtown Anchorage sits on a bluff overlooking the Inlet and on a clear day, visitors can see the Alaska Range and Mount McKinley on the horizon—a distance of nearly 150 miles.

In summer, the city comes alive with numerous festivals and exhibits, millions of flowers, and a seemingly endless array of outdoor activities as the residents and tourists make the most of long hours of daylight and mild temperatures. The municipal area is criss-crossed by a network of 120 miles of paved trails and another 180 miles of wilderness trails popular with mountain bikers, hikers, and runners. Within the city limits, Delaney Park, Earthquake Park, Resolution Park and Kincaid Park provide scenic venues for outdoor entertainment and relaxation. One of the most popular attractions downtown during the summer is the huge outdoor market held every Saturday in the 3rd Avenue parking lot between C and E streets. The Summer Solstice Festival also attracts a lot of tourists and locals with a blend of arts and crafts exhibits, Alaskan food stalls, and local dancers, singers, musicians, and poets to entertain the crowds. Visitors arriving in town other times of the year can learn about Alaska's native art, culture, and history by visiting the Anchorage Museum of History and Art located in the middle of downtown.

Another of Anchorage's main roles is that of a convenient staging area and embarkation point for wilderness exploration and adventure. As Alaska's main rail, air, and road hub, it serves as the gateway to the Kenai Peninsula to the south and Denali National Park and Fairbanks to the north and provides access to hundreds of remote towns and villages via Anchorage International Airport, Merrill Field, and the floatplane base at Lake Hood.

Additional Visitor Information

There are two visitor information centers in Anchorage: downtown at Fourth Ave and F St, phone 907/274-3531; and at the airport, South (Domestic) Terminal Baggage Claim Area, phone 907/266-2437, and North (International) Terminal, phone 907/266-2657.

Public Transportation

People Mover Phone 907/343-6543, www.muni.org.

Airport Ted Stevens Anchorage International Airport. Phone 907/266-2526

Information Phone 907/266-2526

Airlines Air Canada, Alaska Airlines, American Airlines, America West, Asiana Airlines, China Air Lines, Continental Airlines, Delta Air Lines, Era Aviation, Frontier Flying Service, Hawaiian Airlines, Japan Air Lines, Korean Air Lines, Northwest Airlines, PenAir, United Airlines

What to See and Do

Alaska Aviation Heritage Museum. *4721 Aircraft Dr, Anchorage (99502). Phone 907/248-5325. www. alaskaairmuseum.com.* Located on the shores of Lake Hood near Ted Stevens Anchorage International Airport, this private museum aims to preserve and document Alaska's rich aviation history. Interpretive exhibits, vintage photographs, scale models, and an extensive collection of aviation memorabilia offer insight into the evolution of flying in Alaska and the importance it had on the development of the state. An on-site hangar houses an extensive collection of preserved and restored aircraft. (Winter: Fri-Sat 10 am-4 pm, Sun noon-4 pm; summer: Wed-Mon 10 am-6 pm) **$**

Alaska Botanical Garden. *4500 block of Campbell Airstrip Rd, Anchorage (99520). Phone 907/770-3692. www.alaskabg.org.* Encompassing 110 acres of land once used by the Athabascan Indianas, the Alaska Botanical Garden contains more than 480 varieties of cultured plants. Visitors learn about flora in Alaska by exploring the themed gardens, which include two perennial gardens, a rock garden, and an herb garden. The Lowenfels Family Nature Trail, once used by military tanks during World War II maneuvers, features most of the trees native to the area, as well as its wildlife. (Mid-May-mid-Sept: daily 9 am-9 pm; mid-Sept-mid-May: daily dawn-dusk) **DONATION**

Alaska Center for the Performing Arts. *621 W 6th Ave, Anchorage (99501). Phone 907/263-2900 (administrative offices); toll-free 800/GR8-SEAT (tickets and information). www.alaskapac.org.* Opened in 1988, the Alaska Center for the Performing Arts features four state-of-the-art performance spaces and is home to eight resident companies, including the Alaska Dance Theatre, the Anchorage Symphony Orchestra, and the Anchorage Opera. Located in the heart of downtown, the center is within easy walking distance of most major hotels and offers performances throughout the year.

Alaska Native Heritage Center. *8800 Heritage Center Dr, Anchorage (99506). Phone 907/330-8000; toll-free 800/315-6608. www.alaskanative.net.* Opened in 1999, the Alaska Native Heritage Center provides visitors with the opportunity to learn about the native cultures of Alaska through interpretive displays; outdoor demonstrations of traditional hunting, fishing, and construction techniques; traditional villages exhibits;

and live performances of native songs and dances in the 95-seat Welcome House theater. (Mid-May-Sept: daily 9 am-6 pm; Oct-Apr: Sat noon-5 pm) **$$$$** in summer, **$$** in winter

⭐ **The Alaska Zoo.** *4731 O'Malley Rd, Anchorage (99507). Phone 907/346-1088. www.alaskazoo.org.* With annual attendance at more than 200,000 visitors, the Alaska Zoo is one of the most frequently visited places in the state. It exhibits 38 species of arctic and subarctic wildlife on 25 acres of land. Exotic animals include elephants, Bactrian camels, snow leopards, Amur tigers, Tibetan yaks, and llamas, but most of the animals housed here are native Alaskan species, such as black and brown bears, polar bears, harbor seals, Sitka black-tailed deer, mink, moose, red foxes, and wolverines. (Daily 10 am-5 pm; closed Thanksgiving, Dec 25) **$$**

Anchorage Coastal Wildlife Refuge at Potter Marsh. *Mile 117.4, Seward Hwy, Anchorage (99540).* Known locally as Potter's Marsh, this 540-acre refuge at the southern edge of Anchorage is a popular spot for bird-watching. At various times of the year, the marshlands are home to arctic terns, Canada geese, trumpeter swans, Pacific loons, and a variety of other shorebirds. A 1,500-foot wooden boardwalk built out over the marsh enables visitors to venture far from the parking lot without damaging the wetlands or disturbing the wildlife in the area.

Anchorage Fifth Avenue Mall. *320 W 5th Ave, Anchorage (99501). Phone 907/258-5535.* Located in the heart of downtown, the Anchorage Fifth Avenue Mall is one of the largest malls in Alaska, containing 110 shops on the first three levels and a food court on the fourth. Anchored by two large department stores, JCPenney and Nordstrom, it also features smaller national chain stores as well as an array of uniquely Alaskan shops. (Mon-Fri 10 am-9 pm, Sat 10 am-8 pm, Sun 11 am-6 pm)

Anchorage Museum of History & Art. *121 W 7th Ave, Anchorage (99501). Phone 907/343-4326. www. anchoragemuseum.org.* This large museum in the middle of downtown is divided into two distinct parts. The ground floor features six art galleries displaying "art of the North," including works by celebrated Alaskan artist Sydney Laurence. The upper floor focuses on Alaskan history and is packed with artifacts, displays, and exhibits that depict the lives and cultures of the groups that have shaped Alaska,

The Last Great Race on Earth

An event unlike any other, the famed Iditarod Trail Sled Dog Race shakes Alaska out of the winter doldrums, attracting thousands of spectators and volunteers to the state, along with approximately 75 mushers and their respective dog teams. The Iditarod bills itself as "the Last Great Race on Earth." That's a bold claim, but it would be difficult to argue that any race demands more of its competitors. Starting in Anchorage and finishing in Nome, the race covers roughly 1,100 miles along the historic Iditarod Trail. The grueling journey tests the conditioning and resolve of the mushers and their dogs as they endure up to 17 days of subzero temperatures and howling winds, traversing an ever-changing terrain of mountain, forest, tundra, and coastline.

At its core, Alaska's Iditarod is a celebration of sled dogs and their key role in the state's history and development. Sled dogs demonstrated their importance most prominently during the winter of 1925, when diphtheria began to afflict the children of Nome. Medicine could not be delivered to help the ill, as winter storms and a frozen Bering Sea made Nome inaccessible by plane and boat, and neither roads nor railways came near the isolated village in northwestern Alaska. Sled dog teams were called upon to quickly transport a lifesaving serum to Nome. Musher Gunnar Kaasen took the reins for the last leg of the trip, pulled by a team of huskies that was led by a young pup named Balto. The sled dog team rushed toward

Nome at a furious clip, refusing to be slowed by fierce winds, blinding snow, and temperatures as low as 60 degrees below zero. The dogs and their musher pulled it off, delivering the serum in time to save the lives of many children. A statue honoring Balto can be found in, of all places, New York City's Central Park.

In 1973, the first Anchorage-to-Nome Iditarod was held, the event staged to help preserve the state's mushing heritage. Plane travel had, by this time, diminished the need for sled dogs. Dick Walmarth won the 1973 Iditarod, completing the race in just under three weeks—more than twice the pace of today's winning sled teams. Four-time Iditarod winner Martin Buser and his team of Alaskan huskies finished the 2002 race in a record time of 8 days, 22 hours, and 46 minutes. The day after setting the record, Buser, who was born in Switzerland, became a US citizen, taking the oath while standing under the burled-arch finish line in Nome.

The Iditarod is not the ideal spectator sport, with much of the action unfolding in remote wilderness. Nonetheless, crowds gather at the start and finish lines to cheer on the mushers and their dogs. A great way to be a part of the race is to serve as a volunteer, helping with trail communications, caring for the dogs, or transporting supplies. Check out the official Iditarod Web site (www.iditarod.com) for information about volunteer opportunities.

---

from the earliest Native communities to modern-day Alaskans. (Mid-May-mid-Sept: daily 9 am-6 pm, Thurs until 9 pm; mid-Sept-mid-May: Wed-Sat 10 am-6 pm, Sun noon-5 pm) **$$**

Chugach National Forest. *3301 C St, Anchorage (99503). Phone 907/743-9500. www.fs.fed.us/r10/ chugach.* The Chugach National Forest is the second largest forest in the National Forest System. Roughly the same size as Massachusetts and Rhode Island combined, the Chugach (pronounced CHEW-gatch) is the northernmost national forest, only 500 miles south of the Arctic Circle. One-third of the Chugach

is composed of rocks and moving ice. The remainder is a diverse and majestic tapestry of land, water, plants, and animals. The mountains, lakes, and rivers of the Kenai Peninsula, the islands and glaciers of Prince William Sound, and the copious wetlands and birds of the Copper River Delta make this national forest a mecca for adventurers.

Chugach State Park. *Mile 115, Seward Hwy, Anchorage (99540). Phone 907/345-5014.* Chugach State Park is an accessible wilderness in the backyard of Anchorage. Wildlife viewing and mountain scenery are year-round pleasures, and campers can choose developed campgrounds or secluded backcountry valleys. Nearly 30 trails take you throughout the park to see some of its most enchanting views. Many visitors may want to stop at the Eagle River Nature Center for a guided tour or interpretive program. You may want to explore a few of the park's 50 glaciers on your own. And for extreme adventure, try climbing a mountainside or plunging through river rapids. Whatever the case, the 495,000-acre park offers a wide variety of activities in all seasons.

Cyrano's Off Center Playhouse. *413 D St, Anchorage (99501). Phone 907-274-2599. www.cyranos.org.* This small, independent downtown theater is home to the Eccentric Theatre Company, which puts on a wide variety of plays each year, from classic dramas to contemporary comedies. The atmosphere is decidedly informal, the productions first rate. Before and after shows, theatergoers can browse through the shelves of Cyrano's bookstore or enjoy a drink at the small coffee bar.

Delaney Park Strip. *300 W 9th Ave, Anchorage (99501).* Stretching from A to P streets, this narrow park between 9th and 10th avenues was at one time Anchorage's airstrip. Nowadays, it's home to numerous sports fields, playgrounds, the Centennial Rose Garden, and memorials to Alaskan veterans and Martin Luther King Jr. **FREE**

Earthquake Park. *On W Northern Lights Blvd. Phone 907/276-4118.* Located at the west end of Northern Lights Boulevard, this large, forested park was established near the site where a housing development slid into Cook Inlet during the 1964 Good Friday earthquake. The main trail from the parking lot leads to a small interpretive exhibit that explains the geological factors that caused the land beneath the subdivision to collapse. The park also serves as an access point to the Tony Knowles Coastal Trail (see). **FREE**

Eisenhower Alaska Statehood Monument. *2nd Ave and E St, Anchorage (99501).* Located at the end of E Street, this small monument overlooking the Alaska Railroad depot features a bust of President Eisenhower and a plaque commemorating the Alaska Statehood Act that Eisenhower signed on January 3, 1959, making Alaska the 49th state. (Daily)

Eklutna Flats and Palmer Hay Flats. *N of Anchorage at the head of the Knik Arm in Cook Inlet. Phone 907/267-2182.* The Eklutna Flats and Palmer Hay Flats are a tidally influenced wetlands area at the confluence of the Knik and Matanuska rivers. This flat open area provides the broadest view of the Matanuska Valley bordered by the Chugach Mountains, a stone's throw to the east. The ancient Talkeetna Mountains rise in the distance. This area is teeming with waterfowl and other migratory birds in spring and fall. You may even spot a moose during the long winter months. The Palmer Hay Flats State Game Refuge comprises a large portion of this area.

Kepler-Bradley State Park. *Glenn Hwy, Anchorage (99501). Phone 907/269-8400.* A fisherman's paradise, this popular state park comprises several trout-and grayling-filled lakes. Kepler-Bradley State Park is within easy driving distance of Anchorage. The lakes are located in crevasses in between morraine ridges formed by glaciers. Trails from the park connect to the Mat/Su borough Crevasse Morraine Trail System.

Kincaid Park. *Raspberry Rd, Anchorage (99502).* The site of a former Nike missile silo during the early years of the Cold War, this park encompasses nearly 1,400 acres of land at the end of Raspberry Road at the extreme western edge of Anchorage. More than 40 miles of maintained trails provide recreational opportunities for runners and cross-country skiers throughout the year. It marks one end of the Tony Knowles Coastal Trail. **FREE**

Lanie Fleischer Chester Creek Trail. This scenic paved trail follows the course of Chester Creek, providing a green belt connecting eastern Anchorage to the Tony Knowles Coastal Trail (see) and creating a natural divide between downtown Anchorage and the midtown area. With one trailhead at Westchester Lagoon (see) near Cook Inlet and the other at Goose Lake by Alaska Pacific University, it's a popular east-west route across town for bikers, runners, walkers, and cross-country skiers. **FREE**

Matanuska Glacier State Recreation Area. *Glenn Hwy, Anchorage (99501). Phone 907/269-8400.* This newly redeveloped recreation area showcases the Matanuska Glacier with an up-close view that will be forever etched into travelers' memories.

Portage Glacier. *Phone 907/783-3242. www.fs.fed.us.* Many of the world's glaciers are receding. This phenomenon is strikingly evident at Portage Glacier. At Portage, the **Begich-Boggs Visitor Center** used to squarely face the massive blue Portage Glacier directly in front of it. But only a few years after the Forest Service built the visitor center facility, Portage Glacier receded—around a corner of Portage Lake and out of view. Now, tourists must view the glacier's face from a tour boat. (Visitor center open daily 9 am-6 pm Memorial Day-Labor Day, Sat-Sun 10 am-5 pm the rest of the year)

Resolution Park. *300 L St, Anchorage (99501).* Located at 3rd and L streets, this small neighborhood park is named in honor of Captain Cook's ship *Resolution,* which anchored nearby in 1778. With its imposing statue of Cook, summertime flower gardens, and views of Cook Inlet, it's a popular spot for photographers and lunching locals. The Tony Knowles Coastal Trail (see) runs through the park. **FREE**

Ship Creek fishing area. *Ship Creek Ave, just E of the Alaska Railroad depot.* Located in the heart of downtown Anchorage, Ship Creek provides a convenient, though often crowded, place for anglers to try their luck. The king salmon run begins in early June and continues through mid-July; the silver salmon run starts in August. Viewing platforms and a small dam across the river provide excellent spots to observe the action. (Daily)

Tony Knowles Coastal Trail. *900 W 2nd Ave, Anchorage (99501).* This scenic paved trail is popular with bicyclists, skaters, and walkers throughout the long days of summer and with cross-country skiers in the winter. Following the contour of Cook Inlet for most of its length, it runs for 11 miles from 2nd Avenue downtown to Kincaid Park (see), providing unobstructed views of Cook Inlet, Mount Susitna, and the Chugach Range, as well as opportunities to observe moose, bald eagles, and other wildlife. **FREE**

Tours. *Phone toll-free 800/544-2206. www. graylineofalaska.com.* Gray Line of Alaska offers package tours around Alaska (up to 11 days) as well as glacier cruises, bear-viewing tours, sea kayaking, flightseeing, and city and backcountry tours out of Anchorage.

Turnagain Pass. The drive through Turnagain Pass may be one of the most scenic. This is the highest point on the Seward Highway, and wildlife spotting occurs regularly here. Turnagain Pass is located in the south beyond Turnagain Arm. Two large pullouts are easily accessible from the only section of divided highway outside of the Anchorage bowl. Views from the highway here show off the distinctive U-shaped valley created by retreating glaciers. Northbound travelers are treated to spectacular views of Turnagain Arm and Twentymile glaciers as they head down from this 900-foot pass to sea level. This area is especially popular in the winter for skiing and snowmobiling, and in mid-summer for its wildflower displays.

Westchester Lagoon. *1915 Hillcrest Rd, Anchorage (99517).* Located near the west end of 15th Avenue, this large, tree-lined lagoon tucked between the downtown and midtown high rises offers scenic walking and biking trails in the summer and ice skating and cross-country skiing in the winter. It also provides easy access to the Tony Knowles Coastal Trail (see) and the Lanie Fleisher Chester Creek Trail (see). **FREE**

Special Events

Alyeska Blueberry & Mountain Arts Festival. *Alyeska Resort, 1000 Arlberg Ave, Anchorage (99587). Phone 907/754-1111; toll-free 800/880-3880. www. alyeskaresort.com.* This small-town summer festival, held beside the pond at the Alyeska Resort, features live entertainment, local artwork, a poetry jam, homemade foods, and lots of blueberry-flavored treats. Beginning in 2004, the festival merges with the annual Alyeska Mountain Run so that visitors to the festival can sit back and bask in blueberry heaven while watching ultra-fit race participants charge up and down the slopes of Mount Alyeska. The festival date varies by year—contact the Alyeska Resort for the current schedule. **FREE**

Anchorage Fur Rendezvous. *Phone 907/274-1177. www.furrondy.net.* The Anchorage Fur Rendezvous, locally known as the Fur Rondy, was first held in the 1930s with the aim of bringing people together, showing community support, and celebrating the beginning of the end of winter each year. Now running for 18 days from late February to early March, the festival has evolved into a huge midwinter celebration with more than 140 events and activities, including elaborate fancy dress and costume balls, snow-sculpting competitions, a carnival, and live music and theater productions. The festival was expanded in 2004 to serve as a lead-in to Anchorage's most famous winter event: the ceremonial start of the Iditarod Trail Sled Dog race (see), which begins on the corner of 4th and D streets downtown at 10 am on the first Saturday in March. Equally exciting but less well known is the World Championship Sled

Dog Race, a three-day dog sprint event with mushers covering a 25-mile out-and-back course that begins and ends at 4th and D streets downtown. Late Feb-early Mar.

Downtown Saturday Market. *3rd Ave and E St, Anchorage (99501).* Begun in 1992, this wildly popular weekly market features more than 300 vendors offering a wide range of goods, from Alaskan art and souvenirs to locally grown fruits and vegetables. In keeping with its small-town atmosphere, the market features musical performances by local artists as well as booths sponsored by community groups. Held on Saturdays from 10 am to 6 pm regardless of the weather, the market offers something for every taste and style. Mid-May-mid-Sept.

The Iditarod. *Phone 907/376-5155. www.iditarod.com.* A famous dogsled race covering more than 1,150 miles from Anchorage to Nome. It's been run since 1973 and usually takes 9 to 12 days. Early Mar.

Limited-Service Hotels

★ **ANCHORAGE GRAND HOTEL.** *505 W 2nd Ave, Anchorage (99501). Phone 907/929-8888; toll-free 888/800-0640; fax 907/929-8899. www. anchoragegrandhotel.com.* Built in 1950, this newly renovated all-suite hotel is a pleasing blend of "old" Anchorage architecture and modern amenities. All rooms feature full-sized gourmet kitchens, sleeper couches, and large, enclosed closets, and many have excellent views of Cook Inlet and the mountain ranges that surround Anchorage. 31 rooms. Complimentary continental breakfast. Check-in 3 pm, check-out noon. **$$**

★ **ASPEN HOTEL.** *108 E 8th Ave, Anchorage (99501). Phone 907/868-1605; toll-free 888/506-7848; fax 907/868-3520. www.aspenhotelsak.com.* The Anchorage Aspen Hotel caters to a mixture of Alaskan business professionals, local sport groups, and tourists. Its indoor pool, in-room kitchenettes, family suites with bunk beds, and complimentary deluxe continental breakfast—as well as its location near many downtown attractions—make it an inviting place for both families and bargain hunters. 89 rooms. Complimentary continental breakfast. Check-in 3 pm, check-out 11 am. Fitness room. Indoor pool, whirlpool. **$$**

★★ **BEST WESTERN GOLDEN LION HOTEL.** *1000 E 36th Ave, Anchorage (99508). Phone 907/561-1522; toll-free 877/935-5466; fax 907/743-4814. www.bestwesterngoldenlion.com.* The most remarkable thing about this clean, comfortable, and affordable hotel is its "African hunting lodge" décor. Stuffed and mounted African animals dominate the lobby and main staircase and the meeting rooms are called "Kenya" and "Safari." Other noteworthy features are the small but well-designed weight room, the oval sauna, and the in-house hair salon. 83 rooms. Check-in 2 pm, check-out noon. Restaurant. Fitness room. **$$**

★ **CLARION SUITES HOTEL.** *325 W 8th Ave, Anchorage (99501). Phone 907/274-1000; toll-free 888/ 389-6575; fax 907/274-3016. www.choicehotels.com.* This hotel is located within a block of Anchorage's main downtown shopping site, the 5th Avenue Mall. The Anchorage Museum of History and Art is less than a block away, as is the Delaney Park Strip, Anchorage's original airfield, now converted into grassy areas, a rose garden, tennis courts, and ball fields. 111 rooms, all suites. Complimentary continental breakfast. Check-in 3 pm, check-out noon. Fitness room. Indoor pool, whirlpool. **$$**

★★ **COAST INTERNATIONAL INN.** *3333 W International Airport Rd, Anchorage (99502). Phone 907/243-2233; fax 907/248-3796. www.coasthotels.com.* One of the most attractive things about this hotel is that it's close to the airport without being noisy and only yards from Lake Spenard and the network of walking trails that encircle it. Most guest rooms in this upscale, business casual hotel have spectacular mountain and lake views and all of them are comfortable, quiet, and spacious. Corporate travelers, who make up a large part of the client base, frequently stay here because of the quality of the furnishings, the wide range of business amenities offered, and the friendly, professional staff. 141 rooms. Check-in noon, check-out noon. Restaurant. Fitness room. **$$**

★ **COMFORT INN.** *111 W Ship Creek Ave, Anchorage (99501). Phone 907/277-6887; toll-free 800/ 424-6423; fax 907/274-9830. www.choicehotels.com.* The Comfort Inn is located alongside Ship Creek near the site where Anchorage's first settlers lived. Visitors can view salmon spawning in the creek behind the hotel or head uphill into downtown Anchorage for shopping, touring, and dining. With the Alaska Railroad depot a block away, the hotel is an ideal spot for those arriving from or heading to popular rail destinations like Denali National Park and Seward. 100 rooms. Pets accepted. Complimentary continental breakfast. Check-in 4 pm, check-out noon. Fitness room. Indoor pool, whirlpool. **$$**

★ ★ **COURTYARD BY MARRIOTT.** *4901 Spenard Rd, Anchorage (99517). Phone 907/245-0322; toll-free 800/932-2198; fax 907/248-1886. www. courtyard.com.* A five-minute drive from the airport and a ten-minute drive from downtown, this 154-room hotel is within a block of the shores of Lake Spenard and within easy walking distance of a number of restaurants. The Courtyard's main selling point is its on-site recreation facilities, which include a spacious pool area, an indoor sauna, and a well-laid-out exercise room. The small but well-outfitted business center appeals to business travelers. 154 rooms. Check-in 3 pm, check-out noon. Restaurant. Fitness room. Indoor pool, whirlpool. Business Center. **$$**

★ ★ **DAYS INN.** *321 E Fifth Ave, Anchorage (99501). Phone 907/276-7226; toll-free 800/329-7466; fax 907/ 278-6041. www.daysinn.com.* 131 rooms. Pets accepted. Check-in 3 pm, check-out 11 am. Restaurant. **$$**

★ ★ ★ **DIMOND CENTER HOTEL.** *700 E Dimond Blvd, Anchorage (99515). Phone 907/770-5000; toll-free 866/770-5002; fax 907/770-5001. www.dimondcenterhotel.com.* From the outside, this midtown hotel looks more like an office building than anything else. On entering, though, it's a refreshing surprise: it's filled with custom-made hardwood furniture, native Alaskan artwork from the Kachemak Bay region, and upscale amenities in all areas. The rooms, which the hotel bills as being "the most comfortable rooms in the city," are filled with goose-down comforters, original Alaskan artwork, marble counters, deep bathtubs, and custom-made cherry furniture with walnut inlays, all presented in a soothing palette of greens, blues, and earth tones. 109 rooms.

Complimentary continental breakfast. Check-in 3 pm, check-out 11 am. Bar. Children's activity center. Fitness room. **$$**

★ **EXECUTIVE SUITES HOTEL.** *4360 Spenard Rd, Anchorage (99517). Phone 907/243-6366; toll-free 800/770-6366; fax 907/248-2161. www. executivesuitehotel.com.* The Executive Suites Hotel is an independent hotel located near Anchorage International Airport, within yards of Lake Hood. With frequent manager's specials and fourteen different room layouts, it's the kind of place where travelers can always find a bargain. 102 rooms. Pets accepted. Complimentary continental breakfast. Check-in 3 pm, check-out noon. **$**

★ **HAMPTON INN.** *4301 Credit Union Dr, Anchorage (99503). Phone 907/550-7000; toll-free 800/ 426-7866; fax 907/561-7330. www.hamptoninn.com.* 101 rooms. Complimentary continental breakfast. Check-in 3 pm, check-out noon. Fitness room. Indoor pool, whirlpool. **$$**

★ **HAWTHORN SUITES.** *1110 W 8th Ave, Anchorage (99501). Phone 907/222-5005; toll-free 888/469-6575; fax 907/222-5215. www.hawthorn.com.* 111 rooms, all suites. Complimentary continental breakfast. Check-in 3 pm, check-out noon. Fitness room. Indoor pool, whirlpool. **$$**

★ ★ **HILTON GARDEN INN.** *100 W Tudor Rd, Anchorage (99503). Phone 907/729-7000; toll-free 800/ 774-1500; fax 907/729-8000. www.hilton.com.* Just 3 miles from Anchorage International Airport and within two blocks of midtown Anchorage's dining, shopping, and entertainment venues, the Hilton Garden Inn appeals mainly to business travelers, who appreciate the upgraded amenities, spacious rooms, and on-site exercise facilities. The hotel also has a sunny, Alaskan-themed lobby where guests can sit by the fire, watch television, or just relax and read the paper. Another major selling point is the hotel's complimentary shuttle service to the airport, local shopping areas, and downtown. 125 rooms. Check-in

3 pm, check-out noon. High-speed Internet access. Restaurant. Fitness room. Indoor pool, whirlpool. Airport transportation available. **$$**

★ ★ THE HISTORIC ANCHORAGE

HOTEL. *330 E St, Anchorage (99501). Phone 907/272-4553; toll-free 800/544-0988; fax 907/277-4483. www.historicanchoragehotel.com.* This charming and elegant hotel manages to blend the architectural elegance of the 1930s with the demands of the modern traveler. As Anchorage's oldest hotel, its guest rooms are graced with Queen Anne-style furnishings as well as modern amenities such as cable television, microwave ovens, and high-speed Internet access. 26 rooms. Complimentary continental breakfast. Check-in 3 pm, check-out noon. High-speed Internet access. Restaurant, bar. **$$**

★ ★ HOLIDAY INN. *239 W 4th Ave, Anchorage (99501). Phone 907/793-5500; fax 907/258-4733. www.holiday-inn.com.* 251 rooms. Check-in 2 pm, check-out noon. Restaurant. Fitness room. Indoor pool. **$$**

★ HOLIDAY INN EXPRESS. *4411 Spenard Rd, Anchorage (99517). Phone 907/248-8848; toll-free 800/465-4329; fax 907/248-8847. www.hiexpress.com.* 128 rooms. Pets accepted. Complimentary continental breakfast. Check-in 3 pm, check-out noon. Fitness room. Indoor pool, whirlpool. **$$**

★ ★ INLET TOWER HOTEL & SUITES.

1200 L St, Anchorage (99501). Phone 907/276-0110; toll-free 800/544-0786; fax 907/258-4914. www.inlettower.com. A complete renovation in 2003 has recaptured the elegance of this hotel's original 1950s architecture. Renowned New York-based designer Harry Schnaper has created warm and luxurious rooms, but it's the extraordinary views of Cook Inlet, the Chugach Mountains, and the downtown skyline that make this hotel special. 180 rooms. Check-in 4 pm, check-out noon. Restaurant. **$$**

★ LAKESHORE MOTOR INN. *3009 Lakeshore Dr, Anchorage (99517). Phone 907/248-3485; toll-free 800/770-3000; fax 907/248-1544. www.lakeshoremotorinn.com.* Despite its unassuming appearance, this is not a typical motel. The airy and

comfortable lobby pays tongue-in-cheek homage to the fishing and hunting clientele that frequently stay here, and the spacious, crisply clean guest rooms are filled with sturdy wooden furniture, soft fabrics, and local artwork. Better than the usual budget motel, this inn provides a relaxing, refreshing, and affordable place to unwind. 44 rooms. Pets accepted. Complimentary continental breakfast. Check-in 2 pm, check-out 11 am. **$**

★ LONG HOUSE ALASKAN HOTEL. *4335 Wisconsin St, Anchorage (99517). Phone 907/243-2133; toll-free 888/243-2133; fax 907/243-6060. www.longhousehotel.com.* The Long House Alaskan Hotel is set on a quiet street across the road from Lake Hood and within walking distance of many local restaurants. Because of its location, the hotel is a popular stopover for people flying by floatplane to remote hunting and fishing lodges in the Alaskan wilds. 54 rooms. Complimentary continental breakfast. Check-in 4 pm, check-out noon. **$$**

★ MICROTEL INN & SUITES. *5205 Northwood Dr, Anchorage (99517). Phone 907/245-5002; toll-free 888/771-7171; fax 907/245-5030. www.microtelinn.com/anchorageak.* About a mile from the airport and ten minutes from downtown, this budget-friendly 79-room motel is also convenient to some of the main traffic arteries for getting into and out of Anchorage quickly from the south. It's not much to look at from the outside, but the interior is much more appealing, with a small but comfortable lobby, breakfast nook, and large, sunny guest rooms with padded window seats and surprisingly good views. The hotel offers free 24-hour shuttle service to the airport, and guests also appreciate the 1 pm check-out time. 79 rooms. Pets accepted. Complimentary continental breakfast. Check-in 4 pm, check-out 1 pm. Indoor pool. Airport transportation available. **$**

★ PARKWOOD INN. *4455 Juneau St, Anchorage (99503). Phone 907/563-3590; toll-free 800/478-3590; fax 907/563-5560. www.parkwoodinn.net.* This family-friendly motel isn't the plushest in town, but each of the 50 apartment-style rooms has a full-size stocked kitchen, wide balcony, pull-out sofa, and small dining area. Unlike most lodgings in Anchorage, it's busiest in winter, when low rates attract out-of-towners who come to shop, visit family, take care of medical needs,

and escape the hardships of the bush winters. The Parkwood is located close to the city's largest movie theater, the main hospital, Anchorage University, and a large number of restaurants and shops. 50 rooms. Pets accepted. Check-in 2 pm, check-out 11 am. **$**

★ ★ **RAMADA INN.** *115 E 3rd Ave, Anchorage (99501). Phone 907/272-7561; toll-free 800/272-6232; fax 907/279-3879. www.ramada.com.* Opened in the summer of 2003, the Ramada Inn offers clean, quiet, and comfortable rooms decorated with a whimsical Alaskan motif that guests first encounter in the small but tastefully decorated front lobby. Most south-facing rooms have spacious, private balconies, while those facing north have sweeping views of Cook Inlet, Sleeping Lady (Mt. Susitna), and the Alaska Range. 90 rooms. Check-in 3 pm, check-out 11 am. Restaurant, bar. Fitness room. **$$**

★

★ **SPRINGHILL SUITES.** *3401 A St, Anchorage (99503). Phone 907/562-3247; toll-free 877/729-0197; fax 907/562-3250. www.springhillsuites.com.* Located about 4 miles from downtown, in the middle of the city's main shopping and dining area, the SpringHill Suites is down the road from Providence Hospital, close to the University of Alaska, and next door to the State of Alaska offices and Anchorage's largest cineplex. The convenient location makes it popular with tourists during the summer and with government groups, college visitors, and school sports teams the rest of the year. Guest suites are spacious and in excellent condition. 102 rooms, all suites. Complimentary continental breakfast. Check-in 3 pm, check-out noon. Fitness room. Indoor pool, whirlpool. **$$**

★

★ **SUPER 8 MOTEL.** *3501 Minnesota Dr, Anchorage (99503). Phone 907/276-8884; toll-free 800/800-8000; fax 907/279-8194. www.super8.com.* About 2 miles from the airport and 3 miles from downtown, the Super 8 puts guests within a mile of all of midtown Anchorage's main attractions: shopping malls, the large multiplex cinema, and a wide array of restaurants. Prices can be high for a motel with few amenities, especially in summer, but rooms are clean, quiet, and in good condition. 85 rooms. Pets accepted. Complimentary continental breakfast. Check-in 2 pm, check-out noon. **$**

★ ★ **THE VOYAGER HOTEL.** *501 K St, Anchorage (99501). Phone 907/277-9501; toll-free 800/247-9070; fax 907/274-0333. www.voyagerhotel.com.* For 25 years, this small, independent hotel has been focusing on customized service delivered by a friendly and dedicated staff. There is furious attention paid to details here, from the placement of quality china and Alaskan coffee in the galley kitchens to the use of fine carpets and extra-soft pillows in the rooms. The result is a hotel that draws people in and keeps them coming back year after year. 40 rooms. Closed five days during Christmas. Complimentary continental breakfast. Check-out 11 am. Restaurant. **$$**

★ ★ **WESTMARK ANCHORAGE HOTEL.** *720 W 5th Ave, Anchorage (99501). Phone 907/276-7676; toll-free 800/544-0970; fax 907/276-3615. www. westmarkhotels.com.* This hotel is an ideal place to stay for those wanting to be right in the midst of all of the terrific dining, shopping, live theater, and other diversions downtown Anchorage has to offer. The hotel itself is clean, comfortable, and professionally run and, as an added bonus, all rooms have their own large private balconies. 198 rooms. Check-in 3 pm, check-out noon. Restaurant, bar. **$$**

Full-Service Hotels

★ ★ ★ **ANCHORAGE MARRIOTT DOWNTOWN.** *820 W 7th Ave, Anchorage (99501). Phone 907/279-8000; toll-free 800/228-9290; fax 907/ 279-8005. www.marriott.com.* The first thing that strikes visitors about the Anchorage Marriott Downtown is how bright and cheery it is inside. Every guest room has oversized picture windows that flood the rooms with natural light while providing excellent views of either Cook Inlet or the Chugach Mountains. With an upscale on-site restaurant, stylish shopping arcade, sleek indoor pool and fitness center, and a small but well-equipped business center, the hotel is able to provide a high level of comfort and convenience to all of its guests. 392 rooms. Check-in 3 pm, check-out noon. Restaurant, bar. Fitness room. Indoor pool, whirlpool. **$$$**

★

★ ★ ★ **HILTON.** *500 W Third Ave, Anchorage (99501). Phone 907/272-7411; toll-free 800/455-8667; fax 907/265-7042. www.hilton.com.* Located in the heart of downtown, the towers of the Hilton hotel offer sweeping views of the Anchorage area and beyond. On exceptionally clear days, in fact, guests with north-facing rooms can see as far as Mt. McKinley, well over 100 miles away. The main draw of the hotel, though, is its ability to bring a sense of grandiose style and glamour to the edge of the Alaskan frontier. From its spacious, tastefully appointed lobby to its intimate, elegant penthouse restaurant, the Hilton is like a wealthy New York aunt on a visit to the country: she's a little out of place but consistently draws a crowd. 600 rooms. Pets accepted. Check-in 3 pm, check-out noon. Two restaurants. Fitness room. Indoor pool, whirlpool. **$$$**

★ ★ ★ **HOTEL CAPTAIN COOK.** *4th Ave and K St, Anchorage (99501). Phone 907/276-6000; toll-free 800/843-1950; fax 907/343-2298. www. captaincook.com.* The Hotel Captain Cook is located in the middle of downtown Anchorage. As one of Alaska's premier independent hotels, it prides itself on providing the ultimate in service, comfort, and style to all of its guests. All rooms feature twice daily housekeeping service, nightly turndown service, and top-quality furnishings—including down comforters, plush towels, and 250-thread-count sheets. Other highlights of the hotel include three full-service restaurants, a selection of chic boutique shops and art galleries, an on-site athletic club, and a wealth of original artworks and artifacts on display throughout the public areas. 547 rooms. Check-in 3 pm, check-out noon. Three restaurants, bar. Fitness room, fitness classes available. Indoor pool, whirlpool. **$$**

★ ★ ★ **MILLENNIUM ALASKAN HOTEL.**
4800 Spenard Rd, Anchorage (99517). Phone 907/243-2300; toll-free 800/544-0553; fax 907/243-8815. www. millenniumhotels.com. The spectacular lobby of this lakefront hotel really sets the tone for the whole property, as it's filled with dark woods, slate tiles, leather furniture, and a massive rock fireplace. The guest rooms are also luxurious, immaculate, and spacious and those facing the lake offer picturesque views and wonderful summer sunsets. For those looking for upscale accommodations, excellent service, and a scenic location in Anchorage, few properties can rival what this hotel has to offer. 248 rooms. Pets accepted. Check-in 3 pm, check-out noon. Restaurant. Fitness room. Whirlpool. **$$$**

★ ★ ★ **SHERATON ANCHORAGE HOTEL.**
401 E 6th Ave, Anchorage (99501). Phone 907/276-8700; toll-free 800/477-8700; fax 907/276-7561. www. sheratonanchoragehotel.com. This hotel is located in downtown Anchorage, only a short walk from the Anchorage Museum of History and Art, the 5th Avenue Mall, and the Egan Convention and Civic Center. Most of the large, comfortable guest rooms have terrific views of the mountain ranges and tidal flats that surround the city, and with a friendly, professional staff, a 24-hour on-site gym, and a sophisticated bar and lounge, guests need not leave the hotel to enjoy their stay in Anchorage. 375 rooms. Pets accepted. Complimentary continental breakfast. Check-in 3 pm, check-out noon. Restaurant, bar. Fitness room. Whirlpool. **$$$**

Full-Service Resort

★ ★ ★ **ALYESKA PRINCE RESORT.** *1000 Arlberg Ave, Anchorage (99587). Phone 907/754-1111; toll-free 800/880-3880; fax 907/754-2290. www. alyeskaresort.com.* The Alyeska Resort is located in the town of Girdwood, about 45 minutes south of Anchorage on the Seward Highway. It's comprised of a ski area, a golf course (in Anchorage), and the Alyeska Prince Hotel, an appealing blend of Swiss chateau and modern architecture. Everything about this property is first-rate: deluxe guest rooms; world-class skiing, snowboarding, and heli-skiing in winter; extensive hiking and mountain biking in summer; fine-dining restaurants; state-of-the-art fitness facilities; and all-around spectacular views of hanging glaciers, soaring mountains, and miles and miles of pristine wilderness. 307 rooms. Check-in 4 pm, check-out noon. Three restaurants, bar. Fitness room (fee). Indoor pool, whirlpool. Golf, 18 holes. Ski in/ski out. **$$**

Specialty Lodgings

The following lodging establishments are approved by Mobil Travel Guide, but due to their unique and individualized nature have not been given a traditional Mobil Star rating. Included in this listing you may find bed-and-breakfasts, limited-service inns, guest ranches, and other unique hotel properties.

ALASKAN LEOPARD BED & BREAKFAST.
16136 Sandpiper Dr, Anchorage (99501). Phone 907/868-1594; toll-free 877/277-7118. www.alaskanleopard.com. Hillside chalet with spectacular views of the Anchorage Bowl, Cook Inlet, the Kenai Peninsula, and the volcanoes of the Alaska Range. Known for extraordinary breakfasts. 4 rooms, 2 story. **$**

A LOON'S NEST BED & BREAKFAST. *1455 Hillcrest Dr, Anchorage (99503). Phone 907/279-9884; toll-free 800/786-9884. www.aloonsnest.com.* 2 rooms, 2 story. This Frank Lloyd Wright-designed house is poised on a bluff overlooking Westchester Lagoon and features Shaker-style furniture, whirlpool tubs, and wheelchair accessibility. **$**

FIFTEEN CHANDELEERS B & B. *14020 Sabine St, Anchorage (99511). Phone 907/345-3032.* This European-style Georgian mansion is set in a botanical garden. Breakfast is served in a formal dining room with fine china and stemware. 5 rooms, 3 story. **$$**

K STREET BED & BREAKFAST. *1433 K St, Anchorage (99501). Phone 907/279-1443.* A Contemporary cedar-sided home in a residential neighborhood with a garden and solarium, this bed-and-breakfast features homemade breakfast and original Alaskan art. 3 rooms, 2 story. **$**

MAHOGANY MANOR BED & BREAKFAST INN. *204 E 15th Ave, Anchorage (99501). Phone 907/278-1111; toll-free 888/777-0346. www.mahoganymanor.com.* A luxury-oriented bed-and-breakfast in a secluded environment. All rooms feature private baths, entrances, high-speed Internet connections, and DVD players. 6 rooms, 2 story. **$$$**

THE OSCAR GILL HISTORIC BED & BREAKFAST. *1344 W 10th Ave, Anchorage (99501). Phone 907/279-1344. www.oscargill.com.* This 1913 home is located in Delaney Park, bordering the Cook Inlet, and offers views of Denali and Sleeping Lady. Cited as one of Alaska's best lodgings. 3 rooms, 2 story. **$**

PLANET ANCHORAGE BED & BREAKFAST.
1025 H St, Anchorage (99501). Phone 907/770-6732. www.planetanchoragebb.com. 3 rooms, 2 story. This 1950s-style home is five minutes from downtown Anchorage. Fresh homemade breakfasts made with local ingredients are served each morning.

SUSTINA SUNSETS BED & BREAKFAST.
9901 Conifer St, Anchorage (99507). Phone 907/346-1067. www.sustinasunsets.com. Features views of Mt. McKinley with breakfast served in-room or on one of the decks. 3 rooms, 3 story. **$**

Restaurants

★ **THE BAKE SHOP.** *Alyeska Boardwalk, Girdwood (99587). Phone 907/783-2831; fax 907/783-3192. www.thebakeshop.com.* The Bake Shop at Alyeska is a very casual restaurant and bakery serving fresh baked breads, standard breakfast fare, sandwiches, and pizzas. Designed with skiers and outdoor enthusiasts in mind, its counter service and self-seating allows customers to pop in, grab a bite to eat, and get back outdoors without fuss or delay. Deli menu, pizza. Breakfast, lunch, dinner. Casual attire. Outdoor seating. **$**

★ ★ ★ **CAMPOBELLO BISTRO.** *601 W 36th Ave, Anchorage (99501). Phone 907/563-2040.* This midtown bistro features sophisticated Mediterranean cuisine and an impressive wine list and is decorated with modern art. Mediterranean menu. Lunch, dinner. **$$$**

★ ★ ★ **CLUB PARIS.** *417 W 5th Ave, Anchorage (99501). Phone 907/277-6332. www.clubparisrestaurant.com.* The grand belle of Anchorage's downtown restaurant scene, Club Paris is considered by many to be "the" steakhouse in Anchorage. Opened in 1957, this local landmark restaurant has weathered earthquakes, blizzards, and urban renewal and still manages to be as charming and as idiosyncratic as always. Designed on the inside to look like part French bistro, part Alaskan saloon, it's a must for those looking for something out of the ordinary. Seafood, steak menu. Lunch, dinner. Closed Thanksgiving, Dec 25. Bar. Casual attire. **$$$**

★ ★ ★ **CORSAIR RESTAURANT.** *944 W 5th Ave, Anchorage (99501). Phone 907/278-4502; fax 907/274-0333. www.corsairrestaurant.com.* Featuring ultra-private wraparound booths, discreet soft lighting, and a well-trained and knowledgeable staff, Corsair is an ideal destination for those looking for a sophisticated dining experience in the heart of Anchorage. The gourmet menu features continental food with an emphasis on French haute cuisine as well as Alaskan seafood dishes prepared with fresh local ingredients by a well-trained, highly professional staff. Winner of the *Wine Spectator* Best of Award of Excellence and considered one of the top three wine cellars in Alaska, Corsair is above all a wine connoisseur's paradise, with over 700 vintages in its 10,000 bottle cellar. French, seafood menu. Dinner. Closed Sun; holidays. Bar. Casual attire. **$$$**

★ ★ ★ **CROW'S NEST RESTAURANT.** *5th Ave and K St, Anchorage (99501). Phone 907/343-2217.* Featuring one of the best views in Anchorage, this restaurant is best known for its five-course prix fixe menu and an impressive wine list. American menu. Dinner. Closed Sun-Mon. **$$$**

★ **DOLCE EDIBLES CAFE AND BAKERY.** *640 W 36th Ave, Anchorage (99503). Phone 907/770-6680; fax 907/770-6683.* Dolce Edibles is a wonderful find, filled with the tantalizing aroma of fresh-baked pastries, hot bread, and strong coffee. The small seating area's Mediterranean color palette, unobstructed views of the bakers at work, and sturdy wooden chairs and tables create the sense of being a guest in someone's kitchen rather than a customer at a café. American menu. Breakfast, lunch. Closed Sun; holidays. Children's menu. Casual attire. **$**

★ ★ **DOWNTOWN DELI & CAFE.** *525 W 4th Ave, Anchorage (99501). Phone 907/276-7116; fax 907/278-7314.* Downtown Deli & Café has been feeding locals and tourists nonstop since 1979. There's lots of booth and table seating inside the comfortable dining area as well as sidewalk seating during the warmer months. The food is traditional American with a Northwest flavor, including such local favorites as sourdough pancakes, reindeer stew, and Alaskan halibut. American menu. Breakfast, lunch. Closed Thanksgiving, Dec 25. Casual attire. Outdoor seating. **$**

★ ★ ★ **FLYING MACHINE RESTAURANT.** *4800 Spenard Rd, Anchorage (99517). Phone 907/266-2249; fax 907/243-8815. www.millenniumhotels.com.* Located a stone's throw from Lake Spenard and offering exceptional dining with sweeping lake and mountain views, this Millennium Alaskan Hotel (see) restaurant manages to be elegant and warm without being overly formal or pricey. The most appealing aspect of the place is its outdoor patio, which during the summer is filled with diners who soak up sunshine while enjoying the top-quality seafood and steaks the restaurant is known for. Even in winter it's an appealing spot, with snow piling up against the bay windows and a cheery fire burning in the rock fireplace. American, seafood menu. Breakfast, lunch, dinner. Bar. Children's menu. Casual attire. Outdoor seating. **$$$**

★ ★ **GLACIER BREWHOUSE.** *737 W 5th Ave, Anchorage (99501). Phone 907/274-2739; fax 907/277-1033. www.glacierbrewhouse.com.* This casually elegant downtown restaurant, the place "where Alaskans meet Alaskans," features a warm and inviting dining area filled with polished woods, slate tile floors, soft lighting, and a huge rock fireplace. The menu contains a wide range of entreés and appetizers, but the rotisserie-grilled meats and fresh Alaskan seafood are what the restaurant is best known for. American menu. Lunch, dinner. Closed July 4, Thanksgiving, Dec 25. Bar. Casual attire. Reservations recommended. **$$**

★ ★ **GWENNIE'S OLD ALASKA RESTAURANT.** *4333 Spenard Rd, Anchorage (99517). Phone 907/243-2090.* Another of Anchorage's perennial breakfast and brunch favorites, Gwennie's takes pride in its strong ties to Anchorage's history, as evidenced by walls lined with framed newspaper clippings and photos depicting Anchorage's wild and sometimes checkered past. This is a real family restaurant, serving wholesome Alaskan food to generations of tourists and locals. American menu. Breakfast, lunch, dinner. Closed Thanksgiving, Dec 25. Bar. Casual attire. **$$**

★ ★ **HOOPER BAY CAFÉ.** *500 W 3rd Ave, Anchorage (99501). Phone 907/272-7411; fax 907/265-7175.* For travelers looking for prime people-watching venues in Anchorage, the Hooper Bay Café inside the Hilton hotel (see) is the place to go. With only a waist-high wall separating the café from the spacious Hilton lobby, customers are able to keep an eye on all the action while enjoying quality American, Northwestern, and international dishes from a surprisingly adventurous menu. American menu. Breakfast, lunch, dinner. Children's menu. Casual attire. **$$**

★ ★ **HOW HOW CHINESE RESTAURANT.** *207 Muldoon Rd, Anchorage (99504). Phone 907/337-2116; fax 907/338-6569.* Since the early 1970s, this family-owned restaurant has been serving top quality Chinese food to a devoted local clientele as well as legions of weary travelers staying nearby. With an interior filled with carved animals, hanging lanterns, and graceful architectural features, it provides diners with a terrific visual and culinary experience. American, Chinese menu. Lunch, dinner. Closed Thanksgiving, Dec 25. Bar. Children's menu. Casual attire. Outdoor seating. **$$**

★ ★ **JEN'S.** *701 W 36th Ave, Anchorage (99501). Phone 907/561-5367. www.jensrestaurant.com.* Jen's is a chef-owned, fine dining restaurant exquisitely decorated with Alaskan art. Menu changes daily. French menu. Lunch, dinner. Closed Sun. **$$$**

★ ★ ★ **KATSURA TEPPANYAKI.** *1000 Arlberg Ave, Girdwood (99587). Phone 907/754-2237. www. alyeskaresort.com.* This on-site restaurant at the Alyeska Resort in Girdwood serves "world-class Japanese cuisine with flair" and features a u-shaped seating arrangement whereby guests can watch the master chef prepare their food in front of them. With reservations limited to only 18 diners per seating and a menu of four set courses to choose from, the emphasis here is on creating a unique and memorable dining experience in an intimate, upscale environment. Japanese menu. Dinner. Closed Tues-Wed. Bar. Casual attire. **$$$**

★ ★ ★ **KUMAGORO.** *533 W 4th Ave, Anchorage (99501). Phone 907/272-9905.* This is the only restaurant in Alaska to feature a traditional Japanese breakfast and Shabu Shabu dinners. Japanese menu. Breakfast, lunch, dinner. **$$**

★ ★ **LION'S DEN.** *1000 E 36th Ave, Anchorage (99508). Phone 907/743-4814; fax 907/248-1117. www. bestwesterngoldenlion.com.* This midtown restaurant is located in the Best Western Golden Lion Hotel (see). Featuring a bright, airy dining area and a wide selection of American and seafood entreés, it attracts large numbers of locals as well as hotel guests. Twinkle-toed diners are invited to join in free dance lessons held six nights a week in the adjacent lounge. American menu. Breakfast, lunch, dinner. Closed Jan 1, Dec 25. Bar. Casual attire. **$$**

★ ★ ★ **MARX BROTHERS' CAFÉ.** *627 W 3rd Ave, Anchorage (99501). Phone 907/278-2133.* A local favorite, this café was built in 1916 and features progressive American cuisine with an award-winning wine list. American menu. Dinner. Closed Sun. **$$$**

★ ★ **PEPPER MILL.** *4101 Credit Union Dr, Anchorage (99503). Phone 907/561-0800; fax 907/ 563-6382. www.seagalleyalaska.com.* This elegant yet casual steakhouse is one of the most popular in the midtown area, serving top-of-the-line steaks in a private, comfortable setting. It's definitely a unique place to dine, with hundreds of pepper mills on display throughout the dining area, including one so large,

it takes four people to operate. Steak menu. Dinner. Closed Thanksgiving, Dec 25. Bar. Children's menu. Casual attire. **$$$**

★ ★ **PIPERS RESTAURANT & LOUNGE.** *3333 W International Airport Rd, Anchorage (99502). Phone 907/249-4444.* The small, slightly upscale dining room at the Coast International Inn (see) features elegant light fixtures, beautiful architectural highlights, and comfortable booth seating that allows for privacy while dining. During summer, the restaurant's biggest attraction is its outdoor patio, which offers diners the chance to enjoy wonderful lake and mountain views while dining under the midnight sun. American menu. Breakfast, lunch, dinner. Closed Jan 1, Thanksgiving, Dec 25. Bar. Children's menu. Casual attire. Outdoor seating. **$$**

★ ★ **THE POND CAFE.** *1000 Arlberg Ave, Girdwood (99587). Phone 907/754-2236. www. alyeskaresort.com.* The highlight of this family-oriented café at the Alyeska Prince Resort (see) is its sunny, spacious dining room that provides terrific views of the hotel's small pond and the Chugach Mountains that encircle the resort. During the long days of summer, diners can opt to relax and unwind on the covered patio that overlooks the pond. American menu. Breakfast, lunch, dinner. Bar. Children's menu. Casual attire. Outdoor seating. **$$**

★ ★ **PTARMIGAN BAR & GRILL.** *401 E 6th Ave, Anchorage (99501). Phone 907/276-8700; fax 907/ 276-7561. www.sheratonanchorage.com/dining.htm.* This casual, friendly restaurant is located on the ground floor of the Sheraton Anchorage Hotel (see) and specializes in Alaskan cuisine—salmon chowder, reindeer sausage, buffalo meatloaf, and baked halibut. The subtle Alaskan décor and vibrant color scheme in the dining area create a casual, slightly upscale environment that is at once cheerful and inviting. American menu. Breakfast, lunch, dinner. Bar. Casual attire. **$$**

★ ★ **RISTORANTE ORSO.** *737 W 5th Ave, Anchorage (99501). Phone 907/222-3232; fax 907/792-3740. www.orsoalaska.com.* Few, if any, restaurants in Anchorage can rival Ristorante Orso for unique atmosphere and bold continental flair. Designed to resemble the interior of a Tuscan villa, this downtown restaurant is divided into a series of small alcoves and private rooms that enable diners to enjoy fine dining in an intimate setting. Soft lights, warm

Mediterranean colors, and beautiful architectural features combine with the gourmet menu to make a visit here a visual and culinary treat. Mediterranean menu. Lunch, dinner. Closed July 4, Thanksgiving, Dec 25. Bar. Casual attire. **$$$**

★ ★ ★ **SACK'S CAFÉ & RESTAURANT.** *328 G St, Anchorage (99501). Phone 907/274-4022. www. sackscafe.com.* This is an award-winning restaurant specializing in eclectic New American cuisine. American menu. Lunch, dinner. **$$**

★ ★ **SEA GALLEY.** *4101 Credit Union Dr, Anchorage (99503). Phone 907/563-3520; fax 907/563-6382. www.seagalleyalaska.com.* Quality fresh Alaskan seafood is the main draw at this long-time fixture on the midtown restaurant scene, with fresh halibut, Alaska king crab, and fresh oysters flying out the door. A large enclosed atrium permits sunny indoor dining throughout the year, and numerous alcoves make an ideal dining destination for groups, families, and those looking for a bit of privacy. Seafood menu. Lunch, dinner. Closed Thanksgiving, Dec 25. Bar. Children's menu. Casual attire. **$$**

★ ★ ★ **SEVEN GLACIERS.** *1000 Arlberg Ave, Girdwood (99587). Phone 907/754-2237. www. alyeskaresort.com.* Located 2,300 feet above the Girdwood valley floor, the ultra-chic Seven Glaciers restaurant is only accessible by gondola from the Alyeska Prince Resort (see). From this mountainside perch, it provides guests with breathtaking views to the north of seven hanging glaciers on a nearby mountain and to the south, the waters of Turnagain Arm. Winner of the *Wine Spectator* Award of Excellence, the restaurant features award-winning Alaskan cuisine in an exceptionally warm and intimate environment and has a well-deserved reputation for flawless service. Northwestern menu. Dinner. Closed mid-Apr-mid-May and Oct-mid-Nov. Bar. Children's menu. Business casual attire. **$$$**

★ ★ **SIMON & SEAFORT'S SALOON & GRILL.** *420 L St, Anchorage (99501). Phone 907/274-3502.* One of Anchorage's most popular restaurants, Simon & Seafort's Saloon & Grill is located a short walk from the Hotel Captain Hook (see) and offers views of the Cook Inlet from large picture windows. American menu. Lunch, dinner. **$$**

★ ★ **SNOW CITY CAFÉ.** *1034 W 4th Ave, Anchorage (99501). Phone 907/272-2489; fax 907/272-*
6338. *www.snowcitycafe.com.* Voted Anchorage's best brunch in a citywide poll in 2003, Snow City Café serves up hearty meals and fresh-baked pastries to the office workers, tourists, and locals who drop in throughout the day. With strong ties to the local community, it is host to an ever-changing lineup of art exhibits, local community events, and live music. American menu. Breakfast, lunch. Closed Jan 1, Thanksgiving, Dec 25. Casual attire. Outdoor seating. **$**

★ ★ **SNOW GOOSE RESTAURANT & SLEEPING LADY BREWING COMPANY.** *717 W 3rd Ave, Anchorage (99501). Phone 907/272-2489; fax 907/272-6338. www.alaskabeers.com.* The Snow Goose Restaurant is one of only a few moderately priced restaurants in Anchorage that offers scenic outdoor dining to its summertime clientele. During colder months, oversized picture windows enable customers to enjoy the spectacular mountain and inlet views from the warmth of the restaurant and lounge. Art lovers should plan on extra time to enjoy the colorful hand-made Alaskan quilts and stained glass panels that decorate the walls of the restaurant. American menu. Lunch, dinner, late-night. Closed Jan 1, Thanksgiving, Dec 25. Bar. Children's menu. Casual attire. Outdoor seating. **$$**

★ ★ **STUART ANDERSON'S CATTLE COMPANY.** *300 W Tudor Rd, Anchorage (99503). Phone 907/562-2844; fax 907/562-2632. www. stuartandersons.com.* Since opening in Anchorage in 1978, Stuart Anderson's Cattle Company has built a solid reputation for serving up hearty steak and seafood dishes. Weather-beaten boards, enormous wooden rafters, and cowboy memorabilia create a rustic Western feel for the restaurant, but it's the hearty food that draws people back time and again. Steak menu. Lunch, dinner. Closed Dec 25. Bar. Casual attire. **$$**

★ **THAI HOUSE.** *830 E 36th Ave, Anchorage (99503). Phone 907/563-8616; fax 907/562-9490.* Named best Thai food in a local poll a number of years running, Thai House restaurant has loads of charm, with a gracious and attentive waitstaff and an interior filled with an eclectic array of Thai art, intricate wood carvings, and colorful sarongs. Housed in a former Dairy Queen, it's quirky, casual, and inviting. Thai menu. Lunch, dinner. Closed Sun; holidays. Casual attire. **$**

★ ★ ★ **TOP OF THE WORLD.** *500 W 3rd Ave, Anchorage (99501). Phone 907/265-7111; fax 907/265-7175. www.hilton.com.* When it comes to fine dining in Anchorage, Top of the World restaurant's combination of elegance, atmosphere, and location is hard to match. Situated on the 15th floor of the Hilton hotel (see), the restaurant offers a carefully crafted gourmet menu along with impeccable service. The real highlight of the restaurant, though, is its stunning panoramic views, which on a clear day extend as far as Mount McKinley. Guests looking for lighter fare can take a seat in the adjoining lounge, which offers rooftop seating during the summer—a chic and unique place to relax and enjoy the midnight sun. Seafood menu. Dinner. Closed Sun-Tues; Dec 25. Bar. Children's menu. Casual attire. **$$$**

★ **UNCLE JOE'S PIZZERIA.** *428 G St, Anchorage (99501). Phone 907/279-3799. www.unclejoespizzeria .com.* Voted "Best Pepperoni Pizza" by University of Alaska Anchorage students in a 2003 poll, Uncle Joe's Pizzeria offers its customers a wide selection of pizzas, calzones, subs, and gyros "made to order, one at a time with pride." With five locations in and around Anchorage, it's a convenient, casual, and inexpensive place to grab a bite to eat. Pizza. Lunch, dinner. Closed Thanksgiving, Dec 25. Casual attire. **$**

★ **WAYNE'S ORIGINAL TEXAS BAR-B-QUE.** *3400 C St, Anchorage (99503). Phone 907/569-9911; fax 907/569-5582. www.waynesbbq.us.* This ultra-casual family friendly joint focuses on one thing and one thing only: Texas-style barbecue. There's no attempt here to compete with the legions of upscale steakhouses in Anchorage: customers order at a counter and eat and drink from plastic and paper dinnerware. With low prices, a great selection of barbecue favorites, and enormous portions, it's a great place for hungry hombres. Barbecue menu. Lunch, dinner. Closed Jan 1, Thanksgiving, Dec 25. Children's menu. Casual attire. **$**

★ ★ **YUKON YACHT CLUB.** *115 E 3rd Ave, Anchorage (99501). Phone 907/334-8408. www. yukonyachtclub.com.* Proudly billing itself as the northernmost yacht club in North America, the Yukon Yacht Club is open to all with its casual atmosphere, enormous beer selection, live music, and amusing menu. Adventurous customers might consider tackling the 49-ounce Alaskan cut steak, also available in the more "dainty" 22-ounce Texas size. American menu. Breakfast, lunch, dinner. Bar. Children's menu. Casual attire. Outdoor seating. **$$**

Aniakchak National Monument and Preserve

Web site www.nps.gov/ania

The Aniakchak Caldera, a volcanic crater measuring almost 6 miles in diameter, is a spectacular sight and a truly awesome example of nature's power. Created over the last 3,400 years by a series of volcanic eruptions—the most recent occurring in May 1931—the caldera possesses outstanding examples of volcanic features, with numerous explosion pits, lava flows, and cinder cones. The largest cone, Vent Mountain, rises 1,400 feet above the caldera floor. The walls of the caldera vary in height, generally ranging between 2,000 and 4,400 feet. Surprise Lake glistens within the caldera and serves as the source of the Aniakchak River, which offers an unparalleled whitewater rafting experience. The river cuts a 1,500-foot opening, (known as "The Gates") in the caldera wall, and then briskly flows east, winding around the mountains of the Aleutian Range, before spilling out into Aniakchak Bay and the Pacific Ocean. Other popular activities in and around the caldera include camping, fishing, hiking, and wildlife viewing. With its remote location along the Alaska Peninsula, the Aniakchak National Monument and Preserve can be accessed only via floatplane. Phone 907/246-3305.

Barrow (A-4)

Population 4,581
Area Code 907

Barrow, the northernmost city in the United States, is home to a large number of Eskimos, who call the city Ukpeagvik, or "place where owls are hunted." From mid-May to mid-August, the sun never sets—and it never rises above the horizon between mid-December and late January. It's a great place to catch the famous northern lights in winter, and it's also well known as a birding site, with Eider ducks and snowy owls among the 250 species that visit each year. Humorist Will Rogers was killed in Barrow in a plane crash in 1935; two monuments here remember Rogers and the famous pilot of the plane, Wiley Post. No roads connect Barrow to other Alaska cities, but you can catch a (pricey) flight out of Anchorage or Fairbanks. Lodging is available at the King Eider Inn, which was built in 1998 to accommodate the hardy souls who venture here.

What to See and Do

Inupiat Heritage Center. *Phone 907/852-5494. www. nps.gov/inup.* The Inupiat Heritage Center recognizes Alaska Natives who participated in commercial whaling during the late 19th and early 20th centuries. Remotely situated along the Arctic Ocean, the center is an affiliated area of the New Bedford Whaling National Historical Park in Massachusetts. More than 2,000 whaling voyages sailed from New Bedford to the frigid waters near Barrow. Alaska Natives, particularly the Inupiat Eskimo people, contributed greatly to the whaling efforts by hunting for food for the whalers, crewing whaling boats, and sheltering crews that had been shipwrecked off the coast. The Heritage Center features exhibits and artifact collections, as well as a library and gift shop. With its location above the Arctic Circle, Barrow is best reached via a commercial flight from Fairbanks or Anchorage. (Mon-Fri 8:30 am-5 pm)

Bering Land Bridge National Preserve

Web site www.nps.gov/bela

Roughly 13,000 years ago, the continents of Asia and North America were connected by a land bridge thousands of miles wide. Archaeologists believe that the land bridge provided humans the initial means of accessing and populating the Americas. Today, most of this stretch of land, known as the Bering Land Bridge, is submerged beneath the Bering and Chukchi seas. The Bering Land Bridge National Preserve occupies 2.7 million acres along the Arctic Circle in north-western Alaska's Seward Peninsula. One of the most isolated areas in the national park system, the preserve offers visitors the opportunity to explore native villages and learn about traditional subsistence lifestyles. Wildlife viewing is popular within the preserve, which is home to grizzly and polar bears, reindeer, wolves, whales, seals, and more than 170 species of birds. Other popular activities include cross-country skiing, fishing, and dog sledding—the northern terminus of the famous Iditarod Trail can be found just south of

the preserve. Winter temperatures here can sink as low as -55 degrees Fahrenheit. Not surprisingly, then, the Serpentine Hot Springs—with water temperatures between 140 and 170 degrees—have become a favorite stop for visitors to the preserve. Phone 907/443-2522.

Cape Krusenstern National Monument

Web site www.nps.gov/cakr

Cape Krusenstern National Monument sprawls out over 660,000 treeless acres along the Chukchi Sea in northwest Alaska. Isolated above the Arctic Circle, the monument possesses a tundra landscape marked by 114 beach ridges, existing as a record of the sea's ever-changing coastline. The earliest ridges can be found farther inland. Archaeological excavations at these early beach ridges indicate human presence along the coastline 9,000 years ago. Natives still reside in the area, and, within the monument, they are allowed to hunt marine mammals—whales, walruses, and seals. Polar and grizzly bears patrol the limestone hills of the coastline, as do caribou, moose, and wolves. Each fall brings large numbers of migratory birds to the lagoons at Cape Krusenstern. For visitors to the monument, the most popular recreational activities include camping, hiking, and kayaking. The nearest town, Kotzebue, sits 10 miles to the southeast. During the summer months—which are wet, windy, and cool—Cape Krusenstern is accessible by chartered boat or seaplane. Only the hardiest outdoor enthusiasts should consider venturing here during the bitterly cold winter, when a dogsled represents the most effective means of reaching the monument.

Cordova (D-6)

Population 2,454
Area Code 907
Web site www.cordovaalaska.com

Accessible only by boat or plane, Cordova sits on the eastern edge of Prince William Sound, the nearest settlement to the vast Copper River Delta, one of the largest and most important migratory bird habitats in

North America. Originally developed as the southern terminus of the Copper River & Northwestern Railroad, which transported copper from the Kennecott Mine 200 miles to the north, Cordova flourished from 1911 until the mine shut down in 1938. Eventually, the railroad track was torn up and the bed used as a makeshift roadway until the 1964 Good Friday earthquake destroyed the northernmost span of the Million Dollar Bridge across the Copper River, effectively cutting off Cordova's only land-based link to the outside world. The geographic isolation of the town has turned out to be one of its biggest assets, as it remains largely unaffected by the summer tourists who use it as a home base while they hunt, fish, hike, kayak, and explore the vast wilderness that surrounds the town.

What to See and Do

Mount Eyak Ski Area. *Phone 907/424-7766.* Downhill skiing, snowboarding, heli-skiing. Thirty trails; longest run 750 feet. Rentals.

Museum. *First St, Cordova (99574). Phone 907/424-6665.* Exhibits of native artifacts, early explorers, mining, and the railroad. (Mon-Sat 10 am-6 pm, Sun 2-4 pm)

Points North Heli Adventures. *PO Box 1610, Cordova (99574). Phone toll-free 877/787-6784. www.alaskaheliski.com.* Operating out of the Orca Adventure Lodge (see), this tour company helicopters brave skiers and snowboarders into the Chugach Mountains, dropping them directly onto the slopes for amazing runs in exceptional powder. Most skiers average 20,000 to 25,000 vertical feet in a day, consisting of five to eight runs. At more than $500 an hour, the adventure doesn't come cheap, but it's sure to be an experience you won't soon forget. **$$$$**

Special Event

Copper River Wild! Salmon Festival. *Phone 907/424-7260.* Celebrates the annual arrival of Copper River Reds (red salmon)—a major Alaskan export. Early June.

Limited-Service Hotel

★ **PRINCE WILLIAM MOTEL.** *501 Second St, Cordova (99574). Phone 907/424-3201; toll-free 888/796-6835; fax 907/424-2260.* Built on the side of a steep hill overlooking Orca Inlet and Hawkins Island, this small, locally-owned motel is conveniently located in the heart of downtown Cordova. The rooms are large and half of them have kitchenettes, so it's particularly popular with families, budget travelers, and long-term visitors. 16 rooms. Pets accepted. Check-in 2 pm, check-out noon. **$**

Specialty Lodgings

The following lodging establishments are approved by Mobil Travel Guide, but due to their unique and individualized nature have not been given a traditional Mobil Star rating. Included in this listing you may find bed-and-breakfasts, limited-service inns, guest ranches, and other unique hotel properties.

THE CORDOVA LIGHTHOUSE INN. *212 Nicholoff Way, Cordova (99574). Phone 907/424-7080; toll-free 888/424-7080; fax 907/424-7081. www.cordovalighthouseinn.com.* The Cordova Lighthouse Inn is a tiny, ultra-cozy inn on the water's edge in Cordova. Each room is adorned with framed tintype photos on the dressers, home-style bedspreads and pillows, and an eclectic collection of furniture. Rooms at the front overlook Cordova's small boat harbor, while those at the back have views of Odiak Slough and Mt. Eccles. 4 rooms. Check-in 2 pm, check-out 11 am. Restaurant. **$**

ORCA ADVENTURE LODGE. *Cordova (99574). 2 miles N. Phone toll-free 866/424-6722. www.orcaadventurelodge.com.* If you're planning a visit to Cordova, it's likely that you'll find yourself at the Orca Adventure Lodge, even if you don't choose to stay here. Many "adventures" depart from the lodge, including river rafting, kayaking, and fly fishing trips. Situated 2 miles north of town on the shores of Prince William Sound, the 1880s cannery town has been refashioned into a rustic lodging with ocean views. All meals are provided in the cookhouse next door. 37 rooms. Wireless Internet access. Airport transportation available. **$**

Restaurants

★ ★ ★ **AMBROSIA RESTAURANT.** *410 Main St, Cordova (99574). Phone 907/424-7175.* Seafood menu. Lunch, dinner. Bar. Business casual attire. Reservations recommended. **$$$**

★ **THE CORDOVA LIGHTHOUSE INN.** *212 Nicholoff Way, Cordova (99574). Phone 907-424-7080; fax 907-424-7081. www.cordovalighthouseinn.com.* Located across the street from the boat harbor, this snug little restaurant and bakery is filled with the delicious smell of coffee and muffins in the morning, pizzas at night, and fresh-baked bread throughout the day. The range of desserts and pastries they offer makes any thought of a diet impossible. American menu. Breakfast, lunch. Closed holidays; also Sun-Mon in winter. Casual attire. Outdoor seating. **$**

Denali National Park and Preserve

See also Talkeetna

Web site www.nps.gov/dena

Like Alaska and Mount McKinley, Denali is big—really big. It ranks among the largest national parks, covering over 6 million acres of pristine wilderness, a broad expanse of land roughly the same size as Massachusetts. Situated within the 600-mile-long Alaska Range, the park's sharp-edged mountains were carved by sprawling glaciers, many of which are still at work—the park contains more than 20 glaciers that are longer than 5 miles, including one, Kahiltna, that stretches 43 miles. Denali also possesses abundant wildlife, and visitors shouldn't be surprised to spot moose, caribou, Dall sheep, and grizzly bears, as well as smaller mammals such as marmots and snowshoe hares.

Hiking and camping are among the most popular activities at Denali. Although the park has few trails, one worth exploring is the Mount Healy Overlook Trail, a 2.5-mile trek that leads to a stellar view of the fast-flowing Nenana River and majestic peaks of the Alaska Range. The Nenana River offers a stellar whitewater rafting experience that's not for the faint of heart, with stretches of the river categorized as Class IV rapids. Bicycling is another favored activity here, particularly on the 90-mile-long Park Road. Bicycles may be transported on the Park Road shuttle bus, allowing for a one-way bike ride to the center of Denali followed by a one-way bus ride back to the visitor center. For those seeking to truly test their mettle, Mount McKinley stands as one of the most difficult climbs in the world. While not a technically difficult climb, bitterly cold temperatures, fierce winds, and 16,000 feet of snowline make for a daunting expedition. The park is open year-round, and a surprising number of visitors arrive in the winter months to go cross-country skiing or dogsledding.

Deep within Alaska's interior, Mount McKinley boldly emerges from a subarctic desert terrain, the mountain's broad shoulders rising inexorably skyward, culminating at a peak of 20,320 feet—770 feet higher than any other mountain in North America. The massive McKinley is, without question, the star attraction at Denali National Park & Preserve, helping the park to draw nearly 300,000 visitors a year.

Native Alaskans have lived at Denali for many centuries. In fact, Mount McKinley (named for President William McKinley) was originally named Denali, which among the indigenous Athabascan people means "Great One." With the stroke of a pen, President Woodrow Wilson established Mount McKinley National Park in 1917. Congress changed the park's name to Denali National Park & Preserve 63 years later.

Denali is accessible by car. The park's headquarters sit on Highway 3, 125 miles south of Fairbanks and 240 miles north of Anchorage. Denali's mountaineering headquarters are in Talkeetna, about 100 miles north of Anchorage. The highly regarded Alaska Railroad runs the Denali Star line between Anchorage and Fairbanks, with stops in Talkeetna and Denali. (Daily; hours vary by season) **$**

What to See and Do

Tours. *Denali. Phone toll-free 800/544-2206. www.graylineofalaska.com.* Gray Line of Alaska offers package tours around Alaska (up to 11 days) as well as flightseeing, heli-hiking, rafting, horseback, and backcountry wilderness tours of Denali.

Limited-Service Hotels

★ ★ **DENALI BLUFFS HOTEL.** *George Parks Hwy, mile 238.3, Denali National Park and Preserve (99755). Phone 907/683-7000; toll-free 866/683-8500; fax 907/683-7500. www.denalialaska.com/bluffs.* This 112-room hotel is actually a series of low-rise buildings located on a bluff overlooking some of the most scenic wilderness in Alaska. All rooms are tidy and appealing, but it's the views through the windows that really make staying here a memorable experience. The hotel runs a free shuttle service to Denali National Park, only a mile away, and to the little town nearby.

112 rooms. Check-in 3 pm, check-out 11 am. Wireless Internet access. Restaurant, bar. **$$**

★ ★ **DENALI CROW'S NEST LOG CABINS.** *George Parks Hwy, mile 238.3, Denali National Park and Preserve (99755). Phone 907/683-2723. www. denalicrowsnest.com.* Perched on the side of Sugarloaf Mountain 1 mile north of the Denali Park entrance, these one-room log cabins offer magnificent views and cozy, basic accommodations. With neither telephones nor televisions in the rooms, the cabins provide guests with an opportunity to break from routine and enjoy life through nature. 39 rooms. Closed early Sept-mid-May. Check-in 2 pm, check-out 11 am. Restaurant, bar. Whirlpool. **$**

★ **DENALI PARK HOTEL.** *George Parks Hwy, mile 1.5 247, Healy (99743). Phone 907/683-1800; toll-free 866/683-1800; fax 907/683-1801. www.denaliparkhotel .com.* This unassuming complex of long, low buildings offers comparatively inexpensive, comfortable accommodations in a peaceful, rustic setting. Guests check in at a lobby set in a historic Alaska railroad car and then head to their rooms, all of which offer unobstructed views of the Alaska Range and Mount McKinley. Food, souvenirs, and gas are available in the nearby town of Healy. 42 rooms. Closed mid-Sept-mid-May, Pets accepted; fee. Check-in 2 pm, check-out 11 am. **$**

★ ★ **DENALI PRINCESS WILDERNESS LODGE.** *George Parks Hwy, mile 238.5, Denali National Park and Preserve (99755). Phone 907/683-2282; toll-free 800/426-0500; fax 907/683-2545. www. princesslodges.com.* As with all Princess lodges in Alaska, the Denali Princess Wilderness Lodge is an architectural gem set in a stunning Alaskan landscape. From the dramatic two-story rock and wood beam main building, completed in 2004, to the rustic, elegant log buildings that house the guest rooms, the lodge enables its guests to enjoy a taste of Alaskan wilderness without sacrificing comfort or style. The lodge features a number of restaurants, from the casual Lynx Creek Pizza to the unique Music of Denali Dinner Theatre. When not touring, eating, or shopping, guests tend to flock to the lodge's large outdoor deck overlooking the picturesque Nenana River. 440 rooms. Closed mid-Sept-mid-May. Check-in 3:30 pm, check-out 11 am. Three restaurants, two bars. Fitness room. Whirlpool. **$$**

★ ★ **GRANDE DENALI LODGE.** *George Parks Hwy, mile 238.2, Denali National Park and Preserve (99755). Phone 907/683-8500; toll-free 866/683-8500; fax 907/683-8599. www.denalialaska.com.* From its perch at the top of a mountain near the entrance to Denali National Park, this architecturally magnificent lodge dominates the local skyline, literally towering above all other properties in the area. As a full-service, upscale lodge, it features an elegant restaurant, an in-house multi-media theater, and a wide variety of free and fee-based outdoor activities ranging from guided nature walks and mountain bike rentals to tundra wilderness tours and heli-hiking excursions. Most public areas and guest rooms have stunning views of the Denali area, making this one of the most scenic places to stay in the area. 160 rooms. Closed mid-Sept-mid-May. Check-in 3 pm, check-out 10 am. Restaurant, bar. **$$**

★ ★ **MCKINLEY CHALET RESORT.** *George Parks, mile post 239, Denali National Park and Preserve (99755). Phone 907/683-8200; toll-free 800/276-7234; fax 907/683-8211. www.denaliparkresort.com.* Offering upscale rooms and suites, this newly renovated property is located on a hill overlooking the Nenana River and the forested valleys of the Denali wilderness. Guests stay in lodges located near the main building, which houses the resort's restaurants, gift shop, dinner theater, fireside lounge, and interpretive displays. The resort offers guests guided nature walks and twice-daily informational talks given by naturalists familiar with the wildlife and geology of Denali National Park. The centerpiece of the stunning lobby is a large three-dimensional topographical map of the Denali area, which serves as a useful aid in understanding just how big and untamed the Park really is. 345 rooms. Closed mid-Sept-mid-May. Check-in 2 pm, check-out 11 am. Two restaurants, bar. **$$**

★ ★ **MCKINLEY VILLAGE LODGE.** *Mile 23, Denali National Park and Preserve (99755). Phone 907/683-8900; toll-free 800/276-7234; fax 907/258-3668.* Located on the Nenana River 8 miles south of the entrance to Denali National Park, this lodge-style hotel offers family-friendly accommodation in a spectacular setting. Rooms here are filled with comfortable wood furniture, soft, soothing colors, and accent pieces featuring local wildlife, reflecting the attractiveness and beauty of the wilderness outside. Guests of the lodge can spend the day panning for gold, riding the Nenana in a whitewater raft, or hiking local trails through the spruce forests that surround the property.

On-site dining facilities, outdoor sundecks, and a courtesy shuttle into the park add to the allure of the property. 150 rooms. Closed mid-Sept-late May. Check-in 2 pm, check-out 11 am. Restaurant, bar. **$**

★ ★ **MT. MCKINLEY PRINCESS WILDERNESS LODGE.** *George Parks Hwy, mile 133, Denali National Park and Preserve (99683). Phone 907/733-2900; toll-free 800/426-0500; fax 907/733-2922.* This self-described "true wilderness retreat" is located on the Chulitna River inside Denali State Park. Its 334 guest rooms are housed in seventeen separate buildings on the property, ensuring a quiet, relaxing stay for all guests. The main building houses restaurants, a tour desk, an exercise room, and the Great Room, a magnificent social space with floor-to-ceiling windows offering views of Mt. McKinley, a massive stone fireplace, and plenty of cozy chairs for reading and relaxing. The grounds of the lodge feature a network of hiking trails, a spacious outdoor deck perfect for photographers and sun worshippers, and two hilltop whirlpools designed to help guests unwind after a busy day exploring the area. 334 rooms. Closed mid-Sept-mid-May. Check-in 3 pm, check-out 11 am. Restaurant, bar. Children's activity center. Fitness room. Whirlpool. **$$**

★ ★ **TALKEETNA ALASKAN LODGE.** *Talkeeta Spur Rd, mile 12.5, Talkeetna (99676). Phone 907/733-9500; toll-free 888/959-9590; fax 907/733-9545. www.talkeetnalodge.com.* Run by an Alaskan Native corporation, this hilltop lodge on the outskirts of Talkeetna offers unobstructed panoramic views of Denali and the Alaska Range as well as a bird's-eye view of the Susitna River Valley. The lobby features a four-story vaulted ceiling, a massive river rock fireplace, enormous wooden support pillars, and walls of windows that bathe the room in light and provide guests with front-row seats to the breathtaking scenery outside. Guest rooms are exceptionally comfortable and reflect the same attention to quality and detail seen in the public areas of the lodge. The on-site restaurant offers casual upscale dining and has been named a winner of the *Wine Spectator* Award of Excellence. 200 rooms. Closed early Oct-mid-Apr. Check-in 3 pm, check-out 11 am. Two restaurants, bar. **$$$**

★ **WESTMARK DENALI SOURDOUGH CABINS.** *George Parks Hwy, mile 238.8, Denali National Park and Preserve (99755). Phone 907/683-2773; toll-free 800/544-0970; fax 907/683-2357. www.*

denalisourdoughcabins.com. These tiny rustic cabins, surrounded by a heavily wooded forest, soaring mountain peaks, and plenty of wildlife, provide guests with the chance to enjoy Alaska's great outdoors without having to rough it. Each cabin features beautiful cedar paneled walls, a private bathroom and a cozy front porch where guests can sit and take in the sights and sounds of the Denali wilderness. 45 rooms. Mid-Sept-late May. Check-in 2 pm, check-out 11 am. **$**

Specialty Lodgings

The following lodging establishments are approved by Mobil Travel Guide, but due to their unique and individualized nature have not been given a traditional Mobil Star rating. Included in this listing you may find bed-and-breakfasts, limited-service inns, guest ranches, and other unique hotel properties.

SUSITNA RIVER LODGINGS. *13.5 Talkeetna Spur Rd, Talkeetna (99676). Phone 907/733-1505; toll-free 866/733-1505; fax 907/733-5051.* This collection of four cabins and a main lodge is a wilderness oasis set beside the Susitna River on the outskirts of Talkeetna. All rooms are suites with kitchenettes, full baths, and separate living and dining areas. The cabins also feature porches with scenic views and easy access to the communal barbecue and picnic area. 8 rooms, all suites. Check-in 3 pm, check-out noon. **$$**

TALKEETNA ROADHOUSE. *Main St & C St, Talkeetna (99676). Phone 907/733-1351; fax 907/733-1353. www.talkeetnaroadhouse.com.* This historic, family run hotel has been a Talkeetna landmark since 1944 and is a popular stopover for climbers and independent travelers looking for clean, comfortable, budget-friendly accommodations. Guest rooms are small and spartan and guests share a common bathroom, but the highly social, welcoming atmosphere of the hotel and attached restaurant more than compensates for the lack of modern amenities. 8 rooms. Check-in 2 pm, check-out noon. High-speed Internet access, wireless Internet access. Restaurant. Business center. **$**

Restaurants

★ ★ **ALPENGLOW RESTAURANT.** *George Parks Hwy, mile 238.2, Denali National Park and Preserve (99755). Phone 907/683-8720; toll-free 866/683-8500; fax 907/683-8599. www.denalialaska.com.* This spacious, lodge-style restaurant at the Grande Denali Lodge (see) features a menu of Alaskan and traditional American dishes prepared with the freshest ingredients available. A two-story wall of windows dominates the main room, offering guests the chance to marvel at the stunning, rugged wilderness surrounding the lodge as they enjoy some of the best casual fine dining in the area. American menu. Breakfast, lunch, dinner. Closed mid-Sept-mid-May. Bar. Children's menu. Casual attire. Reservations recommended. **$$$**

★ **CREEKSIDE CAFÉ.** *George Parks Hwy, mile 224, Denali National Park and Preserve (99755). Phone 907/683-2277; fax 907/683-1558.* This moderately priced diner-style restaurant is located beside Carlo Creek at McKinley Creekside Cabins. With a casual, rustic décor and good home cooking, it's a popular spot for locals as well as tourists, especially on weekdays when patrons are treated to live acoustic music. One of the café's best-known attractions is its annual chili cook-off, a highly competitive but good-natured event held each summer. American menu. Breakfast, lunch, dinner. Closed mid-Sept-mid-May, children's menu. Casual attire. Outdoor seating. **$$**
🅳

★ ★ ★ **FORAKER RESTAURANT.** *Talkeetna Spur Rd, mile 12.5, Talkeetna (99676). Phone 907/733-9509; toll-free 888/959-9590; fax 907/733-9545. www.talkeetnalodge.com.* Earthy elegance and rustic charm characterize this upscale dining spot named after 17,400-foot Mount Foraker, visible in the distance beside Mount McKinley. Featuring an award-winning wine selection, fresh Alaskan seafood, and panoramic views of the Alaska Range, the restaurant offers diners a memorable fine dining experience in the heart of the wilderness. As part of the Native-owned Talkeetna Alaskan Lodge (see), the restaurant has skillfully incorporated original Native Alaskan artwork into the décor of the dining area, adding artistic drama to the natural beauty of the room. American menu. Dinner. Closed Sept-Apr. Bar. Casual attire. Reservations recommended. Outdoor seating. **$$$**

★ **MOUNTAIN HIGH PIZZA PIE.** *Main St, Talkeetna (99676). Phone 907/733-1234; fax 907/733-7437.* With purple walls and funky hand-painted accents, this pizza joint in the heart of historic Talkeetna is the kind of place people go when they want quality food but don't want the formality of a sit-down meal. There's no pretentiousness here, nor

high prices, and every calzone, pizza, and Italian flat-bread sandwich is hand-made to order. Italian menu. Lunch, dinner, late-night. Children's menu. Casual attire. Outdoor seating. **$**

★ ★ ★ **NENANA VIEW GRILLE.** *George Parks Hwy, mile 238.9, Denali National Park and Preserve. Phone 907/683-8200; toll-free 800/276-7234.* Located at the McKinley Chalet Resort (see) with sweeping views of the Nenana River from both the bar and grill, this restaurant offers some of the best fine dining in the Denali area. Featuring an open kitchen floor plan and a large stone pizza oven, the dining area is filled with beautiful wooden furniture and striking artwork and accent pieces that give the room a sense of rustic elegance. The menu is a mix of haute cuisine, popular Alaskan dishes, and lighter fare and is complemented by an extensive wine selection. American menu. Breakfast, lunch, dinner, late-night. Closed mid-May-mid-Sept. Bar. Children's menu. Casual attire. Reservations recommended. Outdoor seating. **$$$**

★ ★ **THE OVERLOOK BAR AT THE CROW'S NEST.** *George Parks Hwy, mile 238.5, Denali National Park and Preserve (99755). Phone 907/683-2723.* Boasting "the largest beer selection in all of Alaska," this lively bar and grill at the Denali Crow's Nest Log Cabins (see) has become an area institution in the two decades since its founding. Serving burgers, chili, and other kinds of pub grub in its scenic dining area, it is as popular with locals as it is with tourists. American menu. Lunch, dinner. Bar. Casual attire. Outdoor seating. **$**
🅳

★ **PANORAMA PIZZA PUB.** *George Parks Hwy, mile 224, Denali National Park and Preserve (99755). Phone 907/683-2523; toll-free 888/322-2523; fax 907/683-2523. www.denaliparkresorts.com.* Serving piping hot pizzas, hefty burgers, over-sized sandwiches, and fresh-baked pastries prepared from scratch, this little restaurant and pub is an ideal place for a quick, inexpensive meal in the Denali area. Located on Carlo Creek south of the Denali Park entrance, it offers cheerful, friendly service in a beautiful wooded setting. Pizza. Breakfast, lunch, dinner. Children's menu. Casual attire. Outdoor seating. **$**

★ ★ **THE PERCH.** *George Parks Hwy, mile 224, Denali National Park and Preserve. Phone 907/683-2523; toll-free 888/322-2523; fax 907/683-2523. www.denaliperchresort.com.* Part of the Denali Perch Resort, this hilltop restaurant specializes in fine-dining cuisine with an emphasis on popular Alaskan seafood and steak dishes. Multiple bay windows offer dramatic, unobstructed views of the wilderness outside, while the restaurant's rustic architecture and open kitchen provide visual interest inside. Everything here is made from scratch, from the loaves of bread served with meals to the soups, salad dressings, and desserts prepared fresh on site each day. The restaurant also has a full bar featuring Alaskan beers and an extensive wine list. American menu. Dinner. Bar. Children's menu. Casual attire. Outdoor seating. **$$**

Eagle River

This small town 20 minutes north of downtown Anchorage serves as a bedroom community for the city and as a friendly, relaxing, and inexpensive home base for travelers wanting to explore the Anchorage area. The town serves as the one of the main gateways to Chugach State Park, which at nearly half a million acres ranks as the third largest state park in the United States and contains part of the Iditarod National Historic Trail. Twelve miles up Eagle River Road is the Eagle River Nature Center, offering self-guided hiking trails and hands-on interpretive exhibits. Regardless of the season, visitors to Eagle River can find outdoor recreational activities to suit their ages and fitness levels: hiking, biking, fishing, canoeing, rafting, camping, and rock climbing during the summer; ice climbing, dog mushing, downhill skiing, ice skating, and skijoring during the winter. There are also numerous scenic parks and lakes within a short drive of the downtown area that provide excellent family-friendly locales to relax and enjoy the long days of summer.

What to See and Do

Eagle River Nature Center. *32750 Eagle River Rd, Eagle River (99577). Phone 907/694-2108. www.ernc.org.* The Eagle River Nature Center serves as a gateway to the 500,000-acre Chugach State Park. Indoor and outdoor programs offered by the center teach visitors about the kinds of flora, fauna, and geographic features they might encounter inside the park in order to foster greater appreciation of and respect for one of Alaska's most accessible wilderness areas. The center's Web site provides detailed descriptions of program dates, times, and topics. (June-Aug: Sun-Thurs 10 am-5 pm, Fri-Sat 10 am-7 pm; Oct-Apr: Fri-Sun 10 am-5 pm; May, Sept: Tues-Sun 10 am-5 pm) **FREE**

Special Event

Bear Paw Festival. *Various sites, Eagle River. Phone 907/694-4702 (Chugiak-Eagle River Chamber of Commerce). www.cer.org/03bearpw.htm.* First held in 1985, the Bear Paw Festival was created to celebrate the beauty and diversity of the Eagle River and Chugiak area. Visitors to the festival can wander from the Renaissance Village, past the highly popular teddy bear picnic, and end up with prime seats at the Slippery Salmon Olympics. Pet-loving tourists might consider joining the Dog & Owner Look-alike Contest, while faded athletes might gravitate toward an event officially called the "300 Yard* Fun Run (*Because after 300 yards it isn't fun anymore!)." Carnival rides and a grand parade top the list of things to do at this unique small-town event. Contact the Chugiak-Eagle River Chamber of Commerce for detailed information about event dates, times, and locations. **FREE**

Limited-Service Hotels

★ **EAGLE RIVER MOTEL.** *11111 Old Eagle River Rd, Eagle River (99577). Phone 907/694-5000; toll-free 866/256-6835; fax 907/694-1713. www.eaglerivermotel .com.* Summertime prices at this motel are about half of what you'd pay in Anchorage and you get the added bonus of quiet, clean, and comfortable accommodations. It's a family-friendly atmosphere where energetic kids and family pets are very welcome, DVDs can be rented for a nominal fee at the front desk, and guests have access to the motel's laundry facilities. 14 rooms. Pets accepted. Complimentary continental breakfast. Check-in 1 pm, check-out 11 am. **$**

★ **MICROTEL INN & SUITES.** *13049 Old Glenn Hwy, Eagle River (99577). Phone 907/622-6000; toll-free 800/771-7171; fax 907/622-6001. www. eaglerivermicrotel.com.* Located on the main street running through Eagle River, the newer Microtel is very close to the highway on-ramp, enabling guests to leave the motel and be in downtown Anchorage in less than 15 minutes. No restaurant or shop in town is more than a three-minute drive away. The cozy lobby has an appealing river rock fireplace, perfect for lounging on plush couches. With reasonable rates in summer, this is a great choice for families, groups, and travelers looking for reliable accommodations close to Anchorage. 60 rooms. Pets accepted. Complimentary continental breakfast. Check-in 3 pm, check-out noon. **$**

Restaurant

★ ★ **WATERFALLS RESTAURANT.** *12801 Old Glenn Hwy, Suite #7, Eagle River (99577). Phone 907/ 622-6160; fax 907/622-6162.* Serving breakfast, lunch, and dinner seven days a week, the owners of this quiet, comfortable little restaurant on Eagle River's main road serve up a great selection of American and international dishes. Open from early morning to late at night, it's a worthwhile stop for the hungry traveler. American menu. Breakfast, lunch, dinner. Closed holidays. Children's menu. Casual attire. **$$**

Fairbanks (C-5)

Population 30,224
Area Code 907
Information Convention and Visitors Bureau, 550 First Ave, 99701; phone toll-free 800/327-5774
Web site www.explorefairbanks.com

The Fairbanks North Star Borough is about the same size as New Jersey but contains fewer than 90,000 people, a third of whom live in Fairbanks. Centrally located only 120 miles north of Denali National Park and 200 miles south of the Arctic Circle, Fairbanks remains today the largest and most important commercial, social, and tourist center in the Interior.

The origins of modern day Fairbanks can be traced to a series of mishaps that occurred to a would-be goldfield merchant named E. T. Barnette. In 1901, in an attempt to capitalize on the need for supplies at the Tanacross goldfields far up the Tanana River, Barnette loaded a sternwheeler with supplies and set out. After the boat ran aground in the Tanana's shallow waters, Barnette decided to try to reach the area via the nearby Chena River, which proved equally unsuccessful. In defeat, he unloaded the boat on the banks of the Chena and set up a small trading post on the spot, very close to where Italian prospector Felix Pedro struck gold the following year. In the ensuing gold rush, Barnette's business prospered and a town eventually grew up around it. Even today, Fairbanks is still very much a river city, with parks and walkways scattered along the Chena River and tour boats and rental kayaks plying the waters. One of the most popular attractions in the downtown area is a historic sternwheeler that takes passengers for scenic rides on the river during the summer.

One of Fairbanks's main distinctions is that it is subject to some of the widest temperature variations of any city on earth. Summertime temperatures occasionally hit the 90 degree mark, while winter temperatures have dipped as low as -62. Despite this, tourists still visit Fairbanks during winter, primarily because the long hours of darkness and cold night air provides excellent opportunities to view the aurora borealis, Alaska's northern lights. During the summer, the aurora is not visible as the area basks under nearly constant daylight.

What to See and Do

Alaska Highway. *Phone 907/452-1105 (Chamber of Commmerce).* This 1,522-mile-long road from Dawson Creek, British Columbia, to Fairbanks, Alaska was constructed shortly after the attack on Pearl Harbor, when a need for an inland route to Alaska was vital. Highlights along the way include Muncho Lake, Liard Hot Springs, Kluane Lake, and the Trans-Alaska Pipeline Crossing.

Creamer's Field Migratory Waterfowl Refuge. *1300 College Rd, Fairbanks (99708). Phone 907/452-5162. www.creamersfield.org.* This 1,800-acre site on the northern edge of Fairbanks serves as an important stopover point for thousands of Canada geese, pintails, golden plovers, and other birds on their spring and fall migrations. Although spring is the best time to see large numbers and varieties of birds at the refuge, sandhill cranes, shovelers, and mallards remain in the area all summer. Visitors walking any of the three trails on the property might happen upon more than just birds: moose, snowshoe hares, squirrels, voles, and red foxes are frequently spotted in the area. Admission to the refuge is free, as are nature walks departing from the Farmhouse Visitor Center. (Refuge always open. Farmhouse Visitor Center: summer: daily 10 am-4 pm; winter: Sat noon-4 pm. Free guided nature walks in summer: Tues and Thurs 7 pm, Wed and Sat 9 am.) **FREE**

Dalton Highway. Eighty-six miles north of Fairbanks, the Dalton Highway begins after branching off from the Elliott Highway. Also known by its original name, the North Slope Haul Road, the Dalton is 414 miles long, most of it hard-packed gravel, and traverses some of the most remote and rugged terrain of any highway in Alaska. The highway crosses the Yukon

River at mile marker 55.6, just over 129 miles from Fairbanks, and it is at this point that many tourists choose to take a break before turning around and heading back down the road. For the truly adventurous with plenty of free time, adequate provisions, and a properly equipped vehicle, the road continues for another 359 miles, passing between the Kanuti National Wildlife Refuge to the west and the Yukon Flats National Wildlife Refuge to the east before passing Gates of the Arctic National Park and Preserve on the climb up and over the Brooks Range. The road terminates at Deadhorse, also known as Prudhoe Bay, just a few miles from the Arctic Ocean. Because of security concerns at the North Slope oil refineries, private vehicles are not permitted to drive on the final few miles of the road leading from Deadhorse to the water. Commercial tours are available, though, and should be booked in advance along with local accommodations.

El Dorado Gold Mine. *Elliott Hwy, mile marker 1.3, Fairbanks (99709). 9 miles N. Phone 907/479-6673; toll-free 866/479-6673. www.eldoradogoldmine.com.* Run by the same family that operates the Riverboat Discovery (see), the El Dorado Gold Mine provides visitors with a chance to watch a real Alaskan gold mine in operation. The two-hour tour begins with a narrated ride on the Tanana Valley Railroad, a narrow-gauge line which travels through some of Fairbanks' original gold fields. Upon arrival at El Dorado mine, guests are given a guided tour of the facility and are taught how to pan for gold. Reservations are strongly recommended. Shuttle service is available; contact the company for details. (Mid-May-mid-Sept: 9:45 am and 3 pm, except Sat, when there is only a 3 pm departure) **$$$$**

Pioneer Park. *Airport Way and Peger Rd, Fairbanks (99707). Phone 907/459-1087. www.co.fairbanks.ak .us/parks&rec/pioneerpark.* Formerly known as Alaskaland, this 44-acre park set along the Chena River in the middle of Fairbanks is filled with hundreds of artifacts and mementos of the areas' pioneer past. The 230-foot-long sternwheeler *Nenana*, former belle of the Yukon River route, was transported to the park in 1966 and was faithfully restored to its original glory in 1992. The ship's hold now contains a large diorama depicting life on the Yukon and Tanana rivers during the era of the riverboats. Other highlights of the park include Gold Rush Town, a collection of 35 of Fairbanks's historic buildings transported to the park and restored to serve as a link to the town's past. Adult can also spend time exploring the Pioneer Air Museum and the Alaska Centennial Center for the Arts, while younger visitors can play miniature golf, rent bicycles, explore Mining Valley, or take a ride on the narrow-gauge Crooked Creek & Whiskey Island Railroad. (Park: year-round, admission free. Gold Rush Town and museums: Memorial Day through Labor Day, daily 11 am-9 pm; fees.)

Riverboat *Discovery*. *1975 Discovery Dr, Fairbanks (99709). Phone 907/479-6673; toll-free 866/479-6673. www.alaskaone.com/discovery.* Run by an Alaskan family with more than a century of Alaskan riverboating experience, this classic sternwheeler carries tourists on a 3 1/2-hour narrated cruise on the Chena and Tanana rivers. Highlights of the trip include stops at the riverside home of Susan Butcher, four-time winner of the Iditarod Trail Sled Dog race, and at the Old Chena Indian Village, where visitors can experience Alaskan Native culture firsthand and watch a sled dog demonstration. Reservations are required. (Mid-May-mid-Sept: Sun-Fri 8:45 am and 2 pm, Sat 2 pm only) **$$$$**

Tours. *Phone toll-free 800/544-2206. www.grayline ofalaska.com.* Gray Line of Alaska offers package tours around Alaska (up to 11 days) as well as sternwheeler, gold-panning, flightseeing, and other tours around Fairbanks.

University of Alaska Museum of the North. *907 Yukon Dr, Fairbanks (99775). Phone 907/474-7505. www.uaf.edu/museum.* Located on the campus of the University of Alaska Fairbanks, the Museum of the North houses more than 1.3 million artifacts relating to Alaska's history and culture. The museum is divided into five galleries, each representing one of Alaska's ecological regions: Southwest, Southcentral, Southeast, Interior, and Western & Artic Coast. Exhibits in the galleries range from a mummified Ice Age bison, affectionately known as Blue Babe, to intricately woven Aleut baskets and Eskimo ivory carvings. During the summer, visitors can stroll among sculptures in the garden outside or sit and watch construction of the newest museum galleries, scheduled for completion by summer 2005. (Mid-May-mid-Sept: daily 9 am-7 pm; mid-Sept-mid-May: Mon-Fri 9 am-5 pm, Sat-Sun noon-5 pm) **$**

Celebrating the Summer Solstice in Fairbanks

Fairbanks comes alive during the week leading up to the summer solstice on June 21. The **Midnight Sun 10K Run** is held the third Saturday in June. Beginning at the Patty Center on the University of Alaska Fairbanks campus, the course winds through residential and riverside neighborhoods before finishing at Pioneer Park. Despite, or because of, its 10 pm start time, the run draws thousands of runners and walkers each year, and the atmosphere is distinctly festive.

Another highlight of the summer solstice events is the **Midnight Sun Baseball Game** held at Growden Memorial Park (at the corner of 2nd Ave and Wilbur St) each June 21. Fairbanks's home-town boys, the Alaska Goldpanners, hit the field at 10:30 pm for this one-of-a-kind event. Games are held without artificial lights and are stopped only for the singing of the Alaska Flag song during the half-inning break that falls closest to midnight. Detailed information about the team's history and the Midnight Sun Baseball Game can be found at www.goldpanners.com.

The **Midnight Sun Festival** in downtown Fairbanks is held on the day of the solstice and features crafts, food, shopping, a street fair, and live entertainment. Many downtown stores stay open until midnight to accommodate the huge crowds that turn out for this event each year.

Special Event

Aurora Borealis (Northern Lights). One of Alaska's most spectacular and cheapest shows, the best time to see the spectacular streaks of green and red light that make up the Aurora Borealis is from about 10 pm until 2 am on nights with a new moon, although the display is frequently visible at other times. The Web site of the Geophysical Institute at the University of Anchorage (www.gi.alaska.edu) provides daily forecasts for aurora activity, as well as easy-to-under-stand explanations of the causes of the lights. Visitors should keep in mind that this phenomena is visible in Fairbanks only from late August until mid-April; summer visitors won't see it at all, as the sky never gets dark enough for the lights to be visible.

Limited-Service Hotels

★ **ASPEN HOTEL FAIRBANKS.** *4580 Old Airport Rd, Fairbanks (99701). Phone 907/457-2288; toll-free 888/595-2151; fax 907/457-2297. www. aspenhotelsak.com.* Located close to Fairbanks International Airport and the Parks Highway, this clean, comfortable hotel features a wide range of complimentary amenities that appeal to business professionals and families alike. Guests of the hotel enjoy the use of an indoor pool, small exercise room, business center, and coin-operated laundry facility and are treated to a deluxe continental breakfast every morning. 97 rooms. Check-in 3 pm, check-out 11 am. High-speed Internet access. Indoor pool. Airport transportation available. Business center. **$**

✈ 🏊 🏃

★ ★ **BRIDGEWATER HOTEL.** *723 1st Ave, Fairbanks (99701). Phone 907/452-6661; toll-free 800/ 528-4916; fax 907/451-6376. www.fountainheadhotels .com.* This attractive boutique hotel sits on the banks of the Chena River in downtown Fairbanks, only a short walk to the Visitor Center, Alaskan Railroad depot, and Pioneer Park. Light and bright interiors and the use of soft pastels and floral fabrics give it a warm, folksy charm that sets it apart from larger, standardized hotels. 94 rooms. Closed mid-Sept-mid-May. Check-in 2 pm, ch eck-out 11 am. Restaurant. Airport transportation available. **$**

★ ★ **THE CAPTAIN BARTLETT INN.** *1411 Airport Way, Fairbanks (99701). Phone 907/452-1888; toll-free 800/544-7528; fax 907/452-7674. www. captainbartlettinn.com.* Set in the middle of the main shopping and entertainment area of Fairbanks, this large hotel was built to resemble an Alaskan wilder-ness lodge. From the totem poles at the entrance to the stuffed musk ox and brown bear in the lobby, the hotel provides its guests with a strong sense of

Alaska's history, culture, and grandeur. 197 rooms. Pets accepted; fee. Check-in 3 pm, check-out 11 am. Restaurant, bar. Airport transportation available. **$**

★ ★ CHENA HOT SPRINGS RESORT.

Chena Hot Springs Rd, mile 56.5, Fairbanks. Phone 907/451-8104; toll-free 800/478-4681; fax 907/451-8151. www.chenahotsprings.com. One of the Interior's most popular and most easily accessed destinations for wilderness adventure and quiet relaxation, this 440-acre resort an hour's drive northeast of Fairbanks is surrounded by the 250,000-acre Chena River State Recreation Area. With a large selection of cozy rooms to choose from and Alaskan wilderness in all directions, the resort appeals to every budget and every type of adventurer. Originally constructed to allow guests to take advantage of the steaming mineral springs in the area, the resort is now at its busiest during the winter when its remoteness results in fantastic opportunities to see, and sometimes hear, the Aurora Borealis dancing across the cold dark sky. 90 rooms. Pets accepted; fee. Check-in 3 pm, check-out 11 am. Restaurant, bar. Indoor pool, whirlpool. **$$**

★ COMFORT INN CHENA RIVER.

1908 Chena Landings Loop, Fairbanks (99701). Phone 907/479-8080; toll-free 800/228-5150; fax 907/479-8063. www.choicehotels.com. The Fairbanks Comfort Inn hotel stands out from most other hotels in the chain because of its fantastic setting by the Chena River near stands of trees frequented by moose and other wildlife. Located near Pioneer Park and only a short drive from downtown, this sparkling, contemporary hotel has an appealing, backcountry feel that belies its central Fairbanks location. 74 rooms. Pets accepted. Complimentary continental breakfast. Check-in 4 pm, check-out 1 pm. High-speed Internet access. Indoor pool, whirlpool. Business center. **$**

★ FAIRBANKS HOTEL.

517 3rd Ave, Fairbanks. Phone 907/456-6441; toll-free 888/329-4685; fax 907/456-1792. www.fbxhotl.com. Travelers looking for budget accommodation in Fairbanks should check out this small independent hotel, the oldest in Fairbanks. With an eye-catching art deco exterior and small but comfortable rooms, it offers guests basic accommodations, good service, and affordable prices. About one-third of the rooms have private baths; all have wireless Internet access. 36 rooms. Check-in 4 pm, check-out 11 am. Wireless Internet access. Airport transportation available. **$**

★ ★ PIKES WATERFRONT LODGE.

1850 Hoselton Rd, Fairbanks (99703). Phone 907/456-4500; toll-free 877/774-2400; fax 907/456-4515. www.pikeslodge.com. Nestled beside the banks of the Chena River across from the airport, this lodge is a relatively new addition to Fairbanks's accommodation scene. Combining striking architectural features with high-quality Alaskan-themed artwork and furnishings, it creates a sense of rustic elegance in an attractive setting. All rooms are spacious and comfortable; some come with features like fireplaces, whirlpools, balconies, and river views. 208 rooms. Pets accepted; fee. Check-in 3 pm, check-out 11 am. Restaurant, bar. Fitness room. Business center. **$$**

★ ★ REGENCY FAIRBANKS HOTEL.

95 10th Ave, Fairbanks (99701). Phone 907/452-3200; fax 907/452-6505. www.regencyfairbankshotel.com. Situated on the western edge of downtown, this medium-sized hotel contains a variety of different room types, from standard rooms to deluxe suites to rooms with their own whirlpool tubs. All guest rooms, regardless of size, feature full kitchens and designated work areas and guests are encouraged to call the 24-hour bell desk whenever they need assistance or have a special request. 129 rooms. Pets accepted; fee. Check-in 3 pm, check-out 11 am. High-speed Internet access. Restaurant, bar. Fitness room. Business center. **$$**

★ ★ RIVER'S EDGE RESORT.

4200 Boat St, Fairbanks (99709). Phone 907/474-0286; toll-free 800/770-3343; fax 907/474-3665. www.riversedge.net. 94 rooms. Closed mid-Sept-early May. Check-in 3 pm, check-out 11 am. Restaurant, bar. **$$**

★ ★ SOPHIE STATION HOTEL.

1717 University Ave, Fairbanks (99709). Phone 907/479-3650; toll-free 800/528-4916; fax 907/479-7951. www.fountainheadhotels.com. Offering spacious and comfortable lodging close to the airport and

Fairbanks's main shopping areas, this hotel caters to business and leisure travelers not content to settle for average accommodations. All rooms in this hotel are suites with private balconies, full kitchens, and upscale furnishings including artwork by well-known Alaskan artists. The hotel has it's own restaurant, Zach's (see), which is open for breakfast, lunch, and dinner. Other popular amenities include high-speed Internet stations, a free shuttle service to the airport, and discount passes to a well-equipped local gym. 148 rooms, all suites. Check-in 2 pm, check-out 11 am. Restaurant, bar. Airport transportation available. **$$**

⊠

★ ★ **SPRINGHILL SUITES.** *575 1st Ave, Fairbanks (99701). Phone 907/451-6552; toll-free 877/729-0197; fax 907/451-6553. www.springhillsuites.com.* With downtown Fairbanks literally at its doorstep, this all-suite hotel, part of the Marriott chain, offers guests a clean, comfortable place to stay at reasonable rates. Surrounded by shops, restaurants, and numerous riverside walks and attractions, the hotel appeals to just about every taste, from families who appreciate its convenient location, on-site pool, and free continental breakfast to business travelers who are drawn to it for its business center, spacious rooms, and professional staff. 140 rooms, all suites. Complimentary continental breakfast. Check-in 3 pm, check-out noon. High-speed Internet access. Restaurant, bar. Fitness room. Indoor pool, whirlpool. Airport transportation available. Business center. **$$**

🖈 ⚓ 🖈

★ ★ **WEDGEWOOD RESORT.** *212 Wedgewood Dr, Fairbanks (99701). Phone 907/452-1442; toll-free 800/528-4916; fax 907/451-8184. www.fountainheadhotels.com.* Despite being only a mile from downtown, this attractive, campus-style hotel resort on the north side of Fairbanks has a real wilderness feel to it. Guests have the choice of staying in suites or standard rooms, all of which are outfitted with quality furnishings and tasteful accents. The resort is home to the Alaska Bird Observatory and provides easy access to the walking trails and visitor displays found at Creamer's Field Migratory Bird Refuge next door. 157 rooms. Closed mid-Sept-mid-May. Check-in 4 pm, check-out 11 am. Restaurant, bar. Business center. **$$**

🖈

★ ★ **WESTMARK FAIRBANKS HOTEL.** *813 Noble St, Fairbanks (99701). Phone 907/456-7722; toll-free 800/544-0970; fax 907/451-7478. www.westmarkhotels.com.* With the recent completion of an eight-story tower addition, this full-service hotel nearly tripled its capacity and now offers guests some of the newest, most spacious rooms in town. As a key property of the Holland America Line Company, the hotel is held to strict standards relating to the levels of quality, comfort, and service it provides. The result is an upscale hotel staffed by friendly, knowledgeable professionals. Its location near most downtown attractions makes it an appealing place to stay for independent travelers and families. 400 rooms. Pets accepted. Check-in noon, check-out noon. High-speed Internet access. Two restaurants, bar. Fitness room. Airport transportation available. **$$**

🐾 🖈

Full-Service Hotel

★ ★ ★ **FAIRBANKS PRINCESS RIVERSIDE LODGE.** *4477 Pikes Landing Rd, Fairbanks (99709). Phone 907/455-4477; toll-free 800/426-0500; fax 907/455-4476. www.princesslodges.com.* Set along the banks of the Chena River, this large, semi-secluded hotel is one of the most upscale in Fairbanks. The exterior of the property is painted a striking blue and features a huge open deck overlooking the river, perfect for mid-afternoon lazing and wildlife viewing. The interior, in contrast, is much more lodge-like, with intimate dining and lounge areas, log and stone architectural features, and soft, plush furniture. Open year-round, the hotel is a popular spot for cruise ship passengers during the summer months and northern lights watchers in the winter. 325 rooms. Check-in 3:30 pm, check-out 11 am. Restaurant, bar. Fitness room. Airport transportation available. Business center. **$$**

🖈 🖈

Restaurants

★ **BAKERY RESTAURANT.** *69 College Rd, Fairbanks (99701). Phone 907/456-8600; fax 907/456-8602.* This family- and budget-friendly diner-style restaurant just north of downtown serves standard home-style meals all day long. The real draw, though, are the fresh-baked pies, cakes, and other baked goods on display right inside the front door, tempting guests as soon as they walk in. Breakfast is served all day. American menu. Breakfast, lunch, dinner. Children's menu. Casual attire. **$**

★ ★ **BOBBY'S.** *126 N Turner St, Fairbanks (99701). Phone 907/456-3222; fax 907/457-4972.* This cozy, family-owned restaurant near the river in downtown Fairbanks offers a range of traditional Greek and American entrées, including the house specialty, Greek-style rack of lamb. The service is friendly and attentive and the atmosphere decidedly low-key, with attractive leather banquettes and walls covered with pictures of Greece. American, Greek menu. Dinner. Closed holidays. Bar. Casual attire. Reservations recommended. **$$**

★ ★ **CHENA HOT SPRINGS RESORT RESTAURANT.** *Chena Hot Springs Rd, mile 56.5, Fairbanks (99711). Phone 907/451-8104.* Located at Chena Hot Springs Resort (see), an hour northeast of Fairbanks, this log cabin-style restaurant is the perfect place to enjoy a leisurely meal after a day spent exploring the surrounding wilderness or soaking in the resort's hot springs. The menu features regional Alaskan favorites along with standard American fare, and the décor is rustic Alaska, making for a unique, highly enjoyable dining experience. American menu. Breakfast, lunch, dinner. Bar. Children's menu. Casual attire. Reservations recommended. Outdoor seating. **$$**

★ ★ **CHENA'S AT THE RIVER'S EDGE.** *4200 Boat St, Fairbanks (99709). Phone 907/474-3601, ext 229; fax 907/474-8023. www.riversedge.net.* This quaint restaurant at River's Edge Resort (see) offers guests a fascinating glimpse into Fairbanks's pioneer past, with artifacts and furnishings dating from the early 20th century. During summer, the outdoor deck beside the river is a popular place to sit and enjoy the savory Alaskan entrées and extensive dessert menu that have made the restaurant a local favorite for years. American menu. Breakfast, lunch, dinner. Closed mid-Sept-early May. Bar. Children's menu. Casual attire. Reservations recommended. Outdoor seating. **$$**

★ **DILLINGER'S RESTAURANT.** *720 Old Steese Hwy, Fairbanks (99701). Phone 907/456-1830; fax 907/456-1544.* With red leather booths, polished chrome fixtures, and spotlessly clean tables, this family-friendly diner just north of the downtown area is a real local hangout. The menu is typical '50s diner fare, from hamburgers and sandwiches to soft drinks and fries. Outdoor seating is available during the summer. American menu. Breakfast, lunch, dinner. Children's menu. Casual attire. **$**

★ **EL MARIACHI.** *541 3rd Ave, Fairbanks (99701). Phone 907/457-2698; fax 907/457-3394.* For authentic Mexican food in a lively, family-oriented setting, few places in town rival this restaurant. Sombreros, serapes, a Mexican flag, and colorful wall murals adorn the dining room area creating a festive, vibrant atmosphere that serves as a fitting warm-up to the zesty, full-flavored entrées that have earned the place such a loyal following. Mexican menu. Lunch, dinner. Children's menu. Casual attire. **$**

★ **GAMBARDELLA'S.** *706 2nd Ave, Fairbanks (99701). Phone 907/456-3417; fax 907/456-3420. www.gambardellas.com.* The interior of this well-known downtown restaurant has been designed to resemble a small town in the Italian countryside, complete with a *trompe l'oeil* street scene, wrought iron window railings, faux stone walls and foliage, and a full-sized vegetable cart. House specialties include homemade Italian bread, "The Mother of All Lasagnas," and a very addictive tiramisu. Italian menu. Lunch, dinner. Children's menu. Casual attire. Reservations recommended. Outdoor seating. **$$**

★ **GERALDO'S RESTAURANT.** *701 College Rd, Fairbanks (99701). Phone 907/452-2299; fax 907/452-7634.* From the sound of Dean Martin crooning on the sound system to the large original oil painting of Don "The Godfather" Corleone, this restaurant embraces its Italian roots with a passion. Featuring award-winning hand-tossed pizzas, huge servings of traditional Italian entrées, and a special "Bambino's Menu," it's a warm, inviting, place to go for a big meal. Italian menu. Lunch, dinner. Children's menu. Casual attire. Reservations recommended. Outdoor seating. **$$**

★ **GOLDEN SHANG HAI.** *1900 Airport Way, Fairbanks (99701). Phone 907/451-1100; fax 907/425-2530.* Serving a wide variety of Mandarin and Szechuan dishes in an ornate dining room filled with Chinese decorative touches, this midtown restaurant is known for its good food and good values. The 60-item buffet, which includes just about every Chinese dish imaginable as well as a selection of Japanese sushi plates, is particularly popular with diners. Chinese menu. Lunch, dinner. Casual attire. **$**

★ **IVORY JACK'S.** *2591 Goldstream Rd, Fairbanks (99709). Phone 907/455-6665; fax 907/455-4254.* Located about 20 minutes from Fairbanks in Gold Stream Valley, this long-time local hangout is part sports bar, part Wild West saloon. Patrons can choose from a long list of burgers, sandwiches, appetizers, and pizzas or can order from the fine dining menu, which features an assortment of New York strip steaks, fresh Alaskan seafood, and barbecued ribs. Bands play in the saloon on Friday nights; Tuesdays and Saturdays are "open mic" amateur nights. American menu. Breakfast, lunch, dinner. Bar. Children's menu. Casual attire. **$$**

★ ★ **LEMON GRASS THAI CUISINE.** *388 Old Chena Pump Rd, Fairbanks (99709). Phone 907/456-2200.* This appealing little restaurant on the extreme western edge of Fairbanks is a family-owned operation that focuses on serving authentic Thai dishes in a relaxed setting. All meals are prepared entirely from scratch and are served in a Thai-themed dining room filled with hand-carved wooden accent pieces, Thai drums, and ornate works of art. Thai menu. Lunch, dinner. Closed Sun. Casual attire. Reservations recommended. Valet parking. **$**

★ ★ **MUSHER'S ROADHOUSE.** *1411 Airport Way, Fairbanks (99701). Phone 907/452-1888.* Tourists seeking the ultimate in Alaskan-themed restaurants need look no further than this lively roadhouse and saloon located in midtown Fairbanks at The Captain Bartlett Inn (see). The restaurant serves hearty steak, seafood, and Alaskan-inspired dishes in a dining room decked out in dog mushing memorabilia; the attached Dog Sled Saloon, entered through real swinging doors, is equally entertaining and well worth moseying into. American menu. Breakfast, lunch, dinner. Bar. Children's menu. Reservations recommended. Outdoor seating. **$$**

★ ★ ★ **PIKE'S LANDING.** *4438 Airport Way, Fairbanks (99709). Phone 907/479-6500; fax 907/479-6513.* One of Fairbanks's best-known fine dining restaurants, Pike's Landing has long been a favorite destination for people celebrating anniversaries, birthdays, and other special events. The innovative menu varies with the season but normally includes a range of Alaskan seafood dishes such as halibut, salmon, oysters, and other fresh local catches. The chef's special, crab stuffed mushrooms, is a standout

favorite. During the long, warm days of summer, the outdoor deck is often crowded with locals and tourists enjoying close-up views of the nearby Chena River, which provides a soothing natural backdrop for this unforgettable dining experience. American menu. Lunch, dinner, brunch. Bar. Casual attire. Reservations recommended. Outdoor seating. **$$$**

★ ★ **PUMP HOUSE RESTAURANT.** *796 Chena Pump Rd, Fairbanks (99709). Phone 907/479-8452; fax 907/479-8432. www.pumphouse.com.* This restaurant is a must for visitors interested in eating well and learning about the history of the area. Housed in a former pump house once used to help in mine dredging operations, the restaurant is filled with antiques and artifacts of those long ago days. Proud home to the "Farthest North Oyster Bar in the World," the restaurant serves Alaskan cuisine along with less common regional dishes like reindeer steaks and wild musk ox ground sirloin. Throughout the summer, the outdoor riverside patio is a great place to watch the majestic riverboat *Discovery* paddle its way up the river. American menu. Lunch, dinner. Bar. Children's menu. Casual attire. Reservations recommended. Outdoor seating. **$$**

★ **SAM'S SOURDOUGH CAFÉ.** *3702 Cameron St, Fairbanks (99709). Phone 907/479-0523.* Often referred to as "Sourdough Sam's" by the hordes of locals that head there each day, this cheerful diner-style restaurant is located right beside the University of Alaska Fairbanks. As a hometown favorite, it's almost always noisy and chaotic, but in an appealing, small-town, friendly way. Patrons can order lunch and dinner items, but the main draw is unquestionably the breakfast menu, available all day. American menu. Breakfast, lunch, dinner. Casual attire. Outdoor seating. **$**
🖥

★ ★ **SEÑOR FLANNIGAN'S STEAK PIT.** *354 Old Steese Hwy, Fairbanks (99701). Phone 907/451-6100.* This oddly named restaurant serves an eclectic mix of American and Mexican dishes in a faux alfresco dining room complete with plastic foliage and twinkling "star" lights overhead. Adding to the unique décor is a stunning series of illuminated stained glass panels above the long cantina bar depicting pueblo scenes. With reasonable prices, a large menu, and a game room, it's an enjoyable, family-friendly place to dine. American, Mexican menu. Lunch, dinner, late-night. Bar. Children's menu. Casual attire. Reservations recommended. **$$**

★ **SOAPY SMITH'S.** *541 2nd Ave, Fairbanks (99701). Phone 907/451-8380; fax 907/451-8383.* Named after the most notorious criminal in Alaskan Gold Rush history, this downtown restaurant serves reasonably priced standard American cuisine with local influences and is a must for gold rush and pioneer history buffs. Authentic memorabilia, photographs, and newspaper articles about life in Alaska at the turn of the last century crowd the walls, and the proprietor loves to regale diners with tales of Soapy Smith's colorful life. American menu. Lunch, dinner. Closed Sun; holidays. Casual attire. **$$**

★ ★ **TURTLE CLUB.** *2098 Old Steese Hwy N, Fox (99712). Phone 907/457-3883; fax 907/457-4789.* This spacious, low-key restaurant 11 miles north of Fairbanks has earned a solid reputation for great food thanks to a menu featuring fresh Alaskan seafood and choice cuts of prime rib. Adding to the appeal of the place is a large outdoor seating area and an enormous collection of turtle figurines, the inspiration behind the restaurant's name. The on-site bar offers a separate menu and a low-lit, intimate dining area for those looking for privacy. American menu. Dinner. Closed Jan 1, Dec 25; also Tues-Thurs week of Thanksgiving. Bar. Casual attire. Reservations recommended. Outdoor seating. **$$**

★ ★ **TWO RIVERS LODGE.** *4968 Chena Hot Springs Rd, Fairbanks (99712). Phone 907/488-6815. www.tworiverslodge.com.* Located northeast of Fairbanks on Chena Hot Springs Road, this log-cabin style restaurant is set in a pine forest on the shores of a small lake. Open every day during the summer, it really comes alive from Thursday through Sunday when the outdoor Tuscan Garden section is open. Offering a wide range of Mediterranean dishes featuring fresh local produce, imported meats and cheeses, and herbs grown on the property, the Garden serves "healthy and satisfying" cuisine in a beautiful wilderness setting. American menu. Dinner. Bar. Children's menu. Casual attire. Reservations recommended. Outdoor seating. **$$**

★ ★ **VALLATA.** *2190 Goldstream Rd, Fairbanks (99709). Phone 907/455-7773.* Located in Gold Stream Valley, 20 minutes from downtown Fairbanks, this upscale family-run restaurant specializes in fine Italian and American cuisine made fresh to order. Friday and Saturday nights, guests are treated to live piano music as they enjoy sweeping views of the surrounding wilderness from the comfort of the elegant, intimate dining room. Italian, American menu. Dinner. Closed Mon. Bar. Children's menu. Casual attire. Reservations recommended. **$$**

★ ★ **WILD IRIS CAFÉ.** *900 Noble St, Fairbanks (99701). Phone 907/455-4747; fax 907/455-4895.* This small café at the Golden Nugget Hotel offers an appealing range of home-style American entrées in a casual, unpretentious setting. The dining room décor features lots of iris prints and spring colors, while the saloon has a more earthy feel to it, courtesy of an enormous circular stone fireplace, soft lighting, and polished wooden furniture. Both rooms share the same menu and are open long hours during the summer. American menu. Breakfast, lunch, dinner. Bar. Casual attire. **$$**

★ ★ **ZACH'S RESTAURANT.** *1717 University Ave S, Fairbanks (99709). Phone 907/479-3650.* This chic restaurant at the Sophie Station Hotel (see) offers fine continental cuisine served with style in a relaxed, intimate setting. New dishes are constantly being added to the menu, but perennial favorites include the Alaskan halibut fillet and the grilled lamb chops. Dessert favorites include a cheesecake burrito described on the menu as being "shamefully good." During the summer, sheltered outdoor dining is available. American menu. Breakfast, lunch, dinner, brunch. Bar. Children's menu. Casual attire. Reservations recommended. Outdoor seating. **$$**

Gates of the Arctic National Park and Preserve

Web site www.nps.gov/gaar

Sprawling and remote, Gates of the Arctic National Park & Preserve offers solitude and exceptional natural beauty, along with endless opportunities for wilderness adventure. Only the strongest and best-trained outdoor enthusiasts should consider venturing into the park's 8.5 million acres of untamed wilderness. Situated above the Arctic Circle, within the rugged peaks and glaciated valleys of northern Alaska's Brooks Range, Gates of the Arctic possesses no roads or established trails. Before trekking off into the park, recreational travelers are required to complete a backcountry orientation program at either the Bettles Ranger Station, Coldfoot Visitor Center, or Anaktuvuk Pass Ranger Station.

For the trained and hardy, superior wilderness recreation awaits, including river running, dog mushing, and mountaineering. The park is home to Dall sheep, caribou, wolves, moose, grizzlies, black bears, and more than 100 species of birds. Vegetation ranges from boreal forest to alpine tundra. Gates of the Arctic boasts six congressionally designated Wild Rivers and two National Natural Landmarks, as well as a biosphere reserve. The park is best accessed via an air taxi from Fairbanks to either Anaktuvuk Pass or Bettles. Alternately, visitors can take the Dalton Highway from Fairbanks 250 miles north to the Coldfoot Visitor Center, which is open Memorial Day-Labor Day. Phone 907/457-5752.

Girdwood

See also Anchorage

Area Code 907

Forty miles south of Anchorage, nestled among the Turnagain Arm and spectacular Mount Alyeska, Girdwood has evolved from a gold-mining town into Alaska's only year-round resort community. Driving from Anchorage, travelers may see Dall sheep, moose, bald eagles, or Beluga whales in the Turnagain Arm. Girdwood features many bed-and-breakfasts, restaurants, shops, and boutiques and offers many opportunities for outdoor adventure, including kayaking, rafting, hiking, and fishing.

Restaurants

★ **ALPINE BAKERY.** *1 Alyeska Hwy, Girdwood (99587). Phone 907/783-2550.* Offers American and European-style baked goods and light dinner. American menu. Breakfast, lunch, dinner. **$**

★ **THE DOUBLE MUSKIE INN.** *1 Crow Creek Rd, Girdwood (99587). Phone 907/783-2822.*

Renowned local restaurant serving Cajun preparations of local ingredients. Cajun menu. Lunch, dinner. Closed Sun. **$$**

Glacier Bay National Park and Preserve

Web site www.nps.gov/glba

Glacier Bay National Park & Preserve awes visitors with spectacular scenery that is quintessential Alaska, a varied but universally beautiful and pristine landscape of tidewater glaciers, sheltered coves, deep fjords, freshwater lakes, and snow-capped mountain peaks. The explorer George Vancouver led an expedition here in 1794, bringing a survey crew commanded by Lt. Joseph Whidbey, who charted the narrow passage of the Icy Strait. Whidbey's chart showed Glacier Bay to be a small indentation abutting "solid compact mountains of ice." When legendary naturalist John Muir visited the area in 1879, the bay had grown considerably larger, with the glacier retreating more than 30 miles inland. The glacier's retreat has continued ever since, creating a living laboratory for the study of glaciers and the recolonization of newly exposed land. Recolonizing species on the ground include coyotes, wolves, moose, and brown bears, while humpback and killer whales, Stellar sea lions, and otters have moved into the bay. Glacier Bay was set aside as a national monument in 1925, becoming a national park and preserve in 1980. It was recognized as a UN Biosphere Reserve in 1986.

Like many of Alaska's national parks, accessibility can prove challenging. No roads lead to Glacier Bay, so most visitors arrive by boat. Tour boat, cruise ship, and charter boat services are available, and pleasure boats are welcome, although a free permit is required. Many boat tours begin and end in the small town of Gustavus, which sits 75 miles south of Glacier Bay. Air taxis shuttle passengers between Gustavus and Juneau, roughly 50 miles to the east. Glacier Bay has a maritime climate, with cool summers and mild winters—winter lows at sea level rarely dip below 25 degrees Fahrenheit. Phone 907/697-2230.

Haines (E-8)

Population 1,811
Area Code 907

Haines is a town rich in history and natural beauty. Located near the northern end of the Inside Passage, it's surrounded on all sides by soaring mountains, deepwater inlets, and miles and miles of rugged forests and massive glaciers. In 1898, the Klondike Gold Rush flooded the town with prospectors heading up the nearby Dalton Trail on their way north. Soon after the rush ended, the US Army decided to build its first permanent army post in Alaska on the outskirts of town. In 1972, the fort was listed on the National Register of Historic Places and in 1978 it was designated a National Historic Landmark. To this day, it remains a fascinating visual link to Haines's storied past. Visitors interested in learning more about the area can visit the Sheldon Museum, home to a fascinating mix of pioneer and Gold Rush memorabilia as well as an extensive collection of Chilkat Tlingit art and artifacts.

One of the highlights of Haines's event calendar is its annual Alaska Bald Eagle Festival. Held during the middle of November, the festival celebrates the thousands of bald eagles that congregate in the area to feed on late spawning salmon in the Chilkat River. Photographers and birdwatchers can enjoy the spectacle from any number of highway pullouts adjacent to the 48,000 acre Alaska Chilkat Bald Eagle Preserve northwest of town.

What to See and Do

American Bald Eagle Foundation Interpretive Center. *2nd St and Haines Hwy, Haines (99827). Phone 907/766-3094. baldeagles.org.* With a focus on protecting and preserving bald eagles and their habitat, this nonprofit foundation aims to achieve its goals by teaching people about bald eagles and the environmental factors necessary for them to flourish in places like Alaska. Located only 20 miles from the Chilkat Bald Eagle Preserve, where upwards of 3,000 eagles congregate each winter, the interpretive center has incorporated more than 180 specimens of fish and wildlife from the preserve into a massive indoor diorama that depicts the interaction of each species in the local ecosystem. The center also contains a screening room where visitors can watch a video showing scenes from the annual migration of eagles to the area, something that most people would otherwise never have a chance to witness.

Sheldon Museum & Cultural Center. *Corner of First Ave and Main St, Haines (99827). Phone 907/766-2366. sheldonmuseum.org.* Established in 1924, the Sheldon Museum houses a wide variety of historical and artistic artifacts relating to the different cultures that reside in the Chilkat Valley. Through on-site displays and exhibits of rare and elaborate Native handicrafts, visitors are able to learn about the Tlingit culture that predominated in the area before the arrival of white settlers. Evidence of Haines's formative days is also presented, with displays of artifacts from the first permanent white settlement in the valley, a Presbyterian mission established in 1879 on the site the museum now occupies. The museum also focuses on the role Haines played in the Klondike Gold Rush, with exhibits and memorabilia that tell the story of the miners who set off on the nearby Dalton Trail leading into the interior and the gold fields of the Klondike. Most summer afternoons, visitors have the chance to observe master Native craftsmen fashioning totem poles in the front yard of the museum. (Summer: Mon-Fri 11 am-6 pm; Sat-Sun 2-6 pm; winter: Mon-Fri 1-4 pm) **$**

Special Event

Bald Eagle Preserve and Annual Festival. *113 Haines Hwy, Haines (99827). Phone 907/766-3094. baldeagles .org/festival.html.* In October, the world's largest number of bald eagles gathers in Haines to take advantage of the late salmon run. This amazing gathering of eagles is the basis of this annual festival that is held in the eagles' honor. Oct.

Limited-Service Hotels

★ **CAPTAIN'S CHOICE INC. MOTEL.** *108 Second Ave N, Haines (99827). Phone 907/766-3111; toll-free 800/478-2345; fax 907/766-3332. www. capchoice.com.* Built on a steeply sloping lot, this family-run motel has terrific views of Lynn Canal and Portage Cove as well as the Fort Seward area of Haines. The rooms are in excellent shape and filled with solid wood furniture, plank walls, and whimsical nautical accents. Reasonable prices, a great location, and warm, friendly service make it an excellent bargain. 40 rooms. Pets accepted. Check-in 2 pm, check-out 11 am. **$**

★★ **HOTEL HALSINGLAND.** *13 Fort Seward Dr, Haines (99827). Phone 907/766-2000; toll-free 800/359-5627; fax 907/766-2060.* 60 rooms. Closed in winter. Check-in noon, check-out noon. Restaurant, bar. **$**

Specialty Lodging

The following lodging establishment is approved by Mobil Travel Guide, but due to its unique and individualized nature has not been given a traditional Mobil Star rating. Included in this listing you may find bed-and-breakfasts, limited-service inns, guest ranches, and other unique hotel properties.

FORT SEWARD LODGE. *39 Mud Bay Rd, Haines (99827). Phone toll-free 800/478-7772; fax 907/766-2006. www.ftsewardlodge.com.* 10 rooms. Closed Oct-Apr. Check-in 3 pm, check-out noon. **$**

Restaurants

★ **THE BAMBOO ROOM.** *2nd Ave and Main St, Haines (99827). Phone 907/766-2800.* Seafood menu. Breakfast, lunch, dinner. Bar. Children's menu. Casual attire. Reservations recommended. Outdoor seating. **$$**

★★ **FORT SEWARD RESTAURANT.** *39 Mud Bay Rd, Haines (99827). Phone 907/766-2009; toll-free 800/478-7772; fax 907/766-2006. www.ftsewardlodge .com.* Seafood menu. Breakfast, lunch, dinner, brunch. Closed in winter. Bar. Children's menu. Casual attire. Reservations recommended. **$$**

★★ **THE LIGHTHOUSE RESTAURANT.** *2 Front St, Haines (99827). Phone 907/766-2442.* The Lighthouse Restaurant is really a treat: great views and fresh, wholesome steak and seafood dishes without the high prices that often accompany the two. Panoramic views of Lynn Canal and the Chilkoot Range add to the rustic, local charm of the dining room and make for memorable and relaxing dining. Seafood, steak menu. Breakfast, lunch, dinner. Closed Thanksgiving, Dec 25. Bar. Casual attire. **$$**

★★ **THE WILD STRAWBERRY.** *138 Second Ave, Haines (99827). Phone 907/766-3608.* Alaskan seafood menu. Lunch, dinner. Closed in winter. Bar. Casual attire. Outdoor seating. **$$**

Homer (E-5)

Population 3,946
Area Code 907

Homer bills itself as the "Halibut Capital of the World" and is known for having some of the best fishing on the Kenai Peninsula. Set on a hillside overlooking Kachemak Bay and Cook Inlet, it plays host to an enormous number of visitors each year, including hundreds who spend the whole summer camped out on the Homer Spit, a 5-mile-long sliver of land that juts out into the waters of the bay, providing unrestricted access to great halibut and salmon fishing. Homer offers a wide range of other diversions for those uninterested in hooks, bait, and flies. In May, the Kachemak Bay Shorebird Festival takes place, celebrating the tens of thousands of shorebirds that stop over on the local mudflats during their annual migration north. Throughout the summer, boats are available to shuttle passengers across the bay to the small fishing villages and artist communities that dot the rugged coastline. For more athletic types, a network of hiking and biking trails throughout the area provides spectacular views of the mountains, waters, and wildlife that make up this region.

What to See and Do

Alaska Islands and Ocean Visitor Center. *95 Sterling Hwy, Homer (99603). Phone 907/235-6961. www. islandsandocean.org.* Opened in December 2003, the Alaska Islands and Ocean Visitor Center is an educational and research facility that offers visitors an opportunity to learn about the Alaska Maritime National Wildlife Refuge and the Kachemak Bay Research Reserve through interactive exhibits, guided tours, and video presentations. One of the primary goals of the center is to enhance people's awareness of the beauty, fragility, and diversity of the remote 4.9-million-acre refuge, which stretches from the Arctic Ocean all the way to Alaska's southeast panhandle. Another of the center's goals is to make visitors aware of the biologically diverse estuarine and saltwater habitats that exist right outside the windows of the center in the Kachemak Bay region. The center's attractions extend beyond its own walls, too, with trails leading from the back door to nearby Bishop's Beach and

Beluga Slough, where guided and self-guided walks bring visitors face to face with the ecosystems the center is dedicated to preserving and protecting. (Memorial Day-Labor Day, daily 9 am-6 pm) **FREE**

Pratt Museum. *3779 Bartlett St, Homer (99603). Phone 907/235-8635. www.prattmuseum.org.* One of the most attractive things about the Pratt Museum in Homer is that it's not just a historical museum or an art museum or an anthropological museum: it's all of these and more. The interior of this downtown museum houses native and contemporary culture exhibits, natural history artifacts, a gallery of contemporary regional art, and a small room filled with live marine plants and wildlife. Outside, the museum grounds are given over to a fascinating mix of botanical gardens, interpretive forest trails teeming with birds and other wildlife, and historical structures and artifacts from Homer's pioneer days. (Mid-May-mid-Sept: daily 10 am-6 pm; mid-Sept-mid-May: Tues-Sun noon-5 pm; closed Jan) **$$**

Special Event

Kachemak Bay Shorebird Festival. *Phone 907/235-7740. www.homeralaska.org/shorebird.htm.* A popular festival celebrating the arrival of hundreds of thousands of migratory birds each spring. Early May.

Limited-Service Hotels

★ ★ **BELUGA LAKE LODGE.** *204 Ocean Dr Loop, Homer (99603). Phone 907/235-5995.* Beluga Lake Lodge is located halfway between downtown Homer and the start of the Homer Spit, providing easy access to all of Homer's main attractions. With unobstructed views of Beluga Slough and Beluga Lake, it offers nature enthusiasts a unique vantage point from which to view the birds and other wildlife that inhabit the area. 32 rooms. Pets accepted. Check-in 3 pm, check-out 11 am. Restaurant. **$**

★ ★ **BEST WESTERN BIDARKA INN.** *575 Sterling Hwy, Homer (99603). Phone 907/235-8148; toll-free 866/685-5000; fax 907/235-8140. www. bestwestern.com.* Conveniently located at the entrance to Homer, the Bidarka Inn offers rooms with partial views of Kachemak Bay and the Kenai mountains, an impressive new fitness center, conference facilities,

and an on-site restaurant and bar. As the only chain lodging facility in Homer, the motel appeals to travelers looking for a familiar, reliable level of comfort and convenience. 74 rooms. Complimentary continental breakfast. Check-in 2 pm, check-out noon. Two restaurants. Fitness room. **$**

★ ★ **LAND'S END RESORT.** *4786 Homer Spit Rd, Homer (99603). Phone 907/235-0400; toll-free 800/ 478-0400; fax 907/235-0420. www.endofthespit.com.* Land's End Resort, at the end of the 4.5-mile-long Homer Spit, has been providing guests with breathtaking views of the snowcapped Kenai Mountains and the deep blue waters of Kachemak Bay since its opening in 1958. It has grown quite a bit since then, but remains a popular destination for Alaskans and outsiders by continuing to offer guests "beauty, wildlife, serenity, and friendly service." 80 rooms, 2 story. Complimentary continental breakfast. Check-in 4 pm, check-out noon. Restaurant. Fitness room, spa. Indoor pool, whirlpool. **$$**

★ **WINDJAMMER SUITES.** *320 W Pioneer Ave, Homer (99603). Phone 907/235-9761; toll-free 888/730-2770; fax 907/235-9764.* Windjammer Suites is located on Pioneer Avenue in downtown Homer, very close to the junction with the Sterling Highway. Most of the suites are enormous, with large living rooms and full-sized kitchens. Upstairs suites have spacious balconies with sweeping views of the Kachemak Bay region, making them some of the best bargains in Homer. 13 rooms, all suites. Pets accepted. Check-in 2 pm, check-out 11 am. **$**

Specialty Lodgings

The following lodging establishments are approved by Mobil Travel Guide, but due to their unique and individualized nature have not been given a traditional Mobil Star rating. Included in this listing you may find bed-and-breakfasts, limited-service inns, guest ranches, and other unique hotel properties.

ALASKA WATERFRONT HOMER INN & SPA.
895 Ocean Dr, Homer (99603). Phone 907/235-2501; toll-free 800/294-7823. www.alaskawaterfront.com.

Custom seaside suites on beautiful Kachemak Bay featuring a secluded sand beach, hot tub, king-size beds, spectacular ocean and glacier views, and an array of specialty spa treatments. 5 rooms, 2 story. **$$**

ARCTIC SUN LODGING. *61995 Mission Rd, Homer (99603). Phone 907/235-2283; toll-free 888/479-6259. alaskaarcticsun.com.* This inn features clean, comfortable rooms with private baths and views of Kachemak Bay and the Kenai Mountains. 6 rooms, 2 story. **$**

DRIFTWOOD INN. *135 W Bunnell Ave, Homer (99603). Phone 907/235-8019; toll-free 800/478-8019. www.thedriftwoodinn.com.* A mom-and-pop operation in the truest sense, the Driftwood Inn is a collection of funky rooms filled with homey, personal touches. With a small breakfast nook and cozy den on the ground floor, the inn has a real communal feel that seems to encourage guests to stop and chat with one another. The rates are inexpensive, too, making it a great bargain for the independent traveler looking for something unique. 20 rooms. Pets accepted. Check-in 3 pm, check-out noon. **$**

VICTORIAN HEIGHTS BED & BREAKFAST. *61495 Race Ct, Homer (99603). Phone 907/235-6357.* Located in the hills overlooking Kachemak Bay, the Kenai Mountain Range, and several glaciers. All rooms have private baths, comfortable furnishings, and are decorated simply and elegantly. 4 rooms, 2 story. **$**

Restaurants

★ ★ **BELUGA BAY LODGE RESTAURANT.** *204 Ocean Drive Loop, Homer (99603). Phone 907/235-5995.* The Beluga Lake Lodge Restaurant is located adjacent to Beluga Lake, about halfway between downtown Homer and the start of the Homer Spit. It is a popular music venue year round, but really comes alive during the monthly Cajun Bluegrass jam nights, some of which draw crowds from as far away as Anchorage. Seafood, steak menu. Dinner. Closed mid-Sept-early May. Bar. Children's menu. Casual attire. Outdoor seating. **$$**

★ ★ **CHART ROOM.** *4786 Homer Spit Rd, Homer (99603). Phone 907/235-0400; toll-free 800/478-0400; fax 907/235-0420. www.endofthespit.com.* The Chart

Room restaurant at Land's End Resort (see) features traditional steak and seafood dishes prepared with a fresh Alaskan flavor, including long-time favorites halibut & chips and crab & artichoke dip. The best reason to go, though, is to take in the breathtaking views of the snow-capped Kenai Mountains towering over the waters of Kachemak Bay. During the long days of summer, the outdoor patio facing the water is a popular spot to enjoy fine food while taking in the sights, sounds, and scents of the ocean. Seafood, steak menu. Breakfast, lunch, dinner. Bar. Children's menu. Casual attire. Outdoor seating. **$$$**

★ **COAL BAY SANDWICH COMPANY.** *361 Sterling Hwy, Homer (99603). Phone 907/235-3200.* With the motto "Nobody Leaves Hungry," the Coal Bay Sandwich Company is a real find. It's inexpensive, has a wide variety of hearty and healthy sandwiches, and offers fresh clam chowder and chili along with what the menu claims are the best shakes in town. Its convenient location on the main highway through Homer makes it a popular spot for fishermen and daytrippers looking to grab some food before venturing out for the day. Deli, soups. Lunch, dinner. Closed Sun; Jan 1, Thanksgiving, Dec 25. Casual attire. Outdoor seating. **$**

★ ★ **DON JOSE'S.** *127 W Pioneer Ave, Homer (99603). Phone 907/235-7963; fax 907/235-7964.* Since opening its doors in 1982, Don Jose's has become such a favorite in Homer it has expanded to include restaurants in Kenai and Anchorage. Although known primarily as "the place" to get good Mexican food in a relaxed, comfortable setting, it offers Italian food, too, along with traditional American entrées like cheeseburgers and sandwiches. American, Mexican menu. Lunch, dinner. Bar. Children's menu. Casual attire. **$$**

★ ★ **DUNCAN HOUSE.** *125 W Pioneer Ave, Homer (99603). Phone 907/235-5344.* From the eclectic mix of plates, glasses, and mugs that appear on each table to the antiques and Alaskan memorabilia that fill the walls, Duncan House restaurant exudes an authentic down-home charm that makes you want to linger for hours. The menu features large portions of standard American dishes, making it a family-friendly destination for hungry locals and tourists. American menu. Breakfast, lunch. Closed Tues. Children's menu. Casual attire. **$**

★ ★ **FAT OLIVES.** *276 Ohlson Ln, Homer (99603). Phone 907/235-8488.* Fat Olives is a wonderful blend of urban chic and Alaskan informality. The restaurant is filled with warm Mediterranean colors, polished granite table tops, live plants, and a stylish wooden bar back. And yet, the floors are concrete, the walls cinderblock, and the atmosphere ultra-relaxed. The focal point of the restaurant is its wood-fired oven, used to cook everything except the specialty 28" pizzas, which are so large they have to be baked in a traditional pizza oven. Mediterranean menu. Lunch, dinner. Closed Jan 1, Thanksgiving, Dec 25; Feb. Bar. Casual attire. Outdoor seating. **$$**

★ ★ ★ **THE HOMESTEAD.** *East End Rd mile 8.2, Homer (99603). Phone 907/235-8723; fax 907/235-3448.* For the past 11 years, the Homestead Restaurant has been providing a dining experience characterized by owner Lisa Nolan as "white tablecloths without the button-up attitude." It's an elegant place without being "formal," a word that Nolan wrinkles up her nose at. The walls are lined with contemporary Alaskan art, the views are breathtaking, and the service and selection are exceptional. Add to the mix a 1,200-bottle wine cellar filled with premium wines from around the world, and the result is one of Homer's most popular, upscale dining spots. Seafood, steak menu. Dinner. Closed Oct-Mar. Bar. Children's menu. Casual attire. **$$$**

★ ★ **THE ROOKERY.** *Otter Cove, Homer (99603). Phone 907/235-7770; toll-free 800/426-6212. www.ottercoveresort.com.* Located at Otter Cove in Eldred Passage with extensive views of the abundant natural wildlife. Tour and charter boats available. Seafood menu. Lunch, dinner. Closed mid-Sept-late May. Bar. Casual attire. Reservations recommended. Outdoor seating. **$$**

★ **TWO SISTERS BAKERY & CAFÉ.** *106 W Bunnell St, Homer (99603). Phone 907/235-2280. www.twosistersbakery.net.* Two Sisters Bakery & Cafe is located in the small historic district of Homer in a building with wide, wraparound porches where summertime guests can eat, drink, and relax while taking in the views of Kachemak Bay. In winter, the warm Mediterranean colors inside brighten the bakery while art by local artists livens up the walls. The bakery offers a mouthwatering array of pastries and breads baked on-site and uses locally grown ingredients whenever possible. Deli, soups, bakery. Breakfast, lunch. Closed Jan 1, Thanksgiving, Dec 25. Casual attire. Outdoor seating. **$**

Juneau (E-8)

Established 1880
Population 30,711
Area Code 907
Information Juneau Convention & Visitors Bureau, One Sealalaska Plaza, Suite 305, Juneau, 99801; phone 907/586-1737 or toll-free 800/587-2201.
Web site www.juneau.org

Squeezed onto a narrow slip of land between the waters of Gastineau Channel and the base of 3,576 foot tall Mount Juneau, Alaska's capital city is literally and figuratively overshadowed by the vast wilderness that surrounds it. Located in the middle of the Tongass National Forest two thirds of the way up the Inside Passage, Juneau is a former gold rush town that has managed to strike it rich with tourists. Because no roads connect Juneau to the outside world, all visitors must arrive by air or sea. This is an enormous benefit for the city as it is most striking when viewed against a backdrop of massive glaciers, dense forests, towering peaks, and meandering waterways: a sliver of civilization in the wild. In 2002, over three quarters of a million visitors came to this remote region of Alaska, most arriving by cruise ship. The city was originally called Harrisburg, in recognition of Richard Harris, one of the first prospectors to stake a claim in the area. The town's name was later changed to Rockwell for a short time, before being changed in 1881 to Juneau—in honor of Joe Juneau, Harris's partner and cofounder of the settlement. In 1906, the government was moved from Sitka to Juneau and it has remained the state capital ever since despite its geographic isolation from the rest of the state. Although Juneau's population is about 31,000, making it the third largest city in Alaska, it has managed to retain a small town feel, due in large part to the preservation of the historic district around Front and Franklin streets and the casual, friendly attitude of the residents. It may be the capital, but it's still Alaska. With an average of 222 days of rain each year, it's not surprising that the city is brimming with bookstores, coffee houses, restaurants, and bars.

What to See and Do

AJ Mine/Gastineau Mill Mine Tours. *500 Sheep Creek Mine Rd, Juneau (99801). Phone 907/463-5017.* The Alaska Juneau Mine, better known as the AJ Mine, began operation in 1916 and within years became the largest gold mine of its type in the world. At its peak, it was also the most important economic force in Juneau, employing 600 workers and helping the town to grow and prosper. Economic factors caused the mine to close in 1944, but not before it had produced more than $75 million in gold. Nowadays, visitors can take a four-hour tour of the mine and the nearby Gastineau Mill that was used to crush the rock extracted from the mine. Tours, conducted daily beginning in May and continuing to the end of September, include an underground walk, a hard rock mining demonstration, and a chance to pan for gold at the mill site. **$$$$**

Alaska State Capitol. *4th Ave and Main St, Juneau (99801).* Built between 1929 and 1931, the Alaska State Capitol building was known as the Territorial Federal Building for 28 years until Alaska achieved statehood in 1959. The exterior of the building is somewhat nondescript, featuring Alaskan marble and limestone and a replica of the Liberty Bell beside the 4th Avenue entrance. The interior of the Capitol houses the offices of the governor, lieutenant governor, and state legislature as well as legislative chambers and other state government offices. Throughout the year, visitors can take self-guided tours during regular business hours. During the summer, guided tours are offered on weekdays, with tours beginning every 30 minutes between 8 am and 5 pm.

Alaska State Museum. *395 Whittier St, Juneau (99801). Phone 907/465-2901. www.museums.state .ak.us.* Permanent collections and traveling exhibits highlight Alaska's native peoples, its natural history, the Alaska-Yukon gold rushes, and the American period of Alaska's history. Artwork and artifacts include photographs, murals, kayak models, a life-sized eagle tree, and tiny thimble baskets. A children's room features a one-third scale model of the stern of the ship *Discovery,* used by Captain George Vancouver during his famous explorations of Alaska, as well as dress-up clothes and historic exhibits. (Mid-May-mid-Sept: daily 8:30 am-5:30 pm; mid-Sept-mid-May: Tues-Sat 10 am-4 pm; closed holidays) **$**

Governor's House. *716 Calhoun St, Juneau (99801).* Located on the corner of two residential streets, the Governor's House is every bit as unassuming as the State Capitol a short walk away. Built in 1910 in colonial style, it's an attractive, stately building that blends in well with the other attractive homes on the street, giving it an aura of approachability one would not expect to find in a governor's mansion. Public tours of the home are not available, but the governor does host an annual holiday open house for the general public in early December.

Juneau-Douglas City Museum. *4th Ave and Main St, Juneau (99801). Phone 907/586-3572. www.juneau.org /parksrec/museum.* Located across the street from the State Capitol, the Juneau-Douglas City Museum was founded to preserve and display materials relating to the cultural and historical development of the Juneau-Douglas area. The small galleries are packed with artifacts and memorabilia of the groups and events that have influenced the development of the Juneau and Douglas region, from ancient Tlingit tribes to turn-of-the-century mining corporations to modern-day tour companies. The museum also features special exhibits throughout the year, details of which are available on the museum's Web site. (Mid-May-Sept: Mon-Fri 9 am-5 pm, Sat-Sun 10 am-5 pm; Oct-mid-May: Tues-Sat noon-4 pm) **$**

The Last Chance Mining Museum. *1001 Basin Rd, Juneau (99801). Phone 907/586-5338.* Listed on the National Register of Historic Places and Alaska Gold Rush Properties, this museum is housed in a historic compressor building associated with the former Alaska Juneau Gold Mining Company, which operated in Juneau from 1912 until 1944. The museum explores the history of the region's mining industry with exhibits of industrial artifacts associated with hard rock gold mining. (Daily 9:30 am-12:30 pm, 3:30-6:30 pm) **$**

Mendenhall Glacier. *Glacier Spur Rd, Juneau (99801). Phone 907/789-0097. www.fs.fed.us/r10/tongass/districts /mendenhall.* Mendenhall Glacier is located about 12 miles from downtown Juneau at the northern end of the Mendenhall Valley. The glacier originates in the Juneau Icefield and stretches for 13 miles before terminating at the northern end of Mendenhall Lake, the waters of which conceal roughly half of the glacier's 200-foot-thick toe. The visitor center offers excellent views of the glacier as well as interpretive exhibits and displays that explain the movement of glaciers and the way they transform landscapes. Five trails originate in and around the center, providing scenic walks for people of all ages and abilities during the summer months. (Summer, daily 8 am-6:30 pm) **$**

Mount Roberts Tramway. *490 S Franklin St, Juneau (99801). Phone 907/463-3412; toll-free 888/461-8726. www.alaska.net/~junotram.* The Mount Roberts Tramway runs from the cruise ship dock in downtown Juneau up the side of Mount Roberts to an elevation of about 1,800 feet, providing passengers with magnificent views of Juneau, Douglas Island, and the Gastineau Channel. On arrival at the summit, visitors can walk some of Mount Roberts's most popular alpine trails, enjoy a relaxing meal and great views at the summit restaurant, watch a short documentary on Native culture in the Chilkat Theater, browse through the gift shops, or just sit and enjoy the panoramic views of wilderness Alaska. (May-Sept, daily 9 am-9 pm) **$$$$**

Tours. *Phone toll-free 800/544-2206. www. graylineofalaska.com.* Gray Line of Alaska offers package tours around Alaska (up to 11 days) as well as a 2 3/4-hour sightseeing tour of historic Juneau and Mendenhall Glacier.

Limited-Service Hotels

★ **ASPEN HOTEL OF JUNEAU.** *1800 Shell Simmons Dr, Juneau (99801). Phone 907/790-6435; toll-free 866/483-7848; fax 907/790-6621. www. aspenhotelsak.com.* Like other Aspen hotels, this one is extremely clean and comfortable and staffed by a friendly, professional crew. With affordable rooms, a 24-hour business center, and fully equipped meeting rooms, it's a popular spot for business professionals. Families appreciate its deluxe continental breakfast, indoor pool, and family suites featuring a bedroom with bunk beds and a video game console. The hotel is also close to Juneau's two shopping centers, the Nugget Mall and the Mendenhall Mall. 94 rooms. Complimentary continental breakfast. Check-in 3 pm, check-out 11 am. Fitness room. Indoor pool, whirlpool. **$$**

★ **BEST WESTERN COUNTRY LANE INN.** *9300 Glacier Hwy, Juneau (99801). Phone 907/789-5005; toll-free 800/780-7234; fax 907/789-2818. www. bestwestern.com.* Located a half-mile from Juneau International Airport and only a short drive to two local shopping malls and Mendenhall Glacier, this hotel is popular with visitors looking to do a bit of shopping and sightseeing while in town. Rooms are spacious, clean, and quiet and the staff friendly and knowledgeable, making it a good choice for travelers. 55 rooms. Pets accepted. Complimentary continental breakfast. Check-in 2 pm, check-out noon. **$**

★ ★ **BREAKWATER INN.** *1711 Glacier Ave, Juneau (99801). Phone 907/586-6303; toll-free 800/ 544-2250; fax 907/463-4820. www.breakwaterinn.com.* The Breakwater Inn sits across the street from Aurora Harbor about a mile from downtown Juneau. Its rooms—referred to as cabins—are clean and tidy and reflect the nautical theme found in the public areas. The most popular rooms have balconies facing the harbor and about a third of all rooms have kitchenettes. Another draw is The Breakwater Restaurant (see), which serves steak and seafood and is highly regarded for its menu, views, and atmosphere. 49 rooms. Pets accepted. Check-in 3 pm, check-out noon. Restaurant. **$**

★ **THE DRIFTWOOD LODGE.** *435 Willoughby Ave, Juneau (99801). Phone 907/586-2280; toll-free 800/ 544-2239; fax 907/586-1034. www.driftwoodalaska.com.* 63 rooms. Closed Dec 25. Pets accepted. Check-in 2 pm, check-out noon. **$**

★ ★ **FRONTIER SUITES AIRPORT HOTEL.** *9400 Glacier Hwy, Juneau (99801). Phone 907/790-6600; toll-free 800/544-2250; fax 907/790-6612. www. frontiersuites.com.* Whether staying in a suite or a standard room, guests will be pleased with the prices and the amenities: unique Alaskan artwork, DSL access, full kitchens, big dining tables, and large, comfortable chairs and sofas. The Frontier Suites is about half a mile from the airport, within walking distance of a number of moderately priced restaurants, and a ten-minute drive from Mendenhall Glacier, one of Juneau's top tourist draws. 104 rooms. Pets accepted. Check-in 3 pm, check-out noon. High-speed Internet access. Restaurant. Fitness room. **$**

★ ★ **PROSPECTOR HOTEL.** *375 Whittier St, Juneau (99801). Phone 907/586-3737; toll-free 800/ 331-2711; fax 907/586-1204. www.prospectorhotel.com.*

Exploring Juneau's History

The area around Juneau's cruise ship docks is filled with historical statues, memorials, and plaques that commemorate significant historical, social, and cultural events in the city's past.

At the extreme southern end of the cruise ship dock area stands the **Fisherman's Memorial,** dedicated to the memory of local commercial fishermen and women who have died while working in the fishing industry. It is also the site of the annual blessing of the fleet in early May.

The **Archie Van Winkle Memorial** is located nearby in front of the Mount Roberts Tramway terminal. This white granite memorial bears a plaque detailing the gallantry and bravery that led this US Marine Corp Colonel to become Alaska's first Medal of Honor recipient.

Farther north along the waterfront is the **USS *Juneau* Memorial,** dedicated to the memory of the 690 sailors, including the five Sullivan brothers, killed when the USS *Juneau* was torpedoed and sunk during the Battle of Guadalcanal in World War II.

Just beyond the parking garage and public library to the north is Marine Park, which features two far less solemn memorials. The first is the bronze **Patsy Ann statue** commissioned by the Gastineau Humane Society and dedicated in 1992. It honors Patsy Ann, a deaf English bull terrier living in Juneau in the 1930s that was always one of the first at the docks to meet arriving ships. Patsy Ann's uncanny ability to sense the approach of vessels before they came into view made her such a celebrity that the mayor at the time named her "Official Greeter of Juneau, Alaska."

Also in Marine Park, but closer to Marine Way, is the **Hard Rock Miner sculpture** by Juneau artist Ed Way. Created in 1980, the bronze work depicts hard rock miners at work underground, a powerful reminder of the hard-working men and women who transformed Juneau from an isolated gold mining town into one of Alaska's most important cities.

Thanks to extensive upgrades a few years ago, this hotel is in remarkable shape. Located across the highway from Gastineau Channel, comfortable, high quality furnishings are standard here as is thoughtful and attentive service. The hotel is only a short walk from downtown but is far enough from the tourist track to avoid being overrun with daytrippers. 62 rooms. Pets accepted. Check-in 3 pm, check-out noon. Restaurant. **$$**

★ ★ **WESTMARK BARANOF HOTEL.** *127 N Franklin St, Juneau (99801). Phone 907/586-2660; toll-free 800/764-0017; fax 907/586-8315. www. westmarkhotels.com.* This is one of the oldest hotels in Juneau and one of the most famous in Alaska. Built in 1939, this beautiful Art Deco building recently underwent a $3.5 million renovation to return its lobby, lounge, restaurant, and rooms to their original splendor. For over six decades, politicians, lobbyists,

and pundits have called the hotel their home away from home while the legislature is in session, giving the hotel an aura of refinement, dignity, and gravitas unlike any other in Alaska. 196 rooms. Pets accepted. Check-in 3 pm, check-out 11 am. Two restaurants. **$$**

Full-Service Hotel

★ ★ ★ **GOLDBELT HOTEL.** *51 Egan Dr, Juneau (99801). Phone 907/586-6900; toll-free 888/478-6909; fax 907/463-5861. www.goldbelthotel.com.* This hotel is one of the largest in town and has some of the best waterfront views around. A native-owned property, it boasts one of the most extensive collections of Tlingit art found anywhere in Alaska: shields, masks, necklaces, jewelry, baskets, bowls, and many other rare and beautiful items are on display throughout the public areas. The rooms are large and feature upscale amenities and a level of comfort and style that is unsurpassed in Juneau. 105 rooms. Pets accepted. Check-in 3 pm, check-out noon. Restaurant. **$$**

Specialty Lodgings

The following lodging establishments are approved by Mobil Travel Guide, but due to their unique and individualized nature have not been given a traditional Mobil Star rating. Included in this listing you may find bed-and-breakfasts, limited-service inns, guest ranches, and other unique hotel properties.

ALASKA WOLF HOUSE BED & BREAKFAST. *1900 Wickersham Ave, Juneau (99802). Phone 907/586-2422; toll-free 888/586-9053.* Built on the mountainside in a 4,000-square-foot western red cedar log home with open beams, natural skylights, and large windows. A large gourmet breakfast is provided every morning. 5 rooms, 2 story. **$**

THE HIGHLANDS BED & BREAKFAST. *421 Judy Ln, Juneau (99801). Phone toll-free 877/463-5404. www.juneauhighlands.com.* Located in historic downtown Juneau, this bed-and-breakfast features modern amenities, private entrances and baths. 4 rooms, 2 story. **$**

Restaurants

★ **BACAR'S.** *230 Seward St, Juneau (99801). Phone 907/463-4202.* Consistently voted Juneau's best breakfast restaurant in a local poll, BaCar's derives its name from Barry and Carline Shaw, the longtime owners. Located in the middle of downtown Juneau, the place consistently draws crowds coming to enjoy the fresh breads and "fine specialty home cooking" that has made the restaurant a local favorite for years. American menu. Breakfast, lunch. Closed Jan 1, Thanksgiving, Dec 25. Casual attire. **$**

★ ★ **THE BREAKWATER RESTAURANT & LOUNGE.** *1711 Glacier Ave, Juneau (99801). Phone 907/586-6303; toll-free 800/544-2250; fax 907/463-4820. www.madsens.com/breakwater.* In 2003, Elite Dining named this restaurant one of Juneau's top neighborhood favorites "in recognition of excellence in dining." In addition, *Capital City Weekly* magazine has repeatedly awarded it first place for best seafood, best steaks, best quality, and best dining. Offering Black Angus beef, fresh Alaskan seafood, and one of the largest wine selections in Juneau, this intimate, inviting restaurant is a real treat. Seafood, steak menu. Breakfast, lunch, dinner. Bar. Casual attire. **$$$**

★ ★ ★ **CHINOOK'S RESTAURANT.** *51 Egan Dr, Juneau (99801). Phone 907/586-5123; toll-free 888/478-6909; fax 907/463-5861. www.goldbelthotel.com.* This well-known hotel restaurant provides its diners with a sophisticated and elegant contemporary setting in which to enjoy fine food. When the state legislature is in session, the restaurant is a popular place for politicians and their aides to meet, while in the summer, it caters to cruise ship passengers and business professionals. The restaurant's excellent reputation for top-of-the-line seafood is surpassed only by the popularity of its lounge, which is famous for offering 285 different types of martinis. Seafood, steak menu. Breakfast, lunch, dinner. Closed Jan 1, Thanksgiving, Dec 25. Bar. Children's menu. Casual attire. **$$$**

★ ★ **DI SOPRA.** *429 W Willoughby Ave, Juneau (99801). Phone 907/586-3150; fax 907/586-1644. www.thefiddlehead.com/disopra.html.* Since the early 1990s, DiSopra has been providing fine dining to steak and seafood lovers in downtown Juneau. Located upstairs from the equally popular Fiddlehead Restaurant (see), the restaurant is the kind of place to go for a romantic evening, special event, or business dinner. The décor is sleek and modern, the views of Mount Juneau, spectacular. International menu. Dinner. Closed Jan 1, Dec 25; also Sun-Mon in winter. Casual attire. Reservations recommended. **$$**

★ ★ **DRAGON INN CHINESE CUISINE.** *213 Front St, Juneau (99801). Phone 907/586-4888; fax 907/586-8074. www.bestchinesefood.com.* Located on one of Juneau's most vibrant streets, this popular local Chinese restaurant is normally packed with an eclectic mix of young couples, large families, day-tripping tourists, and business professionals. The interior sports a subtle Chinese theme, but the main draw is the extensive menu and the restaurant's reputation for relaxed, casual dining. Chinese menu. Lunch, dinner. Closed Sun; Thanksgiving, Dec 25. Casual attire. **$$**

★ ★ **EL SOMBRERO.** *157 S Franklin St, Juneau (99801). Phone 907/586-6770; fax 907/586-6772.* Winner of numerous local awards for best Mexican food, this busy, vibrant restaurant offers a wide selection of traditional Mexican dishes and caters to a widely disparate clientele: from tradesmen and lunch-daters to business professionals and cruise ship tourists. Open long hours throughout the year, it's a great place to go for casual dining in a relaxed, inviting atmosphere. Mexican menu. Lunch, dinner. Closed Jan 1, Thanksgiving, Dec 25; also Sun in winter. Casual attire. **$$**

★ ★ **FIDDLEHEAD RESTAURANT.** *429 W Willoughby Ave, Juneau (99801). Phone 907/586-3150; fax 907/586-1644. www.thefiddlehead.com/fiddlehead .html.* This fine dining restaurant has a casual, family-friendly feel to it—ideal for those looking for quality food in a relaxed atmosphere. Located on the edge of downtown Juneau, the restaurant is close to the action without being overwhelmed by it. Those with a sweet tooth take note: the pastries and desserts here are considered some of the best in Juneau. Eclectic/International menu. Breakfast, lunch, dinner. Closed Jan 1, Dec 25. Children's menu. Casual attire. **$$**

★ ★ ★ **THE GOLD ROOM.** *127 N Franklin St, Juneau (99801). Phone 907/463-6222; fax 907/586-8315. www.westmarkhotels.com.* This historic restaurant at the Westmark Baranof Hotel (see) is without a doubt one of the most architecturally and artistically attractive restaurants in Alaska. From the exquisite Art Deco skylight rediscovered after a devastating fire in the 1980s to the huge wall mural by Alaskan artist Sydney Lawrence, the restaurant is filled with historical, artistic, and architectural accents that give it an ultra-sophisticated, elegant air. The restaurant's menu is top-rate, too, in keeping with the clientele they serve—a who's who of Alaska's political, social, and business circles. American menu. Dinner. Closed Thanksgiving, Dec 25. Bar. Children's menu. Casual attire. **$$$**

★ ★ **HANGAR ON THE WHARF.** *#2 Marine Way, #106, Juneau (99801). Phone 907/586-5018. www.hangaronthewharf.com.* Juneau's only waterfront restaurant features southeast Alaska's largest selection of microbrew beers in a converted aircraft hangar. American menu. Lunch, dinner. **$**

★ **JOVANY'S.** *9121 Glacier Hwy, Juneau (99801). Phone 907/789-2339; fax 907/790-3234. www.jovanys .com.* This mom-and-pop family restaurant near the airport in the Mendenhall Valley area of Juneau has been in business for many years and serves an eclectic mix of American, Asian, and European dishes. Friendly service, reasonable prices, and consistently superior food make it a long-time local and tourist favorite. Fusion, Italian menu. Lunch, dinner. Closed Jan 1, Thanksgiving, Dec 25. Casual attire. **$$**

★ ★ **MICASA.** *9200 Glacier Hwy, Juneau (99801). Phone 907/789-3636.* Frequent winner of local awards for best Mexican food and best brunch in town, MiCasa Mexican restaurant has been serving the Mendenhall Valley area of Juneau since the late 1970s. Architecturally, it has a subtle southwestern feel to it with an appealing blend of earth tones, painted arches, and decorative tiles reminiscent of those found in Mexican haciendas. Mexican menu. Breakfast, lunch, dinner. Bar. Children's menu. Casual attire. **$$**

★ **PARADISE CAFÉ.** *245 Marine Way, Juneau (99801). Phone 907/586-2253.* Set up in a French bistro style, Paradise Café serves a constantly changing variety of breakfast and lunch dishes and fresh pastries, all prepared on site from scratch. On sunny, warm days, the small outdoor patio at the front is an excellent place to sit and watch the harbor and the local action. American menu. Breakfast, lunch. Closed Dec 25; also three weeks late Dec. Casual attire. Outdoor seating. **$**

★ **PASTA GARDEN.** *9400 Glacier Hwy, Juneau (99801). Phone 907/790-6600; toll-free 800/544-2250. www.madsens.com/riverrockrestr.* There's no garden at the Pasta Garden restaurant, but there is a log-cabin seating area in the middle of the otherwise standard dining room. Despite this unusual architectural feature, the extensive menu, packed with an eclectic mix of Italian, Mexican, Asian, and Alaskan seafood dishes and moderate prices, is a real crowd pleaser. International menu. Breakfast, lunch, dinner. Closed Thanksgiving, Dec 25. Children's menu. Casual attire. **$$**

★ **PIZZERIA ROMA.** *2 Marine Way, Suite 104, Juneau (99801). Phone 907/463-5020.* This small pizzeria is located in the Fisherman's Wharf building at the foot of Main Street in downtown Juneau. Well-known in the area for offering consistently excellent pizza, its great location and solid reputation ensure that it's frequently packed with locals and tourists alike. Pizza. Lunch, dinner. Closed Thanksgiving, Dec 25. Casual attire. **$**

★ ★ **T. K. MAGUIRE'S.** *375 Whittier St, Juneau (99801). Phone 907/586-3711; fax 907/586-1204. www. prospectorhotel.com/restaurant.htm.* Windows in this casually upscale steak and seafood restaurant provide excellent views of Gastineau Channel and Douglas Island. Featuring an understated Irish pub theme, its outdoor deck is a great place to dine on warm, sunny days while taking in the sights and sounds of the waterfront. Fusion menu. Breakfast, lunch, dinner. Closed Jan 1, Memorial Day, Dec 25. Bar. Children's menu. Casual attire. Outdoor seating. **$$**

★ ★ **THANE ORE HOUSE.** *4400 Thane Rd, Juneau (99801). Phone 907/586-3442.* Rustic setting with regional Alaskan specialties and unique seating. Song and dance floor show in adjacent theater. American menu. Lunch, dinner. **$**

Katmai National Park and Preserve

Web site www.nps.gov/katm

Put simply, Katmai is bear country. Katmai National Park and Preserve has one of the world's highest concentrations of brown bears, with more than 2,000 of the giant furry mammals clambering within this remote wilderness along the Alaska Peninsula. The bears are drawn to the area's lakes and rivers, which teem with sockeye salmon. During the months of July and September, it is not uncommon to see dozens of bears gathered at Brooks Falls, feeding on salmon that have migrated up the Naknek River. While the salmon attract bears, the bears in turn attract tourists, thousands of whom make the trip to Katmai via air taxi or boat (no roads lead to the park) to witness North America's largest land predator in its natural habitat. A viewing platform at Brooks Camp enables visitors to safely observe and photograph the brown bears, some of which weigh over 900 pounds. Beyond bears, Katmai is home to numerous other wildlife, including moose, red foxes, weasels, wolves, and porcupines. At the park's southern edge along the Shelikof Strait, hair seals, sea lions, and sea otters inhabit the rugged shoreline, while beluga, killer, and gray whales patrol the waters just off the coast.

Katmai is also famous for its volcanoes, with 14 active volcanoes located in the park. In 1912, the largest volcanic eruption of the 20th century occurred here when the Novarupta Volcano blew its top, launching a plume of smoke and ash 20 miles skyward. The cataclysmic eruption—ten times more powerful than the eruption of Mount St. Helens—created a 40-square-mile ash flow within the Valley of Ten Thousand Smokes, so named by botanist Robert Griggs during a 1916 expedition for National Geographic. Today, the area still resembles a lifeless moonscape, possessing a gray landscape devoid of grasses, trees, and shrubs.

Aside from wildlife viewing, popular activities at Katmai include hiking, sea kayaking, and sport fishing. The park offers a world-class fishing experience, with the Alagnak and Naknek rivers populated by Pacific salmon, rainbow trout, grayling, and northern pike. Visitors to Katmai should be prepared for cold and wet conditions. The weather is often inhospitable, even during the summer months. Phone 907/246-3305.

What to See and Do

Alagnak Wild River. The Alagnak Wild River twists and turns across 67 miles of pristine wilderness in the Aleutian Range of southwestern Alaska. The braided river begins at Kukaklek Lake in the Katmai National Preserve and then flows west, widening along the way, before spilling out into Bristol Bay. In 1980, the Alagnak was included in the national Wild and Scenic Rivers System. Whitewater rafters are drawn to the river's Class I–III rapids and ever changing landscape, ranging from boreal forest to wet sedge tundra. The Alagnak's western stretch, shallow and marked by numerous sandbars, has become a favored destination for fly-fishing. The cool waters of the Alagnak teem with rainbow trout and all five species of Pacific salmon, including the prodigious king salmon, the largest of which can exceed 70 pounds. The Alagnak's designation as a Wild River helps protect the area's abundant wildlife, most notably a large population of brown bears that feed on the salmon. Other wildlife found along the river include bald eagles, caribou, moose, osprey, and wolverines. The Alagnak Wild River is accessible only by boat or seaplane. If you make the trip, be sure to bring heavy-duty rain gear and warm wool clothing.

Kenai (D-5)

Population 6,942
Area Code 907
Information Kenai Convention & Visitors Bureau, 11471 Kenai Spur Hwy, 99611; phone 907/283-1991
Web site www.visitkenai.com

As the oldest settlement on the Alaskan mainland, Kenai has been witness to some of the most significant events in Alaska's history. Originally the home of the Dena'ina Athabascan Indians, the area became a Russian fur trading post in 1791 and remained so for the next 80 years until Alaska was purchased by the US government in 1869. Old Town Kenai, two blocks southeast of the Kenai Visitor Center, contains many artifacts from this period and includes a self-guided walking tour that explores the different cultural and economic influences that have shaped the lives of the Russian, Indian, and American residents of the town over the past two hundred years. In 1947, the Sterling Highway was completed, opening Kenai and the entire Peninsula up to the world and prompting the development of what has become one of the major industries in the area: tourism. Ten years after the Highway was built, oil was discovered at Swanson River northeast of town, opening up a new chapter in the town's history. Despite two centuries of dramatic social, economic, and political change, the Kenai area remains an undeniably appealing place to visit. Set on the edge of Cook Inlet near the mouth of the Kenai River, the town is surrounded on all sides by untamed wilderness, from the muddy shores and frigid waters of the inlet to the pristine lakes, streams, hills, and forests that make up the Kenai National Wildlife Refuge.

With panoramic views across Cook Inlet to three of Alaska's most active volcanoes, Mt. Redoubt, Mt. Spurr, and Mt. Iliamna, few places can match Kenai's ability to put on a show, most recently a series of eruptions of Mt. Redoubt in 1990 and similar eruptions of Mt. Spurr in 1992. Visitors not fortunate enough to witness one of these events can always plan on being in town for the annual Kenai River Festival, held in the Green Strip Park the second weekend in June. The festival celebrates the Kenai River and offers an appealing blend of arts and crafts, environmental exhibits, traditional dance and music, and Alaskan food.

Limited-Service Hotel

★ ★ **UPTOWN MOTEL.** *47 Spur View Dr, Kenai (99611). Phone 907/283-3660; toll-free 800/777-3650; fax 907/283-5833. www.uptownmotel.com.* This downtown Kenai motel is not like most motels. The lobby contains a small, ornate staircase and matching reception desk made of beautiful, dark, polished woods; the hallways have equally attractive wainscoting; and the rooms are accentuated by crown molding and window valances. In all, it's a level of luxury that is entirely unexpected in a motel. 49 rooms. Pets accepted. Check-in 2 pm, check-out noon. Restaurant. **$**

Restaurants

★ ★ **CHARLOTTE'S RESTAURANT.** *115 S Willow St, Kenai (99611). Phone 907/283-2777; fax 907/262-0661.* According to owner Charlotte Legg, Charlotte's serves "contemporary homestyle cooking; comfort food with a flair." It does this by taking foods that people like and making them better: adding extra ingredients or substituting new ingredients to create unexpected, pleasing twists on standard dishes. All of the breads and soups are prepared from scratch and the salads and sandwiches feature vegetables grown on site. California, deli menu. Breakfast, lunch. Closed holidays; also first two weeks in Jan. Children's menu. Casual attire. Outdoor seating. **$**

★ ★ **LOUIE'S STEAK & SEAFOOD.** *47 Spur View Dr, Kenai (99611). Phone 907/283-3660; toll-free 800/777-3650; fax 907/283-5833. www.uptownmotel .com.* Louie's is decorated in an "Alaskan Trophy Room" style, with stuffed native animals, splayed pelts, and mounted fish arranged throughout the room, creating an effect that is far more amusing than shocking. With a long tradition of serving top-quality steak and seafood in a casual fine dining atmosphere, it consistently draws in large crowds of locals and tourists. Seafood, steak menu. Breakfast, lunch, dinner. Closed Dec 25. Bar. Children's menu. Casual attire. **$$$**

★ ★ **OLD TOWN VILLAGE RESTAURANT.** *1001 Mission Ave, Kenai (99611). Phone 907/283-4515.* Seafood, steak menu. Breakfast, lunch, dinner. Closed in winter. Bar. Children's menu. Casual attire. Reservations recommended. **$$**

Kenai Fjords National Park (D-5)

Web site www.nps.gov/kefj.

The Seward Highway, a National Scenic Byway, connects Anchorage and the town of Seward in south-central Alaska. The 127-mile trip to Seward twists around steep ridges, reflective lakes, and alpine valleys, leading to a confluence of mountain, ice, and sea at

Kenai Fjords National Park. The park's inner landscape is dominated by glaciers and ice caps, the most prominent being the 300-square-mile Harding Icefield, the largest ice cap in the United States. The glaciers stretch all the way to the coastline at the park's southern edge. Here, the narrow inlets of Aialik Bay lead out into the cold, choppy waters of the Gulf of Alaska.

Aside from relaxing amid serene surroundings, the most popular activities at Kenai (pronounced "keen eye") Fjords include fishing, hiking, kayaking, and wildlife viewing. The park is home to mountain goats, moose, puffins, sea otters, and sea lions, while humpback whales can be seen surfacing just off the coast. Many commercial guides offer wildlife viewing tours that begin in Seward.

The park has four public-use cabins, three of which (Aialik, Holgate, and Northarm) are situated along the coast. The fourth cabin (Willow) is available only during the winter months, and accessing it requires a 7-mile journey with the help of cross-country skis, snowshoes, a snowmachine, or a dogsled. Visitors can reserve cabins by calling the National Park Service (phone 907/224-3175).

By Alaska standards, the park is easily accessible, with Seward serviced by both the Alaska Railroad and the Alaska Marine Highway. Commercial flights are available as well, and charter boats and cruise ships offer additional alternatives for reaching the majestic scenery and abundant wildlife of Kenai Fjords National Park. Phone 907/224-7500.

Ketchikan (F-9)

Population 7,922
Area Code 907
Information Ketchikan Visitors Bureau, 131 Front St, 99901; phone 907/225-6166 or toll-free 800/770-3300
Web site www.visit-ketchikan.com

Ketchikan is a town of about 8,500 people, but hosts nearly three-quarters of a million visitors during the summer. It's the first Alaskan stop for most cruise ships touring the Inside Passage and proudly declares itself to be "Alaska's First City." Set in the heart of the Tongass National Forest, the town has one of the highest rainfall totals in the state, with 162 inches of rain falling in an average year. It is also the closest community to Misty Fjords National Monument,

a 2.3 million acre wilderness of massive glaciers, deep saltwater fjords, pristine forests, and abundant wildlife. Closer to town, the protected waters of the Inside Passage attract massive runs of salmon each year, leading to Ketchikan's claim to be the "Salmon Capital of the World." The most famous section of the old town area is Creek Street, a former red light district that now houses an appealing blend of restaurants, art galleries, and small shops built on pilings over Ketchikan Creek. It's a pedestrian-only zone and a great place to wander around, do a bit of shopping, and grab a bite to eat. The Ketchikan area is also rich in native culture. Totem Bight State Park, 8 miles north of town, contains a historic collection of totem poles set along a scenic trail on the shores of the Tongass Narrows. Saxman Totem Park, located 2 miles south of town, contains historic totem poles as well as workshops where visitors can watch native carvers fashion totem poles, canoes, and other artwork using the same techniques employed by their ancestors. The Totem Heritage Center in town offers classes in traditional art forms and preserves totems from abandoned villages, and the Southeast Alaska Discovery Center in the middle of downtown has a wide range of exhibits, including a selection of contemporary poles, samples of native basketry, and a model of a traditional fish camp.

What to See and Do

Historic Creek Street and Dolly's House Museum. *#24 Creek St, Ketchikan (99901). Phone 907/225-2279.* One of Ketchikan's most popular tourist destinations is Historic Creek Street, a former red-light district built on pilings over the rushing waters of Ketchikan Creek. Visitors can stroll the narrow, pedestrian-only wooden boardwalks and take time to admire the beauty and architectural grace of the district's turn-of-the-century buildings, most of which have long since been converted into restaurants, art galleries, gift shops, and private residences. Visitors looking for a glimpse into Creek Street's bawdy past should visit the Dolly's House Museum at #24 Creek St. This building was one of Ketchikan's most infamous brothels during the town's early days and was owned and operated by Madam Dolly Arthur. Nowadays, it serves as a tangible link to the past, with fixtures and furnishings seemingly unchanged from the time when Dolly ran the show. (Summer, daily 8 am-5 pm; closed Oct-Apr) **$**

Misty Fiords National Monument. *3031 Tongass Ave, Ketchikan (99901). Phone 907/225-7535. www.fs.fed.us/*

r10/tongass. This area at the southern border of the Tongass National Forest, accessible only by floatplane and boat, derives its name from the almost constant precipitation that occurs in the region; the area receives almost 14 feet of precipitation annually, giving rise to its many lakes, streams, and waterfalls. Behm Canal stretches more than 100 miles through the heart of the area, flowing past active glaciers and towering sea cliffs. Despite the rainy climate, kayaking and camping are popular with adventurers here.

Saxman Native Village. *Mile 2.5, South Tongass Hwy, Ketchikan (99901). Phone 907/225-4846, ext 310. www. capefoxtours.com.* Saxman Native Village, located a short drive south of downtown Ketchikan, offers visitors a chance to immerse themselves in the rich cultural and artistic heritage of the Tlingit tribe of southeast Alaska. The village features a park filled with 28 totems recovered from surrounding villages and restored by members of the Civilian Conservation Corps during the early part of the 20th century. Also on-site is the Beaver Clan House, a replica of a traditional winter house once used by the Tlingits. While in the house, visitors can learn about the history and language of the Tlingits and observe a Native dance demonstration. The highlight of the trip is the Saxman Carving Center, where visitors have the opportunity to observe master totem carvers and their apprentices at work, preserving their cultural heritage while creating objects of great beauty. Although there is no cost to visit the park, there is a fee for guided tours and demonstrations run by the park. Contact Cape Fox Tours for prices and tour availability.

Totem Bight State Historical Park. *Ranger Station, 9883 N Tongass Hwy, Ketchikan (99901). Phone 907/ 247-8574. www.dnr.state.ak.us/parks/units/totembgh .htm.* In 1938, the US Forest Service began salvaging and reconstructing magnificent examples of Tlingit, Haida, and Tsimshian symbolic carvings. Decaying totem poles were copied in freshly cut cedar logs using traditional tools and techniques; even the paints used were made of natural materials like clam shells and salmon eggs. Today, this state park houses the largest collection of totem poles in the world. **$**

Limited-Service Hotels

★ ★ BEST WESTERN LANDING HOTEL.
3434 Tongass Ave, Ketchikan (99901). Phone 907/225- 5166; toll-free 800/428-8304; fax 907/225-6900. www. bestwestern.com. This clean, comfortable, friendly hotel has the added advantage of being close to the main shopping, transportation, and tourist destinations in Ketchikan. With two restaurants, a small fitness center, and a free shuttle service anywhere within the city limits, it's a popular place for tourists looking to avoid the congestion and expense of downtown lodging and dining. 76 rooms. Pets accepted. Check-in 3 pm, check-out noon. Two restaurants. Fitness room. **$**

★ ★ GILMORE HOTEL.
326 Front St, Ketchikan (99901). Phone 907/225-9423; toll-free 800/225-9423; fax 907/225-7442. www.gilmorehotel.com. Built in 1927, the Gilmore Hotel is one of the oldest, best-known hotels in Ketchikan. Located across the street from the cruise ship dock and in the heart of the historic downtown district, it was recently remodeled to bring it up to code while retaining as much of the building's original beauty and charm as possible. The result is a hotel that offers an eclectic mix of modern amenities like cable television and soda machines alongside such traditional features as cast-iron radiators and wooden window frames. Guest rooms are small and can be noisy, as the lounge downstairs is the place to party in Ketchikan. 42 rooms. Pets accepted. Complimentary continental breakfast. Check-in 1 pm, check-out noon. Restaurant. **$**

★ ★ THE NARROWS INN.
4871 N Tongass Hwy, Ketchikan (99901). Phone 907/247-2600; toll-free 888/ 686-2600; fax 907/247-2602. www.narrowsinn.com. The Narrows Inn is the only year-round hotel on the water in Ketchikan and is also one of the most scenic, with many rooms featuring private decks overlooking the water. With its own restaurant, lounge, boat dock, and waterfront grounds, the Inn provides ample opportunities for people to relax and unwind without having to drive anywhere. 47 rooms. Complimentary continental breakfast. Check-in 4 pm, check-out noon. Restaurant. **$**

★ SUPER 8.
2151 Sea Level Dr, Ketchikan (99901). Phone 907/225-9088; toll-free 800/800-8000; fax 907/225-1072. www.super8.com. Located on the water's edge in the same vast parking lot as the main shopping mall, the 82-room Super 8 is one of the best deals in Ketchikan. Rates are lower than at other lodgings in town, and some rooms have great views of Tongass Narrows and the cruise ships and floatplanes

that pass in front of the motel. Rooms lack some common amenities, like coffee makers and ironing boards, but for a basic economy accommodation, it fits the bill just fine. 82 rooms. Pets accepted. Complimentary continental breakfast. Check-in 2 pm, check-out noon. **$**

★ ★ **WESTCOAST CAPE FOX LODGE.** *800 Venetia Way, Ketchikan (99901). Phone 907/225-8001; toll-free 866/225-8001; fax 907/225-8286. www.westcoasthotels.com/capefox.* The views from this architecturally stunning clifftop hotel are spectacular, with south-facing guest rooms overlooking downtown Ketchikan and the Tongass Narrows and north-facing ones looking out on the dramatic mountain range that rises up on the edge of town. The interior is magnificent, too, featuring a grand lobby framed by massive wooden posts and beams, a fireside lounge filled with live plants, museum-quality native artwork displays, and a sweeping central staircase accentuated by a huge totem carving by renowned local artist Nathan Jackson. Guests looking to shop, dine, and sightsee can ride the hotel's funicular from the lobby down the bluff and step off onto Creek Street, the main tourist area downtown. 72 rooms. Pets accepted. Check-in 3 pm, check-out 11 am. Restaurant. **$$**

Restaurants

★ ★ **ANNABELLE'S FAMOUS KEG AND CHOWDER HOUSE.** *326 Front St, Ketchikan (99901). Phone 907/225-6009.* Annabelle's is located in an elegant 1927 dining room complete with mahogany panels, Scottish wool carpets, and beautiful sconce lighting. The attached lounge is impressive, too, with historic murals of old-time Creek Street, pressed tin ceilings, a colorful stained glass ceiling, and a hand-crafted wooden bar. Located on the ground floor of the Gilmore Hotel (see), it's well worth a visit for its architectural, artistic, and historic appeal. American, seafood menu. Lunch, dinner. Closed Thanksgiving, Dec 25; also Sun in winter. Bar. Casual attire. **$$**

★ **DIAZ CAFE.** *335 Stedman St, Ketchikan (99901). Phone 907/225-2257.* American menu. Breakfast, lunch. Closed in winter. Casual attire. **$**

★ **DOCKSIDE DINER.** *1287 Tongass Ave, Ketchikan (99901). Phone 907/247-7787; fax 907/247-7737.* This diner is one of those places tourists are always looking for: a "real" Alaskan restaurant. With a menu offering a wide range of American "homestyle food for family dining" at reasonable prices, it's a place locals like to hang out in to catch up with one another and hear the latest news. American menu. Breakfast, lunch, dinner. Children's menu. Casual attire. Outdoor seating. **$$**

★ ★ ★ **HEEN KAHIDI.** *800 Venetia Way, Ketchikan (99901). Phone 907/225-8001; toll-free 866/225-8001; fax 907/225-8286. www.westcoasthotels.com.* Heen Kahidi, which translates as "House by the River," is perched on the side of a bluff overlooking downtown Ketchikan and the waters of the Tongass Narrows. The dining area has the feel of an après ski lodge, with massive wooden roof beams, a river rock fireplace, subtle lighting, and soft colors that enhance the stylish ambience of the place. Towering literally and figuratively above all of its competitors, this restaurant offers an appealing array of succulent seafood, chicken, and pasta dishes prepared by Chef Tim, the creative mastermind behind the restaurant's success. American, seafood menu. Breakfast, lunch, dinner. Closed Thanksgiving, Dec 25. Bar. Casual attire. **$$**

★ **JEREMIAH'S.** *3434 Tongass Ave, Ketchikan (99901). Phone 907/225-6530; fax 907/225-5526.* Jeremiah was a bullfrog and the inspiration for this restaurant's name as well as its signature drink, the Midori-based "Bullfrog." Designed with style and sophistication in mind, the bistro-style dining area features comfortable booths, a sleek curved wooden bar, soft lighting, and a small outdoor patio overlooking the ferry terminal. Pizza. Lunch, dinner. Closed Dec 25. Bar. Children's menu. Casual attire. Outdoor seating. **$$**

★ **THE LANDING RESTAURANT.** *3434 Tongass Ave, Ketchikan (99901). Phone 907/225-5166; toll-free 800/428-8304; fax 907/225-6900.* This restaurant functions as a popular hangout for people who live at the northern end of Ketchikan. The décor is retro '50s with big, padded booths, stark white floors and walls, glass-block partitions between tables, and plenty of counter seating. Waitresses and customers call each other by name, giving the place a real neighborly, hometown feel. American menu. Breakfast, lunch, dinner. Closed Dec 25. Bar. Children's menu. Casual attire. **$$**

★ **MR. C'S CAFE.** *1630 Tongass Ave, Ketchikan (99901). Phone 907/225-5803.* Mr. C's is an odd but endearing little restaurant. Originally based on the theme of "indoor picnic," it has since evolved into an all-day breakfast and hearty lunch spot decorated with homey knick-knacks and parasol umbrellas. The bright, cheerful dining room and friendly staff add to the appeal, as does the tempting array of fresh-baked desserts they offer. American menu. Breakfast, lunch. Closed Jan 1, Thanksgiving, Dec 25. Casual attire. **$**

★ ★ **THE NARROWS RESTAURANT.** *4871 N Tongass Hwy, Ketchikan (99901). Phone 907/247-5900; fax 907/247-2602. www.narrowsinn.com.* One of the best reasons to visit this restaurant is to take in the exceptional views it offers of the floatplanes, boats, and wildlife that share the waters of Tongass Narrows. The menu is another big selling point, featuring standard American dishes as well as house specialties such as stuffed halibut, Coffman Cove oysters, and Alaskan king crab. American, seafood menu. Breakfast, lunch, dinner. Closed Dec 25. Bar. Children's menu. Casual attire. Reservations recommended. **$$**

★ ★ **NEW YORK CAFE.** *207 Stedman St, Ketchikan (99901). Phone 907/225-0246; toll-free 866/ 225-0246; fax 907/225-1803. www.thenewyorkhotel.com.* American menu. Breakfast, lunch, dinner. Closed in winter. Bar. Children's menu. Casual attire. Reservations recommended. Outdoor seating. **$$**

★ ★ **OCEAN VIEW RESTAURANTE.** *1831 Tongass Ave, Ketchikan (99901). Phone 907/225-7566; fax 907/247-7566.* The décor of this popular local restaurant can best be described as "upscale Mexican villa," with polished wood chairs, petite tea candles, a colorful Mexican bar, and walls and ceilings painted in vibrant oranges, yellows, and reds. Although the emphasis is on Mexican food, the restaurant also serves a wide range of Italian, Greek, and American dishes. Italian, Mexican menu. Breakfast, lunch, dinner. Closed Jan 1, July 4, Dec 25. Bar. Children's menu. Casual attire. Reservations recommended. **$$**

★ **THE PIZZA MILL.** *808 Water St, Ketchikan (99901). Phone 907/225-6646; fax 907/247-8080.* This family-run restaurant proudly bills itself as Ketchikan's original pizza place, having been established in the early 1970s. It offers subs, Mexican food, burgers, and spaghetti, but is most proud of its "pizza with an attitude": thirty-five different pizza choices,

including eleven "Yuppie Pies" with names like Dead Head, Fish Hippie, and Generation X. Pizza. Lunch, dinner, late-night. Casual attire. **$**

★ **RED ANCHOR CAFE & DELI.** *1935 Tongass Ave, #A, Ketchikan (99901). Phone 907/247-5287.* American, deli menu. Breakfast, lunch. Closed Sun. Casual attire. **$**

★ ★ **SALMON FALLS RESTAURANT.** *16707 N Tongass Hwy, Ketchikan (99901). Phone 907/225-2752; toll-free 800/247-9059; fax 907/225-2710.* Seafood menu. Breakfast, lunch, dinner. Closed in winter. Bar. Casual attire. Outdoor seating. **$$**

★ **THAI HOUSE.** *127 Stedman St, Ketchikan (99901). Phone 907/225-8424; fax 907/247-8424.* With window seating on two floors and a small outdoor deck built over the waters of Ketchikan Creek, this bustling restaurant offers guests terrific views of Ketchikan's popular Creek Street as well as savory Thai and Chinese dishes. The atmosphere inside is relaxed and informal, making it a great place to unwind after a long day working or sightseeing. Chinese menu, Thai menu. Lunch, dinner. Closed Thanksgiving, Dec 25. Casual attire. Outdoor seating. **$$**

Kobuk Valley National Park

Web site www.nps.gov/kova

An unexpected sight awaits visitors who venture above the Arctic Circle to Kobuk Valley National Park: sand dunes rising as high as 150 feet. The landscape is not a mirage, and, no, this is not Arizona; the sands were created by the grinding of glaciers during the last ice age and deposited here by shifting sands and water. Squeezed between the Baird Mountains to the north and the Warring Mountains to the south, the Kobuk Valley is perhaps best explored by paddling along the calm, wide waters of the Kobuk River. The ideal time to visit the park is late summer, when more than 300,000 western arctic caribou—the largest caribou herd in North America—cross the river during their migration south. The caribou, known as "the nomads of the north," move constantly across the alpine tundra in search of food to support their body weight, which for a bull ranges from 150 to 300 pounds. Getting to Kobuk Valley is challenging, typically requiring two flights: a commercial flight to either Kotzebue or Nome, followed by an air-taxi ride to the park. There are no roads in or around the park. The Kotzebue Public Lands Information Center offers educational and interpretive programs throughout the year. (Daily; closed holidays) Phone 907/442-3890.

Kodiak (E-5)

Population 6,334
Area Code 907
Information Kodiak Island Convention & Visitors Bureau, phone 907/486-4782 or toll-free 800/789-4782
Web site www.kodiak.org

Located on Chiniak Bay at the northeastern tip of Kodiak Island, the town of Kodiak is home to more than 770 commercial fishing vessels that ply the waters of the Gulf of Alaska and the Bering Sea in search of king crab, salmon, halibut, cod, shrimp, and many other varieties of seafood. Although the Alutiit people have called the island their home for nearly 8,000 years, it wasn't until the arrival of Alexander Baranov in 1792 that a permanent settlement was established next to the sheltered natural harbor he christened St. Paul. In creating a fur trading outpost on the site, he also founded what was to become the first capital of Russian America. By 1804, just twelve years after the Russian's arrival, the sea otters had been hunted to near extinction, so Baranov moved the company's operations far to the west where he founded a new settlement known today as Sitka. With the demise of the fur trade and the 1867 purchase of Alaska by the United States, the local economy shifted to commercial salmon fishing, which has remained a mainstay of the local economy ever since. Two hundred years after the departure of Baranov and his workers, Kodiak still maintains ties to its Russian heritage, most notably in the Holy Resurrection Russian Orthodox Church, with its blue onion-dome spire and Russian cross; in the Baranov Museum nearby, which was built by Baranov's men as an otter pelt warehouse; and in numerous street, place, and business names throughout the town.

Kodiak today offers visitors far more than just fresh Alaskan seafood, liquid sunshine, and spectacular views. An estimated 3,000 Kodiak brown bears live

on the island along with large numbers of deer, foxes, mountain goats, bald eagles, and shore birds and the waters near shore are home to orcas, humpback whales, sea otters, and Stellar seal lions. Visitors need only walk the shores, hike the trails, drive the roads, or paddle the rivers and bays to immerse themselves in the natural wonders that make Kodiak such an extraordinary destination in Alaska.

What to See and Do

Kodiak Island. *Phone 907/486-4782; toll-free 800/789-4782. www.kodiak.org.* Unlike the frozen wilderness that's usually associated with Alaska, Kodiak Island is known as the state's Emerald Isle because of its green snow-tipped mountains and tree-lined fjords. Located off the southern coast of Alaska, it is one of the largest commercial fishing ports in the nation and is famous for its Kodiak brown bears. Outdoor activities here include fishing, kayaking, hiking, biking, and wildlife viewing.

Limited-Service Hotels

★ ★ **BEST WESTERN KODIAK INN.** *236 Rezanof Dr W, Kodiak (99615). Phone 907/486-5712; toll-free 888/563-4254; fax 907/486-3430. www. kodiakinn.com.* Built on the side of a hill on the edge of downtown Kodiak, the Best Western Kodiak Inn has terrific views of Kodiak's two harbors and the orcas, seals, and other wildlife that inhabit the bay. Guests enjoy clean, comfortable, and spacious rooms and access to an outdoor cabana with a whirlpool in it. 80 rooms. Pets accepted. Complimentary continental breakfast. Check-in 2 pm, check-out noon. Restaurant, bar. Whirlpool. **$**

★ ★ **BUSKIN RIVER INN.** *1395 Airport Way, Kodiak (99615). Phone 907/487-2700; toll-free 800/544-2202; fax 907/487-4447.* The Buskin River Inn is an ideal place to stay for those looking for quiet, comfortable accommodations in an idyllic setting, surrounded by excellent fishing, hiking, and sightseeing spots. It's located 6 miles from downtown Kodiak, alongside the Buskin River. Although the river isn't visible from any room in the hotel, west-facing rooms have terrific views of nearby Mount Barometer and other peaks. Wildlife enthusiasts will be in their element here: the area around the hotel is a haven for bald eagles, white-tailed deer, foxes, and other small animals. The hotel's restaurant, the Eagle's Nest (see), is a local favorite. 50 rooms. Pets accepted. Check-in 2 pm, check-out noon. Restaurant, bar. **$**

★ ★ **SHELIKOF LODGE.** *211 Thorsheim Ave, Kodiak (99615). Phone 907/486-4141; fax 907/486-4116. www.ptialaska.net/kyle.* A longtime favorite in downtown Kodiak, the Shelikof Lodge is a popular destination for travelers who use it as their home base while they hunt, fish, and explore Kodiak Island during the summer and fall. Its centralized location, knowledgeable staff, and friendly service make it a good place to go to be in the middle of the action. 38 rooms. Pets accepted. Check-out noon. Restaurant, bar. Airport transportation available. **$**

Restaurants

★ ★ **2ND FLOOR.** *116 W Resanof Dr, Kodiak (99615). Phone 907/486-8555; fax 907/486-8559.* In keeping with its Japanese theme, the interior of this popular restaurant is subtly decorated, with waist-high screens and large plants creating intimate nooks throughout the dining room. Paper lanterns hanging from the ceiling and colorful Japanese prints on the wall create an appealing, casually elegant ambience. Japanese menu. Lunch, dinner. Closed holidays. Children's menu. Casual attire. **$$**

★ ★ **THE CHART ROOM.** *236 Resanof Dr W, Kodiak (99615). Phone 907/486-5712; fax 907/486-3430. www.kodiakinn.com.* Located on the second floor of the Best Western Kodiak Inn, the Chart Room offers captivating views of Kodiak's waterfront and the mountains and bays that surround the town. The restaurant provides casual fine dining in a relaxing, slightly upscale environment. Particularly noteworthy are the pre- and post-tsunami photos of Kodiak that line the entryway. American menu. Breakfast, lunch, dinner. Closed Dec 25. Bar. Children's menu. Casual attire. **$$$**

★ ★ **EAGLE'S NEST RESTAURANT.** *1395 Airport Way, Kodiak (99615). Phone 907/487-2700; toll-free 800/544-2202; fax 907/487-4447.* Eagle's Nest Restaurant is the on-site restaurant at the Buskin River Inn (see). With large picture windows looking out onto a dark green forest and jagged mountains rising above the tree tops, it's a casual, though elegant setting for dining and celebrating. During warmer weather, a large outdoor deck provides an opportunity to dine alfresco with excellent views amid a peaceful setting. American menu. Breakfast, lunch, dinner. Closed Thanksgiving, Dec 25. Bar. Children's menu. Casual attire. Outdoor seating. **$$$**

★ ★ **EL CHICANO MEXICAN RESTAURANT & CANTINA.** *103 Center Ave, Kodiak (99615). Phone 907/486-6116. www.elchicano.com.* El Chicano is the place to go in Kodiak for quality Mexican food in a family-friendly atmosphere in the heart of downtown. With a street-side outdoor patio, extensive menu, and a huge lounge offering live music, karaoke, and weekend DJs, the restaurant is a major player in the local social scene. Mexican menu. Lunch, dinner. Bar. Children's menu. Casual attire. Outdoor seating. **$$**

★ ★ **EUGENE'S RESTAURANT.** *1815 Selief Ln, Kodiak (99615). Phone 907/486-2625; fax 907/486-8589.* This popular Chinese restaurant in downtown Kodiak offers a vast menu selection and ultra-friendly service. There's nothing skimpy or delicate here; owner James Chong is a real meat lover and serves no steaks less than 14 ounces. The only complaint they hear at Eugene's is that the portions are so large, customers can't finish them. Chinese menu. Lunch, dinner. Closed Mon; Thanksgiving, Dec 25, children's menu. Casual attire. **$$**

★ **HENRY'S GREAT ALASKAN RESTAURANT.** *512 Marine Way, Kodiak (99615). Phone 907/486-8844.* American menu. Lunch, dinner. Bar. Children's menu. Casual attire. Reservations recommended. Outdoor seating. **$**

★ **PEKING SIZZLER BURGER RESTAURANT.** *116 W Rezanof Dr, Kodiak (99615). Phone 907/486-3300; fax 907/486-8559.* This newly renovated, oddly named restaurant has been serving an eclectic mix of Chinese food, hamburgers, fish and chips, and shakes to Kodiak locals and tourists since the early 1980s. The extensive menu, inexpensive prices, and convenient downtown location make it a family- and budget-friendly place to grab a bite while on the go. Chinese menu, hamburgers. Lunch, dinner. Closed holidays. Casual attire. **$$**

★ **SHELIKOF LODGE RESTAURANT.** *211 Thorsheim Ave, Kodiak (99615). Phone 907/486-4300; fax 907/486-4116. www.ptialaska.net/kyle.* Billing itself as one of the cheapest restaurants in town, the Shelikof Lodge Restaurant offers a variety of daily specials, fresh soups, and other hearty American and seafood dishes. Although tucked away inside the Shelikof Lodge (see), it's not just hotel guests who eat here—the place is frequently crowded with locals who appreciate the good food and friendly, reliable service. American, Italian menu. Breakfast, lunch, dinner. Closed Thanksgiving, Dec 25. Bar. Children's menu. Casual attire. **$**

Lake Clark National Park and Preserve

Web site www.nps.gov/lacl

Lake Clark National Park & Preserve encompasses 4 million acres of pristine wilderness, extending from Cook Inlet, across the craggy peaks of the Chigmit Mountains, farther west to the tundra-covered hills of Interior Alaska. Two active volcanoes can be found in the park: Mount Redoubt and Mount Iliamna. The park's namesake, Lake Clark, stretches for 40 miles. Teeming with red salmon, grayling, Dolly Varden, and northern pike, Lake Clark offers tremendous fishing opportunities, as do the park's many other lakes and rivers—three of which have been designated National Wild and Scenic Rivers. Fishing season runs from May until October, although a few of the lakes may not fully thaw until June. Hiking is another popular activity, but it requires considerable backcountry experience and know-how. The park contains no trails, and even the most physically fit hikers will be challenged—and slowed—by streams that must be forded and dense vegetation, particularly near the coast. For those willing to take on the challenge, spectacular rewards await: awe-inspiring scenery, incomparable solitude, and frequent wildlife sightings. Dall sheep, moose, and black and brown bears call the park home, as do more than 125 species of birds. Beluga whales, harbor seals, and sea lions can be seen in Chinitna Bay and Tuxedni Bay. No roads lead to the park, but floatplanes regularly shuttle visitors to the waters of Lake Clark from Anchorage, about 150 miles to the northeast. Phone 907/271-3751.

Moose Pass

Settled 1909
Population 206
Area Code 907
Information Moose Pass Chamber of Commerce & Visitors Bureau, PO Box 147, 99631
Web site www.moosepass.net

This tiny hamlet of 200 people on the southern shores of Trail Lake in the middle of the Kenai Peninsula is renown for its scenic beauty and its laid back, rustic charm. Throughout the summer, floatplanes skim in over the mountains and land on the lake, dropping off hikers, hunters, and fishermen who come to take advantage of the town's easy access to wild Alaska. From mid-May to mid-September, the Alaska Railroad winds down the eastern side of the lake, stopping in Moose Pass each day on its journey to and from Seward, 29 miles to the south. In winter, when heavy winter snows close the rail line, the town remains accessible via the Seward Highway, which passes by the edge of town, connecting Anchorage with Seward. Located less than 20 miles from Cooper Landing and the spectacular fishing of the Kenai River, Moose Pass is a popular spot for travelers looking for beauty and tranquility in the heart of one of Alaska's most popular regions.

Limited-Service Hotel

★ ★ **TRAIL LAKE LODGE.** *Seward Hwy, mile 29.5, Moose Pass (99631). Phone 907/288-3101; toll-free 888/395-3624; fax 907/288-3106. www.traillakelodge .com.* The Trail Lake Lodge is actually two buildings: a motel with small, clean rooms and basic amenities and a main building with six newer, more spacious rooms (with telephones) and a restaurant. Located 30 minutes from Seward and 20 minutes from world-class river fishing, it's in a convenient, peaceful, and spectacular setting, ideal for river and lake anglers and daytrippers who don't want to be stuck in a "large" city like Seward. During the winter, it's popular with snowmachiners who like to explore the trails around Moose Pass. In the long days of summer, guests enjoy scenery from the lodge's long, wide veranda. 35 rooms. Check-in 2 pm, check-out 10 am. Restaurant, bar. **$**

Restaurants

★ ★ **SUMMIT LAKE LODGE.** *Seward Hwy, mile 45.5, Moose Pass. Phone 907/244-2031. www. summitlakelodge.com.* American menu. Breakfast, lunch, dinner. Closed in winter. Bar. Children's menu. Casual attire. Reservations recommended. **$**

★ ★ **TRAIL LAKE LODGE RESTAURANT.** *Seward Hwy, mile 29.5, Moose Pass (99631). Phone 907/288-3101; toll-free 888/395-3624; fax 907/288-3106. www.traillakelodge.com.* This small restaurant is one of those warm, inviting, homey places that are so enjoyable to visit while on a road trip. It offers hearty meals at reasonable prices as well as some unexpected treats like jambalaya, quiche Lorraine, and the house specialty and local favorite, quesadillas, listed on the menu as being "World Famous (in Moose Pass)." Eclectic/International menu. Breakfast, lunch, dinner. Closed Oct; also Tues-Thurs Nov-Apr. Bar. Children's menu. Casual attire. **$$**

Noatak National Preserve

Web site www.nps.gov/noat

Far above the Arctic Circle in northwest Alaska, Noatak National Preserve offers an extraordinary float-trip experience for canoeists and kayakers. The Noatak River, designated a National Wild and Scenic River, flows for 350 miles, passing through dense coniferous forests and wide-open tundra as it cuts a path through the rugged peaks of the Brooks Range to Kotzebue Sound, just east of the Bering Strait. Wildlife-watching and photography are other popular activities within the preserve, which is home to musk oxen, grizzly bears, and caribou. There are no trails or roads within the park. Winters are extremely harsh here—only the hardiest of dog mushers should consider a visit during the winter months. Summer days are long and temperatures comparatively mild—July highs often eclipse 60 degrees. Alaska Airlines serves the town of Kotzebue, which is a short air-taxi ride from the preserve. Phone 907/442-3890.

Palmer (D-5)

Population 4,533
Area Code 907
Information Greater Palmer Chamber of Commerce, PO Box 45, 99645; phone 907/745-2880
Web site www.palmerchamber.org

Tucked into a fertile valley between the rugged Talkeetna Range to the north and the towering Chugach Range to the south, Palmer was originally established as a trading post on the Matanuska River by George Palmer around 1890. It remained a sleepy little town until 1935 when it was chosen as the site of a New Deal agricultural experiment called the Matanuska Valley Colony. Two hundred farm families from the American Midwest arrived in the area that year and were given 40-acre tracts of land in the hopes of establishing a permanent agricultural colony that would help in the development of Alaska. Although the colony ultimately proved unsuccessful, descendents of the original colonists continue to live in the area today and many of the original buildings they constructed are listed on the National Register of Historic Places. Nowadays, Palmer is home to the Alaska State Fair, a 12-day event that begins in late August and runs through Labor Day. The Palmer area also offers a broad array of activities year round, ranging from fishing, hiking, and berry picking during the summer to ice-fishing, cross-country skiing, and dog sled racing during the winter.

What to See and Do

Colony House Museum. *316 E Elmwood Ave, Palmer (99645). Phone 907/745-1935.* Housed in a farmhouse constructed as part of the Matanuska Colony during the 1930s, this small historical museum brings to life the story of the Depression-era agricultural experiment that led to the development of modern Palmer. Run by the Palmer Historical Society, the museum offers free guided tours, some led by descendents of the original colonists. (May-Aug: Tues-Sat 10 am-4 pm; closed in winter) **DONATION**

Independence Mine State Historic Park. *On Hatcher Pass Rd between Palmer and Willow. Phone 907/269-8400. www.dnr.state.ak.us/parks/units/indmine.htm.* Located in Hatcher Pass in the heart of the Talkeetna Mountains, Independence Mine is a representative of

Alaska's hard rock gold mining past. As many as 200 miners worked the mine during the 1920s and 1930s until its closure as a result of World War II. Facilities include a museum, hiking trails, and recreation gold panning. It has been proposed that the old tunnels be retrofitted to allow mine tours in the future.

Special Event

Alaska State Fair. *Alaska State Showgrounds, 2075 Glenn Hwy, Palmer (99645). Phone 907/745-4827; toll-free 800/850-FAIR. www.alaskastatefair.org.* This annual state fair is one of the highlights of Alaska's summer season, with 12 days of live entertainment, carnival rides, rodeo events, and exhibitors displaying everything from handcrafted jewelry and local artwork to homemade quilts, cakes, pies, jams, and jellies. One of the most popular highlights of the fair is the agricultural weigh-off, where locally grown cabbages frequently top 100 pounds and carrots have been known to tip the scales at more than 70 pounds. Located less than 45 miles from downtown Anchorage, the fair makes for an easy day trip for visitors to the Anchorage area. Late Aug-early Sept. **$$**

Limited-Service Hotels

★ ★ **COLONY INN.** *325 E Elmwood, Palmer (99645). Phone 907/745-3330; fax 907/746-3330.* This quaint little inn, with only 12 rooms, was built in 1935 as a teacher's dormitory for the Matanuska Colony. Easily accessible from the Glenn Highway, it's located in the middle of downtown Palmer, next to the visitor information center and within sight of most of Palmer's main shops. The lobby features a stately fireplace, period smoking chairs, and tasteful antique furniture and memorabilia, while the former dorm rooms have been transformed into ultra-cozy guest rooms filled with furniture harkening back to the 1930s. For those looking for something elegantly different, it's well worth a visit. Guests register and pick up keys at the Valley Hotel nearby. 12 rooms. Check-out 11 am. Restaurant. **$**

★ ★ **GOLD MINER'S HOTEL.** *918 S Colony Way, Palmer (99645). Phone 907/745-6160; toll-free 800/725-2752; fax 907/745-6173. www.goldminershotel.com.* This hotel began as the town's theater and has been extensively remodeled on numerous occasions since then, which accounts for the unusual floor plan. Overlooking the park area of town, it offers enormous rooms, a convenient mid-town location, and inexpensive rates as well as some magnificent views of Pioneer Peak, Sleeping Lady, and the towering Chugach Range. Seven of the rooms have access to the large rooftop deck, which brings many guests back to the Gold Miner's Hotel year after year. 28 rooms. Pets accepted. Check-in 2 pm, check-out noon. Restaurant. **$**

★ ★ **VALLEY HOTEL.** *606 S Alaska St, Palmer (99645). Phone 907/745-3330; fax 907/746-3330.* One of the most striking new features of this 1948 hotel is the extensive woodwork featured throughout; guest-room headboards, bedside tables, window valances, and hallway moldings and partitions have all been carefully handcrafted by one of the current owners. The result is striking, adding warmth, artistry, and a personal touch to each of the cozy rooms. 43 rooms. Check-out 11 am. Restaurant. **$**

Restaurants

★ ★ **GOLD MINER'S STEAKHOUSE & RESTAURANT.** *918 S Colony Way, Palmer (99645). Phone 907/745-6160; toll-free 800/725-2752; fax 907/745-6173. www.goldminershotel.com.* Combining local history and Alaskan artistry, the owners of this downtown restaurant have incorporated mining memorabilia and a gigantic nature mural into their spacious, rustic dining area. With a relaxed staff, all-day breakfast, and daily all-you-can-eat specials, it's an enticing place to stop for a meal. American menu. Breakfast, lunch, dinner. Closed Thanksgiving, Dec 25. Bar. Children's menu. Casual attire. **$$**

★ ★ **INN CAFÉ.** *325 E Elmwood, Palmer (99645). Phone 907/746-6118.* Located in one of Palmer's oldest buildings, Inn Cafe offers casual dining in a visually and historically appealing setting, with hardwood floors and walls, an understated but elegant lobby, and beautiful six-pane windows that let in plenty of light and provide stunning views of the Chugach and Talkeetna mountain ranges that surround. American menu. Lunch, dinner. Closed Mon; Jan 1, Thanksgiving, Dec 25. Casual attire. **$$**

★ ★ **OPEN CAFE.** *606 S Alaska St, Palmer (99645). Phone 907/745-3330; fax 907/746-3330.* This restaurant is notable for two reasons: it's open 24 hours a day, every day of the year and it offers fresh baked pastries and more than 25 kinds of pie prepared on site by a local pastry chef. With an open-seating plan, lots of windows, and an extensive menu, it's bright, sunny, and family-friendly. American menu. Breakfast, lunch, dinner, late-night. Bar. Children's menu. Casual attire. **$$**

Petersburg (E-8)

Founded 1910
Population 3,224
Area Code 907
Web site www.petersburg.org

Petersburg is both geographically and culturally far removed from the rest of the towns and villages that dot the Inside Passage. In a region with centuries-old ties to Russian and native cultures, this remote fishing port at the northern tip of Mitkof Island proudly celebrates its rich Norwegian heritage. Founded at the end of the 19th century by Norwegian businessman Peter Buschmann, Petersburg soon attracted other Norwegian immigrants who felt at home amid the snowy mountains and deep fjords of the area. Set in the heart of the Tongass National Forest, Mitkof Island features a landscape dominated not by shady forests and craggy peaks but by muskeg bogs, dense brush, and rolling hills. The best time to visit is around May 17, when the town holds its annual "Little Norway Festival" to coincide with Norway's Constitution Day. Visitors can enjoy traditional Norwegian music, dancing, and food, view the works of local artists, and even get their pictures taken with "real" Vikings and Valkyries.

Limited-Service Hotels

★ ★ **SCANDIA HOUSE.** *110 N Nordic Dr, Petersburg (99833). Phone 907/772-4281; toll-free 800/ 722-5006; fax 907/772-4301. www.scandiahousehotel .com.* This hotel offers spacious, bright, and affordable rooms, some of which have terrific views of the water and the mountains around Petersburg. It also provides guests with a large, comfortable lobby along with a wide range of travelers' amenities including wireless Internet access, on-site car and boat rentals, a fish and game freezer, and a hair styling salon. 33 rooms. Pets accepted. Complimentary continental breakfast. Check-in 2 pm, check-out 11 am. Restaurant. Airport transportation available. **$**

★ **TIDES INN.** *307 N 1st St, Petersburg (99833). Phone 907/772-4288; toll-free 800/665-8433; fax 907/ 772-4286. www.tidesinnalaska.com.* Located in the heart of downtown, this motel is convenient to all local attractions and provides its guests with an on-site car rental desk and free email access in the lobby. Some rooms have terrific water and mountain views and all are clean, quiet, and reasonably priced, making it a relaxing and affordable home away from home for guests. 47 rooms. Complimentary continental breakfast. Check-in 1 pm, check-out 11 am. Airport transportation available. **$**

Restaurant

★ **ROONEY'S NORTHERN LIGHTS RESTAURANT.** *203 Sing Lee Alley, Petersburg (99833). Phone 907/772-2900; fax 907/772-2901.* Located on pilings above Hammer Slough overlooking Middle Harbor, this restaurant offers a fairly extensive menu and a line of desserts that are so popular, locals have been known to call ahead and reserve them. Regardless of the weather, the views are terrific, giving guests a chance to watch the local fishermen and tides flow in and out of the harbor. Fusion menu. Breakfast, lunch, dinner. Closed Thanksgiving, Dec 24-25. Children's menu. Casual attire. Outdoor seating. **$$**

Seldovia

Population 286
Area Code 907

Restaurant

★ ★ **THE MAD FISH.** *221 Main St, Seldovia (99663). Phone 907/234-7676. www.madfishalaska .com.* Seafood, steak menu. Lunch, dinner. Closed Mon; also winter. Bar. Children's menu. Casual attire. Reservations recommended. Outdoor seating. **$$**

Seward (D-5)

Population 2,830
Area Code 907
Information Seward Chamber of Commerce, PO Box 749, 99664; phone 907/224-8051
Web site www.sewardak.org

This town of 3,000 people on the shores of Resurrection Bay is named after William H. Seward, the US Secretary of State who was responsible for negotiating the purchase of Alaska from Russia in 1867. The town sits on the eastern side of the Kenai

Peninsula, 127 miles from Anchorage via the Seward Highway. Founded in 1903 as an ocean terminus for the Alaska Railroad, the town's economy originally relied almost exclusively on the fishing and railroad industries. With the opening of the Seward and Sterling Highways on the Kenai Peninsula after World War II, Seward's economy gradually shifted, making tourism and fishing the leading industries today. Throughout the summer, the town vibrates with life as thousands of visitors arrive each day by road, sea, and rail to explore the area. From the bustling small boat harbor, visitors can join halibut and salmon fishing charters, take tour boats to view the abundant wildlife and magnificent tidewater glaciers of Kenai Fjords National Park, or rent kayaks and paddle the shores of Resurrection Bay. After a day on the water, visitors leaving the harbor can either head directly downtown via 4th Avenue or opt to walk part of the Iditarod National Historic Trail that parallels the shoreline all the way to one of Seward's newest and most impressive attractions, the Alaska SeaLife Center. Opened in 1998, it's a combination marine research station, wildlife rehabilitation center, and hands-on interpretive venue. The highlight of the summer is the town's 4th of July celebration, the largest in Alaska. A multi-day event, it's capped off by the Mount Marathon run, a grueling 3 mile out-and-back course in which runners run through the downtown area, claw their way to the top of 3,022-foot-high Mount Marathon, and then turn around and come pounding back down the scree-filled hillside, ending up in the center of town to the cheers of thousands of spectators lining the streets. For athletes and spectators alike, it's a breathtaking event.

What to See and Do

Alaska SeaLife Center. *301 Railway Ave, Seward (99664). Phone 907/224-6300; toll-free 800/224-2525. www.alaskasealife.org.* The Alaska SeaLife Center offers an unrivaled up-close-and-personal experience with Gulf of Alaska marine wildlife. Witness 1,500-pound Stellar sea lions gliding past underwater viewing windows, puffins diving in a carefully crafted naturalistic habitat, and harbor seals hauled out on rocky beaches. Alaskan king crab, sea stars, and Pacific octopus also await you, as well as a variety of intertidal creatures and deep-sea fishes. (Daily; closed Thanksgiving, Dec 25) **$$$**

Benny Benson Memorial Park. *Seward Hwy, mile 1.4, Seward (99664).* This newly renovated roadside park is dedicated to Benny Benson, Seward's most famous

citizen. In 1927, 13-year-old Benson, an orphan living at Seward's Jesse Lee Home, entered and won a competition sponsored by the Alaska Department of the American Legion to design Alaska's territorial flag. In his contest application, Benson described what the flag symbolized: "The blue field is for the Alaska sky and the forget-me-not, an Alaska flower. The North Star is for the future state of Alaska, the most northerly of the union. The dipper is for the Great Bear symbolizing strength." The park is located beside the lagoon at the entrance to town, across the street from the small boat harbor.

Seward Museum. *336 Third Ave, Seward (99664). Phone 907/224-3902.* Operated by the Resurrection Bay Historical Society, the Seward Museum aims to tell the story of Seward's history, from its founding as a railway terminus at the beginning of the 20th century to its role as a strategic port during World War II to its current incarnation as one of the most popular destinations on the Kenai Peninsula. Highlights of the museum include the earthquake exhibits detailing the local devastation caused by the Good Friday Earthquake that rocked Alaska in 1964 and the Iditarod room, which details Seward's role in the development of the Iditarod trail and honors hometown hero Mitch Seavey, winner of the 2004 Iditarod Trail Sled Dog Race. (May-Sept: daily 9 am-5 pm; Oct-Apr, days and hours vary, call for information) **$**

Special Event

Fourth of July Festival and Mount Marathon Race. *Phone 907/224-8051.* Considered by many to be the best Independence Day festival in Alaska. Thousands of people flood into town for parades, food booths, music, and craft fairs. The festival is capped off by the Mount Marathon Race, one of the oldest and toughest footraces in America (a 3.25-mile run from just above sea level to the top of Mount Marathon—3,020 feet—and crashing back down again). Early July.

Polar Bear Jump-Off Festival. *Citywide. Phone 907/224-5688.* Costumed jumpers take the plunge into icy Resurrection Bay in an effort to raise money for the American Cancer Society. Parade, ice bowling, oyster slurping, dogsled race, salmon toss, basketball tournament, and more. Third weekend in Jan.

Limited-Service Hotels

★ ★ **BREEZE INN MOTEL.** *1306 Seward Hwy, Seward (99664). Phone 907/224-5237; toll-free*

888/224-5237; fax 907/224-7024. www.breezeinn.com. Located at Seward's small boat harbor near the train depot, this hotel's convenient location and wide range of room types and prices makes it a popular place for tourists arriving by train or cruise ship and for those going on fishing charters and sightseeing cruises. A well-rounded facility, it has its own gift shops, restaurant, lounge, and espresso shop. 86 rooms. Pets accepted. Check-in 3 pm, check-out 11 am. Restaurant, bar. **$**

★ **HARBORVIEW INN.** 804 Third Ave, Seward (99664). Phone 907/224-3217; toll-free 888/324-3218; fax 907/224-3218. www.sewardhotel.com. This motel is in an excellent location for people going on day trips out of Seward's small boat harbor as well as landlubbers staying in town to go sightseeing and shopping. Guestrooms are relaxing and inviting, with sturdy wooden furniture; colorful bedding and window treatments; and a subtle Alaskan outdoors motif that really adds to the appeal of the place. 37 rooms. Closed Thanksgiving weekend; also late Dec-early Jan. Check-in 3 pm, check-out 11 am. **$**

★ ★ **HOTEL EDGEWATER AND CONFERENCE CENTER.** 202 Fifth Ave, Seward (99664). Phone 907/224-2700; toll-free 888/793-6800; fax 907/224-2701. www.hoteledgewater.com. Built in 1999, this waterfront hotel—the largest and most popular in downtown Seward—is filled with comfortably appointed rooms, some with fantastic views of Resurrection Bay and the southern Chugach Mountains. Architecturally modern from the outside, the hotel's incorporation of simple wood railings, earth tones, and a dramatic three-story central atrium into the interior design evokes romantic images of the frontier hotels of the Wild West. Free shuttle service is available to the Seward small-boat harbor, where glacier cruises and fishing charters depart throughout the day during the summer. 76 rooms. Complimentary continental breakfast. Check-in 2 pm, check-out 11 am. Whirlpool. **$$**

★ **HOTEL SEWARD.** 221 5th Ave, Seward (99664). Phone 907/224-2378; toll-free 800/478-4050; fax 907/224-3112. www.hotelsewardalaska.com. This downtown hotel is physically connected to the much older New Seward Hotel, but charges different rates and offers a more upscale level of accommodation. Bonus features of staying here include in-room VCRs with complimentary videos available at the front desk

and a concierge in the lobby who will make tour and restaurant reservations for guests. 38 rooms. Check-in 3 pm, check-out noon. **$$**

★ **MARINA MOTEL.** Seward Hwy, mile 1, Seward (99664). Phone 907/224-5518; fax 907/224-5553. www.sewardmotel.com. This motel is not the flashiest place in town, but its clean, tidy, sunny rooms reflect the pride the owners take in maintaining and updating the property. Located at Mile 1 of the Seward Highway, it's the closest accommodation to the railroad depot and a short walk to the small boat harbor, making it an excellent bargain in a good location. 18 rooms. Check-in 2 pm, check-out 11 am. **$**

★ **THE VAN GILDER HOTEL.** 308 Adams St, Seward (99664). Phone 907/224-3079; toll-free 800/204-6835; fax 907/224-3689. www.vangilderhotel.com. Built in 1916, this charming 24-room hotel was placed on the National Register of Historical Places in 1980 and is gradually being restored to its former glory. Whenever guests are not in their cozy, tastefully decorated rooms, they are free to relax in the ornate lobby filled with antiques, stained-lass windows, and a magnificent wooden bar from England. Although many of the rooms are small and lack the array of amenities found in more contemporary hotels, the Van Gilder is a popular stopover for independent travelers looking for a unique and memorable lodging. 24 rooms. Check-in 4 pm, check-out noon. **$**

Restaurants

★ ★ **BREEZE INN RESTAURANT.** 1306 Seward Hwy, Seward (99664). Phone 907/224-5237; toll-free 888/224-5237; fax 907/224-7024. www.breezeinn.com. This harborside restaurant is a popular casual dining spot for tourists during the summer and locals throughout the year. Offering standard American and seafood dishes, one of the most popular menu selections is "halibut chunks" made from halibut caught in local waters. In keeping with the restaurant's hometown flair, the walls are lined with photographs and paintings done by local artists. American menu. Breakfast, lunch, dinner. Bar. Children's menu. Casual attire. **$$**

★ **CHRISTO'S PALACE.** 133 Fourth Ave, Seward (99664). Phone 907/224-5255. This chic downtown restaurant serves an eclectic mix of American and international foods in a dining room filled with dark polished woods, soft lights, exposed beams, and dark carpets. The highlight of the dining area, though, is the enormous 150-year-old polished wood back bar that gives the room a sleek and stylish ambience. Diner. Lunch, dinner. Closed Thanksgiving, Dec 25. Bar. Children's menu. Casual attire. **$$**

★ ★ **HARBOR DINNER CLUB.** *220 5th Ave, Seward (99664). Phone 907/224-3012.* This family-run restaurant has been in business since 1958, serving steaks and fresh local seafood such as Alaskan halibut and Kachemak Bay steamer clams to generations of locals and a long line of daytripping tourists. Its casual atmosphere and large outdoor patio make it a popular destination for those seeking good food in a friendly setting. Seafood, steak menu. Lunch, dinner. Closed holidays. Bar. Children's menu. Casual attire. Outdoor seating. **$$$**

★ ★ **LEGENDS RESTAURANT & PUB.** *412 Washington St, Seward (99664). Phone 907/224-3161; fax 907/224-3912.* The menu for this downtown restaurant features an eclectic mix of seafood, steak, Mexican, and American dishes, but it's the amazing views that are the real drawing card. From the dining room, guests have sweeping views of Resurrection Bay and the southern Chugach mountains and from the pub, unobstructed views of Mount Marathon, site of the grueling footrace that is the highlight of the town's Fourth of July celebration. American menu. Breakfast, lunch, dinner. Closed Jan 1, Dec 25. Bar. Children's menu. Casual attire. **$$**

★ **RAY'S WATERFRONT.** *1316 4th Ave, Seward (99664). Phone 907/224-3861.* Seafood menu. Lunch, dinner. Closed in winter. Bar. Casual attire. Outdoor seating. **$**

★ **RESURRECTION ROADHOUSE.** *Herman Leirer Rd, mile 66, Seward (99664). Phone 907/224-7116. www.sewardwindsong.com.* Seafood, steak menu. Lunch, dinner. Closed in winter. Bar. Business casual attire. Outdoor seating. **$$**

Sitka (E-8)

Population 8,835
Area Code 907
Information Sitka Convention and Visitors Bureau, PO Box 1226, 99835; phone 907/747-5940
Web site www.sitka.org

One of the oldest Western settlements in Alaska, Sitka was established at the beginning of the 19th century as a fur trading outpost and fort by the Russian American Company under the leadership of Alexander Baranov. Originally called New Archangel, it served as the capital of Russian Alaska until 1867, when a waning fur trade and domestic economic upheaval led the Russian government to sell its stake in the New World. The transfer of ownership of Alaska from Russian to the United States took place on Castle Hill and a series of plaques on the site now provide visitors with a detailed account of that event. Modern Sitka retains strong ties to its past, as evidenced by the Russian architecture of Saint Michael's Cathedral in the middle of downtown—a replica of the original that burned to the ground in 1966, the restored Russian Bishop's house across from Crescent harbor, and Russian Cemetery at the end of Observatory Street. Evidence of the older, Tlingit civilization in the area can be found on the east end of town at the Sheldon Jackson Museum, which contains a stunning display of native arts and crafts. Further down the road is Sitka National Historic Park, which features a collection of 15 totem poles set along a meandering forest trail. Pamphlets available in the park's visitor center provide detailed explanations of each of the totems, so it's best to stop off there first. The center also houses an extensive native history museum, a collection of delicate wood carvings that could not survive outdoors in Sitka's rainy climate, and a woodworking shop where native Alaskan crafts are fashioned and art classes taught.

What to See and Do

Castle Hill. *Located in downtown Sitka, next to O'Connell Bridge. Parking lot and pathway are located beside the bridge. An additional pathway begins on the Lincoln Street side of the hill.* Officially known as Baranov Castle Hill State Historic Site, this small hill in the middle of Sitka marks the site where Russia formally transferred ownership of Alaska to the United States in October 1867. Easily accessible via wheelchair ramps and stairs, the summit plaza contains numerous interpretive displays recounting the history of Sitka and the role the Castle Hill area played in so many of the town's major developments. The site also offers exceptional views of downtown Sitka and the waterfront area.

Sheldon Jackson Museum. *104 College Dr, Sitka (99835). Phone 907/747-8981. www.museums.state*

.ak.us. This small, oddly shaped museum on the Sheldon Jackson College campus near downtown Sitka houses what is generally regarded as one of the best collections of Native arts and crafts in the state. It is also Alaska's oldest museum, founded in 1887 by Reverend Sheldon Jackson, who sought to create a museum in Alaska that would preserve and exhibit the cultural and artistic history of Native Alaskan cultures. Highlights of the collection include Eskimo masks, Tlingit and Haida headdresses, and a full-sized Aleut baidarka, a specialized form of sea kayak. (Mid-May-mid-Sept: daily 9 am-5 pm; mid-Sept-mid-May: Tues-Sat 10 am to 4 pm) **$**

Sitka National Historical Park. *103 Monastery St, Sitka (99835). Phone 907/747-0110. www.nps.gov/sitk.* Sitka National Historical Park is one of Alaska's smallest but most popular national parks, with nearly 300,000 annual visitors making the trip to the 113-acre park. Located in a temperate rain forest at the mouth of the Indian River on Baranof Island, the park marks the site of the 1804 Battle of Sitka, a fight that pitted the native Tlingit Indians against the Russians. Led by Alexander Baranof, the Russians won the battle, but only after the natives exhausted their supply of gunpowder. The outlines of Tlingit Fort can be seen at the park. Another popular attraction is the Russian Bishop's House, constructed in 1843, a time when the Tsar ruled Alaska. The log structure survives as one of four remaining examples of Russian-period architecture in North America. The park also features a remarkable collection of original and replica totem poles from villages throughout southeastern Alaska. Bold in color and design, the totem poles are exhibited along a scenic coastal trail. The park's visitor center offers interpretive talks, exhibits, and slide programs. Alaska's oldest federally designated park, Sitka National Historical Park is a short drive from downtown Sitka. The Alaska Marine Highway serves Sitka, and the town is a ten-hour ferry ride from Juneau to the north. **$**

Tongass National Forest. *204 Siginaka Way, Sitka (99835). Phone 907/747-6671. www.fs.fed/us/r10/ tongass.* Tongass National Forest, the largest national forest in the US, is the definition of "wilderness"; in fact, one-third of the Tongass (5.7 million acres) is managed as wilderness so that Alaska retains its undeveloped character. Hardy visitors can expect to see eagles, bears, deer, and a variety of other animals, birds, and fish in this vast national forest. Hunting, fishing, cabins (fee).

Limited-Service Hotels

★ ★ **SITKA HOTEL.** *118 Lincoln St, Sitka (99835). Phone 907/747-3288; fax 907/747-8499. www.sitkahotel .com.* Built in 1939 and listed on the National Register of Historic Places, this hotel's Victorian architecture has recently been beautifully restored and preserved, resulting in an atmosphere of graceful elegance and old-time charm. The pressed tin ceilings, real and reproduction Victorian furniture, and period architecture of the lobby and hallways are reminiscent of a time when vacation travel was a slower, more genteel pursuit. The hotel sits on the main commercial road through Sitka's small downtown area, close to the main tourist attractions and within easy walking distance of Sitka's three harbors. 63 rooms. Check-in 2 pm, check-out 11 am. Restaurant. **$**

★ ★ **WESTMARK SHEE ATIKA.** *330 Seward St, Sitka (99835). Phone 907/747-6241; toll-free 800/ 544-0970; fax 907/747-5486. www.westmarkhotels.com.* From the sleek, native-themed lobby and elegant on-site restaurant on the ground floor to the crisp, comfortable rooms on the upper floors, the focus at this hotel is on providing guests with much more than just a place to sleep. Given this emphasis, it's not surprising to find that the hotel recommends making summertime reservations up to a year in advance. Occupying a prominent position on Seward Street in the middle of downtown, the Westmark Shee Atika, owned by the Carnival Cruise Line corporation, is the largest hotel in town. 101 rooms. Check-in 3 pm, check-out 11 am. Restaurant, bar. **$$**

★ **WESTMARK TOTEM SQUARE INN.** *201 Katlian, Sitka (99835). Phone 907/747-6302; toll-free 800/544-0970; fax 907/747-6307.* 59 rooms. Closed Oct-Apr. Check-in 3 pm, check-out noon. **$**

Restaurants

★ **BAYVIEW RESTAURANT.** *407 Lincoln St, Sitka (99835). Phone 907/747-5440.* This charming little restaurant is located on the second floor of a small shopping arcade across the street from Crescent Harbor in downtown Sitka. Popular with tourists and locals alike, guests can choose from a broad menu of traditional American and seafood dishes while enjoying spectacular views of the waters and islands of Sitka Sound. American menu. Breakfast, lunch, dinner. Children's menu. Casual attire. **$$**

★ ★ **THE CHANNEL CLUB.** *2906 Halibut Point Rd, Sitka (99835). Phone 907/747-9916.* American menu. Lunch, dinner. Closed the first three weeks of Jan. Bar. Children's menu. Casual attire. Reservations recommended. **$$**

★ ★ **RAVEN DINING ROOM & KADATAAN LOUNGE.** *330 Seward St, Sitka (99835). Phone 907/747-6241; fax 907/747-5486. www.westmarkhotels.com.* This upscale restaurant has a menu diverse enough to suit most tastes but specializes in fresh local seafood, including the perennial favorite, Halibut Olympia. The layout and décor of the restaurant are very appealing, with large windows providing excellent views of Crescent Harbor and upscale furniture and appointments adding a sense of sleek elegance to the room. Seafood menu. Breakfast, lunch, dinner. Closed Dec 25. Bar. Casual attire. **$$$**

★ ★ **VICTORIA'S.** *118 Lincoln St, Sitka (99835). Phone 907/747-3288; fax 907/747-8499. www.sitkahotel.com/food.htm.* The front windows of this small, quaint restaurant located in the Sitka Hotel look out on the Pioneer Building and Totem Square, both popular destinations for daytrippers. Filled with lace curtains, pressed tin ceilings, antique pictures, and bathed in sunlight, it's the kind of place one can imagine going for breakfast and staying through lunch. American, seafood menu. Breakfast, lunch, dinner. Bar. Casual attire. **$$**

Skagway (D-8)

Population 862
Area Code 907
Information Skagway Convention & Visitors Bureau, PO Box 1029, 99840; phone 907/983-2854
Web site www.skagway.org

Skagway is located at the northernmost point of the Inside Passage near the Canadian border and derives its name from the Tlingit word "skaqua"—windy place. It was a hunting and fishing camp for local Indian tribes for centuries until the discovery of gold 600 miles north at Bonanza Creek in 1896. By 1898, the town had grown to nearly 10,000 people and had become an important staging area for gold prospectors preparing to make the arduous trek through White Pass north of town to seek their fortunes in the Klondike. The nearby settlement of Dyea offered a different route, through Chilkoot Pass,

but both routes merged at Bennett Lake just inside the Canadian border and formed a single route, now referred to as the Trail of '98. Skagway's fortunes declined with the end of the gold rush, but its downtown area still retains its late 1890s charm, with wooden sidewalks, false-fronted wooden buildings, and the restored turn-of-the-century White Pass & Yukon Railroad passenger depot and steam engine. Much of downtown Skagway is now part of Klondike Gold Rush National Historic Park and well-prepared adventurers can once again hike the 33-mile Chilkoot Trail, beginning at the long-abandoned Dyea townsite.

What to See and Do

Klondike Gold Rush National Historical Park. *Second Ave and Broadway St, Skagway (99840). Phone 907/983-2921. www.nps.gov/klgo.* It may be hard to believe, but in 1897, Skagway, a one-building town situated along a narrow inlet in southeastern Alaska, suddenly became the most prosperous city in the Pacific Northwest. In the summer of that year, news spread around the world of a gold strike in the Klondike region of the Yukon Territory. Almost overnight, thousands of stampeders descended on the newly created town of Skagway. The town served as a base during the Klondike Gold Rush, a place to gather supplies and prepare for the arduous 500-mile trek to the gold fields in Canada, where those entering the country were required to be equipped with a year's worth of food. The trip began with a steep climb over Chilkoot Pass, following an aboriginal trail created by Alaska natives many years before the gold rush.

Today, the 33-mile-long Chilkoot Trail is administered by the park, and it makes for a challenging but rewarding three- to five-day hike. Most stampeders abandoned Skagway, along with dreams of instant riches, in 1898. The town now has a year-round population of only 800, although the historical park receives around 750,000 annual visits. From the gold-rush era, approximately 100 buildings remain, 15 of which have been restored by the National Park Service. Nestled within the Taiya Inlet and surrounded by snow-capped mountains, the park offers guided tours of the Skagway Historic District, along with exhibits, ranger presentations, and films. Many visitors arrive in Skagway by boat, as the town is served by the Alaska Marine Highway. **FREE**

Skagway Museum. *City Hall/McCabe Building, 700 Spring St, Skagway (99804). Phone 907/983-2420.*

www.skagwaymuseum.org. Located inside Skagway's historic City Hall, the Skagway Museum is filled with artifacts, photographs, and personal accounts that tell of life in Skagway before and after the Klondike Gold Rush of 1898. A Tlingit canoe and a Bering Sea kayak are just some of the exhibits that paint a picture of the Tlingit culture that once thrived in the area. Displays of gold rush relics, tools, and supplies tell another tale, that of the tens of thousands of gold prospectors who flooded into the region at the end of the 19th century to seek their fortunes in the Klondike. The museum is a few blocks north of most of Skagway's other attractions but is one of the most comprehensive and engaging museums in town. (May-Sept: Mon-Fri 9 am-5 pm, Sat-Sun 1-4 pm; Oct-Apr: hours vary—call for times) **$**

Tours. *Phone toll-free 800/544-2206. www. graylineofalaska.com.* Gray Line of Alaska offers package tours around Alaska (up to 11 days) as well as a historic tour of the city and a combination flightseeing/dogsledding tour.

White Pass & Yukon Route. *White Pass & Yukon Route Depot, Second Ave at Spring St, Skagway (99840). Phone 907/983-2217; toll-free 800/343-7373. www. whitepassrailroad.com.* Built in only 20 months during the Klondike Gold Rush, the White Pass & Yukon Route connecting Skagway with Whitehorse, Yukon Territory remains one of the most spectacular railways in the world and has been designated an International Historic Civil Engineering Landmark. Modern travelers on this rail line can choose from four different excursions, depending on how much time they have. The White Pass Summit Excursion is a three-hour, 40-mile round-trip that climbs 2,865 feet from Skagway to the summit at White Pass. Covering many of the railway's most scenic sections, this tour is the least expensive from Skagway and the most popular. The Lake Bennett Excursion takes 8 1/2 hours and travels an additional 20 miles on the line to Canada's Lake Bennett, where the Chilkoot Trail comes to an end. The railway also offers a Chilkoot Trail Hikers Service for people interested in hiking up the 33-mile historic Chilkoot Trail and then hopping aboard the train as it heads back to Skagway. Another option is the combination bus and train service that transports travelers from Skagway to Whitehorse. Prices and departure times vary, and reservations are required for all excursions.

Special Event

Buckwheat Ski Classic. *Phone 907/983-2544.* Amateurs and professionals alike compete in this cross-country ski race along White Pass Mountain. Late Mar.

Limited-Service Hotels

★ **SGT. PRESTON'S LODGE.** *370 Sixth Ave, Skagway (99840). Phone 907/983-2521; fax 907/983-3500.* Set in the middle of downtown Skagway, this motel has 30 rooms ranging from tiny and very cheap to large and reasonably priced. There's a central courtyard with a BBQ, picnic table, and ice machine for warm weather gatherings and a snug lobby with big couches and residential-style armchairs for wintertime socializing. 30 rooms. Pets accepted. Check-in 2 pm, check-out 11 am. **$**

★ ★ **WESTMARK SKAGWAY.** *3rd and Spring sts, Skagway (99840). Phone toll-free 800/544-0970. www.westmarkhotels.com.* 151 rooms. Closed Oct-Apr. Check-in 3 pm, check-out noon. Restaurant, two bars. **$**

Restaurants

★ ★ **BONANZA BAR & GRILL.** *3rd and Broadway, Skagway (99840). Phone 907/983-6214.* American menu. Lunch, dinner. Closed Nov-Apr. Bar. Children's menu. Casual attire. Outdoor seating. **$**

★ **HAVEN CAFÉ.** *9th Ave and State St, Skagway (99840). Phone 907/983-3553; fax 907/983-3554.* This funky little place focuses on "espresso and light fare," but in a town as small as Skagway, it's a heavy hitter. Owner Susan Jabal has created a very hip, fresh cafe with a real bistro atmosphere. Serving all meals during the summer, its real focus is on its ever-changing, eclectic selection of panini sandwiches, green salads, and fresh-baked pastries. Deli menu. Breakfast, lunch, dinner. Closed Jan 1, Thanksgiving, Dec 25. Casual attire. Outdoor seating. **$**

Soldotna (D-5)

Population 3,759
Web site www.soldotnachamber.com

Soldotna exists due to the confluence of two events in 1947: the granting of homesteading rights on the Kenai Peninsula to veterans of World War II and the selection of the Soldotna area as the site for a highway bridge across the Kenai River. When the Sterling Highway was completed soon after, Soldotna was suddenly connected to the Alaskan road system and rapidly became a major stopping point for travelers and outdoor enthusiasts on the Kenai Peninsula. Nowadays, Soldotna's enormous popularity stems mainly from it's greatest natural asset, the Kenai River, from whose waters the current world record king salmon, weighing in at 97.2 lbs, was pulled in 1985. Other highlights of Soldotna are its two campgrounds, nine parks, and network of trails and walks that provide visitors with plenty of opportunities to enjoy the natural beauty of the area. During the summer, it's possible to go hiking, canoeing, biking, wildlife viewing, and berry picking without straying far from town. During winter, snow machining and cross-country skiing keep locals and off-season visitors active.

What to See and Do

Clam Gulch State Recreation Area. *11 miles SE on Kenai Spur Hwy. Phone 907/262-5581. www.dnr.state.ak .us/parks/units/clamglch.htm.* This area is famous for the hundreds of thousands of razor clams harvested annually from the sandy beaches adjacent to the State Recreation Area. Visitors may dig clams during any low tide, although an Alaskan sportfishing license is required. If you decide to dig, be careful; they are named "razor clams" for good reason! Clam Gulch is located on steep bluffs overlooking Cook Inlet, with sweeping views of the Aleutian Mountains and their three tallest peaks: Mount Iliamna, Mount Redoubt, and Mount Spurr. The park offers tent camping and picnic areas. **$**

Limited-Service Hotels

★ **ASPEN HOTEL SOLDOTNA.** *326 Binkley Cir, Soldotna (99669). Phone 907/260-7736; toll-free 888/ 308-7848; fax 907/260-7786. www.aspenhotelsak.com.* The Kenai River flows at the back of this midtown property, providing fishermen and outdoor enthusiasts with easy access to one of Soldotna's greatest assets. Tourist-friendly features such as an indoor pool, deluxe continental breakfast, in-room kitchens, and free Internet access make it an especially appealing place to stay when visiting the Kenai Peninsula. 63 rooms. Complimentary continental breakfast. Check-in 3 pm, check-out 11 am. Fitness room. Indoor pool, whirlpool. **$**

[image: icons]

★ ★ **BEST WESTERN KING SALMON MOTEL.** *35546A Kenai Spur Hwy, Soldotna (99669). Phone 907/262-5857; toll-free 888/262-5857; fax 907/ 262-9441. www.bestwestern.com.* The main appeal of this modest brand name motel is its convenient location. It's in the heart of the Kenai Peninsula and close to the world-class fishing of the Kenai River, so it tends to attract a steady stream of tourists, fishermen, and outdoor enthusiasts in the summer and an eclectic mix of off-season travelers and hunters in the winter. 49 rooms. Check-in 3 pm, check-out noon. Restaurant. **$$**

★ **KENAI RIVER LODGE.** *393 Riverside Dr, Soldotna (99669). Phone 907/262-4292; fax 907/262- 7332. www.kenairiverlodge.com.* This family-run motel on the Kenai River has been drawing a devoted repeat clientele since its opening in 1969. In an area where "combat fishing" is often the norm, the motel's ability to offer its guests exclusive access to nearly 100 yards of riverbank is a huge draw. Other benefits include BBQ pits and picnic areas, fish cleaning facilities, boat moorage, and river views from all rooms. 25 rooms. Complimentary continental breakfast. Check-in 3 pm, check-out noon. **$**

★ ★ **SOLDOTNA INN.** *35041 Kenai Spur Hwy, Soldotna (99669). Phone 907/262-9169; toll-free 866/ 262-9169; fax 907/262-1099. www.thesoldotnainn.com.* This combination hotel and motel has 18 rooms and ten deluxe suites available for rent by the day, week, or month. All of the rooms are in very good condition and are being steadily upgraded by the new owners. Its excellent downtown location near world-class fishing and outdoor recreation sites and its reasonable rates make it an excellent home base for active tourists. 28 rooms. Pets accepted. Complimentary continental breakfast. Check-in 3 pm, check-out 11 am. Restaurant. Fitness room. **$**

[image: icons]

Restaurant

★ ★ **MYKEL'S RESTAURANT & LOUNGE.** *35041 Kenai Spur Hwy, Soldotna (99669). Phone 907/ 262-4305; fax 907/262-4353. www.mykels.com.* Mykel's bills itself as the finest dining on the Kenai Peninsula and features fresh Alaskan seafood and "choice meats" as part of its imaginative menu. In all, it's the kind of place one would go to celebrate a special occasion or to have a long, leisurely meal with a friend. American menu. Lunch, dinner. Closed Jan 1, Thanksgiving, Dec 25. Bar. Children's menu. Casual attire. **$$$**

Talkeetna (D-5)

See also Denali National Park and Preserve

Population 772
Area Code 907
Information Talkeetna Denali Visitor Center, PO Box 688, 99676; phone 907/733-2499 or toll-free 800/660-2688
Web site www.alaskan.com/talkeetnadenali

Moose Dropping Festival. *Phone 907/733-2487.* This festival ranks high in terms of small-town charm: food and craft booths, slow-pitch softball tournaments, a mini parade, a footrace, pancake breakfasts, and the Mountain Mother Contests, where local women compete for the title of Mountain Mother (crossing a "stream" with a baby doll on their backs, shooting an arrow, casting a fishing pole, cutting firewood, etc.). Mid-July.

Unalaska (F-2)

Settled 1758
Population 4,283
Area Code 907
Web site www.ci.unalaska.ak.us

What to See and Do

Aleutian World War II National Historic Area. *Visitor Center, 2716 Airport Beach Rd, Unalaska (99685). Phone 907/581-1276. www.nps.gov/aleu.* Situated 800 miles west of Anchorage on Amaknak Island, the Aleutian World War II National Historic Area serves to educate present and future generations about the critical role the Aleutian Islands played in the defense of North America during the Second World War. The Historic Area spreads out over 134 acres, encompassing the ruins of the US Army base Fort Schwatka, which stood 1,000 feet above the Bering Sea. During the summer of 1942, the United States and Japan engaged in fierce fighting in the Aleutians, with Japan seizing occupation of the islands of Agattu, Attu, and

Kiska. The US grew increasingly concerned that these islands would be used as a staging area for attacks on the North American mainland. US forces focused their efforts on reclaiming the islands, doing so in May 1943—although both sides suffered significant casualties. The Historic Area also exists to honor the island natives, the Aleut or Unangan people, many of whom were killed or placed in internment camps during the war.

Valdez (D-6)

Population 4,036
Area Code 907
Information Valdez Convention and Visitors Bureau, 200 Fairbanks St, PO Box 1603, 99686; phone 907/835-4636 or toll-free 800/770-5954
Web site www.valdezalaska.org

Valdez was founded in the spring of 1898 by a group of hucksters who printed advertisements touting the speedy, established "All-American Route" from Prince William Sound to the Klondike gold fields. Thousands of prospectors discovered upon arriving that the route they had heard about was little more than a rough-hewn trail up and over a glacier. Despite its ignominious beginnings, Valdez remains today the "Gateway to the Interior," providing a vital link between the Interior and the rest of the world. As North America's northernmost ice-free port, it also serves as the terminus for the Alaska Pipeline. With an average of 325 inches of snow per year, the town boasts some of the best snowcat, helicopter, and extreme skiing in the world as well as world-class ice climbing in nearby Keystone Canyon. In recent years, an extensive network of hiking trails has been developed to provide better access to the wild beauty of the area.

What to See and Do

Tours. *Phone toll-free 800/544-2206. www.graylineofalaska.com.* Gray Line of Alaska offers package tours around Alaska (up to 11 days) as well as flightseeing tours, a jetboat safari, and guided fishing tours.

Valdez Museum and Annex. *217 Egan Dr, Valdez (99686). Phone 907/835-2764. www.alaska.net/~vldzmuse/index.html.* The Valdez Museum is located in the center of downtown Valdez and features displays and exhibits that tell the story of Valdez and the Prince

William Sound area. The museum annex is located in a warehouse at the southern end of Hazelet Avenue, by the ferry dock and Ruth Pond Park. Walking through the museum and its annex, visitors can trace the history of the town, from its origins as a trailhead supply depot during the Klondike Gold Rush of 1897-1898 through its destruction and relocation after the 1964 Good Friday Earthquake to its rejuvenation after being chosen as the southern terminus of the Alaska pipeline. Other exhibits focus on the 1989 *Exxon Valdez* oil spill that occurred in Prince William Sound and detail both the massive cleanup effort that was made and the steps that have been taken locally and nationally to learn from the accident. Visitors to the museum should save time to visit the museum annex located a short walk southeast of the museum. The annex contains an exquisitely detailed 1:20 scale model of Old Town Valdez as it looked just prior to the 1964 earthquake, including more than 400 buildings and covering more than 20 city blocks. Archival news footage and written accounts of the earthquake and its aftermath are also on public display in the annex. (Museum: summer: Mon-Sat 9 am-6 pm, Sun 8 am-5 pm; winter: Mon-Fri 1-5 pm; Sat noon-4 pm. Annex: summer, daily 9 am-4 pm.) **$**

Special Events

Gold Rush Days. *Phone 907/835-4636 (Valdez Convention & Visitors Bureau). www.valdezalaska.org.* Held for five days at the start of August, Valdez's Gold Rush Days festival celebrates the town's rich Gold Rush history. Highlights of the festival include the coronation of the king and queen of Gold Rush Days, a fashion show put on by local residents, roaming costumed can-can dancers, and a free community halibut and salmon fish fry held outdoors in one of the town's parks. Aug.

Last Frontier Theatre Conference. One of the largest theatric conferences in America, with 400 to 800 participants, depending on which famous people agree to take part. Features playwrights, authors, actors, and wannabes. The honorary founder is playwright Edward Albee. Mid-late June.

Limited-Service Hotels

★ **ASPEN HOTEL.** *100 Meals Ave, Valdez (99686). Phone 907/835-4445; toll-free 800/478-4445; fax 907/835-2437. www.aspenhotelsak.com.* This comfortable downtown hotel appeals on different levels to the eclectic mix of people who stay here. Business professionals appreciate the small, private business center and in-room DSL and wireless Internet. Families and groups enjoy the large family suites and the host of freebies the hotel offers: on-site pool and hot tub, small fitness center, email access, and deluxe continental breakfast. 102 rooms. Complimentary continental breakfast. Check-in 3 pm, check-out 11 am. Wireless Internet access. Fitness room. Indoor pool, whirlpool. **$$**

★ ★ **BEST WESTERN VALDEZ HARBOR INN.** *100 Fidalgo Dr, Valdez (99686). Phone 907/835-4391; toll-free 888/222-3440; fax 907/835-2308. www.valdezharborinn.com.* This newly renovated waterfront hotel is located at the Valdez boat harbor with unobstructed views of Prince William Sound and the Chugach mountains. Although it's a popular hotel for people heading out on glacier cruises and fishing charters, its slow-paced, rustic charm makes thoughts of napping and relaxing equally appealing. 88 rooms. Pets accepted. Check-in 2 pm, check-out noon. Restaurant. Fitness room. **$**

★ ★ **TOTEM INN HOTEL.** *144 E Egan Dr, Valdez (99686). Phone 907/835-4443; toll-free 888/808-4431; fax 907/835-4430. www.toteminn.com.* Built in 1973, this well-known family-owned hotel is actually a collection of buildings, the oldest of which houses a restaurant, reception area, and the motel-like original rooms. All rooms on the property are clean, comfortable and in excellent shape; those in the newer buildings offer a more upscale level of accommodation. The inn's restaurant is the place to go for weekend brunch, attracting a steady stream of longtime local customers. 70 rooms. Pets accepted. Check-in 2 pm, check-out 11 am. Restaurant. **$**

Specialty Lodgings

The following lodging establishments are approved by Mobil Travel Guide, but due to their unique and individualized nature have not been given a traditional Mobil Star rating. Included in this listing you may find bed-and-breakfasts, limited-service inns, guest ranches, and other unique hotel properties.

BROOKSIDE INN BED & BREAKFAST. *1465 Richardson Hwy, Valdez (99686). Phone 907/835-9130. www.brooksideinnbb.com.* Built in 1898, this inn is

Alaska's 92-Year Journey to Statehood

Americans today regard Alaska as a national treasure, endowed with spectacular scenery, abundant wildlife, and valuable natural resources. It's ironic to note, then, that Alaska once was viewed by Americans as a "white elephant" and that its procession to statehood, like the glaciers that carved out its magnificent mountains and valleys, moved at a slow pace.

Secretary of State William Seward negotiated a treaty for the purchase of the Alaska territory from Russia in 1867. The US Senate approved the treaty by one vote. Financially devastated by the Crimean War, Russia received a much-needed $7.2 million for the territory, a mere 2 cents per acre but still a considerable sum of money at the time, prompting skeptical Americans to refer to Alaska—thought by many to be a frozen wasteland, devoid of value—as "Seward's Folly."

Over the next 30 years, criticism of the acquisition appeared to be well founded, as the US government made little use of the territory. But Alaska's fortunes improved dramatically at the close of the 19th century with the discovery of gold in Canada's Yukon Territory. Thousands of prospectors descended on the town of Skagway in southeastern Alaska, where they prepared for the arduous trek to the Yukon gold fields. Subsequent gold strikes within the territory itself brought prospectors to towns such as Nome and Fairbanks, providing a boost to the economies in these and other communities—and helping to improve the territory's image in the contiguous states to the south.

The US Congress granted Alaska official territorial status on August 24, 1912. By this time, the heady gold rush days had fizzled, and the territory saw its population decline in the three decades that followed. The territory rebounded during World War II, buoyed by the construction of bases and an influx of military personnel. And at the dawn of the Cold War, Alaska, sitting just across the Bering Strait from Russia, occupied a critical strategic location, and the US military continued to provide a significant boost to the territory's economy.

In July 1958, President Eisenhower inked the Alaska Statehood Act. Six months later, on January 3, 1959—92 years after the US acquired the land from Russia—Alaska was officially proclaimed the nation's 49th state. In retrospect, Seward's purchase—far from being a "folly"—looks like a stroke of genius. Each year, on the last Monday in March, the state celebrates Seward's Day in honor of the man who, many years ago, possessed the foresight to recognize Alaska's tremendous value.

---

located three minutes away from downtown Valdez and Prince William Sound. 6 rooms, 2 story. **$**

L & L'S BED & BREAKFAST. *533 W Hanagita St, Valdez (99686). Phone 907/835-4447. www.lnlalaska .com.* Located minutes from downtown Valdez, the Alaska Marine Ferry Terminal, nature trails, and a visitors center, this bed-and-breakfast offers drop-off and pickup from airport and ferry. 5 rooms, 3 story. **$**

Restaurants

★ ★ **ALASKA'S BISTRO.** *100 Fidalgo Dr, Valdez (99686). Phone 907/835-5688; fax 907/835-4240. www. valdezharborinn.com.* This harborside restaurant is a great location to watch fishing charters return with their catches at the end of the day. A local favorite for fine dining, it features "nouveau Mediterranean" cuisine in a casually upscale dining room. Of the many items on the menu, the crab-stuffed halibut, paella, and homemade cheesecake are far and away the most popular. Mediterranean menu. Breakfast, lunch, dinner. Bar. Casual attire. **$$**

★ ★ **TOTEM INN RESTAURANT.** *144 E Egan Dr, Valdez (99686). Phone 907/835-4443; fax 907/834-4426. ww.toteminn.com.* For decades now, this friendly family restaurant has been serving hearty American dishes along with fresh Alaskan seafood, homemade soups, and fresh-baked biscuits and gravy to hungry tourists and locals. Adding to the appeal of the place is the wood and stone dining room filled with historic photos of Valdez as well as a spectacular array of stuffed Alaskan wildlife. American menu. Breakfast, lunch, dinner. Closed Dec 25. Bar. Children's menu. Casual attire. **$$**

Wasilla (D-5)

Established 1917
Population 5,469
Area Code 907
Information Greater Wasilla Chamber of Commerce, 415 E Railroad Ave, 99654; phone 907/376-1299
Web site www.wasillachamber.org

Like many small towns in Alaska, Wasilla owes its existence to the Alaska Railroad. In 1917, the rail line being constructed between Anchorage and Fairbanks reached Wasilla. Practically overnight, the tiny community that had been little more than a wayside stop on the Carle Wagon Road became a vital commercial and industrial center for the surrounding area. With the completion of the Parks Highway from Anchorage to Fairbanks in 1971, the area once again began an era of rapid growth and change as it suddenly became possible to live amid the scenic beauty and tranquility of the Wasilla area and work in Anchorage, 43 miles away. These days, visitors can learn more about the characters, events, and decisions that shaped the region at the Dorothy Page Museum and Historical Townsite, located in downtown Wasilla. Other noteworthy local attractions are the Iditarod Trail Sled Dog Race Headquarters and the Knik Museum and Dog Mushers Hall of Fame, both of which spotlight the history and evolution of dog sledding through interpretive exhibits and historical artifacts.

What to See and Do

Iditarod Trail Sled Dog Race Headquarters. *Knik Goose Bay Rd, mile 2.2, Wasilla (99687). From the Parks Hwy, head S on Knik Goose Bay Rd for 2.2 miles. Phone 907/376-5155. www.iditarod.com.* This rustic log cabin headquarters and visitor center just south of the Parks Highway contains interpretive displays and historical artifacts relating to the Iditarod dogsled race. Visitors can view videos of past races, wander through the museum, and take dogsled rides during summer months (fee). Unlike many attractions in Alaska, the headquarters stays open all year and really begins to get crowded in the weeks leading up to the race, which officially starts in Wasilla the day after its ceremonial—and much publicized—start in Anchorage. Hours change during the weeks surround-

ing the Iditarod Trail Sled Dog race, so call for details. (Mid-May-mid-Sept: daily 8 am-7 pm; mid-Sept-mid-May: Mon-Fri 8 am-5 pm) **FREE**

Independence Mine State Historical Park. *22 miles S. Phone 907/745-2827. www.dnr.state.ak.us/parks/units/indmine.htm.* This lesser-known area was just one of the places where adventurers flocked to seek out their fortunes in Alaska in the late 1800s and early 1900s. A self-guided historical trail leads visitors through the abandoned mine camp, which includes a comissary, several bunk houses, and a mill complex. Heavy snowfall in winter makes accessing the park difficult (check conditions before attempting the drive) but provides opportunities for cross-country and alpine skiing, as well as snowboarding and sledding. The visitor center (open seasonally 10 am-7 pm) offers guided tours.

Limited-Service Hotels

★ **ALASKAN VIEW MOTEL.** *2650 E Parks Hwy, Wasilla (99654). Phone 907/376-6787; fax 907/376-6726. www.alaskanviewmotel.com.* The primary selling point of this inexpensive, cozy motel is the spectacular, panoramic view it offers of Cook Inlet and the Chugach Range towering above the landscape in the distance. The motel is also only a short distance from Wasilla's main shopping areas and most of the town's restaurants and shops. 24 rooms. Pets accepted. Check-in 4 pm, check-out 11 am. **$**

★ ★ **BEST WESTERN LAKE LUCILLE INN.** *1300 W Lake Lucille Dr, Wasilla (99654). Phone 907/373-1776; toll-free 800/897-1776; fax 907/376-6199. www.bestwestern.com/lakelucilleinn.* Set on the shores of Lake Lucille, every lakeside room has a private balcony with breathtaking views of the wooded lake and the snowcapped Chugach Mountain range soaring into the sky some 15 miles away. Offering comfortable, tranquil lodging in a lodge-like setting, this hotel would be a great place to stop while in transit to or from the Denali area. 54 rooms. Pets accepted. Complimentary continental breakfast. Check-in 3 pm, check-out noon. Restaurant, bar. Fitness room. Whirlpool. **$**

★ ★ **GRAND VIEW INN & SUITES.** *2900 Parks Hwy, Wasilla (99654). Phone 907/357-7666; toll-free 866/710-7666; fax 907/357-6776.* Located at the crest of a hill on the edge of Wasilla, this hotel offers magnificent, unobstructed views of nearby Cook Inlet, the Chugach Mountains, and Knik Glacier. The spacious, comfortable lobby and immaculate rooms provide guests with plenty of room to relax and unwind, but it's the views that make this a terrific place to stop. 79 rooms. Pets accepted. Complimentary continental breakfast. Check-in 3 pm, check-out noon. Restaurant. Fitness room. Indoor pool, whirlpool. **$**

Restaurant

★ ★ **SHORELINE RESTAURANT.** *1300 W Lake Lucille Dr, Wasilla (99654). Phone 907/373-1776; fax 907/376-6199. www.bestwestern.com/lakelucilleinn.* The interior of this popular restaurant is both muted and classy, but the focus here is undeniably on what's outside: strikingly beautiful views of wooded Lake Lucille and the snowy Chugach Range rising behind it. During the long days of summer, the outdoor patio enables guests to dine alfresco while still enjoying the white tablecloth service they would get inside. American menu. Lunch, dinner. Closed Dec 25. Bar. Children's menu. Casual attire. Outdoor seating. **$$**

Wrangell-St. Elias National Park and Preserve

Web site www.nps.gov/wrst

While its name may neither sound familiar nor roll easily off the tongue, Wrangell-St. Elias National Park & Preserve is definitely worth a visit, as it boasts North America's greatest collection of mountain peaks above 16,000 feet, highlighted by 18,008-foot-high Mount St. Elias, the second highest peak in the United States. Wrangell-St. Elias is the nation's largest national park, with over 13 million acres of rugged wilderness, a landscape of towering mountains, sweeping valleys, massive glaciers, and powerful rivers. Wrangell-St. Elias is one of four contiguous parks situated along the US-Canada border, the other three being Glacier Bay National Park & Preserve (Alaska), Kluane National Park Reserve (Yukon Territory), and the Alsek-Tatshenshini Provincial Park (British Columbia). Together, these four parks comprise the world's largest internationally protected area.

Wrangell-St. Elias's headquarters can be found in Copper Center, a four-hour drive from Anchorage on the Alaska Highway. Two gravel roads provide access into the park. Nabesna Road (42 miles long) offers spectacular scenery, while McCarthy Road (60 miles long) leads to exceptional hiking, fishing, and camping. The National Park Service recommends drivers on either of these two roads have a spare tire in tow, as the terrain is quite rough. If you're renting a vehicle for a trip to Wrangell-St. Elias, pass on the midsize sedan and opt for a four-wheel-drive vehicle with a high road clearance. Phone 907/822-5234.

What to See and Do

Petroglyph Beach State Historic Park. *Wrangell. Phone 907/874-2381. www.wrangell.com/visitors/ attractions/history/petroglyph.* Petroglyphs—or rock carvings—were artistic works by Native Americans, and Petroglyph Beach offers some of the best examples that still survive today.

Yukon-Charley Rivers National Preserve

Web site www.nps.gov/yuch

Yukon-Charley Rivers National Preserve is notable for its abundant wildlife. Bordering Canada in east-central Alaska, the preserve has North America's highest nesting density of peregrine falcons. Summer brings a wide variety of other bird species to the area, some traveling from as far away as South America. Grizzlies and black bears roam the hills here, as do herds of caribou and packs of wolves. The preserve protects the entire 1.1 million-acre watershed of the Charley River, as well as 115 miles of the 1,800-mile-long Yukon River. Rafting, kayaking, and canoeing are popular on both rivers, particularly on the Charley, which has been designated a National Wild River. Yukon-Charley Rivers has seven public-use cabins, all available on a first-come, first-served basis. A visitor center in the town of Eagle features exhibits on the preserve's history and ecology. Situated at the northern terminus of Highway 5, Eagle is accessible by car, about a day's drive from Anchorage. Phone 907/547-2233.

Index

Driftwood Lodge, The (Juneau, AK), *320*

Driftwood Shores Resort & Conference Center (Florence, OR), *87*

Driggs, ID, *18–19*

Driving Tour in Deschutes National Forest (Bend, OR), *71–72*

Druids Glen Golf Course (Seattle, WA), *206*

Dubrulle International Culinary & Hotel Institute of Canada (Vancouver, BC), *250*

Duckabush, WA, *145*

Dulces Latin Bistro (Seattle, WA), *221*

Duncan House (Homer, AK), *317*

Dungeness Inn (Sequim, WA), *228*

Dungeness Recreation Area (Sequim, WA), *227*

E

Eagle Gate (Salt Lake City, UT), *42*

Eagle Island State Park (Boise, ID), *10*

Eagle River, AK, *304–305*

Eagle River Motel (Eagle River, AK), *304*

Eagle River Nature Center (Eagle River, AK), *304*

Eagle's Nest Restaurant (Kodiak, AK), *331*

Earth and Ocean (Seattle, WA), *221*

Earthquake Park (Anchorage, AK), *286*

East Linn Museum (Sweet Home, OR), *139*

Eastern Idaho State Fair (Blackfoot, ID), *2, 8*

Eastern Oregon Museum (Baker City, OR), *68*

Eastern Oregon University (La Grande, OR), *99*

Eastern Washington University (Cheney, WA), *161*

Eatonville, WA, *148*

Ecola State Park (Cannon Beach, OR), *76*

Ecomarine Ocean Kayak Centre (Vancouver, BC), *250*

Econo Lodge (Sequim, WA), *227*

Edgewater Inn (Long Beach, WA), *175*

Egyptian Theatre (Boise, ID), *9*

Eisenhower Alaska Statehood Monument (Anchorage, AK), *286*

Eklutna Flats and Palmer Hay Flats (Anchorage, AK), *286*

El Chicano Mexican Restaurant & Cantina (Kodiak, AK), *331*

El Dorado Gold Mine (Fairbanks, AK), *306*

El Gaucho (Seattle, WA), *221*

El Mariachi (Fairbanks, AK), *310*

El Sombrero (Juneau, AK), *322–323*

Elephant Garlic Festival (Portland, OR), *123*

Elk Valley Casino (Crescent City, CA), *142*

Elkins on Priest Lake (Priest Lake Area, ID), *30*

Ellensburg, WA, *165–166*

Ellensburg Inn (Ellensburg, WA), *166*

Elliott Grand Hyatt Seattle (Seattle, WA), *217*

Elmore County Historical Foundation Museum (Mountain Home, ID), *27*

Embarcadero Resort Hotel (Newport, OR), *111*

Embassy Suites (Salt Lake City, UT), *46*

Embassy Suites Downtown (Portland, OR), *126*

Emerald Downs (Auburn, WA), *151*

Emerald Queen Casino (Tacoma, WA), *233–234*

Emigrant Springs State Park (Pendleton, OR), *114*

Empress Hotel (Victoria, BC), *269*

Empress of the North, *281*

Empress Room (Victoria, BC), *276*

Enchanted Forest (Salem, OR), *136*

Enchanted Village (Tacoma, WA), *234*

End of the Oregon Trail Interpretive Center (Oregon City, OR), *113*

English Bay Inn (Vancouver, BC), *263*

English Beach (Vancouver, BC), *251*

English Inn & Resort (Victoria, BC), *274*

Enumclaw, WA, *166–167*

Enzian Inn (Leavenworth, WA), *173*

Ephrata, WA, *167*

Ernesto's Italian Restaurant (Bend, OR), *74*

Esparza's Tex Mex Cafe (Portland, OR), *129*

Espresso Vivace Roasteria (Seattle, WA), *205*

Etta's Seafood (Seattle, WA), *221*

Eugene, Hilton, and Conference Center (Eugene, OR), *85*

Eugene, OR, *83–86*

Eugene's Restaurant (Kodiak, AK), *331*

Everett, Boeing, Facility (Everett, WA), *168*

Everett, WA, *167–168*

Evergreen Floating Bridge (Seattle, WA), *206*

Evergreen Mountain Lookout, *108*

Excelsior Inn (Eugene, OR), *86*

Executive Hotel (Vancouver, BC), *259*

Executive House Hotel (Victoria, BC), *272*

Executive Suites Hotel (Anchorage, AK), *289*

Exhibition Park (Vancouver, BC), *250*

Experience Music Project (Seattle, WA), *206–207*

Experimental Breeder Reactor Number 1 (EBR-1) (Arco, ID), *6*

Ezra Meeker Community Festival (Puyallup, WA), *196*

Ezra Meeker Mansion (Puyallup, WA), *196*

F

F. W. Hastings House Old Consulate (Port Townsend, WA), *194*

F.X. McRory's Steak, Chop & Oyster House (Seattle, WA), *221*

Face Rock State Park (Bandon, OR), *69*

Fairbanks, AK, *305–312, 307, 345*

Fairbanks Hotel (Fairbanks, AK), *308*

Fairbanks Princess Riverside Lodge (Fairbanks, AK), *309*

Fairfield Inn (Beaverton, OR), *71*

Fairfield Inn (Portland, OR), *124*

Fairhaven District (Bellingham, WA), *154*

Fairhaven Park (Bellingham, WA), *154*

Fairhaven Village Inn (Bellingham, WA), *156*

Fairmont Empress, The (Victoria, BC), *272–273*

Fairmont Hotel Vancouver, The (Vancouver, BC), *260*

Fairmont Olympic Hotel, The (Seattle, WA), *217*

Fairmont Vancouver Airport, The (Vancouver, BC), *260*

Fairmont Waterfront, The (Vancouver, BC), *260–261*

Fall Creek Dam and Lake (Eugene, OR), *84*

Fall Festival (Corvallis, OR), *79*

Family History Library (Salt Lake City, UT), *44*

Farewell Bend (Ontario, OR), *112*

Farmer Consumer Awareness Day (Quincy, WA), *197*

Farmers Market (Buhl, ID), *13*

Farragut, ID, *3*

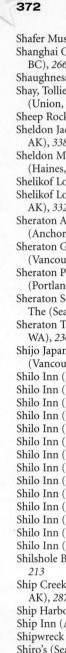

Notes

Notes